NIV BIBLE
HANDBOOK

NIV BIBLE HANDBOOK

ALISTER McGRATH

Mike Beaumont
Associate Editor

Martin H. Manser
Managing Editor

HODDER &
STOUGHTON

Unless indicated otherwise, Scripture quotations are taken from the
Holy Bible, New International Version (Anglicised edition). Copyright ©
1979, 1984, 2011 by Biblica. Used by permission. All rights reserved.

First published in Great Britain in 1995 by Hodder & Stoughton
An Hachette UK company
This revised and updated edition published in 2014

I

A CIP catalogue record for this title is available from the British Library

ISBN 978 1 444 74985 4
eBook ISBN 978 1 444 74987 8

Typeset in Requiem by Hewer Text UK Ltd, Edinburgh

Printed and bound in the UK by Clays Ltd, St Ives plc

Hodder & Stoughton policy is to use papers that are natural, renewable and recyclable products
and made from wood grown in sustainable forests. The logging and manufacturing processes
are expected to conform to the environmental regulations of the country of origin.

Hodder & Stoughton Ltd
338 Euston Road
London NW1 3BH

www.hodderfaith.com

CONTENTS

MAPS, CHARTS AND ILLUSTRATIONS

ABBREVIATIONS FOR BOOKS OF THE BIBLE

The Old Testament

Genesis	Ge	2 Chronicles	2Ch	Daniel	Da
Exodus	Ex	Ezra	Ezr	Hosea	Hos
Leviticus	Lev	Nehemiah	Ne	Joel	Joel
Numbers	Nu	Esther	Est	Amos	Am
Deuteronomy	Dt	Job	Job	Obadiah	Ob
Joshua	Jos	Psalms	Ps	Jonah	Jnh
Judges	Jdg	Proverbs	Pr	Micah	Mic
Ruth	Ru	Ecclesiastes	Ecc	Nahum	Na
1 Samuel	1Sa	Song of Songs	SS	Habakkuk	Hab
2 Samuel	2Sa	Isaiah	Isa	Zephaniah	Zep
1 Kings	1Ki	Jeremiah	Jer	Haggai	Hag
2 Kings	2Ki	Lamentations	La	Zechariah	Zec
1 Chronicles	1Ch	Ezekiel	Eze	Malachi	Mal

The New Testament

Matthew	Mt	Ephesians	Eph	Hebrews	Heb
Mark	Mk	Philippians	Php	James	Jas
Luke	Lk	Colossians	Col	1 Peter	1Pe
John	Jn	1 Thessalonians	1Th	2 Peter	2Pe
Acts	Ac	2 Thessalonians	2Th	1 John	1Jn
Romans	Ro	1 Timothy	1Ti	2 John	2Jn
1 Corinthians	1Co	2 Timothy	2Ti	3 John	3Jn
2 Corinthians	2Co	Titus	Tit	Jude	Jude
Galatians	Gal	Philemon	Phm	Revelation	Rev

INTRODUCTION

Christianity is the best news the world has ever had. It focuses on the hope of a dynamic new life – life that begins right now and that will not end even when we die – made possible through the life, death and resurrection of Jesus Christ. Those who have discovered the joy of the gospel will know the sense of peace and delight that comes from knowing Christ.

The Bible – which Christians often refer to as 'Scripture' – sets out the great historical events on which the Christian gospel is established. It reassures us that the gospel is founded on the bedrock of historical truth. It gives substance to the hope and joy of the Christian life. It allows us to picture the figure of Jesus Christ and realise the enormous attraction he had for ordinary people. Reading the four Gospels fills out our understanding and appreciation of Jesus Christ. There is no better place to start reading Scripture than with one of the Gospels. The Acts of the Apostles also indicates the great joy and delight the good news brought to men and women as it began its explosive expansion in the civilised world.

However, Scripture does more than allow us to appreciate the attraction of the gospel and its central figure, Jesus Christ. It goes behind the coming of Jesus Christ, and helps us understand the great sense of expectation that had built up within Judaism. By reading the Old Testament, we can understand the way in which God was preparing the way for Jesus Christ. We can go back in history and appreciate the hopes and expectations of the Old Testament community of faith, as they looked to the future that they knew would hold the coming of God's long-awaited Messiah. And as we read the gospel accounts of Jesus Christ, we can see how Christ fulfilled those great hopes.

Scripture also helps us to understand the difference knowing Jesus Christ makes to the way Christians think and behave. The New Testament letters help us understand the basic ideas of the Christian gospel – the central doctrines that sum up the Christian understanding of the way things are, and the hope the gospel brings to the world. They also help us learn the way in which knowing Christ should affect the way in which we behave. Paul's letters, for example, are full of wise advice on how Christians ought to live in a pagan world – advice that continues to be relevant and helpful today.

If you've been a Christian for some time, you'll probably feel ready to begin reading the Bible immediately. If you're new to being a Christian, or feel that you could do with a little more information – read on!

This Bible Handbook is designed to help all Christians understand and apply the Bible more. It's in three parts.

Part 1 contains three introductory articles to set the scene:
What Is in the Bible?
Can We Trust What the Bible says?
How Can We Get the Best from Reading the Bible?

Part 2 is the main part of this book: a commentary on all 66 books of the Bible, interspersed with many maps, charts and feature articles on issues of Christian teaching and life.

Part 3 is the reference section containing factual help:
People of the Bible
Places of the Bible
Concordance
For Further Reading

We trust that you will find this book a helpful and reliable guide to your Christian life.

Mike Beaumont
Alister McGrath
Martin Manser

SETTING THE SCENE

WHAT IS IN THE BIBLE?

The Bible is divided into two major sections, referred to as the *Old Testament* and the *New Testament*. The Old Testament consists of 39 books, beginning with Genesis and ending with Malachi. This first section of the Bible deals with the history of the people of God before the coming of Jesus Christ. It helps us understand God's plans for his people, and the way in which he chose to redeem them. It introduces us to the great hopes of divine intervention in history, which will eventually be fulfilled through Jesus Christ. It is impossible to appreciate the full importance and wonder of the gospel without being aware of the preparation for the coming of Christ in the history of the people of God.

The **Old Testament** itself includes a number of different kinds of writings. Appreciating their different natures will help you get more out of reading them. The main sections of the Old Testament are the following:

1. *The Five Books of the Law* (which are sometimes also referred to as *The Five Books of Moses*, or *The Pentateuch*): Genesis, Exodus, Leviticus, Numbers and Deuteronomy. These deal with the creation of the world, the calling of Israel as a people and its early history, including the exodus from Egypt. The story they tell ends with the people of Israel about to cross over the Jordan and enter the promised land. One of the most important themes of these books is the giving of the Law to Moses, and its implications for the life of Israel.

2. *The Historical Books:* Joshua, Judges, Ruth, 1 and 2 Samuel, 1 and 2 Kings, 1 and 2 Chronicles, Ezra, Nehemiah and Esther. These books deal with various aspects of the history of the people of God from their entry into the promised land of Canaan to the return of the people of Jerusalem from exile in the city of Babylon. It includes detailed accounts of the conquest of Canaan, the establishment of a monarchy in Israel, the great reigns of kings David and Solomon, the breakup of the single nation of Israel into two parts (the northern kingdom of Israel and the southern kingdom of Judah), the destruction of Israel by the Assyrians, the defeat of Judah and exile of her people by the Babylonians, and the final return from exile and the rebuilding of the temple. The books are arranged in historical order.

3. *The Prophets:* this major section of the Old Testament contains the writings of a group of individuals, inspired by the Holy Spirit, who sought to make the will of God known to their people over a period of time. There are 16 prophetic writings in the Old Testament, which are usually divided into two categories. First, there are the four *Major Prophets*: Isaiah, Jeremiah, Ezekiel and Daniel. These are followed by the twelve *Minor Prophets*: Hosea, Joel, Amos, Obadiah, Jonah, Micah,

Nahum, Habakkuk, Zephaniah, Haggai, Zechariah and Malachi. The use of the words 'major' and 'minor' does not imply any judgment about the relative importance of the prophets. It refers simply to the length of the books in question. The prophetic writings are arranged roughly in historical order.

Other types of book can be noted, including the *Wisdom Writings*: Job, Proverbs, Ecclesiastes. These works deal with the question of how true wisdom may be found, and often provide some practical examples of wisdom. Another category of writings that lies outside the Old Testament should also be noted – the *Apocrypha*. This is also sometimes referred to as the 'deuterocanonical writings'. It includes a number of later writings from Old Testament times that, although informative, have not been regarded as of binding importance by Christians. Some Bibles include this section of writings; others, like the NIV, do not.

The **New Testament** is of vital importance to Christians, as it sets out the basic events and beliefs of the Christian gospel. The New Testament, which consists of 27 books, is considerably shorter than the Old Testament. It is strongly recommended that new readers of the Bible begin by reading one of the *four Gospels*: Matthew, Mark, Luke and John. The word 'gospel' basically means 'good news'. Each of the four gospel writers – or 'evangelists', as they are sometimes known – sets out the basic events lying behind the good news. These four books describe, from different viewpoints, the life of Jesus Christ, which reaches its glorious climax in his resurrection, as well as presenting his teachings.

The four Gospels have distinctive characteristics – for example, Matthew is concerned to present Jesus' teaching, whereas Mark is more interested in focusing on the last week of his earthly life. Taken together, all four build up to give a comprehensive account of the life, death and resurrection of Jesus Christ. They provide the main building blocks of the Christian faith, allowing readers to understand why Christians believe that Jesus Christ is indeed the Lord and Saviour of the world. You will sometimes find the term *synoptic Gospels* used to refer to the first three Gospels (Matthew, Mark and Luke); this term refers to their similar literary structure. The Gospels are usually referred to simply by the name of their author – such as 'Mark' – rather than the more lengthy phrase 'the Gospel according to Mark'.

The Gospels are followed by an account of the expansion of Christianity. How were events described in the Gospels received at the time? How did the gospel spread from Palestine to Europe? These questions are addressed in the *Acts of the Apostles*, which is almost always referred to simply as 'Acts'. The Gospel of Luke and Acts were written by the same person – Luke.

The next major section of material in the New Testament is the *Letters*, sometimes still referred to by the older English word *Epistles*. These letters provide teaching concerning both Christian beliefs and behaviour, as important today as they were when they were first written. Some of the false teachings that arose in the early period of the church's history continue to arise in present times, and these letters provide important resources for defending the integrity of the Christian faith today.

Most of the letters were written by Paul, whose conversion to the Christian faith led him to undertake a major programme of evangelism and church planting. Many of his letters were written to churches he had planted, giving them advice. All of Paul's letters are written to individuals (such as Timothy or Titus) or churches (such as the churches at Rome, Corinth and Philippi). Although the letters are sometimes referred to as 'Paul's first letter to Timothy' or 'Paul's second letter to the church at Corinth', they are much more usually referred to simply as '1 Timothy' or '2 Corinthians'.

Other letter writers include the apostles Peter and John, as well as the unknown author of the letter to the Hebrews (possibly Barnabas or Apollos). Often, the letters describe the hardship being faced for the gospel, or the joy it brings to the writer and those he is writing to. This reminds us that Christianity is not just about ideas. It is about changed lives! The letters are not dull doctrinal textbooks, but living testimonies to faith, which include doctrinal teaching. Note that all these letters are identified by the person who wrote them, rather than the people they are written to. Although the full titles are sometimes used – such as 'the first letter of Peter' – it is more common to refer to them by shorter forms, such as '1 Peter'.

Two terms should be noted here. The letters of James, John, Jude and Peter are sometimes referred to as the 'general letters' or 'the catholic epistles', to indicate that they have a general readership. Unlike the letters of Paul, they do not seem to be written to a specific audience, but were meant for wide reading. The term *Pastoral Letters* is sometimes used to refer to Paul's two letters to Timothy and his letter to Titus, which deal particularly with issues of pastoral importance (that is, care of people in the church).

The New Testament ends with the Revelation of John – almost always referred simply as 'Revelation', which stands in a class of its own. It represents a vision of the end of history, in which the writer is allowed to see into heaven, and gain a glimpse of the new Jerusalem prepared for believers.

Where do I start?

One possibility might be to start with Genesis – the first book in the Old Testament – and work your way right through to the last book in the New Testament. This is not such a good idea, however. The most appropriate way of reading Scripture is to begin by reading a Gospel. By doing this, you will focus on Jesus Christ, and become familiar with the historical bedrock of the Christian faith. It is often said that 'Christianity is Jesus Christ'. Reading one of the four Gospels will bring you face to face with the central figure of the Christian faith.

So which of the four Gospels should you begin with? Each has a distinctive character. Matthew is especially concerned to bring out how the life, death and resurrection of Jesus Christ fulfil the great Old Testament prophecies of the coming Saviour and Messiah. Mark is brief and fast moving, bringing out clearly the remarkable impact Jesus had upon those around him. Luke is especially interested in bringing out the importance of Jesus for those who are not Jews. John is the most

reflective of all the Gospels, and will give you substantial food for thought. The choice is yours. However, whichever of the Gospels you begin by reading, make sure that you read the other three, in whole or part, at some point.

Where do you go next? You might like to read of the rapid expansion of the gospel by looking at the Acts of the Apostles. This is an especially appropriate thing to do if you have just read Luke's Gospel, as the two works dovetail together. You might also like to try reading one of the letters, to see how the gospel can change people's lives and hopes. Paul's letter to the Philippians is an especially appropriate choice for the next step. It's brief and very easy to read. For those wanting more doctrinal input, the letters to the Romans and Galatians are particularly important.

Having gained an understanding of the gospel, you might then like to go back to the Old Testament, and explore the background to the coming of Jesus Christ. Many translations and editions of the Bible make this easier by providing footnotes or centre-column references to relevant passages in other parts of the Bible.

The best advice, however, is to study the Bible with other people, especially in groups that include older and more experienced Christians. They will be able to explore both the meaning and the implications of biblical passages for Christian life today. Your local church, college or even place of work will probably have a Christian Bible study group attached to it. Find it, and join up! If you haven't started going to a church – do so. Try to find one that takes the Bible seriously. This kind of church will have sermons that examine important biblical passages, and will also have Bible study groups as an integral part of its teaching and support programme.

Why a Bible handbook?

So why a Bible handbook? Why not just read the Bible, and soak in its wisdom? The simplest answer is that the Bible is best read in company. One of the reasons why Bible study groups are so popular is that they allow you to listen to other people talking about their insights into the meaning and relevance of the Bible. A Bible handbook, especially one with a commentary, is like that. This reference tool gives you access to the wisdom of others.

Commentaries and Bible handbooks come in different forms. Some are technical, dealing with the detailed historical backgrounds to the books, and exploring the precise grammatical and theological meaning of the Bible text in depth. Others are devotional, aiming to help readers turn to prayer and adoration as a result of reading Scripture. Some devote entire volumes to a single book of the Bible. Others try to survey the Bible in a shorter space; the commentary section of this handbook is one of them.

The commentary in this handbook is designed to introduce you to the main features of the Bible. It is written by a single author, which ensures that the same level and style of writing will be found throughout the book. Although there is not space in a single volume to deal with all the possible questions, such a book can whet your appetite for more, and give you increasing confidence in your own ability to read and benefit from the Bible.

Referring to biblical books

A further point needs to be looked at. How do you identify the biblical passage you want to study or talk about? To make this as easy as possible, a kind of shorthand way of referring to biblical passages has evolved over the years. Once you understand it, you are set up for the rest of your Christian life. In what follows, we will explore this very briefly.

To locate a verse in the Bible, you need to identify three things: the *book* of the Bible, the *chapter* of that book, and the *verse* of that chapter. To make sure you understand this, turn to the Acts of the Apostles, chapter 27, verse 1. What is the name of the centurion mentioned in this verse? If your answer is not 'Julius', check your reference again. Now try turning to Paul's letter to the Romans, chapter 16, verse 5. Who was the first convert to Christ in Asia? If you answer is not 'Epenetus', check it again.

The above system is cumbersome. Writing out everything – like 'Paul's letter to the Romans, chapter 16, verse 5' – takes up too much space. So it is abbreviated, as follows: Ro 16:5. This is the standard form of reference, with the following features:

1. *An abbreviation of the book* of the Bible being referred to, usually two or three letters in length (such as 1Ki for '1 Kings', Mt for 'Matthew', Ro for 'Romans', and 1Co for '1 Corinthians'). A full list of the books of the Bible, and their standard abbreviations, may be found in a table on page 7.

2. *The number of the chapter* of that book, followed by a colon (:).

3. *The number of the verse* in that chapter.

Below are some further minor points.

First, some biblical books are so brief that they consist of only one chapter (Obadiah, Philemon, 2 John, 3 John, Jude). In this case, only the verse number is cited. Thus Phm 2 is a reference to the second verse of Philemon.

Secondly, a commentary dealing with a passage in a specific biblical book (such as Genesis) may need to refer to another passage *in the same book*. In this case, the book name will be omitted. Thus, in a commentary on Genesis, a reference to Ge 12:1 would appear simply as 12:1.

Thirdly, individual psalms are treated as chapters of the psalter. Thus a reference to Ps 23:1 is a reference to the first verse of the twenty-third psalm.

You will also need to know how to refer to a passage of more than one verse. This is simple. Look at the reference Mt 3:13–17. This reference is to the passage that begins with Mt 3:13, and ends at Mt 13:17. To indicate a passage within a single chapter of a biblical book, you need only identify the opening and closing verse in this way. Sometimes the passage will include material from two or more chapters. The following reference is of this kind: 1Th 4:13–5:11. This refers to a passage that begins at 1Th 4:13, and ends at 1Th 5:11.

CAN WE TRUST WHAT THE BIBLE SAYS?

In today's world – at least in the West – it is fashionable to doubt all authority; how much more then the authority of a book dismissed by many as the writings of a dusty old religion that is completely irrelevant for today? Since this is the atmosphere that Christians live in, it is unsurprising that they too ask – in a way previous generations might not have asked – whether we can really treat the Bible as God's word. And can we really be expected to give it authority over our lives? How might we begin to answer such questions?

Jesus' view of Scripture

For any serious follower of Jesus, the starting place must surely be that Jesus himself trusted these Scriptures and saw them as God's word. For Jesus the Scriptures were both authoritative and binding (e.g., Mt 5:17–19; Jn 10:35); the word of God, not of merely human origin; and he accepted its stories as both instructive and true (e.g., Mt 12:39–42; 19:4–6). In the Gospels we find him frequently quoting from these Scriptures to settle issues (e.g., Mt 19:17–19), authenticate his actions (e.g., Mt 10:34–36; 21:16), support his teaching (e.g., Mt 13:13–15; 21:42) and challenge his opponents (e.g., Mt 15:7–9; 22:41–46). He claimed that his own life fulfilled them (e.g., Mt 26:53–56; Lk 4:18–21; Jn 17:12) and he opened the eyes of the disciples on the Emmaus Road to how they had predicted his life, death and resurrection as, 'beginning with Moses and all the Prophets, he explained to them what was said in all the Scriptures concerning himself' (Lk 24:27). All this must surely carry significant weight in Christians determining their own attitude to the Bible.

The view of Jesus' disciples of Scripture

It is unsurprising therefore that Jesus' disciples adopted the same approach to the Scriptures, not only as any good Jew would have done, but in further interpreting them through their reflections on his life, which they now saw as having clearly fulfilled them (e.g., Mt 1:22; 2:15, 18, 23; 4:15–16; 8:16–17; 12:16–18; 21:4–5; 26:55–56; 27:8–10). Paul summed up the early church's attitude to Scripture like this: 'All Scripture is God-breathed and is useful for teaching, rebuking, correcting and training in righteousness, so that the servant of God may be thoroughly equipped for every good work' (2Ti 3:16–17). The expression 'God-breathed' (*theopneustos* in Greek) means 'breathed out by God' (some English versions translate it as 'inspired by God'). What that means is that God breathed out his Spirit into the writers of Scripture in such a way that what they wrote was exactly what God wanted written. This is why the Bible is often called 'the inspired word of God' ('inspired' comes from the Latin

for 'breathed into') – though in calling it 'inspired' we are not simply saying it is 'inspiring' (many books are that), nor that God gave the authors the general idea of what to write and then left them to it. Rather, we are saying that his Spirit so breathed into them that the words they wrote were the very words he wanted written.

The 'double authorship' of Scripture

This does not exclude genuine human involvement, however. God did not 'take over' the writers in some way, using them as some sort of dictation machine; rather his Spirit used their different characters, styles, experiences, research, even theological reflections, but guided all of that in order to bring his word to us. In that sense, Scripture has 'double authorship': God, the primary author, and the human writers, the secondary.

All this means that it was both *the process* and *the product* that were 'inspired'. Peter summed it up by saying that 'no prophecy of Scripture came about by the prophet's own interpretation of things. For prophecy never had its origin in the human will, but prophets, though human, spoke from God as they were carried along by the Holy Spirit' (2Pe 1:20–21). The expression 'carried along' was used of a ship hoisting its sails to the wind to be carried along by it. In the same way, Peter says, the writers of Scripture 'hoisted their sails' to the wind of God's Spirit who carried them along in their thinking and writing to the exact place where God wanted them to be. Scripture is thus doubly inspired: both its *writings* (2Ti 3:16) and its *writers* (2Pe 1:21) were inspired by God's Spirit. Of course, any such claims of inspiration are limited to the original texts as penned by their authors – what scholars call 'the autographs' – and not to any particular translation, no matter how loved that translation may be.

The process of forming Scripture

But in the quotes we have just examined, both Paul and Peter were referring to the Old Testament. What about the New? On what basis do Christians give this the same level of inspiration and authority? While the first Christians obviously did not yet have the complete Bible (the New Testament was still in the process of being formed), it is clear that they were starting to see some apostolic writings as having the same quality and authority as the Old Testament itself. Hence Peter, writing about Paul, noted that 'his letters contain some things that are hard to understand, which ignorant and unstable people distort, *as they do the other Scriptures*' (2Pe 3:16). This shows that Peter was starting to see Paul's letters on the same level as 'the other Scriptures', by which he would certainly have meant the Old Testament, but quite probably other early apostolic writings, including perhaps the Gospels. Paul – brought up as a devout Jew and formerly a staunch Pharisee – seemed to have no problem in claiming divine authority for what he wrote, just like the Old Testament prophets did, and in seeing those writings as commands of the Lord, as when he told the Corinthians, 'If anyone thinks they are a prophet or otherwise gifted by the Spirit, let them acknowledge that

what I am writing to you is the Lord's command' (1Co 14:37). Since Jesus himself had promised his disciples that 'the Holy Spirit, whom the Father will send in my name, will teach you all things and will remind you of everything I have said to you' (Jn 14:26) this would not have struck the first Christians as surprising. Jesus was simply doing what he had promised.

We should also note that the early church was not casual about which books were included in the New Testament, any more than Jews had been casual about what went into their *Tanak* (the Hebrew name for the Jewish Scriptures, what Christians call the Old Testament). Both Jews and Christians tested the contents of their Scriptures by three key standards. First, the standard of *inspiration*. By that they meant, did the text really sound like it came through the Holy Spirit or was there something 'odd' about it when compared with other acknowledged writings? This is why, for example, early 'Gnostic' writings were excluded from the canon because their picture of Jesus simply didn't line up with the picture of him in the accepted Gospels. Secondly, the standard of *association*. In the Old Testament this meant association with one of the great prophets (among whom Moses was numbered), and in the New Testament, with one of the apostles. Hence Mark's Gospel was accepted because of his close association with the apostle Peter, and Luke/Acts because of Luke's close association with the apostle Paul. Thirdly, the standard of *acceptance*. Did the community of faith at large accept these writings from their earliest appearance? Acceptance by one church or group was insufficient grounds for acceptance. Only when writings had passed these three tests were they accepted into the 'canon' (from the Greek *kanon*, meaning a reed or cane, and ultimately a measuring rod, rule or standard). While the final list of books in the Bible as we know it today was not finalised until the 4th century, it is clear from the writings of the early church fathers that a broad consensus on virtually all the books had been reached as early as the 2nd century. In fact Peter's reference to 'the other scriptures' (2Pe 3:16) indicates some sort of agreement was already forming even in apostolic times.

It is this inspiration – tested and agreed by the community of the faithful at large – that gives Scripture (both Old and New Testaments) its *authority* and *infallibility*. By this we mean that the Bible speaks with the authority of God himself and is therefore fully trustworthy as his revelation of both himself and the way of salvation, and that it will never misinform or mislead us on that which it intends to teach us. This is why the Bible is often called 'the word of God' or 'God's word' (an expression frequently found within the Bible itself), for it reminds us that the Bible carries authority to speak into our lives because of the authority of its ultimate author, God himself. As such, it will never let us down.

Evidence outside the Bible

Of course, all this could be dismissed as mere self-authentication. So are there other factors, outside the Bible, that we can look to as supporting evidence? Yes, for since the Bible's stories are rooted in history we can check its accounts against

external evidence. When we do, we find that *non-biblical records* frequently confirm biblical accounts – for example, the 'Black Obelisk' of Shalmaneser III records his triumph over King Jehu, whose reign is recorded in the Bible, and Tiglath-Pileser III's annals record his invasion of Israel, noted in 2Ki 15:19–20, though using the king's alternative name, Pul; while in the New Testament Luke's consistent use of *accurate geographical and political terms*, confirmed by contemporary sources, reveal what a careful historian he was and how his account may therefore be trusted. *Contemporary customs* described in non-biblical sources show that the Old Testament's portrayal of life, once thought dubious, is in fact utterly realistic – for example, a man's right to father a child by his wife's maid if his wife was barren is affirmed in the Babylonian Code of Hammurabi, while the 20 shekels paid for Joseph is confirmed in contemporary trade tablets as the price of a slave. *Archaeological discoveries* frequently confirm biblical accounts – for example, excavations at Shechem revealed a gate system containing the temple of Baal, destroyed by Abimelek (Jdg 9:46–49), while Sennacherib's siege of Lachish (2Ch 32:9) is confirmed both by reliefs in his palace and excavations on site.

Another common popular argument against taking the Bible seriously is that the original text must have been changed over the years – whether by error or intent – as one scribe copied from another (remember, there was no printing, at least in Europe, until the mid-15th century), and therefore it must be unreliable. But while there are indeed many ancient manuscripts of the Bible, and while those manuscripts do contain variants (though often simply variations in spelling or mislocated words), the study of manuscripts is now so advanced, and techniques for comparing variants so refined, that we can have a high degree of certainty that what we are reading is indeed what the original authors meant us to read. Where there is uncertainty or disagreement, many editions of the Bible make this plain in the footnotes, showing that there is no attempt to deceive or cover up. It should be remembered however that real uncertainty lies with less than 1 per cent of the biblical text.

Trusting the Bible for ourselves

Of course, ultimately there remains an element of faith in receiving the Bible as the word of God. Yet taking this step is not 'blind faith'. As we have seen, there are sound reasons for at least 'trying it out'. This, after all, is what scientists do all the time: take what seems a reasonable, or even possible, theory and test it repeatedly to see if it works. Over the centuries Christians have done just that: stepped out and trusted the Bible, and as they have done so they have discovered that 'your word is truth' (Jn 17:17), just as Jesus affirmed – truth not in a mere academic or philosophical sense, but truth that reveals what God is like (his heart, his character, his purposes, his ways, his plans) and truth that challenges (and changes) us as we follow God's manual for life.

HOW CAN WE GET THE BEST
FROM READING THE BIBLE?

Let's face it: reading and understanding the Bible isn't always easy. After all, it's a collection of 66 books, written by some 40 different authors, in three different languages (Hebrew, Aramaic and Greek), as even its very title reminds us – 'Bible', from the Latin word *biblia*, meaning 'little books', highlighting its nature as an anthology. These writings include many different styles – law, history, prophecy, poetry, wisdom, gospel, letters, apocalyptic – recording events that happened over a period of more than two millennia, the last of which occurred 2000 years ago. To complicate things even more, life changed considerably over that period and has changed even more dramatically since. But if this book is God's eternal and inspired word, given to help us to know him and to live life to its fullest, then it must surely still be understandable and relevant in our own day. So how can we get the best out of it? Two broad areas help answer this question.

A community to help us understand

When it comes to reading and understanding the Bible it is important to remember we are not alone. God has put the community of his people around us to help us. Indeed, it is when Christians read the Bible as though they were alone on a desert island that terribly wrong readings of the Bible occur.

In the West we are so accustomed to reading the Bible personally that we forget that this is not how it would first have been encountered. When the texts were first delivered they would have been to hearers rather than to readers (e.g., Ex 24:7; Ne 8:5–8; Col 4:16). As the Bible was gradually brought together, it was in the form of hand-written manuscripts, and since these were costly they would have been read aloud to a gathered group (no one would have had their own scroll at home). Such corporate encounters with God's word still have their place even in days when every Christian (at least in the West) can have their own copy of the Bible. They enable us to recapture the communal aspect of hearing God's word, probing further together into what has been said, sharing our insights and reflections with one another, asking about parts we did not understand, and seeking to apply it to life today. There are so many opportunities for us to do this – from *the preaching of the word* in our Sunday meetings by someone who has spent hours digging into the passage, grappling with the meaning of the text in order to provide spiritual food for us to reflect on, through *small-group discussions* where we can study the Bible together, share our personal reflections, be shaped in our thinking, lovingly corrected in our misunderstandings, and apply the text specifically to our own lives, to *one-on-one discipleship* which provides

an opportunity for accountability concerning what we have read in order to ensure it does not just stay head knowledge but that we put it into practice. The use of the Bible in small-group discussion has been a repeated feature of growing churches throughout the centuries as Christians have grasped that it is truly 'useful for teaching, rebuking, correcting and training in righteousness, so that the servant of God may be thoroughly equipped for every good work' (2Ti 3:16–17).

Tools to help us understand

Western 21st-century Christians have more tools to help them in their reading and understanding of the Bible than any previous generation. The best place to start is by ensuring you are reading *a good translation*, which is where the NIV excels, since it seeks to be faithful to the original text while finding suitable yet accurate language for today into which to translate it. But comparing it with a different English version can still be helpful as different versions bring out different emphases in words or phrases at times. A good *study Bible* is extremely helpful as its notes will explain difficult historical or theological references that aren't obvious at first reading. *Bible reading notes* are available in abundance, some more devotional, some more textual, but variety in the kind you use is a key to keeping Bible reading 'fresh'. For those who want to go deeper a wide range of *Bible commentaries* is available, exploring the text in more detail, at all levels from the popular to the academic. Browsing in your local Christian bookshop or your minister's library is a good way to find one at the level you are looking for. *The internet* too can be a rich source of information – though you need to be wary about some of what you read there. Remember, here as in every other area, not everything you read on the internet is true or helpful. So get recommendations from trusted Christian friends or ministers. Some sites are amazing, particularly those that reveal more of the background to the Bible in words or photos.

But what about when it comes to actually engaging with the text yourself? Are there things that can help with that? Scholars use tools called *exegesis* (discovering what the text meant *then*) and *hermeneutics* (interpreting what the text means for *today*). It is possible to follow their principles but in a much simpler way by using the following formula: Them – Us – Me.

Them

Begin by asking what this text meant to *them* – to the people who first read or heard this, or who were involved in the story. Even godly imagination can play its part here. But to ensure our imagination doesn't run riot, we can ask five basic questions to keep us on track: Who? When? Where? Why? What? (1) *Who* are the characters involved in this story and what do we know about them? (2) *When* did this event take place and what was happening at that time? (3) *Where* did this event occur? For example, in the promised land with its blessings, or in exile with its challenges? The right answer makes a huge difference, especially to prophecy. (4) *Why?* Why did the writer include

this story? Yes, God wanted it there; but why in this particular place in the Bible? What has happened just before it? What happens next? What is the wider context? And is the writer trying to make a point by putting this particular story in this particular place? (5) *What?* What are the words actually saying, and what do those words mean? The key here is finding out what the passage and its words meant 'there and then' rather than trying to jump quickly to 'here and now'. Start by remembering what kind of writing you are reading, as this is a major key in understanding. Don't interpret history as though it were prophecy, or apocalyptic writing as though it were history. This is where we need to start digging a bit deeper now, and where study Bibles and commentaries can help us. We need to try to understand any cultural or historical features and their significance; we need to see if there are allusions to other parts of the Bible. For example, the Old Testament prophets often allude to the exodus or Israel's time in the desert, and New Testament writers often allude to stories in the Old Testament; seeing that is often a key to understanding. Remember, the key is always to ask yourself what the first hearers would have understood this to mean.

Us

Having discovered what the text first meant to its original hearers or participants, the next step is to bring that up to date and ask ourselves: What is *the exact equivalent meaning of that for today?* If 'the word of God is alive and active' (Heb 4:12) then it is as relevant for now as when God first gave it. Sometimes the meaning for today is plain, straightforward and exactly the same: 'Husbands, love your wives, just as Christ loved the church' (Eph 5:25) means 'husbands love your wives . . .', even if the cultural expression of that love may change according to time and place. Sometimes there is a close equivalent for today. For example, Paul's injunctions to slaves and masters (Eph 6:5–8) are not directly applicable in cultures where slavery does not exist; but the underlying principles of what he writes there (mutual respect, sincerity, working as though for Christ) are just as relevant today for workers and managers, and indeed would be revolutionary if put into practice. But sometimes we might come across something that seems very obscure and that therefore is hard to apply. That is when we need to ask: Is there another passage of Scripture that can throw some light on this? (Footnotes and margin notes can be enormously helpful here.) Is this word or concept used elsewhere? (That's where a concordance comes in useful.) Ultimately, remember that no passage can be interpreted or applied in such a way as to make it contradict the rest of Scripture. If your interpretation does, then you've got something wrong somewhere.

Me

Having taken time to examine what the text meant first to *them*, and then what its exact equivalent meaning is for *us* today, we are ready for our third step, without which Bible study is incomplete. This third step involves turning the focus to *me*. This is where we ask, 'God, what are you saying to *me* through this passage?' Is there some encouragement, challenge, warning or rebuke? Does it bring some guidance I have

been seeking? Or an answer to something I have been praying about? Does it give me a principle by which to live my life today? And what can I see here about God – his heart (what he is like), his purposes (what he is doing), his desire (what he wants), his principles (how he operates)? Unless I take this final step of looking to myself – though note that this should be the final step rather than the first one, for otherwise we are prone to interpret the text wrongly or twist it to meet our own needs – I am treating the Bible no differently from any other book that I might read, rather than what it is: God's word. I am then no better than those whom James challenges when he writes:

> Do not merely listen to the word, and so deceive yourselves. Do what it says. Anyone who listens to the word but does not do what it says is like someone who looks at his face in a mirror and, after looking at himself, goes away and immediately forgets what he looks like. But whoever looks intently into the perfect law that gives freedom, and continues in it – not forgetting what they have heard, but doing it – they will be blessed in what they do. (Jas 1:22–25)

While this process of 'them-us-me' may seem a little challenging at first, especially if you are new to Bible reading, it can really help bring the Bible alive. It is an approach that lends itself to being used when you have only a few minutes (by using godly imagination in the 'them' section) or when you have much longer and can use commentaries to support your learning.

So, yes, reading and understanding the Bible *can* be a challenge – and for some of us, even finding time to read it can be the first challenge (though few of us have trouble finding time to read our emails, access our social networking sites or watch our favourite TV programme). Ultimately, it comes down to how important we really feel it is to hear God speaking to us. If we can grasp that the Bible is truly God's word, however, and that, with the right help, it is not too difficult to understand, then we will be eager not only to read it but also to live it out. After all, this is God's manual for successful living and the account of where he is taking humanity. Who wouldn't want to know that and be part of it?

OLD AND NEW TESTAMENT TIME CHART

For many dates, the year(s) shown are approximate

Biblical period and where it is recorded		World events	
Beginnings of Time Genesis			
Abraham c.2000–1825		Middle Bronze Age	2000 BC
Isaac c.1900–1725		1950–1550	
Jacob c. 1800–1700			
Joseph c. 1720–1550			
Jacob and his eleven sons join Joseph in Egypt c. 1700			
Exodus from Egypt and Conquest of Canaan Exodus–Joshua			
Moses		Pharaoh Rameses II	1300 BC
Exodus 1280/1260		1290–1224	
Desert Wanderings			
Joshua			
Fall of Jericho 1240/1220			
Death of Joshua to the First King Judges–1 Samuel 12			1200 BC
Joshua 1300–1190		PHILISTINES	
The Judges 1220/1200–1050/1045		Iron Age	
Samuel 1075–1035			
Samuel 1050/1045–1010			
Israel's Golden Age 1 Samuel 13–1 Kings II (1 Chronicles 10–2 Chronicles 9)			1000 BC
David 1010–970		PHILISTINES	
Solomon 970–930			
The Two Kingdoms 1 Kings 12–2 Kings 17 (2 Chronicles 10–28)			
Israel: The Northern Kingdom	*Prophets*		930 BC
930–909 Jeroboam I		1950–1550	
909–908 Nadab			
908–885 Baasha			
885–884 Elah			
884 Zimn			
884 Tibni			
884–873 Omni			
873–853 Ahab	Elijah		
853–852 Ahaziah			
852–841 Joram	Elisha		800 BC
841–813 Jehu			
813–798 Jehoahaz			
798–781 Jehoash	?Jonah		
781–753 Jeroboam II	Amos c. 761–753	Tiglath Pileser III	
753–752 Zechariah	Hosea c.750–725	of ASSYRIA 745–727	
752 Shallum			
752–741 Menahem			
741–739 Pekahiah			
739–731 Pekah			
732–722 Hoshea		Shalmaneser V	
Fall of Samaria, capital of Israel 722		of ASSYRIA 727–722	
Judah: The Southern Kingdom	*Prophets*		930 BC
930–913 Rehoboam			
913–910 Abijah			
910–869 Asa			
869–848 Jehoshaphat			
848–841 Jehoram			
841 Ahaziah			800 BC
841–835 Athaliah			
835–796 Joash			
796–767 Amaziah		Tiglath Pileser III	
792–740 Azariah (Uzziah)	Isaiah 740–701	of ASSYRIA 745–727	
739–731 Jotham		Shalmaneser V	
735–715 Ahaz	Micah 725–701	of ASSYRIA 727–722	
Last Days of Judah 1 Kings 18–25 (2 Chronicles 29–36)			
	Prophets		
715–686 Hezekiah	Isaiah/Micah	Sennacherib	
710 Siege of Jerusalem		of ASSYRIA	700 BC

686–641 Manasseh			
641–639 Amon			
640–609 Josiah	Jeremiah/?Zephaniah/ ?Nahum/?Habakkuk/?Joel Lamentations	Fall of Nineveh, capital of ASSYRIA 612	
			600 BC
609 Jehoahaz			
609–598 Jehoiakim		Nebuchadnezzar of BABYLON	
605 Daniel deported to Babylon			
597 Jehoiachin	Ezekiel 593–571		
`First' deportation to Babylon		Babylon defeats Egypt at Carchemish	
597–586 Zedekiah	Obadiah		
586 Fall of Jerusalem			
`Second' deportation to Babylon			
561 Further deportation to Babylon			

Exile and Return Ezra, Nehemiah, Esther, Haggai, Zechariah, Malachi, Isaiah 40–66

	Prophets		
538 Fall of Babylon		Cyrus of PERSIA	
538 Cyrus' Decree			
First return to Jerusalem		Artaxerxes of PERSIA	
520	Haggai 520	Darius of PERSIA	
516 Dedication of second Jerusalem temple	Zechariah 520 Malachi c.500–450		
			500 BC
458 Ezra arrives in Jerusalem			
445 Nehemiah arrives in Jerusalem			

Between the Testaments (1 & 2 Maccabees In the APOCRYPHA)

336–323 Alexander the Great of GREECE		Fall of PERSIA 331	
323 Greek Empire divided into Ptolemaic (Egypt) and Seleucid (Syria and Mesopotamia)			300 BC
328–198 Israel a Ptolemaic state			
198–166 Israel a Seleucid state		Antiochus Epiphanes, SELEUCID king 175–163	200 BC
169 Desecration of Jerusalem temple			
Maccabean Revolt			
165 Jerusalem temple rededicated			
142 Jewish Independence			
63 Pompey of Rome annexes Jerusalem			100 BC
40 BC–AD 4 Herod the Great			

Life of Jesus Matthew, Mark, Luke, John

?4 BC Birth of John the Baptist		27 BC–AD 14 Caesar Augustus of ROME	
?4 Birth of Jesus			
?AD 29 Baptism of Jesus		AD 26–36 Pontius Pilate	AD 30
AD 30/33 Crucifixion			

The Early Church Acts & Letters

	Literature		
32–35 Paul's conversion	53 Galatians	41–54 Claudius	
46–48 Paul's first missionary journey	50–51 1&2 Thessalonians		
	55–56 1&2 Corinthians		
49 Council of Jerusalem	57 Romans		
50–52 Paul's second missionary journey	50–62 James		
	61 Philemon, Colossians, Ephesians		AD 50
53–57 Paul's third missionary journey	64–67 Nero		
56–58 Paul's imprisonment			
64 Death of Paul in Rome	62 Philippians		
70 Fall of Jerusalem to Rome	54–68 1 Peter		
	63–67 1&2 Timothy, Titus		
	64–68 Mark	81–96 Domitian	AD 100
	65–68 2 Peter		
	70 Hebrews		
	70 Matthew		
	65–80 Jude		
	70–80 Luke, Acts		
	70–85 John		
	85–90 1, 2, 3, John		
	81–96 Revelation		

THE OLD TESTAMENT

GENESIS

With the book of Genesis, the curtain lifts over the stage of world history. As the book unfolds, its readers will begin to learn about the great story of God's redemption of his people. Just as an operatic overture will introduce the themes of the opera to its awaiting audience, so Genesis introduces its readers to the great themes that will dominate Scripture. We learn of God's creation of the world, and of its rebellion against him. We learn of God's decision to restore his creation to fellowship with him, and of his calling of a people to serve him and bring this good news to the ends of the earth. In short, Genesis sets the scene for the great drama of redemption that forms the subject of Scripture.

GENESIS 1:1–2:3
The First Creation Account

1:1–25 *The Beginning* The title of this book means 'origins', and it is hence no surprise that Genesis deals with the origins of humanity, and especially its relation to the God who created it. There are two accounts of the creation of the world, each told from different perspectives and with different points of focus. The first creation account in Genesis (1:1–2:3) opens with its famous declaration that God created the heavens and the earth (1:1). Everything has its origins from God. During the six days of creation, everything that is now a familiar part of the world is surveyed, and declared to owe its existence to a sovereign act of creation on the part of God.

The account of the creation of the sun, moon and stars is of special interest. For many ancient peoples, these heavenly bodies represented divine or supernatural powers, and were the object of worship and superstition. Genesis puts them firmly in their place: they are parts of God's creation, and are thus subject to his power. They should not be worshipped, and need not be feared. God has authority and dominion over them. No part of God's creation is to be worshipped. The entire creation is the work of the creator God himself, and he only is to be worshipped.

In a powerful series of affirmations, Genesis declares the goodness of God's creation (1:4, 10, 18, 21). The work of creation is brought to a close with the affirmation that it is 'very good' (1:31), perhaps referring to humanity as the climax of the work of creation, or to the completion of this work as a whole. The theme of the 'goodness' of creation is of central importance. The origins of sin are not due to God, but to the rebellion of his creation against him. The only thing that Genesis explicitly declares not to be good is Adam's loneliness (2:18). Yet even this is remedied immediately, through the creation of woman.

1:26–31 *Humanity Created in the Image of God* The creation of humanity is of special importance. The first creation account places the creation of humanity at the end of God's work of creation (1:26–27). This is the high point of creation, in which the only creature to bear the image of the creator God is introduced. The passage just cited is unusual, in that it opens with something like a fanfare, a declaration that something major is about to take place. It is clear that humanity is meant to be seen as the summit of God's creative action and power. The Hebrew word often translated as 'man' is here to be understood as

---

Did God really create everything in six days?

In the light of what the Bible says about God's nature and power, it is clear that God could easily have created the universe in six days – or six hours, six minutes or six seconds for that matter. But is that what the author of Genesis intended us to think?

The key to understanding Chapter 1 lies in its *genre* (literary category). Every genre (history, poetry, prophecy, etc.) needs reading in a particular way if we are not to misunderstand the message. But while Genesis is clearly presented as history, not myth, its very structure causes us to reflect on the genre of this introductory story. Genesis falls into ten main sections (ten being the Jewish number of completeness). Each begins with the same expression: 'This is the account of . . .' (2:4; 5:1; 6:9; 10:1; 11:10, 27; 25:12, 19; 36:1, 9; 37:2), introducing some new divine initiative. The only section not beginning this way is 1:1–2:3, the story of creation, suggesting that the author himself saw this as somehow different: as truthful in terms of its purpose, yet metaphorical in terms of its language. Its genre is not science, for science had not yet been discovered; rather, it is a powerful picture of what God and his creation are like.

Understanding the passage in this way by no means undermines the Bible's authority (and certainly should not become a test of Christian orthodoxy). Rather, it takes seriously the author's intention as he invites us to think not 'How?' but 'Wow!' Creation is no accident, but the careful work of a creator God who wants us to know him and live in his creation as his representatives.

'humanity' in general, rather than as 'a male human being' in particular.

Humanity, male and female, is created in the image or likeness of God (1:26–27). What does this mean? Two ideas may be noted as being of particular importance. First, being created in the image of God implies a likeness between God and humanity. There is the basis of a relationship here at the origins of the human race. To be made in God's image is to be created with the potential to be able to relate to God personally. Humanity alone, out of all of God's good creation, has the distinctive possibility of being able to enter into a mutual relationship with its creator.

Secondly, the image of God suggests his ownership and authority over his creation. In the ancient world, kings often set up images of themselves throughout their lands in order to assert their authority over them. (There is an important reference to this practice in the book of Daniel, which relates how King Nebuchadnezzar set up a golden image of himself at Babylon, which he commanded to be worshipped; Da 3:1–6.) Being made in the image of God is an assertion of God's ultimate authority over his creation, and a reminder that all human beings are ultimately responsible to God.

2:1–3 God Rests The first creation account concludes by declaring that God 'rested' on the seventh day (2:2). This does not mean that God was physically tired; it is

simply an affirmation that his work of creation was completed. Nothing remained to be done. This theme of 'rest' will recur throughout Scripture. Just as God rested from his work of creation, so his people should rest from their labours on the seventh day (2:3). The Sabbath-rest is thus an important reminder of God's work, and affords an opportunity to reflect on his work of creation and redemption. The image of 'rest' also becomes an image of the salvation that God offers to his people after they have served him in this life (Rev 14:13).

GENESIS 2:4–25
The Second Creation Account

2:4–7 The Breath of Life Breathed into Man The second creation account (2:4–25) takes a different form from the first account, yet makes many of the same points. The second account opens with the creation of humanity (2:7), affirming that humanity is the most important aspect of the creation. It is made absolutely clear that human life is totally dependent upon God. The reference to God breathing the 'breath of life' into humanity (2:7) is of particular importance, in that it both emphasises the God-given origins of life, and also anticipates the important life-giving role of the Holy Spirit. (The Hebrew term *ruach* can mean 'spirit', 'wind' or 'breath', pointing to the close connections between these ideas.) It is only when God breathes upon humanity that it comes to life.

2:8–17 The Garden of Eden We are now introduced to the celebrated garden of Eden (2:8), into which the man is placed. This garden is described in glowing terms (2:9–14). It is not something that humanity has created. Rather, it is something that God has created, and entrusted to humanity. Man is placed in this wonderful garden 'to work it and take care of it' (2:15). The man's responsibility is that of being a steward of God's good creation. This delegated authority extends to the animals and birds. Genesis notes that the man was allowed to give names to 'all the livestock, the birds in the sky and all the wild animals' (2:20). (In the ancient world, naming someone or something was an assertion of authority over that person or thing. Parents named their children as an expression of authority over them.) Yet humanity does not own the garden and all that is in it. Man is simply placed in it, and asked to care for it. Yet, as will become clear only too soon, the man fails totally in this responsibility.

2:18–25 Woman is Created The first Genesis creation account could give rise to the impression that male and female are simply alternative versions of humanity, without necessarily possessing any distinctive characteristics. The second Genesis creation account adds another important insight: male and female are created to complement one another: The Lord God said, 'It is not good for the man to be alone. I will make a helper suitable for him' (2:18). For some people, speaking of the female as a 'helper' may seem to imply that the female is subordinate to the male. Yet according to Genesis 1 and 2, the female was not created to *serve* the male, but to *serve with* the male. Male and female are entrusted with the task of being stewards of God's good creation. It must be

remembered that God himself is referred as a 'helper' at several points in the Old Testament!

This is an extremely important passage. Up to now, God had pronounced his creation to be good. Notice how the refrain 'and God saw that it was good' recurs in Genesis 1. But now, God declares that an aspect of his creation is not good. A humanity without distinction between the sexes is seen as inadequate. The creation of male and female thus produces a complementarity within creation. The Hebrew word translated as 'suitable' implies a correspondence between male and female. Their complementarity is an inbuilt aspect of creation. Male and female are distinct, and are meant to be distinct. Yet both bear the image of God, and both are charged with being stewards of God's creation.

This point is brought out clearly later in this chapter, when Genesis speaks of the male 'being united' to the female: 'That is why a man leaves his father and mother and is united to his wife, and they become one flesh' (2:24). This passage clearly refers to a committed personal relationship between the male and the female, and their union together in emotional and physical love. The passage explicitly uses the Hebrew words for 'male' and 'female', making it unambiguously clear that sexual differences within humanity are to be seen as a good and God-given thing.

It is often pointed out that there are similarities between the Genesis accounts of creation, and some of the creation stories of the ancient Near East. Yet an important point should be noted

here. Genesis 2 presents us with an account of the creation of *woman*, which has no real parallel in any such story.

GENESIS 3:1–24
The Fall of Humanity

3:1–5 The Snake Deceives Having given two complementary accounts of how the world came into being, Genesis now moves on to deal with the origins of sin. How could God's good creation turn into something fallen and sinful, requiring redemption? The answer is provided by Genesis 3, which gives a vivid and powerful account of the rebellion of humanity against its creator. Adam and Eve are treated as representatives of the human race as a whole, as they seek to break free from the authority of God their creator.

The story of the fall opens with the man and the woman enjoying close fellowship with God and with one another in the garden of Eden. It will not last. The figure of the snake is introduced (3:1), possibly as a symbol either of Satan or the lure of worldly wisdom and power. Part of the snake's strategy is to misrepresent God (3:1). Did God *really* say that Adam and Eve were not to eat of the fruit of that special tree? The woman's reply is also interesting; while the serpent calls God's word into question, the woman adds to it (3:3): the command not to touch the tree in the middle of the garden was not part of God's original command.

But the real power of the snake's approach lies in offering them the tantalising possibility of being 'like God' (3:5). The thought of being immortal and divine has been a constant

temptation to humanity throughout its long history. The man and the woman do not want to be told by God what is right and what is wrong. They want to make their own rules. They come to believe that God is trying to keep them in their place, by withholding vital information from them. And so they disobey their creator.

3:6–15 Man and Woman Disobey God

Once their disobedience has been discovered, both the man and the woman try to place the blame on someone else. The man blames the woman; the woman blames the serpent (3:12–13). The woman is deceived first, and subsequently deceives the man. (The passage indicates that God places the primary responsibility for the disobedience on the man, rather than the woman.) However, it is not clear how important the order of this deception is. The passage is quite clear on one point: both consented to the deception. It is quite proper to argue that they were deceived in different ways and at different times. Nevertheless, the passage makes it clear that *both* were deceived.

3:16–20 Relationships with God and Between Man and Woman Are Disrupted   The result of

man and woman's disobedience is clear. The relationship between God and humanity is disrupted. The original intimate relationship of trust is destroyed, and replaced by one of hostility and suspicion. Notice also how the original intimate and cooperative relationship between the man and woman is shattered. Mutual recrimination makes its appearance. The command to reproduce remains. Yet now, childbearing will be a painful matter (3:16). The command to tend God's creation remains. Yet this will now be a painful and tedious matter. In both cases, an existing task that is good, and part of God's intention for his creation – that is, manual labour (3:19) and the bearing of children – become difficult. Work was originally intended to be something pleasurable and enjoyable. It now becomes a burden.

A new theme, which appears to be a direct result of the fall, now makes its appearance: the domination of the female by the male. There is no explicit statement anywhere in Genesis 1 or 2 to the effect that woman was intended or created to be subordinate to man. The theme of complementarity dominates the first two chapters of Genesis. But, as a result of the fall, this situation changes drastically:

To the woman he said,

'I will make your pains in childbearing
  very severe;
with painful labour you will give birth
  to children.
Your desire will be for your husband,
and he will rule over you.'

(3:16)

As a result of the fall, man will 'rule over' woman. There are two main ways of understanding this development.

1. *Subordination (that is to say, males 'lording it over' or 'ruling' females) is a direct result of the fall.* As such, it is one aspect of the influence of sin within the world, and is to be regarded as something that is not itself God's will for his creation, and is thus to be opposed by Christians. The female has become subservient

and the male dominant as a consequence of the entry of sin into the world. Thus it is significant that Adam does not name Eve until after the fall (3:20), suggesting that the authority over her that this implies did not exist before the fall.

2. *A particular form of subordination is a direct result of the fall – namely, subordination based upon force or oppression.* According to this view, woman is naturally subordinate to man, in some sense of the word; the new element introduced by the fall is that this subordination was enforced or imposed by unacceptable means.

The second position has some points in its favour. For example, the Hebrew verb here translated as 'rule' has overtones of domination. There are Hebrew words for the right kind of subordination and the wrong kind of subordination; the word used points to the new element being not the idea of domination itself but the kind of domination that results. An additional consideration is the context in which this verse is located. We noted above that the fall made existing obligations (such as work and childbearing) a pain rather than a pleasure. By extension of this analogy, it would seem that the new element introduced by the fall is that an *existing* obligation (the subordination of female to male) is made unpleasant, through the introduction of the element of force. The kind of domination envisaged would seem to be that which exists between a master and a slave, or between a conquering power and a conquered people, where the latter is forcibly obliged to do things they would otherwise not choose to do.

3:21–24 Adam and Eve Banished from the Garden of Eden Genesis 3 depicts certain other new things as happening as a direct result of the fall. For example, the man and the woman experience *shame* at their nakedness for the first time as a result of their disobedience (3:7, 10–11). Their naked state was already in existence; the new element added is that of shame at this state. There is an easy and natural parallel between shame and subordination, by which a new element is introduced to an existing situation. Complementarity between male and female becomes polarised into domination by the male and submissiveness. The idea of 'inferiority' of women within the created order cannot be traced back to the Genesis creation accounts.

It is interesting to notice the strong parallels within Scripture concerning sin and redemption. Through the disobedience of Adam, humanity lost its fellowship with God; through the obedience of Jesus Christ, the possibility of that fellowship was restored. Eve was a disobedient woman; Mary, the mother of Jesus Christ, was obedient to God. Adam's disobedience took place in a garden (Eden); Christ's obedience to God was made evident in another garden (Gethsemane). Adam's tree of life ended up becoming a tree of death; Christ's tree of death (the cross) ended up becoming a tree of life. In all these respects, Christ's work of salvation can be seen as undoing the damage caused by the disobedience in Eden.

The overall emphasis of the passage under discussion is clear. God did not intend his creation to be spoiled by sin. Nor is God in any way the author of sin.

Sin arises directly from the abuse of the freedom and responsibility that God entrusted to humanity, as the height of his creation. The creation rebels against its loving and caring creator, and decides to go its own way – with tragic results. The essence of this original sin is wanting to be like God. It is not long before the consequences of that sin become clear. The first disobedience is soon followed by the first murder.

GENESIS 4:1–26
Cain and Abel

4:1–7 The Children of Adam and Eve The effect of sin is to disrupt the ordering of God's good creation, and cause it to begin to fall apart. Genesis 3 documented the introduction of sin, distrust and domination. Genesis 4 follows on from this by introducing further symptoms of this breakdown within creation. By the end of this chapter, we shall have encountered the introduction of jealousy, the deliberate killing of human beings, and the denial of responsibility for others.

Cain and Abel are the children of Adam and Eve. Cain's sin demonstrates the manner in which the disobedience of Adam and Eve has now become deeply rooted in human nature. It is not clear why God looks with favour on Abel, but not on Cain (4:4–5). Both bring offerings to God, as an acknowledgment that everything they possess owes its origins to God. Yet, for some reason, Cain's does not find favour. The real significance of the story lies in Cain's reaction to this development: he is angry (4:5). God affirms his own integrity and justice: if Cain does what is right, he will be

accepted. Yet if Cain refuses to do what is right, he will end up being overcome by sin (4:7). What follows confirms the wisdom of these words.

4:8–16 Cain Murders Abel Cain begins his deliberate rebellion against God by deceiving Abel (4:8), and then by attempting to deceive God (4:9). The deliberate murder of an innocent man illustrates the devastating effect of sin upon humanity. Cain tries to deny any responsibility for the deed: Why should he be responsible for his brother? Yet the deed and its motives are known to God, who condemns them in no uncertain terms (4:11–12). Cain recognises that the penalty due for this sin is death (4:14). However, God moves to limit the effects of this sin, by intervening to prevent its full and just penalty being carried out. Cain loses any right to stand in the presence of God, but is spared from death (4:15–16).

4:16–24 Cain's Descendants The catalogue of sin continues in Cain's descendants. Lamech adds polygamy to the list of sins (4:19), and boasts about killing someone who has injured him (4:23–24). He calls this taking of human life vengeance for Cain's disgrace, which can be seen as an act of further defiance against God. Lamech wants to be his own master. By doing so, he furthers the spiral of sin into which humanity has descended.

4:25–26 People Begin to Call on the Lord A note of hope is injected into this account of sin and violence. 'At that time', we are told, 'people began to call on the name of the LORD' (4:26). (The writer uses here the special personal name for God, 'the

LORD', which was revealed much later on, to Moses, Ex 3:14.) Some seem to have realised that there was no hope of salvation in human violence, power or strength. Salvation means turning to the Lord, and trusting in him.

GENESIS 5:1–32
From Adam to Noah

The following section opens with a reaffirmation that men and women are created in the likeness of God, and were blessed by him (5:1–2). In many ways, the material in this section can be seen as bridging the period between Adam's disobedience and God's decision to eradicate sin, and start all over again. The passage includes a number of points of interest. Some of the figures mentioned are described simply as having 'lived' (such as Kenan and Jared, 5:12–14, 18–20). Others, however, are described as having 'walked faithfully with God' (such as Enoch, 5:24). There is a clear distinction being made between simply living at the biological level, and living *for* God. The fact so few are singled out in this way is an important indicator of the continuing rebellion of humanity against God during this period.

The aspect of this section that attracts most comment, however, is the ages recorded for the figures. For example, Methuselah is recorded as having lived for 969 years (5:27), which means that he would have died in the year of the flood described in the following chapter. Scholars are divided as to whether these figures are to be taken literally, or whether they are symbolic. There are certainly indications that the figures may have a deeper meaning: for example, Enoch's

age of 365 years (5:23) could well be a symbol of fullness or completion, based on the 365 days in a year. However, the figures are of relatively little importance in understanding the significance of this passage, which is concerned to bring out the direct line of continuity between Adam and Noah. This latter figure is introduced at the end of this section (5:29), and will be the subject of considerable attention for the next few chapters.

GENESIS 6:1–8
Human Wickedness

6:1–7 God Is Grieved by Humanity The account of the flood opens with a powerful description of human wickedness and sin. Evil has triumphed, corrupting the goodness of God's creation to its very foundations. The meaning of the opening verses (6:1–4) is unclear. One possibility is that the passage refers to the corruption of angelic beings (a possible interpretation of the 'sons of God'); another is that it refers to the spread of intermarriage and the breakdown of traditional family structures. But whatever the explanation of these verses, its spiritual meaning is unambiguous: God's creation is in ruins.

The paradox of all this is that human beings were created in the image of God, and thus with the freedom and ability to love and respect God. Yet this God-given freedom is abused, as human beings turn against their creator. Both in their acts and in the underlying motivation (6:5), humanity has fallen a willing victim to evil. With remarkable candour, the writer of this section describes God's reaction to this situation. He regrets

having created humanity. Painful and distressing though this clearly is to him, God feels that he has to bring his creation to an end (6:7).

6:8 Noah At the end of this account of human wickedness a small word intervenes: 'but' (6:8). The use of 'but' in Scripture can often be dramatic, signalling a new development that opens the way to something that would otherwise be but a dream. And here we find exactly this kind of thing. 'But Noah found favour in the eyes of the LORD.' God's forlorn search for a righteous human being, which will find its climax when he himself provides that righteous person in Jesus Christ, focuses on Noah, who now becomes a sign of hope and redemption.

GENESIS 6:9–8:22
The Flood

Many ancient Near Eastern civilisations knew of a flood at the dawn of civilisation. What is distinctive about the Genesis account of the flood is its interpretation. The flood is God's means of purging sinful humanity from the face of his earth. It is to cleanse his creation from the stain of human evil and sin (6:11–12). Many early Christian writers saw a powerful parallel between the flood and baptism: just as the flood cleansed the world of its sin, so baptism symbolises the cleansing of human sin through the blood of Christ.

6:9–17 Noah Instructed to Build an Ark Noah is identified as a 'righteous man, blameless among the people of his time, and he walked faithfully with God' (6:9).

It is clear that he is not contaminated by the wickedness and sin of the world. There is an important biblical principle here: the obedience of one righteous person can be the means of salvation of others. The issue at stake is finding that righteous person – or, if none can be found, providing one. Noah is the means of salvation of the human race. Noah is directed to construct an ark, which is to bear him and his family, along with the male and female of every living creature, to safety. As the account of the flood progresses, additional points emerge. For example, Noah is ordered to take on board 'seven of every kind of clean animal' (7:2) – those that will be offered as sacrifices in the future. Noah obeys (6:22; 7:5).

6:18–7:10 God's Covenant with Noah A major theme of importance should not be overlooked here. God promises to establish a covenant with Noah (6:18). Here we encounter a biblical theme that will resonate throughout Scripture, and reach its climax in Jesus Christ. A covenant is basically a set of promises made by God, which requires an appropriate response of trust and obedience on the part of those with whom the covenant is established.

7:11–24 The Flood Waters Rise The flood comes, as it rains for 'forty days' (7:17). The phrase 'forty days and forty nights' is often found linked in Scripture with events of major importance in relation to God's redemption of humanity – such as the period of Moses' encounter with God (Dt 9:11), and Christ's temptation in the wilderness (Mt 4:1–11). The flood continues for a further 150 days after the

rains end (7:24). Everything and everyone is wiped out, except the ark and its occupants. (Interestingly, no mention is made of any form of aquatic life: it is clearly assumed that these can and should survive, without the need for special assistance.)

Was the whole world really flooded?

Floods across the world in recent years have shown how suddenly such events can occur and how devastating their results can be. The possibility of a widespread flood, as in Noah's story, is suddenly all the more understandable; and the occurrence of flood stories in other ancient civilisations suggests there was a common folk memory of such an event.

After God had gathered Noah, his family and pairs of animals into the ark, we read that 'all the springs of the great deep burst forth, and the floodgates of the heavens were opened' (7:11). The rain fell for 40 days and the flood lasted 150 days in all, covering 'all the high mountains under the entire heavens' (7:19).

Does this demand, therefore, that we believe the whole earth was flooded, a highly improbable event? At first sight, it seems the author felt the whole earth was indeed covered; and so it was, from his point of view. After all, the known world in those days was simply what we now call the Middle East. So we do not need to imagine a global flood covering the world's highest mountains, something not only scientifically improbable (if not impossible), but simply not required by the story. Much more likely is a massive regional flood in the Middle East (the whole earth of those days), like that proposed by a father of modern archaeology, Sir Leonard Woolley. References to the high mountains being 'covered' (though the Hebrew word can also mean 'drenched') are then a dramatic way of saying that nothing (except what was in the ark) escaped. Assuming that humanity had not yet spread beyond this region, then the flood was geographically limited but anthropologically universal, thus serving God's purpose of making a new beginning.

8:1–22 The End of the Flood As the flood ends, God remembers Noah (8:1). The Hebrew original of this expression conveys far more than just mentally recalling someone or something. It means acting in such a way as to express care and concern. This beautiful phrase sums up God's attitude towards his people. They may forget about God, but he remembers them. Their faithlessness does not cancel his faithfulness. In his wrath, God remembers his mercy, and his covenant with those who remain faithful to him. And so the floodwaters begin to recede, and hope dawns once more. God's judgment has been executed; now the process of reconstruction may begin.

When it is clear that the floodwaters have receded, God commands Noah and the entire company of occupants of the ark to come out. They are told to go and multiply on the earth – a renewal of the creation commandment (1:22). The theme of the renewal of creation emerges as important at this point. There are to

be no more floods (8:21–22). If sin emerges once more as a threat to his creation, God will deal with it in another manner.

GENESIS 9:1–29
God's Covenant with Noah

9:1–17 The Covenant and Its Sign The covenant that God had promised to establish with Noah is now formally pledged. (As becomes clear later, the covenant is actually made with all life on the earth (9:17), and not just Noah and his family.) God commands Noah and his sons to increase, and fill the earth (9:1, 7). Everything is to be entrusted to the faithful remnant of humanity (9:3). The sacredness of human life is affirmed (9:5–6). Then the covenant is proclaimed: never again will there be a flood that will destroy the earth. As a sign of this covenant, God set his rainbow in the clouds (9:13). The idea of a covenant sign is of major importance: it brings to mind God's compassion for his people, his promises towards them and the obligations the covenant places upon them.

9:18–29 Noah's Sin It might be thought that the account of Noah could end happily at this point. Noah has been established as a righteous and obedient human being, through whose righteousness a faithful remnant was preserved. Yet human weakness begins to become apparent almost immediately. Noah plants a vineyard, and becomes drunk on the wine it produced (9:20–21). In this story, the potential weakness of human nature to sin is powerfully exposed. What will happen when other forms of temptation come the way of Noah and his descendants? Even as the account of Noah's triumph reaches its conclusion, we are being forewarned that sin continues to crouch at the door (4:7), awaiting opportunities to master those who foolishly believe they can master sin.

GENESIS 10:1–32
From Noah to Babel

The command to Noah and his descendants was simple: go forth and multiply. The following section of Genesis provides details of how that command was fulfilled. The precise details of the descendants of Noah are not of vital importance to an understanding of the central themes of Genesis. A detailed examination of the information provided indicates that the descendants of Noah spread out over a wide geographical area, probably embracing the eastern Mediterranean region, and extending as far east as the Persian Gulf and the Caspian Sea.

GENESIS 11:1–32
The Tower of Babel

11:1–5 A City and Tower Are Built The repopulation of the world leads to a renewed confidence on the part of humanity. They all speak the same language, and are able to collaborate on various ventures. Sin begins to express itself in their actions. Once more, the same basic human instincts emerge. There is a desire to become famous, to achieve immortality, and to gain total security (11:4). And these aspirations lead to the building of a city on the plain

of Shinar (a term used to refer to what was later known as Babylonia. There is a pun here between the Hebrew word for 'Babylon' (*Babel*) and the Hebrew word for 'to confuse', which sound like each other). The 'tower' in question would probably have taken the form typical of the region, often referred to as a *ziggurat*, consisting of a square base with a series of stepped layers built on top. It was a symbol of defiance. Here was what humanity could do without God. We can even reach heaven by ourselves!

11:6–9 God Confuses Their Language and Scatters the People Once more, sin threatens to frustrate God's purposes for his creation. The tower is a potent symbol of human pride and rebellion against God. Yet God has promised never to destroy the world again. To restrain the power of sin, God scatters the people, and confuses their languages. The collective power of sin is reduced by the simple expedient of limiting the sinful human ability to collude together: 'Let us go down and confuse their language' (11:7). The 'royal we' of this phrase is an expression of authority and dominion, in the face of this human attempt at rebellion against God, and a refusal to accept the limitations placed upon humanity in the created order.

11:10–32 From Shem to Abram After the Babel episode, we are taken back to consider the further descendants of Noah through his son, Shem. The importance of this account lies primarily in the fact that it introduces us to a man named Abram, who had settled in the town of Harran, about 400 kilometres west of Nineveh. Abram was married to Sarai (later to be renamed Sarah, 17:15), who was barren (11:27–30). With these bare details, we are introduced to the first patriarch, later to be renamed Abraham (17:5) who is a central figure in the history of Israel. (The term 'patriarch' is used to refer to Abram, Isaac and Jacob, who are seen as being the great ancestors of the people of Israel.)

GENESIS 12:1–20
The Call of Abram

12:1–9 Abram Called to Go to Canaan Without any reason being given, Abram is called to leave Harran, and go to Canaan. The call of Abram is linked to a promise: that God will make him into a great nation, through whom all the nations on earth will be blessed (12:2–3). Although no explanation of this call was given, Abram clearly feels that he can and should trust and obey this call. So he and his extended household set out for the land of Canaan (12:4–5).

They eventually arrive at Shechem, an important site in the central region of Canaan. At this time, Canaan was the centre of various pagan religious cults. Yet Abram does not worship any of the local gods. Instead, he builds an altar to the Lord in the region of Bethel, and calls upon his name (12:8), in response to the Lord's promise that the region will belong to his descendants.

12:10–20 Abram in Egypt Abram does not settle in the region of Canaan. He continues his wanderings, moving further south and west, as he passes through the Negev into Egypt. A famine had settled over Canaan; Egypt, however, continued to enjoy fertility, on account

of the annual flooding of the river Nile, which ensured fertile and moist land in the neighbourhood of its banks. On account of local customs that are not entirely clear, Abram asks his wife to pose as his sister. The Egyptian monarch, invariably referred to by the royal title of Pharaoh (literally meaning 'a great house'), is attracted to Sarai and treats Abram kindly as a result (12:14–16). On discovering that Sarai is actually Abram's wife, Pharaoh expels the entire household from Egypt (12:20) back to Canaan.

GENESIS 13:1–14:24
The Further History of Abram

13:1–18 Abram and Lot Separate By the time Abram leaves Egypt, he has become quite wealthy. This is especially evident from the references to his large holdings of livestock (13:2). The large number of animals involved lead to friction with his colleague Lot over grazing rights. Lot was introduced earlier in the narrative, and identified as the son of Haran, one of Abram's brothers (11:27). Lot and Abram were thus relatives (13:8). Perhaps it was inevitable that they should go their separate ways. Lot chooses to settle near the cities of the plain, already noted for their sinful behaviour (13:10–13). Abram, however, receives a fresh assurance from the Lord that the land about him will be his inheritance. Thus reassured, he pitches his tents in the area. Once more, Abram responds by building an altar to the Lord, this time at Hebron (13:18).

14:1–24 Abram Rescues Lot While God reassures Abram, Lot finds himself in difficulty. A series of shifting alliances among local kings leads to a major confrontation taking place in the region in which he has settled (14:1–11). In the course of their abortive military action against neighbouring kings, Sodom and Gomorrah and their allies are defeated, and their goods seized and carried off. Lot, who is living in Sodom at this time (14:12), is also taken captive. Abram, learning of the capture of his relative, sets off in pursuit with 318 men, and manages to defeat Lot's captors and release him (14:13–16).

Abram's victory attracts considerable attention, most notably from Melchizedek, who was probably a Canaanite king-priest (14:18–20). Melchizedek probably intended his 'God most high' to refer to a local Canaanite deity. Abram, however, takes it as a reference to the Lord (14:22), and refuses to do anything that might have placed him under an obligation to anyone else.

GENESIS 15:1–17:27
God's Covenant with Abram

15:1–21 The Covenant Abram's act of obedience is immediately followed by God's establishing a covenant with him and his descendants, which goes beyond that established earlier with Noah. Abram is still childless, and has designated his servant Eliezer (15:2) as his legal heir. God, however, promises that Abram will have a son, and that this son will be his heir (15:4). In one of the most poignant moments in this book, God leads Abram outside his tent, and asks him to contemplate the starry heavens. Abram's descendants, he promises, will be as numerous as those stars (15:5). Abram trusts God, and puts his faith in this astonishing promise

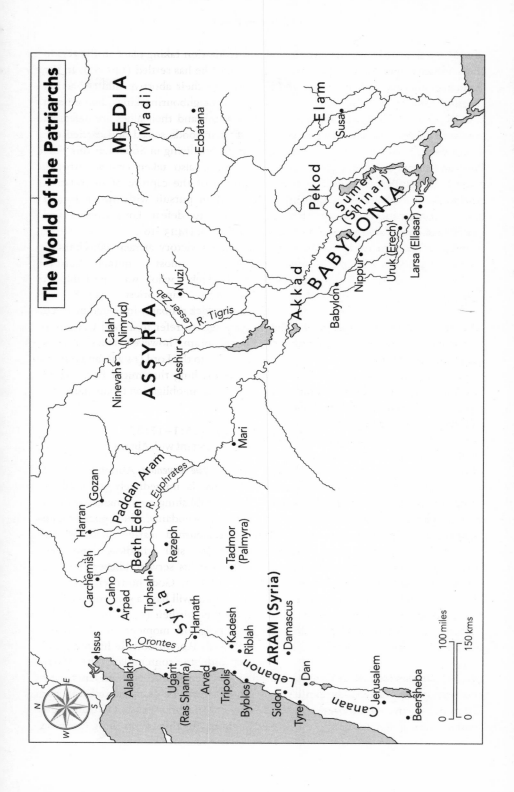

The World of the Patriarchs

MEDIA
(Madi)

Ecbatana

Elam

Susa

Pekod

ASSYRIA

Nuzi

Lesser Zab

R. Tigris

Sumer
(Shinar)

BABYLONIA

Akkad

Calah
(Nimrud)

Ninevah

Asshur

Babylon

Nippur

Uruk (Erech)

Larsa (Ellasar)

Ur

Mari

Gozan

Harran

Paddan Aram

Beth Eden

R. Euphrates

Carchemish

Calno

Arpad

Tiphsah

Rezeph

Tadmor
(Palmyra)

Syria

Hamath

Kadesh

Riblah

ARAM (Syria)

Damascus

Issus

R. Orontes

Alalakh

Ugarit
(Ras Shamra)

Arvad

Tripolis

Byblos

Sidon

Lebanon

Tyre

Dan

Canaan

Jerusalem

Beersheba

N
E
S
W

0   100 miles

0   150 kms

(15:6). Faith is thus seen as the natural and proper response to God's promises, which counts as righteousness in the sight of God.

The promise of a son is followed by the reassurance that Abram will possess the land about him (15:7). Abram asks for reassurance on this point (15:8), and is granted a vision of the future of his people, including the coming exile in Egypt (15:9–16). God then marks the covenant in a variety of ways that, though perhaps strange to modern readers, would have been recognised at the time as involving the most solemn and binding oaths. God's covenant with Abram is for real (15:18), and may be totally relied upon. The covenant will be confirmed and amplified presently. The narrative now switches to the women in Abram's life.

16:1–16 Hagar and Ishmael Sarai continues to be childless (16:1). Following an ancient Near Eastern custom, she suggests to Abram that he ought to sleep with Hagar, a slave whom they may have acquired during their period in Egypt. Abram concurs, and Hagar becomes pregnant (16:2–4). A certain degree of personal hostility now develops between Hagar and Sarai, with the result that Hagar leaves home. However, God speaks to her in a vision, and reassures her of her future. Her son is to be called Ishmael (16:11), and will be the fulfilment of God's promise to Abram. Yet, as becomes clear in the following chapter, God has intentions for Sarai as well.

17:1–27 The Covenant of Circumcision The next major section introduces the next stage of the covenant between God and Abram. The first stage of this covenant

involved the promise of land. Now God affirms that he will be the God of both Abram and his descendants (17:7). As a token of this new relationship, Abram's name is formally altered to Abraham (17:5), just as Sarai is now to be known as Sarah (17:15). Both Abraham and Sarah will be blessed by God, and, despite their advanced years, they will have a son, who is to be called Isaac (17:16–20). God's covenant with Abraham's successors will be through Isaac, not Ishmael (17:19–21). This clear statement that Ishmael is not the child of the promise is, however, tempered by God's evident kindness and mercy towards both Hagar and Ishmael.

The covenant that God now makes with Abraham and Sarah is conditional. Its privileges and benefits are linked with certain obligations, which must be observed if the covenant is to remain in force. Its central feature is circumcision, which is the external sign of this covenant (17:9–14). Circumcision (which is basically the removal of the foreskin of the penis) is to be restricted to male children, and is regarded as an essential sign of being a member of the covenant people of God. Abraham is obedient to this demand, and arranges for himself, his son Ishmael and all the males within his household to be circumcised, as a sign of their new relationship with God (17:23–27).

GENESIS 18:1–19:38
Sodom and Gomorrah

18:1–15 The Three Visitors The next section opens with an account of a visit to Abraham by the Lord, in the form of three visitors who turn out to be the Lord and two angels. (The visit is seen by many commentators as an early hint at

the Christian doctrine of the Trinity.) Although he has no idea who they are, Abraham looks after his visitors with traditional Near Eastern courtesy, ensuring that their feet are washed, and that they are provided with food and drink. The purpose of the visit is to reassure Abraham that his wife Sarah will indeed have a son. Sarah, who knows that both she and her husband are getting old, finds this amusing. But the Lord is adamant: 'Is anything too hard for the LORD?' (18:14).

18:16–33 Abraham Pleads for Sodom As the visitors prepare to leave, they look down on the city of Sodom, notorious for its sinfulness (18:16–22). It is clear that the city is marked for destruction. However, as a matter of justice, two of the three visitors will go on to the city to find out for themselves whether things really are that bad. In the dialogue between Abraham and the Lord that follows (18:23–33), the theme of the preservation of the righteous emerges as being of major importance. The Lord will spare a people for the sake of the righteous remnant with it. Abraham is convinced that God, the Judge of all the earth, is righteous (18:25), and finds this confirmed in God's repeated affirmation that the presence of a small number of righteous people, even in a city as notoriously sinful as Sodom, will ensure its preservation.

What does the Bible say about sexuality?

The Bible's teaching about sexuality is rooted in the creation stories where humanity is blessed by both distinction and complementarity between the sexes. When it speaks of Adam and Eve 'becoming one flesh' (2:24), this isn't a coy way of describing sex, but refers to the ultimate expression of unity and commitment between a man and woman. Any discussion about sexuality in the Bible comes against this background and its declaration that the highest form of relationship is found in one man's commitment to one woman for life. Anything less or other than this – sex before marriage (fornication), sex outside marriage (adultery), and sex instead of marriage (homosexual practice) – is seen as failing to find God's best.

It is against this background that neither the Old nor the New Testament offers any support for homosexual behaviour; indeed, such practices are condemned in both (19:5–11; Lev 18:22; Jdg 19:22–30; Ro 1:24–27; 1Co 6:9–11; 1Ti 1:8–11). The behaviour of Sodom's men, for example, though culturally acceptable – 'all the men from every part of the city' (v.4) were involved – was offensive to both Lot, who came from a different culture and who saw their behaviour as 'wicked' (v.7), and to God, whose angels struck them temporarily blind (v.11). Their desire simply to 'have sex' (v.5) fell far short of God's intention.

However, while portrayed as unacceptable to God, the Bible seems to see homosexuality as no worse than greed or lying, among which it is often simply included in lists of sins (e.g., 1Co 6:9–10). Ultimately, the Christian gospel offers acceptance rather than rejection and hope rather than condemnation.

19:1–29 Sodom and Gomorrah Destroyed
The narrative then moves to Sodom itself. Abraham's relative Lot is sitting in the gate of the city when the angels arrive. This suggests that he was a figure of some importance within the city, as the city gate was the traditional location for the dispensing of justice and handling of local issues. Lot takes them to his house, and offers them the same traditional hospitality as had earlier been shown by Abraham (19:2–3). The visitors then find that their fears about Sodom are confirmed, as they nearly become the victims of homosexual rape (19:4–11). What follows brings out clearly the Lord's concern for the safety of the righteous. Lot and his family are bundled out of Sodom to escape its destruction, and find safety in the nearby town of Zoar (19:20–22), which is spared on account of their presence. The story of Lot's wife looking back seems to have become proverbial, and is even referred to by Jesus Christ himself (Lk 17:32).

19:30–38 Lot's Daughters It soon becomes clear that Lot and his relatives are as weak and fallible as anyone else. The story of how Lot's daughters seduced their father on two successive nights (19:30–38) in order to ensure the continuation of the family line is a forceful reminder of the continuing presence of sin in the world, and the temptations to which God's people are prone.

GENESIS 20:1–25:11
The Later Life and Death of Abraham

20:1–18 Abraham and Abimelek The following section of Genesis focuses on the later period of Abraham's life. The account of Abraham's meeting with Abimelek (20:1–17, and further developed at 21:22–32) is followed by a brief account of the fulfilment of God's promise to Abraham and Sarah: Isaac is born (21:1–7). In response to God's faithfulness, Abraham circumcises his son. Just as God has been faithful to his covenant, so Abraham honours his side of that same covenant. The birth of Isaac leads to growing alienation between Sarah and Hagar, with the result that Hagar and her son Ishmael leave Abraham's home (21:8–21). Yet despite Sarah's hostility towards them, they continue to be watched over and cared for by God.

22:1–24 Abraham Tested After the birth of Isaac, Abraham's commitment to God is put to the test in one of the most famous incidents in the Old Testament. God requires Abraham to take his son Isaac, and sacrifice him as an act of obedience. Earlier, Abraham had declared his faith that the Judge of all the earth would do right: this faith is now put to the test. The story is powerful, moving and disturbing, with strong parallels to the final days of Christ's life. For example, Isaac carries the wood for his own burnt offering (22:6), just as Christ carried his own cross to the place of crucifixion. Abraham is about to sacrifice his son, when he is prevented from doing so. His trust in and obedience to God are now beyond doubt. As Abraham looks around, he notices a ram caught in some thorns (22:13). This ram is then offered as a sacrifice to God in place of Isaac. Christians can hardly read this passage without being reminded of the way in which Jesus Christ as the Lamb of God

was crowned with thorns, and offered himself as a sacrifice to God in the place of sinful humanity (Mk 15:17; Jn 1:29). As a result of Abraham's obedience, God confirms his promises to him. Abraham's descendants will be as numerous as the stars of the sky and the grains of sand on the seashore (22:17). The news of the birth of sons to Abraham's brother Nahor (22:20–23) can be seen as the beginning of the fulfilment of this promise.

23:1–20 The Death of Sarah Sarah and Abraham are now both very old. Sarah dies in the region of Canaan occupied by Hittites at the time. Abraham, who as a 'foreigner and stranger' had no land rights, buys some land from the Hittites as a burial site for his wife. Sarah is finally laid to rest in a cave in a field in Canaan.

24:1–25:11 Isaac and Rebekah; Abraham's Death Aware that his own death cannot be far away, Abraham begins to make arrangements for his son Isaac to take a wife. He despatches the 'senior servant in his household' (possibly Eliezer of Damascus, whom he had earlier considered as his heir, prior to the birth of Isaac) to find a suitable woman. Although they are currently living in Canaan, Abraham does not want Isaac to marry a Canaanite woman, with all the dangers of syncretism that would imply – see on Ezr 9:1–10:44. He wishes him to marry someone from his own home region, and so sends his servant to this region (24:1–11). While preparing to water his camels outside the town of Nahor, the servant meets Rebekah (24:15), who has come to draw water for her family. (This name is sometimes spelled 'Rebecca'.) Convinced that this is the right person, the servant arranges for himself to be introduced to her family (which includes her brother Laban), identifies himself as Abraham's servant and explains why he believes God has guided him in this matter (24:12–49). Both Rebekah and her family are persuaded. Rebekah and her attendants prepare for the long journey to Canaan with Abraham's servant. Finally, Isaac and Rebekah are married (24:50–67). Shortly afterwards, Abraham himself dies, and is buried with Sarah at the cave near Hebron (25:1–11). The era of the first patriarch has ended.

GENESIS 25:12–28:9
Isaac and His Sons

25:12–34 Ishmael's Sons and Isaac's Sons, Jacob and Esau After listing the sons of Ishmael (25:12–18), the following section focuses on the history of Isaac. Initially, Rebekah is childless; after Isaac prays for her, she conceives, and gives birth to twin boys. The first to be born is Esau, so called on account of his hairy appearance; the second is called Jacob, as he emerges from the womb clinging to his brother's heel. As the first to be born, Esau gains the privilege of the birthright – the right to inherit Isaac's property on his death. However, he evidently regards this as being of little importance, and, in a moment of hunger, gives it to Jacob in exchange for a bowl of red lentil stew (25:31–34).

26:1–33 God Renews His Covenant with Isaac During a famine in the following years, the Lord renews his covenant with Isaac (26:1–6), confirming that the same

promises made to Abraham were now extended to Isaac. The same promise is confirmed once more soon afterwards (26:24), after Isaac settles in the Valley of Gerar.

26:34–27:40 Jacob Gets Isaac's Blessing

Relations between Esau and his parents deteriorate. At the age of 40 he marries two Hittite women (26:34); a third wife is mentioned later (28:9). This action is the source of much concern to Isaac and Rebekah; later, they would try to prevent Jacob from marrying a Hittite or Canaanite woman, insisting that he marry someone from their own home region (27:46–28:2). Nevertheless, Esau is the firstborn, and thus has certain rights, including the right to receive his father's blessing. As Isaac's sight begins to fail him, he feels the need to bless Esau. Rebekah, however, is disgusted with Esau, and decides that Jacob will seize this privilege, by disguising himself in such a way as to be taken for Esau. Isaac is deceived, and blesses Jacob (27:5–29). On Esau's return from hunting, the deception is uncovered. Relations between the two brothers become severely strained (27:30–46).

Did God approve of Jacob's cheating?

Jacob's early life was full of deception and cheating. He opportunistically tricked his brother Esau out of his inheritance (25:27–34) and even deceived his father by disguising himself as Esau to get his irrevocable blessing of succession (27:1–40). Perhaps surprisingly this did not stop God from appearing to Jacob and reaffirming to him the promises made to his ancestor Abraham (28:10–22).

Are we therefore to assume that God approved of Jacob's trickery, or at least was prepared to turn a blind eye to it, since it served his purpose? Not at all, as the story goes on to show, for Jacob's deceitfulness caught up with him. Having cheated others, he found himself cheated by Laban, who tricked him into marrying Leah as well as Rachel (29:15–30) and tried to manipulate an agreement about their flocks (30:25–36). All this highlights that God's purpose does not depend on how good we are but on how faithful he is, not on our works but his grace (see Ro 9:10–16). Only after a powerful encounter with God did Jacob's life begin to change (32:22–32).

What this underlines is that individual Bible stories do not always contain the moral within themselves; we must often read on and see the bigger story to get the point. By contrast, the legal and prophetic sections of the Bible are more overt. For example, the eighth commandment specifically commands us not to 'steal' (the Hebrew word also means stealing in the sense of cheating someone out of something) and the Jewish law forbids cheating in business (e.g., Lev 19:35–36; Dt 25:13–16), a repeated theme of Proverbs (e.g., Pr 11:1; 20:10) and the prophets (e.g., Am 8:4–8). The New Testament too condemns outright any sort of cheating (e.g., 1Co 6:7–8; 1Th 4:6; Jas 5:4).

27:41–28:9 Jacob Flees to Laban Relations between Isaac and Jacob also deteriorate. Perhaps partly with a view to getting him away from home for a while, Isaac sends Jacob off to Rebekah's home region of Paddan Aram, with instructions to find a wife from among the daughters of Laban, Rebekah's brother (28:1–5). Rebekah has already advised him to go and stay with her brother, to avoid Esau until his anger towards his younger brother has subsided (27:42–45). Her advice is to stay 'for a while' until things calm down. In the event, Jacob stays there for twenty years (seven years for Leah, seven for Rachel, and six for livestock). The narrative now focuses on Jacob, who emerges as a major figure in his own right.

GENESIS 28:10–36:40
Jacob

28:10–22 Jacob's Dream at Bethel So Jacob sets out for Harran, Abraham's home town. During the course of this journey, he pauses at a place hitherto known as Luz, but which would from then on be known as Bethel. While sleeping, Jacob dreams of a 'stairway' (not a runged wooden ladder, as is sometimes suggested, but probably a brick staircase), on which angels are ascending and descending. In the course of this dream, the Lord extends the covenant he made with Abraham and Isaac to Jacob, promising him land and descendants (28:10–22). Despite all his deceptions, God is prepared to bless Jacob. Thus assured of the Lord's blessing, Jacob continues on his journey to Harran.

29:1–25 Jacob in Paddan Aram On arriving in the region, Jacob asks if anyone knows Laban. Laban is clearly well known in the region. However, the first member of Laban's family whom Jacob meets is the younger and more beautiful of Laban's two daughters, Rachel (29:1–12). After being welcomed into Laban's household, Jacob begins to work to earn his keep. Laban asks him how much he would like as wages. Jacob replies that he would like Rachel's hand in marriage, in return for seven years' work (29:18). Laban consents, but clearly has other plans. On the night of Jacob's wedding feast, Laban gives him his older daughter Leah in place of Rachel. Perhaps it was very dark, perhaps large quantities of wine flowed at the wedding feast. At any rate, Jacob does not notice the substitution. He sleeps with her, and discovers the deception only in the morning (29:25). There is a subtle irony here: having left a trail of deception behind him in Canaan, Jacob himself is now well and truly deceived. As the events recorded later concerning the possession of flocks makes clear (30:25–43), both Laban and Jacob will continue to try to deceive each other.

29:26–30:24 Jacob Marries Rachel and Has Children Laban informs Jacob that he can have Rachel in return for a further seven years of work. The text makes it clear (29:28–30) that Jacob is not required to wait a further seven years before being given Rachel; he is allowed to sleep with her immediately, in return for a promise of seven years of further work. The fact that Jacob has two wives simultaneously is not regarded as unusual or unacceptable. It is only when God establishes his covenant with Moses at Sinai that monogamy becomes the norm for his people. Through Leah, Jacob has a

series of sons; Rachel, however, is barren. By sleeping with Rachel's servant (and later with Leah's, when Leah becomes too old to bear children), Jacob fathers several more sons (30:1–21). Then finally, Rachel conceives, and bears a son. His name is Joseph (30:24).

30:25–31:21 Jacob Flees from Laban After an incident involving mutual deception over flocks (30:25–43), tensions develop between Laban and his family and Jacob. Jacob is obliged to flee from Laban (31:1–55), taking his wives, children and livestock with him. They will return to Isaac. Jacob continues to deceive Laban, by failing to tell him of his intentions (31:20). Interestingly, without Jacob's knowledge, Rachel takes Laban's household gods with her (31:19), possibly reflecting her continuing pagan beliefs, or a belief that the possession of these items would deter Laban from taking lethal action against them.

31:22–55 Laban Pursues Jacob Laban, angry that his daughters and grandchildren have been taken away from him without his knowledge or permission, pursues Jacob and his party, and eventually catches up with them. Yet Laban, despite being a pagan, has a dream in which God tells him not to harm Jacob (31:24). However, he is angry over the theft of his household gods, and demands to have them returned. Jacob, ignorant of Rachel's theft, suggests that they search for them. Rachel, who has concealed the gods in her camel's saddle, tells Laban that she cannot move on account of her period. As a result, the gods remain undetected. After some explanation on the part of Jacob, he and Laban agree to

patch up their differences. Jacob swears that he will take care of Rachel, Leah and their children, and that he will have no more wives. They part reconciled, Laban to return home, and Jacob to visit his brother Esau, who has settled in the region of Edom.

32:1–33:20 Jacob Prepares to Meet Esau Jacob sends messengers to Esau to let him know of their arrival; the messengers duly report back that Esau is on his way to meet them, with 400 men. Fearing the worst, Jacob divides his party into two groups, hoping that one might survive any ensuing attack (32:1–21). As he waits to meet Esau, Jacob has a night meeting with an angel at Peniel (32:22–32). For the first time, the name 'Israel' is used to refer to Jacob, and ultimately to his descendants. The angel refuses to disclose his own name; only at Sinai will God allow his name to be known to Moses. At this stage, Israel is not ready to learn more of the Lord who has called her into being. Finally, Jacob and Esau meet (33:1–20). They have not seen each other for twenty years, and parted on very hostile terms. Esau, however, is overjoyed to see his brother once more (33:4). When they part once more, it is as friends.

34:1–35:15 Jacob Returns to Bethel Trouble now arises on a different front. Dinah, Jacob's daughter by Leah, is raped by Shechem, a local ruler. Jacob and his family are outraged. Two of Jacob's sons suggest that if Shechem and his people agree to be circumcised (a very painful process), they will allow Dinah to marry him, and they will settle in the region. While the men are recovering from the

pain of their circumcision and incapable of resistance, Simeon and Levi put them to the sword, and plunder their possessions (34:1–29). Jacob is appalled, both at the deception and its possible implications. It will no longer be safe for them to live in the region. So they begin the move to Bethel, scene of Jacob's earlier dream, at which the Lord once more reaffirms his commitment to Jacob and his descendants (34:30–35:15).

35:16–36:43 The Deaths of Rachel and Isaac At this stage, Jacob has eleven sons: six sons by Leah, two by Rachel's servant Bilhah, two by Leah's servant Zilpah, and one – Joseph – by Rachel (for the details, see 35:23–26). In the final stages of their journey to the city of Ephrath (also known as Bethlehem), Rachel dies while giving birth to another son, whom Jacob names Benjamin (35:16–18). Rachel is buried near Bethlehem and Jacob returns to the home of his father Isaac near Hebron (35:27–29). Finally, Isaac himself dies, and is buried in the family tomb in the field near Machpelah (see 49:29–32). After listing the various descendants of Esau, and the rulers of the land of Edom in which Esau resided (36:1–43), the narrative now shifts decisively to focus on one of Jacob's twelve sons: Joseph.

GENESIS 37:1–50:26
Joseph

37:1–38:30 Joseph Sold by His Brothers Joseph was Jacob's son by Rachel, whom Jacob had loved. As a result, he seems to have been especially fond of this son, to the intense irritation of his other sons (37:1–4). Joseph himself does little to help his brothers to like him: his dreams,

which suggest that they are inferior to him, merely anger them further (37:5–11). Eventually, they can bear him no longer, and sell him as a slave to a group of passing Midianite traders. Having dipped Joseph's richly ornamented coat in goat's blood, they bring it to Jacob. He concludes that his son has been killed by a wild animal (37:12–35). In fact, Joseph has been sold into slavery in Egypt (37:36). (At this point, the narrative about Joseph is interrupted, to give an account of the marriage of Jacob's son Judah to a Canaanite woman, and his subsequent involvement with his daughter-in-law Tamar: 38:1–30.)

39:1–23 Joseph and Potiphar's Wife The story of Joseph now resumes. Joseph is now a slave in the household of Potiphar, one of Pharaoh's senior officials. God grants Joseph success in his responsibilities, with the result that he gains advancement within the house (39:1–6). However, his attractive features soon get him into trouble with Potiphar's wife, who, failing to seduce him, accuses him of attempted rape (39:7–18). As a result, he is thrown into prison. Yet God remains with Joseph, even in this seemingly hopeless situation (39:20–23).

40:1–23 The Cupbearer and the Baker Joseph is soon joined in prison by two men from Pharaoh's household, a cupbearer and a baker. Each has dreams, which they are unable to interpret. Joseph interprets the former's dream as a prophecy of restoration, and the latter's as a prophecy of condemnation. He asks the cupbearer to remember him when he is restored to his post. In due course, the cupbearer is

restored to Pharaoh's favour, and the baker executed. Yet the cupbearer fails to remember Joseph, who continues to languish in prison, forgotten by all except God.

41:1–57 Pharaoh's Dreams; Joseph in Charge of Egypt Now Pharaoh himself begins to dream, and finds that there is no one who can give a satisfactory interpretation of his dreams. Finally, the cupbearer remembers Joseph, who is summoned from prison, and proves able to interpret the dreams. There will be seven years of rich harvest, followed by seven years of famine. All this has been foretold by God, who has decided that this will take place. Convinced that God has singled out Joseph for this task, Pharaoh places him in charge of Egypt's preparations for the forthcoming famine. As a result, while other nations around languish under a severe famine, Egypt suffers no shortage of food.

42:1–38 Joseph's Brothers Go to Egypt The famine seems to have been especially severe in Canaan. Jacob and his household are affected. Eventually Jacob, hearing that there is grain in Egypt, sends all his sons except Benjamin, Rachel's second son, to buy grain there. On their arrival in Egypt, Joseph recognises them, accuses them of spying, and throws them in prison (42:1–17). After three days, he sets them free, on condition that they return with their youngest brother Benjamin. However, Jacob refuses to allow Benjamin to travel to Egypt. It is too dangerous. He has already lost one of Rachel's two sons, and has no desire to lose the other as well (42:18–38).

43:1–44:34 The Second Journey to Egypt; the Silver Cup The famine persists, and Jacob and his household become dangerously short of food. Finally, the decision is taken: they will have to return to Egypt for more food. This time, Benjamin will have to travel with them (43:1–25). On their arrival, Joseph sees his brother Benjamin for the first time in many years, and is deeply moved (43:29–31). However, as they prepare to return to Canaan, Joseph plants his own special cup in Benjamin's sack of food. As they are leaving, Joseph accuses one of them of stealing his cup. He demands that their sacks be searched. When it is found in Benjamin's sack, the brothers return to Joseph and offer themselves to him as his slaves. They implore him not to take Benjamin away from them. Their father had two sons by Rachel: he has lost one of them, and could not bear to lose the second (44:1–34).

45:1–47:27 Jacob Goes to Egypt Joseph then reveals his identity to the astonished brothers, and embraces them (45:1–15). He tells them of how God has blessed him. Pharaoh, fascinated by these developments, orders that transport should be made available so that Jacob and his household can be moved to Egypt, and allowed to settle in the land as welcome and honoured guests (45:16–24). The brothers return to Canaan, and tell their overjoyed father that Joseph is not merely alive. He is now ruler of all Egypt (45:25–28). So Jacob and his entire family move down to Egypt, and are settled, with Pharaoh's blessing, in one of the richest parts of Goshen (46:1–47:12). Even though the famine

continues in Egypt, Joseph ensures that seed grain is available to all, including the Israelites (47:13–27).

47:28–48:22 *Manasseh and Ephraim* Jacob is now very old. Knowing he must die soon, he asks to be buried in the family tomb in Canaan (47:28–31). He tells Joseph and his two sons of how God had established a covenant with him. After blessing Joseph's two sons Manasseh and Ephraim, Jacob tells Joseph that God will one day take him back to the land of his fathers (48:1–22). God has given Canaan to his descendants. Yet Joseph will die in Egypt. The story of how the people of Israel returned to Canaan has only begun.

49:1–50:21 *Jacob Blesses His Sons and Dies* Finally, Jacob blesses each of his twelve sons individually (49:1–28), and

the tribes that will bear their names. He repeats his request to be buried in the family grave in the field of Machpelah in Canaan, beside Abraham, Sarah, Isaac, Rebekah and Leah. (Rachel, it will be remembered, was buried near Bethlehem.) After these words, Jacob dies (49:29–33). Joseph ensures that his father's dying wishes are honoured, and accompanies the entire family as they return to Canaan to bury him. Afterwards, they go back to Egypt, to remain there permanently (50:1–21).

50:22–26 *The Death of Joseph* Jacob's dying words had included reference to Canaan as the promised land, which one day his offspring would inherit. In the same way, as Joseph himself is dying, he speaks of a day when God will take his people out of Egypt into the land he had

promised to Abraham, Isaac and Jacob. Joseph asks that, when this great day comes, his remains will be buried in that land. Genesis ends by recording the death of Joseph, and his burial in Egypt.

And so the reader is left wondering: Will the people of Israel ever return to the promised land? Or will they remain permanently in Egypt? Will Joseph's remains ever be reburied in Canaan? Will God remain faithful to his promises to Abraham, Isaac and Jacob? It is exactly these questions that are answered in the next book of the Old Testament, to which we now turn.

EXODUS

Exodus tells the story of how the Hebrews, once regarded with great favour in Egypt as a result of the reputation of Joseph, came to be treated as slaves. It describes the birth and calling of Moses and the events that finally lead to Israel being able to make their escape from captivity and begin the wandering in the wilderness. During this period, God gives Israel a new covenant through Moses, including the Ten Commandments, in order that the people of Israel may remain faithful to the God who called them out of Egypt.

EXODUS 1:1–22
Introduction

Exodus opens by describing how the Israelites (as the descendants of Jacob are now known) flourish in the period after Joseph's death. God's promise to the patriarchs of many descendants is more than abundantly fulfilled, to the alarm of the native Egyptians.

Increasingly, the Israelites come to be seen as a threat. The memory of Joseph and his work in Egypt seems to have been forgotten during the period of roughly two hundred years that separates the death of Joseph and the events that will be described in this book.

Finally, a 'new king, to whom Joseph meant nothing' (1:8) comes to power. The Pharaoh in question is often thought to be Ahmose, who is known to have been hostile to Semites. (The term 'Semites', which derives from 'Shem', is often used to refer to peoples of the region of Palestine, and especially to the Israelites.) Alarmed at the growing power of the Israelites, he sets about limiting their numbers and influence. In the first place, the Israelites are forced into slavery (1:11–14); in the second, he attempts to have every male Israelite child killed at birth (1:15–22). Yet the strategy fails; the midwives fear God, and will not carry out his wishes.

EXODUS 2:1–2
The Birth of Moses

In the midst of this attempt to eliminate all Israelite male children, a boy is born to a Levite family. Under Pharaoh's edict, he must be drowned in the river Nile. Unable to bear this thought, his mother places him in a basket amid the reeds by the bank of the river. (The word used for 'basket' is the same as that used at Ge 6:14 to refer to Noah's ark, which was also a means of deliverance from death by drowning.) The child is discovered, and saved – by Pharaoh's daughter. By the grace of God the future deliverer of Israel is saved from death by a member of Pharaoh's own household.

The princess recognises that the child is Israelite. She uses the distinctive term 'Hebrew' (2:6) to refer to the Israelites. The child's sister, whom we later learn is called Miriam, offers to find someone from among the 'Hebrew women' to nurse the child for the princess. Astutely, she finds her mother, and thus achieves reunion of mother and son. When the child is older, he is adopted into Pharoah's household, and given the name Moses.

The story now moves on (2:11–24). Moses has 'grown up', probably having reached the age of 40. Although raised in Pharaoh's household, he has not forgotten his own people. After accidentally killing an Egyptian who is abusing an Israelite, Moses is forced to flee from Egypt (2:15). He settles in the region of Midian, a desolate area to the east of the Gulf of Aqaba, several hundred kilometres from Egypt. While there, he marries a local woman, the daughter of the Midianite priest Jethro, and settles down in that region with his family for many years.

But back in Egypt, the oppression of Israel continues (2:23–25). Yet God has not forgotten his people. The great theme of the covenant between God and Abraham, Isaac and Jacob begins to make its appearance. God's promise to his people remains open. But how can it be

realised? What can be done? The following chapter begins to set the scene for the great act of deliverance that will soon take place.

EXODUS 3:1–6:30
The Calling of Moses

3:1–22 Moses and the Burning Bush Moses is tending the flocks of Jethro in the land of Midian when God calls him by name. In what follows (3:5–10), God reaffirms his commitment to the covenant he made with Abraham, Isaac and Jacob, and his determination to deliver them from slavery in Egypt. He will lead them into 'a land flowing with milk and honey' (3:8). And he has chosen Moses to go to Pharaoh, and bring Israel out of Egypt.

Moses is hesitant about this commission. Why him? And what will the Israelites say when he tries to enlist their support? God reassures him. Moses is to call God by name: 'I AM WHO I AM' (3:14). This is not a name Moses has chosen for God. It is the name by which God wishes to be known by his people. In the Old Testament, to name someone is to have or to claim authority over them. Just as nobody has authority over God, so nobody has the right to name God. God chooses to reveal his name. He is 'the LORD' (3:15). The Hebrew word *Yahweh*, sometimes referred to as the 'tetragrammaton' (the 'four letters' YHWH, sometimes written 'Yahweh', and often written incorrectly as 'Jehovah' in older English translations), is also a personal name for God. The name must not be confused with the general title of 'Lord', which merely refers to the authority of God. 'The LORD' is a special personal name for God, by which he is to be known and addressed in worship and prayer. To avoid confusion, the NIV prints this name like this: 'LORD'. God also affirms that he is the same God who was worshipped and obeyed by Abraham, Isaac and Jacob. His promises to these great patriarchs still stand. He is thus the 'God of Abraham, Isaac and Jacob' (3:16).

Moses is then commanded to return to Egypt, summon the elders (literally, the 'old men' – in the Old Testament, wisdom and age are often regarded as closely linked) of Israel, and tell them what has happened. Their moment of deliverance is not far away. Israel will be liberated from her bondage (3:18–22).

4:1–17 Signs for Moses Moses, however, still hesitates. He can foresee his authority being challenged (4:1–9). He lacks confidence in his ability to speak well (4:10–12). He doesn't want to do it, anyway (4:13–17). But God is adamant. Moses is the man of his choice. If he is worried about his ability to speak, he will use Aaron, Moses' brother, as a mouthpiece (see Ex 4:27–31). But Moses is to be the deliverer of his people Israel. He must get on with the task in hand.

4:18–5:23 Moses Returns to Egypt So Moses obtains Jethro's permission to take his family back to Egypt (4:18–23). Yet, although Moses now clearly stands within the covenant between God and Abraham, he has not yet fulfilled one of its central demands: circumcision of his son (Ge 17:9–14). His wife, more alert to this than her husband, performs the operation on their son (4:24–26). After Moses' arrival in Egypt, he and Aaron call together the elders of Israel. They assure them that the Lord has not forgotten them.

The scene now moves to the confrontation with Pharaoh. Moses and Aaron make their famous demand on behalf of God: 'Let my people go!' Pharaoh is not interested. Who is this Lord that demands that he should act in this way? Irritated at their demands, Pharaoh decides to make life more difficult for the Israelites. No longer will they be given straw to help them make bricks. They will have to find their own (5:1–21). The Israelites are furious with Moses and Aaron for provoking Pharaoh like this. Moses is disconsolate. Why has God treated him in this way (5:22–23)?

6:1–30 *God Promises Deliverance* God reveals himself to Moses once more, and reassures him of his presence and power (6:1–27). The same God who appeared to Abraham, Isaac and Jacob makes himself known again to Moses. He has heard the groaning of his people, and will remain faithful to his covenant. The theme of the 'covenant faithfulness of God', which is of such importance throughout the Old Testament, makes its presence felt strongly in chapters 19 to 24 of Exodus. Yet other themes also feature – such as the refusal of God's people to listen to his chosen servants, and the lack

Why did God send the ten plagues?

For modern readers this story is not easy reading. How can a supposedly good God send such things against people, we ask? But in context, these judgments were meant to provide an opportunity for Pharaoh – a man who had enslaved a whole nation and had ruthlessly had every Jewish baby boy thrown to the crocodiles – to change his mind.

First, the ten plagues happened over a period of months. Many were natural consequences of the previous plague (for example, the Nile turning to 'blood' would cause frogs to leave it; the proliferation of flies would spread disease among the livestock). This increasing pressure was designed to get Pharaoh to realise that his enslavement of a whole nation was unacceptable to God. But Pharaoh's heart was simply 'hardened'.

But not only were the plagues designed to bring increasing pressure on Pharaoh; they were also a direct challenge to Egypt's gods. For everything that was struck was either seen as a god (like the Nile) or represented a god (like the fly). Even Ra, the sun god, one of Egypt's chief gods, was blacked out. One by one, Egypt's gods were shown to be powerless before the living God, yet Pharaoh would not yield. Finally death itself, for which Egyptians took such care in preparing, came without warning and took their firstborn, even as Pharaoh had taken the Hebrew firstborn. At last Pharaoh got the message: the Hebrews' God had won and they were freed.

God was actually therefore very gracious in the time he took and the opportunities he gave Pharaoh to change his cruel policies. Only when the process was complete – represented by ten plagues (ten being seen in ancient times as the number of completion) did Pharaoh at last yield.

of confidence of those servants both in themselves and in the God who has chosen them. For example, when Moses is told to speak to Pharaoh, he quibbles, 'why would Pharaoh listen to me'? (6:28–30). Yet in the end, God is able to use even those with 'faltering lips'.

EXODUS 7:1–11:10
The Judgment Against Pharaoh

If Pharaoh will not listen to Moses' words, then he will have to deal with God's actions instead. The major section which now opens deals with Pharaoh's persistent rejection of God, and obstinate refusal to allow the Israelites to leave their captivity in Egypt. A theme that becomes important in this section is that of the 'hardening of Pharaoh's heart'. This should not be understood to mean that God deliberately makes Pharaoh reject Moses' words or the will of God. Rather, it should be taken to mean that God confirms what is already present within Pharaoh's own heart. For every text which speaks of God hardening Pharaoh's heart (e.g., Ex 7:3; 9:12; 10:20) there is another that speaks of Pharaoh's heart being hardened (e.g., Ex 7:13, 22; 8:15, 32; 9:7). God brings out into the open the secret inner motives and desires of Pharaoh.

7:14–11:10 A Series of Plagues It is clear that Pharaoh has not the slightest intention of allowing the Israelites to leave, despite the obvious signs of the Lord's presence and power (7:1–13). A series of plagues follows, each of which severely disrupts life in Egypt. Each of these plagues can be seen in terms of

natural events. For example, the plague of blood (7:14–24) may have been a severe volcanic eruption that discharges volcanic ash into the Nile, and thus pollutes the drinking water of animals and human beings, as well as darkening the sky. The Israelites, who were localised in the region of Goshen, far away from the Nile, would have been unaffected. Behind these natural phenomena lay the hand of God in judgment. In the order in which they occurred, the plagues are blood (7:14–24), frogs (8:1–15), gnats (8:16–19), flies (8:20–32), livestock (9:1–7), boils (9:8–12), hail (9:13–35), locusts (10:1–20) and darkness (10:21–29). In each case, the same refrain occurs: Pharaoh hardened his heart, and would not let God's people go.

The scene is thus set for the final assault upon Pharaoh's total obstinacy, as the events that would henceforth be celebrated in the Passover festival take place.

EXODUS 11:1–12:30
The Passover

11:1–10 The Plague on the Firstborn The final judgment on Egypt parallels one of the most repressive measures adopted by Pharaoh against the Israelites. Pharaoh had ordered that all newborn male Israelite children were to be killed. Now that same judgment is executed against Egypt, from the royal household downwards. Yet even here, God's judgment is tempered by mercy: where Pharaoh took the life of every male Israelite child, only the firstborn of each Egyptian family is to suffer the same fate. Israel, however, will not suffer from this judgment. She will be marked out as

God's own people, and spared from this act.

12:1–13 The Passover Meal As a sign of the fact that something new is about to happen, Moses is commanded to begin a new religious calendar, based on what now takes place. (The time of year identified here corresponds to the period of March or April in modern calendars.) Each household or group of households is to sacrifice a perfect lamb or goat, and daub its blood across the sides and tops of their doorframes. This will mark them as God's own people. They are to eat a meal, to remind them of their time in Egypt, which is now coming to an end. Both the type of food eaten, and the way in which it is to be eaten, will remind the people of their bitter years in Egypt, as they waited for their redemption. The eating of 'bitter herbs' (12:8) – herbs native to Egypt – symbolise the bitterness

of their bondage, just as the 'bread made without yeast' points to the haste with which the people are being asked to prepare to leave Egypt. The festival is named 'the LORD's Passover', which refers to the fact that God will 'pass over' the houses of his own people as he brings vengeance against the Egyptians.

12:14–28 Commemoration of the Passover In commemoration of this act of deliverance, the Passover is to be celebrated every year as a 'lasting ordinance'. Further regulations concerning its celebration are mentioned later (12:43–49). It is no accident that in the New Testament the 'Last Supper' of Jesus Christ is a Passover meal (Mt 26:17–29; Mk 14:12–25; Lk 22:7–20). In celebrating God's great act of deliverance in the past, Jesus Christ prepares for the great act of deliverance that will take place through his death upon the cross. God's judgment against

THE JEWISH CALENDAR

	Hebrew name	Contemporary equivalent	Festivals
1st month	Aviv, Nisan	March–April	Passover, Unleavened Bread, Firstfruits
2nd month	Ziv, Iyyar	April–May	
3rd month	Sivan	May–June	Weeks (Pentecost)
4th month	Tammuz	June–July	
5th month	Av	July–August	
6th month	Elul	August–September	
7th month	Ethanim, Tishri	September–October	Trumpets, Day of Atonement (Yom Kippur), Tabernacles (Booths)
8th month	Bul, Marcheshvan	October–November	
9th month	Kislev	November–December	Dedication (Hanukkah)
10th month	Tebeth	December–January	
11th month	Shebat	January–February	
12th month	Adar	February–March	Purim

sin, initially made against the firstborn of the Egyptians (12:29–30), eventually leads to the atoning death of his one and only firstborn son.

EXODUS 12:31–18:27
The Exodus

This final act of judgment breaks Pharaoh's resolve. Israel may leave Egypt. Fearful of further calamities, the Egyptians wish the Israelites to get away from their land as quickly as possible (12:31–39). Later (14:5–6) they will change their minds, and decide to force them back into slavery.

13:1–16 Consecration of the Firstborn As the Israelites prepare to leave, the custom is established of offering every firstborn male (whether animal or human) to the Lord. Once Israel has settled in the promised land, she will continue this custom as a means of recalling her imprisonment in Egypt, and the Lord's great power and love in bringing Israel out of that captivity into a 'land flowing with milk and honey'. The custom is there as a reminder, in case Israel should ever forget that the Lord brought her out of Egypt with his mighty hand. The theme of remembering all that God has done for his people occurs frequently throughout Scripture.

13:17–15:21 Crossing the Sea A further theme that will occur frequently in the account of Israel's journey to and entry into the promised land is that of the faithfulness of God to his promises. God promised to give the descendants of Abraham the land of Canaan. He will remain faithful to that promise, despite his people's frequent disobedience and rebellion against him. As a token of this faithfulness of God to his promises, Moses has the bones of Joseph exhumed, and brought with them as they travel (13:19), in order that Joseph may share in the promise of resting in Canaan.

But how are they to reach Canaan? The most direct route would involve heading from Goshen to the coast, and following the coastline through Philistia into Canaan. This, however, was a possible invasion route for Egypt's enemies. As a result, it was defended by a series of fortresses. Guided by a 'pillar of cloud' by day and a 'pillar of fire' by night, the Israelites journey southeast, rather than northeast, avoiding the much-used trade routes of the Sinai peninsula. The road they take leads them to what is traditionally known as the Red Sea, although the Hebrew words *yam suph* really mean 'sea of reeds'. It is not known for certain where this sea was located. The reference need not be to a 'sea' in the strict sense of the term; it is possible that an inland lake may be intended.

By now the Egyptians are regretting their decision to allow the Israelites to leave unhindered (14:1–9). The realisation dawns that they have lost a substantial pool of cheap slave labour. The decision is made: the Israelites will be pursued and recaptured. The search parties set out, and track the fleeing Israelites down to Pi Hahiroth (14:9). Panic breaks out inside the Israelite camp and recriminations flow thick and fast against Moses (14:10–12). Moses, however, urges the people to trust God. In one of the most dramatic and best-known incidents in Scripture, a strong

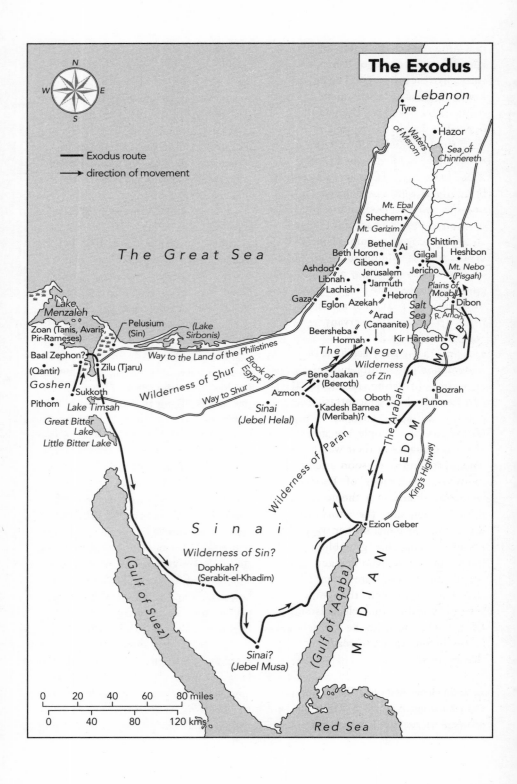

The Exodus

N
W   E
S

— Exodus route
→ direction of movement

Lebanon

The Great Sea

Tyre

Hazor

Sea of Chinnereth

Waters of Merom

Mt. Ebal
Shechem
Mt. Gerizim

Bethel Ai Shittim
Beth Horon Gibeon Gilgal Heshbon
Ashdod Jerusalem Jericho *Mt. Nebo (Pisgah)*
Libnah Jarmuth *Plains of Moab*
Gaza Lachish Azekah Dibon
Eglon Hebron *Salt Sea*

Lake Menzaleh

Zoan (Tanis, Avaris, Pir-Rameses)
Pelusium (Sin)
(Lake Sirbonis)

Baal Zephon?
(Qantir)
Goshen
Zilu (Tjaru)
Sukkoth
Pithom
Lake Timsah

Great Bitter Lake
Little Bitter Lake

Way to the Land of the Philistines

Wilderness of Shur
Way to Shur

Brook of Egypt

Beersheba
Hormah
Arad (Canaanite)

The Negev

Bene Jaakan (Beeroth)
Wilderness of Zin
Azmon
Kadesh Barnea (Meribah)?
Sinai (Jebel Helal)
Oboth Bozrah
Punon

Wilderness of Paran

The Arabah

E D O M

M O A B
R. Arnon
Kir Hareseth

King's Highway

S i n a i

Wilderness of Sin?
Dophkah? (Serabit-el-Khadim)

Ezion Geber

(Gulf of Suez)

(Gulf of 'Aqaba)

M I D I A N

Sinai? (Jebel Musa)

Red Sea

0   20   40   60   80 miles
0   40   80   120 kms

east wind divides the waters of this sea, allowing the people of Israel to pass through to the other side. The Egyptians, however, are swallowed up in the sea. Again, there is a strong element of irony here. The Egyptians wanted to drown every firstborn male child of Israel. They ended up by being drowned themselves. This great act of divine deliverance brings the Israelites to their senses. They now fear and trust God, and are prepared to listen to Moses his servant (14:13–31). In a great song of triumph, Israel exults in the glorious triumph of a God who is faithful to his promises, and who will guide them safely into the promised land of Canaan (15:1–21). For a while, Israel trusts her God and his servant.

15:22–27 The Waters of Marah and Elim But it does not last. Sinful human nature soon tires of trusting and adoring God, and turns back to concentrating on its purely physical needs. Shortly afterwards, the people are grumbling about the quality of their water supply. The problem is soon remedied. However, the reader of Exodus has been introduced to a theme that will recur throughout the story of the wanderings of Israel on her way to the promised land: the grumbling of an impatient people, who demand instant gratification, and are tempted to abandon God when the going gets tough. As will become clear, Israel is a people who need to be refined and tested before they are ready to enter that promised land.

16:1–36 Manna and Quail The grumbling soon starts again (16:1–3). This time, the problem is the food. Israel misses her pots of meat. 'We were better off in Egypt!' becomes something of a recurring theme in the people's long list of complaints against God. God's providential care for his people has already been demonstrated in the way in which they were saved from slavery in Egypt. Yet that care is far from exhausted, as what follows makes clear. For example, God provides quail (16:11–13) for meat. He also ordains that Israel will have 'bread from heaven' (16:4), an aspect of God's goodness that finds its ultimate expression in the coming of Jesus Christ (Jn 6:32–33). The word 'manna' is used to refer to this bread (16:31). It is not entirely clear what manna was. Some have suggested that it may have been a form of honeydew. However, the elaborate provisions concerning the gathering and keeping of the manna suggests that it was not something natural, but rather was ordained by God for the nourishment of his people at this crucial moment in their history. Interestingly, the idea of rest on the seventh day begins to make its appearance (16:23), even though it will not be formally imposed as a covenant requirement until Sinai itself.

17:1–7 Water from the Rock Having had its food sorted out, Israel now begins to complain about the water again (17:1–2). In a marvellous passage, we learn of how Moses struck the rock, and unleashed a stream of water (17:6). This event was commemorated in many of the later writings of the Old Testament (such as Ps 78:15–16 and Isa 48:21) as a sign of God's goodness towards and presence with his people.

17:8–16 The Amalekites Defeated Up to this point, Israel has wandered through the wilderness without facing much in the way of opposition. There have been complaints from among the people about the food and water, but no external threats. Now this situation alters, as Israel finds herself attacked by the Amalekites. The account of how the marauding Amalekites were defeated is of particular importance, in that it introduces us to Joshua. Joshua will eventually lead Israel into the promised land, after the death of Moses. Yet even at this early stage, he is singled out as an obedient and competent person. Later he will be identified as Moses' assistant (24:13), who ascends Mount Sinai with Moses.

18:1–27 Jethro Visits Moses The account of this early period of the wilderness wanderings comes to a close with the meeting between Moses and his father-in-law, Jethro. Midian was not far from the region in which Moses had chosen to camp, and it seems that he sent his wife and children on to Midian to greet Jethro, and arrange a meeting. Jethro was not a worshipper of the Lord, being a priest of Midian. However, the news of the great deeds the Lord has done for his people makes a deep impression on him. He acknowledges that the Lord is God, and offers a sacrifice to him (18:9–12). Jethro, who is now to be regarded as a follower of the Lord, then teaches Moses the essence of the skill of delegation, something that Moses had, by all accounts, yet to master (18:13–27). Moses could not do everything for Israel, and the administration of justice was becoming burdensome and impractical. The beginnings of an organised system of government and law can be seen starting to take shape. It will be consolidated in the future, as Israel presses on towards Sinai. It has been three months since she left Egypt.

EXODUS 19:1–24:18
The Covenant at Sinai

Israel encamps at the foot of Mount Sinai, in the southeastern region of the Sinai peninsula. God summons Moses to the mountain, and declares his intention to make Israel into a 'kingdom of priests and a holy nation' (19:6). She will be set apart from other peoples and nations, and will be dedicated to the service of the Lord. The New Testament picks up on both these ideas, affirming that Christian believers are now God's royal priesthood and people (1Pe 2:5, 9). The distinctiveness of Israel will be safeguarded by the covenant between God and his people, which will establish her distinctive identity as a people.

Moses and Israel prepare to hear God's covenant. In a series of ritual acts, they purify themselves (19:10–25). There is an important insight in this passage: sinners cannot stand before a holy God. Something has to be done if they are to come into God's presence. This idea is developed in the sacrificial system, which stresses the need for purification and holiness on the part of those who wish to draw near to God. However, it reaches its climax in the New Testament: through faith in the atoning blood of Christ, sinners are finally enabled to come with confidence and joy into the presence of a holy God.

Are the Ten Commandments still relevant today?

Spoken aloud by God to all Israel (19:16–20:19), then committed to stone tablets written by God himself (31:18), the Ten Commandments lay at the heart of God's covenant with Israel. So are they relevant to us today? If they are, why don't we keep all the other Jewish laws too?

While the New Testament teaches that Law-keeping isn't a requirement for Gentile Christians (e.g., Gal 5:1–6), there seems to be something 'different' about the Ten Commandments, not least their reaffirmation in some way or other by Jesus. In fact, Exodus itself distinguishes between the 'Ten Commandments' and the rest of the Law. We read that 'Moses went and told the people all the LORD's *words* and *laws*' (24:3) – 'words' referring to the Ten Commandments (elsewhere called the ten 'words', 34:28; Dt 4:12), and 'laws' referring to 'the Book of the Covenant' (24:7), which applied those commandments to various aspects of life, summarised in Ex 21:1–23:19 and further unpacked in the rest of Exodus, Leviticus and Deuteronomy.

The same distinction is found in Deuteronomy where Moses, recalling the Ten Commandments, said, 'These are the commandments the LORD proclaimed . . . *and he added nothing more*' (Dt 5:22). Although a further unpacking then follows, it begins with, 'These are the commands, decrees and laws the LORD your God directed me to teach you to observe *in the land that you are crossing the Jordan to possess*' (Dt 6:1), suggesting that while the Ten Commandments are God's 'words' for everyone, the further laws were specific to Israel for life in the promised land.

The Ten Commandments are therefore God's 'words' not just for Israel, but for everyone – his wise boundaries for fulfilled living, exposing that which dehumanises and destroys, and freeing people to enjoy life as he created it to be.

20:1–21 The Ten Commandments God now delivers the covenant between himself and his people Israel. The basic structure is usually referred to as the 'Ten Commandments', or the 'Decalogue'. There are important similarities between the covenant between God and Israel, and ancient Near Eastern covenants between monarchs and their peoples, which often opened with a declaration of the identity and achievements of the king in question. The covenant opens with a ringing affirmation that the Lord is the God who delivered Israel from her captivity in Egypt. Having identified himself, God lays the following ten conditions upon his people. The first four refer to Israel's relation with God, the remaining six to duties to other Israelites.

20:3 They Are to Have No Other Gods Israel is to be faithful to the one and only God, who delivered her from Egypt. In practice, Israel fails to keep this command: she regularly flirts with other gods and goddesses, especially during the settlement of Canaan. The word 'jealous' is used (e.g., 20:5) to refer to God's demand for total commitment on the

part of his people. It does not refer to petty envy or resentment on God's part, but to his passionate love for his people, and refusal to share them with any other gods.

20:4 Idols Are Forbidden Many of the pagan nations in the region worshipped idols – that is, stone, wooden or metal images of gods. Israel is utterly forbidden to do the same. Only the Lord is to be worshipped. Scripture also condemns other idolatrous practices, including the worship of the sun, moon and stars. Many of the practices associated with idolatry, such as sexual deviancy and the burning of children, are also forbidden. Despite these warnings, Israel lapses into idolatry at many points in her history, including the time of the patriarchs and Moses, the period of the judges, and the period of the monarchy. In addition to identifying the spiritual dangers of idolatry, the Old Testament also brings out the absurdity of the practice. How, it asks, can anyone seriously treat something made of wood as if it were a god?

Underlying this prohibition is another consideration: there is no way in which the Lord can adequately be represented by any human object. It is fatally easy to confuse the creator and the creation, and end up worshipping the latter rather than the former. This commandment ends with a powerful affirmation of the total faithfulness of God to his covenant.

20:7 The Name of the Lord Must Not Be Misused God's holy name is not to be abused, as in the swearing of false oaths.

20:8–11 The Sabbath Is to Be Kept Holy This commandment establishes the seventh day as holy. According to the Old Testament account of creation (Genesis 1), God rested from his work of creation on the seventh day. For this reason, the seventh day of the week (Saturday) was ordained to be a day of rest, a custom that continues in modern Judaism. No manual labour of any kind was permitted on this day, which was to be observed as an occasion for physical rest and giving thanks to God. As Jesus Christ thus pointed out (Mk 2:23–28), the Sabbath was ordained for the benefit of humanity.

By the time of the New Testament, however, the regulations concerning the Sabbath had become expanded considerably. The Sabbath was now subject to various kinds of legalism, with its original intention being overshadowed. Jesus Christ, who openly broke some of the more restrictive Sabbath regulations, declared that the Sabbath was made for humanity, not humanity for the Sabbath. Christ's resurrection from the dead on the first day of the week (Sunday) established this day as being of special importance for Christians. As a result, Christians observe 'the Lord's day' (Sunday) as a period of Sabbath rest, rather than the original Saturday. Christians can maintain the Sabbath principle, without obeying the letter of the Old Testament law.

20:12 Israelites Are to Honour Their Parents As Paul points out (Eph 6:2), this is the first commandment with a promise attached to it. Respect for parents is linked with the wellbeing of Israel in the land that God has promised her. There is a very strong sense of family

obligation here, which is especially noticeable to modern Western readers, who are more accustomed to a very individualist way of thinking. The Old Testament, here as elsewhere, emphasises the responsibilities of the people of God towards each other, and has little time for the ethic of pure self-fulfilment and self-indulgence that is so common in Western society today.

20:13 Murder Is Forbidden The Hebrew word used here would normally have the sense of a deliberate and premeditated act of killing. A distinction was drawn between murder and manslaughter, the chief difference being that the latter was accidental and the former deliberate. However, the commandment was not understood in Old Testament times to prohibit the execution of serious offenders, or the taking of human life in warfare.

20:14 Adultery Is Forbidden This practice is explicitly and repeatedly condemned by Scripture as a breach of trust. It is portrayed as something that is a snare to the unwary, and destructive of both individuals and societies. The Old Testament often compares forms of spiritual faithlessness, such as the worship of other gods or idols, to adultery. The Lord is treated as the husband of his people Israel. Israel's flirtations with other gods, especially Canaanite fertility gods (whose rituals included sexual elements), is therefore regarded as a violation of the covenant between God and his people, in much the same way as adultery is the violation of a marriage covenant.

20:15 Stealing Is Forbidden

20:16 False Testimony – Telling Lies – Is Forbidden

20:17 Coveting Is Forbidden The word 'covet' is a little old-fashioned, and could perhaps be translated as 'be envious about' or 'feel jealous about'. The basic thing that is condemned is longing to have something that belongs to someone else. There is a need to be prepared to accept what we have, without being envious of others. That envy can all too easily lead into violence and murder, and allow sin to express itself in dangerous ways.

The Ten Commandments are then supplemented by a series of additional laws, which expand some of the ideas expressed in the Commandments themselves. These laws relate to the prohibition of idolatry (20:22–26), the way in which servants are to be treated (21:1–11), the way in which personal injuries are to be compensated (21:12–36), the protection of personal property (22:1–15), care for the community at large (22:16–23:9), and regulations for the keeping of the Sabbath rest (23:10–13) and annual festivals (23:14–19).

God affirms his faithfulness to his side of the covenant, provided that Israel continues faithful on her side. In many ways, as we have noted above, there is a direct parallel between the covenant between God and Israel and a marriage covenant, with faithlessness on the part of Israel being compared to adultery or prostitution. God promises to give Israel her promised land, and that he will go ahead of her to sow confusion and terror

within the lands she is to possess (23:20–33). Nevertheless, there is a warning here: Israel can easily become corrupted by the religious beliefs and practices of the peoples already living in that region. The covenant is then confirmed by the people, who declare that they are ready to receive and obey it (24:3). Amid great rituals, Moses reads the Book of the Covenant to the people (24:7), who swear to obey it. Moses then returns with Joshua to Sinai, 'the mountain of God', where Moses will remain for 40 days and nights (24:18).

EXODUS 25:1–31:18
The Tabernacle

Having learned of God's covenant requirements of his people, Moses is now told of the practical details for the worship that is appropriate for Israel. The fine details of this section are complex. For a full appreciation of their functions and importance, they need to be read with care, in the light of a technical commentary. What follows here focuses on the importance of these provisions for Christian readers.

Having called his people, and established them as a 'kingdom of priests and a holy nation' (19:6), God now declares that he will dwell among them in a sanctuary (literally, 'a holy place') which is to be known as the tabernacle (literally, 'a place of dwelling': 25:8–9). The two stone tablets on which the Ten Commandments were engraved are to be an important component of this sanctuary (25:10–22). The box in which the tablets are to be transported during the period of Israel's wanderings is to be known as the 'ark of the covenant law',

although it will also be referred to as the 'ark of the LORD' elsewhere in the Old Testament (as at 2Sa 6:11). The covenant between God and Israel will thus be physically present with Israel as she undertakes her journey through the wilderness. The ark will finally rest in the temple at Jerusalem, after the conquest of this formerly Jebusite city by David.

26:31–35 The Curtain of the Temple Of the remaining details of the tabernacle and its furnishings, some aspects of the design of the tabernacle itself should be noted. The 'curtain of the temple' was an especially important feature of the tabernacle. It was included in order to provide a means of restricting access to the 'Most Holy Place', the part of the tabernacle regarded as sacrosanct. Although the curtain served an important practical function in relation to the worship of Israel, it came to have a deeper significance. The fact that the curtain prevented ordinary worshippers from entering the 'Most Holy Place' came to be seen as pointing to a much deeper separation between God and sinful humanity. The curtain thus came to be a symbol of the barrier placed between God and humanity by human sinfulness. At the time of the crucifixion of Jesus Christ, the curtain of the temple was torn (Mt 27:51). This dramatic event, noted in the Gospels, is seen as a symbol of one of the chief benefits brought about by the death of Christ: the barrier between God and humanity caused by sin has been torn down, so that there is now free access for believers to God on account of Christ's death.

THE TABERNACLE

The Tabernacle can be thought of as a 'portable temple', set within a courtyard that could be moved from one location to another as the Israelites journeyed from Egypt to the Promised Land. It consisted of three parts: the Outer Court, the Holy Place and the Most Holy Place or 'Holy of Holies' (Exodus 25–31; 35–40).

The Courtyard was enclosed by a fence made of linen sheets five cubits high suspended from pillars stabilised by ropes and pegs. The 60 wooden pillars were covered in bronze, and set in copper sockets. The upper parts were overlaid with silver (Exodus 27:9–19; 38:9–17).

The Most Holy Place was located as far as possible from the gate. This small room 10 cubits long, 10 cubits wide, and 10 cubits high, was separated from the Holy Place by a veil. It housed only one item: the Ark of the Covenant (Exodus 25:10–22). Only the High Priest was permitted to enter this place.

The bronze altar, or the altar of burnt offering (Exodus 27:1–8; 38:1–7) was located between the gate and the Holy Place. It was five cubits wide and long, and three cubits high and was made of acacia wood overlaid with bronze, with horns projecting from the top four corners. Poles were used to transport it on the journey through the wilderness.

The Holy Place was a room 20 cubits long, 10 cubits wide and 10 cubits high. It housed a golden lampstand on the left, a table for the 'bread of the presence' on the right, and a golden altar of incense at the back (Exodus 25:23–40; 37:17–29).

The gate to the Tabernacle consisted of four pillars supporting a screen made from blue, purple and scarlet dyed yarns that were woven together with fine linen (Exodus 38:18–20).

N

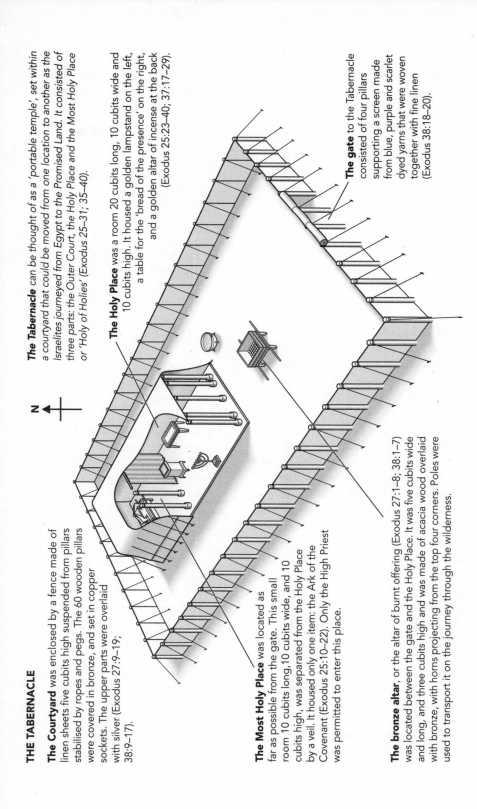

28:1–29:46 The Priesthood The selection
of Moses' brother Aaron and his sons as
priests ensures a continuous supply of
people for the priesthood within Israel.
The details of the priesthood extend to
the clothes that are to be worn by priests
(28:1–43). It is clear that the priests are
to have an especially important and
revered position within Israel, with the
task of ensuring that Israel remains a
holy people. For this reason, special
attention is paid to the manner in which
priests are to be consecrated (29:1–46),
and the care that is to be taken over every
aspect of Israel's worship.

30:1–31:18 Israel's Worship Israel is a holy
nation chosen by a holy God, whose
future depends upon her remaining
holy. This passage is a powerful
affirmation of Israel's need to remain
holy, even as God is holy, if she is to
remain the people of God.

For Christians, many of the details
described in these passages come under
the general category of 'ceremonial law'
or 'cultic law', dealing with the precise
way in which Israel ordered its worship
and sacrifice. Christian writers draw a
distinction between the *moral* law (such
as the Ten Commandments), which
remains valid for and binding upon
Christians, and the 'ceremonial law' or
'cultic law', which is seen as belonging to
a specific period in Israel's history, and as
no longer being binding for Christians.
Christ came to fulfil the Law in such a
way that the cultic law of the 'old
covenant' is no longer binding, having
been superseded by the 'new covenant' of
Jesus Christ. This theme is especially
clearly stated in the letter to the Hebrews.

EXODUS 32:1–34:35
**Rebellion Against God and the Renewal
of the Covenant to Moses**

32:1–35 The Golden Calf We have seen
how the theme of human sin recurs
throughout the narrative of God's
redemption of his people. It now makes
itself felt in one of the best-known
episodes of Israel's wilderness
wanderings: the making of the golden
calf (32:1–4). During Moses' absence,
Israel begins to rebel against the leading
themes of the covenant with the Lord.
Notice how the people attribute the
exodus from Egypt to Moses, not the
Lord (32:1). Despite the total prohibition
of idols within Israel, the Israelites make
themselves a golden calf (probably
designed to look like the Egyptian bull-
god Apis, representations of which they
would certainly have come across during
their time in Egypt). They worship this
idol, declaring that it represents the gods
who brought them out of Egypt (32:4).
Aaron tolerates this lapse into idolatry,
and does nothing to prevent the excesses
that follow (32:5–6).

God is angered by the disobedience of
Israel (32:7–10), and makes it clear that
he wishes to disown her for so flagrantly
violating his covenant. Moses, however,
pleads the case for his people. He asks
God to remember his covenant with
Abraham, Isaac and Jacob, and his
promise to make their descendants
numerous so that they may inherit the
promised land. The Lord agrees to
withhold the judgment on his rebellious
people (32:11–14). On descending the
mountain, Moses is rejoined by Joshua.
As they enter the camp of Israel, they
realise that they are witnessing a total

breakdown of the covenant. As a powerful symbol of this violation of the covenant, Moses breaks the two tablets of stone, upon which God has engraved the law (32:19).

Moses is furious at Israel's rebellion. His first action is to destroy the calf by burning it. (This suggests that the calf may have been made from a thin layer of gold, mounted on a wooden frame.) He confronts Aaron, and demands to know how the calf came into being. Aaron's reply is unconvincing: he threw lots of gold ornaments into the fire, and out popped a golden calf (32:24). The sinful people made him do it. This sly evasion of responsibility merely confirms how deeply ingrained sin has become, even at the highest levels of the people of God. Moses responds by purging Israel of those who have rebelled against God, putting some three thousand idolaters to the sword (32:25–35).

33:1–11 The Faithfulness of the Lord The consequences of sin now become clear. God will not withdraw his promises to the descendants of Abraham, Isaac and Jacob. They will still possess the land he promised on oath to their ancestors. But he himself will not accompany them. His presence will be withdrawn from his people, on account of their sin (33:1–3). This dismays the people, who strip off their ornaments as a sign of mourning and repentance (33:4–6). Moses pleads once more with God to remain with Israel. Despite all her faults, she is still his people (33:13). What point is there in going to the promised land without the presence of the One who promised it to them? What will be different about Israel, if she lacks the presence of her

God? The Lord agrees to be present with his people, because he is pleased with Moses (33:17).

33:12–23 Moses and the Glory of the Lord Moses then requests a personal favour. He wants to see God in all his glory (33:18). Yet no one is capable of seeing God in his full radiance and glory. God will pass by Moses, allowing him to catch a glimpse of him from the rear as he does so. But neither Moses nor anyone else will ever be allowed to see the face of God (33:19–23). Only Jesus Christ has seen the full glory of God, and made this glory known to sinful humanity (Jn 1:18). Having revealed himself in this way, God confirms his covenant with Moses. He will go with his people into the promised land.

34:1–35 The New Stone Tablets However, his people are to avoid any form of compromise with the pagan beliefs of that region (34:1–14). In what follows (34:15–28), the main points of the Ten Commandments are restated. This time it is Moses who engraves the letters. As a result of his encounter with God, Moses' face is transfigured. Having been in the presence of the glory of God, Moses himself is radiant, reflecting that glory (34:29–35). There are important anticipations here of the transfiguration of Jesus Christ (Mt 17:2–4; Mk 9:2–5; Lk 9:29–32), when Moses will be radiant on account of the glory of Christ.

EXODUS 35:1–40:38
Further Regulations and Conclusion

Exodus concludes with a restatement of the regulations that will preserve her

distinctive character as the people of God. The basic features of these regulations for the construction of the tabernacle and worship connected with it have already been set out (see 25:1–28:43; 30:1–5; 31:1–11), and they are repeated here for the purpose of ensuring that they will be remembered and acted upon.

Exodus closes by leaving us with a picture of the people of Israel journeying through the desert, as they move onwards to the land God has promised them. Despite their sin and rebellion, God remains present in their midst. Reassured by the visible presence of God (40:38), Israel presses onwards to her goal. The story of the wilderness wanderings will be continued in the book of Numbers. There is now a brief pause in the narrative, as we learn more of the will of God for his people in the book of Leviticus at this stage in their pilgrimage.

LEVITICUS

The book of Exodus ended with the building of the tabernacle, which would become the focus of Israel's worship as the people journeyed through the wilderness on their way to the promised land. The story of how Israel moved from Mount Sinai to the land of Moab, on the borders of Canaan, is taken up again in the book of Numbers. Attention now shifts to the tabernacle itself, focusing on the laws and regulations for its worship. These are also supplemented by detailed instructions concerning such matters as ritual cleanliness.

The book of Leviticus takes its name from the Levites, who, along with Aaron and his sons, were given the responsibility for the conduct of worship in the tabernacle, and the general maintenance of holiness among the people. A central theme of Leviticus is that of 'holiness'. The people of God must be holy, just as God is holy. The detailed regulations set out in Leviticus bear witness to the need for every aspect of life to be subjected to the will of a holy God.

Of particular importance is the theme of sacrifice, taken up and developed in the New Testament, which affirms that Jesus Christ is the perfect atoning sacrifice for human sin. His perfect sacrifice supersedes the Old Testament sacrificial system and many of the ceremonial or ritual laws associated with it. As the letter to the Hebrews comments, it is impossible for the blood of bulls or goats to take away sins (Heb 10:4). For this reason, Christian readers of Leviticus often find themselves bewildered and confused by its detailed stipulations concerning sacrifice and ritual cleanliness.

So does this mean that Leviticus has no value for the Christian reader? No! Reading Leviticus brings home to Christian readers the utmost importance of holiness on the part of the people of God. It stresses the seriousness of sin, and its damaging effect upon our relationship with God. It emphasises the need for atonement for sin, and affirms God's goodness and faithfulness to his covenant in forgiving such sin. All these themes find their ultimate focus in the sacrificial death of Jesus Christ, through whose blood believers are redeemed. To read Leviticus is to appreciate more fully the background to the coming of Jesus Christ, and the full meaning of his atoning sacrifice (Heb 8:1–6; 10:1–7). With these points in mind, we may begin to explore its themes.

OUTLINE
The sacrificial system
1:1–17 Burnt offerings
2:1–16 Grain offerings
3:1–17 Fellowship offerings
4:1–5:13 Sin offerings
5:14–6:7 Guilt offerings

6:8–7:21 Instructions to priests concerning offerings
7:22–27 Prohibitions against eating fat and blood
7:28–36 The priests allotted a portion of the fellowship offerings
7:37–38 A summary of offerings

The consecration of priests
8:1–13 The anointing of priests
8:14–36 The ordination sacrifice
9:1–10:20 The Aaronic priests

Clean and unclean
11:1–47 Clean and unclean meat distinguished
12:1–8 Purification after childbirth
13:1–14:57 Mildew and defiling skin diseases
15:1–33 Purification after bodily secretions

The Day of Atonement
16:1–2 Instructions for entering the Most Holy Place
16:3–28 Sacrifices on the Day of Atonement
16:29–34 Annual observance of the Day of Atonement

The regulation of the life of Israel
17:1–9 The centralisation of worship

17:10–14 Prohibition against consuming blood
17:15–16 Prohibition against eating animals that have died naturally
18:1–30 Sexual offences
19:1–20:27 Regulations and punishments
21:1–22:16 Regulations concerning the priesthood
22:17–33 Regulations concerning sacrificial animals
23:1–44 Regulations concerning festivals, including the Passover
24:1–9 The oil and bread in the tabernacle
24:10–23 The death penalty for blasphemy
25:1–7 The sabbatical year
25:8–55 The Year of Jubilee
26:1–46 Obedience to God
27:1–34 Redemption of things that have been dedicated

LEVITICUS 1:1–6:7
Types of Offerings to the Lord

Leviticus opens by detailing different types of offerings that may be presented to the Lord. Five are identified and explained.

1:1–17 The Burnt Offering This takes the form of a male animal (such as a bull, ram or goat). However, in the case of poorer people, a male bird (such as a dove) is an acceptable alternative. This type of offering serves a number of purposes. It can be an expression of dedication or commitment to God, an act of worship, or a form of atonement for some type of sin committed

unintentionally. (See also the further details at 6:8–13; 8:18–21.)

Leviticus stresses the need for the offering to be perfect, without defect of any kind (1:3). The idea of a perfect sacrifice, without any blemish, reaches its fulfilment in the New Testament in the obedient death upon the cross of the sinless Jesus Christ, in order that human sin might finally be forgiven, and forgiven fully (see Heb 9:14).

2:1–16 The Grain Offering This form of offering does not involve the taking of any form of animal life, but takes the form of offering agricultural produce of various kinds. Items regarded as suitable include grain, flour and olive oil.

Why don't Christians offer animal sacrifices today?

For most people, the early chapters of Leviticus, with its detailed accounts of sacrifices, aren't easy reading. Some might even wonder if this isn't cruelty to animals (though animals had their throat slit to ensure a speedy death, and the Jewish Law had many rules about animal welfare: e.g., Dt 5:14; 22:1–4, 10).

Although Jews stopped sacrificing animals when the Jerusalem temple was destroyed in AD 70 (for the temple was the only place where sacrifices could be offered), Christians had ceased the practice ever since Christ's death and resurrection. What brought about this incredible change, especially for those Christians from a Jewish background, was their absolute conviction that his death had fulfilled and replaced animal sacrifice. So had all those sacrifices been useless? No. But had they been effective? No. Then what was the point? The writer of Hebrews, writing to Christians from a Jewish background, has a helpful picture. While convinced 'It is impossible for the blood of bulls and goats to take away sins' (Heb 10:4) – that is, that Old Testament sacrifices could never deal with our sin – he saw they still had a purpose. He described them as 'shadows' (Heb 8:5; 10:1). A shadow has no reality in itself – but it does point to a reality beyond itself (whatever casts the shadow). What they had been pointing to was Christ's death on the cross, the one sacrifice that worked because it was the offering of the Son of God himself, his sinless life given in place of our sinful lives. Animal sacrifices could at best make people ceremonially clean; but Christ's death cleansed them for ever (Heb 9:12–14). This final, everlasting, once-for-all sacrifice removed the need for any further sacrifice. The shadow had been replaced by the reality – and Christians have never sacrificed since.

Although this type of offering does not involve the shedding of blood, it is intended to accompany some of the other types of offerings (see 6:14–15; Nu 28:3–8). As these other offerings involve the shedding of animal blood, it will be clear that every offering ultimately involves the taking of life. (See also the further regulations at 6:14–23.)

3:1–17 The Fellowship Offering This offering involves the sacrifice of a male or female animal, usually as an expression of the worshipper's thanksgiving towards the Lord. This type of offering is unusual in one respect, in that the person offering the sacrifice is allowed to eat part of the animal that has been sacrificed (apart from the fat and blood). (See also the further regulations at 7:11–34.)

4:1–5:13 The Sin Offering This type of offering is of major importance in relation to obtaining forgiveness for unintentional sins. Four general classes of individuals are referred to, each of which is required to make a specific sacrifice: priests, the community, leaders and individual members of the community. In each case, the sacrifice has to be perfect and without blemish. When a priest or the entire community sins, a young bull is to be sacrificed. In the case of a leader, a lesser sacrifice is laid down:

a male goat. (Sins on the part of priests were regarded as especially serious, as they brought guilt upon the entire people whom they represented.) In the case of a member of the community sinning unintentionally, a sliding scale of sacrifices comes into operation. Most are required to offer a female goat or lamb. The poor are required to offer a dove or pigeon. Those who are very poor are required to offer 'a tenth of an ephah' (that is, about two litres) of fine flour. (See also the further regulations at 6:24–30; 16:3–22.)

5:14–6:7 The Guilt Offering This sacrifice is obligatory for any unintentional sin that breaks any of the commandments. The sinner is required to sacrifice a ram, make any restitution necessary, and also pay an additional 20 per cent to the priest. Once this has been done, he can rest assured of his forgiveness. (See also the further regulations at 7:1–6.)

LEVITICUS 8:1–10:20
The Priesthood and Its Tasks

This section documents the ordination of Aaron and his sons to the priesthood (8:1–36), and their initial period of ministry (9:1–10:20). A central task of the priesthood relates to the distinction between the clean and unclean. As part of its commitment to holiness, Israel is required to avoid ritual uncleanliness of any kind, through the warnings of the priesthood. Where ritual uncleanness does arise, it is to be cleansed in the appropriate manner by the priests.

LEVITICUS 11:1–15:33
Uncleanness

11:1–47 Clean and Unclean Food The first major area to be discussed focuses on types of food. Certain animals are declared to be unclean. They are not to be eaten, nor should their dead bodies be approached. Examples of such unclean animals include camels, rabbits, pigs and rats. Anyone who becomes ritually unclean by accidentally touching their carcasses must be ritually cleansed by washing their clothes.

12:1–8 Purification After Childbirth However, ritual uncleanliness can also arise in other manners. A woman is unclean after childbirth, and is required to offer a sacrifice to be ritually cleansed (12:1–8). The normal offering would be a lamb. If, however, the woman was poor, she could offer two young pigeons. We thus discover that Mary, the mother of Jesus Christ, was poor, as this was the sacrifice she offered after the birth of her son (Lk 2:24).

13:1–14:57 Infectious Skin Diseases A major source of uncleanness is infectious skin diseases. In biblical times, the term 'leprosy' was used to refer to a group of highly contagious skin diseases, resulting in swellings, rashes or sores. The 'leprosy' in question is not identical with the disease now known by this name (Hansen's disease); the NIV uses the general term 'defiling skin disease' as a means of avoiding this misunderstanding. The Old Testament lays down regulations designed to minimise the risk to society, including the banning of those with leprosy from society in general, and from

Levitical service in particular. The priests are charged with the identification of leprosy, and the enforcing of the isolation of those suffering from it. It is possible for lepers to return to a normal social life only once they have been declared to have been healed of the disease. This declaration has to be made by a priest, after a careful inspection of the leper's skin. Once more, an offering is required before cleansing is complete (13:1–14:57).

15:1–33 Discharges Causing Uncleanness

Any form of bodily emission is regarded as making someone temporarily unclean. A male with any kind of discharge is to be regarded as unclean, as is anyone or anything who comes into direct physical contact with him (15:1–18). Similarly, a woman is to be regarded as unclean during menstruation (15:19–30). In all this, the priests are required to prevent any form of defilement to the tabernacle (15:31–33).

LEVITICUS 16:1–34
The Day of Atonement

One Old Testament ordinance is of particular importance for Jews. This is the Day of Atonement, which is ordained as an annual event for the removal of sin from the people of God. The full ritual is complex, involving the high priest ritually cleansing himself, and then offering a bull as a sacrifice for himself and the other priests. After this, two goats are brought forward. One is selected by lot as a sacrifice, while the other becomes the scapegoat. ('Choosing by lot' refers to the practice of throwing lots – similar to modern dice – and allowing the result of the throw to determine a decision, in much the same way as people today toss coins to make decisions.) The first goat is then sacrificed as an offering for the sins of the people. Afterwards, the dead bull and goat are taken outside the camp, and burned. The high priest then lays his hands upon the head of the second goat, and transfers all the sins of the people to the unfortunate animal. The scapegoat is then driven out into the wilderness, carrying the guilt of the sins of Israel with it. (The 'scapegoat' was so called because it took the sins of the people on its shoulders.)

The Day of Atonement is of major importance as a background to understanding the death of Jesus Christ, a point brought out especially clearly in the letter to the Hebrews (Heb 8:1–6; 10:1–18). Jesus Christ is seen as the perfect high priest, who makes a perfect sacrifice once and for all (instead of the annual ritual of the Day of Atonement). The sacrifice he offers is himself. By his death the sins of the people are transferred to him, and removed from his people. Note especially the fact that Jesus is put to death outside the walls of Jerusalem, just as the bull and goat were finally burned outside the camp of the Israelites. The Levitical ritual sets the scene for the greater and perfect sacrifice yet to come, which brings about what the Old Testament sacrifices could merely point to, yet not deliver.

LEVITICUS 17:1–27:34
Further Regulations

The remainder of Leviticus lays down a series of regulations designed to ensure that Israel retained her distinctive

identity. Some of these are linked with the sacrificial system; others concern personal morality; others relate to festivals Israel is commanded to observe, as a means of recalling the events that gave her a distinctive identity and purpose.

17:1–16 Eating Blood Forbidden The first major regulation concerns blood. A fundamental principle is laid down that is of importance in understanding the Old Testament sacrificial system: 'the life of a creature is in the blood' (17:11). For this reason, the people of Israel were forbidden to eat or drink blood. However, this idea also allows us to understand the importance attached to blood in Old Testament sacrifices. On the Day of Atonement, for example, the blood of the animal sacrifices was sprinkled over the atonement cover (16:15). The considerable emphasis placed by New Testament writers upon the 'blood of Christ' reflects the fact that the shedding of his blood is an atoning sacrifice by which Christ gives up his life in order that human sin might be forgiven.

18:1–20:27 Unlawful Sexual Relations; Various Laws; Punishments for Sin A series of regulations follows concerning forbidden sexual relationships (18:1–30) and other regulations (19:1–37). Once more, the concern is to keep Israel holy, just as God himself is holy. The seriousness with which sin is to be taken can be seen from the punishments laid down for sin (20:1–27). Israel must maintain her distinctive character, and avoid becoming like other nations. 'You must not live according to the customs of the nations I am going to drive out before you . . . I am the LORD your God, who has set you apart from the nations' (20:23–24). The importance of these regulations would become especially clear as Israel entered the promised land, and encountered the religious practices and beliefs of the pagan peoples already present.

21:1–22:22 Rules for Priests The priests, as has already been noted, will play an especially important role in upholding Israel's holy calling. For this reason, special attention is paid to ensuring the holiness of the priests (21:1–22:16), and the correctness of the sacrifices to be offered (22:17–33). A sinful priest will contaminate his people; the priesthood must therefore be free from any such contamination. The emphasis upon the need for a sacrifice without any blemish (22:17–22) anticipates the perfect sacrifice offered by Jesus Christ, who was himself without blemish or sin.

LEVITICUS 23:1–25:55
Major Festivals

A substantial section now deals with the major festivals of Israel. The main ones are the following:

23:3 The Sabbath The seventh day of the week is to be observed as holy.

23:4–5 The Passover Commemorates Israel's delivery from Egypt, and is celebrated annually on the fourteenth day of the first month (March–April in modern calendars).

23:6–8 The Feast of Unleavened Bread This feast recalls the haste in which Israel left Egypt, celebrated annually on the

FESTIVALS IN THE OLD TESTAMENT

Sabbath	7th day of the week	Ex 20:8–11
Sabbath year	7th year	Ex 23:10–11; Lev 25:1–7
Year of Jubilee	50th year	Lev 25:8–54
Passover	1st month (Aviv), 14th	Lev 23:4–8; Dt 16:1–7
Unleavened Bread	1st month (Aviv), 15th–21st	Ex 12:15–20; 13:2–10; 23:4–8, 15
Firstfruits	1st month (Aviv), 16th	Lev 23:9–14
Weeks (Pentecost/Harvest)	3rd month (Sivan), 6th	Ex 23:16; Lev 23:15–22; Dt 16:9–12
Trumpets (Rosh Hashanah)	7th month (Tishri), 1st	Lev 23:23–25
Day of Atonement (Yom Kippur)	7th month (Tishri), 10th	Lev 16; 23:26–32
Tabernacles/Booths	7th month (Tishri), 15th–21st	Ex 23:16; Lev 23:33–44
Purim	12th month (Adar), 14th–15th	Est 9:18–32

following seven days of the first month immediately after the Passover (March–April in modern calendars).

23:9–14 The Feast of Firstfruits Celebrated annually on the sixteenth day of the first month (March–April in modern calendars). This festival celebrates God's goodness in making the land fertile.

23:15–22 The Feast of Weeks Celebrated annually on the sixth day of the third month (May–June in modern calendars). This feast, which would later become known as 'Pentecost', was basically a form of harvest festival, giving thanks for God's provision for food in the land.

23:23–25 The Feast of Trumpets Celebrated annually on the first day of the seventh month (September–October in modern calendars), as a form of New Year Festival. The festival was subsequently known as Rosh Hashanah.

23:26–32 The Day of Atonement As noted earlier, this holy day, observed on the tenth day of the seventh month (September–October in modern calendars), is concerned with the ritual cleansing of priests and people from their sins.

23:33–44 The Feast of Tabernacles Celebrated for a period of seven days beginning on the 15th day of the seventh month (September–October in modern calendars), this feast commemorates the journey of Israel from Egypt to the promised land of Canaan. It would later be known as the 'Feast of Booths'.

25:1–7 The Sabbath Year Every seventh year, land is to be allowed to rest and recover during this fallow period.

25:8–55 The Year of Jubilee The year after a period of seven Sabbath years – in other words, every fiftieth year. In this Year of Jubilee, all debts are to be

cancelled, and all slaves given their freedom. The purpose of this festival appears to have been to prevent the development of long-term poverty within families.

In the midst of these regulations, further details are provided concerning the 'bread of the Presence' (24:1–9), and the use of capital punishment (24:10–23). This section includes the famous phrase 'eye for an eye, tooth for a tooth' (24:20). The point being made here is that there must be a correspondence between the offence and the punishment. Someone who deliberately takes the life of another can be justly sentenced to death. The death sentence, however, would be totally out of place for someone who damaged another person's eye or tooth, or fractured a leg. This famous phrase, which is often misunderstood as implying the need for vengeance, is actually a plea for moderation in punishment. The punishment must be of comparable severity to the offence.

LEVITICUS 26:1–27:34
Reward for Obedience and Punishment for Disobedience

Leviticus ends with a series of regulations, reaffirming the need for Israel to be holy, and observe the commandments the Lord has given to her. The reward for obedience to these commands will be prosperity, the maintenance of national identity and integrity, and the continuing presence of God among his people (26:1–13). However, a failure to remain faithful to these commands will lead to a loss of identity, with Israel being scattered among the nations (26:27–39). Promises and warnings thus converge, to remind Israel that her very existence is totally dependent upon obedience to the God who led her out of Egypt, and who has promised to lead her into the promised land that lies ahead. And with that thought in mind, we return to the narrative of Israel's journey to Canaan, which we left off as Israel was camped at Sinai. The book of Numbers now takes that narrative up again.

NUMBERS

The book of Exodus ended with Israel still in the region of Sinai. Numbers now picks up the narrative, and guides us through the wanderings of Israel as the people proceed on their way to Canaan.

NUMBERS 1:1–4:49
Details of the Tribes

Numbers opens with an account of the numbers of the tribes. (The concern for numbers in the opening chapters of the work gives rise to the book's title.) Aware that the conquest of Canaan will

involve military preparations, a census is taken, in order that Israel's military capability can be established (1:1–46). Arrangements are also made for the specific regions of the camp that are to be occupied by each tribe, with the tabernacle located at the centre of the camp (2:1–34).

The resulting census indicates that some 603,550 men were available for service in the army (1:46; 2:32), which would suggest a total Israelite population in the region of two million. This, however, causes a difficulty, in that the number of the firstborn is elsewhere stated to be 22,273 (3:42), which points to a much lower population. If the larger figure is correct, it would point to a huge increase in the size of Israel since her small beginnings in Egypt. It would be a clear confirmation of God's promise of fruitfulness to Abraham and his posterity.

There is, however, a difficulty with the Hebrew here, which is worth noting. The Hebrew of, for example, 1:41, reads 'forty-one thousands and five hundreds'. The word translated as 'thousands' can also bear other meanings in Hebrew. For example, it can also mean 'chief' (Ge 36:15) or 'family division' (Jos 22:14). It is possible that 1:41 should therefore be translated as 'forty-one chiefs and five hundred men'. However, it is not clear what the ultimate explanation of the numbers recorded in these early chapters might be.

3:1–4:49 The Levites The Levites were not treated as other tribes, but were allocated specifically religious duties (such as those set out earlier in Leviticus). Initially, the Levites were the assistants of Aaron and his sons, and were given specifically religious tasks. During the period of the wilderness wanderings, for example, the Merarites (one branch of the Levites) were responsible for carrying the framework of the tabernacle (4:31–32), while the Kohathites (another branch of the family) were to carry the articles used for ministering in the sanctuary (4:12). In a later section (8:5–26), the role of the Levites is clarified further: they are to be representatives of the people before God. By their ministrations, the community will be kept holy, and thus free from harm of any kind.

NUMBERS 5:1–9:14
Further Regulations

The next section of the work sets out detailed regulations that are concerned to ensure the religious and moral purity of Israel. This concern is of central importance; if Israel loses her distinctive character, she will cease to be the people of God. The precise regulations are ceremonial, moral and legal (5:1–31). The blessing set out at 6:24–26 is well known to many Christians:

> The LORD bless you and keep you;
> the LORD make his face shine on you
> and be gracious to you;
> the LORD turn his face towards you
> and give you peace.

6:1–21 The Nazirite Of particular interest are the regulations concerning the Nazirites (6:1–21). The word 'Nazirite' is derived from the Hebrew word meaning 'to consecrate' or 'to separate from'. The term was used to refer to men and women who had taken the decision to consecrate themselves to

God by 'separating' themselves from certain things through a special vow. This vow could be of a limited duration; occasionally, it was for life. The vow was sealed through certain sacrifices, and by ritual acts performed by a priest. Among the requirements of the Nazirite vow, the following are of special importance: the requirement to abstain from all products of the vine, to refrain from cutting their hair, and to avoid touching dead bodies. The most important Old Testament figure to have taken such vows was Samson (Jdg 13:1–5), who undertook his vows for life; other figures chose to obey their vows for shorter periods of time.

7:1–89 Offerings at the Dedication of the Tabernacle The earlier account of the setting up of the tabernacle (Ex 40) is now supplemented with the precise details of all the offerings made at the dedication of the tabernacle, and a further account of the continuing visible presence of God in the form of a cloud (9:15–23). This is followed by an explanation of the way in which the Levites are to be prepared for their ministry within the tabernacle (8:1–26).

9:1–14 The Passover The regulations concerning the Passover are now clarified further, especially in the case of those who have become unclean (e.g., by touching a dead body). The Passover celebration described here is the second in Israel's history – the first had been celebrated a year earlier, while Israel was still in Egypt. The festival would not be observed again until the entry into Canaan (Jos 5:10).

One of the Passover regulations has special significance for Christians. Moses commands that the bones of the Passover lamb are not to be broken (9:12). The Gospel accounts of the crucifixion of Jesus Christ make it clear that none of his bones were broken (Jn 19:36). Jesus Christ is seen as the true Passover lamb (1Co 5:7), who brings to fulfilment and completion the great act of divine redemption which the Passover marked.

NUMBERS 10:11–12:16
On the Borders of Canaan

After eleven months at Sinai, Israel finally sets out for the land of Canaan (10:11–36). Expectations are clearly high. Moses invites his brother-in-law Hobab (10:29: Hobab is 'son of Reuel': Reuel is another name for Jethro) to join them as they prepare to enter the promised land. As we discover later, he seems to have accepted this invitation; his descendants are among those present in Canaan (Jdg 1:16).

11:1–12:16 Fire and Quail from the Lord; Opposition to Moses This atmosphere of optimism soon begins to evaporate. The people begin to grumble (11:1–35). 'Things were better in Egypt! We're tired of eating manna! Let's have some meat!' The Lord responds by providing droves of quail, blown in from the sea. Moses' problems are made worse by a row with his brother Aaron and sister Miriam (12:1–16), allegedly over the issue of Moses' Cushite wife. (As Moses married Zipporah, a Midianite, it would seem that she may have died, and that Moses subsequently remarried.) The real issue, however, is that of authority. Who has

Why was Canaan the promised land?

Golda Meir, modern Israel's fourth Prime Minister, famously complained that Moses took the Israelites through a desert for 40 years to bring them to the one spot in the Middle East that had no oil. Her humorous comment highlights the question: 'Of all the places God could have picked, why did he choose Canaan as Israel's home?'

It was certainly not because of anything 'mystical' or 'holy'. While often called the 'Holy Land' today, this term occurs only once in the Hebrew Bible (Zec 2:12). The Old Testament more commonly calls it 'the promised land' or simply 'the land'.

The significance of Canaan – named after Canaan, son of Ham and grandson of Noah, whose descendants settled in the region between the Mediterranean and the Jordan – lies in it being the land God promised to Abraham and his descendants for ever (Ge 15:18–20; 17:7–8). Although described as 'a land flowing with milk and honey', unlike surrounding nations it had no great rivers to prosper it and so was utterly dependent on the rains – and therefore on God, perhaps one reason why God chose it. More strategically, Canaan lay at the crossroads of the world, surrounded by great nations: Egypt and Arabia (with its trade routes to the east) to its south; Mesopotamia to its east; Syria, Anatolia and the Hittites to its north. Whoever controlled this tiny strip of land through which all the great trade routes passed, therefore, could control the world, which is why it was frequently the object of territorial ambitions. God's plan was that Abraham's descendants should influence all the nations from here. Sadly, Israel more often ended up being influenced by them instead.

the right to speak in the name of the Lord? In what follows, a firm distinction is drawn between the Lord's revelation to his prophets in visions and dreams, and his relationship with Moses. God speaks to Moses face to face (12:6–8). (After the death of Moses, Israel looked for the coming of a messiah, who, like Moses, would know God in this close manner. This expectation is finally fulfilled in the coming of Jesus Christ who is 'in the closest relationship with the Father'; Jn 1:17–18.)

13:1–33 Exploring Canaan Israel now finds herself in the wilderness of Paran, northeast of Sinai, on the borders of the promised land (13:1–25). Moses sends out spies to reconnoitre the territory that lies ahead. His briefing to the reconnaissance party of twelve (which includes Joshua and a man named Caleb from the tribe of Judah) is thorough: he wants full details of the peoples, land and cities that lie ahead of them, so that the Israelites can prepare for their advance. The spies enter Canaan through its southernmost region (the Desert of Zin), and penetrate as far north as Hebron. Returning to Moses after 40 days, they report on what they discovered (13:26–33). Yes, the land *does* flow with milk and honey! But we can never take possession of this land. Its inhabitants are giants, and will overwhelm us.

14:1–45 The People Rebel The people take fright (14:1–4). They decide that they were better off in Egypt, and announce their intention to choose someone to lead them back to its safety. Joshua and Caleb plead with the people: the land is good, and the Lord will be with Israel (14:5–9). Why should they hold back? But Israel has had enough. The people rebel against Moses, to the anger of the Lord (14:10–19). Moses pleads successfully for his people to be spared, despite their disobedience. But there is a price to pay for Israel's disobedience, as the Lord's response (14:20–38) makes clear.

This section is dramatic, and represents a turning point in the history of Israel. It should be read carefully. As a result of her disobedience on the brink of the promised land, not one of the present people of Israel will live to take possession of the land. Only those who were faithful to God's command (Joshua and Caleb) will live to enter Canaan. Israel will remain in the wilderness for 40 years. Only then will she be allowed to enter into Canaan. By that time, a new Israel will have been born, and a disobedient Israel will have been buried in the desert.

Israel is shocked by this decision (14:39–45). It is clear that the people deeply regret their decision not to obey Moses. They acknowledge their sin, and declare that they are, after all, willing to enter into the promised land. But Moses refuses to listen to them. They would be disobeying the Lord – again. As a result, he will not be with them. What chance would they have on their own? But many are not prepared to tolerate this verdict. They will trust in their own strength. Numbers duly records the catastrophic outcome of their abortive attempt to invade Canaan without the Lord: they are routed by the Amalekites and Canaanites. The invasion is aborted. Israel begins to face up to the grim prospect of enduring 40 years of wandering in the wilderness.

NUMBERS 15:1–19:22
Continued Rebellion Against Moses

Israel has disobeyed the Lord; yet, as what follows makes absolutely clear, the promise of Canaan remains open. The regulations now delivered to the people concern their sacrifices in the promised land itself, which Israel will ultimately enter. Promise and demand are set side by side – the promise of entry into the land, and the demand to do as the Lord commands (15:1–31). Anyone who deliberately disobeys God must be 'cut off from the people of Israel'. As the episode of the Sabbath-breaker makes clear (15:32–36), no disobedience will be tolerated.

16:1–50 Korah, Dathan and Abiram But rebellion against Moses continues. A group of Levites led by Korah and two colleagues accuses Moses of setting himself over and above everyone else. What right has he to do this? They are supported by Dathan and Abiram, who claim that Moses has totally failed to lead them into a land of milk and honey. If anything, all that he has managed to do is lead them *out* of a land flowing with milk and honey, into the desert. The memory of slavery in Egypt seems to have faded, to be replaced by a nostalgic hankering after an idealised Egypt, rich with food and drink. Moses is angered by their

attitude. In the end, Korah, Dathan and Abiram perish in an earthquake shortly afterwards (16:25–40).

The death of Korah, Dathan and Abiram gives rise to new discontent within Israel. Moses and Aaron are accused of having 'killed the LORD's people'. This complaint is not just attributed to a few individuals, but to 'the whole Israelite community' (16:41). It is clear that there is widespread discontent and demoralisation within Israel. An outbreak of a plague is only ended when Aaron makes atonement for his people. Yet discontent remains. It is quelled to some extent by the budding of Aaron's staff (17:1–13), which is seen as a sign of God's approval of Aaron against his critics. Once more, the future hope of Israel is seen as lying in her faithfulness to the Lord. In order to ensure the continuing wellbeing of Israel, the priests and Levites are given religious responsibilities that are intended to prevent the rebellion and disobedience of the past (18:1–19:22).

NUMBERS 20:1–21:9
Preparing to Move on

It is clear that some time has elapsed. The reference to the 'first month' (20:1) is actually the first month of the fortieth year after the exodus from Egypt (see Nu 33:38). Nothing has been recorded of the period Israel spent in the wilderness, rediscovering her identity, purpose and commitment to the Lord. We know nothing of any events that took place during this period, not even the locations at which Israel camped in the course of her wanderings. At the time of her rebellion

against the Lord, Israel was at Kadesh. Now, she is reported as arriving at Kadesh, the scene of that original rebellion. We do not know where Israel has been in between. It is clear that a new Israel is in the process of being formed. Those who rebelled at Kadesh are now old, or have already died. The deaths of Miriam (20:1) and Aaron (20:22–29) are a sign of the passing away of the old Israel. Only Moses remains.

20:1–13 Water from the Rock But Moses will not be allowed to enter the promised land. Israel, as we soon discover, is still prone to grumble (20:2–13). A water shortage causes anger among the community of Israel, who once more express their grievances against Moses and Aaron. Moses is commanded to speak to a rock, and it will give forth water for the people. Yet Moses disobeys, and instead strikes the rock twice with his staff. This disobedience, perhaps prompted by exasperation with the continual grumbling of Israel, angers the Lord, who declares that neither Moses nor Aaron will be allowed to enter the promised land (20:12). Only Joshua and Caleb will have this privilege.

20:14–21 Edom Denies Israel Passage Moses then asks permission for his people to pass through the land of Edom (20:14–21), on their way to Moab. Moab was situated on the east bank of the river Jordan, directly east of the southern region of the land of Canaan, and bordering the eastern shores of the Dead Sea. Instead of entering Canaan from the southwest, which had been

Moses' intention before the rebellion at Kadesh, they will now enter the land by crossing the southern section of the river Jordan, approaching it from the east. The land of Edom lay between Kadesh and the Jordan. Hardly surprisingly, the king of Edom is less than happy about allowing such a vast group of people to pass through his land. He refuses – twice. Aware that words might not be enough, he puts together a large army, and blocks their path. Israel avoids entering Edomite territory, skirting its borders. At Mount Hor (whose location is uncertain), Aaron dies, and is mourned by Israel. However, this sadness does not last long. A marauding Canaanite king based in the Negev attacks Israel, and captures some of her number (21:1–3). Israel retaliates, and defeats him. This reversal of fortunes compared with a generation earlier would have been good news for Israel.

21:4–9 The Bronze Snake Despite this military success, Moses takes the decision to go round, rather than through, Edom. That involves delay, and provokes further grumbling among the people (21:4–9). An outbreak of poisonous snakes adds to their problems, and provokes a mood of repentance among the people. Moses makes a bronze snake, and erects it upon a pole. This offers salvation to those who have been bitten. For Christians, this incident has considerable importance, as it is alluded to by Jesus Christ (Jn 3:14–15). Just as Moses saves Israel by raising up a snake, so Christ will redeem the world by being raised up on the cross for its sake.

NUMBERS 21:10–25:18
From Edom to Moab

21:21–35 The Amorites Defeated Carefully avoiding Edomite territory, Israel traces the course of the Arnon, a dried-up river bed (or *wadi*) that flows into the eastern shores of the Dead Sea, and serves as a border between the Amorites and Moabites. Israel is thus able to avoid Moabite territory altogether. Moses then requests Sihon, king of the Amorites, for permission to travel through his territory (21:21–35). Like the king of Edom, Sihon refuses, and sends an army to meet the Israelites. However, Israel engages with the Amorites, and routs them. As a result, Israel takes possession of a considerable amount of territory north of Moab, stretching as far north as the Jabbok, where Jacob had earlier wrestled with an angel. Finally, Israel prepares to travel across the plains of Moab, in readiness to cross the Jordan and enter Canaan (22:1).

22:1–24:25 Balak Summons Balaam The Moabites, however, have no idea that Israel intends to do nothing more than pass through their land. Having seen what Israel had done to the Amorites, they are terrified (22:2–4). This fear leads to Balak, the king of Moab, summoning the assistance of a well-known pagan expert in divination, Balaam the son of Beor. Balak wishes to persuade Balaam to place a curse on the Israelites, and so invites him to Moab for consultation (22:5–35). On his way to Moab, however, an angel of the Lord blocks Balaam's path. Despite his international reputation as a spiritual expert, Balaam cannot see the angel. The donkey, however, refuses to go any

further, recognising the presence of the angel. Finally, the Lord opens Balaam's eyes, and allows him to see the angel, who commands him to tell Balak only what he is told to.

Meanwhile, Balak journeys to meet Balaam, firmly believing that he will place a curse on Israel, and stop the people in their tracks. Balaam then delivers four messages (22:36–24:25), in which he blesses Israel, to the fury of Balak. The fourth message is the most powerful of all, speaking in strongly messianic terms of a coming victory of the descendants of Jacob over the Moabites (24:17–19). The authority and sovereignty of the Lord is thus demonstrated in his ability to take and use a pagan diviner in declaring his ultimate victory over paganism in the region.

Yet Balaam must not be thought of as a friend of Israel or the Lord. He may have refused to curse Israel at the command of the Moabites, yet he is able to exercise influence over her in other ways. As becomes clear later (31:16), Balaam advises that the best way of destroying Israel is through allowing her men to have sexual relationships with the female worshippers of local Canaanite gods. This is exactly what happens next.

Why did God's people rebel so often?

One sad theme in Numbers is Israel's repeated rebellion and disobedience. Scarcely had they left Sinai (10:11) than they started complaining about their hardships and only having manna to eat (11:1–6). Then Miriam and Aaron opposed Moses (12:1–15); the spies brought a fear-filled report (13:26–33), leading to further rebellion (14:1–4); Korah led a rebellion against Moses (16:1–3); they grumbled over lack of water (20:1–5) and the hardships of desert life (21:4–5); they indulged in sexual immorality and idolatry (25:1–3). The obvious question is 'Why?' Why did people who had experienced such miraculous deliverance in Egypt and such powerful encounters with God at Sinai so quickly, and so often, complain and rebel?

One key answer lies in what it means to be brought into covenant relationship with God. This relationship both originates in and is rooted in God's love; but that love is not controlling and demanding. God doesn't want relationship out of compulsion but out of our love and choice. He wants us to learn how to trust him, especially when things don't go smoothly, and to make right choices at such times as part of our developing relationship with him. He doesn't force trust and obedience from us; he wants us to offer them freely. This means being alert to the reality of temptation and sin, which constantly seek to draw us away from God and into selfish choices, all of which prove to be illusory and empty, as these stories show. Paul referred to these incidents from Numbers in 1 Co 10 as a warning to Christians of the need to be alert to such distractions.

Thankfully, the grace of God always triumphs in Numbers. Though many individuals missed out on their inheritance, God's faithfulness to Israel as a people prevailed. His mercy always triumphed over their rebellion.

25:1–18 Israel Seduced At the military level, Israel sees herself as being favoured by the Lord. Yet sin continues to be a major problem within Israel. A theme that emerges as important throughout Israel's early period in Canaan is the destructive influence of pagan beliefs and practices on the faith of the people of God. This is the case even before Israel crosses into the promised land (25:1–18). While still waiting at Shittim, on the other side of the river Jordan to the Canaanite city of Jericho, Israelite men become involved in various Canaanite fertility cults involving sexual immorality. The Midianites, who had allied themselves with the Moabites against Israel (22:4), were implicated in this spiritual seduction of Israel. As a result, they are declared to be enemies of Israel, despite the historic links of Moses himself with that region.

NUMBERS 26:1–30:16
The Census and Further Regulations

26:1–65 The Second Census Some 38 years have passed since a census was last undertaken. As preparation for the military campaigns that lie ahead, a second census is now undertaken to establish Israel's potential military strength in the light of the forthcoming invasion (26:1–65). A new generation has arisen since the last census: only Moses, Joshua and Caleb remain of those who had originally left Egypt (26:65). The resulting census shows a slight decrease in the numerical strength of Israel during the 40 years of wandering in the wilderness. It is, however, clear that Israel is well prepared for any

military campaign that may lie ahead. Nevertheless, success or failure in such operations is firmly understood to be dependent on the continuing presence and favour of the Lord himself, rather than upon purely human strength.

27:12–23 Joshua to Succeed Moses But who is to lead Israel into the promised land? The privilege and task would once seem to have belonged to Moses. However, Moses' disobedience at Kadesh (20:1–13) had disqualified him. Neither Moses nor Aaron will be permitted to enter Canaan: Aaron was already dead (20:22–29), and Moses will die before the crossing of the Jordan near Shittim. He is, however, allowed to view the land from a mountain range across the Jordan before he dies (Dt 34:1–5). So who will lead Israel? We have already been introduced to Joshua the son of Nun, who has been presented as a man of integrity, courage and obedience. The Lord declares that Joshua is the leader of his choice. The succession is thus settled and safeguarded (27:12–23).

28:1–30:16 Various Regulations In Chapter 27, we are introduced to a dispute about inheritance rights (27:1–11). This leads to the introduction of new regulations concerning these issues, which broadens out into a reaffirmation of regulations concerning various kinds of offerings (28:1–15), and the observance of festivals (28:16–29:40). Some of these regulations have already been encountered in the book of Leviticus, and are repeated here to ensure that they are remembered. A final set of regulations deals with vows (30:1–16).

NUMBERS 31:1–36:13
Final Details

31:1–54 *Vengeance on the Midianites*
Earlier, the alliance between the Midianites and Moabites was noted. Moses' last act is to take vengeance on the Midianites for their actions (31:1–24). Even though Moses had family connections with Midian, he orders a thousand fighting men from each of the twelve tribes to destroy the Midianites in the region. After the division of the spoils (31:25–54), two of the twelve tribes (Reuben and Gad) request permission to remain in the region. They are attracted by the fertility of the lands, and wish to remain on the east bank of the Jordan. This land, they argue, has been given to Israel by God. They should be allowed to remain there, rather than be forced to cross the Jordan and enter into Canaan.

32:1–42 *The Transjordan Tribes* Moses is uneasy about this proposal. The command to conquer and possess Canaan was given to all of the descendants of Abraham, Isaac and Jacob. The refusal of two of the twelve tribes to cross the Jordan could lead to a general refusal on the part of the remainder to enter into Canaan, with unwelcome similarities to the earlier revolt at Kadesh. Israel had been obliged to wander in the wilderness for a generation after that rebellion. In addition, Israel will need all the fighting men at her disposal to conquer and subdue the land.

Eventually, a compromise is reached. Provided that the fighting men of Gad and Reuben go with the main body of Israel to subdue Canaan, their families may remain behind in fortified cities in the region of Gilead. After Canaan has been finally conquered, they will be free to rejoin their families on the other side of the Jordan (32:1–28). So Moses gives the land formerly occupied by Sihon, king of the Amorites, and Og, king of Bashan, to the tribes of Reuben and Gad, and also to the half-tribe of Manasseh, who proceed to build safe cities in the region (32:29–42).

33:1–49 *Stages in Israel's Journey* This episode is followed by a detailed account of the stages in Israel's journey from Egypt to the plains of Moab on the borders of the promised land (33:1–49). Forty locations are identified. Most of these are impossible to locate, as they refer to obscure regions where camps were erected, rather than to existing towns whose location can be established. But the list is important, as it allows the chronology of the later part of the exodus journey to be established (see, e.g., 33:37–38, which identifies the date of the camp at Kadesh, and of Aaron's death).

33:50–35:5 *Boundaries of Canaan* Moses is then commanded to take possession of Canaan, and drive out all its existing inhabitants (33:50–56). The four main boundaries of the land that they are to occupy are carefully defined (34:1–29). Moses then assigns regions of the promised land to each of the remaining nine-and-a-half tribes. Reuben, Gad and the half-tribe of Manasseh had already been allocated territory 'east of the Jordan opposite Jericho, towards the sunrise' (34:15). Particular provision is made for the Levites (35:1–5).

35:6–34 *Cities of Refuge* A feature of considerable interest is the identification of 'cities of refuge'. Six towns, three of which were to be located in Canaan and three on the east bank of the Jordan, are to be designated in this way. The purpose of these cities is related to the accidental killing of an individual, which, by tradition, had to be avenged by someone within the family (the 'avenger of blood'). Someone who finds himself in the position of having accidentally killed another person can take refuge in one of these six cities, and remain there in safety. On the death of the high priest, there will be a general amnesty, as a result of which the person in question can return to his own people without fear of further reprisal.

Further regulations provide safeguards against false accusations of murder, by insisting that more than one witness is required before anyone can be put to death on such a charge. As Israel prepares to change from being a nomadic to a settled people, she can be seen as going through a process of transition from tribal customs of revenge (in which families or clans are responsible for avenging a murder) to government by civil law (in which the state or an assembly of elders is responsible for punishing the guilty, and deterring others from doing the same).

36:1–12 *Inheritance of Zelophehad's Daughters* Numbers ends (36:1–12) by returning to an issue of inheritance rights, which had arisen earlier (27:1–11). The questions involve focus on whether property or goods may be transferred from one tribe to another, in the event of intermarriage between the twelve tribes. Moses declares that intermarriage between the tribes is perfectly acceptable. Tribal land, however, cannot be transferred from one tribe to another, even as an inheritance. In this way, the original allocations of territory within Canaan will be preserved.

36:13 *Conclusion* Israel is now assembled on the plains of Moab, ready to enter the promised land. Moses, however, is still alive. The next book of the Bible, Deuteronomy, can be seen as a renewal of the covenant between God and his people before they go across the Jordan to possess the land that awaits them.

DEUTERONOMY

The title of this book is unusual. The word 'Deuteronomy' comes from two Greek words literally meaning 'the second law', or perhaps 'the repetition of the law'. This unusual title refers to the copy of the Law that Deuteronomy required the king to make for himself (17:18). The work reiterates the law first delivered by the Lord to Moses at Mount Sinai, and recorded in the books of Exodus and Leviticus. The book is virtually entirely composed of addresses by Moses to Israel during the final months of his life, recounting the law given to Israel during the period of her nomadic wanderings in the desert. For this reason, Deuteronomy is best appreciated by reading the first four books of the Bible (or at least Exodus and Numbers) as background material.

In addition to significant sections relating to the Law, Deuteronomy also includes historical sections. These summarise Israel's journey from Sinai to the borders of the promised land, and take the story up to the death of Moses, and the final confirmation of Joshua as his successor. Deuteronomy brings the first major section of the Bible (sometimes referred to as 'The Five Books of the Law' or 'The Pentateuch') to an end.

DEUTERONOMY 1:1–4:43
The Historical Background

1:1–2:6 The Command to Leave Horeb; Rebellion Against the Lord The book opens with Israel assembled on the plains of Moab. Forty years have passed since Israel left Egypt. After the rebellion against God's command that she enter Canaan some 38 years earlier (Nu 14:33–34), Israel had been told that a period of 40 years would elapse between the exodus from Egypt and her entry into Canaan. None of those living at the time of the rebellion against Kadesh, except Joshua and Caleb, would live to enter the promised land. Even Moses is denied that privilege. The mention of the 'fortieth year' (1:3) immediately raises the reader's excitement: this is the year in which Canaan will be entered!

Moses begins by reminding his people that they have been called by God, who gave promises to Abraham, Isaac and Jacob and their descendants. He relates how God finally gave them permission to move on from Sinai (also known as

'Horeb', as here), and to go into the promised land (1:6–8). He relates how spies were sent out from the camp at Kadesh to explore Canaan (1:19–25), and came back with good reports of what they found. But Israel refused to go in and possess the land, rebelling against the Lord (1:26–46). Moses also relates the story of his own failure to obey the Lord, which has led to his being excluded from entering the promised land. Israel was condemned to wander around the 'hill country of Seir' (2:1), just south of the Dead Sea, for a further 38 years. But then the word of the Lord had come: 'You have made your way around this hill country long enough; now turn north' (2:2–3).

2:7–3:29 Division of the Land; Moses Forbidden to Cross the Jordan Moses relates to his people the great story of their triumphs as they marched northwards, defeating all who came between them and their goal (2:7–3:11). This great recital reminds the people of all that God has done for them in the past, and

encourages them to have great expectations for what he will do for them in the future. Canaan has been promised to them by the Lord, who is faithful to his promises and will do what he purposes for an obedient and trusting people.

Moses then relates his own part in the story: how he divided the land conquered east of the Jordan among the tribes of Reuben and Gad (3:12–20). Finally, he relates how, on account of his failure and disobedience, he was not allowed to enter into Canaan. He was allowed to see it from a distance, and assured that his descendants would possess it. He, however, would not enter it himself (3:21–29). The constant emphasis upon 'possession' of the land is a major theme. Abraham, Isaac and Jacob never possessed the land on which they lived. They were nomads, wanderers who lived off the land without ever being able to call it their own. Canaan is to be the possession of their descendants – a land that will belong to them for ever.

4:1–43 Obedience Commanded; Idolatry Forbidden Moses urges his people to remember these great acts of God. Indeed, the call to remember the Lord's great saving deeds is a common theme throughout Deuteronomy. Israel is to remember her days in slavery in Egypt, and to remember how the Lord delivered her from that oppression with a mighty hand (4:1–14). Israel's God is unique, and alone can save. 'Has any god ever tried to take for himself one nation out of another nation, by testings, by signs and wonders, by war, by a mighty hand and an outstretched arm, or by great and awesome deeds, like all the things the Lord your God did for you in Egypt

before your very eyes?' (4:34). He alone is to be obeyed and trusted.

DEUTERONOMY 4:44–28:68
The Lord's Demands for Obedience

4:44–6:3 The Law and the Covenant The next section opens with a declaration that what follows is the law given to Israel by Moses, as she waited in the Moabite region near Beth Peor to enter the promised land (4:44–49). The section begins (5:1–5) with a powerful reminder of the covenant made with Israel at Sinai (here referred to by its alternative name of 'Horeb'). The Ten Commandments have already been explored (see Ex 20:1–17), and the reader should refer back to this discussion for full details (5:6–21). Moses affirms that the Law and the covenant are closely connected (5:22–6:19). God has promised to be with his people; his people are required to obey his laws. Moses clearly states that Israel's safety and prosperity in the promised land depend on obedience to the Law (6:1–3).

6:4–25 Love the Lord Your God The passage that follows has had considerable impact on both Jewish and Christian thought (6:4–9). Moses declares that there is only one God, and gives Israel this commandment: 'Love the Lord your God with all your heart and with all your soul and with all your strength' (v.5). The commandments are to become part of Israel's way of thinking, to be taught to her children and to be talked about whenever possible. We see here a forceful declaration of the importance of the law of God as a means of ensuring the

continuing identity and safety of God's people (a point also stressed in 6:13–19).

Moses stresses that Canaan is God's gracious gift to Israel (6:10–12). It is something Israel by herself could never have gained. For this reason, and others, Israel must never be allowed to forget God, and all that he has done for his people. He has brought them out of slavery into Egypt, and will give them cities they did not build, vineyards they did not plant, and wells they did not dig. These are all part of God's gracious and undeserved provision for his people. So when, in years to come, the children of those who are now living ask about the meaning of the laws that have just been given, they can be told of how these laws are a reminder of all that God has done for his people, and their need to remain faithful to him (6:20–25).

7:1–6 Driving out the Nations God's gracious provision for his people will also be seen in the forthcoming military campaign. Israel's victories will not be due to the might of her armies, but to the presence and power of the Lord. All pagan religious objects are to be destroyed when Israel possesses the land, on account of the threat they pose to the holiness of the people of God. As the subsequent history of Israel makes clear, these warnings were well founded.

Is God one or three?

The words of Dt 6:4 (known as the *Shema* from its opening Hebrew word, meaning 'hear') stand at the heart of Old Testament faith. This declaration that God is one spoke of his *uniqueness*, that there was only one true God, something Israel had already experienced at the exodus where Egypt's 'gods' had proved impotent, yet something they would need constant reminding of in a polytheistic world. But it also spoke of God's *unity*, that he is not made up of separate unrelated 'bits'; his love flows through his justice and his justice flows through his love.

While this *Shema* was recited regularly by every good Jew, including Jesus himself (Mt 22:34–40), his disciples faced a problem, especially after the resurrection. For everything they had believed about God, they had now experienced in Jesus. And after Jesus' ascension and Pentecost, they discovered that the Holy Spirit was to them everything that Jesus himself had been. That is why the New Testament contains unashamed attributions of divinity to both Christ (e.g., Ro 9:5) and the Spirit (e.g., 2Co 3:17).

But how can God's one nature exist in three persons, Father, Son and Holy Spirit, simultaneously? The New Testament never seeks to explain this, though all the raw data is there. It was left to early church theologians to grapple with, and was not until AD 325 at the Council of Nicea that the doctrine was finally formulated. While many illustrations of the Trinity have been proposed, one that is perhaps helpful for today is that of the cube. Just as a cube cannot exist without its three dimensions, so the one God cannot exist without being Father, Son and Holy Spirit all at the same time; such is his greatness and complexity.

7:7–10:22 God's Chosen People One of the most powerful themes of the Bible now becomes apparent: the election or choice of the people of God. God did not choose Israel because of her size or strength. He chose her simply because he loved her (7:7–9). The theme of God showing his love for his people will occur time and time again in Scripture, even where God is correcting his people for their waywardness or rebellion against him. God's love is seen in action in the promises he made to Abraham, Isaac and Jacob. The love of God for his people is an important ground for hope, especially in the light of the threat posed to Israel by other nations (7:9–26).

That love is seen at work in the chastising or correction of Israel in the desert (8:1–20). The rebellion and pain of the desert period is recalled here. God disciplines only those whom he loves, and his chastisement of Israel during her 40 years in the desert is to be seen as a token of his love and care for her. She needed to learn that we do 'not live on bread alone, but on every word that comes from the mouth of the LORD' (8:3). Those lessons had to be learned the hard way. Israel may find that she once more becomes proud, and forgets her God (8:12–14). The lessons from her past should warn her of the dangers of forgetting the God who will never forget her.

Israel will possess the lands across the Jordan, not on account of her own righteousness or merits, but on account of the love of God for his people and his faithfulness to his promises (9:1–6). Israel's past sin, especially the making of the golden calf (9:7–10:22), is so great that she can never expect favours from God as a result of her holiness, but only on account of God's love. Israel is thus commanded to remain faithful to the Lord, and obey his commands.

11:1–32 Love and Obey the Lord This point is repeated so often (e.g., at 11:1–12) that the reader may feel wearied by it. However, the importance of the issues cannot be overstated. The very existence of Israel depends on her faithfulness to God. Without God, she will fail, lose sight of her reason for existence and cease to exist as a nation. The frequent repetition of these promises and demands is an indication of how serious the issues are, and how easily Israel can forfeit her inheritance. Moses stresses how lovely and good the land of Canaan is (11:10–12), and how Israel needs to remain faithful to the Lord if she is to possess and remain in this fertile land. Israel is thus confronted with a choice (11:26–32): she can obey the commands of God, and be blessed; or she can disobey them, and be cursed. Moses pleads with his people to obey God, and receive the riches of God's blessing through their obedience.

12:1–13:18 True Worship The importance of right worship is evident. Moses makes it clear that there is a real danger from syncretism – that Israel will simply take over existing Canaanite religious buildings, objects, beliefs and practices, and by doing so, forget the Lord her God. The people must maintain their distinctiveness (12:1–32). In particular, they must resist any temptation to worship other gods (13:1–18). Any prophet, visionary or seer who declares that God wishes them to follow other

gods is to be rejected as a false prophet. Anyone – even a close relative – who encourages such worship is to be put to death and their property destroyed. So serious are the dangers of worshipping other gods.

14:1–27:26 Rules for Life and Worship

A series of regulations then follows – generally restating or extending regulations already given in Exodus or Leviticus. The reader may find it helpful to read these through with a view to noticing their very precise and practical nature. Israel will be distinct, not simply on account of her religious beliefs, but on account of the way in which these are put into practice. External practice reinforces internal belief and faith. Examples of these regulations include the practice of 'tithing' (14:22–29; 26:1–15). Israel was to set aside one tenth of her produce (the word 'tithe' comes from the Old English word for 'a tenth') for the purpose of maintaining the Levites, foreigners, widows and orphans.

One passage of special importance within this section of detailed regulations is worth particularly close attention. Moses declares (18:14–22) that, after he has died, the Lord will raise up other prophets, who will declare the word of the Lord to his people. This promise may be seen fulfilled in the Old Testament prophets, who ministered to Israel at times of political and religious crisis. However, it also came to have strongly messianic overtones (see Jn 1:21, which refers to this expectation). These hopes are finally fulfilled in the coming of Jesus Christ himself, who declares God's will to his people at first hand, as God himself.

28:1–68 Blessings for Obedience, Curses for Disobedience

This section ends with a further assurance that obeying God will bring blessing (28:1–14). The consequences of disobeying God are then made clear (28:15–68). Israel will be ruined. She will be uprooted from the land of Canaan, and scattered among the nations. Moses therefore offers Israel the opportunity to renew the covenant with the Lord, as she prepares to enter the promised land. This forms the subject of the next section of the book.

DEUTERONOMY 29:1–34:12
The Consecration of Israel as the People of God

29:1–30:20 Renewal of the Covenant

In a ceremony of great solemnity, Moses and Israel renew their covenant with the Lord. Moses begins by reminding the people of Israel of all that God has done for them (29:1–8). The same God who made promises to Abraham, Isaac and Jacob will continue to be the God of Israel. But Israel must be faithful to the Lord, and refuse to worship any other gods (29:9–29). Obedience will lead to prosperity in Canaan, and to security in the face of the many enemies they can expect to encounter. But all this is conditional on obedience to God. Moses declares that two options have been set before the people: life and death. The choice is theirs. If they love God and keep his commands, they will prosper and increase. If they rebel against him and abandon him, they will not live long in the land they are about to possess (30:1–20).

31:1–13 Joshua to Succeed Moses Moses explains that he is not to be allowed to lead Israel across the Jordan into Canaan. In his place, Joshua will take command of Israel, and the Lord will go ahead of the people, and give them victory. In the presence of Israel, Moses reassures Joshua of the continuing presence and favour of the Lord in the future. Moses may be taken from them; the Lord will always remain at their side.

31:14–29 Israel's Rebellion Predicted Even with this assurance of the presence of God, Moses declares that Israel will continue to rebel against him. Despite all the warnings to the contrary, Israel will be attracted to other gods, and worship them. Yet although the Lord foretells this failure and sin, this does not mean that he is prepared to tolerate such rebellion. In order to deal with this situation, Moses is instructed to write down the Book of the Law, and place it alongside the ark of the covenant (31:25–26).

The truth of this prophecy may be seen from events of centuries later. It seems that this 'Book of the Law' lay unnoticed for many years, during which Israel periodically lapsed into paganism. In 622 BC, during the reign of Josiah, it was rediscovered (2Ki 22:1–20). When Josiah realised how much Judah had departed from the terms of the covenant, he ordered that the covenant should be renewed immediately, and reforms were introduced to eliminate the pagan practices and beliefs which had crept into Israel in the period between the death of Moses and his own accession (2Ki 23:1–27). Yet the reforms introduced under Josiah are not enough to save Judah from exile. The theme of the exile begins to become of importance for the first time in 2 Kings, with the forthcoming deportation of both Israel and Judah being seen as the direct consequence of the disobedience and apostasy of their kings.

31:30–33:29 The Song of Moses and the Blessing of the Tribes After passing over all these instructions, encouragements and warnings to his people, Moses sings of confidence in the Lord (31:30–32:43), and charges Israel to be faithful to the law for ever (32:44–47). In the blessing of the tribes that follows (33:1–29), Moses speaks of his hopes for each of the tribes, in much the same way as Jacob earlier blessed his sons (Ge 49:1–28).

In the meantime, Moses has been allowed to have one last glimpse of Canaan. The Lord tells him that he will die on Mount Nebo (32:48–52). On account of his rebellion against God at the waters of Meribah (see Nu 20:1–13), Moses 'will see the land only from a distance', and will not be allowed to enter it (32:52).

34:1–12 The Death of Moses After blessing the tribes, Moses then ascends Mount Nebo, and is allowed to survey all the land around – land that Israel will possess. Moses has been allowed to see it before he dies. On his death, he is buried in Moab, and greatly mourned by the people he has led from Egypt to the border of the new country that awaits them (34:1–9).

Deuteronomy closes with an assessment of the significance of Moses (34:10–12). There has never been

anyone like him, who knew the Lord face to face. Yet with the coming of Jesus Christ, someone greater than Moses came. 'For the law was given through Moses; but grace and truth came through Jesus Christ' (Jn 1:17). Moses was indeed the 'servant of the LORD' (34:5); Jesus Christ was his Son (Heb 3:1–6).

JOSHUA

The book of Deuteronomy brought the first major section of the Old Testament, often known as the 'Five Books of the Law', to an end. But the history of Israel has only just begun. During the period of wandering in the desert, she was given her distinctive identity as a people. Israel knew who she was, who had called her into being, and what she had to do. The narrative now moves on to the conquest of the promised land, as we learn how the people of God, who have wandered for 40 years, enter and set down roots in the promised land.

JOSHUA 1:1–18
The Commissioning of Joshua

With the death of Moses, a new day dawns in the history of Israel. Israel is now free to enter the promised land, and at last to claim the land the Lord promised to their forebears many generations before. It is clear that events now move very quickly. Joshua, the chosen successor, is formally commissioned by the Lord to lead Israel across the Jordan (1:1–9). Joshua is commanded to remain faithful to the laws given to Moses; if he does so, his success and prosperity are assured.

Joshua wastes no time (1:10–18). Allowing three days for mobilisation, he prepares to move across the Jordan. He reminds the Israelites of the great promises made to them, and their responsibilities to ensure that these promises are fulfilled. In the case of the tribes of Reuben and Gad, and the half-tribe of Manasseh, he reminds the men that they must take part in the conquest of the promised land before they will be allowed to return to the

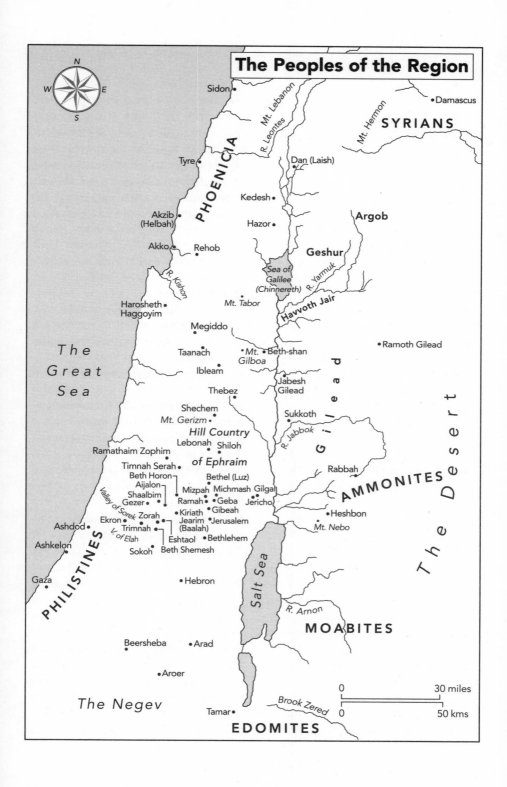

The Peoples of the Region

N
W E
S

Sidon •

• Damascus

Mt. Lebanon
R. Leontes
Mt. Hermon

SYRIANS

PHOENICIA

Tyre •

Dan (Laish) •

Kedesh •

Argob

Akzib
(Helbah) •

Hazor •

Akko •   • Rehob

Geshur

R. Kishon

Sea of
Galilee
(Chinnereth)

R. Yarmuk

Harosheth
Haggoyim •

Mt. Tabor

Havvoth Jair

Megiddo •

Taanach •

• Mt. • Beth-shan
Gilboa

• Ramoth Gilead

Ibleam •

Jabesh
Gilead

Gilead

The
Great
Sea

Thebez •

Sukkoth •

Shechem •
Mt. Gerizm •

Hill Country
Lebonah • Shiloh •

R. Jabbok

of Ephraim

Ramathaim Zophim •

Timnah Serah •

Bethel (Luz) •

Rabbah •

AMMONITES

The Desert

Beth Horon •
Aijalon
Shaalbim •
Gezer •

Mizpah • Michmash Gilgal •
Ramah • Geba • Jericho •

Heshbon •

Valley of Sorek

Ekron • • Zorah
Ashdod •

Trimnah •
V. of Elah

Kiriath
Jearim • Gibeah
(Baalah) • Jerusalem •

Mt. Nebo •

Eshtaol • • Bethlehem

Ashkelon •

Sokoh • Beth Shemesh

Salt Sea

Gaza •

PHILISTINES

• Hebron

R. Arnon

MOABITES

Beersheba •   • Arad

• Aroer

The Negev

0   30 miles
0   50 kms

Tamar •

Brook Zered

EDOMITES

eastern side of the Jordan, and rejoin their wives and families (for the background to this, see Nu 32:1–42). The Israelites acclaim Joshua as their leader, and wish him the same success as that enjoyed by Moses. That success is not long in coming.

JOSHUA 2:1–5:12
The First Days in Canaan

2:1–24 Rahab and the Spies Following a precedent established by Moses 38 years earlier, Joshua sends out spies to report back on what lies ahead of them in Canaan (see Nu 13:1–25). The two spies are requested specifically to provide information concerning the city of Jericho, the first major Canaanite settlement lying in the path of the proposed invasion route. Like most cities of the time, Jericho was a 'city-state', comparable to the Greek city-states of the classical period. It was defended by substantial walled fortifications, making it a difficult military objective. As the text indicates later on, some houses were built on, or into, these walls, including the house of Rahab.

The spies enter the house of a prostitute, named Rahab. It is clear that people in the region are aware of the presence of Israel in Moab, and fearful of what her intentions might be. When the presence of Israelite spies in the city is suspected, Rahab offers them safety and shelter (2:1–7). She explains that everyone is afraid of the Israelites, and affirms her own belief that the Lord has given the land over to Israel. And, just as she has shown kindness to the representatives of Israel, so the Israelites are asked to show kindness to her when they take possession of the city (2:8–14). The spies agree, and ask that a scarlet cord be hung in her window. She and all inside the house will be spared. Just as the red blood of the Passover lamb marked the houses of the people of God at the time of the exodus from Egypt, and ensured that they were spared from destruction, so Rahab's scarlet cord will ensure her safety. Then the spies are allowed to escape down a rope lowered from her window, set in the city's walls. After eluding their pursuers, they report back to Joshua: everyone is terrified of Israel (2:15–24; see also 5:1).

3:1–5:12 Crossing the Jordan; Circumcision at Gilgal Encouraged by this knowledge, Joshua issues orders to cross the Jordan, with the ark of the covenant in the lead (3:1–17). There are obvious similarities between this event and the crossing of the Red Sea, not least the strong sense of expectation that something dramatic is about to happen. Having marked the site of this crossing with twelve stones (4:1–24), Joshua makes arrangements for two of the most central religious practices of Israel to be performed on Canaanite soil. First, all the males within Israel were circumcised. During the period of wandering in the desert, this rite had not been performed; now, this act of obedience to the covenant is carried out in Canaan (5:2–8), followed by the first celebration of the Passover for 38 years (5:9–12). As Israel prepares to take the first steps towards conquering Canaan, she recalls how the Lord delivered her from captivity in Egypt for this very reason.

JOSHUA 5:13–12:24
The Invasion of Canaan

5:13–6:27 The Fall of Jericho Jericho now lies ahead. Encouraged by a vision of a heavenly figure who identifies himself as the 'commander of the army of the LORD' (5:13–15; there are parallels here with the incident of Moses at the burning bush, Ex 3), Joshua prepares to take the city. The story of how he orders his army to march around the city, followed by the ark of the Lord, is recorded in 6:2–27. On the seventh day of the siege, the walls of the city collapse, allowing Israel to gain total control. Rahab and her family are spared. The remainder of the city, including all its inhabitants irrespective of age, is destroyed.

This aspect of the conquest of Canaan causes concern to many reading the story, especially for the first time. How can a loving God permit such slaughter? Why are entire cities put to the sword? Did not God declare that he would spare even Sodom for the sake of a few righteous people in its midst? There are no easy answers to these questions. The ethics of warfare in the ancient world were often fairly basic: kill or be killed.

Did God really command all that killing?

What happened at Jericho was an example of *herem* ('the ban'), the total destruction of a city and everyone and everything within it, rather than taking any captives or plunder, as a way of devoting it all to God. But can such wholesale destruction really have been what God wanted, as Moses said it was (Dt 7:1–7)?

First, it is important to remember that such total destruction was extremely rare – indeed, only two cities in the book of Joshua experienced this: Jericho (6:17–24) and Hazor (11:10–11). Other cities were spared – after all, Israel needed to live in this land.

Secondly, it was always possible to escape such destruction, as Rahab escaped Jericho's destruction because of her faith (2:18–24; 6:24–25).

Thirdly, such commands are not blanket commands throughout the Old Testament. They are extremely rare, occurring only at crucial moments in Israel's history when its very future and survival were at stake.

Fourthly, the cultures that Moses commanded Joshua to destroy (Dt 12:1–3) had an extremely dark side: they followed fertility religions, whose worship involved not only widespread ritual prostitution, but also at times child sacrifice.

Fifthly, this judgment did not come without warning. Generations earlier God had promised to give Canaan to Abraham (Ge 15:12–21) but said he could not do so immediately 'for the sin of the Amorites has not yet reached its full measure' (v.16). Only when their sin was so deep that it was obvious to everybody would God judge them (just as he did not send the flood until the earth was utterly corrupt). But they failed to change their ways, despite knowing who God was and what he had done (e.g., Jos 2:11). Jericho is therefore a solemn reminder of the certainty of coming judgment for those who persistently reject God.

However, one aspect of this matter must be noted, which helps to set it in its proper context.

Israel was entering a unique situation in her history, which she had never faced before and would never face again. She was entering a region populated by peoples of pagan beliefs, which could easily destroy the faith of Israel. As a result, it was regarded as necessary to purge such pagan beliefs and cultures from the land. In no way, then, does what happened at the time of the conquest of Canaan justify the slaughter of innocents at any other time in history. With the coming of Christ, we may rejoice that such episodes are no longer regarded as necessary or justifiable. The situation confronted by Israel as she entered Canaan will never arise again.

7:1–26 Achan's Sin Success is immediately followed by sin. Despite all their pledges and oaths of obedience, Israel disobeys God at the first available opportunity. The sin in question is the theft of some of the booty from Jericho, which was meant to have been dedicated to the Lord. The theft comes to light only on account of a military failure. A band of several thousand men is despatched by Joshua to take the nearby town of Ai, about 25 kilometres away. The town was not heavily populated, and ought to have been an easy objective. In fact, the Israelites suffer serious losses in their abortive attempt to take it. Joshua is devastated. Has God ceased to be faithful to his covenant? Then the truth dawns: it is not God, but Israel, who has been faithless (7:1–15).

Joshua undertakes a major inves-tigation, throwing lots until the guilty party is identified. First, the search is narrowed to the tribe of Judah, then to the Zerahite clan within Judah, then the family of Zimri within the Zerahite clan. Achan, a member of this family, comes forward and admits his guilt. He has stolen some of the booty from Jericho, and hidden it under his tent. For this attempt to deceive both Israel and the Lord, he and his family are stoned to death (7:16–26). Only in this way can the guilt of their crime be purged from the people as a whole.

8:1–29 Ai Destroyed After this purging of the guilt of the people, Joshua turns his attention again to Ai. The town is here described as having a population of 12,000 (8:25), against which Joshua commits 30,000 armed men (8:3). Archaeological evidence suggests that Ai was not a major centre of population around this time, and may even have existed in a ruined or semi-ruined state. There is, however, some slight doubt as to the identification of the archaeological site traditionally identified with the city. At any rate, the attack on the city (which is described in detail) is successful. Once more, the total destruction of the city and its inhabitants raises moral questions noted earlier (see 'Did God really command all that killing?', page 105).

8:30–35 The Covenant Renewed at Mount Ebal The story of how Israel subdues the remainder of the land west of the Jordan will be taken up presently. Even as Israel prepares to engage in warfare with the peoples of the region, Joshua makes space for the people to renew the covenant with the Lord, as Moses had commanded.

This would have been a risky affair: Israel is surrounded by hostile forces, anxious to destroy her in order to neutralise the threat she poses to their security. It is, however, possible that some local peoples have made peace with Israel: the reference to the presence of 'foreigners' (8:33) may refer to the presence of Gibeonites or Hivites from the region, anticipating the developments fully narrated in chapter 9.

The importance of the renewal of the covenant at Mount Ebal is enormous. An altar has been built to the Lord in Canaan, establishing his claim to authority over the land and its peoples. By remaining faithful to the commands of Moses (Dt 27:1–8), Joshua ensures the continuing favour and presence of God in the forthcoming struggle to gain the ascendancy in the region.

9:1–27 *The Gibeonite Deception* Three major sections now follow, which deal with the way in which Israel is able to emerge from her bridgehead in the region of Jericho, and take possession of the land west of the Jordan. The sections deal respectively with the campaigns in the central, southern and northern regions of Canaan. The first section deals with the Gibeonites (9:1–27), a group of peoples to the north of Jerusalem. Realising that they are in danger from the advancing Israelites, the cities send emissaries to Israel. They pretend that they are from a distant region, well away from Canaan. Joshua agrees to enter into a treaty with them, without consulting the Lord. When it turns out that he has unwittingly made a solemn oath of peace with nearby towns, the people are furious. They will not be allowed to

destroy the Gibeonites. Indeed, as it turns out later, they will even have to defend them if they come under attack. However, Joshua deals with the Gibeonites' deceit by pressing them into service as suppliers of wood and water for the altar of the Lord.

10:1–43 *Southern Cities Conquered* The second section relates how Joshua deals with a coalition of kings from the southern regions of Canaan, including the cities of Jerusalem and Hebron (10:1–43). Armies from five Amorite cities lay siege to Gibeon, obliging Joshua to respond to their urgent plea for assistance. After an all-night march from his camp at Gilgal, Joshua takes the Amorite besiegers by surprise, and routs them. The five Amorite kings are tracked down and executed. In a series of assaults, Joshua then lays siege to and sacks the major cities of the southern region of Canaan. In a single campaign, the entire region is subdued. It is important to notice that Joshua's sacking of the region is in response to an attack initiated from its peoples. That same pattern emerges in the account of the subjugation of the northern region of Canaan, which now follows.

11:1–23 *Northern Kings Defeated* After Joshua returns to Gilgal, a coalition of city-states in the northern region of Canaan forms, with the single purpose of neutralising the threat posed by Israel (11:1–23). Armies drawn from the Galilean hill country assemble at a site referred to as Merom, which is thought to be some 12 kilometres to the northwest of Lake Galilee. Joshua defeats the armies, pursuing them to the north, and

eventually turning south again to take and destroy the important city of Hazor. Joshua completes his conquest of the region by defeating the Anakites. With this, the military campaigns end, and 'the land had rest from war' (11:23). Joshua can now divide the land among the tribes, following the allocations laid down by Moses, as described in some detail in later chapters. This account of the conquest of Canaan is followed by a detailed list of those defeated in the campaigns of Moses and Joshua (12:1–24). As will become clear in the following chapter, there are still substantial areas of land to be taken over; however, Israel has now established a firm power base in the region, from which she can expand when the time is right.

JOSHUA 13:1–22:34
The Allocation of Territory to the Tribes

13:1–19:51 Division of the Land This large section deals with the specifics of the allocation of Canaan to the tribes of Israel, giving precise details of the towns and regions they are to occupy. The account opens with details of the regions that remain to be conquered (13:1–7). It then shifts to the land east of the Jordan, which had been allocated to the tribes of Reuben and Gad, and the half-tribe of Manasseh (13:8–32). In accordance with the assignment made by Moses, this allocation is confirmed, and broken down by region. It must be appreciated that this land was not thought of as the 'promised land'; this territory was east of the Jordan. Attention then shifts to the promised land in the strict sense of the term – the areas conquered west of the Jordan, which are now allocated by lot to

the remaining nine-and-a-half tribes (14:1–19:48). Joshua himself is allocated a town in the hill country, where he will later be buried (19:49–50; 24:30).

20:1–21:45 Cities of Refuge; Towns for the Levites The text in this part of the book of Joshua reads rather like a legal document, and may seem a little uninteresting to many readers. However, it must be recalled that this section of Joshua represents the final confirmation of the promise that Israel will possess the land of Canaan. Each tribe is being allocated more than living space or grazing rights: they are being given the right to possess the regions assigned to them. This long section is the concrete fulfilment of the Lord's promise to give the land to the descendants of Abraham, Isaac and Jacob. Now that promise is being fulfilled. Every region and town that is named, including the cities of refuge (20:1–9) and towns for the Levites (21:1–42), is a tangible demonstration of God's faithfulness to his promises: 'So the LORD gave Israel all the land he had sworn to give their ancestors, and they took possession of it and settled there . . . Not one of all the LORD's good promises to Israel failed; every one was fulfilled' (21:43–45).

22:1–34 Eastern Tribes Return Home Finally, with the wars over, Joshua gives permission to the fighting men of the tribes of Reuben and Gad, and the half-tribe of Manasseh, to return home to their families, who had settled on the east bank of the Jordan. However, a misunderstanding develops, which nearly leads to war between the tribes

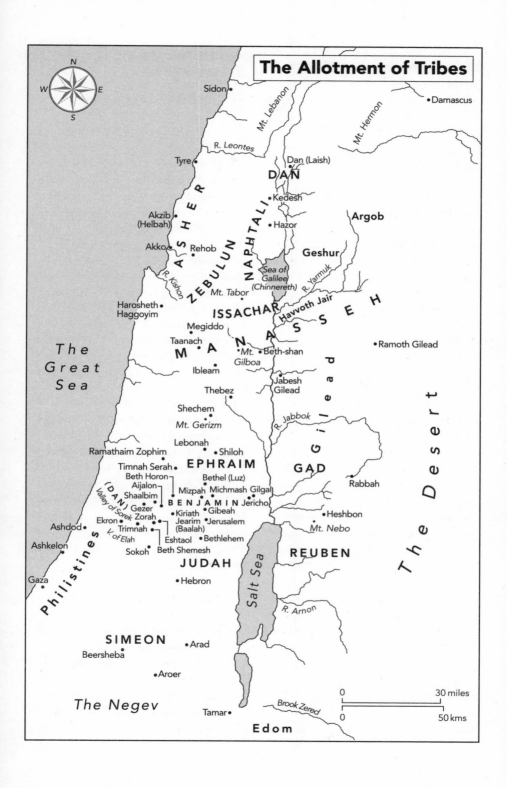

The Allotment of Tribes

N
W E
S

Sidon
Damascus

Mt. Lebanon
Mt. Hermon

R. Leontes

Tyre
Dan (Laish)
DAN

Kedesh
Akzib (Helbah)
ASHER
Hazor
Argob

Akko
Rehob
Geshur
ZEBULUN
NAPHTALI
Sea of Galilee (Chinnereth)

Harosheth Haggoyim
R. Kishon
Mt. Tabor
R. Yarmuk

ISSACHAR

The Great Sea
Megiddo
MANASSEH
Havvoth Jair

Taanach
Mt. Gilboa
Beth-shan
Ramoth Gilead

Ibleam
Jabesh Gilead

Thebez
Gilead

Shechem
R. Jabbok
Mt. Gerizm

Lebonah
GAD
Rabbah
Ramathaim Zophim
Shiloh
EPHRAIM

Timnah Serah
Bethel (Luz)
Beth Horon
Mizpah
Michmash
Gilgal
Aijalon
Shaalbim
(DAN)
BENJAMIN
Jericho
Heshbon
Gezer
Kiriath Jearim (Baalah)
Gibeah
Valley of Sorek
Zorah
Jerusalem
Mt. Nebo
Ekron
Trimnah
V. of Elah
Eshtaol
Bethlehem
Ashdod
Beth Shemesh
REUBEN
Ashkelon
Sokoh
JUDAH
Philistines

Gaza
Salt Sea
The Desert

Hebron
R. Arnon

SIMEON
Arad
Beersheba

Aroer

The Negev
Tamar
Brook Zered

0   30 miles
0   50 kms

Edom

on the east and west banks of the Jordan. Joshua had set up the tabernacle at Shiloh (18:1), about 15 kilometres northeast of Bethel, where it would remain until the time of Samuel (see 1Sa 4:3). However, as the fighting men of Reuben, Gad and Manasseh return to Gilead, they decide to build an altar near the Jordan, on Israelite territory. This provokes an immediate and angry response from the remaining tribes, who interpret this action as an attempt to set up a rival altar to that at Shiloh. This would have been an act of rebellion against the Lord, which would have to be punished. A delegation is sent in an attempt to avert the war that would inevitably have followed.

However, the issue is resolved. The eastern tribes had been concerned that their right to worship the Lord might have been forgotten or denied by those on the western side of the Jordan (22:24–29). As the altar was at Shiloh, in the west, there was a danger that the eastern tribes might have been excluded from any right to worship the Lord, or be part of the covenant community of Israel. Strictly speaking, the land east of the Jordan was not part of the land the Lord had promised to Israel. A case could therefore have been made for suggesting that the tribes who had settled in Gilead were not part of the people of God. The purpose of the altar at Geliloth (22:10) is to assert both their loyalty to the Lord, and their right to worship him, and share in his blessings to his people. Satisfied with this explanation, the delegation returns to Shiloh.

JOSHUA 23:1–24:33
The Death of Joshua

23:1–16 Joshua's Farewell to the Leaders Several years of peace pass, during which Israel is able to consolidate her position. It seems that at least a decade has passed since the wars that led to Israel establishing her permanent presence in Canaan. Now Joshua is becoming old, and is close to death. Using words that recall his own commissioning by the Lord to lead Israel into Canaan (1:7–8), he reminds Israel of the need to remain faithful to the Lord. He forbids intermarriage or any form of association between Israel and the peoples of Canaan, on account of the potential impact that their pagan religions might have on the faith of Israel.

24:1–28 The Covenant Renewed at Shechem Joshua then summons the tribes of Israel to Shechem, to formally and solemnly renew the covenant that had been established at Mount Ebal, shortly after Israel's entry into the promised land (8:30–35). In a powerful and moving speech, Joshua reminds his people of their origins and history (24:1–13). He recounts the calling of Abraham, Isaac and Jacob, and the migration of the people to Egypt. He reminds them of their affliction and misery in that land, and of how the Lord delivered them from their bondage and led them safely to the promised land.

Joshua then asks all who are assembled to renew their pledges to the Lord. Those who do not wish to do so are free to serve other gods (24:14–15). Joshua affirms his own commitment to the Lord, which is

echoed by the people. They freely choose to continue to serve the Lord, with all that this implies (24:16–27). Sadly, as subsequent events will show, they will prove to be as prone to rebellion and disobedience as their ancestors in the desert. Yet this lies in the future. For the moment, the talk is only of commitment and obedience. Joshua dismisses the people, and all of them return to their own region of Canaan (24:28).

24:29–33 Buried in the Promised Land Just as Deuteronomy ended with the death of Moses, so Joshua ends with the death of Moses' faithful successor. Joshua, having been one of the twelve spies sent out by Moses to explore Canaan half a century earlier, at the time of the abortive invasion attempt (Nu 13:16–30), is now buried in his own property in the promised land, in fulfilment of the Lord's promises. The bones of Joseph, brought up from Egypt, are also buried in the promised land, so that he too might find rest in the land promised to his descendants (24:32). And so the account of Israel's wanderings ends. She has found her rest in the promised land. The book of Joshua is thus a story of fulfilled promises and realised hopes.

Yet Joshua has designated no successor. What will happen after his death? Who will lead Israel as she faces the new dangers that lie ahead? Will Israel ever conquer the remaining areas of Canaan? One chapter of the history of Israel now closes, and another prepares to open.

JUDGES

The book of Judges deals with the history of Israel from the death of Joshua to the rise of Samuel, before there is any permanent centralised administration in the land. It chronicles the decline in religious faith and obedience in the land after the death of Joshua, especially its lapse into idolatry and pagan practices. Despite all the warnings and encouragements of Joshua, Israel fails to remain faithful to the Lord.

One of the most noticeable differences between the books of Joshua and Judges concerns the situations that confront Israel. In Judges, Israel has to occupy and subdue Canaan, facing threats from the various peoples already living there. Israel is portrayed as a people acting and working together against these threats from within Canaan. In Judges, however, the main threats come from outside Canaan – from peoples from the east side of the Jordan, such as the Ammonites, Midianites and Moabites. Only on one occasion is there any reference to a threat from within Canaan itself. Israel is no longer a single centralised body of people, but a settled group of tribes who have now established themselves in various regions of Canaan. Although the people share a common faith and a common story, they increasingly tend to think of their identities in terms of individual tribes and clans, rather than being members of Israel as a whole.

The word 'judge' needs a little explanation. During the course of this book, we shall meet a number of individuals, such as Deborah and Samuel, who are referred to as 'judges'. In modern days, this would be understood to mean something like 'an impartial arbitrator in legal debates', or 'someone who passes judgment'. The word is, however, used in a very different sense in this book. Its basic meaning is 'a charismatic leader raised up by God to deliver his people from danger'. The emphasis is upon deliverance from danger rather than impartial legal administration! The 'judges' are actually figures of salvation, rather than judgment. And, as will become clear from what follows, Israel certainly needs that kind of help, as she lapses into sin and rebellion.

OUTLINE

The occupation of the land

The judges

JUDGES 1:1–3:6
Introduction

1:1–2:5 Israel Fights the Remaining Canaanites Judges opens with a survey of the situation within Canaan after the death of Joshua. Large tracts of the promised land remain in the hands of the Canaanites. The first assault on these remaining territories is made by the fighting men of Judah (1:2–10), who make substantial advances. Of particular importance is the capture of the Philistine cities of Gaza, Ashkelon and Ekron and their surrounding territories (1:18). Each of these cities is of major commercial and strategic importance, being located on major trade routes leading from Egypt to the north.

Other successes are scored by other tribes, including the 'tribes of Joseph', a reference to the tribe of Ephraim and the half of the tribe of Manasseh that chooses to settle on the west, rather than the east, of the river Jordan (1:21–26). However, the predominant pattern that emerges is that of establishing an Israelite presence

in the midst of a Canaanite population. Time after time, Judges records Israel's failure to drive out the Canaanites (1:27–36). It seems that Israel's programme of expansion has run out of steam. This is a clear case of failure on the part of Israel, which provokes anger from the Lord (2:1–5).

2:6–3:6 Disobedience and Defeat The narrative then changes pace. An important bridging section deals with events after the death of Joshua, and lays the foundations for an understanding of what goes wrong within Israel during the period of the judges. How can a nation that has shown such dedication and devotion under Joshua lapse into a state of lethargy or rebellion? After the death of Joshua, a generation emerge who know neither the Lord nor what he has done for Israel (2:10). As those who had been present during the nomadic period of Israel's history die, they are replaced by those who know nothing at first hand of the great events that have led to Israel becoming established in the promised land.

Disobedience and apostasy set in. Israelites begin to experiment with native Canaanite pagan religions. In particular, they worship Baal (2:13). Baal is a local god worshipped by the Canaanites, and linked with fertility, both human and agricultural. Linked with Baal is the goddess Ashtoreth (also mentioned at 2:13), who is also linked with fertility cults. Worship of Baal or Ashtoreth often involved cultic prostitution, and is also thought to have involved child sacrifice on occasion. By adopting these forms of worship, Israel clearly abandons her commitment to the Lord. As a result, Israel loses the protection and favour of the Lord, and becomes vulnerable to the attacks of marauders of various kinds. Judges establishes a pattern of rebellion and restoration: Israel worships other gods, and finds herself in distress as a result; she returns to the Lord, and her fortunes are restored. The narrative provided by Judges illustrates this pattern many times.

Israel's misfortunes are thus seen as the direct result of the Lord's decision to try Israel, and see whether she is prepared to remain faithful to him (2:20–23). In particular, the continuing presence of Canaanites in Israelite territory is seen as a result of God's withholding victory from his increasingly wayward and disobedient people (2:23). Yet Israel gradually falls away from God, allowing intermarriage with local peoples, despite Joshua's total prohibition of this practice (3:1–6).

JUDGES 3:7–16:31
Apostasy and Deliverance

3:7–5:31 Disobedience and Deborah's Song
The result of this is neatly summarised

by the opening of the next section: 'The Israelites . . . forgot the LORD their God and served the Baals and the Asherahs' (3:7). As a result of her loss of God's favour, Israel finds herself under the oppression of a local Canaanite king. Deliverance occurs only when she repents, and calls upon the name of the Lord (3:8–11). The same pattern is repeated with a Moabite king (3:12–31), and with Jabin, a king of Canaan (4:1–24). In this final case, at least six tribes of Israel are rallied by the prophet Deborah, and given victory over Sisera, the commander of the forces of Jabin. Sisera himself is eventually killed by a blow from a tent peg by Jael, the wife of Heber (4:17–22). Israel subsequently overcomes Jabin (4:23–24). Deborah's song of triumph (5:1–31) is one of the oldest poems in Scripture, containing many very ancient Hebrew words and expressions. It lays emphasis upon the righteousness of God, which is publicly demonstrated in his victory over the enemies of his people.

6:1–40 Gideon
The narrative moves on to deal with the story of Gideon. Once more, the same pattern is noted: Israel's promises of obedience to the Lord, followed by a lapse into disbelief and disobedience. As a result, Israel finds herself being oppressed by other peoples. In this case, the oppressors are the Midianites, acting in what appears to have been a loose and shifting alliance with other peoples from the east of the Jordan, such as the Amalekites. Eventually, the Israelites are driven to despair and, realising that they cannot manage unaided, call upon the name of

Can God still speak through 'fleeces'?

Some Christians sometimes suggest 'putting out a fleece' as a way of seeking God's will. The expression refers to the incident in Jdg 6:36–40 where Gideon, wanting reassurance of his call to lead Israel into battle, took a wool fleece, laid it on a threshing-floor and then prayed, asking that if God truly wanted to save Israel through him that the next morning dew would cover the fleece but not the ground. When that happened, he asked God to do the same thing, but the other way round, and again it happened. Now convinced God was speaking, he led Israel to great victory.

But is such an approach an authentic way of discovering God's will today? In seeking an answer, we must note the context of Gideon's experience; for actually, this was an expression of his *un*-belief rather than his faith. After all, an angel had already visited him, answering his doubts, commissioning him and assuring him that God would be with him (6:11–16). When his lack of faith had still led him to request a sign, the angel had graciously granted it (6:17–24). God had then protected him the next day when the town was angry with him for cutting down their idols (6:25–32). Yet despite all this, Gideon *still* wanted another sign. This was unbelief, not faith!

So can we still do this sort of thing? God is undoubtedly gracious and no doubt answers such requests at times; but we should remember that it shows the absence of faith rather than its presence. With the Holy Spirit, the Bible and Christian counsel God has provided ample resources for us today to seek and confirm his will without needing to resort to such 'fleeces', which can often be excuses for not facing up to responsibility rather than genuine expressions of courageous faith.

the Lord (6:1–6). They are then reminded of their failures and rebellion, and called to repentance, despite their obstinacy (6:7–10).

The appointed deliverer of Israel is Gideon (6:11–24), a member of the Abiezrite clan of the tribe of Manasseh. Gideon's father, Joash, illustrates well the manner in which Israel has abandoned her faith in the Lord: we learn that he has constructed an altar to Baal, along with an adjoining Asherah pole (6:25). Gideon cannot believe that he is being called by the Lord: Is he not the least important member of a rather insignificant clan? But, as Scripture makes clear, God is in the habit of taking people who regard themselves as being insignificant, and doing great things through them. Gideon is a case in point.

Gideon's mission begins at home. He must purge his family of Baal worship, before he can go any further. He destroys his father's altar to Baal, and replaces it with an altar to the Lord. A popular outcry results, indicating how deeply Baal worship has taken root in the region (6:28–32). However, his real mission relates to the deliverance of Israel from the Midianites and their allies. Gideon rallies first his own clan, then his own tribe, then neighbouring tribes, as he

prepares to deliver Israel. Yet he has genuine hesitations over his calling. Is God really with Israel? Gideon lays out a fleece to reassure himself of the Lord's intentions (6:36–40). Gideon wants to be sure that he will be acting with God's authority and support, not simply on account of some vague feeling that he is being called in this way.

7:1–8:21 Gideon Defeats the Midianites In the end, Gideon's victory over the Midianites (7:1–25) does not depend on human strength, but on the strength of the Lord. The manner of the victory makes this very clear, and prevents Israel from becoming overconfident and arrogant about her own ability and power. Gideon is told to use only 300 of the 10,000 armed men who accompany him in the final assault, which (like his destruction of the altar to Baal) will take place by night. Confused by the darkness, the Midianites gain the impression that a huge Israelite army is in their midst. They scatter, and are subsequently set on and picked off by the larger Israelite force in the vicinity, as well as by others who enter the conflict once they see it is going their way. However, Gideon's success causes resentment and irritation elsewhere (8:1–21).

8:22–9:57 Gideon Dies; Abimelek is Made King Despite this resentment in some quarters, Gideon is recognised as the deliverer of Israel, and the people offer to make him and his descendants kings over them. Gideon refuses: only the Lord will rule over Israel (8:22–27). During the remainder of Gideon's lifetime, Israel enjoys relative peace, on account of her

obedience to the Lord. However, once Gideon is dead, Israel returns once more to Baal worship (8:28–35). Even Gideon's son Abimelek revolts against the memory of his father, murdering his sons and attempting to establish himself as king (9:1–7).

10:1–12:7 Tola, Jair and Jephthah The pattern of disobedience followed by oppression continues. After relative security under Tola and Jair (10:1–5), rebellion again breaks out. Judges records many local gods being worshipped by the Israelites (10:6–14), with a resulting destabilisation in the region. Israel finds herself under attack from the Philistines to the west and the Ammonites to the east. In their situation, they again call on the Lord, and ask for his help (10:10, 15).

The Lord raises up Jephthah the Gileadite (11:1–12:7), who routs the Ammonites. In doing so, he provokes an unfortunate feud with the Ephraimites (12:1–6). This passage is of importance historically, in that it allows us to date the events in question. The reference to Israel having occupied the region for three hundred years (11:26) fits in well with what we know of the chronology of this period.

12:8–13:25 The Birth of Samson After Jephthah, Israel enjoys relative security for a quarter of a century (12:8–15), before the cycle of rebellion and oppression begins once more. This time, the oppressors are the Philistines, based on the western coastal regions of Canaan (13:1). In this case, the deliverer is to be Samson. From the moment of his birth, it is clear that Samson is to be a Nazirite

(13:5). The word 'Nazirite' is derived from the Hebrew word meaning 'to consecrate' or 'to separate from'. The term was used to refer to men and women who had taken the decision to consecrate themselves to God by 'separating' themselves from certain things through a special vow (Nu 6:1–21).

14:1–16:31 *Samson's Vengeance on, and Final Victory over, the Philistines* Samson hardly seems to be qualified as a judge of Israel. Far from being an obedient servant of the Lord, he is prone to do whatever is right in his own eyes – such as marrying a Philistine wife (14:1–3). However, the hand of the Lord is at work in a hidden manner, setting up Samson as the deliverer of his people (14:4).

The story of Samson has many themes of relevance to Israel, not least the way in which Samson is apparently overwhelmed by the Philistines (16:23–30). This can be seen as reflecting the way in which many Israelites think that the Lord has been overwhelmed by local pagan gods, such as Dagon. As the ultimate victory of Samson demonstrates, the Lord is still present with his people, even if they choose to rebel against him.

A further important aspect of the account of Samson is the reference to the 'Spirit of the LORD' coming on him in power (14:19) – an important anticipation of the manner in which God empowers his people to meet the challenges they face. In the New Testament, the coming of the Holy Spirit at Pentecost (Ac 2:1–47) may be seen as standing in a direct line of succession to this incident in the life of Samson.

JUDGES 17:1–21:25
Epilogue

Samson's tendency to do his own thing, rather than be openly obedient, now proves to be typical of the people of Israel as a whole, as the closing remark of this section makes clear (21:25). Israel is portrayed as lacking any centralised administration. The country has no king (18:1; 19:1), and is in the process of degenerating into moral anarchy. The series of incidents related as the book comes to a close are clearly intended to illustrate the moral and religious degeneration of this period in Israel's history. Something has to be done. Israel must be delivered from this state of decay. However, at this stage, it is far from clear what can be done about the state of things.

17:1–18:31 *Micah and the Danites* Two incidents are singled out for special mention, one focusing on religious and the other on moral degeneration. First, the story is told of how a man named Micah sets up a local place of worship in Ephraim, dedicated to some local gods. A Levite is installed to preside over this paganised form of worship (17:1–13), which is taken up and spread by the tribe of Dan as they conquer neighbouring territory, including the city of Laish (18:1–31). The incident, which is not specifically dated, is clearly intended to illustrate how easily pagan practices are picked up by Israel. Even though the altar at Shiloh was the only legitimate site of worship in Canaan, Micah and the tribe of Dan have no difficulty in establishing their own sites of worship, and paganised forms of worship of the Lord.

19:1–30 A Levite and His Concubine The second incident deals with the moral corruption of Israel at the time. In terms that parallel the account of Lot's visit to Sodom (Ge 19:5), local Israelites of the tribe of Benjamin attempt to homosexually rape a traveller in the town of Gibeah, before raping a woman instead, who dies from the shock of the attack. The woman in question was the concubine of a Levite.

20:1–21:25 Israelites Fight the Benjaminites Israel is appalled at this deed, and determines to take her revenge against those in Gibeah who were responsible for the act. However, the tribe of Benjamin defend their city and its inhabitants, despite the fact that it leads directly to the slaughter of their army by the remainder of Israel, and the sack of their cities (20:1–48). The few remaining Benjaminite males are obliged to seize young girls from the region of Shiloh to ensure the continued presence of Benjaminite males in Israel (21:1–23), as no other tribe will allow them to marry their women.

This, then, is the sorry state of Israel at the end of the period of the judges. Religious and moral decay is evident. Everyone does as they please; there is no king to enforce authority (21:25). So will Israel become like the Canaanites, and lose her distinctive beliefs and practices? Or will something happen, to restore the true worship of the Lord, and obedience to him? The story will be taken up in 1 Samuel.

First, we are asked to pause in the midst of this gripping historical narrative, and listen to a love story set in the period of the Judges. It is a love story that will play no small part in the solution of Israel's problems, as will become clear as we turn to the story of Ruth.

RUTH

The book of Ruth, which takes its name from one of its central characters, is set at the time of the Judges. As will be clear from the book of Judges, this was a time of political instability and moral and religious corruption. The background to the book of Ruth is the continuing hostility between the people of Moab and the Israelites, reflecting Moab's lingering resentment against Israel during the period of the conquest. At this time, many Moabite regions and towns had been occupied by Israel. The lands allocated to Judah were directly opposite the land of Moab, on the far side of the Dead Sea.

OUTLINE

Naomi left desolate

1:1–22 Naomi and Ruth The story opens with an account of a famine in Israel, which obliges a family (Elimelek and his wife, Naomi, with their two sons) to move to Moab and find work there. While they are in this region, Elimelek dies, and both sons marry Moabite women, Ruth and Orpah. Eventually, both sons die, leaving Naomi alone with her two daughters-in-law (1:5–6). Hearing that the famine has ended, Naomi decides to return home to Bethlehem, and urges Ruth and Orpah to return to Moab and their own gods. Orpah complies with this wish; Ruth does not (1:7–15). Even though Ruth can expect nothing from Naomi, she insists on remaining by her side. She will share Naomi's faith, as well as her people (1:16–17). As a result, the two women return together to Bethlehem, in time for the barley harvest.

What does God think about the poor?

Jesus' words 'The poor you will always have with you' (Mt 26:11) have sometimes been used to justify poverty. But Jesus was saying anything but that. Responding to his disciples' grumbling, and prompted by a woman's lavish anointing of his feet, he was saying that, while they would always have opportunities to do good to the poor, they would never again have an opportunity to anoint him for burial (Mt 26:6–13). He was quoting from the Law, which said, 'There will always be poor people in the land. *Therefore* I command you to be open-handed towards your fellow Israelites who are poor and needy in your land' (Dt 15:11). The very presence of the poor demands a response from God's people, for God's heart is for them (e.g., Ps 12:5) and the Law is full of commands concerning them.

Ruth's gleaning was possible only because the Law required landowners to leave grain behind when harvesting for the poor (Lev 19:9–10; Dt 24:19–22). God's people were commanded to be generous to the poor (Dt 15:7) and not take advantage of them (Dt 24:14–15). Every third year the tithe was to be used for them (Dt 14:28–29), and every seven years their debts were to be cancelled (Dt 15:1–18). But the Bible's concern is not simply acts of charity; the prophets challenged structural poverty (e.g., Am 8:4–10) and Jesus challenged the love of money that can blind us to others' needs (e.g., Mt 19:16–24). The first Christians set a high standard of care for the poor from the very beginning (Ac 2:45; 4:34–35) and this became a fundamental part of apostolic Christianity (Gal 2:9–10). Paul appealed to Christians to give generously to those in need (2 Co 8–9) and James warned about how easily wealth can blind us to social justice (Jas 5:1–6).

2:1–23 Ruth Meets Boaz We are now told that Naomi has a relative on her husband's side, named Boaz, a person of importance locally. Ruth asks permission of Naomi to go to the local fields, and pick up the leftover grain (2:1–2). She begins to work in some local fields, without knowing either that these fields belong to Boaz, or that Boaz is a relative of Naomi. The code of law given to Moses made provision at several points for the welfare of the poor, widows, orphans and foreigners. One such provision was the insistence that harvesting should leave behind some produce for foreigners, orphans and widows (Dt 24:19–22). Thus sheaves of wheat, olives and grapes would remain in the fields after the harvest, and could be taken and used by those less fortunate than the landowner and his workers. Boaz, on hearing of how Ruth left Moab to remain with Naomi, ensures that she is well cared for (2:3–19).

Returning to Naomi with a substantial amount of grain as a result of her labours, Ruth tells her mother-in-law about the day's events. On learning that Ruth worked in Boaz' fields, Naomi tells her that Boaz is 'one of our guardian-redeemers' (2:20). The importance of this statement needs to be explained in a little detail. The guardian-redeemer was a relative who had the privilege or duty to

restore or preserve the full community rights of family members who had fallen on difficult times. The word 'redeem' here means 'to buy back'. An example of such difficulty is provided by a family member who has had to sell himself into slavery to pay off a bad debt. The particular duties of the guardian-redeemer included the responsibility of redeeming family land where this had to be sold, redeeming enslaved family members, providing an heir for the family, avenging the death of murdered family members and acting as a trustee for family business.

The guardian-redeemer is of particular importance in the book of Ruth. The most likely explanation of what happens here is that Elimelek was obliged to sell his land in Judah before leaving for Moab. Naomi would have retained the right to buy the land back, thus keeping it within the family; however, lacking the funds to do so, she is dependent upon someone in the family buying it back on her behalf. Without this redemption, she cannot possess the land to which she has rights, or benefit from it in any way.

3:1–18 Ruth and Boaz at the Threshing-floor

Naomi then instructs Ruth to go to the threshing-floor, and sleep at Boaz' feet (3:1–6). The actions in question would probably be interpreted as indicating that Ruth wishes to marry Boaz, although it is clear that she also wishes to draw attention to the fact that he is her guardian-redeemer. Boaz is clearly flattered by Ruth's attention (3:10). However, he points out that there is someone else who has priority over him as the guardian-redeemer (3:12–13).

Boaz nevertheless promises to intervene if things do not work out well. Satisfied, Ruth returns to Naomi.

4:1–17 Boaz Marries Ruth

Later, Boaz goes to the town gate, the traditional place for transacting local business and legal matters. The guardian-redeemer eventually turns up, and Boaz raises the subject of the redemption of Elimelek's land. The guardian-redeemer, who is never identified by name, agrees in the presence of witnesses to buy back the land (4:1–4). Boaz then asks him to take Ruth into his home as his wife. The guardian-redeemer declines, probably worried about the legal consequences of any male children he might have by her, who would have had certain inheritance rights concerning the property (4:6). As a result, the guardian-redeemer declines to redeem the property, and hands over all his rights in this matter to Boaz. Boaz publicly declares his intention to redeem the property and to marry Ruth (4:8–12). And so the story ends happily. Ruth marries Boaz, and they have a son, named Obed.

4:18–22 The Genealogy of David

We then learn the full significance of this love story. Obed will himself marry, and have a son named Jesse. And Jesse will have a son named David – the greatest king Israel will ever have. And through David, Boaz and Ruth are ancestors of Jesus Christ himself (Mt 1:5). What may read simply like a love story turns out to be God's providence at work, preparing the way for the renewal of Israel under David, and its redemption through Jesus Christ.

1 AND 2 SAMUEL

The book of Judges gave a graphic account of Israel's degeneration into political, religious and moral corruption after the golden period of Joshua. It left its reader wondering what would happen next. How could order be restored to this situation? How could Israel be brought back to the worship of the Lord? The answer is provided in 1 and 2 Samuel, which were originally one larger book, which was divided into two halves by early translators. The two works together document the development of kingship in Israel. The division (which cannot be regarded as part of the original inspired text of Scripture) is not entirely helpful, and disrupts the flow of the work. To make the reading of the work easier, and to bring out the continuity of the story, we shall treat the two volumes as one work (a practice that will also be adopted in the case of 1 and 2 Kings and 1 and 2 Chronicles).

One of the developments that should be noted in this narrative is the emergence of the terms 'Israel' and 'Judah' to refer to the northern and southern regions of the land that was originally Canaan. The term 'Israel' was originally used to refer to the whole area, up to and during the reign of Saul. However, after the death of Saul, open warfare resulted between the supporters of Saul in the north, and the supporters of David in the south of the country. As David was himself a member of the tribe of Judah, it was probably only to be expected that the term 'Judah' came to refer to both the southern tribes of Simeon and Judah (Jos 19:1–9), who backed David against the house of Saul.

The house of Saul regarded itself as continuing the rule of Saul over all Israel, and thus retained the term 'Israel' to refer to its sphere of influence, despite the fact that this now referred only to the northern region of the country. David is initially proclaimed king of Judah at the southern city of Hebron; it is only as a result of his military campaigns that he becomes king of all Israel. Up to the time of Saul's death, there had been a non-Israelite corridor separating the northern tribes from the southern tribes. This corridor included the city of Jerusalem, which was held by the Jebusites, and the city of Gezer, which was under Egyptian control. David's conquest of Jerusalem united the two halves, a process that was finally completed when Gezer was given to Solomon as a wedding present by Pharaoh (see 1Ki 9:16–17).

When the united kingdom was divided into two after the death of Solomon (930 BC), it was natural that the northern kingdom should retain the name 'Israel', and the southern kingdom, centring on Jerusalem, the name 'Judah'. But this lies far ahead. We must now return to the story of how the monarchy came to be established in the first place.

It will be recalled that the closing chapters of the book of Judges frequently reiterated that 'in those days Israel had no king' (Jdg 17:6; 18:1; 19:1; 21:25). So how did the kingship come to be established? We shall begin to explore the story of how this happened, which begins with the birth of Samuel.

OUTLINE

1 Samuel

The birth and early life of Samuel

The institution of the monarchy

The failure of Saul's kingship

The rise of David

2 Samuel

David anointed as king over Israel

The reign of David

11:26–27 David's marriage to Bathsheba and the birth of their child

12:1–14 Nathan's parable against David's adultery

12:15–31 The death of David's child; birth of Solomon

The rebellion of Absalom

13:1–22 Amnon's rape of Tamar

13:23–29 Absalom murders Amnon

13:30–39 David learns of Amnon's death

14:1–33 Absalom gains entry to David's presence

15:1–6 The growing influence of Absalom

15:7–12 Absalom seizes power

15:13–16:14 David flees from Jerusalem

16:15–17:14 Absalom determines to kill David and his army

17:15–29 David warned of Absalom's plans

18:1–19:8 The battle between the armies of David and Absalom; Absalom killed by Joab

The final period of David's reign

19:9–43 David returns to Jerusalem

20:1–13 The rebellion of Sheba, son of Bikri

20:14–26 The death of Sheba

21:1–14 The Gibeonites avenged on the family of Saul

21:15–22 The defeat of Philistine warriors by David's army

22:1–51 David's song of victory

23:1–7 David's final poem

23:8–39 The list of David's warriors

24:1–17 The census of Israel

24:18–25 David builds an altar to the Lord

1 SAMUEL 1:1–7:1
The Call of Samuel

1:1–2:11 The Birth of Samuel and Hannah's Prayer The story of the beginnings of Israel's kingship opens by introducing us to Elkanah and his two wives, Hannah and Peninnah (1:1–20). Hannah has no children, and is deeply distressed by this fact, not least because Peninnah has children by Elkanah, and taunts her over her infertility. Hannah prays for a child, and promises that she will dedicate him to the Lord as a Nazirite (see Nu 6:1–21). A local priest, named Eli, hears of her plight, and assures her that the God of Israel will grant her this wish. In due course, she conceives and gives birth to a son named Samuel.

As she had promised, Hannah dedicates Samuel to the Lord (1:21–27),

and exults that the Lord has remembered her in her distress and affliction (2:1–10). This remarkable song of thanksgiving and trust is similar in many ways to the song of thanksgiving associated with Mary, on learning that she is to bear a child who will be the Saviour of the world (Lk 1:46–55).

2:12–36 Eli's Sons Samuel ends up serving in the household of Eli, and assists in the service of the sanctuary at Shiloh. The state of religious and moral degeneration within Israel is brought home vividly by the account of the behaviour of Eli's sons. The sons were in the habit of sleeping with servant women in the tent of meeting, in a way that seems to reflect practices current at pagan Canaanite sanctuaries. Samuel, however, is untainted by this abuse, and 'continued

to grow in stature and in favour with the LORD' (2:26). A turning point is reached with the visit of an unnamed 'man of God' to Eli, who passes judgment on Eli and his family, and declares that the Lord will raise up a future 'faithful priest' who will begin to put things to rights (2:27–36).

3:1–21 The Lord Calls Samuel From what we know of Israel's corruption at this stage, it is no cause for surprise that 'in those days the word of the LORD was rare' or that 'there were not many visions' (3:1). Yet something now happens. Samuel, although perhaps only twelve years of age, is called by name by the Lord as he lies near to the ark of God. Initially thinking that it is Eli who is calling, Samuel wakes the older man up. Realising that Samuel is being called by the Lord, Eli urges Samuel to reply to the Lord, and listen to what is said. The message then delivered to Samuel by the Lord is uncompromising: something major is about to happen, at the same time as his judgment against Eli will be carried out. Eli accepts this news calmly. It is not long before Samuel is widely recognised as a prophet. God continues to make himself known to Samuel at Shiloh.

4:1–22 The Philistines Capture the Ark The Israelites, finding themselves in one of their periodic disputes with the

---

Why were the Philistines seen as such a threat?

Today the term 'Philistine' usually means someone uncultured. But in Bible times, nothing could be further from the truth, for the Philistines were a highly cultured people. So why were they seen as such a threat?

During the 13th and 12th centuries BC what Egypt called 'the peoples of the sea' had migrated from Crete and Greece. One of these groups, the Philistines, settled along Canaan's coastal strip in five cities (Gaza, Ashkelon, Ashdod, Gath and Ekron), which they rebuilt and fortified, giving them control of the international coastal highway. But when these cities proved too limiting, they pushed inland, searching for new territory, which inevitably brought them into conflict with the Israelites.

While the Philistines worshipped other gods – Dagon (the grain god), Ashtoreth (Baal's consort) and Baal-Zebul ('Prince Baal') – this was not the main threat they presented to Israel (unlike the Canaanites). In fact, Dagon was shown to be powerless as his statue kept falling down before the captured ark of the covenant (1Sa 5:1–5). The main danger from the Philistines was their military superiority, due to their possession of iron weapons, and they kept their iron-smelting technology a closely guarded secret (1Sa 13:19–22). They therefore proved to be a constant threat during the period of the Judges and the early monarchy. It was not until King David's time that the Israelites gained access to rich iron deposits in Edom (2Sa 8:14), which helped turn things around.

While the Philistines never controlled much of Canaan, their legacy was to leave a name for the region – Palestine.

Philistines, have just received a mauling in their latest engagement. Recognising that their failure is a mark of God's displeasure, the people decide to ensure that God will be with them on their next expedition. They resolve to bring the ark of God into battle with them, assuming that where the ark goes, the Lord is sure to follow. However, as events prove, things are just not that simple. Pagans might believe that their gods are present everywhere their symbols are displayed. The same is not true of the Lord, whose presence is conditional on obedience, trust and repentance. (It will be recalled how God threatened to allow Israel to enter the promised land without his presence, on account of her disobedience in the desert.) The Philistines utterly rout the Israelites, capture the ark of God, and slay the two sons of Eli.

On hearing the news, Eli is so shocked that he falls off his chair, and dies of a broken neck; his daughter-in-law goes into premature labour, from which she dies (4:12–20). The name she chooses for her newborn son as she dies is an apt comment on the state of Israel at the moment: Ichabod (which literally means 'no glory'). As she remarks, the glory of the Lord has departed from Israel (4:21–22).

5:1–7:2 The Ark Returned to Israel The Philistines find that the presence of the ark in their midst brings them no advantages. It is moved from one city to another, as misfortune falls on them (5:1–12). Finally, fed up with their misery, the Philistines arrange for the ark to be returned to Israel; it eventually finds it way to Kiriath Jearim, where it remains for 20 years (6:1–7:2).

Eventually, it will be brought to Jerusalem in triumph by David. That, however, lies far in the future.

7:3–17 Samuel Subdues the Philistines at Mizpah At the moment, Israel's worries focus on the Philistines. Realising that their misfortunes reflect their own disobedience, the people call on Samuel for advice. He demands that they should recommit themselves to the Lord, and get rid of their 'Baals and Ashtoreths' (a pagan Canaanite god and goddess). Once this has been done, Samuel makes a sacrifice to the Lord. The subsequent victory of Israel over a Philistine sneak attack confirms that the Lord is with her once more.

1 SAMUEL 8:1–12:25
The Establishment of Kingship in Israel

8:1–22 Israel Asks for a King Samuel judges Israel for many years. Finally, he hands over to his sons, whom he appoints as judges. Their failings lead to discontent, and to a growing popular demand for a king. Israel demands to be like the other nations around them in this respect. This request displeases the Lord. He is their king. Why should the people set up anyone else in his rightful place? However, through Samuel, he gives a warning of what the establishment of a kingship in Israel may lead to – exploitation and centralised domination. But the people have made up their collective mind. They want a king, like all the other nations. The idea of the distinctiveness of Israel has lost its appeal for them. They want to be like everyone else. And so the Lord reluctantly allows them their way. But who is to be king?

9:1–10:8 Samuel Anoints Saul Samuel is told by the Lord to await the arrival of a young man (who we later learn is aged 30) from the tribe of Benjamin, and to anoint him as king. He will deliver Israel from the oppression of the Philistines. In due course, Saul arrives, and is told that he is to be king (9:1–27). Samuel then anoints Saul with oil, as a sign of being chosen and equipped by God for the task of leadership (10:1–8). This is a private event; the public aspects of his election will come later. So important is the practice of anointing that it needs further comment.

Anointing with oil was a practice widespread in Old Testament times. In everyday contexts, anointing with oil was a form of personal cleansing, or a mark of honour to a distinguished guest. Corpses were also anointed prior to burial, sometimes with very expensive perfumed oils and ointments. In a religious context, anointing was a practice associated with both purification and healing. The practice also had a religious significance, which was of major importance in relation to figures of public office. Kings, priests and prophets were all anointed, as a sign of their having being chosen and appointed by God for these specific ministries. The word 'Messiah' (literally, 'one who is anointed') came to have the sense of 'the one appointed by God' for the redemption of his people. In this developed sense of the word, the term refers to Jesus Christ (the word 'Christ' is the Greek form of 'Messiah').

10:9–11:15 Saul Made King Shortly after his anointing, Saul receives the promised Spirit of the Lord (10:9–11). Samuel then summons all Israel, to formally announce the choice of king. There is widespread, yet not universal, rejoicing over the selection of Saul (10:12–27). However, the choice of Saul does not mean that he is installed in a palace, with servants and rich furnishings. When we next meet him, he is out in a field, behind his oxen. Initial misgivings concerning his selection are soon overcome: Saul leads a successful offensive against an invading Ammonite army (11:1–11). Saul is then publicly confirmed as king of Israel at Gilgal, the site of Joshua's campaigns during the period of the conquest of Canaan (11:12–15).

12:1–25 Samuel's Farewell Speech In a farewell speech, Samuel then reminds Israel of all that God has done for her, drawing the people's attention to his great acts of deliverance and faithfulness. He warns them of the consequences of having a king. The wellbeing of Israel is dependent on the obedience of both king and people to the Lord. A king is no defence against anything or anyone, if Israel does evil in the sight of the Lord.

1 SAMUEL 13:1–31:13
The Reign of Saul

13:1–15 Samuel Rebukes Saul So the 42-year reign of Saul begins. It opens with an attack made by Saul's elder son, Jonathan, against a Philistine outpost, which causes outrage against Israel in Philistia. A huge Philistine army is mustered, equipped with chariots – formidable weapons of war, which Israel will not possess until later in her history. The Israelite army, based at Gilgal, begins to shrink, as men desert in the face of this threat. Finally, after seven days, Saul

offers a sacrifice to God that ought to have been offered by Samuel. Samuel is furious. Saul's disregard of his instructions is tantamount to rebelling against God, whose representative Samuel is.

13:16–14:22 Israel Without Weapons Philistia's advantages over Israel are considerable. Their armies are equipped with chariots and other advanced weapons of war to which Israel will not have access until the time of Solomon. The Philistines have also mastered the production of iron. Realising its military potential, and concerned to ensure that their enemies should not have access to the iron needed to make spears and swords, they have prohibited the setting up of iron works anywhere in Israel. As a result, Israel is at a considerable disadvantage over her enemy (13:16–22). Despite this disadvantage, Israel is able to defeat the Philistines by surprise. In the resulting confusion, the Philistines end up using their iron swords against each other rather than against Israel (13:23–14:22).

14:23–15:35 The Lord Rejects Saul as King Israel's victory is carefully attributed to the Lord, not to Saul or Jonathan (14:23). In what follows, we begin to realise that Saul has a number of serious failings that call into question his competence as king (14:24–48). We learn of his ill-considered oath, which leads to his army first becoming weary with hunger, then gorging itself on blood (something prohibited by the Law of Moses). Even Saul's decision to build an altar to the Lord (the first time he has done such a thing, as the text notes

– 14:35) is something of an afterthought. Despite all Saul's failings, Israel manages to expel the Philistine invaders from her land. Nevertheless, throughout Saul's reign there is continuing war between Israel and the Philistines (14:49–52).

Saul's obedience to the Lord also begins to waver substantially. Samuel, who had anointed Saul as king over Israel, instructs him to rid the land of the Amalekites. Saul deliberately disobeys Samuel over one issue (15:1–35). In the course of a bitter exchange between the two men, Samuel makes it clear that the Lord no longer supports Saul. Saul has rejected the word of the Lord; now 'the LORD has rejected you as king over Israel' (15:26).

16:1–14 Samuel Anoints David Just as Samuel had earlier anointed Saul in secret as king of Israel, in obedience to the Lord, so he is now led to find his replacement. Samuel is told that the Lord has chosen one of the eight sons of the Bethlehemite Jesse (who is, it will be recalled, the grandson of Boaz and Ruth) as future king. To his surprise, it turns out to be David, the youngest son, whom Jesse did not even think worth calling over to meet Samuel. The story of how the Lord chooses David to be king over Israel is packed with important insights. Of these, probably the most important is that it is not outward appearance that matters in the service of the Lord. For example, it is clear that Jesse's son Eliab was strong and tall (16:6); but, in the end, Samuel is led to choose David, the youngest of Jesse's sons, as the future king of his people: 'The LORD does not look at the things people look at. People look at the

outward appearance, but the LORD looks at the heart' (16:7).

Samuel anoints David with oil, and the Spirit of God comes on him in power. He is not yet king of Israel. He is, however, the man whom God has called and equipped for the task that lies ahead of him. Simultaneously, we learn that the Spirit of the Lord has departed from Saul.

16:14–23 David in Saul's Service In the meantime, Saul is still king. David becomes part of Saul's court circle (16:15–23). Unaware of the Lord's intentions, Saul brings within his inner circle the man whom the Lord has chosen to be his replacement. It is clear that David's court appointment is not permanent, with the result that he is often to be found tending his father's flocks. It is during one such occasion that the incident takes place that propels David into the forefront of Israel's life.

17:1–58 David and Goliath In one of his periodic battles with the Philistines, Saul finds himself confronted with the giant Goliath, who is reported as being 'six cubits and a span' high – roughly nine feet or three metres. Goliath terrifies the Israelites, not least by demanding that they send out someone from the Israelite side to face him in single combat. There is a noticeable absence of enthusiasm on the Israelite side about this offer. David, who has been sent by Jesse to ensure that his older brothers are well, volunteers to fight Goliath. Discarding the heavy military armour he is offered for protection, he approaches Goliath

armed only with his sling and five smooth stones as projectiles. He is confident that the Lord will deliver him (17:37). In the event, he fells Goliath with his first shot. Taking Goliath's sword out of its scabbard, he kills the giant with his own weapon. Panic results within the Philistine camp, and the Israelites are able to wreak havoc as the invaders flee.

18:1–30 Saul's Jealousy of David Perhaps the outcome is inevitable. Saul becomes jealous of David, on account of his greater fame. The fight with Goliath has captured everyone's imagination. It is David, not Saul, whom they are talking about. Afraid of him, Saul can do nothing to stop his growing reputation (18:1–16). His attempt to send David to his death in a further confrontation with the Philistines merely leads to David gaining his daughter Michal in marriage, and becoming even more celebrated in his subsequent victories (18:17–30).

19:1–24:22 Saul Tries to Kill David Finally, Saul decides to have David killed. Saul's elder son, Jonathan, who is very fond of David, alerts him to the plot. At one point, Saul attempts to kill David himself. As a result, David becomes a fugitive, and seeks refuge with Samuel at Ramah (19:1–24). He seeks Jonathan's advice and guidance. In a moving scene, the two men swear friendship, before going their separate ways (20:1–42). David now lives a nomadic existence, pursued by Saul (21:1–23:29). At one point, David even has an opportunity to take Saul's life, but decides to spare him. On discovering how close he has come to being killed by David, Saul repents.

However, David suspects that the repentance may not be genuine, and continues to be wary of Saul and his men (24:1–22).

25:1–26:25 Samuel Dies In the midst of this situation, Samuel dies (25:1). It is a moment of considerable uncertainty. Who will succeed him? Who will act as a prophet to Israel in the times ahead? The question remains unanswered. Our attention is immediately drawn back to the continuing feud between Saul and David (25:2–44), which has reached the stage at which Saul has given his daughter Michal, who was earlier married to David, to another man. Once more, Saul's pursuit of David leads to a situation developing in which David is in a position to take Saul's life. Again, he spares it, with the result that Saul repents – at least, for the time being (26:1–25).

27:1–28:25 David Among the Philistines Aware that Saul's repentance tends to evaporate after a few days, David moves to the territory of the Philistines themselves, in the belief that Saul is hardly likely to pursue him in those hostile regions. Taking a small army of six hundred men with him, David settles in the city of Ziklag, whose precise identity and location remain unknown. A condition of safe conduct in the region is that he and his men must serve in the Philistine army on demand (27:1–28:2). Saul, his mood of repentance having duly spent itself, consults a medium to learn of his own future. In a scene that demonstrates Saul's abandonment of the Lord in favour of the occult, the figure of Samuel speaks of Saul's forthcoming doom. Saul is terrified (28:3–25), and returns to his camp at Mount Gilboa to await the inevitable.

29:1–30:31 Achish Sends David Back to Ziklag Meanwhile, David's relations with the Philistines become problematical. While serving in the Philistine army, David and his men are relieved of their duties, on account of the Philistines' fear that David's men may turn against them when they go to war against Saul (29:1–11). When they return to Ziklag, they find that it is in ruins as the result of an attack by the Amalekites. Eventually, David and some of his men track the raiding party down, and recover all the people and items that have been carried off (30:1–31).

31:1–13 Saul Takes His Life The planned Philistine attack against Saul's forces at Mount Gilboa now takes place. In what is clearly a ferocious attack, the Philistines kill three of Saul's sons, including Jonathan. Saul himself is mortally wounded by an arrow, and commits suicide to avoid further humiliation. Panic sets in within Israel as the news of the defeat and deaths becomes known. In a moving gesture, the men of the town of Jabesh Gilead, which Saul had earlier defended against the Ammonites (see 11:1–11), recover their bodies, and bury them at Jabesh. So how can Israel recover from this catastrophic defeat? Will David ever succeed Saul as king of Israel? Is there any Israel left over which he can be king? 2 Samuel immediately takes up the story.

2 SAMUEL 1:1–5:5
David's Accession to the Throne

1:1–27 David's Lament for Saul and Jonathan
While at Ziklag, David learns of the death of Saul and Jonathan from an eyewitness to the events, who claims to have delivered the death blow to Saul. The eyewitness, who is an Amalekite, presumably expects David to be delighted with his alleged action. David orders the man to be executed, and goes into mourning for Saul and Jonathan. Personal grief, however, soon gives way to a sense of duty. If Saul is dead, and he, David, has been anointed king of Israel, should he not be back in Israel, instead of hiding in the territories of the Philistines? The Philistines regard David as an enemy of Saul. They are ignorant of his secret anointing by Samuel to be king of Israel. Had they known of this, they would have moved against him.

2:1–3:38 War Between the Houses of David and Saul David seeks advice from the Lord, and sets out to the city of Hebron, where he is publicly acclaimed and anointed as king over Judah (2:1–7). However, Saul's family have no intention of handing the monarchy over to Saul's enemy David. A surviving son of Saul is given the kingship by one of Saul's commanders, without any authority to do so from the Lord (2:8–10). The scene is thus set for a major confrontation between two claimants to the throne of Israel. Initially, there is a small-scale confrontation between the two parties at Gibeon, a town well away from the Philistine armies. This battle is won by David's men (2:11–32).

This battle turns out to be an indication of the way things will develop in the future. The war between the house of Saul and the house of David, as the two parties are known, goes on for some time, with the house of David gradually gaining the upper hand (3:1–5). A turning point is reached when Abner, the commander who had installed Saul's son Ish-Bosheth as king over Israel, defects to David. An agreement is reached between David and Abner (3:6–21); unaware of this, Joab, one of David's more successful commanders, murders him (3:22–38). David, who has no part in this plot and had promised Abner his life, is outraged by this development, and goes into public mourning.

4:1–5:5 David Becomes King over Israel However morally bankrupt the murder of Abner may have been, it certainly had the effect that Joab probably calculated it would. The house of Saul is totally demoralised. Sensing the way things are moving, two of Ish-Bosheth's commanders murder him, and bring his head to David. David has the commanders killed, and buries Ish-Bosheth's head with Abner in Hebron (4:1–12). With this development, the resistance of the house of Saul to David collapses, and David is publicly anointed as king over the entire people of Israel (5:1–5). He has already been accepted as king by the southern region of Judah; his authority now extends over the entire area.

2 SAMUEL 5:6–10:19
The Early Successes of David's Reign

5:6–25 David Conquers Jerusalem Once he has been established as king of Israel, David moves to consolidate Israel's

position. In a major advance, he captures the Jebusite city of Jerusalem (5:6–16), which he renames the 'City of David'. It will be his capital throughout his reign, and will become heavily reinforced to ensure its safety. Having established his base at Jerusalem, David is able to deal with the threat still posed by the Philistines. As they advance to find and eliminate David (whom they have of course, earlier harboured on their own territory), David seeks the guidance of the Lord as to how to deal with them. Following the guidance given, he is able to rout them, and force them to retreat to their own territory (5:17–25).

6:1–23 The Ark Brought to Jerusalem With his military situation now stabilised, David arranges for the ark of God, which has been left in the house of Abinadab for the previous two decades, to be brought to Jerusalem. There is resistance to this transfer from Abinadab's family. However, the ark eventually arrives to be placed inside a tent in Jerusalem, to great rejoicing (6:1–23).

7:1–29 God's Promise to David David feels that it is quite inappropriate for the ark of God to rest in a tent, while he himself lives in a richly furnished palace (7:1–3). He chooses to consult Nathan, a prophet, who receives a message from the Lord about both the ark of God and the future of David's descendants (7:4–17). David does not need to build God a house. Rather, God will build David a house – that is to say, a dynasty. It is David's descendants who will build the house of the Lord. The Lord promises through Nathan to establish David's throne for ever, and to be his father, just as he would

be the Lord's son (7:14). This strongly messianic prophecy will be the basis of Israel's future messianic hopes, which will eventually find their fulfilment in the coming of Jesus Christ as the Son of God. David responds with a prayer of thanksgiving and adoration (7:18–29), in which he recalls and praises the Lord's goodness and faithfulness.

8:1–10:19 David's Victories God's faithfulness is seen further at work in the great victories David subsequently notches up, in which a series of enemies is defeated. In many ways, David's string of victories – including the defeat of the Jebusites, Philistines, Moabites, Arameans and Ammonites – can be seen as extending the victories won by Joshua at the time of the conquest. Under David, Israel will reach its pinnacle of power, territory and influence. Yet all is not well. In the midst of his military triumphs, David is beginning to show personal weaknesses that will ultimately cause division and weakness within Israel.

2 SAMUEL 11:1–20:26
David's Later Failures

11:1–27 David and Bathsheba The first sign of any disapproval on the part of the Lord for any of David's actions now makes its appearance. The victory against the Ammonites is being followed up by Joab, one of David's most effective commanders. David himself remains in Jerusalem. There he notices Bathsheba, the wife of Uriah the Hittite. (Although the Hittites had long since left the region of Canaan, some had remained behind and settled there, including the Uriah we

meet here, and Ahimelek, noted at 1Sa 26:6.) David, attracted by her, sends for her, and ends up sleeping with her. Soon afterwards, Bathsheba discovers that she is pregnant by David. Under the Mosaic Law, this development means that both David and Bathsheba are liable to the death penalty (Dt 22:22). David summons Uriah home, apparently in the hope that he will sleep with his wife, so that the pregnancy will not be regarded as suspicious, or attributed to him. But Uriah does not sleep with his wife (11:1–13).

Adultery is now supplemented by David's deliberate decision to murder Uriah. David arranges for Joab to ensure that Uriah is given a dangerous task, and placed in a position in which he is certain to be killed. The strategy succeeds. By taking totally unnecessary risks, Joab ensures the death of Uriah, as well as others. David learns of this news, and sends a brief message of condolence to Joab. Then he takes Bathsheba as his wife, and she bears him a son. Yet 'the thing David had done displeased the LORD' (11:27).

12:1–30 Nathan Rebukes David This leads to a confrontation between the prophet Nathan and the king. Nathan, who had

---

Why does the Bible say adultery is wrong?

Just how seriously God sees adultery (sexual relationships where at least one partner is married) is reflected in its prohibition finding a place in the Ten Commandments and being a capital offence in Israel (Dt 22:22). Jesus reaffirmed this prohibition (Mt 19:18) and the early church underlined adultery's ungodliness (Ro 13:8–10; 1Ti 1:9–11; 2Pe 2:13–14).

The story of King David's adultery shows what happens when people fail to take this prohibition seriously. No doubt he thought it was only 'a bit of a fling' or an 'affair'. 'But the thing David had done displeased the Lord' (11:27).

So why does the Bible see adultery as wrong? Isn't it just a private matter between two consenting adults? It is wrong for several reasons. First, because it always involves deceitfulness, lying and increasingly complicated attempts to cover it up, as we see in chapter 12, where events spiral downhill and end in conspiracy to murder – something David would normally never have considered. Secondly, because it always has consequences for others, not just for us. In the rest of 2 Samuel we see how it frequently weakened David's authority to address issues in his own family, which proved disastrous for the whole nation. Thirdly, and perhaps chiefly, it is because it involves breaking covenant (binding, unbreakable commitment). Marriage is not a mere legal contract; it is a covenant between a man and woman to abandon all others and walk faithfully and exclusively together. Breaking this covenant breaks something that lies at the very heart of God's nature and hence is an offence against him, not just others.

Nevertheless, even if we have committed adultery, forgiveness is always possible if we are truly repentant, as this story of David shows.

earlier pronounced God's blessing on David, now chastises him, by telling a parable. In this story, a rich man with many sheep killed the little pet lamb of a poor man, and offered it to his guests as food. David is outraged at the story. Anyone who behaves like that deserves to die. Nathan informs him that he, David, is that man. He has taken Uriah's wife, and delivered him over to a certain death. The Lord is angered by his actions, and will bring disaster on him in consequence. The death of the son of this adulterous relationship follows, to David's intense distress (12:1–23). However, things then seem to begin to go better for David. Bathsheba eventually gives birth to another son, who is named Solomon. And the military campaign against the Ammonites reaches a successful conclusion (12:24–31).

13:1–14:33 Absalom Kills Amnon Other events point to degeneration and moral decay within David's circle. Amnon, David's eldest son, rapes Tamar, David's daughter by another wife. This leads to serious friction between Amnon and Tamar's brother, Absalom, which culminates in Absalom killing Amnon some time later (13:1–39). Absalom flees Jerusalem, but eventually returns through the good offices of Joab. Despite his great love for his son, David refuses to see him initially, on account of his murder of Amnon. Eventually, however, he relents, and kisses Absalom (14:1–33). There is no hint of the treachery that is to come.

15:1–12 Absalom's Conspiracy It soon becomes clear that Absalom is ambitious. Not only does he take possession of a chariot (an advanced weapon of war that has not been used in Israel up to that point), but he will also wait by the city gate for those arriving from outside Jerusalem seeking justice, and gain their affection by promising justice if he ever becomes judge of Israel. After four years, Absalom returns to Hebron, with the objective of proclaiming himself king. While there, he is joined by one of David's closest advisers, Ahithophel (15:1–12).

15:13–16:14 David Flees Finally, David hears of Absalom's growing popularity, and realises that a conspiracy is under way. Aware of the danger he is in, and appalled that his own son has betrayed him in this manner, David flees Jerusalem. However, David requests Hushai the Arkite, a member of David's inner circle, to go back to Jerusalem, insinuate himself within Absalom's advisers, and attempt to frustrate his plans (15:32–37).

16:15–17:29 The Advice of Hushai and Ahithophel When Hushai arrives in Jerusalem, he discovers that Absalom is already totally dependent upon Ahithophel for advice (16:15–23). Absalom's chief concern is to eliminate his father and his armies: he therefore asks both Ahithophel and Hushai (whom he believes to have rebelled against David) what he should do. Ahithophel has no doubts: Absalom should send out 12,000 men immediately with the specific mission of killing David alone. Once David is dead, his supporters will return to Jerusalem, and transfer their allegiance to Absalom. Hushai advises Absalom to mobilise all Israel, and wipe out both David and his army. This will take time,

and give David time to escape. To ensure that David knows what is happening, Hushai sends word to David by messengers, so that he can avoid the action being planned against him (17:1–22).

Ahithophel, on realising that his advice is not being followed, hangs himself (17:23). This can be seen simply as a piqued response to the rejection of his advice. A much more probable explanation, however, is that he realises that if Hushai's advice is followed, Absalom's revolt will fail, with the result that all the conspirators, including himself, will be killed. In the meantime, David makes plans to deal with the impending conflict.

18:1–19:8 Absalom's Death Dividing his army into three independent sections makes it difficult for Absalom to work out which, if any, is protecting David. David urges his commanders to be gentle with Absalom, if they find him. In the event, the dispersion of David's forces leads to Absalom's army spreading out over a wide area, including forests (18:6–8), with the result that Absalom himself became detached from his own forces. Absalom's end is somewhat squalid. He gets stuck in a tree, and is finished off (without David's knowledge or permission) by Joab and his companions (18:9–18).

David is deeply distressed by the news of his son's death, and weeps bitterly (18:19–33). This throws his army into confusion, to the intense irritation of Joab, their commander (19:1–8). The army expects David to be grateful to them for delivering him from Absalom; instead, David is distressed at their achievements. It is clear that Joab is convinced that David has lost his stamina, and is no longer fit to be king.

19:9–20:26 David Returns to Jerusalem David seems to become increasingly incompetent as a king in the period that follows. On his return to Jerusalem, he appears, apparently unwittingly, to favour the men of Judah over the men of Israel by allowing the former to escort him over the Jordan, leading to serious tensions developing between the two groups of men (19:9–43). This tension is exploited by Sheba, who incites the men of Israel to desert David. As a result, David is forced to rely totally on Joab and the men of Judah for support (20:1–5). Joab tracks Sheba down to the northern city of Abel Beth Maakah. Having laid siege to the town, he offers to lift the siege and spare the city, providing its citizens hand Sheba over. In response, the citizens behead Sheba, and throw his head to Joab outside the city (20:6–26).

2 SAMUEL 21:1–24:25
Conclusion

21:1–22 The Gibeonites Avenged; Wars Against the Philistines At this point, the strictly chronological arrangement of material in the books of Samuel ends. The final sections of 2 Samuel contain a number of reports concerning David's reign, arranged as an appendix to the main body of the text. The incident relating to the Gibeonites (21:1–14) clearly dates from before the rebellion of Absalom. There is no reference to the original incident between Saul and the Gibeonites (21:1) that lies behind this episode, and that is understood to be the root cause of the famine. The fate dealt to the

remaining members of the house of Saul can be seen as confirming the rejection of Saul by the Lord. Once Saul's guilt has been purged, the famine ends. This is followed by an account of four incidents in the wars against the Philistines (21:15–22); once more, it is very difficult to date these with any degree of precision.

22:1–23:7 *David's Song of Praise; the Last Words of David* David's song of praise to the Lord (22:1–51) clearly dates from before his adultery with Bathsheba. It is also included in the Psalms (see Ps 18).

The 'last words of David' (23:1–7) are probably not to be understood as the 'last words that David uttered before his death', but as the 'last piece of poetry David composed before his death'. David, as will become clear elsewhere, was a noted poet (see 23:1), and the words that follow are poetry, rather than prose. The section is important in allowing us to see David as a man filled with the Spirit of God (23:2), who knew that the Lord had established an eternal covenant with his house (23:5). The poem looks forward to the day when a king will 'rule over people in righteousness . . . in the fear of God' (23:3). Perhaps David saw this hope fulfilled in himself: the narrative provided by the books of Samuel suggests that David was far from such an ideal king. Only with the coming of Jesus Christ as the true 'king of Israel' would this righteous ruler arise. Yet, as the Gospels make clear, Israel chose to reject and destroy this ruler when he finally entered Jerusalem.

23:8–24:25 *David's Census; an Altar to the Lord* The list of 37 of David's mighty warriors (23:8–39) is clearly drawn from an archive, and may also be found in an expanded form at 1Ch 11:11–41. This is followed by an account of the census of Israel and Judah (24:1–25; also found, with differences, at 1Ch 21:1–17). The dating of the incident referred to in this passage is also uncertain. What is clear is that David decides to determine the number of his troops. Joab, their commander, cannot understand the reason for this. It serves no useful purpose. As the narrative proceeds, it seems that the underlying motive may have been pride on the part of David. Perhaps David wished to gain a sense of personal achievement in the vast number of fighting men he was able to muster – 800,000 in the northern region of Israel, and 500,000 in the southern region of Judah. Subsequently, David regrets this action, which he recognises to have been sinful. The results of this sin are seen in a plague on Israel, which only ends when David erects an altar to the Lord.

David is thus portrayed as an ideal king, embodying the virtues so conspicuously absent from Israel's first king, Saul. The books of Samuel make it clear that his successes are to be attributed to the Lord rather than to David's own wisdom. Nevertheless, David is portrayed in a strikingly honest and direct manner, with no attempt being made to hide his failings and weaknesses. His personal life is shown to be corrupt, and his judgment seriously flawed at points. Yet despite these weaknesses and failures, the Lord is able to take and use David in such a way that his reign will be a standard for later generations.

1 AND 2 KINGS

As with 1 and 2 Samuel and 1 and 2 Chronicles, the two books of Kings were originally one long work, which was divided into two for convenience by translators. The two books of Kings follow on directly from the two books of Samuel, with the result that the four books together provide a continuous account of the development and history of the kingdom of Israel (and subsequently of Israel and Judah) from the establishment of the monarchy until the exile in Babylon. This continuity is brought out more clearly in the title given to the books in the Greek translation of the Old Testament, usually referred to as the 'Septuagint'. In that translation, 1 and 2 Samuel are referred to as '1 and 2 Kingdoms', while 1 and 2 Kings are given the titles '3 and 4 Kingdoms'.

In this commentary, the two books will be treated as a single unit. This has the advantage of allowing the ministry of Elijah to be studied as a continuous unit. Otherwise, it has to be broken into two halves at an unhelpful point in the story. The reader needs to be reminded that the division of Kings into two parts was not part of the original text of Scripture.

A central feature of 1 Kings is the division of the united kingdom of Israel into two parts after the reign of Solomon. What was originally one kingdom, usually referred to as 'Israel', breaks into two components in 930 BC. The northern kingdom of Israel proved to be unstable, and went through a series of political and military crises, until it finally fell to the Assyrians in 722–721 BC. The southern kingdom of Judah, which included the great city of Jerusalem, fared somewhat better. It would remain more or less intact until it fell to the Babylonians. With the fall of Jerusalem in 586 BC, the nation that had been united and given stability under David ceased to exist. Only as the exiles began to return from Babylon in 538 did the nation of Judah begin to take shape once more.

OUTLINE

11:14–25 The rise of Solomon's enemies

11:26–40 The rebellion of Jeroboam against Solomon

11:41–43 The death of Solomon

The division of the kingdom

12:1–24 The northern tribes rebel against Rehoboam

12:25–13:34 Jeroboam re-establishes paganism in Israel

14:1–18 Ahijah's prophecy against Jeroboam

14:19–20 The death of Jeroboam

14:21–31 The reign of Rehoboam (Judah)

15:1–8 The reign of Abijah (Judah)

15:9–24 The reign of Asa (Judah)

15:25–31 The reign of Nadab (Israel)

15:32–16:7 The reign of Baasha (Israel)

16:8–14 The reign of Elah (Israel)

16:15–20 The reign of Zimri (Israel)

16:21–22 The reign of Tibni (Israel)

16:23–28 The reign of Omri (Israel)

16:29–34 The accession of Ahab (Israel)

The ministry of Elijah

17:1–24 Elijah and the ravens; Elijah and the widow

18:1–15 Elijah and Obadiah

18:16–40 Elijah slaughters the prophets of Baal at Mount Carmel

18:41–46 The end of the drought

19:1–8 Elijah flees from Jezebel

19:9–18 God speaks to Elijah at Horeb

19:19–21 The call of Elisha

20:1–34 Ahab defeats the king of Aram

20:35–43 A prophet condemns Ahab

21:1–29 The incident of Naboth's vineyard

22:1–28 The prophecy of Micaiah against Ahab

22:29–40 The death of Ahab

22:41–50 The reign of Jehoshaphat (Judah)

22:51–53 The accession of Ahaziah (Israel)

2 Kings
The ministry of Elisha

1:1–18 Ahaziah and Elijah

2:1–18 Elijah taken to heaven in a whirlwind

2:19–25 The early ministry of Elisha

3:1–27 The accession of Joram (Israel); revolt of Moab

4:1–6:7 Elisha's miracles

6:8–23 The Arameans attempt to capture Elisha

6:24–7:20 The famine in Samaria

8:1–6 The restoration of the Shunammite woman's land

8:7–15 The murder of the king of Aram

8:16–29 The reigns of Jehoram and Ahaziah (Judah)

9:1–13 The anointing of Jehu (Israel)

9:14–37 The death of Joram and Ahaziah; death of Jezebel

10:1–27 The slaughter of Ahab's family and the Baal worshippers

10:28–36 Jehu's sin and death

11:1–3 The reign of Athaliah (Judah)

11:4–21 Joash (Judah) replaces Athaliah

12:1–21 The reign of Joash

13:1–9 The reign of Jehoahaz (Israel)

13:10–25 The reign of Jehoash (Israel); death of Elisha

Israel and Judah from the death of Elisha to the exile of Israel

14:1–20 The reign of Amaziah (Judah)

14:21–22 Azariah (Judah) replaces Amaziah

14:23–29 The reign of Jeroboam II (Israel)

15:1–7 The reign of Azariah (Judah)

15:8–12 The reign of Zechariah (Israel)

15:13–16 The reign of Shallum (Israel)

1 KINGS 1:1–12:24
The Succession and Reign of Solomon

1:1–27 Adonijah Sets Himself up as King The opening section of this book paints a rather unflattering picture of David. Once the great king of Israel, he has now become an old man who cannot keep warm at night (1:1–4). It is obvious that David cannot live for much longer. The question therefore arises: Who will succeed him as king over Israel? David had many wives, and a considerable number of sons. There were thus several leading contenders for the succession. Adonijah, one of these sons, decides that he is the most suitable candidate, and begins plotting to ensure that the kingship passes to him on his father's death (1:5–10). From what follows, it seems that he proclaims himself king, following a pattern established earlier by Absalom. The next step would inevitably be the elimination of the king himself, as well as other possible claimants to the throne.

1:28–53 David Makes Solomon King The prophet Nathan, who played a prominent role in David's early reign, seeks to ensure the succession in a manner pleasing to the Lord. He asks Bathsheba to speak to David about developments, in order to stop them before it becomes too late. David, on hearing of these developments from both Bathsheba and Nathan, makes immediate arrangements for Solomon to be anointed as king over the northern

peoples of Israel and the southern peoples of Judah (1:11–40). Adonijah, realising that he has been outmanoeuvred, submits to the newly anointed king (1:41–53).

2:1–46 David's Charge to Solomon; Solomon's Throne Established Finally, David dies, having solemnly charged Solomon to remain faithful to the Lord. He is buried in his own city of Jerusalem, after reigning for a period of 40 years, usually dated 1010–970 BC (2:1–12). With Solomon firmly established on the throne of Israel, Adonijah begins another attempt to gain the throne. He asks from Bathsheba the right to be married to Abishag, a member of David's harem. Although Bathsheba regards the request as unimportant, Solomon recognises it as an attempt by Adonijah to enhance his credentials as a future king, and orders his execution (2:13–25). More bloodshed follows, as Solomon moves to purge the guilt of past excesses (such as those committed by Joab), and to ensure that potential threats to the throne are eliminated (2:26–46). An alliance with Egypt prevents any likely invasion from that region during his reign (3:1).

3:1–28 Solomon Asks for Wisdom Once his position is secure, Solomon moves to begin fulfilling the promises he made to his dying father. He asks the Lord to give him wisdom, a request gladly granted on the condition that he remains faithful to the Lord during his reign (3:2–15). The wisdom for which Solomon thus becomes famous is to be seen as a gift from the Lord, rather than a natural endowment. That wisdom is immediately shown in

action in the case of the two women who claim to be the mother of the same infant (3:16–28). We later learn that, on account of his wisdom, Solomon is sought out by rulers throughout the world (4:29–34).

4:1–5:18 Solomon's Administration Solomon also proves to be a successful administrator. The names of those who assist him in this task are noted (4:1–19), as are the ways in which this wisdom leads to prosperity for his people (4:20–28). This prosperity leads to the fulfilment of a major promise: the building of the temple. Nathan's prophecy to David had spoken of one of his successors building a fitting house for the Lord at Jerusalem; Solomon now fulfils that promise, committing substantial resources to the project (5:1–18). He is assured by the Lord that this project will be regarded with great favour, and lead to the Lord's continuing presence among his people Israel (6:11–13).

6:1–7:51 Solomon Builds the Temple and His Palace The building of the temple appears to have begun around 966 BC, four years into Solomon's reign, and took seven years to complete. The detailed descriptions provided of the building and ornamentation of the temple indicate that it was a substantial and important building, clearly pointing to the importance attached to the Lord by Solomon (6:1–10, 14–38; 7:13–51). Nevertheless, we are told that Solomon spent nearly twice as much time building his palace as he did building the temple (7:1–12). The implied criticism is clear: perhaps Solomon cared more about the majesty of his own residence than he did about the Lord's. We can see here the

SOLOMON'S TEMPLE

Solomon built the 'House of the Lord' in Jerusalem as a permanent home for the Ark of the Covenant. Construction work on this stone building began in 967 or 966 BC, and was completed seven years later. It was 60 cubits long, 20 cubits wide and 30 cubits high.

Two ornately carved folding wooden doors, decorated with gold, separated the nave from the vestibule (1 Kings 6:33–5).

Solomon erected **two hollow bronze pillars** at the entrance to the Temple. The northern pillar was called 'Boaz', and the southern 'Jachin'. Both were 18 cubits in height.

The bronze altar for burnt offerings was located in the middle of the inner courtyard of the Temple. It was 20 cubits long, 20 cubits wide and 10 cubits high, with a horn on each of its upper corners.

The large basin known as the 'Brazen Sea' measured 10 cubits wide from brim to brim, and was five cubits deep. It rested on the backs of 12 bronze oxen (1 Kings 7:23–6). This was filled with water for the priests to wash in.

The Holy Place contained the golden altar of incense; the golden table for the 'bread of the presence', and 10 golden lampstands – five on the left and five on the right in front of the inner sanctuary (1 Kings 7:48–9).

The Most Holy Place (or the 'Holy of Holies') was an inner sanctuary 20 cubits wide, long and high. Its interior was lined with cedar and overlaid with pure gold. It contained two cherubim made of olive wood on either side of the Ark of the Covenant, each 10 cubits high (1 Kings 6:16–28) with outspread wings 10 cubits long from tip to tip.

Ten bronze wheeled stands, each holding a large water basin for cleaning animal parts that were to be used for burnt offerings (1 Kings 7:27–38).

N

beginnings of some concerns that become more of a problem, as Solomon's reign continues.

8:1–9:9 The Ark and the Dedication of the Temple With great ceremony, the ark of the Lord is brought from the tent in which it was placed by David, and is installed in the temple (8:1–11). In his great prayer of thanksgiving and dedication, Solomon praises the Lord for his faithfulness (8:12–21), and asks for continuing favour and mercy upon his people (8:22–53). Finally, he reaffirms the need for Israel to remain faithful to the Lord (8:54–61). These prayers are then followed by sacrifices on a huge scale, reflecting the large numbers of people from throughout the region who turn out to witness this major moment in the history of their nation (8:62–66). The ark, which was with Israel from the time of the covenant at Sinai to the present day, is finally given the permanent dwelling-place of honour it deserves. The Lord appears to Solomon, confirming his presence with his people at Jerusalem, and reminding Solomon of the continuing need for obedience and faithfulness on the part of Solomon and his sons if the Lord is to remain with his people. Failure to be obedient in this way will inevitably lead to rejection and disaster (9:1–9).

9:10–11:13 Solomon's Wealth; Solomon's Foreign Wives We are then provided with further information about Solomon's immense wealth, and the respect in which he is held internationally (9:10–28). The visit of the queen of Sheba is ample confirmation of this international status and fame (10:1–13). To make sure

that we have fully appreciated his status, we are told of his many possessions and achievements (10:14–29), and his many wives (11:1). Here, however, the note of criticism hinted at in an earlier section becomes much more specific and focused: Solomon's foreign wives led him astray through their pagan religious beliefs and practices. We are told that Solomon genuinely loved his many wives. Nevertheless, as he grew older, his commitment to the Lord wavered. We are told explicitly that Solomon began to experiment with foreign gods such as Ashtoreth and Molek. Worship of the latter is known to have involved child sacrifice on occasion (11:2–8).

Solomon's rebellion against the Lord allows us to see David's weaknesses in their true light. David was prone to all kinds of temptations and misjudgments, as 1 and 2 Samuel make clear. Yet he never abandoned the Lord for foreign gods. The result of Solomon's faithlessness to the Lord is unequivocal. The Lord becomes angry with Solomon for his flagrant violation of the covenant. On account of David's faithfulness to him, the Lord declares that he will not take the kingdom away from Solomon during his lifetime. After his death, however, the kingdom will be divided (11:9–13).

11:14–40 Solomon's Adversaries Solomon's problems now begin. It is clear that his flagrant disobedience in relation to the most fundamental of all of God's commands – to have no other gods – leads to God withdrawing his favour and support. We are told not simply that Hadad and Rezon rise against Solomon; we are told that the Lord raises both of

them up against Solomon. This is no historical accident. This is the judgment of the Lord in action (11:14–25). Jeroboam, one of Solomon's officials, also leads a revolt against Solomon, on the basis of a prophecy delivered by Ahijah, which speaks of the tribes of Israel being divided on account of Solomon's sin. Following an unsuccessful attempt to kill him, Jeroboam seeks refuge in Egypt until it is safe for him to return. Once more, it is made clear that the forthcoming division of Israel into two kingdoms is the direct result of Solomon's disobedience (11:26–40).

11:41–12:24 *Solomon's Death* Finally, Solomon dies, and is succeeded by his son Rehoboam (11:41–43). Jeroboam now deems it safe to return to Israel, and offers his own and his people's allegiance to Rehoboam on condition that he and Israel are treated well by the Judahites. Despite the advice of his court, Rehoboam refuses. If anything, he will make life harder for the northerners. The northerners are outraged, and decide to rebel against the house of David. They install Jeroboam as their king (12:1–24). Aware of the possibility of attack from the south, he fortifies the town of Shechem, and makes it his base.

1 KINGS 12:25–16:34
The Divided Kingdoms to the Ministry of Elijah

12:25–33 *Golden Calves at Bethel and Dan* A problem now arises. Under David and Solomon, the Judahite city of Jerusalem has become the centre of Israel's worship. If northerners were to go south to

worship, they might end up by submitting to the authority of Rehoboam. To avoid this, Jeroboam establishes his own religious cult in the north, borrowing elements from the authentic worship of the Lord, but adding local elements apparently drawn from Canaanite traditions. Jeroboam's concern that Israelites should not attend religious worship in Jerusalem leads to his introducing religious ideas and forms of worship that are totally unacceptable to the Lord. The scene is thus set for the growing influence of paganism in Israel. This is seen initially in the incident of the golden calves at Bethel and Dan (12:25–33).

13:1–14:20 *The Man of God from Judah; Ahijah's Prophecy Against Jeroboam* Condemnation of this lapse into paganism is not slow in coming. An unnamed 'man of God' pronounces judgment against the idolatrous pagan practices now going on within Israel, causing consternation and dismay within Jeroboam's circle (13:1–34). Nevertheless, Jeroboam refuses to alter his practices, and continues to appoint priests at the 'high places' from outside the traditional priestly family of the Levites. The 'high places' in question were basically local sanctuaries outside Jerusalem, where the Lord was worshipped, often along with other gods, using forms of worship that often had pagan overtones. The 'high places' will feature prominently in the prophetic criticism of Israel from now on. They will finally be destroyed only under the reforms introduced by Josiah (foretold at 13:2), some three hundred years later. The prophecy of impending disaster against the kingdom of Israel for

RULERS OF ISRAEL AND JUDAH

Kings of united Israel

Saul	1Sa 8–31; 1Ch 10
David	1Sa 16:1–1Ki 2:12; 1Ch 11–29
Solomon	1Ki 1–11; 2Ch 1–9

Kings and queen of Judah (southern kingdom)

Rehoboam	1Ki 12:1–24; 14:21–31; 2Ch 10–12
Abijah	1Ki 15:1–8; 2Ch 13:1–14:1
Asa	1Ki 15:9–24; 2Ch 14:2–16:14
Jehoshaphat	1Ki 22:41–50; 2Ch 17:1–21:1
Jehoram	2Ki 8:16–24; 2Ch 21:2–20
Ahaziah	2Ki 8:25–29; 2Ch 22:1–9
Queen Athaliah	2Ki 11; 2Ch 22:10–21
Joash	2Ki 12; 2Ch 24
Amaziah	2Ki 14:1–22; 2Ch 25:1–26:2
Uzziah/Azariah	2Ki 15:1–7; 2Ch 26:3–23
Jotham	2Ki 15:32–38; 2Ch 27
Ahaz	2Ki 16; 2Ch 28
Hezekiah	2Ki 18:1–20:21; 2Ch 29–32
Manasseh	2Ki 21:1–18; 2Ch 33:1–20
Amon	2Ki 21:19–26; 2Ch 33:21–25
Josiah	2Ki 22:1–23:30; 2Ch 34:1–36:1
Jehoahaz	2Ki 23:31–34; 2Ch 36:2–4
Jehoiakim	2Ki 23:34–24:7; 2Ch 36:5–8
Jehoiachin	2Ki 24:8–17; 25:27–30; 2Ch 36:9–10
Zedekiah	2Ki 24:18–25:26; 2Ch 36:11–20

Kings of Israel (northern kingdom)

Jeroboam I	1Ki 12:25–14:20
Nadab	1Ki 15:25–31
Baasha	1Ki 15:32–16:7
Elah	1Ki 16:8–14
Zimri	1Ki 16:15–20
Omri	1Ki 16:21–28
Ahab	1Ki 16:29–22:40
Ahaziah	1Ki 22:51–2Ki 1:18
Joram	2Ki 3:1–8:15
Jehu	2Ki 9:1–10:36
Jehoahaz	2Ki 13:1–9
Jehoash	2Ki 13:10–25
Jeroboam II	2Ki 14:23–29
Zechariah	2Ki 15:8–12
Shallum	2Ki 15:13–15
Menahem	2Ki 15:16–22
Pekahiah	2Ki 15:23–26
Pekah	2Ki 15:27–31
Hoshea	2Ki 17:1–6

The Kingdoms of Israel and Judah

N
W • E
S

ARAM

R. Abana

• Damascus

Sidon •

Zarephath •

Ijon •   Beth Rehob

Lebanon

Mt. Hermon

R. Pharpar

Tyre •

Abel Beth •   Dan •

Maacah

• Janoah

Bashan   Argob

Kedesh •

Hazor •

Geshur

• Kamaim

Galilee

Sea of Chinnereth

R. Yarmuk

Mt. Carmel   R. Kishon

Great Plain

Mt. Tabor

• Endor

Jokn(m)eam   • Shunem

Megiddo •

• Jezreel

Lo Debar   Arbel (Irbid)

Tob •

• Rogelim   • Ramoth Gilead

Taanach •   Mt. • Gilboa

• Beth-shan

Ibleam •

Tishbe •   Abel Meholah

Dothan •   Jabesh Gilead •

Brook Cherith

The Great Sea

I S R A   E L

Samaria •   • Tirzah

Zarethan ◉ (Zareden Zererah)

• Shechem

R. Jordan   The Arabah   Gilead

Baal Shalishah •

Hill Country

Gilgal • Shiloh

Jeshanah • • Baal Hazor

of Ephraim

Rabbah •

Beth Horon ⌐   Bethel • • Zemaraim

Aijalon ⌐   • Beeroth   Gilgal

Shaalbim ⌐   Ramah • • Mizpah   Jericho

Gezer ⌐   Baalah •   • Anathoth

Gibbethon ⌐   Gibeon ⌐   • Nob

Ekron •   Zelah •   • Jerusalem

Valley of Elah   • Bethlehem

Ashdod •

Ashkelon •   Azekah ⌐   Beth Shemesh

Sokoh •   • Giloh • Tekoa

Gath •   Adullam ⌐

J U D A H

Gaza •   Keilah ⌐

P H I L I S T I A

AMMON

Salt Sea (Sea of the Arabah)

Hebron •

Keilah •   • Ziph   En Gedi •

Eshtemoa •   • Carmel

• Ziklag   Maon •

R. Arnon

M O A B

Jattir •

Beersheba •   • Arad

Valley of Salt

• Aroer

• Kit-hareseth

The Negev

A m a l e k ?

Arabah

Tamar (Tadmor?)

EDOM

0 ———————— 30 miles

0 ———————— 50 kms

its lapse into paganism continues with the prophecy of Ahijah against Jeroboam (14:1–20).

14:21–15:24 Israel and Judah Lapse Our attention then turns to the southern kingdom of Judah, and its king Rehoboam, the son of Solomon. We discover that Israel is not alone in its lapse into the paganism characteristic of Canaan before the conquest (14:21–31). Judah's lapse into paganism continues under his successor, Abijah (15:1–8). However, an attempt at reform is introduced under Asa (15:9–24), who eliminates at least some of the pagan practices that have crept in under his predecessors.

15:25–16:34 Sin and Rebellion Under Successive Kings The narrative then returns to deal with events in the northern kingdom of Israel. Jeroboam is succeeded as king by his son Nadab. However, Nadab is assassinated by his rival Baasha, who subsequently becomes king. His first major act is to slaughter all of Jeroboam's remaining family, in fulfilment of the prophecy of disaster pronounced against Jeroboam and his family by Ahijah. Yet Baasha continues to encourage pagan beliefs and practices, with the result that the prophet Jehu pronounces condemnation against his household (15:25–16:7). This pattern of continuing sin and rebellion is repeated under successive kings (16:8–28). It reaches a climax under Ahab, who intensifies the introduction of paganism into Israel through his marriage to Jezebel. This marriage was arranged during the reign of Ahab's father, Omri, and seems to have been seen as a means

of consolidating an alliance between Israel and the region of Tyre and Sidon. Jezebel is a Phoenician, and brings her worship of Baal (probably in some form specific to her region) to Israel at the time of her marriage. Once Ahab becomes king, he constructs a temple and altar dedicated to Baal, apparently as a counterpart to the temple and altar dedicated to the Lord at Jerusalem (16:29–34).

So Israel has degenerated into paganism. What can be done about it? The answer lies in the ministry of the prophets Elijah and Elisha, to which we now turn.

1 KINGS 17:1–2 KINGS 8:15
The Ministries of Elijah and Elisha

We are introduced to 'Elijah the Tishbite' without any prior warning. Nothing in the text has prepared the way for his arrival. The scene has been set for the dramatic escalation in Baal worship in Israel under Ahab. Nothing, however, has prepared us for opposition to it. Up to this point, Israel has been departing further and further from the worship of the Lord under successive kings. Only now do we realise that something is about to happen to restrain this development.

17:1–24 Elijah's Early Miracles Our introduction to Elijah makes it clear that he is a man favoured by the Lord (17:1–24). His early miracles are seen by those who encounter him, such as the widow of Zarephath, as confirmation of his credentials as a man of God. There are interesting parallels here between Elijah and Moses, and between Ahab and

Pharaoh. Note, for example, how Ahab refuses to believe in Elijah's warnings of judgment, despite all his signs, just as Pharaoh refused to believe in Moses.

18:1–15 Elijah and Obadiah As the story of Elijah proceeds, we discover the full intensity of Ahab's campaign against the worshippers of the Lord. Jezebel has initiated a campaign of slaughter, by which the prophets of the Lord will be systematically located and killed (18:4, 13). However, there is resistance to this campaign. Obadiah (not the same individual as the prophet who also bore this name), who was a senior official in Ahab's palace, has hidden away a hundred prophets in two secret locations, in order that they may escape the massacre.

18:16–46 Elijah on Mount Carmel In a moment of danger and drama, Elijah confronts Ahab, and delivers his message of judgment. He demands a showdown at Mount Carmel between himself and the prophets of Baal, supported by Jezebel (18:16–20). Elijah demands that the people worship either the Lord or Baal. He does not allow that there is any alternative. Syncretism (worship of several different gods at one and the same time) is excluded: it is either the Lord or Baal who is truly God (18:21–25). The prophets of Baal attempt to invoke Baal through various ritual acts of self-mutilation. Nothing happens (18:26–29). Elijah then calls down the fire of the Lord on the altar he had built (18:30–39). The reaction of the people is immediate and furious. At Elijah's call, they slaughter the prophets of Baal. And in the land that had languished under famine for years, the sound of heavy rain is suddenly heard (18:40–46). The famine was clearly the Lord's judgment for Israel's disobedience.

19:1–18 Elijah Flees to Horeb Yet this great victory brings more danger for Elijah. Infuriated by Elijah's slaughter of her prophets, Jezebel vows to ensure that Elijah himself will not live. Realising his danger, Elijah seeks refuge in the southern kingdom of Judah, beyond Ahab's sphere of authority. Tempted to despair of his situation, Elijah asks that he may be allowed to die. However, he receives an assurance from the Lord, on the basis of which he journeys for 40 days and nights to Mount Horeb (probably another name for Mount Sinai). Just like Moses before him and Jesus Christ after him, Elijah is encouraged and strengthened by God during this period (19:1–8).

At Horeb, Elijah confesses his despair to the Lord. He is the only one left in Israel to remain faithful to the Lord, and his own life is in danger. What can be done about it? We learn here of how the Lord assures Elijah that he is just as much present in the weakness of a gentle whisper as he is in the power of a windstorm, earthquake or fire. The Lord will be able to speak through Elijah, despite his weakness. Furthermore, Elijah is mistaken in his belief that he is entirely on his own; there are in fact, he is reassured, seven thousand people who have not yet submitted to Baal. We see here the theme of a 'faithful remnant' – that is, a small group of faithful people within a much larger group of faithless people, through whom God is able to carry out his saving purposes (19:10–18). This

theme of a 'faithful remnant' is of major importance in the prophecies of Jeremiah and Isaiah as well as in Paul's understanding of the fate of Israel (Ro 9–11).

19:19–21 The Call of Elisha The first such person who is made known to Elijah is Elisha, who is busy ploughing fields. Elijah calls him to serve the Lord. Elisha leaves everything to follow Elijah just as the first disciples of Jesus Christ will leave their nets behind to follow Jesus. In a highly dramatic gesture, Elisha slaughters the oxen that were drawing his plough, and burns the plough itself. There will be no turning back. His commitment is total (19:19–21).

20:1–34 Victory over the Arameans A number of incidents now take place, which are incidental to the ministry of Elijah. We learn that Israel has been at war with the Arameans, and that things have not been going particularly well for Ahab. As a result, when he is offered a settlement by the Arameans, Ahab has little hesitation in accepting, despite the high price demanded for the peace. A new prophet is now introduced. We do not know his name. His purpose, however, is unmistakable. Ahab is being offered a chance to repent. The Lord will give him a victory over the Arameans, despite the small size of Ahab's army. This duly takes place (20:1–34).

20:35–22:40 Ahab Ahab, however, continues to show himself reluctant to take the Lord seriously. A number of incidents illustrate this (20:35–21:28), of which the most important is the episode of Naboth's vineyard. In this incident,

Ahab gains possession of Naboth's vineyard through a deliberate deception on the part of his wife Jezebel. For this, Ahab and his descendants are condemned by Elijah, although judgment will be postponed until after his death and be executed during the days of his son. This prophetic judgment is reinforced through the ministry of Micaiah (22:1–28), and confirmed through the death of Ahab in battle (22:29–40).

22:41–2Ki 1:18 Decline into Paganism Yet paganism continues in both Judah (22:41–50) and Israel (22:51–53). Ahab's son, Ahaziah, takes no steps to reverse Israel's decline into paganism. In fact, he even contributes significantly to the worsening of the situation. Finding himself injured during a rebellion by the neighbouring region of Moab, Ahaziah decides to seek divine guidance about his prospects of recovery. Instead of consulting the Lord, however, he sends messengers to the northernmost Philistine city of Ekron to consult its local deity, Baal-Zebub. (This name, which literally means 'the lord of the flies', was used by Israelites as a derogatory reference to Baal-Zebul, which literally means 'Baal the exalted one'.) Elijah is outraged: why does the king need to ask anything of the gods of the Philistines? 'Is it because there is no God in Israel?' Elijah sends a message back to Ahaziah: for his disobedience, he will die (2Ki 1:1–18).

2:1–25 Elijah Taken up to Heaven With this episode, Elijah's ministry comes to an end. He is succeeded by Elisha, who immediately demonstrates that he is in possession of the same signs of authority

and power that were associated with Elijah (2:1–25). Elijah himself is taken up into heaven in a whirlwind. In later times, the return of Elijah was awaited, as a sign that the Lord would again remember and redeem his people. Elijah would appear before the coming of the Lord (Mal 4:5–6). The ministry of John the Baptist was seen as directly following on from that of Elijah (Lk 1:17). One understanding of the identity of Jesus Christ that is reported in the Gospels is that he was Elijah (Mt 16:14). The appearance of both Moses and Elijah at the transfiguration of Christ (Mt 17:1–13; Mk 9:2–13; Lk 9:28–36) was further confirmation that Jesus Christ came to continue and extend the prophetic ministry of Elijah to his people.

3:1–8:15 Elisha The account of Elisha's ministry continues with details of the miracles by which he confirms his spiritual authority (3:1–8:15). These incidents, which point to Elisha having the same spiritual authority and insight as his predecessor, make for fascinating reading. The account of how the Aramean commander Naaman is cured of his leprosy (5:1–18) is especially important, as it shows how the Lord, the God of Israel, is worshipped and acknowledged by significant people from outside Israel – despite often being ignored and disobeyed by Israel itself.

2 KINGS 8:16–17:41
The Divided Kingdoms to the Fall of Israel

These chapters record the events that take place in the kingdoms of Israel and Judah up to the time of the fall of Israel herself through the invasion of the Assyrians. The narrative can be a little difficult to read, unless its structure is appreciated. The basic structure is that of a survey of events under the kings of Judah and Israel, arranged in a chronological order. This means that the narrative switches from Israel to Judah and back again. The NIV makes the task of reading these sections relatively simple by identifying each section according to king and kingdom. Thus the section entitled 'Pekah king of Israel' (15:27–31) is followed by 'Jotham king of Judah' (15:32–38), making it quite clear that the narrative has shifted from Israel to Judah.

The situation is made somewhat more complicated on account of 'co-regencies' – in other words, periods when Israel or Judah were reigned over by two kings. For example, Jeroboam II was king of Israel during the period 793–753 BC. However, for the first period of his reign (793–782) he reigned alongside Jehoash. The reader who wishes to follow the chronology of the kings of Judah and Israel is referred to the chart on page 144. A further feature of this section of the work is its frequent use of the formula 'As for the other events of the reign of N., and all he did, are they not written in the book of the annals of the kings of Judah/Israel?' Although this formula can be found earlier (e.g., at 1Ki 14:29; 15:7), it is especially noticeable in this later section, on account of the large numbers of kings being surveyed. In addition to the annals of the kings of Judah and Israel, a third source is also noted: the annals of Solomon (1Ki 11:41). The reference is to three collections of documents which have obviously been drawn on by the

writer of 1 and 2 Kings. Some readers make the mistake of confusing this collection of documents, which we no longer possess, with the biblical books 1 and 2 Chronicles. This is especially likely to happen if using versions of the Bible other than the NIV, which often use the word 'chronicles' to translate the Hebrew word here translated as 'annals'.

8:16–9:13 Jehoram King of Judah; Jehu Becomes King of Israel The narrative opens in the year 848 BC, and focuses on the southern kingdom of Judah. We discover that Judah continues to displease the Lord through her rebellion against him (8:16–29). In Israel, however, things begin to change. Elisha orders that Jehu be anointed as king over Israel, despite the fact that Ahaziah is actually king at that time (9:1–13). Just as David was anointed king of Israel while Saul, who had incurred the Lord's displeasure, was reigning, so Elisha indicates that Jehu is the Lord's choice to replace the disobedient Ahaziah, and the instrument of the Lord's judgment against the house of Ahab (see 1Ki 21:21–24).

9:14–10:35 Jehu and the House of Ahab; Baal Worship Events then move quickly. Jehu first kills Ahaziah and Joram (another of Ahab's sons), and then Jezebel herself (9:14–37). Finally, the remainder of Ahab's family and supporters are wiped out in a series of purges (10:1–17). Having eliminated the power base of the house of Ahab, Jehu turns his attention to the Baal worship Ahab had been responsible for encouraging. In a piece of calculated deception, Jehu declares that he will worship Baal to a far greater extent than Ahab ever did. To celebrate

his 'conversion' to Baal worship, Jehu invites the prophets, ministers and priests of Baal to a feast in the temple that Ahab had built to Baal some time earlier (10:18–24). Once Jehu is sure that all these are safely inside the temple, he orders them to be wiped out and the temple itself to be destroyed. Baal worship is thus eliminated from Israel. However, despite this development, Jehu continues some of the practices of Jeroboam, and thus fails to restore the proper worship of the Lord to Israel (10:25–36).

11:1–12:21 Athaliah and Joash Our attention now returns to the southern kingdom of Judah and events that follow the death of its king Ahaziah (not to be confused with the king of Israel to bear that same name, who ruled some 30 years earlier). Ahaziah is eventually succeeded by Joash, despite an attempt by Athaliah, the mother of Ahaziah, to secure the throne for herself by the simple expedient of wiping out the entire royal family (11:1–21). Like Moses, the infant Joash survives the attempt to assassinate him. Finally, he succeeds to the throne at the age of seven, after the assassination of Athaliah. Once more, an attempt at reform is made: the temple at Jerusalem is eventually repaired. However, the high places remained intact, and continue to attract worshippers (12:1–21).

13:1–15:26 Israel and Judah Remain Disobedient The sections that follow document a saga of continuing laxity and disobedience on the part of the kings of Israel and Judah (13:1–15:26). Three points stand out as being of special importance. First, the continuing

references to the 'high places' remaining intact, and continuing to attract worship and sacrifice (14:4; 15:4). It is clear that pagan practices continue in both Israel and Judah throughout the period surveyed in this section. Secondly, there is an important reference to Elisha, in which his final illness is briefly mentioned (13:14–20). On the basis of the chronology that is suggested by this section, it would seem that Elisha's public ministry has either ceased or not been recorded for a period of nearly 40 years. And thirdly, we find the first reference to an attack on the region by

Tiglath-Pileser III, who reigns over the Assyrian Empire for the period 745–727 BC, during which the empire expands considerably in the region of Israel (15:19). (The name 'Pul' is used in the text, which is the Babylonian form of this Assyrian name.)

15:27–31 Threat from Assyria A new, and ominous, section then opens in the history of Israel. In 740 BC, Pekah ascends the throne of Israel, and continues the pagan practices of his predecessors. Now the threat from Assyria has become of major importance,

Why did God use cruel Assyria?

How could God use cruel, polytheistic Assyria to bring judgment on Israel? Even some prophets asked this question (e.g., Hab 1:12–13), though others declared God had not only allowed it but was actively behind it, and Isaiah even called Assyria 'the rod of my anger' (Isa 10:5). Why?

The Assyrians had settled in northern Mesopotamia c.2300 BC, naming their nation and capital after Ashur, their chief god. For centuries they lived as independent city-states and it wasn't until the 14th century BC that they became a nation. By the 8th century BC they were aggressively expanding, thanks to their well-equipped and brutal army. Israel's attempt to throw off their domination led to Samaria's destruction in 722 BC and their citizens were deported across Assyria's empire, ending the history of the northern tribes (2Ki 17:3–6).

So why did God use such a nation? First, according to 2Ki 17:7–23, because of Israel's ongoing disobedience. These events were not simply the world gone mad; God was still on his throne, directing affairs, and calling his people to account. Judgment – righteous response to wrongdoing – is an aspect of God's character that the Bible takes seriously. But this judgment wasn't sudden. The prophets had been calling Israel to abandon its syncretistic worship and godless lifestyle for two centuries. Finally, God's patience ran out and his judgment fell.

But this judgment was not purposeless; rather, it was God's discipline. Amos had prophesied, 'You only have I chosen of all the families of the earth; *therefore* I will punish you for all your sins' (Am 3:1). God disciplines his people because they are his people, not because they aren't; because he loves them, not because he doesn't; because he intends to further his purpose, not abandon it. Discipline proves God's people truly belong to him (Heb 12:1–13), as this moment showed.

with devastating results for Israel. Tiglath-Pileser invades part of the territory of the northern kingdom, and deports its inhabitants to Assyria. The policy of deportation was designed to minimise the risk of rebellion on the part of conquered peoples by resettling them far from their homelands. Pekah is assassinated by Hoshea, who takes the throne in his stead in the year 732.

15:32–16:19 Jotham and Ahaz, Kings of Judah In Judah, things remain quiet, even though the steady deterioration into paganism continues. A relative lull is recorded during the reign of Jotham (15:32–38). In 735 BC Ahaz assumes full authority as king of Judah (it seems that there may have been a co-regency with his father Jotham up to this point). It is immediately made clear that Ahaz is more like the kings of Israel than of Judah. His lapses into paganism are ruthlessly identified, including his entering into an alliance with Assyria against Israel. Ahaz ransacks the temple treasury to secure enough treasure to gain a favourable response from Tiglath-Pileser III. Favourably impressed with a pagan altar he has seen at Damascus, Ahaz orders a similar altar to be built in the temple at Jerusalem. He also tampers with other aspects of the temple furnishings, suggesting a deliberate decision to rebel against the traditional faith of Judah (16:1–19).

17:1–6 Hoshea Last King of Israel The narrative now returns to Israel, and king Hoshea. Having gained the throne through assassination in 732, Hoshea fails to stop Israel's slide into paganism. Tiglath-Pileser III is succeeded by

Shalmaneser V in 727; this latter invades the region of Samaria in 725 BC, and lays siege to it for three years. When the fighting is over, a substantial section of the population of the region is deported to regions deep within the Assyrian Empire. Israel no longer exists as a nation in its own right.

17:7–41 Israel Exiled Because of Sin We are left in no doubt that this deportation and loss of nationhood is a direct result of the disobedience of Israel. The full scale of Israel's rebellion against the Lord is documented. Deportation is God's punishment of a disobedient people, who have failed to honour, respect and obey him. The region of Samaria is then resettled with peoples from other regions of the Assyrian Empire (17:24–41), who mingle pagan beliefs with some elements of the traditional faith of Israel. As a result, Samaria becomes the centre for a degenerate form of worship of the Lord. This factor goes some considerable way to explaining the severe tension between Jews and Samaritans that is encountered in the New Testament period. The Jews may be seen as the descendants of Judah, and the Samaritans as the descendants of the mixed-race population that came into being in Israel as a result of Assyria's conquest of the region.

2 KINGS 18:1–25:30
The Last Days of Judah

18:1–16 Hezekiah King of Judah Israel, then, ceases to exist as a nation in 722 BC. But what of the southern kingdom of Judah? It is clear that a new era in Judah's history opens with the reign of Hezekiah in 729 BC. Initially reigning

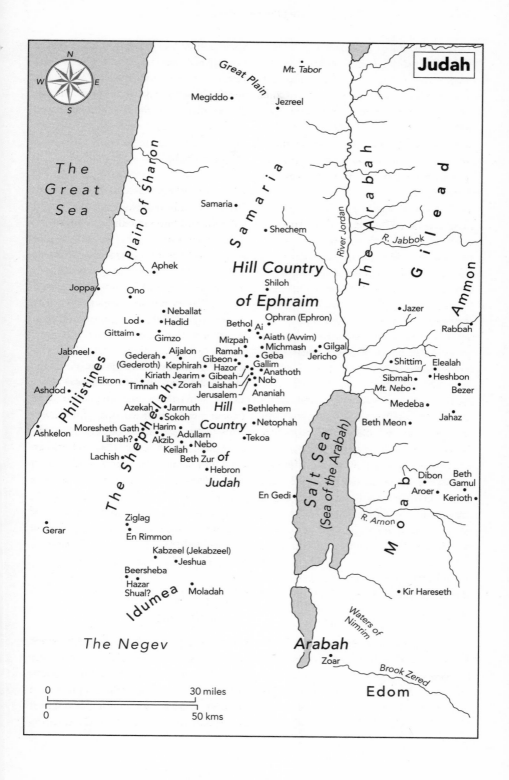

Judah

N W E S

The Great Sea

Great Plain

Mt. Tabor

Megiddo •

• Jezreel

Plain of Sharon

Samaria

Samaria •

• Shechem

Samaria

River Jordan

The Arabah

R. Jabbok

Gilead

Ammon

Aphek •

Hill Country

Shiloh •

of Ephraim

Joppa •

Ono •

• Neballat

• Hadid

Lod •

Gittaim •

• Gimzo

Bethol Ai •

Ophran (Ephron)

• Jazer

Rabbah •

Mizpah •

Ramah •

• Aiath (Avvim)

• Michmash

• Geba

• Gilgal

Jericho

Jabneel •

Gederah (Gederoth) •

Aijalon •

Kephirah •

Gibeon •

Hazor •

Gallim

Anathoth

• Nob

• Shittim

Elealah •

Sibmah •

• Heshbon

Ekron •

Kiriath Jearim

• Gibeah

Mt. Nebo

• Bezer

Ashdod •

Timnah •

Zorah •

Laishah

• Jerusalem

Medeba •

• Jahaz

Ananiah

Philistines

Azekah •

• Jarmuth

Hill Country

• Bethlehem

Beth Meon •

Ashkelon •

Moresheth Gath •

Harim •

• Sokoh

• Netophah

Libnah? •

Akzib •

Adullam •

of

• Nebo

Lachish •

Keilah •

Beth Zur •

• Tekoa

• Hebron

Judah

En Gedi •

Salt Sea (Sea of the Arabah)

Dibon •

Beth Gamul •

Aroer •

• Kerioth

The Shephelah

Gerar •

Ziglag •

En Rimmon •

R. Arnon

Moab

Kabzeel (Jekabzeel) •

• Jeshua

Beersheba •

Hazar Shual? •

• Moladah

Idumea

• Kir Hareseth

The Negev

Waters of Nimrim

Arabah

• Zoar

Brook Zered

0   30 miles

0   50 kms

Edom

alongside his father Ahaz, Hezekiah takes full control in 715. Hezekiah introduces a major programme of reform, which is only briefly described here (a fuller account is provided at 2Ch 29–31). The high places are destroyed, as well as a range of other pagan objects of worship. Among these are the bronze snake held up by Moses (18:4). Once an image of salvation, this has now degenerated into an object of idolatrous worship and superstition.

18:17–19:37 Sennacherib King of Assyria

Yet the Assyrian threat cannot be ignored. Once Israel has been conquered, the Assyrian king Sennacherib turns his attention to the southern region, to attack Jerusalem. Initially, the Assyrians try to use verbal persuasion. Speaking in Hebrew (which the ordinary inhabitants of Jerusalem understand) rather than Aramaic (the international language of diplomacy, which was not understood by ordinary people), the Assyrians tell Hezekiah that he is doomed unless he surrenders. It is clear that they hope to provoke popular pressure against the king's intention to resist them. Yet Hezekiah insists in placing his trust in the Lord. The Assyrians scoff at this. No city has ever been saved from them by its god before.

At this stage, we are introduced to the prophet Isaiah, whom we shall encounter in considerably greater detail later (see Isaiah). He urges Hezekiah to resist the Assyrians, who have incurred the Lord's displeasure. Hezekiah agrees, and prays for guidance and courage. Isaiah then delivers a detailed prophecy against Sennacherib, prophesying his downfall (19:20–34; see also Isa 37:21–38). That

same night, a disaster falls on the encamped Assyrian army. Badly shaken, Sennacherib withdraws to Nineveh, where he will eventually die at the hands of his sons (18:35–37). The prophecy is fulfilled.

20:1–20 Hezekiah and Babylon

Hezekiah receives further encouragement and reassurance from the Lord through Isaiah (20:1–11). Hezekiah appears to overstep the limits of caution in his dealings with some envoys from Babylon. At a time in which the world's horizons were dominated by Assyria, Hezekiah is unreasonably positive towards the Babylonians. As a result, Isaiah prophesies the future downfall of Jerusalem at the hands of the Babylonians (20:12–21).

21:1–25 Manasseh King of Judah

Hezekiah is succeeded by his son Manasseh, who lapses into paganism, even to the extent of rebuilding the high places his father had destroyed and importing pagan objects of worship into the temple. The prophets denounce this sin, and declare the coming of the judgment of the Lord. Judah will suffer the same fate as Israel (21:1–18). Things do not improve under Manasseh's successor, Amon (21:19–26).

22:1–20 Josiah and the Finding of the Books of the Law

Yet things do improve under Josiah, who begins to reign in 640 BC. In the course of some work on the temple, the 'Book of the Law' is rediscovered (22:1–10). It is thought that this is a reference to the book of Deuteronomy, or at least to its central chapters. On hearing it read, Josiah is appalled. He realises that Israel has departed radically

from the Law of Moses, and that something will have to be done about it. This conclusion is reinforced by a prophecy from Huldah, which speaks of the forthcoming destruction of the city and temple (22:11–20). A major programme of reform is set in motion (23:1–25). The catalogue of pagan items removed from the temple in itself is an indication of how compromised the worship of the Lord has become – even at Jerusalem itself, supposedly the central location for the true worship of the Lord by his people. Notice that Josiah even extends his programme of cleansing to the region of Samaria. The pagan holy places of this region are demolished and desecrated.

23:1–30 Josiah Renews the Covenant

A central aspect of the programme of reform undertaken by Josiah is the renewal of the covenant – the declaration on the part of king and people that they will remain faithful to the law of the Lord (23:2–3). The Passover, which has been neglected since the days of the judges, is reinstated, and celebrated at Jerusalem (23:21–23).

Josiah unquestionably finds favour in the sight of the Lord. Yet his obedience is not regarded as an adequate atonement for the sin of Manasseh, who had violated the covenant between God and his people at every turn. The Lord's anger does not focus on Josiah himself, but on Judah. She will suffer the same fate as Israel (23:26–27). It is now merely a matter of time. The reader has been prepared for the fate that will befall Judah. Like Israel, she will be punished for her disobedience. However, that punishment, as it turns out, will take a different form. The exile of Jerusalem will be seen as a time of purification and penance, in which the people of God can rediscover their identity and obligations. But this lies in the future. We turn back to the narrative, knowing that the end of Judah is in sight.

23:31–24:7 Jehoahaz and Jehoiakim, Kings of Judah

After Josiah's death in battle (23:28–30), he is succeeded by Jehoahaz and Jehoiakim (23:31–36). It is during the latter's reign that the first tolling of the bell which marks the end of Judah is heard. In 605 BC, the Babylonian emperor Nebuchadnezzar defeats the massed Egyptian armies at Carchemish, establishing Babylon as the leading military and political power in the region. Along with many other territories in this region, the land of Judah becomes subject to Babylonian rule, possibly in 604 (24:1). Jehoiakim, who clearly fails to remain faithful to the Lord (23:37), decides to rebel against Babylon. It is possible that he may have been encouraged in this move by a successful Egyptian counter-attack against Babylon in 601, which may have seemed to suggest that Babylon's power was on the wane. It proves to be a terrible misjudgment. Judah is invaded by Babylonian forces (24:2–4), which is clearly interpreted as the execution of the promised judgment of the Lord against his faithless people and king. Egypt, once the hope of Judah, is also defeated, and neutralised as a military power (24:7). (These same events are also vividly described and analysed by Jeremiah, the later chapters of whose prophecy should be read in the light of this historical narrative.)

24:8–25:30 *Jehoiachin, Zedekiah and the Fall of Jerusalem* Jehoiakim is succeeded by Jehoiachin (the close similarity of these names being a constant source of confusion to readers) towards the end of 598 BC, shortly before the Babylonians finally lay siege to the city (24:8–20). Early the following year, the king, the royal family and the circle of royal advisors give themselves up to the besieging forces early in 597 (25:1–12). They are deported to Babylon, along with several thousand captives. (Interestingly, a Babylonian ration document mentioning Jehoiachin was discovered some 2,500 years later, during excavations of 1899–1917, confirming this ignominious fate of a king of Judah.) The Babylonians place Zedekiah, a relative of Jehoiakin, on the throne as their vassal, and seem happy to leave things like that for the present.

Yet Zedekiah has other ideas. Probably encouraged by the accession of a new Pharaoh, who seems to offer a real threat to the Babylonians, Zedekiah determines to rebel against Babylon. The Babylonian response is massive and decisive. In January 588, they lay siege to Jerusalem. In July 586, they break through its walls, and take the city. The defending army attempts to flee, but is routed. The next month, a Babylonian official arrives in Jerusalem to supervise the destruction of the defences of the city and its chief buildings, and the deportation of its people (25:1–12). The furnishings of the temple are dismantled, and taken to Babylon as booty. It is distressing to read this account of the destruction of the temple in the light of the account of its erection and ornamentation during the reign of Solomon (25:13–17).

Any hope of a quick end to the exile soon passes. Anyone capable of leading a revolt or taking charge of a government is taken and executed (25:18–21). The assassination of Gedaliah, the governor appointed by the Babylonians, by Ishmael sends shock waves through the remaining inhabitants of the city. Fearing Babylonian reprisals, many flee to Egypt (25:22–26).

Yet this dismal account of the fall of Judah ends on a positive note. In the later period of the exile (from 561), Jehoiachin is treated with increasing kindness by his captors. It is clear that he is to be allowed to live (25:27–30). The house of David will not be wiped out. It will live on in exile, in hope of restoration. It is widely thought that 1 and 2 Kings were written during the period of exile in Babylon. The people had no knowledge that their captivity would one day come to an end. They could only live in hope that the Lord, the God of Israel, would remember and finally deliver his people.

1 AND 2 CHRONICLES

As with 1 and 2 Samuel and 1 and 2 Kings, the two books of Chronicles were originally one long work, which was divided into two for convenience by translators. In this commentary, the two books will be treated as a single unit, as were the two books of Samuel and Kings.

In view of the repetition of material that has been encountered earlier, the commentary on these books will focus on its distinctive interpretation of this material, rather than the historical details themselves. The reader who has been working through the books of the Bible in their canonical order will already be in full possession of the historical details underlying the book, thus making their repetition unnecessary. Anyone who wishes to read Chronicles in isolation is discouraged from doing so, in that it is clear that the writer of the work assumes that his readers will already be familiar with the background to the material in question. It is strongly recommended to read the books of Samuel and Kings first, before trying to tackle Chronicles.

It can be helpful to take an overview of Chronicles, before looking at the text in more detail.

We have already seen how what was originally one kingdom, usually referred to as 'Israel', broke into two components in 930 BC. The northern kingdom of Israel went through a series of political and military crises, until it finally fell to the Assyrians in 722–721 BC. The southern kingdom of Judah, which included the great city of Jerusalem, remained more or less intact until it fell to the Babylonians. With the fall of Jerusalem in 586 BC, the nation which had been united and given stability under

David ceased to exist. Only as the exiles began to return from Babylon in 538 did the nation of Judah begin to take shape once more.

The two books of Chronicles are clearly written with the needs of the restored community in mind. The work is concerned to demonstrate the continuity between the past and the present, and to reassure its readers of the continuing validity of God's covenant promises to his people. In many ways, the books of Chronicles can be regarded as bringing together material spread out across the books of Samuel and Kings. However, additional material is provided in many cases, probably from archive resources. Part of the additional material relates to a much earlier period in Israel's history. Its inclusion stresses the continuity of God's presence and promises throughout the history of his people.

It is also noticeable that Chronicles tends to portray both David and Solomon in a much more favourable light than that found in the books of Samuel and Kings. The incidents that highlight David's weaker side (such as his adulterous relationship with Bathsheba) are not referred to. Nor is his final period as a shivering bedridden old man referred to. Similarly, Solomon is portrayed in a very flattering manner. Any mention of debate or conflict over the succession of Solomon is omitted. The impression could easily be gained that Solomon was the only and the obvious successor to David. No mention is made of his foreign wives or the pagan practices or beliefs they encouraged.

It is clear that one of the purposes of Chronicles is to stress the importance of David and Solomon, and the example and encouragement they provide for the restored community that has now returned from exile in Babylon. They are also seen as pointing ahead to the coming of the Messiah, the ideal king of Israel, who will bring to final fulfilment all that David and Solomon tried to achieve. The work aims to encourage and inspire the nation at a time when its fortunes are often low, and reassure Israel that the God who entered into a covenant with David and Solomon remains faithful to that covenant to this very day. The temple is seen as a major focus for Israel's hope and faith, and particular attention is paid to this theme throughout the work. Thus the account of Solomon's reign is dominated by the building of the temple, which is seen as his major contribution to the wellbeing of his people.

1 CHRONICLES 1:1–9:44
The Genealogies of Israel

The work opens with a detailed analysis of the people who connect God's work of creation and the establishment of the monarchy in Israel. No attempt is made to explore the historical issues involved, such as the way in which Israel made her way from Egypt to the promised land, or how the people took possession of Canaan. The central point being made is that there is a direct and unbroken line of continuity within the people of God between creation and the monarchy. There are also other sections of interest, including details of the descendants of David (3:1–24).

The reader of this section may find much of this material uninteresting, due

to the manner of its presentation. Being confronted with list after list of names is not especially inspiring. However, the reason for these genealogies must be appreciated. This is the family history of Israel, demonstrating the development and continuity of the people of God from the act of creation itself to the restoration. There are also moments of important theological interpretation – for example, the explicit assertion that '[the people of Judah] were taken captive to Babylon because of their unfaithfulness' (9:1). These interpretations help the reader make sense of the history of God's people, and discern the purposes of God behind and within the flow of history itself.

See 'Why does the Bible have so many genealogies?', page 169.

1 CHRONICLES 10:1–29:30
The Reign of David

The scene then changes radically. We are plunged into the world of the early monarchy. No background information is provided as to how the monarchy comes into being in the first place, nor of the role of Samuel in its creation and direction. We are given a very brief account of how Saul takes his life, and thus how the kingship of Israel becomes vacant (10:1–14). The death of Saul is firmly attributed to his disobedience, especially his use of mediums. As a result, the kingdom of Israel passes to David. The struggle that David confronts as he fights to become king of Judah, and then king of all Israel, is passed over. The important point for the writer is the theological interpretation of what happens, rather than the precise historical event – a pattern that will be repeated throughout this work. Historical details are set to one side, in order that the religious significance of events may be fully appreciated. In some cases, as we have hinted, this leads to incidents being passed over. It is the message that is of primary importance.

11:1–16:43 David Becomes King David is acclaimed as king of all Israel. His successes and power are attributed directly to his obedience and faithfulness (11:1–12:40). The episode of the bringing of the ark of the Lord to Jerusalem is given a position of considerable prominence within David's reign, and its spiritual significance is emphasised (13:1–16:43).

17:1–15 God's Promise to David Having brought the ark to Jerusalem, David finds it unacceptable that he, as king, should live in a fine palace, while the ark of the Lord is placed under the shelter of nothing more splendid than a tent. On consulting the prophet Nathan on this matter, he is assured of God's promise to him and his descendants (17:1–15). There is a strongly messianic flavour to this passage, which speaks of one of David's descendants being the 'son of God', and his kingdom being established for ever. This passage underlies some New Testament thinking on the significance of Jesus Christ. It allows us to understand the importance of the opening of Matthew's Gospel, which stresses that Jesus Christ was a descendant of David, as was required of the Messiah.

17:16–20:8 David's Victories David responds to this promise with prayer and delight (17:16–27). As if to demonstrate that these promises are effective immediately, we are told of David's victories in a series of major engagements during his reign (18:1–12). The great victories for which David is renowned are unequivocally attributed to the Lord (18:13). A series of such engagements is singled out for more detailed discussion, including the war with the Ammonites (19:1–20:3) and the Philistines (20:4–8).

21:1–30 David Numbers the Fighting Men The 'census of Israel' assumes a major place in Chronicles. A virtually identical story is told elsewhere (See 2Sa 24:1–25), with one major difference among several minor divergences. In 2 Samuel, David's decision to take a census of Israel is attributed to the Lord. Here it is attributed to Satan (21:1). It is not clear quite how this difference is to be explained. In any case, the Old Testament regarded Satan as an agent who was ultimately responsible to God. Yet it is the location of the story that is of particular interest. In 2 Samuel, the story is part of a group of narratives gathered together at the end of the work. Here it is placed in the main body of the work, explaining the specific location of the future temple in Jerusalem. Chronicles' particular focus on the temple leads to this narrative being placed directly before the account of the preparations for the building of the temple, rather than being relegated to an appendix.

22:1–29:30 Preparations for the Temple Attention then shifts to those preparations for the erection of the temple. The responsibility for building the temple will lie with Solomon, who is identified here as David's chosen heir (22:1–19). David is unable to undertake this task himself. His hands are stained with blood, as a result of the wars he was obliged to wage to ensure Israel's continued safety (22:8–9). Nevertheless, although David is not permitted to begin the building himself, it is clear that he has laid down the basic principles of its administration and worship. Solomon therefore will be responsible for putting into effect the vision and instructions of his father.

Those instructions, along with other details, are then set out in some considerable detail (23:1–27:34). The material in this section is unique to Chronicles, indicating access to archive material not reproduced elsewhere in the Old Testament. The considerable attention given to the fine details of the planned worship and administration of the temple would have been of particular importance to the restored community, as they sought to restore continuity with the worship of the golden age of Israel under David and Solomon. These precise details would have given post-exilic Judaism a much-needed sense of direction as they sought to restore the temple and its worship after years of neglect and disuse.

A major section now follows (28:1–29:30), which details the transition from the reign of David to that of Solomon. David sets out his plans for the temple, and makes it clear that Solomon, his intended heir among his sons, will bring into being his vision for the temple. There is a clear parallel here with Moses (especially clear from the material at

Why did the Jerusalem temple become so important?

While Jerusalem had been important ever since David captured it and made it his capital, Solomon's construction of the temple, and God's acceptance of it by coming down in a cloud (2Ch 5:13–14), made it even more special. The king's rule and God's rule were united. Zion (another name for Jerusalem) came to be seen as the focal point of God's reign on earth (e.g., Pss 2:6–9; 110:1–2) and the temple as his throne (e.g., Ps 132:13–14). This belief was further strengthened by appeal to Moses' command that Israel should worship only at 'the place the LORD your God will choose' (Dt 12:5), now interpreted as the temple. Its importance at this time, as the only place where Israel could offer sacrifice and from where God's rule would be extended, cannot be underestimated.

However, over the years Israel's focus drifted from the God of the temple to the temple of God. They became convinced its very presence would protect them, and its miraculous rescue from Assyrian attack in 701 BC only confirmed this. But as temple abuses grew and godlessness increased, the prophets warned that God needed no temple and would destroy it unless Judah repented (e.g., Jer 7:1–15), something that happened at Babylon's hands in 586 BC. It was rebuilt after the exile, but this much smaller building was replaced by King Herod, who sought to exceed the grandeur of Solomon's temple. Begun in 20 BC, it wasn't finished until AD 64, long after his death – though it too was destroyed by Rome in AD 70 when temple abuses had again become so bad that Jesus called it 'a den of robbers' (Lk 19:46).

The church quickly lost interest in the temple, even before its destruction, understanding that Christians together are now the temple in which God dwells by his Spirit (e.g., 1Co 3:16).

28:12). Just as Moses received the plans for the tabernacle from the Lord, so David receives from the Lord the plans for the temple at Jerusalem. Solomon is acknowledged as David's successor by the people (29:21–25), with the result that, with David's death, Solomon succeeds him as king (29:28).

2 CHRONICLES 1:1–9:31
Solomon and the Building of the Temple

Attention now shifts to the reign of Solomon. This account focuses virtually entirely on Solomon's building of the temple at Jerusalem. Chronicles proceeds directly to Solomon's request for wisdom from the Lord (1:1–17) – a wisdom that is demonstrated especially in the building of the temple. The preparations for this are noted in some detail (2:1–18). A full account of its building is also provided, indicating its massive dimensions and its fine furnishings (3:1–5:1). Although Solomon actually spends longer building his own palace than he does building the temple, all details of the building of the palace are omitted from this account.

The account of how the ark of the Lord is brought to the temple from its

lowly position beneath the tent erected for it by David is documented (5:2–6:11), along with the great affirmation of the faithfulness of the Lord to his people. The dedication of the temple to the Lord (6:12–7:10) is clearly a moment of great joy and celebration. It is followed by the Lord's reaffirmation of his commitment to the house of David and to his people, on condition that they remain faithful to the Law (7:11–22).

So what else did Solomon do during his reign, apart from build the temple? Chronicles seems to have little interest in anything other than the religious aspects of his reign. In a closing section, the work notes some public building works and a military expedition (8:1–10), but does not make much use of them. The religious aspects of Solomon's reign predominate. Indeed, our attention is then immediately redirected to his religious activities, as we learn of his regular sacrifices to the Lord (8:12–15), in obedience to the directives laid down by Moses. Chronicles explicitly brings out the continuity between Solomon and Moses at this point.

Solomon's wisdom, which was a direct gift from God, becomes legendary, and attracts many visitors. Chronicles notes the visit of the queen of Sheba, who testifies to the wisdom of the Lord in placing Solomon upon the throne of Israel (9:1–12). It also records his fabulous wealth (9:13–28). Finally, Chronicles records the death of Solomon after a reign of 40 years (9:29–31), and his succession by his son Rehoboam.

2 CHRONICLES 10:1–36:23
The History of Judah to the Exile

A new section now opens, chronicling the history of Judah from the death of Solomon to the time of the exile in Babylon. There are obvious parallels here with the material that can be found in 1Ki 12–2Ki 25. Nevertheless, important differences must be noted. For example, Chronicles also draws on sources that were not used by the writers of the books of Kings, with the result that we have additional material in our possession relating to the history of Judah at this point.

However, the most important and obvious difference is that Chronicles focuses on the southern kingdom of Judah alone. It must be recalled that one of the purposes of the work appears to have been to help the restored community in Jerusalem gain an understanding of its own history and purposes. In that Israel had ceased to exist as a nation after the Assyrian invasion and deportation of 722, there was no point in referring to the history of the northern kingdom of Israel, except when it related to events in Judah. Thus despite the importance of Elijah, he is only mentioned here indirectly (as the author of a letter: 21:12–15). Chronicles is generally thought to have a special concern to trace the faithfulness of God to his promises to David through the great king's descendants to the time of writing. As this succession takes place only within the kings of Judah, it is natural that the work should focus on this kingdom alone.

10:1–11:4 Israel Rebels Against Rehoboam
The new section opens with an account of the division of the kingdoms, which explains how a serious disagreement between Rehoboam and the Israelite Jeroboam leads to the two nations going their separate ways (10:1–4). The origins of the tension between the two are not explained here. The reader should consult the more detailed account in 1 Kings for the background (1Ki 11:29–33).

11:5–27:9 Rehoboam King of Judah The history of Rehoboam and his successors is then documented (11:5–27:9) as broadly parallel to the accounts in the books of Kings, although there are differences in details or evaluation at points of interest. For example, according to 1Ki 15:14, Asa did not remove all the high places from Judah during the course of his reforms; according to 2Ch 14:3, he did. The difference is almost certainly due to the persistence of the paganism that the high places represented at the time, by which Asa's determined attempts to remove them totally were ultimately frustrated. Chronicles provides a generally positive evaluation of Abijah, whereas the briefer account in 1Ki 15:1–8 is much more negative in tone. Given the complexity of the lives of some of the kings of Judah, this divergence in evaluation is not entirely surprising.

28:1–27 Ahaz King of Judah The figure who is criticised the most severely is Ahaz (28:1–27). The incident that caused particular concern (Ahaz' decision to build an altar in the Jerusalem temple, based on a pagan model he had seen at Damascus: see 2Ki 16:10–16) is not recorded. Nevertheless, his apostasy is fully documented. Ahaz is presented in totally negative terms, as a totally unworthy king of Judah who lapses into paganism and threatens to destroy his kingdom in doing so. Jerusalem is packed with pagan altars, and high places were re-established in every town in his kingdom. So great is his rebellion against the Lord that on his death he is not placed in the tombs of the kings of Israel.

29:1–32:33 Hezekiah King of Judah His successor, Hezekiah, is treated in considerable detail (29:1–32:33), and is clearly identified as a major religious reformer who is able to reverse the lapse into paganism that took place under his father Ahaz. Although Hezekiah is heavily involved in a conflict with Sennacherib at this time, Chronicles focuses on his specifically religious activities. As with Solomon, it is matters of faith and worship that attract the Chronicler's main attention. The restoration of the celebration of the Passover (30:1–27) is of particular importance to the Chronicler, as it stressed the continuity of the Lord's action and presence with his people. The celebration of the Passover would have been an important focus for the identity of the restored community after the end of the exile. This full account of the celebration of the Passover at Jerusalem would have been of considerable importance to the returned exiles, as they sought to re-establish their sense of identity and purpose.

Other events in Hezekiah's reign are noted, including his confrontation with the Assyrian army (32:1–22). Nevertheless, it is clear that it is Hezekiah's faithfulness and obedience that are of special importance here. Hezekiah is portrayed as a worthy king of Judah, a fact that is reflected in his being buried alongside the descendants of David – an honour denied to his faithless father (32:23–33).

33:1–25 Manasseh and Amon, Kings of Judah

Hezekiah is succeeded by Manasseh, who is portrayed in unequivocally negative terms elsewhere (2Ki 21:1–18). Chronicles is kinder to him, and suggests that, despite his disobedience, he has some redeeming features (33:1–20). For example, his attempt to eliminate pagan practices is noted, and their persistence is put down at least in part to the disobedience of the people. Manasseh is recorded as repenting of his earlier sins, an insight not found elsewhere. His successor, Amon, however, continues with the evil ways of his father, and is assassinated (33:21–25).

34:1–35:27 Josiah's Reforms

The reforming reign of Josiah is treated at great length. The narrative tells of the discovery of the Book of the Law (presumably Deuteronomy, or at least part of that book), and its impact on Josiah. Yet even before its discovery, Josiah has engaged in a programme of reform, in which various pagan altars and images are destroyed. In response to the discovery of the Book of the Law, Josiah formally renews the covenant between the Lord and the people,

swearing to follow obediently the law of the Lord (34:29–32). This is followed by a detailed account of Josiah's celebration of the Passover (35:1–19); once more, the importance of this event to the returned exiles should be noted.

35:20–36:14 The Death of Josiah and His Successors

After an extended account of the death of Josiah (35:20–36:1), his immediate successors are given very brief treatment (36:2–14). The surrender of Jehoiachin to the besieging Babylonian army in 597 BC is noted, but is described in terms that avoid mentioning that Jerusalem was under siege in the first place (36:10). Similarly, the fall of Jerusalem in 586 is not explicitly mentioned in the very brief account of the reign of Zedekiah (36:11–14). The destruction of the city is passed over in silence, perhaps as being too painful to mention explicitly.

36:15–23 The Fall of Jerusalem

This silence is ended in a concluding section, which provides a succinct theological analysis of the final days of Jerusalem (36:15–21). The exile to Babylon is God's judgment on his people for their disobedience. Yet this note of judgment is also mingled with a note of hope. While the writer of the book of Kings did not *know* that the exile would not be permanent (however great his hopes may have been, and however much he may have trusted in the Lord), the Chronicler had the benefit of hindsight: he could record the events of the exile, knowing that they would end in deliverance and restoration to Judah. As a result, Chronicles ends on a powerful

note of assurance and hope (36:22–23). The people of Jerusalem will be restored to their city, and the temple of the Lord will be rebuilt.

And on that note, we turn to the account of how that restoration and rebuilding take place, as we prepare to read Ezra.

EZRA

The book of Ezra opens with a thrilling declaration: the exiles in Babylon are to be allowed to return home! The exile is over. Now the inhabitants of Jerusalem can return home, and begin to rebuild their lives, their faith and their city. Written in a style very similar to that of Chronicles and Nehemiah (which suggests that the same person, possibly Ezra himself, wrote them all), the book of Ezra deals with the renewal of worship in Jerusalem, and the decision to rebuild the temple.

EZRA 1:1–6:22
The Return from Exile

1:1–11 Cyrus Helps the Exiles to Return The opening verses of Ezra clearly follow on directly from the end of 2 Chronicles, making it clear that they are to be read together as a continuous narrative. Although we are told little of what happened to the people of Jerusalem during their time in exile, we can nevertheless gain at least some understanding of the difficulties they faced, and their longing to return home. Ezra opens by publishing the proclamation of Cyrus, the founder of the Persian Empire who defeated the Babylonians in 539, which set the exiles free (1:1–4). The proclamation dates from 538 BC, and shows a spirit of generosity and tolerance towards the religion of Israel that had been conspicuously absent from the Babylonians.

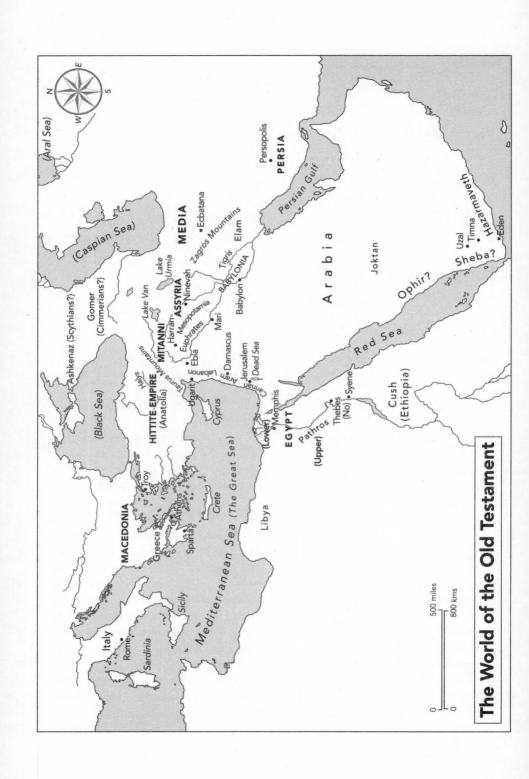

The World of the Old Testament

Why does the Bible have so many genealogies?

One aspect of the Bible that is difficult for modern readers to see the relevance of is its genealogies – family records showing ancestors or descendants. But in Bible times genealogies were crucial for establishing identity, property rights and authority to hold office. This was even truer at key moments in history, like when the exiles returned to the promised land, as recorded in Ezra 2 and, at much greater length, in 1Ch 1:1–9:1.

Sometimes genealogies could be quite short (e.g., Ru 4:18–22), sometimes much longer (e.g., Mt 1:1–16), but the purpose was always the same: establishing an irrefutable link with the past and identity and legitimacy in the present. Genealogies were especially important for hereditary offices like kings and priests. Sometimes, following the custom of those times, genealogies mentioned only key ancestors, so it is not always possible to work out dates by adding up the ages of the people listed, as Bishop Ussher so famously – and so erroneously did – in his attempt to discover the date of creation, which he concluded must have happened in 4004 BC.

In line with Jewish tradition, the early church was careful to show that Jesus was a true descendant of both Abraham and David, which is why his genealogy is listed in Mt 1 and Lk 3. As their descendant he had the legal right to receive the promises God had made to them. But the church also added *an unexpected development*, redefining genealogies by seeing all those who identified with Jesus as Messiah as their true descendants too (Gal 3:29).

2:1–70 The List of the Exiles Who Returned As a result, many of the inhabitants of Jerusalem and Judah prepare to return home, taking the captured treasures of the temple at Jerusalem with them (1:5–11). A long list of exiles who return home in this first major exodus from Babylon is presented at 2:1–70. While this list may seem irrelevant to modern readers, it must be remembered that it would have been of vital importance to the people of God after their return to Judah. It allowed them to trace their family trees back to the time of the exile and stressed their continuity with an earlier generation of the people of God.

3:1–6 Rebuilding the Altar By September or October 537, the returning exiles have settled down in their home towns, and have begun to renew their old patterns of worship. Note that not all the exiles return to Jerusalem; other towns in Judah receive returning exiles. The Feast of Tabernacles is celebrated with an altar built specially for that purpose, despite the risk of alienating peoples in the region around them. There is still no temple at Jerusalem. However, by building an altar dedicated to the Lord, the returning exiles can begin the process of restoring worship to what it had been before the exile.

3:7–13 Rebuilding the Temple But sooner or later, the temple will have to be rebuilt. The ruins of Solomon's temple, which had been razed to the ground by the

Babylonians, will act as the foundations of the new building. Under the direction of Zerubbabel, who emerges as the natural leader in Jerusalem during this period, preparations are made to rebuild the temple in the spring of 536 BC. While many are overjoyed when the foundations are laid, older people (who can remember the great edifice built by Solomon) are distressed. It is clear that the new temple will not be on the same scale as its predecessor.

4:1–24 Opposition to the Rebuilding of the Temple The texts here bring together problems that emerged over a period of several years, spanning the reigns of three Persian kings (Cyrus, Xerxes and Artaxerxes). The first problem noted was clearly a continuing one. As part of the Persians' general strategy for keeping Israel under control, part of the population of the northern kingdom of Israel had been deported to Assyria, and replaced with peoples from elsewhere in the Assyrian Empire. These peoples had brought their pagan practices to the region of Samaria, and had combined them with worship to the Lord. As a result, the Samaritans had evolved a form of religion that combined the worship of the Lord with pagan elements.

Some Samaritans now offer to help rebuild the temple, but are rebuffed by Zerubbabel, who does not wish their degenerate form of worship to have any association with the rebuilt temple. Piqued, the Samaritans do all that they can to prevent the rebuilding of the temple. Their most successful strategy is to inform the Persians that the Jews are rebuilding the walls of Jerusalem in order to turn it into a fortified city, from which they can defy the Persians (4:12–16). As a result, work on the temple is halted for a period of more than 15 years. It will not be until 520 BC, when a new Persian king (Darius) has ascended the throne, that rebuilding can recommence.

5:1–6:12 Tattenai's Letter to Darius and Darius' Decree The decision to go ahead with rebuilding at this stage is linked with the ministry of the prophet Haggai. The local Persian governor objects to the rebuilding, asking what authorisation the Jews have to proceed with such a project. In reply, he is told that Cyrus had explicitly permitted such a project. On consulting his superiors, the governor is told that such a decision had indeed been taken by Cyrus, and that Darius requires the governor to give all assistance to this project.

6:13–18 Completion and Dedication of the Temple With this royal backing, work on the temple proceeds apace. On 12 March 516, the temple is finally completed and is dedicated to the Lord. The first major festival to be celebrated in the new building is the Passover (6:19–22), a festival with strong associations of deliverance from bondage and the commemoration of the faithfulness of the Lord (see Ex 12). It is a fitting moment at which to celebrate the exiles' deliverance from bondage in Babylon, and to recall the Lord's faithfulness to his people.

Jews The use of the term 'Jews' to refer to the returned exiles (4:23; 5:1) is worth commenting on. Up to this time, the people of God have been referred to as 'Israelites' or 'Judahites'. The term 'Jew'

comes to be used in the post-exilic period to designate the people of God, and will be used regularly in later writings for this purpose.

EZRA 7:1–10:44
Ezra's Programme of Reform

7:1–8:14 Ezra and the Exiles Return A new stage in the religious renewal of Judaism after its return from exile begins some sixty years later, with the arrival of Ezra in the city of Jerusalem. Although the new section of the book that now opens does not give details of the precise dates involved, it would seem that Ezra sets out from Babylon in April 458, and arrives in Jerusalem in August of that same year. It is clear from the description provided that Ezra is deeply versed in the Law of Moses, and well placed to ensure that the Jews remain faithful to its instructions (7:1–10). It is also clear that Ezra has full backing from the Persian authorities, as the text of the letter from Artaxerxes makes clear (7:11–28). Returning with Ezra is a sizable body of exiles, detailed at 8:1–14.

8:15–36 The Return to Jerusalem After his journey from Mesopotamia to Palestine (8:15–36). Ezra relates what happens on his arrival at Jerusalem. The sudden switch to the first person at 8:1 indicates that Ezra's personal memoirs are being drawn on at this point, and at what follows. The book of Ezra draws extensively on such documents at several points. Of particular interest is that fact that the section 4:8–6:18, which involves extensive citation from official documents of the period, is written entirely in Aramaic, the international language of diplomacy during this period. Ezra has clearly incorporated these documents directly into his narrative, without feeling the need to translate them.

9:1–10:44 Intermarriage On his arrival in Jerusalem, Ezra is approached by various representatives of the ordinary people, who are deeply anxious concerning the way things are going. They report that their leaders and priests have lapsed from the high standards expected of them by marrying foreigners. Ezra is appalled by this development, seeing it as a direct violation of the law of God (9:1–15).

Why was intermarriage seen as such a serious matter? The answer lies in the need to preserve the distinctive identity of the people of God. As can be seen from the history of Israel and Judah prior to their exile, the marriage between Jews and non-Jews almost invariably led to the importation of foreign pagan religious practices and beliefs into the worship of Israel. Ezra himself identifies eight groups of people, whose religious beliefs found their way into Israel on account of intermarriage (9:1). As the exile was to be seen as God's purification of his people on account of their lapse into paganism, it is hardly surprising that Ezra is outraged. One of the problems that led to the exile being imposed on Jerusalem seemed to be about to occur once more. It is clear that others were also aware of the seriousness of these developments (10:1–4).

Ezra acts to prevent this from taking place (10:5–17). Though the people of Jerusalem have sinned, the harm that has been done can be remedied through repentance. Ezra summons the people of

Jerusalem and all Judah together to the city of Jerusalem. The period in question (November–December 458) would have fallen during the rainy season (10:9). Ezra sets the issue before the assembly, and receives overwhelming support for his proposals to put things right (10:9–15). A committee of investigation is set up (10:16–17); after three months, it publishes its findings (10:18–44). Their report suggests that just over 100 men in the region, including a number of Levites, have married foreign wives. These men would have been required to divorce their wives, even in the case of those with children.

10:44 Conclusion Here the book of Ezra ends abruptly. One of the reasons for this sudden ending has to do with the relation of the books of Ezra and Nehemiah. Although these two books are treated as separate in English versions of the Bible, there is evidence that they were originally a single book. The final event recorded in Ezra (the publication of the committee of investigation) is to be dated to March 457. The narrative is then taken up again in 445, as the contribution of Nehemiah to the rebuilding of Jerusalem is documented. As will become clear, Ezra's ministry continues under Nehemiah, and leads to a major religious revival. How that happens is the subject of the book of Nehemiah, to which the book of Ezra can be seen as an introduction.

NEHEMIAH

The book of Nehemiah continues the story, begun in the book of Ezra, of the rebuilding of Jerusalem and the re-establishment of the worship of the Lord in Judah after the release of the exiles from their captivity in Babylon. It depicts the many discouragements and difficulties faced by Nehemiah, and the way in which he dealt with them. Nehemiah himself, like Ezra, came to Jerusalem from elsewhere in the Persian Empire. Ezra had travelled from Babylon, while Nehemiah journeyed from the major city of Susa, some 300 kilometres east of Babylon. Nehemiah's decision to journey to Jerusalem is to be dated to the spring of 445, some 13 years after Ezra had set out for the same destination.

13:10–14 The provision for the temple staff through tithing
13:15–22 Reinstatement of the Sabbath regulations

13:23–28 Prohibition of mixed marriages
13:29 The purification of the priests and Levites
13:30–31 The provision of firstfruits

NEHEMIAH 1:1–7:73
Nehemiah's Arrival and Administration

1:1–2:10 Nehemiah Returns to Jerusalem It is clear that Nehemiah is moved to travel to Jerusalem on account of reports he has heard concerning the city walls (1:1–11) – almost certainly a reference to the abandoning of construction work in response to Samaritan agitation (Ezr 4:7–23). Nehemiah, as cupbearer to Artaxerxes, was a trusted member of the court, responsible for ensuring that the king's wine had not been drugged or poisoned. He is able to take advantage of this privileged position to request permission to take temporary leave of absence in order to return to his family city of Jerusalem, and rebuild it (2:1–10). This is given, although the temporary leave in question appears to have become extended to a period of twelve years, during which he is granted the status of governor by Artaxerxes.

2:11–20 Nehemiah Inspects Jerusalem's Walls On his arrival in Jerusalem, Nehemiah makes a nocturnal inspection of the southern section of the city's walls. He is unwilling that anyone should know of his purpose in coming to Jerusalem, and so carries out his inspection in secret, under the cover of darkness (2:11–16). Finally, he feels able to let the leading figures of the city know of his purposes (2:17–20). They greet his suggestion with delight. Sanballat, who is clearly Nehemiah's

leading political opponent, pours scorn on the idea.

3:1–4:23 Builders of the Wall; Opposition to the Rebuilding Despite this hostility from Sanballat, work begins on the rebuilding of the walls and gates of the city. Each of the city's ten named gates is identified, along with those who were responsible for their reconstruction (3:1–32). Opposition to the rebuilding of the walls and gates grows, particularly from potential rivals of a rebuilt Jerusalem. Nehemiah learns of their plans to disrupt the work, and posts armed guards to ward off assaults (4:1–23).

5:1–19 Nehemiah Helps the Poor However, the labour-intensive demands of rebuilding the walls and guarding them from assault begin to take their toll. Popular discontent begins to grow, as financial difficulties begin to mount. The situation is complicated by a food shortage, which leads to the price of basic foodstuffs such as grain rising significantly. In the end, Nehemiah can no longer ignore the outcry (5:1–5). He demands – and receives – promises that those who are benefiting financially from the situation pay back interest charges and restore property and goods that have been mortgaged to secure loans (5:6–13). To show his own seriousness, Nehemiah refuses his traditional right as a Persian governor to have superior food. He will share in the situation of his people (5:14–19).

6:1–7:3 The Completion of the Walls

Opposition to the rebuilding continues in other quarters. Sanballat spreads a rumour that Nehemiah proposes to use Jerusalem as the fortified base for a rebellion against Artaxerxes (6:1–14). However, Nehemiah pays no attention to this rumour, and presses ahead with the programme of reconstruction. By October 445, the walls are rebuilt. The entire project has taken 52 days (6:15–19). Shortly afterwards, the gates are installed, and Jerusalem is once more a city that can protect itself (7:1–3). As a precaution against a surprise attack, Nehemiah orders that the gates should not be opened until the heat of the day, thus making it difficult for an enemy to enter without being seen well in advance.

7:4–73 The List of the Exiles Who Returned

Now that the city can defend itself, attention can be paid to reconstructing its interior, and especially its houses. As a preliminary step in this process, Nehemiah decides to establish who is present in the city. In the course of setting up this registration process, he encounters the list of people who returned from exile with Zerubbabel

---

Is there a place for preaching in today's world?

The explanation of God's word in Chapter 8 is an early example of 'preaching'. But in a postmodern world, where authority is viewed with suspicion and educational models favour interaction, is there still a place for preaching today?

Clearly it is God's word that has pre-eminence, rather than any particular form of teaching it. If 'all Scripture is God-breathed' (2Ti 3:16), it is a chief means through which God has ordained to speak to us and interpret his acts in history. But is *preaching* this word essential? Paul certainly esteemed preaching, for having just affirmed Scripture's inspiration (2Ti 3:16–17) he immediately charged Timothy to 'preach the word', using it to 'correct, rebuke and encourage' (2Ti 4:2).

Preaching has important biblical precedents. Ezra read the Law while the Levites explained it (many would not have understood Hebrew by this time) 'so that the people understood what was being read' (Ne 8:8). In New Testament times the synagogue continued to follow this pattern of reading followed by commentary, as Jesus (Lk 4:16–21) and Paul (Ac 13:14–15) did. However Jesus and Paul also used dialogue as a means of teaching (e.g., Jn 8:31–59; Ac 18:28).

If preaching today is retained because of a preacher's fear or desire to control, clearly something is wrong. But the reality is that most Christians go to services unprepared and certainly without having studied the passage as the preacher will have done. While good preaching can still be powerful, if churches are to reach a postmodern generation monologue may not always be the best approach, and openness to participation through questions at agreed moments may well help (though group Bible study can also facilitate this).

Ultimately, authority lies in the word of God, not the one preaching it, nor the method in which we engage with it.

(7:4–73; see Ezr 2:1–70). There are minor differences between the lists provided in each case, suggesting that both accounts draw on the same original source, which may have included abbreviations or ciphers that were interpreted slightly differently at certain points.

NEHEMIAH 7:73–10:39
Ezra and the Dawn of Religious Revival

7:73–9:5 Ezra Reads the Law It is interesting to notice how often religious revival and reform are linked with the public reading of the Law. The public reading of the Book of the Law under Josiah in the period before the Babylonian exile (see 2Ki 23) was one such occasion. The reading of that same book by Ezra is another. It is clear that the 'reading' in question involved both the actual public reading of the Law, as well as exposition of its meaning and implications by Ezra and a team of Levites (8:1–18). The people 'now understood the words that had been made known to them' (8:12). As a result, they are moved to confess their sins and worship the Lord (9:1–3).

9:5–38 The Israelites Confess Their Sins in Prayer The extended prayer used on this occasion is worth detailed study (9:5–8). It surveys the gracious dealings of God with his people from the time of Abraham (see Ge 12–15) through to exodus from Egypt (see Ex 11–15) and wandering in the wilderness, through the conquest of Canaan (see Jos 5–12) up to the present day. The prayer includes powerful affirmations of the graciousness of God, and his total faithfulness to his

promises. Yet the continuing sin of God's people is also openly and fully admitted. Despite God's goodness, his people turned away from him, rebelled against him and disobeyed him.

9:38–10:39 The Agreement of the People As a result of these considerations, the leaders of the people put their agreement in writing to a commitment to reform and renewal (9:38–10:27). This agreement includes a number of major commitments, including a promise not to intermarry (10:30). This is a major concern to Ezra, who has earlier severely criticised the Jews for allowing this practice to continue (Ezr 9:1–15). However, this pledge of obedience goes far beyond this, and includes a commitment to the upkeep of the temple and its ministers (10:31–39).

NEHEMIAH 11:1–13:31
Nehemiah's Later Reforms

11:1–12:26 The New Residents of Jerusalem The narrative now returns to Nehemiah's concern to repopulate the city of Jerusalem. The walls and gates have been rebuilt. It is now necessary to rebuild the population of the once ruined city. It is agreed that the leaders of the people will live within the city. These will be joined by families chosen by lot, who will be required to live in the city rather than remain in the rural areas of Judah. While it is clear that some families volunteer to settle in the city, the majority have to be compelled (11:1–2). The names of the leading Jews who settle in Jerusalem are noted (11:3–36), along with the priests and Levites (12:1–26).

12:27–13:31 Dedication of the Wall of Jerusalem; Nehemiah's Final Reforms In what is clearly an extract from Nehemiah's personal memoirs, Nehemiah records the great event of the dedication of the wall of Jerusalem (12:27–47), and the public reading of the Book of Moses (a reference to Deuteronomy). The section that excludes Ammonites and Moabites from being admitted to the assembly of God is noted (this points to Dt 23:3–6 being among the passages read), and then acted upon (13:1–3). It is clear that there is a new determination to remain faithful to the letter of the Law.

So what had initially seemed an impossible task has been successfully accomplished. Jerusalem is a city once more, with walls and gates. Nehemiah can now rest in the knowledge that he has achieved what he set out to do. He now returns to the court of Artaxerxes (13:6), at some point between 433 and 432 BC, having spent twelve years (see 5:14) as governor of Jerusalem. However, for reasons not made clear, Nehemiah requests permission to spend a further term as governor of Jerusalem, and returns within a year of his departure.

On his return, he learns of a deliberate flouting of his regulations. One of the store-rooms, which he had ordered to be set aside specifically for the safe keeping of tithes and temple offerings, has been reallocated for the personal use of Tobiah. Nehemiah is furious at the manner in which Tobiah has gained such a privilege, and instantly revokes it (13:4–9). But this proves merely to be the tip of an iceberg. The provisions he made to ensure the smooth running of the temple have fallen into disuse, with the result that the Levites have gone back to their fields to support themselves. Nehemiah moves to restore the arrangements, so that worship at the temple can proceed as he intended (13:10–14). Yet other abuses soon emerge. The Sabbath regulations are being openly flouted (13:15–22), and intermarriage is again becoming a major problem (13:23–31).

So the book of Nehemiah ends on a note of caution. Nehemiah is able to list many achievements of his time in Jerusalem. In addition to the rebuilding of the walls and gates of the city, he instigated religious reforms that eliminated many of the pagan practices that had begun to creep back into Jewish worship. But the reader is left with a sense of uneasiness. If such a significant departure from the law of the Lord can take place so soon after the triumphant return from exile, what will the future be like? Can the new community of Israel remain faithful to the Law, if its first period in the restored Jerusalem has seen so many lapses? It seems that one of the most characteristic aspects of human sin is a tendency for people to rebel against God – or at best, to serve him only when this happens to coincide with their own interests.

The history of Jerusalem in the first years of the post-exilic period shows how deeply ingrained sin has become in human nature. And it raises the question 'What can be done?' How can Israel remain faithful to the Lord, let alone ensure that his name is known and honoured throughout the world? And

these questions set the context for the coming of Jesus Christ, as both Lord and Saviour.

But that lies in the future. The biblical narrative now switches to the city of Susa, from which Nehemiah originally came, as we learn the story of Esther and the fate of a Jewish community who remained in that region of the Persian Empire.

ESTHER

The book of Esther deals with the fate of a Jewish community in the city of Susa in the Persian Empire during the reign of Xerxes (486–465 BC). While other Old Testament books dealing with the period tend to focus on events back in Jerusalem at this time, Esther deals with the events focusing on the Jews who remained in the eastern region of the empire. The central character, from whom the book takes its name, is Queen Esther, a Jew who is able to intervene on behalf of her people at a moment of crisis.

Esther is an unusual book in one respect. There is no explicit mention of God, nor any obvious reference to any aspect of worship or prayer. This absence of explicit reference to God should not, however, be interpreted to mean that Esther is a purely secular writing. It is clear that the work is intended as an illustration of God's providential guiding of his people as they face difficult circumstances. There is no need to draw explicit attention to the presence or activity of God. These are both assumed throughout.

OUTLINE

The background to the plot to destroy the Jews

1:1–22 Queen Vashti deposed

2:1–18 Esther made queen

2:19–23 Mordecai uncovers a plot to assassinate the king

The plot to destroy the Jews

3:1–15 Haman's decision to destroy the Jews

4:1–17 Mordecai asks Esther to help him foil the plot

5:1–8 Esther's banquet

5:9–14 Haman builds a gallows to hang Mordecai

6:1–14 The king honours Mordecai

7:1–10 Haman hanged on his own gallows

The institution of the feast of Purim

8:1–17 The king gives the Jews religious freedom and privileges

9:1–17 The Jews kill their enemies in Susa

9:18–32 The institution of Purim

10:1–3 The greatness of Mordecai

1:1–2:23 Queen Vashti Deposed and Esther Made Queen The work opens by setting the scene for its action, vividly depicting the power of Xerxes and the grandeur of his court (1:1–8). We are then introduced to his queen, Vashti (referred to in Greek records of the reign of Xerxes as Amestris). Vashti was deposed in 483 or 484 BC, although the reasons for this are not clear. Her refusal to obey Xerxes' command probably reflects a power struggle within the court, which is only hinted at in this narrative (1:9–22). Eventually, she is replaced by Esther, a beautiful Jewish woman (2:1–1). However,

Esther does not let the fact that she is Jewish be known (2:10, 20).

The dangerous world of court intrigue is then introduced. Mordecai, Esther's adviser and friend, uncovers a plot to assassinate Xerxes, which Esther duly reports to the king (2:19–23).

3:1–4:17 Haman's Plot to Destroy the Jews Mordecai himself then becomes a cause of a plot on the part of Haman, a Persian nobleman, who becomes irritated by Mordecai's failure to pay him due respect. Haman contrives a scheme to eliminate Mordecai and the remaining Jews from the Persian Empire. After casting lots (for which the Hebrew term

is *Purim*), a day is selected for the deed (3:1–7).

Haman persuades Xerxes to issue an order for the annihilation of the Jews (3:8–15). Mordecai, learning of this development, asks Esther to intervene to prevent the massacre, hinting that she may well have been placed in such a prominent position for precisely this purpose (4:1–17). This clear hint at the providence of God in action spurs Esther to take action.

5:1–7:10 Esther's Request to the King; Mordecai Honoured and Haman Hanged Esther asks the king if he will grant her a favour, which she will explain at a

---

What does it mean to say God is sovereign?

The book of Esther is remarkable in that God is nowhere directly mentioned, though it is clear that he is involved throughout the story. It is this unseen hand of God, directing and overruling human affairs, steering them towards his ultimate purpose, and overcoming everything that would resist his will, that is known as God's sovereignty. Paul summed it up by saying, 'In all things God works for the good of those who love him, who have been called according to his purpose' (Ro 8:28). In Esther – one of only two Bible books named after a woman (the other is Ruth) – Haman's plot to exterminate the Jews is foiled by God's behind-the-scenes intervention, bringing together a remarkable series of events and 'coincidences', and thus avoiding a Jewish holocaust.

This is one of many examples in the Bible of God's ability to bring about his purposes, despite all opposition. He can do whatever he wills (e.g., Ps 135:6), as Job declared at the end of his troubles, 'I know that you can do all things; no purpose of yours can be thwarted' (Job 42:2).

Areas in which the Bible reveals God's sovereignty include his sovereignty over creation (e.g., Ps 93), over human affairs (e.g., Isa 40:22–24), over the lives of his people (Jer 18:5–10), in furthering his purposes through Israel (e.g., Ro 9:6–11:36), in his plan of salvation (e.g., Eph 1:11), in bringing good out of suffering (e.g., Job 42:1–17), and even over the smallest details of life (e.g., Mt 10:29–30). Even the devil and all his hosts are subject to God (e.g., Rev 12:7–12).

But all of this is not mere theology in the Bible. This certainty about God's sovereignty is what enables God's people to press on every day, come what may.

banquet she proposes to give the following day, to which only he and Haman will be invited (5:1–8). Haman is delighted at this honour, and decides to make his happiness complete by hanging Moredecai on a purpose-built gallows the following day (5:9–14).

Unfortunately, things do not turn out quite as Haman expected. Xerxes, while browsing through some court records, discovers a record of Mordecai's uncovering a plot against him, and honours him for this service (6:1–14). At the banquet she has prepared for Xerxes and Haman, Esther reveals that she is a Jew, and asks Xerxes to punish the man who has brought the threat of death to her people. Xerxes declares that the man who has perpetrated such an outrage deserves to die. On learning that it is Haman, he orders his immediate execution (7:1–10).

8:1–10:3 Purim Celebrated; the Greatness of Mordecai

Following this, the Jews are given special privileges by Xerxes (8:1–16), and gain vengeance against those who wished to destroy them (9:1–17). A festival is inaugurated by the Jews to commemorate their deliverance, known as Purim after the lots that were thrown to decide the day of their death by Haman. The work ends by noting Mordecai's rise to power at the side of Xerxes (9:18–10:3). There are similarities between these happenings and those recorded in the story of Joseph (see Ge 39–47), in which a Jew also rises to authority in a Gentile – that is, non-Jewish – court.

JOB

The Old Testament includes a number of different types of writings, including works of history (such as 1 and 2 Samuel), prophecy (such as Isaiah) and wisdom. The book of Job (pronounced to rhyme with 'robe' or 'lobe') belongs to this final category of writings. It is one of the most remarkable writings in the Old Testament. It focuses on a question of continuing interest and importance: Why does God allow suffering? Or, more precisely, does the fact that someone is suffering mean that they have fallen out of God's favour? Is suffering the direct result of sin? Is it a mark of disfavour in the sight of God? Important though these issues are, the Christian reader of this book may find that this work does not quite answer these questions. There are two reasons for this.

First, the problem of suffering has become of major importance in Western culture since the time of the Enlightenment – that is, since about 1750. The problem tends to be stated in a very specific form, focusing on the question of the goodness and omnipotence (almightiness) of God. How can a loving, good and all-powerful God allow suffering in his world, or among his people? This specific question is not addressed by the book of Job, which is primarily concerned to affirm that God is *there*, despite all the contradictions and confusion of life. The book makes it clear that nobody can hope to master the mysteries of life, including the apparent prosperity of the wicked and the sufferings of the righteous. Nevertheless, in the midst of all this anxiety, we can be reassured that God is present. There is a sense in which the book of Job must be read from the standpoint of the cross and resurrection of Jesus Christ, in order to appreciate the manner in which a truly righteous person can undergo suffering.

Secondly, the literary form of the book involves an extensive amount of repetition and restatement, which makes its arguments quite difficult to follow. In what follows, we shall aim to identify the main lines of argument and exploration. It is, however, beyond the scope of this work to give a detailed analysis of the at times quite complex ideas being set out in the highly poetic speeches of the five contributors.

The problem of suffering is frequently raised in the Old Testament. Why do the righteous seem to be worse off than the unrighteous? Why is life so unfair? The book of Job explores some of these issues. But in many ways, the book is best seen as pointing ahead to the suffering of another righteous person – Jesus Christ. Why did Jesus have to suffer? Why did he have to die? As the New Testament makes clear, the answer to that question is not that Jesus deserved to suffer and die, but that he chose to suffer and die in order that others might live and be forgiven.

The book of Job has a distinctive structure, which needs to be understood before it can be fully appreciated. The book opens by setting the scene for Job's sufferings, and allowing us to overhear Job's own understanding of his situation. We are then

introduced to his three well-meaning friends, Eliphaz, Bildad and Zophar. As the well-known phrase 'Job's comforters' implies, these end up causing Job more misery and confusion than he had in the first place. Their basic assumption is that Job's suffering results from sin – an assumption that the reader of Job knows to be incorrect, on account of the information supplied in the opening chapters of the work.

The first part of the work consists of three cycles of speeches by the comforters, to which Job replies. This is then followed by some comments by Elihu, who seems to have been an onlooker who wished to contribute to the discussion at this point. Finally God himself responds, clearing up the confusion which has been generated by the theological ramblings of the disputants.

OUTLINE

The prologue
1:1–5 Job is introduced
1:6–2:10 The testing of Job's integrity
2:11–13 Job's three friends come to comfort him

The first cycle of speeches
3:1–26 Job's lament for his situation
4:1–5:27 Eliphaz
6:1–7:21 Job's reply
8:1–22 Bildad
9:1–10:22 Job's reply
11:1–20 Zophar
12:1–14:22 Job's reply

The second cycle of speeches
15:1–35 Eliphaz
16:1–17:16 Job's reply
18:1–21 Bildad
19:1–29 Job's reply
20:1–29 Zophar
21:1–34 Job's reply

The third cycle of speeches
22:1–30 Eliphaz
23:1–24:25 Job's reply
25:1–6 Bildad
26:1–14 Job's reply
27:1–31:40 Job's concluding speech

The four speeches of Elihu
32:1–5 Elihu is introduced
32:6–33:33 Elihu's first speech
34:1–37 Elihu's second speech
35:1–16 Elihu's third speech
36:1–37:24 Elihu's fourth speech

The divine intervention
38:1–40:2 God's first speech
40:3–5 Job's reply
40:6–41:34 God's second speech
42:1–6 Job's reply

Epilogue
42:7–9 God rebukes Job's friends
42:10–17 Job's final vindication

JOB 1:1–2:13
Introduction

The book opens with a powerful description of the character of Job himself. It is left beyond doubt that Job is an upright person of integrity and faith.

It is also clear that Job is prosperous (1:1–5).

1:6–22 Job's First Test The scene then shifts dramatically, to a discussion between the Lord and Satan. The word 'Satan' needs a little clarification. In the book of Job, the

term is not treated as a proper name, and is always preceded by the definite article. The Hebrew is thus better translated simply as 'the accuser' or 'the opposer', and does not have the associations of evil and rebellion against God that are traditionally associated with the proper name 'Satan'. The figure in question is best understood as an angel or member of the heavenly court of the Lord who offers to test Job's faith and integrity (1:6–12). What would happen if Job were to lose all his outward signs of righteousness and integrity – his herds, for example? How would Job interpret such a development? The response is clear (1:13–22). Job has no hesitation in declaring that the Lord has the right to take away what he has given.

2:1–13 Job's Second Test But what would happen if Job were to suffer physically? Once more, Job refuses to criticise God. He is prepared to accept whatever God wishes him to have, whether it is good or trouble (2:1–10). Job's troubles are now, however, made considerably worse by the arrival of his three well-meaning friends. There can be no doubt that they care for him greatly, and wish to help him in his time of trouble (2:11–13). Initially, they simply sit beside him in silence, their presence being a sign of their care and sympathy. As events prove, they might have been well advised to remain silent. Their words of comfort proved to be distinctly unhelpful.

JOB 3:1–14:22
First Cycle of Speeches

3:1–7:21 Job Speaks and Eliphaz Replies The first cycle of speeches opens with Job finally giving expression to his sense of frustration and distress (3:1–26). His misery is such that he wishes that he had never been born. Eliphaz then intervenes, in an attempt to cast light on things. It is quite clear, he argues, that Job's misery results from his sin. God would never allow a righteous person to suffer in this manner. The best course of action would be for Job to be honest about things, and admit that he has sinned. Anyone who experiences the discipline of God ought not to despise it, but should learn from it. The same God who wounded Job will also bind up his wounds and heal him (4:1–5:27). Job's reply to this shows the full extent of his misery and confusion. Why does God create people, when they end up so miserable and unhappy (6:1–7:21)?

8:1–10:22 Bildad and Job Bildad then enters the discussion (8:1–22). Picking up on Job's comment about God's apparent unrighteousness (6:29), Bildad stresses that God is just in all his ways. The fate of Job's children reflects the fact that they were sinners. Yet Job points out in reply that experience suggests that the strong triumph over the weak. It seems to him that there is no real justice underlying what he sees happening in the world (9:1–10:22).

11:1–14:22 Zophar and Job The third comforter, Zophar, then makes his presence felt (11:1–20). It becomes clear that he lacks the gentleness and compassion of Eliphaz and Bildad. His contribution opens with what is clearly a direct criticism of Job for his lack of piety. He should not cast aspersions on God in this manner, nor be allowed to get away with some of his more intemperate

statements. Job doesn't know what he is talking about. What does he know about the mysteries of God? Job ought to confess his sin, and put an end to his misery. If Zophar hoped to reduce Job to silence by this speech, he is soon disappointed. Job reiterates his basic conviction that there is a real tension between this view and his own experience. It is very difficult for him to discern the justice of what is happening to him (12:1–14:22). This speech contains some deeply moving statements concerning the frailty of human life (e.g., 14:1–2), and statements of the unbearable nature of human life without hope (e.g., 14:7–14).

JOB 15:1–21:34
Second Cycle of Speeches

15:1–17:16 Eliphaz and Job The second cycle of speeches inevitably involves at least a degree of repetition. If the first set of speeches from the comforters was based upon the nature and character of God himself, the second set tends to focus more on the experience of life. Eliphaz' second speech (15:1–35) opens by reminding Job that he is not the first person ever to have wondered about the questions they are discussing. He concedes that the wicked may indeed seem to prosper. However, they are troubled by their consciences, and live in fear of the consequences of their deeds. Job replies that his comforters are not the first people ever to have given the world the same unsatisfactory answers to the questions he has raised (16:1–17:16). Again, we find some moving statements concerning the need for hope in the face of death (17:14–16). These statements

will bring home to Christian readers the importance of the resurrection of Jesus Christ, and the new hope it brings to those who know that they will share in its power and glory on the last day.

18:1–21:34 Bildad, Zophar and Job Bildad emphasises the plight of the wicked, who are portrayed as lacking any hope or permanence (18:1–21). Job responds with an assertion of his bewilderment, both at the inconsistencies of the world and the attitude adopted by his comforters, who seem intent on breaking him down (19:1–29). Zophar suggests that it may seem that the wicked escape unpunished, yet this is simply due to a temporary stay of execution. They will get what they deserve in the end, even if for the moment they seem to prosper. Zophar's graphic picture of the fate of the wicked in this life draws out both the material and psychological aspects of their suffering (20:1–29). In reply, Job suggests that this is simply not the case. The wicked are safe in their homes, and their families and flocks prosper. Where is the justice in that? Zophar seems to lack any real experience of the world in making such nonsensical statements (21:1–34).

JOB 22:1–31:40
Third Cycle of Speeches

22:1–25:6 Eliphaz, Bildad and Job The third set of speeches, which is limited to contributions by Eliphaz and Bildad, are noticeably more aggressive than the first two sets. Eliphaz argues that Job is wicked, and that his wickedness is the direct cause of his present misfortune. If Job will only submit to God, he will find

prosperity once more (22:1–30). Job's reply to this does not really address the issues raised by Eliphaz, but focuses once more on the seemingly senseless riddle of life. The wicked seem to prosper, and get away with their evil (23:1–24:25). Bildad's very brief contribution to the debate (25:1–6) adds nothing new.

26:1–31:40 Job Speaks This is followed by an extended series of speeches by Job, which generally recapitulate some of the points he has already made (26:1–31:40). Within this section, 28:1–28 is of special interest, and is worth reading closely. The basic argument is that true wisdom is found only in the fear of God. The section opens with a summary of ancient mining methods, which underscores the difficulty of obtaining the most precious metals and gems. These are located deep within the earth, and their acquisition is both difficult and costly (28:1–11). Yet wisdom is not found in any such mines, nor can it be purchased with any of the precious products of these mines (28:12–19). It is found only in the fear of God. Only God understands everything. He alone views the ends of the earth, and sees everything beneath the heavens (28:24). This insight sets the debate in its proper context, for it brings out that human minds are simply unable to fathom the deepest mysteries – including those under discussion at that moment.

This chapter is followed by Job's nostalgic recollection of his days of happiness and prosperity (29:1–25), reflections on his current miserable state (30:1–31), and a firm declaration of his personal integrity (31:1–40). Job is convinced that, despite all his difficulties and temptation, he has remained faithful to what God requires and expects of him. If anyone can prove otherwise, they must say so. But Job believes, passionately and pathetically, that he is blameless. He cannot understand what is happening.

JOB 32:1–37:24
Elihu's Speeches

We have not been introduced to the fifth contributor to this discussion, who suddenly makes his appearance. In a series of four speeches, Elihu (who is clearly younger than the four other men: 32:6–7) expresses his feeling that what has been said thus far does not really meet the issues. In particular, it is clear that he believes that Job has managed to justify himself, but failed to attempt to justify or explain the ways of God himself (32:12).

The basic theme of Elihu's four speeches seems to be that suffering, such as that experienced by Job, is to be seen as God's way of disciplining his people. It is unthinkable that God should do anything that is in any way unjust (34:10–15). Nothing in the world is hidden from God (34:21–30). Therefore God must be aware of the fact that Job is suffering. The reason for such suffering can only be that Job has sinned (36:5–21). Suffering is thus linked with human hardness of heart and disobedience, and can be alleviated by repentance and amendment of life. In many ways, Elihu's arguments pick up themes that have already been found in the earlier speeches of the three comforters, and add little that is new to the discussion. This discussion is now drawn to its close by the Lord himself.

JOB 38:1–42:17
God's Affirmations and Job's Response

38:1–41:34 The Lord Speaks to Job The Lord now answers Job with a series of questions. In one of the most beautiful pieces of poetry in the Old Testament, the Lord speaks of the wonder and intricacy of creation (38:1–40:2). Aspect after aspect of the created order is explored, as the wonderful complexity of the world is made clear. The survey takes in every aspect of the creation, from the raging of the sea to the wonder of the constellations of the night sky, from the thundering of the rainclouds to the richness of the world's animal life. All of these were created by the Lord. Did Job create these? Does he understand the way the world is? Is he in a position to criticise God?

Job's answer is unequivocal. He has nothing to say. He knows that he has spoken out of turn. He is in no position to argue with the Creator of the world (40:3–5).

The Lord then speaks again (40:6–41:34), affirming his own righteousness and his firm intention to ensure that righteousness prevails within his creation. No explanation is offered for the perplexities of life. Instead, there is a ringing declaration that all is subject to the sovereign justice of the Lord. Job may not understand; but he may trust. Using highly figurative poetic language, the Lord again speaks of his sovereignty over every aspect of his creation. The implication is clear: God may be trusted to take care of every aspect of his world. It is not something that humanity can or need understand. The important thing is to be reassured that the Lord is God, and that all things are ultimately subject to him.

42:1–17 Job Speaks and Prays Job accepts this (42:1–5). He is clearly aware that he has raised questions that are not going to be answered, and that he has ventured into regions where human understanding falters on account of the mysteries it confronts. Yet Job is reassured. The Lord is there, even in the midst of the riddles of life. As a result, he prays for his friends, who tried to comfort him (42:10), and is restored to prosperity.

The overall message of the book of Job is clear. God does not allow his people to suffer without good reason. They may not fully understand what that reason may be. Nevertheless, they may rest assured that the Lord will do what is right. Righteousness does not exempt anyone from suffering. For the Christian, the suffering of Jesus Christ is a powerful reminder that even those who are righteous in the sight of God suffer. Yet it is also a reminder that God is able to do something through apparently pointless suffering. Will not the One who brought about the redemption of the world through the suffering of Christ bring about some good from his people's sufferings?

PSALMS

The book of Psalms (sometimes also known as 'the psalter') is composed of a series of collections of psalms, which was probably arranged in its final form in the 3rd century BC. The psalter as we now have it includes a number of smaller collections, including the 'Psalms of Asaph' (Psalms 73–83), the 'Psalms of the Sons of Korah' (Psalms 84–85; 87–88), and the 'Psalms of David' (Psalms 138–145). The 150 psalms brought together in this collection of collections are arranged in five books, as follows:

Book 1: Psalms 1–41
Book 2: Psalms 42–72
Book 3: Psalms 73–89
Book 4: Psalms 90–106
Book 5: Psalms 107–150

Although the book probably took its final form in the 3rd century BC, most of the material brought together dates from much earlier, generally in the region 1000–500 BC. The task of dating some individual psalms can be difficult, although some can be assigned to dates with a reasonable degree of certainty.

Before commenting briefly on individual psalms, some general comments on the collection of psalms as a whole will be helpful. Many psalms have titles attached to them. For example, Psalm 30 is entitled 'A psalm. A song. For the dedication of the

PSALMS CAN HELP YOU . . . when you are feeling:

Abandoned:	13, 22, 31, 42	Ill or weak:	6, 31, 41, 42, 103
Afraid:	27, 34, 46, 55, 56	Insecure:	27, 46, 71, 93, 125
Angry:	4, 37, 73, 109	Joyful:	33, 47, 66, 92, 103
Bereaved:	23, 27, 71, 116	Lonely:	3, 13, 25, 40, 139
Betrayed:	41, 52, 55	Overwhelmed:	9, 24, 61, 142
Confused:	12, 73, 107	Proud:	36, 49, 75
Depressed:	6, 25, 42, 143	Stressed:	25, 31, 62, 142
Despairing:	13, 42, 130, 142	Tempted:	51, 125, 141
Discouraged:	31, 40, 61, 93, 121	Thankful:	100, 116, 136, 138
Doubting:	10, 27, 53, 77	Threatened:	3, 7, 31, 35, 57
Far from God:	13, 22, 42, 139	Trapped:	25, 27, 31, 88, 118
Guilty:	25, 32, 51, 103, 130	Troubled:	4, 20, 34, 37, 46
Helpless:	27, 42, 46, 71, 121	Undecided:	23, 25, 37, 125

temple. Of David.' This would naturally suggest that this psalm was written by David for the occasion of the dedication of the property and building materials for the temple, as recorded at 1Ch 22:1–23:6. Although the reliability of the individual psalm titles has often been challenged, there are good reasons for believing that they are original and authentic. For example, psalms recorded outside the psalter are generally given titles (such as those found at 2Sa 22:1, Isa 38:9 and Hab 3:1). Furthermore, the historical information preserved in the titles accords well with the content of the psalms in question.

Terms Used

It is known that at the time of the earliest Greek translation of the psalter (around the 2nd century BC), Jewish scholars were no longer familiar with the meanings of some of the technical terms used. This suggests that by this stage the titles were already long established, and were retained by reason of tradition even at this early stage. Examples of these terms include *shiggaion* (a lament?), *maskil* (a meditation?) and *miktam* (a song of expiation?). One term of special interest is *selah*, which occurs 71 times in the psalter, and is found elsewhere only in Habakkuk. The meaning of the word is not entirely clear. The most commonly accepted understanding of the term is that it denotes a pause, perhaps to allow for reflection on what has just been sung. However, it is also possible that it refers to the singing of a refrain, or to the raising of voices while that section of the psalm is sung. (It should be appreciated that the psalms were written to be sung, which explains the numerous musical directions often incorporated in the title.)

Authorship

The authorship of the psalter is a complex issue. The psalm titles themselves mention various people, including David, Asaph and the Sons of Korah. There are also 55 references to an unidentified 'director of music'. The Hebrew text of the titles is often ambiguous. For example, the Hebrew phrase translated as 'a psalm of David' could mean a psalm (a) written by David; (b) written for or dedicated to David; (c) written about David; or (d) written for the use of David. Nevertheless, the association of so many psalms with David is entirely in keeping with the idea that he was 'the hero of Israel's songs' (2Sa 23:1). It is therefore reasonable to conclude that he must have been responsible for the composition of many, if not all, of the psalms that name him in the title.

Structure

The psalms, like much of the Old Testament, are written in poetic form. Unfortunately, there is still considerable debate over the precise nature of Hebrew poetry. Since the original pronunciation of the psalms is no longer known with any degree of certainty, attempts to recover the rhythm or metre have so far proved unconvincing. As a result, scholars have tended to focus on 'parallelism' – the way in which one line of poetry is balanced by another, often either by repeating the same point using slightly different

words ('synonymous parallelism') or by stating the opposite ('antithetic parallelism').
An example of 'synonymous parallelism' is provided in Ps 104:33:

> I will sing to the LORD all my life;
>   I will sing praise to my God as long as
>   I live.

Other patterns can also be discerned. For example, a number of psalms are structured
using an acrostic pattern, based on the letters of the Hebrew alphabet (such as Psalms
25, 34, 37, 111, 112, 119 and 145).

Categories of Psalms

Psalms may be categorised in various ways. Most psalms fall into one of two major
categories: psalms of petition (often referred to as 'laments'), and psalms of praise.
Other minor categories, such as wisdom psalms (such as Psalms 1, 37, 49, 73 and 112)
and liturgies (such as Psalms 15, 24, 68, 82 and 115), may also be noted. We shall
concern ourselves with the first two major categories.

Over one third of the psalms take the form of *prayers of petition*, the largest category
within the psalter. These are mainly prayers addressed to God reflecting thoughts
and emotions arising out of human suffering. This category of psalms may be
divided into two general types: 'plea' and 'complaint'. The former are prayers for
help, made either by individuals (such as Psalms 3, 5, 7, 14, 17, 25 and 26) or
communities (such as Psalms 12, 58, 83, 94 and 123). The latter are complaints that
God has failed to act when he might have been expected to, and are again made by
individuals (such as Psalms 6, 13, 22, 35 and 39) or communities (such as Psalms 9,
10, 44, 60, 74 and 77).

Psalms of praise, like modern hymns, express delight in God as Creator and Saviour.
Such psalms can be divided into two general categories: those that praise the greatness
of God, as it is revealed in nature and history (often referred to as 'hymns', such as
Psalms 8, 19, 29, 33 and 47); and those that express gratitude to God for intervening
in a situation of great distress or suffering (often referred to as 'songs of thanksgiving').
Such 'songs of thanksgiving' may be on behalf of individuals (such as Psalms 18, 30, 32,
34 and 92) or communities (such as Psalms 67, 75, 107 and 124).

Themes

A number of related themes give a unity to the rich diversity of material found in
the psalter. At its heart is the theme of the sovereignty of God over his creation,
reflected not only in the psalms of praise that proclaim his many qualities and
virtues, but also in the psalms of petition. These latter psalms reflect the belief that
God alone is able to meet every request. From beginning to end, the psalms thus
stress, explicitly or implicitly, the universal sovereignty of the Lord God. This theme
is often linked with the kingship of God, especially in those psalms celebrating his
enthronement (such as Psalms 47, 93, 95, 96 and 97). Other aspects of God's

character that are of major importance within the psalter include his holiness, righteousness and goodness.

The psalter also focuses on the royal monarchy, either in the form of David himself or one of his descendants. This reflects the unique position occupied by David and his dynasty. Not only did God choose David to be the shepherd of his people; he designated him as 'son' (see Ps 2:7; 89:26–27). This is linked with the selection of Jerusalem or more precisely Mount Zion as the location for the temple. The temple was widely regarded as God's dwelling-place on earth. God's presence was understood to ensure protection and peace for those living under his rule. The continued prosperity and security of Jerusalem thus became the theme of much praise.

It is not surprising that the themes of praise and prayer should be of major importance within the psalter. These are often linked with specific references to music and musical instruments, and to the human thankfulness and joy that lie at the heart of such praise.

In what follows, we shall explore some of the themes of each of the psalms. In view of the limitations upon space, it will be impossible to explore these themes in the detail or to the depth they so clearly deserve. The psalms are probably best read in an attitude of devotion and meditation. The notes provided are intended to help pick out the points that may be particularly helpful in using the psalms in this devotional manner.

BOOK 1
Psalms 1–41

Psalm 1 may be intended to act as an introduction to the psalter as a whole. It stresses the importance of taking a delight in the law of the Lord, and the benefits that result from this. A particularly powerful image – that of a tree planted by streams of water (1:3) – is employed to illustrate the way in which a close relationship with God leads to spiritual refreshment and renewal. The contrast with those who reject or ignore God will be clear: these are like dried-up chaff, which is blown away by the wind (1:4). A theme that will occur many times in the psalter is that of the Lord watching over his people (1:6), ensuring their wellbeing even in the face of all kinds of adversity.

Psalm 2 belongs to the general category of 'royal psalms', celebrating both the coronation of a new king of Judah and also the kingship of the Lord over his people. The king is anointed by the authority of God, not by human authority. It is impossible to read this psalm without being reminded of, for example, the anointing of David as king over Israel by Samuel. For this reason, other earthly kings and rulers are warned to be on their guard; the king enjoys the protection of the Lord, so that attack on him is futile and misguided.

However, there is also a strongly messianic element to this psalm, which speaks of the king as the 'son' of God (2:7), who enjoys the special protection and favour of the Lord. There is a clear echo here of the great promise made by the Lord to the house of David (2Sa 7:14), to raise up a king from one of his

descendants. For the Christian, this psalm has a special significance in this respect. It is seen by New Testament writers as pointing to the coming of the Son of God, Jesus Christ. This psalm is hinted at on the occasion of the baptism (Mt 3:17) of Jesus Christ. Through his resurrection from the dead, Christ is declared to be the Son in whom God is well pleased (Ac 13:33). Similarly, in relation to both the superiority of Jesus over angels, and his role as the true high priest, the letter to the Hebrews singles out this verse as having major relevance (Heb 5:5).

The title of Psalm 3 points to its having been written at the time that David was facing a serious rebellion from his son Absalom (2Sa 15:13–17:22). The psalm affirms the care and protection of the Lord in the face of enemies, and speaks powerfully of the peace of mind this knowledge brings to God's people. This is the first psalm in a collection that is explicitly attributed to David.

Psalm 4 is also attributed to David, and is again addressed to a situation of distress. It speaks of the assurance of believers that the Lord will hear them in their time of need (4:3). Even though it may seem that all is lost, the Lord may be relied on to remain faithful to those whom he loves. The psalm includes a particularly fine prayer for the light of the face of God to shine on his people (4:6), which echoes the great thanksgiving of Israel during its period of wandering in the desert (Nu 6:25).

Psalm 5 is also a plea for help from the Lord in the face of an enemy. The believer can have confidence in the Lord on

account of the righteousness of God, which will ultimately triumph over the evil of the godless. The ungodly have rebelled against God, and therefore will be dealt with by God himself. There is a clear idea here that the psalmist's difficulties at this moment are caused by his faithfulness to the Lord. In that he has been faithful to the Lord, he can expect the Lord to be faithful in return, and deliver him from his situation. The believer can wait in expectation (5:3), knowing of the protection of the Lord, which is compared to a shield (5:12) that wards off the attacks and missiles of an enemy.

Psalm 6 represents another prayer for the Lord's deliverance in a situation of some difficulty. The psalm sounds a note of anguish, because of the uncertainty of things (6:3), and depicts the psalmist as being in great distress on account of his sorrow (6:6–7). When will the Lord act? The psalm stresses that the only hope of the believer lies in the Lord and not in human strength (6:2), and emphasises the importance of the 'unfailing love' of the Lord in relation to that hope (6:4).

Psalm 7 To judge by its title, this psalm would seem to relate to the period in David's life when he was pursued by Saul, and seemed to be continually in danger of his life. (The term *shiggaion* in the title is not understood. Although it seems to be related to an Akkadian word for 'lament', its inclusion certainly points to the antiquity of the psalm.) The psalm speaks of David's decision to take refuge in the Lord in the face of his dangers, knowing that the Lord will shield and defend the righteous. The psalm ends on a note of confidence, reflecting the

faithfulness of God to his covenant. Even in their darker moments, the people of God may seek refuge in his compassion.

Psalm 8 strikes a very different note. It is a celebration of the place of honour accorded to humanity in the purposes of God. It opens with a ringing declaration of the majesty of God. Yet, as David reflects on the wonder of God's creation, he cannot help but wonder about his own place. It is amazing that God should have given such a place of honour to people such as himself in his great work of creation. For God has set humanity only a little lower than the angels, and given them authority over the world and its remaining creatures. And he cares for them! This is truly a psalm of celebration, and meditation on the wonderful love of God for his creation.

Psalms 9 and 10 should be read together, as they appear originally to have been a single psalm celebrating the steadfast love of the Lord in times of distress and need. The two psalms, together and individually, stress the total faithfulness of the Lord to his people, and his willingness to hear them in their moments of distress.

Psalms 11–14 continue the theme of the threat posed by outside enemies, and the

---

Does God need our praise?

The Psalms are the Bible's hymnbook, still used today by both Jews and Christians. Its Hebrew title is *Tehillim* ('Songs of Praise'), highlighting that the Psalms were primarily songs to be sung. Our title 'Psalms' comes from its title in the Greek translation of the Old Testament: *Psalmos*, meaning 'music played on instruments'. The psalms contain worship, thanksgiving, confession, petition, and even prophecy. Their timeless quality lies in their constant focus on God, his greatness, power, love and faithfulness to his people.

However, unlike in many other ancient religions, the Bible never suggests that God *needs* these prayers or praises. Their gods needed their anger assuaging or their pride bolstering; but there is no suggestion that Yahweh needs such things. He is not some sort of divine battery that constantly needs recharging through the offering of our praise; nor does he need reminding of our needs or informing of our sins, as though he had missed them. God has everything he needs within himself, and our praises and prayers can neither add to him nor take away from him.

So why bother praising or praying? While God doesn't need our worship, he is certainly worthy of it. It is, quite simply, appropriate for us to recognise who he is and what he has done. It pleases him when his children do this, not because of any psychological deficiency on his part, but because in understanding who he is we understand more of who we are too. Likewise, he doesn't need our prayers; but offering them is good for us because it reminds us that we are dependent on him.

The root word for 'praise' in Hebrew means 'making a noise'. In short, if God is good, it is simply appropriate to tell it aloud.

need to look to the Lord for help. In their different, yet complementary ways, these psalms identify the threats posed to faith, and the manner in which the Lord is able to meet those threats. Psalm 14 is of particular interest, on account of its recognition that there are those who deny the existence of God (14:1). It is important to note, as the French philosopher Pascal pointed out many years ago, that Scripture nowhere feels the need to *prove* the existence of God!

Psalm 15 strikes a different note. It represents a fine and poetic analysis of the need for holiness and purity on the part of those who wish to draw near to the Lord. The original reference is specifically to the temple, and relates to those who wish to worship. However, it can also be read from a specifically Christian standpoint, as referring to the need for such holiness on the part of all who wish to gain access to God. Such access is made possible by the atoning death of Christ, which cleanses and purifies sinners and allows them access to God through the blood of Christ.

Psalms 16–18 once more focus on the idea of the Lord as a place of refuge in times of difficulty. Note especially the images used to refer to God that express the idea of stability and permanence. God is a rock and a fortress (18:2) – in other words, a secure place in which one may seek and find safety. Each of the psalms speaks of God's ability to redeem those who turn to him.

Psalm 19 deals with the glory of the Lord, especially as this is made known through the Law. The opening verses (19:1–6)

speak of the way in which the glory of God is revealed in the natural order, especially the heavens. This natural knowledge of God is then supplemented and refined through a knowledge of God through his law, which is declared to be 'more precious than gold . . . sweeter . . . than honey from the honeycomb' (19:10). This is an especially fine psalm to meditate upon on a starry night, or after thinking about the compassion of God as revealed in his word.

Psalms 20 and 21 are generally thought to belong together, and represent the prayer of an army on the eve of battle (20:1–9), and its song of thanksgiving on the day of victory (21:1–13). It is not clear whether the two psalms relate to the same battle, nor precisely which battle they refer to. However, given the violent nature of David's reign and the events that preceded it, the two psalms fit in neatly with what we know of the events of that period.

Psalm 22 is of considerable importance, and needs to be discussed in more detail than the remainder of the book. The importance of this psalm can be judged from the fact that Jesus Christ cites its opening words as he is dying on the cross (Mt 27:46; Mk 15:34). It is the song of a righteous sufferer, in response to the attacks of enemies who at present are gaining the upper hand. He awaits deliverance from the Lord – yet at present there is no sign of any such deliverance. While the original situation refers to one of David's many difficulties, the psalm is of special importance in casting light on the crucifixion of Christ as the righteous suffering servant of God.

The psalm clearly relates to the events of David's lifetime; it is also prophetic, pointing ahead to events that will be fulfilled only in the coming of Jesus Christ. It speaks of the righteous sufferer being scorned and despised, surrounded by those who mocked him (22:6–7) – a perfect description of the fate of Jesus Christ on the cross (Mt 27:41). Those around him taunted him, 'He trusts in the LORD . . . let the LORD rescue him' (22:8) – some of the words of the scoffing crowd who surrounded the dying Christ (Mt 27:43). The description of the sufferer's anguish (22:12–16) corresponds well to the pain experienced by Christ on the cross. The piercing of Christ's hands and feet at crucifixion are prophesied here (22:16; see Jn 20:25), as is the casting of lots for his clothes (22:18; see Mt 27:35; Lk 23:34).

Yet the psalm ends on a note of hope. All is not lost. The Lord has not forgotten nor despised his suffering servant, but will allow him to live to praise his name (22:24–26). The hope of the resurrection shines through this psalm, even in the midst of all this suffering and anguish.

Psalm 23 is one of the most familiar of all the psalms. It is a beautiful statement of the goodness, guidance and care of the Lord for those who trust and obey him. Even in life's darkest moments, believers can rest secure in his tender care.

Psalm 24 is a psalm of celebration, clearly written with the needs of some great religious occasion in mind. The most natural such occasion is David's bringing of the ark of the Lord into the city of Jerusalem (2Sa 6:12–19), an occasion of great rejoicing and praise. The psalm affirms the lordship of God over all his creation, and his continuing presence among his people.

Psalms 25–28 return to the theme of the need to trust the Lord in situations of difficulty, however hopeless the odds against the faithful might be. Each represents a statement of trust in the Lord, and a plea for deliverance from trouble. Psalm 27 is perhaps the finest of this group of psalms, with its powerful use of images of the Lord (27:1–3), and its prayer to be allowed to dwell in the house of the Lord, and contemplate his beauty (27:4). It concludes with a powerful statement of hope. We need not wait until death to see the goodness of the Lord. We can begin to see it while we remain in the land of the living (27:13). With this hope, the uncertainties of the future may be faced, and faced with confidence and trust.

Psalm 29 exults in the lordship of God over his creation. Despite the great power and vast size of the creation, God is still greater and more powerful. The psalm is a powerful statement of the sovereignty of God over the universe, giving believers reason for hope in the face of the great and often frightening forces of nature.

Psalm 30 is a psalm of dedication, which recalls the great saving acts of God, and the radical difference that God's favour makes to the lives of believers. The most likely occasion for the composition of the psalm would seem to be David's dedication of the building material for the temple at Jerusalem (1Ch 22:1–6).

Psalm 31 is an appeal to God, in his righteousness, to deliver believers from their difficult situations. This psalm refers to God as 'rock' and 'fortress', highlighting the strength and stability the Lord brings to life and faith (31:3). The appeal to the righteousness of God (31:1) is important: in the Old Testament, God's righteousness is primarily understood as his faithfulness to his promises to redeem his people.

Psalm 32 focuses on the importance of God not counting sin against individuals, in order that they may experience his saving power (32:1–2). There is a particular emphasis on the way in which God's love surrounds the faithful (32:10), suggesting the image of a protective shield.

Psalm 33 is a psalm of praise, which recalls God's greatness in creation and redemption, and declares the great benefits that result to his chosen people (33:12). The importance of the fear of the Lord is made clear: those who fear the Lord will know his protection, both in this life and in the life to come (33:19). Again, the image of a shield is used to bring out the strongly protective character of knowing God. To know God is to experience his salvation and protection at all times (33:20–22).

Psalm 34 continues the emphasis on the importance of the fear of the Lord (34:9), while also noting the benefits of faith. Once more, the Lord is depicted as protecting the faithful (34:7). Whatever the troubles that the righteous may find themselves going through, they may rest assured of the continuing presence and care of the Lord (34:19–22).

Psalms 35–41 focus on the theme of deliverance. It will be clear that this theme is of major importance throughout this collection of psalms attributed to David, reflecting the enormously difficult situations in which he found himself as he fled for his life from Saul, and subsequently had to evade assassination attempts as king. Each of the psalms, in different ways, represents an acknowledgment of human need and divine graciousness. God alone is a refuge in times of trouble. He alone is a place of safety. Yet in the midst of all these dangers and threats, David knows that his true security lies with the Lord. Nothing can take this from him.

BOOK 2
Psalms 42–72

Psalms 42–43 were originally a single psalm, which speaks of a real sense of the absence of God, linked with a confidence that a sense of his presence will one day be renewed. Its opening verse, which likens the soul seeking for God to a deer that pants for streams of water (42:1) is widely recognised as one of the most beautiful verbal pictures painted by Scripture. The basic message of this great vision of hope is that a knowledge of the presence of God will return, despite its present absence. The decision to remember the great moments of the past (42:4) is an encouragement to hope that these moments will return. God is compared to a rock (42:9) and a stronghold (43:2). The psalms end with a confident declaration that the struggling believer will praise God again, and be reassured of his presence and love (43:5).

Psalm 44 clearly envisages that Israel has been defeated in battle. It is a lament for past failure, and a statement of hope that things will change in the future. Notice how Israel's failure is attributed directly to rejection by God (44:9–16). Just as Israel's victories are due to God's favour (44:4–8), so her failures are due to God's displeasure. Throughout the psalm, there is a sense of bewilderment, comparable to that which permeates the speeches of Job in the book that bears his name. Why has this happened? If Israel had been disobedient, or had forgotten God or rebelled against him, then this calamity could be understood (44:17–22). But it remains a mystery. Israel can only lament her failure, and wonder what the future holds. The psalm ends with a prayer for future deliverance.

Psalm 45 is a festival psalm, clearly written for the occasion of a great royal wedding.

Psalm 46, in contrast, is a declaration of total confidence in God, who is able to meet all our needs. It calls on its hearers to be still, and know that the Lord is God. Believers may rest in the fortress of the Lord, finding a security there that is denied to them everywhere else. The themes of this psalm underlie Martin Luther's hymn 'A Mighty Fortress is our God'.

The theme of the praise of God, which is hinted at in Psalm 46, is picked up and developed in **Psalms 47–48**. The two psalms take delight in the knowledge of the universal reign of God as king, and his power over all nations and peoples. The psalms are saturated with a boldness and confidence that would be unthinkable were they not grounded securely in the nature and purposes of God. Related ideas are developed in **Psalms 49–50**, which note the need to trust in God, rather than in the counsel of the wicked. Psalm 49 stresses the danger of any form of assurance that is grounded in wealth or self-confidence. It points out the inexorable fate of the wealthy, and urges its hearers to avoid these snares. Psalm 50 brings out the need for Israel to acknowledge its dependence on God, particularly through keeping the covenant and offering sacrifices as a token of dependence (50:14).

According to its title, **Psalm 51** was composed by David in the aftermath of his adultery with Bathsheba (see 2Sa 11:1–12:25). It is a psalm of remorse and repentance, which calls on God to forgive a contrite sinner. The psalm brings out the devastating effects of serious sin on David's relationship with God, and his longing to be restored to fellowship with the Lord (51:10–12). The psalm affirms both David's sinfulness and the Lord's willingness to forgive those who truly turn to him in penitence and trust.

Psalms 52–55 represent a group of psalms, each of which is referred to as a *maskil*. The term is not fully understood, as noted in our introductory comments on the Psalms; it is possible that it may refer to the meditative nature of the psalms in question. Psalm 52 is a firm statement of confidence in the Lord, even in times of great difficulty. Psalm 53 focuses on the folly of wickedness, and looks forward to the day when the Lord will restore the fortunes of his people. Psalm 54 again focuses on the importance of trusting in God at moments of distress

Is there anything that God won't forgive?

Most church leaders will have experienced someone telling them they have committed the unforgivable sin. The sin might range from the apparently trivial to something serious, like David's adultery, confessed in Ps 51. But Jesus made it clear there is only one sin that cannot be forgiven – and being worried you may have committed it is a sure sign you haven't.

While reading Scripture in context is always important, it is especially true of the unforgivable sin (Mt 12:22–32; Mk 3:20–30). Yes, Jesus speaks of sin that 'will not be forgiven, either in this age or in the age to come' (Mt 12:32) and of sinners who 'will never be forgiven; they are guilty of an eternal sin' (Mk 3:29). But the context makes his meaning clear. The Pharisees had just attributed his miracles, not to God, but to the devil, and Jesus warns them of the danger of doing this. Rejecting Jesus' victory over the kingdom of darkness is to reject God's long-awaited kingdom that was now breaking in. Not to align with Jesus, therefore, is to align with Satan.

It is this wilful, stubborn, persistent rejection of the Spirit's testimony to Jesus that alone is unforgivable; for if we reject Jesus, and the Holy Spirit who points us to him, how can we hope to be forgiven and saved? All other sins – no matter how bad they are – are forgivable, as David discovered and as Jesus makes clear in this very passage: 'Truly I tell you, people can be forgiven all their sins and every slander they utter' (Mk 3:28).

One of his closest disciples, John, also reassures us, 'If we confess our sins, he is faithful and just and will forgive us our sins and purify us from all unrighteousness' (1Jn 1:9).

and anxiety. Psalm 55 develops this theme, expanding both on the seriousness of the threat from the wicked (55:9–14), and the joy of being able to cast one's cares on the Lord (55:22). The particular danger of a close friend becoming an enemy is noted – a hint of the treachery that would be experienced by Jesus Christ, who was betrayed by one of his close circle, Judas Iscariot.

Psalms 56–60 represent a *miktam* group. It is not clear precisely what this term refers to, but it may denote a type of lament. Once more, the theme of deliverance in times of trouble is evident at every point. At several points, the psalmist expresses himself with total honesty, and asks God to destroy his enemies (e.g., 59:5). Some readers find such sections distasteful. However, they are an important witness to David's willingness to be totally honest and open in his prayers to the Lord, hiding nothing from him. There is some wisdom in this insight. Too often we hold things back from God, when we ought to be more open.

Psalms 61–65 are all described as 'psalms of David', and focus once more on the ability of God to meet all needs, even in the most difficult of situations. Some of the poetic language used to describe the security that God's presence brings

should be noted – for example, the image of resting in the shadow of God's wings (63:7), or of lying awake, thinking about God in the watches of the night (63:6).

Psalm 66 gives indications of having been composed to celebrate Jerusalem's deliverance from the Assyrians due to Hezekiah's obedience to the word of the Lord delivered through the prophet Isaiah (2Ki 19:9–36). The great saving acts of God in the past, including the crossing of the Red Sea (66:5–6), are recalled, as thanks are given for the latest deliverance from the threat of an enemy (66:8–9). Notice how the dangerous experience from which Jerusalem was delivered is referred to as 'refining' (66:10). The experience is like a fire that purifies a precious metal, leaving behind a purer and more valuable resource. A similar note is struck in Psalm 67, which opens (67:1) by recalling the great blessing given to Israel in the wilderness (Nu 6:24–26).

Psalm 68 is a major psalm of praise and celebration, which recalls the great events of Sinai during the desert wanderings of Israel (68:7–10), the conquest of Canaan (68:11–18) and the establishment of Zion (or Jerusalem) as the capital of Israel under David. The psalm seems to have been written for the occasion of a great procession, to celebrate the triumphs of God. Paul picks up the theme of this psalm in speaking of the resurrection and ascension of Christ (Eph 4:8–13).

Psalm 69 again reflects a sense of despair and sorrow in the face of threats from enemies. If this psalm dates from the time of David, it is not clear precisely what threat it concerns. It is more likely that the psalm deals with a dangerous moment in the life of one of David's successors, such as Hezekiah. The psalm's frequent references to suffering at the hands of one's enemies were seen by New Testament writers as pointing ahead to the suffering and death of Jesus Christ (see, e.g., Ro 11:9–10, which takes up the themes of 69:22–23). Similar themes are found in Psalms 70–71, which represent further pleas for God's help in situations of danger and despair. Once more, an appeal is made to the righteousness of God (71:2) – that is, the covenant faithfulness and compassionate love of the Lord. Psalm 72 takes the form of a royal psalm, linked with Solomon, which represents a prayer for the wellbeing of the king and his people.

BOOK 3
Psalms 73–89

This new book of Psalms opens with a series of eleven psalms that are ascribed to, or are somehow associated with, Asaph, one of the leaders of the choirs established by David to provide music for the temple at Jerusalem (1Ch 6:39; 15:17–19; 16:4–7). Psalms 73–83 can thus be seen as a single collection, with a series of common themes providing continuity across the individual psalms. One of the most important themes to be associated with this collection is that of God's sovereign rule over his people and the nations, which is seen as the ground of Israel's hope in the face of anxiety and uncertainty.

The first psalm in the series, Psalm 73, returns to the theme of the apparent

prosperity of the wicked. The ease and wealth of the life of the wicked is depicted in a series of poetic images (73:4–12), which drives the psalmist to despair. He regains a sense of proportion only by returning to the sanctuary of God, and realising the importance of his relationship with God (73:23–28). Other psalms focus on different themes, including expressions of hope that the Lord will deliver his people from oppression by foreign powers (74, 79, 80, 83), acknowledgment that the Lord is the God and Saviour of Israel (75, 76), a recollection of the great deeds by which the Lord delivered his people in the past (77, 78), and the judgment of God on his people and the nations (81, 82).

Psalm 84 is a beautiful meditation on the loveliness of the house of the Lord, and the comfort and solace it brings to those who come there. The image of the swallow finding its nest (84:3) points to the natural resting place of God's people being with the Lord who has redeemed them, and offers them rest.

Psalm 85 may reflect the situation encountered by Ezra or Nehemiah on their return from Babylon to Jerusalem, to begin the long process of rebuilding and spiritual renewal. It represents a plea for revival and restoration, in order that the glory of the Lord may once more dwell in his own land (85:9).

Psalm 86 represents another prayer for help in a time of distress, which combines a strong sense of confidence in the Lord with a sense of urgency over the seriousness of the situation in which the psalmist finds himself.

Psalm 87 is a celebration of the special place of Zion as the 'city of God', which looks forward to the day when all nations will acknowledge its status.

Psalm 88 returns to the themes expressed in Psalm 86. It is an open admission of the terror experienced by the psalmist in the face of his enemies, and the sense of bewilderment he is experiencing. Like Job, he cannot understand what is happening to him, or why God should allow it to take place. Yet he will continue to trust in and pray to the Lord (88:13). The Lord has humbled him. Eventually, the same Lord will restore him.

A similar theme is developed in Psalm 89, which may well date from the time of the Babylonian attack against Jerusalem, which led to the exile of king Jehoiachin (2Ki 24:8–17). The psalm represents a prayer that the Lord will restore his people, in fulfilment of the covenant made with David. The psalmist cannot understand why the Lord seems to have abandoned his people in this way, and pleads for restoration.

BOOK 4
Psalms 90–106

The fourth book of Psalms includes some marvellous songs of praise to the Lord. **Psalm 90** depicts the hopeless state of sinful humanity apart from God, particularly stressing the brevity of human life. **Psalms 91–94** draw attention to the great benefits of knowing the Lord. **Psalm 95** represents a call to worship, which stresses the authority and majesty of God as Creator, and notes the consequences of disobedience and rebellion against him.

A series of psalms then follows that focus on the praise of God as the Creator of the world and the sustainer of his people. **Psalms 96–101** survey the deeds and majesty of God, and exult in his greatness and faithfulness. Psalm 101 is the briefest of these psalms, but expresses well their general content. God is the one who is to be praised and worshipped, and whose great acts are to be responded to with thanksgiving by his obedient and joyful people.

The mood changes abruptly at **Psalm 102**, which is basically the prayer of someone in considerable distress. It is not clear who wrote this psalm, nor under what conditions. But it is clear that it is written with the assurance that, even in the deepest misery and unhappiness, confidence may be placed in the steadfast love of the Lord. This note of confidence is also sounded in **Psalm 103**, which identifies the grounds of such assurance in the deeds of God in the past (103:7) and his inherent nature and character (103:2–5). The psalm rejoices in God's willingness and ability to deal with human sin, so that it need no longer disrupt the relation between God and the believer (103:8–12). The compassion of the Lord for his children is spoken of in the most moving terms: despite our frailty, God still loves and cares for us (103:13–18).

Psalms 104–106 continue this note of confidence and praise, and ground this comprehensively in God's great acts of salvation in the past. Psalm 104 focuses on the whole area of creation, surveying the greatness of the Lord as this is revealed in the works of his creation (104:5–26). Psalm 105 itemises the great acts of redemption that led Israel out of Egypt into the promised land (105:5–45). By recalling God's faithfulness to his covenant in the past, believers can be reassured of his faithfulness to them in the present. Psalm 106 undertakes a similar survey, although noting the rebelliousness of the people during the period of the desert wanderings. This faithlessness on the part of God's people is seen as a warning for the present. God's faithfulness to his covenant must not be abused or taken for granted. There is a need for Israel to keep its side of the covenant.

BOOK 5
Psalms 107–150

The final book of Psalms includes some of the finest psalms of praise in this collection. The themes of God's greatness in creation and redemption, especially as shown in his great acts of deliverance, are referred to frequently. Psalm 107 illustrates this superbly, with its brilliant comprehensive recitation of the great divine acts of deliverance in Israel's history. Who can fail to appreciate the greatness of the love of the Lord by considering these great deeds? Psalm 108 also focuses on the theme of the love of God, and draws on material from Psalms 57:7–11 and 60:5–12 in doing so.

Psalms 109–110 deal with the trustworthiness of God in the face of difficulties and threats. Psalm 109 envisages a case of false accusation, and calls on the Lord to deliver the writer from this situation. Psalm 110 is of considerable importance to the writers of the New Testament. It focuses on a

messianic king or priest, who will be crowned by the Lord. For New Testament writers, this great prophecy is fulfilled in the coming of Jesus Christ as the king of Israel and its true high priest (Heb 6:16–20; 7:20–22). The significance of Melchizedek (first mentioned at Ge 14:18) is the subject of extensive reflection in the letter to the Hebrews, which sees this priest as holding the key to a right understanding of the role of Jesus Christ as high priest. This psalm is also referred to by Jesus Christ himself (Mt 22:44–45).

Psalms 111–118 form a small collection of psalms within this book, often referred to as the 'Hallelujah Psalms' on account of their frequent use of the Hebrew term *hallelu yah*, which literally means 'praise the LORD'. The theme of the goodness of the Lord is constantly stated and explored, especially with reference to his great deeds in the past (surveyed in general terms, e.g., at 111:2–9) and the continued experience of his blessings in the present (see 112:2–8; 113:7–9; 115:9–15). Psalm 117, the shortest of all the psalms, provides a brilliantly neat summary of the leading themes of this group of psalms.

This collection is immediately followed by the longest of the psalms. **Psalm 119** has a complex structure of 176 verses, arranged into 22 groups of 8 verses. There are 22 letters in the Hebrew alphabet, and each of the groups is allocated one letter from this alphabet. Thus 119:1–8 is allocated to aleph, the first letter of the Hebrew alphabet, and 119:25–32 to daleth, the fourth such letter. The basic theme of this great psalm is the wonder and greatness of the word of God. The word of God is seen as something that both demands and offers. It demands obedience, and it offers promises of salvation and wellbeing. This psalm is worth reading at a single session, with a view to appreciating the full richness of the law of God, and all it can mean to believers. To mention just two of the poetic images used to emphasise the importance and pleasure of the law of God: it is like a lamp to guide our feet (119:105), and it is something that tastes sweeter than honey (119:103).

This followed by a collection of 15 psalms known as the 'songs of ascents'. **Psalms 120–134** are generally thought to have been used in connection with the great yearly pilgrimages to Jerusalem, culminating in entry into the Lord's temple. The collection seems to have been arranged in such a way that the opening psalms deal with threats and difficulties of various kinds, such as those one might encounter on a long journey when far from the comforts and safety of home. The collection concludes with entry into the sanctuary itself (134:2), as the purpose of the journey has been triumphantly achieved. The most famous psalm in this collection focuses on the difficulties of the long journey to Jerusalem, and the comfort that the Lord brings to those undertaking such a journey. Psalm 121 represents a powerful promise of God's presence and protection during the journey to Jerusalem. As the pilgrims contemplate the hills they must ascend before they can reach their goal, they can draw comfort from the continual care of the Lord.

Psalms 135–136 focus once more on the Lord's great acts of redemption in the past. The deliverance of Israel from

slavery in Egypt is of particular importance in each case (135:8–12; 136:10–22). However, God's work in and sovereignty over his creation (135:6–7; 136:4–9) and the calling of his people (135:4) are also singled out as important in this respect. Meditation on the works of God in the past gives hope for the present, and calls to mind the great love of God for his people, which endures for ever.

Psalm 137 is a psalm that focuses on the painful exile of Jerusalem in Babylon. The psalm evokes the poignancy of those who are cut off from their homeland, and long for restoration. It ends with a curse that many find offensive. Nevertheless, it is an important testimony to the total honesty of the psalmist, who is prepared to bring his true feelings before the Lord, rather than conceal them in platitudes. Honesty before God concerning one's feelings is one of the hallmarks of the psalter. It is something that should be treasured. In contrast, Psalm 138 returns to the theme of the troubles of the righteous, focusing on God's faithfulness to his revealed purpose.

Psalm 139 is a powerful declaration of the ability of the Lord to see everything within the human heart. Nothing is hidden from the Lord. Nothing and nobody can escape from his presence. The psalmist invites the Lord to search him and expose anything within him that is false. There are clear parallels between the ideas of this psalm and some of Job's speeches, in which he asks God to point out his failings and sins to him. **Psalms 140–144** are psalms of distress, which call to the Lord for deliverance from danger of various kinds. The theme of the constancy of God's love and faithfulness recurs throughout these psalms.

The final set of psalms focuses on the theme of praise. **Psalms 145–150** express praise and thanksgiving to God for all that he is, and all that he has done for his people. Psalms 145–147 recite all the blessings that knowing the Lord brings to his people. It is clear that identifying God's blessings is seen as one of the most effective causes of praise, as each of these psalms ends with outbursts of praise and adoration. Psalm 148 takes a different form, simply inviting all of creation to join in the praise of its great and wonderful Creator. Psalm 149 has an element of 'praise the Lord and pass the ammunition' about it. It acknowledges that the praise of God is always set in the real world, which threatens to destroy the people of God unless they defend both themselves and their God. Finally, the psalter is brought to a glorious end with Psalm 150, one of the finest songs of praise in the psalter, which summons every musical instrument to sound the praise of the great God of Israel, who has done such wonderful things for his people.

PROVERBS

The Old Testament includes a number of different types of writings, including works of history (such as 1 and 2 Samuel), prophecy (such as Isaiah) and wisdom. The book of Proverbs belongs to this final category of writings, which also includes Job and Ecclesiastes. Wisdom was a much-valued resource in the ancient world, and Solomon was fabled for his God-given wisdom. Wisdom should not be confused with prophecy. The purpose of the 'proverbs' is to cast light on the practical side of life, and to pass down to later generations the accumulated wisdom of earlier generations. This wisdom is often based on shrewd observation of everyday life.

The main body of Proverbs (10:1–22:16) consists of a collection of short proverbial sayings, attributed to Solomon. The Hebrew word here translated as 'proverbs' has a much broader range of meaning than the corresponding English word, and can also have the meaning of 'parable' or 'oracle' (both of which suggest God's involvement in the gathering of human wisdom). According to biblical tradition, Solomon was a man of outstanding wisdom. He is credited with having 'spoken' some three thousand proverbs (1Ki 4:32); the sayings collected together in the main body of the work would amount to less than one seventh of these. This suggests that the bulk of Proverbs was written in the 10th century BC, at a time of relative peace and stability suitable for the production of literary works. However, there are indications that not all the material collected in Proverbs may be due directly to Solomon. For example, there is reference to the sayings of two unknown writers, 'Agur son of Jakeh' and 'King Lemuel'. Although the work gives every indication of having been written in the 10th century BC, there are indications in the text itself that it may have received its final form at some point during the reign of Hezekiah (c.715–686 BC).

The proverbs are not intended to be treated as laws that must be adhered to strictly. They are intended to provide practical guidance as to how someone might act in a particular situation. The complexities of human relationships are such that true discernment and wisdom are required to deal with them. Most of the proverbs consist of only two lines, although slightly longer sayings are also encountered occasionally. Frequent use is made of comparisons, often centring on pictures drawn from everyday life. Their basic theme could be summarised as follows: act wisely, and you will prosper; act foolishly, and you will fail.

OUTLINE

PROVERBS 1:1–9:18
The Importance of Wisdom

1:1–7 Prologue The work opens by
declaring the importance of wisdom for
life. It then makes it clear that wisdom
is not some purely secular wisdom, but
is grounded in the fear of the Lord (1:7).
The 'fear' in question should not be
understood as a terror inspired by the
thought of divine vengeance. It is best
understood as a respectful submission
to the word and will of God, in the full
knowledge of his great power.

*1:8–4:27 Exhortations to Embrace
Wisdom* Not everyone is prepared to
accept wisdom. Folly and sin are depicted
as things that are enticing and attractive,
yet that merely lure people to their doom
(1:8–19). In a powerful passage, the dangers of folly are compared with the
benefits of wisdom (1:20–2:18). The final
section of this passage is especially important (2:13–18): wisdom is something for
which it is worth giving up everything.
There are interesting parallels with Jesus
Christ comparing the gospel to the pearl
'of great value' (Mt 13:45–46) – something that satisfies as nothing else can.

By pursuing wisdom and keeping clear
of the dangers of the temptations of the

world, a young person may rest assured
of future happiness and contentment
(2:19–3:18). Wisdom is like a 'tree of life'
(3:18), which will nourish and refresh
those who find and hold fast to her.

The theme of wisdom is now developed
in a new direction. Wisdom is declared to
have been at God's side during the great
work of creation (3:19–20). This theme
will be developed later. The passage now
returns to explore the further benefits of
wisdom (3:21–35). The person who has
wisdom will 'inherit honour' and have
security in the Lord. Parents are understood to have a particularly important role
to play in the process of imparting wisdom
to their children (4:1–27). This is not to
be seen as a paternalist 'the older know
best'. Rather, it is a declaration that parents have a responsibility to ensure that
their children benefit from their accumulated wisdom and experience.

*5:1–7:27 Warnings Against Adultery and
Folly* An extended section now deals with
examples of stupidity. Adultery is condemned, because of its negative effects on
people (5:1–23). The argument here is not
really moral or theological in character. The
tone adopted is practical and pragmatic:
adultery will just make you miserable. After
a series of warnings (6:1–19) against other

Why does the Bible speak of discipline so positively?

Few of us like discipline, especially when we are on the receiving end. But the Bible speaks positively of discipline – loving, corrective training – particularly in Proverbs where it is a recurring theme (e.g., 3:11–12; 5:11–12; 10:17; 12:1; 13:18, 24; 19:18–20; 29:17). Elsewhere in the Bible its benefits are highlighted in story form. For example, Moses reminded the Israelites of the blessings and hardships of the wilderness, seeing the hardships as God's loving discipline (Dt 8:5), and David recognised God's discipline of him in the death of the child of his adulterous relationship (2 Sa 12).

The Bible does not see discipline as something harsh, however, but as an expression of true love, the action of a Father who loves his children too much to let them get away with things. That's why the writer of Proverbs could say:

> My son, do not despise the LORD's discipline,
> and do not resent his rebuke,
> because the LORD disciplines those he loves,
> as a father the son he delights in.
>
> (Pr 3:11–12)

A theme echoed by the writer of Hebrews (Heb 12:1–13). Parents are told to reflect this same loving discipline in the way they raise their children (e.g., Pr 13:24; 22:6; Eph 6:4), for it will produce the fruit they want to see:

> Discipline your children,
> and they will give you peace;
> they will bring you the delights you desire.
>
> (Pr 29:17)

Ignoring discipline is folly not only for ourselves, but also causes us to lead others astray (Pr 10:17).

Discipline is always for our good. Jesus described it as pruning a vine to make it even more fruitful (Jn 15:1–8), and Paul saw life's hardships as discipline intended to make us 'not rely on ourselves but on God, who raises the dead' (2Co 1:9).

kinds of stupidity (such as the negative effects of laziness or telling lies), the text returns to its main theme (6:20–7:27).

8:1–9:18 Wisdom's Call The nature of wisdom herself now comes to the fore. Wisdom is spoken of in personal terms (8:1–36), a process described as 'personification' or 'hypostatisation'. Wisdom is portrayed as a woman who seeks to attract people to her, in order that they may benefit from her counsel. Wisdom is the basis of true human government, and underlies all just laws. The role of wisdom in the creation of the world is then described (8:22–31).

KEY THEMES IN PROVERBS
Speech
What we say reveals what we're really like. Many proverbs are about controlling our speech: a wise person will be known by their words.

> Those who guard their mouths and their tongues keep themselves from calamity.
> (Pr 21:23)

> Gracious words are a honeycomb, sweet to the soul and healing to the bones.
> (Pr 16:24)

See also Pr 12:18; 25:11.

Quarrels
Relationships feature a good deal in Proverbs. A wise person knows how to behave appropriately with different kinds of people: parents, children, people in authority, neighbours. Loyalty and self-control are the key qualities. Quarrels are to be avoided.

> Starting a quarrel is like breaching a dam; so drop the matter before a dispute breaks out.
> (Pr 17:14)

See also Pr 20:3; 26:17.

Friends
Loyalty features in many proverbs. We need to appreciate a good friend.

> A friend loves at all times, and a brother is born for a time of adversity.
> (Pr 17:17)

> One who has unreliable friends soon comes to ruin, but there is a friend who sticks closer than a brother.
> (Pr 18:24)

See also Pr 27:6.

Laziness
People are accountable for how they use their time and skills. Proverbs has some humorous things to say about laziness – but is candid about its dangers.

> Go to the ant, you sluggard; consider its ways and be wise!
> (Pr 6:6)

See also Pr 6:10–11; 26:14.

Women
Proverbs has a lot to say about women: both good women and bad. The adulterous woman is warned against and condemned. On the other hand, the ideal woman is a skilled, confident, entrepreneurial businesswoman and mother. She is attractive because of her compassion, character and skill . . . but, above all, because of her respect for God.

He who finds a wife finds what is good and receives favour from the LORD.
(Pr 18:22)

A wife of noble character who can find? She is worth far more than rubies.
(Pr 31:10)

See also Pr 6:20–25; 7:1–27; 19:14; 31:14, 17, 20, 25–26, 30.

Money

Proverbs is realistic about money – for example, the rich have many friends. It also advises generous giving but notes that it is better to be poor and to respect God than to be rich and to have trouble.

The poor are shunned, even by their neighbours, but the rich have many friends.
(Pr 14:20)

Better a little with the fear of the LORD than great wealth with turmoil.
(Pr 15:16)

See also Pr 10:15; 19:17; 22:7, 9; 23:4; 28:6.

Wisdom and folly

Proverbs has sharp warnings against fools – those who ignore God's will.

The fear of the LORD is the beginning of wisdom.
(Pr 9:10)

Fools give full vent to their rage, but the wise bring calm in the end.
(Pr 29:11)

See also Pr 1:32; 18:6–7; 26:11.

Wisdom is once more personified, and depicted as God's assistant and skilled master worker in the process of creation. Wisdom came into being before anything else. Anyone who has wisdom has access to the secrets of the creation, and will be able to find favour in the sight of the Lord (8:32–36).

The personal aspects of wisdom are further emphasised in the following section (9:1–18), which compares wisdom and folly to two women. Wisdom calls to all who hear her voice, and invites them to enter her house and feast at her table (9:1–6). Whoever accepts that invitation will find life. In contrast, folly seeks merely to lure fools to their death (9:13–18).

PROVERBS 10:1–22:16
The Proverbs of Solomon

The collection of Solomonic proverbs that follows cannot easily be summarised, and is best read through to gain an understanding of the kind of wisdom being commended. The proverbs generally

take the form of single statements, one verse in length, in two parts. For example, 'Better a little with righteousness than much gain with injustice' (16:8). The two parts of the proverb often express a contrast, with the word 'but' joining the two parts to make this contrast clear.

The proverbs are often written in the form of commands, for example:

Stay away from a fool,
for you will not find knowledge on
their lips.
(14:7)

These proverbs, it must be stressed, are not to be placed on the same level as the Old Testament law! The force of the proverb cannot be compared with the absolute prohibition of, for example, the worship of idols or murder. The general status of such proverbs is best understood along the lines of 'anyone who is wise will stay away from a fool'. The proverbs are about human advice, not commands from the Lord. Hence, to give one especially interesting example, the authority of God cannot be sought for the physical punishment of children (13:24).

PROVERBS 22:17–31:31
Further Collections of Proverbs

22:17–24:34 *Sayings of the Wise* The remainder of the book of Proverbs is taken up with shorter collections of proverbs, not all of which are attributed to Solomon himself. The 'Sayings of the Wise' and its appendix (24:23–34) are snippets of worldly wisdom, generally longer in form than the shorter and pithier sayings of Solomon himself. While some of the proverbs represent worldly wisdom (e.g., 23:6–8), at other points spiritual insights are clearly involved (e.g., 22:22–23). The reference to 'thirty sayings' (22:20) could be understood to refer to the remainder of this section (22:22–24:22), which breaks down into 30 sections, most of which are two verses long.

25:1–29:27 *More Proverbs of Solomon* This further collection of proverbs, attributed to Solomon himself, consists of pithy sayings of wisdom, generally one verse in length. Many of these proverbs focus on issues of government and management.

30:1–31:31 *Sayings of Agur and Lemuel; Epilogue* The short collection of 'Sayings of Agur' and 'Sayings of King Lemuel' is drawn from collections of material attributed to these writers, about whom nothing is known for certain. The book ends with a poem that extols the virtue of 'a wife of noble character' (31:10–31), which consists of 22 verses, each of which begins with a successive letter of the Hebrew alphabet.

ECCLESIASTES

The book of Ecclesiastes is perhaps the most pessimistic in the Old Testament. Like Proverbs and Job, it belongs to the category of wisdom literature. The book takes the form of a collection of proverbs and observations, some long and some very brief. Many readers find the book puzzling, as it seems to be dominated by views that do not fit easily into the general pattern of biblical outlooks. The book is best understood as a powerful and convincing commentary on the meaninglessness of life without God, and the utter despair and cynicism that will inevitably result from lacking a biblical faith. It represents a graphic portrayal of the misery and futility of human life without God, and the inability of human wisdom to discover God in all his fullness.

The author of this work introduces himself as 'the teacher' (*Ekklesiastes* in the Greek translation of the Old Testament), and is traditionally identified as Solomon on account of the reference to 'son of David, king of Jerusalem' (1:1). This designation could, however, be used of any descendant of David. The book itself occasionally indicates that it was written by a subject rather than a ruler, and the style of Hebrew used suggests that the book dates from later than the time of Solomon. There is no general consensus on any particular date, and it is probable that we shall never know with certainty when the book was written.

1:2–3:22 *Everything Is Meaningless* The book opens with a dramatic declaration of the meaninglessness of life (1:2). This is illustrated by an analysis of all kinds of happenings (1:3–11). What is the point of it all? Death brings life to an end, and extinguishes the memory of those who once lived. So why go on? To the Christian reader, these deeply gloomy and bleak words are transcended by the hope of the resurrection to eternal life in Jesus Christ. Ecclesiastes provides an agonised picture that allows us to understand how utterly hopeless is life without God or without hope in eternal life. It is a powerful reminder of the importance of the Christian hope.

However, the work continues its gloomy analysis. It is not merely the events of life that seem devoid of any meaning. Human wisdom is a waste of time. What use is it? If anything, it just creates more misery (1:12–18). The same goes for pleasure (2:1–16). The writer's experiments with the seeking of pleasure were disastrous. Everything proved to be little more than a meaningless 'chasing after the wind' (2:11). In fact, just about every human achievement is pointless. What is the point in becoming wise, when wisdom cannot save anyone from death (2:12–16)? And what is the point in labouring over something, when everything is a waste of time (2:17–26)? It is all utterly and totally useless (3:1–22). Humans are just like animals: they live and die, and that is the end of the

matter. Once more, the Christian reader of these words will turn with joy to the hope of the resurrection, and the sense of purpose and peace this brings.

4:1–9:12 *A Common Destiny for All* Having painted this bleak picture, the writer now fills it out with further details and examples of the futility he has in mind. The oppression of the world (4:1–12), the pursuit of promotion (4:13–16), the accumulation of riches (5:8–12), and the pursuit of wisdom are all a waste of time (7:1–8:1). Even wisdom has its limits. While acknowledging that wisdom is worth possessing, the writer raises a serious doubt. Can anyone really possess wisdom in the first place? Wisdom seems very far away, and very elusive (7:23–25). People might as well eat, drink and be happy (8:1–17); there is nothing else to look or hope for. Everyone, whether wise or foolish, sinner or saint, will meet the same miserable end: death (9:1–12).

9:13–12:8 *Remember Your Creator While Young* The writer then returns to his musings on the nature of wisdom (9:13–10:20). While wisdom may well be an excellent thing, why is it that fools seem to end up in all the best positions? In the end, all these things are beyond human understanding (10:1–6). The work ends with a sustained reflection on the futility of life. Youth passes very quickly, leaving nothing but memories in the midst of present futility (11:7–12:8).

12:9–14 *The Conclusion of the Matter*
The work closes with some final reflections on the hopelessness of things (12:9–14). The 'teacher' himself was wise – but his wisdom led him only to despair and a deep sense of meaninglessness. In the end, the only source of real wisdom is the fear of the Lord. The duty of all people is to 'fear God and keep his commandments' (12:13). If there is any hope or meaning, it lies in God alone.

The Christian, reading this work from the standpoint of God's wonderful act of deliverance and hope through Jesus Christ, can end the study of this bleak and gloomy work by echoing some words of Peter: 'Praise be to the God and Father of our Lord Jesus Christ! In his great mercy he has given us new birth into a living hope through the resurrection of Jesus Christ from the dead' (1Pe 1:3). If only the writer of this book had lived to see that glorious day!

SONG OF SONGS

This brief work, sometimes referred to as the 'Song of Solomon', is generally regarded as an outstanding love poem. The title literally means 'the greatest of songs'. The work is traditionally understood to have been written by Solomon, although there is insufficient evidence within the text of the work itself to confirm this with certainty. The book is loosely structured around five meetings between the lover and the beloved, with reflection on the periods during which they are obliged to be apart.

Many Christian writers have seen this work as an allegory of the love between Christ and his church. Others have seen it as a figure (that is, a sign or symbol) of the relation between Christ and individual believers. In other words, the work was not interpreted as a celebration of human love, but as a poetic or figurative way of speaking of the spiritual love of Christ for the church or for individual believers. More recently, however, there has been an increased willingness on the part of most Christian interpreters of this book to see it simply as a superb account of human love – a love that echoes the love of God for his people, but that focuses on the deep feelings of love between a man and a woman.

The song is divided into a number of sections, of which the most well marked are the five meetings of the lover and beloved (1:2–2:7; 2:8–3:5; 3:6–5:1; 5:2–6:3; and 6:4–8:4). The most helpful way to read this work is to take each of the five meetings at a time, and try to appreciate the anticipation of meeting and joy of fulfilment. There is an unquestionable parallel between the joy of the meeting of lovers and the believer coming home to God, and there is no reason why the book should not be read as an allegory of the love of God for his people.

OUTLINE

1:1 Title

1:2–2:7 The first meeting of the lover and beloved

2:8–3:5 The second meeting of the lover and beloved

3:6–5:1 The third meeting of the lover and beloved

5:2–6:3 The fourth meeting of the lover and beloved

6:4–8:4 The fifth meeting of the lover and beloved

8:5–14 Conclusion

1:2–2 The First Meeting We are introduced to the young woman, who is anticipating her first meeting with her beloved. She is anxious. Will he like her? Or will he notice that she has been working in the sun too long, which has darkened her skin? One of the major themes in this opening section is the human need for love. Without love, life is bleak and meaningless. Love is 'more delightful than wine' (1:2). The young woman will be enfolded by love, which strengthens

and supports her. The identity of her beloved is not made clear. There are clues throughout the passage that he is noble and of high social status, fitting in with the traditional understanding that he is Solomon himself.

2:8–3:5 The Second Meeting   The relationship is now developing. Yet the young woman is troubled by anxiety and doubt. The beloved finds her, and asks her to come away with him into the countryside. Although there are hints that he is noble, her beloved behaves as one who loves her, rather than one who rules over her. She is anxious that she was too reserved, leading her to dream that she loses him, and has to set out on a journey to find him and rekindle his love.

3:6–5:1 The Third Meeting The anxiety of the last meeting is past. The young woman is now reassured of her beloved's commitment, which is shown in the fact that a grand carriage made of precious wood from the Lebanon is sent to collect her, and bring her to Jerusalem. She will be accompanied by a guard of honour. The passage allows us to see how the young woman's status has changed completely. As she prepares to marry her beloved, her own status rises. She will share in his status and wealth. This imagery is repeated in the New Testament, which uses similar language to describe the believer's sharing in the attributes of Christ (2Co 5:21).

5:2–6:3 The Fourth Meeting The mood now changes. The lovers are married, and the woman finds herself cooling towards her beloved when he comes in from the fields. Instantly, she regrets her coldness towards him. But he has gone. Once more, she finds herself dreaming of searching the city for her beloved. Wondering if she has lost him, she begins to recall his beauty and strength and reaffirms her love for him.

6:4–8:4 The Fifth Meeting In the fifth and final encounter, the young woman reflects on her relationship with her beloved. Disillusioned by wealth and splendour, she wants to return to the place of their first love – to the countryside, the villages and the vineyard. Their relationship is renewed.

8:5–14 Conclusion The couple now return to Jerusalem, wiser and closer. The overall story is that of the importance of love to give meaning to life, and how it needs to be tended. Even the most loving relationship needs care and renewal. If something really matters, it needs constant attention. It is not surprising that so many Christian writers saw the Song of Songs as casting light on the need for believers to sustain their relationship with Christ, and not take it for granted.

ISAIAH

The book of the prophet Isaiah is the first of the four 'Major Prophets' (the other three books being Jeremiah, Ezekiel and Daniel). Isaiah lived and worked in Jerusalem in the latter part of the 8th century BC. His call to prophesy came in 740 BC, the year of king Uzziah's death (6:1), and he is known to have prophesied up to at least 701 BC, when the northern kingdom of Israel fell to Assyria. At this stage, Judah and Israel were both moving out of a longer period of peace and prosperity into one of uncertainty and danger. Assyria is becoming aggressive in the region, and Israel, Judah and Syria are uncertain as to how to react to this threat. It is against this context of political and military uncertainty that Isaiah's ministry is set. The reader will find it helpful to read the story of Jerusalem during this period, as set out in 2 Kings. This will provide important background material to the earlier parts of this major prophecy.

However, the prophecy is not restricted to this period in the history of Jerusalem. The later parts of the book concern prophecies of hope and restoration for the Babylonian exiles. The early parts of the prophecy cover the period between the fall of the northern kingdom of Israel in 722, and the extreme danger to Judah from Assyria in 701 BC. An important section of the work (chapters 36–39) deals with Judah's survival of this threat. A major later section (chapters 40–55) goes on to prophesy Judah's later enslavement to Babylon and her eventual deliverance from exile in that land. The final perspective of the book looks beyond events in Judah's immediate future to a glorified Jerusalem, set amid 'new heavens and a new earth'.

14:24–32 Judgment against Assyria and Philistia

15:1–16:14 Judgment against Moab

17:1–14 Judgment against Syria and Israel

18:1–20:6 Judgment against Ethiopia and Egypt

21:1–17 Judgment against Babylon, Edom and Arabia

22:1–25 Judgment against Judah and some of her officials

23:1–18 Judgment against Tyre

The Lord's final victory over all evil

24:1–23 Judgment against all evil in heaven and earth

25:1–12 The banquet on the mountain of the Lord

26:1–21 The hope of resurrection

27:1–13 The exiles of Israel will be gathered together

Oracles of judgment against Jerusalem and others

28:1–29:24 The Lord will punish unbelief among his people

30:1–33 Condemnation of Israel

31:1–9 Israel is to trust in the Lord, not in Egypt

32:1–33:24 The promise of a king reigning with peace and righteousness in Jerusalem

34:1–17 Judgment against Edom

35:1–10 Salvation for those restored to Jerusalem

Jerusalem and the siege of Sennacherib, 701 BC

36:1–37:13 The Assyrians lay siege to Jerusalem

37:14–20 Hezekiah prays for deliverance from the siege

37:21–35 Isaiah prophesies deliverance of the city

37:36–38 The death of Sennacherib; lifting of the siege

38:1–22 Hezekiah's illness and recovery

39:1–8 Isaiah warns of future exile in Babylon

The release of the Babylonian exiles and their restoration to Jerusalem

40:1–31 The exiles' punishment has ended

41:1–29 The Lord will bring an enemy to defeat Babylon

42:1–25 The servant of the Lord will bring salvation

43:1–44:8 The exiles will join in a new exodus and new creation

44:9–20 The futility of the worship of idols

44:21–45:25 God's means of restoring the exiles will be Cyrus, king of Persia

46:1–48:22 Babylon and her gods will be brought low and the exiles released

49:1–26 The servant of the Lord will bring salvation to the nations

50:1–11 The faithfulness of the servant

51:1–23 The Lord calls the exiles out of Babylon

52:1–12 There will be rejoicing at this deliverance

52:13–53:12 The innocent servant will be afflicted and suffer for the sins of others

54:1–17 The blessings of the redeemed people

55:1–13 The call to accept the salvation offered

The vision of the restored community

56:1–12 The call to keep the Sabbath

57:1–21 The salvation of the righteous

58:1–14 The importance of fasting

59:1–21 Injustice will bring God's judgment

60:1–22 The glorious return of the exiles

ISAIAH 1:1–12:6
Prophecies of Hope and Judgment

The work opens by declaring that what follows represents the prophecies of Isaiah concerning both Judah and Jerusalem, during the reigns of several kings which span the period 792–686 BC. Note that Isaiah's ministry is only to the southern kingdom of Judah, and its capital city Jerusalem. No mention is made of the northern kingdom of Israel (1:1). At this stage, we have no idea about who Isaiah was, or how he came to be called as a prophet. Those details will be provided later. It is clear that Isaiah sees his role as that of declaring the word and will of the Lord to a people who were generally inclined to disobey him.

1:2–31 A Rebellious Nation This is made clear from the first major prophetic oracle recorded in this book (1:2–31), which stresses that the Lord's own people have rebelled against him. Israel – a term used throughout this prophecy to refer to the people of God, rather than to the northern kingdom of the same name – has forsaken the Lord (1:4). Even dumb animals show more sense than the people of God. Israel may offer all the right sacrifices, and do all the right things at the temple. But the heart of the people is far from the Lord (1:10–17). Outward observance of the religious cult is not accompanied by a love for the Lord and

obedience to him. Note carefully the refrain 'Hear the word of the LORD' (1:10), a characteristic prophetic turn of phrase, indicating that the prophet is speaking under inspiration on behalf of the Lord, and not for his own sake. Yet this opening oracle of judgment ends on a note of hope. God will refine his people (1:25–26), removing all their impurities as a furnace refines a precious metal, and restore his people to their former glory.

2:1–5 The Mountain of the Lord The second major oracle reaffirms the rebelliousness and disobedience of the people of God. This oracle opens with a remarkable vision (the essentials of which are also found at Mic 4:1–3) concerning the 'mountain of the LORD' (2:1–4). This refers to Mount Zion, which will become a focus of worship, peace and prosperity when the Lord's saving work has been accomplished. This passage includes a reference to beating swords into ploughshares (2:4), as it graphically portrays the reign of peace the Lord will usher in.

2:6–4:1 The Day of the Lord But that is in the future. In the present, the 'descendants of Jacob' (a reference to the people of God) have rebelled against the Lord in all kinds of ways. Particular criticism is directed against the increasing influence of paganism in Jerusalem (2:6–8), which the Lord is not prepared to

tolerate. The prophet then speaks of a coming 'day of the LORD' in which all these practices will be swept away, as the Lord comes in majesty and power to purify his people (2:12–22). This judgment is depicted graphically (3:1–4:1), as the future fall of a proud and haughty Jerusalem is predicted. By failing to obey the Lord, both Judah and Jerusalem have condemned themselves.

4:2–6 The Branch of the Lord The judgment will be stated more specifically presently, but a brief passage promising redemption now breaks in. The thoroughgoing message of judgment now being delivered is tempered with the future hope of salvation for those who remain faithful to the Lord.

5:1–30 The Song of the Vineyard A major passage of judgment now opens, focusing on the image of a vineyard (5:1–7). Israel is compared to a vineyard, established, planted and protected at great trouble by its owner. Not unreasonably, he expected the vineyard to produce some good grapes; in the end, all that he got for his trouble was bad fruit. The story is a parable of Israel, which God called into being, loved and tended. He expected Israel to be righteous and obedient, but found only bloodshed and distress. Things have gone very seriously wrong. This verdict is then amplified (5:8–30), as the crimes and injustices that give rise to the Lord's anger with his people are documented. For their lack of obedience and understanding, the people of God must face exile (5:13).

6:1–13 Isaiah's Commission At this point, we finally discover more about Isaiah himself. The year of king Uzziah's death

was 740 BC. In that year, Isaiah had a vision of the Lord in all his holiness and majesty. It is possible that the prophet had this vision in the temple itself. The vision centres on the holiness of the Lord. It terrifies Isaiah: As a sinner, how can he live after seeing God? In an act of purification, he is touched by a burning coal by one of the seraphim (a term used only in this passage; its full meaning is not clear). His guilt has now been removed, and he is free to speak of the Lord to his people. He is then called and commissioned to bring the word of the Lord to the people, in the full knowledge that they will be hardened by what they hear and refuse to respond to it.

It is not clear why this account of Isaiah's call as a prophet occurs so late in this work. It might have seemed more natural to place it at the beginning. However, its present location within the book heightens the importance of the preceding material, and prepares the reader for more oracles yet to come.

7:1–25 The Sign of Immanuel A new historical section now opens, set at the time of the Syro-Ephraimite war of 735 BC. In the face of growing Assyrian expansion, Aram and the northern kingdom of Israel (often referred to as 'Ephraim') try to persuade Judah to join an anti-Assyrian coalition. Ahaz, who is then king of Judah, is tempted to side with the Assyrians. As a result, Jerusalem finds itself under attack from the north.

Isaiah urges Ahaz to stand firm, in the knowledge that the Lord will deliver him from this threat (7:1–12). As a sign, Isaiah speaks of a virgin giving birth to a son who will be called Immanuel. In this specific historical context, Isaiah

What was the role of the prophet?

Behind the Bible's understanding of prophecy is the conviction that, unlike pagan gods, Yahweh is a God who speaks, and it was through his prophets that he spoke.

In Old Testament times, prophets had two main roles – forth-telling (declaring God's truth) and fore-telling (declaring God's plans). Their message focused around three key points: first, God, who alone was Creator, Redeemer and Lord and to whom they called Israel to return; secondly, the nation, whom they challenged to be holy and live as a light to the Gentiles; thirdly, the land, held in trust for God and from which all political, economic and social abuses must therefore be removed – messages that frequently caused them to be rejected.

Unlike ecstatic pagan prophets, Israel's prophets remained in full control of their words and behaviour. In fact, God used their different backgrounds, personalities and styles to bring his message. Peter explained it like this: 'Prophecy never had its origin in the human will, but prophets, though human, spoke from God as they were carried along by the Holy Spirit' (2Pe 1:21). The term 'carried along' was used of a ship's sail catching the wind. Peter meant that the prophets 'hoisted their sail of faith' to catch the wind of God's Spirit and were led to say exactly what God wanted them to say – though even then their words needed testing (Dt 18:14–22; 1Co 14:29).

In New Testament times, prophecy underwent a significant change. As God's Spirit was now given to all believers, prophecy, dreams and visions were now open to all of them to receive (Ac 2:17, quoting Joel 2:28). With the gift broadened – so much so that Paul could say, 'You can *all* prophesy' (1Co 14:31) – its purpose also broadened, now focusing on 'strengthening, encouraging and comfort' (1Co 14:3).

probably meant primarily that within nine months, the threat posed to Jerusalem would be ended. It is possible that the events of 8:3 are related to this. However, the great prophetic implications of the passage cannot be ignored. It clearly points ahead to the birth of another child called Immanuel (Mt 1:23), who would deliver his people from sin.

8:1–9:7 To Us a Child is Born After a discussion of the role of Assyria in the purposes of the Lord (8:1–22), Isaiah returns to the coming salvation promised by the Lord. He focuses attention on the region of Galilee. It is there that 'the people walking in darkness have seen a great light'. Here Isaiah uses a literary device sometimes referred to as 'the prophetic perfect', by which an event that has yet to happen is spoken of as if it has already come to pass. A child will be born, who will be the Prince of Peace. The passage speaks of hope in the coming of a deliverer at a dark moment in the life of the people of God (9:1–7). For New Testament writers, this great prophecy finds its fulfilment in the coming of Jesus Christ (see Lk 2:14) and his ministry in the region of Galilee.

9:8–10:34 The Lord's Anger Against Israel; the Remnant of Israel Yet this message of hope is again set in the context of judgment and condemnation for Israel's sins (9:8–10:4). Although Isaiah is clear that God will judge Assyria (10:5–19), it is clear that he proposes to use Assyria as his 'rod of anger' by which the people of God will be punished for their disobedience and rebellion. In its turn, Assyria will rebel against God, and refuse to recognise that he has the right to use it as his instrument (10:15–19). Only a faithful remnant of Israel will remain, who will trust in the Lord (10:20–34).

11:1–12:6 The Branch from Jesse; Songs of Praise From this remnant a redeemer will emerge, and usher in a new period of hope in the history of the people of God (11:1–10). This strongly messianic prophecy finds its ultimate fulfilment in the coming of Jesus Christ, who is filled with the Spirit of God. When this redeemer finally arrives, the people of God will be exultant (12:1–6), just as Simeon was exultant when he realised that Jesus Christ was the long-awaited saviour of Israel (Lk 2:25–32).

ISAIAH 13:1–23:18
Judgment against Israel's Neighbours

Thus far, Isaiah's judgment has been directed primarily against Judah and Jerusalem. While Assyria has been judged, it is on account of its future and foreseen refusal to accept its limited role as the agent of God's judgment, and its attempt to set itself up as a supreme power in itself. Attention now shifts to the surrounding nations. Each of these nations comes under the righteous survey of God, and is condemned for its failings.

The series of international condemnations is interrupted only to deliver a prophecy concerning Jerusalem (22:1–25). The date of the events referred to by this prophecy is unclear. It could refer to the attack mounted on Jerusalem by the Babylonians shortly before its fall and deportation of much of its population in 586 BC. However, it is also possible that it refers to the earlier siege against Jerusalem mounted by Sennacherib in 701 BC. The latter siege is referred to explicitly at several points later in this work, and it is possible that this passage anticipates these later sections. However, the prophecy could also be seen as anticipating the devastation wrought on Jerusalem by Babylon over the period 588–586 BC, initially during the siege and subsequently during the occupation and destruction of the city.

The reader of this section should read each prophecy carefully, noting the fundamental theme that underlies them all: in the end, only the Lord will triumph, and they will pass into the dust of history. The structure of the sections is as follows.

13:1–14:23	Babylon
14:24–32	Assyria and Philistia
15:1–16:14	Moab
17:1–14	Syria and Israel
18:1–20:6	Ethiopia (also known as Cush) and Egypt
21:1–10	Babylon
21:11–17	Edom and Arabia
22:1–25	A Prophecy concerning Jerusalem
23:1–18	Tyre

The basic theme of the ultimate victory of the Lord over all earthly and spiritual powers is then asserted in the following section, to which we may now turn.

ISAIAH 24:1–27:13
The Lord's Final Victory

24:1–25:12 The Lord's Devastation of the Earth The section opens (24:1–23) with a survey of the total victory the Lord will gain over every force that opposes him, both in heaven above and on earth below (24:21–23). The judgment is universal, and none can hope to escape. Yet this judgment will bring deliverance for the people of God, who have been subjected to oppression by the forces whose comprehensive and total rout has just been foretold. Isaiah can see the jubilation and delight these great events will bring (25:1–12). The people of God will finally find that their trust in the Lord has been totally vindicated.

26:1–27:13 A Song of Praise and Deliverance of Israel A song of praise, to be sung on that day, portrays the faith of Israel as a fortified city, which can withstand all assaults on it through the faithfulness of the Lord. Israel will be delivered from all her turmoil and suffering, and can rest assured that the Lord will watch over and safeguard her in the future (26:1–21). The guilt of the people of God will be purged in an act of atonement. This atonement is almost certainly the coming period of exile, which is seen as God's way of punishing the guilt and purging the stain of the sin of his people (27:1–13). All pagan practices and beliefs will finally be removed from the people of

God. As becomes clear in the following section, Jerusalem badly needs exactly that sort of purging.

ISAIAH 28:1–35:10
Judgment against Jerusalem

28:1–30:33 Woe to David's City The next section opens with a clear declaration (28:1–29:24) that the Lord will punish unbelief among his people. The religious life of Jerusalem has become totally debased, even to the point at which its priests and prophets stagger in a drunken state through drinking too much wine and beer (28:7–8). If Jerusalem will not hear the word of the Lord in their own language, they will have to listen to the language of foreigners (28:11–13) – a clear reference to the coming of the Assyrians, and the threat of deportation. The fact that Jerusalem is David's own city does not excuse the degeneration within its walls, and will not save it from the coming judgment (29:1–10). This message of condemnation continues (30:1–33) by describing the miseries that await Jerusalem on account of its disobedience. Nevertheless, this prophecy of judgment is softened by the promise of restoration (30:19–26).

31:1–9 Woe to Those Who Rely on Egypt As the following section makes clear, Isaiah is insistent that Israel must trust in the Lord, not in its own strength, or in alliances with foreign nations. Isaiah's particular concern focuses on Egypt, which was seen by many as the only source of help against the Assyrian menace at this stage. Isaiah's point is clear: 'the Egyptians are mere mortals and not God; their horses are flesh and

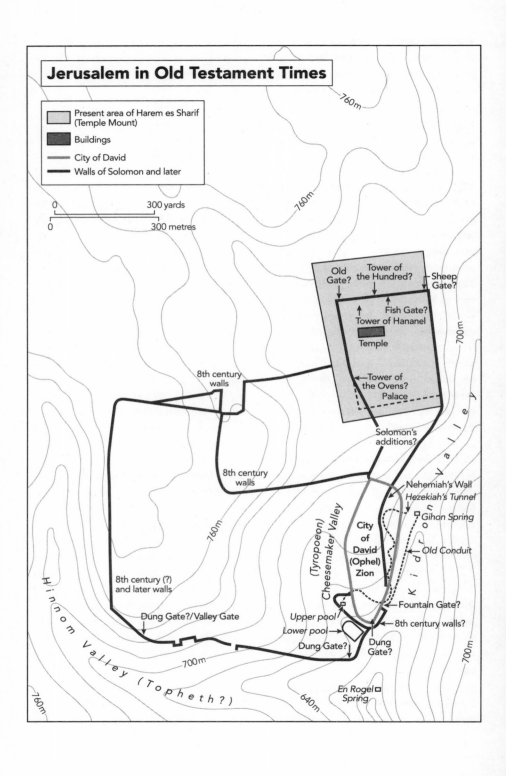

Jerusalem in Old Testament Times

Present area of Harem es Sharif
(Temple Mount)

Buildings

City of David

Walls of Solomon and later

0   300 yards

0   300 metres

760m

760m

760m

700m

Old
Gate?

Tower of
the Hundred?

Sheep
Gate?

Fish Gate?

Tower of Hananel

Temple

Tower of
the Ovens?

Palace

8th century
walls

Solomon's
additions?

8th century
walls

Nehemiah's Wall

Hezekiah's Tunnel

Gihon Spring

(Tyropoeon)
Cheesemaker Valley

City
of
David
(Ophel)
Zion

Old Conduit

K
i
d
r
o
n
  V
a
l
l
e
y

8th century (?)
and later walls

Dung Gate?/Valley Gate

Upper pool

Lower pool

Dung Gate?

Fountain Gate?

8th century walls?

Dung
Gate?

H
i
n
n
o
m
  V
a
l
l
e
y
  (T
o
p
h
e
t
h ?)

760m

760m

700m

700m

640m

En Rogel
Spring

not spirit' (31:3). Jerusalem's ultimate hope and security do not lie in foreign powers, but in obedience and trust in the Lord. In the end, Isaiah declares, Assyria will fall – but it will fall before a sword that is ultimately not mortal (31:8), a clear reference to the action of God to deliver his people.

32:1–35:6 The Kingdom of Righteousness; Joy of the Redeemed This is followed (32:1–33:24) by the promise of a future king who will reign with peace and righteousness in Jerusalem. This reign will be accompanied by the outpouring of the Holy Spirit (32:15). The prophecy also includes a message of judgment directed against a 'destroyer' (33:1–9), which is probably to be identified with Assyria. This is followed (34:1–17) by an oracle of judgment against Edom, and a prophecy of salvation for those restored to Jerusalem (35:1–10).

This final prophecy looks ahead to the day when all nature will rejoice with the entry of the Lord's redeemed people into Zion. The prophecy includes mention of several signs of the messianic age (35:5–6), which the New Testament indicates as having been brought to fulfilment in the ministry of Jesus Christ (e.g., Mt 12:22).

ISAIAH 36:1–39:8
Jerusalem and the Siege of Sennacherib

Prophecy now gives way to history, as we learn of the events that took place during the reign of Hezekiah. This section, which can also be found in a similar version at 2Ki 18:13–20:19, explains the political crisis against which part of Isaiah's ministry is set. The occasion is the major assault mounted by the Assyrian king Sennacherib against a series of cities in Judah. The background to this event is important, and needs to be explained a little.

The Assyrian king Shalmaneser V invaded Samaria, the capital of the northern kingdom, in 725 BC, and laid siege to it for three years. When the fighting was over, a substantial section of the population of the region was deported to regions deep within the Assyrian Empire. The northern kingdom of Israel existed no longer as a nation in its own right. Shortly before this catastrophe, a new era in Judah's history opened with the reign of Hezekiah in 729 BC. Initially reigning alongside his father Ahaz, Hezekiah took full control in 715. Once Israel had been conquered, the Assyrian king Sennacherib, who had succeeded Shalmaneser, turned his attention to the southern region of Judah. In the course of this, he decided to attack Jerusalem. It is this development that forms the background to this section of Isaiah.

36:1–37:20 Sennacherib Threatens Jerusalem; Hezekiah Prays It is clear that the Assyrians intend to take Jerusalem by the simplest means possible. Initially, the Assyrians try to use verbal persuasion. Speaking in Hebrew (which the ordinary inhabitants of Jerusalem understood) rather than Aramaic (the international language of diplomacy, which was not understood by ordinary people), the Assyrians tell Hezekiah that he is doomed unless he surrenders. It is clear that they hope to provoke popular pressure against the king's intention to resist them. Yet Hezekiah insists in placing his trust in the Lord. The Assyrians scoff at this. No

city has ever been saved from them by its god before (36:4–22). Hezekiah is distraught, and prays for guidance (37:1–20).

37:21–38 Sennacherib's Fall Isaiah urges Hezekiah to resist the Assyrians, and delivers a detailed prophecy against Sennacherib, prophesying his downfall (37:21–35). That same night, a disaster falls on the encamped Assyrian army. Badly shaken, Sennacherib withdraws to Nineveh, where he will eventually die at the hands of his sons (37:36–38). The prophecy is fulfilled.

38:1–39:8 Hezekiah's Illness; Envoys from Babylon At the time of an apparently fatal illness, Hezekiah receives further encouragement and reassurance from the Lord through Isaiah (38:1–22). Hezekiah appears to overstep the limits of caution in his dealings with some envoys from Babylon. At a time when the world's horizons were dominated by Assyria, Hezekiah is unreasonably positive towards the Babylonians (39:1–4). As a result, Isaiah prophesies the future downfall of Jerusalem at the hands of the Babylonians (39:5–7). Hezekiah believes these events to lie far in the future. He seems unaware that his own failings will contribute to the punishment and purification of his people through exile in Babylon.

ISAIAH 40:1–55:13
Prophecies of Restoration from Exile in Babylon

The situation now changes radically. The grim prophecies of coming exile have been fulfilled. Jerusalem is in exile in Babylon. The great prophecies of restoration found in this new section may be the work of a prophet active during the time of exile, and speaking directly to the exiled community. Alternatively, they may be the words of an earlier prophet, foretelling both the exile and subsequent restoration. Some scholars believe that we are dealing with a new writer at this point, speaking the Lord's words of comfort and hope to an exiled community whose exile was shortly to end, by the grace of God. If this is the case, we are dealing with a 'Second Isaiah', to be distinguished from the prophet who operated earlier during the reign of Hezekiah.

The exile of the people of Jerusalem began in 586 BC, and ended nearly 50 years later in 538 BC, when the first group of exiles returned to Jerusalem – an event described in the opening chapters of the book of Ezra.

40:1–41:29 Comfort for God's People The new vision of hope opens with words of comfort (40:1–2). Jerusalem's time of exile is over. Its sin has been paid for. It is free to return home. The prophet sees the Lord going ahead of his returning people, making a highway in the desert for the people of the Lord to travel along on their way back (40:3–5). All the obstacles to their path will be swept away, as the Lord guides his people home. The frailty of human power, evident in the forthcoming collapse of Babylonian power, is proclaimed. Only the word of God remains for ever. Everything else will fade away (40:6–8).

The prophet now relates his glorious vision of the Lord returning in triumph to his own city of Jerusalem, and the

excitement this return will bring to its inhabitants (40:9–11). The Lord will act like a shepherd, gathering up his tired flock and carrying them home. The prophet reflects on the greatness of God (40:12–26). No one can rival him. Jerusalem can rest assured that its God is beyond comparison. So why, he asks, does Jerusalem believe that the Lord has forgotten it? Does it not know that the Lord will comfort and support it (40:27–31)? The whole world will see this great act of deliverance, and appreciate the greatness of the God of Israel. No idol ever achieved redemption in this manner! There is no other redeemer (41:1–29).

42:1–25 The Servant of the Lord; Song of Praise to the Lord

The prophet's attention now turns to the figure of the 'servant of the LORD', who will possess the Spirit of God and bring justice to the nations (42:1–4). Further details of this servant will be provided in later chapters. The prophet returns to his theme of the greatness of the Lord, and the wonderful nature of the redemption that will soon come to the exiled people of Jerusalem (42:5–25).

43:1–44:28 Israel's Only Saviour; Israel the Chosen

The following sections stress that the Lord is the Redeemer and Saviour of Israel. There is no other saviour apart from the Lord (43:1–28). This point is especially important in relation to the New Testament, which unhesitatingly declares that Jesus Christ is the Saviour of the world – in the full knowledge that only God is Saviour. As God, Jesus Christ is indeed the true Saviour of the world.

Alongside the theme of redemption we find that of election. God has chosen Israel as his own people (44:1–8). This is followed by a superb critique of idolatry (44:9–20). How can idols be taken seriously, when the same piece of wood can be used both to make an idol for worship, and to light a fire by which to keep warm? It is too ridiculous to be taken seriously. And Jerusalem must remember that it is the Lord, and no idol, who has done all these great things for it (44:21–28).

So how is this great act of deliverance to be achieved? Earlier, we learned that Assyria was the rod of the Lord's punishment against Israel. In other words, Assyria was the human agency through which Jerusalem was punished for its disobedience. In that it exceeded its authority (note how Jerusalem is said to have suffered twice as much as was necessary: 40:2), Assyria itself must now be humbled.

45:1–48:22 The Fall of Babylon and Israel Freed

We are now introduced to the human agency by which this humbling will come about: Cyrus the Great, king of Persia (559–530 BC), who conquered Babylon in 539 BC. Cyrus has been chosen and anointed by the Lord to break Assyria and set his people free (45:1–7).

The prophet reflects on the joy and delight that this deliverance will bring to the patiently waiting people of God (45:8–25). All the gods of the nations will be shown up for what they really are. The gods of Babylon proved to be powerless to prevent the downfall of their city and empire. But the Lord will lead his people home in triumph (46:1–13). The fall of Babylon will be as spectacular as it is certain (47:1–15).

Jerusalem's captivity was not the result of any weakness on the part of the Lord; it was due to the stubbornness of Israel, which required that she should be punished and refined (48:1–22).

49:1–7 The Servant of the Lord We now learn more about the coming 'servant of the LORD' (49:1–7). This servant, chosen by the Lord, will carry on the mission of Israel where Israel herself had failed. The servant is clearly a messianic figure, with a mission to restore the people of God. He is also to be 'a light for the Gentiles', through whom salvation will be brought to the ends of the earth (49:6). This remarkable prophecy was seen by Simeon as having been fulfilled through Jesus Christ (Lk 2:32).

49:8–26 Restoration of Israel The theme of the restoration of Israel is then explored in some detail, as the prophet foresees the great joy that this news will bring to the people of God, and the consternation that it will cause their enemies. This passage also uses a very powerful and moving image to emphasise the Lord's love for his people. Just as a mother can never forget the infant to whom she gave birth and suckled at her breasts, so the Lord can never forget his own people, the people he brought into being and loves (49:15–16). This theme is then developed further.

50:1–52:12 The Servant's Obedience; Everlasting Salvation for Zion The exile in Babylon did not mean that God had abandoned his people, broken his covenant bond with them (a process here compared to a divorce), or sold them to anyone. They remain his people (50:1–3), whom he will redeem and lead to their proper home.

We are then told more about the 'servant of the LORD' (50:4–9). In this third of the four 'servant songs' (as the pieces in question are generally known), we learn that he is to be mocked and despised. This theme will be developed most fully in the fourth 'servant song', which occurs soon after this in the text. In the meantime, the prophet's thoughts turn back to the joy that the return of the exiled community to their homes in Jerusalem will bring, and the effect that this will have on those who once tormented them (50:10–51:23).

This theme is then intensified, as the prophet pictures in his mind the overwhelming pleasure that forthcoming events will bring to Jerusalem (52:1–12). The Lord will be seen in all his strength and power. The watchmen of Jerusalem will hear the bearers of the good news of Jerusalem's release, and will shout for joy at what they learn (52:7–10). Perhaps they never expected to hear such joyous news in their lifetimes. Perhaps they never expected the exiled people Jerusalem to return. Yet suddenly, the realisation will dawn: they are coming home! (This same image is used at Na 1:15, in the prophet's vision of the great rejoicing that will accompany the fall of the city of Nineveh.)

52:13–53:12 The Suffering and Glory of the Servant We now come to the fourth 'servant song', which is generally regarded as one of the most important pieces of Old Testament prophecy concerning Jesus Christ. It opens by describing the total transformation of the way in which

Could Isaiah really have foreseen Jesus?

Isaiah's vision, language and prophetic insight makes him tower over other prophets. But could he really have foreseen all that the book claims for him? To see round the corner is one thing; but could he really have predicted events 150 years ahead, and then stood within that time and seen another 70 years ahead? And could he really have looked ahead 700 years and seen so much about Jesus?

Some are doubtful, maintaining his prophecies were written by later followers after the event (though against this, his language, terminology and style are consistent throughout, suggesting one author). Others believe the church simply took his prophecies and read the life of Jesus back into them.

Such approaches rest on assumptions that predictive long-range prophecy is impossible. But supposing it isn't? Probably no Old Testament book is more messianic *in its whole nature* than Isaiah, focusing around three messianic portraits: King (Isa 1–37), Servant (Isa 38–55) and Conqueror (Isa 56–66). In such a messianic-orientated book it shouldn't surprise us, therefore, if God revealed profound truths about the Messiah's coming. Yes, Isaiah's words were always relevant to his listeners; but he also saw deeper than this to God's ultimate answer to Israel's (and our) problem: the coming of the messianic king who would unite God and humanity in a unique way – of David's line, but also the root from which David came (11:1), suggesting existence before him; knowing human frailty (53:2–3), but also 'the arm of the LORD' revealed (53:1–3); in fact no one less than the 'Wonderful Counsellor, Mighty God, Everlasting Father, Prince of Peace' (9:6), whose kingdom would never end (9:7). He also foresaw, in amazing detail, the Messiah's suffering to achieve all this (53:4–9). All this was more than any contemporary Jewish author could ever have conceived of. The simple truth is: Isaiah indeed saw ahead to Jesus.

people view this servant. Once he was despised, having a disfigured appearance. Yet now he is seen in a totally new light. Something has happened to change the way he is seen (52:13–15). So what is this all about? Who is this disfigured and despised servant? The full details are then provided (53:1–12). The reader should take this passage very slowly, and savour the powerful manner in which this most moving of passages finds its fulfilment in the suffering, death and resurrection of Jesus Christ.

The servant is someone who possessed no physical beauty. He was despised and rejected by others. He knew what it was like to suffer. Yet he did not suffer for himself; he bore the suffering and pain of others. He was pierced (just as Christ's body was pierced by the nails of the cross) for the sins of others. His wounds brought healing for others. Everyone else had lost their way. Yet the Lord laid on this servant the iniquity of the human race. The servant suffers for others, and bears their iniquities or sins. Although he was righteous, he was nevertheless 'numbered with the transgressors'. It is of the utmost importance that Jesus Christ was crucified between two

criminals (Lk 22:37; 23:32–33). Could there be any more powerful demonstration that he, in fulfilment of this prophecy, was 'numbered with the transgressors'? He bore their sin, and ours. The servant even prayed for those who sinned, just as Jesus Christ prayed for those who were crucifying him as he died on the cross (Lk 23:34).

54:1–55:13 The Future Glory of Zion The prophecy then moves on, to dwell once more on the forthcoming wonderful reunion between God and his people (54:1–17), and the reliability of the word of God. Having promised that this would happen, the Lord will bring it all to fulfilment (55:9–11). This wonderful prophecy of restoration would soon be fulfilled, demonstrating the faithfulness of the Lord to his word, and encouraging believers to take God's promises more seriously and trustingly.

ISAIAH 56:1–66:24
The Vision of the Restored Community

The prophecy now changes tone slightly. The great prophecies of the coming of restoration come to an end. In their place, we find a series of prophecies that set out a vision for the future of the restored community, describing its role in the future plans of the Lord.

56:1–8 Salvation for Others This new section opens by describing the return from Babylon in terms that suggest it is a counterpart to the exodus from Egypt (56:1–8). The set of regulations laid down parallel those given to Israel after she left her bondage in Egypt. Emphasis is placed on the need for Jerusalem to maintain covenant faithfulness with the Lord if she is to benefit fully from his blessings.

It is not only Jerusalem who is to benefit from the Lord. All nations will be blessed by him. The temple at Jerusalem will become a house of prayer for all nations, not just Judah. And just as the Lord gathered together the exiles of Israel, so he will gather to them other peoples (56:7–8). In other words, Israel has a mission to bring a knowledge of the Lord to the nations, in order that all might find blessing in him. Yet, as we learn from the history of Israel in later years, quite the reverse would actually happen. Israel would become increasingly exclusivist, regarding the Law of God as a charter of national privilege for the Jews, rather than as a manifesto of grace for the world.

56:9–57:21 God's Accusation Against the Wicked; Comfort for the Contrite The Lord's criticism is now directed against the wickedness of his people, who have deserted him for other lovers. Strongly critical though this passage is, the hope of grace is firmly stated (56:9–57:13). Those who are lowly and sincerely contrite will know the comfort of his grace and forgiveness (57:14–21).

58:1–59:21 True Fasting, Sin, Confession and Redemption The importance of true worship, obedience, repentance and confession on the part of Jerusalem is emphasised. Human sin is a barrier to God's blessing. Yet the Lord will remain faithful to his covenant, and provide both a redeemer for his people, and the gift of the Holy Spirit.

60:1–22 The Glory of Zion Zion (another term for Jerusalem) will be greatly honoured and revered throughout the world on account of the greatness of its God. The material prosperity of its people will be matched by the consolation of knowing that the Lord, the God of Israel, will remain with her for ever (60:1–22). Israel will draw the nations to herself, so that they may learn of her God. Israel thus has a mission to the nations.

61:1–11 The Year of the Lord's Favour This theme is developed further in a great passage of prophecy, which proclaims the 'year of the LORD's favour'. The prophecy speaks of a messianic figure, on whom the Spirit of the Lord will rest, who will come to bring liberation and health to his people. The opening verses of this great prophecy were cited by Jesus Christ when he preached in the synagogue at Nazareth (Lk 4:16–21); in his ministry, the great signs and wonders spoken of in this prophecy were brought to fulfilment. The prophecy is especially focused on the restoration and rebuilding of Jerusalem, perhaps with the situations of Ezra or Nehemiah in mind. But the passage has a much wider significance, pointing to the dawning of a new era of consolation and joy for those who hitherto had known only sadness and despair. For the Christian, the references to Jesus Christ are unmistakable.

62:1–63:6 Zion's New Name The prophecy continues with a great vision of the future greatness of Zion (62:1–12), in which Jerusalem will be acknowledged throughout the world as the place in which the Lord's redeemed dwell. The Lord stresses his total commitment to Jerusalem and its people. Yet that commitment reflects his intentions for both city and people. They are to be a light that will illuminate the nations, and draw people to the Lord their God. The Lord affirms that he will deal with the enemies of his people, symbolised by Edom, one of the historic enemies of both Israel and Judah (63:1–6). The Lord will take his revenge against those who oppress his people, and none will be able to resist him.

63:7–64:12 Praise and Prayer The prophet then turns to a glorious rehearsal of the great deeds of the Lord in history, focusing especially on the way in which the Lord delivered his people from captivity in Egypt. He alone is the God of history. The people are moved to repentance at the realisation of their failure to remain faithful to him (64:6–7). Their hope lies solely in the goodness and mercy of the Lord, by which he takes compassion on his suffering people.

65:1–25 Judgment and Salvation; New Heavens and a New Earth The prophecy of judgment against those who have forsaken the Lord continues (65:1–12). Yet the promise of restoration of those who remain faithful to him is affirmed once more (65:13–16). A time is coming when the Lord's faithful people will know peace. It will be a time of renewal (65:17–19), in which tranquillity will reign in the land. People can build houses and know that they will live in them. They can plant vineyards, knowing that they will eat their fruit. The wolf and the lamb will lie down together (65:20–25). As the Christian

knows, this great vision of hope and encouragement will find its fulfilment only when the Lord brings history to an end, and his faithful people rest in the new Jerusalem (Rev 21:1–14).

66:1–24 *Judgment and Hope* This great prophecy comes to an end with a final vision of restoration and hope. The Lord will execute judgment against those who oppose him and show mercy and compassion to those who trust and obey him. There will come a day when all people will acknowledge the Lord as God – including the nations of the world. In this new era, Gentiles – non-Jews – will be chosen to be priests of the Lord.

So we leave Isaiah, in the full knowledge that many of the great themes, promises and privileges of the gospel of Jesus Christ have been anticipated by his faithful people during the time of the old covenant. Christians can rejoice that they have had the privilege of seeing many of these great promises and hopes finally come to fulfilment in and through Jesus Christ.

JEREMIAH

The book of the prophet Jeremiah is the second in the series of four 'Major Prophets'. It is not just the longest of these major prophets. It is the longest book in the whole Bible. Jeremiah was called to be a prophet to Jerusalem in the year 626 BC. He would continue his ministry during the remainder of the reign of Josiah (who died in battle against the Egyptians in 609 BC), and during the reigns of Jehoahaz (609), Jehoiakim (609–598), Jehoiachin (598–597) and Zedekiah (597–586 BC). These were turbulent years. The reader wishing to know more about these events in some detail is recommended to read the story of the last days of Judah, as presented either in 2 Kings or 2 Chronicles. This will provide an understanding of the historical events that form the backdrop to Jeremiah's prophetic ministry.

The basic sequence of events during the period of Jeremiah's ministry can be summarised as follows. Josiah, who has instigated a series of religious reforms that lead to a purification and refining of Judah's religious life, dies in 609, attempting to oppose an Egyptian advance to aid the ailing Assyrian forces, who are about to fall to the sustained attacks of the Babylonians and their allies the Medes. The capital city of Assyria, Nineveh, falls to their armies in 612. It is just a matter of time before Babylon establishes itself as supreme in the region. The death of Josiah is something of a personal tragedy for Jeremiah, as it is clear that the king has been sympathetic both to the prophet and to his message from the Lord. Josiah's successors are consistently hostile towards him, and often openly contemptuous of his prophetic message.

On the international stage, the power of Babylon continues to grow. The Egyptians, the only remaining power of importance in the region, are routed by Babylonian armies at Carchemish in 605 BC. The Egyptians withdraw to lick their wounds, and will play no further role of importance in international politics during the time of Jeremiah. In 605, during the reign of Jehoiakim, the Babylonians lay siege to Jerusalem, and subdue it for a while. Following further unrest within the city, the Babylonians attack it again in 598–597 BC, taking away Jehoiachin, who has succeeded Jehoiakim at that time.

The Babylonians install Zedekiah as king, but he rebels against Babylon, possibly believing that a new Egyptian Pharaoh may be able to overthrow the Babylonian domination of the region. It is a disastrous miscalculation. The Babylonians attack Jerusalem in 588 BC, and take full possession of the city two years later. Gedaliah is appointed governor. Jeremiah finds himself within the circle of the governor, which is shattered by his assassination shortly afterwards. Jeremiah seeks refuge in Egypt, where he is believed to have died. According to a Jewish tradition, reflected at Heb 11:37, he was killed by being stoned while in exile in Egypt.

The general argument of the book of Jeremiah is difficult to follow at points because of the arrangement of the material within the book. The work is not arranged in a strictly

chronological order, making it difficult to follow events through from one reign to another. For this reason, considerable care will be taken to ensure that readers appreciate the approximate date and historical context of key passages, so that their full significance can be appreciated. For example, if a purely chronological arrangement were adopted, chapter 26 would come between 7:15 and 7:16, and chapter 45 between 36:8 and 36:9. The book is in fact a complex collection of documents, requiring some patience to follow at points. However, the effort involved is unquestionably justified by the results.

OUTLINE

Jeremiah's call to preach judgment and repentance

1:1–19 The call of Jeremiah

2:1–37 Judah's lack of faithfulness to the covenant

3:1–4:4 The call to repentance

4:5–6:30 The coming wrath of the Lord

7:1–8:3 The charge against Judah of false worship

8:4–9:26 Jeremiah's grief over the apostasy of his people

10:1–25 God is to be worshipped as Creator and judge

11:1–13:27 The rebellion of Judah against God

14:1–15:21 The coming judgment against Judah

16:1–17:27 Judgment announced through Jeremiah's life and preaching

18:1–19:15 Jeremiah's visits to the potter's house

20:1–18 Jeremiah's misery over his life and fate

21:1–23:40 The rejection of King Zedekiah

24:1–10 The exile as a necessary time of purging

25:1–38 The fall of Babylon foretold

26:1–29:32 The Babylonian exile foretold

30:1–33:26 The prophecy of the restoration of the remnant of the people, with the renewal of the covenant

34:1–36:32 Further resistance to Jeremiah

37:1–21 Jeremiah falsely accused and imprisoned

38:1–28 Jeremiah rescued from the pit

The fall of Jerusalem and its results

39:1–18 The fall of Jerusalem

40:1–16 Jeremiah remains with the remnant in Palestine

41:1–18 The murder of the governor Gedaliah

42:1–22 Jeremiah's prophecy against going to Egypt

43:1–13 The flight to Egypt

44:1–30 Jeremiah's prophecy that Egypt will be overthrown by Babylon

45:1–5 Baruch's reward

Judgment against the nations

46:1–28 Judgment against Egypt

47:1–7 Judgment against Philistia

48:1–47 Judgment against Moab

49:1–6 Judgment against Ammon

49:7–22 Judgment against Edom

49:23–27 Judgment against Damascus

49:28–33 Judgment against Kedar and Hazor

49:34–39 Judgment against Elam

50:1–51:64 Judgment against Babylon

52:1–34 Appendix: a further account of the fall of Judah

JEREMIAH 1:1–19
The Call of Jeremiah

The book opens with events that take place in 626 BC, the thirteenth year of the reign of Josiah, the great reforming king of Judah whose rediscovery of the 'Book of the Law' had led to one of the greatest religious shake-ups in Judah's history (1:1–2). The call of Jeremiah is described in terms of the coming of the word of the Lord (1:2, 4). Jeremiah is told that he has been set apart by God and appointed as a prophet to the nations. Two visions follow in rapid succession, as part of the calling itself. First, Jeremiah sees the branch of an almond tree. The Hebrew word for 'almond tree' is very similar to that for 'watching', and leads to the interpretation of this vision in terms of the Lord's concern for his people (1:11–12).

Secondly, he sees a boiling pot or cauldron, which is tilted from the north. The Hebrew for 'boiling' is very similar to that for 'will be poured out', leading to this vision being interpreted as a future disaster befalling Judah from the north (1:13–14). Jeremiah is asked to remain faithful to the Lord, despite the great opposition he will face (1:17–19). The great loneliness and sense of isolation experienced by Jeremiah during his ministry are here put down to his faithful proclamation of the word of God against people in Judah who do not wish to hear it.

JEREMIAH 2:1–6:30
Jeremiah's Earliest Prophecies

2:1–3:5 Israel Forsakes God The first set of Jeremiah's prophecies dates from the reign of Josiah himself. The basic message is as simple as it is uncomfortable for the inhabitants of Judah. Judah has fallen away from the Lord. As a result, God will punish and refine his people through an invasion by foreigners. The prophecy opens by recalling the close relationship that existed between God and his people in their early period. But something has gone wrong. Jeremiah reproaches his own people for abandoning the Lord without any good cause, and asserting their own independence. They have forsaken the Lord, and done what pleased them (2:1–30). But what has the Lord done to deserve this? What has he failed to do for his people? Why has Israel forgotten her God? Israel has behaved like a prostitute (2:31–3:5).

3:6–4:4 Unfaithful Israel A substantial section now deals with the specifics of Judah's faithlessness. Judah has become just like her sister Israel, the northern kingdom that was wiped out by Assyria on account of its apostasy and disobedience. Judah has forgotten the Lord. The imagery of prostitution and adultery is used extensively to highlight the full extent of Judah's faithlessness to her faithful God. The Lord begs her to return to him in repentance, for he will gladly have her back (3:21–4:4).

4:5–6:30 Disaster from the North If Israel will not repent and return, she will suffer disaster from the north. Even now, a mighty army is on the move, intent on laying waste the land and cities of Judah (4:5–31). Yet Jerusalem is full of wicked and deceitful people, who have rejected the Lord. As a result, a distant nation will overwhelm them. Yet even in the face of this threat, Jeremiah knows that he will

not be heard. People prefer to ignore God than to face up to the truth of what is happening (5:1–31).

This section ends with a prophetic vision of Jerusalem under siege from an aggressor from the north, with the Lord urging the besiegers on as they punish his disobedient people (6:1–30). The image of the Lord encouraging those who seek to destroy Judah would have been deeply distressing to his audience, who imagined that they had special privileged status in the sight of the Lord, which somehow exempted them from the requirements of faith and obedience to him.

JEREMIAH 7:1–35:19
Further Judgment Against Judah

7:1–29 False Religion Worthless Jeremiah's prophecy continues with a cutting critique of the religious life of Judah. The first set of oracles centres on the temple, the great focus of the religious life of Judah (7:1–10:25). The word of the Lord comes to Jeremiah, telling him to prophesy at the gate of Solomon's temple (7:1–2). The basic theme of his temple oracles can be summarised like this. Jerusalem cannot trust in the temple for its salvation and continued favour in the sight of God. The tabernacle had been established in Shiloh at the time of the conquest of Canaan. Yet the presence of the tabernacle did not prevent Shiloh from being overrun by the Philistines. The house of the Lord has become little more than a den of robbers (7:11) – a theme to which Jesus Christ returns in his ministry in Jerusalem during the final week of his life (Mt 21:13).

7:30–9:26 The Valley of Slaughter; Sin and Punishment Jeremiah ruthlessly exposes the deep inroads made by paganism in the religious life of Judah. Pagan idols have been placed in the temple. High places have been re-established. Even the pagan practice of child sacrifice has been introduced (7:30–34). The Lord will not tolerate this state of affairs, and will bring judgment to his rebellious and disobedient people. Yet the people seem unaware of the seriousness of their situation. They pretend that their wounds are not serious, when they are in fact fatal. They talk about peace, when there is no peace to be had at all (8:11).

Jeremiah takes no pleasure in his own prophetic denunciation of his people. He is horrified by the extent of their sin, and the punishment that will be its inevitable and just reward. He is moved to weep over the state of his people (8:21–9:6). A time of refinement and purification must follow, in which the dross of paganism and sin will be removed from Judah (9:7–9). The devastation wrought will be terrible. In a series of curt and blunt images, Jeremiah portrays the carnage that will result when Jerusalem is laid waste (9:17–26).

10:1–25 God and Idols Jerusalem's lapse into idolatry is as senseless as it is pointless. Idols cannot save anyone; nor did they create the world. So why trust them? By abandoning the Lord, Jerusalem has brought judgment on her head. A storm is brewing in the north, which will eventually bring destruction to the towns of Judah, and leave them as heaps of ruins, populated only by marauding jackals.

11:1–17 The Covenant Is Broken
The style of writing now alters. Prose may replace poetry, but the message remains the same. Judah has broken her covenant with the Lord, and will herself be broken in consequence. This passage stresses the conditionality of the covenant. The Lord will remain faithful to his people. Yet the people must remain faithful to him – something they have conspicuously failed to do in the past (11:1–17). By their lapse into paganism, the people of Judah have provoked the righteous anger of the Lord.

11:18–13:27 Plot Against Jeremiah; His Complaint and God's Answer
At this point, we learn once more of the personal cost to Jeremiah of his ministry of judgment on behalf of the Lord. We learn of an attempt on his life (11:18–23), and of the prophet's bewilderment at the events taking place around him (12:1–4). Yet the Lord reassures Jeremiah that there is no alternative: Judah has sinned grievously, and will suffer disaster as a result (12:5–17). If she continues to behave in this way, she will be uprooted, abandoned and forsaken by the Lord himself. Jeremiah is then given a sign, in the form of a linen belt that was initially new, yet then become rotten (13:1–11). In the same way, the people of God have lost their initial cleanness in the sight of God, and become soiled and stained by sin. Once more, Jeremiah proclaims the coming of judgment from the north (13:20), bringing with it devastation and destruction.

14:1–15:21 Drought, Famine, Sword
The prophecy then shifts slightly in its tone, and focuses on what was clearly a severe drought in the land (14:1–15:9). Jeremiah sees in this further confirmation of the anger of the Lord against his people. To those false prophets who speak of lasting peace in the land, Jeremiah issues a rebuke on behalf of the Lord: there will be no peace – only destruction, famine and plague. Escape from this ordained destruction is utterly impossible. Jeremiah is distressed at this thought, as can be seen from the 'confession' that follows (15:10–21), in which he admits to his personal pain. However, the Lord assures Jeremiah of his presence and support, as the prophet seeks to remain faithful to his calling and not speak the soothing and comforting words that the people want to hear.

16:1–17:18 Day of Disaster
The Lord gives Jeremiah a bleak message of judgment, dominated by the theme of disaster. Although moments of comfort may be discerned within this prophecy of doom, its dominant theme is that of forthcoming distress and destruction. Judah will be thrown out of her own land, and placed in a foreign land (16:13). If Judah has forsaken the Lord, then the Lord is perfectly free to forsake Judah. Yet even as this sombre note of future exile is sounded, a promise of restoration is placed alongside it (16:14–15). Just as the Lord brought his people up out of Egypt in the exodus, so he will also gather them in from their places of exile and banishment.

17:19–19:15 At the Potter's House
After a brief section reiterating the importance of keeping the Sabbath as a sign of the covenant between the Lord and his people (17:19–27), we come to the series

of incidents in which Jeremiah visits a potter's house.

At the bidding of the Lord, Jeremiah visits the house of a potter, and watches him at work. The first of the incidents focuses on the way in which the potter reworks his clay. Dissatisfied with the first attempt at making a pot, he breaks down the clay, and refashions it, until he is finally content with the outcome. In this action, Jeremiah sees a parable of God's dealings with his people. Just as the potter is at liberty to do what he pleases with his clay, so the Lord is equally at liberty to break and remould the people of Judah (18:1–17).

Meanwhile, Jeremiah faces increased hostility and criticism, which he clearly feels keenly (18:18–23). Yet he remains faithful to his commission to proclaim the word of the Lord. The next episode again centres on a visit to the potter's house, this time to purchase a clay jar. He is ordered to smash the jar in public, as a sign of the way in which the Lord will smash his people for their disobedience. Both Judah and Jerusalem will be broken to pieces, on account of the paganism of their peoples (19:1–15).

20:1–18 Jeremiah and Pashhur; Jeremiah's Complaint This action irritates one of the priests, who arranges for Jeremiah to be beaten and humiliated (20:1–6). Although Jeremiah prophesies exile in Babylon for his

---

Does God mind if we are honest with him?

'You deceived me, LORD, and I was deceived' (20:7), Jeremiah complains. His accusation is even stronger when one realises the word 'deceived' can also mean 'seduced'. Jeremiah accuses God of having sweet-talked him into becoming a prophet through false promises (1:4–19); the reality, he feels, is far from this. He has had enough – though deep down he knows he can't give up (20:9). However, the moment he offloads his complaint, something changes in him. It is as if he is free to rise in faith again. So within a few verses we read, 'But the LORD is with me like a mighty warrior . . .' (v.11).

Jeremiah wasn't alone in bringing plain-speaking, grievances, hurts, disappointments and anger to God. Moses complained that God had made things worse for the Hebrew slaves (Ex 5:22–23); Elijah complained that not only had his work been fruitless, but Jezebel was out to kill him for it (1Ki 19:1–4); Job complained that he was suffering without cause and demanded God showed the charges against him (Job 10:1–7); Habakkuk complained that God was using unholy Babylon to judge his people (Hab 1:12–2:10); Jonah even complained that God had been too kind (Jnh 4:1–3)!

Through all these examples the Bible shows that God is well able to handle our telling him what we really think. We don't need to dress up prayer in religious or unreal language. In fact, the surprising thing about prayer in the Bible is that, unlike other ancient religions, there are no special words for use in prayer. What God wants from us is the open and honest sharing of our hearts. As David put it, 'Pour out your hearts to him, for God is our refuge' (Ps 62:8).

assailant, he is unnerved by the experience. In a passage that reveals great self-questioning and uncertainty (20:7–18), Jeremiah speaks of his deep-seated feeling that he has been deceived by the Lord. His prophecies have brought him nothing but ridicule and ruin. Yet he knows that he cannot remain silent. He must speak the word of the Lord, in the knowledge that this is the Lord's will. Yet the whole process has made him so miserable that he wishes he had never been born.

21:1–14 *God Rejects Zedekiah's Request* A new section now opens. Much of the previous material has concerned the reign of Josiah. The new material now abruptly moves forward, to deal with events in the reign of Zedekiah, the final king of Judah. Zedekiah has been installed by the Babylonians as their ruler in Jerusalem. Zedekiah, perhaps misreading the military and political climate, feels the time has come to rebel against Babylon. It is to prove a disastrous judgment on his part. The situation envisaged in this passage suggests that it dates from around 588 BC, when the Babylonians laid siege to Jerusalem in response to Zedekiah's rebellion.

Zedekiah asks Jeremiah for a favourable response from the Lord in response to this situation of emergency. But Jeremiah will have none of this. The Lord will use the Babylonians to punish Jerusalem for its disobedience and rebellion. Resistance will lead only to death. Submission to exile in Babylon will lead to life. Jerusalem will be laid waste.

22:1–23:8 *Judgment Against Wicked Kings; the Righteous Branch* Jeremiah sees future travellers going past the ruins of the city, and talking about the disobedience of its people and the response of their God to these things (22:1–9). Jeremiah's prophecy condemns both present and past kings of Judah for their failures (22:10–30).

A note of hope is sounded in the midst of this unrelenting prophecy of doom. A remnant will remain, and a new king will rise in the line of David, who will redeem his people (23:3–8). This passage reaches its ultimate fulfilment only in Jesus Christ.

23:9–24:10 *Two Baskets of Fruit* After a powerful passage denouncing false prophets, who merely say what people want to hear (23:9–40), we come to another prophetic vision. This time, the vision concerns two baskets of figs, one containing good fruit, and the other rotten fruit. Jeremiah interprets the former as a symbol of the people of Jerusalem who have been carried off into exile in Babylon, and the latter as Zedekiah and his court, who have remained behind in Jerusalem. The former will one day return to their home city; but the latter have no further place in the purposes of God (24:1–10).

25:1–14 *Seventy Years of Captivity* Jerusalem must face 70 years of exile in Babylon, after which the Lord will punish Babylon in its turn, and set his people free. Babylon, who has enslaved so many nations, will in turn be enslaved by others. The period of 70 years can be regarded as beginning with the limited deportations of 605 BC, and ending with the first return of the exiles in 538 BC.

25:15–26:24 The Cup of Wrath; Jeremiah Threatened with Death A further vision follows, in which Jeremiah sees the cup of God's wrath. The nations drink of it, and stagger. While they are drunk, they will die by the sword (25:15–38). A storm is gathering, which will sweep away the nations – a clear reference to the advances of the Babylonians. Jeremiah once more faces threats as a result of the unremittingly negative nature of his prophecy. These threats come from the highest level, and it is clear that Jeremiah is in serious danger of being killed (26:1–24). The threat is averted, but it is obvious that Jeremiah's words are not finding either favour or attention at the highest levels in Jerusalem. The false prophets (including Hananiah and Shemaiah, whom we shall meet presently), who proclaim that Jerusalem will be spared from Babylon and enjoy a period of peace, have the ear of the king. Perhaps the Lord wants Jerusalem to rebel against Babylon, and regain its freedom?

27:1–22 Judah to Serve Nebuchadnezzar The prophecies that follow make it clear that Jeremiah knows of these false prophecies, and the false and unjustified sense of security they bring to the royal court. Jerusalem will be forced to submit to Babylon. There is no alternative. Exile is a God-given punishment for Jerusalem. The people's only hope lies in accepting what God has ordained for them, in the knowledge that it will eventually lead to restoration.

28:1–17 The False Prophet Hananiah The false prophets will have none of this. One of their number is now mentioned specifically by name: Hananiah declares that the Lord will soon break the power

of Babylon, and restore all the items from the temple which had been taken there by the Babylonians. Jeremiah, who is wearing a yoke as a symbol of the need to submit to Babylon, opposes Hananiah's prophecy, to the latter's intense annoyance. Hananiah breaks Jeremiah's yoke as a protest. Yet Jeremiah clearly wins the argument. Within two months, the false prophet is dead.

29:1–31:40 A Letter to the Exiles Jeremiah then writes to those in exile in Babylon, urging them to settle down, buy land and houses, and marry. Their exile will be long term (29:1–23). This flatly contradicts the optimistic utterances of the false prophets, including Shemaiah. Although we are not told the precise nature of his prophesying, we learn that Shemaiah has falsely claimed to be a prophet, and sought to discredit Jeremiah (29:24–32). Israel will indeed be restored from exile and the Lord will establish a new covenant with her (30:1–31:40) – but not yet. There must first be a time of purification and refinement.

32:1–44 Jeremiah Buys a Field To demonstrate his God-given conviction that the Lord will indeed restore his people to Jerusalem, Jeremiah purchases a plot of land in his home town of Anathoth. To the curious and bewildered onlookers this would have seemed absurd. Why buy a field, when the Babylonians are about to capture Jerusalem? Yet Jeremiah's conviction remains firm: although exile is fast approaching, on account of Judah's sin, the people will one day again own land in their own country.

33:1–35:19 Promise of Restoration; a Warning to Zedekiah Restoration will follow exile (33:1–26). The messianic prophecy of 23:5–6 is repeated, to underscore the reliability of what has been said (33:15–16). The covenant will be restored and renewed. This major section ends with further warnings of the seriousness of the situation of Judah and Jerusalem (34:1–35:19). None can escape – not even Zedekiah.

JEREMIAH 36:1–38:28
The Woes of Jeremiah

36:1–32 Jehoiakim Burns Jeremiah's Scroll It is clear that Jeremiah's message is deeply unpopular, especially in court circles. This is reflected in the way in which he is treated, documented in this section of the book. The first incident recorded relates to 605 BC, the fourth year of Jehoiakim's reign. During this year, Jeremiah openly speaks of Jerusalem going into captivity for a period of 70 years (25:1–14). Jeremiah is ordered by the Lord to write down all his prophecies. Jeremiah proceeds to do so, making use of Baruch both as his secretary and his public spokesman. Jeremiah's prophecies are thus written down on a scroll. After reading Jeremiah's prophecies aloud from a room near the temple, Baruch is invited to read them again to a group of court officials. Terrified by the judgments they hear pronounced, they insist that the king should hear them.

The king, however, is not impressed. As each section of the prophecy is read, he cuts off that section of the scroll, and throws the pieces on to a burning brazier. Neither the king nor his inner circle is in the least moved or concerned by

Jeremiah's prophecy. In fact, their immediate reaction is to arrest and silence both Jeremiah and Baruch. In the meantime, Jeremiah has to repeat his prophecies, so that Baruch can copy them down once more. No copy has been taken. At this dictation session, it seems that Jeremiah adds additional prophecies to those originally delivered (see the 'many similar words' at 36:32).

37:1–21 Jeremiah in Prison This pattern of studied indifference to Jeremiah's prophecies continues under Zedekiah. Initially, Zedekiah allows Jeremiah a considerable degree of freedom (37:1–5), perhaps assuming that, with Egyptian troop movements forcing the Babylonians to withdraw, he has no need to be anxious about the future. However, the Babylonians repel the Egyptian advance, and are soon able to resume their siege of Jerusalem. At this point, which is generally dated to 588 BC, Jeremiah delivers a prophecy of judgment that speaks of the end of Jerusalem (37:6–10). Perhaps unwisely, he then attempts to leave the city during the period of the Babylonian withdrawal and attend to family property matters in the region of Benjamin, in which his home town of Anathoth is located. He is accused of deserting to the Babylonians, and thrown into prison (37:11–21).

The situation resembles the story of Joseph in many ways, especially in relation to the period spent languishing in prison. Zedekiah eventually summons him from prison and asks him whether there had been any word from the Lord. He expects to hear good news. The word of judgment that follows, speaking of his own capture by the Babylonians, is clearly

not what he expects. However, Zedekiah arranges for Jeremiah to be held under more humane conditions, and to receive a supply of fresh bread.

38:1–28 Jeremiah Thrown into a Cistern Jeremiah's new style of imprisonment involves being obliged to remain within the courtyard of the guard. Although he is not allowed to leave, he is nevertheless allowed visitors. It is clear that the visitors ask him for his words of prophecy, and pass them on to those outside. Jeremiah urges his hearers to submit to Babylon as the only hope of salvation (38:1–3). Alarmed at the result of these prophecies on the morale of the city, the officials ask for him to be silenced, preferably permanently. Eventually, they settle on a course of action that allows the prophet to live, at least for a while, but not to prophesy. He is thrown into a deep muddy cistern within the courtyard of the guard (38:4–6).

The king, on hearing of Jeremiah's fate, arranges for him to be released from the cistern. Jeremiah once more informs the king in private that the only course of action open to him is to surrender to the Babylonians. He is then returned to the courtyard of the guard, where he remains until the city finally falls. Zedekiah has ignored his advice (38:7–28).

JEREMIAH 39:1–45:5
The Fall of Jerusalem

39:1–40 The Fall of Jerusalem; Jeremiah Freed The next major section of the book chronicles the final fall of Jerusalem in July 586. It is the most detailed account of the fall of the city to be provided anywhere in the Old Testament, and should be read carefully. Zedekiah is taken prisoner. The main buildings of the city are set on fire. The people of the city and all those who have already surrendered are carried off to exile in Babylon (39:1–10). Some are left behind in the land and the city, mostly poor people who will cause no problems for the occupying Babylonians.

Jeremiah is held back, however, for different reasons. He has come to the attention of Nebuchadnezzar (39:11–18), for reasons that are not clear. Perhaps he has learned of Jeremiah's advice to surrender to the Babylonians, and regards him as an ally. At any rate, Jeremiah is not to be allowed to leave Jerusalem. Instead, he is to live in the house of Gedaliah, whom the Babylonians have appointed as governor. Gedaliah is based at the town of Mizpah, north of Jerusalem. The events leading up to this transfer from prison to the governor's house are then related in more detail, from the standpoint of the Babylonian commander Nebuzaradan (40:1–6).

40:7–43:13 Gedaliah Assassinated and the Flight to Egypt It might seem that all is now well for Jeremiah. But disaster is about to befall him. Gedaliah is assassinated, along with a small detachment of Babylonian soldiers who are responsible for his safety (40:7–41:15). There are fears of a massive Babylonian reprisal against the Jews remaining in the region. Many want to leave the region immediately, and seek safety in Egypt. Jeremiah is asked to pray for guidance. His prophecy speaks of doom for those who abandon their country to flee to safety in Egypt. If they

remain where they are, they will not face the wrath of Babylon (41:16–42:22).

This is not what many of the senior military figures want to hear. They accuse Jeremiah of lying, and prepare to set out for Egypt. It is clear from what follows that Jeremiah, Baruch and the remaining Jews in the region are given no choice in this matter: they are forced to leave Judah for Egypt (43:1–7).

So there are now two remnants of Judah: one that has been deported to Babylon, and the other that has fled to Egypt. It is clear that Jeremiah continues to act as a prophet to the exiled Jewish community in Egypt, predicting the destruction of Egypt itself at the hands of the Babylonians (43:8–13).

44:1–30 *Disaster Because of Idolatry* Jeremiah's final recorded prophecy focuses on the new threat of idolatry that arises in Egypt. Jeremiah reports the anger of the Lord against his people. Not only have they abandoned Judah, where they should have remained as a remnant. They have adopted the pagan religious practices and beliefs of the Egyptians themselves. As a result, they will face disaster (44:1–14).

Jeremiah's Jewish audience is not impressed. They argue that their problems began when they were forced to stop sacrificing to pagan gods by Josiah. Everything was going well while they worshipped the 'Queen of Heaven' (a Babylonian term used to refer to the goddess Ishtar). When Josiah put a stop to that, things went disastrously wrong (44:15–19). Jeremiah is outraged at these suggestions, and prophesies the total destruction of the Jewish community in Egypt (44:20–30).

45:1–5 *A Message to Baruch* Nothing more is heard of Jeremiah. He is assumed to have died in Egypt. This section of the book then ends with a brief account of Jeremiah's words to Baruch, although he had written down the prophet's words many years earlier.

JEREMIAH 46:1–52:34
Oracles Against the Nations

The book of Jeremiah concludes with a series of oracles against the nations (46:1–51:64). The dating of these prophecies is unclear. Although the location of the oracles might suggest that they were delivered during the time that Jeremiah was in Egypt, the general content of the oracles suggests that they date from an earlier period in his career. The general theme of impending disaster at the hands of the Babylonians suggests that they date from around 605 BC, the date of the battle of Carchemish, at which the Egyptians were totally routed by the Babylonians. They have probably been gathered together in this section of the book on account of the similarities between each of the oracles, which survey a range of nations, beginning with Egypt and ending with Babylon.

By far the greatest attention is paid to Babylon itself (50:1–51:64), but the same themes can be discerned throughout these chapters: destruction is on its way for the nations around Babylon. Babylon is the Lord's instrument of vengeance and judgment against the nations of this region, yet Babylon herself will not escape judgment. She too will fall.

The work ends with a further account of the fall of Jerusalem (52:1–34), which seems to draw upon the same source as

2Ki 24:18–25:30. However, at several points (such as the account of the fate of Zedekiah, 52:10–11), the account in Jeremiah is more detailed. It is generally thought that this section of the work was compiled by Baruch, to provide further historical information concerning the events around the time of the fall of Jerusalem, showing how Jeremiah's prophecies were fulfilled by events. It also means that this book ends on a positive note, with the hope of restoration. Jeremiah and the second wave of exiles may have disappeared into Egypt. But the hope of restoration of the Babylonian exiles is kept alive.

LAMENTATIONS

The book of Lamentations consists of five poems or 'laments' over the destruction of Jerusalem by the Babylonians in 586 BC. Four of the five poems take a very similar form, and are based on the 22 letters of the Hebrew alphabet. According to an ancient tradition, they were written by Jeremiah himself. While this cannot be proved, the book certainly seems to have been written at some point between 586 and 538 BC. The fact that the book provides such a graphic portrayal of the destruction of Jerusalem suggests that most of the material is to be dated shortly after the fall of the city in 586 BC, when the events described would still have been vivid in the memory of those who lived through them.

OUTLINE

1:1–22 First lament: the Lord's rejection of Jerusalem

2:1–22 Second lament: the Lord's anger against Jerusalem

3:1–66 Third lament: repentance and the hope of renewal

4:1–22 Fourth lament: the sin of the leaders of the people

5:1–22 Fifth lament: a prayer for restoration

1:1–22 The First Lament focuses on the Lord's rejection of Jerusalem. It conveys a vivid picture of a desolate city. Once a great nation, Judah has been utterly humiliated and trodden under foot. There is nobody present to comfort her at the moment of her downfall. Even the Lord seems to have abandoned his own people to the wrath of the Babylonian invader. This is no accident of history. This is the deliberate and considered infliction of punishment on a disobedient people by the God who once loved them. The rebellion of the people is openly acknowledged. God, in his righteousness, has every right to do this. The lament emphasises the misery that Judah's disobedience has brought in its wake. In this first lament, no note of hope is sounded. The dominant theme is that of merited punishment, and the shame and pain it has brought to a once-proud people.

2:1–22 The Second Lament deals with a related theme. It is a meditation on the Lord's anger against Jerusalem. The destruction of Jerusalem is a result of her justly incurring the anger of the Lord. He has laid waste his own dwelling-place. Jerusalem's prophets and priests have failed her. They did not warn her of the seriousness of her sins, nor of the future devastation that she would suffer in consequence. (Jeremiah was very much the exception to this rule: most of the 'prophets' expected Babylon to fall, and leave Judah in peace.) Yet why does the Lord treat his people in this way? The pain and sadness of the situation is impossible to bear.

3:1–66 The Third Lament strikes a different, and much more positive tone. It deals with the need for personal and corporate repentance, and the resulting hope of renewal. This section is substantially longer than the other four laments, and takes the form of three groups of 22 verses. Within each group, the verses are again arranged according to the order of the Hebrew alphabet. Although this lament is presented as the words of an individual, it is clear that the individual in question (who may well be Jeremiah himself) is speaking on behalf of his people. The lament reflects on the affliction the people have suffered, their need to return to the Lord, and the wonderful compassion of the Lord to those who return to him (note especially 3:21–33).

4:1–22 The Fourth Lament turns to deal with the sin of the leaders of the people. After reviewing once more the distress of the people, the lament turns to allocate blame for this misery. The fault lies with the prophets and priests (4:13–14), who ought to have known better. Their failure has led to the downfall of the nation. A wider failure on the part of the people themselves is also acknowledged (4:17). Yet this lament also ends on a note of hope: although Zion is being punished for her sins, that punishment will come to an end (4:22).

5:1–22 The Fifth and Final Lament takes the form of a prayer for the restoration of the people of God. It builds on the hints of hope found in the previous two laments. While once more pointing to the devastation of Jerusalem, the lament pleads with the Lord for restoration and renewal (5:21). Nevertheless, the compassion of the Lord cannot be taken for granted. The lament ends with an acknowledgment that the just anger of the Lord may lead to his total rejection of his people. Lamentations thus ends on a dark note. However, as history will show, that rejection is not total. The day is not that far ahead when the Lord will again turn the fortunes of Zion, and restore his people to their homeland.

EZEKIEL

The book of Ezekiel is the third of the four 'Major Prophets', and centres on the great issues of apostasy, sin and exile that also dominated both Isaiah and Jeremiah. Ezekiel deals with the period in the history of Judah in which the threat of exile became both real and urgent. Following the Babylonian defeat of the Egyptians at the battle of Carchemish (605 BC), the way was clear for the Babylonians to dominate the entire region that included Judah. This development is the background to some of Jeremiah's major prophecies concerning the threat of exile. That threat would be fulfilled in its totality in 586 BC, when the besieging Babylonian army would finally conquer Jerusalem and deport its population. However, an earlier deportation took place in 597 BC, when Jehoiachin and a group of about ten thousand of the population were deported. This group included Ezekiel.

Ezekiel thus prophesies about the state of affairs in Jerusalem from his exile near Babylon. There is no evidence that Ezekiel himself ever left Babylon. The exiles settled in Babylon along the 'river Kebar' (1:1), which was actually an irrigation canal. We learn that Ezekiel had been born into a priestly family, and would have expected to serve in the temple at Jerusalem. In 593, when he would normally have begun his priestly duties in the temple, Ezekiel is called to be a prophet to the exiles. This prophetic ministry is carried out entirely in Babylon, and covers the period 593–573 BC.

During the first period of his ministry, the temple at Jerusalem is still standing. The bulk of the book relates to this phase. Ezekiel's initial visions centre on the idolatrous worship that has been introduced into the temple. His message is simple: Jerusalem will fall for her sins. With the final fall of the city, and the destruction of the temple (586 BC), a new phase begins in his ministry (33:21–22). A ministry characterised by condemnation and judgment gives way to one of encouragement and reassurance. He gives the exiles oracles concerning the future restoration of his people. There will be a new temple, and a new land for the people of God.

11:1–25 The threat of divine punishment

12:1–28 Ezekiel departs with baggage as a sign of exile

13:1–23 The accusations against the false prophets

14:1–23 The penalty for idolatry

15:1–8 Jerusalem compared to a burned vine branch

16:1–63 Jerusalem and Samaria like harlots

17:1–24 An allegory of two eagles and a vine

18:1–32 Each is responsible for their own life before God

19:1–14 A lament for the fate of Israel

20:1–49 The hardness of heart of Israel

21:1–32 Babylon as the sword of the Lord

22:1–31 Israel's sins to be purged as in a furnace

23:1–49 Judgment against Jerusalem and Samaria

24:1–14 The end of Jerusalem

24:15–27 The death of Ezekiel's wife and the destruction of the temple at Jerusalem

Judgment against the nations

25:1–17 The oracles against Ammon, Moab, Edom and Philistia

26:1–28:19 The oracle against Tyre

28:20–26 The oracle against Sidon

29:1–32:32 The oracle against Egypt

Oracles of comfort and reassurance for the future

33:1–20 Ezekiel as the watchman for the house of the Lord

33:21–33 The fall of Jerusalem reported and explained

34:1–31 The oracle against false shepherds

35:1–15 The oracle against Edom

36:1–38 Israel's enemies will be overthrown

37:1–14 A vision of dry bones: the resurrection of the people

37:15–28 The vision of national reunification

38:1–39:29 The Lord's victory over all his enemies

The visions of a new temple and a new land

40:1–42:20 The vision of the new temple

43:1–27 The glory of the Lord returns to the temple

44:1–31 The consecration of the priests and Levites

45:1–25 The allocation of land and the celebration of the Passover

46:1–24 The responsibilities of the prince

47:1–12 A river of life fills the land

47:13–48:35 The land is allocated to its people

EZEKIEL 1:1–3:27
The Call of Ezekiel

1:1–28 The Living Creatures and the Glory of the Lord In his thirtieth year, Ezekiel is called by the Lord to be a prophet while in exile in Babylon (1:1). His age is significant: thirty was the age at which a priest would expect to begin service in

the temple. Ezekiel thus begins a service to the Lord of a rather different kind than he would have expected. The deportation that took Ezekiel to Babylon occurred in 597 BC; his call to be a prophet dates from 593 (1:2). His calling is set in the context of a vision of God (1:4–28), which brings out clearly the glory of God, a major theme for Ezekiel.

2:1–3:15 *Ezekiel's Call* The Lord then calls Ezekiel, referring to him as a 'son of man' – a term that will be used frequently (some 93 times) in this work. The Lord commands Ezekiel to tell the people exactly what he is told, whether they like it or not (2:7). As a token of his calling, he is given a scroll, on which are written words of 'lament and mourning and woe'. Ezekiel is told to eat this scroll, and discovers that it tastes sweet. But the words that Ezekiel is commanded to speak to the exiles at this stage are far from sweet. They are words of judgment and condemnation concerning Jerusalem. Overwhelmed by this vision and calling, Ezekiel rests for seven days. Then he is given details of what he is to say.

3:16–27 *Warning to Israel* Ezekiel is to be a 'watchman for the house of Israel' (3:17). Just as men were posted on the walls of Jerusalem to warn of impending attack or the arrival of messengers, so Ezekiel is to warn of impending judgment for his people through the word of the Lord. If Ezekiel fails to warn his people of this judgment, he will be held responsible for the consequences. If he warns them and they refuse to listen, their subsequent fate is their own responsibility (3:18–21). Ezekiel thus prepares for his prophetic ministry, forewarned that he will be dealing with a 'rebellious people', who are unlikely to listen to his words, however much authority they may possess.

EZEKIEL 4:1–24:27
The Judgment Against Jerusalem

4:1–5:17 *Siege of Jerusalem Symbolised* The oracles of judgment against Jerusalem now begin. A series of dramatic symbolic acts conveys the seriousness of the sin of Jerusalem. First, Ezekiel takes a block of clay on which he is to draw Jerusalem under siege (4:1–3). He is then asked to lie first on his left, and then on his right, side (4:4–8). This action symbolises the sin of the northern kingdom of Israel and the southern kingdom of Judah. It is not quite clear what the numbers 390 and 40 signify. It is possible that 390 refers to the number of years between Solomon's lapse into disobedience and the fall of Jerusalem, and that 40 refers to the number of years for which Manasseh encouraged pagan practices in Judah.

The next image involves Ezekiel imitating the conditions that exist inside a city under siege (4:9–17), in which the population is reduced to eating a diet of grain and vegetables, and using dung as fuel. This is followed by the shaving of Ezekiel's head, in which a third of his hair is burnt, a third cut with a sword, and a third scattered in the wind (5:1–4). This action symbolises the fate of the population of Jerusalem. For the benefit of those who see these actions but fail to understand their meaning, a detailed explanation is then provided (5:5–17). Jerusalem will be besieged. A third of her population will die of the plague or famine, a third will be killed and a third will be scattered among the nations.

6:1–7:27 *Prophecy Against the Mountains of Israel* Ezekiel turns his attention to the mountains of Israel, where the high places and other sites of pagan worship and practices are located (6:1–14). These will all be destroyed, along with those who worship at them. Only some of the people will be allowed to survive. A disaster is about to happen, and the

population of Judah will be carried off in chains (7:1–27). The detestable pagan practices that are going on in Judah at this moment will·be the cause of her downfall and total humiliation.

8:1–9:11 Idolatry in the Temple; Idolaters Killed Detestable practices are not found merely in the high places of the mountains of Israel. They are even taking place inside the temple at Jerusalem, supposedly the most holy place in Judah (8:1–18). Ezekiel relates how he is caught up by the Spirit, and taken to Jerusalem, where he sees the glory of the Lord in the temple. Yet around the temple all kinds of pagan rites are taking place. The inhabitants of Jerusalem are even worshipping Tammuz, the Babylonian fertility god (8:14). Ezekiel is appalled. However, he is not alone. It is clear that some in Jerusalem are shocked at what has happened. In his vision, Ezekiel sees these faithful people being marked on the forehead with the letter 'taw' – the last letter of the Hebrew alphabet, which looks like a cross (9:4). (This represents a fascinating anticipation of the Christian practice of marking believers with a cross in baptism.) They will be spared from the destruction that follows.

10:1–11:25 The Glory Departs from the Temple, but the Return of Israel Promised Ezekiel then sees the glory of the Lord departing from the temple (10:1–20). In a series of images that recall the opening vision of the prophecy by the river Kebar, Ezekiel sees the glory of the Lord filling the temple. But it does not stay there. Slowly and majestically it crosses the threshold of the temple. The Lord has left his temple. No longer is it protected

through his presence. As if to confirm the appalling spiritual state of Jerusalem, Ezekiel is then allowed to overhear the leaders of the city talking. They are confident that the threat of Babylonian attack has receded. They can build houses once more. However, the reality is utterly different. Destruction is on its way to the house of Israel (11:1–15). Nonetheless, a note of consolation creeps in at this point (11:16–25). Israel will be scattered among the nations, but the Lord will bring the people back home. Their hearts of stone will be replaced by hearts of flesh. The covenant will be renewed once more.

12:1–14:23 The Exile Symbolised; Judgment Inescapable However, the theme of exile comes to the fore once more. Ezekiel is commanded to perform a symbolic act to bring home the ultimate fate of his people. He is told to pack his belongings, and put them over his shoulder. This will be a symbol of the long trudge into exile on the part of his people (12:1–28). Despite all the platitudes and smooth words of the false prophets, there can be no escape from the punishment of exile. These false prophets speak of peace when there is no peace. They have no authority to speak on God's behalf (13:1–16), and idolatry cannot be tolerated. The people of Jerusalem have deserted the Lord for foreign idols. Now the Lord will cut off such people from himself (13:17–14:11). There can be no escape from the forthcoming judgment. There will be survivors, but the resulting devastation will make it undeniably clear that the Lord is in control (14:12–23).

15:1–8 Jerusalem, a Useless Vine A series of prophecies then focuses on Jerusalem

itself. Jerusalem is likened to a vine – an image that is often used to refer to Israel (Ps 80:8–13; see also the related image of Israel as an unproductive vineyard in Isa 5:1–7). Where other prophets, such as Isaiah, at least allowed that Israel brought forth *some* fruit (even if it was poor in quality), Ezekiel seems to treat Jerusalem as utterly useless. At best, the vine of Jerusalem will make good firewood.

16:1–63 An Allegory of Unfaithful Jerusalem

A further parable follows, which likens Jerusalem to an infant abandoned at birth, without any proper afterbirth care or attention. Yet the Lord took compassion on this abandoned child, gave her good food, and tended her throughout her youth. And the Lord's reward for all this? The child he tenderly nourished has become a prostitute (16:1–19). The implication of this prophecy seems to be that Jerusalem's origins lay in paganism. The city was only captured from the Jebusites by David (2Sa 5:6–9). Ezekiel's prophecy seems to suggest that her pagan past is reasserting itself. This is certainly the implication of the description of Jerusalem's infidelity to the Lord with surrounding nations (16:20–34).

The result of this degeneration is then made unambiguously clear: Jerusalem will be stripped naked in front of her lovers, so that they may see her in all her shame. The nations on whom she trusted will see her besieged and destroyed. What Jerusalem has done makes Sodom look respectable (16:35–52). Yet even in this prophecy of judgment, a ray of hope appears. Jerusalem will eventually be restored – but not before these things have happened (16:53–63).

17:1–24 Two Eagles and a Vine

This prophecy is followed by a parable of two eagles and a vine (17:1–24). The two eagles in question are Nebuchadnezzar (17:3) and an Egyptian pharaoh (17:7; the most likely candidate is Hophra). Ezekiel's vision is that of the Babylonians carrying off some of the inhabitants of Jerusalem (the 'Lebanon' of 17:3) to Babylon (the 'city of traders'). There they flourish. But the remaining inhabitants of Jerusalem become involved with Egypt, and will wither. The meaning of the parable is explained in detail (17:11–21). However, the Lord himself will ensure that his people will prosper. He will replant them, and ensure their security and prosperity (17:22–24).

18:1–19:14 The Soul Who Sins Will Die

A powerful affirmation of individual responsibility and the reality of the Lord's forgiveness follows. Sons will not be punished for the sins of their fathers. And those who truly repent will live. Ezekiel makes it clear that the Lord is pleased when the wicked turn from their ways and live (18:1–32). The Lord takes no pleasure in the death of sinners. He wishes them to repent, and enjoy the privilege of continued life. The implication is clear. Jerusalem has only herself to blame for her present sorry state. There is little point in listing the sins of the past. It is the disobedience of the present that matters. Yet repentance remains a real possibility if only they will realise the extent of their sin, and turn away from it. Otherwise, their princes will be uprooted and destroyed (19:1–14).

20:1–49 Rebellious Israel; Judgment and Restoration The rebellious nature of Israel is again asserted in uncompromising terms (20:1–29). The prophecy in question dates from 591 BC, and takes a familiar form. Ezekiel traces the history of Israel's rebellion against the Lord from the time of their stay in Egypt to the entry into the promised land. It is a continuous catalogue of failure and rebellion on the part of Israel, and pity and compassion on the part of the Lord. But now the time has come for judgment. Yet, once more, a note of hope is sounded. There will be restoration after this judgment (20:30–49).

21:1–23:49 Babylon, God's Sword of Judgment Babylon is now unambiguously identified as the sword by which the Lord will punish his people (21:1–32). Even now, the sword is about to be drawn from its scabbard, and used against both the righteous and the wicked in Jerusalem. Ezekiel's vision of destruction suggests that all will perish in the consuming wrath of the Lord. The house of Israel has sinned to such an extent that she has become dross in the sight of the Lord. The precious metal of the people of God will be refined in a fierce heat, in order that she may be purified (22:1–31). In the parable that follows (23:1–49), Judah's political alliances with foreign powers are compared in detail with prostitution. Judah and Israel, who seem to be represented by the sisters, have abandoned the Lord in favour of other lovers. Now the price must be paid.

24:1–27 The Cooking Pot The next prophecy dates from early in 588 BC. The news from Jerusalem is grim. The Babylonians have laid siege to Jerusalem. Ezekiel's prophecy makes use of the image of a cooking pot. The pot represents Jerusalem, which was earlier congratulating itself on the very small scale of the deportations of 597 BC. All the best pieces of meat were left in the pot. But now the heat has been turned up. The pot will boil dry. The remaining meat will burn. In other words, Jerusalem will be destroyed (24:1–14). This section ends with the death of Ezekiel's wife (24:15–27).

EZEKIEL 25:1–32:32
Oracles Against the Nations

The next major section of the prophecy deals with the nations around Judah. This pattern of oracles has already been found in the prophecies of Isaiah and Jeremiah. Judgment on Judah does not in any way mean that her neighbours are exempted. The basic theme set out in the prophetic writings is that judgment begins within the household of faith, but is not restricted to it.

The seven oracles here presented deal with traditional enemies of Judah – the nations of Ammon (25:1–7), Moab (25:8–11), Edom (25:12–14), Philistia (25:15–17), Tyre (26:1–28:19), Sidon (28:20–26) and Egypt (29:1–32:32). The oracles against Tyre and Egypt are substantially more lengthy than the remainder. The basic theme is that the nations shall know that God is the Lord through his mighty acts, including the devastation that will come to them. Babylon is not included in this list of nations. It is, however, referred to as the agent through which the Lord will bring punishment to these proud nations,

such as Tyre (26:7–14) and Egypt (30:10–12).

It is important to notice that Ezekiel, in common with the other great prophets, sees the Lord as working out his purposes through pagan nations. Even though they do not acknowledge him as Lord, they are nevertheless instruments of his providence. For Isaiah, Assyria was the rod of God's wrath against his faithless people; yet when Assyria become arrogant, she was punished by Babylon. Once more, a pagan nation served to bring about God's purposes in history. Likewise, when Babylon had exceeded her usefulness to the Lord, she in turn was brought down by Cyrus the Great – again, seen as the instrument of God's justice. Indeed, Isaiah even goes so far as to declare that Cyrus was 'his anointed' (Isa 45:1), using language normally reserved for the kings and priests of Israel. Jeremiah also sees Babylon as God's chosen instrument for the discipline and purification of his people.

EZEKIEL 33:1–39:29
The Promise of Future Comfort and Restoration

33:1–20 Ezekiel a Watchman The next major section of the book is to be dated from after the fall of Jerusalem. Up to this point, Ezekiel's prophecies have been dominated by the themes of judgment and exile. Now, the themes of hope and restoration begin to gain the ascendancy. Although a number of passages are of a more critical and judgmental nature, there is a distinct change of mood. The section opens with a call for repentance on the part of the people. The Lord takes no pleasure in the death of anyone, and

would much rather that sinners turn to him in repentance, and live. The tone of the prophecy is still critical, however.

33:21–33 Jerusalem's Fall Explained Up to this point, there has been no confirmation of any of the events Ezekiel has prophesied. Jerusalem was at a great distance from Babylon. It took Ezra some four months to make the journey (Ezr 7:8–9) under what were clearly regarded as good conditions. The only means by which news of the fall of Jerusalem could reach Babylon was by messenger. The two key events are the fall of the city walls and the burning of the temple (2Ki 25:3–4, 8–9), which can be dated to 18 July and 14 August 586. The earliest that any confirmation of these events could be expected to reach the exiles in Babylon would thus have been in December 586. In a prophecy that is to be dated to 8 January 585, nearly five months after the destruction of the temple, Ezekiel receives confirmation from someone who has managed to escape from Jerusalem that these events have indeed taken place (33:21–22). Now that the fall of the city is public knowledge, Ezekiel is free to speak of the hope of restoration.

34:1–31 Shepherds and Sheep The first major prophecy of restoration soon follows. The Lord declares that the 'shepherds of Israel' (a term that clearly includes Israel's kings, priests and prophets) have failed her utterly. As a result, the Lord's people (who are here compared to sheep) have been scattered. After severely criticising the shepherds for their lack of responsibility, the Lord declares that he himself will be the shepherd of his people. He will gather

them from the places to which they have been scattered and restore them. He will lead them to safe pastures, bind up their wounds, bring back the strays and strengthen the weak. This great passage echoes themes developed elsewhere (such as Ps 23:1–6), especially in the coming of Jesus Christ as the good shepherd, who will lay down his life for his sheep (Jn 10:11–18).

35:1–36 A Prophecy to the Mountains of Israel
The prophecy then turns to condemn Edom for rejoicing over the fate of Israel (35:1–15). In a great prophecy of restoration, addressed to the 'mountains of Israel', the Lord promises that he will again restore them to their former state. They will be inhabited again, and their ruins will be rebuilt (36:1–12). The Lord will bring his people home from the places to which they have been scattered. National restoration will be accompanied by personal renewal, as hearts of stone are replaced by hearts of flesh (36:13–38).

37:1–14 The Valley of Dry Bones
The great theme of restoration of the people then reaches a climax with the vision of the dry bones. The prophet receives a vision of a valley full of dry bones. It is clear that they are totally dead and seem to be beyond any hope of coming back to life, in much the same way as the people of God seem to be beyond any hope of resuscitation. Yet the Lord has other ideas. In a remarkable act, which has direct parallels with the account of the creation of Adam (Ge 2:7), the Lord assembles the bones into bodies and breathes life into them. In the same way, the Lord will breathe new life into his

people and restore them. The situation may seem hopeless: nevertheless, the same Lord who can restore life to dry bones will also restore his people.

Although the primary focus of this prophecy is the rescue of Jerusalem from Babylon, and its restoration to its homeland, it is impossible to read the later parts of this passage (37:12–14) without anticipating the great gospel hope of resurrection to eternal life.

37:15–39:29 One Nation Under One King
The vision is then supplemented with a prophecy concerning a future king who, like David, will rule over his people. Under his rule, Jerusalem will again know all the benefits of the covenant of the Lord, including the presence of the Lord among his people (37:15–28). This section concludes with a detailed prophecy against 'Gog' (38:1–39:29). It is not clear who this figure is. What is clear, however, is the firm commitment on the part of the Lord to bring his people back from captivity, and pour out his Spirit on them (39:25–29).

EZEKIEL 40:1–48:35
The New Temple and the New Land

40:1–42:20 The New Temple
The final part of this great prophecy now opens. Dating from 573 BC, the prophecy centres on visions of the restored temple and people. The first vision concerns the temple. Ezekiel's vision of the temple suggests a building comparable to Solomon's great architectural achievement, but with an expanded courtyard area. It is clear that Ezekiel's vision points to the restoration of a temple at least as impressive as Solomon's, but devoid of all the pagan

influences that had crept into the temple area and worship under successive kings of Judah.

43:1–48:35 *The Glory Returns to the Temple* The climax of this vision is now reached. Earlier, Ezekiel had suffered the pain of seeing the glory of the Lord leaving the temple, as a sign of the Lord's forsaking his rebellious people (10:1–22). He had spoken of the restoration of that presence (e.g., 37:27); and now, in his vision, Ezekiel sees that presence being restored. The glory of the Lord returns to the new temple (43:1–5). The Lord will again dwell among his people. The vision of the restored temple now continues (43:6–48:35), embracing every aspect of the life of the nation – its princes, priests and boundaries. But it is clear that the central theme is that the Lord once more will dwell among his people. And that is why, the prophet concludes, the city of Jerusalem shall henceforth be called by a different name: 'THE LORD IS THERE' (48:35).

DANIEL

The book of Daniel is the fourth and final part of the 'Major Prophets'. The book deals with events that take place while Jerusalem is in exile in Babylonia. Under successive Babylonian kings, a series of deportations takes place from Judah. The most significant is in 586 BC, when Jerusalem is laid waste after the final fall of the city. However, there have also been earlier deportations, including that of 597, when Jehoiachin and about ten thousand people (including the prophet Ezekiel) were deported. Although this would seem to be the most natural date for the deportation of Daniel and his colleagues, the book of Daniel itself suggests that there were limited deportations in the aftermath of the battle of Carchemish in 605 BC. The Babylonians, having heavily defeated the Egyptians, turned their attention to subduing what they termed 'Hatti-land', which included Judah. This policy of subjugation may have included deportation.

The book of Daniel emphasises the importance of remaining faithful to God, even under difficult circumstances, and illustrates this from the story of Daniel and his three companions in Babylon. The later part of the book consists of visions of coming judgment and retribution, which often include symbols of peoples and nations. This style of writing, which is usually referred to as 'apocalyptic', emphasises God's sovereign control over history, and his ultimate victory over forces that may seem to have gained the upper hand for the time being.

The final chapters of the book have often been the subject of considerable speculation, with some writers finding in them precise prophecies of modern events, such as the rise of Nazi Germany or the Soviet Union. It is, however, best to see these visions as relating to the rise and fall of empires in the ancient world, rather than attempting to use them to predict the future. The primary purpose of these visions is to reassure those who initially received them.

OUTLINE

Daniel and his friends in exile

1:1–21 Daniel and his three friends exiled to Babylon

2:1–49 Nebuchadnezzar has a dream, which Daniel, where others failed, succeeds in interpreting to him

3:1–30 Shadrach, Meshach and Abednego refuse to worship an image and are thrown into a furnace

4:1–37 Nebuchadnezzar's second dream

5:1–30 Belshazzar's feast interrupted by writing on the wall, which Daniel interprets

6:1–28 Darius prohibits prayer to any but himself; Daniel's disobedience leads to his being thrown into the lions' den

Daniel's visions of the future

7:1–28 The vision of the four beasts and the son of man

8:1–27 The vision of the ram defeated by the goat

DANIEL 1:1–6:28
The Story of Daniel

1:1–21 Daniel's Training in Babylon We are introduced to Daniel and his three companions, who have been deported to Babylon during recent Babylonian attacks on the region by Nebuchadnezzar. There are obvious similarities between the stories of Joseph and Daniel. Both concern Jews who find themselves carried off to foreign countries, and eventually manage to work their way into important positions within the royal administration of these countries. Despite the refusal of Daniel and his friends to compromise their obedience to the God of Israel by eating the royal

---

Does my work matter to God?

Although the workplace is where most of us spend most of our time, we can sometimes feel that our work there is less important than work 'in church', and certainly less important than the work of church leaders. But such thinking is quite unbiblical.

Jesus said his Father was 'always at his work' (Jn 5:17), unlike in ancient religions whose gods lazed around while human slaves served them. When we first encounter God in the Bible, he is working on creation. Work was a gift to Adam, not a curse (Ge 2:15), part of being created in God's image. Work isn't the same as 'our job', however (otherwise the stay-at-home parents and carers, the unemployed and the retired would be excluded from its blessing). Work is any kind of productive activity, and as such is an expression of worship to God.

The clergy–laity divide that arose in the church, valuing 'church' work more highly than 'secular' work', is unbiblical. None of the key people God used in the Bible were 'clergy'. Abraham was a nomad; Amos was a shepherd and farmer; Daniel was a servant in a pagan royal household; Paul was a tentmaker – and all continued their 'secular' work while God used them.

The sacred–secular divide crept into the church from Greek culture where work was seen as a curse or, at best, a necessary evil, an idea that was deeply entrenched by the Middle Ages. But Martin Luther rejected this as unbiblical, reclaiming the idea of vocation (divine calling) for all who worked in whatever way, seeing this as a means of serving both God and neighbour. God wants his people today to reclaim the workplace, not just as a mission field but as a place to demonstrate his kingdom rule, confident he is with them and blessing what they do.

food and wine (which could well have been offered to idols), they are valued on account of their wisdom, and are consulted regularly by the king.

2:1–49 *Nebuchadnezzar's Dream* Like Pharaoh before him, Nebuchadnezzar has a dream, which neither he nor his pagan astrologers can make sense of. And, just as Pharaoh consulted Joseph, so the king eventually consults Daniel (2:1–26). Daniel's interpretation of the dream is prophetic: the great power and authority of Nebuchadnezzar will eventually give way to a series of lesser realms. In the end, God himself will establish a kingdom that shall not be destroyed (2:27–45). This interpretation of the dream pleases the king, and he rewards Daniel for his efforts (2:46–49).

3:1–30 *The Image of Gold and the Blazing Furnace* Yet the favour found by Daniel in the sight of the king seems to have been relatively short-lived. The king orders an enormous image of himself to be made, and set up near Babylon. He requires all his officials to bow down and worship the image, as a sign of obedience to the king himself (3:1–7). All duly do – except Daniel and his companions, who remain faithful to the command not to worship any image (Ex 20:3–5). This failure to comply with the king's instructions is reported by the astrologers, presumably piqued at Daniel's success at interpreting the dream that had baffled them. As a result, Daniel's companions (here referred to by their Babylonian names, Shadrach, Meshach and Abednego) are summoned before the king and ordered to comply.

(Daniel himself is not mentioned in this narrative.) On their refusal, they are condemned to death, and thrown into a furnace. Their deliverance from its heat moves the king to acknowledge the greatness of their God (3:8–30).

4:1–5:30 *Nebuchadnezzar's Dream of a Tree and the Writing on the Wall* Daniel now shows himself once more to be a divinely inspired interpreter of dreams (4:1–37). The dream relates to the downfall of Nebuchadnezzar, and his insanity. A further instance of Daniel's God-given ability to interpret things that baffle everyone else then follows.

The event in question is a banquet, thrown by Belshazzar, Nebuchadnezzar's successor as king (5:1–30), which is disrupted by the appearance of a hand writing upon the wall. Deeply shocked, the king invites the astrologers and magicians to attempt to interpret the words the hand has written. They fail. Daniel is then summoned, and interprets the words as referring to God's judgment on the king. The words are MENE, MENE, TEKEL and PARSIN, ambiguous terms that Daniel interprets as referring to the overthrow of Belshazzar by the Medes and Persians. The subsequent assassination of the king and the rise of 'Darius the Mede' (possibly the name by which Cyrus the Great was known in Babylon) demonstrates once more the extent of Daniel's wisdom.

6:1–28 *Daniel in the Den of Lions* Under Darius, Daniel continues to prosper, being appointed as one of a triumvirate who is to administer his extensive realms. So successful is Daniel that it seems likely he will become the king's favourite. However,

professional jealousy puts an end to all this. His rivals attempt to end his promotion prospects (not to mention his life). The only grounds for accusation lie in the worship of God. In all other respects he is blameless (6:1–5). There is an important point here, also echoed in 1 Peter: believers must ensure that the only charges the world can lay against them relate to their faith in God, and not to their moral conduct.

Daniel's rivals gain the king's approval (without alerting him to their vendetta against Daniel) for a new law which will lay down that no one may worship any other god than Darius himself. Daniel duly disregards this order, and prays to God. (Notice, however, that he does so in private, so as not to draw public attention to his actions and render himself guilty of some kind of public posturing.) However, knowing that he will pray to God in this way, his enemies burst in on him, discover him at prayer, and demand that the king should throw him into the lion's den. The king is clearly reluctant to do so and demonstrates his affection for Daniel; but it must be done (6:6–18). However, Daniel is delivered from certain death by God, to the evident relief of the king. Moreover, there is an evangelistic dimension to this action: Darius, deeply impressed with the power and faithfulness of the God of Daniel, orders that this God should now be worshipped in his realm (6:19–28).

DANIEL 7:1–12:13
The Visions of the End

The style of the book now changes. A series of visions received by Daniel is set out at some length. In reflecting on these images, we must be careful not to misinterpret them, or to apply them without thought to other periods in history, such as our own. The prophecies here recorded were given to Daniel, with his own situation in mind. They cannot

Visions in Daniel

Chapters 7–12 contain Daniel's series of strange – sometimes nightmarish – visions. This is sometimes referred to as apocalyptic material – symbolic, visionary, and prophetic literature concerned with the supernatural realm and the end of the world. The symbolism is very complicated, but basically the visions speak about God's perspective on Israel's role among the nations around that time, and also point to the *end* of time when God will finally reveal his power. They show that God is in control of history. (They also contain references to a mysterious son of man figure that Jesus interpreted as references to himself.):

- a vision of four beasts (Chapter 7)
- a vision of two animals (Chapter 8)
- a vision of an angel (Chapter 9:21–27)
- a vision of a man (Chapter 10:5–14) – possibly part of the preceding vision
- a vision of the panorama of the centuries – ending with the last act in world history (Chapter 11–12)

be treated as a detailed prediction of every major event of world history up until the present day. Rather, they are to be seen as allowing Daniel a vision of the future of the empire that has taken him captive, so that he may face the present in the knowledge of what God has prepared for him and his people.

7:1–28 Daniel's Dream of Four Beasts The first major vision is of four beasts: a lion, a bear, a leopard and an unidentified beast which is clearly terrifying in its appearance. Each of the beasts represents an empire: the lion corresponds to the Babylonian Empire, the bear to the Medo-Persian Empire, the leopard to the empire established by Alexander the Great, and the fourth beast appears to symbolise the Roman Empire. The basic point being made is that Babylon will give way to other empires, which will eventually all be succeeded by the reign of God himself, who will give victory to his people.

This vision is of particular importance to Christian readers, for two reasons. First, the vision speaks of 'one like a son of man' (7:13–14), who comes on the clouds and is given authority by God (here referred to as the 'Ancient of Days') to rule over the nations, who worship him. Jesus Christ understood this to refer to himself, especially his coming in triumph to judge the world at the end of time (see Mt 24:27–31; Mk 14:62; Rev 1:17). Secondly, the reference to the fourth beast appears to be a reference to the Roman Empire – the empire that persecuted the followers of Jesus Christ. The Christian reader of this prophecy can see the fulfilment of this prophecy as a reign of terror, but also has the assurance that such terror will not triumph over the people of God.

8:1–27 Daniel's Vision of a Ram and a Goat The second vision features a ram and a goat. The ram represents the Medo-Persian kings, and the goat the king of the empire established by Alexander the Great (here referred to as the 'king of Greece'). The latter will overwhelm and displace the former. A later part of the prophecy (8:23–25) refers to the coming of Antiochus IV, one of the most vicious persecutors of the Jews.

9:1–11:1 Daniel's Prayer The impact of these visions is clearly considerable, especially when the news of the fall of Jerusalem comes through. In response, Daniel prays one of the most thoughtful and helpful prayers of the Old Testament (9:1–27). The prayer is an affirmation of the compassion, greatness, love and faithfulness of God, even in the face of the sin and rebellion of his people. The prayer appeals to God in his righteousness and mercy to deliver his people from their predicament. Daniel makes it clear that the grounds of this prayer lie not in any appeal to human righteousness, but to the great mercy of God himself (9:18). In response, Daniel receives an assurance concerning the future of Jerusalem, and the coming of the 'Anointed One' (9:25). This sense of hope is confirmed by a vision (10:1–11:1), in which he feels himself to be strengthened and encouraged by God.

11:2–12:13 The Kings of the South and the North; the End Times Finally, Daniel

receives another vision, focusing on later kings, who will reign during the period of Greek rule in the region (11:2–12:13). Of particular importance is the reference to the 'abomination that causes desolation' (11:31). This is widely regarded as a prophecy of destruction within the Jerusalem temple or acts of desecration against it, such as those that took place under Antiochus IV in 169 BC. This is followed by prophecies concerning an unknown king (11:36–45), and a final assurance that, whatever may happen in the future, the Lord will remain faithful to his people (12:1–13).

Daniel himself can rest assured that, even though he is in exile in Babylon, he will one day receive his 'allotted inheritance' (12:13). This passage is particularly important, on account of its clear references to a resurrection to life. In his closing words, the prophet looks ahead to the secure knowledge of resurrection and eternal life, which is one of the greatest joys of the Christian gospel.

HOSEA

A new section of the Old Testament now opens, usually referred to as 'the Minor Prophets'. This term does not in any way imply that their prophecies are of lesser value than those of the 'Major Prophets', such as Isaiah. It simply refers to the fact that the twelve books that now follow are shorter than works such as Isaiah or Jeremiah.

Hosea, the first of these writings, dates from the middle of the 8th century BC. It is clear that Hosea, like Amos, comes from the northern kingdom of Israel, and prophesies to it during its final days before it is destroyed by the Assyrians, and its peoples are taken off into exile. Despite this, however, the book itself appears to have been written in the southern kingdom of Judah, suggesting that Hosea may have fled to the safety of this region after the fall of Israel.

HOSEA 1:1–3:5
The Faithlessness of Israel

1:1–11 Hosea's Wife and Children The book opens by describing Hosea's family life. In response to the Lord's prompting, Hosea marries Gomer, a woman who is already guilty of adultery. After bearing Hosea a son, she subsequently has two further children. The wording of the passages referring to these two later children is significant (1:6, 8): they are not attributed to Hosea. It seems that they are the children of another man. In this story of past and present unfaithfulness, we are to see a symbol of Israel's unfaithfulness to the Lord. Each of the children is given a name that symbolises the problems that have arisen between the Lord and his people. In

particular, Lo-Ruhamah (which literally means 'not loved') points to the utter exasperation of the Lord at the rebelliousness of his own people, which leads to his decision to reject them – a decision that can be seen summarised in the name of the third child Lo-Ammi (which literally means 'not my people').

The covenant formula is thus reversed. Where the Lord once declared that he was Israel's God, and they were his people, we now find a terse statement to the effect that 'you are not my people, and I am not your God' (1:8). However, this is immediately followed by a promise of future restoration (1:9–11). This follows a pattern, which is evident in the writings of the major prophets, of tempering anger with compassion. Even though Israel is being judged for her unfaithfulness, she is being promised that restoration lies on the far side of that judgment.

2:1–23 Israel Punished and Restored Hosea is totally dominated by the theme of the unfaithfulness of the northern kingdom of Israel to her Lord. This is clear from the song that follows, which speaks of Israel's abandonment of the God who loves her, in order to chase after other

Does marriage still matter to God?

In days when there is great diversity in domestic and family arrangements, does marriage still matter? If two people (of whatever sex) love each other, isn't it enough for them just to live together?

While not wishing to judge others' lifestyles, Christians are called to follow the Bible's teaching about relationships. The Bible makes clear that God's intention for intimate relationships is for one man to live faithfully with one woman throughout their lives, the two becoming one (Ge 2:24), something both Jesus and Paul reaffirmed (Mt 19:4–6; Eph 5:31), and something Hosea was determined to live out. When Jewish leaders looked to find ways around this, Jesus made the challenge of marriage even more demanding, such was his high esteem of it (Mt 19:1–12).

Of course, Adam and Eve didn't have a wedding ceremony; and throughout the biblical period the actual way of getting married seems to have varied. But at the heart of marriage always lay the concept of *covenant* – a binding commitment to relationship. This is the word that the Bible uses of God's relationship with people – one he has no intention of breaking and in which he gives himself fully and permanently. And this is what he calls a man and woman to in marriage: a lifelong, binding, committed relationship, declared in public, with both parties resolved to make it work, no matter what happens. Any relationship without such a covenant at its heart is therefore a pale reflection of what God intends for marriage and cannot expect his blessing on it.

The Bible's high view of marriage is reflected in the New Testament's describing the church as 'the bride of Christ' (2Co 11:2; Eph 5:25–32; Rev 19:7; 21:2, 9), a powerful image of the union between Jesus and his church, and a model for every married couple.

gods – a clear reference to Israel's frequent lapses into paganism, which are such a conspicuous feature of her national life at this stage. Canaanite religious practices and beliefs have crept into every aspect of national life, and have compromised her special relationship with the Lord. Yet the Lord speaks of his intention to woo Israel once more. He will court her once more, in an attempt to bring back the days of their first love in Egypt (2:14–19).

3:1–5 Hosea's Reconciliation with His Wife

Hosea's final reconciliation with his wife is thus to be seen as more than the happy resolution of a domestic situation. It is a symbol of the reconciliation the Lord desires to have with his faithless people Israel. Indeed, it is more than that. It is also a statement of hope that what once seemed an impossible outcome in the context of a personal relationship might also be possible between the Lord and his people.

HOSEA 4:1–10:15
Israel's Disobedience and Punishment

4:1–5:15 The Charge Against Israel The prophecy of Hosea is dominated by the accusation that Israel has flouted her covenant relationship with the Lord. Gomer's adultery is to be seen as a symbol of the state of Israel's relationship with the Lord. She has abandoned him for other short-term relationships, in which instant gratification has overshadowed all other considerations. What follows documents in some detail Israel's religious adultery and faithlessness. They have deserted the Lord for idols and pagan altars (4:1–19). Their priests have failed to stop this lapse into paganism. Their leaders have even turned to Assyria for help, when they ought to have trusted in the Lord (5:1–15).

6:1–7:16 Israel Unrepentant One of the most beautiful passages in Hosea's prophecy then follows. It speaks of the Lord's love for his people, and his passionate desire to bind their wounds and restore them. It is the Lord who has wounded his people. It is he who will restore them. The coming of the Lord is compared to the arrival of the rains that water the earth and give it nourishment. In this passage, the prophet envisages his people turning in repentance to the Lord (6:1–3). However, this is only a dream. We are immediately returned to the harsh reality, in which Israel stubbornly refuses to do anything of the sort (6:4–7:16). Judgment must therefore follow.

It is interesting to notice the asides to Judah in this prophecy. Although the prophecy is directed against the northern kingdom of Israel, every now and then reference is made to Judah – usually along the lines 'and this applies to you as well, Judah'. An example of this is seen at 6:11; others can be found at 4:15, 5:5, 5:10 and 11:12. In no way is Judah being allowed to gloat over either the misfortune or the sins of her northern neighbour. She is just as vulnerable.

8:1–10:15 Israel to Reap the Whirlwind Israel's violation of the covenant with the Lord is then detailed. Israel has lapsed into idolatry, chosen kings whom the Lord did not want and forgotten the God who has so clearly not forgotten her (8:1–14). A day of reckoning is at hand

(9:1–9). Even so, the Lord returns to tender memories of Israel in her youth, when she first came out of Egypt (9:10). She was young and innocent in those days. Then she entered Canaan, and lapsed (9:11–17). As Israel increased in prosperity, she came to rely more and more on that prosperity and her material resources, and less and less on the Lord. The people turned to worship tangible gods, such as idols (10:1–15).

HOSEA 11:1–14:9
The Promise of Restoration

11:1–11 God's Love for Israel This alienation makes the memory of the first period of the love between the Lord and his people, as they left Egypt together, all the more difficult to bear. In those days, the Lord and his people were close (11:1). Like a growing child, however, Israel grew away from the Lord and forgot the Lord's kindness during her youth (11:2–4). Why has Israel forsaken the Lord for such things? Justice demands that Israel be punished. Yet the Lord, in his compassion, is reluctant to do so. How can he turn against his own people? The Lord thus looks forward to the restoration that lies beyond the punishment that must inevitably come to his disobedient people (11:5–11).

11:12–14:9 Repentance to Bring Blessing Israel's sin is then affirmed once more (11:12–12:14), with further illustrations of its nature and extent. Israel has gained in wealth, not always through honest means; and the people have used their wealth to pay tribute to foreign powers. What about the Lord? Why do they not pay tribute to him? Israel has become crippled through her worship of foreign gods and submission to foreign powers. The people of Israel demanded a king of the Lord; and when the Lord granted them that request, they ended up by trusting in kings rather than in him (13:1–16). Yet this catalogue of sin and proclamation of judgment is not the last word of the Lord to his people. In a tender vision, the prophet can still see his people declaring their intention to return to the Lord, having admitted that they need him badly. In his compassion, the Lord will heal their wounds and restore them to fellowship with him (14:1–9).

JOEL

Little is known about Joel, apart from the name of his father. The prophecy contained in this book is difficult to date, as there are no clear references to any historical events that would allow even a provisional date to be assigned to this work. Some have suggested that the work may date from as early as the 9th century. Others point to a later date, suggesting that the work may have been written after the return from exile.

1:1–2:11 An Invasion of Locusts The central theme of the work is the coming of the 'Day of the LORD'. The occasion of the opening prophecies can be found in a disaster that had taken place. A rural economy, which was heavily dependent on crops for both human and animal feed, had been devastated through a plague of locusts. Joel describes the havoc and misery caused by the locusts in some detail, and interprets this as a sign of a coming judgment, in which the Lord will devastate his people (1:1–20). A day of darkness is at hand, in which destruction will come to Zion (2:1–11). Although the reference is primarily to the coming of a vast cloud of locusts, it is clear that Joel sees in this catastrophe a sign of the Lord's judgment.

2:12–27 The Lord's Answer This disaster is intended to move a complacent people to repentance. This repentance must be heartfelt and thorough. The Lord does not want outward signs of repentance (such as the tearing of clothes). What is being demanded is inner transformation: 'Rend your heart and not your garments'

(2:13). Even at this late stage, with the threat of judgment and destruction there for all to see, it is not too late to repent. This section is followed by a prophecy of restoration, which is clearly related to the demand for repentance. The land may have been devastated. It will be restored. The ground will once more produce grain, wine and oil. The army of locusts will die and rot (2:18–20). Soon the misery and shame of the years of the locusts will be forgotten.

2:28–32 The Day of the Lord This promise of restoration is then supplemented with a still greater hope: the Spirit of the Lord will be poured out on all people – male and female, old and young. This will be a day of salvation, on which everyone who calls on the name of the Lord will be saved. This great prophecy would be fulfilled at Pentecost, when the Holy Spirit came with great power and inaugurated the public ministry and preaching of the Christian church (Ac 2:16–21). On account of the resurrection, Jesus Christ has been publicly declared to be Lord. As a result, anyone who calls on his name will be saved. This prophecy of Joel provides one of the most important pointers to the great work of God that lay ahead as a result of the coming of Jesus Christ.

3:1–21 Blessings for God's People The final chapter of the book looks ahead to the restoration of both Judah and Jerusalem, in which all nations will be brought to judgment (3:1–3). The sins of the enemies of Israel are listed, including selling children into prostitution and Jews to the Greeks. With the restoration of Israel, the achievements of her enemies have been undone. The enemies of Israel will be routed and destroyed by the Lord in his judgment (3:4–16). So the prophet turns to contemplate the future, in which a restored Jerusalem, delivered from the fear of all her enemies, reigns supreme (3:17–21). Her material prosperity contrasts with the sterility and poverty of her enemies. The nations will be punished for their guilt; Jerusalem, however, will be pardoned. The Lord will dwell in Jerusalem, ensuring its safety and wellbeing.

This prophecy might seem to be little more than a nationalist aspiration, in which a Jewish prophet looks ahead to the domination of the world by Jerusalem. However, this is clearly not so. The gift of the Spirit is clearly intended to be made to all nations – a prophecy that was fulfilled in the coming of the Spirit at Pentecost. Although the Spirit did indeed descend on people at Jerusalem, he was given to people of all nations and not simply to Jews. Reading this prophecy from the standpoint of the New Testament, we may see it as a glorious anticipation of the coming of the Holy Spirit on the entire people of God – that is, those for whom Jesus Christ died and who respond to his saving death in repentance and faith. Far from being a nationalist manifesto, the book of Joel looks ahead to the universal gifting of all believers.

AMOS

Although born in the southern kingdom of Judah, Amos appears to have ministered primarily to the northern kingdom of Israel during the reigns of Uzziah, king of Judah 792–740 BC, and Jeroboam II, king of Israel 793–753. While little is known about Amos for certain, we know that he was from the region of Tekoa in Judah, and is referred to as both a shepherd (1:1; 7:14–15; note, however, that the Hebrew term may mean 'a sheep breeder') and someone who takes care of sycamore-fig trees (7:14). He was probably a wealthy farmer who left his home in Judah to prophesy to the northern kingdom of Israel. The main part of his ministry was probably carried out over a two-year period at some point during the years 767–753, centring on the shrine at Bethel. There is not enough archaeological information available to allow the date of the earthquake mentioned in the opening verse to be established with any degree of certainty.

The prophecy takes the form of judgment against both the nations and Israel for their sins. Israel is declared to be no better than the surrounding nations. In fact, she bears an even greater responsibility for her sins on account of being God's chosen people. It is clear from several references in the prophecy that this was a time of national prosperity. There were few indications of the disaster that Israel would suffer at the hands of Assyria in 722–721, which would lead to the fall of the northern kingdom. The prophecy particularly complains about the lack of social justice in Israel, and her failure to remain faithful to the covenant. Although the dominant theme of Amos' prophecy is that of condemnation and judgment, the book ends with an assurance of restoration for a remnant of the people.

OUTLINE

The oracles against the nations
1:1–2 Title and announcement of God's judgment
1:3–8 Oracles against Damascus and Philistia
1:9–15 Oracles against Tyre, Edom and Ammon
2:1–5 Oracles against Moab and Judah
2:6–16 The oracle against Israel herself

The judgment against Israel
3:1–15 Israel is meant to be God's chosen people
4:1–13 Israel is unrepentant of her sins

5:1–17 Injustice is widespread within Israel
5:18–27 The Day of the Lord will bring judgment
6:1–14 The inevitability of judgment

The visions of Amos
7:1–3 The vision of the plague of locusts
7:4–6 The vision of judgment by fire
7:7–9 The vision of the plumbline
7:10–17 The judgment against Amaziah and his family
8:1–3 The vision of ripe fruit
8:4–6 Condemnation of social injustice
8:7–10 The decree of punishment

AMOS 1:1–2:16
Oracles Against the Nations

1:1–2:5 Judgment on Israel's Neighbours The prophecy opens with a series of declarations against Israel's neighbours. To appreciate the impact this series of oracles would have made on his audience, the reader should appreciate that the condemnation of Damascus (1:3–5), the Philistine city of Gaza (1:6–8), Tyre (1:9–10), Edom (1:11–12), Ammon (1:13–15) and Moab (2:1–3) would have met with widespread approval on the part of Amos' audience. These were the historic enemies of the people of God,

---

Is God concerned about social justice?

While Greek civilisation gave us many good things, one unhelpful matter was its separation of sacred and secular. By contrast, the Bible sees no such separation. All of life is seen as given by God and is therefore to be both enjoyed and stewarded, in the knowledge that one day we will be accountable to him.

In the light of this, the Old Testament prophets had no doubt that God was concerned with social justice. They fearlessly confronted Israel's lack of compassion to the needy and its maintenance of unjust social structures (e.g., Isa 3:13–15; Am 4:1–3; 5:10–17; 8:4–14). They refused to let people think they could be religious, yet neglect justice. Amos even said that God could stand their worship no longer (Am 5:21–23), demanding, 'Let justice roll on like a river, righteousness like a never-failing stream!' (Am 5:24). Nor was Judah any better, as prophets like Micah reminded them that what God wanted was for them 'to act justly and to love mercy and to walk humbly with your God' (Mic 6:8).

All that the prophets were doing in speaking like this was calling God's people back to the Law, for it required justice for the poor (Ex 23:6), care for widows and orphans (Dt 14:28–29), generous lending without interest (Lev 25:35–38), writing off debts after seven years (Dt 15:1–11; 24:6) – things that would make most modern-day economies tremble. Nor was this confined to the Old Testament. Social justice and care for the poor was an intrinsic part of apostolic Christianity from the beginning (Ac 2:45; 4:34–35; Gal 2:9–10).

Both prophets and apostles would undoubtedly be appalled at the sort of Christianity that focuses only on 'getting saved' without demanding from people a fundamental commitment to social justice like the justice that God himself demonstrates.

who had made life difficult for them during the period of the united kingdom and afterwards. The fact that they were being condemned for their arrogance would be widely applauded by those within Israel who heard them.

Yet a distinct feeling of unease would have resulted from the next oracle, which pronounces judgment against Judah (2:4–5). In this oracle, we find the southern kingdom being condemned in almost exactly the same way as Tyre and Moab, yet Judah was part of the people of God. And the city of Jerusalem, which is here declared to be marked for destruction (2:5), was the site of the temple, the house of God. This sense of unease would have been replaced by a sense of despair or outrage as the prophet turned his attention to Israel itself.

2:6–16 Judgment on Israel The judgment against Israel is longer and more detailed than the condemnation against the other nations. Amos declares that there has been a breakdown of social justice within Israel, with a series of lamentable sins being given as illustrations. Israel has become just as bad as her pagan neighbours. The consequences of this failure to keep the law of the Lord will be severe: Israel is to be crushed, and not even her finest soldiers or weapons of war will save her.

AMOS 3:1–6:14
The Condemnation of Israel

3:1–15 Witnesses Summoned Against Israel The charges made against Israel are now pursued with vigour. First, Israel's privileged position is emphasised. What

other nation did the Lord bring out of Egypt? What other people did he choose as his own (3:1–2)? Although both Judah and Israel are included in this understanding of the privileges of being the people of God, it is clear that Amos' message is directed specifically against Israel. Being the people of God has its obligations – and Israel has failed to honour them. The Lord summons all the nations around to hear his judgment against Israel. The particular sins singled out for mention here are the reversion to pagan practices associated with the shrine of Bethel under Jeroboam I (1Ki 12:26–33), and the excessive wealth of Israel's merchants, which led to the building of extravagant mansions (3:13–15).

4:1–5:17 A Lament and Call to Repentance The basic theme of Amos' message then develops further, with mention of the sins that have arisen within Israel, and give rise to the Lord's judgment against his people (4:1–12). Israel may have kept many of the covenant requirements, but boasted about doing so. To humble his people, the Lord sent on them famine and drought, but to no apparent avail. Once more, the Lord urges his people to return to him, to repent and to live (5:1–17). The message 'seek the LORD and live' recurs throughout this passage. Israel has turned away from him. The time has come to turn back, before the Lord adopts more drastic ways of forcing his people to return to him.

5:18–6:14 The Day of the Lord The prophet now turns to the theme of the 'Day of the LORD'. This phrase is used extensively in

The Day of the Lord

The prophets often spoke about a coming *Day of the Lord*. It was the day when God would judge his people and establish his reign on the earth. People looked forward to that day and often spoke about it – but the prophets warn that for people who do wrong there is nothing to look forward to. It is the day when accounts will be settled. God will intervene in justice. The *Day of the Lord* is a reminder that time is running out, that people should not let anything stop them from turning to God while there is still time.

the prophetic writings of the Old Testament to refer to the great day of victory in which the Lord will triumph over his enemies and establish his rule over the nations. It is clear that many in Israel were looking forward to that day, seeing it as a clear sign of hope. The Day of the Lord would be good news for Israel. Not so, declares Amos (5:18–27). The Lord will judge Israel, just as he will judge everyone else. That day will be 'darkness, not light'. Why does Israel long for this day? Does she not realise what it will bring to her?

Amos exposes the complacency and smugness of Israel, who seems to think that her great religious festivals and sacrificial offerings are enough to ensure her continued good standing in the sight of God. However, the favour of God depends on social justice and righteousness in his eyes, not mechanical observance of cultic rituals. If the 'Day of the LORD' brings anything to Israel, it will be exile in a land beyond Damascus. The complacency (6:1–7) and pride (6:8–14) of Israel are further explored, giving added weight to the severity of this judgment.

AMOS 7:1–9:10
Visions of Judgment

7:1–17 Locusts, Fire and a Plumbline The next section of the prophecy centres on a series of visions, in which Amos is shown what the future holds for Israel. The first set of visions begins with a swarm of locusts, which the Lord has prepared as a judgment on his people (7:1–3). In response to Amos' plea for mercy, this judgment is withheld. The same thing happens concerning another judgment, this time by fire (7:4–6).

This is followed by a vision of a plumbline (7:7–9), which shows how far out of line Israel has become. Israel was called into being by the Lord, true to what he intended for her. But now the plumbline shows up the extent to which she has departed from her intentions. This message of judgment is not well received by Amaziah, the priest in charge of the sanctuary at Bethel. It is clear that Amaziah feels that his professional status is undermined by the words of this amateur (the word 'seer' seems to be used contemptuously). Amos replies that he is not a professional prophet: he is just someone whom the Lord has called to speak to the people of Israel, and that message is about forthcoming exile.

Amaziah may want him to be quiet. The Lord, however, wants him to speak out (7:10–17).

8:1–9:10 A Basket of Ripe Fruit This programme of declaring what the Lord has made known to Amos continues with the vision of the basket of ripe fruit (probably figs). The ripe fruit points to the time being ripe for the judgment of Israel (8:1–14), whose sins are again identified and commented on.

The nature of the judgment involved is clarified through a further vision (9:1–10), in which Amos sees the Lord ready to begin judging his people from the altar of his temple. Israel expected the altar to be a place of security; instead, it turns out to be the starting point for the Lord's punishment of his people. His rebellious people will be ruthlessly hunted down, wherever they may seek to escape from the coming judgment. Israel cannot depend on her special status in the sight of God to save her from this judgment. Israel might feel that she is safe, on account of the Lord having brought her out of Egypt. However, the Lord was responsible for other major migrations of people in history (9:7), and no longer chooses to regard Israel as being special in this respect.

9:11–15 Israel's Restoration This unrelenting movement towards judgment, however, will ultimately lead to restoration. In a strongly messianic passage, Amos looks ahead to the coming of another day that will dawn after the dreadful day of judgment. In this day, the ruined cities of the land will be rebuilt, and the countryside will again bring forth wine and produce in abundance. A restored Israel will once more be planted in the land, never to be uprooted again. In particular, the house of David (here referred to as a 'shelter' ('tent' or 'hut') to indicate the sorry state into which it has declined will be restored, with new authority over the nations (9:11–12). Israel's enemies (of which only Moab is mentioned) will be subject to the reign of this restored house of David. With the coming of Jesus Christ as the king of Israel and the Lord of all nations, this prophecy can be seen finally to have been fulfilled.

OBADIAH

Very little is known about either this prophet or the circumstances under which he prophesied. There are no references to historical events within the prophecy that can be dated with absolute certainty. The most likely date for the prophecy would seem to be some point during the period 605–586 BC. This period saw Babylonian attacks on Judah and Jerusalem, culminating in the fall of Jerusalem and the deportation of its people in 586 – presumably to the delight of the people of Edom, historic enemies of Judah, who feature prominently in this prophecy. However, it must be stressed that we can only guess that this is the most likely background to the book, which is the shortest in the Old Testament.

vv.1–14 After the fall of Jerusalem, Edom had taken possession of some territories once belonging to Judah (Eze 35:3–15). Now, Edom itself has been ravaged by foreigners. Obadiah sees in this a just punishment of Edom for her pride. On account of her pride, Edom will be humbled (2–4), and utterly destroyed through the complicity of her former friends and allies (5–7). The nation which refused to assist Judah in her hour of need, and which benefited from the fall of Jerusalem, will now itself feel the pain of defeat and humiliation (8–14).

vv.15–21 Obadiah then takes up the theme of the coming 'Day of the LORD' (15–21). Amos had seen this coming day as bringing judgment, rather than hope, for Israel (Am 5:18). Obadiah, however, sees it in much more positive terms. Jerusalem has paid for her sins. The coming of the 'Day of the LORD' can now mean only restoration and deliverance for Jerusalem, and the punishment of those who have ravished and humiliated her. The Lord is both just and powerful. Therefore his people may rely on him.

JONAH

The book of the prophet Jonah differs significantly from the remaining eleven minor prophets. Whereas the other eleven books are primarily concerned with the *words* of the prophet in question, the book of Jonah is much more concerned with his *deeds*. There is a sense in which it is what Jonah does, rather than anything he says, that is of importance to the reader of the book. Indeed, we are given virtually no indication of exactly what Jonah says: it is the story that really matters.

The book indicates that the events to which it refers probably took place in the period 800–750 BC. The city that features so prominently in the narrative is Nineveh, a leading city of Assyria, which became the capital of the Assyrian Empire at some point around 700 BC. By the later stage of the 9th century, Nineveh was widely thought of as the hub of the civilised world on account of its military importance. The book itself was probably written at a later stage, and may even date from the post-exilic period. However, the dating of the book is not of central importance to its message.

OUTLINE

Jonah flees from God
1:1–2 God commissions Jonah
1:3 Jonah's flight to Tarshish
1:4 The great storm at sea
1:5–10 Jonah exposed as the cause of the storm
1:11–15 Jonah is thrown overboard by the ship's crew
1:16 The crew of the ship worship the Lord
1:17 Jonah is swallowed by a huge fish

Jonah's prayer
2:1 Jonah prays from inside the fish
2:2–7 Jonah's plight and God's response
2:8 The futility of idolatry
2:9 Jonah's thanksgiving
2:10 The fish throws up Jonah

Jonah in Nineveh
3:1–2 God repeats the commission of Jonah
3:3 Jonah goes to Nineveh
3:4 Jonah's message to the Ninevites
3:5–9 The repentance of the Ninevites
3:10 God spares Nineveh

Jonah's reaction to God's mercy
4:1 Jonah's anger at God's decision
4:2–4 Jonah's prayer and God's response
4:5–7 Jonah and the leafy plant
4:8–9 Jonah's prayer and God's response
4:10–11 God's compassion on Nineveh

1:1–16 Jonah Flees from the Lord The book opens with an account of the call of Jonah to go to Nineveh and preach to it. Jonah's response is immediate: he promptly boards a ship heading in precisely the opposite direction. ('Tarshish' is usually thought to be the city of Tartessus, which was established in Spain by the

Phoenicians. It would have represented the most distant place on earth from Babylon for the writer of this prophetic book.) The voyage is disrupted by a violent storm, which causes panic among the pagan sailors. By throwing lots, they identify Jonah as the cause of their predicament, and throw him overboard (1:1–16). It is important to notice how the pagan sailors refer to God by the specific title 'LORD' (1:14), thus acknowledging his sovereignty in this matter.

The practice of casting lots was a means of reaching decisions that was widespread in the ancient Near East, and was used by Old Testament believers wishing to have divine guidance – for example, in allocating territory to Israel within Canaan (Jos 18:10). However, it was also used specifically to identify guilty individuals, as in the case of exposing the sin of Achan (Jos 7:13–18). Even though the lots were thrown by pagans, the Lord was responsible for the selection of Jonah.

1:17–3:3 Jonah's Prayer Jonah has not been abandoned to destruction, however. He will be given an opportunity to reconsider his actions and repent. He is swallowed by 'a huge fish' (1:17) which may have been a whale. The period of three days during which Jonah remains inside the fish foreshadows Jesus Christ remaining in the bowels of the earth until his resurrection on the third day (Mt 12:40). During this period, Jonah reflects on his situation, his thankfulness for deliverance being mingled with repentance for his own failure. As the prayer comes to an end, Jonah comes to his conclusion: he will make good his

failures, and do what he promised. As a result, Jonah finds himself back on dry land. When the Lord's call comes again, asking him to go to Nineveh, he obeys (2:1–3:3).

3:4–10 Jonah Goes to Nineveh We are given no indication of the manner in which Jonah proclaims the Lord to the people of Nineveh. The words he uses and the occasions on which he speaks are not indicated. The real point of the account of Jonah lies elsewhere. The point is that the pagan people of Nineveh respond to the Lord. Although they do not use the special name 'the LORD' to refer to God, it is clear that they acknowledge him. The Lord accepts their repentance. There are clear parallels here with two other Old Testament books, Esther and Daniel, both of which document Gentiles responding positively to the claims of the Lord.

4:1–11 Jonah's Anger at the Lord's Compassion Jonah, however, is irritated at the Lord's compassion. The reason for this is not made clear by the text itself. But it is highly likely that Jonah's attitude reflects a form of Israelite nationalism which believed that the great benefits of knowing the Lord should be available only to the people of God – in other words, to the Jews. Why should the Lord have compassion on Gentiles, especially when they are hostile towards Israel? On the basis of this nationalist theology, the Lord should be compassionate towards Israel, and punish those outside her bounds. The Lord has little time for Jonah's rather petulant attitude (4:1–4).

The account of Jonah ends, perhaps a little abruptly, with the incident of the

leafy plant (possibly a castor oil plant). The point being made in this concluding section of the work seems to be this. Jonah is hot and uncomfortable. In his grace, the Lord alleviates his discomfort by providing a shady plant. When this dies, Jonah becomes angry with the Lord. Yet his situation is precisely the same as before the plant's arrival. He is uncomfortable once more.

There is no hint of gratitude on Jonah's part for the temporary comfort the plant brings to him. As the story makes clear, Jonah seems inclined to complain, no matter what happens. If the Lord was compassionate enough to alleviate Jonah's discomfort for a while, would not that compassion also demonstrate itself in forgiving repentant people of a great city? We can see in this concluding section a powerful statement of the universal love and forgiving grace of God, from which we have all benefited (4:5–11). The universality of the grace and compassion of God is proclaimed to the full in the New Testament, with its passionate plea to make disciples of all nations (Mt 28:17–20).

MICAH

Micah, who came from a village in the Judaean foothills, prophesied in the southern kingdom of Judah at some point during the period 750–686 BC. His clear prediction of the fall of Samaria, the capital of the northern kingdom of Israel, points to at least part of his ministry having taken place before 722–721 BC, when the Assyrians finally ended the independent existence of Israel. There are important parallels between Micah and parts of Isaiah, which partly reflect the fact that both were prophesying around the same time. In particular, both prophets mingle prophecies of destruction with prophecies of hope, as a means of pointing to the restoration that lies beyond the inevitable punishment of Judah for her sins.

1:1–16 *Judgment Against Samaria and Jerusalem* The work opens by identifying the reigns during which Micah prophesied, and notes that his oracles concern both Samaria (the capital of Israel) and Jerusalem (the capital of Judah). What

follows is a powerful and spirited attack on the corruption of life in the great cities of the two kingdoms. Perhaps Micah's origins in a small village lead him to be especially critical of the way of life in cities. Nevertheless, the sins he identifies and opposes represent serious violations of the covenant between the Lord and his people. The Lord's judgment on his people is coming.

2:1–3:12 False Prophets For Micah, both Judah and Israel are guilty of a series of unacceptable offences, including the oppression of the weak by the strong, the dispossession of people from their lands by powerful landowners, and the enslavement of helpless children (2:1–5). The priests and prophets, who ought to have been speaking out against these events, have totally failed to do so. They have taken comfort from the unacceptable idea that no harm can come to the people of God. Anyone who promised plenty of wine and beer would be acceptable as a prophet to this smug people. The leaders of the people are just as complacent, preferring reassuring prophecies of peace to the harsh realities of the coming judgment the Lord will bring upon his people (2:6–3:12).

4:1–13 The Mountain of the Lord This oracle of judgment is supplemented by a vision of hope. It is significant that Micah echoes some words of his near-contemporary, Isaiah (Isa 2:2–5), as he looks forward to a golden age in which peace and prosperity will reign. Does this mean that Micah is akin to one of the false prophets whom he condemns for speaking of peace? No. It means that Micah is looking beyond the calamity of

impending judgment, and seeing the hope that lies beyond. In those days, people will be drawn to the mountain of the Lord, and will turn their swords into ploughshares. There will be an end to war (4:1–5). The remnant of Jerusalem will be brought home in triumph. Even though Jerusalem will lose her monarchy (an event that took place as a result of the fall of Jerusalem in 586), she will be redeemed out of the hands of all her enemies (4:6–13).

5:1–4 A Promised Ruler from Bethlehem This leads Micah to speak of the coming ruler of Judah and Israel. This ruler will arise from the town of Bethlehem, in the region of Ephrathah, and will give peace and security to his people. For Christians, this great prophecy has finally been fulfilled in Jesus Christ. Christ, himself a descendant of David, is born in this royal city. His origins are indeed 'from of old'; in fact, he was present with God at creation. We can see here a clear anticipation of the coming of Jesus Christ as the shepherd of his people, leading them to a safety that transcends any peace the world can give them.

5:5–6:16 Deliverance and Destruction The need for this coming deliverer is then clearly indicated. The Assyrian is coming, and will devastate the land. The remnant of Jacob (in other words, those who survive within Israel, and remain faithful to the Lord) will be scattered among the nations. By scattering them in this way, through the Assyrians, the Lord will put an end to their pagan forms of worship (5:5–15). The Lord does not want elaborate sacrifices, but humility and obedience from the people whom he

loves (6:1–8). Israel must abandon her fraudulent use of inaccurate weights and measures, and pursue justice for her people. If she does not, Israel will not survive to benefit from her own produce. An intervening act of judgment will allow others to benefit from the food, wine and oil she has produced and stored (6:9–16).

7:1–20 Israel Will Rise In the midst of all this misery and corruption, Micah's faith in the Lord remains firm. He will watch in hope for the coming of the Lord (7:1–7), just as he finally expects Israel to be delivered and restored (7:8–13). For this reason, the work ends on a note of praise, as Micah sees the Lord shepherding his people, to the envy of all those surrounding them. The Lord will show compassion to his people. His anger does not last for ever, and he will finally deliver his people from the sins and iniquities that have ensnared them (7:14–20). Here again, we may see a glorious prophetic hint of the gospel of Jesus Christ, and all the benefits it brings to the people of God.

NAHUM

Little is known about Nahum. He operated in the southern kingdom of Judah in the period following the fall of the northern kingdom of Israel to the Assyrians. The book may be dated with a reasonable degree of certainty to the period between the fall of the Egyptian city of Thebes (663 BC) and the fall of the Assyrian capital of Nineveh (612 BC). The former is treated as a past event, and the latter as something yet to happen. Although the book is clearly written with the needs of Judah in mind, a substantial part of its prophecy is actually directed against Nineveh itself. It is clear that Judah felt increasingly threatened by the Assyrian Empire in the period following the fall of Israel and its capital city Samaria.

1:1–15 The Lord's Anger Against Nineveh It is against this background of fear and anxiety that Nahum's prophecy is to be set. The opening prophecy envisages the joy that will accompany the overthrow of Nineveh. Using an image that is used by Isaiah to stress the joy of the restoration of Jerusalem from captivity in Babylon (Isa 52:7), Nahum looks ahead to the rejoicing that will accompany the news that Nineveh has fallen (1:15). The Lord will break the stranglehold of Assyria over his people, and deliver them from its threat. Unlike Isaiah and Jeremiah, who saw Assyria as the Lord's appointed instrument of judgment and punishment of his rebellious people, Nahum treats Assyria simply as a foreign oppressor, whose yoke must be cast off.

2:1–3:19 Nineveh to Fall The second prophecy (2:1–13) looks forward both to the restoration of Israel to its former glory, and also the awe-inspiring fall of Nineveh. In his vision, the prophet can see the terror that falls upon the once-great city, as its inhabitants flee for their lives, realising that the greatness and security of the past has vanished for ever. The Lord is against Assyria. Therefore it

will fall. In the third section of the prophecy (3:1–19), Nahum compares the coming fall of Nineveh to the past fall of Thebes, the capital of Upper Egypt. So hated is Assyria that there will be nobody to mourn her end. The world, and not just Judah, will be a better place without the tyranny of Assyria.

HABAKKUK

Habakkuk prophesied in the southern kingdom of Judah at some time around the battle of Carchemish (605 BC). This battle, which resulted in the total defeat of the Egyptian armies, marked the end of any serious resistance to the Babylonian advances in the region. It was not long before Judah found herself under threat from Babylon – a threat that would lead to an attack on Jerusalem and partial deportation of its inhabitants in 597 BC, and a final onslaught in 588, eventually leading to the fall of the city and deportation of most of its population in 586 BC. The text of the book itself does not allow us to date the prophecy with any great precision.

OUTLINE

1:1 Title
1:2–4 Habakkuk's first complaint to God: sin goes unpunished
1:5–11 God's reply: the Babylonians are his agent of punishment
1:12–17 Habakkuk's second complaint: the excesses of God's agents of punishment
2:1 The prophet as a watchman
2:2–20 God's response: the punishment of the wicked
3:1–19 Habakkuk's psalm of praise

1:1–11 Habakkuk's Complaint The book opens with a complaint: Why does the Lord allow so much evil to take place within Judah? It seems that justice is not observed, and that violence has become an everyday occurrence (1:1–4). The Lord's response to this complaint is dramatic. Something is indeed about to be done about this unacceptable state of affairs. He will summon the Babylonians as agents of his punishment. The Babylonians are not righteous. Indeed, they are people who regard their own strength as a god. But they will be his agent of punishment for the sins of Judah.

1:12–2:20 Habakkuk's Second Complaint Habakkuk's second complaint picks up on this point (1:12–2:1): How can a righteous God use such a wicked people as the agents of his punishment? After all, Judah is sinful – but the Babylonians are even worse. So why use an evil nation to punish a people who, though sinful, are more righteous than they are? The answer given focuses on the fate of Babylon (2:2–20). The Babylonians will also be punished for their wickedness. A series of woes is directed against Babylon, making it clear that the Lord in no way condones any aspect of their behaviour. The righteous must learn to live by faith (2:4; see also Ro 1:17). In other words, they must learn to put their trust in the Lord, and realise that his ways, although apparently lying beyond human understanding, are nevertheless righteous, and will achieve their goals.

The knowledge of the Lord will cover the earth, just as the waters cover the sea (2:14).

3:1–19 Habakkuk's Prayer The prophecy ends with a prayer of Habakkuk, in response to all that he has learned. Like many of the psalms, the prayer takes the form of a song. It recalls the great deeds of the Lord in the past, and the devastation that was caused by his presence. The song focuses on the way in which the Lord acted to deliver his people from their oppressors, such as in the crossing of the Red Sea (3:13–14). No matter what happens, Habakkuk declares that he will continue to praise and trust the Lord. He alone is Saviour and Lord and gives hope to his people.

Why do bad things happen in life?

If there is a good God, why do bad things happen? This perennial question troubled Habakkuk greatly. Like others, he didn't really get an answer; but he did get a fresh revelation of God in the light of which he was content to wait, see what God would do and trust in him in the meantime. But human inquisitiveness has led many to search for fuller answers – a search known as *theodicy*.

Theodicy seeks to reconcile belief in God as good and sovereign with the existence of evil in the world – bad people, actions, events, experiences, which all destroy human happiness. Do such things demonstrate God doesn't care, or that he cares but is powerless to intervene, or that he doesn't exist? Various theodicies have been proposed: that evil is not real, only illusory; that it is a punishment for sin (something Jesus denied, Jn 9:1–3); that God permits it to help us discover more of our humanity and to purify our character. But there is still a nagging 'Why?'

The Bible never fully answers this question. It certainly roots evil in the Fall, which led to pain, toil and death (Ge 3:14–19), and recognises the devil's activity in seeking to oppose God's plans for humanity. But most of all, it tells us that God doesn't leave us alone in our pain. In Christ, he entered our world and shared our suffering to redeem us. One day all evil and suffering *will* be removed and 'there will be no more death or mourning or crying or pain' (Rev 21:4). In the meantime, God walks with us, giving us courage and confidence as we trust in him. And as we do, we begin to find that, even in the bad things, 'God works for the good of those who love him' (Ro 8:28).

ZEPHANIAH

It is clear from his own description that Zephaniah belonged to the royal family of Judah, being a direct descendant of Hezekiah, king of Judah, 715–686 BC. Zephaniah prophesied during the reign of Josiah (640–609 BC), which was one of the most important periods of religious reform in Judah. The rediscovery of the 'Book of the Law' led to a major religious reformation, and a corporate renewal of the covenant with the Lord that had been violated by the paganism which flourished under earlier monarchs.

1:1–13 Warning of Coming Destruction It would seem that Zephaniah's prophecies are delivered before these reforms. It is quite clear from their general tone that the religious life of Judah has reached an all-time low, and that the threat of imminent divine judgment is required to spur the king and nation into any kind of reform and renewal. The great warning of destruction in Judah speaks of a continuing legacy of Baal worship, worship of the stars and devotion to the god Molek, who was chiefly noted for the cult of child sacrifice associated with his name. These practices are totally unacceptable.

1:14–2:3 The Great Day of the Lord The prophet then turns to the coming 'Day of the LORD', a common theme among

many of the prophets of this period. The coming of the Lord to such a corrupt and rebellious people can only bring judgment. It will be a time of distress and anguish, as the Lord brings a long overdue punishment to his disobedient people. Nothing can stand in the way of this judgment: wealth and power are useless. Only righteousness and humility on the part of Judah offer any hope of this dreadful judgment not being inflicted.

2:4–3:20 The Future of Jerusalem This prophecy is followed by a series of oracles against the nations around Judah (2:4–15), detailing the judgment that will surely come against these nations. Yet Jerusalem itself, supposedly the site of the house of God, is also condemned (3:1–8). The Lord is angered that Jerusalem refuses to fear him, or accept his correction. As a result of its refusal to take any notice of him, it will be punished for its sins.

That punishment, however, will be followed by a new period in its history. It will be purified, purged both of its pagan ways and of its inhabitants who were proud and haughty. The purification of the city will result in its being inhabited only by the meek and the humble, who trust in the Lord (3:9–13). These people will rejoice, knowing that the period of their punishment is over, and that they can again be an object of delight and love to their Lord (3:14–17). They will be brought home from the lands to which they had been sent in shame, and will have the satisfaction of seeing themselves restored in the full gaze of the surrounding nations.

HAGGAI

The prophet Haggai is specifically mentioned by name in the account of the rebuilding of the temple at Jerusalem after the return from exile. Along with Zechariah, Haggai belongs to the period of post-exilic prophecy, in which the Lord made his ways and will known to his people after their return from exile in Babylon, after the fall of Jerusalem. The background to Haggai's ministry lies in the decision of Cyrus the Great, the conqueror of the Babylonian Empire, to allow peoples who had been deported to return to their homelands (Ezr 1:2–4). In the case of the inhabitants of Jerusalem, permission was given to begin the rebuilding of the temple. Yet work soon stalled, for various reasons. Haggai's prophecy concerns the need to begin the work of rebuilding as a matter of obligation to the Lord.

1:1–14 A Call to Build the House of the Lord The date of the prophecy, which consists of four messages from the Lord, can be established with accuracy. The call to prophesy (1:1) can be dated to the end of August 520. The last message is dated from the middle of December 520, nearly four months later. The first message (1:2–11) is a command to rebuild the temple. Why are the people of Jerusalem building expensive houses for themselves, while failing to build a house for the Lord? Is it any wonder that Jerusalem is in such a miserable state,

when the people treat their God in such a way? Until the Lord's house is rebuilt, Jerusalem will remain a wilderness. It is clear that this message has its desired effect. The rebuilding of the temple begins under Zerubbabel (1:12).

2:1–9 The Promised Glory of the New House
The second message is as remarkable as it is simple: the Lord is with his people. This deeply reassuring affirmation can be – and is almost certainly meant to be – interpreted in two ways. First, it is a declaration that the Lord is on the side of his people. No longer is he against them, as he was when he summoned the Assyrians or Babylonians as the agents of his wrath against Israel and Judah. And second, it is an assurance of the physical presence of the Lord among his people. Just as Ezekiel's vision of the restored temple included a dramatic moment in which the glory of the Lord returned to the temple it had earlier deserted, so Haggai is assured that the Lord will be with his restored people. The new temple will surpass in glory the old building, which had been destroyed by the Babylonians. It will bring peace to the people.

2:10–19 Blessings for a Defiled People
The third message concerns the defilement of the people. It seems that some among the returning exiles may have gained the impression that, on account of their exile in Babylon, they are now free from sin. If such an idea had gained widespread assent, it would ultimately have led to a lack of concern for the law of the Lord, and a failure to be concerned about obeying him. Haggai demonstrates that sin is spread far more easily than holiness. There is a real danger that the people of God will become defiled through a lack of interest in holiness. Yet holiness on the part of the people is, Haggai argues, an essential precondition for blessings from the Lord. By rebuilding the temple, the people will demonstrate their commitment to the Lord. He will then return the compliment, and bless the people.

2:20–23 Zerubbabel the Lord's Signet Ring
The fourth and final message is brief. It affirms the Lord's commitment to Zerubbabel. The Lord has chosen Zerubbabel and will make him 'like my signet ring' – an apparent reference to Zerubbabel himself being seen as a pledge or guarantee of the faithfulness of the Lord to his people. That faithfulness is not in question but it is clear that the people need to be reassured of it, and to have physical signs of the promises of the Lord. Here we can see an important anticipation of one of the many purposes of the work of Jesus Christ – to reassure us of God's faithfulness, by both his words and his work. As Paul points out, all of God's promises find their 'Yes' in him (2Co 1:20) – and him alone.

ZECHARIAH

Like his contemporary Haggai, Zechariah is to be dated to the period immediately after the return to Jerusalem from exile in Babylon. Haggai's calling can be dated to August 520 BC. Zechariah's calling took place a few months later, in October or November of the same year. Although Haggai's visions took place only over a few months, Zechariah's prophetic ministry was spread out over a much longer period. Zechariah was among the large group of exiles who returned to Judah in 538 BC under the leadership of Zerubbabel. Like Ezekiel, he was also a priest. However, Zechariah was born during the Babylonian captivity. He had never seen Jerusalem before 538.

Like Haggai, Zechariah wishes to encourage the people of Jerusalem to rebuild the temple. Alongside these messages of encouragement and rebuke for inaction there are to be found a series of strongly messianic prophecies.

ZECHARIAH 1:1–6:15
The Eight Night Visions

1:1–6 A Call to Return to the Lord The work opens by identifying its author as the grandson of Iddo, who is found named in Nehemiah's list of those returning from Babylon (Ne 12:4). The date of the call of the prophet can be placed in October or November 520, some time after the initial return of the exiles. The opening words of the prophecy declare both the need and the possibility of returning to the Lord. Israel may have returned to Jerusalem; she has yet to return fully to the Lord who exiled her as a punishment, and then restored her. Surely the people's experience of exile would have taught them to listen to the prophets of the Lord?

1:7–21 The Man Among the Myrtle Trees There then follows a series of night visions, the first of which dates from about three months after the call of the prophet. The first vision (1:7–17) is that of a horseman among a group of myrtle trees. The Lord had punished his people by sending them into exile for 70 years. Yet Judah has been punished more than she deserves by the nations about her (1:14–15; a similar idea is found at Isa 40:1–2). Now the Lord's tender mercy and compassion will be made known to his people. Their towns will prosper, and the house of the Lord will be rebuilt at Jerusalem.

The second vision (1:18–21) demonstrates that the great powers who were responsible for the chaos that descended on Judah, Israel and Jerusalem will themselves be overthrown.

2:1–3:10 A Man with a Measuring Line The third vision is that of a man with a measuring line (2:1–13). This extended vision points to the city of Jerusalem being rebuilt. The Lord himself will dwell with his people. The Lord has chosen Jerusalem as his dwelling-place, and will be its chief glory. In addition to its declaration that Jerusalem will be rebuilt, the vision also points to Zechariah's relative youth (2:4).

The fourth vision (3:1–10) points ahead to the cleansing of the sin of Israel, and her restoration as a priestly nation to the Lord. The symbolism involved in the vision is especially important. Joshua, the high priest who with Zerubbabel had brought the people back from Babylon (Ezr 2:2; Ne 7:7) – not the earlier leader who supervised the conquest of Canaan – initially is seen wearing filthy clothes. Then the high priest's filthy clothes are removed, and are replaced by clean ones. In the same way, Israel's sins will be removed by the Lord and be replaced with his righteousness.

4:1–14 The Gold Lampstand and the Two Olive Trees The fifth vision is of a solid gold lampstand. The 'seven channels' are best

understood as referring to channels through which the supply of olive oil for the lamp is fed. The image then emphasises the constancy and abundance of the oil that keeps the lamp alight. This is reinforced by the reference to the two olive trees, which will provide a constant source of oil. However, there is a deeper meaning to this vision. Oil was used for anointing, especially for the anointing of priests and kings, who had a special role to play in the history of the people of God. The vision identifies Zerubbabel and Joshua as continuing the kingly and

priestly functions of earlier generations, which will ultimately be fulfilled in the coming of the Messiah.

5:1–6:15 Further Visions The final visions are briefer. The sixth vision takes the form of a flying scroll (5:1–4), symbolising the universal validity of the law of the Lord, and the condemnation it will bring to those who ignore or disobey it. The seventh (5:5–11) focuses on a basket, in which the sins of the nation will be removed from the land and transferred to Babylon. The eighth and final vision

Does fasting have any value?

The words of Zec 7:4–10 (like those in Isa 58) seem to suggest that God has no interest in fasting and would rather have people show mercy and kindness. But both prophets were confronting people who thought that the mere practice of fasting, rather than the heart behind it, would achieve the desired result, a view far from what the Bible teaches.

Fasting is abstaining from food, partially or totally, for a certain time to devote oneself more fully to God and seek him in prayer. The Hebrew word means 'to submit oneself humbly to God'. By missing meals and devoting more time to prayer, the person fasting is saying that nothing is more important than seeking God and finding his answer for their situation. Varying in type (partial or complete) and in length (one, three or seven days were the norm), fasting was used to express grief (2Sa 1:12) or repentance (1Sa 7:5–6), to seek guidance (Ac 13:1–3) or express dependence on God (Ezr 8:21–23), and to pray for a breakthrough (Ne 1:1–5; Est 4:1–3; Da 9:1–3).

Fasting was voluntary, only one fast being commanded, on the Day of Atonement (Lev 16:29–31). But after the exile Jews introduced other fasts, like those in Zec 7:5 that were linked with Jerusalem's destruction. By New Testament times fasting had become a twice-weekly requirement for pious Jews (Lk 18:12) and its ostentatious outward show was condemned by Jesus (Mt 6:16). Nevertheless, Jesus still fasted (Mt 4:1–2) and expected his followers would do so (Mk 2:19–20), though in a different spirit (Mt 6:17–18). The early church certainly continued the practice (Ac 13:2–3; 14:23).

Many Christians still practise fasting, either as a regular part of their spiritual routine or at times of earnestly seeking God. The medical values of fasting have also been highlighted recently.

(6:1–8) repeats the basic themes of the first vision, stressing the ultimate victory of the Lord over all his enemies.

In what follows, Zechariah sees Joshua, the high priest, being crowned (6:9–15). This action identifies him as the one who will be responsible for the rebuilding of the temple. However, there are strongly messianic overtones to this passage, which points to the coming Messiah being both a priest and a king (6:13) – a prophecy that is fulfilled in the coming of Jesus Christ as the perfect high priest, and the true king of Israel.

ZECHARIAH 7:1–14:21
Repentance and Restoration

7:1–9:8 The Lord Promises to Bless Jerusalem Some two years after the eight night visions related above, the word of the Lord comes to Zechariah again. After condemning Jerusalem for a lack of true justice, mercy and compassion (7:1–10), the Lord declares the importance of listening to and obeying him (7:11–14). Yet despite all its faults, Jerusalem remains special in the sight of the Lord. He has chosen and loved it. In an important turn of phrase, the Lord declares that he is 'jealous for Zion' (8:2) – meaning that his love for it is such that he cannot bear the thought of Jerusalem loving anyone else.

In the past, Jerusalem has been the object of cursing; now it will be the object of blessing. The same Lord who ordained exile as a punishment for his people now ordains blessing for Jerusalem. Those around will notice and will want to discover this Lord for themselves, so that they may share in its joy (8:1–23). Its enemies will be destroyed. In a panoramic survey of the region, the prophet identifies all the historic enemies of God's people, and sees their downfall (9:1–8).

9:9–11:17 The Coming of Zion's King A strongly messianic passage now opens (9:9–13). In a great vision of hope, the prophet sees the great messianic king, the descendant of David, entering the city in triumph, bringing salvation with him. Markedly, he will not enter on a war-horse, but with humility. He will be seated on a donkey, just as David and his sons were content to ride on mules (2Sa 18:9). This great passage will reach its ultimate fulfilment in the triumphant entry of Jesus Christ into Jerusalem (Mt 21:1–11). The Lord will come and save his people (9:14–11:3). Furthermore, the messianic oracle just noted is now supplemented by another, in which the messianic shepherd-king is deemed to be worth a mere 30 pieces of silver (11:4–17). The fulfilment of this prophecy in the betrayal of Jesus

---

Prophecies of the Messiah in Zechariah fulfilled in Jesus

Prophecy	In Zechariah	Fulfilment in New Testament
To enter Jerusalem as a king	9:9	Mt 21:1–11; Jn 12:12–16
To be sold for 30 silver coins	11:14–17	Mt 26:14–15; 27:9–10
To have his hands, feet and side pierced	12:10	Jn 19:34, 37; 20:27

Christ by Judas Iscariot is a reminder of what Israel thought of her long-awaited Messiah, when he finally appeared.

12:1–9 Jerusalem's Enemies to Be Destroyed
The book comes to a close with a vision of the end, in which Jerusalem is once more under siege. The besiegers are no longer the Babylonians, but great armies drawn from all over the earth. Perhaps this prophecy refers to the siege of Jerusalem in AD 70, when the city was destroyed by the Romans. However, the references to the victory of Jerusalem over her enemies can also be understood in terms of the final establishment of the New Jerusalem in heaven, which none can overthrow.

12:10–13:6 Mourning for the One They Pierced; Cleansing from Sin Two themes now appear, which can be understood in their full sense only in the light of the New Testament. The first is the reference to the inhabitants of Jerusalem looking on the 'one they have pierced', and whose death is mourned as that of a firstborn son or an only child (12:10). These themes are fulfilled in the crucifixion of Jesus Christ, who was nailed to the cross and then pierced by a spear (Jn 19:34, 37), surrounded by onlookers. Here was the death of the only Son of God (Jn 3:16), the firstborn of all creation (Col 1:15, 18).

The second theme is the prophecy of a fountain that will cleanse the descendants of David from all their sin and impurity (13:1), which is clearly linked with a future prophet who is wounded by his friends (13:6). These verses clearly anticipate the betrayal of Jesus Christ, whom many recognised as a prophet (Mk 8:28; Jn 4:19) by one of his friends. It also points ahead to the cleansing from sin that is possible through the death of Christ (Ac 22:16; 1Co 6:11; Rev 22:14).

13:7–9 The Shepherd Struck; the Sheep Scattered The strongly messianic prophecies continue, as Zechariah looks ahead to the coming of a future shepherd who will be struck down, with the result that his sheep are scattered. The shepherd is a favourite messianic image, pointing to the coming of a king-shepherd like David. Once more, the Christian reader of this passage will immediately recognise the fulfilment of this prophecy in the events surrounding the death of Jesus Christ: at the time of the crucifixion, his disciples were scattered, like sheep without a shepherd (Mt 26:31, 56; Mk 14:27, 49–50).

14:1–21 The Lord Comes and Reigns Finally, the prophecy returns to the theme of the 'Day of the LORD'. On that day, there will once more be assaults on Jerusalem and its people. Yet the Lord will triumph in the midst of this calamity, and will finally overcome all the enemies of Jerusalem.

Although it is possible to see this prophecy as a piece of crude nationalism, looking forward to the Jewish domination of the world, it is clear that this is not the intended sense of the words at all. From a Christian perspective, the prophecy is clearly pointing ahead to the tribulation of the Christian church in the world, and assuring believers of the final victory of the Lord over the enemies of faith. Zechariah's vision of the purity of the temple (14:21) will be fulfilled only in the

New Jerusalem. There is no temple in the New Jerusalem, because the Lord dwells there in all his fullness. But no impurity of any kind will be found there (Rev 21:22–27). God will reign supreme, and his people will rest from their labours and their fears.

MALACHI

Like Haggai and Zechariah, Malachi appears to have prophesied in the post-exilic period, at some point soon after the return of the exiles from Babylon to Jerusalem. This is suggested by a number of considerations, including the close similarity between the sins condemned in this book and those singled out for condemnation by Nehemiah. It is generally thought that Malachi (whose name literally means 'my messenger') was the final prophet of the Old Testament period. If this is the case, the work represents an important point of transition between the Old Covenant and the New, pointing ahead to the coming of the Lord to his people in Jesus Christ.

1:1–5 Jacob Loved, Esau Hated The prophecy opens with an affirmation of the love of God for his people Israel. (It should be noted that the term 'Israel' is used here to mean 'the people of God' rather than 'the northern kingdom'. Long after the collapse of the northern kingdom through the Assyrian conquest in 722–721 BC, the term 'Israel' continued to be used in this inclusive sense by some of the later prophets, and also in the writings of the New Testament.) That love is contrasted with the Lord's rejection of Esau and his descendants, the Edomites (see the prophecy of Obadiah). Israel is special in the sight of God, in a way that other nations and peoples are not.

1:6–2:9 Blemished Sacrifices Despite this special relationship between the Lord and Israel, all is not well. Israel is beginning to show a degree of contempt for the Lord by cheating on her sacrificial regulations. Who cares what kind of animal is sacrificed? Anything will do. The Lord declares his disgust at the emergence of such attitudes within his own people (1:6–14). The priests of Israel are severely criticised for their failures in this respect (2:1–9). Israel has violated the covenant with the Lord in many ways, of which two are singled out for special comment.

2:10–16 Judah Unfaithful In the first place, Israelite men are marrying foreign women. By doing so, they are introducing

people with alien religious beliefs into Israel. To marry a foreign woman is to import her gods into the land of the Lord. Nehemiah had vigorously opposed this practice (Ne 13:23–29), and enforced a strict policy that prohibited such intermarriage. In the second place, Israelite men are divorcing their wives, despite the solemn covenant of commitment that undergirds the marriage. Indeed, it is possible that these two issues are related: perhaps Israelite men are divorcing their Israelite wives in order to marry foreign women instead.

2:17–3:5 The Day of Judgment Israel's sins thus anger and weary the Lord. Something will have to be done about it. The Lord proposes that he will send 'my messenger' (for which the Hebrew is the term used as the title of the prophecy, *Malachi*) to prepare the way for a great and dramatic event: the coming of the Lord himself to his temple. On account of her sin, Israel will not be able to cope with this development. The coming of the Lord will not bring consolation, but a refiner's fire, which will indeed purify – but will hurt as well. The coming of the Lord will lead to the purification of his

Should Christians still tithe?

Malachi confronted God's people with failing to pay their tithes, as required by the Law, which said that one-tenth of their income through harvest or livestock *belonged* to God (Lev 27:30). Not to give that tithe, therefore, was to rob God, Malachi said (3:9). But is tithing still relevant to Christians, who are no longer under that Law?

Although tithing wasn't commanded until the Law, the Patriarchs tithed *before* that Law was given (Ge 14:18–20; 28:20–22). While well established in other ancient cultures, practised almost as a tax, the patriarchs' tithing was rather a spontaneous expression of worship and thanksgiving. The tithe was used for various purposes: supporting the Levites' ministry, providing for the needy, even being enjoyed by the worshippers (Dt 14:22–29). But to these basic laws the rabbis gradually added many others, which the Pharisees turned into opportunities for self-righteousness (Lk 18:11–12). It was this, rather than tithing as such, that Jesus attacked. As a Jew he would have tithed, and he certainly never abolished tithing, simply insisting it be done with right attitudes (Mt 23:23–24). But he also went further, commending a widow who gave all she had (Lk 21:1–4).

The New Testament makes no reference to Christians tithing. What is stressed is the importance of *generous giving*, a major theme in 2 Co 8–9 and frequently occurring elsewhere (e.g., Ac 11:29; Ro 12:13; 1Co 16:1–2; Gal 2:10; Php 4:14–17; 1Ti 5:17–18). While we cannot prove Christians tithed, it is hard to imagine them understanding 'generous giving' as *less* than they gave under the Law. There was certainly no compulsion, for 'God loves a cheerful giver' (2Co 9:7); but Paul saw generous giving as a natural expression of new life in Christ.

Giving, at whatever level, requires faith; but that is what being a Christian is all about.

people, a process that will be as painful as it is necessary.

3:6–4:6 Robbing God; the Day of the Lord

Nonetheless, the promise of forgiveness and restoration still stands. Despite Israel's obvious sin, the promise of reconciliation remains real and open. If Israel returns to the Lord, he will return to Israel (3:6–18). If Israel will only keep to what is required of her (e.g., in respect of tithes), all will be well. However, the signs are not good. As a result, the Lord proclaims the coming of the 'Day of the Lord' (4:1). In that day, the arrogant will be wiped out, while the righteous will bask in the light of the sun of righteousness (4:2).

When will this great day be? When will the Lord visit his temple? When will the Lord come? Malachi does not say.

What he does say, however, is that the Lord will send the prophet Elijah before that day comes, to prepare the way for his coming (4:5–6). So if Elijah should come again, people will know that a great day is about to dawn – a day that offers both a threat and a promise. Many years later, perhaps when some had given up hope, John the Baptist appeared by the Jordan, dressed in the manner of Elijah and declaring that he had come to prepare the way for someone greater than himself. You can understand the reason for the great sense of anticipation that developed.

This brings us to the great event of the coming of Jesus Christ and its implications for the world – the subject of the New Testament, to which we may now turn, eagerly awaiting the fulfilment of the great hopes of Israel.

THE NEW TESTAMENT

MATTHEW

Matthew is the first of the four Gospels. Each of the Gospels has distinctive characteristics. Perhaps the most noticeable feature of Matthew's Gospel is its concern to demonstrate the way in which Jesus Christ fulfils both the prophecies and expectations of the Jewish people. It seems that Matthew was especially concerned to show his readers how Jesus Christ was exactly the person towards whom the Old Testament was pointing.

The first three Gospels include a lot of material in common. This is widely believed to be due to the fact that all three draw on several common sources, such as collections of the sayings of Jesus that were committed to memory at a very early stage. Some material is common to all three Gospels. Some is common to Matthew and Luke (which are much longer than Mark). And some is found only in Matthew or Luke. In each case, the evangelist (as the gospel writers are known) has drawn on his own set of historical sources to allow his readers access to the details of the central figure of the Christian faith. The overlap between the first three Gospels is reflected in the name that is sometimes given to them: the 'Synoptic Gospels', from the Greek word *synopsis*, which means 'account' or 'summary'.

The earliest written documents of the Christian church are not the Gospels themselves, but some of the letters of Paul. So why should the Gospels have been written later than the letters? For the first few decades of its history, the Christian church relied on memorised accounts of the words and deeds of Jesus. Mark's Gospel is usually regarded as the first to have been written down, probably in the mid 60s. Matthew is often thought to have been written in the 70s, although the case for it having been written earlier is still upheld by some scholars. Luke's Gospel is also dated in the 70s by many scholars, although the possibility of an earlier date remains open.

16:1–12 The Pharisees and Sadducees

16:13–20 Peter recognises Jesus as the Christ and Son of God

16:21–28 Jesus Christ predicts his coming suffering

17:1–13 The transfiguration

17:14–27 Further ministry in Caesarea Philippi

18:1–35 Further parables of the kingdom

19:1–12 Teaching on divorce

19:13–15 Jesus Christ blesses the children

19:16–30 The rich young man

20:1–16 The parable of the workers in the vineyard

20:17–19 Further predictions of the death of Jesus Christ

20:20–28 Teaching on servant leadership

20:29–34 The healing of the blind men

The final week of Jesus Christ's earthly ministry

21:1–11 The entry into Jerusalem

21:12–17 The cleansing of the temple

21:18–23:39 Controversy with Jewish religious leaders

24:1–25:46 Teaching concerning the last times

26:1–29 The Last Supper

26:30–56 The betrayal in Gethsemane

26:57–27:26 The trial before the Jewish leaders and Pilate

27:27–66 The death and burial of Jesus Christ

28:1–20 The resurrection of Jesus Christ

MATTHEW 1:1–2:23
The Birth of Jesus Christ

1:1–17 The Genealogy of Jesus Matthew's immediate concern is to tell his readers about the background to the central figure of the gospel – Jesus Christ. He therefore opens by considering the background to his birth. First, he traces the family tree. Jesus is shown to be descended from the great Old Testament figures David and Abraham. This point would have been especially important to Jewish readers of this Gospel. They would realise that Jesus had the necessary family connections to be the 'Messiah' – that is, 'God's Anointed One' (1:17), who would bring in a new period in the history of God's people. Jesus is identified (1:1) as 'the son of David' (a strongly messianic title). Notice also that Joseph is referred to as the 'husband of Mary' (1:16), rather than the 'father of Jesus'.

Matthew is preparing his readers for the unusual circumstances surrounding the birth of Jesus, to which he will turn presently.

There are some interesting differences between the genealogies presented here and in Luke's Gospel (Lk 3:23–38). Matthew tends to trace Jesus' descent through Joseph, whereas Luke's preference is to trace it through Mary. This corresponds with Matthew's particular interest in Joseph, and Luke's in Mary. Matthew tells the story of the birth of Jesus, for example, from Joseph's perspective, whereas Luke relates it from Mary's. Matthew thus brings out the fact that, legally speaking, Jesus is the son of David.

Notice also how Matthew points out how the birth of Jesus is strategically located in the history of the people of God (1:17). Abraham marks the origins of Israel. God called him to leave his

home and become 'a great nation' (Ge 12:1–3). Fourteen generations later, the history of Israel entered a glorious new phase, with the reign of King David. This was followed fourteen generations later by the exile of Jerusalem to the great city of Babylon. This was seen by the Old Testament prophets as another turning point in the history of Israel, marking a new period in God's dealings with his people. It was a time of renewal, purification and judgment. And fourteen generations after this exile, Jesus Christ was born. The implication is clear: another turning point in God's dealings with his people is about to take place.

The word 'Christ' is worth further thought. Too often, it is treated as a surname, so that 'Jesus Christ' seems to be on the same level as 'John Smith'. Yet the second word is actually a title. The best translation of the name of the central figure of the Gospels is 'Jesus the Christ' or 'Jesus the Messiah' (the Greek word *christos*, from which we get the word 'Christ', means 'Anointed One' or 'Messiah').

The claim that the Messiah has finally come (1:17) would indeed be good news to many Jews. It is therefore important to demonstrate the grounds of this belief. What is there about the life of Jesus that

---

Did the Virgin Birth really happen?

In these scientific days surely we cannot believe that Jesus was born of a virgin, can we? And anyway, do we need to? After all, only Matthew mentions it. Many have therefore dismissed it as both impossible and unintended. Surely Matthew was simply using a literary device to show Jesus was somehow 'special', the fulfilment of Old Testament longings and promises.

But that is exactly the point. For the Old Testament itself said that *God* would one day come to redeem his people, a point underlined by John the Baptist who announced the coming of no one less than the LORD himself, the living God (e.g., Mt 3:1–12; Isa 40:3–5).

It is in the light of this promise that God himself would come that we must read the story of the Virgin Birth. While it is strange, even humanly speaking 'impossible', it surely cannot be ruled out if *God* chooses to come to us. Through the Virgin Birth he enabled his eternal Son to lay aside his divine powers and become truly human, having a brand new humanity created by the Spirit (rather than by human procreation) just like Adam at the beginning. This is why Paul calls Jesus 'the second man' (1Co 15:47). It was this creation of a new humanity that meant Jesus did not inherit Adam's sin like us – crucially important, for it was this sinlessness that made it possible for Jesus to die in our place, the sinless for the sinful.

Note also that neither Mary nor Joseph believed this at first; both required further revelation (Joseph) or a sign (Mary) to convince them. But others, not just Matthew, came to see its truth and importance, summed up in classic passages by Paul (Php 2:6–8) and John (Jn 1:1–14).

points to this conclusion? In many ways, Matthew's Gospel can be thought of as aiming to help its readers appreciate that the long-awaited Messiah has finally come in the person of Jesus of Nazareth.

1:18–25 The Birth of Jesus Christ Mary was 'pledged to be married' to Joseph, but had never had any sexual relations with him. When she is found to be pregnant, Joseph obviously fears the worst, and prepares to have the necessary divorce papers drawn up in private. Out of kindness to Mary, he resolves to avoid a public trial, which would have led to her being stoned to death (Dt 22:23–24). Yet even as he was considering this course of action, an 'angel of the Lord' speaks to him in a dream, and sets out the facts of the matter. Mary is pregnant through the Holy Spirit. The child who is to be born is no ordinary child. He is to be called 'Jesus, because he will save his people from their sins' (1:21). Note that Joseph is not allowed to choose the name of the child. For biblical writers, to name someone is to have authority over them (as when Adam was allowed to name the living creatures, Ge 2:19–20). Joseph is told to name the child 'Jesus', because the name is a vital indication of the significance of the child who will bear it. He is to be a saviour.

Matthew then introduces us to a major theme of his Gospel: the fulfilment of prophecy. At twelve points, Matthew shows how the events of Jesus' life and death fulfil the great prophetic hope of the Old Testament. Here Matthew points out how the birth of Jesus fulfils Isa 7:14, which speaks of a virgin bearing a child as a sign to God's people. Again, the name given to the child is enormously significant: he is called 'Immanuel', which means 'God with us' (1:23). This name conveys two vital ideas, which are central to the Gospel: 'God with us' means both that 'God is on our side' in our struggle against sin, despair and death; and that 'God is among us' in that he has chosen to dwell with men and women in the world. This central Christian idea (usually known as the 'doctrine of the incarnation') is of special importance in John's Gospel (see Jn 1:14). By fulfilling this great prophecy (and the others that follow), Jesus shows himself to be the culmination of the great hopes and expectations of the Old Testament.

2:1–12 The Visit of the Magi Matthew then details further events surrounding the birth of Jesus, which continue the theme of the fulfilment of prophecy. The birthplace of Jesus is identified as 'Bethlehem in Judea' (2:1), a village about 8 kilometres south of Jerusalem. The significance of this location is explained later (2:4–6), which points to the prophecy (Mic 5:2) of a future ruler and shepherd of God's people being born in this royal city. Yet the first worshippers of the newborn Christ are not Jews. They are Gentiles. Although they bring three gifts (2:11), we do not know that there were 'three wise men', as the Christmas tradition has it. The 'Magi' (2:1) were almost certainly astrologers from lands east of Judea, such as Persia. The reference to the 'star' (2:2, 9–10) is important. It clearly points to an unusual and significant heavenly event, which some scholars have interpreted as possibly a supernova, or perhaps two or more planets occupying positions very close to each other. But it also picks up

Judea in New Testament Times

N
W E
S

Sidon

Zarephath

Damascus

Abilene

Mt. Hermon

Tyre

Phoenicia

PROVINCE OF SYRIA

Iturea

Caesarea Philippi
(Paneas)

Ptolemais

L. Huleh
(Semechonitis)

Chorazin

TETRARCHY

Trachonitis

OF

PHILIP

Batanaea

Galilee

GALILEE

Sea of
Galilee

Gaulanitis

Mt. Carmel

R. Kishon

Cana?

Sepphoris

Cana?

Nazareth   Mt. Tabor

Nain?

The Great
Plain
(Esdraelon)

R. Yarmuk

Gadara

DECAPOLIS

Chorazin

Capernaum

Bethsaida

Gennesaret

Sea of
Galilee
(Gennesaret
Tiberias)

Taricheae
(Magadan)

Gergesa?

Tiberias

Hippos

Ceaesarea

Scythopolis

Salim?

Pella

Aenon?

The
Great
Sea

Samaria

Samaria

R. Jordan

Antipatris

R. Jabbok

Joppa

Arimathea?

PEREA

Lydda

Ephraim?

Philadelphia

Emmaus?

Jerusalem   Jericho

Emmaus?   Bethpage

Azotus

Bethany

Qumran

A   B

Ashkelon

Hill

country

NABATEAN

Gaza

of

Hebron

Judea

Machaerus

KINGDOM

Idumea

Wilderness of Judea

Dead
Sea
(Salt Sea)

R. Arnon

Masada

Beersheba

NABATEAN
KINGDOM

0   30 miles

0   50 kms

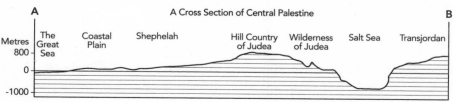

A   B

A Cross Section of Central Palestine

Metres   The   Coastal   Shephelah   Hill Country   Wilderness   Salt Sea   Transjordan
800   Great   Plain   of Judea   of Judea
         Sea

0

-1000

the great Old Testament theme of the star that 'will come out of Jacob' (Nu 24:17), widely seen as a messianic prophecy.

Both the future worship of Jesus Christ by the Gentiles and God's victory over the worship of heavenly objects is anticipated in this marvellous account of how the Magi 'bowed down and worshipped him' (2:11). The gifts they offer him are precious, an entirely appropriate means of honouring a future king. Yet King Herod (also known as 'Herod the Great') is deeply threatened by this development, which he clearly feels will lead to a loss of his own authority. If the real 'king of the Jews' (2:2) has now been born, what place will there be for Herod, who was installed as king of Judea by the Roman authorities? Herod moves to have Jesus eliminated, and orders the massacre of all young boys in Bethlehem under the age of two (2:16). This incident can remind readers of the story of Moses, who was also delivered from the massacre of young boys ordered by a frightened king (Ex 1:22–2:10).

2:13–18 The Escape to Egypt Warned in a dream of Herod's intention to kill Jesus, Joseph takes Mary and Jesus to Egypt for safety. Matthew points out how this action fulfils another Old Testament prophecy (Hos 11:1). Israel went into Egypt at the time of Joseph, and would finally be led out by God at the time of the exodus. Matthew sees the same pattern in the life of Jesus. And so the second chapter of this Gospel ends with an account of how Joseph, Mary and Jesus settle down in the small village of Nazareth, in the region of Galilee.

MATTHEW 3:1–4:11
The Opening of the Ministry of Jesus

3:1–12 John the Baptist Prepares the Way Some years now pass. Matthew opens his introduction to the ministry of Jesus by introducing John the Baptist, the son of Zechariah and Elizabeth (Lk 1:5–80). It is obvious that John creates a sensation, with crowds streaming out into the deserts to hear him speak. John is recognised as the forerunner of Jesus. In fulfilment of Old Testament prophecy, John comes as the one who was promised to 'prepare the way for the Lord' (3:3, citing Isa 40:3 and Mal 3:1). John, who clearly meets with considerable resistance from the Jewish religious authorities (3:7–10), sees his role as preparing the way for someone greater than himself. John can baptise only with water. The one who is to come will baptise with the Holy Spirit (3:11). So who is this mysterious person?

3:13–17 The Baptism of Jesus Matthew does not keep us in suspense for long. Jesus appears on the scene (3:13). John refuses to baptise him. The sinless Jesus does not need to be baptised, which is a symbol of repentance. But Jesus insists. The result is one of the most powerful moments in the ministry of Jesus: the Holy Spirit descends on him, as he receives an endorsement from God, who affirms that Jesus is his well-beloved Son (3:17). Note that Jesus does not *become* the Son of God at his baptism. God confirms what is already the case.

4:1–11 The Temptation of Jesus Just as Israel spent 40 years in the wilderness, being tested and prepared for their final

---

Is the Old Testament still important for Christians?

While many Christians feel the Old Testament must be important (after all, it's in the Bible), they aren't really sure why, and certainly aren't confident reading it. So is it still relevant today?

It is important to note, first, that the New Testament never rejects the Old Testament, nor sees it as less important than the New Testament. Paul sums up the early church's view: 'All Scripture is God-breathed and is useful for teaching, rebuking, correcting and training in righteousness' (2Ti 3:16) – and by 'all Scripture' he meant the Old Testament. Both he and Peter (2Pe 1:20–21) believed the Old Testament had huge abiding value because it was still God's word. But something had now changed; Jesus, the One for whom the Old Testament had prepared, had now come and this changed everything. The Old Testament now had to be read in the light of his coming. So Jesus said he hadn't come to abolish the Law and the Prophets (a common designation for the Old Testament) but rather to 'fulfil them' (Mt 5:17) – that is, 'to bring them to full completion'. He did this by fulfilling all its laws, rituals and sacrifices for us, which means we no longer need to try to do what he has already done for us. But those parts of the Bible are still important, for they constantly point us to Jesus, often prefiguring what he did.

But more than this, the Old Testament *as a whole* remains important, for it gives us the context for Jesus' coming, as it steadily unfolds God's plan of salvation. Salvation history did not begin with Jesus, even less with our particular church; and the Old Testament shows us how we fit into the bigger drama of what God is doing.

---

entry into the promised land, so Matthew tells us how Jesus is prepared for his mission to Israel through his temptation – a period of 40 days and nights in the wilderness, in which Jesus confronts and successfully resists temptation. The testing centres on whether Jesus will use his power and authority as the Son of God for his own advantage, or for the ends for which they have been given. There are important anticipations of the cross in this passage, especially the section dealing with the temptation to throw himself from the highest point of the temple, knowing that he would be saved (4:6). Will Jesus come down from the cross, and escape death? Or will he remain there, faithful to the end, and redeem those for whom he came to die? By the end of this period, it is clear that Jesus will be obedient to the will of his Father. He is ready to begin his public ministry.

MATTHEW 4:12–13:58
Jesus' Ministry in Galilee

4:12–17 Jesus Begins to Preach Jesus' ministry now begins in the region of Galilee. In fulfilment of Old Testament prophecy (4:14), Jesus begins to preach his message in this region. It has two central themes (4:17): the need for repentance, and the coming of the kingdom of God. Matthew relates how this message finds a response in the

calling of the first disciples, Peter, Andrew, James and John (4:18–22). They are fishermen – not academics, not religious teachers, not even educated people. They illustrate superbly the remarkable attraction that Jesus proves to have over people – an attraction that Matthew then documents from the early healing ministry of Jesus (4:23–25). Even at this early stage, Jesus creates a sensation.

5:1–7:29 The Sermon on the Mount But Jesus is not a mere healer. He has come to bring the good news of the kingdom of God. Immediately, Matthew introduces us to a major section of the teaching of Jesus, which is generally known as the 'Sermon on the Mount' (5:1–7:29). One of the most distinctive characteristics of Matthew's Gospel is the way in which the teachings of Jesus are conveniently arranged into five blocks of material, of which this is the first. Each block ends with similar words (7:28; 11:1; 13:53; 19:1; 26:1). The fivefold division may suggest that the author sees his work as a new Law (reflecting the five books of the Pentateuch: Genesis–Deuteronomy) and Jesus as a new and greater Moses. The sermon stresses the high demands that Christians are called to work towards, while realising that it is impossible to meet them without the grace of God himself.

For many commentators, the sermon sets out a series of standards that Christians should aim towards, even if they ultimately fail to reach them in their own lives. This does not mean that the demands are perfectionist or hopelessly idealistic. It just points to the fact that being a Christian makes a difference to the way in which such people live, and indicates the goals they should be aiming at, even if they cannot achieve them all. It is like being set on the right road, and encouraged to begin walking down it. Even if believers don't reach the end of that road, at least they know that they are walking in the right direction.

5:1–12 The Beatitudes The sermon opens with a set of pronouncements widely known as 'the Beatitudes'. Each pronouncement opens with the words 'Blessed are . . .'. The word 'blessed' is easily misunderstood. It does not really mean 'happy' or 'fortunate'. It is possible, as Jesus points out, to be blessed even if you are unhappy. Someone is 'blessed' if they have found favour and acceptance in the sight of God. Even if the believers' worldly status or situation is humble or distressing, they can know that they have found favour in the sight of God – which is much more important. Notice how many of the beatitudes emphasise that a lowly situation (such as meekness), or a situation of need (such as mourning or persecution) is seen as leading to blessing.

5:13–16 Salt and Light Believers are then compared to salt (5:13) and light (5:14–16). Believers are the 'salt of the earth', in that they can bring a new quality to the world. Perhaps with rock salt in mind (where water could easily wash out the salt, leaving only rock behind), Jesus stresses how easily believers can lose their 'saltiness' unless they take care to preserve it. Believers are also like lamps, who are able to bring light to a dark world, leading people to find and praise God.

5:21–48 The Fulfilment of the Law The coming of Jesus Christ is then declared to be in fulfilment of the Law, not contradiction of it. In no way does the coming of Jesus abolish the Law. He has come to fulfil it (5:17–20). In Christ, the purposes and intentions of the Law reach their climax and final fulfilment. He is the one to whom the Law and the Prophets point. While in no way endorsing the precise and detailed interpretations of the Law that prevailed in the Judaism of the time, Jesus is clearly indicating that the Old Testament continues to play an important role in the life of believers. The relation between the Old Testament law and the life of faith is explored in some detail in the writings of Paul, and will be returned to later in this work (see Romans 1–8).

Indeed, far from abolishing the Law, Jesus intensifies it. Murder is not simply about the physical action of killing. It is about the motivation that underlies this action. Adultery is not simply about the physical action of sleeping with someone else's partner. It is about the motivation for that action. If someone is asked to walk one mile, Jesus asks them to walk two. The basic theme is clear: the righteousness that is the ultimate goal of the new covenant actually *exceeds* that of the old covenant. There is thus no basis in the teaching of Jesus for any accusation of 'antinomianism' (that is, a disregard or contempt for the moral law) in the Christian life. Christians are obliged to do good. Yet Jesus insists that the motivation for doing such good deeds must not be to gain public favour, but to please God, who sees and rewards in secret (6:1–4). This also applies to prayer. Jesus is critical of loud, long and pompous public prayers, and declares that the prayers of individuals (by which he does not mean the public worship of the church) should ideally be in private, to avoid this temptation. In any case, the effectiveness of prayer is not dependent on its verbosity (6:5–8)!

6:9–15 The Lord's Prayer Having set the context in which prayer should be offered, Jesus hands down a model prayer, which has become an integral part of the life of Christian believers down the ages. It is generally known as 'The Lord's Prayer'. Its simplicity, brevity and intimacy set a model for the kind of prayer Jesus wishes his followers to adopt. The prayer affirms the fatherhood of God, reminding us that we owe our origins to him, and that he cares for his children. It reminds us that God is holy (the term 'hallowed' has the basic meaning of 'kept holy'), and that this holiness must be reflected in the way in which believers address God in prayer, speak of him to the world, and worship him. It asks God to bring about his sovereign will in the lives of believers – a dangerous prayer, given what God sometimes wants his people to do for him. The prayer then turns to the needs of believers – to their physical need for food, and their spiritual need for forgiveness, comfort and protection from temptation.

At this point, the prayer ends. However, some later versions of the text of Matthew's Gospel add a final concluding section offering glory to God, which reads as follows in the Authorised or King James Version: 'For thine is the kingdom, and the power, and the glory, for ever. Amen.' This longer version has

found its way into the traditional forms of public worship of many Christian denominations. Yet although the prayer has ended, Jesus' comments on its importance have not. In a passage that must not be overlooked, Jesus makes the point that God's forgiveness of our sins is linked with our forgiveness of the sins of others (6:14–15), a point illustrated by a parable later in this Gospel (18:21–35).

6:16–34 Fasting and the Providence of God Jesus now returns to the theme of giving glory to God, not currying favour with religious people (6:16–18). Underlying this point is the basic principle that it is more important to lay up an imperishable treasure in heaven, than to labour for something here on earth which will not endure (6:19–24). Believers must learn to trust in the providence of God, a lesson Jesus illustrates from the birds of the air and the lilies of the field. The important thing is to look towards God, not the world, and to trust in his goodness and seek his righteousness (6:25–34).

7:1–23 Judging Others; Answers to Prayer; Right Behaviour The sermon continues with a reminder of the sinfulness of human nature, which leads us to criticise others when we ought to be examining ourselves (7:1–6). Jesus affirms both the importance of prayer and God's goodness in responding to our needs. Just as human fathers, inadequate though they are, still want to do good for their children, so God takes delight in answering the requests of his children (7:7–12). The importance of right behaviour is stressed in a number of ways (7:13–23). Just as the good tree brings forth good fruit, so the

person who has really come to faith will naturally produce good works.

7:24–29 The Wise and Foolish Builders The sermon ends with the parable of the house built on the rock and the house built on the sand (7:24–27). Jesus here makes it clear that it is vitally important that the house of faith is built on a solid foundation, which will survive the worst storms life can produce. Only by building on Jesus Christ and his gospel can we be sure of the stability and peace that God intends for our lives.

The crowd are deeply impressed by this teaching, and recognise Jesus as someone who, unlike their own teachers, taught with authority (7:28–29). That authority is now confirmed by a series of events, before we come to the second major section of teaching (10:5–42). In a series of remarkable healings, Jesus demonstrates that there is something about him that distinguishes him from everyone else. All the signs of spiritual authority and power are present in his ministry – both in what he says and what he does. The 'Sermon on the Mount' focuses on what Jesus says; our attention is now drawn to what he does.

8:1–17 Jesus Heals Many The healing of the man with leprosy (8:1–4) illustrates the ability and willingness of Jesus to heal, as well as his affirmation of the Old Testament law – note how the healed leper is sent to the priest for confirmation of the healing. The healing of the centurion's servant (8:5–13) demonstrates the importance of faith for healing. As Jesus' words make clear, it also shows both that Gentiles are drawn to Jesus Christ and that they can benefit from his

ministry. (As a senior officer, the centurion would have been a Roman, not a Jew.) All these healings, together with many others, are in direct fulfilment of Old Testament prophecy (8:14–17).

8:18–9:8 Jesus' Authority After stressing the cost of following him, Jesus continues to demonstrate his authority over the natural and spiritual order – whether by stilling a storm, casting out demons or healing someone who is paralysed (8:18– 9:8). The crowds are amazed at his authority. Significantly, the demons recognise his true identity, hailing Jesus as the 'Son of God' (8:29).

9:9–13 The Calling of Matthew The calling of Matthew (widely regarded as the compiler of this Gospel) is of special interest (9:9–13). Matthew – referred to by his original name of 'Levi son of Alphaeus' in Mark's account of the same incident (Mk 2:13–17) – was a tax collector, and was thus a member of a group of Jews who were widely despised and regarded as outcasts by their fellows. At this time, the region of Palestine was occupied by the Romans. Not only did the tax collectors associate with the Gentile occupying power. They also charged more taxes than they were entitled to, as a way of ensuring their own wellbeing. As a result, they were detested by Jews, and regarded as traitors. Yet Jesus calls one of them to his inner circle. In this action, we can see one of the most important aspects of Jesus' ministry – his acceptance of those regarded as beyond hope of redemption by Judaism, including prostitutes, Gentiles and tax collectors. Jesus summarises this with his declaration that he has come to call

sinners, not the righteous (9:13). There is unquestionably a strong trace of irony in this declaration. Perhaps those, such as the Pharisees, who think they are righteous are merely self-righteous? The glorious new wine of the gospel cannot be contained by the tired old wineskins of Judaism (9:14–17).

9:18–38 Jesus Heals A series of further healings is then recorded. One is of particular interest. The woman who had been bleeding for twelve years (9:20) would have been regarded as unclean by Jews, on account of the discharge of a bodily fluid. Yet Jesus has no hesitation in healing her. What Judaism regards as unclean, Jesus sees as someone worth saving.

10:1–42 Jesus Sends out the Twelve A new phase in Jesus' ministry now develops. Jesus gives his twelve disciples authority to continue his ministry (10:1–4), and instructs them as he sends them out. They are to bring the good news of the coming of the kingdom of God, along with its attendant signs of healing and renewal, to the people of Israel (10:5– 42). Notice that initially Jesus sends his disciples only to the Jews, and instructs them to avoid others, such as Samaritans. It is clear that Jesus regards the Jews as the people of God, who have the right to hear the good news of what God is doing for his people before anyone else. As events prove, the rejection of Jesus and the gospel by Judaism leads to the opening up of the gospel and all its benefits to all peoples, a theme that is especially important for Paul (see Ro 1–11). Anticipating this rejection, Jesus makes it clear that his disciples can

expect to have a tough time as they preach this good news in Israel. But he reassures them of the continuing protection and provision of God as they set out. In moments of great stress, the Holy Spirit will even give them the words they need to speak.

11:1–19 Jesus and John the Baptist The story now shifts back to John the Baptist, who had been thrown in prison by Herod (see 14:3–4). John sends his followers to ask Jesus whether he is the long-expected Messiah, or whether they will have to wait for someone else (11:2–3). In reply, Jesus lists the great signs of the coming of the Messiah that had been prophesied in the past (Isa 35:4–6; 61:1). As can be seen from his ministry at this stage, they have all been fulfilled. It is clear that the Messiah has indeed arrived. Jesus declares that John marks the end of an age. He is the Elijah, whom the Old Testament promised would come before the coming of the Lord himself (Mal 4:5). Jesus' words leave us with no option but to conclude that he himself is the Lord.

11:20–12:14 Lack of Repentance; Sabbath-rest Although many respond to Jesus, it is clear that many refuse to repent (11:20–24). But for those who do repent, Jesus offers rest and refreshment (11:25–30). This theme of rest is developed in the account of Jesus breaking the Sabbath laws by picking corn and healing people on the day of rest (12:1–13). Two points are brought out clearly here. First, Jesus has authority over the Sabbath. Secondly, the Sabbath was instituted in order to give people refreshment, rather than to add still further to their burdens.

12:15–50 Old Testament Prophecy, and Jesus' Authority Over Evil Spirits The theme of the relation of Jesus to Old Testament prophecy is then taken up once more. Matthew shows how Jesus' ministry fulfils one of the great messianic prophecies of the Old Testament (12:15–21; see Isa 42:1–4). He also reports how the resurrection of Jesus will bring to fulfilment the 'sign of Jonah' (12:38–42) through his resurrection from the dead. Yet the theme of the authority of Jesus over evil spirits is also significant in this section (12:22–37; 43–45). It is clear that Jesus has authority over such spirits. The question then arises concerning the basis of this authority. The crowds attribute this authority to his messianic status. His opponents attempt to cast aspersions on Jesus by suggesting that he has authority over demons because he is in league with 'Beelzebul, the prince of demons' (12:24). This assertion is the unforgivable sin – the blasphemy against the Holy Spirit, by which the great acts of God are attributed to Satan.

13:1–52 Parables of the Kingdom A third major section of teaching now opens (13:1–58), which includes some 'parables of the kingdom'. The fact that Jesus teaches in parables is itself significant, as it points to the fulfilment of another Old Testament prophecy (13:35; see Ps 78:2; Hos 12:10). The Hebrew word hinted at here has a number of meanings, including 'riddle' or 'dark saying'. As becomes clear, these 'dark sayings' can be understood only by those who have been given the privilege of understanding them. Some may hear them, and yet totally fail to understand what they are all about. They will see, but not perceive (13:10–17).

JESUS' PARABLES

Parable	Matthew	Mark	Luke
A lamp under a bowl	5:14–15	4:21–22	8:16; 11:33
Wise and foolish builders	7:24–27		6:47–49
New cloth on an old garment	9:16	2:21	5:36
New wine in old wineskins	9:17	2:22	5:37–38
The sower and soils	13:3–8	4:2–20	8:4–8
Mustard seed	13:31–32	4:30–32	13:18–19
Weeds	13:24–30		
Yeast	13:33		13:20–21
Hidden treasure	13:44		
The valuable pearl	13:45–46		
The net	13:47–48		
A house owner	13:52		
Lost sheep	18:12–13		15:4–6
The unmerciful servant	18:23–34		
Workers in the vineyard	20:1–16		
Two sons	21:28–31		
Tenants	21:33–41	12:1–9	20:9–16
Wedding banquet	22:2–14		
The fig-tree	24:32–33	13:28–29	21:29–32
Ten virgins	25:1–13		
Bags of gold (minas)	25:14–30		19:12–27
Sheep and goats	25:31–46		
Growing seed		4:26–29	
A money-lender			7:41–43
The good Samaritan			10:30–37
A friend in need			11:5–8
The rich fool			12:16–21
Watchful servants			12:35–40
The unfruitful fig-tree			13:6–9
The lowest place at the feast			14:7–14
The great banquet			14:16–24
The cost of discipleship			14:28–33
A lost coin			15:8–10
The lost son			15:11–32
The shrewd manager			16:1–8
A rich man and Lazarus			16:19–31
A master and his servant			17:7–10
A persistent widow			18:2–8
A Pharisee and a tax collector			18:10–14

The first such parable is the *parable of the sower* (13:1–9, 18–23). This parable notes how the same seed falls on different kinds of ground. What eventually happens to it depends on the quality of the soil. In the same way, Jesus sows the seed of the word of God through his preaching. The effect it has on people depends on how they respond to it. If someone should fail to respond, or fall away, it is not on account of any failure on the part of the seed.

The second parable focuses on a *field of wheat*, in which an enemy of the farmer has sown some weeds (13:24–30, 36–43). Wheat and weeds thus grow alongside one another. Rather than risk damaging the wheat by getting rid of the weeds at this stage, the farmer decides to wait till the harvest. They will be separated out then. And so there will be good and evil people in the world. They will be separated out only at the last judgment. Rather than risk injuring the righteous, God will wait until the end to sort things out – and sort them out permanently. The same point is also made in the parable of the net (13:44–50).

Two brief parables – the growth of *a seed* and *the spread of yeast in dough* – illustrate the way in which the kingdom of God can expand from small beginnings (13:31–33). The value and attraction of the gospel are then illustrated by the parables of buried treasure and the pearl of great price (13:44–45).

13:53 A Prophet Without Honour This section of Matthew's Gospel concludes by reporting the rejection of Jesus by his own people at Nazareth. Despite all the signs of spiritual authority and power, the people of Nazareth are dismissive of him. Because of their lack of faith, Jesus performs no miracles in his home town. This points to an important general principle: no faith, no miracles. Faith is the precondition of benefiting from Christ.

MATTHEW 14:1–20:34
The Final Phase of Jesus' Ministry

14:1–36 John the Baptist Beheaded; the Popularity of Jesus A new phase begins with the execution of John the Baptist (14:1–12). As a result of this, Jesus attempts to withdraw from his public ministry. However, the crowds will not allow him to be on his own. The feeding of the five thousand (14:13–21) illustrates the huge size of the crowds now following him, as much as it points to the compassion and power of Jesus. His authority over the natural order is again emphasised through his walking on the water and the ensuing stilling of the storm. Again, we learn of the huge interest in Jesus, evident in the large crowds that gather everywhere he moves (14:22–36).

15:1–39 Jesus and Judaism The relationship of Jesus to the Judaism of his day now comes into focus once more. The issue of ritual cleanliness emerges as important, with the Pharisees protesting against the disciples' failure to observe ritual cleanliness traditions (15:1–19). Jesus argues that the Pharisees are putting human traditions above the word of God. The evil thoughts of the heart, not eating food with unwashed hands, make a person unclean. This rebuke directed against the traditionalism of the Pharisees is followed by an incident that

shows how people outside Judaism (in this case, a woman from the region of Tyre and Sidon) were attracted to Jesus, and put their faith in him (15:21–28). The feeding of the four thousand (15:29–39), which is very similar to the earlier account of the feeding of the five thousand, once more points to both the appeal and authority of Jesus.

16:1–12 Pharisees and Sadducees and the Demand for a Sign

But not everyone is prepared to accept the authority of Jesus. The Pharisees and Sadducees (the two main religious parties) put him to the test, and demand a sign by which this authority can be verified (16:1–4). Jesus points them to the 'sign of Jonah', a clear reference to his forthcoming resurrection (see 12:39–40). After warning his disciples against the influence of the Pharisees and Sadducees (16:5–12), Jesus and his disciples press on to the region of Caesarea Philippi. It is here that one of the most important incidents in the ministry of Jesus takes place. This time, however, it is the disciples rather than Jesus who are the focus of attention.

16:13–20 Peter's Confession of the Messiah

Jesus asks his disciples the basic question 'Who do people say that I am?' (He uses the technical term 'Son of Man' to refer to himself in this case.) The disciples report back on the various opinions they have heard: Jesus is one of the prophets, or John the Baptist come back to life, or perhaps Elijah. But Jesus presses them: 'What about you? Who do *you* say that I am?' This is a vitally important question. Unlike the crowds, the disciples have been with Jesus throughout most of his ministry. They have watched him and listened to him. Now they are being asked what their conclusion is.

Peter speaks for them all when he replies that he believes that Jesus is the Messiah, the Son of the living God (16:13–20). Jesus is the long-awaited Messiah, who has come to his people. Jesus declares that Peter is correct. This is no conclusion that he could have reached unaided. He has been assisted by God himself in reaching this momentous conclusion. Presumably anxious that the title 'Messiah' might be understood in a purely political sense, Jesus asks the disciples not to tell anyone of their realisation of his true identity. The Messiah could too easily be misunderstood as a triumphalist political leader, concerned only to liberate the country from its Roman occupying force.

16:21–28 Jesus Predicts His Death

But it is clear that the disciples themselves also have misunderstandings concerning Jesus. Immediately after their confession that he is the Messiah, Jesus declares that he must go to Jerusalem, suffer, be put to death and finally rise from the dead. He is under compulsion to do this. It is part of his calling. He must do it. But the disciples cannot cope with this. It was no part of their traditional view of the Messiah that he should suffer and die. Peter protests – and is rebuked by Jesus (16:21–28).

17:1–13 The Transfiguration

An important anticipation of the resurrection now follows. The account of the transfiguration (17:1–13) demonstrates both the continuity of Jesus with the ministries of Moses and Elijah, while at the same time providing an anticipation

of the resurrection glory of Christ. An endorsement of Jesus' identity and authority from heaven confirms his ministry and mission.

17:14–18:20 Humility and Sin Within the Church

After reports of further healing and teaching in the region (17:14–27), we come to the fourth major block of teaching in this Gospel (18:1–35). This teaching focuses on the importance of humility (18:1–9), and the importance of individual Christian believers (18:10–14). Jesus makes clear the way in which sin within the church is to be handled, and affirms that where two or three are gathered together in his name, he himself is present among them (18:15–20).

18:21–35 The Parable of the Unmerciful Servant

This section of teaching includes a major parable relating to forgiveness. Jesus speaks of a person who is a servant to a king, who runs up a huge debt. So great is the debt that he and his entire family will have to be sold into slavery in order to meet his obligations. The servant begs for his debt to be cancelled. In his mercy, the king agrees. Yet the servant promptly demands immediate payment of a trivial debt owed him by another servant. When this unfortunate man proves unable to pay, he is thrown into prison. The king is outraged by this behaviour, and revokes his forgiveness of the huge debt. This parable supplements the important concluding sections of the Lord's Prayer (6:14–15), and speaks of our forgiveness depending upon our forgiving others 'seventy-seven times' (or perhaps 'seventy times seven'). In other words, forgiveness is to be offered time and time again, without any limits.

19:1–30 Divorce, Little Children; the Rich Young Man

After this, Jesus crosses the Jordan, and undertakes a teaching and healing ministry in the area. Part of that teaching ministry includes clarification on Moses' teaching concerning divorce (19:1–12), and an important affirmation of young children (19:13–15). This is followed by the meeting with the rich young man (19:16–30), in which the question of the conditions for salvation are discussed. After discovering that the young man has faithfully kept the commandments, Jesus asks him to sell all he has, and follow him. This dismays the young man, who departs with great sadness. Notice that Jesus does not make any attempt to compromise his position. It is difficult for someone who is rich to enter the kingdom of God. But Jesus does not say that it is impossible. It is clear that wealth poses a real obstacle to coming to God. Nevertheless, as Jesus makes clear, with God anything is possible. Nobody lies outside the saving purposes of God, who has promised salvation to those who put their faith in Jesus Christ.

20:1–16 The Parable of the Workers in the Vineyard

This theme of the faithfulness of God to his promises is taken up in the parable of the workers in the vineyard (20:1–16). The parable focuses on a landowner who offers some workers a denarius – the usual daily wage – to work in his vineyard for a day. Later he hires some more, promising them the same wage, even though they will work for a shorter period. He does the same again at noon, and in the middle of the afternoon. At dusk he pays all the workers the same wage, despite the fact that some have

How does God see divorce?

Trying to catch Jesus out, the Pharisees asked for his views on divorce, a topic hotly debated by rabbis. Two main schools had developed, both claiming to be true interpretations of Moses' teaching in Dt 24:1, which spoke of a man finding 'something indecent' in his wife and using this to divorce her. Rabbi Shammai interpreted this as adultery, while Rabbi Hillel interpreted it more liberally, seeing it as anything the husband found unacceptable, including a burnt dinner. The Pharisees wanted to know whom Jesus supported.

His answer was – neither. Both were misinterpreting Moses who, in context (Dt 24:1–4), was not teaching a principle about divorce but rather saying that *if* a man divorced his wife he could not remarry her later. He wasn't justifying divorce (in fact, he completely forbade frivolous divorce, Dt 22:13–19), but simply recognising it sometimes happened – a permission, not a command, as Jesus reminded them (Mt 19:7–8). But Jesus then raised the bar higher, reminding them that even this permission was not God's plan from the beginning (see Ge 2:24) and that divorce and remarriage on any grounds other than marital unfaithfulness was therefore adultery in God's sight. This teaching was so stark that even his disciples reacted to men being robbed of their traditional and easy way of opting out of the marriage commitment (v.11). To this sole ground for divorce, Paul adds one other: where someone (man or woman) becomes a Christian and their spouse refuses to stay married because of it (1Co 7:12–16).

Clearly this is challenging teaching (though no more so today than in Jesus' day), but being a Christian means following Jesus' teaching in this area as much as any other, despite cultural norms. However, while God hates divorce (Mal 2:13–16), he does not hate the divorced. With him there is always hope of forgiveness and redemption.

laboured all day, and some for only a matter of two or three hours. The workers who had been hired at the beginning of the day are furious: it's not fair, they declare. Yet the landowner had remained faithful to his promises.

The importance of the parable for believers lies at two different levels. First, it allows them to see that even though God called the Gentiles later than the Jews, both are still entitled to the same reward of salvation. And it also reminds them that the promise of forgiveness and salvation remains open, even though some may respond to that offer only late in the day.

20:17–19 Jesus Predicts His Death as a Ransom for Many Readers are then reminded once more of the high price of that salvation, as Jesus once more predicts his betrayal, suffering and resurrection. These passages remind us also that Jesus' death is no accident. It is something that has been purposed and foretold. Jesus dies because he has to die – there is no other way in which sinful humanity can be redeemed. The crucifixion has to happen.

This prediction of suffering and death is followed by a deeply moving declaration on the part of Jesus. He has come to serve, and to give his life as a ransom for many (20:20–28). The word 'ransom' indicates a payment made by which freedom is gained. Through the death of Jesus Christ, believers are liberated from bondage to sin. Secular rulers may lord it over people. Christian leaders, however, are to serve their peoples, as Christ served before them. The compassion of Jesus in his ministry is then further demonstrated by his healing of two blind men (20:29–34).

MATTHEW 21:1–28:20
The Final Week

21:1–11 The Triumphal Entry While all this has been going on, Jesus and his disciples have been drawing nearer and nearer to Jerusalem. According to Dt 16:16, all Jewish men were required to celebrate the Passover feast in Jerusalem itself. On this occasion, the Passover would take on a special significance for Jesus, who turns out to be the true Passover lamb, sacrificed for the sins of the world. Jesus had told his disciples that he must go to Jerusalem, to be betrayed and crucified. Now Jesus prepares to enter the great city itself (21:1–4). Jesus enters in humility, mounted on a donkey, in fulfilment of a great messianic prophecy of the Old Testament (Zec 9:9). Jesus enters Jerusalem as its king, an event especially celebrated by Christians on Palm Sunday. It is clear that there were many who were looking forward to this event. He is greeted by crowds, honouring him and singing his praises (21:5–11). Although Jesus is treated as a king, the crowds refer to him as a prophet (21:11). They have yet to discover that he is both prophet and king – and also a saviour.

21:12–22 Conflict with the Religious Authorities The final week of Jesus' life is packed with teaching and conflict with the religious authorities. The first major incident is the celebrated cleansing of the temple, in which Jesus ejects the merchants and overturns the tables of the money-changers and sellers of doves (21:12–17). The protest is probably only partly against the commercialisation of the temple areas. It almost certainly represents Jesus' anger that any form of payment or purchase is necessary before an individual may worship God. The cursing of the fig-tree (21:18–22) represents Jesus' anger against the Judaism of his time, which was barren when it ought to have borne much fruit.

21:23–46 Jesus Is Questioned and Rejected Controversy now develops with increasing intensity. Once more the authority of Jesus is questioned by his critics (21:23–27), who prove unable to give an adequate response to Jesus' challenge to them. Jesus stresses that it is more important to do the will of God than to talk about it. Prostitutes and tax collectors will be given preference over the Pharisees for this reason (21:28–32). This point is reinforced by the parable of the tenants (21:33–46), which is a superb and distressing illustration of the way in which Judaism had rejected the prophets of God, and was also about to reject the Son of God. The final killing of the son reminds us of Jesus' predictions of his own death in Jerusalem, through which his final rejection by Judaism will be sealed.

The question of who will enter the kingdom of God is then addressed through the parable of the wedding feast (22:1–14). A great wedding feast is prepared, and a select few invited. When these refuse or fail to turn up, the invitation is extended to all around. The point of the parable is simple. The gospel invitation is first offered to Israel. When she fails to respond, or rejects the invitation, it is thrown open to the Gentiles. Yet the invitation is not unconditional. Just as the wedding guests must dress in an appropriate way for the feast, so repentance and faith are needed to enter the kingdom of God.

22:15–46 More Controversial Questions

Jesus then addresses a series of controversial questions raised by the Pharisees and Sadducees, who attempt to outwit him. An initial attempt is made by the Pharisees to trap Jesus by embroiling him in a controversy that relates to the Roman authorities (22:15–22). Should Jews pay taxes to the Romans or not? The Pharisees are opposed to paying such taxes. The Herodians (who are strongly pro-Roman) are in favour. Both groups are opposed to Jesus. Whichever way he replies, Jesus will lose out, either by supporting treason or by supporting the Romans. Jesus takes neither option, evading the trap set for him. He draws attention to the image of Caesar on the coins used to pay the tax. What is Caesar's should be given to Caesar. What is God's should be given to God. As humanity is created in the image of God (Ge 1:26–27), this reply is actually a declaration of the need for people to dedicate themselves to him.

This is followed by a question raised by the Sadducees concerning marriage at the resurrection (22:23–33). In an attempt to trap Jesus into conceding that there is no resurrection, they ask a question, based on marriage in heaven, designed to demonstrate the logical impossibility of resurrection. Jesus points out that, as there is no marriage in heaven, their argument falls to the ground. Since the Sadducees are reduced to silence over this, the Pharisees quiz him over which of the commandments in the Law is the greatest (22:34–40). This is not specifically a question about the Ten Commandments. The Law was generally regarded as having 613 commandments. Jesus was being asked to single one out as being of supreme importance. By bringing together Dt 6:5 and Lev 19:18, Jesus provides a succinct answer to this question – and then puts one of his own to the Pharisees (Mt 22:41–46). As stated, the question has no easy answer, and reduces Jesus' opponents to silence.

23:1–39 Seven Woes

Jesus continues his controversial ministry in Jerusalem by condemning the religion of his day for its many faults (23:1–39). Particular criticism is directed against the external and formal character of the religion of the Pharisees. All too often, they have become preoccupied with trivial matters, and have neglected the great issues of justice and faith. They 'strain out a gnat but swallow a camel' (23:24). (The reference here is to the smallest and largest types of unclean creatures.)

24:1–35 Signs of the End of the Age

Jesus now opens the fifth and final section of his teaching. This section focuses on the

end of the age (24:1–25:46). This section, which is sometimes referred to as the 'Olivet discourse', alerts the disciples to the troubles that lie ahead. The distress and pain that lie in the future are vividly described. Many of these sayings will find at least partial fulfilment in the destruction of Jerusalem by the Roman armies in AD 70. This will be a time of betrayal, of persecution and of false teaching. It is, however, clear that Jesus' ultimate reference is to the end of the world itself, at a time and date unknown to all save the Father. Not even the Son knows this (24:36). It will come like a thief in the night (24:42–44) – a saying of Jesus that Paul picks up and uses in 1Th 5:2.

24:36–25:13 The Day and Hour Unknown The sudden coming of the end leads Jesus to place a particular emphasis on the need for watchfulness. Unlike the householder who was not prepared for the thief who broke into his property, believers must not be taken unawares by the coming of the Lord. This point is made with clarity in the parable of the ten virgins (25:1–13), which exhorts its hearers to 'keep watch, because you do not know the day or the hour'.

25:14–30 The Parable of the Bags of Gold The theme of the return of the Lord is also explored in a different direction in the parable of the bags of gold (25:14–30). Attention here focuses on what the servants do during the master's absence. The parable tells of a master who entrusts his bags of gold to his servants during his absence, and of the variety of ways in which the servants make use of that money. The main point

being made is that the master will return, without warning, to see what has happened in his absence.

Yet in addition to this, three other points are made by this parable. First, talents are gifts from God. The servants had no claim on the money: it was their master's, entrusted to them during his absence. They were stewards, rather than possessors, of the money. They were responsible for its wise use during the master's absence. Secondly, God's gifts are given in order to be used. The returning master is furious with the servant who buried his bag of gold, and refused to use it. Believers are responsible thus for using these gifts in the world, and will be held accountable for the way in which they are used. And thirdly, God's gifts increase through being used. The parable tells of three servants, two of whom use their bags of gold, and the third who buries it in the ground. This final bag of gold remains unaltered in its hole in the ground. It was not used and therefore did not grow. The two other servants, however, found that the money with which they had been entrusted increased through being used wisely. Faith does not deepen through being allowed to stagnate, but through being applied.

25:31–46 The Sheep and the Goats This is followed by the parable of the sheep and the goats, which develops the theme of judgment. The parable points to the ultimate separation of the good and the wicked, developing the ideas already found in the parable of the weeds (13:24–30, 36–43) and the net (13:47–50). The parable brings out clearly the importance of good works in the

Christian life as a mark of true commitment to Christ.

26:1–13 Preparations for Jesus' Death

The pace of the narrative now quickens dramatically. It is two days from the Passover, and Jesus foretells once more his forthcoming crucifixion. In the meantime, arrangements are made by the Jewish authorities for the arrest of Jesus, culminating in Judas Iscariot's decision to go to the chief priests and offer to hand Jesus over to them. Jesus himself is anointed in preparation for burial as this is happening.

26:17–30 The Last Supper

Having hinted at the forthcoming death of Jesus in many ways, Matthew now narrates the events of the Last Supper. This event is a Passover meal, which takes place the evening before the crucifixion. For Jews, the meal acted as a reminder of the great act of deliverance through which God led his people out of Egypt (see Ex 11–12). Jesus celebrates this meal with the twelve disciples. It is clearly an occasion of great intimacy. Yet Jesus then announces that one of them – one of his closest colleagues – will betray him. The disciples are shocked at this. Yet Jesus insists that this must happen. It has been foretold in Scripture (as in Ps 41:9, Isa 53:1–12), and so must come to pass. But this does not in any way excuse his betrayer, who is now publicly identified as Judas. (Note how Judas refers to Jesus merely as 'Rabbi' or teacher, while the others refer to him as 'Lord'.) Jesus then offers his disciples broken bread as a sign of his soon-to-be-broken body, and wine as a sign of the new covenant that will be established through his blood, and through which forgiveness of sins will be possible. By continuing to eat bread and drink wine in remembrance of Jesus Christ, Christians ensure that the full significance of his saving death will never be forgotten.

26:31–46 Peter's Denial; Jesus and the Disciples at Gethsemane

The group then moves to the Mount of Olives, where Jesus explains that the disciples will fall away on account of the events that are about to take place, in fulfilment of the messianic prophecy of Zec 13:7 (26:31–35). Yet in this moment of darkness and gloom, a ray of light shines. Jesus declares that after he has risen, he will go ahead of the disciples to Galilee. Peter refuses to believe this. No matter what happens, he will stand by his Lord. Yet Jesus gently rebukes him: that night, Peter will deny him three times. The weakness of the disciples immediately becomes apparent, when they move on to Gethsemane (26:36–46). Clearly deeply distressed at the knowledge of what lies ahead, Jesus turns to prayer. The disciples just fall asleep.

Jesus' prayer is especially important. He prays that, if possible, 'this cup' may be taken from him. In this context, the cup is a symbol of sorrow and suffering. It is clear that the full humanity of Jesus expresses itself in this prayer. He does not want to die. But if God has purposed that he should die, then he will bear its pain. Many commentators see in this prayer evidence that the full weight of human sin is beginning to bear down on Jesus, cutting him off from his Father. On the cross, he will experience a sense of being totally abandoned by God, on account of the burden of human sin.

Here in Gethsemane we can begin to see our sin being transferred to Christ.

26:47–56 Jesus Arrested Finally, the moment of betrayal arrives. The fact that it has been foretold in no way diminishes its tragedy and pathos. Judas, again greeting Jesus as a mere 'Rabbi', betrays him with a sign of love – a kiss. Jesus is resigned to this. Scripture must be fulfilled. Obedient to the will of his Father, here as always, Jesus allows himself to be led away, as his disciples scatter – like sheep whose shepherd has been struck down (26:47–56).

26:57–68 Before the Sanhedrin Jesus is then dragged before representatives of the Jewish religious establishment. (A religious trial before the high priest will be followed by a civil trial in front of the Roman governor Pontius Pilate.) He is followed, at a safe distance, by Peter. Under Jewish law, two male witnesses were required to secure a conviction of any kind. This poses some problems, as no witnesses are forthcoming. Eventually, two come forward with a somewhat garbled version of some of Jesus' words. It might have been possible to convict him on the basis of this obvious distortion. However, the high priest asks Jesus specifically whether he is 'the Messiah, the Son of God'. In answer to this direct question, Jesus replies in the affirmative. Notice that Jesus himself never *himself* claims to be the Messiah. But when others realise who he is (as with the disciples at Caesarea Philippi, 16:13–17), or ask him specifically whether he is the Messiah, he admits to being so. The high priest is outraged that anyone should make such claims, and declares

that he is guilty of blasphemy. And so anyone doing so would be – unless they *were* the Messiah and Son of God. The penalty for blasphemy was death. However, with one exception, the Romans had deprived the Sanhedrin (that is, the 71-member supreme Jewish court, consisting of the chief priests, elders and teachers of the Law) of the right to sentence anyone to death. This was a matter for the Roman authorities. And so Jesus is taken to the Romans. They will decide what to do next.

26:69–75 Peter Disowns Jesus The narrative now switches to Peter, who has been waiting outside in the courtyard, keeping his distance from what is going on inside the house. It is obvious that he is very apprehensive. He is noticed by some of the servants, who challenge him. Hasn't he been with Jesus? Surely he is one of his followers? But Peter denies having anything to do with Jesus – three times. After the third denial, the cock crows, and Peter realises that he has not only failed Jesus, but that Jesus' prediction of his failure has come true.

It is worth making a comment on the 'cock crowing'. The Romans divided the night into four 'watches' – 'evening' 6:00–9:00 p.m., 'midnight' 9:00–12:00 midnight, 'when the cock crows' 12:00 midnight–3:00 a.m., and 'dawn' 3:00–6:00 a.m. These four watches are referred to at Mk 13:35. The 'cock crowing' may in fact be a reference to the trumpet blast that marked the end of the third watch of the night, rather than to the cry of a cockerel.

27:1–10 Judas Hangs Himself But Peter's failure is totally overshadowed by that of

Judas, who has betrayed Jesus for 30 pieces of silver, in fulfilment of Old Testament prophecy (the prophecy in question seems to bring together both Jer 19:1–13 and Zec 11:12–13). He is burdened down with his guilt, and clearly wants to repent and receive forgiveness for what he has done. But the Jewish leaders, who here may be taken as a symbol of Judaism at that time, have no forgiveness to offer. They tell Judas that it is his responsibility. We see in this passage one of the greatest paradoxes of the Gospel: Judas, who probably needs forgiveness more than anyone, is the one who brings about the death of the one through whom forgiveness ultimately comes.

27:1–31 Jesus Before Pilate The narrative now returns to Jesus, who has been brought before Pontius Pilate, Roman governor of Judea AD 26–36. Pilate confronts Jesus with the charges brought against him, and is amazed when Jesus makes no reply. However, we may see in this the fulfilment of an important Old Testament prophecy: that the suffering Messiah would be silent before his accusers (Isa 53:7). Pilate's inclination, which would have been reinforced by his wife's belief in Jesus' innocence, would probably have been to order some token punishment, but take things no further. However, the crowd is whipped up into a frenzy by agitators. They demand that Jesus be crucified.

Pilate, who has the right to release a prisoner at Passover, offers to release either Jesus or a convict named Barabbas. The crowd demands the release of Barabbas, and the death of Jesus. Barabbas is thus the first to benefit

directly from the death of Christ. He ought to have died. Jesus dies in his place. Washing his hands of the whole affair, Pilate sends Jesus off to be flogged and crucified. Jesus is then humiliated by the Roman soldiers, who dress him up in a caricature of royal costume, including a crown of thorns.

The floggings administered by the Romans were vicious. They had been known to cause the death of victims before they were crucified. Under Jewish law, victims were allowed to be flogged only with 40 strokes. This was invariably reduced to 39, as an act of leniency. But under Roman law, there were no limits to the extent of the suffering to be inflicted. The whips used for this purpose generally consisted of several strands of leather with small pieces of metal or broken bones at the end. These tore apart the skin of those being whipped, with the result that many did not survive the ordeal.

27:32–43 The Crucifixion Jesus is clearly severely weakened by his beating, and proves unable to carry his own cross. Simon from Cyrene is forced to carry it for him. Finally, they reach Golgotha, the place of execution. This place is also often referred to as 'Calvary', from the Latin word *calvaria*, meaning 'the skull' – the literal meaning of 'Golgotha'. As Jesus hangs on the cross, he is mocked by those watching him die, while the Roman soldiers cast lots for his clothes. These events fulfil the great Old Testament prophecy of the fate of the righteous sufferer of Psalm 22 (see Ps 22:7–8, 18). The identity of Jesus with this sufferer is confirmed by his cry of utter desolation (27:46), which draws on the opening

verse of this important psalm. It is here that Jesus experiences the sense of the absence of God. The sin he is bearing on behalf of his people has now cut him off from his Father.

27:45–56 The Death and Burial of Jesus

Finally, Jesus dies. Darkness settles over the land, perhaps pointing to the fact that the 'light of the world' (Jn 8:12) has been extinguished. A series of events then takes place, pointing to the significance of what has just happened. The opening of the tombs points ahead to the resurrection of Christ. However, the tearing of the 'curtain of the temple' is of particular interest. The 'curtain of the temple' was an especially important feature of the Old Testament tabernacle (Ex 26:31–35). It was included in order to provide a means of restricting access to the 'Most Holy Place', the region of the tabernacle regarded as sacrosanct. Although the curtain served an important practical function in relation to the worship of Israel, it came to have a deeper significance. The fact that the curtain prevented ordinary worshippers from entering the 'Most Holy Place' came to be seen as pointing to a much deeper separation between God and sinful humanity. The curtain thus came to be a symbol of the barrier placed between God and humanity by human sinfulness. The tearing of this curtain at the crucifixion (27:51) is a symbol of one of the chief benefits brought about by the death of Christ: the barrier between God and humanity caused by sin has been torn down, so that there is now free access for believers to God on account of Christ's death (Ro 5:1–2).

The disciples, we now discover, are nowhere to be found. Matthew carefully identifies some witnesses of the death of Jesus. Not a single disciple is mentioned. It seems that they, like sheep without a shepherd, have scattered – just as Jesus predicted. The witnesses who are identified are the Roman centurion, who declares that Jesus is the 'Son of God' (27:54) – a vitally important testimony, coming from a Gentile. The chief priest, symbolising his own Jewish people, has refused to accept that Jesus is the Son of God. Yet here we can see the acceptance of this fact among the Gentiles, anticipating both the mission to the Gentiles, and the enormous appeal that the gospel would prove to have to those outside Judaism. The other witnesses are women. Notice how Matthew names them (27:55–56), so that they will not be forgotten. Finally, Jesus is buried in a borrowed tomb (27:57–61). The women are still there, keeping vigil by the tomb, at the end of this long day – the first Good Friday.

The prophecy of resurrection has not been forgotten, however – at least, not by the Jewish leaders. In order to forestall any attempt on the part of the disciples to steal the body of Christ, and thus spread false rumours of his resurrection, they request Pilate to place a guard on the tomb (27:62–66).

See 'Did the resurrection really happen?', page 338.

28:1–15 The Resurrection

And so we come to the third day – the Sunday. In a brief account of the discovery of the empty tomb, we learn that Jesus has risen from the dead, and has gone ahead of his disciples to Galilee. The women who

were the first to discover the empty tomb are afraid at what has happened (28:1–10). So are the Jewish leaders, who realise the implications of the resurrection. The Jesus whom they have accused of blasphemy and demanded to be crucified will have turned out to be the Messiah and their Lord. Rumours are planted to attempt to discredit the resurrection (28:11–15). Yet, as we learn from the other Gospels and from Acts, it is all to no avail.

28:16–20 The Great Commission And so Matthew's Gospel comes to its conclusion. Even though some disciples continue to doubt that he has been raised from the dead, Jesus reassures them both of the reality of his resurrection, and of his continuing presence until the end of time itself. The great commission is entrusted to the eleven disciples: they are to go and make disciples of all nations, reaching out beyond the bounds of Israel to the farthest places of the earth. And the fact that you are reading this Gospel is a testimony to their effectiveness in doing just that. There is a link between Christian faith today and that great commission all those years ago. Believers may preach the gospel with the full authority of the risen Christ, resting assured of his presence and power until he comes again.

MARK

Mark's Gospel is the second of the three Synoptic Gospels, and is widely regarded as being the first to have been written down. The Gospel is generally accepted to have been written by the 'John Mark' who is known to have accompanied both Peter (1Pe 5:13) and Paul (Ac 12:12, 25). The Gospel is thought to have been written in Rome, drawing extensively on the memories of Peter. The vivid details that are such a distinctive feature of this Gospel (such as the specific reference to the 'cushion' in the boat at 4:38), and the occasionally critical portrayal of the disciples (as at 8:14–21) are best understood if Peter was the source of the stories in question. For these and other reasons, scholars tend to regard Mark's Gospel as the first of the Gospels to be written down, with Matthew and Luke expanding his accounts of the life of Jesus on the basis of additional sources available to them. Peter was executed during the Roman emperor Nero's persecution of the Christians during the period AD 64–68, and it is possible that the death of Peter was the stimulus Mark needed to ensure that the Gospel was committed to writing.

One of the most noticeable features of the Gospel is its emphasis on the deeds of Jesus, rather than his teaching. Mark's focus on the cross, rather than the teaching, of Jesus gives his Gospel a distinctive emphasis. Nevertheless, Mark passes down some major parables and sayings of Jesus.

OUTLINE

The revelation of Jesus as the Messiah

1:1 Title
1:2–8 The ministry of John the Baptist
1:9–11 The baptism of Jesus Christ
1:12–13 The temptation of Jesus Christ
1:14–20 The calling of the first disciples
1:21–45 The authority of Jesus Christ in his deeds
2:1–22 Ministry in Capernaum
2:23–3:12 The Sabbath controversy
3:13–19 The calling of the Twelve
3:20–35 Growing controversy surrounding Jesus Christ
4:1–34 The parables of the kingdom
4:35–5:43 Miracles around Galilee
6:1–6 Unbelief in Nazareth
6:7–13 The Twelve sent out to continue the work

6:14–29 The execution of John the Baptist
6:30–56 Further miracles
7:1–23 Teaching on uncleanness
7:24–8:10 Miracles in Gentile territory
8:11–21 The lack of understanding of the Pharisees and the disciples
8:22–26 A blind man sees
8:27–30 Peter confesses Jesus to be the Messiah

The revelation of the suffering of Jesus the Messiah

8:31–38 Jesus Christ defines discipleship as the way of the cross
9:1–13 The transfiguration
9:14–29 Jesus Christ heals a demoniac
9:30–50 Teaching on servant leadership
10:1–12 Teaching on divorce

MARK 1:1–6:29
The Galilean Ministry of Jesus

1:1–8 John the Baptist Prepares the Way While Matthew and Luke provide details of the birth of Jesus, Mark plunges us directly into the events of his ministry, beginning with its background in John the Baptist. The great prophecy of the coming of the Lord to his people is recalled, especially as it points to the coming of someone in advance to prepare his way. We are then introduced immediately to John the Baptist, who is to be seen as fulfilling this Old Testament prophecy. The description of John is significant; there are strong similarities with that of Elijah (2Ki 1:8). As Elijah was expected to return before the final coming of the Lord to his people (Mal 4:5) in order to prepare the way for this great event, this description has considerable importance. As John himself makes clear, he is only here to prepare the way. Someone greater than himself is coming.

1:9–13 The Baptism and Temptation of Jesus Although we can guess who he is talking about, Mark then confirms what we suspect. Jesus appears, and is baptised by John in the Jordan (1:9). With breathless pace, Mark takes us through the events of Jesus' preparation for ministry. Matthew and Luke provide far greater detail (e.g., about the temptation of Jesus, to which Mark devotes a line). Mark rushes on, as if he is anxious that we should waste no time in discovering who Jesus Christ is, and why he is of such great importance.

1:14–20 The Calling of the First Disciples It seems that the stimulus to the ministry of Jesus is the imprisonment of John the Baptist. Once this has happened, Jesus begins to proclaim the 'good news of God'. The kingdom of God is drawing near. There is an urgent need to repent. The phrase 'kingdom of God' should not be understood in a geographical or territorial sense. It does not refer to an area of land ruled by God, but to the kingly rule of God himself. The first evidence of the breaking through of this kingly rule of God can be seen in the calling of the first disciples. In response to Jesus' call, the disciples leave everything, and follow this man. There seems to be something about him that draws them. He has authority, which they obey.

The twelve disciples of Jesus

Andrew Simon Peter's brother; former disciple of John the Baptist (Mt 4:18–20; Mk 1:16–18, 29); he introduced people to Jesus (Jn 1:35–41; 6:8–9; 12:22).

James, son of Alphaeus (Mt 10:3; Mk 3:18; Lk 6:15; Ac 1:13).

James, son of Zebedee Son of Zebedee, and brother of John; fisherman (Mt 4:21–22; 10:2; Mk 1:19–20; 3:17; Lk 5:10). With Peter and John, especially close to Jesus: at raising of Jairus' daughter (Mk 5:37; Lk 8:51); transfiguration (Mt 17:1–2; Mk 9:2; Lk 9:28–29); in Gethsemane (Mt 26:36–38; Mk 14:32–34). His mother's request (Mt 20:20–28; Mk 10:35–45). He was killed by Herod (Ac 12:2).

John Son of Zebedee and brother of James. With Peter and James, especially close to Jesus at raising of Jairus' daughter (Mk 5:37; Lk 8:51); transfiguration (Mt 17:1–2; Mk 9:2; Lk 9:28–29); in Gethsemane (Mt 26:36–38; Mk 14:32–34). His mother's request (Mt 20:20–28; Mk 10:35–45). He was called 'the disciple whom Jesus loved' and was close to Jesus at the Last Supper (Jn 13:23; 21:20) and at the crucifixion (Jn 19:25–27). He was a leader in the Jerusalem church (Gal 2:9; 2Jn 1; 3Jn 1). He wrote the fourth Gospel, letters and the book of Revelation (Rev 1:1, 9; 22:8; Jn 20:2; 21:7, 24).

Judas Iscariot The treasurer for the disciples (Jn 12:6; 13:29), known as Jesus' betrayer (Mt 10:4; Mk 3:19; Lk 6:16; Jn 6:71; 12:4); he agreed to betray Jesus for 30 silver pieces (Mt 26:14–16; Mk 14:10–11; Lk 22:3–6) and kissed Jesus to identify him (Mt 26:47–49; Mk 14:43–45; Lk 22:47–48); later he was filled with remorse and committed suicide (Mt 27:3–5; Ac 1:16–25).

Judas, son of James (Lk 6:16; Jn 14:22; Ac 1:13); also known as Thaddaeus (Mt 10:3; Mk 3:18).

Matthew A tax collector; also called Levi (Mt 9:9–13; Mk 2:14–17; Lk 5:27–32; Mt 10:3; Mk 3:18; Ac 1:13). He wrote the Gospel named after him.

Nathanael From Cana in Galilee, he was brought to Jesus by Philip (Jn 1:45–51; 21:2). Possibly to be identified with Bartholomew, who is also linked with Philip (Mt 10:3).

Peter His name means 'rock'; in Aramaic he was known as Cephas (Jn 1:42). Brother of Andrew, and also called Simon (Mt 4:18; Mk 1:16–18; Lk 5:3–11; Jn 1:40–42; Mt 10:2; Mk 3:16; Lk 6:14; Ac 1:13). With James and John, he was especially close to Jesus at raising of Jairus' daughter (Mk 5:37; Lk 8:51), the transfiguration (Mt 17:1–2; Mk 9:2; Lk 9:28–29) and in Gethsemane (Mt 26:36–38; Mk 14:32–34). He confessed Jesus as the Messiah (Mt 16:13–20; Mk 8:27–30; Lk 9:18–21). His denial of Christ was predicted (Mt 26:33–35; Mk 14:29–31; Lk 22:31–34; Jn 13:37–38). He followed Jesus after Jesus' arrest (Mt 26:58; Mk 14:54; Jn 18:15) but denied Jesus (Mt 26:69–75; Mk 14:66–72; Lk 22:54–62; Jn 18:17–27). He was recommissioned by Jesus after his resurrection (Jn 21). He exercised leadership in the early church (Ac 1:15; 2:14; 5:3–11), preached on the day of Pentecost (Ac 2) and healed a lame man at the

temple gate (Ac 3). He received a vision, went to Cornelius and supported the mission to the Gentiles (Ac 10–11; 15:7–11).

Philip From Bethsaida; he brought Nathaniel to Jesus (Mt 10:3; Mk 3:18; Lk 6:14; Jn 1:43–45; Ac 1:13).

Simon Called 'the Zealot' (Mt 10:4; Mk 3:18; Lk 6:15; Ac 1:13).

Thomas (Mt 10:3; Mk 3:18; Lk 6:15; Ac 1:13); called Didymus, the Twin (Jn 11:16). He asked where Jesus was going (Jn 14:5) and doubted the resurrection (Jn 20:24–25); he then saw Jesus alive and confessed him as Lord and God (Jn 20:26–29).

1:21–45 Jesus Drives out an Evil Spirit and Heals Many The narrative now moves from Galilee to Capernaum, where the first public recognition of his true identity takes place. The reader already knows that Jesus is the Son of God (1:1, 11). This fact is now publicly acknowledged by an evil spirit (1:21–28), over whom Jesus clearly has authority. This incident makes a deep impression on those looking on. Quickly, word spreads. Something dramatic is happening. This is confirmed by a series of healings, through which Jesus becomes much sought after (1:29–45). No matter how much Jesus may try to avoid publicity, his name is on everyone's lips. Yet in the midst of all this activity, Jesus clearly sees it as being important to nourish his relationship with God through prayer (1:35).

2:1–12 Jesus Heals a Paralytic But who is Jesus Christ? And what authority does he possess? This question comes to the fore in the following chapter. What at first seems to be another healing turns out to have major implications for a right understanding of the identity of Jesus. As part of his healing of a paralytic, Jesus declares that the man's sins are forgiven. The teachers of the Law are outraged by this. Only God can forgive sins! They accuse Jesus of blasphemy. And, in one sense, they are right to do so. Only God can forgive sins. By claiming this authority, Jesus puts himself in the place of God. But the Christian reader of this passage will notice two things. First, that the man is healed. Jesus clearly possesses the ability to heal – and hence the authority to forgive. And secondly, the later resurrection of Jesus from the dead affirms that he is indeed the Son of God (Ro 1:3–4), and thus possesses the necessary authority to forgive sin. But at this early stage in his ministry there is no hint of what is to come. That will soon change – but not yet.

2:13–17 The Calling of Levi Jesus then adds a tax collector to his group of inner disciples, to the outrage of the onlookers. (Mark and Luke both refer to the person concerned by his original name, 'Levi' or 'Levi son of Alphaeus'. In Matthew's account of the same incident, the apostolic name 'Matthew' is used.) Tax collectors were widely despised and regarded as outcasts by their fellows. At this time, the region of Palestine was occupied by the Romans. Not only did the tax collectors associate with the

Gentile occupying power. They also charged more taxes than they were entitled to, as a way of ensuring their own wellbeing. As a result, they were detested by Jews, and regarded as traitors. Yet by calling one of them to his inner circle, Jesus demonstrates his acceptance of those regarded as beyond hope of redemption by Judaism, including prostitutes, Gentiles and tax collectors. Jesus summarises this with his declaration that he has come to call sinners, not the righteous (2:17). There is unquestionably a strong trace of irony in this declaration. Perhaps those, such as the Pharisees, who think they are righteous are merely self-righteous?

2:18–22 Jesus Questioned About Fasting
The criticism continues. Not only does Jesus call outcasts into his inner circle. He does not impose rigorous fasting requirements on them. Jesus responds by pointing out that there is no need for fasting while the bridegroom – an obvious reference to himself – is still among his guests. The glorious new wine of the gospel cannot be contained by the tired old wineskins of Judaism (2:22).

2:23–3:6 Lord of the Sabbath Yet the criticism goes on, relentlessly. The Pharisees criticise Jesus for picking corn on the Sabbath. Jesus retorts that the Son of Man (a reference to himself) has authority over the Sabbath. The clear implication is that the Creator has authority over his creation. In any case, Jesus points out that the Sabbath was ordained for the benefit of people, not the other way round, and cites the example of David to show that his actions

have excellent precedents. He also insists that he has a right to heal on the Sabbath, and challenges any who think otherwise to prove it. There is a long silence. Furious at this, the Pharisees (who are generally nationalistic and anti-Roman in their politics) and the Herodians (who are strongly pro-Roman), who normally have nothing to do with each other, begin to plot to destroy Jesus.

3:7–19 The Appointing of the Twelve Apostles
Yet while they are doing so, the crowds are gathering round Jesus, who is acknowledged as Son of God by the evil spirits over whom he has authority (3:7–12). At this point, Jesus calls to himself twelve disciples (3:13–19), whom he designated as 'apostles' – a word that literally means 'those who are sent'. These twelve are given authority to speak and act in Jesus' name, and will play a central role in the ministry of Jesus. Even at this stage, the grim act of future betrayal is noted (3:19). After Judas had betrayed Jesus and committed suicide, he was replaced with Matthias (Ac 1:15–26), thus keeping the number at twelve. Why is this number so important? One possibility is that it picks up the theme of the 'Twelve Tribes of Israel', with Jesus being the One who will restore the people of God to what God intended them to be.

3:20–35 Jesus and Beelzebul The question then arises concerning the basis of Jesus' obvious authority. Finding it impossible to deny that such authority exists, his opponents suggest that this authority over demons is grounded in some link with Beelzebul 'the prince of demons'. Jesus declares that this is the unforgivable

sin – the blasphemy against the Holy Spirit, by which the great acts of God, seen in and through the ministry of Jesus, are attributed to Satan.

4:1–34 A Series of Parables A series of parables then follows, focusing on the image of seeds. The first in the series is *the parable of the sower* (4:1–20), which draws on the image of a sower scattering seed on the ground as an image of the preaching of the word of God in the world. Jesus notes how it is the same seed that falls onto different kinds of ground. What eventually happens to it depends on the quality of the soil. In the same way, Jesus sows the seed of the word of God through his preaching. The effect it has on people depends on how they respond to it. If someone should fail to respond, or fall away, it is not on account of any failure on the part of the seed.

The second parable about *a lamp on a stand* departs briefly from the theme of seeds, and draws on the imagery of light (4:21–25). Just as a lamp is allowed to illuminate a room, so the effects of the gospel are to be felt in the world. The theme of *growing seeds* then returns,

---

Did Jesus really perform miracles?

The New Testament clearly claims that 'miracles' – events transcending the usual ways of nature – were a fundamental part of Jesus' ministry. The Gospels recount 35 specific miracles, as well as referring to many more; in fact, almost one-third of Mark concerns miracles. Peter's first sermon declared that 'Jesus of Nazareth was a man accredited by God to you by miracles, wonders and signs' (Ac 2:22), and the rest of the New Testament claims Jesus continued to do miracles through his church (e.g., Ac 8:13; 19:11; Gal 3:5; Heb 2:4). Even Josephus, a 1st-century Jewish-Roman historian, acknowledged that Jesus 'was a doer of startling deeds'.

But doesn't science show that miracles simply don't happen? That, at best, they were the result of advanced psychological insights, and at worst, manipulative tricks to get the naive to believe?

Jesus' miracles were far from this common parody. In fact, it is clear that Jesus didn't perform miracles to attract followers – they were just as likely to lead to his rejection (e.g., Mt 11:20; Mk 6:1–6). Rather, their purpose was to demonstrate the present reality of God's kingdom with its demands that people radically change how they live – hardly an attractive message. Moreover, Jesus simply healed the wrong sorts of people to attract serious religious attention: lepers, outcasts, non-Jews – in the Pharisees' eyes, people whose religious impurity excluded them from God's blessing. No number of miracles would convince the religious that what he was doing was therefore from God.

Perhaps what really needs examining, therefore, is the modern – at least modern Western – automatic dismissal of miracles, as though these are things that could never possibly occur. For if this man were truly God, then miracles should not surprise us. After all, if God cannot control his creation, who can?

allowing two points to be made. First, that the absence of any sign of growth does not necessarily mean that the seed has failed to establish itself (4:26–29). The kingdom of God may grow in secret, before its presence becomes visible to the world. Secondly, a small seed such as a *mustard seed* may give rise to a very large plant (4:30–34), just as the kingdom of God will grow from its small beginnings.

4:35–5:20 Jesus' Authority Confirmed

A series of events then takes place in quick succession, confirming Jesus' authority over the natural and supernatural order. In a story packed with fine detail, suggesting that Mark had access to a first-hand account of the incident, we learn of Jesus' authority over the wind and the waves, to the astonishment of his disciples (4:35–41). And in the healing of a man who was possessed by demons (5:1–20), we see once more that evil spirits recognise the identity of Jesus as Son of God, and submit to his authority. Once more, amazement and fear mingle among the onlookers, who are stunned by what they see taking place before their eyes.

5:21–43 A Dead Girl and a Sick Woman

Finally, Jesus demonstrates that he has authority over death itself, by bringing the young daughter of Jairus, a prominent member of the local synagogue, back to life (5:21–24, 35–43). Alongside this miracle we also learn of another healing incident. Jesus heals a woman who had been bleeding for many years, and who was widely regarded as being beyond any hope of cure. Yet this is more than an act of healing. It is also an important act of affirmation. The woman would have been regarded as unclean by Jews, on account of the discharge of a bodily fluid. Yet Jesus has no hesitation in healing her. What Judaism regards as unclean, Jesus sees as someone worth saving. This is one of the few gospel passages that records – and explains – the precise Aramaic words used by Jesus (another being Mk 7:34).

6:1–13 A Prophet Without Honour; Jesus Sends out the Twelve

Yet despite all these great happenings and acts of spiritual authority and power, Jesus finds that he is not accepted by his own people (6:1–6). Despite all the signs of spiritual authority and power, the people of Nazareth are dismissive of him, and refuse to acknowledge him. Jesus himself is amazed at their lack of faith. Because of their lack of faith, Jesus performs no miracles in his home town. This points to an important general principle: no faith, no miracles. Faith is the precondition of benefiting from Christ. The faith of the disciples, however, is then affirmed. The Twelve are sent out to preach the gospel, with the result that demons are driven out and the sick healed (6:7–13). This clearly points to faith, both on the part of the disciples and those to whom the good news is proclaimed.

6:14–29 John the Baptist Beheaded

The narrative then returns to John the Baptist. We learn of the manner in which the daughter of Herodias (named Salome, according to the Jewish historian Josephus) secures the execution of John the Baptist by putting Herod under obligation to her. Her mother Herodias disliked John, on account of his opposition to her marriage to Herod.

She had left her first husband, Philip, in order to marry his brother, who was Herod himself. John had pointed out that this was strictly against the Law of Moses, thus causing considerable resentment on Herodias' part.

6:30–56 Jesus Feeds the Five Thousand and Walks on the Water

We then return to the ministry of Jesus (6:30–34). After the disciples return from their mission, Jesus attempts to find time to be alone with them. However, the crowds will not allow them to be on their own. The feeding of the five thousand illustrates the huge size of the crowds now following him, as much as it points to the compassion and power of Christ. The authority of Jesus over the natural order is again emphasised through his walking on the water, and the ensuing stilling of the storm (6:45–56). Again, we learn of the huge interest in him, evident in the large crowds that gather everywhere he moves.

This major section of Mark's Gospel thus ends by demonstrating the remarkable authority of Jesus. This authority is obvious in his teaching, and his ability to command both the natural and supernatural orders. It is clear that Jesus is someone very special. But is he just a wonder worker? Is he just a great teacher? Or is there something more to Jesus than this? As Mark's Gospel continues to unfold, the full significance of his identity begins to emerge.

MARK 7:1–10:52
The Later Ministry of Jesus

7:1–23 Clean and Unclean

The relationship of Jesus to the Judaism of his day now comes into focus once more. The issue of ritual cleanliness emerges as important, with the Pharisees protesting against the disciples' failure to observe ritual cleanliness traditions. Jesus argues that the Pharisees are putting human traditions above the word of God. It is not eating food with unwashed hands, but the evil thoughts of the heart, that make a person unclean. Mark emphasises that Jesus declares all foods to be clean.

7:24–37 The Faith of a Syro-Phoenician Woman

This rebuke directed against the traditionalism of the Pharisees is followed by an incident which shows how people outside Judaism (in this case, a Syro-Phoenician woman from the region of Tyre and Sidon) are attracted to Jesus, and put their faith in him (7:24–30). The important point of this incident is the reality of the woman's faith. Despite not being a Jew, the woman is able to benefit from Christ. After leaving this region and returning to Galilee, Jesus continues to heal and demonstrate his authority (7:31–37). Nothing that Jesus does silences the crowds, who continue to proclaim his deeds across the country.

8:1–26 The Authority of Jesus Demonstrated and Questioned

The feeding of the four thousand (8:1–10), which is very similar to the earlier account of the feeding of the five thousand, once more points to both the appeal and authority of Jesus. But not everyone is prepared to accept that authority. The Pharisees put him to the test, and demand a sign by which this authority can be verified (8:11–13). Jesus refuses to give them any such sign, and warns his disciples against the malevolent influence of the Pharisees and the

Herodians (8:14–21). A further healing miracle then takes place, in which the sight of a blind man is restored (8:22–26).

8:27–30 Peter's Confession of the Messiah

Jesus and his disciples then press on to the region of Caesarea Philippi. It is here that one of the most important incidents in the ministry of Jesus takes place. This time, however, it is the disciples rather than Jesus who are the focus of attention. Jesus asks his disciples the basic question 'Who do people say that I am?' The disciples report back on the various opinions that they have heard: Jesus is one of the prophets, or John the Baptist, come back to life, or perhaps Elijah. But Jesus presses them: 'What about you? Who do *you* say that I am?' This is a vitally important question. Unlike the crowds, the disciples have been with Jesus throughout most of his ministry. They have watched him and listened to him. Now they are being asked what their conclusion is.

Peter speaks for them all when he replies that he believes Jesus is the Messiah (8:27–30), the long-awaited One who has come to his people. Presumably anxious that the title 'Messiah' might be understood in a purely political sense, Jesus asks the disciples not to tell anyone of their realisation of his true identity. The Messiah could too easily be misunderstood as a triumphalist political leader, concerned only to liberate the country from its Roman occupying force.

8:31–9:1 Jesus Predicts His Death

But it is clear that the disciples themselves also have misunderstandings concerning Jesus. Immediately after their confession that he is the Messiah, Jesus declares that he must go to Jerusalem, suffer, be rejected, be put to death and finally rise from the dead. It is an integral part of his calling. He must do it. But the disciples cannot cope with this. It was no part of their traditional view of the Messiah that he should suffer – and die. Peter protests against what Jesus tells them – and is rebuked by Jesus. It is clear that the cross is going to be a major theme in Mark's account of the ministry of Jesus.

9:2–13 The Transfiguration

Yet an important anticipation of the resurrection now follows. The account of the transfiguration demonstrates the continuity of Jesus with the ministries of Moses and Elijah, while at the same time providing an anticipation of the resurrection glory of Christ. An endorsement of Jesus' identity and authority from heaven confirms his ministry and mission. Notice the reaction of the disciples: they are frightened (9:6). Precisely this same emotion is aroused by the resurrection itself (16:8), of which the transfiguration is a foretaste.

9:14–32 The Healing of a Boy with an Impure Spirit

After a further demonstration of the power of Jesus over evil spirits (9:14–29), the theme of the coming suffering of Jesus reappears (9:30–32). The disciples continue to be bewildered by this prediction. It does not accord with their expectations of what the Messiah will be like. The Messiah was expected to be a figure of triumph, not suffering. Yet Jesus makes it clear that the forthcoming triumph of the resurrection can take place only through the cross.

It must also be appreciated that the references to Jesus 'rising' would have

been incomprehensible to the disciples. It is easy to suppose that the disciples were accustomed to the idea of resurrection. In fact, however, neither of the two main Jewish beliefs of the period about rising from the dead bears any resemblance to the resurrection of Jesus. The Sadducees denied the idea of a resurrection altogether (a fact that Paul was able to exploit at an awkward moment: Ac 23:6–8), while the majority expectation was of a general resurrection on the last day, at the end of history itself. The resurrection of Jesus simply did not conform to contemporary expectations. The disciples would probably have interpreted Jesus' words as referring to his final resurrection on the last day – not to his resurrection in history. Such an event would have been incomprehensible. We have got used to the idea of Jesus' resurrection – but we need to appreciate how difficult it would have been for the disciples to take this idea in at the time.

9:33–50 Status, Temptation and Being Like Salt

A section of teaching then opens. After noting the unimportance of matters of status and the importance of servant leadership (9:33–41), Jesus deals with the problem of sin and the need to be alert to the issue of temptation (9:42–49). Care should be taken to avoid temptation in one's own life, as well as to avoid causing others to stumble through temptation. The disciples are said to be like salt, in that they can bring a new quality to the world (9:50). Perhaps with rock salt in mind (where water could easily wash out the salt, leaving only rock behind), Jesus stresses how easily believers can lose their 'saltiness' unless they take care to preserve it.

10:1–31 Teaching and Healing in Judea

After this, Jesus undertakes a teaching and healing ministry in the region of Judea. Part of that teaching ministry includes clarification on Moses' teaching concerning divorce (10:1–12), and an important affirmation of young children (10:13–16). This is followed by the meeting with the rich young man (10:17–31), in which the question of the conditions for salvation are discussed. After discovering that the young man has faithfully kept the commandments, Jesus asks him to sell all he has, and follow him. This dismays the young man, who departs with great sadness.

Notice that Jesus does not make any attempt to compromise his position. It is difficult for someone who is rich to enter the kingdom of God, as the comparison between someone who is rich entering the kingdom of God and the camel passing through the eye of a needle makes clear. But Jesus does not say that it is *impossible*. It is clear that wealth poses a real obstacle to coming to God. Nevertheless, as Jesus makes clear, with God anything is possible. Nobody lies outside the saving purposes of God, who has promised salvation to those who put their faith in Jesus Christ.

10:32–34 Jesus Again Predicts His Death

Readers are then reminded once more of the high price of that salvation, as Jesus once more predicts his betrayal, suffering and resurrection. These words remind us once more that Jesus' death is no accident. It is something that has been purposed and foretold. Jesus dies because he has to die – there is no other way in which sinful humanity can be redeemed.

The crucifixion has to happen. This is the third prediction of his passion in Mark's Gospel.

10:35–52 The Request of James and John; the Healing of Blind Bartimaeus This prediction of suffering and death is followed by a deeply moving declaration on the part of Jesus. In response to a petty squabble among the disciples over who is the greatest, Jesus points out that rank in the kingdom of God is determined by God, and is gained through the suffering he is about to undergo himself. Jesus also affirms the importance of servant leadership. He has come to serve, and to give his life as a ransom for many (10:35–45). The word 'ransom' indicates a payment made by which freedom is gained. Through the death of Jesus Christ, believers are liberated from bondage to sin. Secular rulers may lord it over people. Christian leaders, however, are to serve their peoples, as Christ served before them. The compassion of Jesus in his ministry is then further demonstrated by his healing of a blind man. Although physically blind, he is possessed of spiritual sight: he immediately acknowledges Jesus as the Son of David (10:46–52).

Throughout this, Jesus and the disciples have been drawing nearer and nearer to Jerusalem – the city in which Jesus predicted his own betrayal and death would take place. The healing of the blind man took place at Jericho, a mere 20 kilometres from Jerusalem. The entry into Jerusalem, with all that this implies, is now imminent.

MARK 11:1–16:8
The Passion, Death and Resurrection of Jesus

11:1–11 The Triumphal Entry Jesus now prepares to enter the great city itself (11:1–1). Jesus enters in humility, mounted on a donkey, in fulfilment of a great messianic prophecy of the Old Testament (Zec 9:9). Jesus enters Jerusalem as its king, an event especially celebrated by Christians on Palm Sunday. It is clear that there were many who were looking forward to this event. He is greeted by crowds, who honour him and sing his praises. However, Mark makes it clear that Jesus is concerned about the temple. Immediately after the entry into Jerusalem, Jesus goes to the temple and examines it (11:11). Nothing happens that evening. Jesus is tired, and goes on to Bethany, about 3 kilometres away. But on the next day, the action begins.

11:12–25 Jesus Clears the Temple; the Withered Fig-tree A hint of the origins of Jesus' anger against the temple may possibly be gained from the incident of the fig-tree (11:12–14). As he walks from Bethany to Jerusalem, Jesus sees a fig-tree, which gives the impression of being in fruit, but, on closer inspection, turns out not to be so. Perhaps we can see in this incident the grounds of Jesus' anger against the temple. The tree that is meant to bear fruit has borne only leaves. The temple, which is meant to be a house of prayer for all nations – pointing to the coming of the good news of God to the Gentiles – has degenerated into a symbol of Jewish nationalism and religious privilege.

Entering the temple, Jesus ejects the merchants and overturns the tables of

the money-changers and sellers of doves (11:15–17). The protest is probably only partly against the commercialisation of the temple areas. It almost certainly represents Jesus' anger that any form of payment or purchase is necessary before an individual may worship God. But at a deeper level, we may see Jesus proclaiming the failure of Israel to bring the good news of her God to the world – a point affirmed by the citation of Isa 56:7. As Jesus and the disciples return to Bethany that evening, they notice that the fig-tree has withered (11:20–25), just as Israel has withered spiritually by failing in her responsibilities.

11:27–12:12 The Authority of Jesus Questioned

Controversy now develops with increasing intensity. Once more, the authority of Jesus is questioned by his critics (11:27–33), who prove unable to give an adequate response to Jesus' challenge to them. The parable of the tenants (12:1–12) illustrates the way in which Judaism had rejected the prophets of God, and is a prediction of the way in which they will also reject the Son of God. The killing of the son reminds us of Jesus' predictions of his own death in Jerusalem.

12:13–17 Paying Taxes to Caesar

Jesus then addresses some controversial questions raised by the Pharisees and Sadducees, who attempt to trap him into making incautious remarks. An initial attempt is made by the Pharisees to trap Jesus by involving him in a long-standing controversy that relates to the Roman authorities. Should Jews pay taxes to the Romans or not? The Pharisees are opposed to paying such taxes. The Herodians (who are strongly pro-Roman) are in favour. Both groups are opposed to Jesus. Jesus will end up supporting either treason or the Romans – both of which will result in his discrediting in the eyes of many, and can also lead to his possible arrest for sedition.

Jesus takes neither option, evading the trap set for him. He draws attention to the image of Caesar on the coins used to pay the tax. What is Caesar's should be given to Caesar. What is God's should be given to God. As humanity is created in the image of God (Ge 1:26–27), this reply is actually a declaration of the need for people to dedicate themselves to him.

12:18–27 Marriage at the Resurrection

This is followed by a question raised by the Sadducees, who do not believe in the resurrection, concerning marriage at the resurrection. They attempt to trap Jesus into conceding that there are insuperable logical difficulties associated with the idea of a resurrection. The question focuses on marriage in heaven, raising the issue of what happens to a woman with many husbands. Jesus points out that, as there is no marriage in heaven, their argument falls to the ground.

12:28–34 The Greatest Commandment

Jesus is then challenged by one of the teachers of the Law over the issue of which of the commandments in the Law is the greatest. It should be appreciated that this is not a question about the Ten Commandments, but about the much larger range of commands contained in the Law of Moses. The Law was generally regarded as having 613 commandments: Jesus is being asked to name the one that

was of supreme importance. In his famous answer, Jesus combines Dt 6:5 and Lev 19:18, to provide a brilliant statement of the fundamental purpose and goal of the Old Testament law.

12:35–44 Whose Son Is the Christ? The Widow's Offering Having met the challenges of his opponents, Jesus then puts a question of his own to the Pharisees (12:35–40). The question focuses on the interpretation of one of the messianic psalms (Ps 110), and proves to be unanswerable. Having baffled his opponents, Jesus then criticises the teachers of the Law for their all too human weaknesses – in contrast with a poor widow, who is highly praised for her generosity and selflessness (12:41–44). The widow places two 'very small copper coins' in the chests that are along the walls of the Court of the Women. The point Jesus makes is simple, yet fundamental: the woman, although giving little, nevertheless gives 'all she had'.

13:1–31 Signs of the End of the Age Jesus continues his ministry in Jerusalem by focusing on the end of the age. This section, which is sometimes referred to as the 'Olivet discourse', alerts the disciples to the troubles that lie ahead. The distress and pain that lie in the future are vividly described. Many of these sayings would have found at least partial fulfilment in the destruction of Jerusalem by the Roman armies in AD 70. This will be a time of betrayal, of persecution and of false teaching. It is, however, clear that Jesus' ultimate reference is to the end of the world itself, at a time and date unknown to all save

the Father. Not even the Son knows this (13:32). The sudden coming of the end leads Jesus to place a particular emphasis on the need for watchfulness.

14:1–26 Jesus Anointed at Bethany; the Lord's Supper It is only two days from the Passover, and Jesus foretells once more his forthcoming crucifixion. Jesus is anointed by an unnamed woman in preparation for burial as this is happening (14:1–11). The disciples are outraged at the extravagance of this gesture. Jesus, however, rebukes them. The woman's action will be remembered wherever the gospel is preached. As Judas prepares to betray Jesus – the first indication we have had that this predicted action is about to take place – Jesus returns to the theme of remembrance, as he celebrates a Passover meal with his disciples (14:12–26).

Having hinted at the forthcoming death of Jesus in many ways, Mark now presents his account of the Last Supper. This is a Passover meal, which takes place the evening before the crucifixion. For Jews, the Passover meal was a reminder of the great act of deliverance through which God led his people out of Egypt (see Ex 11–12). Jesus celebrates this meal with the twelve disciples in an upper room, which has been prepared for them in advance. To the dismay of the disciples, Jesus declares that one of them – one of his closest colleagues – will betray him. This must happen. It has been foretold in Scripture (as in Isa 53:1–12), and so must come to pass. But this does not in any way excuse his betrayer.

Jesus then turns to the theme of remembrance. The Passover meal included both bread and wine. Jesus now

gives a new meaning to each of these two elements. The bread is declared to be his body, and the wine his 'blood of the covenant, which is poured out for many'. There is a clear reference here to Jesus' earlier declaration that he will give his 'life as a ransom for many' (10:45). This passage is rich in allusions to the establishment of the covenant between God and Israel at Sinai, and points to the establishment of a new covenant between God and his people through the death of Christ.

14:27–42 Jesus Predicts Peter's Denial; Gethsemane

The group then moves to the Mount of Olives, where Jesus predicts that the disciples will fall away on account of the events that are about to take place, in fulfilment of the messianic prophecy of Zec 13:7 (14:27–31). Peter refuses to believe this. No matter what happens, he will stand by his Lord. Yet Jesus gently rebukes him: that night Peter will deny him three times. The weakness of the disciples immediately becomes apparent, when they move on to Gethsemane (14:32–42). Clearly deeply distressed at the knowledge of what lies ahead, Jesus turns to prayer. He asks his disciples to keep watch. They, however, fall asleep. They lack the physical strength to stay awake.

Jesus' prayer is especially important. The intimacy of the prayer is evident from the use of the word *Abba* (14:36), an Aramaic word for 'Father' that is found only at this one point in the Synoptic Gospels. Jesus prays that, if possible, 'this cup' may be taken from him. In this context, the cup is a symbol of sorrow and suffering. It is clear that the full humanity of Jesus expresses itself in this prayer. He does not want to die. But if God has purposed that he should die, then he will bear its pain. Many commentators see in this prayer evidence that the full weight of human sin is beginning to bear down on Jesus, cutting him off from his Father. On the cross, he will experience a sense of being totally abandoned by God, on account of the burden of human sin. Here in Gethsemane, we can begin to see our sin being transferred to Christ.

14:43–52 Jesus Arrested

Finally, the moment of betrayal arrives. The fact that it has been foretold in no way diminishes its tragedy and pathos. Judas, greeting Jesus as a mere 'Rabbi', betrays him with a sign of love – a kiss. Jesus is resigned to this. Scripture must be fulfilled. Obedient to the will of his Father, here as always, Jesus allows himself to be led away, as his disciples scatter. The tantalising reference to a young man who flees naked from the scene is seen by some commentators as a possible reference to Mark himself, who may well have been present at the scene of betrayal.

14:53–65 Before the Sanhedrin

Jesus is then forcibly taken before the Sanhedrin (that is, the 71-member supreme Jewish court, consisting of the chief priests, elders, and teachers of the Law), representing the Jewish religious establishment. This religious trial before the high priest would be followed by a civil trial in front of the Roman governor Pontius Pilate, if this proved necessary. Under Jewish law, two male witnesses were required to secure a conviction of any kind. This poses some problems, as no consistent witnesses against him are

forthcoming. Eventually, two come forward with a distorted version of some of Jesus' words. It might have been possible to convict him on the basis of this obvious misrepresentation. The high priest asks Jesus to respond to these vague accusations, and is amazed when Jesus makes no reply. However, we may see in this the fulfilment of an important Old Testament prophecy: that the suffering Messiah would be silent before his accusers (Isa 53:7).

However, the high priest then asks Jesus specifically whether he is 'the Messiah, the Son of the Blessed One'. In answer to this direct question, Jesus replies in the affirmative. Notice that Jesus never *himself* claims to be the Messiah. But when others realise who he is (as with the disciples at Caesarea Philippi, Mt 16:13–17), or ask him specifically whether he is the Messiah, he admits to being so. The high priest is outraged that anyone should make such claims, and declares that he is guilty of blasphemy. And so anyone doing so would be – unless they *were* the Messiah and Son of God. The penalty for blasphemy was death. However, with one exception, the Romans had deprived the Sanhedrin of the right to sentence anyone to death. This was a matter for the Roman authorities.

14:66–72 Peter Disowns Jesus The narrative now switches to Peter, who has been waiting outside in the courtyard, keeping his distance from what is going on inside the house. He is noticed by one of the servant-girls, who challenges him. Hasn't he been with that Nazarene Jesus? Surely he is one of his followers? But Peter denies having anything to do with Jesus – three times. After the third denial, the cock crows, and Peter realises that he has not only failed Jesus, but that Jesus' prediction of his failure has come true. He breaks down, and weeps.

The reference to the 'cock crowing' is important. The Romans divided the night into four 'watches' – 'evening' 6:00–9:00 p.m., 'midnight' 9:00–12:00 midnight, 'when the cock crows' 12:00 midnight–3:00 a.m., and 'dawn' 3:00–6:00 a.m. These four watches are referred to earlier in this Gospel at 13:35. The 'cock crowing' may in fact be a reference to the trumpet blast that marked the end of the third watch of the night, rather than to the cry of a cockerel. Although some versions of the text of Mark make reference to the cock crowing twice, many early manuscripts refer to it only as crowing once.

15:1–32 Pilate and the Crucifixion of Jesus The narrative now returns to Jesus. It is early in the morning of the Friday that is to prove to be the last day of Jesus' life. The Sanhedrin finally reaches its decision, and hands Jesus over to Pontius Pilate, Roman governor of Judea from AD 26 to 36. Pilate confronts Jesus with the charges brought against him. Initially, he demands to know if Jesus is the 'king of the Jews'. Pilate's interest in this question was probably political. If Jesus had been making any kind of claims to be a Jewish king, it would probably have amounted to an open call to the Jews to rebel against Rome. Pilate then turns to the specifically religious charges brought against Jesus by the chief priests. To his amazement, Jesus refuses to respond to these accusations. Again, we may see in this the fulfilment of the crucial Old

Testament prophecy that the Messiah would be silent before his accusers (Isa 53:7). It is clear that Pilate can find nothing about Jesus that merits the death penalty. However, he is placed under enormous pressure by the crowd, who insist on his crucifixion.

Pilate has the right to release a prisoner at Passover. He offers to release either Jesus or a convict named Barabbas. The crowd demands the release of Barabbas, and the death of Jesus. Barabbas is thus the first to benefit directly from the death of Christ. He ought to have died. Jesus dies in his place. Pilate sends Jesus off to be flogged and crucified. Jesus is then humiliated by the Roman soldiers, who dress him up in a caricature of royal costume, including a crown of thorns. He is ritually humiliated as the 'king of the Jews' (15:16–20), a title that will also be included in the charge against him, which would have been written on a wooden board and placed above his head upon the cross.

The floggings administered by the Romans were vicious; they had been known to cause the death of victims before they were crucified. Jesus was clearly severely weakened by his beating, and proves unable to carry his own cross. Simon of Cyrene is forced to carry it for him. Finally, they reach Golgotha, the place of execution. This place is also often referred to as 'Calvary', from the Latin word *calvaria*, meaning 'the skull' – the literal meaning of 'Golgotha'. As Jesus hangs on the cross, he is mocked by those watching him die, while the Roman soldiers cast lots for his clothes. These events fulfil the great Old Testament prophecy of the fate of the righteous sufferer of Psalm 22 (see Ps 22:7–8, 18).

The identity of Jesus with this sufferer is confirmed by his cry of utter desolation (15:34), which draws on the opening verse of this important psalm. It is here that Jesus experiences the sense of the absence of God. The sin he is bearing on behalf of his people has now cut him off from his Father. The crowds around Jesus demand that he come down from the cross and save himself. However, he remains there, and saves sinful humanity instead (15:21–32).

15:33–41 The Death of Jesus Finally, Jesus dies. Darkness settles over the land, perhaps pointing to the fact that the 'light of the world' (Jn 8:12) has been extinguished. The 'curtain of the temple' is torn from top to bottom, an event with important significance in the light of the saving significance of the death of Christ. The 'curtain of the temple' was an important feature of the Old Testament tabernacle (Ex 26:31–35). It was included in order to provide a means of restricting access to the 'Most Holy Place', the region of the tabernacle that was regarded as sacrosanct. Although the curtain served a practical function in relation to the worship of Israel, it came to have a deeper significance. The fact that the curtain prevented ordinary worshippers from entering the 'Most Holy Place' came to be seen as pointing to a much deeper separation between God and sinful humanity. The curtain thus came to be a symbol of the barrier placed between God and humanity by human sinfulness. The tearing of this curtain at the crucifixion is a symbol of one of the chief benefits brought about by the death of Christ: the barrier between

Did the resurrection really happen?

If the resurrection didn't happen, then Christianity is meaningless and untrue, and Christians remain unforgiven and without hope (1Co 15:12–19). But claims of resurrection were central to Christianity from earliest times (1Co 15:3–4). So could it really have happened? Doesn't science show such things are impossible (a view shared by the first witnesses, remember)?

Good science cannot rule out conclusions at the beginning, no matter how implausible. But resurrection seems all we are left with when we examine the alternatives. Grave robbers cannot have stolen the body, for Roman guards were posted to prevent this; disciples cannot have stolen it to start rumours of resurrection for the same reason – and anyway as Jews they believed that resurrection would happen only at the end of the age; the authorities cannot have removed it, for they could have produced it later to thwart claims of resurrection; the women cannot have mistaken the tomb, for the authorities could have gone to the right tomb; Jesus could not simply have fainted on the cross and revived in the cool tomb, for the execution party was convinced he was dead – and even if he wasn't, he would have had to roll back the stone, overcome the guards, walk to Jerusalem in his weakened state and appear as the glorious conqueror of death. Nor can we explain the resurrection as a purely 'spiritual' experience, for the first Christians stressed its physical nature (e.g., Jn 21:26–29).

The most likely explanation is the one the New Testament gives, the one for which Christians were ready to die: that Jesus was indeed raised from the dead, confirming he was indeed the Messiah and that God's new age was breaking in. His resurrection is the confirmation that our own resurrection will happen one day.

God and humanity caused by sin has been torn down, so that there is now free access for believers to God on account of Christ's death (Ro 5:1–2).

Mark now draws our attention to the testimony of the Roman centurion, who declares that Jesus is the 'Son of God' (15:39) – a vitally important testimony, coming from a Gentile. As Mark's Gospel is often thought to have been written in Rome (notice, e.g., the reference to the 'Praetorium' at 15:16), the importance of the testimony of this Roman officer would have been of special relevance to his intended readership.

15:42–47 The Burial of Jesus Mark also draws our attention to the role of three women: Mary Magdalene, Mary the mother of James and Joseph (Joses), and Salome (15:40–41). Although the disciples are nowhere to be seen, the women remain as witnesses to the death of Christ – just as these same women would be the first witnesses to the resurrection. Finally, Jesus is buried in a borrowed tomb (15:42–47). The disciples are not mentioned. The burial arrangements are made by a prominent Jewish religious leader, Joseph of Arimathea, who is clearly sympathetic towards Jesus. Two of the three women

are still there, keeping vigil by the tomb, at the end of this long day – the first Good Friday.

16:1–8 The Resurrection Early on the morning of the Sunday, the three women go once more to anoint the dead body of Jesus at the tomb. The previous day had been the Sabbath, on which such activity would have been disallowed. Once more, there is no mention of the disciples, who are clearly totally demoralised. As they draw near to the tomb, the women realise that it is empty, and learn that Jesus has been raised. Terrified, they run away (16:1–8).

It should be noted that all four Gospels attribute the discovery of the empty tomb to women. The only Easter event to be explicitly related in detail by all four of the Gospel writers is the visit of the women to the tomb of Jesus. Mark tells us the names of these women witnesses – Mary Magdalene, Mary the mother of James, and Salome – *three times* (Mk 15:40, 47; 16:1). Yet Judaism dismissed the value of the testimony or witness of a woman, regarding only men as having significant legal status in this respect. The greatest news the world has ever known is thus first disclosed to people whose status as witnesses was negligible! This point is of considerable importance in relation to the historical reliability of the Gospels. Would anyone invent a story in which its climax was first witnessed by people whose testimony would carry so little weight at the time? Yet the Gospels have no hesitation in reporting the facts as they were, without doctoring them to make them more acceptable and credible.

16:9–20 Ending of the Gospel According to Later Manuscripts And at this point, Mark's Gospel breaks off. Some later versions of the text include the section 16:9–20, which relates the appearance of Jesus to his disciples, and includes (16:12) a reference to the incident on the road to Emmaus (described in detail at Lk 24:13–35). But most scholars are agreed that the text ends at 16:8. The women are terrified at their discovery. What can it mean? Just as the disciples were terrified at the transfiguration, so the resurrection initially evokes fear. That will give way to joy – but only once the full reality of what has happened has been appreciated.

LUKE

Luke is the third of the Synoptic Gospels. Luke's Gospel is the first part of a two-part work, the second being the Acts of the Apostles. Taken together, these two works constitute the largest piece of writing in the New Testament. Both works are dedicated to a man named Theophilus (literally meaning 'a lover of God'), who may well have been a wealthy and influential Christian sympathiser at Rome. Luke himself was probably a Gentile by birth, with an outstanding command of written Greek. He was a physician, and the travelling companion of Paul at various points during his career. Luke's Gospel has clearly been written with the interests and needs of non-Jewish readers in mind, apparently with a special concern to bring out the relevance of the 'good news' for the poor, oppressed and needy.

It is not clear when Luke's Gospel was written. The abrupt ending of the account of Paul's imprisonment in the Acts of the Apostles suggests an early date for the two-part work, such as some time in the period 59–63. However, many scholars argue that Luke draws on Mark's Gospel at points, suggesting that the third Gospel is to be dated later than the second, and pointing to the 70s as a possible time of writing.

OUTLINE

LUKE 1:1–2:52
The Birth of Jesus Christ

1:1–4 Introduction Luke opens his Gospel by setting out his intention of giving as accurate as possible an account of the events that lie behind the Christian gospel, drawing on eyewitness accounts. The same method will be used in both the Gospel and Acts: reliable sources are checked out and brought together, to create a coherent account of both the foundations and the subsequent spread of the Christian gospel.

1:5–25 The Birth of John the Baptist Luke, drawing on sources not available to the other evangelists (as the writers of the

Gospels are known), then provides us with detailed information concerning the birth of John the Baptist (1:5–25). John is born into a priestly family. There are clear similarities between the situation of Zechariah and Elizabeth and that of Elkanah and Hannah (see 1Sa 1:1–2:11). In each case, a child, born through the providence of God, becomes a prophet. There are also similarities between John the Baptist and the prophet Samuel: for example, both take Nazirite vows of obedience, which include a vow to abstain from alcohol (Nu 6:1–4; Jdg 13:4–7; 1Sa 1:11).

Even before he is born John is thus marked out as a special figure within the providence of God. He will be like

Are the records of Jesus' life really reliable?

While the Gospels clearly have a point to make about who Jesus is and why he came, as they acknowledge (e.g., Jn 20:30–31), this doesn't mean they are unreliable. In fact, Luke notes his careful historical research (Lk 1:1–4); and wherever we can check his facts, they are accurate. Even apparent 'conflicts' can easily be explained by the preachers' practice of repeating stories and illustrations on different occasions but with slight variations.

But what of the claim that some things must have been changed before the Gospels were written? We should note that oral transmission of information in those days was extremely accurate and reliable. In addition, Jesus' teaching style, with its bite-size chunks and graphic illustrations, made this all the more easy. The first Christians spread his message through preaching that followed a pattern (e.g., Ac 2:14–36; 3:11–26; 10:34–43; 13:16–41), again aiding memorisation and transmission. Even the letters, addressing specific situations, were based on the earliest traditions (e.g., 1Co 15:3–5), thus maintaining continuity. Only when it became clear that Jesus would not return soon did the church feel the need to commit his message to writing in the Gospels.

But did these Gospels reflect more of the church's thoughts than Jesus' teaching? It is true that their life-situation helped shape their *selection* and *presentation* of the material, but the *content* remained true to Jesus' teaching. After all, they believed they were handling the teaching of God incarnate, so they would have been very careful not to change or add to it, and would certainly never have created material to suit their needs in his name. In fact, the apostles understood well the importance of distinguishing between their own teaching and his (e.g., 1Co 7:10, 12).

We can therefore have a high level of confidence that what we read in the Gospels is indeed an accurate reflection of Jesus' life and teaching.

Elijah (1:17), and go before the Lord to prepare his way. The Old Testament prophet Malachi had declared that the Lord would send the prophet Elijah to prepare the way for his coming (Mal 4:5–6). So if Elijah should come again, a great day would be about to dawn, in which the Lord would come to his people with judgment and salvation. And so even at this early stage, we have a strong indication that the coming of the Lord to his people is not that far away.

1:26–45 Jesus' Birth Foretold; Mary Visits Elizabeth This is confirmed by the visit of the angel Gabriel to Mary shortly afterwards, in which he announces that she will bear a child (1:26–38). In a message that brings together many of the great messianic hopes of the Old Testament, the angel tells Mary that she has found favour in the sight of God, and will bear a son who is to be named Jesus. He will stand in succession to David as the ruler of his people. Though Mary is a virgin, she will have a child through the power of the Holy Spirit. Mary then

visits her relative Elizabeth, as they share the news of all that has happened to them both (1:39–45). From what follows (1:56), it is clear that Mary remains with Elizabeth until the ninth month – that is, until the final birth of John.

1:46–56 Mary's Song In the great song of praise that follows, Mary expresses her joy at the news she has had, and all that it will mean for Israel (1:46–55). The song, often referred to as the 'Magnificat' (from its opening word in the standard Latin translation of the text), bears a strong resemblance to the great song of praise of Hannah, as she exulted in the knowledge that she would bear a child (1Sa 2:1–10). Mary's song dwells on the great faithfulness of God to his people, and of his mercy and favour to those who, like her, are humble and meek. It is clear that a great act of divine deliverance lies to hand.

1:57–66 The Birth of John the Baptist This sense of anticipation is heightened by the birth of John the Baptist, and the realisation on the part of the people that the hand of the Lord is on him. In his song that celebrates the birth of his son, Zechariah proclaims the great faithfulness of God to his people (1:67–80). The song – often referred to as the 'Benedictus' (from the opening word of the standard Latin translation of the text) – declares that, in his great faithfulness to his people, the Lord God of Israel has raised up a new hope of salvation within his people. His son, John, will go before the Lord to prepare the way for his coming. Salvation and forgiveness are near to hand.

2:1–20 The Birth of Jesus Luke now leads directly into the climax of these first two chapters: the birth of Jesus himself. The section opens by relating the events of salvation history to those of world history (2:1–7). Luke dates the birth of Jesus with reference to the reigns of two figures. First, it took place during the time of Caesar Augustus, the first Roman emperor, whose reign spanned the period 31 BC to AD 14. Secondly, it occurred during the governorship of Quirinius in Syria. This is slightly more difficult to date, with a range of dates a few years before and after AD 1 being suggested. At this time, a census was held, presumably for taxation purposes, as a result of which Joseph and Mary went to the royal city of Bethlehem. While there, Jesus was born. The action of the imperial authorities thus led to the fulfilment of the great messianic prophecy of Mic 5:2. Traditionally, the site of his birth has been identified as a stable on the basis of the reference to a 'manger' (2:7), which is basically a feeding trough for animals.

The narrative now shifts to a group of shepherds in nearby fields at night (2:8–20). An angel declares the birth of a Saviour, who is the Messiah, the Lord. Luke's Greek text is quite complex at this point, and it is probably best interpreted as follows: a child has been born, who at one and the same time is Saviour, Messiah and Lord. In other words, the angel is proclaiming that one who will save his people, who is the long-awaited Messiah, and who is Lord, has been born. As a result, the shepherds go and find the newborn child, and spread the word of his birth.

2:21–40 Jesus Presented in the Temple The child is named Jesus, in obedience to the message of the angel to Mary (2:21–24).

In obedience to the Law of Moses, the child is circumcised, and, as the firstborn male of the family, is dedicated to the Lord. Mary offers a sacrifice for her purification after the interval of 40 days specified by the Law is complete (Lev 12:2–8). The sacrifice in question is that specified for the poorest of people, pointing to the state of poverty in which Mary and Joseph live.

Two incidents now take place, which further confirm the spiritual significance of the child Jesus. Simeon, who has been granted a special gift of discernment through the Holy Spirit, recognises Jesus as the coming Messiah (2:25–35). His song of praise, often referred to as the 'Nunc Dimittis' (from its opening words in the standard Latin translation of the text), speaks of the Lord finally allowing him to see the coming of salvation to Israel, for both the glorification of God's people and the revelation of God to the Gentiles. This is followed by an encounter with the prophetess Anna (2:36–40), who proclaims the significance of Jesus to 'all who were looking forward to the redemption of Jerusalem'.

2:41–52 The Boy Jesus at the Temple This section of Luke's Gospel concludes with an account of how Mary and Joseph lose Jesus during a visit to the temple some twelve years later (2:41–50). The story, which is told from the perspective of Mary and Joseph, reflects their bewilderment at Jesus' wisdom, and his statement that he had to be in his Father's house. Only later will the full significance of this statement become clear. This pattern is encountered throughout the Gospels. Jesus' words and deeds often assume their full significance and meaning only in the light of his cross and resurrection – for example, his comments about the rebuilding of the temple (Jn 2:19–22), and his prediction of his own betrayal and death (Mk 9:31–32). Yet even at this early stage, the clues are there for those with the wisdom to see them.

So where does Luke get all this information from? Who is his source for all this information? The most obvious source is Mary herself, who would have been an eyewitness to much of what we read about in this section. The remarks that Mary 'treasured up all these things and pondered them in her heart' (2:19) and that she 'treasured all these things in her heart' (2:51) are a clear hint that Mary committed everything to memory, and that Luke has drawn on her memories in compiling these two opening chapters of his narrative. Where Matthew tends to tell the story of the birth and early life of Jesus from Joseph's point of view, Luke relates it from Mary's.

LUKE 3:1–9:62
Jesus' Ministry in Galilee

3:1–20 John the Baptist Prepares the Way Luke once more takes care to relate the events of salvation history to those of world history. Following the tradition of ancient historians, including those of the Old Testament, the opening of the ministry of Jesus Christ is dated with reference to the years of the reign of regional and international rulers (3:1–2). Some of these are relatively easy to date. Pontius Pilate was Roman governor (or, more strictly, procurator) of Judea AD 26–36. The 'fifteenth year of the reign of Tiberias' can be dated to the period AD

28–29. Other dates are more difficult to fix, due to the imprecision of our knowledge concerning the people involved. Although they would be well known to Luke's readers, whether Jews or Gentiles, there is now some difficulty in ascertaining the dates with certainty. Nevertheless, it is clear that Jesus' ministry begins, according to Luke, just before AD 30. Luke later notes that Jesus was 'about thirty years old' when he began his ministry (3:23).

This ministry begins with an encounter with John the Baptist. Luke provides a substantial degree of background information concerning John (3:3–20). It is obvious that John creates a sensation, with crowds streaming out into the deserts to hear him speak. John is recognised as the forerunner of the Messiah; indeed, there is even a suggestion – which John is quick to refute – that he himself might be that Messiah (3:15–17). In fulfilment of Old Testament prophecy, John comes as the one who was promised to 'prepare the way for the Lord' (3:4, citing Isa 40:3 and Mal 3:1). John sees his role as preparing the way for someone greater than himself. John can baptise with water only; the one who is to come will baptise with the Holy Spirit (3:16). In an aside, Luke then informs us of what will later happen to John, as a result of his criticism of Herod's seduction of Herodias, his brother's wife (3:19–20).

3:21–38 The Baptism and Genealogy of Jesus Luke then tells us that Jesus was among those who were baptised by John (3:21–22). A voice from heaven affirms the identity of Jesus as the Son of God, in fulfilment of the great messianic hope set out in Ps 2:7. Jesus does not *become* the Son of God at his baptism. God confirms what is already the case. Yet although Jesus is in reality the Son of God, Luke points out that most people just think of him as the son of Joseph.

In his genealogy of Jesus, Luke makes the point that Jesus traces his descent from Adam, not just Abraham (3:23–28). Where Matthew stresses the Jewish origins of Jesus, Luke points to his wider significance for the human race as a whole. While not in any way denying Jesus' special importance for Judaism, Luke wants to bring out his universal significance. There are differences between the genealogies presented here and in Matthew's Gospel (Mt 1:2–16). The differences in the genealogies from David onwards are best explained on the basis of the assumption that Matthew traces Jesus' descent after David through Joseph, whereas Luke's preference is to trace it after David through Mary. As we noted earlier (Mt 1), this corresponds with Luke's particular interest in Mary, and Matthew's in Joseph.

4:1–13 The Temptation of Jesus Just as Israel spent 40 years in the wilderness, being tested and prepared for their final entry into the promised land, so Luke tells us how Jesus is prepared for his mission to Israel through his temptation – a period of 40 days and nights in the wilderness, in which Jesus confronts and successfully resists temptation. The testing centres on whether Jesus will use his power and authority as the Son of God for his own advantage, or for the ends for which they have been given. By the end of this period, it is clear that Jesus will be obedient to the will of his Father. He is ready to begin his public ministry.

4:14–44 *Jesus Rejected at Nazareth* That
ministry now opens with his public
rejection by his own people at Nazareth.
Luke has emphasised that Jesus was filled
with the Spirit (4:1, 14). Thus inspired,
he returns to Jerusalem, already the
object of intense discussion, to worship
at the local synagogue. Although the text
does not explicitly state this, it seems
that Jesus had already ministered
extensively before coming to Nazareth.
By this stage, he has become well known,
and was clearly a frequent teacher in
synagogues throughout the region. But at
Nazareth, he finds open rejection.
Reading the great messianic prophecy of
Isa 61:1–2, he declares that this prophecy
has been fulfilled in himself.

The prophecy makes reference to the
preaching of good news and the healing
of the blind – essential elements of Jesus'
ministry. This suggests strongly that
Jesus applies these words to himself, in
the knowledge that the details of his
public ministry will confirm them. But
instead he finds outrage and rejection. As
the following episodes make clear,
Jesus is even accepted as the 'Holy One
of God' (4:31–37) and 'Son of God'
(4:38–44) by demons, where his own
people will not hear him. Despite this
rejection, Jesus continues to preach in
synagogues, clearly receiving a warm
welcome by others.

5:1–11 *The Calling of the First Disciples* Jesus
then calls his first disciples. Although it is
clear that he has been greatly admired by
many people to date, he now invites some
to assume a specially favoured position
alongside him. The first disciples are
ordinary fishermen, whom Jesus declares
will 'fish for people'.

5:12–26 *Jesus' Healing Ministry Continues*
The healing of the man with leprosy
(5:12–16) illustrates the ability and
willingness of Jesus to heal, as well as his
affirmation of the Old Testament law –
note how the healed leper is sent to the
priest for confirmation of the healing.
What at first seems to be another healing
(5:17–26) turns out to have major
implications for a right understanding of
the identity of Jesus. As part of his
healing of a paralytic, Jesus declares that
the man's sins are forgiven. The teachers
of the Law are outraged by this. Only
God can forgive sins! They accuse Jesus
of blasphemy. And, in one sense, they are
right to do so. Only God can forgive sins.
By claiming this authority, Jesus is
putting himself in the place of God. But
the Christian reader of this passage will
notice two things. First, that the man is
healed. Jesus clearly possesses the ability
to heal – and hence the authority to
forgive. And secondly, the later
resurrection of Jesus from the dead
affirms that he is indeed the Son of God
(Ro 1:3–4), and thus possesses the
necessary authority to forgive sin. But at
this early stage in his ministry, there is no
hint of what is to come. That will soon
change – but not yet.

5:27–32 *The Calling of Levi* Jesus then adds
a tax collector named Levi to his group of
inner disciples, to the outrage of the
onlookers. (Mark and Luke both refer to
the person concerned by his original
name, 'Levi' or 'Levi son of Alphaeus'; in
Matthew's account of the same incident,
the apostolic name 'Matthew' is used.)
Tax collectors were widely despised and
regarded as outcasts by their fellows. At
this time, the region of Palestine was

JESUS' MIRACLES

Miracles of healing	Matthew	Mark	Luke	John
A man with leprosy	8:2–3	1:40–42	5:12–13	
A centurion's servant	8:5–13		7:1–10	
Peter's mother-in-law	8:14–15	1:30–31	4:38–39	
Two Gadarenes	8:28–34	5:1–15	8:27–35	
A paralysed man	9:2–7	2:3–12	5:18–25	
A woman with bleeding	9:20–22	5:25–29	8:43–48	
Two blind men	9:27–31			
A mute demon-possessed man	9:32–33			
A man with a shrivelled hand	12:10–13	3:1–5	6:6–10	
A blind, mute, demon-possessed man	12:22		11:14	
A Canaanite woman's daughter	15:21–28	7:24–30		
A demon-possessed boy	17:14–18	9:17–29	9:38–43	
Bartimaeus and another blind man	20:29–34	10:46–52	18:35–43	
A deaf mute		7:31–37		
A demon-possessed man at the synagogue		1:23–26	4:33–35	
A blind man at Bethsaida		8:22–26		
A crippled woman			13:11–13	
A woman with an abnormal swelling			14:1–4	
Ten men with leprosy			17:11–19	
The high priest's servant			22:50–51	
An official's son at Capernaum				4:46–54
A sick man at the pool of Bethesda				5:1–9
A man born blind				9:1–7
Miracles over nature				
Calming the storm	8:23–27	4:37–41	8:22–25	
Walking on water	14:25	6:48–51		6:19–21
Feeding the 5,000	14:15–21	6:35–44	9:12–17	6:5–13
Feeding the 4,000	15:32–38	8:1–9		
Coin in a fish's mouth	17:24–27			
A fig-tree withered	21:18–22	11:12–26		
Catches of fish			5:1–11	21:1–11
Water turned into wine				2:1–11
Miracles of raising the dead				
Jairus' daughter	9:18–25	5:22–42	8:41–56	
A widow's son at Nain			7:11–15	
Lazarus				11:1–44

occupied by the Romans. Not only did the tax collectors associate with the Gentile occupying power. They also charged more taxes than they were entitled to, as a way of ensuring their own wellbeing. As a result, they were detested by Jews, and regarded as traitors. Yet by calling one of them to his inner circle, Jesus demonstrates his acceptance of those regarded as beyond hope of redemption by Judaism, including prostitutes, Gentiles and tax collectors. Jesus summarises this with his declaration that he has come to call sinners, not the righteous (5:32).

5:33–6:11 The Authority of Jesus Questioned

The criticism of Jesus continues relentlessly. Not only does Jesus call outcasts into his inner circle. He does not impose rigorous fasting requirements on them. Jesus responds by pointing out that there is no need for fasting while the bridegroom – an obvious reference to himself – is still among his guests. The glorious new wine of the gospel cannot be contained by the tired old wineskins of Judaism (5:33–39).

Yet the criticism goes on (6:1–11). The Pharisees criticise Jesus for picking corn on the Sabbath. Jesus retorts that the Son of Man (a reference to himself) has authority over the Sabbath. The clear implication is that the Creator has authority over his creation. In any case, Jesus points out that the Sabbath was ordained for the benefit of people, not the other way round, and cites the example of David to show that his actions have excellent precedents. He also insists that he has a right to heal on the Sabbath, and challenges any who think otherwise to prove it.

6:12–49 Sermon on the Plain

After calling the twelve disciples together (6:12–16), Jesus then delivers what is sometimes referred to as the 'Sermon on the Plain', which includes some of the material to be found in the 'Sermon on the Mount' (Mt 5:1–7:29). The sermon, which is spoken to the disciples rather than those whom Jesus has just healed, stresses the high demands that Christians are called to work towards, while realising that it is impossible to meet them without the grace of God himself.

6:20–26 Blessings and Woes

The sermon opens with a set of pronouncements widely known as 'the Beatitudes' (6:20–23). Each pronouncement opens with the words 'Blessed are . . .'. The word 'blessed' can easily be misunderstood to mean 'happy' or 'fortunate'. Yet it is possible, as Jesus points out, to be blessed even if you are unhappy. Someone is 'blessed' if they have found favour and acceptance in the sight of God. Even if the believers' worldly status or situation is humble or distressing, they can know that they have found favour in the sight of God – which is much more important. This point is stressed in the series of 'woes' that follow (6:24–26); those who have found worldly security and satisfaction may easily forfeit favour in the sight of God.

6:27–45 Love for Enemies; Judging Others; A Tree and Its Fruit

The high standards expected within the kingdom of God are then set out. The strongly self-sacrificial character of the redeemed life is brought out in a series of commands, each illustrating the radical nature of the gospel demands. For many commenta-

tors, the sermon sets out a series of standards that Christians should aim towards, even if they ultimately fail to reach them in their own lives. This does not mean that the demands are perfectionist or hopelessly idealist. It just points to the fact that being a Christian makes a difference to the way in which such people live, and indicates the goals they should be aiming at, even if they cannot achieve them all. The sermon continues with a reminder of the sinfulness of human nature, which leads us to criticise others when we ought to be examining ourselves (6:37–42). Just as the good tree brings forth good fruit, so the person who has really come to faith will naturally produce good works (6:43–45).

6:46–7:10 The Wise and Foolish Builders; Faith in Jesus

The sermon ends with the parable of the house built on the rock and the house built on the sand. Jesus here makes it clear that it is vitally important that the house of faith is built on a solid foundation, which will survive the worst storms that life can produce. Only by having faith in Jesus Christ and his gospel can we be sure of the stability and peace that God intends for our lives. As if to make this point absolutely clear, Luke then relates a series of incidents that bring out the importance of faith in Christ. The faith of the Roman centurion in the ability of Jesus to heal his servant is noted, commended and rewarded (7:1–10), as is that of a sinful woman (7:36–50). Her faith, Jesus declares, has saved her (7:50).

7:11–32 Jesus and John the Baptist

The question of the identity of Jesus then emerges once more. After raising a widow's son (7:11–17), Jesus is approached by two disciples of John the Baptist, who is languishing in prison (7:18–32). John wishes them to ask Jesus if he is the Messiah whose coming he had proclaimed, or whether he should wait for someone else. Jesus responds by pointing out that all the great signs to be associated with the coming of the Messiah have been fulfilled through him. A list of messianic prophecies, including that quoted from by Jesus at Nazareth, are clearly seen as having been fulfilled in the ministry of Jesus (7:22; see Isa 29:18–19; 35:4–6; 61:1–2). Jesus affirms that he is indeed the One for whom John had been sent to prepare the way, in fulfilment of prophecy.

7:33–50 Jesus Criticised as a Friend of Sinners

Yet criticism continues. Jesus continues to be criticised for being the 'friend of sinners' (7:33–35). In response, Jesus makes the point that the greater the sin, the greater the gratitude at its forgiveness (7:36–50). In forgiving the sin of a local woman, Jesus again raises the question of his authority. Only God can forgive sins – so who, people wonder, is this 'who even forgives sins?' (7:48–49; see 5:20–26). Drawn to Jesus, the Twelve and a group of women, many of whom are specifically named (8:1–3), follow him around and minister to him.

8:4–15 The Parable of the Sower

The parable of the sower draws on the image of a sower scattering seed on the ground as an image of the preaching of the word of God in the world. Jesus notes how it is the same seed that falls onto different kinds of ground. What eventually happens to it depends on the quality of

the soil. In the same way, Jesus sows the seed of the word of God through his preaching. The effect it has on people depends on how they respond to it. If someone should fail to respond, or fall away, it is not on account of any failure on the part of the seed.

8:16–21 A Lamp on a Stand A second parable draws on the imagery of light. Just as a lamp is allowed to illuminate a room, so the effects of the gospel are to be felt in the world. In a saying that reinforces the importance of faith, and action as a result of that faith, Jesus affirms that his brothers are 'those who hear God's word and put it into practice' (8:19–21).

8:22–39 Jesus' Authority Confirmed A series of events then takes place which confirms Jesus' authority over the natural and supernatural order. Through his stilling of a storm, Jesus is shown to have authority over the wind and the waves, to the astonishment of his disciples (8:22–25). And in the healing of a man who is possessed by demons (8:26–39), we see once more that evil spirits recognise the identity of Jesus as 'Son of the Most High God', and submit to his authority. Once more, amazement and fear mingle among the onlookers, who are stunned by what they see taking place before their eyes.

8:40–56 A Dead Girl and a Sick Woman Finally, Jesus demonstrates that he has authority over death itself, by bringing the young daughter of Jairus, a prominent member of the local synagogue, back to life. Jesus also heals a woman who had been bleeding for many years, and who was widely regarded as being beyond any

hope of cure. Yet this is more than an act of healing. It is also an important act of affirmation. The woman would have been regarded as unclean by Jews, on account of the discharge of a bodily fluid. Jesus refuses to acknowledge this barrier to his ministry. No artificial human obstacles will be placed between the healer and those whom he has come to save.

9:1–17 Jesus Sends out the Twelve and Feeds Five Thousand The Twelve are sent out to preach the gospel, with the result that demons are driven out and those who are ill healed (9:1–6). This and other reports come to the attention of Herod, who had earlier beheaded John the Baptist (an incident recounted at length in Mk 6:14–29). Herod, like so many others, is confused over the identity of Jesus. Is he John the Baptist come back to life? Or is he Elijah? (9:7–9). After a brief interlude, in which Luke recounts the feeding of the five thousand (9:10–17), this theme is pursued again: Who is Jesus?

9:18–27 Peter's Confession of the Messiah This is precisely the question that Jesus puts to the disciples. The disciples report back on the various opinions that they have heard: Jesus is one of the prophets, or John the Baptist come back to life, or perhaps Elijah. But Jesus presses them: 'What about you? Who do *you* say that I am?' This is a vitally important question. Unlike the crowds, the disciples have been with Jesus throughout most of his ministry. They have watched him and listened to him. Now they are being asked what their conclusion is.

Peter speaks for them all when he replies that he believes that Jesus is

'God's Messiah' (9:20). Presumably anxious that the title 'Messiah' might be understood in a purely political sense, Jesus asks the disciples not to tell anyone of their realisation of his true identity (9:21). The Messiah could too easily be misunderstood as a triumphalist political leader, concerned only to liberate the country from its Roman occupying force. Immediately after Peter's confession that he is the Messiah, Jesus declares that he must go to Jerusalem, suffer, be rejected, be put to death and finally rise from the dead. It is an integral part of his calling. He is to be a suffering Messiah.

9:28–45 The Transfiguration; Jesus' Power Over Evil Spirits

An important anticipation of the resurrection now follows, in the account of the transfiguration (9:28–36). This demonstrates both the continuity of Jesus with the ministries of Moses and Elijah, while at the same time providing an anticipation of the resurrection glory of Christ. An endorsement of Jesus' identity and authority from heaven confirms his ministry and mission. After a further demonstration of the power of Jesus over evil spirits (9:37–43), the theme of the coming suffering of Jesus reappears (9:44–45). The disciples continue to be bewildered by this prediction. It does not accord with their expectations of what the Messiah would be like. The Messiah was expected to be a figure of triumph, not suffering.

9:46–62 Who Will Be the Greatest? The Cost of Discipleship

This early period of Jesus' ministry comes to an end (9:46–62) with a discussion among the disciples as to who will be the greatest among them. Jesus' reply makes it clear that worldly standards of supremacy and rank carry no weight in the kingdom of God. This is followed by a series of uncompromising statements concerning the cost of discipleship. Everything else must take second place to following Christ (9:57–62).

LUKE 10:1–19:27
Jesus' Later Ministry

10:1–37 Jesus Sends out the Seventy-two

Jesus now commissions 72 disciples to carry on the work of proclamation of the good news of the kingdom of God (10:1–24). They are authorised to speak in his name, and return joyfully to report of the results of their ministry. Jesus himself is then asked what must be done for someone to inherit eternal life (10:25–28). Jesus allows his questioner to answer this for himself, and then affirms the importance of love of God and love of one's neighbour, bringing together Dt 6:5 and Lev 19:18. However, the questioner has another issue to raise: Who is my neighbour? Jesus answers this question with the parable of the good Samaritan (10:30–37), which draws on the traditional hatred between Jews and Samaritans to make the point that mercy must not be compromised by social or national prejudices.

10:38–11:13 Mary and Martha; the Lord's Prayer

The episode with Mary and Martha (10:38–42) is generally thought to illustrate the importance of spending time with Jesus, enjoying the luxury of his presence and teaching, instead of fussing around and being anxious about other things. These can wait! The theme

of spending time with the Lord is then further developed in a section dealing with prayer. Jesus hands down a model prayer, generally known as 'The Lord's Prayer'. Its simplicity, brevity and intimacy set a model for the kind of prayer Jesus wishes his followers to adopt (11:1–4). The prayer affirms the fatherhood of God, reminding us that we owe our origins to him, and that he cares for his children. It reminds us that God is holy (the term 'hallowed' has the basic meaning of 'kept holy'), and that this holiness must be reflected in the way in which believers address God in prayer, speak of him to the world, and worship him. The prayer then turns to the needs of believers – to their physical need for food, and their spiritual need for forgiveness, comfort, and protection from temptation. Just as even sinful human fathers wish well for their children, so God will give his Holy Spirit to those who ask him (11:5–13).

11:14–32 Jesus and Beelzebul; Sign of Jonah

His opponents then attempt to cast aspersions on Jesus by suggesting that he has authority over demons because he is in league with 'Beelzebul, the prince of demons' (11:14–28). Jesus vigorously rejects this attempt to attribute his authority to Satan. The unbelief of his critics is further underscored by their demands for a sign, by which his authority might be justified. Jesus points them to the 'sign of Jonah', a clear reference to his forthcoming resurrection (11:29–32; see Mt 12:39–42).

11:33–12:2 Jesus Criticises the Pharisees

A series of teachings then follows, dealing with questions that arise at this stage during Jesus' ministry. In particular, Jesus criticises the Pharisees for their hypocritical conduct, which focuses on externals and neglects internal matters of faith and motivation. Lacking any real doctrine of grace, they merely lay burdens on others without doing anything to assist them. The disciples are to be on their guard against such people, and the threat they pose.

12:13–13:9 Watchfulness

This is followed by a series of teaching focusing on the theme of watchfulness. The disciples are not to be like the rich fool (12:13–21), who stored up wealth on earth without considering the eternal dimensions of life. Nor are they to worry too much about the physical aspects of life (12:22–34): if God takes care of the birds of the air and the lilies of the field, will he not also take care of them? What the disciples should be worried about is being taken unawares by the coming of the Lord. A series of illustrations brings out the importance of being prepared for the return of an absent master (12:35–48), pointing to the coming of Christ. This theme of 'being prepared for the end' is then developed in a number of different directions. The coming of Jesus will bring division, not peace (12:49–53). The disciples are to watch for the signs of the end, as people watch for signs of a change in the weather (12:54–59). The need for urgent repentance is illustrated by the incident of the tower of Siloam and the fruitless tree threatened with destruction unless it bears fruit (13:1–9).

13:10–14:35 Jesus Continues to Heal and to Teach

The healing and teaching continue. Jesus' vigorous refutation of those who criticise his healing on the Sabbath meets

with widespread approval. The parable of the mustard seed points to how the kingdom of God can grow rapidly from small beginnings (13:19). The theme of healing on the Sabbath is explored further when he is invited to eat at the house of a local Pharisee (14:1–14). He uses this occasion to emphasise the difference between worldly and spiritual understandings of rank and importance.

The theme of food leads on to the parable of the great banquet (14:15–24). This parable deals with a feast to which a select few are invited, but who, for various reasons, fail to attend. The invitation is then extended to all. The parable clearly deals with the extension of the good news of the kingdom from the narrow bounds of Israel to the Gentiles. Yet Jesus makes it clear that the kingdom of God is not simply about feasting. Becoming and being his disciple will involve pain, suffering and loss. It is something that must be thought about carefully, and not undertaken lightly (14:25–35).

15:1–32 Parables of the Lost
Three parables then follow, each of which focuses on the joy of recovering something that is lost, and rebuts the objections of the Pharisees and teachers of the Law against the welcome Jesus offered to so-called 'sinners'. Why should not God be overjoyed at the return of the lost? The first parable centres on the recovery of a *lost sheep* (15:3–7); the second on the finding of a *lost coin* (15:8–10); the third – which is the celebrated parable of *the prodigal (lost) son* – or the return of a wayward son to his father (15:11–32). This third parable superbly illustrates the joy experienced by the father at the return of his son, whom he had given up as lost. It also points to the sense of irritation felt by the father's older son, who fails to understand fully the grounds of the father's delight at the restoration of his brother.

16:1–18:14 The Parables Continue
A series of parables then follows, interspersed with accounts of incidents on the way to Jerusalem (16:1–19:27). The parable of *the shrewd manager* (16:1–15) points to the need to plan for the future, particularly in the light of coming judgment. The parable in question is difficult to interpret, and is probably best understood as follows. It was common practice to overcharge buyers. The steward was in fact reducing the debts from the inflated prices charged by the master to the real price the items were worth. As a result, the master could take some comfort from what he had done, and the clients would regard the steward favourably.

The story of *the rich man and Lazarus* (16:19–31) illustrates both the evils of riches and the importance of the resurrection in establishing the authority of Jesus. However, Jesus suggests that humanity is so sinful that it is unlikely even to listen to someone who returns from the dead in this manner. Perhaps that sin is inevitable. Nevertheless, there is a real need to avoid *being the cause of sin to anyone* (17:1–4). The importance of faith is then stressed (17:5–10), and illustrated by the incident in which *ten men are healed of leprosy* (17:11–19). Only one – a Samaritan – has the grace to thank Jesus for what he has done. Jesus commends him for doing so, and assures him that his faith has restored him. Jesus then returns to the theme of *the coming of the kingdom,*

and especially emphasises the need for watchfulness (17:20–37).

Two parables then illustrate aspects of the good news. The parable of *the persistent widow* (18:1–8) illustrates how even an unjust judge responds to persistent requests. How much more so, he suggests, will God – who is a good and merciful judge – respond to the persistent prayer of his people. This is followed by the parable of *the Pharisee and the tax collector* (18:9–14), which brings out the importance of humility. The Pharisee thanks God for his many virtues. The tax collector openly admits his misery and sin. There is no hint that the Pharisee was a hypocrite. It is virtually certain that he did everything he mentioned, which exceeded the demands of the Law. For example, fasting was commanded by the Law on the Day of Atonement only – yet he fasted twice a week. The point being made is simple: humility leads to mercy and forgiveness.

18:15–30 Little Children; Jesus and the Rich Ruler The kind of lowliness that is commended is then illustrated through two different incidents. In the first, Jesus declares that people must receive the kingdom of God with the trust, delight and dependence of little children (18:15–17). In the second, the meeting with the rich young ruler (18:18–30) brings out the obstacle that riches pose to acceptance in the sight of God. After discovering that the young man has faithfully kept the commandments, Jesus asks him to sell all he has, and follow him. This dismays the young man, who departs with great sadness. It is clear that wealth poses a real obstacle to coming to God. Nevertheless, as Jesus makes clear, with

God anything is possible. Nobody lies outside the saving purposes of God, who has promised salvation to those who put their faith in Jesus Christ.

18:31–43 Jesus Again Predicts His Death; A Blind Beggar Receives His Sight Readers are then reminded once more of the high price of that salvation, as Jesus once more predicts his betrayal, suffering and resurrection (18:31–34). This passage reminds us that Jesus' death is no accident. It is something that has been purposed and foretold. Jesus dies because he has to die – there is no other way in which sinful humanity can be redeemed. The crucifixion has to happen. This prediction of suffering and death is followed by the healing of the blind man (18:35–43), which illustrates both the importance of faith and the spiritual discernment of this physically blind man, who recognises the 'Son of David' as he passes.

19:1–10 Zacchaeus the Tax Collector The personal impact of Jesus is then demonstrated in the encounter with Zacchaeus the tax collector. As noted earlier, tax collectors were hated on account of their dishonesty and collaboration with the Roman authorities. Zacchaeus is, however, attracted to Jesus. Despite his despised social status, Jesus welcomes him and visits his home – to the outrage of onlookers. Yet the encounter proves to be transformative. Zacchaeus repents of his dishonesty, and offers more than adequate restoration of anything he has dishonestly received. For Jesus, this provides yet another illustration of his mission to seek and reach the lost.

Why did Israel's leaders reject Jesus?

When the promised and long-awaited Messiah finally arrived, one might have expected Israel's religious leaders and scholars to have welcomed him. Instead, they rejected him, because his message about God's kingdom radically cut across their expectations.

The Pharisees rejected him because his view of the Jewish Law was so different. Deeply aware that disobedience had led Israel into exile centuries earlier, they believed that meticulous obedience to that Law was now called for, as the only way to prepare for God's kingdom; and obedience not just to the Law, but also to all the many oral traditions built upon it. It was their insistence on the latter – things like ritual washings, obligatory fasting, rules for keeping the Sabbath, avoiding anything 'defiling' – that brought them into constant conflict with Jesus who had no time for such merely human rules, declaring they undermined the very heart of what God had intended (Mt 5:21–48).

The scribes were the ones who had created those oral traditions as they had sought to interpret and apply the Law during the exile, and by Jesus' day these interpretations were seen as important as the Law itself. They rejected Jesus because he would not line up with their interpretations, and strongly reacted to his accusations that they had let go of God's commands in favour of human traditions (Mk 7:8) and were so concerned with details that they missed the most important things (Mt 15:1–20).

The Sadducees rejected Jesus for completely different reasons, however. Although they had theological differences with him, their main concerns were political. They had become hugely influential in Jerusalem, controlling the temple and the high priesthood and were afraid that Jesus might upset the delicate political balance that would lead to their losing influence if Rome clamped down.

19:12–27 The Parable of the Ten Minas The theme of the return of the Lord is then explored in the parable of the ten minas, which corresponds broadly to the parable of the bags of gold (talents): Mt 25:14–30. Attention here focuses on what the servants do while the master is away. The parable tells of a master who entrusts his minas (quantities of silver, which act as money) to his servants during his absence, and of the variety of ways in which the servants make use of that money. The main point being made is that the master will return, without warning, to see what has happened in his absence.

LUKE 19:28–24:53
The Passion, Death and Resurrection of Christ

19:28–44 The Triumphal Entry While all this has been going on, Jesus and his disciples have been drawing nearer and nearer to Jerusalem. Jesus had told his disciples that he must go to Jerusalem, to be betrayed and crucified. Now Jesus prepares to enter the great city itself. Jesus enters in humility, mounted on a donkey, in fulfilment of a great messianic prophecy of the Old Testament (Zec 9:9). Jesus enters Jerusalem as its king, an

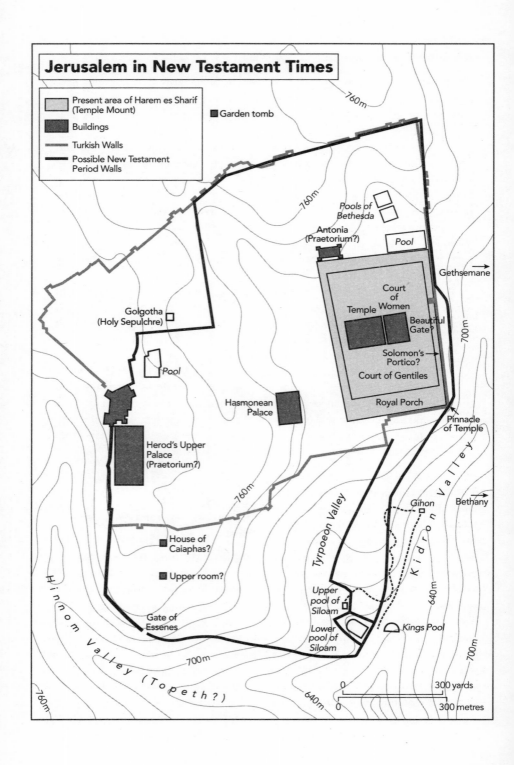

Jerusalem in New Testament Times

Present area of Harem es Sharif (Temple Mount)

Buildings

Turkish Walls

Possible New Testament Period Walls

Garden tomb

760m

760m

Pools of Bethesda

Antonia (Praetorium?)

Pool

Gethsemane

Court of Women

Temple

Beautiful Gate?

Golgotha (Holy Sepulchre)

Solomon's Portico?

Court of Gentiles

Pool

700m

Hasmonean Palace

Royal Porch

Herod's Upper Palace (Praetorium?)

Pinnacle of Temple

760m

Bethany

Gihon

Tyrpoeon Valley

Kidron Valley

House of Caiaphas?

Upper room?

640m

Upper pool of Siloam

Gate of Essenes

Kings Pool

Lower pool of Siloam

Hinnom Valley (Topeth?)

700m

700m

760m

640m

0   300 yards

0   300 metres

event especially celebrated by Christians on Palm Sunday. It is clear that there are many who were looking forward to this event. He is greeted by crowds, honouring him and singing his praises, to the obvious annoyance of the Pharisees.

19:45–48 Jesus at the Temple The final week of Jesus' life is packed with teaching and conflict with the religious authorities. The first major incident is the cleansing of the temple, in which Jesus ejects the merchants and overturns the tables of the money-changers and sellers of doves. The protest is probably only partly against the commercialisation of the temple areas. It almost certainly represents Jesus' anger that any form of payment or purchase is necessary before an individual may worship God.

20:1–19 The Authority of Jesus Questioned Controversy now develops with increasing intensity. Once more, the authority of Jesus is questioned by his critics (20:1–8), who prove unable to give an adequate response to Jesus' challenge to them over the authority of John the Baptist. The parable of the tenants (21:9–19) represents a superb and distressing illustration of the way in which Judaism had rejected God's prophets – and was also about to reject the Son of God. The final killing of the son reminds us of Jesus' predictions of his own death in Jerusalem, through which his final rejection by Judaism will be sealed. Yet even though he has been rejected, this will not be the end of the story, as the prophetic remark concerning the rejected stone makes clear (20:17; see Ps 118:22). (The 'cornerstone' refers to

the first stone placed in a building, which determined the position of every stone that followed it.)

20:20–26 Paying Taxes to Caesar Jesus then addresses a series of controversial questions raised by the agents of the religious authorities, who attempt to outwit him. An initial attempt is made to trap Jesus by embroiling him in a controversy that relates to the Roman authorities. Should Jews pay taxes to the Romans or not? The Pharisees are opposed to paying such taxes. The Herodians (who are strongly pro-Roman) are in favour. Both groups are opposed to Jesus. Whichever way he replies, Jesus will lose out, either by supporting treason or by supporting the Romans. Jesus takes neither option, evading the trap set for him. He draws attention to the image of Caesar on the coins used to pay the tax. What is Caesar's should be given to Caesar. What is God's should be given to God. As humanity is created in the image of God (Ge 1:26–27), this reply is actually a declaration of the need for people to dedicate themselves to him.

20:27–44 The Resurrection and Marriage This is followed by a question raised by the Sadducees concerning marriage at the resurrection (20:27–40). In an attempt to trap Jesus into conceding that there is no resurrection, they ask a question, based on marriage in heaven, designed to demonstrate the logical impossibility of resurrection. Jesus points out that, as there is no marriage in heaven, their argument falls to the ground. He further adds to the embarrassment of his opponents by showing up their inability to make sense

of the messianic prophecy of Ps 110:1 (20:41–44).

20:45–21:38 Signs of the End of the Age

After stressing the importance of humility and commending the generosity of a poor widow (20:45–21:4), Jesus turns his attention to the end of the age (21:5–38). This section alerts the disciples to the troubles that lie ahead. The distress and pain that lie in the future are vividly described. Many of these sayings will find at least partial fulfilment in the destruction of Jerusalem by the Roman armies in AD 70. This will be a time of betrayal, of persecution and of false teaching. It is, however, clear that Jesus' ultimate reference is to the end of the world itself, when he, as the 'Son of Man' will come again in glory to judge the world. His point is that the disciples must not be frightened when these things happen. When they come to pass, it will be a sign that their hour of final redemption has arrived.

22:1–38 The Last Supper

Luke then sets the scene for the final days of Christ's earthly life at the time of the Passover, when Israel remembered the great act of deliverance by which God rescued their ancestors from bondage in Egypt (22:1–12). According to Dt 16:16, all Jewish men were required to celebrate the Passover feast in Jerusalem itself. On this occasion, the Passover will take on a special significance for Jesus, who turns out to be the true Passover lamb, sacrificed for the sins of the world. Redemption is drawing near.

As Luke begins to tell the story of Christ's final days in Jerusalem, we become aware of the power of sin in the present. Luke relates how the Jewish leaders plot to get rid of Jesus, Satan enters into Judas Iscariot, and the love of money triumphs over the love of God. The Passover was indeed a celebration of a past act of deliverance. Yet the power of sin remained. Something needed to be done to achieve a once-for-all victory over sin. In what follows, we learn of how the death of Christ holds the key to this vital development.

As the Jewish people were preparing to sacrifice their Passover lambs, Jesus prepares to die. While Israel remembered a past act of redemption, God was achieving a new and greater work of redemption in their midst. Having gathered together in the upper room, Jesus and his disciples celebrate Passover (22:14–23). With great solemnity, Jesus tells the apostles that he will never celebrate Passover again 'until it finds fulfilment in the kingdom of God'. The Passover is seen as something that points beyond itself, to something greater that is yet to find its fulfilment. And as the meal proceeds, the full meaning of his words begins to become clear. Just as the Passover lamb was slain, so Jesus will be slain. His body will be broken, and his blood shed. And through his death, a 'new covenant' will be established.

Jesus' words are momentous: the Passover is about to find its fulfilment in and through him. But what does a 'new covenant' mean? The Greek word used here has the sense of 'testament' as in 'last will and testament'. It points to a set of promises and an inheritance, which become effective with the death of the testator. Jesus is declaring that through his death, the promises of

forgiveness and eternal life come into effect, allowing believers to receive the inheritance of eternal life. Yet these words of promise are followed by a reminder of the reality and presence of sin, as Jesus declares that one of his disciples will betray him.

Luke continues to tell the tale of Christ's final days on earth by returning to the theme of the presence and power of sin (22:24–38). Even at this solemn moment, as Christ's death draws near, the disciples begin to bicker among themselves. Is Luke telling his readers how much even the apostles needed redemption? Is he hinting at how weak unredeemed human nature is? If so, it allows us to understand and appreciate all the more Christ's death on the cross, to liberate sinful humanity from the power of sin. The lingering presence of sin can be seen in Peter's confident denial that he could ever let Jesus down. 'I am ready to go with you to prison and to death' (22:33). In the light of what eventually happens, those words sound rather superficial and hollow.

Jesus declares that he has come to be a servant among his people. He is a servant king, unlike the power-loving kings of the Gentiles. And that service is seen supremely in the fact that he is willing, in fulfilment of prophecy, 'to be numbered with transgressors'. A sense of new urgency breaks in, as Jesus speaks of this great prophecy 'reaching its fulfilment'. This calls to mind other sections of that prophecy, such as, 'the Lord has laid on him the iniquity of us all' (Isa 53:6, 12). Even though Jesus is sinless, he is content to be treated as if he were a sinner, so that he can redeem sinners.

22:39–53 *Jesus Arrested on the Mount of Olives* Jesus and the disciples then leave the warmth and safety of the upper room, and go out into the night (22:39–53). Many commentators see the burden of human sin beginning to weigh upon Jesus at this point. The Lamb of God has taken the weight of human sin on his shoulders, and become affected by it. Does he begin to share in the human condition of being uncertain about God? Certainly, his deeply moving prayer suggests hesitation about the future mingled with total obedience: 'Father, if you are willing, take this cup from me; yet not my will, but yours be done' (22:42). (The 'cup' is a traditional Old Testament reference to suffering.) Luke brings out Jesus' pain and anguish at this point, noting that 'his sweat was like drops of blood falling to the ground'. We must not think of Christ's passion as having begun only at the moment of crucifixion. Luke makes it clear that Jesus went through mental agony, as he reflected on what lay ahead of him. Part of that agony concerns his betrayal by one of his closest friends.

We now come to the story of the betrayal of Jesus by Judas' kiss. Many commentators have pointed to the irony of the event: a gesture of affection becomes an act of betrayal. There is a moral here. The history of the church reminds us that those who declare love for Christ may still betray him by their actions. Even in his moment of betrayal, the kindness of Jesus still shines through. In a moment of foolishness, one of his followers cuts off the ear of the high priest's servant. Jesus heals this man, just as he had healed so many others during his ministry. Even as his crucifixion draws

near, he still shows the compassion of God for those who need healing.

22:54–62 Peter Disowns Jesus

Luke then relates another story of failure. Jesus has just been betrayed by a disciple. Now he will be disowned by another. Peter, the closest to Jesus of the apostles, has been confident of his own commitment to Christ. He has declared that he will willingly face prison, or even death, for him. But when things get tough, Peter discovers that he is a total failure. He repeatedly denies having anything to do with Christ. Then, in a moment of utter despair, he remembers his brave words, and feels shamed. In Luke's words, 'He went outside and wept bitterly.'

22:63–67 The Guards Mock Jesus; the Chief Priests Question Him

Having faced betrayal and denial, Jesus is then confronted with mockery, as his guards begin to taunt and ridicule him. All this is in fulfilment of prophecy: 'He was despised and rejected by mankind, a man of suffering and familiar with pain' (Isa 53:3). Finally, he is faced with disbelief and rebellion, as he is brought before the chief priests. They demand to know whether he is 'the Messiah' (22:67) or 'the Son of God' (22:70). According to the Jewish beliefs of the time, the appearance of the Messiah would lead to his people falling down in worship before him. Yet when Jesus admits that he is the Son of God, all that the chief priests do is to hand him over to the Romans for execution. Luke reminds us that sin, with its deepseated tendency to rebel against God, had permeated to the very heart of Israel. Israel could not save itself. It needed a redeemer. The sheer tragedy of the sinful human situation is seen in this: when a redeemer finally came, he was rejected with contempt.

23:1–25 Jesus Before Pilate and Herod

Jesus is now led to face the Roman governor, Pontius Pilate (23:1–12), accused of being 'Messiah, a king' by his Jewish opponents (23:2). Once more, Luke draws our attention to the irony of the situation. The Messiah's people should have knelt at his feet. Instead, they rise up. They ought to have adored him. Instead, they accuse him. The accusations brought against Jesus can be seen as deliberately slanted to make Pilate take the worst possible view of Jesus. He is charged with opposing the 'payment of taxes to Caesar' and claiming to be a king. Both of these are calculated to rouse the suspicions of a Roman governor, anxious to suppress any sedition or rebellion in his territories. By restating Jesus' religious message in political terms, the chief priests hope to discredit him. In the event, they fail. Pilate has no hesitation in declaring that Jesus 'has done nothing to deserve death' and when he sends Jesus to Herod, Herod mocks him but can find no basis for the charges brought against Jesus. Yet this does not satisfy the crowds, who are clearly intent on destroying him.

We are now introduced to Barabbas, who 'had been thrown into prison for an insurrection in the city, and for murder' (23:19). Luke presents Barabbas as a man guilty of rebellion and murder, someone who, according to the Law, deserves to die. The crowds demand the death of Jesus and the release of Barabbas. Pilate repeats his firm belief that Jesus does not deserve

death for any reason. Yet, in the end, he is not totally in control of the situation. He finally yields to the enormous pressure that is being applied to him by the crowds. Barabbas is released, and Jesus led away to execution.

22:26–46 The Crucifixion and Death of Jesus And so we come to Luke's account of the suffering and death of Jesus Christ – a section of Luke's Gospel often referred to as 'the passion narrative', from the Latin term *passio*, 'suffering' (23:26–46). Jesus is so tired that Simon from Cyrene has to carry his heavy cross on his shoulders (23:26). Jesus is put to death between two criminals (23:33), praying for those who are putting him to death (23:34) – again, in fulfilment of prophecy (Isa 53:12). He is mocked and taunted by those whom he has come to redeem (23:35). The crowds scorn him: 'let him save himself if he is God's Messiah, the Chosen One'. The soldiers mock him, and call on him to save himself (23:36–37). One of the criminals curses him, and demands that he save himself (23:39). But Christ remains on that cross. Instead of saving himself, he saves sinful humanity. One of the two criminals is deeply moved by what takes place, and puts his faith in him, receiving an assurance of going with Christ to paradise (23:42–43).

Finally, Jesus dies. Luke notes some events accompanying his death, and leaves his readers to ponder their meaning. 'Darkness came over the whole land' (23:44). The light of the world had been extinguished. 'The curtain of the temple was torn in two' (23:45). The curtain symbolised the barrier placed between God and humanity through sin.

With the death of Christ, this barrier has been torn down.

23:47–56 The Innocence of Jesus Luke then returns to the central theme of the innocence of Christ. Having already cited Pontius Pilate as a witness to his guiltlessness, Luke now calls on the support of the senior Roman officer present: 'Surely this was a righteous man' (23:47). The declarations of Pilate and the centurion are thought to be of vital importance for Luke: his Gospel was probably aimed at partly Roman readership, which may have heard rumours of Jesus as an executed criminal or political rebel. Luke puts the record straight: Jesus did not die for his own sins, but for the sins of others. Luke also makes the point that not every senior Jewish religious figure approved of what had happened, noting Joseph of Arimathea (23:50–51) as an example of someone who was deeply uneasy over the course that events had taken.

23:50–56 Jesus' Burial Finally, Luke records the burial of Christ. This whole passage is tinged with sadness. There is not a hint of an expectation of the resurrection. The promise of Jesus' resurrection seems to have been forgotten. The picture Luke paints for us is that of a dedicated and caring group of people ensuring that their dear friend Jesus is buried with quiet dignity. Luke stresses that 'the women' were witnesses to all that he describes (23:49, 55).

See 'Did the resurrection really happen?', page 338.

24:1–12 *The Resurrection* 'He has risen!' (24:6). With these words, the lives of all those who saw Christ die are turned upside down. As Luke tells us the story of that first Easter Day, we can sense the total surprise and disbelief of all concerned. Here is no group of gullible disciples, determined, at any cost, to believe that Christ is risen. Here is a group of hardheaded men and women, confronted with evidence that throws their world into confusion, as they try to take in the momentous implications of what is going on. The man they have known and loved; the man they have seen killed; the man they have buried themselves is risen! The Gospels insist that the initial reaction to the resurrection is fear (24:5): the disciples cannot take in what is happening.

Yet the angel reminds them of the great promise Christ had made to them before his death (24:6–7). He had prophesied that he would be betrayed, crucified and finally rise again. And in a moment of wonder, the disciples remember (24:8). But again, Luke stresses that the disciples are not going to be rushed to hasty conclusions. They want time to think about things, and take in their momentous implications. The words of the women 'seemed to them like nonsense' (24:11). Even Peter went away, 'wondering to himself what had happened' (24:12).

24:13–35 *On the Road to Emmaus* In the midst of all this excitement and confusion, Luke leads us away to a quiet road, leading from Jerusalem to Emmaus (24:13–35). Two disciples, one of whom is named Cleopas, are discussing the day's events, and marvelling at them

(24:13–17). Again, Luke lets us know that they are still not sure what to make of them (24:19–24). And as they talk, a third man joins them. The risen Christ is present with them, yet they do not recognise him.

The stranger then opens up the Scriptures to them, explaining how Jesus had 'to suffer these things and then enter his glory' (24:26). Again, we encounter the theme of the necessity of Christ's death. This was no accident. He had to suffer and die, to buy freedom and forgiveness for his people. And Jesus takes these marvelling disciples through the Old Testament prophecies, as 'he explained to them what was said in all the Scriptures concerning himself' (24:27).

But they still do not realise who he is. The moment of truth dawns shortly afterwards, when he makes himself known to them through the breaking of the bread (24:30–31). And suddenly, everything falls into place. They realise who he is, and all that this implies. Two things happen as a result. They *understand* who he is, and make sense of all that he has told them about Scripture (24:32). And they begin to *witness* to the reality of the resurrection (24:33–35).

24:36–53 *Jesus Appears to the Disciples, and the Ascension* Luke then takes us back to Jerusalem, to the company of the apostles (24:36–53). Jesus appears to them. Once more, the reaction is that of fear, rather than of joy (24:37). The apostles still cannot really believe what has happened. Yet Jesus, knowing their unspoken doubts, reassures them. It really is him. The marks on his hands and feet are there to prove it (24:39). And again, Jesus patiently

explains that all this had to happen to him (24:44–47). The reality of his suffering and death is now surpassed by the power of his risen presence. Gradually, fear gives way to joy and amazement (24:41). Their doubts are resolved.

Reassurance of the resurrection then leads directly into the apostles being commissioned to proclaim this good news to the world. What has happened is not just good news for the disciples, who have regained a friend. It is good news for the world, which has gained a Saviour. The apostles are to go forth into that world. 'You are witnesses of these things' (24:48). It is only when the disciples really believe that Christ is risen themselves, that they are told to go and tell others the news. Luke's point is clear: the resurrection of Jesus is something that is trustworthy.

Yet the disciples are not to witness unaided. The power by which God raised his Christ from the dead will be channelled into the apostles' witness and preaching. They will be 'clothed with power from on high' (24:49), a reference to the promised coming of the Holy Spirit, who will empower his people to proclaim the good news of the risen Christ to all nations. And, having been blessed by their Lord at Bethany, the disciples 'returned to Jerusalem with great joy' (24:52). The good news they have been entrusted with is not burdensome to share, for it brings joy. And Christians today have been called to share in the apostles' witness to the risen presence of Christ in their lives. They can turn from Luke, reassured of the trustworthiness of the gospel, and the joy it can bring to a world that needs to hear it. In the second part of his work, the book of Acts, we shall learn of how that world responded to this news.

JOHN

John's Gospel is noticeably different from the first three Gospels, both in terms of its style of writing and also the way in which it presents its material. It is often thought to be the Gospel most suited to devotional reading, as it uses powerful imagery to bring home to its readers the full impact of Jesus Christ on believers, and his significance for the world.

The Gospel itself testifies that its author is 'the disciple whom Jesus loved' (e.g., 13:23–26; 18:15–16). Tradition has identified this as the apostle John, although it should be noted that the text of the Gospel itself does not make this statement explicitly. There are reasons for thinking that the Gospel may have been written for churches in the region of Ephesus. The date of writing of the Gospel remains unclear. Most scholars suggest a date towards the end of the 1st century (perhaps around AD 85), although the possibility of an earlier date remains open.

JOHN 1:1–51
The Background to the Ministry of Jesus

1:1–18 The Word Became Flesh It is immediately obvious that there is something different about John's Gospel. Matthew, Mark and Luke all open their Gospels by pointing to important events in history that cast light on the background to Jesus' ministry – such as his ancestors, the events surrounding his birth or the coming of John the Baptist. But John is different. We are immediately taken behind the scene of history, to learn of the background to the coming of Jesus Christ, as seen from the perspective of God himself.

The Gospel opens with a section referred to as the 'Prologue' (1:1–18) – a sort of 'foreword', which sets the scene for the coming of Christ. Even before we are introduced to any event in history, we know the background to the coming of Jesus. Jesus is none other than 'the Word' become 'flesh' (1:14). The Prologue opens by recalling the great words of the Genesis creation account, taking us right back to the beginning of time (1:1; see Ge 1:1). The term 'Word' (Greek *logos*) is used to refer to Christ. The use of this word is enormously important, as it points to God's ability to communicate himself, and make himself known through Jesus Christ – a major theme of John's Gospel.

It is immediately clear that there is a direct relationship between God's work of creation and his work of redemption. The passage makes it clear that creation was the work of God through Christ (1:3), just as redemption is also the work of God through Christ. And this process of redemption involves Christ entering into the world. The imagery now shifts from word to light, as John brings out the judgment that the coming of Christ brings to the world. Light shows up things as they really are, and thus brings both judgment and the hope of cleansing. Even though the world is dark, it cannot overcome the light that now breaks into its gloom (1:3–5).

We are now prepared for the coming of John the Baptist (1:6–9). John was a witness to the coming of the light into the world. He himself was not that light. Nevertheless, he pointed to its coming. Yet when that light finally entered the world, the world chose to reject it (1:11–13). His own people rejected him – a clear reference to the refusal on the part of Judaism to acknowledge the Messiah when he finally came. Yet those who did recognise and acknowledge Christ were granted the privilege of becoming children of God.

John then summarises the importance of Jesus in his declaration that 'the Word became flesh and made his dwelling among us' (1:14). The glory of Christ is the same as the glory of God himself – a glory that we have been allowed to see and experience through Christ. Many Christian writers use the term

'incarnation' to refer to the coming of Christ. The word means 'being in the flesh', and refers to God coming into his world in the person of Jesus Christ. The testimony of John the Baptist is then anticipated: this is indeed the person to whom he was sent to bear witness. Even though nobody has seen God face to face (Moses, after all, only caught a glimpse of the back of God disappearing into the distance), God has determined to make himself known through Jesus Christ (1:15–18). And why is Jesus Christ able to make God known in this way? For John, the answer is simple and crucial: Jesus makes God known, because Jesus himself is God.

1:19–28 John the Baptist Denies Being the Christ We now enter the realm of human history. The scene has been set for the coming of Jesus Christ. Now we prepare to hear how he made his appearance on the stage of history. John opens his account by drawing our attention to the ministry of John the Baptist, who affirms that his purpose is to prepare the way for the coming of the Lord. He emphatically denies being anyone of any importance himself. He is not, for example, the long-awaited prophet, nor the Messiah. He is simply there to point to someone else.

1:29–34 Jesus the Lamb of God But who? We already know the answer to this

---

Did Jesus really think he was God?

John certainly believed that Jesus was no one less than God come into our world. But wasn't such an idea the church's creation? Surely no sane person proclaims he is God, and no good Jew would believe him if he did.

First, we should note Jesus' own awareness of a special relationship with God from an early age. When his parents lost him, aged 12, they eventually found him in the temple, talking with rabbis. To their understandable rebuke, he simply replied, 'Didn't you know I had to be in my Father's house?' (Lk 2:49). No Jew would dare say such words; God was the Father of Israel, yes, but not of individuals. By the time his ministry began, he was claiming that this relationship wasn't just special, but unique, prompting his opponents to seek his death, for 'he was even calling God his own Father, making himself equal with God' (Jn 5:18).

While Jesus never openly proclaimed, 'I am God!' he made unmistakable claims of unique relationship with the Father. He did this through his miracles, which demonstrated the freedom only God can bring (Lk 4:18–19); through his forgiveness, claiming authority to forgive sins, and healing to confirm it (Mk 2:1–12); through his words, which he claimed fulfilled the Law (Mt 5:17) and would determine people's destiny (Mk 8:38); through his actions, like riding into Jerusalem on a donkey, fulfilling messianic prophecy (Mt 21:1–11; Zec 9:9); through his intimacy with God, calling him 'Abba' ('daddy'), unparalleled in Jewish literature. Moreover, whenever people grasped he was God, he never rebuked them, but only blessed them (Mt 16:13–17; Jn 20:28).

Jesus clearly knew who he was: no one less than God come to us.

from the Prologue. We now see this answer actualised in history, as Jesus comes towards John (1:29–34). John immediately bears witness to Christ, making it clear that this is the person whose coming he was sent to proclaim. This is none other than the Son of God himself. Some of John's own disciples are attracted to Jesus, and spend some time with him. Although they initially refer to him as 'rabbi' (the term used to refer to a teacher), as a result of their encounter with Jesus they begin to refer to him as the Messiah (1:35–42).

1:35–51 Jesus' First Disciples Further encounters with Jesus follow, as his first disciples begin to spread the news of him around the neighbourhood (1:43–51). Philip is explicitly clear about the significance of Jesus: he is 'the one Moses wrote about in the Law, and about whom the prophets also wrote' (1:45). In other words, he is the fulfilment of all the great hopes and expectations of the Old Testament. Nathanael, to whom Philip has explained all these things, is sceptical, and wonders if anything good can come out of Nazareth. Philip's reply is simple: 'Come and see' – in other words, have your doubts resolved by encountering Jesus for yourself. This is an important model for evangelism, as it directs people's attention away from arguments and disputes, and leads them directly to the person of Christ. And sure enough, when Nathanael meets Jesus, he is convinced. Here is the 'Son of God' and the 'King of Israel' (1:49).

JOHN 2:1–12:11
The Public Ministry of Jesus Christ

2:1–11 Jesus Changes Water to Wine The public ministry of Jesus begins with a celebration – a wedding feast at Cana in Galilee. The occasion is remarkable on account of the miracle Jesus performs on that occasion. The feast threatens to grind to a halt on account of the wine running out. Nearby, there were six large stone vessels full of water, which was meant to be used for Jewish purification rites. Jesus changes this water to wine, to such good effect that the 'master of the banquet' regards it as being even better than the wine they had originally been using.

It is, of course, easy to treat this simply as a miracle. There is no doubt that it was this: John describes it as 'the first of the signs' (2:11). But it is also more than that. It can be read at a number of symbolical levels. For example, the comment about the new wine being better than the old can be read as pointing to the superiority of the new covenant over the old covenant. Equally, it is important that the water thus transformed was originally to be used for the purpose of purification rites. A religion of ritual cleansing is thus transformed into a faith that 'gladdens human hearts' (as Ps 104:15 describes the effect of wine).

2:12–25 Jesus Clears the Temple The scene now changes. It is the season of Passover, and Jesus goes up to Jerusalem for the feast. According to Dt 16:16, all Jewish men were required to celebrate the Passover feast in Jerusalem itself. Later, the Passover would take on a special significance for Jesus, whom we shall

discover to be the true Passover lamb, sacrificed for the sins of the world. But on this occasion, Jesus directs his attention towards the temple, and the abuses that have found their way within its precincts. John places the incident of the cleansing of the temple at the opening of the ministry of Jesus, whereas the Synoptic Gospels (that is, Matthew, Mark and Luke) place it during the final week of Jesus' ministry. The reason for this divergence is not entirely clear, although two reasons can easily explain the difference. First, it could be suggested that we are dealing with two different attempts to clean up the temple, one of which dates from the opening and the other from the close of his ministry. This is supported by differences in detail between the accounts (e.g., John mentions the selling of cattle and sheep and the use of a whip, which are not noted in the Synoptic Gospel accounts of the same incident). Alternatively, it could be suggested that John has placed the account of the cleansing of the temple at the opening of Jesus' ministry to bring out the theological importance of the event. By placing the account at the opening of the ministry, John brings out the fact that Jesus was exercising judgment throughout his ministry, and not simply at its end.

The incident is particularly important on account of a misunderstanding that arises over some words of Jesus. His reference to destroying the temple (2:19) is misunderstood to refer to the physical building in which his protest has taken place. This charge reappears at the time of his trial before the high priest (Mt 26:60–61). The onlookers protest that building the temple has taken 46 years

thus far (it would finally be completed in AD 64, work having started around 20 BC – a fact which suggests that this incident took place around AD 26). But the real meaning of Jesus' words becomes clear only after the resurrection itself. His reference to raising it again in three days is a reference to himself. This is important, as it points to the way in which many of Jesus' sayings and deeds can be understood fully and properly only in the light of his resurrection.

3:1–21 Jesus Teaches Nicodemus It is clear that many people are attracted to Jesus on account of his miraculous signs (2:23). Yet this could be little more than a superficial attraction, based on passing interest. Jesus demands a far more radical commitment than this on the part of those who wish to be his followers, as the meeting with Nicodemus makes clear. This meeting deserves careful study.

Nicodemus, like so many others, is attracted to Jesus. On account of his senior status within Judaism, he visits Jesus by night, so that his interest will not compromise his position within the Sanhedrin, the 71-member supreme Jewish court, consisting of the chief priests, elders and teachers of the Law. He declares that he, and others, know that there is something special about Jesus. Only someone with a special relationship with God could perform such miraculous signs.

Jesus' response clearly mystifies Nicodemus. Only someone who is 'born again' can see the kingdom of God. Nicodemus assumes that this refers to a physical rebirth, in which it is necessary to re-enter his mother's womb. Yet Jesus' words have a deeper significance. As

becomes clear, he is referring to a spiritual rebirth, in which someone who already possesses life at the physical level comes to birth at the spiritual level. They are alive already, in the sense that they physically exist. Yet they have yet to discover life in all its fullness, which comes only through being born again. The references to the flesh and spirit (3:6) make this point clear. Yet there is more to the idea than this. The Greek word translated as 'again' (*anō*) can also mean 'from above' (we find it used in this sense in Matthew's account of the curtain of the temple being torn from 'top to bottom' – literally, from above to beneath – at Mt 27:51). This rebirth does not take place from below, but from God himself. To see the kingdom of God, it is necessary to be born of both water and the Spirit (3:5), a reference to both the physical and spiritual side of life. It is also possible that Jesus intends to distinguish between the external cleansing of water, and the internal renewal brought by the Holy Spirit.

So what authority does Jesus have to make such statements? This question is dealt with by Jesus, who makes the point that only someone who has descended from heaven – and will ascend there again – has the authority and the ability to speak about heavenly things (3:13). Here we see a clear statement of the importance of the resurrection in establishing Jesus' authority. In the incarnation, Jesus comes down to earth, already in full possession of the authority to speak about God. The resurrection demonstrates this authority publicly, as well as being the means by which 'the one who came from heaven' will return there.

Jesus then proclaims the crucial link between his own forthcoming death and the full benefits of the gospel. In a reference to Moses delivering Israel from a plague of snakes (Nu 21:8–9), Jesus speaks of the deliverance of believers from death through the gift of eternal life that will become possible through his death. The 'eternal life' in question must not be thought of as if it were some kind of infinite extension of everyday existence. Rather, it refers to a new quality of life, begun here and now through faith, which is consummated and fulfilled through resurrection. This eternal life is only made possible through the love of God, which is shown in the astonishing fact that he loves his world so much that his only Son should die for it (3:16).

There are important echoes here of the trauma experienced by Abraham, when he was asked to give up his only son Isaac (Ge 22:1–14). What Abraham was not, in the end, required to do, God willingly did in order that sinful humanity might have the hope of eternal life. The death of the Son of God is thus the price of eternal life. Yet, despite the wonderful gift that God offers, the world will not want anything to do with it (3:19–21). It prefers darkness to light, and the gloomy prospect of death to the glorious hope of eternal life.

3:22–36 John the Baptist's Testimony About Jesus

The story now shifts to the countryside of Judea, in which John is continuing his ministry (3:22–36). Hearing the reports of the growing fame and influence of Jesus, John stresses that this rests on the authority of Jesus to speak for God – an authority that John

clearly does not regard himself as possessing. Jesus speaks the words of God, and has supreme authority. For this reason – and perhaps we can sense a tinge of sadness here – Jesus must become still greater, while John himself will fade into the background.

4:1–26 Jesus Talks with a Samaritan Woman As Jesus and his disciples move from Judea to Galilee, they are obliged to pass through Samaria, traditionally hostile to Jews (4:1–4). Jesus, tired by the journey, decides to rest by the traditional site of Jacob's well (which is not specifically identified in Scripture), while his disciples go to get some food from the nearby town of Sychar. While he rests, a Samaritan woman comes to draw water at the well. A dialogue results (4:9–26).

The Samaritan woman is initially astonished that Jesus should want to speak to her. She was both a Samaritan (with whom Jews traditionally had no dealings) and a woman (and hence avoided in public by Jewish men, in order to avoid any form of sexual temptation or impropriety). The conversation initially focuses on the theme of thirst. Jesus offers to provide 'living water' (as opposed to the stagnant water of the well) which would satisfy her in such a way that she would never thirst again (4:13). The woman is puzzled by this. Nevertheless, she is deeply impressed by Jesus' knowledge of the secrets of her private life (4:16–18). There is clearly something special about him. But what?

The woman draws the conclusion that Jesus is a prophet (4:19). But she soon discovers that even this is inadequate to do justice to the significance of Jesus. She speaks of her faith in the future coming of the Messiah, and the insight that he would bring. Jesus then declares that he himself is none other than this Messiah (4:26). The woman thus began by finding a thirsty man, then a prophet, and finally, the long-awaited Messiah.

4:27–42 The Disciples Rejoin Jesus On their return, the disciples are shocked to find Jesus speaking with a Samaritan woman. However, the effects of his dialogue are obvious. The Samaritans in her village have heard her report, and are converging on Jesus in order to find out more about him. Initially, their interest is aroused by her reports about him. Yet, when they meet him for themselves, their faith becomes grounded in Jesus himself, rather than the woman's testimony concerning him. They recognise that he is the Saviour of the world.

4:43–5:15 Jesus Heals the Official's Son; the Healing at the Pool This faith in Jesus as the Saviour of the world is then amply justified in a healing miracle in the Galilee region involving an official's son, which leads to faith on the part of all who are witnesses to the event (4:43–54). This healing incident is then identified as the 'second sign Jesus performed', the first having been the changing of the water into wine at Cana in Galilee. It is followed some time later by a healing miracle in Jerusalem (5:1–15). This incident is important for a number of reasons. It demonstrates the authority of Jesus both to heal the infirm, and also to heal on the Sabbath – an important echo of the theme that the 'Son of Man is Lord even of the Sabbath' (Mk 2:23–28).

But it is also important to notice the question (5:6) that Jesus puts to the

invalid: Do you want to be healed? Healing follows only once the invalid has admitted his need to be healed, recognised Jesus' ability to heal and accepted the healing that Jesus offers. In the same way, the forgiveness that Jesus makes possible can be received only by those who acknowledge their need of forgiveness, acknowledge the ability of Jesus to forgive their sins, and finally accept and receive that forgiveness.

5:16–47 Life Through the Son This act of healing causes controversy. But Jesus continues to assert his authority. His authority rests on his relationship with his Father. There is the closest of relationships between Father and Son, with the result that the Son has full authority to act for the Father, especially in relation to judgment. The Father has also declared that his life – a reference to eternal life – will be made available to the world through the Son. This important statement will, of course, be fully justified through the resurrection. However, Jesus makes these declarations at this early stage in order to make it clear that he has authority to speak for God throughout his ministry.

Jesus is particularly critical of those who fail to respond to the witness borne to him by others, such as John the Baptist. John was like a lamp preparing the way for the greater light that was to come. Yet there is another testimony that Jesus believes people should have understood and acknowledged – the testimony of Scripture. Jesus is here referring to the Old Testament. Earlier, we saw how Nathanael recognised Jesus as 'the one Moses wrote about in the Law, and about whom the prophets also wrote' (1:45).

But why have others not done the same? Jesus points out that there are many who think that eternal life is gained by studying Scripture as an end in itself. In fact, eternal life is gained through an encounter with the One to whom Scripture points – Jesus Christ himself. If these people bothered to study Moses' writings properly, they would realise that he had written about Jesus.

6:1–24 Jesus Feeds the Five Thousand and Walks on Water Our attention then turns again to the miracles of Jesus. John provides an account of the feeding of the five thousand, illustrating once more the authority of Jesus over the natural order (6:1–15). The response to this miracle is significant: people begin to draw the conclusion that he 'is the Prophet who is to come into the world' (6:14). The reference here is to the Prophet, promised by Moses, whom God would raise up in the future (Dt 18:15–19). Jesus' authority over the natural order is then demonstrated once more, through his walking on the water (6:16–24). However, the real importance of these passages lies in their leading into the great discourse on the 'bread of life', which develops themes already raised by the miracle of the feeding of the five thousand.

6:25–59 Jesus the Bread of Life The theme that Jesus explores focuses on the theme of bread. Why do people spend so much effort pursuing bread, when this will simply perish? Why not work for something that will endure for ever? Instead of eating bread that will satisfy physically, and then only for a while, why not eat bread that will lead to eternal

life? The crowds around initially think that Jesus is referring to manna, the food that was providentially provided for Israel as she wandered through the wilderness. But Jesus is referring to himself, as what follows makes clear.

Jesus declares that he is the 'bread of life' (6:35). This saying is of particular importance, as it is the first of the 'I am' sayings. The form of these sayings is grammatically unusual, making them stand out from the remainder of the text. This point is difficult to appreciate for readers not familiar with Greek. However, the importance of the point is that there is a direct similarity between these sayings and Ex 3:14, in which God reveals himself to Moses as 'I AM WHO I AM'. There is thus an implicit declaration of divinity on the part of Jesus within each of these sayings. The seven 'I am' sayings in this Gospel are as follows:

6:35, 48	The Bread of Life
8:12; 9:5	The Light of the World
10:7, 9	The Gate for the Sheep
10:11, 14	The Good Shepherd
11:25	The Resurrection and the Life
14:6	The Way, the Truth and the Life
15:1, 5	The True Vine

Jesus, then, is the 'bread of life', who has come down to heaven, and will give life to the world (6:33). Everyone who feeds on him will be raised up on the last day, and have eternal life. The bread that Jesus will offer the world is his own flesh. He is the 'bread of life' (6:48). Those

who ate manna in the wilderness died. But those who feed on Christ will have eternal life. Again and again we find Jesus reiterating that he has come down from heaven, in order to bring life to the world. So how does someone benefit from this bread? What do the references to 'eating' this bread mean? Jesus makes it clear that he is speaking about faith. Anyone 'who believes has eternal life' (6:47). The image of eating points to the closest of relationships between Jesus and the believer, in which Christ becomes part of the believer's life.

6:60–71 Many Disciples Desert Jesus These sayings cause division, however. Many of those who were attracted to Jesus cease to follow him. Yet this is something to be expected. Jesus points out that only those who are enabled to by the Father will come to him. It is not a purely human choice. Yet the Twelve remain with him. As Peter points out, Jesus alone has the words of life. There is nobody else to compare with him. The theme of sin then enters briefly, as Jesus declares that one of the Twelve will betray him.

7:1–24 Jesus Goes to the Feast of Tabernacles A major section now opens (7:1–8:59), which focuses on the growing opposition to Jesus, and his response to this. The initial occasion for this is the Feast of Tabernacles, the major Jewish festival that celebrated God's providential provision for his people during the period of wandering in the wilderness, as Israel moved from Egypt to the promised land (7:1–13; see Lev 23:33–43). Jesus' disciples go from Galilee to Jerusalem to observe the festival. Jesus follows later in

secret, knowing that he will be the subject of critical scrutiny. Halfway through the festival, Jesus appears in the Jerusalem temple precincts, and begins to teach (7:14–24). The initial reaction is amazement: how can this man know so much, when he has never undertaken any formal study? A similar reaction can be seen in Luke's account of the 12-year-old Jesus' remarkable knowledge of the Law: Lk 2:46–47). Yet Jesus declares that his wisdom does not have its origins in himself. It derives directly from God, who has sent him in the first place.

7:25–52 Is Jesus the Christ? This point is then stated with greater intensity, and provokes considerable controversy. Jesus' claims to have been sent by God and to speak with his authority provoke some to be tempted to physical violence against him, and others to put their faith in him. Some believe that he is the coming Prophet, others that he really is the Messiah. Others counter this suggestion. The Messiah will be a descendant of David, and come from Bethlehem; Jesus, however, comes from the region of Galilee. Although Jesus indeed spent most of his life in Nazareth (which was

Why didn't the Jews accept Jesus as their Messiah?

The Jewish messianic hope had reached fever pitch by Jesus' day. 'Messiah' means 'anointed one' and was rooted in the practice of anointing priests, prophets and kings to commission them for their work, though it increasingly came to be seen as a title for Israel's king (e.g., Ps 2:2). After the exile, hope grew for a renewed Davidic monarchy (e.g., Zec 12:2–13:1), and by the late 4th or early 3rd centuries BC 'Messiah' meant the one God would use to restore Israel's independence, glory and righteousness – though this figure was always human, never divine. Many speculations arose; but key to them all was the belief that the Messiah would overthrow the Gentile invaders, free Israel, cleanse the land and prepare the way for God's kingdom.

This is why Jesus was so reluctant to use this title, sometimes even commanding secrecy to those who had been healed, for there was too great a danger of popular misunderstanding, and many such would-be messiahs had arisen (e.g., Ac 5:36–37). But Jesus' messiahship would be of a completely different kind – exercised not through a sword, but through a cross.

The religious leaders had even more problems with Jesus. After all, he didn't keep their religious rules, and his theology was often suspect. How could such a man bring God's kingdom? And when he was crucified, that settled the matter; after all, such a man was under God's curse (Dt 21:23) and so couldn't possibly be Messiah. And so leaders and people alike rejected him.

Christians still refer to Jesus as Messiah, though in a form they don't normally recognise. The Greek translation of the Hebrew *masiah* is *Christos* – our word Christ. When we speak of Jesus 'Christ', we are remembering that he is the One whom God anointed to save people and establish his kingdom.

in the region of Galilee), it is clear that these onlookers were unaware of the circumstances of his birth, or his historical pedigree (see Mt 1:1–2:1). This ignorance is also reflected in the comments of the Pharisees, who dismiss Jesus as a nonentity. No prophets will come out of Galilee (7:45–52).

The passage is also of importance on account of Jesus' references to the future coming of the Spirit (7:37–39). The Spirit will come only when Jesus has been glorified – a clear reference to the resurrection. And when the Spirit does come, he will be like 'rivers of living water' within believers, bringing them new life and refreshment.

7:53–8:11 A Woman Caught in Adultery

A section now follows which is not present in the earliest manuscripts of John's Gospel. Those manuscripts that do include it occasionally place it at other points – such as towards the end of John 21, or even towards the end of Luke 21. The incident in question does, however, fit in entirely with what we know of the ministry of Jesus. The incident deals with a woman who is about to be put to death by stoning for adultery. Should this sentence be carried out? The question bears a close resemblance to the question about whether it was proper to pay taxes to Caesar. If Jesus declared it was not proper to do so, he would have been in open conflict with the law. As it happens, Jesus upholds the law, while imposing a condition on its execution that makes this impossible. Whoever is 'without sin' (not the specific sin of adultery, but any sin in general) may carry out the sentence. And the woman's accusers slink away, beginning with the oldest

(who presumably have accumulated the greatest burden of sin). The passage provides a superb illustration of the manner in which sin has permeated human nature.

8:12–59 The Validity of Jesus' Testimony

Further controversy now ensues (8:12–59). Jesus declares that he is the 'light of the world' (8:12) – the second of the great 'I am' sayings. The point being made is that, in a world of darkness and sin, Jesus is the light by which people are saved from their lostness. Father and Son together testify that this is the truth. Human beings, even if they are the descendants of Abraham, are slaves to sin, and are unable to break free from its bondage. Only Jesus himself is free from sin (8:46), and able to make known the truth that will set people free. Abraham and the prophets were great people – but they died like everyone else. But there will be something different about Jesus – a clear reference to the resurrection. His audience is shocked by the boldness of this claim.

This claim is further developed with dramatic assertion on the part of Jesus: 'before Abraham was born, I am!' (8:58). Like the 'I am' saying that opened this section (8:12), the Greek structure of this statement picks up the name of God revealed to Moses (Ex 3:14), and hints strongly at the eternity of Jesus Christ. The Christian reader of John's Gospel already knows this. The Prologue (1:1–18) contains a strong statement of the pre-existence of Christ, and of his involvement in the work of creation itself. Before Abraham or the world came into being, Jesus Christ was already existent and active. To the Christian, this

is a glorious affirmation of the divinity of Christ. To many Jewish onlookers at the time, it was nothing less than blasphemy. And so they tried to stone Jesus, just as they had earlier sought to stone the woman taken in adultery.

9:1–41 Jesus Heals a Man Born Blind Jesus then continues to demonstrate his authority to heal and teach. In a fitting confirmation of his claim to be the 'light of the world' (8:12; 9:5), Jesus heals a man who is born blind. This great healing becomes the focus for Jesus' declaration that the world is spiritually blind, and needs to be healed if it is to see and benefit from the light of the world. Controversy results, over both the healing itself and its implications. The Pharisees, who try to play down its importance, find themselves humiliated by the insistence on the part of the healed blind man, who wants to tell everyone about his healing and the one who healed him. Totally frustrated, they 'threw him out' (9:34) – a probable reference to some kind of excommunication. Yet the formerly blind man comes to faith in Jesus Christ, and worships him (9:38) – an acknowledgment of the divinity of Christ, in that Jews were permitted to worship only God, and none other (Ex 20:4–5). He had been rejected by his own people, yet he found acceptance with Jesus.

10:1–21 The Shepherd and His Flock The narrative now shifts from a discussion of Jesus as the 'light of the world' to Jesus as 'the good shepherd'. This section includes two of the seven 'I am' sayings. The section opens by establishing the imagery of the people of God as sheep – an image that would be familiar through its extensive use in the Old Testament (e.g., see Ps 74:1; 78:52; 79:13; 100:3; 119:176). In much the same way, God himself was often portrayed as the shepherd of his people (e.g., see Ge 49:24; Ps 23:1; 80:1; Jer 31:10). Basing himself on this well-known imagery, Jesus declares, in the third of the 'I am' sayings, that he is the 'gate for the sheep' (10:7, 9). This powerful image makes the following point: there is only one way in which sheep can find safety, and that is through him. Only through Jesus Christ can anyone come in from the dangers of a fallen world, and find safety and rest inside. Anyone who enters through Jesus will find salvation, pasture and life (10:9–10).

The discussion then turns to the image of a shepherd. In the past, Israel had suffered from irresponsible, uncaring and self-seeking leaders, referred to as 'false shepherds'. In his great prophetic vision of the future of Israel, Ezekiel looked forward to the day when the Lord himself would shepherd his people (Eze 34:1–17). In referring to himself as the 'good shepherd' (10:11), Jesus declares that this moment has arrived. His care for his sheep is such that he will – and, as events will prove, *does* – lay down his life for his sheep. He does this willingly and voluntarily, in obedience to his Father, who will then restore him to life.

10:22–42 The Unbelief of the Jews These sayings, and many others, anger some of his Jewish audience. They accuse him of blasphemy. 'You, a mere man, claim to be God' (10:33). Jesus rejects this argument. There is no blasphemy in his declaring himself to be the 'Son of God' if his

words and deeds demonstrate that this is indeed the case. If his critics will not listen to what he says, will they not at least ask what his great miracles point to? Yet despite the official hostility, many continue to put their faith in him.

11:1–44 The Death of Lazarus The authority of Jesus is then confirmed dramatically in the raising of Lazarus. Lazarus is the brother of Mary and Martha, two sisters from the village of Bethany, both of whom are mentioned elsewhere in the New Testament (Lk 10:38–42). It is clear that the family is known to Jesus. On hearing that Lazarus is ill, Jesus eventually travels to be with them. When they finally arrive at the village, Lazarus has been dead for four days. This period is important, as it emphasises that Lazarus is totally past any hope of resuscitation.

On his arrival, Jesus is greeted by Martha. He assures her that her brother will rise again. Martha's reply makes reference to the general Jewish belief (not shared, however, by the Sadducees) that the dead will rise at the end of time (11:23–24). Jesus then dramatically declares, in the fifth of the 'I am' sayings, that he is 'the resurrection and the life' (11:25). This terse statement declares more than the central Christian belief that resurrection and eternal life are made possible through Jesus Christ. It declares that Jesus himself *is* the life that is made possible through his resurrection. Eternal life is about being with Christ. Resurrection is about being raised with Christ, to be with Christ. Jesus Christ is not simply the basis of the gospel. He is also its content.

What Jesus said here is enormously significant, and needs to be looked at carefully. First, he declares that anyone 'who believes in me will live', even if they die (11:25). This part of the statement makes it clear that anyone who puts their faith in Jesus Christ has the hope of resurrection and eternal life, and need no longer fear death. The second part of the statement amplifies this somewhat: anyone who 'lives by believing in me will never die' (11:26). This makes a slightly different point: that to have faith in Jesus is to begin something *now*, so that, at least in one sense, such a person will never die. Death implies separation. Jesus' point is that a relationship may be begun with him now through faith, and that death cannot in any way separate the believer from Christ.

Martha's response to this is immediate. She puts her trust both in the messenger and the message, and acknowledges that he is indeed the Messiah, the Son of God who has come into the world (11:27). That trust is immediately justified. Jesus shows that he has authority even over death, as he brings Lazarus back from the dead, to the amazement of all. Even the dead hear his voice, and respond to it. And so do the living: deeply impressed by what they see, many of Mary's friends put their faith in him (11:45).

11:45–57 The Plot to Kill Jesus However, when the Sanhedrin, the supreme Jewish court, consisting of the chief priests, elders and teachers of the Law, hears of these developments, they do not respond with faith. Instead, they make plans to destroy Jesus (11:46–57). Caiaphas, the high priest at the time, is clearly worried about the threat of Roman intervention if things get out of hand, and many respond to Jesus. He argues that the

death of Jesus for his people would be preferable to the entire nation being wiped out. His words are a simple statement of political realism. But they have a deeper meaning than he intends or imagines. For Jesus does indeed die for his people – not in order to avert the threat of Roman intervention, which came about with a massive vengeance in AD 70, but in order to make it possible for their sins to be forgiven.

12:1–11 Jesus Anointed at Bethany The closeness of Jesus' death is then brought home by his being anointed with expensive oil by Mary. As the Passover draws near, Jesus prepares to die for his people.

JOHN 12:12–17:26
The Farewell Discourses of Jesus Christ

12:12–19 The Triumphal Entry The triumphal entry into Jerusalem takes place against this background of threats against Jesus on the part of the Jewish religious authorities. Yet despite all their threats and criticisms, more and more are coming to faith in him. As we read the account of this entry, we again come across a theme we noted earlier – that the disciples do not fully understand what is happening at the time, and only come to a full appreciation of its importance in the light of the resurrection (12:12–19).

12:20–36 Jesus Predicts His Death Jesus then predicts his own death, and declares that this is the ultimate reason for his coming into the world. When he is lifted up from the earth on the cross, he will draw everyone to himself (12:32). This

verse represents a dramatic clarification of Isaiah's great prophecy of the coming of a suffering servant (Isa 52:13–53:12). This had spoken of this servant being 'raised and lifted up and highly exalted' (Isa 52:13). This could have been misunderstood to mean 'made important, and given an important status in the world'. Now we realise that it means something rather different. The suffering servant will be raised up on a cross, for all to see. The hope of resurrection for that servant is indeed there – but first, he must be raised up on the cross, and die in the full gaze of a scornful public.

12:37–50 The Jews Continue in Their Unbelief So why do so few believe in him? Why this atmosphere of pervasive unbelief? Has not Jesus shown his authority in all that he has said and done? John now draws our attention to the fact that this rejection and unbelief were foretold in the great prophetic writings of the Old Testament. Noting the prophecies of Isaiah in particular, John declares that Isaiah saw the glory of Jesus himself, and was speaking about Christ in the prophecies in question.

13:1–17 Jesus Washes His Disciples' Feet The section now moves on to the great 'farewell discourses' – the words spoken by Jesus to his closest disciples as he prepares to be taken from them and put to death. Once Judas has left the assembled company, Jesus can speak openly to those who remain about what lies ahead. But first, John sets the scene for these discourses (13:1–30). It is 'just before the Passover', when Israel recalled God's great act of deliverance in the past, by which he set his people free from their

bondage in Egypt. A Passover lamb was sacrificed in memory of this great event. With great skill, John draws his readers' attention to a central insight of the gospel. A new act of divine deliverance is about to take place, with Jesus as the true Passover lamb who gives his life as a sacrifice for the sins of his people. John stresses that Jesus knows he has to die (13:1, 3). His death is no accident, no premature end to a promising career as a religious teacher. Here is the Saviour of the world, preparing to die for those whom he loves.

The passage stresses the humility of Jesus. He is prepared to wash his disciples' feet (13:4–5). At a Christian seminary in India, there is a statue of Jesus washing Peter's feet. Hindu visitors to the seminary often pause to admire it. They assume it depicts a disciple falling down in worship at Jesus' feet. They are astonished to learn that it is Jesus who is kneeling. 'How he must love his disciples,' some of them remark.

Having washed his disciples' feet, Jesus explains the importance of this action (13:12–17). We see here a superb illustration of the idea of 'a servant king' – someone who has authority, but exercises it by serving, rather than dominating others.

13:18–30 Jesus Predicts His Betrayal One of the great themes of the New Testament is that Jesus brings to fulfilment the great prophecies of the Old Testament. Many of these prophecies are positive in tone, speaking of the coming of the Messiah to his people, and the marvellous things he will achieve. But some are more melancholy, speaking of the betrayal of the Messiah by one who is close to him. Once more, John makes it clear that the

betrayal of Jesus is no accident. Sadly, it is something that has to happen. Jesus explains this to his disciples, so that they will not be dismayed when it does (13:19). Not only is he to be betrayed. Perhaps most shockingly of all, he is to be betrayed by one of those with whom he is sharing that last supper. Here John notes Jesus' own distress (13:21), as he faces up to the grim events that lie ahead. We must never think that death was an easy thing for Jesus to face.

But which of the disciples is it to be? Who will betray him? One of themes we find earlier in John's Gospel is that Jesus knows the inmost secrets of people's hearts. We find, for example, both Nathanael and the Samaritan woman amazed that he knows their innermost thoughts so intimately. It comes as no surprise to find that he knows who is to betray him (13:22–27): it will be Judas.

In a poignant passage, Jesus tells Judas to go and do what has to be done (13:27). As Judas leaves the room and the presence of Christ, John makes the comment 'And it was night' (13:30). Judas has left the presence of the Light of the World, and has gone into the darkness of a fallen and sinful world. Through Judas, the Light of the World will be extinguished. Through the power of God, however, it will rekindled.

13:31–38 Jesus Predicts His Death and Peter's Denial With the departure of Judas, Jesus can speak frankly and openly to the faithful disciples. The 'farewell discourses' that now follow represent moments of great intimacy between Jesus and his disciples, as he explains what is going to happen, and prepares them for the future. First, Jesus repeats

what he said earlier: he is soon to be taken from them (13:33). Yet this will lead both to his own glorification and the glorification of God through him. Yet the main emphasis of this passage falls on the need for disciples to love one another (13:34–35). Jesus loves them so much that he will die for them; that same quality of love is to be evident in the lives of Christian believers. Love of this quality cannot be ignored by the world (13:35).

Peter then asks Jesus to explain where he is going, and asks to be allowed to come with him (13:36–38). Jesus explains that Peter will have this wish in due course. But not yet. When Peter protests, Jesus predicts that he will be denied by Peter three times 'before the cock crows'. The reference to the 'cock crowing' needs a little comment. The Romans divided the night into four 'watches' – 'evening' 6:00–9:00 p.m., 'midnight' 9:00–12:00 midnight, 'when the cock crows' 12:00 midnight–3:00 a.m., and 'dawn' 3:00–6:00 a.m. (see Mk 13:35). The 'cock crowing' may in fact be a reference to the trumpet blast that marked the end of the third watch of the night, rather than to the cry of a cockerel.

14:1–4 Jesus Comforts His Disciples It is clear that the disciples are distressed at the thought of Jesus leaving them. Knowing this, Jesus comforts them. The disciples must learn to trust him. He knows what he is doing, and where he is going. And in the midst of this reassurance, we find a promise: that where Christ goes, his disciples will follow. They will not be separated from him, but will know the joy of being reunited with him. They – and all believers – will be privileged guests in his Father's house.

14:5–14 Jesus, the Way to the Father But how can they find their way there? Thomas raises the kind of awkward common-sense question that may have gone through the minds of others (14:5). Jesus replies with a powerful and helpful statement: 'I am the way and the truth and the life' (14:6). Jesus does not show the way, and then leave his disciples to make their own way unaided. He takes them there, accompanying them as they travel. He is far more than a good religious teacher, who tells his followers what to do and who to believe. He is the good shepherd, who loves, tends, feeds and guides his sheep.

But how can we know what God is like? Once more, Jesus provides a powerful answer (14:7–13). God is Christlike. To have seen Jesus is to have seen the Father (14:9). To give an example, the love of Jesus for his disciples is shown by his being prepared to give his life for them. There is no love greater than this. And that is what the love of God is like. Jesus is like a snapshot of God, the 'image of the invisible God', as Paul puts it (Col 1:15). Yet the love of Christ for believers must also be shown in the love that believers show towards each other.

14:15–31 Jesus Promises the Holy Spirit However, the main theme of this section of the passage is the giving of the Holy Spirit. Christians will not be on their own, in the midst of a disbelieving and hostile world. They will be given 'another advocate' (14:16), who will be sent by the Father. This is an enormously encouraging thought. The word

Who is the Holy Spirit?

As Jesus prepared his disciples for his imminent departure, he spoke increasingly about the Holy Spirit – the one who would take his place, describing him as '*another advocate*' (Jn 14:16). There were two Greek words for 'another': one meaning 'another of a different kind'; the other, 'another of the same kind'; it is the latter that is used here. Jesus was saying that the Spirit would be to them everything that he himself had been – an 'advocate' (often translated 'counsellor' or 'comforter', but literally 'someone called alongside to help').

But who is the Holy Spirit? We first meet him at the beginning of the Bible's story, involved with God in creation (Ge 1:2). We continue to see him throughout the Old Testament, inspiring prophets and performing God's mighty acts. But, perhaps because of the imagery used of him (like wind, fire, water), people tended to think of the Spirit as simply God's power in the world. What Jesus made clear, however, is that the Spirit is not a *power* but a *person* – a truth so important that the New Testament breaks the rules of grammar to make the point; for while the Greek word for Spirit (*pneuma*) is *neuter*, it uses a *masculine* pronoun when writing of him. The Spirit is a person, the third person of the Trinity.

This is what makes Jesus' promise that the Spirit would come to live within his followers (e.g., Jn 14:17) so amazing. He meant that no one less than *God himself* would live within them – something that happened for the first time at Pentecost.

It is the gift of the Spirit that makes Christianity so different. While other religions call people to become more holy to know God better, Jesus says God sends his Spirit first to make us more holy.

'advocate' has a number of meanings, including 'counsellor' and 'comforter'. The root meaning suggests someone who encourages, reassures and stimulates believers to do things they otherwise could never do. Without such divine assistance, Christians would be unable to live and work effectively for God in the world. When God issues a command, he also provides gifts that equip his people for the tasks that lie ahead. Christians are not like 'orphans' (14:18). They can rest assured of the continuing presence and care of God as they live out their calling in the world. The Holy Spirit is God's gift to his people, to enable believers to obey Christ's commands (14:21).

But perhaps Jesus is just saying these things to encourage his disciples. Perhaps they are without any basis in reality. Possibly aware of such thoughts, Jesus moves to reassure them. These are not his own words. They are the words of his Father (14:24), who sent him. As the resurrection confirms, Jesus speaks as one who has the right to make promises on God's behalf – promises that can be trusted.

Developing the idea of the Holy Spirit as the 'Advocate', Jesus assures his disciples that the Spirit will bring to mind all that he has taught them (14:26). He then speaks some enormously consoling words to his disciples. 'My

peace I give you' (14:27). This is not peace as the world understands it. Secular ideas of peace may include an absence of conflict, but cannot bring any comfort or peace of mind in the face of death. The peace that Jesus offers brings hope in the face of death, and a reassurance that his love will never let his people go. For this reason, the disciples need not be 'troubled' or 'afraid'. Once more, as the resurrection makes clear, this is no wishful thinking, but an assurance based on the power of a loving God. Finally, Jesus assures his disciples of one remaining issue. Even though 'the prince of this world is coming' (14:30), he has no hold over Jesus. The reference is to Satan and his allies, such as sin and death. Jesus will die. But that is not to be the end of the story. The best wine is yet to come.

15:1–17 The Vine and the Branches

In this passage, Jesus declares that he is the 'true vine' (15:1, 5). The image of a vine has deep Old Testament roots. Jesus uses it to emphasise the importance of 'remaining in him', or, as older English translations rendered, 'abiding in him'. Believers are attached to Jesus, as branches are attached to a vine. And just as a branch can bear fruit only if it remains attached to the vine, so believers can bear fruit only if they remain in Christ. If they fail to do so, they will wither and die (15:6). There seems to be no intended reference to eternal punishment in the image of a dead branch being 'thrown into the fire and burned'. The point being made is simply that there is nothing much that can be done with a dead branch, except use it for firewood. But believers are not meant to

be like this. By remaining close to Christ, they will bear much fruit, as God intends them to. But apart from – that is, removed from – Christ, they can do nothing (15:5).

The image of a vine is also important because of the idea of pruning (15:2). This is one of the most important New Testament ways of dealing with suffering. Just as a father disciplines only those whom he loves, so the Father prunes only those branches he expects to bear fruit. Christians must learn to see suffering, difficulty or adversity as a form of God's pruning, by which he will make them better Christians, and more effective witnesses to him in the world. Useless branches are discarded. Only those that are worth the trouble are pruned.

We now return to the theme of the love of Christ for his disciples, and the love that these disciples must have for each other. If this theme seems familiar, it is on account of its importance. There is a natural connection between the love of the Father for the Son, the love of the Son for believers, and the love of believers for each other (15:9–10, 17). In much the same way, there is a close connection between obedience, love and joy (15:10–12). Obedience to the love of Christ is the only route to lasting joy.

Jesus then speaks words that we need to rediscover and savour the full meaning of: 'Greater love has no one than this: to lay down one's life for one's friends' (15:13). There is nothing more that anyone can give than life itself. And that is what Jesus will give for those whom he loves. He can give no more, and he willingly gives his life in order that others might live. It is a deeply moving thought, which reminds believers of how

precious they are in the sight of Christ. But there is more to this great affirmation. Those for whom Jesus dies are not so much his 'servants', as his 'friends' (15:14–16). In washing his disciples' feet, Jesus makes it clear that he is not prepared to lord it over them. They are not his menial servants, but his friends – those whom he has chosen, and those whom he loves.

Believers are not those who have chosen Jesus, but those whom Jesus has chosen (15:16). This may seem strange, at first. Believers may feel, 'Surely we *did* choose to follow him? Surely it *was* our decision?' But Jesus here points to the deeper insight that God draws people to him, preparing the way as they come home to him. As they look back over how they came to faith, Christians can sometimes see the hand of God at work, moving them in certain ways, which eventually led them to discover him. Christians are believers because they are *meant* to be believers.

15:18–16:4 The World Hates the Disciples

Jesus now turns to deal with the hostility of the world towards believers. Although the world was created by God, it has now rebelled against him, refusing to recognise his authority over it. The world thus hates Jesus, who asserts God's claims over his creation and declares it to be sinful. 'If I had not come and spoken to them, they would not be guilty of sin; but now, they have no excuse for their sin' (15:22). And its hate for Jesus extends to the disciples: 'if the world hates you, keep in mind that it hated me first' (15:18). The world's hostility towards Christ is thus transferred to his servants. To be a Christian is potentially to suffer on

account of Christ, who suffered first in order that believers be called by his name. To be a Christian is to be called out of the world (15:19), and bear the force of its fury at having lost its control of us.

16:5–33 The Work of the Holy Spirit; Grief into Joy

We now learn of the mixed feelings of joy and sadness experienced by the disciples on account of their knowledge of the imminent suffering and death of Christ. On the one hand, they are horrified that the man whom they love and adore is to be taken from them to die in such a horrific manner. On the other, they know that his death will bring about the salvation of the world. The 'Lamb of God, who takes away the sin of the world' (1:29) must be slain before he can take that sin away. In this passage, Jesus confronts those mixed feelings, and reassures his disciples, 'You are filled with grief but very truly I tell you, it is for your good that I am going away' (16:6–7).

Jesus now returns to the great theme of the coming of the Holy Spirit – the 'Advocate' or 'Comforter', whose presence and power will guide and empower the disciples, as they face the future for Christ. The task of persuading the world of its sin is not something that Christians must accomplish unaided. They will be assisted by the Spirit (16:8–9). The coming of the Spirit at Pentecost may be seen as fulfilling this prophecy.

Finally, Jesus speaks of his resurrection (16:16). It is immediately clear that Jesus' words cause his disciples some confusion. They just cannot take in all that he is saying. It doesn't seem to make sense. They are bewildered. Yet Jesus knows what they are thinking (16:19). He uses

an analogy to bring out how grief can be changed to joy. The analogy is that of a woman giving birth to a child (16:20–22). The physical pain of giving birth gives way to the joy of knowing that a new life has come into the world. In the same way, the physical pain of Christ's death will give way to the joy of knowing that the hope of eternal life has dawned in a sad and dark world.

Finally, Jesus assures his disciples of his continuing love and care for them, and grants them the privilege of being able to approach the Father in his name (16:23–24). Whatever they ask in his name will be given to them. This does not mean that God will give believers anything they want, providing they simply add the word 'in Jesus' name' mechanically onto their prayers. Rather, it means that God will grant them all that they need to 'abide in Christ', and bear much fruit in his name. The Christian tasks of evangelism and care may be great – but so are the gifts God provides to minister in his name.

The subject now changes slightly, as Jesus deals with his own mission: 'I came from the Father and entered the world; now I am leaving the world and going back to the Father' (16:28). Christ humbled himself so that he could come into this world, and redeem sinful humanity. 'God so loved the world that he gave his one and only Son, that whoever believes in him shall not perish but have eternal life' (3:16). After his mission has been accomplished, he will be exalted by the Father.

But this is in the future. In the meantime, the disciples will be scattered after Jesus' death and will have trouble and sorrow in this world. But in the midst of all these difficulties, they may have the consolation of knowing that Jesus has overcome the world (16:33). Its apparent triumph is temporary. The death of Jesus seems to point to the world's victory over Christ. The resurrection shows that it is the world that has been defeated, and that Christ is the victor. Christians need that kind of perspective, as they contemplate the sadness and despair of the world. This knowledge brings an assurance of peace. The world may cause all kinds of anxieties to believers as they wonder what is going on, and whether God is *really* there. But Christ reassures his disciples, 'Take heart! I have overcome the world.'

17:1–26 Jesus Prays This section is followed by an extended prayer of Jesus (17:1–26), which is often referred to as the 'high priestly prayer' on account of the themes of offering and sacrifice that can be seen throughout it. The time has now come (17:1). Earlier in the Gospel, Jesus had often stated that the time had *not* yet come (e.g., 2:4; 7:6; 7:30; 8:20). But now that moment has arrived. God gave Jesus the authority to bring knowledge of him to the world, and in doing so to bring eternal life. That task has now been accomplished. It is time to go.

But what of those he leaves behind? What of the disciples? Jesus offers a prayer on their behalf. They have put their trust in him, and will remain behind in the world after he has been taken from it. Jesus prays that they might know God's protection and unity in all that lies ahead for them. They are no longer 'of the world'. Yet Jesus' prayer is not that they be taken *out* of the world, but that

they be protected and encouraged while they witness to and in that world.

Yet Jesus also looks ahead down the great road of history, to those who will put their faith in him on account of the disciples' witness. He prays for them as well, that they might know unity and the joy of being able to go where he is about to go, and be with him. Jesus prays that the love the Father had for the Son might be present among them in whatever lies ahead for them (17:25–26).

JOHN 18:1–21:25
The Passion, Death and Resurrection of Christ

18:1–11 Jesus Arrested The farewell discourses now come to an end. Words give way to actions, as Jesus prepares to meet his death. Jesus and his disciples cross the Kidron Valley to the east of Jerusalem, and enter an olive grove. It is there that they are confronted by Judas and a detachment of soldiers. The moment of betrayal has come. Brushing aside a pathetic attempt on the part of Peter to prevent the arrest, Jesus affirms that he is prepared to 'drink the cup' the Father has given him. He will go through with the suffering that is an integral part of the mission for which God has sent him into the world.

18:12–21 Jesus Taken to Annas; Peter's Denial Jesus is then forcibly taken before Annas and Caiaphas, followed by Peter and 'another disciple' – possibly John himself. Although Caiaphas was the high priest, there appears to have been lingering popular affection for Annas, who was deposed as high priest by the Romans in AD 15. Although he no longer

had any official position of seniority, he nevertheless continued to exercise considerable influence (18:12–14). While the process of interrogation proceeds, Peter finds himself denying anything to do with Jesus. The challenge does not come from anyone of any importance, merely a servant-girl. Yet Peter still denies having anything to do with Jesus. He will deny him two more times, before the cock crows (18:25–27; see 13:38).

18:19–40 The High Priest Questions Jesus; Jesus Before Pilate In the meantime, Jesus is being subjected to questioning by the high priest. Initially, Jesus makes the point that the high priest and his officials had ample opportunity to question him about his teaching while he taught openly in the temple area. Why all this secrecy? Why not challenge him openly? John's Gospel does not go into any detail about the precise charges brought against Jesus by his accusers. However, it is clear that they are sufficiently serious to warrant his being turned over to the Roman authorities (18:28–40). Pilate, Roman governor of Judea AD 26–36, is clearly puzzled by the charges brought against Jesus. The Jewish leaders want to avoid entering the Roman palace, so that they are not affected by the ritual uncleanliness that would result from this contact with Gentiles on the eve of the major religious festival of the Passover. Pilate is therefore obliged to leave the palace, and confront the crowd outside.

The issue Pilate has to determine is whether there is any basis for a death sentence against Jesus. He explores the issue of whether Jesus is a king, and receives the reply that Jesus' kingdom is

'not of this world' (18:36). Pilate takes this as meaning that Jesus admits to being a king, and will now refer to Jesus, perhaps scathingly, as the 'king of the Jews'. Being in a position to set a prisoner free at Passover, Pilate offers to release Jesus. The crowd, however, demands the release of Barabbas, who took part in an insurrection against Rome.

19:1–27 Jesus Sentenced to Be Crucified After ordering that Jesus be flogged, Pilate brings him before the crowds again. He informs them that there is no legal basis for the death sentence. He is not prepared to crucify him. Yet the clamour increases. The crowd insist that, since Jesus claims to be the Son of God, he deserves to die. They follow up their advantage by pointing out the negative impact that any report of someone claiming to be 'king of the Jews' would have on Caesar, the Roman emperor. At this, Pilate caves in. As the Jews declare that they have no king but Caesar, Pilate hands Jesus over to be crucified (19:1–16). Over the place of his execution, the charge against him is written for all to see: 'Jesus of Nazareth, King of the Jews'. In many paintings and representations of the crucifixion, this inscription is represented by four letters: INRI – the initial letters of the Latin phrase *Iesus Nazarenus Rex Iudaeorum*, meaning 'Jesus of Nazareth, King of the Jews'.

The soldiers in charge of the execution throw lots for his clothes. In doing so, they unconsciously fulfil the great prophecy of Ps 22:18, which speaks of the destiny of a righteous sufferer. In drawing attention to this psalm, John also intends his readers to note the many other parallels between the prophetic description of the sufferings of this righteous person, and the actual events of the crucifixion itself. And, watching from a safe distance is the disciple Jesus loved – widely regarded as a reference to the author of this Gospel, John, who is thus identified as an eyewitness of the events that take place.

19:28–42 The Death and Burial of Jesus Finally, Jesus dies (19:28–37). His last words are 'It is finished'. The Greek original of these words has the sense 'It is accomplished', or perhaps, in certain contexts, 'It has been settled or paid'. This is no cry of despair. This is a cry of achievement. What had to be done is done. For John, Jesus is the true Passover lamb, who dies on the cross at more or less the moment when the Passover lambs are being slain. Just as the Passover lamb has to be perfect and without any broken bones (Ex 12:46), so it is in the case of Jesus, the sinless Passover lamb who is slain for the sin of the world. It appears to have been normal practice to break the legs of the victims of crucifixion, to hasten their end by denying them any means of supporting themselves on the cross. Yet in Jesus' case, this is not necessary – again, leading to an unwitting fulfilment on the part of the Roman soldiers of a great Old Testament prophecy. Instead, Jesus is stabbed with a spear to make sure that he is dead, as a result of which 'a sudden flow of blood and water' emerges – apparently a description of clotted blood. There can be no doubt that Jesus is dead. Joseph of Arimathea, accompanied by Nicodemus, arranges for his burial in a nearby borrowed tomb (19:38–42). As the

following day is the Sabbath, there is nothing more that can be done. Further arrangements will have to wait until the Sunday.

See 'Did the resurrection really happen?', page 338.

20:1–9 The Empty Tomb The Sunday arrives. Mary Magdalene is the first to visit the tomb 'while it was still dark'. Mark's account places this visit 'just after sunrise' (Mk 16:2), when darkness would gradually have been giving way to the first light of day. It is clear, however, that something dramatic has happened during the night. It is clear that Mary's initial reaction is that the authorities – whether Jewish or Roman – have removed Jesus' dead body. There is no hint of an expectation of resurrection – a point that John explains to his readers (20:9). All that they can see is that the dead body of Jesus is there no more. The gravecloths in which Jesus had been wrapped remain inside the tomb. Jesus, however, has gone (20:1–9).

20:10–23 Jesus Appears to Mary Magdalene and to His Disciples The disciples return home (20:10). There is no hint of joy at the thought of the resurrection of Jesus. The atmosphere is that of utter disconsolation. Not only is Jesus dead. They have not even been allowed to bury him properly, and pay their final respects to the man who mattered so much to them. Yet Mary remains behind, lingering at the site of the empty tomb. Unaware of what has really taken place, she is astonished to find a figure behind her, whom she takes to be 'the gardener' – that is, the person in charge of the garden

(19:41) within which the tomb was located (20:11–15).

The 'gardener' then speaks to her. And just as the sheep know the voice of the good shepherd (10:3–5), so Mary recognises who is speaking to her. Overjoyed, she rushes to tell the others of what – or, more accurately, whom – she has seen (20:16–18). Although they are initially obliged to rely on her testimony, they soon discover for themselves the reality of the resurrection, as Jesus stands among them in his risen glory that same evening (20:19–23). There is a fascinating parallel here with the story of the Samaritan woman. Just as the people of her village initially believed in Jesus on account of her report, but then discovered it to be true for themselves (4:42), so the disciples also trust Mary, before having all she said confirmed by Jesus himself.

20:24–29 Jesus Appears to the Disciples But not Thomas. He is absent from the meeting at which Jesus appears to his disciples, and is deeply sceptical of their reports about the resurrection. He wants proof. He wants to see the nail marks in Christ's hand, and to touch his wounds, both from the nails and the spear. On being confronted with the risen Christ, he kneels in adoration. His confession is of the utmost importance: 'my Lord and my God'. It is one of the clearest statements in the New Testament of the divinity of Jesus Christ. But it is also important to notice how Jesus looks ahead, to the doubts of those who will come to faith later. Thomas has it easy. He can have his doubts dispelled by an encounter with Christ. Those who come later – including all the readers of this

section – are more blessed than he, for they have believed without access to this sort of proof.

20:30–31 An Explanation

This section of the Gospel ends with an explanation (20:30–31). John has had to be selective in what he included in his Gospel. There is so much more that could have been included. But what we find in this Gospel has been written for a reason – to bring us to faith in this same Jesus Christ, so that we might, along with those we have read about, believe that he is the Messiah and the Son of God, and thus come to have the same eternal life which has been the subject of this Gospel.

21:1–23 Jesus and the Miraculous Catch of Fish; His Reinstatement of Peter

The Gospel as a whole now comes to a close with an epilogue, stressing once more the reality of the resurrection (21:1–14). All the doubts about the resurrection are dispelled. It is clear that Jesus has been risen, and that this news, along with all that it implies for the world, must be proclaimed. But attention focuses on two disciples: Peter, and the 'disciple whom Jesus loved' (almost certainly a reference to John himself). In a moving dialogue (21:15–23), Jesus both charges Peter with the responsibility of taking care of his sheep, and looks ahead to the day of Peter's own death (Peter is thought to have been martyred at Rome under the emperor Nero around AD 64). Despite his denial of Jesus, he is now reinstated. Jesus speaks the words of reinstatement and recommissioning: 'Follow me!' It does not matter what happens to others, as Jesus' comments about the other disciple (21:20–22) make clear. The important thing is to follow Jesus, irrespective of where that same following may lead others.

21:24–25 Conclusion

John then ends his Gospel. It is clear that there is so much more that he wants to tell his readers. There is simply not enough space for him to say all that he would like. But there is more than enough to give food for thought, and to convey the full significance of Jesus Christ, who is the 'light of the world' and the 'bread of life' to a hungry people who up to now have walked in darkness.

ACTS

'Acts' or 'The Acts of the Apostles' as it is often called, is the second instalment of Luke's account of the origins of the Christian church, and follows on from the Gospel that is attributed to him. Taken together, Luke's Gospel and history of the early church is the largest single document in the New Testament. In his Gospel, Luke told Theophilus (probably a well-placed Roman official who had become interested in Christianity) about the life, death and resurrection of Jesus. However, the story does not stop there. By the time that Luke was writing, Christianity was well on the way to becoming a major force in the Roman Empire. So how did Christianity progress from its humble origins in Palestine to the hub of the Roman Empire? How did it come to wield such influence in so short a time?

Luke sets out to show how the gospel spread like wildfire throughout the Roman Empire. He is careful to make a distinction between the divine power that lies behind the gospel (such as the resurrection of Christ, and the gift of the Holy Spirit), and the human agents who served to spread it (such as Peter and Paul). Acts opens with a vivid account of the ascension of the risen Christ and the coming of the Holy Spirit in power. Although the work is entitled 'Acts of the Apostles', it could probably equally well be described as the 'Acts of the Holy Spirit'. Having allowed us to appreciate the power of the gospel, Luke moves on to deal with the people who were committed to it. The first twelve chapters focus on Peter, and the dramatic series of events that led to the Christian gospel becoming firmly rooted in Jerusalem and the surrounding regions.

Having shown how the gospel became rooted in Palestine, Luke moves on to show how it gradually became established in much of the Roman Empire. The remainder of the work focuses on Paul. Luke explains Paul's background, and shows how he became first a Christian, and then the 'apostle to the Gentiles'. He gives a vivid account of the impact that Paul had on the expansion of the Christian church from Palestine into the regions of modern-day Turkey and Greece. It gives details of the three missionary journeys he undertook in the eastern Mediterranean, and ends with a description of his final voyage as a prisoner to Rome itself. Luke gives us access to some of Paul's sermons, allowing us to appreciate the way in which he presented the gospel in a variety of different situations.

OUTLINE

Peter and the church in Jerusalem

1:1–14 The ascension of Jesus Christ

1:15–26 The election of Matthias to replace Judas

2:1–47 The day of Pentecost

3:1–4:31 Peter and John heal in the name of Jesus Christ

4:32–5:11 The early Christian fellowship

5:12–42 The authorities fail to suppress the church

ACTS 1:1–12:25
The First Days of the Church

1:1–11 The Gift Provided Luke begins his second work by reminding his readers of the great events of Easter, and Christ's command not to leave Jerusalem, but to wait for the gift that God had promised (1:4). But what is this gift? And when would it come?

Immediately, Luke answers this question, by reminding his readers that John the Baptist merely baptised his followers with water, whereas Jesus would baptise 'with the Holy Spirit' (1:5). John's baptism symbolised regeneration. The baptism Jesus offers brings real renewal and rebirth. The disciples have been called to be Christ's 'witnesses in Jerusalem, and in all Judea and Samaria, and to the ends of the earth' (1:8). This is a great and daunting responsibility. Christians are not to stand around idly, wondering where Jesus has gone (1:10–11). Their task is to make that same Christ known to the world.

However, Luke makes it clear that this great challenge is matched by an equally great enabling gift. The disciples will 'receive power when the Holy Spirit comes' on them (1:8). Here we find one of the great themes of the New Testament: God gives gifts to enable his people to meet the challenges and tasks he gives them. The church still needs those gifts badly, as she confronts the new challenges and opportunities awaiting her.

1:12–14 Fellowship This opening passage closes with a vivid portrayal of the close-knit fellowship that is enjoyed by the early church (1:13–14). Though small in number, they are full of confidence and anticipation. Where once they had been a band of demoralised and dismayed men and women who had seen their leader executed, they are now an excited group

of evangelists, waiting to proclaim the good news of their risen Saviour to the world. And, as we shall see, they do not have long to wait.

At this stage, the Christian church is small in number. Luke mentions the figure of 120 believers (1:15). It is all too easy for the casual reader of Acts to lose sight of the importance of this point. We know from history that the church would grow enormously. But try to imagine that you don't know this. Try to imagine that you are reading this for the very first time, not knowing what is going to happen. In a period in which new religions were born every minute, what chance would so small a group of people have? Would their message survive at all? The fact that it did is, as Paul points out, a reminder that the gospel does not rest on human wisdom, but on the power of God.

1:15–26 Matthias Chosen to Replace Judas The passage goes on to describe the search for a replacement for Judas. But why was a replacement needed? One suggestion is that the twelve apostles were the New Testament equivalent of the Twelve Tribes of Israel. Further, just as Peter sees the betrayal of Jesus foreshadowed in Old Testament prophecy (1:20), so he also sees there the need for a replacement. Note how the authority of Scripture is linked with the action of the Holy Spirit (1:16).

What qualifications were thought of as being necessary for someone to share in the 'apostolic ministry' (1:25)? The basic requirement seems to have been that an apostle is one who was present with the remaining eleven apostles from the point at which Jesus was baptised by John to the moment of the ascension (1:21–22). Matthias is then chosen by the casting of lots (1:26). This is an exceptional course of action in exceptional circumstances, reminding believers that God must be involved in the selection of church leaders. It follows a well-established Old Testament precedent, in which matters of major spiritual importance were sometimes determined by allowing the Lord to decide things through throwing lots.

2:1–13 The Holy Spirit Comes at Pentecost We now come to one of the most important passages in the New Testament. Earlier, we saw how the disciples would 'receive power when the Holy Spirit comes' on them (1:8). In this momentous passage, the fulfilment of that promise is described. 'All of them were filled with the Holy Spirit' (2:4). There is no indication that the disciples were expecting anything like this to take place. They seem to have been taken by surprise, as they gathered together on the day of Pentecost (2:1). Luke struggles with words, as he attempts to describe what happened when the Spirit came. It was 'like the blowing of a violent wind' (2:2). What 'seemed to be tongues of fire' (2:3) rested on those present.

It is obvious that something dramatic and unexpected has taken place, for which no existing way of speaking is adequate. Luke has to forge new images and analogies, as he tries to convey the unprecedented events that unfold. Peoples from throughout the civilised world of the time hear and understand the gospel (2:5–12). They are 'amazed and perplexed' (2:12) by what they hear. It is clear that something astonishing is

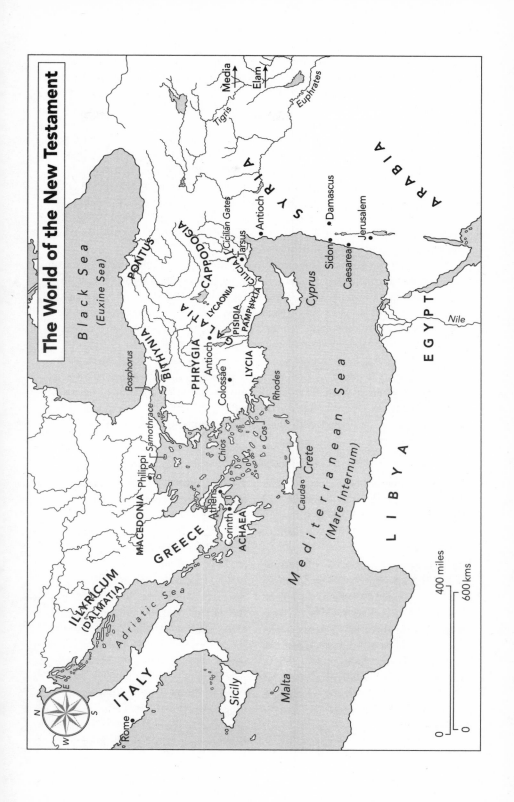

The World of the New Testament

N W E S

Black Sea
(Euxine Sea)

ILLYRICUM
(DALMATIA)

ITALY

Rome

Adriatic Sea

MACEDONIA
Philippi

GREECE

Sicily

Malta

Athens
Corinth
ACHAEA

Samothrace

Chios

Cos

Rhodes

Crete

Cauda

Mediterranean Sea
(Mare Internum)

LIBYA

EGYPT

Nile

BITHYNIA

PONTUS

GALATIA

CAPPODOCIA

PHRYGIA

LYCAONIA

PISIDIA

PAMPHYLIA

Antioch

Colossae

LYCIA

Cilician Gates

Tarsus

CILICIA

Antioch

SYRIA

Cyprus

Sidon

Damascus

Caesarea

Jerusalem

ARABIA

Tigris

Euphrates

Media

Elam

Bosphorus

400 miles

600 kms

0

0

What is meant by speaking in tongues?

Of the many tangible manifestations of the Spirit's coming at Pentecost that Luke struggles to describe, one was 'speaking in other tongues' (Ac 2:4). This clearly was not overexcited babbling or ecstatic praying, but the disciples speaking real 'languages' (the word 'tongues' simply means 'languages'), languages that pilgrims to Jerusalem from many other nations could readily understand (2:11). However, its primary purpose does not seem to have been evangelistic – the evangelism didn't start until Peter began preaching, and he did that in his own language. Rather, Luke says that they were 'declaring the wonders of God' (Ac 2:11) – in other words, they were praising not preaching. But it was praising of a new kind and quality that drew the gathered pilgrims to want to find out more.

This gift of tongues wasn't just a dramatic event for Pentecost however. In fact, on all but one occasion in Acts, whenever the giving of the Spirit is recorded, the gift of tongues always accompanies it; and it is a gift that was still being used by at least the Corinthian church some 25 years later (1Co 14:1–25) – and while Paul needed to correct the way they were using it in their meetings, he never sought to stop them. In fact, it was a gift of the Spirit that he himself gladly exercised (1Co 14:18).

While the theological framework of some Christians today leads them to say the gift of speaking in tongues died out with the early church, millions of other Christians – whether from Pentecostal denominations or charismatic wings of other mainstream denominations – still use this gift to help them in their praising and praying, or, combined with the gift of interpretation, to bring words of encouragement and insight from God.

taking place before their eyes. The barriers of culture and language are broken down, as God draws to himself a new people, drawn from every nation under heaven.

Yet even the greatest works of God are mocked by those who fail to understand. Those standing around the dying Christ poked fun at him. And those witnessing the outpouring of the Spirit do the same. The disciples have had too much to drink (2:13), they sneer. Even today, people make fun of Christians on account of their conversion experiences or religious beliefs. As Luke reminds us, this is nothing new!

2:14–41 Peter Addresses the Crowd In the midst of the excitement and confusion, Peter preaches the first recorded Christian sermon. As his audience is largely Jewish, he makes considerable use of Old Testament prophecy, showing how it points to both the death and resurrection of Jesus, and the coming of the Holy Spirit. A similar approach is often used by Matthew in his Gospel, as he draws attention to the many ways in which Jesus fulfils Old Testament prophecy.

Peter begins by disposing of the suggestion that he or his colleagues are drunk: it is, after all, only nine o'clock in the morning (2:15). Something far more

significant is happening. Peter explains its meaning by appealing to one of the great prophecies of the Old Testament (Joel 2:28–32), which speaks of God pouring out his Spirit upon all people 'in the last days' (2:17). In his prophecy, Joel speaks of the coming of a future day, in which God will come to his people in power, and reassure them of his presence and care (Joel 2:27). The fortunes of Judah and Jerusalem will be restored, and all nations will be gathered together (Joel 3:1–2). On that day, God will 'pour out' his 'Spirit on all people' (Joel 2:28). The gift of the Spirit will lead to prophecy and vision. The pouring out of the Spirit is thus seen as a sign of this long-hoped-for 'day of the Lord'. The coming of the Spirit is thus seen as a sign of a vitally important moment in the history of the people of God, in which 'everyone who calls on the name of the Lord will be saved' (Joel 2:32). As Peter makes clear, this means that salvation is now available to all.

In the first part of this sermon, Peter shows how the coming of the Holy Spirit is in fulfilment of Old Testament prophecy. He now focuses on the person of Jesus, and his significance for the world. Peter begins this new section of the sermon by declaring that Jesus was 'a man accredited by God' (2:22), God performed a series of miracles, wonders and signs through him – things that everyone knew about, and recognised as being from God. Peter stresses that Christ's death upon the cross was no accident, but something that took place 'by God's deliberate plan and fore-knowledge' (2:23). While this does not remove human responsibility for the death of Christ, it nevertheless sets that

death in a very different context. God purposed to achieve something through the death of Christ. What Israel rejected, God sealed with his approval, through the resurrection.

The theme of the resurrection dominates this part of Peter's sermon. Two distinct ideas can be disentangled in the midst of its rich network of themes. First, the sheer joy that Jesus is alive. Death was not able to hold him (2:24, 26, 32). Secondly, the realisation that the resurrection means that Jesus has been 'exalted to the right hand of God' (2:33). More than that: the Holy Spirit is given *through* Christ. 'He has received from the Father the promised Holy Spirit' (2:33). Peter brings this section of the sermon to a climax by pointing out how two messianic passages from the Psalms can refer only to Jesus (2:25–35). 'God has made this Jesus, whom you crucified, both Lord and Messiah' (2:36). Jesus is the long-promised Messiah, who has authority over his people.

The impact of Peter's preaching on his audience is immediate and shattering: 'What shall we do?' (2:37). The crowd realises that Peter's conclusion demands a response – not just agreement with what he has been saying, but a real change in heart and mind. Two words summarise the response he asks of his hearers. First, they are to *repent* (2:38). Repentance is about an inner reorientation, a turnabout in one's life away from sin and towards God. The outward and public sign of this inward change is *baptism*, which Peter urges on his hearers (2:38, 41). Secondly, having accepted the need for repentance, the way is open to *receiving* (2:38) the gift of the Holy Spirit. Repentance and renewal go hand in hand, as part and

parcel of the promise of God to his people. Peter makes it clear that this promise is for all. There is no small print, restricting it to only a chosen few, a privileged elite, or a national group (2:39). The message is appealing and transforming. At nine o'clock that morning, there had been 120 believers. By the evening of that same day, three thousand had been added to their number (2:41).

2:42–47 The Fellowship of the Believers Luke also gives us insights into the quality of the fellowship of the converts at this time. The new believers grow through the teaching of the apostles (such as that presented in many of the sermons recorded in Acts), fellowship, the breaking of the bread, and prayer (2:42). It is a time of great excitement and expectation (2:43). People expect things to happen – and, as Luke makes clear, they do, with the result that the church grows daily (2:47). The image of believers having everything in common (2:44) has served as a model for many Christian communities. Even if it sounds idealistic today, it continues to remind believers that all they have has been given to them by God for the common good.

3:1–10 Peter Heals a Lame Beggar The story now changes pace. We move away from the frenetic activity of Pentecost, to an occasion when Peter and John meet a man lame from birth at one of the temple gates (3:2, 10). His situation is hopeless. Nothing can be done for him. His only hope for survival is to beg for money. In many ways, he can be regarded as representing the pitiful condition of fallen humanity: we are unable to change our situation, and our only hope is to cope with it. Peter, however, offers the man what he really needs: healing. 'Silver or gold I do not have, but what I do have I give you' (3:6). Here is a powerful and moving illustration of the hope that the gospel brings to the world.

The New Testament often uses the term 'healing' to refer to the salvation that comes through Christ. The word immediately suggests the idea of a restoration to wholeness, including both physical illness and broken personal relationships. It is a word that has a deep meaning for our modern world, which is aware of its ills, yet often lacks both the resources and the will to do anything about them. It is an especially important term for Luke, who was a physician by background.

Perhaps the most powerful aspect of this incident concerns the reaction of those who know the lame man (3:9–10). It is obvious that his situation has changed. Something has happened to him. No longer is he a sullen beggar. He is seen 'walking and jumping, and praising God' (3:8).

3:11–26 Peter Speaks to the Onlookers The impact made by the healing of the crippled beggar is enormous. A crowd gathers, curious to find out more about what has happened (3:11). The opportunity is too good to miss: Peter preaches a sermon. His initial concern is to dismiss the idea that he has some special powers that healed the lame man. There is nothing special about Peter himself (3:12). On the other hand, there is something special about the risen Christ, which led to that afternoon's spectacular event. 'By faith in the name

of Jesus, this man whom you see and know was made strong' (3:16). Once more, we see how personal transformation is one of the most powerful and telling forms of witness to the gospel. Arguments about whether God exists or not tend to get bogged down very quickly. It is, however, difficult to argue with someone who wants to talk about the difference that Christianity has made to their lives. Perhaps Christians today can learn from this example.

Peter again stresses the importance of the resurrection of Christ (3:15), and the way in which the suffering Messiah fulfilled the great prophetic hopes of the Old Testament (3:18–26). The Old Testament points ahead, looking beyond itself to the coming of the Messiah and 'times of refreshing' (3:19) for the people of God. Peter's message is direct and simple: those times have now come. The great hopes of the prophets and patriarchs have now been fulfilled. 'You are heirs of the prophets and of the covenant God made with your fathers' (3:25). Yet this promise requires a response from those who hear it. Peter asks his audience to turn from their wicked ways (3:26). It is important to appreciate that the gospel changes people's lives, not just the way people think.

4:1–4 Preaching the Resurrection of Jesus

The events after Pentecost attract a lot of attention, and ensure a ready hearing for the gospel among the people. The number of believers has by now grown to five thousand (4:4), as a result of the preaching of the gospel. But not all are pleased about these new developments. Some are distinctly threatened by them.

The religious authorities of the time are outraged by the apostolic preaching of the resurrection of Jesus (4:2). Even today, some people suggest that Christians should not preach the resurrection, as it belittles other religious teachers (who have not been raised from the dead!). Acts reminds us that for Christians the resurrection of Jesus is non-negotiable, something so important that it must be proclaimed, whatever the results. 'We cannot help speaking about what we have seen and heard' (4:20).

4:5–22 Peter and John Before the Sanhedrin

After a night in jail, Peter and John are hauled before a religious court to account for their actions (4:5–7). But the authorities are faced with a dilemma. Everyone knows about the healing of the lame man. It is not something that can be denied. Arguments can be refuted; miracles are rather more difficult to deal with. (Once more, note the importance of personal transformation as a form of witness!) Peter and John defend themselves by declaring that they can remain faithful only to what they have seen and heard. 'It is by the name of Jesus Christ of Nazareth, whom you crucified but whom God raised from the dead, that this man stands before you healed' (4:10). He alone brings salvation (4:12). How can they remain silent? They may only be 'unschooled, ordinary men' (4:13); but their testimony has a power and inner conviction that cannot be denied – not least when the healed man is to hand to back them up (4:14).

4:23–31 The Believers' Prayer

Peter and John return to the church, to report on what happened to them (4:23). It is clear

that the assembled believers are deeply troubled by the reports of hostility towards the gospel (4:24). Instinctively, they turn to prayer. They recall God's sovereignty and goodness, and take comfort from the fact that inspired Old Testament writers spoke of such hostility against God and his Messiah (4:25–28). Obeying God is never going to earn approval from the world. The current opposition to the gospel fits into this pattern of defiance and resistance on the part of worldly and religious rulers. So the assembled believers ask God for the necessary strength and determination to face the future, with its great challenges and opportunities (4:29–30).

As Luke makes clear, they get the encouragement and reassurance they need. Luke records how they were 'all filled with the Holy Spirit and spoke the word of God boldly' (4:31). Yet this is no human boldness, such as some kind of bravado. It is a secure confidence in the power and purpose of God to uphold those – then and now – who obey him, and preach his gospel with conviction and steadfastness.

4:32–5:11 The Believers Share Their Possessions

At several points, Luke sets out the vision that fired the early Christians – a vision that can still challenge and inspire today. As we have seen, those first Christians were infectiously enthusiastic about their faith. But they were also concerned to put that faith into action, inside and outside the church. This important section gives us a glimpse of the social concerns of the church, and challenges Christians today to consider their own attitudes to other believers and society at large.

Luke sets out the way in which the first Christians are transformed by the gospel.

Although the apostles continue faithfully to preach the resurrection of Christ (4:33), that preaching is supplemented by the fostering of Christlike attitudes inside the church: 'No one claimed that any of their possessions was their own, but they shared everything they had' (4:32). Possessions are seen as a gift from God, given for the good of the church. They are to be shared, for the common good. As a result, no one was in need (4:34–35). This is not communism. This is simply Christian love in action. Luke then provides some examples, positive and negative, of Christian attitudes towards possessions. Barnabas is praised for his unselfish attitudes (4:36–37). Ananias and Sapphira, on the other hand, pretend to give all the proceeds from a land sale to the church, but secretly hold back part of the money (5:1–2). When confronted with their deceit, both die, possibly from heart attacks (5:5, 10). This passage raises anxieties for some readers, on account of its apparent harshness, and especially Peter's severe words to both. However, it is clear that Ananias and Sapphira are being criticised for their lack of honesty, and an attempt to mislead the apostles.

ACTS 5:12–8:40
Increasing Success and Growing Persecution

As the narrative of the early church continues, it becomes clear that the gospel continues to have enormous appeal during these early days. People hold Christians in respect, yet are frightened to join them (5:13). Perhaps we see here something like the problem faced by Nicodemus. Although attracted

to Jesus, he was fearful of this becoming public knowledge. As a result, he visited Jesus at night, so that none would know (Jn 3:1–16). Nevertheless, despite this reticence on the part of many, it is clear that some are able to overcome the stigma of following Christ, and publicly declare their faith (5:14).

5:17–42 The Apostles Persecuted But this success brings with it resentment on the part of the high priest and his associates, who are 'filled with jealousy' (5:17) at each new success of the gospel. This theme becomes increasingly frequent in Acts, as Luke documents the growing hostility towards the gospel by the Jewish authorities, at every level. Interestingly, Luke often places reports of official hostility towards believers alongside reports of popular support (5:26), indicating that the ordinary people do not share their leaders' prejudices.

The initial instinct of the religious authorities is to suppress the movement by force, throwing its leaders in prison. This backfires. The apostles, set free by divine providence, merely move on to preach the gospel within the court of the temple itself (5:19–20), bringing the full message of this new life to an even wider audience.

Eventually the apostles are persuaded to appear before the Sanhedrin, an assembly of senior religious figures (5:26). The high priest's irritation with them is obvious (5:28). Why are they still talking about Jesus? Why don't they keep quiet? Life would be a lot easier for everyone. Peter's reply is important: 'We must obey God rather than human beings' (5:29). It is, he argues, impossible to be silent about the truth of what God

has done in Christ. No one can be silent about the exaltation of Christ, and the promise of repentance and forgiveness of sins to Israel (5:31). The apostles are witnesses to these things. They cannot bear false witness!

The situation becomes nasty. The original idea was to put the apostles in the dock. However, it now turns out to be the Sanhedrin itself that is put on trial, through its apparent failure to respond to God when he came to his people. However, the tension is defused through an intervention from Gamaliel, a respected teacher of the Law (5:34). His argument wins the day, and is of considerable importance. If this movement is from God, he declares, it will be unstoppable (5:38–39). There have been many spurious religious teachings in the past. If this one is for real, it will survive. 'If it is from God, you will not be able to stop these men; you will only find yourselves fighting against God' (5:39). As we look ahead to the further expansion of the church, as Luke describes it in this work, we can see the wisdom of his advice, and have to reckon with the conclusion to which it points – that the gospel is indeed 'from God'.

6:1–15 The Choosing of the Seven At this stage, the expansion of the church requires that further measures be taken to ensure that none of its missionary and pastoral tasks are neglected (6:1–7). The choosing of the seven is an indication of the growing appeal of the gospel to Jews outside and the resulting increase in this section of the population within the church. All seven, including Stephen, have Greek names, suggesting that all were drawn from this section of the

church. However, this increasing growth is met by growing opposition from certain Jewish bodies, with the result that Stephen finds himself accused of blasphemy, and brought before the Sanhedrin – that is, the 71-member supreme Jewish court, consisting of the chief priests, elders, and teachers of the Law (6:8–15).

7:1–53 Stephen's Speech to the Sanhedrin In his defence, Stephen delivers an impassioned speech to the Sanhedrin (7:1–53). The speech is a remarkable summary of the manner in which God has prepared the way for the gospel. It begins with the calling of Abraham (7:1–8), and traces the development of the people of God from their descent into and eventual exodus from Egypt (7:9–44), through the entry into the promised land (7:45) and the establishment of the monarchy (7:46). It is important to note the considerable portion of this sermon that is devoted to Moses, who is seen as establishing the fact that the people of Israel are prone to disobey God. Have things changed? Israel is just the same today, Stephen declares (7:51). Whenever a prophet appeared in her midst, her instant reaction was to kill him, rather than listen to him (7:52–53). Her killing of Jesus Christ is just the latest example in a long chain of rebellion and disobedience.

7:54–8:1 The Stoning of Stephen This outrages the Sanhedrin, who determine to stone him to death for blasphemy there and then (7:54–8:1). Before they have a chance to do this, Stephen declares that he has had a vision in which he can see the 'Son of Man' – a reference to Jesus himself – standing at the right hand of God. This indicates not merely that Jesus has been accepted and vindicated by God. It implies that Jesus now has equal status with God – which adds further to the outrage of the traditionalists. And so Stephen dies, the first Christian martyr. Luke now mentions in passing that among those who witness and approve of his death is a man called Saul, who will feature prominently in the remainder of Luke's account of the early church.

8:1–3 The Church Persecuted and Scattered As a result of this martyrdom, the church is subjected to vicious persecution, leading to its members being scattered throughout the region (8:1–40). Saul is identified as one of the ringleaders of this attempt to destroy Christianity. However, the process of persecution merely disperses the apostles throughout the region, and allows them to witness to the gospel over a far wider area than before. We read of Philip preaching in the northern region of Samaria, and subsequently Philip heading south towards Gaza. In each case, they meet with a positive response. (Later, we learn that the gospel penetrates even to Cyprus and Antioch as a result of this dispersion: 11:19–21.)

8:4–25 Philip in Samaria, and Simon the Sorcerer The establishment of the gospel in Samaria leads to an incident of considerable importance – a confrontation with a sorcerer named Simon (also referred to as 'Simon Magus'). As the gospel meets with an overwhelmingly positive result in Samaria, through the preaching of the

word and the working of signs and wonders, Simon became attracted to the idea of purchasing some of the spiritual gifts of the apostles for himself. He is severely chastised by Peter for this suggestion.

8:26–40 Philip and the Ethiopian In the meantime, Philip, who had headed south, has a meeting with a senior official in the household of the queen of the Ethiopians (8:26–40). The Ethiopian may have been a Jewish proselyte (notice how he had travelled to Jerusalem to worship, and his familiarity with the Old Testament). Now on his way home, he finds himself puzzled by a portion of the prophet Isaiah, which he is reading in his chariot. The passage in question is Isa 53:7–8, a section dealing with the coming of the 'suffering servant'. Philip asks him if he can understand what he is reading. The Ethiopian invites Philip to join him, and explain the text. Philip then shows how this text, and others, point to the good news of Jesus Christ. As a result, the Ethiopian makes the decision to be baptised there and then, and goes on his way rejoicing.

9:1–19 Saul's Conversion But a more momentous conversion is in the offing. The narrative now returns to Saul. By his attempt to eliminate the church, he has succeeded merely in dispersing it, with the result that the gospel spreads far beyond Jerusalem. As he continues his attempt to eliminate Christianity, he shifts his sights from Jerusalem to Damascus (9:1–19). As he travels along the road to Damascus, with a view to ridding the city of its growing Christian presence, he experiences an encounter with the risen Jesus Christ. He hears Christ speak his name, and ask Saul why he is persecuting him. Blinded by the vision, he is obliged to be led into Damascus by his attendants.

However, Ananias, one of the growing number of Christians in the city, receives a vision in which Saul is identified and located. He is asked to take care of Saul, who is to be the Lord's 'chosen instrument . . . to the Gentiles' (9:15). On finding Saul, Ananias lays his hands on him, with the result that he regains his sight. As a token of his new-found faith, he is baptised. This account of the conversion of Paul is found three times, with minor variations, in Acts (see also 22:3–16; 26:9–18). It is also found in an abbreviated form in Paul's own writings (Gal 1:13–17). The brevity of this account reflects the fact that Paul clearly assumes that his readers are broadly familiar with the story of his conversion, and he wishes simply to use the account to establish his credentials as an apostle.

9:20–31 Saul in Damascus and Jerusalem So Saul, who was once a persecutor of the church, now becomes its defender. Luke notes how Saul is able to demonstrate irrefutably that Jesus is the Messiah, to the amazement of those who know his background, and the irritation of the Jewish population of Damascus. During his period in the region (which he elsewhere identifies as being three years in length: Gal 1:17–18), he clearly grows considerably in stature and wisdom. As a result, he comes under threat of death from those whom he once supported. Learning of an attempt to kill him, Saul is lowered down the city wall in a basket, escapes from the city and makes his way

to Jerusalem, where he continues his evangelistic ministry until his own personal safety makes it imperative that he be moved to Tarsus.

9:32–42 Peter in Lydda and Joppa

Attention now shifts from Saul to Peter (9:32–43), who is continuing his work of evangelism and healing in the region to the northwest of Jerusalem, around the towns of Joppa (now the modern city of Jaffa) and Lydda. In each case, he performs miracles of healing among Jews. But a major crisis is about to develop. Thus far, the good news has been taken to Jews, whether Grecian or Hebraic. But what about the Gentiles? Will they benefit from the gospel?

10:1–48 Cornelius calls for Peter, and Peter's Vision

This issue is raised for Peter by a message he receives from a Roman centurion named Cornelius (10:1–8). Though not a Jew, he is 'God-fearing' – a term used to refer to a Gentile sympathetic to Judaism, but who has not formally become a proselyte. In a vision, Cornelius learns of the presence of Peter, and sends messengers to him to arrange a meeting. As the messengers approach Joppa, Peter himself has a vision (10:9–16; see also 11:5–14) in which he sees various creatures being lowered in what looks like a sheet. Some of these are unclean, and hence forbidden to Jews. Yet Peter hears a voice commanding him to eat them. He refuses. He will not eat anything unclean or impure. Yet he is told in return that nothing that God has created is unclean or impure. Wondering what the vision means, Peter goes to meet the messengers who are waiting for him.

The meaning of the vision soon becomes clear (10:17–48). The vision is a declaration that the Gentiles are no longer to be treated as impure or second class. When Peter arrives at Cornelius' house, he has understood the meaning of the vision. Even though Cornelius is a Gentile, and even though the Law prohibits Jews from having contact with Gentiles, Peter declares that these barriers are now broken down: 'God does not show favouritism but accepts from every nation the one who fears him and does what is right' (10:34).

As Peter speaks of the great work of God through the death and resurrection of Jesus Christ, a remarkable thing happens. The Holy Spirit descends on all who are listening to him – Jews and Gentiles. It is clear that the same Spirit is being experienced by all present. The Spirit refuses to make any distinction between Jew and Gentile, causing them to speak in tongues and praise God. Any lingering doubts on Peter's part are now removed: he baptises them in the name of Jesus.

11:1–18 Peter Explains His Actions

This action is not well received by the church back in Jerusalem. They call Peter to account for his actions. Why did Peter go into the house of Gentiles (something regarded as defiling by Jews)? The Jewish Christians are outraged, in that Peter has clearly violated parts of the Law of Moses (11:1–3). Peter responds by relating the vision he had at Joppa (11:4–14), and its consequences. His line of thought is clear: nobody has the right to resist God. If God has given the same gift to the Gentiles as he gave to the Jews, what right did he, Peter, have

to stand in the way of its full recognition? The company of believers is not merely persuaded by this argument; they are delighted that God has allowed the Gentiles to share in the great benefits of Christ (11:15–18).

11:19–30 The Church in Antioch Our attention now returns to the effects of the persecution initiated by Saul some time before. As a result of this, the disciples have been scattered throughout the region, leading to the more rapid spread of the gospel than would otherwise have been the case. As so often proves to be the case, a time of persecution becomes a time of expansion. We now learn of the establishment of Christian communities in the region of Antioch (11:19–30). This development is of strategic importance. At this stage in its history, the Roman Empire is dominated by three cities. First and foremost is Rome itself. The second greatest city of the empire is the Egyptian city of Alexandria. The third greatest is Antioch. In due course, the gospel will establish itself in all three cities. We now learn of the foothold established in the city of Antioch. Luke's readers, familiar with the politics of the eastern region of the Roman Empire, would immediately have realised the significance of this development, and the great comfort it would have brought at a time of persecution elsewhere. We also learn of another important development associated with Antioch: it is in this city that the word 'Christians' is first used to refer to believers (11:26). Up to this point, a variety of words have been used. This term will now pass into general usage.

12:1–19 Peter's Miraculous Escape from Prison The rapid growth in the church at this stage is seen as a threat by many within the Jewish community. It is also a cause of concern to the Herodians, a group of Jews who support the Roman presence in the region. Luke now documents a number of developments that relate specifically to the Herodians (12:1–25). 'King Herod' (12:1) refers to Agrippa I, a nephew of the Herod who had beheaded John the Baptist. (The term 'Herod' was often used to refer to members of the Herodian dynasty without identifying which of the various family members was intended.) Having beheaded James, the brother of John (Mt 4:21), it is clear that Herod intends to deal with Peter in much the same way as Jesus before him: he will be publicly tried at Passover. The inevitable result of this trial would have been death, probably by crucifixion. But it is not God's will that Peter should die at this time. In an act of deliverance, Peter is set free from his chains, and escapes from imprisonment, to the outrage of Herod.

12:21–23 Herod's Death The subsequent death of Herod is then documented (12:21–23). While celebrating a festival in honour of the emperor Claudius in AD 44, Herod is acclaimed as a god – an acclamation that Herod makes no attempt to deny. He is immediately struck down with violent pains, from which he dies a few days later. Luke's account of events corresponds well with that presented by the Jewish historian Josephus, confirming Luke's reliability as a historian.

12:24–25 *Christianity Continues to Spread* Yet despite all these official and semi-official attempts to suppress the gospel, Christianity continues to spread. The remainder of Acts focuses on the ministry of one individual who, with his companions, will prove instrumental in the spread of the gospel throughout the eastern Mediterranean world – Saul, who, as we shall see (13:9), soon becomes known by his more familiar name of Paul. Having gained a foothold in the third city of the empire, the gospel now moves on inexorably, to gain ground in its greatest city, Rome itself. Although Paul is not responsible for establishing the gospel in Rome, he nevertheless writes to the church in that city, probably in the spring of AD 57, and will eventually be received and supported by this church when he arrives there in the spring of AD 59. But this is to look into the future. Our attention returns to Luke's account, which now goes back to Antioch.

ACTS 13:1–28:31
The Spread of the Gospel from Antioch to Rome

13:1–3 *Barnabas and Saul Sent off* While the leading members of the church are

---

Is it right to evangelise in a pluralistic world?

In today's pluralistic, postmodern world it is widely believed that there is no overarching explanation of anything, no 'truth' that is true for everyone, and that all paths are acceptable as long as they don't hurt someone else. To claim there is one religious reality, universally true for everyone, is therefore seen as bigoted and oppressive. So can Christians evangelise in such a culture, claiming Christ as the only way to God?

First we should remember that our world is not greatly different from the world of New Testament times. When the church sent out Barnabas and Paul (Ac 13), it was breaking into a Greco-Roman world with as pluralistic a culture as today, with as many conflicting philosophies, spiritualities and religions. Rome was happy to let all such views coexist, as long as once a year its citizens offered sacrifice to Caesar and declared 'Caesar is Lord'. After that, they could believe whatever they liked.

Yet Christians refused to compromise and make this declaration, for 'there is but one Lord, Jesus Christ' (1Co 8:6); and this refusal to acknowledge that Caesar was Lord, that Christianity was just one option among many, led thousands to martyrdom. They believed compromise was not possible for Jesus had said, 'I am the way and the truth and the life. No one comes to the Father except through me' (Jn 14:6). Other religions were simply not a valid option therefore. Even Jews needed Christ, so how much more the adherents of other religions.

While Christians today will therefore treat followers of other religions with respect and kindness, it seems impossible to be faithful to Jesus' claims and commission and accept other religions as equally valid paths to God. Christians have no choice but to share the truth as they have found it in Jesus.

Paul's First Missionary Journey

worshipping and fasting, the Holy Spirit identifies Barnabas and Paul as having a special commission to perform for the Lord (13:1–3). After the leaders of the church have laid hands on them, they begin their journey of preaching, teaching and evangelism. This is the first of Paul's missionary journeys (13:4–14:28), which would probably have taken place at some time around AD 46–48. At this stage, Paul would probably have been around 44 years old. Some 14 years have passed since his conversion, during which time he has been occupied primarily with missionary work in the region of Syria (Gal 1:21). Now he is called to undertake a much more ambitious missionary project. For this journey, Paul and Barnabas are joined by John Mark (referred to simply as John at 13:5, but more usually known as Mark). Mark was

a cousin of Barnabas (Col 4:10), and is generally thought to have been the author of the Gospel now known by his name.

13:4–52 On Cyprus and in Pisidian Antioch

So in AD 46, these three companions set out on their way to the south coast of Asia Minor, a region of the northeastern Mediterranean coast which constitutes modern-day Turkey. Their journey initially takes them to the island of Cyprus (13:4–12). Although Luke does not mention this during his narrative, at some point in this early stage of the journey, Paul suffers from his 'thorn in the flesh' (1Co 2:3; 2Co 12:7), which may have taken the form of an illness such as malaria. At this stage in the journey, Mark leaves the group, and returns to Jerusalem (13:13). It is not clear why this

takes place. At any rate, Paul and Barnabas then proceed alone to another city named Antioch, located in the province of Galatia, and usually referred to as 'Pisidian Antioch' to distinguish it from the Syrian city of the same name (13:14–52).

During his time in Pisidian Antioch, Paul preaches a Sabbath sermon at a local synagogue, proclaiming that Jesus is the long-awaited Messiah. Through Jesus Christ, God has made forgiveness of sins available in a way that the Law of Moses could never allow. The message meets with an enthusiastic response. Paul is invited to speak again on the following Sabbath at the same synagogue. Some of its members, unable to wait that long to hear more, seek out Paul and Barnabas for further discussions. This irritates some of the local Jewish leaders, who manage to have Paul and Barnabas expelled from the region.

14:1–28 In Iconium and Again in Antioch in Syria

The same pattern of events is repeated at Iconium (14:1–6). In nearby Lystra and Derbe, the apostles are received with such enthusiasm that they are taken for gods themselves – an impression that they are able to dispel, while at the same time proclaiming the good news (14:7–18). This time, however, local Jewish opposition is more violent, with an attempt being made to stone Paul to death (14:19–20). Undaunted, Paul establishes small Christian communities in the area, and then revisits those he has already planted as he traces his steps back to Antioch (14:21–28). The gospel is now firmly rooted outside Palestine.

15:1–40 The Council at Jerusalem

But inside Palestine, things are becoming difficult. Divisions are beginning to open up within the church over the issue of circumcision. A section of the church is arguing that it is essential that male Christians are circumcised. In effect, they seem to regard Christianity as an affirmation of every aspect of contemporary Judaism, with the exception of one additional belief – that Jesus is the Messiah. Unless males are circumcised, they cannot be saved (15:1). In Paul's absence, things have become serious, with a real threat of division within the church.

In order to resolve this issue, Paul and Barnabas set out to Jerusalem from Antioch. Luke provides us with an account of the first General Council of the Christian church – the Council of Jerusalem in AD 49 (Acts 15:2–29). The debate is initially dominated by converted Pharisees, who insist on the need to uphold the Law of Moses, including the circumcision requirements. Yet Paul's account of the amazing impact of the gospel among the Gentiles causes the wisdom of this approach to be questioned. If so many Gentiles are being won for the gospel, why should anything unnecessary be put in their way? Paul concedes the need to avoid food that has been sacrificed to idols – an issue that features elsewhere in his letters (1Co 8:7–13). But there is no need for circumcision. This position wins widespread support, and is summarised in a letter that is circulated at Antioch (15:30–35).

Yet although the issue is resolved at the theoretical level, it will remain a live issue for many churches in the future, as the relation between the new wine of the

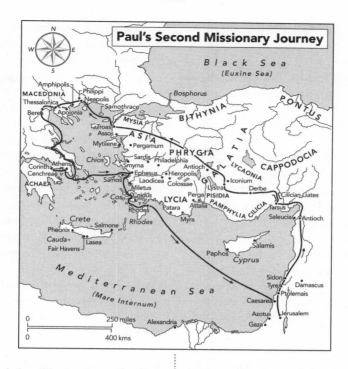

Paul's Second Missionary Journey

gospel and the old wineskins of Judaism continues to be controversial. Having sorted out this issue in Palestine, Paul determines to return to Galatia to make sure the churches he has planted know of this decision. (Incidentally, it should be noted that Paul's letter to the Galatians is dominated by this issue.) A second missionary journey is therefore undertaken (15:36–18:22), around AD 50–52. Initially, Paul expects to be accompanied by Barnabas. However, the latter wants to take Mark along with him, which Paul refuses to countenance – again, for reasons that are not clear, but that seem to relate to Mark's premature departure from the first missionary journey.

16:1–15 Timothy Joins Paul and Silas The
first stage of the journey takes them overland to Galatia (15:36–41). At Lystra,

they are joined by Timothy, who will become one of Paul's most trusted colleagues (16:1–5). They then proceed to the northwestern tip of Asia Minor. At Troas, close to the site of the ancient city of Troy, they are joined by Luke himself, who is unquestionably a major eyewitness source for many of the accounts relating to this part of the journey (notice the use of 'we' in many of the reports from this section). Crossing the Aegean Sea, they land in the area of Macedonia, where they spend some time in the city of Philippi, a major Roman colony. For the first time, the good news is being preached on the continent of Europe. It is here that Lydia, a well-to-do business woman, is converted and baptised (16:13–15). Her house subsequently becomes a centre for missionary activity in the region. Not surprisingly, Paul later

writes to the church that was planted during his time in the city.

16:16–17:10 Paul and Silas Imprisoned and Released Inevitably, opposition results from this success, with the result that Paul and Silas are thrown in jail (16:16–40). However, once the authorities have discovered that they are Roman citizens, they are hastily released, and are able to return to Lydia's house, before moving on to the region of Thessalonica. Here Paul may have taken temporary employment as a tentmaker (1Th 2:9) to support himself while undertaking missionary work in the region. As a result of his preaching in the local synagogue (17:1–9), a church is established (to which he will later write his first two letters, 1 Thessalonians and 2 Thessalonians).

17:10–34 In Berea and in Athens After passing through Berea (17:10–14), the group finally arrive in Athens, still widely regarded as the intellectual centre of the ancient world (17:15–34). The city had a reputation for its short-lived interest in the latest ideas and intellectual fashion, and appears to have seen in Paul the source of some exciting new ideas. It is here that Paul delivers his address on the Areopagus, or 'Mars Hill'. Rather than get caught up in some petty theological arguments, Paul declares that it is common knowledge that there is a creator God, who has authority over men and women. But who is this God? And how may he be known? Having noted an altar in the city dedicated to 'an unknown god', Paul declares that what the Athenians worship as something unknown, he will proclaim as someone who can be known. Having thus laid the

foundations for the gospel, he develops the basic Christian message of the need for repentance. The reception accorded to his address is not particularly enthusiastic. Nevertheless, the gospel has now been proclaimed in Athens.

18:1–28 In Corinth There is no letter from Paul to the Athenians. It seems that no church was founded in this city. But in the port city of Corinth, further south, Paul gains a much more sympathetic hearing (18:1–28). All that time Corinth was a huge seaport, with many openings for evangelism within the local Jewish community, as well as within the vastly larger Gentile population. Paul stayed there for 18 months. It was clearly an important time. Encouraged by the reports of church growth in the region of Macedonia, Paul wrote both his letters to the Thessalonian Christians. Aided by Priscilla and Aquila, the church grew considerably, drawing in both Jewish and Gentile converts.

19:1–41 Paul in Ephesus But Paul is anxious to move on. At some point in AD 53, Paul sets off on his third missionary journey (18:23–21:17). The conversion of Apollos, a Jew from the Egyptian city of Alexandria, leads to renewed evangelistic activity elsewhere in the region. However, Apollos seems to leave out a number of aspects of the gospel. While his preaching persuades many that Jesus is the Christ, there seems to have been no mention of the gift of the Holy Spirit. For example, baptism seems to be understood as little more than an external token of cleansing, without any real understanding of spiritual renewal. Yet once this

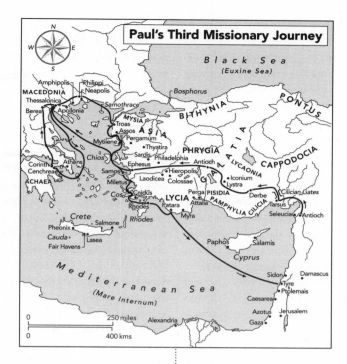

Paul's Third Missionary Journey

misunderstanding is cleared up, Apollos is able to undertake a major evangelistic ministry in Corinth.

Paul, however, is now involved in evangelism in the city of Ephesus. The city is a stronghold of pagan superstition, centring on the goddess Diana. This cult is supported by the local merchants, who rely on it for their living. Yet, on account of Paul's ministry, the city will become a stronghold of the Christian church (19:8–20). Yet this is not without its difficulties. A local silversmith manages to provoke a riot, which is eventually subdued by some diplomacy from a local official (19:23–41).

20:1–21:16 The Church in Jerusalem Paul's attention now turns to the church in Jerusalem, the work of which he wishes to support. Travelling by land, Paul sets off for Jerusalem, with the object of collecting money to support the work of the church in the city (20:1–16). At the town of Miletus, near Ephesus, Paul brings members of the Ephesian church together in order to bid farewell to them (20:17–38). As he journeys on to Jerusalem, he appears to have become aware of difficulties awaiting him at Jerusalem. A series of warnings received along the way point to hostility lying ahead (21:1–16). Yet on his arrival in the city, he is warmly received by the Christians in the city (21:17–26). He is advised by local Christian leaders to show respect for the Jewish laws, and to avoid giving offence. As is clear from his actions, Paul decides to adopt this advice.

But it does not work. Almost immediately, Paul is made an object of hate by some local Jewish fanatics. In a

scene that at times resembles the Gospel accounts of the arrest and trial of Jesus, the crowds get out of control. The local Roman commander orders Paul to be arrested (21:27–36). Paul's attempt to defend himself to his Jewish accusers, using the Aramaic language, only enrages them all the more (21:37–22:21). In this defence, Paul provides an account of his Jewish credentials, and tells how his own conversion took place. Things seem to go well, until Paul speaks of his own mission to bring this good news to the Gentiles (22:21). At this point, the crowd becomes uncontrollable. His attempt to defend himself before the Sanhedrin exposes the divisions between the Pharisees and Sadducees over the question of the resurrection, and again leads to rioting.

22:22–24:1 *Paul in Custody* For his own safety, Paul is placed in protective custody, and sent under escort to the headquarters of the Roman procurator of Judea, based at Caesarea (22:22–23:33). He will spend a period of two years – AD 56–58 – in custody at Caesarea. The length of this imprisonment reflects the recall of the procurator Antonius Felix for alleged cruelty to Jewish rebels and his eventual replacement by Porcius Festus.

24:1–27 *The Trial Before Felix* Initially, Paul is tried before Felix. This trial is inconclusive. The account of the proceedings provides its readers with a third version of Paul's conversion, and also indicates that there is no particular hostility on the part of this senior Roman citizen towards Christianity. It is clear that Felix is anxious concerning the impact of Christianity in the highly volatile region he is responsible for

administering. Yet he has no quarrel with any of its basic ideas. This point would have been important for Luke's readers, many of whom would probably have been Roman – perhaps including Theophilus himself.

25:1–12 *The Trial Before Festus* The trial then seems to have been adjourned, as a result of the recall of Felix. After some two years, Felix is replaced by Festus (24:27), and the trial can resume. It is clear that the Jewish leaders regard Paul as a serious threat, and wish to pursue the case against him as forcefully and rapidly as possible (25:1–12). Yet Paul outmanoeuvres his opponents. Knowing that they wish him to be tried before a Jewish religious court in Jerusalem, he makes the point that he is guilty of no crime in the sight of Rome – again, an important point for Luke's Roman readers. Paul claims the right to be tried in a Roman court, before the emperor or his representative – a privilege to which every Roman citizen had the right.

25:13–26:32 *King Agrippa* Unsure as to how to proceed, Festus consults with Herod Agrippa II (referred to as 'king' here, but in reality little more than a figurehead), who is on a goodwill visit to the region (25:13–27). Agrippa is interested in hearing Paul for himself, and gives him an audience (26:1–32). Once more, Paul relates how he was converted, leading Agrippa to ponder whether he will become converted himself. Since there is clearly nothing treasonable in what Paul says, Agrippa is in favour of setting him free. But Paul has demanded a trial in Rome. The matter is now out of their hands, and he will have

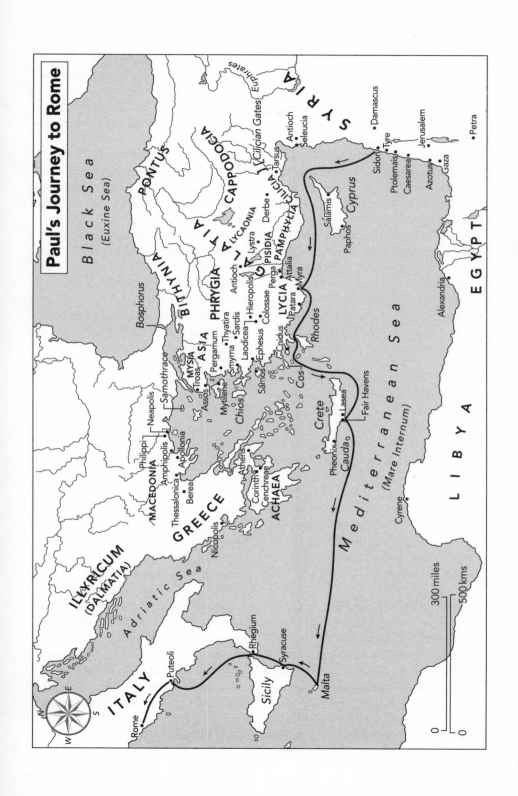

Paul's Journey to Rome

Black Sea
(Euxine Sea)

PONTUS

BITHYNIA

GALATIA

CAPPODOCIA

Cilician Gates

Euphrates

SYRIA

Antioch
Seleucia

Damascus

Jerusalem

Petra

Tyre
Sidon
Ptolemais
Caesarea
Azotus
Gaza

PHRYGIA

Bosphorus

Salamis
Paphos

Cyprus

Tarsus

CILICIA

LYCAONIA

PISIDIA

Derbe
Lystra
Antioch
Iconium

PAMPHYLIA

Perga
Attalia
Myra
Patara

LYCIA

Rhodes

Alexandria

EGYPT

MYSIA

ASIA

Pergamum
Thyatira
Sardis
Smyrna
Hierapolis
Laodicea
Colossae
Ephesus

Troas
Assos
Mytilene

Samothrace

Chios

Samos
Cos
Cnidus

Mediterranean Sea
(Mare Internum)

LIBYA

Neapolis
Philippi
Amphipolis
Apollonia

MACEDONIA

Thessalonica
Berea

Athens
Corinth
Cenchreae

GREECE

ACHAEA

Nicopolis

Crete

Lasea
Fair Havens
Pheonix
Cauda

Cyrene

ILLYRICUM
(DALMATIA)

Adriatic Sea

Rhegium
Syracuse

ITALY

Puteoli

Rome

Sicily

Malta

N
E
S
W

to go to Rome. Once more, the impact of this development on Luke's Roman readers must be appreciated. Paul's transference to Rome is, in effect, the result of a technicality, rather than any proven guilt on his part.

27:1–28:10 Paul Sails for Rome And so Paul sets sail for Rome, at some point in the later part of AD 58 (27:1–28:10). It is clear that Luke is present on this voyage – note the constant use of the word 'we'. Luke is an honest historian, and allows his reader to understand which parts of Acts are due to his own eyewitness reporting, and which are due to the reports of others. The account of the trip, with its many dangers culminating in the shipwreck on Malta, is a masterpiece of narrative, in which fine detail after fine detail is woven into the tapestry of the story. After being forced to spend the winter on the island of Malta, they eventually arrive at Puteoli in the Bay of Naples in the spring of the following year. There they are greeted by members of the local churches, who have clearly been looking forward to greeting this famous Christian leader from the eastern region of the Roman Empire. As they approach Rome itself, they are joined by more Christians from the great city, who have travelled to meet him.

28:11–16 Arrival at Rome The symbolic importance of this point must not be underestimated. Paul has already written his great letter to the Roman Christians (probably in the spring of AD 57) and hence would be known to the churches in the region. The gospel has already taken a firm hold in the 'eternal city', and the compassion and care shown towards him

by Paul's fellow believers is an important testimony to the growing influence of the gospel in the region.

28:17–31 Paul Preaches at Rome Under Guard Although under restrictions, Paul is able to live a relatively open life in the city as he awaits his trial. In typical Pauline fashion, the apostle begins an evangelistic ministry to his chief critics – the Jews (28:17–28). In his address, Paul emphasises that the coming of Jesus represents the fulfilment of the Law and the Prophets, in much the same way as the refusal of official Judaism to respond to the Messiah on his arrival was in fulfilment of the scriptural predictions of the hardheartedness and rebelliousness of Israel. For this reason, Paul has become an apostle to the Gentiles, who are prepared to listen to him.

Then, suddenly, the account ends. Luke affirms that Paul is free to move and speak, and that he exercises a successful evangelistic ministry for two years (28:30–31). Even though he is technically awaiting the arrival of charges from his accusers, so that he can face trial in Rome, he is nevertheless at liberty to speak about Christ. So what happens next? Why this abrupt end to Acts?

Nobody knows. From some of his letters, we know that Paul expected to be released soon (Php 2:24; Phm 22), leaving open the possibility that, after his time in Rome, Paul travelled elsewhere, perhaps on a fourth missionary journey. For example, the letter to the Romans hints at a possible visit to Spain (Ro 15:24, 28). Early Christian writings outside the New Testament canon certainly know of a tradition that he arrived there. If Paul was indeed released

in AD 61 or 62, there is no reason why he should not have undertaken such a journey. Indeed, there are references in the Pastoral Letters (1Ti 1:3; 3:14; 2Ti 4:13, 20; Tit 1:5) that point to travels in regions that Luke does not record him visiting on previous occasions – such as Crete, Nicopolis and Colossae. Furthermore the early historian of the church, Eusebius, states that Paul was released after his first period of imprisonment. But we do not know.

There is another explanation. During the persecution of Christians at Rome under the emperor Nero, a number of leading believers were martyred in AD 64. It is widely believed that both Peter and Paul were among them. Luke's Roman readers would have known of this, and realised that Paul was guilty of no crime in the eyes of Roman law. He would have been martyred for one reason, and one reason only – his faith.

ROMANS

Paul probably wrote his letter to the Christians at Rome in the early spring of AD 57, during his time at Corinth in the course of his third missionary journey. No apostle had ever visited Rome before. The letter therefore provides the church at Rome with the basic elements of Christian teaching. Although most of Paul's letters were directed to churches he had personally established and taught, the church at Rome had never been instructed by anyone of his stature. For this reason, this letter is of special importance to Christians today.

1:1–7 Introduction The letter opens with a declaration of Paul's personal authority as an apostle (1:1). The subject of his letter is to be the gospel concerning Jesus Christ. Immediately, Paul emphasises that the gospel was promised beforehand in the Old Testament. This is no novelty, but a long-promised and long-awaited act of salvation, which brings to a climax the great work of preparation in the Old Testament (1:2). And that gospel centres on the good news concerning Jesus Christ, the Son of God, whose credentials in this respect were established first

through his being a direct descendant of David, and secondly through his resurrection from the dead (1:3–4). Paul is entrusted with the task of calling all people to respond to this good news – good news he will explore during the course of this letter.

1:8–15 Paul's Longing to Visit Rome After greeting his readers as fellow Christians, Paul tells them of his delight at the witness of the Roman church, and his longing to be with them, so that he can be of some use to them. He has been able to serve congregations elsewhere in the world. Now he longs to come to Rome

itself, and proclaim the gospel in all its fullness at the hub of the Roman Empire (1:8–13). Paul regards himself as being under an obligation to proclaim this good news to everyone, irrespective of nationality or social status (1:14–15).

ROMANS 1:16–8:39
The Main Themes of the Gospel

1:16–17 Paul Gives Full Expression to His Delight at the Gospel It is difficult to avoid noticing Paul's obvious joy here. The power of God is at work for the salvation of everyone who believes. Notice the emphasis on 'everyone'. There are to be

Does God really get angry?

We probably all recoil when we read of 'the wrath of God' (1:18). Isn't this Paul simply attributing human emotions to God, we ask? Doesn't this conflict with Jesus' picture of God?

We need to be clear what Paul is saying here. In speaking of God's wrath Paul isn't thinking of the human kind of anger, which is *reactive* to something said or done that offends us. God's anger is not *reactive* but *responsive*. It is like our response when we walk past a drain with a bad smell and instinctively turn away in disgust. God's wrath is his absolutely right response to human sin because, being holy and perfect, he cannot bear with it, so great is its stench.

But Paul wasn't the first to say such things. The prophets often spoke of God's righteous judgment against sin. A common image was 'the cup of God's wrath' (e.g., Isa 51:17–23; Jer 25:15–28), symbolising the fullness of God's holy anger and judgment against sin that was being kept for the moment when sinners would have to drink from it. And it was not only the prophets who spoke of judgment; so did Jesus. Yes, he spoke of God's love and mercy, but he also spoke of a Day of Judgment when everyone would have to give account (e.g., Mt 12:36; 25:31–46). Judgment and mercy are not irreconcilable opposites, therefore, but two sides of the same coin.

And that's what Paul is saying here. Yes, he speaks clearly of God's wrath (1:18); but he has already spoken of the good news of the gospel first. That's how it is in the Bible: the bad news comes last, the good news comes first. Judgment is real, and judgment is for all; but it is God's last word, not his first.

no human barriers placed in the way of the gospel. Through faith, a righteousness that comes from God is made available to all who have faith – a righteousness that, as Paul will explain later in this letter, places those who believe in the gospel in a right relationship with God. Paul sees this great gospel affirmation as bringing to fulfilment the vision of the prophet Habakkuk (Hab 2:4), in which the righteous would live by faith in God.

1:18–32 God's Wrath Against Humanity To understand the full importance of this revelation of the righteousness of God, Paul analyses the sinful situation in which humanity finds itself (1:18–32). The glory of God has been made known to all through his wonderful work of creation. Yet humanity has not merely ignored God. It has deliberately chosen to rebel against him. Instead of worshipping the Creator himself, it has worshipped aspects of his creation. Humanity has fallen away radically and totally from what God intended for it. Even those who feel that they stand above such things are in reality contaminated by them. They have simply failed to realise how deeply their judgments and motives are affected by sin. Everyone, irrespective of whether they are Jews or Gentiles, has fallen short of the glory of God (2:1–11).

2:1–29 God's Righteous Judgment Paul lays emphasis on one particular theme at this point. It is clear that he is concerned to counter the idea that seems to have gained influence among at least some Jews – the idea that the Law of Moses was some kind of charter of national privilege, which exempted Israel from God's judgment. The Gentiles would be condemned by God on account of their sin. But because Israel possessed the Law, she was immune from such judgment. Paul dismisses this kind of argument. If anything, God's judgment will be directed against the Jews first, because they ought to have known better. Circumcision does not ensure acceptance in the sight of God. It is merely an external sign. What really matters is the inward reality of faith and trust in God – something that is demanded of Jews and Gentiles alike (2:12–29).

3:1–20 No One Is Righteous This does not mean that being a Jew is without its good points (3:1–8). What it does mean is that the Jew has no privileged access to God. All, whether Jew or Gentile, are sinners. All, whether Jew or Gentile, need God's forgiveness. Paul assembles an impressive array of biblical citations to bring out the fact that humanity is totally contaminated by sin (3:9–20). The Law of Moses is powerless to deliver from sin. Although it is able to identify sin and raise human consciousness of being sinful, it cannot do anything about what it uncovers. The Law is thus like medical practitioners who have diagnosed a fatal illness, which they are unable to remedy in any way. At least it shatters any illusions we may have. But it cannot improve things.

3:21–31 Righteousness Through Faith Until now. All this has changed through the coming of Jesus Christ. The Law and the Prophets pointed to this great development, in which God's righteousness would be made known outside the limits of the Law. Just as all have sinned, so all will be freely justified by the grace of God. Through faith in

Jesus Christ everyone can share in this righteousness. Jesus Christ was presented by God as 'a sacrifice of atonement' (a term also translated as 'propitiation'). In other words, the death of Christ is the one and only means by which the sin of humanity can be cleansed and forgiven. And just as all have sinned, so all can benefit from the death of Christ.

4:1–25 Abraham Justified by Faith Paul then demonstrates that Abraham himself was 'justified' (that is, put in a right relationship with God) through his faith. The great patriarch was not put in a right relationship with God through circumcision. That came later. That relationship with God was established through Abraham's faith in God's promise to him (Ge 15:6). Circumcision was simply the external sign of that faith. It did not establish that faith, but confirmed something that was already there. The great promise of God to Abraham was made before either circumcision or the Law of Moses were delivered. Thus all who share in the faith of Abraham are the children of Abraham. It is possible for the Gentiles to share Abraham's faith in the promises of God – and all the benefits that result from this faith – without the need to be circumcised, or be bound to the fine details of the Law of Moses. It is Christ's death and resurrection, not external observance of the Law, that constitute the ultimate grounds of relationship with God.

5:1–11 Peace and Joy Therefore, Paul affirms, believers may rejoice in the knowledge that they have been justified by faith (5:1–5). Through faith in God, believers have access to his presence, and the hope, peace and love that can come only through the saving work of Christ on the cross. Even though sinners were powerless to do anything about their situation, God graciously chose to intervene at the right moment. Paul exults in the amazing love of God for sinners. Maybe we could understand why someone might want to give their lives for a very good person. Yet the love of God is shown through Christ giving his life for sinners! Through his death, we now have reconciliation with God (5:6–11).

5:12–21 Death Through Adam, Life Through Christ Having already used Abraham as an example of faith, Paul now explores the relationship between Christ and Adam (5:12–21). In this very helpful comparison, we can see the way in which God chose to reverse the work of Adam through the work of Christ. Adam's disobedience led to sin, condemnation and death. Yet Christ's obedience led to forgiveness, justification, and eternal life. Just as all humanity shares in the sinful state that resulted from Adam's fall, so all those who put their faith in Christ will share in the glorious joy of grace and peace that result from his obedience to the will of his Father.

6:1–14 Dead to Sin, Alive in Christ As a result, believers have died to sin, and risen to new life in Christ (6:1–7). This change, which is symbolised in baptism, does not mean that the resurrection has already taken place. Rather, it means that the believer has 'died to sin' – that is, that the power of sin over the believer has been broken, with the result that the believer can now experience a new life of faith in which it is Christ, rather than sin,

---

Does it matter if I sin since I will be forgiven anyway?

If all Paul has said so far is true – that Christ has taken God's wrath upon himself and paid the price for it at the cross – then surely it doesn't matter if we keep on sinning since that sin is already paid for? And if it's true that 'where sin increased, grace increased all the more' (5:20), then doesn't it follow that if we sin more we will receive more grace? Doesn't Paul's teaching on justification by faith lead to a careless attitude to sin? These are the questions Paul now imagines his readers asking.

To such questions Paul's answer is an unmistakable 'No!' In fact, the Greek words translated 'By no means!' (6:2) are very strong – something like, 'God forbid!' 'We are those who have died to sin; how can we live in it any longer?' Paul continues. And this 'death' was expressed in our baptism (6:3–14). Just as we don't keep the body when someone has died but rather bury it, so we 'buried' our old life in baptism; it simply wasn't needed any more. (Paul's analogy shows he is thinking here of the baptism of converts by immersion.) Burial is the acknowledgment that the past is over. That's what baptism symbolises, Paul says. We buried our old life so we could rise to a new life with Jesus (6:4); so how can we think of returning to it? And to underline his argument he uses two illustrations, one from slavery (6:15–23), and another from marriage (7:1–6).

Becoming a Christian doesn't mean you suddenly stop struggling with sin (7:7–25); but it does mean you recognise it is no longer your friend but your enemy. Sin will not rob you of relationship with God, but it can rob you of intimacy with God and fruitfulness for him.

---

who reigns. Just as Christ was crucified, so the believer's old nature, along with its bondage to sin, has been put to death, in order that a new nature might come to birth. Paul thus assures believers that they may count themselves as 'dead to sin but alive to God in Christ Jesus' (6:8–14). They are no longer under law, but under grace.

6:15–7:25 Slaves to Righteousness; Struggling with Sin
There has thus been a change of allegiance through faith (6:15–23). On account of faith, believers are no longer 'slaves to sin' but are now 'slaves to righteousness'. Instead of being loyal to sin, which leads only to the reward of

death, Christians owe their loyalty to God, who offers the gift of eternal life in Christ. Believers have died to the authority of the law on account of their faith (7:1–6). As a result, they are released from its power only to condemn, so that they can discover the grace offered through the gospel. So there is nothing wrong with the Law. It does not cause sin. It simply exposes the reality and power of sin, and prevents people from lapsing into a false security concerning their own situation and abilities (7:7–12).

Paul then discusses the problem of sin (7:13–25). This passage is difficult to interpret, as it is not clear whether Paul is here referring to his life as a pious Jew

before his conversion, or to his life as a Christian after his conversion. His reference to being 'sold as a slave to sin' (7:14) certainly suggests that he is referring to his life as a non-Christian. However, the use of the present tense throughout this section suggests that Paul is referring to something that was still applicable at the time of writing. The debate is complex, and cannot easily be resolved.

Whatever the answer may be to this question, it is clear that Paul brings out the power of sin, and the utter inability of human nature to break free from its stranglehold. Even if people wanted to break free from sin, they would find that their good intentions were frustrated by sin (7:17–23). So what can be done about this? If we had to rely on our own resources, the answer would be simple: nothing. Yet, as Paul declares, we have not been left on our own. Who will rescue us? God will! Through the death and resurrection of Jesus Christ, the powerful hold of sin has been broken.

8:1–17 *Life Through the Spirit* As a result, the joys of the Christian life are available to believers. There is no condemnation now for believers. They have been set free through Christ. That which the Law could never do, God did through sending Christ to die for sinners. As a result, believers are 'children of God', a fact that is objectively grounded in Christ, and is confirmed by the internal witness of the Holy Spirit (8:1–17). Through faith, they have been adopted into the family of God, and as a result of this, they now share the full inheritance rights of the natural Son of God, Jesus Christ. Christians are thus 'heirs of God and co-heirs with Christ'. This gives them hope, because it affirms that they will share in all that he has already received – whether it is suffering or glory.

8:18–39 *Future Glory; More Than Conquerors* And this glory is worth waiting and suffering for (8:18–27). Paul likens the life of faith to a woman who is about to give birth. She is in pain, but knows that new life will result. All the suffering and pain of the present life will be seen in its proper perspective once believers have been glorified with Christ. Christians can rest assured that God works for their good in all things (8:28–30), even if they do not fully understand what is happening. Believers can know that there is nothing in all of creation or the world to come that can ever separate them from the wonderful love of God, made known in Christ (8:31–39).

ROMANS 9:1–11:36
The Problem of the Rejection of Israel

Having now presented the main themes of the gospel, Paul turns to deal with a difficult question that has been hinted at, but not fully dealt with, in what he has said so far. Why did Israel reject the Messiah? And why did Israel – Paul's own people – find themselves rejected by God? This question will preoccupy Paul for a substantial portion of the letter (9:1–11:36). As we prepare to explore this section of the letter, it must be understood that Paul is not dealing specifically with the issue of predestination (the question of God deciding human happiness or misery in advance, from eternity). This word is not used once throughout this section. The

key question that Paul is wrestling with relates to God's purpose in raising up Israel as the bearer of his good news – and then seeming to reject Israel once the Messiah arrived. Why did this happen?

The answer Paul gives is complex, and needs to be considered carefully. Paul's mood should also be noted: he is clearly sorrowful and distressed over this issue, and greatly wishes that his own people will be saved. After all, they have received God's covenants and law, and the Messiah has emerged from within their ranks (9:1–5). Yet, being a physical descendant of Abraham does not guarantee being in a right relationship with God (9:6–18). As Paul puts it, 'not all who are descended from Israel are Israel'.

Yet God has raised up, guided and preserved Israel because he intends to use her as a means of bringing knowledge of himself to all nations. This has been the reason for bringing her into being in the first place. Israel is, from beginning to end, the creation and possession of God. And just as a potter has the right to rework his creation to ensure that it does what he intended it to, so God is entitled to refashion Israel to ensure that his intended objectives are met (9:19–29). The use of the image of the potter is significant (9:21). The same image was used by Jeremiah (Jer 18:6) to make sense of the way in which God was dealing with Jerusalem at the time of the Babylonian invasion.

9:30–10:21 Israel's Unbelief Yet Israel decided to trust in her own righteousness, based on possession of the Law (10:1–21). Rather than submit to the righteousness of God – which, for Paul, comes through the gospel – she chose to rely on the Law, unaware that Christ was the ultimate culmination of that Law (10:4). Yet Israel was meant to proclaim this righteousness of God to the world – and if Israel failed to proclaim it, how was anyone going to get to hear about it? Israel knew about the coming of Christ – but she did nothing to make this known (10:14–15). As a result, this good news has been entrusted to the Gentiles, in fulfilment of Old Testament prophecy.

11:1–10 The Remnant of Israel Yet this does not mean that God has rejected each and every member of Israel (11:1–36). Paul is absolutely clear that the gospel is offered to Jew and Gentile, without distinction. Individual Jews, like individual Gentiles, can have access to God through faith, on account of what Christ has done. Yet being a member of Israel in itself does not ensure this access. It is faith, not nationality or the external sign of circumcision, that matters. In developing this point, Paul draws on the idea of a 'remnant' within Israel, an idea that is illustrated by the seven thousand Israelites at the time of Elijah who did not worship Baal (see 1Ki 19). Despite the rejection of Christ by the leaders and institutions of Israel, many Jews have come to faith in Christ. They are the new faithful remnant.

11:11–36 The Model of an Olive Tree So what, then, is the relation between Jew and Gentile? Paul uses the model of an olive tree, onto which new branches have been grafted. The stump of the tree is Israel, and the grafted branches the

Gentiles. They have been brought into Israel on account of their faith. The church is thus what Israel was meant to be – the community of faithful people who, like Abraham, trust in the promises of God, and who will proclaim this news to the world. The church is built on the foundation of God's saving work and revelation in and through the history of Israel. Without this preparation in the history of Israel, there would be no church – and so Gentiles owe their salvation to God's work in and through the Jewish people. There can be no place for Jewish nationalism or Gentile hostility towards the Jews within the church. Yet God's work has now reached far outside the narrow confines of

God spoke to them through Romans
Paul's letter to the Romans has had a profound effect on individuals and through them the church and the whole world.

Augustine
In the summer of 386, Augustine sat in a friend's garden in Milan. He was in tears because he lacked the will to break with the old life and begin the new. He heard some children next door playing, singing a song that included the words 'Pick up and read.' He reached for the nearest book – a New Testament, which lay open at a passage from Paul's letter to the Romans. On reading the passage, he said, 'A clear light flooded my heart, and all the darkness of doubt vanished away.' He became a great leader of the church and one of its most influential thinkers.

Martin Luther
In 1513, Martin Luther, an Augustinian monk and a professor at Wittenberg University, became deeply concerned about his own salvation. He thought deeply about Romans: 'Night and day I studied until I grasped the truth – what being right with God really means. It is when in his loving kindness and great mercy, God makes us right with himself through our faith,' he said. 'From that moment I felt reborn – as if I had gone through an open door into heaven.' Luther was one of the great architects of the Reformation.

John Wesley
One day in 1738, Luther's introduction to Romans was being read at a meeting in London. It was 24 May and about 8.45 in the evening. A young man in the audience, John Wesley, was very interested. The words from Luther were describing how God changes our hearts when we put our trust in Jesus Christ. John found his heart 'strangely warmed'. He wrote, 'I felt I did trust in Christ, Christ alone for salvation. An assurance was given me that he had taken *my* sins and saved *me* from the law of sin and death.' John Wesley was able to speak to many and bring many to faith in Jesus Christ.

Judaism, which has become a religion of national privilege.

ROMANS 12:1–15:14
Practical Advice

12:1–21 *Living Sacrifices* Having dealt with this theoretical issue, which was a live concern in the church at Rome as it was elsewhere in the churches, Paul turns to give practical advice to his fellow believers at Rome. In the light of their death to sin through faith, he urges them not to be conformed to the world, but to be transformed and renewed (12:1–3). Paul then develops the qualities he particularly expects to find in believers. These include an awareness of the various roles played by individual Christians in the life of the church (12:4–8), and the showing of love in many different aspects of the Christian life (12:9–21).

13:1–14 *Submission to the Authorities* One question that was particularly important to the church at Rome was the relation between believers and the secular power. How should Christians respond to a non-Christian government? Rome was the centre of the empire, and it was therefore natural that believers in the city would come face to face with this issue in their everyday lives. Paul's advice remains of fundamental importance: believers should submit to the governing authorities, in that these have been established by God to bring order to his world (13:1–7).

However, it is clear that Paul assumes that the secular government will remain within its allocated sphere of authority. What happens if the government should exceed that authority, by rebelling against God and persecuting his people? Paul does not deal with this question. However, the implication of his line of thought would suggest that by doing this, the government would have exceeded its limits, and could no longer expect Christians to respect or obey it.

Following Jesus Christ, Paul reaffirms the importance of the Law, and its summary in terms of loving neighbours as oneself (13:8–14; see also Mt 19:19; Mk 12:31; Lk 10:27). He also affirms that the future Christian hope gives a new meaning to life in the present. Believers are walking in the dark, in the sure knowledge that the day of salvation is nearer than when they first believed. This hope gives them confidence as they travel in the life of faith, knowing that the day of eternal life is at hand. (A similar point is made by many of the gospel parables relating to the theme of watching.)

14:1–15:13 *The Weak and the Strong* Paul then turns to deal with the question of giving offence to other believers, whose faith may be weaker. This continues to be an important issue today for many Christians. What, Paul asks, can be said to someone who, for example, refuses to eat meat? The basic lines of his argument can be set out as follows, and remain of vital importance in the life of the church. All food is clean, so there is no need for anyone to refuse to eat meat or drink wine on the grounds of faith. However, some do refuse to eat or drink such items on the grounds of conscience. So why destroy the work of God for the sake of such a trivial issue? If their faith is so weak that they feel the need for such scruples, those whose faith is strong must respect the

views of those whose faith is weaker. Those who are strong in their faith must bear with the failings of those who are weak. As a result, Christians must learn to accept and respect one another, in order that God's work may be advanced.

15:14–16:27 Conclusion The letter then draws to a close. Paul sets forth his own understanding of his special mission to the Gentiles (15:14–22), and the results of his ministry in the eastern Mediterranean region. He declares his hope to be able to visit the church at Rome, in order to share in their fellowship (15:23–33). He then commends the many Christians whom he knows (16:1–23). What is especially noticeable about this impressive list of individuals is how many of them are women. One of them (Junia: 16:7) may even be described as an apostle, suggesting that she was recognised as a preacher of the gospel in the region, although the Greek text is ambivalent at this point. The letter ends with a doxology – or exclamation of praise – in which Paul gives thanks to God for revealing his gospel to all nations (16:25–27).

1 CORINTHIANS

Corinth was one of the most important cities of Greece, often being estimated as having a population of more than 500,000 people. It was a leading seaport and commercial centre, and was evangelised by Paul during his third missionary journey. The letter is written from the city of Ephesus in Asia Minor, and probably dates from some point before the feast of Pentecost in AD 55. It was prompted by a number of factors, including a visit from some prominent members of the Corinthian church, and a letter brought by some other Corinthian visitors requesting guidance on a number of points. Although the resulting Pauline letter is primarily pastoral in its orientation, it includes a vigorous defence of some of the central themes of the gospel.

1:1–9 Greetings and Thanksgiving The letter opens with Paul sending his greetings to his Christian brothers and sisters in Corinth (1:1–3), followed by a strong statement of the Christian hope of resurrection, based on the total faithfulness of God (1:4–9). Here, as elsewhere, we are reminded that the faith of believers is securely grounded in a relationship with a trustworthy and faithful God.

1:10–17 Divisions in the Church Immediately, Paul proceeds to one of his chief causes for concern – the divisions that are emerging at Corinth. The Greeks were notorious for forming factions. While this made Greek politics much more interesting than they otherwise might have been, it was potentially disastrous in the case of the church. The factions seemed to centre on

What is an apostle?

The Greek for 'apostle' originally simply meant 'sent one' or 'messenger'; but the New Testament lifts the role to a higher status. Some scholars think its roots lie in the rabbinic šālîaḥ (Hebrew for 'messenger'), an agent authorised to act on behalf of the one who sent him. However it is in the ministry of Jesus that we find its most likely roots. After all, Jesus often spoke of being sent from the Father (Mt 10:40; Mk 9:37; Lk 4:43; Jn 5:36), and Hebrews describes him as 'our apostle' (Heb 3:1). And Jesus in turn sent his disciples (Mk 3:14–15; Jn 20:21). At the heart of the concept is this idea of being sent with authority to perform a mission.

The term was used in several ways, summarised in 15:5–9, where Paul speaks of Jesus appearing to 'Cephas [Peter] . . . the Twelve . . . James . . . all the apostles, and last of all he appeared to me . . . For I am the least of the apostles.' This shows that 'the apostles' meant not just 'the Twelve' but several others, including Paul – what he calls 'apostles of Christ' (1Co 1:1; 1Th 2:6), those commissioned by Christ himself (in Paul's case, in a post-ascension appearance) and therefore carrying special authority. Such apostles were the foundation of the church (1Co 12:28).

But the term also had a wider use. Other 'apostles' are mentioned, like Epaphroditus, the messenger (literally, 'apostle') of the Philippian church (Php 2:25); Barnabas, an apostle alongside Paul (Gal 2:8–9); James the brother of Jesus (Gal 1:19); Andronicus and Junia (Ro 16:7). Even Paul's warning about 'false apostles' (2Co 11:13) shows there must have been more than twelve or there would have been no problem identifying them. In this wider sense – those sent to plant churches or work between churches – the term can clearly still apply today.

personalities: Paul here notes three – himself, Apollos (see Acts 18:24–28) and Cephas (another name for Peter, and possibly referring to Christians who placed a particular emphasis on their Jewish heritage). Paul, as one of the personalities on which this personality cult has come to centre, is outraged. The gospel must not be divided by its human agents. There is a real danger that the cross of Christ will be emptied of its power as a result.

1:18–2:16 Christ the Wisdom and Power of God
This thought leads Paul directly into a major discussion of the place of the cross in the Christian life (1:18–2:5). Paul points out how the cross lays down a challenge to human ideas of wisdom and power. The Jews insisted on looking for signs of some sort, and the Greeks demanded wisdom. But in the end, neither got what they were looking for. For Paul, Christianity is all about 'Christ crucified' – a phrase that can mean either 'the crucified person of Jesus Christ' or 'a crucified Messiah'. The second interpretation of the phrase is likely, as it represents a total contradiction of the Jewish belief that the Messiah would be a figure of triumph, which was totally contradicted by the cross.

For Paul, human standards of wisdom – such as those associated with the

Greeks – are overturned by the cross. Christian believers need not worry when they are, by worldly standards, weak or foolish. They are weak and foolish only when judged by the world. In the light of the cross, they are strong and wise. God has chosen what is weak and lowly in the sight of the world, in order to show up the total folly of worldly standards.

Paul also makes the important point that the gospel does not rest on human wisdom, but on the power of God. This means that the resilience and strength of the gospel do not lie in the eloquence of its preachers, but in the power of the God who upholds and sustains both the gospel and those who proclaim it (2:1–5). In the end, true wisdom comes only from God, through the Holy Spirit. Wisdom is something that God reveals, rather than something that human beings can hope to find for themselves (2:6–16). This emphasis on the importance of the Holy Spirit will occur many times during this letter, and is of major importance to Paul. But further exposition of the role of the Holy Spirit will have to wait until later in the letter. Paul now returns to the divisions that have opened up within the Corinthian church.

3:1–4:21 On Divisions in the Church One of the problems faced by the church at Corinth was its spiritual immaturity. It was a young church, perhaps only a few years old. As a result, Paul was able to offer them only some Christian basics, rather than a full exposition of the gospel (3:1–2). Just as a newborn child cannot cope with solid food, and relies on milk, so Paul found that he could offer the Corinthians only milk rather than solid food. They were not mature enough to cope with anything else. And this immaturity is reflected in the carrying over of worldly disputes and attitudes into the church. Factions are simply the transference of worldly conflicts to the church (3:3–4).

But why is this being allowed to happen? Paul and Apollos, two centres of such personality cults, have each had different roles to play in establishing the church at Corinth. Initially, the imagery is that of growing seeds. Paul got things going (Acts 18:4–11); Apollos followed things up (Acts 18:24–28). Yet they were both engaged in the same overall task. God is the one who really matters. They were just working in the background (3:5–9). So why don't the Corinthians realise this? The imagery now shifts from seeds to houses. The Christian life is ultimately grounded in Christ himself. Christ is the only foundation on which the life of faith can be built (3:10–15).

Continuing this theme of Christians as 'buildings', Paul affirms that individual believers are temples of God, and that the Holy Spirit dwells within them individually (3:16–23). One of the many important points made by this comparison is that the relationship with God established by conversion changes people. It is not simply something external, but a transforming relationship in which God comes to dwell within his people.

Paul now moves on to chasten gently the Corinthian church for its failure to respond fully and faithfully to the gospel that had been entrusted to it (4:1–21). Paul has no intention of humiliating his Corinthian brothers and sisters. Nevertheless, he feels that he must

somehow draw their attention to these issues. They did not learn to behave in this way from him. In each case, the problems that arise result directly from the importation of secular values into the church.

5:1–6:20 Sexual Immorality Paul begins by addressing the growth of sexual immorality within the Corinthian church (5:1–13). The church has become even worse than the world in some respects. Paul makes it clear that this kind of behaviour is not to be tolerated. While believers have to live in the world, despite its corruption, they should make every effort to avoid being contaminated by those who are clearly sexually immoral. Paul returns to this theme a few paragraphs later (6:9–20), where he identifies the theological basis of this immorality. Some Corinthian believers clearly believe that their faith frees them from any moral obligations. In response, Paul makes the fundamental point that they are not totally at liberty. They have been bought at a price, and are therefore required to be obedient to their master, who is none other than God himself.

6:1–8 Lawsuits Among Believers Paul then notes with despair that the secular obsession with lawsuits has found its way into the church (6:1–8). Can they not sort things out for themselves, without parading their differences in front of unbelievers? It is clear that Paul believes this to be an appalling witness to the world.

7:1–40 Marriage The issue of marriage then arises. Paul seems to open this discussion by quoting from a letter the Corinthians have written to him. The phrase 'It is good for a man not to have sexual relations with a woman' seems to be quoted by Paul, rather than endorsed by him. Paul is known to have been strongly in favour of marriage (see Eph 5:22–33; Col 3:18–19); indeed, at one point he even identifies the refusal to marry as a kind of heresy (1Ti 4:1–3). The phrase should thus probably be included in quotation marks, along with other quotations or slogans accepted at Corinth (such as at 6:12–13). In what follows, Paul offers a strong defence both of marriage and of full sexual relations within marriage. Marriage is not a sin, and nobody should be discouraged from marrying. Each believer must work out what is best for him or her, in order that they may serve the Lord as effectively and wholeheartedly as possible.

8:1–13 Food Sacrificed to Idols Paul then deals with an issue that was an issue for many believers in Greek and Roman cities: should food that has been offered to idols be avoided? At least twelve pagan temples were known to have been in existence around this time, although not all may have been used for worship of this kind. Paul's answer is simple. There is no problem about the food. The problem lies with the believer who has a scrupulous conscience over this issue. Although believers may eat such food without anxiety, they must respect the consciences of weaker believers, who may find this scandalising. Faith is too precious a gift to risk compromising in this manner. Although there is nothing wrong with eating such food, it should not be eaten if doing so will give offence to other believers.

9:1–11:1 *Confidence in the Christian Life; the Lord's Supper* After discussing the rights and responsibilities of apostleship, Paul turns to the theme of confidence in the Christian life (10:1–11:1). There is no room for complacency of any kind, he warns. Israel was complacent during the period of wilderness warnings – and look at what happened to her as a result. The grace of God is something that must never be taken for granted. It must not be imposed upon. However, Paul couples this warning with an assurance: although God will break down human pride, he will do so in such a way that takes account of how much each believer can bear, and allow a way out for those who need it (10:11–13).

Paul is particularly concerned about the abuse of the Lord's Supper (10:14–22) and abuses of Christian freedom (10:23–11:1). In response to the latter, he emphasises the importance of responsibility towards others. The Christian life is corporate, and this means that individual believers must pay attention to the scruples and concerns of others – a principle that has already been stated clearly in dealing with the question of meat offered to idols.

11:2–16 *Propriety in Worship* Having mentioned the Lord's Supper, Paul now turns to deal with issues of worship in general. This section offers a number of problems to its readers, which need to be noted. First, Paul lays down that women should cover their heads during public worship (11:2–16). The major question that arises here is this: Is Paul laying down a local regulation for the church at Corinth around AD 55, or a permanent regulation for the entire Christian church in every time and place? Most interpreters of this passage believe that Paul is laying down a local rule, in response to local circumstances. Similarly, Paul's stipulations about the length of hair are widely regarded as a response to local factors at Corinth, and probably reflect the fact that long hair in a man and short hair in a woman were regarded as a sign of homosexuality – something Paul would not tolerate within his church. In this, Paul declares that he is simply following common practice.

11:17–34 *The Lord's Supper* Paul then provides further explanation concerning the Lord's Supper. Concerned that this meal is being treated with disrespect, Paul explains why it was instituted in the first place. He wishes to pass on what he has received (11:23), using language which clearly implies that Paul is passing on a solemn and unalterable practice or belief, which goes back to Jesus Christ himself. The words Paul quotes bear a strong similarity to those used by Jesus Christ himself at the Last Supper (see Lk 22:17–20). Eating the bread and drinking the wine are reminders of the saving death of Christ, and must not be taken lightly. In particular, there is a need for believers to examine themselves, to ensure that they do not come under judgment.

12:1–11 *Spiritual Gifts* Paul now turns to deal with the charismatic aspects of worship, dealing specifically with the role of the Holy Spirit. The gift of the Holy Spirit is given for the good and upbuilding of the church as a whole. The one Spirit works in many ways, depending on the individual in question. Each of these

ways is equally valid. The important thing is that the 'manifestations of the Spirit' lead to the common good, not to individual gratification.

12:12–31 *One Body, Many Parts* Paul stresses this point through his analogy of the church as a body. Just as a human body has many parts, each with different functions, so the church has many members, each with their different roles to play. They are all needed. Their interdependence is considerable, with the result that when one member suffers, all suffer. There is no room for arrogance within the body, nor can one member declare that others are not required.

Having established this general point, Paul then turns to the specific issue of the 'manifestations of the Spirit'. Some are entrusted with the spiritual gift (or 'gift of the Spirit' – the Greek can be translated both ways) of prophecy, others of teaching, others of being an apostle, and so on. All are necessary for the good of the church. Not everyone speaks in tongues – but so what? The important point is that some do, and thus contribute to the life of the church as a whole. Paul thus lays the foundation for a theology which acknowledges the great diversity of the gifts of the Spirit, without declaring that any one is of supreme importance, or that any can be dispensed with as unnecessary.

13:1–13 *Love* Yet Paul does draw attention to one aspect of the work of the Spirit that he regards as being of vital importance to the life of the church – love. Paul selects four spiritual gifts (13:1–3), and makes the point that all are without real value unless they are accompanied by love. Yet love is not to be thought of as a gift of the Spirit. More strictly, it is a fruit of the Spirit (Gal 5:22) – something that is the natural result of the Spirit's presence in the life of a believer. Not all are given the gift of speaking in tongues – but all ought to show the fruit of love. The need for some of the gifts of the Spirit will pass away. However, love will remain for ever. Long after prophecy has ceased and people have stopped speaking in tongues, love will continue to be of vital importance within the church.

14:1–40 *Gifts of Prophecy and Tongues and Orderly Worship* Having shown the importance of love, Paul returns to the theme of the gifts of the Spirit in more detail (14:1–39). (Paul perhaps implied that the Corinthians had many gifts of the Spirit, but lacked love.) While affirming the importance of speaking in tongues and prophecy, Paul expresses some anxieties about the manner in which these take place at Corinth. The issue of good order in public worship emerges as being of major importance, not least on account of the impression that speaking in tongues might create on outsiders or visitors. There is a need to speak in words that can be understood. Otherwise, the church will not be built up in faith. Everything must be done in a fitting and orderly way (14:40).

One aspect of Paul's teaching on public worship has attracted special attention – the requirement that women should be silent in worship, and ask their husbands to explain things they don't understand when they get home (14:33–40). Once more, this seems to be a local rule reflecting local conditions. Paul's concern

is clearly for order in worship, which would be disrupted by talking within the congregation. Scholars have suggested that the Corinthian congregation would have included many well-educated men, but few educated woman. The need for the women to have things explained to them by their husbands should therefore be seen as specific to this congregation, rather than a universal comment on the ability of women to understand.

15:1–58 The Resurrection of Christ But such issues are put in perspective when Paul turns to address his major concern at Corinth – the denial of the resurrection of Christ (15:1–58). Using very solemn language, Paul declares that the resurrection is a non-negotiable element of the Christian faith. The central affirmation of the Christian faith is that Christ died for our sins, and was then raised again (15:1–4). Paul makes the

The significance of the resurrection

Christians believe that the resurrection of Jesus Christ from the dead is the foundation of the Christian faith. According to Chapter 15, if Christ has not been raised from the dead, then Christian preaching and the Christian faith are without value; Christians are misrepresenting God; Christ's death is in vain and has no significance; Christians who have died have perished and are still 'in their sins'; and Christians are in fact deluded.

But if the resurrection did take place, then the opposite conclusions follow: Christian preaching and the Christian faith have meaning; Christians are accurately representing God; there is a resurrection for Christians who have died, and being a Christian is seen as a privilege.

The resurrection of Jesus Christ does the following:

- *It shows that Jesus is God.* It proves that Christ's claims to be God are true.
- *It shows that Christ's death on the cross was an effective sacrifice for sin*, and that his death was accepted as a complete atonement for sin.
- *It showed God's power over evil.* Jesus Christ stripped the spiritual powers of their authority, 'triumphing over them by the cross' (Col 2:15). In his resurrection Jesus conquered Satan and his forces.
- *It points the way to the resurrection of Christians.* Jesus Christ is described as the first one of all those who will be raised from death to life again.

For Christians, the resurrection has relevance for present experience. Because Jesus was resurrected, he is alive today and can be known personally. Christians are those who 'want to know Christ . . . [and] the power of his resurrection' (Php 3:10). For Paul, the resurrection is the basis for a changed perspective on life: 'Since, then, you have been raised with Christ, set your hearts on things above, where Christ is, seated at the right hand of God. Set your minds on things above, not on earthly things' (Col 3:1–2).

point that this was a public event, to which there were many witnesses, some of whom are still living at the time he is writing.

And even he, Paul, can testify to the reality of the resurrection (15:5–7). No matter which of the apostles people ask, they will get the same answer: Christ has been raised from the dead. And the Corinthians accepted this as well, to start with (15:8–11).

But now some of them are denying the resurrection of Christ. But why? Not only is the witness to that event highly reliable, as Paul has just shown. Without it, the Christian faith makes no sense (15:12–19). The whole Christian hope would be lacking in any foundation. Without the resurrection, there is no hope of eternal life and no forgiveness of sins (see Ro 4:24–25). An 'eat, drink and be merry for tomorrow we die' attitude would be the only realistic approach. Yet the reality is totally different: Christ has been raised from the dead. There can be and need be no doubt about this. And because Christ has been raised, believers will be raised as well. Paul uses the term 'firstfruits' (15:20) to refer to Christ's resurrection. In other words, Christ is the first in the great resurrection harvest, which will include all believers.

Having vigorously defended the reality of the resurrection, Paul then moves on to discuss the nature of the resurrection body of believers (15:35–58). The point that Paul is making in this difficult passage is that there is a direct connection between earthly and resurrection bodies, even though they will be totally different. The seed that dies in the ground gives rise to a plant that looks nothing like the seed – yet there is a direct link between seed and plant. In the same way, the death of the natural body will give way to the resurrection body, which need look nothing like the present body. Yet the connection remains!

But this kind of speculation has limited importance for Paul. The vitally important thing is that the resurrection of Christ *did* occur, and that the believers' resurrection *will* occur. The Christian life may be lived in this secure and certain hope of resurrection. Christians know that God has given them the victory over sin and death through Jesus Christ. And knowing that, they may serve him with all their abilities.

16:1–18 Conclusion Finally, Paul brings his letter to an end by asking his readers to contribute to the churches at Jerusalem (16:1–4), and making a few personal requests relating to his future missionary plans (16:5–18). In the course of these requests, he mentions by name those who have supported and assisted him in his missionary tasks. Finally, Paul passes on greetings from the churches in the region of Asia (that is, the area around Ephesus). It is clear that many of these were house churches, including that which met in the house of Aquila and Priscilla (16:19–20).

The letter probably ended with Paul adding a few lines in his own handwriting. The bulk of the letter would have been written by a professional secretary or scribe. Now Paul added some items in his own hand (16:21–24). These final words look ahead with passionate longing for the coming of the Lord, as he commends his dear brothers and sisters to the love and grace of their common Saviour and Lord, Jesus Christ.

2 CORINTHIANS

Paul's second letter to the church at Corinth was written at some point late in AD 55, before winter had finally set in. The letter was written from Macedonia, the region to the north of the Roman province of Achaia (in which both Corinth and Athens were located). The mood of the letter is sombre, and it is clear that things have not improved all that much at Corinth since Paul's first letter of about six months earlier. Perhaps some of the difficulties noted in that first letter have been sorted out. Now, new problems have arisen in their place.

1:3–11 The God of All Comfort The letter opens with greetings to his readers (1:1–3), which Paul clearly expects to include Christians in the whole region of Achaia, rather than Corinth itself. The theme which dominates the early verses of the letter is that of the consolation God offers to believers (1:4–7). Terms such as 'compassion' and 'comfort' are used to refer to the deep sense of peace that believers are able to experience, through knowing God's consoling presence in the midst of suffering. For Paul himself has been through a very difficult time (1:8–11). Although he does not identify the hardships he has experienced, it is clear that he expects his readers to have heard at least something about them.

1:12–2:17 Paul's Change of Plans He now turns to deal with a distressing accusation that is being made against him by some at Corinth – that of a lack of sincerity towards the Corinthian church, through his cancellation of a planned visit to the city (1:12–2:11). Paul makes clear that it was only after great thought that he had cancelled this visit. He wished to spare the church from any pain such a visit might bring, on account of the criticisms

he might have been obliged to make. However, since the church itself has taken action against his critics, he considers the incident closed. In any case, Paul clearly regards the hand of God as having been on his travel plans (2:12–17), just as he is aware of the gracious assistance of God at every point in his ministry. He has been given the privilege of preaching the good news of Christ, allowing the fragrance of Christ to be present in the stench of a decaying world.

3:1–18 The New Covenant

Paul now turns to deal with the theme of the joyful privilege of being a minister of the new covenant (3:1–6). The contrast with the old covenant is clear at every point. Although the covenant given through Moses can be said to reflect the glory of God, that of the new covenant exceeds it at every point. The old covenant did not succeed in establishing a right relationship between humanity and God, whereas the new is able to do precisely this (3:7–11). Just as a veil was placed over the scrolls of the Law in synagogues, so the Law placed a veil between the people and God. But now, through Christ, that veil has been removed (3:12–18).

4:1–5:10 Treasures in Jars of Clay

Yet the treasure of the gospel has been entrusted to weak and frail human beings. This is a major theme in this letter – the sufficiency of the grace of God to compensate for the weakness of believers. For Paul, one of the great joys of the gospel is that God has chosen to make known the good news of redemption in Christ through the ministry of ordinary people (4:1–18). The treasure of the gospel has been placed in jars of clay. Even though believers are aware of their weakness and subjected to all kinds of persecution and harassment, they can rest assured that they will be upheld by God himself. In any case, human mortality will eventually give way to immortality, on account of the gospel of grace (5:1–10). The flimsy tent of earthly lives will give way to the solid building of resurrected bodies.

5:11–6:13 The Ministry of Reconciliation

Having dwelt on the weakness and mortality of the ministers of the gospel, Paul now turns to the gospel itself (5:11–21). He declares that on account of the gospel, sinners become a new creation through their conversion. Something happens to transform them. And that transformation has its ground in God himself, who 'was reconciling the world to himself in Christ'. As a result of Christ's work, our sin has been transferred to him, and his righteousness has been transferred to us. And the ministry of proclaiming this good news has been entrusted to believers, who are called on to be 'Christ's ambassadors' in the world. They are 'God's fellow workers' (6:1–2). Paul then documents his own personal hardships once more (6:3–13). He has had to suffer for the gospel. Others must expect to do the same.

6:14–7:1 Do Not Be Yoked with Unbelievers

A brief passage then deals with a practical concern relating to Christian conduct. It is clear that Paul is anxious about the results of believers being 'yoked together with unbelievers'. This could be understood as a specific

Should a Christian marry a non-Christian?

The Bible consistently says that God's people should not marry outside the family of faith. In 6:14 Paul writes, 'Do not be yoked together with unbelievers.' While he was perhaps thinking here of business or religious partnerships, his statement reflects Old Testament teaching that God's people should avoid mixture and remain distinctive, so almost certainly includes the most fundamental of partnerships, marriage.

This is largely common sense. For committed Christians, their relationship with Jesus is the most fundamental aspect of life; yet marrying a non-Christian would mean excluding this from the marriage – hardly a good basis for shared life. Paul had been clear in 1 Corinthians that someone who became a Christian should not divorce their unbelieving spouse but pray for them to be saved (1Co 7:12–16); but this is wholly different from a believer choosing to marry an unbeliever. To do this – even with evangelistic intentions – is to go against God's word. For at the end of 1 Co 7 Paul specifically says that the one criterion governing a Christian's choice of spouse is that 'he must belong to the Lord' (1Co 7:39). This is in line with other biblical commands; for example, just before the Israelites entered the promised land where they would meet many beliefs, Moses commanded them, 'Do not give your daughters to their sons or take their daughters for your sons, for they will turn your children away from following me to serve other gods' (Dt 7:3–4). This same message was repeated after the return from exile when there were practical pressures to intermarry with unbelievers; yet Ezra and Nehemiah forbade God's people to do so (Ezr 9:12; Ne 13:25).

If Christians are 'the temple of the living God' (2Co 6:16), then the question of marrying a non-Christian should clearly not be an option.

reference to mixed marriages between believers and unbelievers, in line with the prophetic criticism of inter-marriage between Jews and Gentiles. But it is more likely that Paul is concerned about the use of pagans within the church, including in teaching roles. Just as the Old Testament prophets were anxious that pagan practices would contaminate Israel's faith through intermarriage between Jews and pagans (see Ezra 9–10), so Paul is concerned to ensure that Christian faith is not adulterated by paganism in the same way.

7:2–9:15 The Jerusalem Collection It is clear that Paul is concerned that his earlier letter to Corinth may have caused some offence to its readers. If this is the case, he is saddened by the offence given, but nevertheless believes that he was right to raise the issues with them. However, it is clear that Paul believes, to his obvious delight, that the issues which had troubled him earlier have now been resolved (7:2–16). With these issues behind him, he is able to raise once more the question of the collection that he intends to be used to help support the church at Jerusalem. Just as the

Lord Jesus Christ became poor for the sake of believers, so believers ought to give to support the work of ministry elsewhere (8:1–15). Paul declares his intention to take every precaution to ensure that the money is administered properly, and notes that his colleague Titus will visit Corinth presently to oversee matters (8:16–9:5). Paul also makes reference to an unnamed 'brother' (8:22), who may well have been Luke or Barnabas.

Underlying this appeal for money is the belief that Christians throughout the world ought to support each other in every way possible (9:6–15). The theme of stewardship is developed here. Although Paul's concern is to raise money for the Jerusalem collection, the general principles apply throughout the Christian life. God's gifts do not *belong* to those to whom they have been given. They are *entrusted* to them, with the expectation that they will be used. In order for the gospel to be advanced, generous giving and sowing are required of all. As it is God who provides the seed in the first place, believers are simply using God's own gifts in his service. By giving generously in this way, believers are doing two things – meeting the needs of God's people, and giving thanks and glory to God. The implication of Paul's comments seems to be that the Macedonian churches, who were much less wealthy than the Achaian churches, had given generously – so why should the Corinthians not be equally generous?

10:1–11:33 Paul's Defence of His Ministry

The tone of the letter now changes abruptly. The first nine chapters are gentle in character, probably reflecting a growing appreciation of Paul and his ministry within the Corinthian church. But Paul still has opponents, and he now moves to confront them and their criticisms of his ministry. The first accusation he confronts is that he is not 'spiritual' enough to be a true apostle (10:1–6), or that he has an exaggerated sense of his own speaking ability (10:7–11). Paul rejects such criticisms. He will be judged by the effectiveness of his ministry in Corinth and elsewhere, and the extent to which God has been pleased to work through him (10:12–18). There is no room for boasting here. There is, however, a real need to be honest about what God has done in and through his ministry.

Paul then makes the point that he preached the gospel in Corinth without any support from them. Would they have been more persuaded of his apostolic claims if he had lived off their generosity? He was supported by the Macedonian churches while he undertook his evangelistic ministry in Corinth. In no way can he be accused of having exploited the Corinthians (11:1–15). Paul then provides an impressive catalogue of the hardships he has suffered during his missionary journeys (11:16–33). On reading this list of hardships, we realise how little Luke has told us of Paul's personal sacrifices for the sake of the gospel. Luke's account of Paul's evangelistic ministry makes reference to some difficulties, but does not have the detail that Paul provides. Paul's point in this passage is that he has suffered greatly as he exercised his apostolic ministry. So why is he being criticised for claiming to be an apostle?

12:1–10 Paul's Thorn Paul mentions particular hardship – the 'thorn in the flesh'. Paul makes the point that there are some who have something to boast about – like someone who has had a mystical experience of God, being caught up into the heavens. But boasting can lead to arrogance, rather than humility. Paul brings out the importance of humility from his own experience, making reference to the 'thorn'. It is not clear what this 'thorn' actually was. The most likely explanation is that it refers to an illness Paul contracted during the course of his missionary journey, which severely limited his actions. An obvious possibility would be malaria.

But it is the spiritual relevance of the 'thorn', rather than its precise identity, that really matters. It taught Paul to rely on the grace of God, rather than his own strength. It also brought home to him that his own weakness was more than compensated for by the strength of God. Paul heard the Lord speak these words, which summarise these points superbly: 'My grace is sufficient for you, for my power is made perfect in weakness' (12:9).

12:11–13:11 Paul's Concern for the Corinthians Having failed to visit Corinth in the recent past (as we have seen, to the irritation of some in the church: 1:15–2:1), Paul now affirms his intention to visit Corinth for a third time (12:14–21). His ministry will be self-supporting, and will make no demands on the Corinthian church. In a moment of self-disclosure, Paul confesses his anxieties over this forthcoming visit: he might find things at Corinth that would distress him (12:21). Yet, no matter how difficult it may be, Paul is determined to maintain discipline within the church (13:1–10). Challenges to his apostolic authority will not deter him from insisting on the moral responsibilities of believers. Paul can live with challenges to his own personal prestige. However, he will not tolerate violations of Christian conduct.

13:11–14 Final Greetings The letter thus comes to an end on a negative note. Paul's need to express his concern about the church at Corinth leads to the final section of this letter having a critical tone. Yet in his final greeting (13:11–14), Paul affirms the graciousness of God. Despite all human weakness, the grace of God is at work in the churches. And so Paul ends with a form of words that has passed into Christian use down the ages, and is now known simply as 'the grace' (13:14). By using these words in their prayers, Christians today remind themselves of their continuity with that early Christian community in Corinth. Though they lived nearly two thousand years earlier, they share the same Lord and faith as believers today. Every time they use this prayer, Christians affirm that time and space are no barriers to sharing a common faith in Christ.

GALATIANS

Paul's letter to the Galatians dates from some point around AD 53. It is not clear whether the churches in question were clustered in the northern or central area of Galatia, or whether they were based on the southern Galatian cities Paul had visited during his first missionary journey, such as Pisidian Antioch, Iconium and Derbe. Another possibility is that the letter dates from shortly after the Council of Jerusalem (Acts 15), which raised questions very similar to those that Paul addresses in this letter.

1:1–2:10 Paul's Apostleship and the Gospel

The letter opens with a greeting, and an affirmation of Paul's status as an apostle (1:1–2). His apostolic authority does not derive from any human agency, but from a direct commission by the risen Christ – a clear reference to the circumstances surrounding his conversion, to which he will return presently. After a brief statement of some of the great themes of the gospel (1:3–5), including salvation from sin through Christ, Paul turns to the issue that is troubling him. The Galatian churches – churches he had planted himself – are in the process of abandoning the gospel.

Paul insists that anyone who preaches a gospel different from the one he delivered to them is to be ignored (1:6–10). Paul begins by establishing his authority as an apostle, providing details of his conversion. Paul derives the gospel directly and personally from the risen Christ. He is not guilty of repeating some purely human tradition, or of inventing a gospel to suit his own taste. He is being obedient to the same Christ whom he encountered at the moment of his conversion (1:11–12).

For the benefit of those who do not know his personal history, Paul provides a very brief account of his conversion (1:13–24). This provides a summary of the events documented in more detail at

Ac 9:1–31. It is not intended to be exhaustive, but simply to demonstrate that Paul has authority from Christ to preach the gospel in his name, and that this authority is recognised by the other apostles (2:1–10). They acknowledge that Paul has been entrusted with the task of proclaiming the gospel to the Gentiles, just as Peter has the equally important task of preaching the gospel to the Jews. Paul is thus emphatic concerning both the divine foundations of his calling, and its public recognition by the remaining apostles.

2:11–21 Paul Opposes Peter However, he admits to differences with Peter. Paul here gives us an important insight into a real tension within the early church, which has now made its presence felt at Galatia as well. The development Paul is worried about is the emergence of a Judaising party – that is, a group within the church who insist that Gentile believers should obey every aspect of the Law of Moses, including the need to be circumcised. According to Paul, the leading force behind this party is James – not the apostle James, who died in AD 44, but the brother of Jesus Christ who was influential in calling the Council of Jerusalem, and wrote the New Testament letter known by his name.

For Paul, this trend is highly dangerous. If Christians can gain salvation only by the rigorous observance of the Law, what purpose does the death of Christ serve? It is faith in Christ, not the scrupulous and religious keeping of the Law of Moses, that is the basis of salvation. Nobody can be justified (that is, put in a right relationship with God) through keeping the Law. The righteousness on which human salvation depends is not available through the Law, but only through faith in Christ.

3:1–14 Faith or Works of the Law Aware of the importance and sensitivity of this issue, Paul then explores this question in greater detail (3:1–29). The Galatians have fallen into the trap of believing that salvation came by doing works of the Law, or by human achievement. So what has happened to faith? Did the gift of the Holy Spirit ever come through keeping the Law? Paul then makes an appeal to the example of Abraham to make his point.

Paul argues that Abraham was 'justified' (that is, put in a right relationship with God) through his faith (3:6–18). The great patriarch was not put in a right relationship with God through circumcision. That came later. That relationship with God was established through Abraham's faith in God's promise to him (Ge 15:6). Circumcision was simply the external sign of that faith. It did not establish that faith, but confirmed something that was already there. Nor does the Law, or any aspect of it, abolish the promises God had already made. The promise to Abraham and his seed – which includes believers – remains valid, even after the introduction of the Law.

So the basic point is that the promise of God to Abraham was made before either circumcision or the Law of Moses was delivered. Thus all who share in the faith of Abraham are the children of Abraham. It is possible for the Gentiles to share Abraham's faith in the promises of God – and all the benefits that result from this faith – without the need to be

circumcised, or be bound to the fine details of the Law of Moses. It is Christ's death and resurrection, not external observance of the Law, that constitute the ultimate grounds of relationship with God. Paul clinches his case by citing from the prophet Habakkuk (Hab 2:4), who declares that the righteous shall live by faith.

Yet in the middle of this detailed analysis of the relation between the Law, the promise and faith, we find an important interpretation of the meaning of the death of Christ (3:10–14). Paul notes that the Law declares that everyone who dies on a tree – a category that includes execution by crucifixion – is cursed (Dt 21:23). Yet, as the resurrection makes clear, Christ did not die under a curse. Christ therefore became a curse 'for us' (3:13). In other words, the curse that affected the cross did not relate to Christ himself, but to believers, in that Christ chose to bear their curse for them. The guilt of sin was thus assumed by Christ himself on the cross.

3:15–25 The Law and the Promise

So what purpose did the Law serve? Paul is clear that the Law had a positive role to play. The whole world, according to Scripture, is held captive to sin, preventing anyone from achieving righteousness. But the Law was able to point ahead to the coming of Christ, who would be the means by which deliverance from sin would finally be achieved. The Law was thus like a guardian, teacher or mentor, who took charge until the coming of the gospel. But now that faith has finally come, the Law need no longer have this function.

3:26–4:7 Children of God

So what, then, does faith achieve? Paul has already emphasised that the righteousness that puts believers in a right relationship with God (which is the basic meaning of the word 'justification') comes only through faith. But what are its other benefits? Paul now identifies one of the many blessings faith brings (3:26–4:7). Faith in Christ gives believers the status of being children of God. As a result of this new status in Christ, all other differences are totally overshadowed. They are not abolished. They are just seen in their proper light. Differences of nationality, social status or gender are seen to be of no ultimate significance. Believers remain different from one another – but those differences are seen to be unimportant in relation to issues of salvation or Christian living.

As a result of being sons of God, believers are in full possession of all the legal rights of sonship – including both liberty and inheritance rights. The Holy Spirit confirms this, allowing believers to refer to God as 'Abba' – a remarkably intimate term for a father, reflecting the close relationship between the believer and God.

4:8–5:15 Freedom in Christ

Yet the Galatians want to squander these privileges. They want to revert to being slaves to the dictates of the Law of Moses, rather than exulting in the glorious liberty of the gospel (4:8–20). Why should the fine detail of Jewish regulations get in the way of Christian living? Why should believers be obliged to observe special Jewish festivals and regulations? Paul confesses himself to be bewildered by their lapse into some form

of legalism. Who wants to be a slave, when you can be a child? Paul illustrates this point by an exposition of Ge 16:1–16 and Ge 21:2–5, which, although difficult to follow, makes the point that there is no need for believers to lapse back into slavery, when they have the right to the privileges of sonship (4:21–31).

Paul thus declares that Christ has come in order to liberate believers. They have been set free, and must never allow themselves to be lured back into slavery (5:1–15). If anyone feels that they must be circumcised, then they are under obligation to the Law in its totality – and Christ might as well not have come, as far as they are concerned. The issue is that of freedom. This does not mean a freedom to indulge in sin, but rather a freedom to love without limits. As Paul puts it, the entire Law can be summarised in terms of love.

5:16–6:10 Life by the Spirit Yet this love does not rest upon legalism. Believers are moved by the work of the Spirit to love others (5:16–26). The command to love is necessary, as an objective statement of what it means to be a Christian. Yet the basic motivation to love in this way is subjective, arising through the renewing work of the Holy Spirit within believers. Just as the sinful nature naturally leads to all kinds of immorality, so the Spirit naturally leads to love, joy, peace, forbearance, kindness, goodness, faithfulness, gentleness and self-control. Paul refers to these as 'the fruit of the Spirit', meaning that they will arise naturally in the life of faith, just as fruit grows on a tree. The old sinful nature has been put to death on the cross. Now, believers are able to come to life, through the renewing work of the Spirit.

Paul then carefully explains how these principles will work out in the Christian life (6:1–10). Throughout Paul's letters, we find theology being used as the basis of ethics and pastoral care. Paul's emphasis on the need for believers to lead loving lives is grounded on the belief that the Spirit of the risen Christ will assist and empower believers. They will not be acting on their own!

6:11–18 Not Circumcision but a New Creation Finally, Paul brings this letter to an end. The closing sections are written in his own handwriting. The rest of the letter would have been written by a professional scribe. In these concluding remarks, he again makes the point that circumcision is useless. The important thing is to experience the new creation that comes only through faith in Christ. And, rejoicing in this thought, he commits the Galatian believers to the care of the Lord Jesus Christ.

EPHESIANS

Ephesus was the chief city of the region of Asia Minor, and the scene of some of Paul's most difficult evangelistic work. This letter does not have the usual specific greetings that are customary in Paul's letters. This has led some scholars to conclude that the letter was meant to be circulated throughout the churches of the region, rather than addressed to any one congregation. Even the specific reference to Ephesus (1:1) is omitted by many manuscript versions of the text.

The letter does not deal directly with any specific false teaching, which further suggests that the letter was intended to circulate throughout the churches of Asia Minor, rather than deal with the specific problems of any one congregation. It is difficult to date the letter precisely, due to the lack of personal details that are usually found in Paul's letters. However, a date in the early 60s would fit in with what we know of Paul's movements and situation at this time.

1:1–14 *Spiritual Blessings in Christ* The letter opens with an affirmation of Paul's credentials as an apostle (1:1–2), followed by a remarkably powerful statement of the glory of the risen Christ (1:3–14). Paul declares that believers have been chosen from the foundation of the world to be adopted as sons of God, through the death and resurrection of Jesus Christ. God's purposes have been made known through Jesus Christ, so that believers might know what God intends for them. And their election is sealed – that is, confirmed – by the indwelling of the Holy Spirit.

Paul uses this image to bring out the fact that the presence of the Holy Spirit represents God's seal of ownership on believers. But the Spirit is more than this; he is also a 'deposit', which guarantees inheritance of salvation. Paul here uses what seems to have been a commercial or trading term, meaning 'an initial payment that secures possession of something, with the promise to pay the full amount later'. Paul is thus declaring that the presence of the Spirit in believers' lives is both a sign of God's ownership and sovereignty, and the confirmation of a promise to give more in the future.

The boundless riches of Christ

Certain phrases in Ephesians that concern Christians being rich in Christ:

'. . . the riches of God's grace that he lavished on us' (1:7–8).

'. . . the riches of his glorious inheritance in his holy people' (1:18).

'. . . God, who is rich in mercy, made us alive with Christ even when we were dead in transgressions' (2:4).

'. . . the incomparable riches of his grace, expressed in his kindness to us in Christ Jesus' (2:7).

'. . . the boundless riches of Christ' (3:8).

'I pray that out of his glorious riches he may strengthen you with power . . .' (3:16).

1:15–23 Thanksgiving and Prayer Having rejoiced in the wonder of the gospel, Paul now turns and gives thanks for the believers in the region. Knowing that they already believe in the Lord Jesus Christ, Paul prays that they might come to the full knowledge of his glory in every respect. Paul's language strains to its limits as he tries to express his sense of wonder at the richness of the gospel, which he and his readers have in common. The power of the risen Christ, under whose authority God has placed the present age, is available to believers through faith.

2:1–10 Made Alive in Christ The letter then turns to celebrate the benefits of faith in Christ. Paul rejoices in the fact that the power of the rulers and spirits of the present age have been overcome through the resurrection of Christ. Through faith, believers have been delivered from

the death of sin, and made alive in Christ. They have begun to taste the life of heaven, as they are raised up with Christ in the heavenly realms. By this, Paul does not mean that Christians are physically removed from this world. He is simply pointing to the way in which faith allows believers to experience the presence and power of Christ in a way that anticipates their fullness in heaven. And this great hope does not rest on any human achievement, but on the handiwork of God within believers, as he works to refashion them in his service.

2:11–22 One in Christ God has broken down all barriers, in order that all might find the peace and joy that come only through faith in Christ. There is no place for any human distinctions within the Christian community – for example, between Jew and Gentile. Christ died in order to break down once and for all such

divisions, and to enable all to come to him. Both Jew and Gentile are able to come to God through Christ. In the church, both groups are equally valued and welcome. Both are fellow citizens within the household of God, which has been built securely on the teaching and witness of the prophets and apostles, with Jesus Christ himself as the cornerstone.

3:1–13 Paul the Preacher to the Gentiles Paul continues this theme of the Jews and Gentiles being brought together in one body, as he explains his own special calling to be the bearer of God's good news to the Gentiles (3:1–13). Paul stresses that he was given access to the mystery of the gospel by a special revelation, a clear reference to the events of his conversion, in which he had a personal encounter with the risen Christ. And an integral part of the gospel message is the proclamation that Jews and Gentiles alike can share in and benefit from the promises of Jesus Christ.

For Paul, the fact that he has been singled out in this way does not in any way reflect a special talent or merit on his part. His calling is purely a matter of God's grace. Even though Paul is intensely aware of his own weakness and failings, he is nonetheless called and equipped to be an apostle. He is convinced that his calling was a matter of grace, not human merit. Christians may approach God with confidence on account of his grace and the work of Jesus Christ.

3:14–21 A Prayer for the Ephesians Paul thus prays that his readers might be strengthened through Christ coming to dwell within their hearts in power. At this point, Paul pauses to try to put into words the full extent of the love of Christ for his people, glorying in its width, length, height and depth (3:14–21). Human words cannot adequately express this love and yet it is available in all its fullness to those who put their faith in Jesus Christ. Believers need to discover that God 'is able to do immeasurably more than all we ask or imagine'.

4:1–16 Unity in the Body of Christ They also need to discover their unity. There is only one Lord, only one faith and only one baptism. As a result, there is a need for believers to discover that, beneath any differences, there is a common unity in Christ. Through the death of Christ, God has broken down all divisions. Believers must ensure that they do not create new divisions, and thus undo the work that Christ has already done. Paul emphasises that, despite its different component parts, there is only one church. All its various members, in their different roles, share the same common task of building up the body of Christ (one of Paul's favourite terms for the church), and leading each and every believer to the fullness of Christ. For it is Christ who holds the entire church together, as its head. (There is an important parallel here with the image of the vine and the branches: Jn 15:1–7.)

4:17–5:21 Living as Children of Light One vitally important aspect of this process of maturing in Christ is maintaining Christian integrity in a fallen world (4:17–5:21). In this section, Paul stresses that Christian faith must lead to a Christian lifestyle, in which believers

stand out from the world in terms of their moral conduct. They must discard their old selves and former natures, and clothe themselves with the new nature that comes through Jesus Christ. Paul identifies a series of specific failings that Christians must take care to avoid (4:25–31).

In particular, Paul emphasises the importance of forgiveness. Just as God forgave their sins in Christ, so believers must forgive the sins of others (4:32). The church is thus, in contrast to the world, to be a community of compassion and forgiveness. Here we see Paul bringing out the need to be like God himself: believers are to be imitators of God, patterning their lives on God as he has made himself known through Christ. Anything that comes in the way of this process of becoming like God, or that threatens to make believers become like the fallen world, is to be avoided. Christians have been called out of darkness into light, and must not return to that darkness. For this reason, they must encourage and support one other – for example, through song and prayer – in order that they may remain faithful and close to their risen Lord (5:1–20).

5:21–32 Wives and Husbands Paul then turns his attention to the practical business of relationships within the church and family. His argument here is that God has ordered the world in a certain way, and that this ordering must reflect itself in human relationships. The word 'submit' is used several times in this section (5:21–6:9), not with the sense of 'obeying an earthly superior', but rather with the meaning of 'discovering and accepting God's intentions'. For example,

at no point are wives told to obey their husbands. Paul's instructions to his female readers do not employ this term at all – although he does lay down that children should obey their mothers and fathers (6:1). The mutual relationship between man and woman in marriage is defined in terms of love and submission – that is, the same quality of self-giving love that took Christ to the cross for his church, and the same committed willingness to be faithful to the demands of a relationship.

6:1–9 Children and Parents, Slaves and Masters The relations of man and woman, children and parents, slave and master are all defined in terms that at first sight seem to be conventional 1st-century terms. Yet, on closer inspection, some vital qualifications are introduced. We have already noted the way in which husbands are told to love their wives. Parents are also instructed not to exasperate their children, just as masters are reminded that their superiority over slaves has an earthly, not a heavenly, basis. In all this, we may see the basic principle set out in Gal 3:28 being explored – that in Christ, there are no fundamental distinctions of race, gender or social status. These exist on earth – but they must be seen from a heavenly perspective. Life within the church must begin to mirror the life of heaven, in which such distinctions will play no part.

6:10–20 The Armour of God Having instructed his congregations to avoid sin and remain faithful to the Lord, Paul then provides his readers with guidance on how this may be achieved. His basic

---

What the does the Bible say about drinking alcohol?

Different Christian traditions have different attitudes to alcohol, and sometimes there are differences even within the same denomination or in different parts of the world. To answer the question is therefore to step into a minefield. However, if we stay simply with what the Bible itself teaches, it seems clear that nowhere is drinking alcohol forbidden, whether beer or wine.

In Bible times 'wine' meant fermented juice (generally from grapes, but also from other fruits); no non-alcoholic beverage was ever called 'wine'. It was consumed at daily meals (e.g., Jdg 19:19; 1Sa 16:20; Isa 55:1), usually mixed with water. Jesus drank wine (e.g., Lk 7:33–34) and anticipated doing so in his Father's kingdom (Mt 26:29), and Paul encouraged Timothy to 'stop drinking only water, and use a little wine because of your stomach and your frequent illnesses' (1Ti 5:23). Beer, made from barley, was also drunk. Drinking such beverages was never frowned upon; indeed, abundant wine was seen as a sign of God's blessing (e.g., Ge 27:28; Am 9:13–14). Abstinence from it was purely voluntary, normally for reasons of religious ritual purity (e.g., Da 1:8) or as part of a vow (e.g., Nu 6:1–4).

However, the danger of alcohol is also noted, often through stories with disastrous consequences. For example, Lot's daughters became pregnant by their father, having got him drunk (Ge 19:30–38), and their offspring would trouble Israel for years to come; and David tried to mask his adultery by getting Bathsheba's husband drunk (2Sa 11:12–13), ultimately leading to his murder. Christians are commanded not to get drunk (Eph 5:18), and drunkenness or addiction to drink excluded people from church leadership (1Ti 3:3, 8; Tit 1:7).

While alcohol is therefore not forbidden, but rather seen as a blessing, we are warned to beware of its dangers and make appropriate choices.

---

point is that it is impossible to manage these demands without the grace of God. An integral element of the Christian life is the cultivation of the practice of turning to God, and using the resources he has put at believers' disposal. This leads Paul to his image of the 'full armour of God' (6:10–18).

Paul clearly understands the Christian life to involve conflict. As will be clear from his own career, that conflict often arises through the opposition of secular and religious authorities to the message of the gospel. But it is clear that Paul also recognises another level of conflict, which could be referred to as 'spiritual warfare'. The Christian is obliged to struggle, not just against 'flesh and blood' (in other words, purely human opponents), but against 'the powers of this dark world and against the spiritual forces of evil in the heavenly realms' (6:12).

To resist these onslaughts, Christians must make the best use of the defences God himself provides – such as truth, righteousness, faith and salvation. Notice that all the types of armour, except one that Paul mentions, are defensive – that is, intended to defend the wearer against

the attacks of others. The only offensive weapon is the 'sword of the Spirit', which allows the Christian, armed with the Spirit of the living God, to launch a counter-attack against such spiritual forces.

6:21–24 Final Greetings Finally, Paul asks his readers to pray for him, as he ends his letter by dwelling on the themes of grace and peace – two central themes of the Christian gospel, which allow believers to live and work in the world, knowing that their faith rests securely on a rock that God himself has established. Whatever difficulties believers may find themselves in (and recall that Paul himself is in chains at this point: 6:20), they may know that they have peace with God.

PHILIPPIANS

Paul's letter to the church at Philippi is generally thought to have been written during a period of imprisonment, probably in Rome, around AD 61. The circumstances of the letter fit in well with those described in Ac 28:14–31, when Paul was under house arrest, but was still permitted to see visitors and enjoy at least some degree of freedom.

Philippi, an important Roman colony in Macedonia, was evangelised by Paul during his second missionary journey (Ac 16:11–40). It was the first European city in which Paul proclaimed the gospel. There were so few Jews in the region that there was no synagogue (Ac 16:16 refers only to a 'place of prayer', not a synagogue). This may explain both why Paul does not cite the Old Testament at all during this letter, and also why the letter is virtually free of argument. It is one of the most positive and delightful of Paul's letters, which sets out the sheer joy of the gospel to its readers.

1:1–11 Thanksgiving and Prayer The letter opens with an outpouring of delight and thanksgiving. Paul is filled with joy at the reports he has heard of the church in the region. He speaks of their 'partnership in the gospel' with him, and of his great confidence in all that God will do through them in the years that lie ahead. It is clear that Paul longs to be with them, sharing in their work and witness. But he knows that he may entrust them to the Lord, confident of his guidance and protection.

1:12–30 Paul's Chains Advance the Gospel Just as Paul has heard reports about the Philippians, so the Philippians have clearly learned about Paul's imprisonment (1:12–14). Paul reassures them that the cause of his imprisonment is his faith. There are no other accusations being brought against him, other than the stand he has taken for the gospel. And the fact that he has taken this stand is itself a powerful act of witness for the gospel. The contingent of Roman guards, from which his guards are drawn, are aware of his faith in the gospel, and that his imprisonment is for Christ, and Christ alone. And Paul's stand on this matter has given new confidence to other

Does God ever give up on us?

If anyone had grounds for feeling God had given up on him, it was Paul. Jailed several times, including once in Philippi (Ac 16), and having experienced many hardships (2Co 11:23–28), he was now under house arrest in Rome (Ac 28:30), from where he wrote this letter to the Philippians. But nowhere is there any hint that these hardships were signs that God had given up on him, or on the Philippians. Despite everything, Paul had huge confidence that 'he who began a good work in you will carry it on to completion until the day of Christ Jesus' (1:6). He was confident that what God starts, he always completes, for the gospel is all about *God's* faithfulness, not ours. Doubting this turns Christianity into a religion of human effort.

But what if we sin badly? Might not God give up on us then? Far from it. John assures us that, 'If we confess our sins, he is faithful and just and will forgive us our sins and purify us from all unrighteousness' (1Jn 1:9), and Paul writes that 'if we are faithless, he remains faithful, for he cannot disown himself' (2Ti 2:13). No matter how badly we fail, God doesn't give up on us and is always ready to welcome us back, as the parable of the lost son makes clear (Lk 15:11–31) and as other key passages affirm (e.g., Jn 10:27–28; 1Co 1:8–9; 1Th 5:23–24; 1Pe 1:3–5). This conviction that God never gives up on his people became known as 'the perseverance of the saints'.

This is not an excuse for carelessness, however, as some passages make clear – though these need reading in context: Heb 6:4–6 is a warning to Jewish Christians not to abandon Jesus and return to Judaism, and 2Pe 2:20–23 is a warning about false teachers.

Christians, as they seek to witness to the Lord. Even in this apparently miserable situation, Paul is able to bear witness to his faith.

Yet not all preach Christ from such good motives. Paul admits that some preach the gospel for questionable reasons (1:15–18). But for Paul, the important thing is that the gospel is preached. Even the most base motive can be used in the spreading of the gospel. And this thought encourages Paul, as he contemplates his own situation. He may be in prison. The gospel, nevertheless, continues to be preached. Paul declares his personal conviction that whatever happens to him will turn out for the good, under God's grace. It does not matter whether he lives or dies. If he lives, he will be able to preach the gospel. If he dies, he will go to be with Christ – which is even better. He will be content to accept whatever the Lord wills for him, knowing that Christ will be exalted, whether through Paul's life or his death (1:19–26). Believing in Christ may lead to suffering for Christ. This is already happening in the case of Paul. It may also happen to the Philippians (1:27–30). Yet Paul declares that it is a privilege to suffer in this way (note 1:29; the phrase 'it has been granted' implies a special favour).

2:1–11 Imitating Christ's Humility With this point in mind, Paul urges his readers to think about the example of Jesus Christ, who provides a model for Christian behaviour (2:1–4). The particular point that Paul wishes to bring out is the importance of humility, which he sees illustrated to perfection in the life and death of Jesus Christ. Paul now draws on a Christian hymn, which was evidently known to his readers, in making these points (2:5–11). It will be useful to note the main features of this remarkably helpful statement of the meaning of the death and resurrection of Christ.

The hymn begins by affirming that Jesus Christ had the nature of God from the beginning. However, he chose to 'make himself nothing' or 'empty himself', by becoming a servant in the form of a human being. We can see here a clear reference to the incarnation – that is, to Christ becoming a human being, and entering into our world of time, space and suffering (Jn 1:14). Christ humbled himself. Not only did he set aside his majesty to come to dwell among us human beings, but he was willing to subject himself to death on a cross for our salvation.

Yet God chose to exalt him to the highest place – a clear reference to the resurrection and ascension of Christ. These great events publicly demonstrated that Christ was divine, and that every knee should bow at his name and confess

A hymn about Christ

Who, being in very nature God,
did not consider equality with God something to be used to his own advantage;
    rather, he made himself nothing
by taking the very nature of a servant,
being made in human likeness.
And being found in appearance as a man,
he humbled himself
by becoming obedient to death –
even death on a cross!

In 2:6–11, Paul includes a hymn about Jesus. Paul may have written it himself, or it may be by someone else. It is all about how Christ 'emptied' himself, shedding his privileges one by one until he faced the ultimate degradation – death on a cross. But because he humbled himself, God raised him up to the highest place:

> 'Therefore God exalted him to the highest place and gave him the name that is above every name, that at the name of Jesus every knee should bow, in heaven and on earth and under the earth, and every tongue acknowledge that Jesus Christ is Lord, to the glory of God the Father' (2:9–11).

Christians, Paul says, should think and act like Christ: they should be humble, and think more about others than themselves.

that he is indeed Lord. An Old Testament text that originally referred to God (Isa 45:23) is here applied to Jesus Christ. On account of the resurrection, Jesus Christ has been demonstrated to be divine, so that this transposition is fully justified. But the main point that Paul wishes to make here is simply that this attitude of humility ought to be part of the Christian life.

2:12–18 Shining as Stars Paul then urges his readers to 'work out' their salvation (2:12–18). Yet in doing so, Paul is not implying that the Christian life is totally dependent on human effort. A close inspection of his comments (2:12–13) reveals that there are two contributors to the Christian life – the believer and God. Paul asks his readers to do their best. He then makes the point that God is at work in the lives of believers, enabling them to desire and achieve his purposes. Christians are not on their own. God does not make demands, and leave believers to get on with them on their own. He assists them, as they do what they can for him.

2:19–30 Timothy and Epaphroditus We then learn of Paul's plans for the future, and especially for Timothy and Epaphroditus. They have both been with Paul in Rome, and it is his intention to send them both to Philippi and to follow them, when this becomes possible. This suggests that Paul expects to be released from his house arrest at Rome in the near future, and be able to resume his missionary and pastoral activity.

3:1–11 No Confidence in the Flesh Having informed the Philippians of his plans for the future, Paul returns to the theme of confidence and joy in the gospel. There is no ground for confidence in any human achievement or qualification – such as being a Jew (3:1–6). Paul makes the point that, if there were any such ground for confidence, he would be a very confident man indeed, on account of his excellent standing within Judaism. But all of this is worthless in comparison with the joy and privilege of knowing Christ. To know Christ overshadows everything, and shows it up in its proper light (3:7–11). Once more, we find Paul making the point that righteousness does not come by observing the Law, but by faith in Christ. Yet alongside this theological argument, we can detect Paul's sense of utter delight at being able to share in the fellowship of Christ – both in his sufferings and, eventually, in his resurrection. This thought gives him comfort and hope as he contemplates the future (3:12–16).

3:12–4:1 Pressing on Towards the Goal The fact that Philippi was a Roman colony also comes in useful to Paul. It gives him a model for his thoughts about the relation between the present situation of believers and their future state in heaven (3:17–4:1). For believers, their 'citizenship is in heaven'. In other words, the church is a colony of heaven, whose people look forward to the day when they can return to their homeland. The true homeland of believers is heaven. They are presently exiled on the earth, but have the full assurance that they will one day return home. Christ will come from heaven, and gather his people to him, and transform them so that they share both his glorious likeness and also his habitation in heaven.

4:2–20 *Exhortations and Thanks* The letter now begins to draw to a close. Paul asks his readers to rejoice, no matter what their circumstances (4:1–9). All their concerns and requests can be made known to God, who will grant them peace in the midst of this turbulent world. Paul praises the Philippians for their kindness towards him, including the gifts they had sent through Epaphroditus, and reassures them that he has found the secret of being content, no matter what his situation. Wherever he is, and whatever his situation, he can draw strength from the God of peace. God will meet all his needs (4:10–20).

4:21–23 *Final Greetings* The letter ends with Paul wishing God's blessing on his readers (4:21–23). Yet one little phrase in the closing paragraph merits a little closer attention. Paul sends greetings to Philippi from 'those who belong to Caesar's household' (4:22) – a clear reference to the presence of Christians within the palace area itself. The gospel has not merely reached Rome. It has begun to find its way to the heart of its seat of power. It would be many years before the emperor became a Christian. Nevertheless, the foundations for this dramatic development were already being laid during Paul's own lifetime.

COLOSSIANS

Colossians, like Philippians, is a letter written by Paul while he was under house arrest at Rome, probably at some point around AD 60. The city of Colossae was located on the river Lycus in Asia Minor. Paul himself had not evangelised this city during any of his missionary journeys. However, Epaphras, one of Paul's converts during his Ephesian ministry (Ac 19:10), had travelled to the city in order to preach the gospel there. The letter is particularly concerned to deal with a false teaching that has arisen within this young church.

In view of the importance of this false teaching to the letter, it is important to consider what it was. Although this false teaching is never specifically expounded, its main features can be worked out from Paul's response to it. These appear to have been three. First, an emphasis on some secret or mystical knowledge (a theme that would become a major theme of the movement known as Gnosticism, which became especially influential in the 2nd century). Secondly, a strict set of rules concerning what it was legitimate to eat and drink, linked with an emphasis on asceticism. Thirdly, a tendency to play down the importance of Jesus Christ, and to worship angels. In many ways, the ideas seem to represent a mingling of Jewish and Greek ideas. Paul counters the teaching by emphasising that all that needs to be known about God and his purposes has been revealed supremely, uniquely and adequately in Jesus Christ.

1:1–14 Thanksgiving and Prayer The letter opens with the traditional greetings, and giving thanks for all that God has done in and through the church at Colossae. The main themes of the gospel are stated: God has rescued believers from darkness, and brought them into the kingdom of his Son. Through Christ they have redemption and forgiveness of sins. Paul assures the believers in the city of his continued prayers for their spiritual wellbeing and development.

1:15–23 The Supremacy of Christ Paul then launches into one of the major themes of the gospel, which is of particular importance in the light of the Colossian error. The theme is that of the majesty of

Jesus Christ. Christ is declared to be the image of the invisible God. In other words, although God himself cannot be seen, he has chosen to make himself known in a visible and tangible form in Jesus Christ. Everything is subject to Christ: he possesses God's total authority. God dwells fully in Christ. Through him, and through him only, we can have reconciliation with God. Throughout this section, the implication is clear: Christ is the unique bearer of divine revelation. Nobody else possesses his spiritual authority.

1:24–2:5 *Paul's Labour for the Church* Paul then affirms his own authority. He has been commissioned by God (not by any human being!) to proclaim this gospel (and no other gospel!) to every living creature. It is his mission to make known this gospel in all its fullness. God has fully disclosed all that needs to be known for salvation. He, Paul, will make sure that the 'glorious riches of this mystery' are known to all. The term 'mystery' really means something that is so wonderful that we cannot fully get our minds around it. The gospel has been made known, fully and completely, in Christ. It makes available 'the full riches of complete understanding'. And anyone who says anything else, even in 'fine-sounding arguments', is trying to deceive them.

2:6–3:4 *Freedom from Human Regulations Through Life with Christ* This brings Paul directly to his concern about the false teachings that are gaining a hearing at Colossae. This section provides the real heart of the letter, and would have been read with particular care and attention by its original recipients. He urges his readers to avoid the 'hollow and deceptive philosophy' that is grounded in secular human culture, rather than in the self-revelation of God in Christ. In Christ, and in Christ alone, the fullness of God has been made known in physical form.

Relentlessly, Paul presses home his point. It is Christ, and Christ alone, who is supreme. Believers need look to no one and nothing else in their search for wisdom and knowledge. He alone can deliver humanity from its bondage to sin and death. Through his cross, he has disarmed the powers and authorities. It is possible that the Colossians were being urged by the false teachers to worship such powers and authorities. Paul, however, insists that their power has been broken by Christ. Why worship a defeated power, when one can and should worship the one who triumphed over them?

Paul declares that believers are under no obligation whatsoever to observe fussy regulations concerning food or drink. Nobody has the authority to lay such obligations on them. These are purely human commands and regulations, without any basis in the will of God. They may seem to be wise and spiritual – yet they threaten to destroy the basis of faith, by diverting believers away from Jesus Christ himself.

But believers have been raised with Christ. By this, Paul does not mean that they are already in heaven. He means that their future place in heaven is assured, on account of Christ, and that the anticipation of the joy of heaven can be experienced now. And for that reason, they should raise their eyes heavenward, where Christ has gone (3:1–4). Paul's

What are angels?

The Colossians not only believed in angels – mentioned throughout the Bible from the garden of Eden to Revelation – they had turned them from God's servants to intermediaries whom they worshipped (2:18), wrongly thinking God was so transcendent you couldn't worship him directly.

Angels aren't God's intermediaries, a role reserved for Christ alone who is far higher than any angel (Heb 1:1–14); they are simply God's servants. 'Angel' means 'messenger'; so we often find angels carrying God's message to people (e.g., Lk 1:26–38; 2:8–20). But the message often brought God's blessing (Ge 24:40), intervention (Ge 22:9–12), guidance (Ex 23:20), commission (Jdg 6:11–16), help (Da 6:22), deliverance (Ac 12:6–11), direction (Ac 8:26), even judgment (Ge 19:1–29). And children – seen as unimportant in the ancient world – are not excluded (Mt 18:10). In short, angels are 'ministering spirits sent to serve those who will inherit salvation' (Heb 1:14). But their chief role is the continual worship of God (e.g., Isa 6:1–3; Rev 5:11–13).

Angels are not eternal, but are rather created, spiritual beings – though they often take human form to do their work and are frequently mistaken for people (e.g., Ge 19:1–5). Despite their depiction in Christian art, they do not have wings, something ascribed only to cherubim (Eze 10:3–5) and seraphim (Isa 6:2).

But not all angels are good. Some rebelled and were cast out of heaven (2Pe 2:4; Jude 6). From earliest times the church saw prophecies of Isaiah and Ezekiel about human kings as mirroring what had happened. Satan had been a guardian cherub whose pride led to his being cast down to earth (Eze 28:13–17; Isa 14:12–15). John describes a similar scene in Revelation (Rev 12:7–9). Since Satan took only one-third of the angels with him, that means there are still two angels for every demon – an encouraging thought!

point here is that this exercise will remind believers of the ultimate authority of Christ. He, and he alone, has been raised in this manner. Christ alone has been raised from the dead, and Christ alone possesses the authority that results from being raised in this way.

3:5–4:1 Rules for Holy Living In the light of this, Paul asserts the need for moral behaviour on the part of believers (3:5–17). Yet these moral demands differ totally from the demands of the false teachers. Paul calls believers to be like Christ. As God's chosen people, they should demonstrate God-like qualities to the world. Interestingly, Paul notes the importance of praise in sustaining the Christian life (3:16). In a brief section, he provides a summary of his views on appropriate Christian approaches to the relation of wives and husbands, children and parents, and masters and slaves (3:18–4:1; for an expanded account, see Eph 5:21–6:9, where the same values are noted, but with a more detailed theological foundation being provided).

4:2–6 Further Instructions Paul then turns his attention to his own needs. He asks for prayer, in order that doors may be opened for his preaching of the gospel in their region. He asks for prayer, in order that he may communicate the gospel as effectively and faithfully as possible. Once more, it seems that Paul has every expectation of being released from protective custody at Rome in the near future, so that he will be free to travel and proclaim the gospel once more.

4:7–18 Final Greetings The letter then moves to its close, with a series of personal greetings. Paul commends Tychicus to them. He will bring the Colossian believers further news about Paul, as may John Mark, if he ever gets to Colossae. The form of the reference to Tychicus suggests that he may have been the bearer of the letter (and possibly of others as well, such as Ephesians and Philemon). Epaphras – who brought the gospel to Colossae in the first place – is mentioned to them, as is Luke. Notice the reference to the letter being 'read to you' (4:16): it was the practice to read such letters aloud in the churches, so that all might hear what Paul had to say. Once more, Paul ends this letter with a concluding section in his own hand (4:18; see also 1Co 16:21; Gal 6:11; Phm 19), asking his readers to remember that he is being held captive for the sake of the gospel.

1 THESSALONIANS

Paul's first letter to the Christians at Thessalonica was written from Corinth, probably at some point in AD 51. The date cannot be fixed with absolute certainty. It is widely accepted, however, that this is the earliest of Paul's letters in the New Testament. Thessalonica was the largest city in Macedonia, and was evangelised by Paul during his second missionary journey (Ac 17:1–14). Paul was able to stay in the city only briefly, being obliged to flee from the city and seek refuge in nearby Berea, before moving on to Athens and then Corinth. While in Corinth, Paul wrote to the Christian church at Thessalonica, to offer her encouragement and guidance.

1:1–10 *Greetings and Thanksgiving* The letter opens with greetings from Paul, Silas and Timothy – the three evangelists who had founded the church in the city (1:1–2). Although all three are mentioned, what follows makes it clear that the letter is Paul's work. He begins by offering thanks and praise for the remarkable growth of the church in the city, and the extent to which its reputation has spread throughout the regions of Achaia and Macedonia (1:3–10). Thessalonica was a busy seaport located on the Egnatian Way, one of the major trade routes in the region. It was thus an ideal centre for mission. It is clear that many in the city had turned away from various forms of paganism in order to accept Jesus Christ, and that these developments were attracting attention throughout the region.

2:1–16 *Paul's Ministry in Thessalonica* Paul's stay in Thessalonica had been brief, and probably did not allow him time to say all that needed to be said to the fledgling church. This letter gives Paul the opportunity to put into writing some of the points that need to be made. The first major section of the letter deals with a series of matters relating to ministry, and especially the proclamation of the gospel.

The first major point concerns motivation. The gospel is not proclaimed from a desire to please people – the evangelist is no demagogue! Nor does it arise from greed, a desire for personal gain, or winning praise from people. The most fundamental motivation for evangelism is a desire to please and serve God. Paul and his companions were entrusted with the gospel message by God himself, and were carrying out their responsibility to him by preaching the gospel at Thessalonica.

This attitude on the part of those who proclaimed the gospel was met with a corresponding attitude on the part of those who received it. The Thessalonians realised that this was no human wisdom, having its origins in the human mind, but something that was grounded in the word of God itself. Despite all the opposition, whether from Jew or Gentile, the gospel had been preached and believed.

2:17–3:13 Timothy's Report; Paul's Longing to See the Thessalonians Paul then begins to tell of his own experiences. He relates how he had to leave Thessalonica abruptly, leaving behind a church that was unsettled. Paul had sent Timothy to encourage them, and had then made inquiries about them, to ensure that all was well. But now, he has learned from Timothy that all is as it should be. It is easy to see Paul's relief at the report that Timothy has brought to him, both concerning the morale of the Thessalonian church, and also of their memories of him. It is clear that the Thessalonians bore Paul no grudge for his hasty departure, which left them to face opposition without any real guidance or support. He assures them of his prayers for them, and his longing to see them again.

4:1–12 Living to Please God He now turns to deal with ethical matters, stressing the importance of right conduct. It is vitally important that the Thessalonians should live upright and attractive lives, so that others from outside the church might be drawn into its fellowship on account of their witness.

4:13–5:11 The Coming of the Lord As the letter comes to a close, Paul chooses to explain some aspects of Christian belief concerning the end of all things. In a section that shows familiarity with some of the gospel passages dealing with the need for believers to be ready for the coming of the Lord, Paul stresses that Christ may return at any moment, and his people must be prepared for this event. Nobody can be sure precisely when this will happen, and there is a need to be watchful. The day of the Lord will come like a thief in the night, when people are unprepared for it.

It is possible that some believers at Thessalonica had died since Paul's visit, leading to a discussion about their fate, and that of those who were still living. Paul reassures them of the hope of resurrection, and that the great promises of eternal life are open to those who are still alive when Christ comes. It seems that the Thessalonians were convinced that those who died in faith would indeed rise again to eternal life. The problem concerned those who were still alive at the time of the second coming. What will happen to them? Will they be able to share in the resurrection?

What happens when we die?

The ancient Hebrews, like most of their contemporaries, believed that after death everyone, good and bad alike, went to the underworld – *Sheol* (in Greek, *Hades*), what Job describes as 'the place of no return . . . the land of gloom and utter darkness . . . the land of deepest night, of utter darkness and disorder' (Job 10:21–22). Just occasionally we find the hope of something better – as when Job himself declares that 'after my skin has been destroyed, yet in my flesh I will see God; I myself will see him with my own eyes – I, and not another' (Job 19:26–27), or when one of the prophets received revelation (e.g., Isa 26:19; Da 12:2); but by and large such glimpses were rare. By New Testament times Jewish opinion had developed but also divided, with some (like the Sadducees) firmly rejecting any idea of resurrection, and others (like the Pharisees) accepting it.

In contrast to such uncertainty, Jesus proclaimed clear hope for the future (e.g., Mt 25; Jn 14:1–3). His resurrection broke the fear of death for his followers (Heb 2:14–15), convincing them of the reality of a future life (e.g., 1Co 15:50–57; Php 3:7–14; 1Th 4:13–18). Death was not the end, but simply a 'departure' (Php 1:23; 2Ti 4:6–8; 2Pe 1:13–15) in which we leave our physical bodies, for which we have no further use, and immediately enter God's presence. That was why Jesus could promise the man crucified alongside him, '*Today* you will be with me in paradise' (Lk 23:43) – no delay, purgatory, soul-sleep or reincarnation, but rather immediately being 'with Christ, which is better by far' (Php 1:23). This was why John could reassure believers that not even martyrdom could rob them of victory. In his privileged glimpse into heaven he had seen the believers who had gone ahead and knew they were safe, with Christ (e.g., Rev 7:9–10; 14:1–5).

This confidence in life after death is the birthright of all true Christians.

See also, 'Where will we spend eternity?', page 498.

Paul reassures them on this point. Whether they are alive or dead at that time, they will all be taken to be with the Lord. Both those who are 'awake or asleep' (terms Paul uses here to mean 'living' and 'dead') will live with Christ (5:10). Yet confusion would arise at Thessalonica as a result of his letter over this point, obliging Paul to write once more to correct a misunderstanding that had resulted.

5:12–28 Final Instructions Paul then brings his first surviving letter to a close. After offering some advice on relationships within the church, Paul reassures his readers of the total faithfulness and reliability of God. The God who has called them is faithful, and will see them through to the end (5:24). After asking that the letter be read aloud in the congregation, Paul commends those who read the letter to the grace of God.

2 THESSALONIANS

Paul's second letter to the church at Thessalonica probably dates from about six months after the first. It was written from Corinth, in late AD 51 or early 52. Like the first letter, the work opens with a dedication from Paul, Silas and Timothy, who were responsible for establishing the church in the city in the first place (Ac 17:1–14). The bulk of the letter deals with a misunderstanding that has arisen as a result of one section of the first letter.

1:1–12 Thanksgiving and Prayer After an opening greeting (1:1–2), Paul once more gives thanks for the growth and witness of the Christian community in the great city of Thessalonica (1:3–12). It seems that the church is going through a period of oppression, and Paul reassures them that this is to be expected. Suffering for the kingdom of God is a sure sign of being counted worthy of that kingdom. But Paul soon turns his attention to the real issue, which has to do with the second coming of Christ.

2:1–12 The Coming of the Lord It seems that the Thessalonians were unsettled by Paul's first letter (or possibly by a different letter, circulating under Paul's name, but not written by him; however, the view Paul describes could easily arise through a misunderstanding of the contents of 1Th 4:13–5:3). Some appear to have understood Paul to mean that the day of the Lord has already come – that is, that the end-time is under way, leading up to the final coming of Christ in the very near future (2:1–12).

It is possible that this belief may underlie the idleness Paul castigates later in the letter (3:6–15). Some may have argued that, as the end of the world will happen at any moment, there is no point in doing anything. Paul argues that his own ministry shows how false this attitude is. He himself was not idle, but threw himself totally into the business of preaching the gospel. The instruction regarding not allowing an idle person to eat (3:10) should probably be seen in this context of end-time speculation.

In response to this feeling that the final days have begun, Paul declares that there will be warning signs, evident to all, before this final period in the history of

The man of lawlessness

The identity of this man, the Antichrist, is a mystery. Paul says that he will be characterised by pride – he will play at being God and demand people's worship. He will go into the temple at Jerusalem. He will be successful and powerful – and even perform miracles. But the source of his power will be Satan, not God, and only those who reject God will fall for his tricks.

Paul may have been referring to the Roman emperor Gaius, who in AD 40 planned to set up his statue in the Jerusalem temple. In Daniel the 'abomination that causes desolation' (Da 11:31) alludes to the desecration of the Jerusalem temple by a pagan oppressor in 167 BC. That image is re-applied by Jesus in Mk 13:14 and here by Paul to further acts of aggression against the temple and hostility towards God. Some Christians believe that these events have yet to unfold. They point to advances in technology that make it possible for individuals and corporations to hold sway over millions. (References to the Antichrist are also found in the book of Revelation.) What is certain is that Paul believes that, before Christ returns, things will get very black indeed. The man of lawlessness will epitomise that dark time.

the world begins (2:1–12). In particular, he draws attention to the dawn of a period of open rebellion against God (see Mt 24:10–12) and the coming of 'the man of lawlessness' (2:3). This person, who seems to correspond to the 'antichrists' mentioned in John's letters (see 1Jn 2:18), will claim to be God. When these events have taken place, the end days will have begun. But they have not happened yet.

2:13–3:15 Stand Firm Paul is quite clear that he taught the Thessalonians these things when he was with them (2:5). They have either forgotten them, or have been led astray in some way. For this reason, Paul emphasises the need to remain faithful to the teachings he passed on to them, whether by word of mouth or by letter (2:13–17). He asks for the prayers of his readers, so that he and his colleagues may be able to preach the gospel in safety (3:1–5). Yet Paul is careful to make it clear that his ultimate ground of security lies in the faithfulness of Christ, in whom he knows he may have total confidence (3:3–5). His prayer is thus partly that his readers may come to share that same faith and hope so characteristic of his own ministry as a servant of the Lord.

3:16–18 Final Greetings And so Paul ends his letter, once more commending his readers to the 'Lord of peace'. As with so many of his letters, Paul ends this letter with a few sentences he has penned himself. The rest of the letter would have been written by a professional scribe. But Paul, wanting to authenticate the letter and add a personal touch, wrote these final words himself.

1 TIMOTHY

Paul's two letters to Timothy and the letter to Titus form a special group. They are distinguished by the fact that they are written to specific individuals, rather than to churches, and also by their strongly pastoral tone. This latter is seen in their concern with issues of church government and practical Christian living. For this reason, these three letters are often referred to collectively as 'The Pastoral Letters'. The pastoral letters date from a time after the events described in Ac 28. The most obvious explanation is that Paul was released from his house arrest in Rome at some point around AD 63, and that these letters were written after this release.

The first two such letters are written to Timothy, who had played a significant role in Paul's missionary work (especially in Achaia and Macedonia: see Ac 17:14–15; 18:5), and is referred to with great affection in several of Paul's letters (Php 2:19–22). In addition, no fewer than six of Paul's letters name him in their opening greetings (2 Corinthians, Philippians, Colossians, 1 Thessalonians, 2 Thessalonians, and Philemon). Paul refers to Timothy as his 'true son in the faith', raising the possibility that Paul was himself responsible for Timothy's conversion.

1:1–11 Warning Against False Teachers After greeting Timothy (1:1–2), Paul warns of the dangers that can arise through false teachings (1:3–11). The general description of the false teachings which follow suggest that Timothy has encountered doctrines similar to those that had troubled the Christian churches at Ephesus and especially Colossae, mingling some Jewish ideas with others that had been borrowed from paganism. Paul stresses the need of remaining faithful to the basics of the gospel, which have been entrusted to him, as an apostle.

1:12–20 The Lord's Grace to Paul Paul then spends some time talking about these basics, noting with some sadness that some have departed from them totally (1:19–20). Paul stresses the importance

of grace, explaining why it is of such importance to him personally. It was only by the grace of God that he, who had been a blasphemer and persecutor, was shown mercy. This mercy results directly from the death of Christ. In fact, Christ came into the world with the specific intention and purpose of saving sinners – of whom Paul was among the worst (1:15). Paul's point is that if the grace of God can deliver him from sin, it can deliver anyone. Paul's personal testimony is thus to be an encouragement to others to discover the depths of God's forgiving grace.

2:1–15 Instructions on Worship

Having emphasised the importance of right doctrine, Paul then explores the importance of correct forms of worship. Public prayer for people in authority is commended – even if these are not believers. Paul seems to regard such people as *potential* Christians, drawing attention to the fact that Christ died for them. God wants everyone to be saved, and sent Christ into the world in order that he might be a mediator between God and the world. Paul uses the idea of a ransom to explain the meaning of the death of Christ – that is, Christ's death is to be seen as a payment that ensures the liberation of those who were formerly in captivity.

Paul then lays down some guidelines about the role of men and women in worship. Paul, apparently speaking in a personal capacity rather than in his capacity as an apostle, insists on propriety in public worship. In particular, he states his opposition to women being allowed to teach. Some scholars hold that this is to be understood as meaning that Paul did not allow any woman to be an official teacher in the church. Others suggest that he has a particular type of woman (perhaps unqualified or self-appointed teachers) in mind.

This is followed by a statement that has been the subject of considerable debate, on account of both its translation and interpretation (2:15). Paul states that women (Eve? A woman in general?) will be 'saved' or 'restored' through bearing a child. This could mean, for example, that Eve's disobedience is countered by Mary's obedience in bearing Jesus Christ (just as Adam's sin was countered by the obedience of Christ), or that any sin imputed to woman in general has been cancelled through the birth of Christ. It could also mean that a woman who has faith in Christ can find salvation simply through her calling as a mother.

3:1–16 Overseers and Deacons

Paul then turns to the issue of church order, and the qualifications of those who are to minister. The change in Paul's language makes it clear that he is no longer speaking in a purely personal capacity, but is speaking for the church at large. By this stage, the need for an official ministry within the church to carry on the work of the apostles had become increasingly clear. So how were they to be chosen? Paul sets out a series of guidelines that are to govern the selection of ministers.

Two basic offices or ministries are identified in this section: bishops, overseers, elders, or superintendents and deacons. It is clear that Paul expects such people to be of exemplary conduct and character, and to be strong and knowledgeable in their faith. In the end, however, Paul points out that the church

rests on the foundation of Jesus Christ, not its ministers.

4:1–16 Instructions to Timothy Having laid down guidance for the church at large, Paul now turns to offer counsel to his much-loved coworker Timothy himself. He stresses the importance of solid doctrine and fidelity to the gospel, as it has been passed down to him. Timothy is to avoid the false teachings of the age, and to place his full trust in the gospel of salvation in Christ. For Paul, the doctrinal orthodoxy of the churches can be maintained in part through the public reading of Scripture, preaching and teaching. Timothy is thus called upon to

develop such a ministry, for his own benefit as well as that of his hearers.

5:1–6:2 Advice About Widows, Elders and Slaves Again, we find Paul returning to the practical pastoral wisdom for which these letters are especially noted. Having stressed the importance of both life and doctrine (4:16), Paul offers guidance as to how to deal with a series of pastoral issues (5:1–6:2). His emphasis on the priority to be given to the pastoral care and support of widows is particularly significant. In the pagan culture of this period, widows and orphans were often left totally without any form of support. Paul clearly believes that the church has a

What does the Bible say about money?

Like so many other things, money in itself is neither good nor bad. It is how people handle it and what they do with it that matters. God doesn't seem to mind people having money; after all, there are many wealthy people in the Bible – whether Abraham in the Old Testament, who had many flocks and herds, or Lydia in the New Testament, a dealer in high-fashion purple cloth. But there are also many poor people in the Bible – not least Jesus who had no place to lay his head and who had to borrow a donkey when he needed one. Neither the presence nor the absence of money therefore can be taken as an indicator of God's blessing, or the lack of it.

However, those who do have money (whether much or little) are called to handle it with wisdom and according to godly principles, understanding it can so easily blind and deceive us (Lk 18:18–30; 1Ti 6:9–10). Some of the key principles the Bible gives us concerning our handling of money include the exhortation to (1) *Get our money honestly* (e.g., Eph 4:28), always working with diligence and integrity; (2) *Enjoy our money gratefully* (Ecc 5:19), receiving it as God's blessing rather than our right (Pr 10:22); (3) *Handle our money carefully*, by providing for ourselves and our family (Pr 13:22), seeking to avoid debt (Pr 22:26–27), paying all our dues, both to God and the state (Lk 20:22–25; Ro 13:6–8), and living as faithful stewards of all we have (e.g., Mt 25:14–20; Lk 16:10–12); (4) *Share our money generously*, both by helping the poor (e.g., Pr 19:17) and sowing into the work of God's kingdom (2Co 9:6–12). Without these principles we may be rich in the world's eyes, but we are poor in God's eyes.

duty to support its female widowed members. The advice to believers who are slaves with believing masters is also significant. Paul urges them to behave with even greater diligence towards such masters.

6:3–10 Love of Money Yet it is the lure of possessions, and especially money, that causes Paul special concern (6:3–10). The love of money, he remarks, is the root of all evil. Note that it is not money in itself. Paul treats this as something that is neutral. It is the attitude people have towards money that is the problem. Paul urges Timothy to seek contentment in what he has, and avoid the pursuit of wealth with all its attendant dangers. Later, he also points out that the only riches really worth seeking are those that are grounded in God himself (6:17–19).

6:11–21 Paul's Charge to Timothy Finally, Paul charges Timothy to fight the good fight that lies ahead of him, secure in the confidence of the eternal life God has promised him (6:11–16). He is to remain faithful to what has been entrusted to him – a charge that could refer both to the churches to whom he is called to minister, and also to the gospel he is to preach and teach. Perhaps Paul is aware that the time is drawing near when he must pass on the work of proclaiming and defending the faith to others (6:20–21). Timothy, he is sure, will be a faithful servant in the years that lie ahead.

2 TIMOTHY

Paul's second letter to Timothy presupposes a situation rather different from his first. Paul is now in prison once more, possibly for the last time. It is difficult to assign a date to the letter, although some date during the reign of the emperor Nero, possibly AD 65–67, would seem to be reasonable. Perhaps Paul is aware of the death of Peter, which may have convinced him of the urgency of writing to Timothy for the last time. The letter is saturated with an atmosphere of finality. Paul clearly believes that he has not much longer to live, and as a result wants to pass on his final instructions to the man who would have to exercise a role of leadership in the churches that Paul will leave behind. At several points during the letter, Paul hints at his loneliness. He feels abandoned by those who were once his colleagues and friends, but who have now lost interest in him or disowned him.

1:1–3:9 *Encouragement to Be Faithful* The letter opens with the traditional apostolic greeting (1:1–2). It is clear that Timothy was greatly loved by Paul. He had earlier referred to him as his 'true son in the faith' (1Ti 1:2), suggesting that Paul may have led Timothy to faith. Paul's detailed knowledge of Timothy's family background certainly suggests a deep affection for the younger man (1:3–5). But there is no time for sentimental reflection. Paul wants to pass on to Timothy his instructions for the churches, as they face new difficulties in the future. The implication, especially of some of the material in the final chapter, is clear: Paul will not be around to guide the churches for very much longer.

Paul begins by reminding Timothy of the main points of the gospel, especially that salvation is by the grace of God, rather than by human effort. This grace, which had been purposed from all eternity, was made known only through the coming of Jesus Christ as Saviour. Paul reminds Timothy of how he had been called to be an apostle of this good news for humanity. Despite all the

suffering this brought him, including being abandoned by those whom he thought to be his friends, he remained absolutely determined to defend and safeguard the gospel entrusted to him (1:6–18). This theme of being entrusted with the gospel is of central importance in this letter. When Paul speaks of 'his gospel' (e.g., 2:8), he does not mean 'the gospel that he possesses and owns', but 'the gospel that has been entrusted to him for safe keeping'.

Paul therefore urges Timothy to be strong, and endure whatever hardship may lie ahead of him (2:1–6). Death and suffering are not to be feared. The resurrection of Jesus Christ allows them to be seen in their true light. They will not get in the way of the believer's final reward in heaven. The example of Jesus Christ himself is of vital importance here, giving hope to believers in their present hardships. To make this point, Paul quotes from an early Christian hymn, with which Timothy would have been familiar (2:11–13). This hymn affirms that those who have died with Christ will be raised to life with him, on account of his total faithfulness to his promises. The image of 'dying with Christ' is used elsewhere in Paul's writings to refer to conversion and its resulting benefits (Ro 7:6), and occasionally to baptism, which is the public demonstration of this conversion (Ro 6:3–7).

Having reassured Timothy of the certainty of the reward awaiting him, and all who believe in Christ, Paul stresses the importance of moral living and avoiding false teaching (2:14–26). Indeed, Paul declares that an outbreak of false teaching and personal greed are to be expected in the last days (3:1–9).

3:10–4:8 Paul's Charge to Timothy Having forewarned Timothy of all the dangers and difficulties that lie ahead, Paul solemnly charges him with the responsibility of guiding the churches through the uncertain period that is coming. Paul points to his own problems as an illustration of the kind of thing that Timothy can expect to happen to him. He must be under no illusions. But he will not be without protection and guidance. In particular, Paul stresses the importance of Scripture as a God-given and God-breathed resource for ministry and teaching (3:14–17). It will protect Timothy from false teaching, and equip him to meet all the challenges that lie ahead. It will be clear that this resource continues to be of vital and supreme importance to Christians today, as they try to learn more about their Saviour and their salvation, and all that Scripture implies for their lives.

Having stressed the importance of Scripture, Paul charges Timothy to preach and teach, countering false teachings and reassuring believers of the grounds and nature of the Christian faith and hope. In this fickle and fallen world, people will want to hear other ideas. Timothy must be prepared to carry on preaching and teaching, even if he meets with hostility or scorn. Paul expresses his own deep sense of contentment at having fought the good fight, and being able to rest in the knowledge of the crown of righteousness that is held in store for him – and for all who share his own faithfulness to their calling.

4:9–22 Personal Remarks and Final Greetings
Finally, Paul ends with the personal remarks and greetings that are so characteristic a feature of his letters. The letter includes a commendation of John Mark (4:11), the travelling companion of Paul and Barnabas for part of the first missionary journey before his decision to leave them for Jerusalem (Ac 13:13). It is thought that Mark wrote his Gospel at some point around this time, probably in Rome. It is clear that, despite the gloomy tone of parts of his letter, Paul expects to meet Timothy again. Unlike many of the friends who failed to support him, he is confident that Timothy will remain faithful. But in the end, Paul's hopes rest on the faithfulness of God, not of any human being. And so he commends Timothy to the grace of the faithful God whom they both serve and love.

TITUS

Titus was one of Paul's many Gentile converts, and is known to have served him well and faithfully at several major stages in his ministry. Luke does not mention Titus at any point during Acts. However, there are frequent references to him elsewhere in the New Testament, indicating his importance to the early churches. In this letter, Paul again deals with the issues of pastoral ministry and teaching that he had addressed in the two letters to Timothy. The letter seems to have been written following the release of Paul after his imprisonment in Rome, described in Acts, and is probably to be dated around AD 64. However, there are no references to events within the letter to allow more precise dating.

1:1–4 Greetings The letter opens with a traditional apostolic greeting, linked with a vigorous statement of hope in the gospel. The total faithfulness and reliability of the gospel are affirmed in exultant tones, making it clear that, despite all his difficulties, Paul remains absolutely and joyfully committed to the gospel (1:1–3). He has no doubt either of his calling to be an apostle or of the power of the gospel.

1:5–16 Titus' Task on Crete Paul then explains the background to his decision to leave Titus on the Mediterranean island of Crete. Luke does not record Paul as having any ministry in this region, although the visit in question may have taken place after Paul's eventual release from imprisonment in Rome. It is clear that, in Paul's absence, Titus has been preoccupied with establishing and organising the churches on the island. Paul's advice to Titus relates chiefly to the fine details of church organisation, including the personal qualities that are to be looked for in the ministers of the church. He is especially concerned with the roles of elders and overseers – or, more traditionally, bishops. From Paul's comments, it seems that he expects Titus to have some difficulty in finding suitable persons within Crete, which he clearly regards to be peopled with liars and cheats.

2:1–3:11 What Must Be Taught to Various Groups The strongly pastoral tone of the letter continues, as Paul advises Titus on how to deal with various groups within

the church. It is important to note how one of Paul's chief concerns is to obtain a favourable public hearing for the gospel among potential converts and present critics. His advice to Christian slaves with unbelieving masters is particularly interesting, as it makes clear how important personal witness can be in gaining a positive response to the good news. In this context, Paul brings out how negative and unhelpful disagreements can be (3:9–11).

Underlying this pastoral wisdom is some important theological reflection. Paul emphasises that the gospel rests on the work of 'our great God and Saviour, Jesus Christ' (2:13), who gave himself up in order that believers might be saved and purified, becoming the people of God. There is a strong emphasis on the transformational aspects of the gospel: to be a believer is to be a changed person. Salvation involves washing and renewal. The themes of purification and transformation are both linked with the grace of God, the death of Christ, and the renewing work of the Holy Spirit – without these, the Christian life would be an impossibility. Believers may rest assured that they have been justified through the grace of God, and are heirs to all that lies ahead for them in heaven. Recognising that some will find these ideas objectionable, Paul urges Titus to defend them, irrespective of the response they evoke from those who hear them.

3:12–15 Final Remarks Finally, Paul sends his personal greetings to those around Titus, mentioning his travel plans. As always, we realise that the gospel is not simply about ideas – it is about men and women whose lives have been changed by the gospel, and who share in a fellowship that knows no national boundaries.

PHILEMON

This short letter was written by Paul from Rome, during the period in which he was held under house arrest (around AD 60). It is a highly unusual letter, in that it deals with the fate of a runaway slave, rather than with the leading ideas of the gospel. However, the inclusion of the letter in the New Testament reminds us that the gospel is not just about ideas, but about real life and the moral decisions which are part of that life. And Paul's concern is to show how the gospel bears on the situation of a single slave, who has come to put his faith in Christ. The message is simple: every believer counts, whether slave or master.

OUTLINE

1–3 Introduction and greeting

4–7 Thanksgiving and prayer

8–21 Paul's plea for Onesimus

23–25 Final greetings and blessing

vv.1–7 Greeting and Thanksgiving The letter opens (1–3) with a traditional apostolic greeting, which identifies Philemon both as a believer and a friend. (Since the letter is so brief, references are given only by verse number, there being no chapters to refer to.) Paul takes great delight in the reports he has heard concerning Philemon's faith, and the impact this is having on those around him (4–7).

vv.8–22 Paul's Plea for Onesimus Paul then gets down to the real purpose of the letter. He does not want to impose on Philemon, let alone preach at him. But he does have a favour to ask, which he believes Philemon will realise to be grounded in the love that the gospel illustrates and commends. This favour concerns Onesimus, a slave who became Paul's son – a reference to conversion – while Paul was in prison at Rome. The name 'Onesimus' means 'useful', and Paul exploits this meaning in a pun (11), which is clearly designed to win over Philemon to the favour in question. This favour turns out to be a request to treat Onesimus mercifully.

Onesimus clearly had stolen some property from his master, and then run away. Under Roman law, the penalty for this was death. However, Onesimus had now become a Christian, through the ministry of Paul, and Paul asks Philemon to be merciful. Onesimus is no longer a slave, but a brother. Paul has told him to return to his master. In response, he hopes that Philemon will forgive him for his past behaviour (12–21).

vv.22–25 Final Greetings After expressing his hope that he will be able to meet Philemon again (22), he sends his own greetings, along with those of four others, including Mark and Luke. We have no way of knowing what the outcome of this letter was. However, the letter would

Does the Bible approve of slavery?

Slavery was very common in ancient times. Some became slaves through conquest, capture or poverty, while others were born into it. Although many were treated harshly (Ex 1:8–22), others were entrusted with huge responsibilities (Ge 39:1–6) – though ultimately the slave was always their master's property. Slavery in ancient Israel was completely different. It was 'economic slavery' whereby debtors sold themselves as slaves to pay off their debt (2Ki 4:1). Such slavery wasn't permanent, limited to seven years, after which the debt was considered paid (Ex 21:2–4; Dt 15:12–15, 18).

By Roman times slavery was widespread (85–90 per cent of Italy's population were slaves or from slave origins). Slaves who absconded or rebelled were normally executed if caught. Paul therefore faced a dilemma. As a Roman citizen, he was obliged to hand over Onesimus; but as one of God's people, he was obliged to give him sanctuary (Dt 23:15–16). So since Onesimus had become a Christian, Paul appealed to Philemon to take back the runaway, not as a slave to be punished but as a brother to be welcomed, forgiven even as Philemon himself had been forgiven by Christ – a request exceeding anything found in any other contemporary documents.

Paul was being tactical. He knew he couldn't change an entrenched structure like slavery overnight; but he could start to undermine it. So he encouraged slaves to gain their freedom if possible (1Co 7:21), said slave-trading was incompatible with Christianity (1Ti 1:9–11), and said masters and slaves alike should function in the light of their common relationship to Christ (Eph 6:5–9; Col 3:22–25). Above all he reminded everyone that 'there is neither Jew nor Gentile, neither slave nor free, nor is there male and female, for you are all one in Christ Jesus' (Gal 3:28). Such teaching sounded the death knell for slavery in due course.

have been carried to Philemon by Onesimus, and the very fact that it is included in the New Testament suggests that Philemon decided to act on its contents.

HEBREWS

The 'letter to the Hebrews' is one of the most fascinating letters in the New Testament, stressing how Jesus Christ represents the fulfilment of the Old Testament sacrificial system. It is not clear who the intended readers of the letter would have been. The most appropriate readers would have been Greek-speaking Jewish converts to Christianity, who wanted to know the relationship between their new faith and the old ways and ideas of Judaism. This information is provided in a superb manner by this letter.

The author of the letter is also unknown. Some older English translations suggest that the author is Paul. However, the text makes no such claim. In any case, the style of the writing is very different from that of Paul. The two people who are most likely to have written the work are Barnabas and Apollos, both of whom would have had the deep familiarity with the Old Testament and the excellent command of the Greek language that this book demonstrates. However, the question of authorship is not of major importance to appreciating the importance and relevance of this letter. The writer will simply be referred to as 'the author' in this commentary.

1:1–2:4 *The Son Superior to Angels* The letter does not open with a greeting. Instead, it plunges directly into a declaration of the superiority of Jesus Christ over every other form of divine revelation. Noting that God has indeed revealed himself, to some extent and in different ways, in the past, the author declares that God has now chosen to reveal himself completely and definitively through his Son Jesus Christ. Jesus Christ is the 'exact representation' of God. In other words, to see Christ is to see God. Jesus is like the mirror image or the definitive imprint of God's own nature.

Having made this point, the author proceeds to demonstrate the superiority of Jesus over a range of people who might be considered rival claimants to the title of 'supreme revelation of God'. In due course, he will deal with Moses, a figure of special importance to Jewish readers. But his attention first focuses on the angels, regarded by some Jews as the mediators of God's revelation. In an analysis of a series of biblical passages, he demonstrates how they point to the coming of Jesus Christ as the Son of God. God spoke to no angel like this! Angels serve God – and therefore serve Jesus Christ, to whom they are inferior.

2:5–18 *Jesus Made Like His Brothers* In addition, the Son has authority over the world to come. In an important exposition of Psalm 8, the author demonstrates how the psalm's reference to the son of man being made 'a little lower than the angels' is a reference to the incarnation of Jesus Christ (2:5–9). In other words, the psalm looks ahead to Jesus Christ becoming man, and hence willingly accepting a status lower than that of the angels in order to achieve the salvation of humanity. And as a result of his incarnation, Jesus was made perfect through suffering (2:10–18).

For the author, this is a vitally important point, bringing hope to any who are going through suffering, or being tempted. Jesus had to become like us human beings, in order to redeem us. If he was to be an effective high priest who would be able to deal with our sins, he had to become like those whom he intended to redeem. Although Jesus is none other than God himself – a point the author establishes in his opening

chapter – this does not mean that he is totally different from us. He is both God and a man. Being God does not prevent him from being human as well. Hence the author insists on the likeness between Jesus and us, and the great spiritual comfort that this brings. Jesus knows what it is like to suffer – and so can sympathise with us when we suffer.

3:1–6 *Jesus Greater than Moses* The author now turns his attention to the greatest figure of the Old Testament, through whom God gave the Law to Israel – Moses. Great though Moses was, he is overshadowed and outranked by Jesus. Just as a son is superior to a servant within a household, so Jesus (as the Son of God) is superior to Moses (as the servant of God) in God's saving plans and purposes.

3:7–19 *Warning Against Unbelief* The author now turns his attention to the need for redemption. He points out how, even after Israel had been given the Law, she continued to sin. In an important exposition of Psalm 95, the author draws attention to the devastating impact of Israel's rebellion against God, and the continued promise of a 'rest' for the people of God. The idea of a 'rest' is used here as a symbol of the redemption that God offers to his people. Yet that rest cannot be entered, on account of unbelief. So what can be done about this?

4:1–13 *A Sabbath-rest for the People of God* The author begins by stressing that the hope of a Sabbath-rest for the people of God remains open, despite all the sin of the past. The vital role of the word of God is noted: it is able to bring out the

Old Testament allusions

Hebrews uses Old Testament concepts to explain Christ's work. There are references to:

- a *Sabbath rest*. According to Hebrew tradition, God 'rested' on the seventh day of creation, and expected his people to keep the seventh day holy by not doing any work. Hebrews uses this as a picture of the salvation that Christ brings.
- the *covenant*. The contract or agreement that God gives to his people. For the Jews, this agreement was expressed in the Law of Moses. But now God has given a better agreement to his people through Christ.
- Christ as a *high priest*. Under the Law of Moses, the high priest represented the people to God and sacrificed animals to secure forgiveness of their sins. God has provided a perfect high priest who offered not animals, but himself.
- *the Most Holy Place*. A room within the tent of meeting (or tabernacle) that contained the ark of the covenant. Only the high priest was allowed to enter it, once a year, to offer sacrifices. Hebrews sees it as a picture of heaven, where Christ enters into God's presence.

---

reality of human sin, penetrating to the very depths of human nature. From his brief overview of Israel's history, the author brings out the fact that those who are obedient can expect to receive this promised rest.

4:14–5:10 Jesus the Great High Priest
Having identified the promise of rest, and the problem of sin, the author now turns to the means by which this promise may be fulfilled through Jesus Christ, the great high priest. Although some aspects of this theme will be explored later, the author makes a number of points immediately, as he sets out the significance of Jesus Christ. First, he makes the point that Jesus Christ is a sympathetic high priest. He is like us in every way (except for sin), so that we can draw near to God through him with confidence. Secondly, he draws attention to the need to be called to the office of high priest. In the case of Jesus Christ, this

calling comes directly from God himself. By learning obedience through suffering, Jesus demonstrated himself to be the perfect high priest, who would be able to make the necessary sacrifice for sin.

5:11–6:20 The Certainty of God's Promise
This theme will be taken up again presently. The author now turns to deal once more with the problem of unbelief (5:11–6:12), stressing the serious threat it poses to a believer's relationship with God. He then returns to the theme of the promises of God, and deals with their utter reliability (6:13–20). In making a promise, people swear by the authority of someone greater than themselves to bring home their commitment to the promise. But in God's case, there is none who is superior to him. As a result, God swears by himself as way of affirming his total faithfulness to his promises. God cannot lie: therefore, believers can have total

trust in his promises. The author uses the image of an anchor to bring out the way in which the Christian life is firmly 'anchored' in God himself. And the ultimate grounds of this hope? For the author it is that believers may rest assured of their salvation on account of the work of Jesus as high priest (6:19–20).

7:1–28 Melchizedek the Priest This leads the author to explore the high priesthood of Jesus in more detail. He begins by focusing on the mysterious figure of Melchizedek (Ge 14:18–20), who blessed Abraham on his return from defeating the five kings. This action implies the superiority of Melchizedek over Abraham, which is confirmed by the latter's paying tithes to the former. Now the Levitical priests were descended from Abraham, and failed to deal with the sin of the people. For this reason, there is a need for a different priest, descended from Melchizedek rather than Abraham, who can deal with the sinful situation of humanity. The author then argues that Jesus Christ is a high priest after the order of Melchizedek (picking up a theme from the strongly messianic Ps 110:4).

So what failings were there with human high priests? The author points

---

Can Christians lose their salvation?

Such a question normally comes from someone fearing God has given up on them, or troubled by someone drifting away from Jesus, or who has read Heb 6:4–6. While this difficult passage has been interpreted in many ways, it must be remembered for whom Hebrews was written: Christians from a Jewish background who, under pressure, were considering reverting to Judaism. The writer therefore reminds them of Jesus' superiority to everything Jewish (Heb 1–5), asking how they hope to be saved if they abandon Jesus – the Jesus they turned to precisely because they saw their old Judaism couldn't save them. Would they really go back to what couldn't save them? How then could they hope to be saved, he asks? Yet his immediately going on to speak of God's faithfulness (Heb 6:13ff) suggests this will not – could not – happen.

Indeed the New Testament often speaks of God's faithfulness to keep his people. Jesus promised his sheep that 'they shall never perish; no one will snatch them out of my hand' (Jn 10:28). Paul wrote that 'he who began a good work in you will carry it on to completion until the day of Christ Jesus' (Php 1:6). The doctrine of justification by faith underlines that we already have God's end-time 'not guilty' verdict right now and that nothing can ever change this.

Yes, the Bible has some challenging passages – challenges to not become faithless, careless or lazy; but such passages are not meant to discourage, but rather to provoke us to press on with God in challenging and hard times so that we do not miss out on what God wants to do in us through them. Ultimately, the Bible assures us that 'if we are faithless, he remains faithful, for he cannot disown himself' (2Ti 2:13).

out how these high priests had to make sacrifices for their own sins, before dealing with those of their people. And this very action demonstrated that they needed forgiveness, as much as everyone else. The need, therefore, is for a sinless high priest. And this is only met through Jesus Christ.

8:1–9:10 The High Priest of a New Covenant Jesus is therefore the high priest of the new covenant, which replaces the old covenant established through Moses (8:1–13). Using a series of Old Testament passages, the author demonstrates that the old covenant had to pass away, to make way for a better covenant, mediated only through Jesus Christ. And so the ceremonial regulations of the old covenant, important in their own time, are now outmoded (9:1–10). A distinction is drawn between the eternally valid aspects of the Old Testament (such as the promises of forgiveness), and those that are superseded through the coming of Christ (such as external matters of worship, or regulations concerning food and drink).

9:11–28 The Blood of Christ In a reference to the ritual associated with the Old Testament Day of Atonement (Lev 16:11–19), the author points out how the blood of bulls and goats was able to achieve only outward cleansing. But the blood of Christ is able to achieve eternal redemption, thus bringing about the internal cleansing and purification that the Law had pointed to, but was unable to deliver (9:11–14). Through his blood, Christ is the mediator of a new covenant, through which those who have been called may receive their eternal heritage (9:15).

The author now draws out the parallel between the old and new covenants, and human wills (the same Greek word is used to refer to both, in much the same way as the English word 'testament'). A will becomes operative once the person who made it has died. And through the death of Christ, the promises of forgiveness have finally been realised. At his first coming, Christ was sacrificed for us, so that he might bear our sins. At his second coming, he will bring the final salvation for those who have put their trust in him, and have been sanctified through his blood (9:16–28).

10:1–18 Christ's Sacrifice Once for All As the author continues to develop the contrast between the sacrifices of the Old Testament, and the perfect sacrifice of Christ, he points out how the Old Testament sacrifices did not actually achieve what they pointed to. If the sacrifices had to be repeated year after year, it is clear that they had not achieved their objective. To put it simply: the blood of bulls and goats cannot take away sins (again, note the clear reference to the Day of Atonement ritual, Lev 16:11–19). The priest offers the same old sacrifices year after year, without ever managing to take away people's sins – but Christ made a perfect and once-for-all sacrifice, which obtains full forgiveness of sins, and thus does away with any need for further sacrifices. Christ's perfect sacrifice makes the sacrifices of the old covenant obsolete. There is no need for them any more, in that what they pointed to – but could not deliver – has now been achieved.

10:9–39 A Call to Persevere With this thought in mind, the author urges his readers to appreciate what God has done for them, and the great hope to which it leads. On account of the death of Christ, a way has been opened through the curtain of the temple – that is, through the barrier that separates the people from God on account of their sin. It is now possible to draw near to God, with full assurance that sins have been cleansed and forgiven through the blood of Christ. And this thought, the author argues, ought to enable believers to persevere in the Christian life.

11:1–40 By Faith A further stimulus to perseverance is provided by the great figures of faith of the Old Testament. In one of the most famous passages in the letter, the author provides his reader with a spectacular panorama of trust, as he surveys the great believers of the Old Testament. Faith is about being able to see through to the world of spiritual realities. It is about being certain of things that we cannot actually see, but nevertheless know to be true – such as the truth and trustworthiness of the promises of God. The author then surveys the great men and women of faith, allowing us to see that a central feature of Christian faith – a trust in the promises, presence and power of God – was present in the past.

So what advantage does the Christian believer have over these great Old Testament figures of faith? The author is clear: they trusted in the great promises of God, *but did not receive what they promised.* The Christian believer also believes in those same promises, but has the advantage both of *knowing* that they have

been fulfilled in Jesus Christ, and of *receiving* the benefits that were promised (11:39–40).

12:1–13 God Disciplines His Children With this thought in mind, the author encourages his readers to take heart from the witness of the past. He provides believers with a powerful image to encourage them to keep going in the Christian life. He argues that it is like being in a race, and cheered on by a crowd of believers from the past. They are shouting encouragement, just as crowds urge on runners in a marathon, so that believers will make the effort to finish the course. And if that thought is not enough, the author asks believers to fix their eyes on Jesus, and appreciate how he was prepared to accomplish all that was asked of him (12:1–3). Jesus is here referred to as the 'pioneer and perfecter of faith' (12:2). By this, the author wants to bring out the fact that Jesus has gone before believers in the life of faith, blazing a trail they are being asked to follow. Jesus is both the basis of their faith, and an example of faith. He has made the Christian life possible through his sacrificial death. He also provides an example, from which believers may take encouragement.

And just as discipline is an important element in long-distance running, so it is in the Christian life. In order to finish the marathon of the Christian life, believers need to be disciplined by God. The author thus asks his readers to expect and welcome discipline from God. Discipline is to be seen as a mark of commitment and love. After all, fathers discipline only their own children. God's discipline affirms believers, by informing

them that they are his children
(12:4–13).

12:14–13:19 Encouragement to Keep Going
The letter now begins to draw to its
close. It does so with an extended passage
of encouragement, urging its readers to
devote time and attention to their
relationship with God, not to be
discouraged by their weaknesses, and to
seek comfort and strength in Jesus
Christ. Life may change, but he will
remain the same for ever. There is a real
need to advance to Christian maturity,
and shake off the sin that can so easily be
an obstacle to faith.

13:20–25 Concluding Prayer The author
concludes with a powerful prayer of
commitment and personal greetings. In
his prayer, he entrusts his readers to the
care of a greater pastor than himself, who
can be relied on to care for his sheep, and
bring them safely through to their final
salvation. The same God who raised
Christ from the dead will work in the
lives of believers, and bring them through
whatever lies ahead.

JAMES

The letter of James is the first of a group of letters sometimes referred to as the 'catholic letters' or 'epistles general'. These unusual terms draw attention to the fact that the letters in question are not written to specific individuals, or specific churches, but seem to be intended to be read by a wide range of people. Their intended readership is thus general or universal. (The word 'catholic' basically means 'universal' or 'general'.)

The letter of James was probably not written by James the apostle, but by James the brother of Jesus, who played an important role in the Council of Jerusalem (Ac 15:13). This council was especially concerned with clarifying whether Christian believers would be under any obligation to respect the Law of Moses, especially its requirement that males should be circumcised. In the end, the council decided that this should not be a requirement (see Ac 15). However, no reference is made to this controversy in the letter.

The absence of any reference to the controversy over whether Gentile believers should be circumcised points to an early date for the letter. However, James appears to be concerned to correct a possible misunderstanding of Paul's doctrine of justification by faith, which would suggest a date at some point in the late 50s or early 60s. We shall probably never know precisely when the letter was written. The letter is packed full of practical advice, as invaluable today as it was when it was first written. At a number of points, it seems to draw on, or reflect knowledge of the themes of, the Sermon on the Mount.

OUTLINE

1:1 Addressed to Jewish Converts The letter is addressed to 'the twelve tribes scattered among the nations' (1:1). This way of referring to believers suggests that they are primarily Jewish converts. The letter is probably the most Jewish writing in the New Testament. It seems to reflect a very early period in the history of the church, when a large proportion of believers were converted Jews, and the meeting-place of Christians is still referred to as a 'synagogue' (2:2, in the Greek).

1:2–2:13 Trials and Temptations James open his letter by stressing the need to resist doubt and temptation. The role of riches in causing temptation is

particularly noted. Believers are not simply people who hear the word of God. They are those who obey it (1:19–27). Faith is something that expresses itself in practical, not just theoretical, ways. James is particularly concerned to ensure that the standards of the world do not contaminate the church (1:27). The example he chooses to bring out the way in which the church can be swayed by worldly attitudes is that of a rich man who turns up for a meeting, and is given preference in every way over a poor man (2:1–13).

2:14–26 Faith and Deeds Probably the most important section of the letter now follows. It is possible that James has encountered a misunderstanding of Paul's doctrine of justification by faith, which suggested that if someone believes in Christ, they are freed from any obligation to do good works. Whether this is the case or not, there can be no doubt that James is concerned to emphasise the moral consequences of faith. Even the demons believe that there is a God – but that faith does not justify them!

James declares that the kind of faith that matters is a faith that shows itself in action. This does not mean that anyone is put right with God by doing good works. Rather, it means that good works are the natural result of a real faith. James appeals to two examples from the Old

---

Why does the Bible have so much to say about the tongue?

From the very beginning of the Bible we see that words are powerful, for good or for bad. At creation God simply spoke and powerful things happened. All he said was, 'Let there be . . .' and what he spoke came into being (e.g., Ge 1:3). But equally words can be used for evil, as when the serpent questioned what God had said, seeking to undermine both God and his truth (Ge 3:1), with devastating results for humanity. It was this power – for good or for evil – that James was aware of when he wrote these words about the tongue (3:1–12). And it is why the Bible calls on God's people to be very careful how they use their words.

Proverbs – the Bible's book of practical wisdom – has much to say about the tongue. It stresses that wise people hold their tongue rather than speaking out quickly, for talking too much leads to sin (10:19). Guarding what you say is one of the clearest signs of wisdom, and can spare you from disaster (21:23) or even save your life (13:3) – though it is not just about us, for wise words can bring healing to others too (12:18).

The Bible has many examples of the negative use of the tongue, highlighting the destructive power of things like gossip, ridicule, slander, mockery, criticism and cynicism. Yet the value of the tongue is also seen, in things like encouragement, comfort, blessing, prophecy, singing, worship and teaching. Christians more than anyone should guard how they speak, knowing they represent the one who was called 'the Word' (Jn 1:1), the very presence of God incarnate in the world (Jn 1:14) to bring his message of forgiveness, hope and new beginnings.

Testament to make this point – Abraham and Rahab. Both believed in God, and did certain things as a result.

3:1–4:12 Taming the Tongue; Learning Humility

The emphasis now returns to practical wisdom. The tongue needs careful controlling (3:1–12). The tongue can just as easily praise and curse. There is a real need to take care over what is said, given the enormous consequences of careless and thoughtless words. The importance of wisdom is noted, and its true source in God himself affirmed (3:13–18). Believers should submit themselves to God, and learn his humility (4:1–12). Once more, the dangers of worldliness are pointed out. Anyone who chooses to become a friend of the world will end up by being an enemy of God.

4:13–17 Boasting About Tomorrow

As an example of this worldliness, James gives the example of someone who confidently predicts the future course of his life. For James, this is unacceptable. Our futures lie with God, who alone knows what will take place. Anyone planning the future should add the phrase 'if it is the Lord's will' to their words, as a reminder as to who is in control (4:13–17). (This phrase is often represented by the letters D.V., representing the Latin form of this phrase, *deo volente*.)

5:1–12 Warning to the Rich; Patience in Suffering

The criticism of attitudes towards riches apparent earlier in the letter now emerges once more. James makes the point that riches come from somewhere, and are generally gained at someone else's expense. For this reason, the Lord is angry with those who are rich (5:1–6). In marked contrast, James encourages those who are suffering in any way, in order to increase their patience. The example of Job is commended: suffering can lead to blessings (5:7–12).

5:13–20 The Prayer of Faith

The letter draws to its conclusion with some practical advice on prayer (5:13–20). The importance of prayer is noted, especially the prayers of the righteous, whether for forgiveness or for healing. The practice of anointing the sick with oil in the name of the Lord is commended. Finally, the importance of supporting and correcting one other in the faith is pointed out. And so this very practical and moral letter comes to its end.

1 PETER

The first letter of Peter is addressed to Christians scattered throughout the general region of Asia Minor, who are facing the threat of persecution. Although that persecution has yet to begin, it is clearly seen as a major threat by those to whom Peter was writing. The situation that the letter presupposes could easily fit in with what we know of the difficulties faced by Christians in the reign of Nero (AD 54–68). Peter indicates that he was in 'Babylon' when he wrote the letter (5:13), which is widely interpreted as a reference to Rome itself (although a town of that name also existed on the river Euphrates around this time).

1:1–2 *Authorship and Readership* The letter opens with an affirmation that its writer is Peter, the apostle, and that his intended readership is believers in the general area of Asia Minor. The descriptions used for believers are very important. They are 'God's elect' (in that they have been chosen by God) and 'exiles' (in that although they live in the world, they are not of that world). Father, Son and Holy Spirit are all identified as being involved in the salvation of believers.

1:3–12 *Praise to God for a Living Hope* Peter then expresses his joy at the Christian hope (1:3–4:9). He and his readers have the enormous privilege of being born again into a hope that nothing can ever take away from them. They are being shielded by God's power, so that they will finally inherit all the riches that are being stored for them in heaven. And they can rest assured of this inheritance, on account of the resurrection of Christ. Even though the threat of suffering looms on the horizon, it cannot take away their hope in Christ.

The salvation that believers now enjoy is something the great prophets of the Old Testament longed to see. They knew that God would send a Messiah, whose sufferings and glory the people of God would share (1:10–12). Many New Testament writers, especially Matthew and the writer of the letter to the Hebrews, stressed the way in which the coming of Jesus Christ brought to fulfilment the great hopes and expectations of the Old Testament, often allowing the true meaning of a passage to be understood for the very first time.

Isn't the picture of Jesus' death as a sacrifice outdated?

Isn't seeing Jesus' death as a sacrifice not only obscure, but also unhelpful for today? After all, language like sacrifice, blood and atonement are meaningless to most modern Western readers, while God just comes across as angry. But the picture cannot be so easily discarded.

First, because we don't need to. The imagery of sacrifice is still well understood, as when firefighters sacrifice their lives to rescue someone. While the biblical picture goes much deeper than this, it is at least a starting point for discussion with non-Christians. But secondly, because Jesus' death as a sacrifice isn't just a *picture*; it's a *reality*. Sacrifice is a theme running deeply through the whole of Scripture and as such is significant. Jesus placed his own death firmly in line with this, especially at the Last Supper when he declared, 'This is my blood of the covenant, which is poured out for many' (Mk 14:24) – a clear reference to Moses' sealing his covenant with sacrificial blood (Ex 24:6–8) and to priests 'pouring out' blood onto the altar to effect various sacrifices (e.g., Lev 4:27–31). Since this was a Passover meal – the recollection of the averting of God's wrath (Ex 12:12–13) – it seems clear how Jesus saw his death: as an atoning sacrifice to avert God's righteous anger against sinners by paying the price of their sin. This was no mere picture, but reality.

Yes, sacrifice is only one explanation of the cross; others include redemption or ransom, cleansing, reconciliation, victory and justification. None is the sole explanation; rather like facets of a diamond they together display the splendour of the whole. Equally, none are pictures; all are realities. Dispensing with any of them is to dispense with a fundamental aspect of salvation and leave us prone to doubting accusations about our forgiveness.

1:13–2:3 The Reality and Cost of Redemption

Peter then stresses both the reality and the cost of redemption. The cost of the redemption of believers cannot be measured in terms of silver and gold. These are not precious enough to compare to the true price of our redemption. The price of salvation is nothing less than the blood of Christ, 'a lamb without blemish or defect' – a clear reference to the perfect lamb that had to be selected for the Passover celebration, which recalled God's great act of deliverance in which he freed his people from bondage in Egypt.

And nothing can snatch this hope away from believers. In the midst of a transient world, believers can rest assured of the reality of the hope of final redemption and resurrection. Christian faith rests securely on the word of God, which will stand for ever. And, given the total faithfulness of God to his people, Peter urges them to show an equal faithfulness to God, by dedicating themselves to his service and ridding themselves of all sinful desires. They must go on to maturity, just as infants progress from milk to solid food (2:1–3).

2:4–12 *The Living Stone, and a Chosen People* Peter then explains the privileges of being the people of God. He develops the image of believers as stones that are being built up into a house. Although this image differs from Paul's analogy of the human body with its various parts, the same point is being made: the Christian life is meant to be corporate, rather than individualist. And these stones are being laid on an absolutely solid and dependable foundation, which is none other than Jesus Christ himself. Unbelievers may fail to understand how someone who was rejected by his own people could come to have such importance. But Christ, though rejected by his own people, was affirmed by God through his resurrection, and was thus declared to be the Son of God.

And believers, as a body, are called to be the people of God. Peter brings together a small galaxy of Old Testament themes and allusions, as he demonstrates how the calling of believers brings to fulfilment a whole series of hopes and prophecies. They have been chosen by God. They have been made into a royal priesthood (a reference to the king-priests of the Old Testament, who were endowed with special gifts of the Spirit). They are holy, like God himself, and belong to him, in that he has purchased them through the blood of his only Son. God has called them from the darkness of a sinful world into his own wonderful light. In every respect, Peter brings out the dramatic consequences of being called out of the world to serve God through Christ. But as a result of their calling, they are now foreigners and exiles in the world (2:11). Although they live in the world, they look beyond it to their homeland in heaven. It is a great privilege to be a Christian.

2:13–25 *Submission to Earthly Authorities* Part of that privilege is to suffer for Christ. Peter urges his readers to submit to earthly authorities, so that any resulting persecution will obviously be due to the fact that they are Christians. Christ has already suffered, and left this example for believers to follow. It is therefore important that believers should be seen to suffer *for Christ*, and not for some civil offence for which some form of punishment would be fully merited. Peter wants to gain the maximum evangelistic potential from any persecution of Christians.

However, as he explores the theme of suffering, Peter meditates further on the death of Christ. Drawing on Isaiah's words concerning the future suffering servant of God (Isa 52:13–53:12), he shows how the suffering of Christ on the cross fulfilled this great prophecy. Christians believe that Christ bore their sins on the cross. It is by his wounds that they have been healed. They were like sheep that had gone astray, yet through Christ, they have returned to God.

3:1–7 *Wives and Husbands* As we noted earlier, Peter is concerned to gain the maximum evangelistic potential for the gospel. Apparently as part of this strategy, Peter urges husbands and wives to behave towards each other in ways that would be acceptable to the world at large. Peter's plan is clear: he wants Christian wives to be able to win over their non-believing husbands. However, it is clear that Peter believes that both men and women have an equal share in the 'gracious gift of life'

(3:7). While Peter is recommending that wives adopt an attitude of submission to their husbands, this is seen as a tactic to enable them to win over their husbands to their faith. For Peter, gender has no bearing on eternal life – an attitude echoed and endorsed by Paul (Gal 3:28).

3:8–4:19 Suffering for Doing Good
The theme of suffering now returns. To be a believer is potentially to be a suffering believer. Peter begins his discussion of this sombre theme by emphasising the need to suffer for the gospel, rather than for doing wrong. What is the point of suffering for doing wrong? The important thing is to make sure that any suffering that comes the way of believers is a direct result of their faith, rather than of wrongdoing. The example of Christ is supremely important in this respect.

Peter then elaborates on some aspects of the meaning of the death of Christ (3:18–22), which deserve special attention. The death of Christ is the means by which sin is forgiven, and access to the presence of God is gained. Christ is now raised on high and seated at the right hand of God, with all heavenly beings and powers in submission to him. However, before his resurrection, Christ 'went and made proclamation to the imprisoned spirits' (3:19). The full meaning of this passage is not clear. However, one possible interpretation is of interest, and may be noted here. According to this interpretation, the passage refers to Christ preaching the good news to those who died before his coming, so that none might be deprived of hearing the gospel.

This section also includes an important interpretation of Noah's ark. The waters of the flood point both to judgment (in that they resulted from the sin of the world) and salvation (in that they offered a means of deliverance through the ark). In much the same way, the water of baptism symbolises both the judgment resulting from sin, and the cleansing and forgiveness that result only from the death and resurrection of Jesus Christ.

Peter then encourages his readers to prepare for suffering (4:1–11), in the sure knowledge that God will sustain and support them, and that their fortitude under suffering will lead to the praise of God. Believers must not be surprised by this threat of suffering. Perhaps Peter has in mind the 'common-sense' view that the righteous will not suffer – a view contradicted by the cross, on which the only truly righteous person suffered and died. Believers must expect to suffer for their righteousness. Whatever heavenly reward it will gain, it is likely to lead only to mocking, scorn and persecution on earth.

5:1–11 To Elders and the Flock
Peter makes it clear that he writes as someone who himself had been a witness to the sufferings of Christ (5:1). He now asks his readers to prepare themselves, as individuals and as communities, for any such ordeals. After some advice to elders and those who are younger (5:2–5), he emphasises that believers may cast all their cares on the God who cares for them (5:6–7). Although the threat of satanic attack remains real, it may be resisted by standing firm in the faith, in the sure knowledge that God will comfort and restore them (5:8–11).

5:12–14 Final Greetings
The letter then concludes. Peter acknowledges the

assistance of Silas in writing the letter (5:12). It is highly likely that Silas did more than write the letter down. Secretaries were often given the task of putting a writer's thoughts into better Greek than the writer himself could manage. The letter is written in excellent Greek – much better than would be expected from a former Galilean fisherman! Silas may well have ensured that Peter's practical advice and theological wisdom were stated in the best possible manner. (Interestingly, 2 Peter is written in much poorer Greek, and no reference is made to Silas: perhaps we may see Peter's unaided writing style in this later letter?) Finally, Peter offers the greetings of John Mark, who is widely credited with recording Peter's memories of Jesus in the form of the Gospel of the same name.

2 PETER

The second letter of Peter differs from the first in a number of ways. Perhaps the most obvious is the style of Greek used, which is noticeably less 'professional' than that of the first letter – a point that is often explained through the involvement of Silas in the composition of the earlier letter. The letters also differ significantly in terms of their subjects: 1 Peter was especially concerned with the threat of suffering and hardship; 2 Peter is more concerned with the threat posed by false teaching.

1:1–11 *Making One's Calling and Election Sure*
The letter opens with a call to believers: they must work to ensure their election or salvation, by pressing on towards Christian maturity. God has promised that those who remain faithful will share in his own nature, and escape from this sinful world. Believers need to press on, to ensure that they benefit from this secure promise (1:1–11). Yet there is a real threat to this security of faith from false teachers. Before providing further details of these teachers, Peter emphasises his own personal credentials as an apostle (1:12–21). He has been an eyewitness to what he reports. He has not invented anything, but merely faithfully and truthfully reported what he has seen and heard, guided and sustained by the Holy Spirit.

2:1–22 *False Teachers and Their Destruction*
This contrasts sharply with the dishonesty of the false teachers. Peter makes the point that there have always been false teachers within the household of faith, even in the days of the Old Testament prophets. The rise of false teachers within the church thus falls into a well-established pattern. However, it also poses a serious threat to the gospel, by denying or calling into question the fundamentals of the Christian faith. Peter makes it clear that many false teachers are motivated by personal ambition, and care nothing for the welfare of believers.

Although Peter never specifically identifies the false teachings that so concern him, it is clear he expects his readers to know what they are. The false teachings in question are like dried-up springs, which seem to offer refreshment, but on closer inspection turn out to be arid. They offer freedom to their hearers – but in reality they threaten to enslave them once more, by dragging them back into the world from which they have

been liberated by the gospel (2:17–20). The hints he provides suggest that the false teachings are related to those that emerged at Colossae, which would later find their full expression in the movement known as 'Gnosticism' in the 2nd century. Peter's concern is more to emphasise the fate of the false teachers than to provide an analysis and refutation of their teaching.

3:1–13 The Day of the Lord Peter then turns to deal with a question that seems to have been troubling some of his readers. When will the second coming take place? It seems that many who expected to live to see this coming had died, causing bewilderment to some. Peter stresses the total reliability of the Lord's promise to return. He will return – but nobody knows for certain when this will be. In any case, there may be a disparity between divine and human understandings of time. After all, a thousand years is like a day in the sight of the Lord. The important thing, Peter argues, is to look forward with certainty to the hope of the new heaven and new earth, rather than become preoccupied with precise dates and times.

3:14–18 Trust in the Lord Peter then asks his readers to trust in the Lord, knowing that the Lord in his patience wants people to be saved. The delay of the second coming will give more people the opportunity to repent. The fact that the second coming has not yet happened is not an indication of God's failure or faithlessness, but rather an expression of his patience, and desire to save as many people as possible. This point, Peter argues, is made in the writings of Paul, although he concedes that these are not as easy to understand as one might like (3:14–16).

Finally, Peter reassures his readers of the total reliability of 'our Lord and Saviour Jesus Christ' (3:17–18). He can be trusted – unlike the false teachers!

1, 2, 3 JOHN

The three letters of John are best taken together, as they are very similar in content and style. Their common author is the apostle John, who was also responsible for writing the fourth Gospel and the book of Revelation. It is generally thought that the letters date from the end of the 1st century, perhaps having been written from the city of Ephesus around AD 85–90. The identity of the readership of the first two letters is not clear. They are addressed to believers in general, and may have been intended as circular letters for the use of travelling evangelists. The third letter is specifically addressed to Gaius, although his identity is not clear.

1 JOHN
OUTLINE

1:1–4 Prologue: the word of life incarnate

1:5–2:11 Walking in the light: Christian living

2:12–14 The new status of the people of God

2:15–17 The people of God and the world

2:18–27 A warning against antichrists

2:28–3:3 The hope of the children of God

3:4–10 The Christian hope and resisting sin

3:11–24 Brotherly love as a mark of true Christian faith

4:1–6 True and false spirits distinguished

4:7–5:5 Divine and human love

5:6–12 God's testimony concerning assurance in Jesus Christ

5:13–21 Conclusion: Christian certainties

1 John

The first letter, in addition to affirming some central features of the gospel, is concerned to deal with false teachings that had arisen within the church at this time. The basic features of the false teachings (which seem to be an early form of Gnosticism) include a denial of the incarnation of Jesus Christ, and the belief that there is no need for believers to act morally. It opens with John affirming that he is an eyewitness to the coming of Jesus Christ (1:1–4). The basic theme of the gospel is that the light of life has broken into a dark world. Through the blood of Christ, the lives of believers may be purified from the taint of sin (1:5–7).

1:8–10 Sin Having introduced the theme of sin, John now develops it in more detail. The universal extent of sin is vigorously affirmed: nobody is free from its stains, and all need cleansing from its contamination (1:8–10). John's purpose in writing is partly to encourage believers to resist sin, but also to assure them that, if they do sin, they have forgiveness through the atoning sacrifice of Christ. In other words, the death of Christ enables God

How can I be sure God has forgiven me?

'If we confess our sins, he is faithful and just and will forgive us our sins and purify us from all unrighteousness' (1:9). This was something John's readers really needed to hear, having fallen into sin through embracing false teaching. Could God really forgive them now, they wondered? John's reply contains two key words that are the grounds of Christian confidence, no matter what we've said or done: *faithful* and *just*. Both are to do with God; neither is to do with us. This is the heart of the Christian message: it is all about God, not us. This is why we can be sure of forgiveness. If it depended on our efforts, we might have doubts, as John's readers did. But John turns their eyes from themselves to God – God who is 'faithful and just'.

First, it is because God is *faithful* that we have confidence. This is the constant message of the Bible, and countless stories affirm this: Abraham, forgiven though he lied; Moses, forgiven though he murdered; David, forgiven though he committed adultery; Jonah, forgiven though he disobeyed. God did not give up on them. But not only is God faithful; he is also *just*. He always does what is righteous and right. And what is right is to forgive those who trust in Christ, for Christ has paid the price of our sin – past, present and even future – through his substitutionary death on the cross, so that there remains no price for us now to pay. God's right verdict over us, now cleansed by Christ's blood, can be only 'Not guilty!' And this is his final, just word on the matter.

Assurance of forgiveness has nothing to do with us, but everything to do with God. And this is why we can be so confident.

to cancel the guilt of sin, and purge us from its stain (2:1–2).

2:3–14 Love It is clear that some of John's readers have been told that there is no need for them to concern themselves with morals. John rejects this opinion, and insists on the need for morality, and especially love, in the Christian life (2:3–14). This does not mean that believers should love the world, but rather love the God who created the world, and those whom God has redeemed from that world into the community of believers (2:15–17).

2:18–27 Warning Against Antichrists The theme of false teaching is now explicitly introduced. John declares that the churches are in danger of being seduced by 'antichrists' (2:18–27). The word is plural, and refers to a general category of people who oppose the claims of Jesus Christ to be the Messiah (note especially 2:22). John makes it clear that Jesus is to be acknowledged both as Son of God and as Messiah. To fail to do this is to miss out on the benefits of the gospel, including knowing the Father. (There are strong echoes of some themes of John's Gospel here, especially its insistence that the Father is made known through the Son: Jn 14:6, 9.)

2:28–4:21 Love One Another The theme of the 'love of God' is now examined in greater detail (2:28–4:21). All those who are called 'children of God' must live up to this calling, especially by resisting sin. Although at points John may seem to suggest that the life of believers is characterised by a complete absence of sin (e.g., 3:9), a closer reading indicates that his meaning is slightly different. The lives of believers must not be characterised or dominated by sin. In other words, believers must live towards God, not towards sin.

On a more positive note, John stresses the importance of love within the Christian community (3:11–24). The same love that was shown in Jesus laying down his life for his people must also be at work in the lives of believers. The world may hate believers. Believers, however, must love each other. John summarises the gospel in a nutshell as follows: to believe in Jesus the Son of God, and to love each other as he commanded us (3:23).

In a brief digression, John now warns his readers against a further specific false teaching – the denial of the basic Christian belief that 'Jesus Christ has come in the flesh' or that Jesus is from God (4:1–6). (This is similar to the

---

Who or what is Antichrist?

No figure has dominated end-time Christian thinking more than 'Antichrist' – remarkable, considering the term is used just four times (1Jn 2:18, 22; 4:3; 2Jn 7), and not at all in Revelation. Similar figures appear under different names however – 'false messiahs [Christs]'. However Antichrist is never seen as being *solely* an end-time phenomenon. John says that anyone who doesn't acknowledge Jesus as God incarnate and Messiah is 'the antichrist' (2Jn 7) and that 'many antichrists' were active in his day (1Jn 2:18; 4:2–3). Clearly he had in mind far more than one end-time figure.

It is helpful to understand the meaning of 'Antichrist'. We use 'anti' in the sense of something standing *against* something else; but in Greek 'anti' means 'instead of' or 'in place of'. Antichrist is therefore not merely a figure who will battle *against* Christ; he is also a person (or even a worldview or '-ism') that seeks to be established *in place of Christ*. He seeks not just to fight him but to replace him. Hence, in Rev 13 John sees the beast seeking to rival Christ in everything – his crown (13:1, contrast 19:12), his name (13:1, contrast 19:11–16), his authority (13:2, contrast 12:5), his worship (13:4, contrast 5:6–14), his death and resurrection (13:3, contrast 1:18). This same idea of competing against Christ is seen in Mk 13:22 and 2Th 2:4.

The New Testament doesn't waste time, therefore, on trying to identify 'Antichrist'; for Antichrist is anything or anyone in any time that seeks to replace Christ, against which Christians should always be on guard. But ultimately, we are assured, Antichrist and all antichrists will be overthrown (2Th 2:3; Rev 19:19–20; 20:10). In the meantime, fruitless end-time interpreting might be better replaced by exposing the 'antichrists' of our day.

error noted in an earlier chapter, which refused to accept that Jesus was the Christ or Messiah.) He then returns to the theme of the love of God. The reason for the digression then becomes clear.

God is love. But what is the love of God *like*? John declares that the love of God is shown in action (4:7–21). Everyone knows that actions speak louder than words. God, John declares, showed his love in action by sending his son Jesus Christ as an atoning sacrifice, so that believers might live through him. And it will be clear that if Jesus Christ is not from God, the basis of this declaration is void. Only if Jesus is from God is the love of God shown in the death of Christ on the cross. And believers can know and share in this love. God loved them first. Their love is simply a response to his.

5:1–12 Faith in the Son of God John then emphasises once more the importance of accepting that Jesus is the Messiah (or Christ). This is no human belief, but one that has been revealed by God himself. Believing that Jesus is the Son of God is the only basis for Christian living and hope of eternal life. This great truth is confirmed by the witness of the Holy Spirit (a reference to the Spirit's witness at the baptism of Jesus, Jn 1:32–34). God himself has declared that Jesus Christ is his Son. To fail to acknowledge this is to make God out to be a liar. (The same point was made earlier, when John declared that anyone who denied their sinfulness made God out to be a liar, 1:8–10.)

5:13–21 Concluding Remarks The first letter of John then concludes by declaring once more the total reliability of the gospel. John wants his readers to know that they have eternal life. Sin is indeed an obstacle to God – but not every type of sin leads to spiritual death or the loss of the hope of eternal life. Believers must resist sin, and trust in Jesus Christ as the Son of God. By doing so, they can rest assured that God will hear and respond to their prayers, and finally bring them to eternal life.

2 JOHN
OUTLINE
1–4 Greetings and commendation

5–11 Warnings against false teachings

12–13 Conclusion

2 John
The second and third letters of John are so brief that, like Philemon and Jude, references are made only to verse numbers. The second letter is probably written to a specific church and its members in Asia Minor, here referred to as 'the lady chosen by God and . . . her children' (1; the reference to the 'sister . . . chosen by God' at 13 is probably a reference to another local church).

After stressing the importance of love in the life of the Christian believer and community (4–6), John again deals with the false teaching he addressed at greater length in his first letter – namely, the denial that Jesus Christ had come in the flesh (7–11). It is clear that John's intention here is to oppose the teachers, rather than analyse and criticise the teaching (this may be found in the first letter).

3 JOHN
OUTLINE

3 John

The third letter is specifically addressed to Gaius, who is clearly a prominent Christian believer. The letter encourages him to be faithful in his Christian work. The references to hospitality (6–8) probably reflect the care shown to travelling missionaries, who used the houses of local Christian believers as staging posts on their evangelistic journeys. After reporting unfavourably on one local believer (probably the leader of a church, who appears to have been something of a prima donna, 9–10), and favourably on another, John ends his letter by passing on his greetings to all whom he knows.

JUDE

The letter of Jude is shrouded in mystery. It is not clear who 'Jude' is: the most likely contenders for authorship would be Judas the apostle (whom Luke carefully distinguished from Judas Iscariot: Lk 6:16; Ac 1:13), and Judas the brother of the Lord (Mt 13:55; Mk 6:3). Nor is it clear whom he was writing for. The main theme of the letter is a false teaching that has arisen, and appears to have become widespread. Variations on the same theme can be found in numerous other New Testament works, including Colossians, 2 Peter and 1 John.

OUTLINE

1–2 Address and greetings

3–4 The reason for writing

5–16 Warnings about false teachers

17–23 The need to persevere

24–25 Concluding prayer

vv.1–16 False Teaching The letter opens with Jude greeting his readers (1–2), followed by an immediate condemnation of false teaching. Jude had intended to write a very different letter, in which he would have written about the salvation that is the common heritage of all Christians. However, the 'faith that was once for all entrusted to God's holy people' is under threat from false teaching. The basic themes of the false teaching, to judge from Jude's very brief analysis (4) is a denial of the lordship of Jesus Christ and the rejection of the need for morality (teachings which are also examined and rejected in 1 John).

What follows is quite difficult to understand (5–16). It is clear that Jude is well read in Jewish writings, including a number of works that are not included in the Old Testament, and sees parallels between some of the incidents related in these works and the problems of his own day. Just as Paul occasionally quoted from secular Greek writers to illustrate a point to a Greek audience, so Jude clearly feels that his (presumably largely Jewish) readership will benefit from these comparisons, and realise how serious the problems are. In a series of images, Jude emphasises the sterility and self-serving motives of the false teachers, without going into detail concerning the nature of their teachings (12–13).

vv.17–25 A Call to Persevere; a Doxology Having stressed the dangers posed by such teachers, Jude urges his readers to persevere in the true faith (17–23). The rise of false teachers is only to be expected. Believers must strengthen their own faith through prayer. As for those who are weak in faith, they are to be treated mercifully (22–23). The letter ends with a doxology or exclamation of praise in which Jude affirms the glorious hope the gospel offers to believers, and the steadfastness of the God who has called believers to faith in his name (24–25).

REVELATION

The book of Revelation, which brings the New Testament to its close, is probably the most difficult book in the New Testament to understand. It is generally regarded as having been written by John the apostle, who was also responsible for the Gospel and three letters bearing his name in the New Testament. The book seems to have been written at a late date, probably during the later part of the reign of the Roman emperor Domitian (AD 81–96), when the Roman authorities were attempting to suppress Christianity in certain regions of their empire.

In many ways, the bulk of the book of Revelation resembles the second half of the prophecy of Daniel. It is composed of visions, making extensive use of symbolism and highly figurative language. In some cases, it is reasonably clear what the symbols represent. In many cases, however, the interpretation of the visions is difficult and speculative. It is no accident that the visions of Revelation have proved to be a hunting ground for some of the more bizarre religious sects and cults in recent years, who have found it easy to interpret some of the visions in line with their own highly unusual understanding of the end of the world. Readers of the visionary parts of the book must be clear that it is highly speculative to interpret any aspects of these visions in terms of the political world of today.

REVELATION 1:1–3:22
The Messages to the Churches

1:1–8 Greetings and Doxology The book opens by declaring that it is a 'revelation from Jesus Christ' (1:1). The word 'revelation' (Greek *apokalypsis*) – which gives the book its name 'The Apocalypse' – literally means 'the removing of a veil'. John addresses himself to the seven churches of Asia Minor, each of which will be addressed individually in the course of this section of the work. The work opens by giving thanks to God for all that he has done for believers through Jesus Christ. God is declared to be 'the Alpha and the Omega' (1:8), a reference to the first and last letters of the Greek alphabet. He is the beginning and end of history, its source and its ultimate goal.

1:9–20 One Like a Son of Man John then describes the circumstances under which the revelation came to him (1:9–20). After noting that he shares in the sufferings of the churches, he relates how he experienced a vision of the risen Christ. This incident took place on a Sunday on the island of Patmos, off the coast of Asia Minor, when John was 'in the Spirit' (1:10) – a reference to a state of inspiration, comparable to that associated with the Old Testament prophets.

Using language that recalls the vision of the prophet Daniel (Da 7:13), John relates how he saw the risen Christ standing among seven golden lampstands, holding seven stars in his right hand. These aspects of the vision are then interpreted to him: the seven stars represent the angels associated with each of the churches to be addressed in the work, just as the lampstands represent the churches themselves.

This opening vision, however, seems to set the scene for the whole book. John is told to write of 'what you have seen, what is now and what will take place later' (1:19). This suggests a threefold structure. First, 'what you have seen', a clear reference to the opening vision (1:9–20). Secondly, 'what is now', a reference to the state of the seven churches, which will be addressed in the letters to the seven churches (2:1–3:22). And thirdly, John is told to relate 'what will take place later', referring to the great vision of the end that takes up the bulk of this distinctive work (4:1–22:21).

2:1–11 To the Churches in Ephesus and Smyrna John now relays to the seven churches of Asia Minor the messages that were entrusted to him in his vision. The church at *Ephesus* is commended for its perseverance, and also for its rejection of the 'practices of the Nicolaitans' (2:1–7). This group appears to have been characterised by a doctrine of Christian liberty that allowed its adherents to become involved with idolatry and fall into various forms of moral laxity. However, the church has lost its enthusiasm for the gospel, which it needs to rediscover. The church at *Smyrna* has been going through a hard time, apparently being discriminated against by both the Roman authorities and a large Jewish presence in the city (2:8–11). Yet their sufferings will not destroy their faith, and they may rest assured that they will inherit eternal life at the end.

2:12–29 To the Churches in Pergamum and Thyatira The church at *Pergamum* is praised for its faithfulness in the face of the official Roman cult of emperor worship, which had a regional centre in the city (2:12–17). However, the church has tolerated the presence and teachings of the Nicolaitans (see above), which has compromised its integrity. As a result, there is a need for repentance and change within the church. The church in *Thyatira*, although commended in some ways, is criticised for allowing toleration of paganism within its ranks (2:18–29). This tendency is clearly associated with some prominent woman within the congregation, who is given the name Jezebel to bring out her affinity with the pagan queen of that same name, who led Israel astray at the time of the ministry of Elijah (2Ki 9:30–37).

3:1–13 To the Churches in Sardis and Philadelphia The church in the wealthy city of *Sardis*, despite its outward appearance of strength, is declared to be inwardly weak (3:1–6). It needs to recover its vision and sense of identity, by returning to the roots of its faith. This message includes the first reference in this work to the 'book of life' (3:5), a register of all those who are citizens of heaven, and thus have a right to reside within it. To have one's name blotted out from this book would be to imply loss of all citizenship rights – and hence the right to dwell within heaven. The church in the city of *Philadelphia* is praised for its faithfulness and spiritual strength during what has clearly been a very difficult time (3:7–13). The 'synagogue of Satan' is probably a reference to an aggressive Jewish community, intent on eliminating Christianity from the region. The church is reassured of the continuing protection and presence of God, in order that it may survive what lies ahead.

3:14–22 To the Church in Laodicea Finally, the church at *Laodicea* is addressed. This is perhaps the most celebrated of the seven messages to the churches in the region. The church in this city is declared to be lukewarm in its faith, and in urgent need of repentance and revival. It has trusted in its own strength, rather than the power of the Lord. The city was noted in the ancient world for its wealth, its textiles and a local eye ointment. The criticism of the church alludes to all three (3:18) in terms which make it clear that the risen Christ alone can supply what the church needs. The message concludes with the declaration that Christ is knocking at the door of this church, seeking readmission. If the door is opened, he will enter and eat with those inside – a clear statement of restoration of fellowship.

REVELATION 4:1–22:21
The Visions of the End

4:1–11 The Throne in Heaven The tone of the book now alters radically. We are caught up in a prophetic vision of heaven. John enters into heaven as through an open door, and is confronted with a glorious vision of God, very similar to that granted to Isaiah (see Isa 6:3, cited here). This vision of the worship of heaven prepares the way for the remainder of the vision, which relates events in heaven to the situation of the persecuted church on earth in Asia Minor.

A fascination with numbers

There are lots of numbers in Revelation – all of them symbolic. The number *seven* symbolises completeness and perfection: there are seven churches, seven angels, seven trumpets, seven plagues, seven peals of thunder, seven seals, and seven lamps. The number *six*, on the other hand, falls completely short of perfection. The mysterious number '666' is the number of the beast in 13:18 and could be decoded to apply to the emperor Nero, who symbolised all the evils of the Roman Empire.

In Rev 14 John sees 144,000 people following the Lamb (Jesus). The number 144,000 is 12 × 12 × 1,000, and probably symbolises completeness. It is an inclusive, rather than an exclusive, number. John does not mean that only 144,000 people will be saved, but that all Christ's followers will be brought safely to him.

5:1–14 The Scroll and the Lamb As he contemplates the vision of God, John becomes aware of the presence of a lamb. This lamb is none other than Jesus Christ, who was slain in order to redeem sinful humanity for God. The lamb is an important symbol here: it picks up the theme of the slaughtered Passover lamb, whose blood marked off Israel from her enemies (Ex 12:1–7), the lamb who was slain for others (Isa 53:7), and the lamb who takes away the sins of the world (Jn 1:29). The use of the number seven may also be noted here: there are seven seals (5:1) seven horns, and seven eyes (5:6). The number is here used as a symbol of the completeness of heaven. Other examples of its use include the seven churches (1:4), seven crowns (12:3), seven hills (17:9), seven kings (17:10), seven plagues (15:6), and seven trumpets (8:2).

6:1–11:19 The Seals and the Trumpets The scene now changes. The Lamb is granted authority to open the seven seals, setting loose forces of destruction and devastation upon the earth (6:1–17).

Before the opening of the final seal, all of the people of God are marked with a sign to demonstrate that they are God's own. A total of 144,000 – 12,000 from each tribe of Israel – are marked in this way (7:1–17). This important chapter makes the point that a faithful remnant of Israel will be saved, along with countless others whose sins have been purged by the saving death of Christ. (The number 144,000 should probably be regarded as symbolic rather than actual.)

With the sealing of the people of God, the final seal is opened. Initially, there is a reverential silence. Then the forces of destruction are unleashed, to the accompaniment of seven trumpet blasts (8:1–11:19). At the sound of the seventh and final trumpet, voices from heaven declare the dawning of the reign of God.

12:1–20:15 A Series of Visions But disbelief and rebellion against God continue. In a vivid series of visions, John sees a series of figures and beasts, symbolising the forces of evil and Satan (12:1–13:18). The final beast to be mentioned has the

mystical number 666 (13:18). It is far from clear how this number is to be interpreted. Given that seven is seen as a perfect number, it is possible that 666 is to be seen as a 'trinity of imperfection' or a numerical code for an enemy of the church, perhaps spelling out the name Nero Caesar (that is, the emperor Nero). The reference to the mark of the beast (13:16–17) is important, as it indicates the importance of the mark of Christ (the cross) in sealing a believer's redemption. The mark of the beast probably refers to a symbol of the emperor cult, which forced individuals to worship the Roman emperor as a god as a means of demonstrating loyalty to Rome.

Yet the end is now very near. After a vision which demonstrated that the 144,000 drawn from the twelve tribes of Israel were safe, and were intended to be the firstfruits of those redeemed from the earth (14:1–5), John is presented with a vision of the final destruction of evil and unbelief (14:6–20:15), culminating in the destruction of Satan himself. The time scale referred to in this section has been the subject of frequent speculation, particularly the 'thousand years' for which Satan is bound (20:2, 7). However, the figure is best seen as symbolic, rather than as a precise indication of time. The book of Revelation is not a timetable, but a prophetic vision, concerned above all with demonstrating the final and total victory of God, despite all the trials and tribulations of his people at present.

21:1–22:21 The New Jerusalem and Final Victory

Now the tone of the book changes radically once more. John presents us with his vision of a new heaven and a new earth, and the new Jerusalem (21:1–5). The vision can be regarded as the ultimate fulfilment of the great Old Testament prophecies of renewal and regeneration of the world, and the ushering in of a new age in which suffering and pain are abolished for ever. The vision of the new Jerusalem continues by affirming that there is no temple in the city. There does not need to be, for God himself is present in its midst (21:6–27). This must be seen in the light of the prophecy of Ezekiel, who saw the 'glory of the LORD' depart from the temple as a result of Judah's disobedience. Now, God's presence has been restored to his people for ever. God's people will finally be granted a vision of his face, something that not even Moses was permitted on earth (22:1–6; see Ex 33:20; Jn 1:18).

So what is the value of this vision? What comfort would it bring to the seven churches of Asia Minor? The answer becomes clear in the closing section of the book (22:7–21). It is an assurance that things will not go on for ever, and that the suffering of today will finally give way to the hope of heaven – which nothing can take away. Those who have been sealed by God may rest assured that, whatever trials and difficulties they are facing, God will remain faithful. Believers will be delivered from the presence and threat of all those who are seeking their destruction. Behind the façade of events on earth, a train of events is being set in motion in heaven that will bring the forces of evil to an end. Christ will come again, and bring all things to an end. And then 'There will be no more death or mourning or crying or pain, for the old order of things has

Where will we spend eternity?

If you ask average Christians this question, they will almost certainly say, 'In heaven.' But this answer is shaped more by tradition, art and hymnology than by what the Bible actually says. For while heaven is indeed real – the dwelling-place of Christians who die before Christ's return (see 1Th 4 and 'What happens when we die?', page 456) – it is actually just their temporary home. What the Bible says is that we shall spend eternity, not in heaven, *but on a new earth*.

If that sounds surprising, consider where the final scenes of the Bible are set – not in heaven but on a renewed earth. After Satan's destruction and the last judgment, John sees 'the Holy City, the new Jerusalem, *coming down out of heaven from God*' (Rev 21:2), hears a voice saying, 'Look! God's dwelling-place is now *among the people*' (v.3), and sees a magnificent city (vv.10–27), shaped like a cube (v.16). Anyone familiar with the Old Testament would immediately think of another cube: the Most Holy Place in the tabernacle, where God dwelt. What John was seeing was that the whole city, the whole new creation, will become God's dwelling in the age to come. Contrary to common opinion, God is not going to take us to be with him in heaven; rather he is going to come to us on a renewed earth. Yet the extent of this radical transformation is such that it is right to speak of this as a 'new creation', showing both continuity and discontinuity with the old order.

This is wholly in line with the prophets, who saw God *restoring* the earth, not destroying it (e.g., Isa 65:17–25); and while Peter says fire will come upon the earth at the end (2Pe 3:10), fire is often used as an image of purification as much as of destruction. Such a renewal of the earth makes sense of Paul's teaching that God will give us 'resurrection bodies' at Christ's return (1Co 15:35–57), for bodies would not be needed for a purely spiritual existence in some transcendent realm, and of Christ's teaching that there is useful work to be done in the age to come – responsibilities to be carried (Mt 25:14–23) and cities to be ruled (Lk 19:11–19) – a far cry from the sentimental idea of sitting on clouds, playing harps throughout eternity.

The Christian's future hope lies on a renewed earth, with God himself in our midst, truly paradise regained.

passed away' (21:4). And that vision remains just as important for Christians today. Believers can take comfort in the sure and certain knowledge that, whatever the woes and pains of this life, their future joy and life lie with the risen Christ.

REFERENCE

PEOPLE OF THE BIBLE

AARON
Brother of Moses; appointed as his spokesman (Ex 4:14–16; 7:1–2). Held up Moses' hands in battle (Ex 17:12). Consecrated as priest (Ex 28:1–4; 29; Lev 8; Heb 5:4). Made golden calf (Ex 32); opposed Moses (Nu 12:1–3). Priesthood challenged (Nu 16); staff budded as confirmation of his call (Nu 17). With Moses, excluded from Canaan (Nu 20:12). Death (Nu 20:22–29).

ABEDNEGO
Formerly Azariah; member of Jewish nobility taken to Babylon with Daniel, Meshach and Shadrach (Da 1:3–7). Refused unclean food (Da 1:8–16); appointed as administrator (Da 2:49). Refused to worship golden image; kept safe in fiery furnace (Da 3).

ABEL
Second son of Adam. Shepherd (Ge 4:2); offered sacrifice acceptable to God (Ge 4:4; Heb 11:4); killed by his brother Cain (Ge 4:8).

ABIATHAR
Son of Ahimelek; priest in time of Saul and David. Escaped Saul's massacre of priests who helped David (1Sa 22:20–23). Faithful to David (1Sa 23:6; 2Sa 15:24–29). Supported Adonijah (1Ki 1:7); deposed by Solomon (1Ki 2:26).

ABIGAIL
1. David's sister (1Ch 2:16–17).
2. Wife of Nabal (1Sa 25:3); entreated David to spare his life (1Sa 25:14–35). Married David after Nabal's death (1Sa 25:40–43); mother of Kiliab (Daniel) (2Sa 3:3; 1Ch 3:1).

ABIMELEK
1. King of Gerar in time of Abraham. Took Sarah, Abraham's wife, thinking she was his sister (Ge 20). Made covenant with Abraham (Ge 21:22–34).
2. King of Gerar in time of Isaac. Rebuked Isaac for deceit (Ge 26:8–10); later made covenant with him (Ge 26:26–31).
3. Son of Gideon (Jdg 8:31). Murdered brothers (Jdg 9:5); crowned king at Shechem (Jdg 9:6). Death (Jdg 9:54).

ABISHAI
Son of David's sister, Zeruiah; brother of Joab (1Sa 26:6; 1Ch 2:16). One of David's leading warriors (1Ch 11:15–21; 18:12; 2Sa 18:2; 20:6). Wanted to kill Saul (1Sa 26:7–8), Shimei (2Sa 16:9; 19:21).

ABNER
Saul's cousin and commander of his army (1Sa 14:50; 17:55). Made Ishbosheth king after Saul's death (2Sa 2:8–9). Killed Asahel, Joab's brother (2Sa 2:18–25). Defected to David (2Sa 3:6–21).

Murdered by Joab and Abishai to avenge Asahel's death (2Sa 3:26–30).

ABRAHAM

Formerly Abram ('exalted father'). Descendant of Shem and son of Terah (Ge 11:10–27); married to Sarah (Ge 11:29). With Terah, travelled from Ur to Harran. Obeyed God's call to continue journey to Canaan (Ge 12:1–5). In Egypt (Ge 12:10), passed Sarah off as his sister (Ge 12:11–20). Divided the land with his nephew, Lot (Ge 13:5–17); settled at Hebron (Ge 13:18). Rescued Lot (Ge 14:1–16); blessed by Melchizedek (Ge 14:18–20). Name changed to Abraham ('father of many') (Ge 17:5; Ne 9:7). Father of Ishmael by Hagar (Ge 16). Entertained angelic visitors (Ge 18:1–8); promised a son by Sarah (Ge 18:9–15; 17:16). Pleaded for Sodom (Ge 18:22–32). In Gerar (Ge 20:1), passed Sarah off as his sister (Ge 20:2–18). Father of Isaac (Ge 21:1–7); dismissed Hagar and Ishmael (Ge 21:8–14). Made treaty with Abimelek (Ge 21:22–34). Tested by God's command to sacrifice Isaac (Ge 22). Secured wife for Isaac (Ge 24). Death (Ge 25:7–11). God's covenant with (Ge 12:1–3; 15; 17; 22:15–18; Ex 2:24; Lk 1:72–73; Heb 6:13–15). Example of faith (Heb 11:8–12); faith credited as righteousness (Ge 15:6; Ro 4:3; Gal 3:6–9). Described as father of God's people (Isa 51:2; Ac 13:26; Gal 3:26–29); God's servant (Ge 26:24); God's friend (2Ch 20:7; Isa 41:8; Jas 2:23).

ABSALOM

Son of David (2Sa 3:3). Had Amnon killed for raping his sister, Tamar (2Sa 13:23–29); fled from David (2Sa 13:37–38). Returned (2Sa 14:21–23); reconciled to David (2Sa 14:33). Conspired against David (2Sa 15:1–12); proclaimed king (2Sa 16:15–22). Defeated, killed by Joab (2Sa 18:6–10); mourned by David (2Sa 18:33).

ACHAN

Sinned by keeping spoils after conquest of Jericho, thus causing Israel's defeat at Ai; stoned as punishment (Jos 7).

ACHISH

King of Gath, with whom David sought refuge and feigned insanity (1Sa 21:10–15), and later feigned loyal service (1Sa 27:2–12).

ADAM

First man. Created by God (Ge 1:27); placed in Eden (Ge 2:15); given Eve as helper (Ge 2:19–24). Disobeyed God (Ge 3; Ro 5:14) and so brought sin into world (Ro 5:12, 15–19). Jesus is described as 'the last Adam' (1Co 15:45).

ADONIJAH

1. Son of David, by Haggith (2Sa 3:4; 1Ch 3:2). Attempted to succeed David as king (1Ki 1); killed by Solomon's order after he requested Abishag for his wife (1Ki 2).

2. Levite and teacher of the Law (2Ch 17:8–9).

AGRIPPA

1. Herod Agrippa I, grandson of Herod the Great. Jewish king, killed apostle James and imprisoned Peter (Ac 12:1–4); sudden death (Ac 12:20–23).

2. Herod Agrippa II, son of Herod Agrippa I, before whom Paul appeared at Caesarea (Ac 25:13–26:32).

AHAB

1. Son of Omri; evil king of Israel (1Ki 16:29–30). Married Jezebel; encouraged worship of Baal (1Ki 16:31–33). Opposed by Elijah (1Ki 17:1; 18:17–20). Defeated Arameans (1Ki 20); condemned for sparing Ben-Hadad (1Ki 20:42). Murdered Naboth and stole his vineyard (1Ki 21). Opposed by Micaiah (1Ki 22:1–28); killed (1Ki 22:34–38).
2. False prophet (Jer 29:21–22).

AHAZ

Son of Jotham; king of Judah (2Ki 16). Worshipped foreign gods (2Ki 16:3–4, 10–18; 2Ch 28:2–4, 22–25). Attacked by Aram and Israel (2Ki 16:5–6; 2Ch 28:5–8). Turned for help to Assyria rather than God (2Ki 16:7–9; 2Ch 28:16; Isa 7:3–17).

AHIMELEK

1. Priest at Nob who helped David (1Sa 21:1–9); killed by Saul (1Sa 22:9–19).
2. One of David's soldiers (1Sa 26:6).

AHITHOPHEL

David's counsellor; gave support to Absalom (2Sa 15:12; 16:21–23). Hanged himself when his advice was ignored (2Sa 17).

AMASA

David's nephew (1Ch 2:17). In charge of Absalom's army (2Sa 17:24–25); made commander of David's army (2Sa 19:13); treacherously killed by Joab his cousin (2Sa 20:9–10; 1Ki 2:5).

AMNON

David's firstborn son (2Sa 3:2). Raped Absalom's sister, Tamar (2Sa 13:1–22); killed by Absalom's men (2Sa 13:23–29).

AMOS

1. Prophet from Tekoa (Am 1:1); spoke against Israel (Am 7:10–17).
2. Ancestor of Jesus. (Lk 3:25).

ANANIAS

1. With wife Sapphira, died for lying to God (Ac 5:1–11).
2. Disciple, sent to heal and baptise Saul (Paul) in Damascus (Ac 9:10–19).
3. High priest before whom Paul appeared (Ac 22:30–23:5; 24:1).

ANDREW

Apostle; brother of Simon Peter (Mt 4:18–20; 10:2; Mk 1:16–18, 29); introduced boy with loaves and fish to Jesus (Jn 6:8–9); brought Greeks to Jesus (Jn 12:22). Former disciple of John the Baptist (Jn 1:35–40); brought Simon to Jesus (Jn 1:41).

ANNA

Widow; prophetess of the tribe of Asher; recognised the baby Jesus as the Messiah when he was brought into the temple (Lk 2:36–38).

ANNAS

High priest (Lk 3:2). Questioned Jesus (Jn 18:13, 19–24); questioned Peter and John (Ac 4:5–7).

APOLLOS
Disciple from Alexandria, well versed in the Scriptures (Ac 18:24–25); instructed by Priscilla and Aquila in Ephesus (Ac 18:26). Ministered in Corinth (Ac 18:27–19:1; 1Co 1:12; 3:5–9) and on Crete (Tit 3:13).

ARTAXERXES
King of Persia. Stopped work on walls of Jerusalem (Ezr 4:17–23). Provided resources for temple worship under Ezra (Ezr 7); reversed earlier decision to allow rebuilding of walls under Nehemiah (Ne 2:1–10).

ASA
King of Judah (1Ki 15:9–10). Removed idols and reformed worship (1Ki 15:11–15; 2Ch 14:2–5; 15). Rebuilt Judah's cities (2Ch 14:6–7). Relied on God against the Cushites (2Ch 14:9–15); relied on Aram, instead of God, against Israel, rebuked by Hanani the seer (1Ki 15:15–22; 2Ch 16). Death (2Ch 16:12–14).

ASAHEL
David's nephew; brother of Joab and Abishai (1Ch 2:16). One of David's leading warriors (2Sa 23:24; 1Ch 11:26; 27:7). Killed by Abner after a rash pursuit (2Sa 2:18–23); avenged by Joab (2Sa 3:26–27).

ASAPH
1. Levite, in charge of music in the tabernacle and temple (1Ch 6:39; 15:17–19; 16:4–7, 37; 1Ch 25:6; Ne 12:46). Composed several psalms (2Ch 29:30; Ps 50; 73–83). His sons set apart for musical and prophetic ministry (1Ch 25; 2Ch 20:14; 35:15; Ezr 2:41; 3:10; Ne 11:17).

2. Keeper of the king's forest (Ne 2:8).

3. Hezekiah's recorder (2Ki 18:18, 37; Isa 36:3, 22).

ASHER
1. Son of Jacob by Zilpah (Ge 30:12–13; 35:26; Ex 1:4; 1Ch 2:2); blessed by Jacob (Ge 49:20).

2. Tribe descended from Asher. Blessed by Moses (Dt 33:24–25). Included in census (Nu 1:40–41; 26:44–47); apportioned land (Jos 19:24–31; Eze 48:2). Supported Gideon (Jdg 6:35; 7:23) and David (1Ch 12:36) but not Deborah (Jdg 5:17).

ATHALIAH
Daughter of Ahab; wife of Jehoram, king of Judah; mother of Ahaziah (2Ki 8:18, 26; 2Ch 22:2). Encouraged idolatry (2Ki 8:18, 27). After Ahaziah's death, killed royal family (except Joash) and reigned for six years (2Ki 11:1–3; 2Ch 22:10–12). Killed by order of Jehoiada, who made Joash king (2Ki 11:4–16; 2Ch 23:1–15).

BALAAM
Prophet, requested by Balak to curse Israel (Nu 22:4–11; 2Pe 2:15); forbidden by God (Nu 22:12); rebuked by his donkey (Nu 22:21–34). Curse turned to blessing (Nu 23–24; Dt 23:4–5; Jos 24:9–10). Advice led to Israel's seduction (Nu 31:15–16). Killed in Israel's defeat of Midianites (Nu 31:8; Jos 13:22).

BARABBAS
Criminal, released by Pilate instead of Jesus (Mt 27:15–26; Mk 15:6–15; Lk 23:18–25; Jn 18:40).

BARAK
Summoned by Deborah to lead Israel against Canaanites (Jdg 4–5; 1Sa 12:11; Heb 11:32).

BARNABAS
Name (meaning 'son of encouragement') given to Joseph, a disciple from Cyprus (Ac 4:36). Apostle (Ac 14:14) and missionary (Gal 2:9). Introduced Paul to Jerusalem apostles (Ac 9:27). Sent to Antioch where he worked with Paul (Ac 11:22–26). With Paul on first missionary journey (Ac 13–14) and at Council of Jerusalem (Ac 15:2–35); parted company over his cousin John Mark (Ac 15:36–40).

BARTHOLOMEW
One of the twelve apostles (Mt 10:2–3; Mk 3:16–18; Lk 6:13–14; Ac 1:13). May also have been known as Nathanael.

BARTIMAEUS
Blind beggar healed by Jesus (Mk 10:46–52; Lk 19:35–43; Mt 20:29–34).

BARUCH
Secretary and companion of Jeremiah. Wrote down Jeremiah's prophecies and read them to the people (Jer 36). Jeremiah gave him deeds of field in Anathoth (Jer 32:12–16). Accused of influencing Jeremiah; taken with him to Egypt (Jer 43:1–7). God's word to (Jer 45).

BATHSHEBA
Wife of Uriah; committed adultery with David and became his wife (2Sa 11).

Secured succession for her son, Solomon (1Ki 1:11–40). Included in Jesus' genealogy (Mt 1:6).

BELSHAZZAR
King of Babylon at time of its overthrow by Darius. Downfall announced by Daniel, who interpreted writing on the wall (Da 5).

BELTESHAZZAR
Name given to Daniel in Babylon (Da 1:7).

BENJAMIN
1. Jacob's youngest son; second by Rachel, who died in childbirth (Ge 35:16–18, 24; 46:19). Jacob's favourite after loss of Joseph. Father reluctant to allow him to go to Egypt (Ge 42:38; 43); brothers' concern about led Joseph to make himself known (Ge 44–45). Blessed by Jacob (Ge 49:27).

2. Tribe descended from Benjamin. Blessed by Moses (Dt 33:12). Included in census (Nu 1:36–37; 26:38–41). Apportioned land (Jos 18:11–28; Eze 48:23); did not take full possession (Jdg 1:21). Almost destroyed by other tribes (Jdg 20–21). Tribe of Saul (1Sa 9:1); followed Ishbosheth (2Sa 2:8–9); later gave support to David (1Ch 12:29; 1Ki 12:21). Tribe of Esther (Est 2:5) and Paul (Php 3:5).

BEZALEL
Craftsman of the tribe of Judah (1Ch 2:20; 2Ch1:5) chosen, with Oholiab, to organise building of the tabernacle (Ex 31:1–6; 35:30–36:7). Credited with making the ark (Ex 37:1–9).

BOAZ

Wealthy and benevolent landowner from Bethlehem; married Ruth, the widow of a relative, fulfilling the responsibility of kinsman-redeemer (Ru 2–4). Ancestor of David (Ru 4:17–22; 1Ch 2:5–15) and of Jesus (Mt 1:5).

CAIAPHAS

High priest at time of Jesus' arrest (Mt 26:57–68; Jn 18:13, 24). Unknowingly foretold the significance of Jesus' death (Jn 11:49–52; 18:14). Questioned Peter and John (Ac 4:5–7).

CAIN

Eldest son of Adam and Eve (Ge 4:1). Farmer (Ge 4:2); murdered his brother, Abel, when sacrifice not accepted by God (Ge 4:3–8; 1Jn 3:12). Given mark of protection to limit punishment (Ge 4:9–16).

CALEB

One of spies sent to explore Canaan (Nu 13:6); with Joshua encouraged the people to go in (Nu 13:30; 14:6–9). Allowed to enter land because of his faith (Nu 26:65; 32:12; Dt 1:36). Given possession of Hebron (Jos 14:6–15; 15:13–19).

CORNELIUS

God-fearing Roman centurion stationed at Caesarea (Ac 10:1–2). Sent for Peter (Ac 10:1–8, 19–33); heard gospel, received Holy Spirit, baptised (Ac 10:34–48); first Gentile convert.

CYRUS

King of Persia. Issued edict to allow exiles to return to rebuild Jerusalem temple (2Ch 36:22–23; Ezr 1:1–4; 5:13; 6:3); gave back articles taken from temple (Ezr 1:7–11; 5:14–15; 6:5) and provided funds for building work (Ezr 3:7; 6:4). Place in God's purpose foretold by Isaiah (Isa 44:28–45:7, 13).

DAN

1. Son of Jacob by Bilhah (Ge 30:4–6; 35:25); blessed by Jacob (Ge 49:16–17).

2. Tribe descended from Dan. Blessed by Moses (Dt 33:22). Included in census (Nu 1:38–39; 26:42–43). Apportioned land (Jos 19:40–48; Eze 48:1); unable to take full possession (Jdg 1:34), most of tribe migrated northwards to Laish (Jdg 18). Tribe of Samson (Jdg 13).

DANIEL

1. Son of David and Abigail (1Ch 3:1).

2. Ancient figure regarded as an outstanding example of righteousness and wisdom (Eze 14:14, 20; 28:3).

3. Hebrew of noble descent among those taken as captives to Babylon to be trained in the king's service (Da 1:3–6); renamed Belteshazzar (Da 1:7); refused to eat unclean food (Da 1:8–16). Possessed great understanding (Da 1:17, 20); interpreted Nebuchadnezzar's dreams (Da 2:24–45; 4:19–27), writing on wall (Da 5:13–29). Held government posts under Nebuchadnezzar (Da 2:48), Belshazzar (Da 5:29), Darius (Da 6:1–2). Refused to obey king's decree; thrown into lions' den (Da 6). Visions predicting coming of Messianic kingdom (Da 7–12).

DARIUS

1. Mede, who became ruler of Babylon

(Da 5:31; 9:1). Appointed Daniel as leading official (Da 6:2, 28). Possibly to be identified with Cyrus.

2. Darius the Great, king of Persia (Hag 1:1; Zec 1:1); revived Cyrus' edict allowing work on rebuilding temple to continue (Ezr 4:24–6:15).

3. Darius II, king of Persia (Ne 12:22).

DAVID

Israel's second and greatest king; ancestor of Jesus (Mt 1:1; Ro 1:3; Rev 22:16); type of promised Messiah (Isa 11:1; Eze 34:23–24; 37:24–25).

Singer of psalms and songs (2Sa 23:1; Am 6:5). Son of Jesse of Bethlehem (Ru 4:17; 1Sa 17:12). Anointed king by Samuel (1Sa 16:1–13). Entered Saul's service as musician (1Sa 16:14–23). Killed Goliath (1Sa 17:32–54). Friendship with Jonathan (1Sa 18:1–4; 19:1–7; 20; 23:16–18; 2Sa 1:25–26). Fled because of Saul's hostility (1Sa 19; 21–23). Spared Saul's life (1Sa 24; 26). Among the Philistines (1Sa 21:10–15; 27–29). Lament for Saul and Jonathan (2Sa 1).

Anointed king of Judah at Hebron (2Sa 2:1–7). War with Saul's family (2Sa 2–4). United northern and southern tribes as king over all Israel (2Sa 5:1–4; 1Ch 11:1–3; 12:38–40). Captured Jerusalem from Jebusites (2Sa 5:6–10; 1Ch 11:4–9); installed ark there (2Sa 6; 1Ch 15–16). Promised lasting dynasty by God (2Sa 7; 1Ch 17; Ps 89; 132). Established empire: defeated Philistines (2Sa 5:17–25; 1Ch 14:8–17; 2Sa 21:15–22; 1Ch 20:4–8), Moabites, Arameans, Edomites (2Sa 8:1–14; 1Ch 18:1–13), Ammonites (2Sa 10; 1Ch 19).

Committed adultery with Bathsheba;

murdered Uriah (2Sa 11); rebuked by Nathan (2Sa 12:1–14); repented (Ps 51).

Married Bathsheba and other wives (1Sa 18:27; 25:39–43; 2Sa 5:13; 11:27); father of Solomon, Absalom, Adonijah, etc. (2Sa 3:2–5; 1Ch 3:1–9). Absalom's revolt (2Sa 15–18). Preparations for temple (1Ch 22; 28–29). Appointment of Solomon as successor (1Ki 1:28–48). Death (1Ki 2:10–12; 1Ch 29:26–28).

DEBORAH

1. Prophet, one of Israel's judges. Appointed Barak to lead Israel against Canaanites (Jdg 4–5).

2. Rebekah's nurse (Ge 35:8).

DELILAH

Betrayed Samson (Jdg 16:4–22).

DEMAS

Fellow-worker with Paul (Col 4:14; Phm 24), whom he later deserted (2Ti 4:10).

DEMETRIUS

1. Christian commended by John (3Jn 12).

2. Silversmith who stirred up a riot against Paul in Ephesus (Ac 19:23–41).

DINAH

Daughter of Jacob by Leah (Ge 30:21; 46:15). Raped by Shechem; avenged by Simeon and Levi (Ge 34).

DORCAS

Also known as Tabitha. Disciple in Joppa, known for her good works (Ac 9:36, 39). Died (Ac 9:37); raised to life by Peter (Ac 9:38–42).

EDOM

1. Another name for **Esau.**

2. Nation descended from Esau (Ge 36).

ELEAZAR

Third son of Aaron (Ex 6:23; Nu 3:2; 1Ch 6:3–4); anointed as priest (Lev 8–9; Nu 3:2–4); leader of Levites, responsible for care of sanctuary (Nu 3:32; 4:16). Succeeded Aaron (Nu 20:28; Dt 10:6); assisted Moses (Nu 26:1–4, 63; 27:2; 31:12; 32:2). With Joshua, apportioned land (Nu 32:28; 34:17; Jos 14:1; 19:51). Death (Jos 24:33).

ELI

Priest at Shiloh; blessed Hannah (1Sa 1:9–17), who brought Samuel to him (1Sa 1:24–27); raised Samuel (1Sa 2:11, 18–21, 26). Wickedness of sons (1Sa 2:12–17, 22–25); rebuked by prophet (1Sa 2:27–36). Directed Samuel to the Lord (1Sa 3). Death of Eli and his sons (1Sa 4:10–18).

ELIJAH

Prophet; predicted drought in Israel (1Ki 17:1; Lk 4:25; Jas 5:17). Fed by ravens at brook Kerith (1Ki 17:2–6), and by widow of Zarephath (1Ki 17:9–16); raised widow's son (1Ki 17:17–24). Contest with prophets of Baal on Mt Carmel (1Ki 18:18–46). Fled from Jezebel to Horeb (1Ki 19); called Elisha (1Ki 19:19–21). Denounced Ahab over Naboth's vineyard (1Ki 21:17–29). Prophesied God's judgment on Ahaziah and called down fire (2Ki 1:1–17). Divided Jordan (2Ki 2:7–8); taken up to heaven in chariot of fire and whirlwind (2Ki 2:11–12); mantle taken by Elisha (2Ki 2:9–10, 13–15).

Appeared with Moses at Jesus' transfiguration (Mt 17:2–3; Mk 9:2–4; Lk 9:28–31). Return prophesied (Mal 4:5–6; Mt 17:10; Mk 9:11); identified with John the Baptist (Mt 11:13–14; 17:11–13; Mk 9:12–13; Lk 1:17).

ELISHA

Prophet; succeeded Elijah (1Ki 19:16–21); took his cloak and divided Jordan (2Ki 2:13–14). Purified bad water (2Ki 2:19–22); cursed youths who mocked him (2Ki 2:23–25); helped defeat Moab (2Ki 3:11–19); provided oil for widow (2Ki 4:1–7); raised Shunammite woman's son (2Ki 4:8–37); purified food (2Ki 4:38–41); fed 100 men with 20 loaves (2Ki 4:42–44); healed Naaman (2Ki 5); made axe-head float (2Ki 6:1–7). Captured Arameans (2Ki 6:8–23). Life threatened (2Ki 6:31–33). Prophesied end of siege of Samaria (2Ki 7:1–2). Visit to Damascus (2Ki 8:7–15). Sent prophet to anoint Jehu as king (2Ki 9:1–3). Death (2Ki 13:14–20); miracle with bones (2Ki 13:21).

ELIZABETH

Wife of Zechariah; mother of John the Baptist (Lk 1:5–25, 57–60). Related to Mary (Lk 1:36); blessed Mary when she visited (Lk 1:39–45).

ENOCH

1. Cain's first son; city named after him (Ge 4:17–18).

2. Descendant of Seth; father of Methuselah (Ge 5:18–21). Prophesied (Jude 14–15); walked with God, and taken by him (Ge 5:22–24).

EPAPHRODITUS

Christian from Philippi; brought gifts from Philippians to Paul (Php 4:18); fellow-worker with Paul; almost died serving Christ (Php 2:25–29).

EPHRAIM

1. Joseph's second son (Ge 41:52); blessed by Jacob as firstborn (Ge 48:13–20).

2. Tribe descended from Ephraim. Blessed by Moses (Dt 33:13–17). Included in census (Nu 1:32–33; 26:35–37). Apportioned land (Jos 16:1–9; Eze 48:5); unable to take full possession (Jos 16:10; Jdg 1:29). Occupied prestigious position among tribes (Jdg 8:2–3).

ESAU

Also known as Edom (Ge 25:30). Son of Isaac; older twin of Jacob (Ge 25:24–26); hunter, favoured by Isaac (Ge 25:27–28). Sold birthright (Ge 25:29–34; Heb 12:6); lost blessing as eldest son (Ge 27). Married foreign wives (Ge 26:34–35; 28:8–9; 36:2–3). Reconciled to Jacob (Ge 32:3–21; 33:1–16). Occupied land of Seir (Ge 36:8; Dt 2:4–12); ancestor of Edomites (Ge 36:9–43). Rejection by God contrasted with gracious choice of Jacob (Mal 1:2–3; Ro 9:13).

ESTHER

Jew living in Persia, also called Hadassah; brought up by cousin Mordecai (Est 2:7). Became Xerxes' queen (Est 2:8–18). Persuaded by Mordecai to help foil Haman's plot to destroy Jews (Est 3–4); risked life by approaching Xerxes (Est 4:9–11; 5:1–8); revealed Haman's plans (Est 7). Encouraged Jews to slaughter enemies; initiated feast of Purim in celebration (Est 9).

EVE

First woman; created from Adam as wife and helper (Ge 2:20–24). Deceived by serpent (Ge 3:1–6; 2Co 11:3; 1Ti 2:13–14). Punished (Ge 3:16). Mother of Cain and Abel (Ge 4:1–2).

EZEKIEL

Member of priestly family; deported to Babylon with Jehoiachin (Eze 1:1–3). Vision and call to be prophet to exiles (Eze 1:4–28; 2–3). Listened to, but words not acted upon (Eze 8:1; 14:1; 20:1; 33:30–32). Sudden death of wife (Eze 24:15–18).

Visions: idolatry of Jerusalem (Eze 8–11); valley of dry bones (Eze 37); new temple (Eze 40–47). Prophetic symbolism (Eze 4–5; 12). Oracles: against Israel (Eze 13–24; 33); against nations (Eze 25–32; 35; 38–39); of restoration (Eze 34; 36).

EZRA

Priest and teacher of the Law of Moses (Ezr 7:6, 10–28); commissioned by Artaxerxes to lead a return of exiles to Jerusalem, to provide resources for temple worship and to establish observance of Law (Ezr 7–8). Addressed problem of intermarriage (Ezr 9–10); read Law at Feast of Tabernacles (Ne 8); took part in dedication of city walls (Ne 12:36).

GABRIEL

Angel; sent to Daniel to interpret vision (Da 8:15–26) and deliver prophetic

message (Da 9:20–27); announced birth of John the Baptist (Lk 1:11–20) and of Jesus (Lk 1:26–38).

GAD
1. Son of Jacob by Zilpah (Ge 30:9–11; 35:26); blessed by Jacob (Ge 49:19).

2. Tribe descended from Gad. Blessed by Moses (Dt 33:20–21). Included in census (Nu 1:24–25); 26:15–18). Apportioned land east of Jordan (Nu 32; 34:14–15; Jos 18:7; 22); crossed into Canaan to fight alongside other tribes (Nu 32:16–32). Place in restored land (Eze 48:27–28).

3. Seer at David's court (1Sa 22:5; 2Sa 24:11–19).

GAMALIEL
1. Leader from Manasseh; helped Moses with census (Nu 1:10; 2:20; 7:54–59; 10:23).

2. Pharisee and respected rabbi and teacher of the law who intervened in trial of apostles (Ac 5:34–40). Acknowledged by Paul as his teacher (Ac 22:3).

GEHAZI
Elisha's servant. Suggested Shunammite woman be rewarded with a son (2Ki 4:14); obtained money from Naaman falsely, contracted leprosy as punishment (2Ki 5:19–27); recounted Elisha's raising of Shunammite's son (2Ki 8:1–6). May be unnamed servant (2Ki 4:43; 6:15).

GIDEON
Judge, called to save Israel from Midianites (Jdg 6:11–24). Broke down altar of Baal (Jdg 6:25–32). Sign of fleece (Jdg 6:36–40); army reduced to 300 (Jdg 7:2–8); defeated Midianites (Jdg 7:16–8:28). Refused throne (Jdg 8:22–23); ephod made from spoil became source of idolatry (Jdg 8:24–27). Death (Jdg 8:32).

GOLIATH
Philistine giant (1Sa 17:4–7); challenged Israel (1Sa 17:8–11, 23–26); killed by David (1Sa 17:32–50). Sword kept at sanctuary at Nob; given to David (1Sa 21:9).

HABAKKUK
Prophet to Judah (Hab 1:1; 3:1).

HAGAR
Sarah's Egyptian maidservant given to Abraham as his wife (Ge 16:1–3). Became pregnant; fled from Sarah (Ge 16:4–8); encouraged by God (Ge 16:9–14). Gave birth to Ishmael (Ge 16:15–16; 25:12); driven away by Sarah (Ge 21:9–21). Symbol of those in slavery through dependence on law for justification (Gal 4:21–31).

HAGGAI
Prophet; encouraged returned exiles to continue rebuilding temple (Ezr 5:1; 6:14; Hag 1:1–11; 2).

HAM
Son of Noah (Ge 5:32; 6:10; 1Ch 1:4). Saved in ark (Ge 7:13; 9:18–19). Father of Canaan, Cush (Ethiopia), Put (Libya) and Mizraim (Egypt) (Ge 9:18; 10:6; 1Ch 1:8). Dishonoured Noah by looking at his nakedness; brought curse on Canaan (Ge 9:20–27). Associated with Egypt (Ps 78:51; 105:23, 27; 106:22).

HAMAN

Agagite, honoured by Xerxes (Est 3:1–2). Angered by Mordecai's defiance (Est 3:3–5; 5:9–14); planned to exterminate Jewish people (Est 3:6–15). Ordered to honour Mordecai (Est 6:1–12). Plot exposed by Esther (Est 7:1–7); hanged on gallows built for Mordecai (Est 7:9–10).

HANNAH

Wife of Elkanah; childless (1Sa 1:1–8). Prayed for a child (1Sa 1:9–18); gave birth to Samuel (1Sa 1:19–20); dedicated Samuel to God (1Sa 1:21–28). Her prayer (1Sa 2:1–10). Blessed with other children (1Sa 2:19–21).

HEROD

1. Herod the Great. King of Judea at time of Jesus' birth (Mt 2:1; Lk 1:5). Received Magi (Mt 2:1–8); slaughtered infants in attempt to kill Jesus (Mt 2:16–18).

2. Son of Herod the Great, also called Antipas. Tetrarch of Galilee. Arrested and executed John the Baptist (Mt 14:1–12; Mk 6:14–29; Lk 3:19–20; 9:7–9); questioned Jesus (Lk 23:6–12, 15).

3. See **Agrippa 1, 2.**

HERODIAS

Granddaughter of Herod the Great. Divorced Philip to marry his brother Herod Antipas, bringing condemnation from John the Baptist (Mt 14:3–4; Mk 6:17–19); prompted daughter to ask for John's head (Mt 14:6–12; Mk 6:21–29).

HEZEKIAH

King of Judah; outstanding for piety (2Ki 18:5–6; 2Ch 31:20–21). Reformed Judah's religious life (2Ki 18:3–4; 2Ch 29–31). Rebelled against Assyria (2Ki 18:7); sought and received help from God (2Ki 19:1–4, 14–37; Isa 37:1–7, 14–38). Healed (2Ki 20:1–11; Isa 38:1–22; 2Ch 32:24). Built up Jerusalem's defences (2Ch 32:2–5, 30). Isaiah challenged dependence on human resources (Isa 22:8–11) and pride in displaying wealth to envoys from Babylon (2Ki 20:12–18; 2Ch 32:31; Isa 39:1–8); repented (2Ch 32:26). Included in Jesus' genealogy (Mt 1:9–10).

HIRAM

King of Tyre. Helped with building of David's palace (2Sa 5:11–12; 1Ch 14:1). Made treaty with Solomon (1Ki 5:12); provided materials and expertise for building temple (1Ki 5; 2Ch 2) and navy (1Ki 9:26–27; 2Ch 8:18; 1Ki 10:22; 2Ch 9:21).

HOSEA

Prophet to Israel. Relationship with unfaithful wife, Gomer, and readiness to forgive her mirrored relationship between God and unfaithful Israel (Hos 1–3).

HOSHEA

1. Former name of Joshua.

2. Last king of Israel. Assassinated and succeeded Pekah (2Ki 15:30). Imprisoned when withheld tribute from Assyria; Israel was invaded and king and people exiled (2Ki 17:3–6; 18:9–12).

ISAAC

Son of Abraham and Sarah. Birth announced by God (Ge 17:15–19;

18:10–15; 21:1–7); heir through whom God's promises to Abraham continued (Ge 17:19, 21; 21:12; 26:2–5; Ro 9:6–9; Heb 11:9); patriarch (Ge 50:24; Ex 3:6; Dt 29:13; Mt 8:11).

Offered by Abraham (Ge 22; Heb 11:17–19; Jas 2:21). Married Rebekah (Ge 24); father of Esau and Jacob (Ge 25:21–26; 1Ch 1:34). In Gerar, passed Rebekah off as his sister (Ge 26:6–11). Made treaty with Abimelek (Ge 26:26–31). Deceived by Rebekah; blessed Jacob as firstborn (Ge 27:1–29; 28:1–4). Death (Ge 35:28–29).

ISAIAH

Prophet to Judah (Isa 1:1); commissioned by God (Isa 6). Married prophetess (Isa 8:3), had two sons whose names were clues to message (Isa 7:3; 8:3). Warned Ahaz; gave sign of Immanuel (Isa 7). Called for trust in God rather than human resources (Isa 7:9; 22:7–11; 31:1); rebuked Hezekiah's pride (2Ki 20:12–18; 2Ch 32:31; Isa 39:1–8). Announced deliverance from Assyria (Isa 10:12–19, 24–27; 14:24–27; 36–37; 2Ki 19). Hezekiah's sickness and recovery (2Ki 20:1–11; 2Ch 32:24–26; Isa 38). Recorded Judah's history (2Ch 26:22; 32:32).

ISHMAEL

1. Son of Abraham by Hagar (Ge 16:15; 1Ch 1:28); circumcised (Ge 17:23–26); blessed by God, but not as heir of promise (Ge 17:19–21; 21:10–13; Gal 4:21–30). Hostility towards Isaac (Ge 16:12; 21:9; 25:18; Gal 4:29); driven away by Sarah (Ge 21:10–14); cry heard by God (Ge 21:15–21). With Isaac, buried Abraham (Ge 25:9). Children (Ge 25:12–16; 1Ch 1:29–31). Death (Ge 25:17).

2. Son of Nethaniah; killed Gedaliah, governor of Judah, and his followers (2Ki 25:22–26; Jer 40:7–9; 41:1–16). Pursued by Johanan; escaped to Ammon (Jer 41:10–15).

ISSACHAR

1. Son of Jacob by Leah (Ge 30:17–18; 35:23); blessed by Jacob (Ge 49:14–15).

2. Tribe descended from Issachar. Blessed by Moses (Dt 33:18–19). Included in census (Nu 1:28–29; 26:23–25). Apportioned land (Jos 19:17–23; Eze 48:25).

JACOB

Son of Isaac; younger twin of Esau (Ge 25:21–26). Favoured by Rebekah (Ge 25:27–28). Bought birthright from Esau (Ge 25:29–34); tricked Isaac into blessing him as firstborn (Ge 27); fled to Harran (Ge 27:41–28:5).

Dream at Bethel (Ge 28:10–22); heir to promises of Abrahamic covenant (Ge 28:13–15; 48:3–4; Lev 26:42; Heb 11:9); patriarch (Ex 3:15–16; Jer 33:26; Mt 22:32; Mk 12:26). Gracious choice by God contrasted with rejection of Esau (Mal 1:2–3; Ro 9:13).

Worked for Laban to win Rachel; tricked into marrying Leah; married Rachel in return for further labour (Ge 29:16–30). Children (Ge 29:31–30:24; 35:23–26; 1Ch 2–9). Wealth increased (Ge 30:25–43); returned to Canaan (Ge 31); wrestled with God; called Israel (Ge 32:22–32); reconciled to Esau (Ge 33). Returned to Bethel (Ge 35:1–15).

Showed favouritism to Joseph (Ge 37:3–4). Sent sons to Egypt for food (Ge 42:1–5). Settled in Egypt with family (Ge 46; Ex 1:1–5). Blessed Ephraim and

Manasseh (Ge 48:8–20; Heb 11:21); blessed sons (Ge 49:1–28). Death (Ge 49:29–33); burial in Canaan (Ge 50:1–14).

JAEL
Wife of Heber the Kenite; killed Sisera, commander of Canaanite army, after his defeat by Deborah and Barak (Jdg 4:17–22; 5:24–27).

JAIRUS
Synagogue ruler whose daughter was raised to life by Jesus (Mt 9:18–26; Mk 5:22–43; Lk 8:41–56).

JAMES
1. Apostle; son of Zebedee, brother of John (Mt 4:21–22; 10:2; Mk 1:19–20; 3:17; Lk 5:10). With Peter and John, especially close to Jesus: at raising of Jairus' daughter (Mk 5:37; Lk 8:51); transfiguration (Mt 17:1–2; Mk 9:2; Lk 9:28–29); in Gethsemane (Mt 26:36–38; Mk 14:32–34). Mother's request (Mt 20:20–28; Mk 10:35–45). Killed by Herod (Ac 12:2).

2. Apostle; son of Alphaeus (Mt 10:3; Mk 3:18; Lk 6:15; Ac 1:13).

3. Brother of Jesus and Jude (Mt 13:55; Mk 6:3; Gal 1:19; Jude 1); saw risen Lord (1Co 15:7) and with disciples before Pentecost (Ac 1:13); leader of church in Jerusalem (Ac 12:17; 15:13–21; 21:18; Gal 2:9); wrote letter (Jas 1:1).

JAPHETH
Son of Noah (Ge 5:32; 6:10; 1Ch 1:4). Saved in ark (Ge 7:13; 9:18–19). Blessed by Noah (Ge 9:27); descendants (Ge 10:2–5; 1Ch 1:5–7).

JEHOIACHIN
King of Judah; succeeded father, Jehoiakim; after three months taken as captive to Babylon (2Ki 24:8–17; 2Ch 36:8–10); removed from prison to royal palace (2Ki 25:27–30; Jer 52:31–34).

JEHOIAKIM
King of Judah. Son of Josiah, formerly called Eliakim; made king by Pharaoh Necho (2Ki 23:33–36; 2Ch 36:4). Killed prophet Uriah (Jer 26:20–23); burned Jeremiah's scroll (Jer 36). Became Babylonian vassal; subsequent rebellion brought invasion; died on way into captivity (2Ki 24:1–4; 2Ch 36:5–8; Da 1:1–2).

JEHOSHAPHAT
King of Judah; son of Asa (1Ki 22:41). Devoted to God; removed idols; sent officials to teach Law (2Ch 17:3–9). Strengthened kingdom (2Ch 17:2, 10–19). Allied with Israel (1Ki 22:44; 2Ch 18:1; 20:35–36); helped Ahab against Aram (1Ki 22:1–33; 2Ch 18:1–19:1) and Joram against Moab (2Ki 3). Alliances rebuked (2Ch 19:1–2; 2Ch 20:35–37). Appointed judges (2Ch 19:4–11). Trusted God for victory over Moab and Ammon (2Ch 20:1–30). Death (2Ch 21:1).

JEHU
1. Prophet; rebuked Baasha (1Ki 16:1–7) and Jehoshaphat (2Ch 19:1–2).

2. King of Israel. Choice by God announced to Elijah (1Ki 19:16–17); anointed by servant of Elisha; instructed to destroy Ahab's house (2Ki 9:1–13). Killed Joram, Ahaziah (2Ki 9:14–29),

Jezebel (2Ki 9:30–37), Ahab's family (2Ki 10:1–17), ministers of Baal (2Ki 10:18–29). Succession promised for four generations (2Ki 10:30). Death (2Ki 10:34–36).

JEPHTHAH

Judge. Social outcast, called on to deliver Israel from Ammonites (Jdg 11:1–32). Rash vow led to sacrifice of daughter (Jdg 11:30–40). Victory over Ephraim (Jdg 12:1–6). Death (Jdg 12:7). Example of faith (Heb 11:32–34).

JEREMIAH

Prophet to Judah (Jer 1:1–3). Called by God while still young (Jer 1). Persecuted (Jer 11:18–23; 12:6; 18:18); put in stocks (Jer 20:2); threatened with death (Jer 26:7–11); scroll burned (Jer 36); imprisoned (Jer 37); thrown into cistern (Jer 38:6–13). Warned of Babylonian exile (Jer 25:8–11; 34:1–3); challenged false prophets (Jer 6:10–15; 23:9–40; 28). Promised restoration (Jer 25:12–14; 30; 33); announced new covenant (Jer 31); bought field (Jer 32). Taken to Egypt with fleeing remnant (Jer 43).

JEROBOAM

1. Israel's first king. Former official of Solomon; rebelled and fled to Egypt (1Ki 11:26–40). After Solomon's death, led northern tribes in rebellion against Rehoboam (1Ki 12:1–20; 2Ch 10). Established idolatrous worship (1Ki 12:25–33); set evil example for successors (1Ki 15:34; 16:19, 26, 31; 22:52). Rebuked by prophets (1Ki 13–14). Death (2Ch 13:20).
2. Jeroboam II. Son of Jehoash. Restored Israel's boundaries; brought economic prosperity (2Ki 14:23–29). Spiritual decay challenged by Amos (Am 1:1; 2:6–8; 5:21–24; 6:1–8; 7:9–11).

JESSE

From Bethlehem; father of David (Ru 4:17, 22; 1Sa 16; 17:12–20; 1Ch 2:12–17; Isa 11:1, 10; Ro 15:12).

JESUS

Life: genealogy (Mt 1:1–17; Lk 3:23–38); birth (Mt 1:18–2:12; Lk 1:26–38; 2:1–20); presented in temple (Lk 2:21–40); fled to Egypt (Mt 2:13–18). Brought up in Nazareth (Mt 2:19–23); visited Jerusalem temple (Lk 2:41–52).

Baptised by John (Mt 3:13–17; Mk 1:9–11; Lk 3:21–23; Jn 1:29–34); tempted (Mt 4:1–11; Mk 1:12–13; Lk 4:1–13); began public ministry (Mt 4:12–17; Mk 1:14–15; Lk 4:14–30); called first disciples (Mt 4:18–22; Mk 1:16–20; Lk 5:2–11; Jn 1:35–51); preached in Galilee (Mt 4:23–25; Mk 1:39). Appointed and sent out disciples (Mt 9:35–10:16; Mk 3:13–18; 6:7–11; Lk 9:1–6; 10:1–17).

Acknowledged by Peter as Christ (Mt 16:13–23; Mk 8:27–33; Lk 9:18–22). Transfigured (Mt 17:1–8; Mk 9:2–8; Lk 9:28–36). Set out for Jerusalem (Mt 16:21; 20:17–19; Mk 10:32–34; Lk 18:31–34).

Last week in Jerusalem: entered city (Mt 21:1–11; Mk 11:1–11; Lk 19:29–44; Jn 12:12–15); cleared temple (Mt 21:12–13; Mk 11:15–19; Lk 19:45–48; Jn 2:13–16); anointed at Bethany (Mt 26:6–13; Mk 14:3–9); shared Last Supper (Mt 26:17–30; Mk 14:12–26; Lk 22:7–23); washed disciples' feet (Jn 13:1–17); prayed in Gethsemane (Mt 26:36–46; Mk 14:32–42; Lk 22:40–46); arrested and tried (Mt

26:47–68; 27:11–26; Mk 14:43–65; 15:1–15; Lk 22:47–53; 22:66–23:25; Jn 18:1–19:16); crucified and buried (Mt 27:27–66; Mk 15:16–47; Lk 23:26–56; Jn 19:17–42).

Raised to life; appeared to followers (Mt 28; Mk 16; Lk 24; Jn 20–21; Ac 1:1–4; 1Co 15:1–8); commissioned disciples (Mt 28:16–20; Ac 1:4–8); ascended (Lk 24:50–53; Ac 1:9).

Miracles: See p. 347.

Teaching: Announced God's kingdom (Mt 4:17; 10:7; 12:24–29; Lk 11:14–22; Mt 16:28; Mk 9:1; Mk 1:15; Lk 4:43; 9:11); Sermon on the Mount (Mt 5–7; Lk 6:20–49); pronounced woe on Pharisees (Mt 23; Lk 11:37–54); signs of the end of the age (Mt 24; Mk 13; Lk 21); conversations with Nicodemus (Jn 3), Samaritan woman (Jn 4); the bread of life (Jn 6:25–58); the good shepherd (Jn 10:1–20); discourse in Upper Room (Jn 13–17).

Parables: See p. 309.

JETHRO
Father-in-law of Moses (Ex 3:1; 4:18), also called Reuel (Ex 2:18). Visited Moses at Horeb; advised him to delegate administration of justice (Ex 18).

JEZEBEL
1. Daughter of Sidonian king; wife of Ahab (1Ki 16:31). Encouraged his sin (1Ki 21:25): promoted worship of native god, Baal (1Ki 16:32–33; 18:19); killed Lord's prophets (1Ki 18:4, 13); threatened Elijah (1Ki 19:1–2); had Naboth killed (1Ki 21). Death prophesied by Elijah (1Ki 21:23); killed by Jehu (2Ki 9:30–37).

2. Designation of prophet in church at Thyatira who was leading believers astray (Rev 2:20).

JOAB
Nephew of David; brother of Abishai and Asahel (1Ch 2:16). Led David's army against Abner (2Sa 2:13–32); killed Abner to avenge death of Asahel (2Sa 3:26–27, 30). Led attack on Jerusalem (1Ch 11:4–6); made commander-in-chief (2Sa 8:16; 18:2; 20:23). Defeated Ammon (2Sa 10:7–14; 1Ch 19:8–15), Rabbah (2Sa 12:26–27). Followed David's order to kill Uriah (2Sa 11:14–17); killed Absalom (2Sa 18:14–15); killed Amasa (2Sa 20:9–10). Supported Adonijah (1Ki 1:17–19); killed by Benaiah (1Ki 2:5–6, 28–34).

JOASH
1. Father of Gideon (Jdg 6:11, 29–31; 8:32).

2. King of Judah; son of Ahaziah. Hidden from Athaliah (2Ki 11:1–3; 2Ch 22:10–12); crowned king by Jehoiada (2Ki 11:4–21; 2Ch 23). Repaired temple (2Ki 12; 2Ch 24:1–14); returned to idolatry after Jehoiada's death (2Ch 24:17–24). Defeated by Aram (2Ch 24:23–24); murdered by officials (2Ki 12:20; 2Ch 24:25).

JOB
1. Wealthy, God-fearing man from Uz (Job 1:1–8). Uprightness tested by Satan, with God's permission (Job 1:6–12; 2:1–6). Suffered loss of family and wealth (Job 1:13–19), and physical affliction (Job 2:7–8). Remained patient (Job 1:20–22; 2:9–10); protested when innocence challenged by friends (Job

3–31). Rebuked by the Lord (Job 38–41); finally vindicated, healed and restored to greater wealth (Job 42:7–17).

2. Job's friends: Eliphaz (Job 4–5; 15; 22), Bildad (Job 8; 18; 25) Zophar (Job 11; 20) and Elihu (Job 32–37). Came to offer sympathy (Job 2:11–13); tried and failed to explain Job's suffering in terms of conventional wisdom.

JOEL

Prophet (Joel 1:1). Saw plague of locusts as depiction of God's judgment (Joel 1:2–2:12); called for repentance (Joel 2:13–17). Future blessing included pouring out of Spirit (Joel 2:18–32; Ac 2:16–21).

JOHN

1. The Baptist; son of Zechariah and Elizabeth (Lk 1:5–25, 57–80). Prepared way for Jesus (Mt 3:1–12; Mk 1:3–8; Lk 3:2–17; Jn 1:6–8, 15, 19–36; 3:27–30); baptised Jesus (Mt 3:13–15; Mk 1:9; Lk 3:21). Opposed Herod's marriage to Herodias; arrested (Mt 14:3–5; Mk 6:17–18); reassured and commended by Jesus (Mt 11:2–19; Lk 7:18–35). Executed (Mt 14:6–12; Mk 6:21–29). Identified with Elijah (Mt 11:14; 17:11–13; Mk 9:12–13; Lk 1:17).

2. Apostle; son of Zebedee; brother of James. With Peter and James, especially close to Jesus: at raising of Jairus' daughter (Mk 5:37; Lk 8:51); transfiguration (Mt 17:1–2; Mk 9:2; Lk 9:28–29); in Gethsemane (Mt 26:36–38; Mk 14:32–34). Mother's request (Mt 20:20–28; Mk 10:35–45). Called 'the disciple whom Jesus loved': close to Jesus at Last Supper (Jn 13:23; 21:20); at crucifixion (Jn 19:25–27). Leader in Jerusalem church (Gal 2:9; 2Jn 1; 3Jn 1). Wrote fourth Gospel, letters, book of Revelation (Rev 1:1, 9; 22:8; Jn 20:2; 21:7, 24).

3. See **Mark**.

JONAH

Prophet during reign of Jeroboam II (2Ki 14:25). Ran from God's call to preach against Nineveh (Jnh 1:2–3, 10). God sent storm; thrown overboard; swallowed by fish (Jnh 1:4–17). Prayed; disgorged onto dry land (Jnh 2); deliverance a 'sign' prefiguring Jesus' death and resurrection (Mt 12:39–41; Lk 11:29–32). Obeyed second call (Jnh 3); response to Nineveh's repentance rebuked (Jnh 4).

JONATHAN

Eldest son of Saul (1Sa 13:16; 14:49; 1Ch 8:33). Courageous warrior (1Sa 14:1–23; 2Sa 1:22–23). Violated Saul's oath (1Sa 14:24–45). Friendship with David (1Sa 18:1–4; 19–20; 23:16–18; 2Sa 1:26). Killed (1Sa 31:1–2); mourned by David (2Sa 1:19–27).

JOSEPH

1. Son of Jacob by Rachel (Ge 30:22–24; 35:24; 1Ch 2:2). Father's favouritism aroused brothers' hostility (Ge 37:3–4). Dreams (Ge 37:5–11). Sold by brothers (Ge 37:12–36); became slave of Potiphar (Ge 39:1–6). Resisted attentions of Potiphar's wife; falsely accused; imprisoned (Ge 39:7–23). Interpreted dreams of cupbearer and baker (Ge 40); Pharaoh (Ge 41:1–36). Put in charge of Egypt (Ge 41:37–57). Tested brothers when came to buy grain (Ge 42–44);

made himself known (Ge 45:1–15); settled family in Egypt (Ge 45:16–47:12). Sons blessed (Ge 48); received Jacob's blessing (Ge 49:22–26). Death (Ge 50:22–26; Ex 13:19; Jos 24:32; Heb 11:22). Descendants divided into tribes of Ephraim and Manasseh (Jos 14:4; 16–17; Eze 47:13); blessed by Moses (Dt 33:13–17).

2. Husband of Jesus' mother, Mary (Mt 1:16, 18–25; Lk 1:27); descendant of David (Lk 2:4); carpenter (Mt 13:55). Dreams (Mt 1:20–23; 2:13, 19–20).

3. Disciple from Arimathea; member of Jewish council. Asked for Jesus' body; gave tomb for burial (Mt 27:57–60; Mk 15:42–46; Lk 23:50–54; Jn 19:38–42).

4. See **Barnabas**.

JOSHUA

1. Son of Nun, formerly called Hoshea (Nu 13:8, 16; 1Ch 7:27). Fought Amalekites (Ex 17:9–14). Moses' assistant: on Sinai (Ex 24:13; 32:17); at tent of meeting (Ex 33:11). One of spies sent to explore Canaan (Nu 13:8); with Caleb encouraged people to go in (Nu 14:6–9); so allowed to enter land (Nu 26:65; 32:12). Succeeded Moses (Dt 1:38; 3:28; 31:1–8; 34:9). Commissioned and encouraged by God (Jos 1:1–9). Crossed Jordan (Jos 3–4). Victory at Jericho (Jos 5:13–6:27); defeat then victory at Ai (Jos 7–8); renewed covenant at Mt Ebal (Jos 8:30–35); deceived by Gibeonites (Jos 9); sun stood still to enable victory over five kings at Gibeon (Jos 10); conquered southern Canaan (Jos 10:29–43), northern Canaan (Jos 11). Apportioned land among tribes (Jos 13–22). Gave final instructions (Jos 23); renewed

covenant at Shechem (Jos 24:1–27); death (Jos 24:29–31; Jdg 2:8–9).

2. High priest at time of restoration (Hag 1:1); encouraged by Haggai to finish work on temple (Hag 1:12–2:9). Representative of sinful Israel saved by God's grace (Zec 3); crowning foreshadowed reign of Messiah (Zec 6:9–15).

JOSIAH

King of Judah; son of Amon (2Ki 21:26; 1Ch 3:14; 2Ch 33:25). Birth prophesied (1Ki 13:2). Godliness commended (2Ki 22:2; 2Ch 34:2–3; Jer 22:15–16). Removed idols (2Ch 34:3–7); repaired temple (2Ki 22:3–7; 2Ch 34:8–13). Repented, following discovery of Book of the Law (2Ki 22:8–20; 2Ch 34:14–28); renewed covenant (2Ki 23:1–3; 2Ch 34:29–32); purified temple (2Ki 23:4–12); destroyed high places (2Ki 23:13–20, 24–25; 2Ch 34:33). Celebrated Passover (2Ki 23:21–23; 2Ch 35:1–19). Killed while fighting Pharaoh Necho (2Ki 23:29–30; 2Ch 35:20–27).

JUDAH

1. Son of Jacob by Leah (Ge 29:35; 35:23; 1Ch 2:1). Urged brothers to sell, not kill, Joseph (Ge 37:26–27). Father of Perez and Zerah, by daughter-in-law Tamar (Ge 38). Offered himself in place of Benjamin (Ge 44:18–34). Blessed by Jacob as ruler (Ge 49:8–12).

2. Tribe descended from Judah. Blessed by Moses (Dt 33:7). Included in census (Nu 1:26–27; 26:19–22). Apportioned land (Jos 15; Eze 48:7); unable to take full possession (Jos 15:63; Jdg 1:1–20). Anointed David as king (2Sa 2:4); remained loyal to Davidic

kings (1Ki 12:21; 2Ch 11:12). Tribe of Jesus (Mt 1:3; Heb 7:14).

JUDAS

1. Brother of Jesus (Mt 13:55; Mk 6:3); also called Jude, author of letter (Jude 1).

2. Disciple; son of James (Lk 6:16; Jn 14:22; Ac 1:13); also known as Thaddaeus (Mt 10:3; Mk 3:18).

3. Apostle; also called Iscariot; known as Jesus' betrayer (Mt 10:4; Mk 3:19; Lk 6:16; Jn 6:71; 12:4); treasurer for disciples (Jn 12:6; 13:29). Agreed to betray Jesus for 30 silver pieces (Mt 26:14–16; Mk 14:10–11; Lk 22:3–6); kissed Jesus to identify him (Mt 26:47–49; Mk 14:43–45; Lk 22:47–48); filled with remorse; committed suicide (Mt 27:3–5; Ac 1:16–25).

4. Prophet; also called Barsabbas. Sent, with Silas, by apostles in Jerusalem to Antioch with decision about circumcision (Ac 15:22–34).

KORAH

1. Son of Esau; Edomite chief (Ge 36:5, 14, 18).

2. Grandson of Kohath (1Ch 6:22); ancestor of group of musicians (Ps 42; 44–49; 84; 85; 87; 88) and temple gatekeepers (1Ch 9:19; 26:1, 19); led rebellion against Moses; killed by God (Nu 16; 26:9–11; Jude 11).

3. Son of Hebron (1Ch 2:43).

LABAN

Brother of Rebekah (Ge 24:29); gave permission for sister to marry Isaac (Ge 24:50–51). Received Jacob (Ge 29:13–14); gave daughters, Leah and Rachel, in exchange for service (Ge 29:15–30).

Deceived by Jacob (Ge 30:25–31:21); pursued and made covenant with him (Ge 31:22–55).

LAZARUS

1. Beggar in Jesus' parable (Lk 16:19–31).

2. Brother of Mary and Martha; raised to life by Jesus (Jn 11:1–12:11).

LEAH

Daughter of Laban; wife of Jacob (Ge 29:16–23); bore six sons and one daughter (Ge 29:31–35; 30:16–21; 34:1; 35:23).

LEVI

1. Son of Jacob by Leah (Ge 29:34; 35:23); with Simeon killed Shechemites to avenge rape of sister Dinah (Ge 34); blessed by Jacob (Ge 49:5–7).

2. Tribe descended from Levi. Blessed by Moses (Dt 33:8–11). Numbered separately (Nu 1:47–49; 3:14–39; 26:57–62); responsible for tabernacle (Nu 1:50–53; 3:14–37; 4; 8; 18:2–4); dedicated to God in place of firstborn (Nu 3:11–13, 40–41). Given towns (Nu 35; Jos 21) but not land (Nu 18:20–24; 26:62; Dt 10:9; Jos 13:14); allocated land in new division (Eze 48:13–14).

3. See **Matthew.**

LOT

Nephew of Abraham (Ge 11:27); accompanied him from Harran (Ge 12:4–5; 13:1). Settled in Sodom (Ge 13:5–13); rescued by Abraham (Ge 14), and by two angels (Ge 19; 2Pe 2:7–8). Wife became pillar of salt (Ge 19:26). Fathered Ammon and Moab by his two daughters (Ge 19:30–38).

LUKE

Doctor; coworker and close companion of Paul (Col 4:14; 2Ti 4:11; Phm 24). Writer of third Gospel and Acts.

LYDIA

God-fearing woman living in Philippi; accepted Paul's message; baptised; offered hospitality (Ac 16:14–15, 40).

MALACHI

Prophet; name means 'my messenger' (Mal 1:1).

MANASSEH

1. Joseph's elder son (Ge 41:51; 46:20); blessed by Jacob but not as firstborn (Ge 48:13–20).

2. Tribe descended from Manasseh. Blessed by Moses (Dt 33:13–17). Included in census (Nu 1:34–35; 26:29–34). Apportioned land on both sides of Jordan: east (Nu 32:33, 39–42; Jos 13:8, 29–31); west (Jos 17:1–11; Eze 48:4); failed to possess fully (Jos 17:12–13).

3. King of Judah; son of Hezekiah (2Ki 20:21; 2Ch 32:33). Led Israel into idolatry (2Ki 21:2–9; 2Ch 33:2–9); sin held responsible for exile (2Ki 21:10–15; Jer 15:3–4). Deported to Babylon; repented; carried out limited reform (2Ch 33:10–19). Death (2Ki 21:18; 2Ch 33:20).

MARK

Also called John (Ac 12:12). Cousin of Barnabas (Col 4:10). Accompanied Paul and Barnabas (Ac 12:25) but later deserted them (Ac 13:13). Cause of disagreement (Ac 15:37–39). Reconciled to Paul (2Ti 4:11) and a fellow-worker (Phm 24); close to Peter (1Pe 5:13). Wrote second Gospel.

MARTHA

Sister of Mary and Lazarus (Lk 10:38–39; Jn 11). Concerned with practical things (Lk 10:40–41; Jn 12:2).

MARY

1. Mother of Jesus; wife of Joseph (Mt 1:16–25; Lk 1–2). Visited by Gabriel (Lk 1:26–38); praised God (Lk 1:46–55). With Jesus at wedding in Cana (Jn 2:1–11). Witnessed crucifixion (Jn 19:25); entrusted to John's care (Jn 19:26–27). With disciples after resurrection (Ac 1:14).

2. Magdalene. Demoniac delivered by Jesus (Lk 8:2; Mk 16:9). At crucifixion (Mt 27:55–56; Mk 15:40–41, 47; Jn 19:25); visited tomb (Mt 28:1; Mk 16:1; Lk 24:1–10; Jn 20:1); met by risen Jesus (Jn 20:10–18).

3. Sister of Martha and Lazarus (Lk 10:38–39; Jn 11); commended for devotion (Lk 10:39–42); anointed Jesus' feet (Jn 12:3; 11:2).

4. Mother of James and Joses; wife of Clopas. At crucifixion (Mt 27:55–56; Mk 15:40–41, 47; Jn 19:25); visited tomb (Mt 28:1; Mk 16:1; Lk 24:1–10).

5. Mother of John Mark whose home was used by one Jerusalem church (Ac 12:12–17).

6. Believer in Rome (Ro 16:6).

MATTHEW

Apostle; tax collector, also called **Levi** (Mt 9:9–13; Mk 2:14–17; Lk 5:27–32; Mt 10:3; Mk 3:18; Ac 1:13). Wrote first Gospel.

MELCHIZEDEK

King of Salem and priest of God Most High who blessed Abraham and received tithe from him (Ge 14:18–20; Heb 7:1–10). Presented as a type of Christ (Ps 110:4; Heb 5:6, 10; 6:20; 7:11–17).

MEPHIBOSHETH

1. Son of Jonathan; also called Merib-Baal (1Ch 8:34; 9:40). Crippled by a fall (2Sa 4:4); shown kindness by David (2Sa 9:1–13). Slandered by Ziba (2Sa 16:1–4); reconciled to David (2Sa 19:24–30).

2. Son of Saul, executed by the Gibeonites (2Sa 21:8–9).

MESHACH

Formerly Mishael; member of Jewish nobility taken to Babylon with Daniel, Shadrach and Abednego (Da 1:3–7). Refused unclean food (Da 1:8–16); appointed as administrator (Da 2:49). Refused to worship golden image; kept safe in fiery furnace (Da 3).

METHUSELAH

Son of Enoch; grandfather of Noah; lived to be 969 (Ge 5:21–27; 1Ch 1:3; Lk 3:36–37).

MICAH

1. Prophet from Moresheth (Jer 26:18–19; Mic 1:1).

2. Ephraimite whose idols and priest were taken by migrating Danites (Jdg 17–18).

3. Micaiah. Prophet (1Ki 22:4–28; 2Ch 18:1–27).

MICHAEL

Archangel (Jude 9). Heavenly guardian of Israel against power of Greece and Persia (Da 10:13, 21; 12:1). Defeated Satan and cast him from heaven (Rev 12:7–9).

MICHAL

Daughter of Saul (1Sa 14:49). Became David's wife (1Sa 18:20–29); warned him of Saul's plot (1Sa 19:11–17). Given to Paltiel (1Sa 25:44); returned to David (2Sa 3:13–16). Despised David (2Sa 6:16–23; 1Ch 15:29).

MIRIAM

Sister of Moses and Aaron (Nu 25:59; 1Ch 6:3). Watched Moses in bulrushes; suggested mother as nurse (Ex 2:4–8). Prophet; led dancing and sang at Red Sea (Ex 15:20–21); criticised Moses, became leprous (Nu 12:1–15; Dt 24:9). Death (Nu 20:1).

MORDECAI

1. Benjamite exile; brought up cousin, Esther, as own daughter (Est 2:5–7, 15, 20). Reported plot to kill Xerxes (Est 2:21–23). Refused to bow to Haman, resulting in plot against Jews (Est 3:1–6); mourned; persuaded Esther to help (Est 4). Honoured (Est 6); given Haman's position as next in rank to king (Est 8:1–2; 10). Saved Jews; instituted feast of Purim (Est 8–9).

2. Jewish exile who returned with Zerubbabel (Ezr 2:2; Ne 7:7).

MOSES

Levite; brother of Aaron (Ex 6:20; 1Ch 6:3). Put into Nile in basket; found and

raised by Pharaoh's daughter; killed Egyptian; fled to Midian; married Zipporah (Ex 2; Ac 7:20–29). Called by God at burning bush (Ex 3–4; Ac 7:30–36); confronted Pharaoh (Ex 5:1–4; 7:1–13); plagues (Ex 7–11; Ps 105:26–36). Led people out of Egypt (Ex 12–13), through Red Sea (Ex 14). Brought water from rock (Ex 17:1–7); raised hands to enable victory over Amalekites (Ex 17:8–16); appointed judges (Ex 18; Dt 1:9–18). Given Law on Mount Sinai (Ex 19–23); spoke to people; confirmed covenant (Ex 19:7–8; 24:1–11; Heb 9:19); returned to mountain to receive stone tablets (Ex 24:12–18; 31:18). Broke tablets over golden calf (Ex 32:15–19; Dt 9:7–17); interceded for people (Ex 32:10–14; Dt 9:25–29). Saw God's glory (Ex 33:18–23); given new tablets (Ex 34; Dt 10:1–5); face shone (Ex 34:29–35).

Supervised building of tabernacle (Ex 35–40; Heb 8:5); consecrated Aaron and sons as priests (Ex 28–29; Lev 8–9). Took census (Nu 1–4; 26). Opposed by Aaron and Miriam (Nu 12), Korah (Nu 16; Jude 11). Sent spies into Canaan (Nu 13; Dt 1:19–25). Forbidden to enter Canaan for striking rock (Nu 20:12; 27:12–14; Dt 3:27; 32:48–52). Lifted up bronze snake (Nu 21:4–9). Allocated land east of Jordan (Nu 32). Last words to Israel (Dt 31–33); death (Dt 34); succeeded by Joshua (Dt 3:28; 34:9; Jos 1:1–9). Faithfulness as God's servant commended (Heb 3:3–5). Prayer of Moses (Ps 90); songs of Moses (Ex 15:1–18; Dt 32; Rev 15:3–4).

NAAMAN
Commander-in-chief of Aramaean army; leprosy healed by Elisha (2Ki 5).

NABOTH
Jezreelite, killed by Jezebel so Ahab could take possession of his vineyard (1Ki 21:1–16).

NAHUM
Prophet; spoke against Nineveh (Na 1:1).

NAOMI
Mother-in-law of Ruth. With husband Elimelek, moved from Bethlehem to Moab during famine; returned with Ruth after death of husband and sons (Ru 1). Encouraged Ruth's marriage to Boaz (Ru 2:19–3:6); nursed Ruth's son (Ru 4:16–17).

NAPHTALI
1. Son of Jacob by Bilhah (Ge 30:8; 35:25; 1Ch 2:2). Blessed by Jacob (Ge 49:21).

2. Tribe descended from Naphtali. Blessed by Moses (Dt 33:23). Included in census (Nu 1:42–43; 26:48–50). Apportioned land (Jos 19:32–39; Eze 48:3); unable to take full possession (Jdg 1:33).

NATHAN
1. Prophet; announced God's promise to David of lasting dynasty (2Sa 7:1–17; 1Ch 17:1–15); rebuked David's sin with Bathsheba (2Sa 12:1–14). Supported Solomon's succession (1Ki 1:8–40). Chronicled reigns of David and Solomon (1Ch 29:29; 2Ch 9:29).

2. Son of David (2Sa 5:14; Zec 12:12); included in Jesus' genealogy (Lk 3:31).

NATHANAEL
Apostle from Cana in Galilee; brought to Jesus by Philip (Jn 1:45–51; 21:2).

Possibly to be identified with Bartholomew, who is also linked with Philip (Mt 10:3).

NEBUCHADNEZZAR
King of Babylon. Defeated Egyptians at Carchemish (Jer 46:2); invaded and subdued Judah; took exiles to Babylon; destroyed Jerusalem (2Ki 24–25; 2Ch 36; Jer 39; Da 1:1–5). Dreams interpreted by Daniel (Da 2; 4); fiery furnace (Da 3); madness and restoration; worshipped God (Da 3:28–29; 4:34–35).

NECHO
Pharaoh. Reluctantly fought and killed Josiah, who opposed support for Assyria (2Ki 23:29–30; 2Ch 35:20–25). Deposed Jehoahaz, appointed Jehoiakim as vassal (2Ki 23:31–35; 2Ch 36:2–4). Defeated by Nebuchadnezzar at Carchemish (Jer 46:2).

NEHEMIAH
Cupbearer to Artaxerxes (Ne 1:10). Prayed over state of Jerusalem (Ne 1); allowed to return to rebuild city walls (Ne 2–6); appointed governor (Ne 5:14; 8:9). Called Ezra to read Law (Ne 8); confessed nation's sin (Ne 9); dedicated wall (12:27–47); made other reforms (Ne 13).

NICODEMUS
Pharisee, member of Sanhedrin who visited Jesus at night (Jn 3:1–15). Argued against condemning Jesus without a hearing (Jn 7:50–51). With Joseph anointed and buried Jesus (Jn 19:38–42).

NOAH
Righteous man (Ge 6:8–9; 7:1; Eze 14:14, 20; Heb 11:7). Obeyed God's command to build ark (Ge 6:11–22). God's covenant with (Ge 6:18; 9:8–17). Planted vineyard; became drunk, dishonoured by Ham (Ge 9:20–23); cursed Canaan; blessed Shem and Japheth (Ge 9:24–27). Death (Ge 9:28–29).

OBADIAH
1. Official in charge of Ahab's palace; believer; hid 100 prophets from Jezebel (1Ki 18:1–16).

2. Prophet; spoke against Edom (Ob 1).

OMRI
King of Israel; father of Ahab (1Ki 16:30). Army commander, appointed king after Zimri assassinated Baasha (1Ki 16:15–28). Sinned against God (1Ki 16:25–26).

ONESIMUS
Runaway slave belonging to Philemon; converted by Paul and dear to him (Col 4:9; Phm 10–16).

PAUL
Apostle (Gal 1:1); also called Saul (Ac 13:9). From Tarsus (Ac 9:11; 21:39; 22:3; Php 3:5); Pharisee (Ac 23:6; 26:5; Php 3:5); taught by Gamaliel (Ac 22:3).

Approved of Stephen's death (Ac 7:58; 8:1); persecuted church (Ac 8:3; 9:1–2; 1Co 15:9; Gal 1:13). Saw Jesus on Damascus road (Ac 9:3–9; 22:6–11; 26:12–18); healed and baptised by Ananias (Ac 9:17–19; 22:12–16). Into Arabia (Gal 1:17); escaped from Damascus in a basket (Ac 9:23–25; 2Co

11:32–33). Introduced to apostles in Jerusalem by Barnabas; sent to Tarsus (Ac 9:26–30; Gal 1:18–21).

Brought to Antioch by Barnabas (Ac 11:22–26). Visited Jerusalem; message and commission confirmed by apostles (Ac 11:30; Gal 2:1–10). First missionary journey, with Barnabas (Ac 13–14). Stoned at Lystra (Ac 14:19–20). At Council of Jerusalem (Ac 15). Disagreed with Barnabas over Mark (Ac 15:36–39). Second missionary journey, with Silas (Ac 15:40–18:22). Called to Macedonia (Ac 16:9–10); miraculously released from prison in Philippi (Ac 16:16–40); in Athens (Ac 17:16–34); in Corinth (Ac 18). Third missionary journey (Ac 18:23). In Ephesus (Ac 19); raised Eutychus to life (Ac 20:7–12); farewell to Ephesian elders (Ac 20:13–37). Travelled to Jerusalem (Ac 21); arrested (Ac 21:27–36); appealed as Roman citizen (Ac 22:25–29); before Sanhedrin (Ac 22:30–23:10). Taken to Caesarea (Ac 23:12–35); before Felix, Festus and Agrippa (Ac 24–26). Journeyed to Rome (Ac 27–28); shipwrecked on Malta (Ac 27:27–28:10); under house arrest in Rome; preached gospel (Ac 28:16–31).

Letters: Romans, 1 & 2 Corinthians, Galatians, Ephesians, Philippians, Colossians, 1 & 2 Thessalonians, 1 & 2 Timothy, Titus, Philemon.

PETER

Name means 'rock'; in Aramaic, Cephas (Jn 1:42). Apostle; brother of Andrew, also called Simon (Mt 4:18; Mk 1:16–18; Lk 5:3–11; Jn 1:40–42; Mt 10:2; Mk 3:16; Lk 6:14; Ac 1:13). With James and John, especially close to Jesus at raising of Jairus' daughter (Mk 5:37; Lk 8:51);

transfiguration (Mt 17:1–2; Mk 9:2; Lk 9:28–29); in Gethsemane (Mt 26:36–38; Mk 14:32–34). Confessed Jesus as Christ (Mt 16:13–20; Mk 8:27–30; Lk 9:18–21). Caught fish with coin (Mt 17:24–27). Denial predicted (Mt 26:33–35; Mk 14:29–31; Lk 22:31–34; Jn 13:37–38). Followed Jesus after arrest (Mt 26:58; Mk 14:54; Jn 18:15); denied Jesus (Mt 26:69–75; Mk 14:66–72; Lk 22:54–62; Jn 18:17–27). Commissioned by Jesus after resurrection (Jn 21).

Exercised leadership in early church (Ac 1:15; 2:14; 5:3–11). Preached on day of Pentecost (Ac 2). Healed lame man at temple gate (Ac 3); before Sanhedrin (Ac 4). In Samaria (Ac 8:14–25). Received vision; went to Cornelius (Ac 10); supported Gentile mission (Ac 11; 15:7–11); lapsed and rebuked by Paul at Antioch (Gal 2:11–21). Miraculously released from prison (Ac 12). Wrote 1 & 2 Peter.

PHILEMON

Coworker with Paul (Phm 1); owner of runaway slave, Onesimus (Phm 8–11).

PHILIP

1. Apostle (Mt 10:3; Mk 3:18; Lk 6:14; Ac 1:13); from Bethsaida; brought Nathanael to Jesus (Jn 1:43–45).

2. Deacon (Ac 6:1–7). Evangelist (Ac 21:8); in Samaria (Ac 8:4–13); spoke to Ethiopian official (Ac 8:26–40).

PHINEHAS

1. Son of Eleazar; grandson of Aaron (Ex 6:25). Priest (Nu 31:6; Jdg 20:28). Held back God's judgment by killing Israelite and pagan Midianite woman (Nu

524 NIV Bible Handbook

25:6–11; Ps 106:28–31); zeal rewarded by everlasting covenant of priesthood (Nu 26:12–13). In charge of temple gatekeepers (1Ch 9:20).

2. Disreputable son of Eli (1Sa 1:3; 2:12–17). Condemned with his brother (1Sa 2:34). Both died in battle (1Sa 4:11).

PILATE

Roman governor of Judea (Lk 3:1). Questioned Jesus (Mt 27:11–14; Mk 15:2–5; Lk 23:2–5; Jn 18:33–38); gave way to crowds: freed Barabbas; washed hands and gave Jesus up to be crucified (Mt 27:15–26; Mk 15:6–15; Lk 23:13–25; Jn 19). Released Jesus' body to Joseph (Mt 27:57–58; Mk 15:43–46; Lk 23:50–54); allowed guard on tomb (Mt 27:62–66).

POTIPHAR

Egyptian official who bought Joseph (Ge 37:36; 39:1) and made him chief steward (Ge 39:2–6). Sent Joesph to prison (Ge 39:7–20).

PRISCILLA

Also called Prisca. Wife of Aquila. Disciples from Rome (Ac 18:2); coworkers with Paul (Ro 16:3; 1Co 16:19; 2Ti 4:19), accompanied him to Ephesus (Ac 18:18–19); instructed Apollos (Ac 18:26).

RACHEL

Daughter of Laban (Ge 29:9–13); became Jacob's wife (Ge 29:28); mother of Joseph and Benjamin (Ge 30:22–24; 35:16–18, 24); died in childbirth; buried by Jacob (Ge 35:16–20; 48:7).

RAHAB

1. Prostitute in Jericho; sheltered Israelite spies and helped them escape (Jos 2; Jas 2:25); spared when city fell (Jos 6:22–25; Heb 11:31). Mother of Boaz (Mt 1:5).

2. Female chaos monster (Job 26:12; Ps 89:10; Isa 51:9); figurative name for Egypt (Ps 87:4; Isa 30:7).

REBEKAH

Sister of Laban (Ge 25:20); left Harran with Abraham's servant to marry Isaac (Ge 24). Mother of Esau and Jacob (Ge 25:21–26). In Gerar, pretended to be Isaac's sister (Ge 26:1–11). Helped Jacob deceive Isaac and steal blessing (Ge 27).

REHOBOAM

Son of Solomon; succeeded him as king (1Ki 11:43; 2Ch 9:31). Refusal to ease burden on people led to breaking away of northern tribes under Jeroboam (1Ki 12; 2Ch 10). In his evil reign temple plundered by Egyptians (1Ki 14:21–28; 2Ch 12:9–16).

REUBEN

1. Jacob's firstborn, by Leah (Ge 29:32; 35:23; 46:8). Wanted to save Joseph (Ge 37:19–30). Lost position as slept with Bilhah (Ge 35:22; 49:4). Blessed by Jacob (Ge 49:3–4).

2. Tribe descended from Reuben. Blessed by Moses (Dt 33:6). Included in census (Nu 1:20–21; 26:5–11). Apportioned land east of Jordan (Nu 32; 34:14–15; Jos 18:7; 22); crossed into Canaan to fight alongside other tribes (Nu 32:16–31). Place restored in land (Eze 48:6).

RUTH

Moabitess at time of Judges; widow of Naomi's son, Mahlon (Ru 1:4–5; 4:10). Refused to leave Naomi; accompanied her to Bethlehem (Ru 1:11–22). Gleaned in field of Boaz and treated kindly (Ru 2). Claimed protection from Boaz as kinsman-redeemer (Ru 3). Married Boaz; gave birth to Obed, grandfather of David (Ru 4).

SAMSON

Judge. Birth promised (Jdg 13:2–3); set apart as Nazirite (Jdg 13:4–7); great strength linked with uncut hair (Jdg 16:17, 22). Married Philistine (Jdg 14); killed lion, 30 Philistines (Jdg 14:6, 19). Took vengeance on Philistines when wife given away (Jdg 15); killed 1,000 with jawbone (Jdg 15:15–16). Carried off gates of Gaza (Jdg 16:1–3). Betrayed by Delilah and captured (Jdg 16:4–21); died when brought temple of Dagon down on Philistines (Jdg 16:23–30).

SAMUEL

Judge and prophet (Ac 3:24; 13:20). Born to Hannah, who vowed to dedicate him to God (1Sa 1:9–20). Taken to temple to be raised by Eli (1Sa 1:21–28; 2:11, 18–21). Called by God (1Sa 3). Led Israel to victory over Philistines (1Sa 7). Asked by people for a king (1Sa 8); anointed Saul (1Sa 9–10). Farewell speech (1Sa 12). Rebuked Saul (1Sa 13:8–14; 15); and announced his rejection by God (1Sa 13:13–14; 15:22–26). Anointed David (1Sa 16:1–13); protected David (1Sa 19:18–24). Death (1Sa 25:1). Spirit called up by Saul (1Sa 28:11–19).

SANBALLAT

Horonite; governor of Samaria; leading opponent of Nehemiah in his task to rebuild walls of Jerusalem (Ne 2:10, 19; 4:1–9; 6).

SARAH

Wife of Abraham; formerly Sarai; barren (Ge 11:29–30). Taken by Pharaoh when pretending to be Abraham's sister (Ge 12:10–20). Gave Hagar to Abraham (Ge 16:1–3). Name changed; promised a son (Ge 17:15–21; 18:9–10; Ro 9:9; Heb 11:11); laughed in disbelief (Ge 18:10–15). Taken by Abimelek when pretending to be Abraham's sister; returned (Ge 20:1–18). Gave birth to Isaac (Ge 21:1–7); sent away Hagar and Ishmael (Ge 21:8–14). Death and burial (Ge 23).

SAUL

1. Benjamite; Israel's first king. Chosen by God (1Sa 9:15–16); anointed by Samuel (1Sa 10:1); acknowledged publicly (1Sa 10:17–25). Defeated Ammonites (1Sa 11). Rebuked by Samuel, when offered sacrifices (1Sa 13) and for disobedience (1Sa 15); rejected as king (1Sa 13:13–14; 15:23, 26–28; 28:17). Defeated Philistines (1Sa 14). Troubled by evil spirit; soothed by David's playing (1Sa 16:14–23). Sent David to fight Goliath (1Sa 17). Gave David his daughter Michal as wife (1Sa 18:20–21). Became jealous; tried to kill David (1Sa 18:1–11; 19:1–10). Anger at Jonathan (1Sa 20:26–34). Pursued David; killed priests at Nob (1Sa 22); life spared by David (1Sa 24; 26). Consulted medium at Endor; rebuked by Samuel's spirit (1Sa 28). Defeated by Philistines on Mt Gilboa; wounded, took own life (1Sa 31;

1Ch 10). Mourned by David (2Sa 1:19–27). Children (1Sa 14:49–51; 1Ch 8).

2. See **Paul.**

SENNACHERIB

King of Assyria. Attacked Judah and laid siege to Jerusalem (2Ki 18:13–19:13; Isa 36:1–37:13; 2Ch 32). Pride brought God's judgment (Isa 10:12–19). Fall prophesied by Isaiah, following Hezekiah's prayer (2Ki 19:14–34; Isa 37:14–35); defeat and death (2Ki 19:35–37; Isa 37:36–38).

SHADRACH

Formerly Hananiah; member of Jewish nobility taken to Babylon with Daniel, Meshach and Abednego (Da 1:3–7). Refused unclean food (Da 1:8–16); appointed as administrator (Da 2:49). Refused to worship golden image; kept safe in fiery furnace (Da 3).

SHECHEM

Son of Hamor, a ruling Hivite (Ge 34:2). Raped Jacob's daughter, Dinah, and asked to marry her (Ge 34:2–12). Shechemites treacherously killed by Simeon and Levi in revenge (Ge 34:13–31).

SHEM

Son of Noah (Ge 5:32; 6:10; 1Ch 1:4). Saved in ark (Ge 7:13; 9:18–19). Blessed by Noah (Ge 9:26); descendants (Ge 10:21–31); ancestor of Abraham (Ge 11:10–32).

SILAS

Prophet and a leader in Jerusalem church; sent to Antioch from Council of Jerusalem (Ac 15:22–32). Accompanied Paul on second missionary journey (Ac 15:40–18:22; 2Co 1:19). Assisted Peter with first letter (1Pe 5:12), and Paul (1Th 1:1; 2Th 1:1).

SIMEON

1. Son of Jacob by Leah (Ge 29:33; 35:23; 1Ch 2:1). With Levi killed Shechemites to avenge rape of sister Dinah (Ge 34). Left in Egypt as hostage (Ge 42:24–43:23). Blessed by Jacob (Ge 49:5–7).

2. Tribe descended from Simeon. Included in census (Nu 1:22–23; 26:12–14). Given territory in restored land (Eze 48:24).

3. Righteous and devout man in Jerusalem; recognised the child Jesus as the Messiah when he was brought into the temple (Lk 2:25–35).

SIMON

1. See **Peter.**

2. Apostle; called 'the Zealot' (Mt 10:4; Mk 3:18; Lk 6:15; Ac 1:13).

3. Brother of Jesus (Mt 13:55; Mk 6:3).

4. Leper from Bethany, in whose house Jesus was anointed with oil (Mt 26:6; Mk 14:3).

5. Pharisee, in whose house Jesus' feet were washed with tears (Lk 7:40).

6. Man from Cyrene, forced to carry Jesus' cross (Mk 15:21).

7. Sorcerer, who amazed Samaritans with his magic (Ac 8:9–11). Believed Philip and was baptised (Ac 8:12–13); rebuked by Peter for trying to buy spiritual power (Ac 8:18–24).

8. Tanner, with whom Peter lodged (Ac 9:43).

SOLOMON

Third king of Israel; son of David and Bathsheba (2Sa 12:24). Appointed by David; anointed by Nathan and Zadok (1Ki 1; 1Ch 29:21–25). Given charge by David (1Ki 2:1–9); had Adonijah, Joab and Shimei killed (1Ki 2:13–46). Asked God for wisdom (1Ki 3:5–15; 2Ch 1:7–12); gave wise judgment (1Ki 3:16–28); noted for his wisdom (1Ki 4:29–34; 10:23–24). Wrote proverbs (1Ki 4:32; Pr 1:1; 10:1–22:16; 25–29); psalms (Ps 72:1; 127:1); Song of Songs (SS 1:1). Built temple (1Ki 5–7; 2Ch 2–4); brought ark; prayer of dedication (1Ki 8–9; 2Ch 5–7). Established trading fleet (1Ki 9:26–28; 2Ch 8:17). Visited by Queen of Sheba (1Ki 10:1–13; 2Ch 9:1–12; Mt 12:42; Lk 11:31). Acquired great wealth (1Ki 10:14–29; 2Ch 1:14–17; 9:13–28). Foreign wives turned his heart from God (1Ki 11:1–10), causing him to break covenant with God and so to lose part of kingdom (1Ki 11:11–13, 29–39). Death (1Ki 11:41–43; 2Ch 9:29–31).

STEPHEN

Deacon (Ac 6:5–6). Performed miracles; aroused opposition; arrested (Ac 6:8–15). Defence to Sanhedrin (Ac 7:1–53); killed by stoning (Ac 7:54–8:1; 22:20).

TAMAR

1. Married in turn to Judah's sons Er and Onan (Ge 38:6–10). Pretended to be prostitute and became pregnant by Judah when he withheld third son (Ge 38:11–30). Mother of Perez and Zerah (Ge 38:27–30; Ru 4:12).

2. Daughter of David. Raped by Amnon; avenged by brother Absalom (2Sa 13).

THOMAS

Apostle (Mt 10:3; Mk 3:18; Lk 6:15; Ac 1:13); called Didymus, the Twin (Jn 11:16). Asked where Jesus was going (Jn 14:5). Doubted resurrection (Jn 20:24–25); saw Jesus alive; confessed him as Lord and God (Jn 20:26–29). Present at miraculous catch of fish after resurrection (Jn 21:2–14).

TIMOTHY

Disciple from Lystra (Ac 16:1); convert of Paul (1Ti 1:2), probably during first missionary journey (2Ti 3:10–11). Circumcised by Paul and taken with him on second missionary journey (Ac 16:2–18:22; 2Co 1:19). Ministry confirmed by prophetic utterances (1Ti 1:18) and laying on of hands (1Ti 4:14; 2Ti 1:6). Sent by Paul to Thessalonica (1Th 3:2); Macedonia (Ac 19:22); Corinth (1Co 4:17). Accompanied Paul to Jerusalem (Ac 20:4–16). Remained in Ephesus to give leadership to church (1Ti 1:3). Imprisoned and released (Heb 13:23).

Timid (1Co 16:10–11; 2Ti 1:7), needing encouragement (1Ti 4:12; 2Ti 1:8; 2:1); but warmly commended by Paul as coworker and son in the faith (Ro 16:21; 1Co 4:17; Php 2:19–22; 1Th 3:2; 2Ti 1:1–5). Associated with Paul in the writing of the letters to the Thessalonians (1Th 1:1; 2Th 1:1) and to Philemon (Phm 1).

TITUS

Gentile convert and companion of Paul (Tit 1:4; 2Ti 4:10; 2Co 8:23). Accompanied Paul and Barnabas to Jerusalem (Gal 2:1–3). Sent to Corinth to deal with difficulties; brought good news to Paul in Macedonia (2Co 7:6–16).

In Corinth again to complete collection (2Co 8:6, 16–17). Left by Paul in Crete to consolidate work (Tit 1:5).

URIAH
Hittite. Husband of Bathsheba; killed on David's order (2Sa 11).

UZZIAH
Also called Azariah. King of Judah; son of Amaziah (2Ki 14:21–22; 15:1–2; 2Ch 26:1–3). Commended, though failed to remove high places (2Ki 15:3–4; 2Ch 26:4–5). Extended power and prestige; strengthened Jerusalem's defences (2Ch 26:6–15). Pride in assuming priestly authority led to affliction with leprosy and isolation (2Ki 15:5; 2Ch 26:16–21). Death (1Ki 15:7; 2Ch 26:23; Isa 6:1).

VASHTI
Queen of Persia; wife of Xerxes. Deposed for refusal to appear at banquet (Est 1). Replaced by Esther (Est 2:1–17).

XERXES
King of Persia (Ezr 4:6; Est 1:1–2); father of Darius (Da 9:1). Deposed Vashti; married Esther (Est 1–2). Assassination attempt uncovered by Mordecai (Est 2:21–23). Gave assent to Haman's edict to kill Jews (Est 3); allowed Esther to see him without calling her (Est 5:1–8); hanged Haman (Est 7). Exalted Mordecai (Est 8:1–2; 9:4; 10); allowed Jews to defend themselves (Est 8–9).

ZACCHAEUS
Tax collector; climbed tree to see Jesus (Lk 19:2–10).

ZADOK
Priest; descendant of Aaron (1Ch 6:3–8). With Abiathar, served David (2Sa 8:17; 1Ch 15:11; 16:39–40); in charge of ark (2Sa 15:24–29). Anointed Solomon as David's successor when Abiathar supported Adonijah (1Ki 1:8, 32–48). Descendants served as chief priests (2Ch 31:10; Eze 40:46; 43:19; 44:15).

ZEBULUN
1. Son of Jacob by Leah (Ge 30:20; 35:23; 1Ch 2:1). Blessed by Jacob (Ge 49:13).

2. Tribe descended from Zebulun. Blessed by Moses (Dt 33:18–19). Included in census (Nu 1:30–31; 26:26–27). Apportioned land (Jos 19:10–16; Eze 48:26); unable to take full possession (Jdg 1:30).

ZECHARIAH
1. King of Israel; son of Jeroboam II; assassinated (2Ki 14:29; 15:8–12).

2. Prophet who, with Haggai, encouraged rebuilding of temple (Ezr 5:1; 6:14; Zec 1:1).

3. Priest; father of John the Baptist; struck dumb because of unbelief at the angel Gabriel's announcement of the birth of a son (Lk 1:5–22, 59–79).

ZEDEKIAH
1. Last king of Judah. Son of Josiah, formerly Mattaniah. Installed by Nebuchadnezzar (2Ki 24:17–18). Evil denounced (Jer 24:8–10; Eze 21:25); dealings with Jeremiah (2Ch 36:12; Jer 37; 38:14–28). Rebellion and broken oath led to fall of Jerusalem (2Ki 24:20–25:7; 2Ch 36:13–21; Jer 39; Eze 17:12–15).

2. Leader of false prophets at Ahab's court (1Ki 22:11–24; 2Ch 18:10–23).

ZEPHANIAH
Prophet during reign of Josiah; descended from Hezekiah (Zep 1:1).

ZERUBBABEL
Leader of returning exiles (Ne 12:1; Hag 1:1; 2:2); began work on temple (Ezr 3); after delay, encouraged to continue by Haggai (Ezr 5:1–2; Hag 1:2–15; 2) and Zechariah (Zec 4:6–10).

ZIPPORAH
Daughter of Jethro; wife of Moses (Ex 2:21–22; 18:2); circumcised son to save Moses' life (Ex 4:20–26).

PLACES OF THE BIBLE

ABARIM, MOUNTAINS OF
Mountain range east of the Jordan and Dead Sea. Includes Mount Nebo at its northern point. From here Moses viewed the promised land (Nu 27:12; Dt 32:49) and the death of Jehoiakim was proclaimed (Jer 22:20).

ACHAIA
Roman province, with capital Corinth (2Co 1:1); governed by a pro-consul (Ac 18:12). Linked with Macedonia to denote the whole of Greece (Ac 19:21; Ro 15:26; 1Th 1:7–8); may refer specifically to Corinth. Christians from here contributed to Paul's collection for the poor in Jerusalem (Ro 15:26–27). Visited by Paul during his second and third missionary journeys (Ac 18:1–18), and Apollos (Ac 18:27). The household of Stephanas were the first converts here (1Co 16:15).

ACHOR, VALLEY OF
Not far from Jericho at the entrance to the promised land. Name, meaning 'trouble', given because Achan and family were killed here for hoarding spoil from Jericho (Jos 7:24–26). Becomes a symbol of hope for God's restored people (Hos 2:15; Isa 65:10).

ADULLAM
Canaanite city whose king was defeated by Joshua (Jos 12:15). Allotted to the tribe of Judah (Jos 15:35), it was fortified by Rehoboam as part of his southern defences (2Ch 11:7). David and his men hid from Saul in Adullam's caves (1 Sa 22:1; 2 Sa 23:13; 1 Ch 11:15).

AI
1. Canaanite town east of Bethel, near to Abram's camp and altar (Ge 12:8; 13:3–4). Attacked and finally defeated by Joshua (Jos 8), although Achan's sin led to earlier failure (Jos 7:4–5). Also called Aiath (Isa 10:28) and possibly Aija (Ne 11:31). See **Achor, Valley of.**

2. Ammonite city east of the Jordan in Moab (Jer 49:3). Exact location unknown.

ALEXANDRIA
Port on west of Nile delta on Mediterranean coast. Capital city of Egypt in Greco-Roman period; second city of Roman Empire with large Jewish community. Jews who argued with Stephen came from here (Ac 6:9), as did Apollos (Ac 18:24).

AMMON
Territory inhabited by Ammonites east of the Jordan between Aarnon and Jabbok rivers; with capital Rabbah. Western part captured by the Amorites, later occupied by Israel (Dt 2:21–23; Jdg 11:13–23). Its inhabitants frequently warred against the Israelites (1 Sa 11:1; 2 Sa 10:6–14; 12:26–28; 2 Ch 27:5) and its

destruction prophesied (Jer 49:1–6; Eze 21:28–32; Am 1:13–15; Zep 2:8–11).

ANATHOTH

Levite village northeast of Jerusalem, in Benjamin territory (Jos 21:18). Home of Abiezer (2Sa 23:27), Jehu (1Ch 12:3), Abiathar (1Ki 2:26) and Jeremiah (Jer 1:1; 29:27). Its inhabitants threatened Jeremiah and so faced God's punishment (Jer 11:21–23). During Babylonian siege of Jerusalem, God instructed Jeremiah to purchase a field here as an assurance of eventual redemption (Jer 32:1–15). The Assyrian army passed through here en route to Jerusalem (Isa 10:30).

ANTIOCH

1. Cosmopolitan capital city of Roman province of Syria, on bank of river Orontes, about 15 miles inland from Mediterranean port of Seleucia. Home of Nicolas, one of the first 'deacons' (Ac 6:5). Persecuted believers arrived from Jerusalem to evangelise Jews (Ac 11:19) and Greeks (Ac 11:20–21). Barnabas and Paul also came here (Ac 11:22–26). Term 'Christian' first used here (Ac 11:26). Became the base for Paul's three missionary journeys (Ac 13:1–3; 15:35–41; 18:23). Dispute arose here about circumcision (Ac 15:1–2), which was later decided at the Council of Jerusalem.

2. City in province of either Pisidia or Phrygia (disputed) in southern Asia Minor. On first missionary journey, Paul preached in its synagogue, and though many Gentiles were converted, he experienced Jewish opposition and was expelled (Ac 13:14–51). Paul returned on his way home (Ac 14:21), and possibly again on his second journey (Ac 16:6). He refers to his persecution here in a letter to Timothy (2Ti 3:11).

ANTIPATRIS

See **Aphek** 1.

APHEK

1. City on coastal Plain of Sharon whose king was defeated by Joshua (Jos 12:18). Used as a Philistine encampment (1Sa 4:1; 29:1). Later rebuilt as Roman city Antipatris, where Paul was taken on his way to Caesarea (Ac 23:31).

2. Town east of Galilee, where Ahab overcame the Aramean army (1Ki 20:26–30). Elisha predicted another Aramean defeat at Aphek (2Ki 13:17).

3. Canaanite city (also known as Aphik) in Asher's territory (Jos 19:30–31; Jdg 1:31–32).

ARABAH

Valley stretching from Mount Hermon in the north to the Gulf of Aqaba in the south, including the Sea of Galilee, river Jordan and Dead Sea. On their journey to the promised land, the Israelites travelled and camped in this region (Dt 2:8). Sea of Arabah (Dt 3:17, etc) = Dead Sea.

ARAM

Region north of Palestine, from Lebanon to beyond the river Euphrates. Known also as Paddan Aram and Aram Naharam and by its Greek name Syria. Named after son of Shem (Ge 10:22), whose descendants spread rapidly around this area. Rebekah, Leah, Rachel and Jacob lived here (Ge 25:20; 27:43–44; 28:2;

29:16–28). Balaam came from here (Nu
23:7; Dt 23:4). The Israelites often served
its gods (Jdg 10:6; 2Ch 28:23), and suffered
at the hand of its army (1Ki 11:25; 2Ki 6:8;
13:4). At one stage Judah and Syria teamed
up against Israel (1Ki 15:18–20) but at
other times Israel and Syria joined together
against Judah (2Ki 16:5). Its downfall was
prophesied (Isa 7:1–8; Am 1:5). Roman
province in New Testament times (Mt
4:24) of which Quirinius was governor
(Lk 2:2). Paul travelled through here (Ac
15:41; 18:18; 21:3).

ARAM NAHARAIM
See Aram; Mesopotamia.

ARARAT, MOUNTAINS OF
Range between Black Sea and Caspian
Sea, from which streams converged to
form rivers Tigris and Euphrates.
Traditionally the resting place of Noah's
ark (Ge 8:4). Sennacherib's two sons fled
here after murdering him (2Ki 19:37; Isa
37:38). One of the kingdoms God would
use to punish Babylon (Jer 51:24–27).

ARNON GORGE
Swift river stream running from the
mountains of Gilead into the Dead Sea.
It separated Moab from the Amorite
Kingdom (Nu 21:13; 22:36; Jdg 11:18),
and later Moab and Israel (Nu 21:25–26;
Dt 2:24; 3:8, 16; Jos 12:1–2; Jdg 11:21–22).
After Moab's destruction, fugitives fled
here (Isa 16:2–4).

AROER
1. Amorite city on northern bank of Arnon
Gorge (Dt 2:36; 4:48; Jos 12:2). Captured
by Israel and given to Reuben and Gad

(Dt 3:12). Taken during Jehu's reign by
King Hazael of Syria (2Ki 10:32–33).
   2. Town in Gilead, facing Rabbah, on
the boundary between Gad and the
Ammonites (Jos 13:25). Restored and
enlarged by descendants of Gad (Nu
32:34). 20 towns between Aroer and
Minnith destroyed by Jephthah (Jdg
11:32–33). Exact location unknown.
   3. Town in southern Judah (1Sa
30:28). Possibly the same place as Adadah
(Jos 15:22) or modern Ararah (12 miles
southeast of Beersheba).

ASHDOD
Probably the capital of the five philistine
cities. Three miles from the
Mediterranean coast and 20 miles north
of Gaza. Its inhabitants survived Joshua's
advances against them (Jos 11:22). Its
people suffered punishment when the
captured ark of the covenant was placed
in Dagon's temple here (1Sa 5:1–7).
Captured by King Uzziah of Judah (2Ch
26:6), but generally remained
independent. Amos prophesied against it
(Am 1:8), and Sargon of Assyria attacked
and captured it (Isa 20:1). Later prophets
also predicted its fall (Jer 25:20; Zep 2:4;
Zec 9:6). Its inhabitants opposed the
rebuilding of Jerusalem (Ne 4:7–8), and
Israelites were rebuked for intermarrying
with them (Ne 13:23–25). Later known
as Azotus, and evangelised by the deacon
Philip (Ac 8:40).

ASHER
1. Territory along Mediterranean coast of
Palestine, between Tyre and Mount
Carmel. Its boundaries and towns were
clearly listed (Jos 19:24–31). Allotted to
descendants of Jacob's eighth son, failed to

drive out all the Canaanites (Jdg 1:31–32).

2. Town east of Shechem and west of river Jordan, in territory of Manasseh (Jos 17:7).

ASHKELON
One of the five Philistine cities, on the Mediterranean coast about 12 miles north of Gaza. It posed a regular threat to the judges of Israel, though the men of Judah captured it for a while (Jdg 1:18). Samson later killed 30 of its men (Jdg 14:19). Named in David's lament about Saul and Jonathan's deaths (2Sa 1:20). Amos prophesied its destruction (Am 1:8), which saw fulfilment when King Sargon of Assyria attacked and captured it (Isa 20:1).

ASHUR
See **Assyria**.

ASSYRIA
Originally a city on the west bank of the river Tigris, also known as Ashur (Ge 2:14), probably named after a son of Shem (Ge 10:22). It grew into a powerful empire with capital city Nineveh. Its king, Tiglath-Pileser III invaded Israel (2Ki 15:19), and deported Israelites (2Ki 15:29), and this continued under Sargon (2Ki 17:6, 23). Then Sennacherib invaded Judah (2Ki 18:13), but this ultimately failed (2Ki 19:35–36; Isa 37:36–37). The prophets predicted its fall (Isa 10:12; 30:31; Mic 5:4–6; Zep 2:13).

ATHENS
Political and cultural centre of Greek state of Attica visited by Paul. Paul argued with the Athenians about their idolatry (Ac 17:16–32).

BABYLON
1. City on the Euphrates in the Land of Shinar, founded by Nimrod (Ge 10:10). Became capital city of Babylonian Empire; known for its great splendour (Da 4:30). Its destruction was prophesied (Isa 47; Jer 50). The city was taken by the Persians.

2. Name used generally for Babylonia.

3. Used figuratively for Rome to emphasise its opposition to God (Rev 14:8; 16:19).

BABYLONIA
Located on the plain between the Euphrates and Tigris rivers. Also called 'land of Shinar' (Ge 10:10) and 'land of the Chaldeans' (Jer 24:5). Following the fall of Jerusalem, the people of Judah were exiled here (2Ki 25:21; 2Ch 36:20) just as Isaiah had prophesied (2Ki 20:16–18; Isa 39:5–7). They left here 50 years later (Ezr 1).

BEERSHEBA
Chief city of the Negev, in territory of Simeon (Jos 19:1–2). Site of well where Abimelek made an oath with Abraham (Ge 21:31) and Isaac (Ge 26:32–33). Hagar (Ge 21:17–19), Abraham (Ge 21:33), Isaac (Ge 26:23–24) and Jacob (Ge 46:1–4) encountered God here. It became a focus for pilgrimage (Am 5:5), rivalling Bethel and Gilgal. Samuel's sons were judges here (1Sa 8:1–2); Elijah passed through as he fled from Jezebel (1Ki 19:3).

BENJAMIN
Hilly territory west of the river Jordan, with Ephraim to the north, Judah to the

south and Dan to the west. Its boundaries and towns were clearly listed (Jos 18:11–28). Allotted to descendants of Jacob's youngest son, who failed to drive out the Jebusites from Jerusalem (Jdg 1:21). Its people were almost destroyed by the other tribes of Israel, because of their sin at Gibeah (Jdg 19–21).

BEREA

City in Macedonia, about 50 miles southwest of Thessalonica. Paul fled to here with Silas after trouble in Thessalonica (Ac 17:10). Its people were receptive to the gospel and searched the Scriptures daily (Ac 17:11). Jews from Thessalonica followed Paul here, forcing Paul to leave; Silas and Timothy continued the work (Ac 17:13–14). Home of Paul's helper Sopater (Ac 20:4).

BETHANY

1. Village on eastern slope of the Mount of Olives, about 2 miles east of Jerusalem (Jn 11:18). Home of Mary, Martha and Lazarus (Jn 11:1). Jesus was anointed here in the home of Simon the Leper (Mt 26:6–7; Mk 14:3). Near to the site of Jesus' ascension (Lk 24:50–51).

2. Town on eastern side of the river Jordan where John was baptising (Jn 1:28). Exact location uncertain.

BETHEL

1. Town about 12 miles north of Jerusalem, originally known as Luz (Ge 28:19). Abraham built an altar close by (Ge 12:8; 13:3–4). Jacob renamed the city after his vision (Ge 28:19) and later settled here (Ge 35:1). Conquered by Joshua (Jos 8:17); allotted to Benjamin

(Jos 18:22) but taken by the house of Joseph (Jdg 1:22–26). Because the ark of the covenant was kept here (Jdg 20:27), it became a place of divine enquiry (Jdg 20:18; 21:2–3). Centre of worship for northern kingdom, and site for one of Jeroboam's golden calves (1Ki 12:27–29). Denounced for its idolatry (Hos 10:15; Am 5:5–6); Josiah broke down its altar (2Ki 23:15).

2. City in the territory of Simeon near Ziklag (1Sa 30:26–31). Bethul (Jos 19:4) and Bethuel (1Ch 4:30) are probably variants. Exact location unknown.

BETHLEHEM

1. Town in Judah about 5 miles south of Jerusalem. Also known as Ephrath (Ge 35:16, 19; 48:7), Ephrathah (Ru 4:11; 1Ch 4:4; Ps 132:6) and Bethlehem Ephrathah (Mic 5:2). Rachel buried near here (Ge 35:19; 48:7); book of Ruth set here. David's birthplace where he was anointed (1Sa 16:1–13). Micah predicted Messiah's birth here (Mic 5:2; Mt 2:6), fulfilled by Christ's birth in the 'town of David' (Lk 2:11).

2. Town in territory of Zebulun, about 7 miles northwest of Nazareth (Jos 19:15). Probably the home of Ibzan (Jdg 12:8).

BETHPHAGE

Town near Bethany, on slopes of Mount of Olives, near the road from Jerusalem to Jericho. Here the disciples found a colt for Jesus to ride into Jerusalem (Mt 21:1; Mk 11:1; Lk 19:29).

BETHSAIDA

1. City north of Sea of Galilee, east of river Jordan. Originally a small town, but

Philip the Tetrarch raised its status to a city and called it Julias. Home of Peter, Andrew and Philip (Jn 1:44), and possibly James and John (Lk 5:10).

2. City east of the Jordan, about 2 miles north of the Sea of Galilee. Site associated with the feeding of the 5,000 (Lk 9:10–17), and healing a blind man (Mk 8:22–26).

(Possibly these two descriptions relate to the same place.)

BETH SHEMESH
1. Town in Valley of Sorek, about 15 miles southwest of Jerusalem, on the border of Judah (Jos 15:10). Probably also called Ir Shemesh (Jos 19:41). Allotted to tribe of Dan and assigned to the Levites (Jos 21:16; 1Ch 6:59). The stolen ark of the covenant was sent here by the Philistines, where it remained until it was taken to Kiriath Jearim (1Sa 6:10–7:2). Located in one of Solomon's twelve districts (1Ki 4:9), it was the scene of battle between Jehoash and Amaziah (2Ki 14:11–14; 2Ch 25:21–23). Captured by the Philistines in the time of Ahaz (2Ch 28:18).

2. Town between Mount Tabor and the river Jordan, on the border between the territories of Issachar and Naphtali (Jos 19:22).

3. Fortified town in Naphtali (Jos 19:35, 38), from which Canaanite inhabitants were not driven out (Jdg 1:33).

CAESAREA
Mediterranean port about 30 miles north of Joppa and capital of Judea. Herod Agrippa I died here (Ac 12:19–23); Agrippa II visited with Bernice (Ac 25:13). Home of Cornelius, to whom Peter ministered (Ac 10:1, 24), and Philip the evangelist (Ac 6:5). Paul passed through on his journeys (Ac 9:30; 18:22; 21:8) and was imprisoned here for two years before being sent to Rome (Ac 23:23, 33; 25:4; 27:1).

CAESAREA PHILIPPI
City north of Sea of Galilee, on southwest slope of Mount Hermon. Known as Paneas (after the god Pan) until Philip the Tetrarch renamed it. Northernmost limit of Jesus' ministry, where Simon Peter proclaimed him the Messiah (Mt 16:13–16; Mk 8:27–29).

CANA
A Galilean village where Jesus changed water into wine (Jn 2:1–11) and healed the son of a royal official (Jn 4:46–54). Home of Nathanael (Jn 21:2).

CANAAN
Region between river Jordan and Mediterranean Sea, originally occupied by descendants of Ham's youngest son (Ge 9:18). God promised to give it to Abram and his descendants (Ge 12:1–7), so they settled here (Ge 13:12; 31:18; 33:18). It was a fruitful land in Moses' time (Nu 13:27–29) but God promised it to the Israelites, who captured it under Joshua (Jos 1:1–3), and it became the land of Israel.

CAPERNAUM
City on northern shore of Sea of Galilee, where Jesus resided after leaving Nazareth (Mt 4:13; 9:1). Jesus taught in its synagogue (Mk 1:21; Lk 4:31; Jn 6:59),

and performed significant miracles here (Mk 1:34), e.g., healing centurion's son (Mt 8:5–13; Lk 7:1–10), Peter's mother-in-law (Mk 1:30–31; Lk 4:38–39), a paralytic (Mt 9:1–8; Mk 2:3–12; Lk 5:18–26) and a man possessed by an evil spirit (Mk 1:21–26; Lk 4:31–35). Though a base for Jesus' ministry, he cursed it for its unbelief (Mt 11:23–24; Lk 10:15).

CARMEL

1. Wooded mountain range overlooking Mediterranean coast, west of Sea of Galilee. Site of contest between Elijah and prophets of Baal (1 Ki 18:19–39). The Shunammite woman found Elisha here (2 Ki 4:25). Used figuratively on account of its fruitfulness (SS 7:6; Isa 33:9; 35:2; Jer 46:18; 50:19; Am 1:2; 9:3; Na 1:4).

2. Town in hill country of Judah, about 8 miles south of Hebron. Site of Saul's monument to himself (1Sa 15:12). Home of Nabal's widow Abigail (whom David married, 1Sa 25), and one of David's mighty men (2Sa 23:35; 1Ch 11:37).

CENCHREAE

Eastern port of Corinth. Paul cut his hair off before sailing from here (Ac 18:18). Phoebe served the church based here (Ro 16:1).

CILICIA

Region along southern coast of Asia Minor, whose capital Tarsus was the birthplace of Paul (Ac 21:39; 22:3). Cilician Jews argued with Stephen in Jerusalem (Ac 6:9). Paul came here soon after his conversion (Gal 1:21), and again on his second missionary journey (Ac 15:41).

COLOSSAE

City in Phrygia, in Lycus Valley, about 12 miles east of Laodicea. Paul wrote to the church here (Col 1:2), possibly established by Epaphras (Col 1:7; 4:12), and led by Archippus (Col 4:17; Phm 2). Home of Onesimus (Col 4:9).

CORINTH

Capital of Achaia, an important trading port between Rome and the East. Paul worked with Aquila and Priscilla here (Ac 18:1–2), and appeared before Proconsul Gallio (Ac 18:12–17). Paul left for Syria (Ac 18:18), and Apollos came to preach (Ac 18:27–19:1). Paul wrote to the church (1Co 1:2; 2Co 1:1), and returned at least twice (2Co 12:14; 13:1–3).

CRETE

Large island in the Mediterranean Sea, about 60 miles south of Greece, where Paul's ship sheltered from a storm (Ac 27:8). Titus organised the church here (Tit 1:5).

CUSH

1. Country south of Egypt. Land of precious stones (Job 28:19) and tall smooth-skinned people (Isa 18:2, 7). Linked with Egypt in war, sometimes against Israel (2Ki 19:9; 2Ch 12:3; Jer 46:9; Eze 38:5). Prophets proclaimed judgment upon Cush (Isa 18:1; Zep 2:12), but some of its inhabitants would join the people of God (Ps 68:31; Isa 11:11; 18:7).

2. Land bordering the Gihon River that flowed from Eden (Ge 2:10–14). Exact location unknown.

CYPRUS

Large island in Mediterranean Sea, about 60 miles west of Syria. Mentioned by Isaiah and Ezekiel (Isa 23:1, 12; Eze 27:6). Home of Barnabas (Ac 4:36); refuge for believers (Ac 11:19). Barnabas came here with Paul (Ac 13:4), and then Mark (Ac 15:39). Home of Mnason (Ac 21:16).

DAMASCUS

Capital city of Syria (Aram) (Isa 7:8), at foot of Mount Hermon, northeast of Sea of Galilee. Home of Abram's servant Eliezer (Ge 15:2). Base for attacks on Israel; captured by David (2Sa 8:5–6; 1Ch 18:5), but later rebelled (1Ki 11:23). Recaptured by Jeroboam II (2Ki 14:28), but became Rezin's base for attack on Jerusalem (2Ki 16:5). Prosperous (Eze 27:18), due to rivers Abana and Pharpar (2Ki 5:12). Final destruction prophesied (Isa 17:1; Am 1:5), and fulfilled through Assyria. Became part of kingdom of Aretas (2Co 11:32). Paul (Saul) converted near here (Ac 9:1–8), and met Ananias here (Ac 9:10–22). Jewish inhabitants were angered by Paul's preaching (Ac 9:25; 2Co 11:32–33). Paul returned later (Gal 1:17).

DAN

1. Territory given to tribe of Dan on Mediterranean coast (hence shipping trade, Jdg 5:17). Smallest portion of land allotted to a tribe (Jos19:40–48). Due to Amorite activity, some Danites forced to migrate north (Jdg 1:34).

2. City near the sources of river Jordan. As the city at Israel's most northern point, it appears to describe the extent of the land (Jdg 20:1; 1Sa 3:20; 2Sa 3:10; 17:11; 24:2, 15; 1Ki 4:25; 1Ch 21:2; 30:5). Known originally as Leshem (Jos 19:47) or Laish (Jdg 18:7). Jeroboam set up a golden calf here (1Ki 12:28–30). Conquered by Ben-Hadad of Aram (1Ki 15:20; 2Ch 16:4).

DEAD SEA

At southern end of Jordan Valley, about 50 miles long and averaging about 10 miles wide. Up to 1,300 feet below sea level with salt and potash deposits more concentrated than in any other lake or sea in the world. Known as Salt Sea, Eastern Sea and Sea of the Arabah. Mostly mentioned as a boundary – to the land of Israel (Nu 34:3, 12; 2Ki 14:25; Eze 47:18), tribal territory (Dt 3:17; Jos 15:2, 5; 18:19), neighbouring kingdoms (Dt 4:49; Jos 12:3). Its source was cut off when Israelites crossed into promised land (Jos 3:16). Israel's enemies will be driven into it (Joel 2:20), and living water will flow into it from Jerusalem (Zec 14:8).

DERBE

Town in Lycaonia in Asia Minor, about 16 miles east of Lystra. Paul and Barnabas fled here from trouble in Iconium (Ac 14:6), and gained converts (Ac 14:20–21). Paul visited again on second missionary journey (Ac 16:1). Home of Gaius (Ac 20:4).

DOTHAN

Town about 12 miles north of Samaria, on trade route between Syria and Egypt. Joseph betrayed by brothers near here (Ge 37:17). Elisha encountered Aramean soldiers here (2Ki 6:8–19).

EBAL, MOUNT
North of Shechem, facing Mount Gerizim to the south. Highest peak of Samaria, at centre of Canaan. The LORD's curses were to be proclaimed from here (Dt 11:29), and an altar erected (Dt 27:4). Joshua carried out these instructions (Jos 8:30, 33).

EDEN
1. Wooded garden including tree of life and tree of knowledge of good and evil (Ge 2:9). First home of Adam and Eve (Ge 2:8) who took care of it (Ge 2:15). River flowed from Eden into the garden, and split into four (Ge 2:10–14). After disobeying God (Ge 2:17; 3:1–6), Adam and Eve banished from here (Ge 3:23–24). Used figuratively for God's paradise (Isa 51:3; Eze 28:13; 31:9; 36:35). Alluded to in vision of New Jerusalem (Rev 22:2–3).

2. Market town providing Tyre with choice items (Eze 27:23), captured by Assyrians (2Ki 19:12; Isa 37:12). Probably in Mesopotamia.

EDOM
Region south of Dead Sea and East of Arabah, known also as land of Seir and Esau. Home of Esau (also called Edom) (Ge 32:3; 38:8). Esau's descendants expelled the Horites (Dt 2:12, 22). During her exodus, Israel not permitted to pass through (Nu 20:14–21; 21:4; Jdg 11:17–18). Its people battled against Saul (1Sa 14:47), but were conquered by David (2Sa 8:13–14; 1Ki 11:15–16), enabling Solomon to develop a port here (1Ki 9:26). Revolted against Jehoram (2Ki 8:20–22), but retaken by Amaziah (2Ki 14:7). Azariah captured port of Elath (2Ki 14:22), but it was later recaptured (2Ki 16:6). Inhabitants joined with Babylonians against Judah (Ps 137:7; 35:5; 36:5; Ob 10–16), thus becoming subject of prophetic judgment (Isa 34; 63:1–6; Jer 49:7–22; Eze 25:12–14; 35; Joel 3:19; Ob; Mal 1:3–5). Later referred to as Idumea (Mk 3:8).

EGYPT
Country lying south of the Mediterranean Sea and southwest of Palestine. Habitable land limited to Valley of the river Nile. A place of refuge in time of famine or oppression for Abram (Ge 12:10), Jacob and his sons (Ge 42:1–3; 45:16–20), Hadad (1Ki 11:17), Jeroboam (1Ki 11:40), Uriah (Jer 26:21), Ishmael (Jer 41:15–18), and Mary, Joseph and Jesus (Mt 2:13). Also a place of oppression and servitude for many, e.g., Joseph (Ge 37:28), Jacob's descendants (Ex 1:1–11), Jehoahaz (2Ch 36:4), and the remnant of Judah (Jer 44:12–14, 27). Jacob and Joseph both died here (Ge 50). Moses led Israelites out of slavery in Egypt (Ex 3–12). They were tempted to return to its relative security (Ex 13:17; 14:11–12; Nu 14:2–4; Ac 7:39). Figuratively a place of false security and hope (2 Ki 18:21; Isa 20:5–6; 30:1–3; 31:1–3; 36:6; Jer 2:18; Eze 17:15–17). A centre of idolatry (Lev 18:3; Ezr 9:1; Isa 19:1, 3; Eze 20:7–8). Its downfall prophesied (Isa 19; Jer 46; Eze 29–32), but it will eventually turn to the Lord (Isa 19:19; Zec 14:16–19).

EKRON
Most northern of five principal Philistine cities, about 35 miles west of Jerusalem. Not conquered by Joshua (Jos 13:1–3), but allotted to Judah (Jos 15:45), and

later Dan (Jos 19:43). Ark of covenant brought here (1Sa 5:10), and the five Philistine rulers return here (1Sa 6:16). Philistine army fled here from Israelite army (1Sa 17:52). Baal-Zebub worshipped, and consulted by Ahaziah who dies as a result (2Ki 1). Its judgment is pronounced (Jer 25:20; Am 1:8; Zep 2:4; Zec 9:5, 7).

ELAM

Region east of Babylonia, named after son of Shem, ancestor of the Elamites (Ge 10:22; 1Ch 1:17). Capital city is Susa or Shushan (Da 8:2). Its king captured Lot in Sodom (Ge 14:1–17). Some Israelites exiled here by Assyria (Isa 11:11; Ac 2:9) and Elamites settled in Samaria (Ezr 4:9). Its part in Babylon's downfall was prophesied (Isa 21:2; 22:6), but it would receive God's judgment (Jer 25:115–126; 49:34–39; Eze 32:24–25).

EMMAUS

Village in Judea about 7 miles from Jerusalem (Lk 24:13). After his resurrection, Jesus appeared to Cleopas and another disciple on the Emmaus road (Lk 24:15). He explained scriptures concerning himself but was not recognised until he broke bread at the evening meal (Lk 24:30–31). Exact location unknown.

ENDOR

Town about 4 miles south of Mount Tabor, allotted to tribe of Manasseh (Jos 17:11). Home of the medium whom Saul consulted (1Sa 28:7). Fleeing Midianites perished here (Ps 83:10).

EPHESUS

Capital city and important port of Asia Minor, opposite island of Samos. Famous for temple of Artemis (Ac 19:35). Paul visited on second missionary journey leaving Priscilla and Aquila here (Ac 18:19). Apollos joined them (Ac 18:24–26). Paul returned on third missionary journey (Ac 19:1) and stayed for between two and three years (Ac 19:10; 20:31), preaching in the synagogue (Ac 19:8), in the school of Tyrannus (Ac 19:9) and in private homes (Ac 20:20). His effective preaching threatened reputation of Artemis and associated trade (Ac 19:23–27), and trouble ensued (Ac 19:28–41). Paul wrote to Corinth from here (1Co 16:8; 15:32). He left Timothy, Onesimus and Tychicus to continue the work (1Ti 1:3; 2Ti 1:18; 4:12), and wrote to the church (Eph 1:1). One of the seven letters of Revelation is addressed to Ephesus (Rev 1:11), in which they receive both praise and criticism (Rev 2:1–7).

EPHRAIM

1. Territory west of river Jordan, between Manasseh, and Benjamin. Allotted to the descendants of Joseph's younger son. Territories of Ephraim and Manasseh, often treated together (Jos 16:1–17:2). Canaanites not driven out (Jos 16:10), but enslaved (Jos 17:13). Known for its beauty and fertility, contrasting with its moral decay (Isa 28:1, 4; Hos 9:13; 10:11; 12:8).

2. Became synonym for northern kingdom (Ps 78:9–16, 67–68; Isa 7:1–17; Jer 7:15; Hos 5; 11).

3. Town where Jesus withdrew with his disciples (Jn 11:54). Exact location unknown, probably also known as Ophrah.

EPHRATH
See **Bethlehem** 1.

EPHRATHAH
See **Bethlehem** 1.

ETHIOPIA
See **Cush** 1.

EUPHRATES, RIVER
Longest river of western Asia (about 1,780 miles), which joins with the river Tigris. Known as the River (Ex 23:31) and the Great River (Ge 15:18). Babylon and Ur situated on its bank. One of the four rivers of Paradise (Ge 2:14); the northeast boundary of the promised land (Ge 15:18; Dt 1:7; Jos 1:4). David fought here (2Sa 8:3; 1Ch 18:3), and Josiah was killed here (2Ch 35:20–24). It features in prophecies about the exile (Isa 11:15; Jer 46:6; 51:63) and in John's vision (Rev 9:14; 16:12).

GAD
Territory east of river Jordan, with Manasseh to the north, and Reuben to the south. Its boundaries and towns were listed (Jos 13:24–28; Nu 32:34–36). Allotted to the descendants of Jacob's seventh son, who liked it for its good grazing (Nu 32:1).

GALATIA
Central region of Asia Minor. Paul passed through on second missionary journey (Ac 16:6) and due to illness stayed and preached (Gal 4:13–14). Returned during third journey to encourage the churches here (Ac 18:23), and sent letter here (Gal 1:2; 3:1). Crescens left Paul to go here (2Ti 4:10). Peter addressed his first letter to Galatian church (1Pe 1:1).

GALILEE
1. Lake situated 60 miles north of Jerusalem, measuring approximately 13 by 8 miles, fed by river Jordan. Known as Sea of Galilee (Mt 4:18), Sea of Kinnereth (Nu 34:11), Sea of Tiberias (Jn 6:1) and Lake of Gennesaret (Lk 5:1). In Old Testament mentioned as a boundary (Nu 34:11; Jos 12:3; 13:27). Fishing industry thrived here: Jesus called some fishermen to become disciples (Mt 4:18; Mk 1:16); he made use of boats (Lk 5:3; Jn 6:1); he provided disciples with a large catch of fish (Jn 21:1–6); he calmed a storm (Mk 4:35–41).

2. Region between the lake and the Mediterranean Sea. Contained refuge city of Kedesh (Jos 20:7; 21:32). Solomon gave 20 of its towns to Hiram (1Ki 9:11). It was later captured by Tiglath-Pileser III of Assyria (2Ki 15:29), and flooded with immigrants (2Ki 17:24). It became known as Galilee of the Gentiles. It would be honoured through the coming Messiah (Isa 9:1; Mt 4:15); Jesus lived and ministered here (Mt 2:22; 4:12–13; Lk 23:5; Ac 10:37). He became known as Jesus of Galilee (Mt 26:69).

GATH
One of five chief cities of the Philistines, about 10 miles east of Ashdod (Jos 13:3; 1Sa 6:17). Inhabited by the Anakim, even after Joshua had driven them out of the hill country of Judah (Jos 11:22). Home to Goliath (1Sa 17:4) and another giant (2Sa 21:20). Its inhabitants were struck by plague when ark of covenant brought here (1Sa 5:8–9), so sent a guilt offering

to Israel (1Sa 6:17). David took refuge here from Saul (1Sa 21:10; 27:2–4), and later captured it (1Ch 18:1). Rehoboam fortified it (2Ch 11:8), but Hazael of Aram captured it on his way to attacking Jerusalem (2Ki 12:17). Was destroyed by the time of Amos (Am 6:2). Exact location unknown.

GAZA

Most southern of five principal Philistine cities, and the oldest, having been a Canaanite border town (Ge 10:19). Reached during Joshua's conquests (Jos 10:41), but not subdued (Jos 11:22). Captured briefly by men of Judah (Jdg 1:18), but back in Philistine hands when Samson tormented its people (Jdg 16:3, 21, 30). Destruction was prophesied (Jer 25:20; Am 1:6–7; Zep 2:4; Zec 9:5). Ethiopian eunuch converted on road from Jerusalem to here (Ac 8:26).

GERAR

Border town between Egypt and Philistia (Ge 10:19), where Abraham stayed and pretended Sarah was his sister (Ge 20:1–7). Isaac also dug wells here (Ge 26). Asa's army pursued the Cushites to here, killing them and plundering the surrounding villages (2Ch 14:13–14).

GERIZIM, MOUNT

South of Shechem, facing Mount Ebal to the north. The LORD's blessings were to be announced (Dt 11:29; 27:12), fulfilled by Joshua (Jos 8:33–35). Place where Jotham addressed the people of Shechem (Jdg 9:7). In Jesus' day the Samaritans worshipped on Mount Gerizim (Jn 4:20–21).

GIBEAH

1. City in territory of Benjamin (Jos 18:28; Jdg 19:14); inhabitants brutalised the concubine of a Levite of Ephraim (Jdg 19:22–25). War with the Benjamites ensued (Jdg 20:12–48). Occupied by Philistines for a while (1Sa 10:5). Also Saul's home (1Sa 10:26; 15:34) and base (1 Sa 11:4; 22:6; 23:19; 26:1). Spirit of God came upon Saul here (1Sa 10:10) and seven of his descendants were killed here by Gibeonites (2Sa 21:6).

2. Town southeast of Hebron in territory of Judah (Jos 15:57). Exact location unknown.

3. Town in territory of Phinehas, where Aaron's son Eleazar was buried (Jos 24:33).

GIBEON

Chief of four fortress cities, inhabited by the Hivites (Jos 9:17) and allotted to the tribe of Benjamin (Jos 21:17). Gibeonites tricked Joshua into signing a peace treaty, but they became Israel's woodcutters and water carriers (Josh 9). Joshua defended them from the Amorite alliance; during the battle the sun stood still (Jos 10:1–14). Saul violated treaty (2Sa 21:1), so his descendants killed by Gibeonites (2Sa 21:9). Place where Saul's and David's men fought (2Sa 2:12–16); David slaughtered the Philistines (2Sa 5:25; 1Ch 14:6) and Solomon offered sacrifices (1Ki 3:3–5; 1 Ch 16:39; 21:29; 2Ch 1:3–5, 13). Inhabitants helped rebuild Jerusalem (Ne 3:7; 7:25). Home of Hananiah (Jer 28:1).

GILBOA, MOUNT

Range between plain of Jezreel and river Jordan. Site of battle between Israelites and Philistines (1Sa 28:4), when Israel

was defeated (1Sa 31:1; 1Ch 10:1), and Saul and his sons killed (1Sa 31:8; 1Ch 10:8). Cursed by David (2Sa 1:21).

GILEAD

1. Mountainous region east of river Jordan, between Sea of Galilee and Dead Sea. Place of refuge for Jacob from Laban (Ge 31:21), Israelites from the Philistines (1Sa 13:7) and David from Absalom (2Sa 17:22, 26). Midianite merchants, who bought Joseph, were travelling from here (Ge 37:25). Ideal region for raising livestock, so Reuben and Gad desired it (Nu 32:1). Half was allotted to them and the rest to Manasseh (Dt 3:12–13).

2. A city of wicked men (Hos 6:8). Location unknown.

3. Mountain in the Jezreel Valley, where Gideon had to reduce the size of his army (Jdg 6:2–3).

GILGAL

1. First encampment for Israelites in the promised land, on the eastern side of Jericho (Jos 4:19). Monument set up as a memorial (Jos 4:19–20): here Israelites were circumcised and celebrated Passover (Jos 5:2–10). Israelite base camp for Joshua's conquest (Jos 6:11; 10:15; 14:6), until it moved to Shiloh (Jos 18:1). Here the Gibeonites tricked Joshua (Jos 9:6), and from here he marched to their aid (Jos 10:7). Samuel held court here (1Sa 7:15–16) and it became a sanctuary (1Sa 10:8; 13:8–10; 15:21). Here Agag died (1Sa 15:33), and Saul was both proclaimed King (1Sa 11:15) and rejected as King (1Sa 15:12–23). David was greeted here by the men of Judah (2Sa 19:15). Became a centre of idolatry (Hos 4:15; 9:15; 12:11; Am 4:4; 5:5).

2. Village from which Elijah travelled (2Ki 2:1). Elisha visited here (2Ki 4:8). Probably in hill country of Ephraim, near Bethel and Shiloh.

3. Royal city associated with Dor (Jos 12:23), about five miles north of Antipatris.

GOMORRAH

City in the Valley of Siddim (Ge 14:2–3), usually paired with Sodom. Its king and army were defeated by a Mesopotamian alliance (Ge 14:8–11). Faced God's judgment on account of gross sin (Ge 18:20–21; 19:24–25). Used to exemplify human depravity and God's judgment (Dt 29:23; Isa 13:19; Jer 23:14; 49:18; Am 4:11; Mt 10:15; Ro 9:29; 2Pe 2:6). See **Sodom.**

GOSHEN

1. Northeastern region of Nile Delta in Egypt. Jacob's family brought here by Joseph during famine (Ge 45:10; 46:28–29, 34; 47:1, 4, 6). They flourished here (Ge 47:27), and Jacob died here (Ge 49:33). It was protected from the plagues (Ex 8:22; 9:26).

2. Region of southern Palestine, between Gaza and Gibeon. Joshua's conquests reached to here (Jos 10:41; 11:16).

3. Town in the mountains of southwest Judah (Jos 15:51).

GREAT SEA

Known also as the Mediterranean Sea, it was called the Great Sea (Nu 34:6–7; Jos 1:4; 9:1; 15:12, 47; 23:4; Eze 47:10–20; 48:28), the Western Sea (Dt 11:24; 34:2; Joel 2:20; Zec 14:8), and the Sea of the Philistines (Ex 23:31). Formed a natural boundary, so often used as a territorial marker.

HAMATH

City and region in Syria on southern bank of river Orontes. Its king congratulated David for defeat of Hadadezer (2Sa 8:9–10; 1Ch 18:9–10). Solomon controlled it, and built storage depot there (2Ch 8:4). Was lost to Israel but recovered by Jeroboam (2Ki 14:28). After Assyrian capture, some inhabitants moved to Samaria (2Ki 17:24; Isa 36:18–19; 37:13), and some Israelites moved to Hamath (Isa 11:11). Its people worshipped Ashima (2Ki 17:30), and were guilty of syncretism (2Ki 17:29–33). In Amos' time the city was in ruins (Am 6:2).

HARRAN

City in northern Mesopotamia, where Terah and Abram stayed and Terah died (Ge 11:31–32; Ac 7:2, 4). Abram received God's promise here (Ge 12:1–4). Here Jacob fled (Ge 28:10), then found and married Rachel (Ge 29:4–28). Captured by Assyrians (2Ki 19:12; Isa 37:12). Its merchants traded with Tyre (Eze 27:23–24).

HEBRON

Town in the highlands of Judah, between Beersheba and Jerusalem. Originally known as Kiriath Arba (Ge 23:2; Jos 14:15). Abram's home, where he built an altar (Ge 13:18), received promise of birth of Isaac (Ge 18:1–15), and where Sarah died (Ge 23:2). Isaac and Jacob lived here (Ge 35:27) and Moses' spies came here (Nu 13:22). Joshua killed its king (Jos 10:3–27); Caleb drove out its inhabitants (Jos 14:12–15). Designated a city of refuge (Jos 20:7). Abner killed and buried here (2Sa 3:27–32). David

made king here (2Sa 5:1–5); base for Absalom's rebellion (2Sa 15:7–12). Fortified by Rehoboam (2Ch 11:10–12).

HERMON, MOUNT

At the most northerly point conquered by Joshua (Dt 3:8; Jos 11:3, 17; 12:1, 5; 13:5, 11), also known as Mount Sirion, Mount Senir (Dt 3:9; 1Ch 5:23), Mount Siyon (Dt 4:48) and Mount Baal Hermon (Jdg 3:3; 1Ch 5:23) because of its role in Baal worship. Used figuratively in Hebrew poetry (Ps 42:6; 89:12; 133:3; SS 4:8). Possibly the site of Jesus' transfiguration.

HESHBON

Capital city of Sihon, king of Amorites (Nu 21:26), situated about 25 miles east of northern Dead Sea. Captured by Israelites when Sihon blocked their path (Nu 21:25–30; Dt 2:24–33; Jos 13:10–27). Allotted to Gad and Reuben, who rebuilt it (Nu 32:37), became a Levite town for the Merarites (Jos 21:39). Occupied by Moabites (Isa 15:4; Jer 48:34, 45) and Ammonites (Jer 48:2; 49:3). Known for its pastures (Nu 32:1–4), vineyards (Isa 16:8–9) and pools (SS 7:4).

HINNOM VALLEY

Deep ravine on southern slope of Jerusalem, known also as Ben Hinnom. Part of boundary between Judah and Benjamin (Jos 15:8; 18:16; Ne 11:30). Scene of abominable practice of sacrificing children to Molek (2Ch 28:3; 33:6; Jer 7:31–32; 19:6; 32:35), which Josiah tried to prevent (2Ki 23:10) and Jeremiah denounced (Jer 19:2–6).

HOR, MOUNT
1. On border of Edom (Nu 20:23; 33:37), where Aaron died (Nu 20:22–29; 33:38–39; Dt 32:50).

2. On northern border of Palestine, exact location unknown (Nu 34:7–8).

HORMAH
Canaanite town near Ziklag in southern Judah (Jos 12:14). Originally called Zephath, until renamed either by the Israelites (Nu 21:3) or the men of Judah and Simeon (Jdg 1:17). Israelites defeated near here by the Amalekites and Canaanites (Nu 14:45; Dt 1:44). Allotted to Simeon, though in the territory of Judah (Jos 19:14; 1Ch 4:30). David sent a share of Amalekite spoils to here (1Sa 30:30).

ICONIUM
Capital city of Lycaonia in Asia Minor. Visited by Paul and Barnabas who enjoyed successful ministry here until Jews forced them out (Ac 14:1–7) and pursued Paul to Lystra to stone him (Ac 14:19). Paul later returned (Ac 14:21) and was well received (Ac 16:2), but he remembered the persecution (2Ti 3:11).

ISRAEL
The new name given to Jacob (Ge 32:28; 35:10) was soon used of the land where his descendants settled (Ge 34:7; 49:7), giving rise to the twelve tribes of Israel (Ge 49:28). While in Egypt and the wilderness, it was used only of the people (Ex 5:2), but once resettled in Canaan it was used of the land and kingdom (Lev 20:2; 22:18; Dt 17:4, 20; 18:6; Jdg 5:2, 7). It reached its full potential (Nu 34:1–15; Eze 47:13–21) under the reigns of David and Solomon. After the kingdom divided it designated the ten tribes of the northern kingdom (1Ki 11:31, 35), as opposed to Judah in the south (which had absorbed Simeon). For two centuries Israel was in conflict with Judah (1Ki 12:19), until it fell to the Assyrians (2Ki 17). Reunification was prophesied (Jer 3:18; Eze 37:16–17).

ISSACHAR
Fertile territory southeast of Sea of Galilee, with Naphtali to the north and Manasseh to the south. Allotted to the descendants of Jacob's ninth son. Its towns were listed, but its borders were rather vague (Jos 19:17–23).

JABBOK
An eastern tributary of river Jordan, about 22 miles north of Dead Sea. Jacob crossed at its ford, before wrestling with an angel (Ge 32:22–24). It was a natural boundary (Nu 21:24; Dt 2:37; 3:16; Jos 12:2; Jdg 11:13, 22).

JABESH GILEAD
Town in Gilead about 10 miles southeast of Beth Shan, 2 miles east of the Jordan. Its people would not fight against Benjamin, so they were put to the sword (Jdg 21:8–15). It was besieged by the Ammonites, but rescued by Saul (1Sa 11:1–11). Its people later rescued Saul's body from the Philistines and gave him a proper burial here (1Sa 31:1–13; 1Ch 10:11–12). Also known by abbreviated name Jabesh (1Ch 10:12).

JAHAZ

Town on plains of Moab about 17 miles east of Dead Sea. Sihon the Amorite was defeated by Israel here (Nu 21:23–24; Dt 2:32–33; Jdg 11:20). Allotted to tribe of Reuben (Jos 13:18) and set aside for the Levites (Jos 21:34–36). Became part of Moab, about which the prophets proclaimed disaster (Isa 15:4; Jer 48:34). Variant name Jahzah (1Ch 6:78; Jer 48:21).

JAZER

Town east of the Jordan, in the south of Gilead. Captured by Israel from Amorites (Nu 21:32). Both Gad and Reuben laid claim to it (Nu 32:1–3), but Gad was given it, and fortified it (Nu 32:35; Jos 13:25). Later designated as a Levite town (Jos 21:39; 1Ch 6:81). Included in David's census (2Sa 24:5; 1Ch 26:31). Became part of Moab, about which the prophets proclaimed disaster (Isa 16:8–9; Jer 48:32).

JERICHO

One of the oldest and lowest-lying cities in the world, situated in Jordan Valley, about 15 miles northeast of Jerusalem. The Israelites camped opposite here, before crossing the Jordan (Nu 22:1; 26:3, 63; 31:12; 33:48, 50; 35:1; 36:13; Dt 32:49; 34:1, 3; Jos 3:16; 13:32). Joshua's spies focused on this city and escaped with Rahab's help (Jos 2:1–7). Israel's army camped near here to prepare for battle (Jos 4:13), and defeated the city (Jos 6). Allotted to the tribe of Benjamin (Jos 18:21). David's men waited here while their beards grew back (2Sa 10:5; 1Ch 19:5). Joshua's curse was fulfilled on Hiel, who rebuilt Jericho (Jos 6:26; 1Ki 16:34).

It became a community of prophets (2Ki 2:5). Known also as the City of Palms (2Ch 28:15). Zedekiah was captured by the Babylonians near here (Jer 39:5; 52:8). Place where Jesus healed blind men (Mt 20:29; Mk 10:46; Lk 18:35) and met with Zacchaeus (Lk 19:1). Referred to in a parable (Lk 10:30).

JERUSALEM

City in northern Judea, about 18 miles west of Dead Sea. Its king was defeated by Joshua (Jos 10:1–26; 12:10). Allotted to tribe of Judah, and later Benjamin, but they could not expel the Jebusites (Jos 15:63; 18:28; Jdg 1:21). Chosen by David as capital of his kingdom (2Sa 5:5; 1Ch 3:4) and captured from the Jebusites. He put the ark of the covenant here (2Sa 6:12–15). He planned to build a great temple for the Lord here (2Sa 7; 1Ch 17), but this was Solomon's task (2Ch 2–7). Known as the City of David (2Sa 5:7), it remained capital of Judah after the kingdom split, until it was destroyed by the Babylonians (2Ki 25:10). Since the time of David the word 'Zion' has been used to refer either to the hill on which the temple stood or to Jerusalem in its entirety. The prophets and the Psalms use 'Zion' to convey the idea that Jerusalem is the central place of Israelite religion and as a special place of God's presence it has security and renown (Ps 48; Isa 2:2–4). Historically the city of Jerusalem was rebuilt by Nehemiah after the exile (Ne 2:5); the temple rebuilt by Zerubbabel (Ezr 6:13–15). In New Testament times Jerusalem was associated with kings (Mt 2:1–2), and another temple stood in place of Zerubbabel's. Jesus came here at 12 years

of age (Lk 2:41–42), and later confronted the temple sellers (Lk 19:45–46). He entered the city triumphantly (Lk 19:28), but was soon arrested (Lk 22:47), tried (Lk 22:66–23:25) and crucified (Lk 23:26–55). After Stephen was martyred here (Ac 7:59), many believers left and scattered (Ac 8:1). It remained the place for settling disputes (Ac 15:2). In AD 70 the city was destroyed, fulfilling Jesus' prophecy (Lk 19:41–44). A new Jerusalem is envisioned at the heart of God's new kingdom on earth inhabited by Christ and the church (Rev 3:12; 21:2, 10).

JEZREEL

1. City in hill country of Judah (Jos 15:56), where Ahinoam was probably born (1Sa 25:43; 27:3). Exact location uncertain.

2. City in northern Israel, about 56 miles north of Jerusalem (Jos 19:18), in a valley named after it (Jos 17:16), with nearby spring (1Sa 29:1). Ahab had a palace here, overlooking Naboth's vineyard (1Ki 21:1–16). Joram recovering from battle was visited by Ahaziah here (2Ki 8:29; 2Ch 22:6). Place of bloodshed during Jehu's revolt (2Ki 9:1–10:11). Hosea's son named Jezreel to announce God's judgment on the house of Jehu (Hos 1:4–5).

JOPPA

Mediterranean seaport about 35 miles northwest of Jerusalem, important for trade. Allotted to the tribe of Dan who had difficulty possessing it (Jos 19:46–47). Solomon and Zerubbabel used the port when building their temples (2Ch 2:16; Ezr 3:7). Jonah sailed from here when fleeing the Lord (Jnh 1:3). Home of Tabitha, whom Peter restored to life (Ac 9:36–40). While staying with Simon the tanner, Peter had a vision from God (Ac 10:5–17).

JORDAN, RIVER

Largest river in Palestine, with principal source near Mount Hermon. Flows southwards from Sea of Galilee through a deep valley into the Dead Sea. Lot desired the fertile land around it (Ge 13:10–11). A natural boundary crossed to escape enemies, e.g. by Jacob (Ge 32:10), and David (2Sa 17:21–22). Israelites camped to its east (Jos 3:1), before crossing it on dry ground to take the promised land (Jos 3:11–17). Used strategically in battle by Ehud (Jdg 3:28), Gideon (Jdg 7:24) and the Gileadites (Jdg 12:5). Elijah and Elisha crossed it on dry ground (2Ki 2:8, 14), and Elisha instructed Naaman to wash in it (2Ki 5:10). Mentioned in Isaiah's Messianic prophecy (Isa 9:1), and is the site of Jesus' baptism (Mt 3:13; Mk 1:9).

JUDAH

Southern kingdom of Judah. Following the breakdown of relationships between the northern and southern tribes, Palestine was divided (about 931 BC) and Judah suffered two centuries of conflict with the northern kingdom of Israel (1Ki 12–2Ki 17). Judah survived because Israel fell to the Assyrians (2Ki 17:18). But Judah herself fell to the Babylonians about 134 years later (2Ki 25) and the people of Judah were exiled. Following the fall of Jerusalem (586 BC) Judah lost its kingdom status and became a small province of the Persian Empire. By New Testament

times this area was known as Judea, an annex of the Roman province of Syria, in which Jesus was born (Mt 2:1).

KADESH BARNEA

Oasis town in northern Sinai 50 miles south of Beersheba. Originally known as En Mishpat and abbreviated to Kadesh. Kedorlaomer defeated the Amalekites and Amorites here (Ge 14:7). An angel appeared to Hagar near here (Ge 16:14), Abram settled close by (Ge 20:1) and the people camped here during the exodus (Nu 20:1; 33:36; Dt 1:19, 46). Here Miriam died and was buried (Nu 20:1), the spies reported back (Nu 13:26; Jos 14:7), the people complained (Nu 20:2–5) and messengers were dispatched to Edom and Moab (Jdg 11:17).

KEBAR, RIVER

Runs through Babylonia; the exiled people lived along its banks (Eze 1:1; 3:15); Ezekiel received his vision here (Eze 1:3; 3:23; 10:15, 20, 22; 43:3).

KEILAH

Town about 18 miles southwest of Jerusalem allotted to Judah (Jos 15:44). David rescued it from Philistine attack (1Sa 23:1–5), then left here to escape from Saul (1Sa 23:7–14). In Nehemiah's time it had two rulers who helped rebuild Jerusalem (Ne 3:17–18).

KERITH RAVINE

An almost dry river bed east of the Jordan. Elijah hid here (1Ki 17:2–3, 5), was fed by ravens and drank from the small brook (1Ki 17:4). When the brook dried up, he went to Zarephath (1Ki 17:7–9).

KIDRON VALLEY

On eastern slope of Jerusalem, towards Mount of Olives, through which flows a small brook. David crossed here to escape from Absalom (2Sa 15:23), and so did Shimei, in disobedience of Solomon (1Ki 2:37–46). Here Asa burned Maakah's Asherah pole (1Ki 15:13; 2Ch 15:16), and the priests burned and tipped articles dedicated to Baal and Asherah (2Ki 23:4, 6, 12; 2Ch 29:16; 30:14). It became the site of a cemetery (2Ki 23:6; Jer 31:40). Nehemiah inspected the walls of Jerusalem from here (Ne 2:15). Jesus crossed it to reach Gethsemane (Jn 18:1).

KIR

1. Region of Mesopotamia to which Tiglath-Pileser III deported the Aramaeans (2Ki 16:9) and from which God later rescued them (Am 9:7). Appears in prophecy about Jerusalem (Isa 22:6).

2. Walled city of Moab that withstood Israelite attack (2Ki 3:25) but would be destroyed (Isa 15:1; 16:7, 11; Jer 48:31, 36). Also known as Kir Hareseth.

KIRIATH JEARIM

One of four Gibeonite fortress cities (Jos 9:17), also known as Baalah (Jos 15:9), Kiriath Baal (Jos 15:60) and Kiriath (Jos 18:28). First allotted to Judah (Jos 15:60) then to Benjamin (Jos 18:28). 600 Danites camped here on their way to attack Laish (Jdg 18:12). After the Philistines returned the ark of the

covenant it was kept here in Abinadab's house for 20 years (1Sa 6:21–7:2). Home of Uriah the prophet (Jer 26:20).

KIRIATHAIM

1. City of refuge in territory of Naphtali, assigned to the Levites (1Ch 6:76). Also known as Kartan (Jos 21:32).

2. Town east of Dead Sea, in hill country of Moab. The Emites were expelled from here (Ge 14:5). Taken by the Israelites and allotted to Reuben (Jos 13:19), who fortified it (Nu 32:37). Became Moabite territory, sharing in its downfall (Jer 48:1, 23; Eze 25:9).

KISHON

River flowing northeast from Mount Gilboa, past Mount Carmel to the Mediterranean Sea. Scene of Deborah's victory over Sisera (Jdg 4:7, 13; Ps 83:9), when the Canaanite chariots became bogged down by the flooded river (Jdg 5:21). Elijah brought the prophets of Baal here to be slaughtered (1Ki 18:40).

LACHISH

Canaanite royal city in the lowlands of Judah near Libnah. Its king joined the alliance against Joshua but the alliance was defeated and the city was taken (Jos 10:1–35). Allotted to Judah (Jos 15:39). Fortified by Rehoboam (2Ch 11:5–9). Amaziah fled here from Jerusalem (2Ki 14:19; 2Ch 25:27). Captured by Sennacherib, it became base for negotiations with Hezekiah (2Ki 18:13–17; 2Ch 32:9; Isa 36:1–2). It was one of two fortified cities left in Judah during the Babylonian invasion (Jer 34:7). Denounced by Micah for its sin (Mic 1:13).

LAODICEA

City in Phrygia, in the Lycus Valley, about 12 miles west of Colossae. Its church was probably not established by Paul (Col 2:1; 4:12–13), but he addressed a letter to them (Col 4:16). Accused of being lukewarm in one of the seven letters of Revelation (Rev 3:14–22).

LEBANON

Mountainous region to the north of Palestine, along the Mediterranean coast. Regarded as part of the promised land (Dt 1:7; 3:25; 11:24; Jos 1:4; 13:5–6; 1Ki 9:19; Zec 10:10), but occupied by the Hivites (Jdg 3:3–5; 1Ki 9:20–21; 2Ch 8:7–8). Renowned for its forests of cedar and cypress (Jdg 9:15; 1Ki 4:33; 2Ki 14:9; 19:23; 2Ch 25:18), which were used by Solomon (1Ki 5; 7:2; 2Ch 2:8, 16), and Zerubbabel (Ezr 3:7). Used figuratively to speak of righteousness (Ps 92:12), pride (Isa 2:13), glory (Isa 60:13), security (Hos 14:5), etc.

LIBNAH

1. A place where the Israelites camped during the exodus from Egypt (Nu 33:20–21).

2. Canaanite town in lowlands of Judah, near Lachish. Captured by Joshua (Jos 10:29–32, 39), allotted to Judah (Jos 15:42) and designated a Levitical city (Jos 21:13; 1Ch 6:57). Participated in revolt against Jehoram (2Ki 8:22; 2Ch 21:10) and attacked by Sennacherib (2Ki 19:8; Isa 37:8). Home of Hamutal, the mother of Jehoahaz and Zedekiah (2Ki 23:31; 24:18; Jer 52:1).

LOD

City in Plain of Sharon, 11 miles southeast of Joppa. Built by the sons of Elpaal (1Ch 8:12) and occupied after the exile by the Benjamites (Ne 11:35). Known later as Lydda, Peter healed Aeneas here (Ac 9:32–35).

LYSTRA

City in Lycaonia 18 miles from Iconium. Paul and Barnabas fled here (Ac 14:6) and healed a crippled man (Ac 14:8–10). Jews from Pisidian Antioch and Iconium arrived to stone Paul, but he survived and left for Derbe (Ac 14:19–20), returning later (Ac 14:21–22). Timothy lived here (Ac 16:1). Paul reminded Timothy of the persecution here (2Ti 3:11).

MACEDONIA

Country north of Greece, with capital Philippi. Paul visited here after being invited in a vision (Ac 16:9–10); also Silas and Timothy (Ac 18:5) and Erastus (Ac 19:22). Home of Paul's companions Gaius and Aristarchus (Ac 19:29). Paul returned during his third journey (Ac 19:21; 20:1–6; 1Co 16:5; 2Co 1:16; 2:13; 7:5) and may have returned again later (1Ti 1:3). The church here was generous in supporting Jerusalem (Ro 15:26; 2Co 8:1–5; Php 4:15–18) and Paul himself (2Co 11:9).

MAHANAIM

Town in Gilead, east of the Jordan, on the south bank of the Jabbok. Named by Jacob when he saw the angels of God (Ge 32:1–2). On border between Manasseh and Gad (Jos 13:26, 30); assigned to the Levites (Jos 21:38; 1Ch 6:80). Here Ish-Bosheth reigned (2Sa 2:8, 12, 29) and David found refuge from Absalom (2Sa 17:24, 27; 19:32; 1Ki 2:8). Became capital of one of Solomon's districts (1Ki 4:14).

MAKKEDAH

Canaanite royal town (Jos 12:16) in the lowlands of Judah. Joshua captured the city and its inhabitants. The five Amorite kings were executed after hiding in a cave nearby (Jos 10:16–27). Allotted to Judah (Jos 15:41).

MALTA

Island in Mediterranean, between Sicily and Africa where Paul was shipwrecked (Ac 28:1). He stayed for three months surviving a snake attack, healing the sick and receiving hospitality (Ac 28:1–11).

MAMRE

Wooded area north of Hebron where Abram set up camp and built an altar (Ge 13:18). Here Abram heard of Lot's capture (Ge 14:13) and received promise of a son (Ge 18:1, 10). He bought a field and cave here (Ge 23:17): the burial site for Sarah (Ge 23:19), Abraham (Ge 25:8–9), Isaac (Ge 35:27–29), Rebekah, Leah and Jacob (Ge 49:29–33; 50:12–13).

MANASSEH

Territory to the west and to the east of river Jordan south of the Sea of Galilee. Allotted to the descendants of Joseph's older son. Territories of Manasseh and Ephraim often treated together (Jos 16:1–17:1, 14). Its towns and borders listed, to the east (Jos 13:8, 29–31) and to

the west (Jos 17:7–11). Territory divided by the Jordan, so its inhabitants were treated as two half-tribes (Jos 13:6–8). The eastern half had good grazing (Nu 32:1). In the western half the Canaanites were not driven out but enslaved (Jos 17:12–13).

MEDIA

Mountainous country south of Caspian Sea. Some people of Samaria deported here (2Ki 17:6; 18:11). Darius searched its city Ecbatana for Cyrus' decree to rebuild Jerusalem (Ezr 6:2). Absorbed into Persian Empire, its military leaders were invited to dine with King Xerxes (Est 1:3, 14). Mordecai's greatness was recorded in its annals (Est 10:2). Its defeat of Babylonian Empire was prophesied (Isa 13:17; 21:2; Jer 51:11, 28; Da 5:28) and its own eventual defeat by Greece (Jer 25:25; Da 8:20–21). Its people were in the crowd at Pentecost (Ac 2:9). See **Persia**.

MEDITERRANEAN SEA

See **Great Sea**.

MEGIDDO

Canaanite royal town, southeast of Carmel, on trade route between Egypt and Syria. Conquered by Joshua (Jos 12:21), allotted to the tribe of Manasseh (Jos 17:11; 1Ch 7:29). Scene of Deborah's victory over Sisera (Jdg 5:19). One of Solomon's 12 districts (1Ki 4:12) and fortified by him (1Ki 9:15). Ahaziah fled here from Jehu (2Ki 9:27). Josiah was mortally wounded here (2Ki 23:29–30; 2Ch 35:20–24). Zechariah prophesies that a great battle will take place near

here (Zec 12:11), often identified with the battle of Armageddon (Rev 16:16).

MEMPHIS

Egyptian royal city on west bank of the Nile, about 13 miles south of Cairo. Referred to by the prophets as a place of false hope (Isa 19:13; Jer 2:16; 44:1; 46:14, 19; Eze 30:13, 16; Hos 9:6).

MERIBAH

1. Place of a spring near Rephidim, in the Desert of Sin. Means 'strife'. Here the Israelites grumbled against Moses because of lack of water and God provided water when Moses struck a rock (Ex 17:1–7). Also known as Massah (Ex 17:7; Dt 6:16; 9:22; 33:8; Ps 95:8).

2. Place of a spring near Kadesh, in the Desert of Zin. Once again the Israelites grumbled about lack of water, and water was provided despite Moses' rebellion (Nu 20:1–13). Also known as Meribah Kadesh (Nu 27:14; Dt 32:51).

MESOPOTAMIA

Means 'between the rivers', used in the New Testament to refer to the region around the Euphrates and Tigris. In the Old Testament it was known as Aram Naharaim, Paddan Aram or simply as 'beyond the river'. Original home of Abraham, where he worshipped other gods (Jos 24:14–15) and where God first appeared to him (Ac 7:2; Jos 24:2–3). Home of Rebekah (Ge 24:10; 25:20), Leah and Rachel (Ge 28:2, 5–7; 29:1–28) and several sons of Jacob (Ge 35:26; 46:15). Jacob lived here for a time (Ge 27:43–44; 28:2) but left to return to Canaan (Ge 31:17–18; 33:18). Home of Balaam (Dt

23:4). Its armies fought with Aram (Jdg 3:8; 2Sa 10:16; 1Ch 19:16), defeating the Israelites (Isa 7:20), and scattering them across this region (1Ki 14:15). Its people were in the crowd at Pentecost (Ac 2:9).

MICHMASH
A town of Benjamin north of Jerusalem. Scene of battle between Israel and the Philistines where Jonathan's men won a great victory (1Sa 13:2, 5–7; 14:4–15, 31). The Assyrians stored supplies here (Isa 10:28).

MIDIAN
Land inhabited by Midian's descendants (Ge 25:1–2; 1Ch 1:32–33), on eastern side of Gulf of Aqaba. Moses fled here (Ex 2:15; Ac 7:29) and married Zipporah (Ex 2:16–21). Here God spoke to Moses from a burning bush (Ex 3:1–10; 4:19). Its elders were consulted by the Moabites about the approaching Israelites (Nu 22:4). Israel defeated its army (Nu 31:7–12) but its people soon recovered and oppressed Israel (Jdg 6:2, 6–7). God used Gideon to save the Israelites (Jdg 6:11–8:28) and the victory was remembered in later poetry (Ps 83:9; Isa 9:4; 10:26; Hab 3:7).

MIGDOL
Fortified town in the northeast of Egypt, where the Israelites camped after leaving Egypt (Ge 14:2; Nu 33:7) and Jewish refugees moved after Jerusalem was destroyed (Jer 44:1). Its downfall was foretold (Jer 46:14).

MILETUS
Seaport on eastern coast of Asia Minor, about 37 miles south of Ephesus. Paul visited here (Ac 20:15). He summoned Ephesian elders and addressed them here (Ac 20:16–38). Possibly Paul revisited it leaving Trophimus sick here (2Ti 4:20).

MIZPAH
1. A town of Benjamin (Jos 18:26), where the Israelites assembled before the Lord (Jdg 20:1, 3; 21:1, 5, 8). Here Samuel and the Israelites defeated the Philistines (1Sa 7:5, 7, 11) and Saul was proclaimed king (1Sa 10:17–25). Fortified by Asa (1Ki 15:22; 2Ch 16:6), who built a cistern that was used by Ishmael for Gedaliah and others whom he slaughtered (Jer 41:1–9).

2. Town in Gilead, east of Jordan, where Jacob set up a memorial to his covenant with Laban (Ge 31:48–49). Probably an Israelite camp (Jdg 10:17) and home of Jephthah (Jdg 11:11, 34). Also known as Ramath Mizpah (Jos 13:26).

3. Region near foot of Mount Hermon, where Jabin's allies the Hivites lived (Jos 11:1–3), whom Joshua defeated (Jos 11:8).

4. Town in Moab, where David took his parents for safety from Saul (1Sa 22:3).

5. Town in the lowlands of Judah (Jos 15:38).

MOAB
Country east of the Dead Sea, inhabited by descendants of Lot's son (Ge 19:36–37). Also called the plains of Moab; captured by the Amorites before the Israelites conquered it (Nu 21:17–31). Here God instructed Moses how to allot the promised land (Nu 33:50–36:12), Moses expounded the commandments (Nu 36:13; Dt 1:5) and made the covenant

with God (Dt 29:1). Moses viewed promised land from Moab's Mount Nebo before he died here (Nu 27:12–23; Dt 34:1–6). Birthplace of Ruth (Ru 2:6). Its people were defeated by Israelites under Ehud (Jdg 3:29–30), Saul (1Sa 14:47) and David (2Sa 8:2). The tension continued under Jehoshaphat (2Ch 20:1–23), Jehoram (2Ki 3:4–27) and Jehoiakim (2Ki 24:2). The prophets announced its destruction (Isa 15–16; Jer 48).

MORIAH, MOUNT

Abraham was instructed by God to sacrifice Isaac here (Ge 22:2). Exact location unknown, but visible after a three-day journey from Beersheba (Ge 22:4). Probably also the site of Solomon's temple at Jerusalem (2Ch 3:1).

NAIN

Town in southwest Galilee where Jesus raised a widow's son to life (Lk 7:11–15).

NAPHTALI

Territory to the west of Sea of Galilee, with Zebulun and Asher to the west, and Issachar to the south. Allotted to the descendants of Jacob's fifth son. Its towns and borders were clearly listed (Jos 19:32–39). Canaanite inhabitants not driven out but enslaved (Jdg 1:33). Conquered by Assyria before fall of Samaria and its people deported (2Ki 15:29). Isaiah predicted great honour for this land (Isa 9:1), fulfilled in Jesus' ministry there (Mt 4:13–16).

NAZARETH

Town in Galilee between Sea of Galilee and Mediterranean. Home of Mary and Joseph (Lk 1:26; 2:4, 39); home of Jesus (Mt 2:23; 21:11; Lk 2:51), which he left to begin his preaching (Mt 4:13–17; Mk 1:9). Jesus returned here (Lk 4:16) but was rejected (Lk 4:29). He was often called Jesus of Nazareth (Mt 26:71; Mk 1:24; 10:47; Lk 4:34; 18:37; 24:19; Jn 1:45; 18:5, 7; 19:19; Ac 2:22; 3:6; 4:10; 6:14; 10:38; 22:8; 26:9) or the Nazarene (Mt 2:23; Mk 14:67; 16:6). The town had a poor reputation (Jn 1:46).

NEBO

1. Mountain of the Abarim range in Moab (Nu 33:47). Here Moses viewed the promised land, and then died (Dt 32:49–50; 34:1–6).

2. Town in Moab allotted to and rebuilt by tribe of Reuben (Nu 32:3, 37–38; 1Ch 5:8). Named by the prophets in their laments (Isa 15:2; 46:1; Jer 48:1, 22).

3. Possibly a town in Judah whose inhabitants returned from exile (Ezr 2:29). Called by Nehemiah 'the other Nebo' (Ne 7:33).

NEGEV

The southern desert region of Judah (Jos 15:21). Abraham (Ge 12:9; 13:1, 3; 20:1) and Isaac (Ge 24:62) camped here. Twelve spies approached Canaan from this direction (Nu 13:17, 22). The home of the Canaanite King Arad (Nu 21:1; 33:40). Part of the promised land (Dt 1:7; 34:3), which Joshua conquered (Jos 10:40; 11:16; 12:8). Land here given by Caleb to his daughter (Jos 15:19; Jdg 1:15), and some land was reallocated to the tribe of Simeon (Jos 19:8). It was prone to attack from Amalekites (1Sa 30:1, 14), and Philistines (2Ch 28:18). Included in David's census (2Sa 24:7).

Used poetically to portray hardship (Ps 126:4; Isa 30:6) and referred to by the prophets (Jer 13:19; 17:26; 32:44; 33:13; Ob 19–20; Zec 7:7).

NILE, RIVER

Running about 3,500 miles from central Africa, northwards to the Egyptian delta on the Mediterranean coast. Appears in Pharaoh's dream that Joseph interpreted (Ge 41:1, 3, 17). All Hebrew baby boys were to be drowned here (Ex 1:22); Moses escaped and was discovered by Pharaoh's daughter (Ex 2:5–10). During the plagues its water was turned to blood (Ex 4:9; 7:17–25; Ps 78:4), and its frogs invaded the land (Ex 8:3, 9, 11). Used symbolically by the prophets because of its importance and regular flooding (Isa 19:7–8; 23:3, 10; Jer 46:7–8; Eze 29:3, 9; 30:12; Am 8:8; 9:5; Na 3:8; Zec 10:11).

NINEVEH

City on bank of river Tigris, built by Nimrod, in Assyria (Ge 10:11–12). Sennacherib's capital city, where he was murdered by his sons (2Ki 19:36; Isa 37:37–38). God instructed Jonah to preach here; its people repented and turned to God (Jnh 1:2; 3:2–10; 4:11). Nahum pronounced God's judgment upon it (Na 1:1, 8, 11, 14; 2:1, 8; 3:7); Zephaniah foretold its destruction (Zep 2:13). Jesus compared its people in Jonah's time with his own stubborn generation (Mt 12:41; Lk 11:32).

NOB

Priestly town (1Sa 22:19) in territory of Benjamin (Ne 11:32), about 2 miles east of Jerusalem. David fled here from Saul (1Sa 21:1) and was given consecrated bread and Goliath's sword (1Sa 21:1–9). All of its priests were then executed by Saul (1Sa 22:11–19). The Assyrian army camped here before assaulting Jerusalem (Isa 10:32).

OLIVES, MOUNT OF

East of Jerusalem, across the Kidron Valley. David climbed it on hearing of Absalom's revolt (2Sa 15:30). In the end-times, the Lord will stand here, and it will split in two from east to west (Zec 14:4). In Jesus' time, Bethany and Bethphage were located here (Mt 21:1; Mk 11:1; Lk 19:29). Jesus talked with his disciples here (Mt 24:3; 26:30; Mk 13:3; 14:26; Lk 19:37; 21:37; Jn 8:1), and prayed here on the night of his arrest (Lk 22:39). Probably the site of Jesus' ascension (Ac 1:12).

ON

Town in Egypt about 20 miles northeast of Memphis, east of river Nile. Home of Joseph's wife Asenath (Ge 41:45, 50; 46:20). Later known by its Greek name Heliopolis (Eze 30:17), when its capture by Nebuchadnezzar was foretold.

OPHIR

Region famous for gold and precious stones; location is uncertain. Reached by sea (1Ki 9:28; 10:11; 22:48; 2Ch 8:18), its gold was brought to Solomon for his building projects (1Ki 9:28; 10:10–21; 1Ch 29:4; 2Ch 8:18; 9:10). Used figuratively on account of its great wealth (Job 22:24; 28:16; Ps 45:9; Isa 13:12).

OPHRAH

1. City of Benjamin (Jos 18:23), attacked by Philistines (1Sa 13:17). Probably also known as Ephraim (Jn 11:54) and Ephron (2Ch 13:19). Exact location unknown.

2. City of Manasseh, occupied by Abiezrites (Jdg 6:11). Here Gideon built an altar (Jdg 6:24), placed the golden ephod (Jdg 8:27) and was buried (Jdg 8:32). Abimelek came to his father's home here and murdered 70 sons of Jerub-Baal to take the throne (Jdg 9:5). Exact location unknown.

PADDAN ARAM

See Aram; Mesopotamia.

PAMPHYLIA

Province along southern coast of Asia Minor, between Lycia and Cilicia. Capital city was Perga (Ac 13:13). Its people were represented in Jerusalem at Pentecost (Ac 2:10). Paul's point of entry into Asia Minor on his first journey (Ac 13:13–14); he returned on his way back to Jerusalem (Ac 14:24–26). Paul sailed near here on his way to Rome (Ac 27:5).

PAPHOS

Port on southwestern coast of Cyprus. Paul and Barnabas visited here, and its governor was converted (Ac 13:6–13). From here they sailed to Perga in Pamphylia (Ac 13:6–13).

PARAN

1. Wilderness region in Sinai Peninsula, known also as El-Paran (Ge 14:6). Here Hagar fled with Ishmael (Ge 21:21) and the Israelites stayed after leaving Egypt (Nu 10:12; 12:16). From here the spies were sent into Canaan (Nu 13:3, 26).

2. Mountain in Seir (Edom), associated with God coming to help his people (Dt 33:2; Hab 3:3). Hadad passed through here on his way to Egypt (1Ki 11:18).

PATMOS

Island in the Aegean where the Romans banished criminals. Here John wrote the book of Revelation (Rev 1:9).

PENIEL

Place along the Jabbok where Jacob wrestled with God (Ge 32:22–32; Hos 12:4); means 'the face of God'. Its inhabitants refused to give Gideon bread for his men, so he destroyed the city and its tower (Jdg 8:8–9, 17). Later fortified by King Jeroboam (1Ki 12:25).

PERGA

Capital city of Pamphylia, on southern coast of Asia Minor. Paul and Barnabas passed through here twice. John Mark left them during the first visit (Ac 13:13–14); they returned later to preach (Ac 14:25).

PERGAMUM

Capital city of Asia Minor where Antipas was martyred (Rev 2:13). One of the seven letters of Revelation was addressed to the church here, which was praised for its faithfulness and warned about false teaching (Rev 2:12–15).

PERSIA

Ancient empire that began east of Persian Gulf, but under Cyrus absorbed Media and Babylonia (2Ch 36:20). Its kings allowed the exiled Jews to return to Jerusalem to rebuild the temple (2Ch 36:22–23; Ezr 1:1–11; 7:1–28; 9:9). Its military leaders were guests of King Xerxes (Est 1:3, 14). Mordecai's greatness was recorded in their Kings' annals (Est 10:2). Persians served in the armies of Tyre (Eze 27:10) and Magog (Eze 38:5). Its defeat of the Babylonian Empire was prophesied (Da 5:28), as was its own eventual defeat by Greece (Da 10–11). See **Media**.

PHILADELPHIA

City of the province of Lydia in western Asia Minor. One of the seven letters of Revelation was addressed to its church, which was praised for its endurance (Rev 3:7–13).

PHILIPPI

City in eastern Macedonia, near northern shore of the Aegean. Paul stayed here several days and preached to the women, including Lydia, who believed and was baptised (Ac 16:12–15). A fortune-teller was released from spirit possession by Paul resulting in his own imprisonment and the jailer's conversion (Ac 16:16–34). Paul wrote to the Christians here expressing fondness for them (Php 1:1–8).

PHILISTIA

Also known as 'the land of the Philistines' or 'the region of the Philistines'. It extended from the river Shihor (Brook of Egypt) northwards to Ekron (Jos 13:2–3). The term 'Philistia' is common in poetry (Ex 15:14; Ps 60:8; 87:4; 108:9; Isa 11:14).

PHRYGIA

Mountainous region of Asia Minor, between Asia and Galatia. Its people were represented in Jerusalem on the Day of Pentecost (Ac 2:10). Paul travelled through this province on his journeys (Ac 16:6; 18:23), but does not appear to have founded the churches here (Col 2:1).

PISGAH

Headland near Mount Nebo in the Abarim range, where Moses viewed the promised land (Nu 21:20; Dt 3:17, 27; 4:49; 34:1). Probably a sacred 'high place'; Balaam built seven altars here (Nu 23:14). Originally ruled by King Sihon (Jos 12:3), but eventually allotted to tribe of Reuben (Jos 13:20).

RABBAH

1. Chief city of the Ammonites on eastern border of the territory of Gad (Dt 3:11; Jos 13:24–25; 2Sa 12:26; 17:27; Jer 49:2; Eze 21:20). Uriah the Hittite was slain here under orders from David (2Sa 11:1, 15). Eventually conquered by David (2Sa 12:27–31; 1Ch 20:1). Its eventual destruction was prophesied (Jer 49:2–3; Eze 21:20; 25:5; Am 1:14).

2. City in the Judean hill country, mentioned with Kiriath Jearim (Jos 15:60). Exact location unknown.

RAMAH

1. Town in territory of Benjamin (Jos 18:25), near Gibeah (Jdg 19:13–14).

Deborah held court between here and
Bethel (Jdg 4:5). On border between the
divided kingdoms, so was heavily fortified
(1Ki 15:17; 2Ch 16:1), but Judah weakened
its defences (1Ki 15:22; 2Ch 16:6). On
Nebuchadnezzar's invasion route (Isa
10:29; Hos 5:8); he detained Jewish
captives here (Jer 31:15; 40:1).

2. Town in territory of Ephraim, exact
location unknown. Known also as
Ramathaim (1Sa 1:1). Home and burial
place of Samuel (1Sa 7:17; 25:1), where
the people demanded a king (1Sa 8:4–6).
David fled here from Saul (1Sa 19:18).

3. Town on border of territory of
Asher (Jos 19:29). Exact location
unknown.

4. Fortified town in territory of
Naphtali (Jos 19:36).

5. Town in territory of Simeon in the
Negev (Jos 19:8). Exact location
unknown.

RAMATHAIM
See Ramah 2.

RAMOTH GILEAD
Fortified city in territory of Gad, about
25 miles east of river Jordan. Designated
as a town of refuge (Dt 4:43; Jos 20:8),
and assigned to the Levites (Jos 21:38;
1Ch 6:80). Its people received Amalekite
plunder from David (1Sa 30:27), and it
was one of Solomon's twelve districts
(1Ki 4:13). Ahab tried to retake the city
from the Arameans, rejecting Micaiah's
advice and was killed by a random arrow
(1Ki 22:1–38; 2Ch 18:2–34; 22:5–6).
Ahab's son Joram also fought the
Arameans here and was injured (2Ki
8:28–29). Jehu was anointed king here
(2Ki 9:1–6).

RED SEA
Sometimes called 'Sea of Reeds' as this is
an alternative translation of the Hebrew
expression. Stretch of water separating
Arabia from Egypt and Ethiopia. Locusts
sent upon Egypt were carried away to
here (Ex 10:19). When Moses led the
Israelites out of Egypt, its waters parted
for them to cross over (Ex 14:16; Jos 2:10;
4:23) and then returned to drown the
pursuing Egyptians (Ex 15:4; Dt 11:4;
24:6–7). The southern border of the
promised land (Ex 23:31) and an
important trade route for Israel
(1Ki 9:26).

REUBEN
Territory east of Dead Sea, and south of
territory of Gad. Allotted to the
descendants of Jacob's eldest son, who
liked it for its good grazing (Nu 32:1). Its
towns and borders were clearly listed
(Jos 13:15–23).

RIBLAH
1. Town on river Orontes, between
Hamath and Damascus. Pharaoh Necho
put Jehoahaz in chains here to prevent
him from ruling in Jerusalem (2Ki 23:33).
During his siege of Jerusalem,
Nebuchadnezzar established his base
here (2Ki 25:6, 20–21; Jer 39:5–6; 52:9–
10, 26–27).

2. Landmark given by Moses for the
eastern boundary of Israel, between
Shepham and the Sea of Kinnereth
(Nu 34:11).

RIMMON
1. Town in the Negev region of southern
Judah (Jos 15:32; Zec 14:10), later

reassigned to the tribe of Simeon (Jos 19:7; 1Ch 4:32).

2. Town marking the eastern border of the territory of Zebulun (Jos 19:13).

3. A rock in the territory of Benjamin, where 600 of the tribe found refuge from the other Israelite tribes, after they had sinned at Gibeah (Jdg 20:45, 47). They were eventually offered peace (Jdg 21:13).

ROME

Capital city of Roman Empire, about 15 miles from Mediterranean coast of Italy. Its inhabitants were at Pentecost (Ac 2:10). Aquila and Priscilla were ordered out of here by Claudius (Ac 18:2). Paul possessed Roman citizenship (Ac 16:37; 22:28) and resolved to preach here (Ac 19:21; 23:11; Ro 1:15; 15:24). After appealing to Caesar for justice (Ac 25:11) he was brought here as a prisoner (Ac 25:24–25; 28:16). The fall of Rome is anticipated in Revelation (Rev 17–18).

SALT SEA
See **Dead Sea**.

SAMARIA

1. City built by King Omri on hill of Samaria, which he bought from Shemer (1Ki 16:24). It replaced Tirzah as capital of northern kingdom (1Ki 16:23, 28–29), and remained the royal residence until the Assyrian conquest (2Ki 17:5–6). Site of ornate palace built by Ahab (1Ki 22:39; Am 3:15), and also his temple to Baal (1Ki 16:32–33). Prophets condemned its pride and idolatry (Isa 9:9; Jer 23:13; Eze 16:46–55; Am 6:1; Mic 1:1). The prophets Elisha (2Ki 5:3) and Oded (2Ch 28:9) lived here. Site of assassinations of Ahab's sons (2Ki 10:1–17), Shallum (2Ki 15:14) and Pekahiah (2Ki 15:25). Twice under Syrian siege (1Ki 20:1; 2Ki 6:24), but did not fall until the Assyrian conquest. Became inhabited by refugees from other conquered countries (2Ki 17:24); led to intermarriage with remaining Jews, and the birth of a despised people (Jn 4:9). Philip preached here (Ac 8:5) and Peter and John were sent to support the new church (Ac 8:14; 9:31).

2. The name of the city extended to include the surrounding region, which became a province under Roman occupation (Lk 17:11; Ac 1:8; 8:1; 9:31; 15:3).

SARDIS

Capital city of Lydia in Asia Minor, situated on river Pactolus east of Smyrna. One of the seven letters of Revelation was addressed to the church here (Rev 1:11), which was encouraged to turn from complacency (Rev 3:1–6).

SEIR
See **Edom**.

SHARON

1. Large plain on Mediterranean coast of Palestine, stretching from the foot of Mount Carmel to Joppa. Rich in pasture (1Ch 27:29; Isa 65:10) and known for its fruitfulness and beauty (SS 2:1; Isa 33:9; 35:2). Peter enjoyed a fruitful ministry here (Ac 9:35).

2. District to the east of river Jordan, occupied by tribe of Gad; boasted good pasture land (1Ch 5:16).

SHEBA

1. City in territory of Judah, assigned to tribe of Simeon (Jos 19:2).

2. Kingdom of the Sabeans, location uncertain but probably in southwest Arabia. Its queen travelled to Jerusalem to test Solomon's reputed wisdom (1Ki 10:1–13; 2Ch 9:1–12; Mt 12:42; Lk 11:31). Renowned for the quality of its goods (Job 6:19; Ps 72:10, 15; Isa 60:6; Jer 6:20; Eze 27:22–23).

SHECHEM

Town in hill country of Ephraim, between mounts Ebal and Gerizim. Where the Lord promised Abram the land (Ge 12:6–7). Abram erected an altar, so it became an important sanctuary (Ge 12:7). Jacob built an altar here to mark his return from Paddan Aram (Ge 33:18–20), and later buried foreign gods under its great oak tree (Ge 35:4). Jacob gave it to Joseph for his burial site (Jos 24:32; Ac 7:16). Allotted to the tribe of Ephraim; became a city of refuge (Jos 20:7; 1Ch 6:67). Here Joshua drew up the covenant and laws (Jos 24). Home of Abimelek (Jdg 8:31; 9:1), who was crowned here after executing the sons of Jerub-Baal (Jdg 9:1–6). Jotham chastised its people for this (Jdg 9:7–20), and so they revolted against Abimelek (Jdg 9:22–57). Rehoboam was crowned here (1Ki 12:1; 2Ch 10:1). Jeroboam made it the capital of the northern kingdom (1Ki 12:25). After the exile, inhabited by Samaritans, and became Sychar, where Jesus met a woman at Jacob's well (Jn 4:5–40).

SHILOH

City in hill country of Ephraim, north of Bethel, and east of the road that connects Bethel to Shechem (Jdg 21:19). The tent of meeting was first set up here; it became an important sanctuary (Jos 18:1, 8–10; 19:51; 21:2; 22:9, 12; Jdg 18:31; 21:12, 19, 21). Samuel grew up here under Eli's care (1Sa 1:24–28; 3:19–21). The ark of the covenant was kept here until it was captured by the Philistines (1Sa 4:1–22), and it never returned (2Sa 6:2–17). Base for Ahijah the prophet (1Ki 14:2, 4), who pronounced the downfall of Jeroboam (1Ki 14:7–16). Lay in ruins during the time of Jeremiah's ministry (Jer 7:12–14; 26:6, 9).

SHITTIM

An abbreviation of Abel Shittim. Israel's last encampment east of river Jordan, before entering promised land (Nu 33:49–50). Here the Israelites sinned (Nu 25:1–3) and were punished with a plague (Nu 25:4–9). Joshua sent out spies from here (Jos 2:1) before all the people left to cross the river Jordan (Jos 3:1; Mic 6:5).

SHUNEM

Town in territory of Issachar (Jos 19:18), where the Philistines camped before meeting Saul in battle (1Sa 28:4). Home of Abishag, who cared for the aged David (1Ki 1:3). Elisha occasionally lodged here with a wealthy couple, and foretold the birth of their long-desired son (2Ki 4:8–17). He later restored the boy to life (2Ki 4:32–37).

SHUR

Desert region between Egypt and the Negev. Hagar was on her way here when the angel found her (Ge 16:7). Abraham

stayed near here (Ge 20:1). Ishmael's descendants settled here (Ge 25:18). Moses led the Israelites through this parched land (Ex 15:22). Saul pursued the Amalekites this far (1Sa 15:7); David attacked its inhabitants (1Sa 27:8).

SIBMAH

Town east of Jordan, near Heshbon. Probably also known as Sebam. One of the towns requested by the Reubenites and Gadites (Nu 32:1–3). Eventually allotted to the tribe of Reuben, who rebuilt it (Nu 32:37–38; Jos 13:19). Renowned for its vines (Isa 16:8–9; Jer 48:32).

SIDON

Ancient city on Mediterranean coast of Lebanon, about 20 miles north of Tyre, founded by the son of Canaan (Ge 10:15; 1Ch 1:13). Israel pursued the defeated Canaanites to here (Jos 11:8); it formed the northernmost border of Asher's territory (Jos 19:28). Asher failed to drive out its Canaanite inhabitants (Jdg 1:31) and Israel was punished for serving their gods (Jdg 10:6,12). The city's importance grew so the King of Tyre was known as 'king of the Sidonians' (1Ki 16:31), and its name was used for that whole area (1Ki 17:9). Despite its power, wealth and security (Ezr 3:7; Isa 23:2), the prophets emphasised its fragility (Isa 23:12; Jer 27:3, 6; 47:4; Eze 28:21–26; Joel 3:4–8; Zec 9:1–4). Jesus spoke of it more favourably than some of the towns of Galilee (Mt 11:21–22; Lk 4:26; 10:13–14). Here he praised a Canaanite woman's faith and healed her daughter (Mt 15:21–28; Mk 7:24–31). Its people went to Galilee to hear Jesus preach (Mk 3:8; Lk 6:17); they sought peace with King Herod (Ac 12:20); and Paul found kind hospitality here (Ac 27:3).

SIMEON

Territory at southernmost end of Palestine, in the Negev Desert. Allotted to the descendants of Jacob's second son, taken from Judah's territory, which was more than was needed (Jos 19:1–9).

SIN, DESERT OF

Wilderness area 'between Elim and Sinai' (Ex 16:1), near the Red Sea and Dophka (Nu 33:11–12), exact location unknown. Here the Israelites grumbled to Moses, but were fed with quails and manna (Ex 16).

SINAI

1. Mountain situated in Sinai Peninsula, also known as Horeb, exact location contested. Here God spoke to Moses from the burning bush (Ex 3:1–4; Ac 7:30), and later provided water for the Israelites (Ex 17:6). God appeared here again after the exodus (Ex 19; Nu 3:1), revealing to Moses the law (Ex 31:18; 34:29; Lev 7:38; 25:1; 26:46; 27:34; Nu 28:6; Ne 9:13; Ac 7:38). Used figuratively by Paul when writing about slavery to the law (Gal 4:24–25).

2. Wilderness area around the mountain (Ex 19:1), where the Israelites camped while God met with Moses (Ex 19:2; Lev 7:38). Here the Tent of Meeting was set up (Nu 1:1) in which Moses was instructed to take a census of the people (Nu 1:2, 19; 3:14; 26:64). Two of Aaron's sons were struck down for making an unauthorised offering (Nu 3:4). The people celebrated Passover (Nu 9:1, 5)

before moving on (Nu 10:12). They returned to this place later (Nu 33:15–16).

SMYRNA

Wealthy city in western Asia Minor, about 40 miles north of Ephesus. One of the seven cities John addressed in which they are described as 'in poverty' due to their afflictions and are encouraged to persevere (Rev 2:8–11).

SODOM

City in Valley of Siddim (Ge 14:2–3), at south end of the Dead Sea, exact location contested. Often paired with Gomorrah as a place of wickedness. Lot and his family chose to settle near here (Ge 13:12). When its king and army were defeated by a Mesopotamian alliance (Ge 14:8–11), Lot was captured (Ge 14:12) and then rescued by Abram (Ge 14:14–16). God threatened to destroy it (Ge 18:20–21) but Abraham pleaded on its behalf (Ge 18:23–33). It was destroyed because of its depravity but Lot and his daughters survived (Ge 19:1–29). Frequently used as an example of man's depravity and God's judgment (Dt 29:23; Isa 1:9–10; Jer 23:14; La 4:6; Eze 16:46–56; Am 4:11; Zep 2:9; Mt 10:15; Lk 10:12; Ro 9:29; 2Pe 2:6; Jude 7; Rev 11:8). See Gomorrah.

SUKKOTH

1. Town east of the Jordan in territory of Gad (Jos 13:27), where Jacob stayed after reconciliation with Esau (Ge 33:16–17). Gideon punished its inhabitants for not helping his troops when they pursued the Midianites (Jdg 8:5–16). Solomon had foundries in this valley (1Ki 7:46; 2Ch

4:17). The psalmist mentions it to emphasise God's sovereignty (Ps 60:6; 108:7). Exact location unknown.

2. Region where the Israelites first encamped, having left Egypt (Ex 12:37; 13:20; Nu 33:5–6). Located in the northeast of the Egyptian delta, close to Rameses.

SUSA

Capital city of Elam, situated about 150 miles north of the Persian Gulf. Favoured by the kings of Persia as a winter residence, and therefore the backdrop to the book of Esther. Some of its deported officials wrote to Artaxerxes warning of the rebuilding of Jerusalem (Ezr 4:9–10). Here Nehemiah served as Artaxerxes' cupbearer (Ne 1:1) and Daniel received his vision about Belshazzar (Da 8:2).

SYCHAR

City in Samaria near Jacob's well where Jesus spoke with a Samaritan woman (Jn 4:5–43). Probably built on the site of the ancient town of Shechem (Ge 33:18).

SYRIA

See Aram.

TAANACH

Royal city of the Canaanites, situated in the hills south of Valley of Jezreel, about 5 miles southeast of Megiddo. After its defeat by Joshua (Jos 12:21), it was allotted to the tribe of Manasseh (Jos 17:11; 1Ch 7:29) and assigned to the Levites (Jos 21:25). Its Canaanite inhabitants were never driven out, so it retained some independence (Jdg 1:27). Canaanite kings fought against Deborah

and Barak here (Jdg 5:19). Part of one of Solomon's twelve districts (1Ki 4:12).

TABOR

1. Isolated mountain on the border between Issachar, Zebulun and Naphtali (Jos 19:22), about 6 miles east of Nazareth. Here Barak gathered his troops to attack the Canaanite army of Sisera (Jdg 4:6, 12, 14), and Gideon's brothers were killed by the Midianite kings (Jdg 8:18–19). Its greatness was equated with Mount Carmel (Jer 46:18) and Mount Hermon (Ps 89:13), but it became a sanctuary for idolatry (Hos 5:1).

2. Levite city in the territory of Zebulun (1Ch 6:77).

3. Site of a great tree where Samuel told Saul he would receive a sign of God's favour (1Sa 10:3).

TAHPANHES

City on the eastern side of the Nile Delta, often associated with Memphis (Jer 2:16; 44:1; 46:14). The Judeans fled here after the murder of Gedaliah (Jer 43:7) and Jeremiah was instructed by God to warn the people against putting their faith in Egypt, for it too would fall (Jer 43:7–13; Eze 30:18–19).

TAMAR

Town at south end of the Dead Sea. Precise location unknown but near the border of Judah and Edom. It would form part of the southern boundary of the restored land (Eze 47:19). Also known as Tadmor (1Ki 9:18; 2Ch 8:4), which Solomon rebuilt.

TARSHISH

City or territory at western end of Mediterranean Sea, possibly in southern Spain, renowned for its shipping (Ps 48:7; Isa 23:1, 14; 60:9; Eze 27:25) and valuable merchandise (Ps 72:10; Jer 10:9; Eze 38:13). Jonah tried to flee here from God's call to Nineveh (Jnh 1:3; 4:2).

TARSUS

Principal city of Cilicia in Asia Minor. Birthplace of Paul (Ac 9:11; 21:39; 22:3), he was sent here to escape a Jewish death threat (Ac 9:30). Barnabas fetched him and took him to Antioch (Ac 11:25).

TEKOA

Town in hill country of Judah, about 6 miles south of Bethlehem, and 10 miles south of Jerusalem. Home of the wise woman used by Joab to bring reconciliation between David and Absalom (2Sa 14:2–21). Also home of David's bodyguard Ira (2Sa 23:26). Rehoboam fortified it (2Ch 11:6) because it was a strategic warning point overlooking Jerusalem (Jer 6:1). Birthplace of Amos, where he received his call from God (Am 1:1).

TEMAN

Town and region in the south of Edom, probably named after one of Esau's grandsons (Ge 36:11; 1Ch 1:36). Its inhabitants were famous for their wisdom (Jer 49:7; Ob 8), one being Job's advisor (Job 2:11). Its destruction was foretold along with all of Edom (Eze 25:13).

THEBES

City in Upper Egypt, on eastern bank of the Nile, also known as No or No-Amon. Its destruction was foretold (Jer 46:25; Eze 30:14–16), to emphasise that no city, however great, could escape God's judgment (Na 3:8).

THESSALONICA

Chief seaport of province of Macedonia. Paul established a church here (Ac 17:1–4; 1Th 1:9–10). A deep affection grew between Paul and the church (1Th 2:1–12). Home of two of his coworkers, Aristarchus and Secundus (Ac 20:4; 27:2); Demas moved here after deserting Paul (2Ti 4:10).

THYATIRA

Town in province of Lydia in western Asia Minor. Home of Lydia, a dealer in purple cloth (Ac 16:14). Though not large, this town was known for its thriving manufacturing industry and the pagan customs of some of its trade guilds. One of the seven letters of Revelation was addressed to its church warning against the immoral teaching of Jezebel (Rev 2:18–29).

TIBERIAS

City on the western shore of the Sea of Galilee, which is sometimes referred to as the Sea of Tiberias (Jn 6:1; 21:1). Some of its inhabitants travelled to hear Jesus (Jn 6:23–25) but there is no record of Jesus visiting here.

TIGRIS, RIVER

Major river in southwest Asia (about 1,150 miles), which with the river Euphrates gives Mesopotamia its name. One of the four rivers of Eden (Ge 2:14). Daniel was standing on its banks when he received his vision (Da 10:4–7).

TIMNAH

1. Town in hill country of Judah (Jos 15:57) where Judah was going when he was tricked by Tamar (Ge 38:12–18).

2. Town on border of territory of Judah (Jos 15:10), belonging to Dan (Jos 19:43). Here Samson met and married a Philistine woman (Jdg 14:1–8), who was subsequently killed by her own people (Jdg 15:6). The town was captured and occupied by the Philistines (2Ch 28:18).

TIRZAH

Ancient Canaanite town about 8 miles east of Samaria and 5 miles northeast of Shechem. Captured by the Israelites under Joshua (Jos 12:24). It replaced Shechem as the capital of the northern kingdom, and remained so until Omri moved his capital to Samaria (1Ki 16:23–28). From this base Menahem launched his coup against King Shallum in Samaria (2Ki 15:14). Known for its beauty (SS 6:4).

TROAS

Port on coast of Mysia in northwestern Asia Minor. Paul had a vision here and was called to Macedonia (Ac 16:8–11). On his travels he revisited here, the first time hoping to find Titus (2Co 2:12–13), and the second time reviving a man from a fatal accident (Ac 20:5–12). He probably returned on at least one further occasion (2Ti 4:13).

TYRE

Important sea port on Mediterranean coast, about 25 miles south of Sidon and 35 miles north of Carmel. A fortress built upon a rock (Eze 26:4, 14) with a commanding position over the sea (Eze 26:17; 27:3). Renowned for its strength and prosperity (Ps 45:12). Good trade relations existed between Tyre and Israel at the time of David and Solomon's building works (2Sa 5:11; 1Ki 5:1; 7:13–14; 9:11–12; 1Ch 14:1; 2Ch 2:3, 11–14), and during Zerubbabel's rebuilding (Ezr 3:7). Its dramatic fall was foretold by the prophets because of its pride and faithlessness (Isa 23; Eze 26–28; Joel 3:4; Am 1:9–10; Zec 9:2–3). Despite its wickedness, Jesus spoke of it more favourably than some of the towns of Galilee (Mt 11:21–22; Lk 10:13–14). While visiting, he praised a Canaanite woman's faith and healed her daughter (Mt 15:21–28; Mk 7:24–31). Many of its people went to Galilee to hear Jesus (Mk 3:8; Lk 6:17). Its people sought peace with King Herod (Ac 12:20), and Paul used its port on his third missionary journey (Ac 21:3,7).

UR

City in southern Mesopotamia, home of Abram's family (Ge 11:28–32), from which God brought him to the promised land (Ge 15:7; Ne 9:7).

ZAREPHATH

.City on Mediterranean coast, between Tyre and Sidon. Here Elijah was given hospitality by a widow whose son he restored from death (1Ki 17:9–24). Jesus praised this widow's faith, and contrasted it with the faith of those from his home town (Lk 4:26).

ZEBULUN

Mountainous territory at northern end of Palestine, between Asher and Naphtali. Allotted to the descendants of Jacob's tenth son, its towns and borders were clearly listed (Jos 19:10–16). Its former Canaanite inhabitants were not driven out but enslaved (Jdg 1:30). Isaiah predicted a time of great honour for this land (Isa 9:1). This was fulfilled in the coming of Christ (Mt 4:13–16).

ZIKLAG

Town in the Negev, about 10 miles north of Beersheba. Allotted by Joshua to the tribe of Judah (Jos 15:31), but later assigned to Simeon (Jos 19:5; 1Ch 4:30). Achish gave it to David as a refuge from Saul (1Sa 27:6; 1Ch 12:1, 20). Here the Amalekites took captive Israelite wives and children (1Sa 30). After Saul's death David stayed here for two days (2Sa 1:1), executing the man who claimed he had killed Saul (2Sa 1:8–15). After the exile it was occupied by Judeans (Ne 11:28).

ZIN, DESERT OF

Desert region south of the Negev, through which the Israelites wandered on their way from Egypt to the promised land (Nu 13:21; 33:36). Here Miriam died and was buried (Nu 20:1), and Moses and Aaron disobeyed God's instructions (Nu 27:14; Dt 32:51). Part of it was included in the promised land (Nu 34:3–4), and was eventually allotted to the tribe of Judah (Jos 15:1, 3).

ZION
See Jerusalem.

ZIPH
1. Town in southernmost corner of Judah, on the border with Edom (Jos 15:21, 24).

2. Town in hill country of Judah, about 4 miles southeast of Hebron. Probably named after Caleb's grandson (1Ch 2:42), and later fortified by Rehoboam (2Ch 11:8). Saul searched for David here, after a tip-off from some of its inhabitants, but he did not find him (1Sa 23:19, 24).

3. Desert region surrounding 2 above, where David hid to escape Saul's pursuit (1Sa 26:1–2), and where Jonathan brought him encouragement (1Sa 23:14–15).

ZOAN
Ancient city in Egypt, on the northeast side of the Nile Delta. Its people witnessed the miracles of God at the exodus (Ps 78:12, 43), and its wise men were counsellors to Pharaoh (Isa 19:11, 13). However, God's power and wisdom surpasses any found within Egypt (Isa 30:1–5; Eze 30:14).

ZOAR
City in Jordan Valley, south of the Dead Sea, near Sodom and Gomorrah (Ge 13:10). Originally known as Bela (Ge 14:2, 14), God refrained from destroying it along with Sodom and Gomorrah, so that Lot could find refuge there (Ge 19:22–23). Lot did not stay long, however, preferring the safety of the mountains (Ge 19:30). A landmark at the southernmost point of the promised land (Dt 34:3), on the border with Moab (Isa 15:5; Jer 48:34).

ZORAH
City in the lowlands of Judah near Eshtaol (Jos 15:33), in territory of Dan (Jos 19:41). Home of Manoah and his son Samson (Jdg 13:2–3, 24), who were both buried between here and Eshtaol (Jdg 16:31). Its warriors were sent to spy out Laish for the Danites (Jdg 18:2, 8, 11). Later Rehoboam strengthened its fortifications (2Ch 11:10).

CONCORDANCE

a

accept, -s, -ed, -able, -ance

Ex	23:	8	'Do not a a bribe,
Job	42:	9	the LORD a-ed Job's prayer
Pr	19:	20	Listen to advice and a discipline,
Jn	13:	20	whoever a-s anyone I send a-s me;
Ro	15:	7	A one another ... just as Christ
Php	4:	18	a-able sacrifice, pleasing to God
1Th	2:	13	you a-ed it not as a human word,
1Ti	1:	15	saying that deserves full a-ance:
Jas	1:	21	humbly a the word planted in you,
1Pe	2:	5	spiritual sacrifices a-able to God

adoption

Ro	8:	15	brought about your a to sonship
	8:	23	wait eagerly for our a to sonship
	9:	4	Theirs is the a to sonship;
Gal	4:	5	receive a to sonship
Eph	1:	5	predestined us for a to sonship

advocate

Job	16:	19	in heaven; my a is on high
Jn	14:	16	he will give you another a
	14:	26	But the A, the Holy Spirit
	15:	26	When the A comes,
	16:	7	the A will not come to you
1Jn	2:	1	an a with the Father

afraid

Ge	15:	1	'Do not be a, Abram.
	26:	24	Do not be a, for I am with you;
Ex	3:	6	because he was a to look at God
	14:	13	'Do not be a. Stand firm
Ps	56:	4	in God I trust and am not a.
Isa	43:	5	Do not be a, for I am with you;
Mt	1:	20	'Joseph son of David, do not be a
	10:	31	So don't be a;
Mk	5:	36	'Don't be a; just believe.
	6:	50	'Take courage! It is I. Don't be a.
Lk	1:	13	'Do not be a, Zechariah;
	1:	30	'Do not be a, Mary,
	2:	10	'Do not be a. I bring you good
	12:	32	'Do not be a, little flock,
Jn	14:	27	hearts be troubled and do not be a
Heb	13:	6	Lord is my helper; I will not be a.

Almighty

Ge	17:	1	'I am God A; walk before me
Ex	6:	3	to Isaac and to Jacob as God A,
Ru	1:	20	the A has made my life very bitter
Job	33:	4	the breath of the A gives me life
Ps	24:	10	The LORD A – he is the King of glory.
	89:	8	Who is like you, LORD God A?
	91:	1	rest in the shadow of the A
Isa	6:	3	'Holy, holy, holy is the LORD A;
	47:	4	Our Redeemer – the LORD A is his
Rev	4:	8	'Holy, ... holy is the Lord God A,
	15:	3	'Great ... your deeds, Lord God A.

altar

Ge	8:	20	Then Noah built an a to the LORD
	12:	8	There he built an a to the LORD
	22:	9	Abraham built an a there
	26:	25	Isaac built an a there and called
Ex	17:	15	Moses built an a and called it
Jdg	6:	24	Gideon built an a to the LORD there
2Sa	24:	25	David built an a to the LORD there
2Ch	33:	16	Then he restored the a of the LORD
Ezr	3:	2	to build the a of the God of Israel
Isa	6:	6	he had taken with tongs from the a
Mt	5:	24	your gift there in front of the a.
	23:	18	'If anyone swears by the a,
Ac	17:	23	found an a with this inscription:
Heb	13:	10	We have an a from which those who
Jas	2:	21	he offered his son Isaac on the a
Rev	6:	9	I saw under the a the souls

angel, -s

Ge	22:	15	The a of the LORD called to Abraham
Ex	23:	20	I am sending an a ahead of you
Ps	34:	7	The a of the LORD encamps around
Mt	2:	13	an a of the Lord appeared to Joseph
	18:	10	their a-s in heaven always see
	25:	41	prepared for the devil and his a-s
Lk	1:	26	God sent the a Gabriel to Nazareth,
	2:	9	An a of the Lord appeared to them,
Ac	6:	15	his face was like the face of an a
1Co	6:	3	know that we will judge a-s?
	13:	1	in the tongues of men or a-s?
2Co	11:	14	Satan himself masquerades as an a
Heb	1:	4	as much superior to the a-s
	1:	6	'Let all God's a-s worship him.
	1:	7	'He makes his a-s spirits,
	2:	9	made lower than the a-s,
	12:	22	thousands of a-s in joyful assembly
	13:	2	hospitality to a-s without knowing it
1Pe	1:	12	a-s long to look into these things
2Pe	2:	4	For if God did not spare a-s
Rev	12:	7	Michael and his a-s fought against

anger, -ed

Ex	32:	11	'why should your a burn against
	34:	6	slow to a, abounding in love
2Ki	22:	13	Great is the LORD's a that burns
Ps	30:	5	For his a lasts only a moment,
	90:	11	If only we knew the power of your a!
Pr	22:	24	do not associate with one easily a-ed
1Co	13:	5	it is not easily a-ed,
Eph	4:	26	'In your a do not sin': do not let
Jas	1:	20	our a does not produce the righteousness

anoint, -ed, -ing

Ex	30:	30	'A Aaron and his sons
1Sa	15:	1	a you king over his people Israel;
Ps	23:	5	You a my head with oil;
	45:	7	by a-ing you with the oil of joy
Isa	61:	1	LORD has a-ed me to proclaim good
Mk	6:	13	and a-ed with oil many people
Lk	4:	18	he has a-ed me to proclaim good news
Ac	10:	38	how God a-ed Jesus of Nazareth
Heb	1:	9	by a-ing you with the oil of joy.
Jas	5:	14	to pray over them and a them with oil
1Jn	2:	20	have an a-ing from the Holy One,

answer, -s, -ed

1Ki	10:	3	Solomon a-ed all her questions;

	18:	24	The god who *a-s* by fire – he is God
Ps	34:	4	I sought the LORD, and he *a-ed* me
	38:	15	LORD, I wait for you; you will *a*
	69:	13	God, *a* me with your sure salvation
	69:	17	*a* me quickly, for I am in trouble
	86:	1	and *a* me, for I am poor and needy
	119:145		*a* me, LORD, and I will obey
	143:	7	*A* me quickly, LORD; my spirit
Pr	15:	1	A gentle *a* turns away wrath,
	24:	26	An honest *a* is like a kiss
	26:	5	*A* a fool according to his folly,
Isa	65:	24	Before they call I will *a*;
Jnh	2:	2	I called to the LORD, and he *a-ed*
Jn	19:	9	but Jesus gave him no *a*
1Pe	3:	15	be prepared to give an *a* to

apostle, -s

Ac	1:	26	so he was added to the eleven *a-s*
	2:	43	signs performed by the *a-s*
Ro	11:	13	I am the *a* to the Gentiles,
1Co	15:	9	For I am the least of the *a-s*
2Co	11:	13	masquerading as *a-s* of Christ
Eph	2:	20	built on the foundation of the *a-s*
	4:	11	Christ himself gave the *a-s,*
1Ti	2:	7	I was appointed a herald and an *a* –
Heb	3:	1	our *a* and high priest

appear, -s, -ing, -ed, -ance

1Sa	16:	7	People look at the outward *a-ance,*
2Ch	1:	7	That night God *a-ed* to Solomon
Mal	3:	2	Who can stand when he *a-s*?
Mt	1:	20	an angel of the Lord *a-ed* to him
	24:	30	will *a* the sign of the Son of Man
Lk	2:	9	An angel of the Lord *a-ed* to them,
	24:	34	The Lord has risen and has *a-ed*
Ac	1:	3	He *a-ed* to them over a period
1Co	15:	6	he *a-ed* to more than five hundred
2Co	5:	10	we must all *a* before the judgment
Col	3:	4	When Christ, who is your life, *a-s,*
1Ti	6:	14	until the *a-ing* of our Lord Jesus
2Ti	4:	8	all who have longed for his *a-ing.*
Tit	2:	13	the *a-ing* of the glory of our great God
Heb	9:	24	now to *a* for us in God's presence
	9:	28	and he will *a* a second time,
1Pe	5:	4	And when the Chief Shepherd *a-s,*
1Jn	3:	2	when Christ *a-s,* we shall be like him,

appoint, -ed

Ezr	1:	2	he has *a-ed* me to build a temple
Mt	26:	18	my *a-ed* time is near.
Jn	15:	16	I chose you and *a-ed* you
Ac	13:	48	all who were *a-ed* for eternal life
	14:	23	Paul and Barnabas *a-ed* elders
1Co	4:	5	judge nothing before the *a-ed* time;
Eph	1:	22	*a-ed* him to be head over everything
1Th	5:	9	God did not *a* us to suffer wrath
Tit	1:	5	and *a* elders in every town,
Heb	1:	2	his Son, whom he *a-ed* heir of all

ark

Ex	25:	21	Place the cover on top of the *a*
Dt	10:	5	and put the tablets in the *a*
1Sa	4:	11	The *a* of God was captured,
	7:	2	the *a* remained at Kiriath Jearim,
2Sa	6:	6	reached out and took hold of the *a*
1Ki	8:	9	There was nothing in the *a* except
1Ch	13:	10	put his hand on the *a.* So he died
2Ch	35:	3	'Put the sacred *a* in the temple
Heb	9:	4	the gold-covered *a* of the covenant.
Rev	11:	19	within his temple was seen the *a*

army, -ies

Jos	5:	14	as commander of the *a* of the LORD
1Sa	17:	36	defied the *a-ies* of the living God
	17:	45	the God of the *a-ies* of Israel,

1Ch	12:	22	a great *a*, like the army of God
2Ch	14:	11	we have come against this vast *a.*
	20:	12	no power to face this vast *a*
	32:	7	the king of Assyria and the vast *a*
Ps	33:	16	king is saved by the size of his *a;*
	44:	9	you no longer go out with our *a-ies*
Rev	19:	14	*a-ies* of heaven were following him,
	19:	19	and their *a-ies* gathered together

ask, -s, -ing, -ed

Ex	8:	13	And the LORD did what Moses *a-ed.*
1Ki	3:	11	you have *a-ed* for this and not
Ps	27:	4	One thing I *a* from the LORD,
Isa	7:	11	'*A* the LORD your God for a sign,
	65:	1	to those who did not *a* for me;
Jer	6:	16	*a* for the ancient paths,
Mt	6:	8	knows what you need before you *a*
	7:	7	'*A* and it will be given to you;
	7:	8	For everyone who *a-s* receives;
	7:	11	give good gifts to those who *a* him
	9:	38	*A* the Lord of the harvest,
	18:	19	agree about anything you *a* for,
	21:	22	whatever you *a* for in prayer.
Mk	10:	35	do for us whatever we *a.*
	10:	38	don't know what you are *a-ing,*'
	11:	29	'I will *a* you one question.
Lk	6:	30	Give to everyone who *a-s* you,
	11:	13	give the Holy Spirit to those who *a*
	20:	3	'I will also *a* you a question.
Jn	9:	21	*A* him. He is of age; he will speak
	11:	22	God will give you whatever you *a.*
	14:	13	will do whatever you *a* in my name,
	14:	16	And I will *a* the Father,
	15:	7	*a* whatever you wish,
	16:	23	you will no longer *a* me anything.
	21:	17	Jesus *a-ed* him the third time,
Ro	10:	20	to those who did not *a* for me.
Eph	3:	20	immeasurably more than all we *a*
Jas	1:	5	should *a* God, who gives generously
	1:	6	But when you *a*, you must believe
	4:	2	because you do not *a* God
1Pe	3:	15	give an answer to everyone who *a-s*
1Jn	5:	14	if we *a* anything according

b

battle, -s

1Sa	17:	47	for the *b* is the LORD's,
2Sa	1:	25	'How the mighty have fallen in *b*!
	22:	35	He trains my hands for *b*;
2Ch	20:	15	For the *b* is not yours, but God's
	32:	8	God to help us and to fight our *b-s*
Ps	18:	39	You armed me with strength for *b*;
	24:	8	the LORD mighty in *b*
	144:	1	my hands for war, my fingers for *b*
Ecc	9:	11	or the *b* to the strong,
Isa	31:	4	Almighty will come down to do *b*
Eze	13:	5	stand firm in the *b* on the day
Jas	4:	1	your desires that *b* within you
Rev	16:	14	for the *b* on the great day
	20:	8	Gog and Magog – and to gather them for *b*

bear, -s, -ing

1Ki	8:	43	house I have built *b-s* your Name
Isa	53:	11	and he will *b* their iniquities
Mt	7:	18	A good tree cannot *b* bad fruit,
Jn	15:	16	so that you might go and *b* fruit
Ro	7:	4	that we might *b* fruit for God
1Co	10:	13	tempted beyond what you can *b.*
Gal	6:	17	I *b* on my body the marks of Jesus
Eph	4:	2	*b-ing* with one another in love
Col	1:	10	*b-ing* fruit in every good work,

	3:	13	*B* with each other and forgive
Heb	13:	13	*b-ing* the disgrace he bore

beauty, -iful

Ps	27:	4	to gaze on the *b* of the LORD
	48:	2	*B-iful* in its loftiness,
SS	1:	15	How *b-iful* you are, my darling!
Isa	52:	7	How *b-iful* on the mountains are
	53:	2	He had not *b* or majesty to attract
Mk	14:	6	She has done a *b-iful* thing to me
Lk	21:	5	adorned with *b-iful* stones
Ac	3:	10	at the temple gate called *B-iful*,
Ro	10:	15	As it is written: 'How *b-iful* are
1Pe	3:	4	*b* of a gentle and quiet spirit,

believe, -s, -ing, -d, -r, -rs

Ge	15:	6	Abram *b-d* the LORD,
Isa	53:	1	Who has *b-d* our message and to whom
Mt	21:	22	If you *b*, you will receive
Mk	1:	15	Repent and *b* the good news!
	9:	24	do *b*; help me overcome my unbelief
Lk	8:	50	'Don't be afraid; just *b*,
Jn	1:	12	to those who *b-d* in his name,
	3:	16	whoever *b-s* in him shall not perish
	3:	18	Whoever *b-s* in him is not condemned
	3:	36	Whoever *b-s* in the Son has eternal
	6:	35	who *b-s* in me will never be thirsty
	6:	47	the one who *b-s* has eternal life
	11:	25	The one who *b-s* in me will live,
	11:	27	'I *b* that you are the Messiah,
	12:	38	'Lord, who has *b-d* our message
	14:	11	*b* on the evidence of the works
	20:	27	Stop doubting and *b*.'
	20:	31	and that by *b-ing* you may have life
Ac	15:	32	to encourage and strengthen the *b-rs*
	16:	31	'*B* in the Lord Jesus, and you
Ro	1:	16	salvation to everyone who *b-s:*
	4:	11	he is the father of all who *b*
	10:	4	righteousness for everyone who *b-s*
	10:	9	*b* in your heart that God raised him
	10:	11	'Anyone who *b-s* in him will never
Gal	2:	4	false *b-rs* had infiltrated our ranks
	3:	6	So also Abraham '*b-d* God,
1Th	4:	14	we *b* that Jesus died and rose again
1Ti	4:	10	and especially of those who *b*
2Ti	1:	12	because I know whom I have *b-d*,
Heb	11:	6	comes to him must *b* that he exists
Jas	1:	6	But when you ask, you must *b*
	2:	19	Even the demons *b* that –
1Jn	4:	1	Dear friends, do not *b* every spirit
	5:	1	Everyone who *b-s* that Jesus is the
3Jn		10	he even refuses to welcome other *b-rs*

belong, -s

Ge	40:	8	'Do not interpretations *b* to God?
Dt	5:	21	anything that *b-s* to your neighbour
	29:	29	The secret things *b* to the LORD
Ps	47:	9	for the kings of the earth *b* to God
Mk	10:	14	kingdom of God *b-s* to such as these
Jn	8:	47	*b-s* to God hears what God says.
	15:	19	you do not *b* to the world,
Ro	7:	4	that you might *b* to another, to him
	12:	5	each member *b-s* to all the others
	14:	8	live or die, we *b* to the Lord
1Co	12:	15	Because I am not a hand, I do not *b*
Gal	3:	29	If you *b* to Christ, then you are
Col	3:	5	whatever *b-s* to your earthly nature
1Th	5:	8	But since we *b* to the day, let us
1Jn	2:	19	but they did not really *b* to us.

birth

Dt	32:	18	you forgot the God who gave you *b*
Ps	51:	5	Surely I was sinful at *b*,
	71:	6	From my *b* I have relied on you;

Mt	1:	18	This is how the *b* of Jesus the Messiah
Jn	3:	6	Flesh gives *b* to flesh,
Gal	1:	15	when God, who set me apart from *b*
Jas	1:	15	conceived, it gives *b* to sin;
	1:	18	He chose to give us *b*
1Pe	1:	3	he has given us new *b* into a living

bless, -ing, -ed

Ge	1:	22	God *b-ed* them and said, 'Be
	2:	3	Then God *b-ed* the seventh day
	12:	3	all peoples on earth will be *b-ed*
Nu	6:	24	The LORD *b* you and keep you
Ps	32:	2	*B-ed* is the one whose sin the LORD
Pr	3:	13	*B-ed* are those who find wisdom,
	16:	20	*b-ed* is the one who trusts in the LORD
	31:	28	Her children ... call her *b-ed;*
Eze	34:	26	there will be showers of *b-ing*
Mt	5:	3	'*B-ed* are the poor in spirit,
	5:	4	*B-ed* are those who mourn,
	5:	5	*B-ed* are the meek,
	5:	6	*B-ed* are those who hunger
	5:	7	*B-ed* are the merciful,
	5:	8	*B-ed* are the pure in heart,
	5:	9	*B-ed* are the peacemakers,
	5:	10	*B-ed* are those who are persecuted
	21:	9	'*B-ed* is he who comes in the name
Mk	10:	16	placed his hands on them and *b-ed* them
Lk	1:	42	'*B-ed* are you among women,
	1:	48	all generations will call me *b-ed*
	6:	28	*b* those who curse you,
Jn	20:	29	*b-ed* are those who have not seen
Ac	3:	25	all peoples on earth will be *b-ed.*
	20:	35	more *b-ed* to give than to receive."
Ro	4:	8	*B-ed* is the one whose sin the Lord
	12:	14	*B* those who persecute you;
Gal	3:	8	'All nations will be *b-ed*
Eph	1:	3	every spiritual *b-ing* in Christ.
Tit	2:	13	while we wait for the *b-ed* hope –
Rev	1:	3	*B-ed* is the one who reads aloud
	14:	13	*b-ed* are the dead who die in the

blood

Ge	4:	10	Your brother's *b* cries out to me
	9:	6	'Whoever sheds human *b*,
Ex	7:	20	all the water was changed into *b*
	12:	13	when I see the *b*, I will pass over
Lev	16:	15	and take its *b* behind the curtain
	17:	11	the life of a creature is in the *b*,
Dt	12:	16	But you must not eat the *b;*
Joel	2:	31	to darkness and the moon to *b*
Mt	26:	28	This is my *b* of the covenant,
	27:	4	'for I have betrayed innocent *b*.
	27:	8	it has been called the Field of *B*
	27:	24	'I am innocent of this man's *b*,
Lk	22:	44	and his sweat was like drops of *b*
Jn	6:	54	and drinks my *b* has eternal life,
Ac	2:	20	to darkness and the moon to *b*
	15:	20	of strangled animals and from *b*
	20:	28	which he bought with his own *b*
	22:	20	the *b* of your martyr Stephen
Ro	3:	25	atonement, through the shedding of his *b*.
	5:	9	we have now been justified by his *b*
1Co	11:	25	cup is the new covenant in my *b;*
Eph	1:	7	we have redemption through his *b*,
Col	1:	20	by making peace through his *b*,
Heb	9:	12	once for all by his own *b*
	9:	22	of *b* there is no forgiveness.
	10:	4	it is impossible for the *b* of bulls
	12:	24	*b* that speaks a better word
	13:	20	the *b* of the eternal covenant
1Pe	1:	19	but with the precious *b* of Christ,
1Jn	1:	7	the *b* of Jesus, his Son, purifies
Rev	1:	5	freed us from our sins by his *b*

5:	9	and with your *b* you purchased
7:	14	white in the *b* of the Lamb
12:	11	him by the *b* of the Lamb

body, -ies, -ily

Dt	21: 23	must not leave the *b* hanging
Mt	6: 22	'The eye is the lamp of the *b*.
	26: 26	'Take and eat; this is my *b*.
Jn	2: 21	temple he had spoken of was his *b*
Ac	2: 31	nor did his *b* see decay
Ro	8: 11	give life to your mortal *b-ies*
	12: 1	your *b-ies* as a living sacrifice,
1Co	6: 19	*b-ies* are temples of the Holy Spirit,
	9: 27	I strike a blow to my *b* and make it my slave
	11: 24	'This is my *b*, which is for you;
	12: 12	Just as a *b*, though one, has many
	12: 13	baptised by one Spirit so as to form one *b*
	12: 27	Now you are the *b* of Christ,
	13: 3	and give over my *b* to hardship
	15: 44	natural *b*, there is also a spiritual *b*
Gal	6: 17	I bear on my *b* the marks of Jesus
Php	3: 21	will transform our lowly *b-ies*
Col	1: 18	the head of the *b*, the church;
	2: 9	of the Deity lives in *b-ily* form
1Th	4: 4	should learn to control your own *b*
Heb	10: 5	but a *b* you prepared for me
Jas	2: 26	the *b* without the spirit is dead,
1Pe	2: 24	bore our sins' in his *b* on the cross,

book, -s

Ex	32: 33	against me I will blot out of my *b*
Dt	29: 21	covenant ... in this *B* of the Law
	31: 26	Take this *B* of the Law and place it
2Ki	22: 8	'I have found the *B* of the Law
Ne	13: 1	the *B* of Moses was read aloud
Ecc	12: 12	Of making many *b-s* there is no end,
Jn	20: 30	which are not recorded in this *b*
Gal	3: 10	written in the *B* of the Law.
Php	4: 3	whose names are in the *b* of life
Rev	21: 27	written in the Lamb's *b* of life

born

Ps	87: 6	'This one was *b* in Zion.'
	90: 2	Before the mountains were *b*
Ecc	3: 2	a time to be *b* and a time to die,
Isa	9: 6	For to us a child is *b*,
Lk	2: 11	a Saviour has been *b* to you;
Jn	3: 3	unless they are *b* again.
	3: 7	"You must be *b* again.
	18: 37	the reason I was *b*,
Ac	22: 28	'But I was *b* a citizen,'
Gal	4: 4	God sent his Son, *b* of a woman,
1Pe	1: 23	For you have been *b* again,
1Jn	3: 9	because they have been *b* of God
	5: 4	for everyone *b* of God overcomes

bread

Ex	12: 18	to eat *b* made without yeast,
	16: 4	'I will rain down *b* from heaven
Dt	8: 3	man does not live on *b* alone
Ps	41: 9	one who shared my *b*, has lifted up
Pr	31: 27	and does not eat the *b* of idleness
Mt	4: 3	tell these stones to become *b*.
	4: 4	'Man shall not live on *b* alone,
	6: 11	Give us today our daily *b*
	7: 9	if your son asks for *b*,
	14: 17	only five loaves of *b* and two fish
	26: 26	Jesus took *b*, and when he had given thanks
Jn	6: 31	"He gave them *b* from heaven to eat.
	6: 33	the *b* of God is the *b*
	6: 35	'I am the *b* of life.
	13: 18	"He who shared my *b* has lifted up
Ac	2: 46	They broke *b* in their homes

	20: 7	we came together to break *b*.
1Co	11: 23	the night he was betrayed, took *b*

break, -s

Jdg	2: 1	I will never *b* my covenant with you
Ps	2: 9	will *b* them with a rod of iron
Isa	42: 3	A bruised reed he will not *b*,
	45: 2	I will *b* down gates of bronze
Mt	6: 20	where thieves do not *b* in and steal
	12: 20	A bruised reed he will not *b*,
Jn	19: 33	they did not *b* his legs
Ac	20: 7	we came together to *b* bread.
1Co	10: 16	the bread that we *b* a participation
Heb	2: 14	by his death he might *b* the power
1Jn	3: 4	Everyone who sins *b-s* the law;

broke, -n

Ps	34: 20	not one of them will be *b-n*
	51: 17	My sacrifice, O God, is a *b-n* spirit
Ecc	4: 12	three strands is not quickly *b-n*
	12: 6	severed, and the golden bowl is *b-n;*
Mt	21: 44	who falls on this stone will be *b-n*
	26: 26	when he had given thanks, he *b* it
Mk	6: 41	he gave thanks and *b* the loaves.
Lk	24: 35	was recognised by them when he *b*
Jn	10: 35	and Scripture cannot be *b-n*
	19: 36	'Not one of his bones will be *b-n,*
Ac	2: 46	They *b* bread in their homes and ate
Ro	11: 20	were *b-n* off because of unbelief,

brother, -'s, -s

Ge	4: 9	he replied. 'Am I my *b-'s* keeper?
Pr	17: 17	and a *b* is born for a time of adversity
	18: 24	a friend who sticks closer than a *b*
Mt	5: 22	anyone who is angry with a *b*
	7: 3	speck of sawdust in your *b-'s* eye
	12: 48	and who are my *b-s?*
	18: 35	forgive your *b* or sister from your heart.
	19: 29	*b-s* or sisters or father or mother
	22: 25	Now there were seven *b-s* among us.
	23: 8	only one Master and you are all *b-s*
	25: 40	the least of these *b-s* and sisters of mine,
Mk	3: 35	Whoever does God's will is my *b*
	6: 3	*b* of James, Joseph, Judas and Simon
Lk	15: 32	*b* of yours was dead and is alive
	17: 3	'If your *b* or sister sins against you
Jn	7: 5	his own *b-s* did not believe in him
Ro	8: 29	the firstborn among many *b-s*
	14: 10	why do you judge your *b* or sister?
	14: 13	obstacle in the way of a *b*
	14: 21	that will cause your *b* or sister to fall
1Co	6: 6	one *b* goes to law against another
	8: 13	if what I eat causes my *b*
Col	1: 2	the faithful *b-s* and sisters in Christ
1Th	3: 2	our *b* and co-worker in God's service
	5: 25	*B-s* and sisters, pray for us,
1Ti	4: 6	point these things out to the *b-s*
	5: 1	Treat younger men as *b-s*
Phm	16	better than a slave, as a dear *b*.
Heb	2: 11	is not ashamed to call them *b-s*
	13: 1	Keep on loving one another as *b-s*
Jas	2: 15	a *b* or a sister is without clothes
	4: 11	Anyone who speaks against a *b*
1Jn	2: 10	Anyone who loves their *b* and sister
	2: 11	anyone who hates their *b* or sister
	3: 10	does not love their *b* and sister
	3: 17	possessions and sees a *b* or sister in need
	5: 16	If you see any *b* or sister commit a sin
Rev	12: 10	For the accuser of our *b-s* and sisters,

build, -s, -ing

2Sa	7: 5	are you the one to *b* me a house
1Ki	6: 1	he began to *b* the temple

2Ch	36:	23	he has appointed me to *b* a temple
Ezr	1:	3	and *b* the temple of the LORD,
Ps	127:	1	Unless the LORD *b*-*s* the house,
Pr	14:	1	The wise woman *b*-*s* her house,
Ecc	3:	3	a time to tear down and a time to *b*
Jer	31:	4	I will *b* you up again
Mt	16:	18	and on this rock I will *b* my church
Ac	20:	32	his grace, which can *b* you up
Ro	15:	2	for their good, to *b* them up
1Co	3:	9	you are God's field, God's *b-ing*
	3:	10	each one should *b* with care.
	14:	12	excel in those that *b* up the church
2Co	10:	8	for *b-ing* you up rather than
Eph	4:	16	grows and *b-s* itself up in love,
	4:	29	what is helpful for *b-ing* others up
Jude		20	*b* yourselves up in your most holy

built

1Ki	6:	14	So Solomon *b* the temple
	8:	27	How much less this temple I have *b*
Pr	24:	3	By wisdom a house is *b*,
Mt	7:	24	like a wise man who *b* his house
	7:	26	like a foolish man who *b* his house
Ac	17:	24	not live in temples *b* by human hands
1Co	3:	14	If what has been *b* survives,
2Co	5:	1	in heaven, not *b* by human hands
Eph	2:	20	*b* on the foundation of the apostles
	2:	22	in him you too are being *b* together
	4:	12	that the body of Christ may be *b* up
Col	2:	7	rooted and *b* up in him,
1Pe	2:	5	are being *b* into a spiritual house

burn, -ing, -ed, -t

Ge	19:	24	rained down *b-ing* sulphur on Sodom
Lev	6:	9	regulations for the *b-t* offering:
Dt	7:	5	and *b* their idols in the fire
2Sa	6:	7	The LORD's anger *b-ed* against Uzzah
	24:	22	Here are oxen for the *b-t* offering,
1Ki	9:	25	Solomon sacrificed *b-t* offerings
	10:	5	*b-t* offerings he made at the temple
Ps	18:	28	You, LORD, keep my lamp *b-ing*;
Pr	25:	22	heap *b-ing* coals on his head,
Mt	13:	30	and tie them in bundles to be *b-ed*;
Lk	3:	17	but he will *b* up the chaff
	12:	35	and keep your lamps *b-ing*
	24:	32	Were not our hearts *b-ing* within us
Ac	19:	19	scrolls together and *b-ed* them
Ro	12:	20	heap *b-ing* coals on his head.
1Co	3:	15	If it is *b-ed* up, the builder
	7:	9	to marry than to *b* with passion
Heb	6:	8	In the end it will be *b-ed*
Rev	8:	7	A third of the earth was *b-ed* up,
	19:	20	the fiery lake of *b-ing* sulphur

C

call, -s, -ing, -ed

Ge	13:	4	Abram *c-ed* on the name of the LORD
	26:	25	altar there and *c-ed* on the name of
1Sa	3:	4	LORD *c-ed* Samuel. Samuel answered,
2Sa	22:	7	In my distress I *c-ed* to the LORD;
2Ch	7:	14	my people, who are *c-ed* by my name,
Ps	50:	15	*c* on me in the day of trouble; I
Isa	40:	3	voice of one *c-ing*: 'In the wilderness
	55:	6	while he may be found; *c* on him
	65:	24	Before they *c* I will answer; while
Joel	2:	32	who *c-s* on the name of the LORD
Mt	26:	53	think I cannot *c* on my Father, and
Mk	12:	37	David himself *c-s* him "Lord". How
Lk	1:	32	be *c-ed* the Son of the Most High.
	5:	32	I have not come to *c* the righteous,

	15:	19	longer worthy to be *c-ed* your son
Jn	1:	23	'I am the voice of one *c-ing* in
	10:	3	sheep listen to his voice. He *c-s*
	11:	43	*c-ed* in a loud voice, 'Lazarus,
Ac	2:	21	And everyone who *c-s* on the name
	11:	26	were *c-ed* Christians first
Ro	8:	30	predestined, he also *c-ed*; those he *c-ed*
	10:	13	Everyone who *c-s* on the name of the
	11:	29	gifts and his *c* are irrevocable.
1Co	1:	1	Paul, *c-ed* to be an apostle of
	1:	2	Jesus and *c-ed* to be his holy
	1:	24	God has *c-ed*, both Jews and Greeks,
	1:	26	of what you were when you were *c-ed*
	7:	20	they were in when God *c-ed* them
	15:	9	even deserve to be *c-ed* an apostle,
Gal	1:	6	quickly deserting the one who *c-ed*
	1:	15	set me apart from birth and *c-ed* me
Eph	1:	18	the hope to which he has *c-ed* you,
	4:	1	live a life worthy of the *c-ing* you
	4:	4	just as you were *c-ed* to one hope
1Th	2:	12	live lives worthy of God, who *c-s*
	4:	16	the trumpet *c* of God, and the dead
	5:	24	The one who *c-s* you is faithful
2Th	1:	11	may make you worthy of his *c-ing*,
	2:	14	*c-ed* you to this through our gospel
1Ti	6:	12	eternal life to which you were *c-ed*
2Ti	1:	9	saved us and *c-ed* us to a holy
Heb	2:	11	is not ashamed to *c* them brothers
1Pe	1:	15	But just as he who *c-ed* you is holy
	1:	17	Since you *c* on a Father who judges
	2:	9	declare the praises of him who *c-ed*
	3:	9	to this you were *c-ed* so that you
	5:	10	the God of all grace, who *c-ed* you
2Pe	1:	3	of him who *c-ed* us by his own glory
	1:	10	confirm your *c-ing* and election.
Rev	6:	16	*c-ed* to the mountains and the rocks

care, -s

Ps	8:	4	human beings that you *c* for them?
	55:	22	Cast your *c-s* on the LORD and he
Mk	4:	38	'Teacher, don't you *c* if we drown?
Lk	10:	34	brought him to an inn and took *c* of
	10:	40	'Lord, don't you *c* that my sister
Jn	10:	13	because he is a hired hand and *c-s*
Ac	13:	40	Take *c* that what the prophets have
1Co	4:	3	*c* very little if I am judged by you
1Ti	3:	5	how can he take *c* of God's church?
	6:	20	what has been entrusted to your *c*.
Heb	2:	6	them, a son of man that you *c* for
1Pe	5:	2	God's flock that is under your *c*,
	5:	7	anxiety on him because he *c-s* for

carry, -ies, -ied

Ex	19:	4	I *c-ied* you on eagles' wings
Nu	11:	14	I cannot *c* all these people
Dt	1:	31	as a father *c-ies* his son,
1Ki	18:	12	the Spirit of the LORD may *c* you
Isa	40:	11	*c-ies* them close to his heart;
Mt	3:	11	whose sandals I am not worthy to *c*.
	12:	29	a strong man's house and *c* off
Mk	15:	21	they forced him to *c* the cross
Lk	14:	27	whoever does not *c* their cross
Jn	8:	44	to *c* out your father's desires.
	19:	17	*C-ing* his own cross, he went out
	20:	15	'Sir, if you have *c-ied* him away,
Ac	5:	9	they will *c* you out also.
Ro	7:	18	I cannot *c* it out
2Co	4:	10	We always *c* around in our body
Gal	6:	2	*C* each other's burdens,
Php	1:	6	will *c* it on to completion
Heb	13:	9	Do not be *c-ied* away
2Pe	1:	21	*c-ied* along by the Holy Spirit

cause, -s, -d

Ge	2:	21	God c-d the man to fall into a deep
Ex	33:	19	'I will call my goodness to pass
Isa	8:	14	a stone that c-s people to stumble
	53:	10	the LORD's will to crush him and c
La	3:	52	Those who were my enemies without c
Da	11:	31	abomination that c-s desolation
Mt	5:	29	If your right eye c-s you to sin,
	18:	8	hand or your foot c-s you to stumble,
	24:	15	abomination that c-s desolation,"
Ro	9:	33	I lay in Zion a stone that c-s people
1Co	8:	13	if what I eat c-s my brother or sister
Jas	4:	1	What c-s fights and quarrels among
1Pe	2:	8	'A stone that c-s people to stumble

change, -s, -d

Ex	7:	15	staff that was c-d into a snake
Ps	110:	4	The LORD has sworn and will not c
Da	2:	21	He c-s times and seasons;
	4:	16	his mind be c-d from that of a man
Mal	3:	6	'I the LORD do not c.
Mt	18:	3	unless you c and become like
Lk	9:	29	the appearance of his face c-d,
Ac	6:	14	c the customs Moses handed down
1Co	15:	51	sleep, but we will all be c-d
Heb	1:	12	like a garment they will be c-d
	7:	12	when the priesthood is c-d,
	7:	21	has sworn and will not c his mind:
	12:	17	he could not c what he had done.
Jas	1:	17	does not c like shifting shadows

charge, -s

Job	13:	19	Can anyone bring c-s against me?
Isa	50:	8	Who then will bring c-s against me?
Da	2:	48	placed him in c of all its wise men
Mt	24:	47	him in c of all his possessions
	25:	21	I will put you in c of many things.
	26:	63	c you under oath by the living God
Mk	15:	26	The written notice of the c
Jn	13:	29	Since Judas had c of the money,
Ac	25:	20	stand trial there on these c-s
Ro	8:	33	bring any c against those whom God
1Co	9:	18	the gospel I may offer it free of c
Gal	3:	24	the law was put in c of us
Col	2:	14	cancelled the c of our legal
1Ti	5:	21	I c you, in the sight of God
	6:	13	made the good confession, I c you

child, -ren, -ren's

Ge	17:	17	Will Sarah bear a c at the age
Dt	4:	9	Teach them to your c-ren
	4:	40	may go well with you and your c-ren
Ps	8:	2	Through the praise of c-ren and infants
	37:	25	or their c-ren begging bread
	103:	13	father has compassion on his c-ren,
	127:	3	C-ren are a heritage from the LORD
Pr	17:	6	C-ren's c-ren are a crown
	22:	6	Start c-ren off on the way they should go,
Isa	9:	6	For to us a c is born, to us a son
	11:	6	and a little c will lead them
Jer	31:	29	the c-ren's teeth are set on edge.
Hos	11:	1	'When Israel was a c, I loved him,
Mal	4:	6	of the parents to their c-ren,
Mt	2:	18	Rachel weeping for her c-ren
	5:	9	they will be called c-ren of God.
	7:	11	to give good gifts to your c-ren,
	11:	25	and revealed them to little c-ren
	15:	26	not right to take the c-ren's bread
	18:	2	He called a little c
	18:	3	change and become like little c-ren
	19:	29	or c-ren or fields for my sake
	23:	37	I have longed to gather your c-ren
	27:	25	blood is on us and on our c-ren!
Lk	1:	17	to their c-ren and the disobedient

	2:	5	and was expecting a c
	14:	26	wife and c-ren, brothers and sisters
Jn	1:	12	the right to become c-ren of God
	8:	39	'If you were Abraham's c-ren,'
	16:	21	woman giving birth to a c has pain
Ac	2:	39	promise is for you and your c-ren
	13:	10	'You are a c of the devil
Ro	8:	14	led by the Spirit of God are the c-ren
	8:	16	our spirit that we are God's c-ren
	8:	17	if we are c-ren, then we are heirs –
	8:	19	for the c-ren of God to be revealed
	8:	21	freedom and glory of the c-ren
	9:	7	are they all Abraham's c-ren.
1Co	13:	11	When I was a c, I talked like a
Gal	3:	7	who have faith are c-ren of Abraham
	3:	26	you are all c-ren of God
Eph	6:	1	C-ren, obey your parents in the
	6:	4	do not exasperate your c-ren;
Php	2:	15	blameless and pure, 'c-ren of God
1Ti	3:	12	manage his c-ren and his household
Heb	11:	23	they saw he was no ordinary c
	12:	7	treating you as his c-ren. For what c-ren
1Jn	3:	1	we should be called c-ren of God!

chose, -n

Dt	7:	6	The LORD your God has c-n you
Isa	41:	9	You are my servant"; I have c-n you
Mt	22:	14	many are invited, but few are c-n.
Lk	9:	35	'This is my Son, whom I have c-n;
	10:	42	Mary has c-n what is better,
Jn	6:	70	'Have I not c-n you, the Twelve?
	15:	16	You did not choose me, but I c you
Ac	9:	15	'Go! This man is my c-n instrument
Ro	8:	33	against those whom God has c-n?
	11:	5	there is a remnant c-n by grace
1Co	1:	27	God c the foolish things
Eph	1:	4	he c us in him before the creation
	1:	11	also c-n, having been predestined
1Th	1:	4	loved by God, that he has c-n you
2Th	2:	13	God c you as firstfruits
Jas	1:	18	He c to give us birth
	2:	5	has not God c-n those who are poor
1Pe	1:	2	c-n according to the foreknowledge
	1:	20	He was c-n before the creation
	2:	9	a c-n people, a royal priesthood,

Christ, -'s

Jn	1:	17	grace and truth came through Jesus C
	1:	41	found the Messiah' (that is, the C
	17:	3	the only true God, and Jesus C,
Ro	3:	24	redemption that came by C Jesus
	5:	1	with God through our Lord Jesus C
	6:	3	baptised into C Jesus
	8:	1	no condemnation ... who are in C
	8:	35	separate us from the love of C?
	13:	14	yourselves with the Lord Jesus C,
1Co	1:	13	Is C divided?
	1:	23	we preach C crucified:
	2:	2	except Jesus C and him crucified.
	8:	6	there is but one Lord, Jesus C,
	10:	4	that rock was C
2Co	4:	5	not preach ourselves, but Jesus C
	5:	17	if anyone is in C, the new
Gal	2:	20	I have been crucified with C
	3:	28	you are all one in C Jesus.
Eph	2:	6	God raised us up with C
	2:	10	created in C Jesus to do good works
	2:	20	C Jesus himself as the chief
	3:	8	the boundless riches of C,
	5:	23	head of the wife as C is the head
Php	1:	6	until the day of C Jesus
	1:	21	to live is C and to die is gain
	2:	5	the same mindset as C Jesus

	2:	11	acknowledge that Jesus *C* is Lord,
	3:	8	garbage, that I may gain *C*
	3:	10	to know *C* – yes, to know the power
Col	1:	22	reconciled you by *C-'s* physical
	1:	27	*C* in you, the hope of glory.
	2:	10	in *C* you have been brought
1Th	4:	16	the dead in *C* will rise first
1Ti	1:	15	*C* Jesus came into the world to save
	2:	5	God and mankind, the man *C* Jesus
2Ti	2:	3	like a good soldier of *C* Jesus.
Heb	9:	14	*C,* who through the eternal Spirit
1Pe	1:	19	the precious blood of *C,* a lamb
	3:	15	revere *C* as Lord.
2Pe	1:	16	coming of our Lord Jesus *C*
1Jn	2:	1	Jesus *C,* the Righteous One.
	2:	22	denies that Jesus is the *C.*
Rev	1:	1	The revelation from Jesus *C,*
	20:	4	reigned with *C* for a thousand years

church

Mt	16:	18	on this rock I will build my *c,*
	18:	17	tell it to the *c;*
Ac	14:	23	appointed elders for them in each *c*
	20:	28	Be shepherds of the *c* of God,
1Co	4:	17	I teach everywhere in every *c*
	5:	12	to judge those outside the *c?*
	14:	4	who prophesies edifies the *c.*
Eph	3:	10	through the *c,* the manifold wisdom
	5:	23	Christ is the head of the *c,*
	5:	25	Christ loved the *c* and gave
Col	1:	24	sake of his body, which is the *c.*
1Ti	3:	5	how can he take care of God's *c?*
Heb	12:	23	the *c* of the firstborn,

clothes

Ge	27:	27	Isaac caught the smell of his *c,*
Dt	8:	4	Your *c* did not wear out
Mt	6:	30	If that is how God *c* the grass
	22:	11	who was not wearing wedding *c*
	25:	36	I needed *c* and you clothed me,
	28:	3	and his *c* were white as snow
Ac	14:	14	they tore their *c* and rushed out
1Ti	2:	9	gold or pearls or expensive *c*
Jas	2:	2	wearing a gold ring and fine *c,*
1Pe	3:	3	gold jewellery and fine *c*
Rev	3:	18	and white *c* to wear,

cloud, -s

Ex	13:	21	in a pillar of *c* to guide them
1Ki	18:	44	'A *c* as small as a man's hand
Pr	25:	14	Like *c-s* and wind without rain
Da	7:	13	coming with the *c-s* of heaven.
Mt	24:	30	the Son of Man coming on the *c-s*
Lk	9:	35	A voice came from the *c,* saying,
1Th	4:	17	in the *c-s* to meet the Lord
Heb	12:	1	such a great *c* of witnesses,
Jude		12	They are *c-s* without rain,
Rev	1:	7	Look, he is coming with the *c-s,*

come, -s, -ing

Ge	17:	6	kings will *c* from you
	39:	12	'*C* to bed with me!'
Ex	3:	5	'Do not *c* any closer,' God said.
Job	1:	7	to Satan, 'Where have you *c* from?
Ps	19:	5	like a bridegroom *c-ing* out
	24:	7	the King of glory may *c* in
	40:	7	I have *c* – it is written about me
	91:	7	it will not *c* near you
	121:	1	where does my help *c* from?
Ecc	5:	15	everyone *c-s* naked from their mother's
			womb,
Isa	1:	18	'*C* now, let us reason together,
	11:	1	A shoot will *c* up from the stump
	37:	32	out of Jerusalem will *c* a remnant,

	55:	1	thirsty, *c* to the waters;
	60:	1	Arise, shine, for your light has *c*
	62:	11	'See, your Saviour *c-s!*
	64:	1	rend the heavens and *c* down,
Da	7:	13	son of man, *c-ing* with the clouds
Hos	6:	1	'*C,* let us return to the LORD.
Mic	5:	2	*c* for me one who will be ruler
Zec	9:	9	See, your king *c-s* to you,
Mal	3:	1	will *c* to his temple;
	3:	2	can endure the day of his *c-ing?*
Mt	2:	2	rose and have *c* to worship him.
	2:	6	out of you will *c* a ruler
	3:	11	*c-s* one who is more powerful
	4:	4	that *c-s* from the mouth of God."
	4:	19	'*C,* follow me,' Jesus said,
	6:	10	your kingdom *c,* your will be done
	7:	15	They *c* to you in sheep's clothing,
	10:	34	I have *c* to bring peace
	11:	28	'*C* to me, all you who are weary
	15:	11	but what *c-s* out of their mouth
	19:	14	'Let the little children *c* to me,
	20:	28	Son of Man did not *c* to be served,
	21:	5	'See, your king *c-s* to you,
	23:	39	who *c-s* in the name of the Lord."
	24:	30	the Son of Man *c-ing* on the clouds
Mk	6:	31	'*C* with me by yourselves
Jn	1:	15	"He who *c-s* after me has surpassed
	1:	32	I saw the Spirit *c* down from heaven
	1:	39	'*C,*' he replied, 'and you will
	4:	29	*C,* see a man who told me everything
	5:	25	has now *c* when the dead will hear
	5:	40	you refuse to *c* to me to have life
	6:	37	*c-s* to me I will never drive away
	10:	10	The thief *c-s* only to steal
	11:	43	'Lazarus, *c* out!
	12:	15	your king is *c-ing,* seated
	14:	6	No one *c-s* to the Father
Ac	1:	11	will *c* back in the same way
	3:	19	refreshing may *c* from the Lord
	16:	9	'*C* over to Macedonia and help us.
Ro	10:	17	faith *c-s* from hearing the message,
1Co	2:	1	I did not *c* with eloquence
	11:	26	the Lord's death until he *c-s*
	16:	22	person be cursed. *C,* Lord!
2Co	1:	22	guaranteeing what is to *c*
	5:	17	the new creation has *c:*
	6:	17	*C* out from them and be separate,
Gal	4:	4	when the set time had fully *c,*
Eph	5:	6	God's wrath *c-s* on those
Col	2:	17	the things that were to *c;*
1Th	4:	16	the Lord himself will *c* down
	5:	2	will *c* like a thief in the night
2Th	2:	3	for that day will not *c* until
Heb	10:	7	I have *c* to do your will, my God."
	12:	22	you have *c* to Mount Zion,
	13:	14	looking for the city that is to *c*
Jas	4:	8	to God and he will *c* near to you.
2Pe	1:	16	the power and *c-ing* of our Lord
1Jn	2:	18	many antichrists have *c.*
Rev	1:	7	he is *c-ing* with the clouds,
	3:	3	I will *c* like a thief,
	3:	11	I am *c-ing* soon.
	3:	20	I will *c* in and eat with that person
	16:	15	'Look, I *c* like a thief!
	19:	7	the wedding of the Lamb has *c,*
	22:	17	Let the one who is thirsty *c;*
	22:	20	'Yes, I am *c-ing* soon.'
	22:	20	Amen. *C,* Lord Jesus.

command, -s, -ed

Ge	2:	16	And the LORD God *c-ed* the man,
Ex	7:	2	You are to say everything I *c* you,

Dt	5:	32	the LORD your God has *c-ed* you;
	30:	16	I *c* you today to love the LORD
Jos	1:	9	Have I not *c-ed* you? Be strong
Ps	19:	8	The *c-s* of the LORD are radiant,
	91:	11	he will *c* his angels concerning
	112:	1	find great delight in his *c-s*
	119:	98	Your *c-s* are always with me
Pr	3:	1	but keep my *c-s* in your heart
Mt	4:	6	"He will *c* his angels concerning
	15:	3	do you break the *c* of God
	28:	20	obey everything I have *c-ed* you.
Mk	7:	8	You have let go of the *c-s* of God
	7:	9	setting aside the *c-s* of God
	10:	3	'What did Moses *c* you?'
Lk	8:	25	He *c-s* even the winds
Jn	10:	18	This *c* I received from my Father.
	13:	34	'A new *c* I give you: love
	14:	15	'If you love me, keep my *c-s*.
	15:	14	my friends if you do what I *c*
Ac	17:	30	now he *c-s* all people everywhere
Ro	13:	9	summed up in this one *c*: 'Love
1Co	7:	10	To the married I give this *c*
	9:	14	Lord has *c-ed* that those who preach
	14:	37	writing to you is the Lord's *c*
Gal	5:	14	fulfilled in keeping this one *c*:
1Th	4:	16	with a loud *c*, with the voice
1Ti	1:	5	The goal of this *c* is love,
	1:	18	I am giving you this *c* in keeping
	6:	17	*C* those who are rich
Heb	11:	3	the universe was formed at God's *c*,
1Jn	2:	3	to know him if we keep his *c-s*
Rev	3:	10	have kept my *c* to endure patiently,

commit, -s, -ted

Ex	20:	14	'You shall not *c* adultery
1Ki	8:	61	may your hearts be fully *c-ted*
Ps	31:	5	Into your hands I *c* my spirit;
	37:	5	*C* your way to the LORD;
Mt	5:	27	"You shall not *c* adultery.
	11:	27	'All things have been *c-ted* to me
	27:	23	'Why? What crime has he *c-ted*?'
Mk	10:	11	marries another woman *c-s* adultery
Ac	14:	23	*c-ted* them to the Lord,
	20:	32	I *c* you to God and to the word
Ro	1:	27	*c-ted* shameful acts with other men,
1Co	10:	8	We should not *c* sexual immorality,
2Co	5:	19	he has *c-ted* to us the message
Heb	9:	7	for the sins the people had *c-ted*
1Pe	2:	22	'He *c-ted* no sin, and no deceit
1Jn	5:	16	see any brother or sister *c* a sin

compassion, -s, -ate

Ex	33:	19	*c* on whom I will have *c*
	34:	6	LORD, the *c-ate* and gracious God,
Ps	103:	8	the LORD is *c-ate* and gracious,
La	3:	22	for his *c-s* never fail
Mt	9:	36	saw the crowds, he had *c* on them,
Lk	15:	20	filled with *c* for him;
Ro	9:	15	I will have *c* on whom I have *c*
Eph	4:	32	Be kind and *c-ate* to one another,
Col	3:	12	clothe yourselves with *c*,
Jas	5:	11	The Lord is full of *c* and mercy

condemn, -s, -ing, -ed, -ation

Pr	17:	15	Acquitting the guilty and *c-ing*
Isa	50:	9	Who will *c* me?
Mt	12:	41	with this generation and *c* it;
Jn	3:	17	Son into the world to *c* the world,
	3:	18	believes in him is not *c-ed*,
	5:	29	done what is evil will rise to be *c-ed*
Ro	3:	7	why am I still *c-ed* as a sinner?
	5:	16	one sin and brought *c-ation*,
	8:	1	there is now no *c-ation* for those
	8:	34	Who then is the one who *c-s*?

	14:	22	*c* himself by what he approves
Gal	2:	11	because he stood *c-ed*.
1Jn	3:	20	if our hearts *c* us, we know

conscience, -s

Ac	24:	16	always to keep my *c* clear
Ro	2:	15	their *c-s* also bearing witness,
	9:	1	I am not lying, my *c* confirms it
1Co	4:	4	My *c* is clear, but that does not
	10:	25	without raising questions of *c*
1Ti	1:	19	faith and a good *c*,
	4:	2	whose *c-s* have been seared
2Ti	1:	3	ancestors did, with a clear *c*,
Heb	9:	14	cleanse our *c-s* from acts that
	10:	22	to cleanse us from a guilty *c*
	13:	18	sure that we have a clear *c*
1Pe	3:	16	keeping a clear *c*,
	3:	21	a clear *c* towards God.

consider, -ed

1Sa	16:	7	'Do not *c* his appearance or
Job	1:	8	'Have you *c-ed* my servant Job?
Ps	8:	3	When I *c* your heavens,
Lk	12:	27	'*C* how the wild flowers grow.
Ac	20:	24	I *c* my life worth nothing to me;
Php	2:	6	did not *c* equality with God
	3:	7	*c* loss for the sake of Christ
1Ti	1:	12	he *c-ed* me trustworthy, appointing me
Heb	10:	24	*c* how we may spur one another on
	12:	3	*C* him who endured such
Jas	1:	2	*C* it pure joy, my brothers and sisters

continue, -s, -d

Ps	78:	17	But they *c-d* to sin against him,
	119:	90	Your faithfulness *c-s* through all
2Co	10:	15	as your faith *c-s* to grow,
Gal	2:	10	we should *c* to remember the poor,
Php	2:	12	*c* to work out your salvation
Col	1:	23	if you *c* in your faith,
	2:	6	Jesus as Lord, *c* to live
2Ti	3:	14	*c* in what you have learned
1Jn	3:	6	No one who *c-s* to sin
Rev	22:	11	let the holy person *c* to be holy.

court, -s

Ps	84:	2	faints, for the *c-s* of the LORD;
	84:	10	Better is one day in your *c-s*
	100:	4	and his *c-s* with praise;
Am	5:	15	maintain justice in the *c-s*.
Mt	5:	25	adversary who is taking you to *c*.
	26:	55	Every day I sat in the temple *c-s*
Lk	2:	46	they found him in the temple *c-s*,
Jn	2:	14	*c-s* he found people selling cattle,
Ac	3:	2	those going into the temple *c-s*
Jas	2:	6	ones who are dragging you into *c*

covenant, -s

Ge	6:	18	I will establish my *c* with you,
	9:	12	'This is the sign of the *c*
	17:	7	my *c* as an everlasting *c*
Ex	2:	24	he remembered his *c* with Abraham,
Dt	4:	13	his *c*, the Ten Commandments,
Job	31:	1	'I made a *c* with my eyes
Jer	31:	31	I will make a new *c* with the house
Mal	2:	14	the wife of your marriage *c*
Mk	14:	24	'This is my blood of the *c*,
Ro	9:	4	theirs the divine glory, the *c-s*,
1Co	11:	25	the new *c* in my blood;
2Co	3:	6	ministers of a new *c* –
	3:	14	when the old *c* is read.
Gal	4:	24	the women represent two *c-s*.
Eph	2:	12	foreigners to the *c-s* of
Heb	7:	22	the guarantor of a better *c*
	9:	18	first *c* was not put into effect
	12:	24	Jesus the mediator of a new *c*,

cover, -s, -ing, -ings, -ed, -up

Ge	3: 7	made *c-ings* for themselves
Ex	25: 17	'Make an atonement *c* of pure gold
	33: 22	in a cleft in the rock and *c* you
	40: 34	the cloud *c-ed* the tent of meeting,
Ps	32: 1	whose sins are *c-ed*
Isa	6: 2	two wings they *c-ed* their faces,
Lk	23: 30	and to the hills '*C* us!'
Ro	4: 7	whose sins are *c-ed*
1Co	11: 15	hair is given to her as a *c-ing*
Jas	5: 20	*c* over a multitude of sins
1Pe	2: 16	do not use your freedom as a *c-up*
	4: 8	love *c-s* over a multitude of sins

creation

Mt	13: 35	hidden since the *c* of the world.
Ro	1: 20	since the *c* of the world God's
	8: 19	the *c* waits in eager expectation
	8: 39	all *c*, will be able to separate us
2Co	5: 17	in Christ, the new *c* has come:
Gal	6: 15	what counts is the new *c*
Eph	1: 4	he chose us in him before the *c*
Col	1: 15	the firstborn over all *c*
Heb	4: 13	Nothing in all *c* is hidden
1Pe	1: 20	He was chosen before the *c*
Rev	13: 8	slain from the *c* of the world

cross

Mt	10: 38	Whoever does not take up their *c*
	27: 40	Come down from the *c*, if
Jn	19: 17	Carrying his own *c*, he went out
Ac	2: 23	by nailing him to the *c*
	5: 30	you killed by hanging him on a *c*.
	13: 29	they took him down from the *c*
1Co	1: 18	message of the *c* is foolishness
Gal	6: 12	persecuted for the *c* of Christ
	6: 14	May I never boast except in the *c*
Php	2: 8	to death — even death on a *c*
Col	1: 20	his blood, shed on the *c*
Heb	12: 2	joy that was set before him he endured the *c*,
1Pe	2: 24	bore our sins' in his body on the *c*,

crucify, -ied

Mt	20: 19	mocked and flogged and *c-ied*.
	27: 26	and handed him over to be *c-ied*
	28: 5	Jesus, who was *c-ied*
Jn	19: 15	Take him away! *C* him!'
Ro	6: 6	our old self was *c-ied* with him
1Co	1: 23	we preach Christ *c-ied*:
	2: 2	except Jesus Christ and him *c-ied*
	2: 8	not have *c-ied* the Lord of glory
Gal	2: 20	I have been *c-ied* with Christ
Rev	11: 8	where also their Lord was *c-ied*

cry, -ies, -ing, -ied

Ex	2: 23	in their slavery and *c-ied* out,
Ps	22: 2	O my God, I *c* out by day,
	84: 2	my flesh *c* out for the living God
	107: 13	*c-ied* to the LORD in their trouble,
	130: 1	Out of the depths I *c* to you,
Pr	21: 13	shuts their ears to the *c* of the poor
Isa	6: 5	'Woe to me!' I *c-ied*.
Mt	12: 19	He will not quarrel or *c* out;
	27: 50	when Jesus had *c-ied* out again
Lk	19: 40	the stones will *c* out.
Jn	20: 11	Mary stood outside the tomb *c-ing*.
Ro	8: 15	And by him we *c*, 'Abba, Father.
Heb	5: 7	with fervent *c-ies* and tears
Jas	5: 4	The *c-ies* of the harvesters have
Rev	21: 4	no more death or mourning or *c-ing*

curse, -ing, -d

Ge	3: 14	*C-d* are you above all livestock
	3: 17	'*C-d* is the ground because of you;

Ex	22: 28	blasphemies against God or *c* the ruler
Job	2: 9	*C* God and die!
Mt	25: 41	'Depart from me, you who are *c-d*,
Lk	6: 28	bless those who *c* you,
Ro	9: 3	wish that I myself were *c-d*
	12: 14	bless and do not *c*
1Co	12: 3	Spirit of God says, 'Jesus be *c-d*
Gal	1: 8	let them be under God's *c*
	3: 10	rely on the law are under a *c*,
Jas	3: 10	same mouth come praise and *c-ing*.

cut, -ting

1Sa	24: 11	I *c* off the corner of your robe
1Ki	3: 25	'*C* the living child in two
Isa	53: 8	*c* off from the land of the living;
Mt	3: 10	*c* down and thrown into the fire
	5: 30	*c* it off and throw it away.
	24: 22	If those days had not been *c* short,
Lk	12: 46	*c* him to pieces and assign
	13: 9	If not, then *c* it down."
Jn	18: 10	*c-ting* off his right ear.
Ac	3: 23	*c* off from their people.
	18: 18	he had his hair *c* off at Cenchreae
Ro	9: 3	I myself were cursed and *c* off
	11: 22	you also will be *c* off
1Co	11: 6	might as well have her hair *c* off;
Gal	5: 7	Who *c* in on you to keep you

d

dark, -ness

Ge	1: 2	*d-ness* was over the surface
	1: 4	separated the light from the *d-ness*
Ex	20: 21	the thick *d-ness* where God was
2Sa	22: 29	the LORD turns my *d-ness* into light
Ps	139: 12	the *d-ness* will not be *d* to you
SS	1: 5	*D* am I, yet lovely, daughters
Isa	9: 2	people walking in *d-ness* have seen
Joel	2: 31	The sun will be turned to *d-ness*
Mt	4: 16	people living in *d-ness* have seen
	8: 12	thrown outside, into the *d-ness*,
	27: 45	*d-ness* came over all the land
Jn	1: 5	The light shines in the *d-ness*,
	3: 19	people loved *d-ness* instead of light
Eph	5: 8	For you were once *d-ness*, but now
Col	1: 13	from the dominion of *d-ness*
1Jn	1: 5	in him there is no *d-ness* at all
	2: 11	hates a brother ... is in the *d-ness*

daughter, -s

Ge	6: 2	saw that the *d-s* ... were beautiful,
	19: 30	Lot and his two *d-s* left Zoar
Ex	2: 10	she took him to Pharaoh's *d*
Ps	45: 10	Listen, *d*, consider and pay careful
	137: 8	*D* Babylon, doomed to destruction
SS	1: 5	*d-s* of Jerusalem,
Isa	62: 11	'Say to *D* Zion, "See,
Joel	2: 28	Your sons and *d-s* will prophesy,
Zec	9: 9	Rejoice greatly, *D* Zion!
Mt	21: 5	'Say to *D* Zion, "See,
Lk	13: 16	this woman, a *d* of Abraham,
	23: 28	'*D-s* of Jerusalem, do not weep
Ac	2: 17	Your sons and *d-s* will prophesy,
	21: 9	four unmarried *d-s* who prophesied
2Co	6: 18	and you will be my sons and *d-s*,

day, -s

Ge	1: 5	God called the light '*d*',
	1: 14	to separate the *d* from the night,
	2: 3	God blessed the seventh *d*
Ex	16: 26	Six *d-s* you are to gather it,
	16: 30	the people rested on the seventh *d*

	20:	8	'Remember the Sabbath *d*
Nu	14:	14	in a pillar of cloud by *d*
Dt	17:	19	to read it all the *d-s* of his life
	32:	7	Remember the *d-s* of old;
	33:	25	your strength will equal your *d-s*
Jos	1:	8	meditate on it *d* and night,
	5:	12	The manna stopped the *d* after
1Ki	17:	14	until the *d* the LORD sends rain
	19:	8	forty *d-s* and forty nights
2Ki	7:	9	This is a *d* of good news
1Ch	29:	15	Our *d-s* on earth are like a shadow
2Ch	15:	5	In those *d-s* it was not safe
Ne	8:	17	From the *d-s* of Joshua son of Nun
Est	3:	4	*D* after *d* they spoke to him
Job	3:	1	I cursed the *d* of his birth
	8:	9	our *d-s* on earth are but a shadow
	14:	1	'Mortals, born of woman, are of few *d-s*
Ps	21:	4	length of *d-s*, for ever and ever
	23:	6	all the *d-s* of my life,
	46:	5	God will help her at break of *d*
	84:	10	Better is one *d* in your courts
	90:	4	in your sight are like a *d*
	90:	9	All our *d-s* pass away
	90:	10	Our *d-s* may come to seventy years,
	90:	12	Teach us to number our *d-s*,
	118:	24	The LORD has done it this very *d*;
	119:	97	I meditate on it all *d* long
	119:	164	Seven times a *d* I praise you
	121:	6	the sun will not harm you by *d*,
	139:	12	the night will shine like the *d*,
	144:	4	their *d-s* are like a fleeting shadow
Pr	27:	1	you do not know what a *d* may bring
Ecc	9:	9	the *d-s* of this meaningless life
	12:	1	Creator in the *d-s* of your youth,
Isa	13:	9	See, the *d* of the LORD is coming –
	38:	20	all the *d-s* of our lives
	43:	13	Yes, and from ancient *d-s* I am he.
	49:	8	in the *d* of salvation I will help
Jer	46:	10	But that *d* belongs to the Lord,
Da	7:	9	the Ancient of *D-s* took his seat.
	7:	22	until the Ancient of *D-s* came
Joel	2:	29	pour out my Spirit in those *d-s*
	2:	31	great and dreadful *d* of the LORD
Ob		15	'The *d* of the LORD is near
Jnh	1:	17	three *d-s* and three nights
Zec	14:	1	A *d* of the LORD is coming
Mal	4:	5	dreadful *d* of the LORD comes
Mt	4:	2	for forty *d-s* and forty nights,
	6:	34	Each *d* has enough trouble
	7:	22	Many will say to me on that *d*,
	24:	38	For in the *d-s* before the flood,
	27:	63	"After three *d-s* I will rise again.
Lk	11:	3	Give us each *d* our daily bread
Jn	5:	17	always at his work to this very *d*,
	6:	40	I will raise them up at the last *d*.
	9:	4	As long as it is *d*,
Ac	2:	17	'In the last *d-s*, God says,
	5:	42	*D* after *d*, in the temple courts
	17:	11	examined the Scriptures every *d*
	17:	17	as well as in the market-place *d* by *d*
2Co	4:	16	we are being renewed *d* by *d*
Eph	4:	30	sealed for the *d* of redemption
Php	1:	6	until the *d* of Christ Jesus
1Th	5:	2	the *d* of the Lord will come like
	5:	4	so that this *d* should surprise
	5:	8	But since we belong to the *d*,
2Th	2:	2	the *d* of the Lord has already come
2Ti	3:	1	terrible times in the last *d-s*
Heb	1:	2	these last *d-s* he has spoken to us
	7:	27	need to offer sacrifices *d* after *d*
2Pe	3:	3	in the last *d-s* scoffers will come,
	3:	8	with the Lord a *d* is like

	3:	10	*d* of the Lord will come like a
1Jn	4:	17	confidence on the *d* of judgment,
Rev	1:	10	On the Lord's *D* I was in the Spirit
	4:	8	*D* and night they never stop saying:
	6:	17	For the great *d* of their wrath
	7:	15	serve him *d* and night in his temple
	16:	14	on the great *d* of God Almighty

dead

Dt	18:	11	or spiritist or who consults the *d*
2Sa	9:	8	you should notice a *d* dog like me?
Ecc	9:	4	dog is better off than a *d* lion
	10:	1	*d* flies give perfume a bad smell,
Isa	8:	19	Why consult the *d* on behalf of
Jnh	4:	9	I'm so angry I wish I were *d*
Mt	8:	22	and let the *d* bury their own dead.
	9:	24	The girl is not *d* but asleep.'
	10:	8	Heal those who are ill, raise the *d*,
	11:	5	the deaf hear, the *d* are raised,
Mk	12:	27	He is not the God of the *d*
Lk	15:	24	this son of mine was *d* and is alive
Jn	20:	9	that Jesus had to rise from the *d*.
Ac	10:	42	as judge of the living and the *d*
Ro	6:	11	count yourselves *d* to sin but alive
	8:	11	who raised Christ from the *d*
1Co	15:	16	For if the *d* are not raised,
	15:	52	the *d* will be raised imperishable,
Eph	2:	1	you were *d* in your transgressions
Col	2:	13	When you were *d* in your sins
1Th	4:	16	and the *d* in Christ will rise first
Jas	2:	26	so faith without deeds is *d*
Rev	14:	13	blessed are the *d* who die
	20:	13	The sea gave up the *d*

death

Dt	30:	19	I have set before you life and *d*,
Ps	44:	22	for your sake we face *d* all day
	56:	13	For you have delivered me from *d*
	116:	15	is the *d* of his faithful servants
Ecc	7:	2	*d* is the destiny of everyone;
SS	8:	6	for love is as strong as *d*,
Isa	53:	12	he poured out his life unto *d*,
Jer	21:	8	the way of life and the way of *d*
Eze	18:	23	pleasure in the *d* of the wicked?
Da	9:	26	the Anointed One will be put to *d*
Hos	13:	14	Where, O *d*, are your plagues?
Jn	5:	24	has crossed over from *d* to life
	8:	51	obeys my word will never see *d*.'
Ro	4:	25	delivered over to *d* for our sins
	5:	14	*d* reigned from the time of Adam
	6:	23	For the wages of sin is *d*,
	7:	24	rescue me from this body of *d*?
	8:	13	put to *d* the misdeeds of the body,
	8:	36	'For your sake we face *d* all day
1Co	15:	21	since *d* came through a man
	15:	26	The last enemy to be destroyed is *d*
	15:	55	'Where, O *d*, is your victory?'
Php	3:	10	becoming like him in his *d*
Col	3:	5	Put to *d*, therefore, whatever
2Ti	1:	10	Christ Jesus, who has destroyed *d*
Heb	2:	14	him who holds the power of *d*
1Jn	3:	14	we have passed from *d* to life,
	5:	16	There is a sin that leads to *d*.
Rev	1:	18	And I hold the keys of *d* and Hades
	2:	10	Be faithful, even to the point of *d*
	20:	14	Then *d* and Hades were thrown into
	21:	4	There will be no more *d*

deliver, -ed, -er, -ance

Ex	14:	13	the *d-ance* the LORD will bring you
2Sa	22:	2	my rock, my fortress and my *d-er*
2Ch	20:	17	see the *d-ance* the LORD will give
Ps	3:	8	From the LORD comes *d-ance*.
	18:	2	my rock, my fortress and my *d-er*;

	32:	7 surround me with songs of *d-ance*.
	34:	4 he *d-ed* me from all my fears
	40:	17 You are my help and my *d-er;*
	72:	12 For he will *d* the needy who cry out
	140:	7 Sovereign LORD, my strong *d-er,*
Da	3:	17 God we serve is able to *d* us
Mt	6:	13 but *d* us from the evil one.
Lk	24:	7 *d-ed* over to the hands of sinners,
Ro	4:	25 *d-ed* over to death for our sins
	11:	26 'The *d-er* will come from Zion;
2Co	1:	10 he will continue to *d* us,

demon, -s

Mt	7:	22 and in your name drive out *d-s*
	8:	31 The *d-s* begged Jesus,
	12:	27 And if I drive out *d-s* by Beelzebub
Jn	8:	49 'I am not possessed by a *d,'*
Ro	8:	38 neither angels nor *d-s,*
1Co	10:	20 are offered to *d-s,* not to God,
1Ti	4:	1 spirits and things taught by *d-s*
Jas	2:	19 Good! Even the *d-s* believe that –

desert

Ps	107:	4 Some wandered in *d* wastelands,
	107:	35 He turned the *d* into pools of water
Isa	32:	2 like streams of water in the *d*

desire, -s, -d

Ge	3:	16 Your *d* will be for your husband,
Ps	20:	4 May he give you the *d* of your heart
	73:	25 earth has nothing I *d* besides you
	103:	5 satisfies your *d-s* with good things
Pr	19:	22 What a person *d-s* is unfailing love;
Hos	6:	6 For I *d* mercy, not sacrifice,
Hag	2:	7 what is *d-d* by all nations will come,
Mt	9:	13 learn what this means: "I *d* mercy,
Ro	8:	5 minds set on what the Spirit *d-s*
1Co	12:	31 Now eagerly *d* the greater gifts.
Gal	5:	16 not gratify the *d-s* of the flesh.
Php	1:	23 I *d* to depart and be with Christ,
Col	3:	5 impurity, lust, evil *d-s* and greed,
2Ti	2:	22 Flee the evil *d-s* of youth
Jas	1:	15 *d* has conceived, it gives birth
	4:	1 your *d-s* that battle within you
1Jn	2:	17 The world and its *d-s* pass away,

destroy, -s, -ing, -ed

Ge	9:	11 a flood to *d* the earth.
	18:	32 'For the sake of ten, I will not *d*
	19:	29 God *d-ed* the cities of the plain,
Est	9:	24 plotted against the Jews to *d* them
Job	19:	26 And after my skin has been *d-ed,*
Ps	5:	6 You *d* those who tell lies.
Isa	11:	9 nor *d* on all my holy mountain,
Jer	51:	55 The LORD will *d* Babylon;
Da	2:	44 a kingdom that will never be *d-ed,*
Mt	6:	19 on earth, where moth and rust *d,*
	10:	28 One who can *d* both soul and body
Mk	1:	24 Have you come to *d* us?
	14:	58 "I will *d* this temple made
Lk	6:	9 to do evil, to save life or to *d* it
	17:	27 the flood came and *d-ed* them all
Jn	2:	19 Jesus answered them, '*D* this
Ac	6:	14 Jesus of Nazareth will *d* this place
	8:	3 But Saul began to *d* the church.
Ro	14:	15 not by your eating *d* someone
	14:	20 Do not *d* the work of God
1Co	3:	17 If anyone *d-s* God's temple,
	6:	13 and God will *d* them both.
	10:	10 and were killed by the *d-ing* angel
	15:	26 The last enemy to be *d-ed* is death
Gal	1:	13 the church of God and tried to *d* it
Eph	2:	14 two groups, one and has *d-ed* the barrier
2Ti	1:	10 Christ Jesus, who has *d-ed* death

2Pe	3:	10 the elements will be *d-ed* by fire,
1Jn	3:	8 appeared was to *d* the devil's work

devil, -'s

Mt	4:	1 the wilderness to be tempted by the *d*
	4:	8 the *d* took him to a very high
	4:	11 Then the *d* left him,
	13:	39 the enemy who sows them is the *d.*
	25:	41 the eternal fire prepared for the *d*
Lk	4:	3 The *d* said to him, 'If you are
	8:	12 then the *d* comes and takes away
Jn	6:	70 Yet one of you is a *d!*
	8:	44 You belong to your father, the *d,*
	13:	2 the *d* had already prompted Judas
Ac	10:	38 who were under the power of the *d,*
Eph	4:	27 and do not give the *d* a foothold
	6:	11 your stand against the *d-'s* schemes
1Ti	3:	6 under the same judgment as the *d*
Heb	2:	14 the power of death – that is, the *d*
Jas	4:	7 Resist the *d,* and he will flee
1Pe	5:	8 Your enemy the *d* prowls around
1Jn	3:	8 was to destroy the *d-'s* work
Rev	12:	9 that ancient snake called the *d,*
	20:	10 And the *d,* who deceived them,

die, -s, -d

Ge	2:	17 you eat of it you will certainly *d*
	3:	3 must not touch it, or you will *d.'*
	3:	4 'You will not certainly *d,'*
Ex	11:	5 Every firstborn son in Egypt will *d*
Ru	1:	17 Where you *d* I will *d,* and there
2Sa	12:	5 the man who did this must *d!*
1Ch	10:	13 Saul *d-d* because he was unfaithful
Job	2:	9 Curse God and *d!*
	14:	14 If someone *d-s,* will they live again?
Pr	10:	21 but fools *d* for lack of sense
Ecc	3:	2 a time to be born and a time to *d,*
Isa	6:	1 In the year that King Uzziah *d-d,*
	22:	13 you say, 'for tomorrow we *d!*
	66:	24 their worm will not *d*
Eze	3:	18 that wicked person will *d* for their sin,
	18:	4 one who sins is the one who will *d*
	18:	31 Why will you *d,* house of Israel
Mt	26:	52 draw the sword will *d* by the sword
Mk	9:	48 where ' "their worm does not *d,*
Jn	11:	25 in me will live, even though they *d*
	11:	26 by believing in me will never *d.*
	11:	50 it is better for you that one man *d*
	12:	24 wheat falls to the ground and *d-s,*
Ro	5:	6 Christ *d-d* for the ungodly
	5:	7 will anyone *d* for a righteous person
	5:	8 still sinners, Christ *d-d* for us
	6:	8 Now if we *d-d* with Christ,
	6:	10 The death he *d-d,* he *d-d* to sin
	7:	4 brothers ... you also *d-d* to the law
	14:	8 and if we *d,* we *d* to the Lord.
1Co	15:	3 that Christ *d-d* for our sins
	15:	22 For as in Adam all *d,* so in Christ
	15:	32 eat and drink, for tomorrow we *d*
2Co	5:	14 are convinced that one *d-d* for all
Php	1:	21 to live is Christ and to *d* is gain
Col	2:	20 Since you *d-d* with Christ
	3:	3 you *d-d,* and your life is now
1Th	4:	14 we believe that Jesus *d-d* and rose
2Ti	2:	11 If we *d-d* with him, we will also
Heb	9:	27 Just as people are destined to *d* once,
1Pe	2:	24 so that we might *d* to sins and live
Rev	2:	8 who *d-d* and came to life again
	14:	13 the dead who *d* in the Lord

disciple, -s, -s'

Mt	10:	1 Jesus called his twelve *d-s* to him
	10:	42 little ones who is my *d,*
	26:	26 broke it and gave it to his *d-s,*

	26:	56	all the *d-s* deserted him and fled
	28:	19	go and make *d-s* of all nations,
Mk	4:	34	when he was alone with his own *d-s*,
Lk	14:	27	cross and follow me cannot be my *d*.
	19:	37	*d-s* began joyfully to praise God
	22:	11	I may eat the Passover with my *d-s*?
Jn	2:	11	and his *d-s* put their faith in him
	4:	2	not Jesus who baptised, but his *d-s*
	6:	66	many of his *d-s* turned back
	8:	31	my teaching, you are really my *d-s*
	12:	16	At first his *d-s* did not understand
	13:	5	and began to wash his *d-s'* feet,
	13:	35	everyone will know that you are my *d-s*,
	15:	8	showing yourselves to be my *d-s*
	19:	26	the *d* whom he loved standing
	19:	38	a *d* of Jesus, but secretly
	20:	2	the other *d*, the one Jesus loved,
Ac	6:	1	the number of *d-s* was increasing,
	11:	26	*d-s* were called Christians first
	14:	22	strengthening the *d-s*

drink, -s, -ing

Ex	17:	2	Give us water to *d*.' Moses replied
	32:	6	they sat down to eat and *d*
Pr	5:	15	*D* water from your own cistern,
	25:	21	he is thirsty, give him water to *d*
Mt	6:	25	your life, what you will eat or *d*;
	11:	19	Son of Man came eating and *d-ing*,
	20:	22	*d* the cup I am going to drink?'
	25:	37	thirsty and give you something to *d*
	26:	27	saying, '*D* from it, all of you
	27:	48	and offered it to Jesus to *d*
Mk	14:	25	I will not *d* again of the fruit
Lk	5:	30	*d* with tax collectors and sinners?
	12:	19	Take life easy; eat, *d* and be merry
Jn	4:	14	whoever *d-s* the water I give them
	6:	54	and *d-s* my blood has eternal life,
	7:	37	who is thirsty come to me and *d*
	18:	11	Shall I not *d* the cup the Father
1Co	10:	4	and drank the same spiritual *d*;
	10:	7	'The people sat down to eat and *d*
	11:	27	or *d-s* the cup of the Lord
	12:	13	were all given the one Spirit to *d*
Php	2:	17	being poured out like a *d* offering
Rev	14:	10	will *d* of the wine of God's fury,

dust

Ge	2:	7	the man from the *d* of the ground
	3:	14	and you will eat *d* all the days
	3:	19	for *d* you are and to *d* you will
Ps	22:	15	you lay me in the *d* of death
	90:	3	'Return to *d*, you mortals.
	103:	14	he remembers that we are *d*
	113:	7	He raises the poor from the *d*
Mt	10:	14	shake the *d* off your feet
Ac	13:	51	So they shook the *d* off their feet
1Co	15:	47	The first man was of the *d*

dwell, -s, -ing, -ings

Dt	12:	11	will choose as a *d-ing* for his Name
2Sa	7:	5	the one to build me a house to *d* in
1Ki	8:	27	'But will God really *d* on earth?
Ps	15:	1	LORD, who may *d* in your sacred
	23:	6	I will *d* in the house of the LORD
Lk	16:	9	be welcomed into eternal *d-ings*
Jn	5:	38	nor does his word *d* in you,
1Co	3:	16	and that God's Spirit *d-s* among you
2Co	5:	2	be clothed ... with our heavenly *d-ing*
Eph	3:	17	that Christ may *d* in your hearts
Col	1:	19	to have all his fullness *d* in him
	3:	16	Let the message of Christ *d* among you
2Pe	3:	13	new earth, where righteousness *d-s*
Rev	21:	3	God's *d-ing*-place is now among the people,

e

ear, -s

Ex	21:	6	pierce his *e* with an awl.
2Ch	6:	40	your *e-s* attentive to the prayers
Job	42:	5	My *e-s* had heard of you
Ps	40:	6	my *e-s* you have opened –
	44:	1	We have heard with our *e-s*, O God;
Isa	6:	10	make their *e-s* dull and close
Mt	11:	15	Whoever has *e-s*, let them hear
Ac	28:	27	they hardly hear with their *e-s*,
1Co	2:	9	'What no eye has seen, what no *e* has heard,
	12:	16	And if the *e* should say,
2Ti	4:	3	their itching *e-s* want to hear
Rev	2:	7	Whoever has *e-s*, let them hear

earth, -'s, -ly

Ge	1:	1	God created the heavens and the *e*
	1:	28	fill the *e* and subdue it.
	7:	24	The waters flooded the *e*
	8:	22	*e* endures, seedtime and harvest,
Jos	23:	14	to go the way of all the *e*.
1Ki	8:	27	will God really dwell on *e*?
Job	38:	4	when I laid the *e-'s* foundation?
Ps	2:	8	the ends of the *e* your possession
	8:	1	majestic is your name in all the *e*!
	24:	1	The *e* is the LORD's,
	46:	2	though the *e* give way
	96:	13	he comes to judge the *e*.
	97:	1	LORD reigns, let the *e* be glad;
	103:	11	as the heavens are above the *e*,
Isa	6:	3	the whole *e* is full of his glory.
	40:	22	enthroned above the circle of the *e*
	45:	22	be saved, all you ends of the *e*;
	55:	9	the heavens are higher than the *e*,
	65:	17	create new heavens and a new *e*.
Da	4:	17	sovereign over the kingdoms on *e*
Hab	2:	14	For the *e* will be filled
Mt	6:	10	be done, on *e* as it is in heaven.
	16:	19	whatever you bind on *e* will be
	24:	35	Heaven and *e* will pass away,
	28:	18	All authority in heaven and on *e*
Lk	2:	14	and on *e* peace to those
Jn	3:	12	have spoken to you of *e-ly* things
	12:	32	when I am lifted up from the *e*,
Ro	1:	3	his Son, who as to his *e-ly* life
1Co	10:	26	'The *e* is the Lord's
	15:	40	there are *e-ly* bodies;
Eph	3:	15	in heaven and on *e* derives its name
	4:	9	to the lower, *e-ly* regions
	6:	5	Slaves, obey your *e-ly* masters
Php	2:	10	in heaven and on *e*
	3:	19	Their mind is set on *e-ly* things
Col	3:	2	things above, not on *e-ly* things
	3:	5	belongs to your *e-ly* nature:
Heb	9:	1	and also an *e-ly* sanctuary
Jas	3:	15	heaven but is *e-ly*, unspiritual,
1Pe	4:	2	*e-ly* lives for evil human desires,
2Pe	3:	13	a new heaven and a new *e*,
Rev	20:	11	*e* and the heavens fled from his presence,
	21:	1	Then I saw 'a new heaven and a new *e*

eat, -s, -ing

Ge	2:	16	free to *e* from any tree
	2:	17	*e* from the tree of the knowledge
	3:	14	*e* dust all the days of your life
Lev	7:	27	Anyone who *e-s* blood must be cut off
Dt	8:	16	gave you manna to *e* in the wilderness,
1Ki	19:	5	'Get up and *e*.
Ps	22:	26	The poor will *e* and be satisfied;
Pr	25:	21	enemy is hungry, give him food to *e*
Isa	51:	8	moth will *e* them up like a garment;
	55:	1	have no money, come, buy and *e*!

	65: 25	lion will *e* straw like the ox,
Eze	3: 1	'Son of man, *e* what is before you
Da	4: 25	you will *e* grass like the ox
Mt	6: 25	what you will *e* or drink;
	14: 16	You give them something to *e*.
	24: 38	before the flood, people were *e-ing*
	25: 35	you gave me something to *e*,
	26: 26	'Take and *e; this is my body.'
Jn	4: 32	food to *e* that you know nothing
	6: 31	gave them bread from heaven to *e*."
	6: 52	this man give us his flesh to *e*?
	6: 54	*e-s* my flesh and drinks my blood
Ro	14: 17	not a matter of *e-ing* and drinking,
1Co	5: 11	Do not even *e* with such people.
	8: 13	if what I *e* causes my brother or
	10: 31	So whether you *e* or drink or
	11: 20	it is not the Lord's Supper you *e*
	11: 26	whenever you *e* this bread and drink
	15: 32	'Let us *e* and drink, for tomorrow
Col	2: 16	judge you by what you *e* or drink,
2Th	3: 10	unwilling to work shall not *e*.
Rev	3: 20	I will come in and *e* with that person,

Egypt, -ians

Ge	12: 10	Abram went down to *E* to live there
	15: 18	the Wadi of *E* to the great river,
Ex	1: 15	of *E* said to the Hebrew midwives,
	3: 7	seen the misery of my people in *E*.
	3: 12	brought the people out of *E*,
	7: 5	*E-ians* will know that I am the
	10: 22	total darkness covered all *E*
	12: 40	people lived in *E* was 430 years
	20: 2	God, who brought you out of *E*,
Nu	11: 18	We were better off in *E*!'
	14: 4	choose a leader and go back to *E*.
Dt	5: 15	Remember that you were slaves in *E*
2Ki	18: 21	you are depending on *E*,
Ps	80: 8	You transplanted a vine from *E*;
Isa	19: 23	a highway from *E* to Assyria.
	31: 1	Woe to those who go down to *E*
Hos	11: 1	out of *E* I called my son
Mt	2: 13	his mother and escape to *E*.
	2: 15	'Out of *E* I called my son.
	2: 19	a dream to Joseph in *E*
Heb	11: 27	By faith he left *E*,
	11: 29	but when the *E-ians* tried to do so,

elder, -s

Nu	11: 16	'Bring me seventy of Israel's *e-s*
Mt	15: 2	break the tradition of the *e-s*?
Ac	4: 8	'Rulers and *e-s* of the people
	14: 23	Paul and Barnabas appointed *e-s*
	15: 4	church and the apostles and *e-s*,
	20: 17	Paul sent to Ephesus for the *e-s*
1Ti	5: 17	The *e-s* who direct the affairs
	5: 19	an accusation against an *e*
Tit	1: 6	An *e* must be blameless,
Jas	5: 14	Let them call the *e-s*
Rev	4: 4	on them were twenty-four *e-s*.
	7: 13	Then one of the *e-s* asked me,
	19: 4	The twenty-four *e-s* and the four

encourage, -ing, -d, -ment

Ac	4: 36	Barnabas (which means 'son of *e-ment*
	9: 31	*e-d* by the Holy Spirit,
	11: 23	*e-d* them all to remain true
	14: 22	*e-ing* them all to remain true
Ro	1: 12	mutually *e-d* by each other's faith
	12: 8	if it is to *e*, then give *e-ment*;
	15: 4	taught in the Scriptures and the *e-ment*
Php	2: 1	any *e-ment* from being united
1Th	4: 18	*e* one another with these words
	5: 14	*e* the disheartened, help the weak,
2Ti	4: 2	*e* – with great patience

Heb	3: 13	But *e* one another daily,
	10: 25	but *e-ing* one another –
	12: 5	forgotten this word of *e-ment*

end, -s

Job	19: 25	redeemer lives, and that in the *e*
Ps	2: 8	inheritance, the *e-s* of the earth
	46: 9	He makes wars cease to the *e-s*
Pr	16: 25	but in the *e* it leads to death
Ecc	12: 12	making many books there is no *e*,
Isa	9: 7	there will be no *e*. He will reign
	40: 28	Creator of the *e-s* of the earth.
	45: 22	be saved, all you *e-s* of the earth;
Mt	13: 39	The harvest is the *e* of the age,
	24: 13	stands firm to the *e* will be saved
Jn	11: 4	This illness will not *e* in death.
	13: 1	he loved them to the *e*
1Co	15: 24	Then the *e* will come,
Heb	3: 14	if we hold firmly till the *e*
Rev	21: 6	the Beginning and the *E*.

endure, -s, -ing, -d, -ance

Ge	8: 22	long as the earth *e-s*, seedtime
2Sa	7: 16	your kingdom shall *e* for ever
Ps	107: 1	his love *e-s* for ever
Da	4: 3	his dominion *e-s* from generation
Mal	3: 2	who can *e* the day of his coming?
Jn	6: 27	for food that *e-s* to eternal life,
Ro	15: 4	so that through the *e-ance* taught
2Ti	2: 10	Therefore I *e* everything for
Heb	12: 2	set before him he *e-d* the cross,
	13: 14	here we do not have an *e-ing* city,
1Pe	1: 25	the word of the Lord *e-s* for ever.'

enemy, -ies

Nu	10: 35	May your *e-ies* be scattered;
Jos	5: 13	for us or for our *e-ies*?
1Ki	21: 20	you have found me, my *e*!'
Ps	8: 2	a stronghold against your *e-ies*,
	23: 5	me in the presence of my *e-ies*.
	69: 4	many are my *e-ies* without cause,
	110: 1	I make your *e-ies* a footstool
Pr	24: 17	Do not gloat when your *e* falls;
	25: 21	*e* is hungry, give him food to eat;
La	3: 52	my *e-ies* without cause
Mic	7: 8	Do not gloat over me, my *e*!
Mt	5: 43	Love your neighbour and hate your *e*
	10: 36	a man's *e-ies* will be the members
	13: 25	his *e* came and sowed weeds
	13: 28	"An *e* did this," he replied.
	22: 44	I put your *e-ies* under your feet.'
Lk	1: 71	salvation from our *e-ies*
	10: 19	overcome all the power of the *e*;
Ro	5: 10	God's *e-ies*, we were reconciled
	12: 20	'If your *e* is hungry, feed him;
1Co	15: 25	all his *e-ies* under his feet
	15: 26	last *e* to be destroyed is death
Gal	4: 16	Have I now become your *e*
Php	3: 18	many live as *e-ies* of the cross
Col	1: 21	*e-ies* in your minds because
Heb	1: 13	I make your *e-ies* a footstool
1Pe	5: 8	Your *e* the devil prowls around

enter, -s, -ed

Ps	73: 17	I *e-ed* the sanctuary of God;
	95: 11	"They shall never *e* my rest.
	100: 4	*E* his gates with thanksgiving
Isa	51: 11	They will *e* Zion with singing;
Mt	5: 20	not *e* the kingdom of heaven
	7: 13	and many *e* through it
	7: 21	"Lord, Lord," will *e* the kingdom
	12: 29	how can anyone *e* a strong man's
	15: 17	whatever *e-s* the mouth goes into
	18: 8	It is better for you to *e* life

	19:	23	for someone ... rich to *e* the kingdom
Mk	9:	43	to *e* life maimed
Lk	24:	26	to suffer these things and then *e*
Jn	3:	4	*e* a second time into their mother's
	10:	1	anyone who does not *e* the sheepfold
Ac	14:	22	many hardships to *e* the kingdom
Ro	5:	12	sin *e-ed* the world through one man
Heb	3:	11	"They shall never *e* my rest."
	9:	12	did not *e* by means of the blood
	9:	24	Christ did not *e* a sanctuary
	10:	19	confidence to *e* the Most Holy

establish, -es, -ed

Ge	6:	18	I will *e* my covenant with you,
2Sa	3:	10	*e* David's throne over Israel
Ps	9:	7	has *e-ed* his throne for judgment
	96:	10	The world is firmly *e-ed*,
Isa	2:	2	the LORD's temple will be *e-ed*
	62:	7	no rest till he *e-es* Jerusalem
Mt	18:	16	"every matter may be *e-ed*
Ro	13:	1	except that which God has *e-ed*.
Gal	3:	15	covenant that has been duly *e-ed*,
Eph	3:	17	being rooted and *e-ed* in love

eternal

Ge	21:	33	name of the LORD, the *E* God
Dt	33:	27	The *e* God is your refuge,
Ps	16:	11	*e* pleasures at your right hand
	119:	89	Your word, LORD, is *e*;
Da	4:	3	His kingdom is an *e* kingdom;
Mt	18:	8	and be thrown into *e* fire
	19:	16	good thing must I do to get *e*
	25:	41	the *e* fire prepared for the devil
Jn	3:	16	shall not perish but have *e* life
	4:	14	water welling up to *e* life.
	6:	54	and drinks my blood has *e* life,
	10:	28	I give them *e* life,
	17:	3	Now this is *e* life:
Ac	13:	48	appointed for *e* life believed
Ro	6:	23	the gift of God is *e* life
2Co	4:	17	achieving for us an *e* glory
	4:	18	but what is unseen is *e*
Eph	3:	11	according to his *e* purpose
1Ti	1:	17	the King *e*, immortal, invisible,
Heb	5:	9	became the source of *e* salvation
	9:	14	through the *e* Spirit offered
	13:	20	through the blood of the *e* covenant
1Jn	5:	11	God has given us *e* life,

evil

Ge	2:	9	of the knowledge of good and *e*
	3:	5	like God, knowing good and *e*.
	6:	5	heart was only *e* all the time
Jdg	2:	11	Israelites did *e* in the eyes of
1Sa	16:	14	an *e* spirit from the LORD
1Ki	11:	6	Solomon did *e* in the eyes
Job	1:	1	he feared God and shunned *e*
Ps	23:	4	I will fear no *e*,
	51:	4	done what is *e* in your sight,
	52:	3	You love *e* rather than good,
Pr	3:	7	fear the LORD and shun *e*
Isa	1:	13	I cannot bear your *e* assemblies
	5:	20	Woe to those who call *e* good
Hab	1:	13	eyes are too pure to look on *e*;
Mt	5:	11	falsely say all kinds of *e* against
	6:	13	deliver us from the *e* one.
	7:	11	If you, then, though you are *e*,
Jn	3:	19	light because their deeds were *e*
	5:	29	those who have done what is *e*
Ro	1:	29	wickedness, *e*, greed and depravity.
	6:	12	mortal body so that you obey its *e*
	7:	19	the *e* I do not want to do – this
	12:	9	Hate what is *e*;
	12:	17	Do not repay anyone *e* for *e*.

1Co	13:	6	Love does not delight in *e*
Eph	5:	16	because the days are *e*
1Ti	6:	10	money is a root of all kinds of *e*.
1Pe	1:	14	do not conform to the *e* desires
	2:	16	freedom as a cover-up for *e*;
1Jn	2:	13	you have overcome the *e* one.

eye, -s

Ge	3:	5	your *e-s* will be opened,
Ex	21:	24	*e* for *e*, tooth for tooth,
Dt	32:	10	guarded him as the apple of his *e*,
Jdg	16:	21	gouged out his *e-s*
Job	42:	5	now my *e-s* have seen you
Ps	19:	8	giving light to the *e-s*
	33:	18	the *e-s* of the LORD are on those
	118:	23	and it is marvellous in our *e-s*
	121:	1	I lift up my *e-s* to the mountains –
Pr	15:	30	messenger's *e-s* brings joy to the heart,
SS	1:	15	Your *e-s* are doves
Isa	5:	21	who are wise in their own *e-s*
	6:	10	ears dull and close their *e-s*.
	35:	5	the *e-s* of the blind be opened
	40:	26	your *e-s* and look to the heavens:
	64:	4	ear has perceived, no *e* has seen
Hab	1:	13	Your *e-s* are too pure to look
Mal	2:	17	evil are good in the *e-s*
Mt	5:	29	your right *e* causes you to stumble,
	5:	38	"*E* for *e*, and tooth for tooth.
	6:	22	'The *e* is the lamp of the body.
	7:	3	sawdust in your brother's *e*
	18:	9	to have two *e-s* and be thrown
	19:	24	to go through the *e* of a needle
	21:	42	and it is marvellous in our *e-s*"
Lk	2:	30	my *e-s* have seen your salvation
Jn	4:	35	open your *e-s* and look
	9:	15	'He put mud on my *e-s*,'
	12:	40	'He has blinded their *e-s*
Ac	1:	9	taken up before their very *e-s*,
	4:	19	Which is right in God's *e-s*
	9:	18	like scales fell from Saul's *e-s*,
Ro	3:	18	no fear of God before their *e-s*.
1Co	2:	9	'What no *e* has seen, what no ear
	12:	16	'Because I am not an *e*,
	15:	52	in the twinkling of an *e*,
Eph	1:	18	that the *e-s* of your heart
	6:	6	favour when their *e* is on you,
Heb	4:	13	laid bare before the *e-s* of him
	12:	2	fixing our *e-s* on Jesus,
1Pe	3:	12	For the *e-s* of the LORD are on
1Jn	1:	1	which we have seen with our *e-s*,
Rev	1:	7	every *e* will see him,
	1:	14	his *e-s* were like blazing fire
	7:	17	every tear from their *e-s*.

f

face, -s

Ge	32:	30	'It is because I saw God *f* to *f*
Ex	3:	6	At this, Moses hid his *f*,
	33:	11	LORD would speak to Moses *f* to *f*
	33:	20	'you cannot see my *f*
	34:	30	saw Moses, his *f* was radiant,
Nu	6:	25	the LORD make his *f* shine on you
1Ch	16:	11	seek his *f* always
2Ch	7:	14	and pray and seek my *f* and turn
Ps	27:	8	My heart says of you, 'Seek his *f*!
	44:	22	for your sake we *f* death all day
Pr	15:	13	A happy heart makes the *f* cheerful,
Isa	50:	7	have I set my *f* like flint,
	54:	8	I hid my *f* from you for a moment,
	59:	2	your sins have hidden his *f*

Mt	17:	2	His *f*shone like the sun,
	18:	10	always see the *f* of my Father
Jn	19:	3	And they slapped him in the *f*
Ro	8:	36	'For your sake we *f*death all day
1Co	13:	12	then we shall see *f*to *f.*
2Co	3:	18	who with unveiled *f-s* contemplate
	4:	6	God's glory displayed in the *f*of Christ
Rev	1:	16	His *f*was like the sun shining
	22:	4	They will see his *f,* and his name

faith

Isa	7:	9	If you do not stand firm in your *f,*
Mt	6:	30	– you of little *f?*
	8:	10	anyone in Israel with such great *f.*
	9:	22	'your *f*has healed you.'
	15:	28	'Woman, you have great *f!*
	17:	20	'Because you have so little *f.*
	21:	21	if you have *f*and do not doubt,
Mk	11:	22	Have *f*in God,' Jesus answered
Lk	17:	6	*f*as small as a mustard seed,
	18:	8	will he find *f*on the earth?
Jn	2:	11	his disciples put their *f*in him
Ac	3:	16	By *f*in the name of Jesus,
	6:	5	Stephen, a man full of *f*
	11:	24	full of the Holy Spirit and *f,*
	15:	9	for he purified their hearts by *f*
	26:	18	those who are sanctified by *f*in me
Ro	1:	5	to the obedience that comes from *f*
	1:	17	a righteousness that is by *f*
	3:	25	blood – to be received by *f*
	3:	26	justifies those who have *f*in Jesus
	4:	5	their *f*is credited as righteousness
	4:	12	the *f*that our father Abraham had
	4:	16	Therefore, the promise comes by *f,*
	5:	1	we have been justified through *f,*
	10:	17	*f*comes from hearing the message,
	12:	6	prophesy in accordance with your *f;*
	14:	1	Accept the one whose *f*is weak,
	14:	2	person's *f*allows them to eat
1Co	12:	9	to another *f*by the same Spirit,
	13:	2	a *f*that can move mountains,
	13:	13	three remain: *f,* hope and love.
	15:	14	is useless and so is your *f.*
2Co	10:	15	as your *f*continues to grow,
Gal	2:	20	I live by *f*in the Son of God,
	3:	11	'the righteous will live by *f.*
	3:	26	you are all children of God through *f*
Eph	2:	8	you have been saved, through *f*
	3:	17	may dwell in your hearts through *f.*
	4:	5	one Lord, one *f,* one baptism;
	4:	13	until we all reach unity in the *f*
	6:	16	take up the shield of *f,*
Php	1:	27	striving together as one for the *f*
Col	1:	23	if you continue in your *f,*
1Th	3:	10	supply what is lacking in your *f*
1Ti	4:	1	some will abandon the *f*
	4:	6	nourished on the truths of the *f*
	6:	11	pursue righteousness, godliness, *f,*
	6:	12	Fight the good fight of the *f.*
	6:	21	so doing have departed from the *f.*
2Ti	1:	5	reminded of your sincere *f,*
	3:	15	salvation through *f*in Christ Jesus
	4:	7	I have kept the *f*
Heb	4:	14	hold firmly to the *f*we profess
	11:	1	*f*is being sure of what we hope for
	11:	6	And without *f*it is impossible
Jas	2:	26	so *f*without deeds is dead
1Pe	1:	9	receiving the end result of your *f,*
2Pe	1:	5	add to your *f*goodness;
1Jn	5:	4	has overcome the world, even our *f*
Jude	:	3	and urge you to contend for the *f*
Rev	2:	19	I know your deeds, your love and *f,*

faithful, -ness

Dt	7:	9	the *f*God, keeping his covenant
2Sa	22:	26	To the *f*you show yourself *f*
Ps	16:	10	will you let your *f*one see decay
	51:	6	you desired *f-ness* even in the womb;
	57:	10	your *f-ness* reaches to the skies
	85:	10	Love and *f-ness* meet together;
	100:	5	his *f-ness* continues through all
	116:	15	death of his *f*servants
	145:	13	promises and *f*in all he does
Pr	3:	3	Let love and *f-ness* never leave you
Isa	55:	3	my *f*love promised to David
La	3:	23	every morning; great is your *f-ness*
Hab	2:	4	righteous person will live by his *f-ness*
Mt	25:	21	"Well done, good and *f*servant!
Ro	12:	12	patient in affliction, *f*in prayer
1Co	10:	13	God is *f;*
Gal	5:	22	kindness, goodness, *f-ness*
1Th	5:	24	The one who calls you is *f*
Heb	3:	5	Moses was *f*as a servant
	3:	6	But Christ is *f*as the Son
1Jn	1:	9	confess our sins, he is *f*and just
Rev	2:	10	Be *f,* even to the point of death,

fall, -s, -en

Dt	32:	2	Let my teaching *f* like rain
2Sa	1:	27	'How the mighty have *f-en!*
Ps	37:	24	though he may stumble, he will not *f,*
	46:	5	God is within her, she will not *f;*
	69:	9	of those who insult you *f*on me
Pr	11:	14	For lack of guidance a nation *f-s,*
	16:	18	a haughty spirit before a *f*
Isa	14:	12	How you have *f-en* from heaven,
	40:	7	The grass withers and the flowers *f*
Eze	33:	21	to me and said, 'The city has *f-en!*
Da	3:	5	must *f*down and worship the image
Hos	10:	8	and to the hills, '*F*on us!
Mt	13:	21	they quickly *f*away
	26:	31	This very night you will all *f*away
Lk	8:	13	in the time of testing they *f*away
	10:	18	'I saw Satan *f*like lightning
	23:	30	say to the mountains, '*F*on us!'
Ro	3:	23	and *f*short of the glory of God
	14:	21	cause your brother or sister to *f*
	15:	3	who insult you *f*on me.
1Co	10:	12	be careful that you don't *f*
Gal	5:	4	you have *f-en* away from grace
Heb	10:	31	*f*into the hands of the living God
1Pe	1:	24	the grass withers and the flowers *f*
Rev	14:	8	"*F-en! F-en* is Babylon the Great,

false, -ly, -hood

Ex	20:	16	'You shall not give *f*testimony
La	2:	14	The visions of your prophets were *f*
Mt	7:	15	'Watch out for *f*prophets.
	19:	18	you shall not give *f*testimony
	24:	24	*f*messiahs and *f*prophets
Mk	14:	56	Many testified *f-ly*against him,
2Co	11:	26	in danger from *f* believers
Eph	4:	25	put off *f-hood*and speak truthfully
1Ti	1:	3	not to teach *f*doctrines any longer
1Jn	4:	1	many *f*prophets have gone out
	4:	6	of truth and the spirit of *f-hood*

family, -ies

Ge	7:	1	into the ark, you and your whole *f,*
Ps	68:	6	God sets the lonely in *f-ies,*
Pr	31:	15	she provides food for her *f*
Mk	3:	21	When his *f* heard about this,
Lk	9:	61	go back and say good-bye to my *f.*
	12:	52	in one *f*divided against each other
Ac	10:	2	He and all his *f*were devout
Gal	6:	10	who belong to the *f*of believers
Eph	3:	15	every *f*in heaven and on earth

1Th	4:	10	love all of God's *f* throughout Macedonia
1Ti	3:	4	He must manage his own *f* well
	5:	4	by caring for their own *f*
Heb	2:	11	who are made holy are of the same *f*

father, -'s, -s

Ge	2:	24	a man will leave his *f* and mother
	17:	4	you will be the *f* of many nations
Ex	20:	12	'Honour your *f* and your mother,
	21:	17	'Anyone who curses their *f* or mother
Dt	1:	31	carried you, as a *f* carries his son
	27:	16	who dishonours their *f* or mother.
	32:	6	Is he not your *F*, your Creator,
2Sa	7:	14	I will be his *f*, and he will be
2Ki	2:	12	'My *f*! My *f*! The chariots
1Ch	22:	10	will be my son, and I will be his *f*
Job	29:	16	I was a *f* to the needy;
Ps	2:	7	my Son; today I have become your *F*
	27:	10	Though my father mother forsake me,
	68:	5	A *f* to the fatherless,
	89:	26	"You are my *F*, my God, the Rock
	103:	13	As a *f* has compassion
Pr	10:	1	A wise son brings joy to his *f*
	23:	22	Listen to your *f*, who gave you life
Isa	9:	6	Everlasting *F*, Prince of Peace
	51:	2	look to Abraham, your *f*,
	63:	16	But you are our *F*, though Abraham
Jer	3:	4	"My *F*, my friend from my youth
	31:	9	because I am Israel's *f*,
Eze	18:	18	his *f* will die for his own sin,
Mal	1:	6	If I am a *f*, where is the honour
Mt	3:	9	"We have Abraham as our *f*."
	5:	16	glorify your *F* in heaven
	6:	9	you should pray: '"Our *F* in heaven
	6:	26	yet your heavenly *F* feeds them.
	10:	37	Anyone who loves their *f* or mother
	11:	27	no one knows the *F* except the Son
	15:	4	"Honour your *f* and mother"
	19:	5	a man will leave his *f* and mother
	19:	19	honour your *f* and mother,
	28:	19	in the name of the *F* and of the Son
Lk	2:	49	I had to be in my *F*-'s house?
	9:	59	first let me go and bury my *f*.'
	11:	11	'Which of you *f*-s, if your son
	14:	26	does not hate *f* and mother,
	15:	12	"*F*, give me my share of the estate
	15:	21	"*F*, I have sinned against heaven
	22:	42	'*F*, if you are willing, take this
	23:	34	'*F*, forgive them, for they do not
Jn	1:	14	who came from the *F*, full of grace
	3:	35	The *F* loves the Son and has placed
	4:	21	you will worship the *F* neither on
	5:	18	he was even calling God his own *F*,
	5:	20	For the *F* loves the Son
	5:	22	the *F* judges no one, but
	6:	44	No one can come to me unless the *F*
	6:	46	No one has seen the *F* except
	8:	19	'You do not know me or my *F*,'
	8:	44	You belong to your *f*, the devil
	10:	29	My *F*, who has given them to me,
	10:	30	I and the *F* are one.'
	10:	38	the *F* is in me, and I in the *F*
	12:	28	*F*, glorify your name!'
	14:	2	My *F*-'s house has plenty of room;
	14:	6	No one comes to the *F* except
	14:	11	I am in the *F*
	14:	23	My *F* will love them,
	15:	9	'As the *F* has loved me, so have I
	16:	15	All that belongs to the *F* is mine.
	16:	27	the *F* himself loves you because
	17:	1	'*F*, the hour has come.
	17:	11	Holy *F*, protect them by the power

	20:	17	"I am ascending to my *F* and
Ac	1:	4	wait for the gift my *F* promised,
Ro	4:	11	he is the *f* of all who believe
	8:	15	by him we cry, 'Abba, *F*
Eph	5:	31	a man will leave his *f* and mother
	6:	2	'Honour your *f* and mother'
	6:	4	*F*-s, do not exasperate your
Php	2:	11	to the glory of God the *F*
Col	3:	21	*F*-s, do not embitter your children
Heb	1:	5	today I have become your *F*'?
	7:	3	Without *f* or mother, without
1Pe	1:	2	the foreknowledge of God the *F*,
1Jn	1:	3	our fellowship is with the *F*
	2:	13	I write to you, because you
	2:	24	remain in the Son and in the *F*.
	4:	14	the *F* has sent his Son to be the
2Jn		3	Jesus Christ, the *F*-'s Son,
		9	teaching has both the *F* and the Son
Jude		1	who are loved in God the *F*
Rev	14:	1	his name and his *F*-'s name written

fear, -s, -ed

Dt	6:	13	*F* the LORD your God,
Job	1:	9	'Does Job *f* God for nothing?'
	28:	28	'The *f* of the Lord – that is wisdom,
Ps	19:	9	The *f* of the LORD is pure,
	23:	4	I will *f* no evil,
	27:	1	my salvation – whom shall I *f*?
	34:	4	he delivered me from all my *f*-s
	76:	7	you alone who are to be *f*-ed.
	103:	13	compassion on those who *f* him
	147:	11	LORD delights in those who *f* him,
Pr	8:	13	To *f* the LORD is to hate evil;
	9:	10	The *f* of the LORD is the beginning
Ecc	12:	13	*f* God and keep his commandments,
Isa	11:	3	will delight in the *f* of the LORD.
	41:	10	So do not *f*, for I am with you;
Lk	12:	5	I will show you whom you should *f*:
Ac	5:	11	Great *f* seized the whole church
	9:	31	Living in the *f* of the Lord
Ro	8:	15	so that you live in *f* again;
2Co	5:	11	we know what it is to *f* the Lord,
Php	2:	12	your salvation with *f* and trembling
Heb	2:	15	held in slavery by their *f* of death
1Pe	3:	6	and do not give way to *f*
1Jn	4:	18	But perfect love drives out *f*,

feast, -s

Mt	26:	5	'But not during the *F*,' they said,
Lk	13:	29	at the *f* in the kingdom of God
	14:	8	someone invites you to a wedding *f*,
	14:	15	eat at the *f* in the kingdom of God
	15:	23	Let's have a *f* and celebrate
Jn	7:	37	the last and greatest day of the *F*,
Jude		12	blemishes at your love *f*-s,

feet

2Sa	9:	3	he is lame in both *f*.
Ps	8:	6	you put everything under their *f*
	110:	1	your enemies a footstool for your *f*
	119:	105	Your word is a lamp to my *f*
Isa	52:	7	the *f* of those who bring good news,
Mt	10:	14	shake the dust off your *f*
	22:	44	I put your enemies under your *f*.'
Lk	10:	39	Mary, who sat at the Lord's *f*
	24:	39	Look at my hands and my *f*. It is I
Jn	12:	3	she poured it on Jesus' *f* and wiped
	13:	5	and began to wash his disciples' *f*,
Ac	2:	35	your enemies a footstool for your *f*
	3:	7	man's *f* and ankles became strong
	13:	51	So they shook the dust off their *f*
Ro	10:	15	'How beautiful are the *f* of those
	16:	20	will soon crush Satan under your *f*.
1Co	12:	21	And the head cannot say to the *f*,

Eph	1:	22	God placed all things under his *f*
1Ti	5:	10	washing the *f* of the Lord's people,
Rev	1:	15	His *f* were like bronze glowing

festival, -s

Ex	5:	1	a *f* to me in the wilderness
	23:	14	you are to celebrate a *f* to me
	23:	15	Celebrate the *F* of Unleavened Bread
	23:	16	'Celebrate the *F* of Harvest
	34:	22	'Celebrate the *F* of Weeks
Lev	23:	2	'These are my appointed *f-s*,
Hos	9:	5	on the day of your appointed *f-s*
Am	5:	21	I despise your religious *f-s*;
1Co	5:	8	Therefore let us keep the *F*
Col	2:	16	or with regard to a religious *f*

field, -s

Ge	4:	8	Abel, 'Let's go out to the *f*.'
Lev	19:	19	"Do not plant your *f* with two kinds
Ps	103:	15	flourish like a flower of the *f*
Isa	40:	6	faithfulness is like the flowers of the *f*
Hab	3:	17	and the *f-s* produce no food,
Mt	6:	28	See how the flowers of the *f* grow.
	9:	38	workers into his harvest *f*.
	13:	24	a man who sowed good seed in his *f*
	13:	38	The *f* is the world,
	24:	40	Two men will be in the *f*;
	27:	10	used them to buy the potter's *f*,
Mk	10:	30	sisters, mothers, children and *f-s* –
	13:	16	Let no one in the *f* go back
Lk	2:	8	shepherds living out in the *f-s*
	14:	18	said, "I have just bought a *f*,
Jn	4:	35	open your eyes and look at the *f-s*
Ac	1:	18	Judas bought a *f*; there he fell
	4:	37	sold a *f* he owned and brought
1Co	3:	9	you are God's *f*, God's building

fight, -s, -ing

Ex	2:	13	went out and saw two Hebrews *f-ing*.
	14:	14	The LORD will *f* for you;
2Ch	20:	17	You will not have to *f* this battle.
Ne	4:	20	Our God will *f* for us!
Ps	35:	1	*f* against those who *f* against me
Jn	18:	36	If it were, my servants would *f*
Ac	5:	39	find yourselves *f-ing* against God.
1Co	9:	26	I do not *f* like a boxer beating
2Co	10:	4	The weapons we *f* with are not
1Ti	6:	12	*F* the good *f* of the faith.
2Ti	4:	7	I have fought the good *f*,
Jas	4:	1	What causes *f-s* and quarrels among

fill, -s, -ed

Ge	1:	28	increase in number; *f* the earth
1Ki	8:	11	glory of the LORD *f-ed* his temple
Ps	16:	11	you will *f* me with joy
	81:	10	Open wide your mouth and I will *f*
	107:	9	and *f-s* the hungry with good things
Hab	2:	14	earth … *f-ed* with the knowledge
Mt	5:	6	for they will be *f-ed*
Lk	3:	5	Every valley shall be *f-ed* in,
Jn	2:	7	servants, '*F* the jars with water'
Ac	2:	4	were *f-ed* with the Holy Spirit
	2:	28	you will *f* me with joy
	4:	31	were all *f-ed* with the Holy Spirit
	9:	17	and be *f-ed* with the Holy Spirit.
	13:	52	the disciples were *f-ed* with joy
	14:	17	food and *f-s* your hearts with joy.
Ro	15:	13	May the God of hope *f* you with
Eph	1:	23	fullness of him who *f-s* everything
	4:	10	in order to *f* the whole universe.
	5:	18	Instead, be *f-ed* with the Spirit
Col	1:	9	to *f* you with the knowledge
	1:	24	and I *f* up in my flesh

find, -s

Ge	18:	26	'If I *f* fifty righteous people
Nu	32:	23	your sin will *f* you out
Dt	4:	29	you will *f* him if you seek him
Ps	62:	5	Yes, my soul, *f* rest in God;
Pr	8:	17	and those who seek me *f* me
	8:	35	For those who *f* me *f* life
Jer	6:	16	and you will *f* rest for your souls.
	29:	13	You will seek me and *f* me
Mt	2:	8	As soon as you *f* him, report to me,
	7:	7	seek and you will *f*; knock
	7:	8	asks receives; the one who seek *f-s*
	7:	14	leads to life, and only a few *f* it
	10:	39	Whoever *f-s* their life will lose it,
	11:	29	and you will *f* rest for your souls
	12:	43	seeking rest and does not *f* it
Lk	2:	12	you will *f* a baby wrapped in cloths
	18:	8	will he *f* faith on the earth?
	24:	3	they did not *f* the body of the Lord
Jn	7:	34	look for me, but you will not *f* me
	10:	9	come in and go out, and *f* pasture.
	21:	6	of the boat and you will *f* some.'
Eph	5:	10	*f* out what pleases the Lord
2Ti	1:	18	that he will *f* mercy from the Lord

fire

Ex	3:	2	LORD appeared to him in flames of *f*
	13:	22	the pillar of *f* by night
Dt	4:	12	the LORD spoke to you out of the *f*.
1Ki	18:	38	Then the *f* of the LORD fell
	19:	12	but the LORD was not in the *f*.
2Ki	2:	11	a chariot of *f* and horses of *f*
2Ch	7:	1	*f* came down from heaven
Isa	43:	2	When you walk through the *f*,
Jer	23:	29	'Is not my word like *f*,'
Da	3:	25	four men walking around in the *f*,
Mal	3:	2	For he will be like a refiner's *f*
Mt	3:	11	with the Holy Spirit and with *f*
	5:	22	in danger of the *f* of hell
	7:	19	cut down and thrown into the *f*
	25:	41	eternal *f* prepared for the devil
Lk	9:	54	to call *f* down from heaven
	12:	49	I have come to bring *f* on the earth
	16:	24	because I am in agony in this *f*.
Jn	15:	6	thrown into the *f* and burned
Ac	2:	3	saw what seemed to be tongues of *f*
1Co	3:	13	and the *f* will test the quality
2Th	1:	7	revealed from heaven in blazing *f*
Heb	1:	7	his servants flames of *f*
	12:	29	for our 'God is a consuming *f*.
Jas	3:	6	The tongue also is a *f*,
2Pe	3:	10	the elements will be destroyed by *f*
Jude		7	suffer the punishment of eternal *f*
		23	save others by snatching them from the *f*
Rev	1:	14	and his eyes were like blazing *f*
	20:	14	The lake of *f* is the second death

firm, -ly

Ex	14:	13	'Do not be afraid. Stand *f* and you
2Ch	20:	17	stand *f* and see the deliverance
Ps	93:	1	the world is established, *f* and secure
Isa	7:	9	If you do not stand *f* in your faith
Lk	21:	19	Stand *f*, and you will win life
1Co	1:	8	He will also keep you *f* to the end,
	15:	2	you are saved, if you hold *f-ly*
2Co	1:	24	it is by faith you stand *f*
Eph	6:	14	Stand *f* then, with the belt of
1Th	3:	8	you are standing *f* in the Lord
Heb	4:	14	let us hold *f-ly* to the faith
1Pe	5:	10	make you strong, *f* and steadfast
2Pe	1:	12	*f-ly* established in the truth

first

Ge	1:	5	and there was morning – the *f* day

Isa	44:	6	I am the *f* and I am the last;
Mt	5:	24	*F* go and be reconciled
	6:	33	But seek *f* his kingdom
	7:	5	hypocrite, *f* take the plank out
	10:	2	the twelve apostles: *f*, Simon
	19:	30	But many who are *f* will be last,
	20:	27	wants to be *f* must be your slave
	22:	38	the *f* and greatest commandment
Jn	8:	7	sin be the *f* to throw a stone
	20:	1	Early on the *f* day of the week,
Ac	11:	26	were called Christians *f* at Antioch
	20:	7	On the *f* day of the week
Ro	1:	16	*f* to the Jew, then to the Gentile
1Co	12:	28	placed in the church *f* of all apostles,
	15:	45	'The *f* man Adam became a living
	16:	2	On the *f* day of every week,
Eph	1:	12	who were the *f* to put our hope
	6:	2	the *f* commandment with a promise
1Th	4:	16	and the dead in Christ will rise *f*
1Ti	2:	13	For Adam was formed *f*, then Eve
Heb	10:	9	He sets aside the *f* to establish
1Jn	4:	19	We love because he *f* loved us
3Jn		9	Diotrephes, who loves to be *f*,
Rev	1:	17	I am the *F* and the Last
	2:	4	forsaken the love you had at *f*

flesh

Ge	2:	23	bone of my bones and *f* of my *f*;
	2:	24	and they will become one *f*
Mt	19:	5	and the two will become one *f*
	26:	41	is willing, but the *f* is weak.
Jn	1:	14	The Word became *f*
	6:	51	This bread is my *f*,
	6:	55	For my *f* is real food
Ro	7:	5	when we were in the realm of the *f*
	8:	4	us, who do not live according to the *f*
	8:	5	*f* have their minds set on what the *f* desires
	8:	9	realm of the *f* but are in the realm of the Spirit
1Co	5:	5	man over to Satan for the destruction of the *f*
	6:	16	'The two will become one *f*.
	15:	39	Not all *f* is the same:
2Co	12:	7	I was given a thorn in my *f*,
Gal	5:	16	Spirit ... will not gratify the desires of the *f*
	5:	17	the *f* desires what is contrary to the Spirit
	5:	19	the acts of the *f* are obvious:
	5:	24	belong to Christ Jesus have crucified the *f*
Eph	2:	3	gratifying the cravings of our *f*
Col	2:	11	Your whole self ruled by the *f* was put off
1Ti	3:	16	he appeared in the *f*, was vindicated
1Jn	4:	2	that Jesus Christ has come in the *f*

flock, -s

2Sa	7:	8	from tending the *f*, and appointed
Ps	77:	20	You led your people like a *f*
Isa	40:	11	He tends his *f* like a shepherd.
Jer	31:	10	watch over his *f* like a shepherd.
Eze	34:	16	I will shepherd the *f* with justice
Mt	26:	31	sheep of the *f* will be scattered.
Lk	2:	8	keeping watch over their *f*-s
	12:	32	'Do not be afraid, little *f*,
Jn	10:	16	shall be one *f* and one shepherd
Ac	20:	28	all the *f* of which the Holy Spirit
1Co	9:	7	Who tends a *f* and does not drink
1Pe	5:	2	God's *f* that is under your care,
	5:	3	but being examples to the *f*

follow, -s, -ing, -ed

Ex	23:	2	'Do not *f* the crowd in doing wrong.
Lev	22:	31	'Keep my commands and *f* them.
Nu	32:	15	If you turn away from *f*-ing him,
Dt	5:	1	Learn them and be sure to *f* them
1Ki	11:	6	he did not *f* the LORD completely,

Ps	23:	6	Surely goodness and love will *f* me
	119:	14	I rejoice in *f*-ing your statutes
Mt	4:	19	'Come, *f* me,' Jesus said,
	4:	20	they left their nets and *f*-ed him
	8:	22	But Jesus told him, '*F* me,
	9:	9	and Matthew got up and *f*-ed him
	16:	24	and take up their cross and *f* me
Mk	10:	52	received his sight and *f*-ed Jesus
Lk	9:	61	'I will *f* you, Lord; but first
	18:	28	'We have left all we had to *f* you!
Jn	6:	66	turned back and no longer *f*-ed him
	8:	12	*f*-s me will never walk in darkness,
	10:	4	his sheep *f* him because they know
	10:	27	I know them, and they *f* me
	12:	26	Whoever serves me must *f* me;
	13:	36	'Where I am going, you cannot *f*
	21:	22	what is that to you? You must *f* me.
1Co	1:	12	'I *f* Paul'; ... 'I *f* Apollos
	11:	1	*F* my example, as I *f*
	14:	1	*F* the way of love
2Th	3:	7	know how you ought to *f* our example
1Ti	4:	6	good teaching that you have *f*-ed
	5:	15	already turned away to *f* Satan
1Pe	2:	21	that you should *f* in his steps
Jude		16	they *f* their own evil desires;
Rev	14:	4	They *f* the Lamb wherever he goes.

food, -s

Ge	1:	30	I give every green plant for *f*'
	9:	3	that lives and moves will be *f*
Ps	104:	21	and seek their *f* from God
	111:	5	provides *f* for those who fear him;
	127:	2	stay up late, toiling for *f* to eat —
Pr	9:	5	'Come, eat my *f* and drink the wine
	9:	17	*f* eaten in secret is delicious!
	22:	9	for they share their *f* with the poor
	25:	21	enemy is hungry, give him *f* to eat;
	31:	15	she provides *f* for her family
Isa	58:	7	to share your *f* with the hungry
Mt	3:	4	His *f* was locusts and wild honey
	6:	25	Is not life more important than *f*,
Mk	7:	19	Jesus declared all *f*-s clean.
Jn	4:	34	'My *f*,' said Jesus, 'is to do
	6:	27	Do not work for *f* that spoils,
	6:	55	For my flesh is real *f* and my blood
Ac	15:	29	abstain from *f* sacrificed to idols,
1Co	3:	2	I gave you milk, not solid *f*,
	8:	1	Now about *f* sacrificed to idols:
	8:	8	But *f* does not bring us near to God
Heb	5:	14	But solid *f* is for the mature,

forget, -ting, -got, -gotten

Dt	4:	23	Be careful not to *f* the covenant
	6:	12	careful that you do not *f* the LORD
1Sa	12:	9	'But they *f*-got the LORD their God
Ps	103:	2	and *f* not all his benefits
	137:	5	If I *f* you, Jerusalem,
Isa	49:	15	'Can a mother *f* the baby
Lk	12:	6	not one of them is *f*-gotten by God
Php	3:	13	*f*-ting what is behind and straining
Heb	6:	10	not unjust; he will not *f* your work
	13:	2	Do not *f* to show hospitality

forgive, -s, -ing, -n, -ness

Ex	34:	7	*f*-ing wickedness, rebellion and sin
Nu	14:	18	abounding in love and *f*-ing sin
2Ch	7:	14	and I will *f* their sin and will heal
Ps	19:	12	*F* my hidden faults
	32:	1	one whose transgressions are *f*-n,
	103:	3	who *f*-s all your sins and heals
Jer	31:	34	'For I will *f* their wickedness
Mt	6:	12	*f* us our debts, as we also have
	6:	15	But if you do not *f* others their sins
	12:	31	against the Spirit will not be *f*-n.

	18:	21	many times shall I *f* my brother
	18:	35	*f* your brother or sister from your heart.
	26:	28	for many for the *f-ness* of sins
Mk	2:	7	Who can *f* sins but God alone?
Lk	6:	37	*F*, and you will be *f-n*
	23:	34	Jesus said, 'Father, *f* them,
Jn	20:	23	If you *f* anyone's sins,
Ac	2:	38	for the *f-ness* of your sins.
Ro	4:	7	those whose transgressions are *f-n*,
Eph	1:	7	his blood, the *f-ness* of sins,
Col	1:	14	redemption, the *f-ness* of sins.
	3:	13	Bear with each other and *f*
Heb	9:	22	shedding of blood ... no *f-ness*
1Jn	1:	9	faithful and just and will *f* us

found

Ge	2:	20	for Adam no suitable helper was *f*
	6:	8	But Noah *f* favour
	39:	4	Joseph *f* favour in his eyes
Ru	2:	10	'Why have I *f* such favour
1Sa	10:	21	looked for him, he was not to be *f*
2Ki	22:	8	'I have *f* the Book of the Law
1Ch	28:	9	you seek him, he will be *f* by you;
Job	28:	12	But where can wisdom be *f*?
Isa	55:	6	Seek the LORD while he may be *f*;
	65:	1	I was *f* by those who did not seek
Da	5:	27	weighed on the scales and *f* wanting
Mt	8:	10	I have not *f* anyone in Israel
	13:	44	When a man *f* it, he hid it again,
Lk	1:	30	Mary, you have *f* favour with God
	2:	46	After three days they *f* him
	15:	6	I have *f* my lost sheep.
	15:	24	alive again; he was lost and is *f*'
Ac	4:	12	Salvation is *f* in no one else,
Ro	10:	20	'I was *f* by those who did not seek
Php	2:	8	And being *f* in appearance as a man
	3:	9	and be *f* in him,
Col	2:	17	reality, however, is *f* in Christ
Heb	3:	3	Jesus has been *f* worthy
	11:	5	He could not be *f*, because God had

friend, -s, -ship

Ex	33:	11	as one speaks to a *f*.
Pr	16:	28	and a gossip separates close *f-s*
	18:	24	*f* who sticks closer than a brother
	27:	6	Wounds from a *f* can be trusted,
Isa	41:	8	you descendants of Abraham my *f*
Zec	13:	6	was given at the house of my *f-s*.
Mt	11:	19	*f* of tax collectors and sinners
Lk	11:	8	you the bread because of *f-ship*
Jn	15:	13	lay down one's life for one's *f-s*
	15:	14	You are my *f-s* if you do what I
Jas	2:	23	and he was called God's *f*
	4:	4	*f-ship* with the world means enmity
3Jn		14	The *f-s* here send their greetings.

fruit, -ful

Ge	1:	22	'Be *f-ful* and increase in number
Ps	1:	3	which yields its *f* in season
Isa	11:	1	from his roots a Branch will bear *f*
	32:	17	*f* of that righteousness will be peace;
Mt	3:	8	*f* in keeping with repentance
	7:	17	good *f*, but a bad tree bears bad *f*
	26:	29	not drink of this *f* of the vine
Jn	15:	5	and I in you, you will bear much *f*;
	15:	16	go and bear *f* – *f* that will last
Gal	5:	22	But the *f* of the Spirit is love,
Php	1:	22	this will mean *f-ful* labour for me
Col	1:	6	gospel is bearing *f* and growing,
	1:	10	bearing *f* in every good work,
Heb	13:	15	the *f* of lips that openly profess
Rev	22:	2	yielding its *f* every month.

fulfil, -led, -ment

Ps	116:	14	I will *f* my vows to the LORD
Jer	25:	12	when the seventy years are *f-led*,
Mt	1:	22	to *f* what the Lord had said
	2:	17	the prophet Jeremiah was *f-led*
	5:	17	not come to abolish them but to *f*
	8:	17	This was to *f* what was spoken
	13:	14	*f-led* the prophecy of Isaiah:
	27:	9	by Jeremiah the prophet was *f-led*:
Lk	4:	21	'Today this scripture is *f-led*
	24:	44	be *f-led* that is written about me
Jn	15:	25	to *f* what is written in their Law:
	19:	28	that Scripture would be *f-led*,
Ac	13:	27	yet in condemning him they *f-led*
Ro	13:	10	love is the *f-ment* of the law
Gal	6:	2	you will *f* the law of Christ

full, -y, -ness

1Ki	8:	61	may your hearts be *f-y* committed
Ps	127:	5	the man whose quiver is *f* of them.
	130:	7	and with him is *f* redemption
Isa	6:	3	the whole earth is *f* of his glory.
Mt	6:	2	have received their reward in *f*
Lk	4:	1	Jesus, *f* of the Holy Spirit,
	5:	7	so *f* that they began to sink
	10:	21	*f* of joy through the Holy Spirit,
Jn	1:	14	*f* of grace and truth
	10:	10	have life, and have it to the *f*
Ac	6:	5	*f* of faith and of the Holy Spirit;
Gal	4:	4	But when the set time had *f-y* come,
Eph	1:	23	the *f-ness* of him who fills
	3:	19	all the *f-ness* of God
	4:	13	measure of the *f-ness* of Christ
Col	1:	19	to have all his *f-ness* dwell in him
	2:	9	all the *f-ness* of the Deity lives
	2:	10	have been brought to *f-ness*.
Heb	10:	22	in *f* assurance of faith,

g

gate, -s, -keeper

Ps	24:	7	Lift up your heads, you *g-s*;
	100:	4	Enter his *g-s* with thanksgiving
Pr	31:	23	husband is respected at the city *g*,
Eze	43:	4	entered the temple through the *g*
Mt	7:	13	'Enter through the narrow *g*.
	16:	18	*g-s* of Hades will not overcome it
Lk	16:	20	At his *g* was laid a beggar
Jn	10:	1	not enter the sheepfold by the *g*,
	10:	3	The *g-keeper* opens the *g*
	10:	7	I am the *g* for the sheep
Ac	3:	2	to the temple *g* called Beautiful,
	16:	13	outside the city *g* to the river,
Heb	13:	12	suffered outside the city *g*
Rev	21:	25	will its *g-s* ever be shut,

gather, -ed

Ecc	3:	5	time to *g* them, a time to embrace
Isa	11:	12	and *g* the exiles of Israel;
Jer	3:	17	all nations will *g* in Jerusalem
	23:	3	'I myself will *g* the remnant
Zep	3:	20	At that time I will *g* you;
Mt	12:	30	who does not *g* with me scatters
	13:	30	then *g* the wheat and bring it
	23:	37	I have longed to *g* your children
	24:	31	*g* his elect from the four winds,
	25:	32	nations will be *g-ed* before him,
Lk	17:	37	the vultures will *g*.
Ac	4:	26	rulers *g* together against the Lord
	14:	27	they *g-ed* the church together

gave

Ge	2: 20	man *g* names to all the livestock,
	3: 6	She also *g* some to her husband,
	35: 12	The land I *g* to Abraham and Isaac
Ne	9: 20	You *g* your good Spirit
Job	1: 21	The LORD *g* and the LORD has taken
Ps	106: 15	he *g* them what they asked for,
Ecc	12: 7	the spirit returns to God who *g* it
Da	1: 17	God *g* knowledge and understanding
Mt	1: 25	And he *g* him the name Jesus.
	25: 35	you *g* me something to eat,
	26: 26	he broke it and *g* it to his disciples
	27: 50	he *g* up his spirit
Jn	1: 12	he *g* the right to become children
	3: 16	he *g* his one and only Son,
	6: 31	"He *g* them bread from heaven
	17: 4	finishing the work you *g* me
	19: 30	his head and *g* up his spirit
Ro	1: 24	Therefore God *g* them over
	8: 32	Son, but *g* him up for us all
2Co	5: 18	*g* us the ministry of reconciliation
	8: 5	they *g* themselves by the will of God
Gal	1: 4	who *g* himself for our sins
	2: 20	who loved me and *g* himself for me
Eph	4: 8	captives and *g* gifts to his people
	5: 25	loved the church and *g* himself
1Ti	2: 6	who *g* himself as a ransom
1Jn	3: 24	we know it by the Spirit he *g* us

Gentile, -s

Isa	42: 6	a light for the *G-s*
Lk	2: 32	a light for revelation to the *G-s*
Ac	9: 15	to proclaim my name to the *G-s*
Ro	1: 16	first to the Jew, then to the *G*
	2: 14	when *G-s*, who do not have the law,
	3: 9	Jews and *G-s* alike are all under
	11: 13	I am the apostle to the *G-s*
	11: 25	full number of the *G-s* has come in
	16: 26	so that all the *G-s* might come
1Co	1: 23	Jews and foolishness to *G-s*
Gal	2: 8	an apostle to the *G-s*
	3: 8	God would justify the *G-s* by faith
Eph	2: 11	formerly you who are *G-s* by birth
	3: 6	*G-s* are heirs together with Israel,
Col	1: 27	to make known among the *G-s*

gift, -s

Ps	68: 18	you received *g-s* from people,
Mt	2: 11	*g-s* of gold, frankincense and myrrh
	5: 23	offering your *g* at the altar
	7: 11	give good *g-s* to your children,
Jn	4: 10	'If you knew the *g* of God and who
Ac	2: 38	receive the *g* of the Holy Spirit
Ro	6: 23	the *g* of God is eternal life
1Co	12: 1	about the *g-s* of the Spirit, brothers
2Co	9: 15	God for his indescribable *g*
Eph	2: 8	it is the *g* of God
	4: 8	captives and gave *g-s* to his people.
1Ti	4: 14	Do not neglect your *g*,
Jas	1: 17	good and perfect *g* is from above,
1Pe	4: 10	whatever *g* you have received to serve
Rev	22: 17	the free *g* of the water of life

give, -s, -ing, -n, -r

Ex	20: 16	'You shall not *g* false testimony
	33: 14	I will *g* you rest.
Nu	6: 26	face towards you and *g* you peace.
Ps	7: 17	I will *g* thanks to the LORD
	19: 8	*g-ing* joy to the heart.
	37: 4	*g* you the desires of your heart
	100: 4	with praise; *g* thanks to him
	107: 1	*G* thanks to the LORD, for he is
	119:130	unfolding of your words *g-s* light;
	146: 8	the LORD *g-s* sight to the blind,

Pr	2: 6	For the LORD *g-s* wisdom;
	28: 27	*g* to the poor will lack nothing,
Ecc	6: 2	God *g-s* some people wealth,
Isa	7: 14	Lord himself will *g* you a sign:
	9: 6	to us a son is *g-n*,
	40: 29	He *g-s* strength to the weary
Eze	36: 26	I will *g* you a new heart
Da	2: 21	He *g-s* wisdom to the wise
	7: 14	He was *g-n* authority, glory and
Mt	6: 4	your *g-ing* may be in secret.
	6: 11	*G* us today our daily bread.
	6: 33	these things will be *g-n* to you
	7: 7	'Ask and it will be *g-n* to you;
	10: 8	Freely you have received, freely *g*.
	10: 42	anyone *g-s* even a cup of cold water
	13: 12	Whoever has will be *g-n* more,
	15: 36	had *g-n* thanks, he broke them
	21: 43	away from you and *g-n* to a people
	22: 21	'G* back to Caesar what is Caesar's,
	28: 18	on earth has been *g-n* to me
Lk	6: 38	*G*, and it will be *g-n* to you.
	12: 48	everyone who has been *g-n* much,
	22: 19	'This is my body *g-n* for you;
Jn	1: 9	light that *g-s* light to everyone
	3: 34	God *g-s* the Spirit without limit
	5: 27	*g-n* him authority to judge because
	6: 37	All whom the Father *g-s* me will
	6: 63	The Spirit *g-s* life;
	10: 28	I *g* them eternal life,
	10: 29	My Father, who has *g-n* them to me,
	14: 27	*g* to you as the world *g-s*.
	17: 22	I have *g-n* them the glory
Ac	4: 12	no other name under heaven *g-n*
	17: 25	he himself *g-s* everyone life and
	17: 31	has *g-n* proof of this to everyone
	20: 35	more blessed to *g* than to receive.
Ro	5: 5	Holy Spirit, who has been *g-n* to us
	12: 6	according to the grace *g-n* to each of us.
	12: 8	if it is *g-ing*, then *g* generously;
	13: 7	*G* to everyone what you owe
1Co	4: 2	those who have been *g-n* a trust
	12: 7	Spirit is *g-n* for the common good
	12: 13	all *g-n* the one Spirit to drink.
	15: 57	He *g-s* us the victory through our
2Co	3: 6	but the Spirit *g-s* life
	4: 11	*g-n* over to death for Jesus' sake,
	9: 7	for God loves a cheerful *g-r*
Eph	1: 16	I have not stopped *g-ing* thanks
	3: 2	God's grace that was *g-n* to me
	3: 8	this grace was *g-n* me: to preach
	4: 7	each one of us grace has been *g-n*
	5: 20	always *g-ing* thanks to God
Php	4: 13	through him who *g-s* me strength
Col	1: 12	*g-ing* joyful thanks to the Father,
1Ti	6: 13	God, who *g-s* life to everything,
Jas	1: 15	it *g-s* birth to sin; and sin,
	1: 25	the perfect law that *g-s* freedom
	4: 6	But he *g-s* us more grace.
1Pe	1: 3	he has *g-n* us new birth
2Pe	1: 3	divine power has *g-n* us everything
1Jn	5: 11	God has *g-n* us eternal life,
Rev	6: 4	rider was *g-n* power to take peace
	6: 11	each of them was *g-n* a white robe,
	13: 4	he had *g-n* authority to the beast,
	13: 7	It was *g-n* power to wage war
	21: 23	for the glory of God *g-s* it light,

glorify, -ies, -ing, -ied

Ps	34: 3	*G* the LORD with me: let us exalt
Mt	5: 16	and *g* your Father in heaven
Lk	1: 46	'My soul *g-ies* the Lord
	2: 20	The shepherds returned, *g-ing*

Jn	7:	39	since Jesus had not yet been *g-ied*
	11:	4	God's Son may be *g-ied* through it.
	12:	23	for the Son of Man to be *g-ied*
	17:	1	that your Son may *g*you
Ac	3:	13	has *g-ied* his servant Jesus.
Ro	1:	21	they neither *g-ied* him as God
	8:	30	those he justified, he also *g-ied*
1Pe	2:	12	see your good deeds and *g*God

glorious

Ps	87:	3	*G*things are said of you, city
Isa	12:	5	for he has done *g*things;
Mt	19:	28	Son of Man sits on his *g*throne,
Ac	2:	20	the great and *g*day of the Lord
Eph	3:	16	I pray that out of his *g*riches
Php	3:	21	they will be like his *g*body
1Pe	1:	8	an inexpressible and *g*joy
Jude	:	24	present you before his *g*presence

glory, -ies

Ex	16:	7	you will see the *g*of the Lord,
	24:	16	the *g*of the Lord settled on Mount
	33:	18	'Now show me your *g*.'
	33:	22	When my *g*passes by, I will put
	40:	34	the *g*of the Lord filled the
Nu	14:	10	Then the *g*of the Lord appeared
Jos	7:	19	'My son, give *g*to the Lord,
1Sa	4:	21	'The *G*has departed from Israel'
Ps	8:	1	set your *g*above the heavens
	8:	5	crowned them with *g*and honour
	19:	1	The heavens declare the *g*of God;
	24:	7	that the King of *g*may come in
	29:	2	Ascribe to the Lord the *g*due
	73:	24	afterwards you will take me into *g*
	96:	7	ascribe to the Lord *g*and strength
Isa	6:	3	the whole earth is full of his *g*.
	40:	5	*g*of the Lord will be revealed,
Eze	1:	28	appearance of the likeness of the *g*
Da	7:	14	given authority, *g*and sovereign
Hag	2:	9	The *g*of this present house will be
Mt	16:	27	in his Father's *g*with his angels,
	24:	30	with power and great *g*
Lk	2:	9	*g*of the Lord shone around them,
	2:	14	'*G*to God in the highest,
	24:	26	these things and then enter his *g*?
Jn	1:	14	We have seen his *g*, the *g*of
	2:	11	through which he revealed his *g*,
	17:	4	I have brought you *g*on earth
	17:	5	*g*I had with you before the world
	17:	24	where I am, and to see my *g*,
Ac	7:	2	The God of *g*appeared to our father
Ro	1:	23	*g*of the immortal God for images
	3:	23	fall short of the *g*of God
	5:	2	boast in the hope of the *g*of God
	5:	3	but we also *g*in our sufferings,
	8:	18	not worth comparing with the *g*
	8:	21	freedom and *g*of the children of God
	9:	4	theirs the divine *g*,
	9:	23	to make the riches of his *g*known
1Co	2:	8	crucified the Lord of *g*
	10:	31	do it all for the *g*of God
	11:	7	he is the image and *g*of God;
	15:	43	it is raised in *g*; it is sown
2Co	3:	18	faces contemplate the Lord's *g*,
	4:	17	achieving for us an eternal *g*
Eph	1:	12	might be for the praise of his *g*
Php	2:	11	to the *g*of God the Father
	4:	19	the riches of his *g*in Christ Jesus
Col	1:	27	Christ in you, the hope of *g*
1Ti	1:	11	the *g*of the blessed God,
	3:	16	in the world, was taken up in *g*
Heb	1:	3	Son is the radiance of God's *g*
	2:	7	you crowned them with *g*and honour

1Pe	1:	11	sufferings of Christ and the *g-ies*
	5:	1	share in the *g*to be revealed
	5:	10	called you to his eternal *g*
Jude		25	to the only God our Saviour be *g*,
Rev	4:	11	to receive *g*and honour and power,

God, -'s

Ge	1:	1	In the beginning *G*created
	1:	3	*G*said, 'Let there be light,'
	1:	26	*G*said, 'Let us make mankind
	2:	3	*G*blessed the seventh day
	2:	22	Then the Lord *G*made a woman
	5:	24	Enoch walked faithfully with *G*;
	6:	2	sons of *G*saw that the daughters
	14:	19	'Blessed be Abram by *G*Most High,
	17:	1	'I am *G*Almighty;
	20:	11	no fear of *G*in this place,
	22:	8	'*G*himself will provide the lamb
	32:	30	because I saw *G*face to face,
	35:	11	*G*said to him, 'I am *G*Almighty;
	39:	9	and sin against *G*?
	46:	3	'I am *G*, the *G*of your father
	50:	20	but *G*intended it for good
Ex	2:	24	*G*heard their groaning
	3:	6	'I am the *G*of your father,
	8:	19	'This is the finger of *G*.'
	20:	1	*G*spoke all these words
	20:	5	the Lord your *G*, am a jealous *G*
	20:	7	the name of the Lord your *G*,
	20:	10	a sabbath to the Lord your *G*.
	34:	14	for the Lord ... is a jealous *G*
Lev	19:	2	I, the Lord your *G*, am holy
Nu	22:	38	speak only what *G*puts in my mouth
	23:	19	*G*is not human, that he should lie
Dt	4:	24	Lord your *G*is a consuming fire,
	6:	4	the Lord our *G*, the Lord is one.
	6:	5	Love the Lord your *G*with all
	6:	16	put the Lord your *G*to the test
	9:	10	inscribed by the finger of *G*.
	10:	20	Fear the Lord your *G*
	11:	22	to love the Lord your *G*,
	14:	2	a people holy to the Lord your *G*.
	18:	15	*G*will raise up for you a prophet
	31:	6	the Lord your *G*goes with you;
	33:	27	The eternal *G*is your refuge,
Jos	1:	9	your *G*will be with you wherever
	14:	8	Lord my *G*wholeheartedly
	23:	14	promises the Lord your *G*gave you
	24:	19	He is a holy *G*; he is a jealous
Jdg	13:	8	let the man of *G*you sent to us
	13:	22	'We have seen *G*!
Ru	1:	16	my people and your *G*my *G*
1Sa	2:	2	there is no Rock like our *G*
	4:	11	The ark of *G*was captured,
	12:	9	they forgot the Lord their *G*;
	14:	44	'May *G*deal with me,
	17:	26	defy the armies of the living *G*?
	30:	6	found strength in the Lord his *G*
2Sa	6:	6	took hold of the ark of *G*,
	22:	30	with my *G*I can scale a wall
	22:	31	'As for *G*, his way is perfect;
1Ki	8:	27	But will *G*really dwell on earth?
	17:	24	I know that you are a man of *G*
	18:	21	If the Lord is *G*, follow him;
	18:	24	answers by fire − he is *G*.'
	18:	39	'The Lord − he is *G*!
	19:	10	zealous for the Lord *G*Almighty.
2Ki	2:	3	because there is no *G*in Israel
	17:	39	worship the Lord your *G*;
1Ch	17:	20	there is no *G*but you,
2Ch	5:	14	of the Lord filled the temple of *G*
	6:	18	will *G*really dwell on earth

Ezr 5: 13 to rebuild this house of *G*
　　 7: 9 gracious hand of his *G* was on him
　　 8: 22 'The gracious hand of our *G*
Ne 1: 5 *G* of heaven, the great and awesome
　　 2: 20 *G* of heaven will give us success.
Job 1: 1 he feared *G* and shunned evil
　　 1: 5 cursed *G* in their hearts.'
　　 1: 9 'Does Job fear *G* for nothing?'
　　 2: 9 Curse *G* and die!
　　 2: 10 Shall we accept good from *G*,
　　 13: 3 to argue my case with *G*
　　 19: 6 *G* has wronged me
　　 19: 26 in my flesh I will see *G*
　　 25: 4 can a mortal be righteous before *G*?
Ps 5: 4 a *G* who is pleased with wickedness;
　　 9: 17 all the nations that forget *G*
　　 14: 1 in his heart, 'There is no *G*.'
　　 18: 2 my *G* is my rock,
　　 18: 30 As for *G*, his way is perfect;
　　 19: 1 heavens declare the glory of *G*;
　　 22: 1 my *G*, why have you forsaken me?
　　 33: 12 the nation whose *G* is the LORD,
　　 36: 1 no fear of *G* before their eyes
　　 40: 8 I desire to do your will, my *G*;
　　 42: 1 so my soul pants for you, my *G*
　　 43: 5 Put your hope in *G*,
　　 45: 6 throne, O *G*, will last for ever
　　 45: 7 *G*, your *G*, has set you above
　　 46: 1 *G* is our refuge and strength,
　　 46: 4 streams make glad the city of *G*,
　　 46: 10 Be still, and know that I am *G*;
　　 51: 1 Have mercy on me, O *G*,
　　 51: 10 Create in me a pure heart, O *G*,
　　 53: 1 in his heart, 'There is no *G*.'
　　 57: 7 My heart, O *G*, is steadfast,
　　 63: 1 You, *G*, are my *G*,
　　 68: 20 Our *G* is a *G* who saves;
　　 73: 1 Surely *G* is good to Israel,
　　 73: 17 I entered the sanctuary of *G*;
　　 73: 26 but *G* is the strength of my heart
　　 81: 10 I am the LORD your *G*,
　　 84: 2 cry out for the living *G*
　　 84: 10 a doorkeeper in the house of my *G*
　　 90: 2 to everlasting you are *G*
　　100: 3 Know that the LORD is *G*.
　　139: 23 Search me, *G*, and know
Ecc 5: 4 When you make a vow to *G*,
　　 12: 13 fear *G* and keep his commandments,
Isa 9: 6 Wonderful Counsellor, Mighty *G*,
　　 40: 1 comfort my people, says your *G*
　　 40: 3 a highway for our *G*
　　 40: 8 the word of our *G* endures for ever.
　　 40: 18 With whom, then, will you compare *G*?
　　 40: 28 The LORD is the everlasting *G*,
　　 41: 10 do not be dismayed, for I am your *G*
　　 45: 22 I am *G*, and there is no other
　　 52: 7 'Your *G* reigns!
　　 53: 4 we considered him punished by *G*,
　　 55: 7 to our *G*, for he will freely pardon
　　 57: 21 'There is no peace,' says my *G*
　　 59: 2 separated you from your *G*;
　　 61: 2 the day of vengeance of our *G*,
Jer 30: 22 I will be your *G*."
Eze 1: 1 I saw visions of *G*
　　 11: 20 and I will be their *G*
Da 2: 19 Daniel praised the *G* of heaven
　　 2: 28 *G* in heaven who reveals mysteries.
　　 3: 17 the *G* we serve is able to deliver us
　　 6: 16 'May your *G*, whom you serve
　　 6: 22 My *G* sent his angel,
　　 9: 4 Lord, the great and awesome *G*,
Hos 1: 10 "children of the living *G*"

Jnh 1: 9 worship the LORD, the *G* of heaven,
　　 4: 2 a gracious and compassionate *G*,
Mic 6: 8 to walk humbly with your *G*
　　 7: 18 Who is a *G* like you,
Hab 3: 18 I will be joyful in *G* my Saviour
Zec 4: 7 shouts of "*G* bless it!'
Mal 3: 8 Will a mere mortal rob *G*? Yet you rob me.
　　 3: 14 "It is futile to serve *G*.
Mt 1: 23 Immanuel' ... means '*G* with us
　　 3: 16 he saw the Spirit of *G* descending
　　 4: 3 'If you are the Son of *G*
　　 4: 4 that comes from the mouth of *G*."
　　 5: 8 pure in heart, for they will see *G*
　　 5: 9 for they will be called children of *G*
　　 6: 24 You cannot serve both *G* and Money
　　 12: 28 by the Spirit of *G* that I drive
　　 14: 33 'Truly you are the Son of *G*.
　　 15: 3 why do you break the command of *G*
　　 16: 16 Messiah, the Son of the living *G*.
　　 19: 6 what *G* has joined together,
　　 19: 24 rich to enter the kingdom of *G*
　　 22: 21 Caesar's, and to *G* what is *G*-'s.
　　 22: 29 the Scriptures or the power of *G*
　　 22: 37 Love the Lord your *G* with all your
　　 27: 43 He trusts in *G*. Let *G* rescue him
　　 27: 46 my *G*, why have you forsaken me?
Mk 1: 15 'The kingdom of *G* has come near.
　　 2: 7 Who can forgive sins but *G* alone?
　　 9: 47 enter the kingdom of *G* with one eye
　　 10: 6 creation *G* "made them male
　　 10: 18 'No one is good – except *G* alone
　　 11: 22 'Have faith in *G*,' Jesus answered
　　 12: 27 He is not the *G* of the dead,
　　 12: 29 the Lord our *G*, the Lord is one.
　　 16: 19 he sat at the right hand of *G*
Lk 1: 19 I stand in the presence of *G*,
　　 1: 30 Mary, you have found favour with *G*
　　 1: 37 For no word from *G* will ever fail
　　 1: 47 my spirit rejoices in *G* my Saviour,
　　 2: 14 'Glory to *G* in the highest
　　 3: 6 all people will see *G*-'s salvation."
　　 9: 60 proclaim the kingdom of *G*.
　　 9: 62 for service in the kingdom of *G*.
　　 11: 20 drive out demons by the finger of *G*
　　 11: 42 you give *G* a tenth of your mint,
　　 12: 20 'But *G* said to him, "You fool!
　　 12: 28 how *G* clothes the grass
　　 13: 29 feast in the kingdom of *G*
　　 17: 21 the kingdom of *G* is in your midst.
　　 23: 40 'Don't you fear *G*,'
Jn 1: 1 and the Word was with *G*,
　　 1: 1 and the Word was *G*.
　　 1: 2 He was with *G* in the beginning
　　 1: 6 There was a man sent from *G*
　　 1: 12 the right to become children of *G*
　　 1: 18 No one has ever seen *G*,
　　 1: 29 'Look, the Lamb of *G*,
　　 1: 49 'Rabbi, you are the Son of *G*;
　　 3: 3 no one can see the kingdom of *G*
　　 3: 16 For *G* so loved the world
　　 3: 17 For *G* did not send his Son
　　 4: 24 *G* is spirit,
　　 6: 28 the works *G* requires?
　　 6: 33 bread of *G* is the bread that comes
　　 8: 42 'If *G* were your Father,
　　 9: 31 *G* does not listen to sinners.
　　 11: 40 you will see the glory of *G*?
　　 13: 31 *G* is glorified in him
　　 14: 1 Trust in *G*; trust also in me
　　 20: 28 'My Lord and my *G*!
Ac 2: 24 But *G* raised him from the dead,
　　 2: 39 whom the Lord our *G* will call.

	3: 15	but *G* raised him from the dead.
	3: 19	Repent, then, and turn to *G*,
	5: 4	lied just to human beings but to *G*
	5: 29	'We must obey *G* rather than human beings
	7: 2	The *G* of glory appeared
	7: 55	saw the glory of *G*, and Jesus
	10: 46	speaking in tongues and praising *G*.
	13: 30	But *G* raised him from the dead
	15: 8	*G*, who knows the heart,
	17: 23	inscription: to an unknown *g*
	17: 24	'The *G* who made the world
	17: 30	past *G* overlooked such ignorance,
	20: 28	Be shepherds of the church of *G*,
	22: 14	*G* of our ancestors has chosen you
	26: 20	repent and turn to *G*
Ro	1: 4	appointed the Son of *G* in power
	1: 16	it is the power of *G*
	1: 17	righteousness of *G* is revealed,
	1: 18	The wrath of *G* is being revealed
	1: 20	world *G-'s* invisible qualities
	1: 23	the glory of the immortal *G*
	1: 24	Therefore *G* gave them over
	3: 4	Let *G* be true,
	3: 18	'There is no fear of *G*
	3: 21	the righteousness of *G* has been made
	3: 23	fall short of the glory of *G*
	5: 8	*G* demonstrates his own love for us
	6: 23	the gift of *G* is eternal life
	8: 7	by the flesh is hostile to *G*.
	8: 28	in all things *G* works for the good
	8: 29	For those *G* foreknew
	8: 39	separate us from the love of *G*
	11: 33	wisdom and knowledge of *G*!
1Co	1: 25	the foolishness of *G* is wiser
	2: 9	*G* has prepared for those who love
	3: 6	but *G* has been making it grow.
	6: 20	Therefore honour *G* with your bodies
	10: 13	*G* is faithful;
	10: 31	do it all for the glory of *G*.
	15: 10	by the grace of *G* I am what I am,
2Co	2: 17	peddle the word of *G* for profit.
	4: 4	Christ, who is the image of *G*
	5: 19	*G* was reconciling the world
	9: 7	for *G* loves a cheerful giver
Gal	3: 6	'believed *G*, and it was credited
	4: 4	*G* sent his Son, born of a woman,
Eph	2: 4	*G*, who is rich in mercy
	4: 6	one *G* and Father of all,
	4: 30	do not grieve the Holy Spirit of *G*
Php	2: 6	who, being in very nature *G*,
	4: 19	And my *G* will meet all your needs
Col	1: 15	is the image of the invisible *G*,
1Th	1: 9	how you turned to *G* from idols
1Ti	1: 17	immortal, invisible, the only *G*,
	2: 5	there is one *G* and one mediator
	4: 4	For everything *G* created is good,
2Ti	1: 6	fan into flame the gift of *G*,
Heb	1: 1	In the past *G* spoke
	1: 8	'Your throne, O *G*, will last
	10: 22	let us draw near to *G*
	10: 31	into the hands of the living *G*
Jas	1: 13	should say, '*G* is tempting me.'
	4: 8	Come near to *G* and he will come
1Pe	2: 4	rejected by humans but chosen by *G*
	3: 18	to bring you to *G*.
	5: 2	be shepherds of *G-'s* flock
2Pe	1: 21	spoke from *G* as they were carried
1Jn	1: 5	*G* is light; in him there is no
	4: 9	*G* showed his love among us:
	4: 16	rely on the love *G* has for us.
Jude		21 keep yourselves in *G-'s* love

Rev	7: 10	'Salvation belongs to our *G*,
	19: 10	Worship *G*!
	19: 13	his name is the Word of *G*
	22: 19	*G* will take away from you

god, -s

Ge	31: 19	stole her father's household *g-s*
Ex	15: 11	Who among the *g-s* is like you,
	20: 3	shall have no other *g-s* before me
Dt	32: 17	sacrificed to false *g-s*, which are not
	32: 39	There is no *g* besides me
Ps	82: 6	'I said, "You are '*g-s*';
	86: 8	Among the *g-s* there is none like you,
	106: 37	and their daughters to false *g-s*
Da	2: 47	'Surely your God is the God of *g-s*
	3: 25	looks like a son of the *g-s*.
Jn	10: 34	"I have said you are '*g-s*'
Ac	14: 11	*g-s* have come down to us in human
	17: 18	seems to be advocating foreign *g-s*.'
1Co	8: 5	even if there are so-called *g-s*,

gold

Ge	44: 8	why would we steal silver or *g*
Ex	11: 2	for articles of silver and *g*.
	25: 17	an atonement cover of pure *g* –
	32: 31	have made themselves gods of *g*
1Ki	20: 3	"Your silver and *g* are mine,
Ezr	5: 14	from the temple of Babylon the *g*
Job	23: 10	I shall come forth as *g*
Ps	19: 10	They are more precious than *g*,
Pr	11: 22	Like a *g* ring in a pig's snout
SS	5: 11	His head is purest *g*;
Da	3: 1	Nebuchadnezzar made an image of *g*,
Zec	13: 9	like silver and test them like *g*.
Mal	3: 3	refine them like *g* and silver.
Mt	2: 11	presented him with gifts of *g*
Ac	3: 6	'Silver or *g* I do not have,
1Co	3: 12	builds on this foundation using *g*,
Jas	2: 2	wearing a *g* ring and fine clothes,
1Pe	1: 7	faith – of greater worth than *g*,
	1: 18	silver or *g* that you were redeemed
Rev	3: 18	I counsel you to buy from me *g*
	14: 14	with a crown of *g* on his head
	21: 21	street of the city was of *g*,

good, -ness

Ge	1: 4	God saw that the light was *g*
	1: 31	God saw ... made, and it was very *g*
	2: 18	not *g* for the man to be alone.
1Ki	8: 56	failed of all the *g* promises
1Ch	16: 34	for he is *g*; his love endures
Ne	9: 20	You gave your *g* Spirit
Job	2: 10	Shall we accept *g* from God,
Ps	14: 1	there is no one who does *g*
	16: 2	apart from you I have no *g* thing.
	23: 6	Surely your *g-ness* and love will follow
	27: 13	I will see the *g-ness* of the LORD
	34: 8	Taste and see that the LORD is *g*;
	73: 1	Surely God is *g* to Israel,
	84: 11	no *g* thing does he withhold
	100: 5	LORD is *g* and his love endures
Pr	15: 30	*g* news gives health to the bones
	22: 1	A *g* name is more desirable
Isa	52: 7	feet of those who bring *g* news,
	61: 1	to proclaim *g* news to the poor.
La	3: 25	The LORD is *g* to those whose hope
Mic	6: 8	shown you, O mortal, what is *g*.
Mt	4: 23	proclaiming the *g* news of the
	5: 45	sun to rise on the evil and the *g*,
	7: 11	to give *g* gifts to your children,
	13: 8	Still other seed fell on *g* soil,
	16: 26	What *g* will it be for someone
	19: 17	'There is only One who is *g*.
Mk	1: 1	The beginning of the *g* news about Jesus

	3:	4	the Sabbath: to do *g* or to do evil,
Jn	1:	46	Can anything *g* come from there?'
	5:	29	done what is *g* will rise
	10:	11	'I am the *g* shepherd.
Ac	10:	38	he went around doing *g*
Ro	2:	7	persistence in doing *g* seek glory,
	3:	8	Let us do evil that *g* may result
	3:	12	no one who does *g*, not even one.
	5:	7	though for a *g* person someone might
	7:	18	I know that *g* itself does not dwell
	8:	28	in all things God works for the *g*
	12:	2	his *g*, pleasing and perfect will.
	12:	9	cling to what is *g*.
1Co	7:	1	It is *g* for a man not to have
	12:	7	Spirit is given for the common *g*
	15:	33	'Bad company corrupts *g* character.
2Co	5:	10	in the body, whether *g* or bad
Gal	5:	7	You were running a *g* race.
	5:	22	kindness, *g-ness*, faithfulness
	6:	9	Let us not become weary in doing *g*,
	6:	10	let us do *g* to all people,
Eph	2:	10	created in Christ Jesus to do *g*
Php	1:	6	he who began a *g* work in you will
1Th	5:	15	always strive to do what is *g*
1Ti	1:	8	We know that the law is *g*
	4:	4	everything God created is *g*,
	6:	12	Fight the *g* fight of the faith.
2Ti	3:	17	equipped for every *g* work
	4:	7	I have fought the *g* fight,
Heb	10:	1	The law is only a shadow of the *g*
	10:	24	on towards love and *g* deeds
	13:	21	everything *g* for doing his will,
Jas	1:	17	Every *g* and perfect gift
	2:	14	What *g* is it, my brothers
1Pe	2:	3	have tasted that the Lord is *g*
2Pe	1:	5	to add to your faith *g-ness;*
3Jn		11	imitate what is evil but what is *g*.

gospel

Mt	24:	14	this *g* of the kingdom will be
Mk	8:	35	for me and for the *g* will save it
Ro	1:	16	I am not ashamed of the *g*
1Co	9:	16	when I preach the *g*, I cannot boast
	15:	2	By this *g* you are saved,
2Co	4:	3	And even if our *g* is veiled,
Gal	1:	8	preach a *g* other than the one
	2:	14	in line with the truth of the *g*,
Eph	3:	6	*g* the Gentiles are heirs together
Php	1:	27	manner worthy of the *g* of Christ.
Col	1:	6	the *g* is bearing fruit and growing
1Th	1:	5	*g* came to you not simply
1Ti	1:	11	conforms to the *g* concerning the glory
2Ti	1:	10	immortality to light through the *g*
	2:	8	descended from David. This is my *g*
1Pe	4:	17	who do not obey the *g* of God
Rev	14:	6	he had the eternal *g* to proclaim

grace

Jn	1:	14	full of *g* and truth
	1:	17	*g* and truth came through Jesus
Ac	4:	33	God's *g* was so powerfully at work
	13:	43	them to continue in the *g* of God.
	15:	11	through the *g* of our Lord Jesus
Ro	3:	24	justified freely by his *g*
	5:	2	this *g* in which we now stand.
	5:	15	how much more did God's *g*
	5:	20	*g* increased all the more,
	5:	21	so also *g* might reign through
	6:	1	sinning, so that *g* may increase?
	6:	14	you are not under the law, but under *g*
	11:	5	there is a remnant chosen by *g*
1Co	15:	10	by the *g* of God I am what I am,
2Co	8:	9	the *g* of our Lord Jesus Christ,

	12:	9	'My *g* is sufficient for you,
	13:	14	May the *g* of the Lord Jesus Christ,
Gal	2:	21	I do not set aside the *g* of God,
	5:	4	you have fallen away from *g*
Eph	1:	6	to the praise of his glorious *g*,
	1:	7	with the riches of God's *g*
	2:	5	it is by *g* you have been saved
	2:	7	the incomparable riches of his *g*,
	2:	8	it is by *g* you have been saved,
	4:	7	to each one of us *g* has been given
Col	4:	6	conversation be always full of *g*,
2Ti	2:	1	strong in the *g* that is in Christ
Tit	3:	7	having been justified by his *g*
Heb	2:	9	*g* of God he might taste death
	4:	16	approach God's throne of *g* with
Jas	4:	6	But he gives us more *g*.
1Pe	1:	10	spoke of the *g* that was to come
	5:	10	And the God of all *g*,
2Pe	3:	18	But grow in the *g* and knowledge

grain

Ge	41:	35	store up the *g* under the authority
Ex	29:	41	*g* offering and its drink offering
Dt	25:	4	ox while it is treading out the *g*
Mk	4:	7	so that they did not bear *g*
	4:	28	then the full *g* in the ear
Lk	6:	1	in their hands and eat the *g*
Jn	12:	24	unless a *g* of wheat falls
1Co	9:	9	ox while it is treading out the *g*.
1Ti	5:	18	ox while it is treading out the *g*,

great, -er, -est, -ly

Ge	12:	2	'I will make you into a *g* nation
	15:	1	your shield, your very *g* reward.
1Ch	16:	25	For *g* is the LORD and most worthy
Ps	19:	11	in keeping them there is *g* reward
	48:	1	*G* is the LORD, and most worthy
	51:	1	according to your *g* compassion blot
	126:	3	LORD has done *g* things for us,
Jer	31:	34	least of them to the *g-est*,'
	33:	3	tell you *g* and unsearchable things
	45:	5	seek *g* things for yourself?
La	3:	22	LORD's *g* love we are not consumed,
	3:	23	*g* is your faithfulness
Na	1:	3	slow to anger but *g* in power;
Zep	1:	14	The *g* day of the LORD is near –
Mal	4:	5	*g* and dreadful day of the LORD
Mt	2:	18	weeping and *g* mourning, Rachel
	4:	16	in darkness have seen a *g* light;
	5:	12	because *g* is your reward in heaven,
	12:	6	one *g-er* than the temple is here
	13:	46	When he found one of *g* value,
	18:	1	'Who, then, is the *g-est* in the kingdom
	19:	22	because he had *g* wealth
	22:	36	which is the *g-est* commandment
Jn	1:	50	will see *g-er* things than that.
	4:	12	Are you *g-er* than our father
	10:	29	*g-er* than all; no one can snatch
	13:	16	no servant is *g-er* than his master,
	14:	28	for the Father is *g-er* than I
	15:	13	*G-er* love has no one than this:
1Co	12:	31	eagerly desire the *g-er* gifts.
	13:	13	But the *g-est* of these is love
Heb	6:	13	no one *g-er* for him to swear by,
	7:	7	lesser is blessed by the *g-er*
1Pe	1:	6	In all this you *g-ly* rejoice,
	1:	7	faith – of *g-er* worth than gold,
1Jn	3:	20	that God is *g-er* than our hearts,
3Jn		4	I have no *g-er* joy than to hear

ground

Ge	1:	10	God called the dry *g* 'land',
	2:	7	a man from the dust of the *g*
	3:	17	'Cursed is the *g* because of you;

Ex	3:	5	where you are standing is holy g.
Ecc	12:	7	dust returns to the g it came
Isa	40:	4	the rough g shall become level,
Hos	10:	12	break up your unploughed g;
Mt	10:	29	not one of them will fall to the g
Jn	8:	6	to write on the g with his finger
	12:	24	wheat falls to the g and dies,
Eph	6:	13	you may be able to stand your g,

guard, -s

Ps	91:	11	angels concerning you to g you
	141:	3	Set a g over my mouth, LORD;
Pr	4:	23	Above all else, g your heart,
	13:	3	who g their lips preserve their lives,
Mal	2:	15	So be on your g,
Lk	4:	10	angels concerning you to g you
	11:	21	a strong man, fully armed, g-s
Ac	20:	31	So be on your g! Remember
1Co	16:	13	Be on your g; stand firm
Php	4:	7	g your hearts and your minds
1Ti	6:	20	g what has been entrusted
2Ti	1:	12	able to g what I have entrusted
	1:	14	G the good deposit that was

guilt, -y

Ex	23:	7	I will not acquit the g-y
	34:	7	does not leave the g-y unpunished;
Lev	5:	15	It is a g offering
Ps	38:	4	My g has overwhelmed me
Isa	6:	7	your g is taken away and your sin
Mk	3:	29	but is g-y of an eternal sin.
Jn	8:	46	any of you prove me g-y of sin?
1Co	11:	27	g-y of sinning against the body
Heb	10:	22	cleanse us from a g-y conscience
Jas	2:	10	stumbles at just one point is g-y

h

hand, -s, -ed

Ex	3:	20	I will stretch out my h
	6:	1	because of my mighty h
	6:	8	I swore with uplifted h
	7:	19	stretch out your h over the waters
	17:	11	As long as Moses held up his h-s,
	33:	22	rock and cover you with my h
Dt	4:	34	by a mighty h and an outstretched
1Ki	18:	44	'A cloud as small as a man's h
1Ch	13:	9	his h to steady the ark,
Ezr	8:	18	gracious h of our God was on us,
Job	1:	11	now stretch out your h and strike
	40:	14	your own right h can save you
Ps	16:	8	With him at my right h,
	16:	11	eternal pleasures at your right h
	19:	1	skies proclaim the work of his h-s
	22:	16	pierced my h-s and my feet
	24:	4	clean h-s and a pure heart,
	31:	5	Into your h-s I commit my spirit;
	31:	15	My times are in your h-s;
	47:	1	Clap your h-s, all you nations;
	73:	23	you hold me by my right h
	89:	21	My h will sustain him;
	90:	17	establish the work of our h-s
	98:	8	Let the rivers clap their h-s,
	102:	25	heavens are the work of your h-s
	110:	1	'Sit at my right h until
	110:	5	The Lord is at your right h;
	121:	5	your shade at your right h
	144:	1	who trains my h-s for war,
Pr	6:	10	little folding of the h-s to rest
	10:	4	Lazy h-s make for poverty,
	21:	1	LORD's h the king's heart
	31:	13	flax and works with eager h-s

Ecc	9:	10	Whatever your h finds to do,
Isa	6:	6	with a live coal in his h,
	11:	8	will put its h into the viper's
	35:	3	Strengthen the feeble h-s,
	36:	6	pierces the h of anyone
	40:	2	received from the LORD's h double
	40:	12	the waters in the hollow of his h,
	41:	10	you with my righteous right h
	49:	16	engraved you on the palms of my h-s
Jer	32:	21	mighty h and an outstretched arm
La	2:	15	clap their h-s at you;
Eze	10:	21	looked like human h-s
Da	5:	5	fingers of a human h appeared
Am	7:	7	with a plumb-line in his h
Zec	2:	1	with a measuring line in his h
Mt	3:	12	His winnowing fork is in his h,
	5:	30	if your right h causes you to stumble,
	6:	3	do not let your left h know
	9:	25	and took the girl by the h,
	12:	10	man with a shrivelled h was there.
	15:	2	They don't wash their h-s before
	22:	44	'Sit at my right h until
	24:	9	be h-ed over to be persecuted
	26:	45	delivered into the h-s of sinners
	26:	64	Son of Man sitting at the right h
Lk	9:	62	who puts a h to the plough
	24:	40	he showed them his h-s and feet
Jn	3:	35	placed everything in his h-s
	10:	12	The hired h is not the shepherd
	10:	28	will snatch them out of my h
	20:	20	he showed them his h-s and side.
	20:	25	see the nail marks in his h-s
Ac	2:	23	This man was h-ed over to you
	2:	33	Exalted to the right h of God,
	2:	34	to my Lord: 'Sit at my right h
	7:	55	standing at the right h of God
	17:	24	live in temples built by human h-s
Ro	8:	34	is at the right h of God
	10:	21	held out my h-s to a disobedient
1Co	5:	5	h this man over to Satan
	12:	15	'Because I am not a h,
2Co	5:	1	in heaven, not built by human h-s
Eph	1:	20	seated him at his right h
Col	3:	1	Christ is, seated at the right h
1Ti	2:	8	pray, lifting up holy h-s
	5:	22	hasty in the laying on of h-s,
2Ti	1:	6	through the laying on of my h-s
Heb	1:	3	the right h of the Majesty
	10:	12	he sat down at the right h of God
	10:	31	fall into the h-s of the living God
1Pe	5:	6	under God's mighty h,
1Jn	1:	1	looked at and our h-s have touched –
Rev	1:	16	right h he held seven stars,
	6:	5	holding a pair of scales in his h

hard, -er, -ship, -ships

Ge	18:	14	Is anything too h for the LORD?
Ex	7:	13	Yet Pharaoh's heart became h
Mt	19:	8	because your hearts were h.
	19:	23	h for someone who is rich to enter
	25:	24	"I knew that you are a h man,
Jn	6:	60	'This is a h teaching.'
Ac	14:	22	'We must go through many h-ships
	26:	14	It is h for you to kick against
Ro	8:	35	Shall trouble or h-ship or
1Co	15:	10	I worked h-er than all of them
Heb	12:	7	Endure h-ship as discipline;
1Pe	4:	18	'If it is h for the righteous
2Pe	3:	16	things that are h to understand,

hate, -s, -ing, -d, -red

Ex	20:	5	generation of those who h me
Ps	5:	5	you h all who do wrong

	69:	4	Those who *h* me without reason
	139:	21	Do I not *h* those who *h* you,
Pr	6:	16	There are six things the LORD *h-s,*
	13:	24	Whoever spares the rod *h-s* their children,
	15:	17	than a fattened calf with *h-red.*
Ecc	3:	8	a time to love and a time to *h,*
Isa	1:	14	festivals I *h* with all my being
Mal	1:	3	but Esau I have *h-d,*
	2:	16	'I *h* divorce,' says the LORD God
Mt	5:	43	"Love your neighbour and *h*
	10:	22	*H-d* by everyone you because of me,
Lk	14:	26	does not *h* father and mother,
Jn	3:	20	Everyone who does evil *h-s* the
	7:	7	The world cannot *h* you,
	15:	18	If the world *h-s* you, keep in mind
Ro	9:	13	'Jacob I loved, but Esau I *h-d.*
Gal	5:	20	idolatry and witchcraft; *h-red,*
Eph	5:	29	no one ever *h-d* their own body,
1Jn	2:	9	in the light but *h-s* a brother,
	4:	20	yet *h-s* a brother or sister,
Jude		23	*h-ing* even the clothing stained by

head, -s

Ge	3:	15	he will crush your *h,*
Jdg	13:	5	whose *h* is never to be touched
Ps	22:	7	hurl insults, shaking their *h-s*
	23:	5	You anoint my *h* with oil;
	24:	7	Lift up your *h-s,* you gates;
	133:	2	like precious oil poured on the *h,*
Pr	25:	22	will heap burning coals on his *h,*
Isa	59:	17	helmet of salvation on his *h;*
Mt	5:	36	do not swear by your *h,*
	8:	20	Son of Man has nowhere to lay his *h*
	10:	30	hairs of your *h* are all numbered
	14:	8	the *h* of John the Baptist.
	27:	29	thorns and set it on his *h.*
Jn	13:	9	my hands and my *h* as well!
Ac	18:	6	'Your blood be on your own *h-s!*
Ro	12:	20	will heap burning coals on his *h.*
1Co	11:	3	the *h* of every man is Christ,
	11:	4	prophesies with his *h* covered
	11:	10	have authority over her own *h*
Eph	1:	22	*h* over everything for the church
	5:	23	the husband is the *h* of the wife
Col	1:	18	And he is the *h* of the body,
	2:	10	He is the *h* over every power
2Ti	4:	5	keep your *h* in all situations,
Rev	4:	4	crowns of gold on their *h-s*
	10:	1	with a rainbow above his *h;*
	13:	3	One of the *h-s* of the beast
	19:	12	and on his *h* are many crowns.

heal, -s, -ing, -ed

Ex	15:	26	I am the LORD, who *h-s* you.
2Ch	7:	14	forgive their sin ... *h* their land
Job	5:	18	he injures, but his hands also *h*
Ps	103:	3	and *h-s* all your diseases
	147:	3	He *h-s* the broken-hearted
Ecc	3:	3	a time to kill and a time to *h,*
Isa	6:	10	and turn and be *h-ed.*
Mal	4:	2	rise with *h-ing* in its rays.
Mt	4:	23	*h-ing* every disease and illness
	8:	8	my servant will be *h-ed*
	9:	21	touch his cloak, I will be *h-ed.*
	10:	1	to *h* every disease and illness.
Lk	4:	23	'Physician, *h* yourself!'
Jn	12:	40	nor turn – and I would *h* them.
1Co	12:	9	to another gifts of *h-ing*
Jas	5:	16	so that you may be *h-ed.*
1Pe	2:	24	by his wounds you have been *h-ed*
Rev	22:	2	for the *h-ing* of the nations

hear, -s, -ing, -d

Ge	3:	10	'I *h-d* you in the garden,
Ex	2:	24	God *h-d* their groaning
Dt	6:	4	*H,* O Israel: the LORD our God,
1Sa	15:	14	this lowing of cattle that I *h?*
1Ki	8:	30	and when you *h,* forgive
Job	42:	5	My ears had *h-d* of you
Ps	18:	6	From his temple he *h-d* my voice;
	19:	3	no sound is *h-d* from them
	34:	2	let the afflicted *h* and rejoice
	34:	6	and the LORD *h-d* him;
	80:	1	*H* us, Shepherd of Israel,
	95:	7	Today, if only you would *h*
Isa	6:	9	"'Be ever *h-ing,* but never
	29:	18	the deaf will *h* the words
	30:	21	will *h* a voice behind you
	40:	28	Have you not *h-d?* The LORD
	42:	18	'*H,* you deaf; look, you blind
	59:	1	nor his ear too dull to *h*
Jer	31:	15	'A voice is *h-d* in Ramah,
Eze	34:	7	shepherds, *h* the word of the LORD
Hab	3:	2	LORD, I have *h-d* of your fame;
Mal	3:	16	the LORD listened and *h-d.*
Mt	2:	18	'A voice is *h-d* in Ramah,
	5:	21	'You have *h-d* that it was said
	7:	24	who *h-s* these words of mine
	11:	15	Whoever has ears, let them *h*
	12:	19	No one will *h* his voice
	13:	13	though *h-ing,* they do not *h*
	13:	20	people who *h* the word and at once
	24:	6	You will *h* of wars and rumours
Mk	12:	29	"*H,* O Israel: the Lord our God,
Lk	4:	21	is fulfilled in your *h-ing.*
	8:	10	*h-ing,* they may not understand.
	11:	28	those who *h* the word of God
Jn	3:	8	You *h* its sound, but you cannot
	3:	29	he *h-s* the bridegroom's voice.
	3:	32	to what he has seen and *h-d,*
	5:	24	whoever *h-s* my word and believes
	5:	25	when the dead will *h* the voice
Ac	2:	8	*h-s* them in our native language
	19:	2	*h-d* that there is a Holy Spirit.
	28:	26	ever *h-ing* but never understanding;
Ro	10:	14	one of whom they have not *h-d?*
	10:	17	faith comes from *h-ing* the message,
1Co	2:	9	'What no eye has seen, what no ear has *h-d,*
Heb	3:	7	'Today, if you *h* his voice
	5:	7	was *h-d* because of his reverent
Jas	1:	25	not forgetting what they have *h-d*
2Pe	1:	18	We ourselves *h-d* this voice
1Jn	1:	1	which we have *h-d,*
	5:	14	according to his will, he *h-s* us
Rev	1:	3	blessed are those who *h* it
	2:	7	let them *h* what the Spirit says
	3:	20	If anyone *h-s* my voice
	21:	3	I *h-d* a loud voice from the throne
	22:	17	let the one who *h-s* say, 'Come!'

heart, -'s, -s

Ge	6:	5	thoughts of the human *h* was only evil
Ex	4:	21	I will harden his *h* so
	8:	32	Pharaoh hardened his *h* and would
Lev	19:	17	Do not hate a fellow Israelite in your *h*
Dt	4:	29	seek him with all your *h*
	6:	5	God with all your *h* and
1Sa	1:	13	Hannah was praying in her *h,*
	13:	14	sought out a man after his own *h*
	16:	7	but the LORD looks at the *h.*'
1Ki	3:	9	give your servant a discerning *h*
	8:	17	in his *h* to build a temple
	8:	39	you alone know every human *h*
Ps	7:	9	God who probes minds and *h-s.*

	13: 5	my *h* rejoices in your salvation
	14: 1	fool says in his *h*,
	19: 14	the meditation of my *h* be pleasing
	37: 4	will give you the desires of your *h*
	45: 1	My *h* is stirred by a noble theme
	51: 10	Create in me a pure *h*, O God,
	51: 17	a broken and contrite *h* you, God,
	66: 18	If I had cherished sin in my *h*,
	73: 1	to those who are pure in *h*
	73: 26	My flesh and my *h* may fail,
	84: 2	my *h* and my flesh cry out
	86: 11	give me an undivided *h*,
	95: 8	Do not harden your *h-s* as you did
	119: 11	I have hidden your word in my *h*
	139: 23	Search me, O God, and know my *h*;
Pr	3: 5	Trust in the LORD with all your *h*
	4: 23	Above all else, guard your *h*,
	12: 25	Anxiety weighs down the *h*,
	17: 3	but the LORD tests the *h*
	19: 21	Many are the plans in a person's *h*,
SS	3: 1	I looked for the one my *h* loves;
Isa	14: 13	You said in your *h*, 'I will ascend
	40: 11	and carries them close to his *h*;
Jer	17: 9	The *h* is deceitful above all things
	31: 33	write it on their *h-s*.
Eze	36: 26	I will give you a new *h*
Hos	10: 2	Their *h* is deceitful,
Joel	2: 13	Rend your *h* and not your garments.
Mal	4: 6	He will turn the *h-s* of the parents
Mt	5: 8	Blessed are the pure in *h*,
	5: 28	adultery with her in his *h*
	6: 21	there your *h* will be also
	11: 29	I am gentle and humble in *h*,
	12: 34	mouth speaks what the *h* is full
	13: 15	people's *h* has become calloused
	15: 8	their *h-s* are far from me
	15: 19	For out of the *h* come evil thoughts
	22: 37	Lord your God with all your *h*
Lk	24: 32	Were not our *h-s* burning within us
Jn	14: 1	'Do not let your *h-s* be troubled.
Ac	16: 14	The Lord opened her *h* to respond
Ro	1: 21	their foolish *h-s* were darkened
	10: 1	Brothers and sisters, my *h-'s* desire
	10: 6	say in your *h*, "Who will ascend
	10: 9	believe in your *h* that God raised
2Co	3: 15	a veil covers their *h-s*
	4: 6	made his light shine in our *h-s*
Eph	3: 17	Christ may dwell in your *h-s*
	6: 6	doing the will of God from your *h*.
Col	3: 1	set your *h-s* on things above,
	3: 15	peace of Christ rule in your *h-s*,
Heb	3: 8	do not harden your *h-s*
	3: 12	a sinful, unbelieving *h*
	10: 16	I will put my laws in their *h-s*,
	10: 22	having our *h-s* sprinkled
1Pe	3: 15	in your *h-s* revere Christ
1Jn	3: 20	if our *h-s* condemn us,

heaven, -s, -ly

Ge	1: 1	God created the *h-s* and the earth
	14: 19	Creator of *h* and earth
2Sa	22: 10	He parted the *h-s* and came down;
1Ki	8: 27	The *h-s*, even the highest *h*,
2Ki	1: 12	'may fire come down from *h*
1Ch	29: 11	everything in *h* and earth is yours.
2Ch	7: 14	I will hear from *h*, and I will forgive
Ps	2: 4	The One enthroned in *h* laughs;
	8: 3	When I consider your *h-s*,
	8: 5	a little lower than the *h-ly* beings
	19: 1	The *h-s* declare the glory of God;
	29: 1	Ascribe to the LORD, you *h-ly* beings
	73: 25	Whom have I in *h* but you?

	103: 11	For as high as the *h-s* are above
	119: 89	it stands firm in the *h-s*
	139: 8	up to the *h-s*, you are there;
Isa	14: 12	How you have fallen from *h*,
	40: 22	He stretches out the *h-s*
	55: 9	'As the *h-s* are higher than
	64: 1	Oh, that you would rend the *h-s*
	66: 1	'*H* is my throne, and the earth is
	66: 22	'As the new *h-s* and the new earth
Mal	3: 10	throw open the floodgates of *h*
Mt	3: 2	for the kingdom of *h* has come near.
	3: 17	And a voice from *h* said,
	5: 3	theirs is the kingdom of *h*
	5: 18	until *h* and earth disappear,
	5: 34	Do not swear at all: either by *h*,
	5: 45	may be children of your Father in *h*.
	6: 9	you should pray: ' "Our Father in *h*
	13: 33	'The kingdom of *h* is like yeast
	16: 19	bind on earth will be bound in *h*,
	24: 35	*H* and earth will pass away,
	26: 64	coming on the clouds of *h*.
	28: 18	'All authority in *h* and on earth
Lk	10: 20	that your names are written in *h*,
	15: 7	there will be more rejoicing in *h*
Jn	1: 32	'I saw the Spirit come down from *h*
	12: 28	a voice came from *h*,
Ac	2: 2	a violent wind came from *h*
	2: 19	I will show wonders in the *h-s* above
	4: 12	no other name under *h* given
	7: 56	'I see *h* open and the Son of Man
Ro	1: 18	is being revealed from *h*
1Co	15: 49	the image of the *h-ly* man
2Co	5: 2	clothed instead with our *h-ly* dwelling
	12: 2	caught up to the third *h*.
Gal	1: 8	if we or an angel from *h*
Php	3: 20	our citizenship is in *h*.
1Th	4: 16	will come down from *h*,
Heb	1: 3	right hand of the Majesty in *h*
	4: 14	priest who has ascended into *h*,
	9: 24	he entered *h* itself, now to appear
	11: 16	a better country – a *h-ly* one.
1Pe	1: 4	kept in *h* for you
2Pe	3: 5	by God's word the *h-s* came
	3: 13	looking forward to a new *h* and
Rev	4: 1	a door standing open in *h*.
	21: 1	Then I saw 'a new *h* and a new earth,
	21: 2	coming down out of *h* from God,

help, -ing, -ed, -less, -er

Ge	2: 18	will make a *h-er* suitable for him.
Dt	33: 29	He is your shield and *h-er*
Ps	18: 29	*h* I can advance against a troop;
	46: 1	an ever-present *h* in trouble
	121: 1	where does my *h* come from?
Mt	9: 36	they were harassed and *h-less*,
	15: 5	used to *h* their father or mother
	15: 25	'Lord, *h* me!' she said.
	25: 44	in prison, and did not *h* you?
Mk	9: 24	believe; *h* me overcome my unbelief!
Lk	1: 54	He has *h-ed* his servant Israel,
Ac	4: 20	*h* speaking about what we have seen
	9: 36	doing good, and *h-ing* the poor.
	16: 9	'Come over to Macedonia and *h* us.
	20: 35	we must *h* the weak, remembering
1Co	12: 28	gifts of healing, of *h-ing*
2Co	6: 2	in the day of salvation I *h-ed* you.
1Th	5: 14	encourage the disheartened, *h* the weak
Heb	2: 18	to *h* those who are being tempted
	4: 16	grace to *h* us in our time of need
	13: 6	'The Lord is my *h-er*; I will not

hid, -den

Ge	3:	8	they *h* from the LORD God
Ps	19:	12	Forgive my *h-den* faults
	119:	11	I have *h-den* your word in my heart
Isa	59:	2	sins have *h-den* his face from you,
Mt	5:	14	A city on a hill cannot be *h-den*
	10:	26	*h-den* that will not be made known
	11:	25	*h-den* these things from the wise
	13:	44	like treasure *h-den* in a field.
	25:	18	ground and *h* his master's money
Ac	1:	9	a cloud *h* him from their sight
Ro	16:	25	mystery *h-den* for long ages past
1Co	2:	7	a mystery that has been *h-den*
Eph	3:	9	ages past was kept *h-den* in God,
Col	1:	26	mystery that has been kept *h-den*
	2:	3	*h-den* all the treasures of wisdom
Heb	4:	13	Nothing in all creation is *h-den*

hide, -s

Ge	18:	17	'Shall I *h* from Abraham what
Ex	2:	3	when she could *h* him no longer,
Job	14:	13	only you would *h* me in the grave
Ps	10:	1	Why do you *h* yourself in times
	51:	9	*H* your face from my sins
Isa	45:	15	you are a God who has been *h-ing*
	50:	6	I did not *h* my face from mocking
	53:	3	one from whom people *h* their faces
Lk	8:	16	'No one lights a lamp and *h-s* it
Rev	6:	16	'Fall on us and *h* us from the face

high, -est

Ge	14:	18	He was priest of God Most *H*
	14:	19	'Blessed be Abram by God Most *H,*
Lev	26:	30	I will destroy your *h* places,
2Ch	2:	6	*h-est* heavens, cannot contain him?
Ps	50:	14	fulfil your vows to the Most *H*
	68:	18	When you ascended on *h,* you took
	91:	1	in the shelter of the Most *H*
	103:	11	For as *h* as the heavens are above
Isa	6:	1	the Lord, *h* and exalted,
Mt	26:	51	the *h* priest, cutting off his ear
	26:	57	took him to Caiaphas the *h* priest,
Mk	5:	7	Jesus, Son of the Most *H* God?
Lk	1:	32	be called the Son of the Most *H.*
	1:	35	power of the Most *H* will overshadow
	24:	49	clothed with power from on *h.*
Ac	7:	48	the Most *H* does not live in houses
	16:	17	men are servants of the Most *H* God,
Eph	4:	8	he ascended on *h,* he took many captives
Php	2:	9	God exalted him to the *h-est* place
Heb	2:	17	a merciful and faithful *h* priest
	3:	1	as our apostle and *h* priest
	4:	15	have a *h* priest who is unable
	5:	1	Every *h* priest is selected
	6:	20	He has become a *h* priest for ever,
	8:	1	We do have such a *h* priest,

hill, -s

Ps	50:	10	and the cattle on a thousand *h-s*
Isa	40:	4	every mountain and *h* made low;
Mt	5:	14	A city on a *h* cannot be hidden
Lk	3:	5	every mountain and *h* made low.
	23:	30	and to the *h-s* 'Cover us!'
Ac	1:	12	the *h* called the Mount of Olives,
Rev	17:	9	seven *h-s* on which the woman sits

hold, -s

Ps	73:	23	you *h* me by my right hand
Ac	2:	24	for death to keep its *h* on him
1Co	15:	2	if you *h* firmly to the word
Php	2:	16	as you *h* firmly to the word of life.
1Ti	6:	12	Take *h* of the eternal life
Heb	2:	14	him who *h-s* the power of death –

	4:	14	let us *h* firmly to the faith
Rev	2:	1	him who *h-s* the seven stars
	2:	4	Yet I *h* this against you:

holy

Ge	2:	3	the seventh day and made it *h,*
Ex	3:	5	you are standing is *h* ground.
	20:	8	Sabbath day by keeping it *h*
	26:	33	*H* Place from the Most *H* Place.
Lev	10:	3	I will be proved *h;*
	11:	45	be *h,* because I am *h*
Dt	7:	6	a people *h* to the LORD your God.
Jos	5:	15	where you are standing is *h.'*
1Sa	2:	2	'There is no one *h* like the LORD;
Ps	2:	6	my king on Zion, my *h* mountain.
Isa	6:	3	*H, h, h* is the LORD Almighty
	40:	25	who is my equal?' says the *H* One
Zec	14:	5	and all the *h* ones with him
	14:	20	*h* to the Lord will be inscribed
Mk	1:	24	you are – the *H* One of God!
Ac	2:	27	will not let your *h* one see decay
Ro	1:	2	his prophets in the *H* Scriptures
	7:	12	So then, the law is *h,*
	12:	1	sacrifice, *h* and pleasing to God
1Co	1:	2	Christ Jesus and called to be his *h* people
Eph	1:	4	to be *h* and blameless in his sight.
1Th	4:	7	be impure, but to live a *h* life.
1Ti	2:	8	to pray, lifting up *h* hands
2Ti	1:	9	and called us to a *h* life –
	3:	15	you have known the *H* Scriptures,
Heb	7:	26	one who is *h,* blameless, pure,
	10:	14	those who are being made *h*
	10:	19	to enter the Most *H* Place
	12:	14	peace with everyone and to be *h;*
1Pe	1:	16	'Be *h,* because I am *h*
	2:	9	a royal priesthood, a *h* nation,
2Pe	3:	11	You ought to live *h* and godly lives
Rev	4:	8	"*H, h, h* is the Lord God
	21:	2	the *H* City, the new Jerusalem,

home, -s

Dt	6:	7	Talk about them when you sit at *h*
Ps	84:	3	Even the sparrow has found a *h,*
Mt	10:	12	*h,* give it your greeting
	13:	57	honour except in his own ... *h*
Mk	10:	29	'no one who has left *h* or brothers
Lk	15:	30	*h,* you kill the fattened calf
	18:	14	went *h* justified before God.
Jn	14:	23	to them and make our *h* with them
Ac	2:	46	They broke bread in their *h-s*
	16:	15	she invited us to her *h.*
1Co	11:	22	Don't you have *h-s* to eat
	14:	35	ask their own husbands at *h;*
2Co	5:	6	at *h* in the body we are away
	5:	8	body and at *h* with the Lord
Tit	2:	5	to be busy at *h,*

honour, -s

Ex	20:	12	'*H* your father and your mother,
1Sa	2:	30	Those who *h* me I will *h,*
Ps	8:	5	crowned them with glory and *h*
Mal	1:	6	'A son *h-s* his father,
Mt	13:	57	prophet is not without *h* except
	15:	4	For God said, "*H* your father
	15:	8	These people *h* me with their lips,
Jn	5:	23	that all may *h* the Son just as
	12:	26	My Father will *h* the one
Ro	2:	7	seek glory, *h* and immortality,
	12:	10	*H* one another above yourselves
1Co	6:	20	Therefore *h* God with your bodies
Eph	6:	2	'*H* your father and mother' –
Heb	2:	7	you crowned them with glory and *h*

hope, -s, -d

Job	13:	15	slay me, yet will I *h* in him;
Ps	25:	3	No one who *h-s* in you will ever
	42:	5	Put your *h* in God,
	71:	14	as for me, I shall always have *h;*
	130:	7	Israel, put your *h* in the LORD,
Pr	13:	12	*H* deferred makes the heart sick,
Isa	40:	31	who *h* in the LORD will renew
Mt	12:	21	the nations will put their *h.*
Lk	24:	21	we had *h-d* that he was the one
Ac	26:	6	my *h* in what God has promised
Ro	4:	18	Against all *h,* Abraham in *h*
	5:	2	in the *h* of the glory of God
	5:	4	character; and character, *h.*
	8:	24	Who *h-s* for what they already have
	12:	12	joyful in *h,* patient in affliction,
	15:	4	they provide we might have *h*
	15:	13	May the God of *h* fill you with
	15:	13	so that you may overflow with *h*
1Co	13:	13	three remain: faith, *h* and love.
	15:	19	for this life we have *h* in Christ,
Eph	1:	12	were the first to put our *h* in Christ,
	2:	12	without *h* and without God
Col	1:	23	not move from the *h* held out
	1:	27	Christ in you, the *h* of glory
1Th	4:	13	the rest of mankind, who have no *h*
	5:	8	the *h* of salvation as a helmet.
1Ti	4:	10	have put our *h* in the living God,
Tit	2:	13	we wait for the blessed *h* –
Heb	6:	19	this *h* as an anchor for the soul,
	10:	23	unswervingly to the *h* we profess,
	11:	1	faith is being sure of what we *h*
1Pe	1:	3	new birth into a living *h*
	3:	15	the reason for the *h* that you have.
1Jn	3:	3	this *h* in him purify themselves,

house, -s, -hold, -holds

Ge	28:	17	none other than the *h* of God;
Ex	20:	17	not covet your neighbour's *h.*
Jos	24:	15	as for me and my *h-hold,*
2Sa	7:	2	Here I am, living in a *h* of cedar,
	7:	13	who will build a *h* for my Name,
	23:	5	'If my *h* were not right with God,
1Ch	17:	12	the one who will build a *h* for me,
Ps	23:	6	dwell in the *h* of the LORD
	27:	4	I may dwell in the *h* of the LORD
	69:	9	zeal for your *h* consumes me,
	84:	10	a doorkeeper in the *h* of my God
	122:	1	'Let us go to the *h* of the LORD.
	127:	1	Unless the LORD builds the *h,*
Pr	15:	27	The greedy bring ruin to their *h-holds*
	25:	24	share a *h* with a quarrelsome wife
Jer	18:	2	'Go down to the potter's *h,*
Hag	1:	4	to be living in your panelled *h-s,*
	2:	9	'The glory of this present *h*
Mt	7:	24	a wise man who built his *h*
	10:	36	the members of his own *h-hold.*
	12:	25	city or *h-hold* divided against
	12:	29	anyone enter a strong man's *h*
	12:	44	"I will return to the *h* I left."
	21:	13	"My *h* will be called a house
Lk	2:	4	to the *h* and line of David
	2:	49	I had to be in my Father's *h*?
	11:	17	*h* divided against itself will fall.
	19:	·5	I must stay at your *h* today.
	20:	47	They devour widows' *h-s*
Jn	2:	17	'Zeal for your *h* will consume me.
	14:	2	My Father's *h* has plenty of room;
Ac	2:	2	heaven and filled the whole *h*
	7:	48	Most High does not live in *h-s*
	16:	31	be saved – you and your *h-hold.*
	16:	33	he and all his *h-hold* were baptised

	16:	34	believe in God – he and his whole *h-hold*
Ro	16:	5	church that meets at their *h.*
2Co	5:	1	an eternal *h* in heaven,
Eph	2:	19	members of his *h-hold*
1Ti	3:	12	manage his children and his *h-hold*
	5:	8	and especially for their own *h-hold*
2Ti	2:	20	In a large *h* there are articles
Heb	3:	3	builder of a *h* has greater honour
	3:	6	faithful as the Son over God's *h.*
	10:	21	a great priest over the *h* of God
1Pe	2:	5	being built into a spiritual *h*
	4:	17	judgment to begin with God's *h-hold.*

human, -s

Ge	1:	26	'Let us make *h* beings in our image,
	6:	5	how great the wickedness of the *h* race
	9:	6	Whoever sheds *h* blood, by *h-s*
Nu	23:	19	God is not *h,* that he should lie
1Sa	2:	25	If anyone sins against another *h* being,
Job	4:	17	Can *h* beings be more pure
Isa	29:	13	*h* rules they have been taught
Da	2:	34	cut out, but not by *h* hands
Mt	15:	9	teachings are merely *h* rules
Ac	5:	29	'We must obey God rather than *h* beings
Ro	1:	23	images made to look like a mortal *h* being
	9:	20	But who are you, a *h* being,
1Co	2:	5	might not rest on *h* wisdom,
Heb	2:	17	made like them, fully *h*
Jas	5:	17	Elijah was a *h* being, even as we are
2Pe	1:	21	but prophets, though *h,* spoke from God

husband, -s

Isa	54:	5	your Maker is your *h* –
Hos	2:	2	and I am not her *h.*
Jn	4:	16	'Go, call your *h* and come back.
Ro	7:	2	a married woman is bound to her *h*
1Co	7:	3	*h* should fulfil his marital duty
Eph	5:	22	to your own *h-s* as you do to the Lord
	5:	23	the *h* is the head of the wife
	5:	25	*H-s,* love your wives, just as
1Pe	3:	7	*H-s,* in the same way
Rev	21:	2	beautifully dressed for her *h*

i

idol, -s

Ex	32:	4	an *i* cast in the shape of a calf,
1Ch	16:	26	the gods of the nations are *i-s,*
Ps	115:	4	their *i-s* are silver and gold,
Isa	40:	19	As for an *i,* a metalworker casts it,
Jer	2:	11	their glorious God for worthless *i-s*
Ac	15:	20	abstain from food polluted by *i-s,*
	17:	16	the city was full of *i-s*
1Co	8:	1	Now about food sacrificed to *i-s:*
2Co	6:	16	between the temple of God and *i-s*?
1Th	1:	9	how you turned to God from *i-s*
1Jn	5:	21	keep yourselves from *i-s*

image, -s

Ge	1:	26	make mankind in our *i*
Ex	20:	4	not make for yourself an *i*
Isa	40:	18	To what *i* will you liken him
Da	3:	1	Nebuchadnezzar made an *i* of gold
Ro	1:	23	for *i-s* made to look like a mortal
	8:	29	conformed to the *i* of his Son
2Co	3:	18	transformed into his *i*
	4:	4	Christ, who is the *i* of God
Col	1:	15	the *i* of the invisible God

inheritance

Ge	21:	10	share in the *i* with my son Isaac.
Ex	32:	13	it will be their *i* for ever."
Ps	2:	8	I will make the nations your *i,*

	33:	12	the people he chose for his *i*
Mt	21:	38	let's kill him and take his *i*.
	25:	34	blessed by my Father; take your *i*,
Lk	12:	13	tell my brother to divide the *i*
Gal	3:	18	if the *i* depends on the law,
Eph	1:	14	a deposit guaranteeing our *i*
	1:	18	his glorious *i* in his holy people
Heb	9:	15	receive the promised eternal *i* –
1Pe	1:	4	into an *i* that can never perish,

instruct, -ion, -ions

Ex	12:	24	these *i-ions* as a lasting ordinance
Ne	9:	20	gave your good Spirit to *i* them.
Pr	1:	8	Listen ... to your father's *i-ion*
	9:	9	*I* the wise and they will be wiser
Isa	8:	20	Consult God's *i-ion* and the testimony
	40:	13	or *i* the LORD as his counsellor?
Ac	1:	2	*i-ions* through the Holy Spirit
Ro	15:	14	competent to *i* one another.
1Co	2:	16	the Lord so as to *i* him?
Gal	6:	6	the one who receives *i-ion* in the word
Eph	6:	4	the training and *i-ion* of the Lord

intercede, -s, -ing

Ge	23:	8	*i* with Ephron son of Zohar
1Sa	2:	25	who will *i* for them?'
	7:	5	I will *i* with the LORD for you.
1Ki	13:	6	*I* with the LORD your God
Ro	8:	26	the Spirit himself *i-s* for us
	8:	34	and is also *i-ing* for us
Heb	7:	25	because he always lives to *i* for them

Israel

Ex	4:	22	*I* is my firstborn son
	5:	2	obey him and let *I* go?
	14:	30	LORD saved *I* from the hands
	24:	10	and saw the God of *I*.
Nu	32:	13	The LORD's anger burned against *I*
Dt	6:	4	Hear, O *I*: the LORD our God,
Jos	10:	14	the LORD was fighting for *I*
Jdg	21:	25	In those days *I* had no king;
1Sa	4:	22	'The glory has departed from *I*,
	9:	2	as could be found anywhere in *I*
	15:	26	rejected you as king over *I*!
	15:	29	He who is the Glory of *I*
	17:	46	there is a God in *I*
2Sa	3:	18	I will rescue my people *I*
	7:	8	you ruler over my people *I*
	20:	1	Every man to his tent, *I*!'
1Ki	9:	5	royal throne over *I* for ever,
	17:	1	'As the LORD, the God of *I*, lives,
	18:	18	'I have not made trouble for *I*,'
	22:	17	'I saw all *I* scattered
2Ki	1:	3	because there is no God in *I*
	2:	12	The chariots and horsemen of *I*!'
2Ch	18:	16	'I saw all *I* scattered
Ezr	3:	11	his love towards *I* endures for ever.'
Ps	14:	7	that salvation for *I* would come
	22:	3	you are the praise of *I*
	73:	1	Surely God is good to *I*,
	78:	41	they vexed the Holy One of *I*
	80:	1	Hear us, Shepherd of *I*,
	118:	2	Let *I* say: 'His love endures
	149:	2	Let *I* rejoice in their Maker;
Isa	41:	8	'But you, *I*, my servant, Jacob
	54:	5	Holy One of *I* is your Redeemer;
Jer	3:	11	'Faithless *I* is more righteous
	3:	23	God is the salvation of *I*
	50:	17	'*I* is a scattered flock
	50:	19	bring *I* back to their own pasture
Eze	3:	17	a watchman for the house of *I*;
	8:	4	the glory of the God of *I*,
	12:	6	a sign to the house of *I*.
	18:	31	Why will you die, house of *I*

	21:	2	Prophesy against the land of *I*
	34:	2	against the shepherds of *I*;
	39:	23	*I* went into exile for their sin,
	39:	29	my Spirit on the house of *I*,
Hos	8:	14	*I* has forgotten his Maker
	10:	1	*I* was a spreading vine;
	11:	1	'When *I* was a child, I loved him,
	14:	5	I will be like the dew to *I*;
Am	2:	6	'For three sins of *I*, even
Mic	5:	2	one who will be ruler over *I*,
Mt	2:	6	who will shepherd my people *I*."
	8:	10	I have not found anyone in *I*
	10:	6	Go rather to the lost sheep of *I*
	19:	28	judging the twelve tribes of *I*.
Mk	12:	29	Hear, O *I*: the Lord our God,
	15:	32	Messiah, this king of *I*,
Lk	2:	25	waiting for the consolation of *I*,
	4:	25	many widows in *I* in Elijah's time,
	24:	21	one who was going to redeem *I*.
Jn	1:	31	he might be revealed to *I*.
	1:	49	you are the king of *I*.
	12:	13	'Blessed is the king of *I*!
Ac	1:	6	to restore the kingdom to *I*?
	5:	31	bring *I* to repentance and forgive
Ro	9:	4	the people of *I*. Theirs is
	9:	6	who are descended from *I* are *I*.
	9:	31	*I*, who pursued the law as the way
	11:	26	this way all *I* will be saved.
Gal	6:	16	– to the *I* of God
Eph	3:	6	heirs together with *I*,
Heb	8:	8	new covenant with the house of *I*

Israelite, -s

Ex	1:	7	the *I-s* were exceedingly fruitful
	3:	15	Moses, 'Say to the *I-s*,
	14:	22	the *I-s* went through the sea
	29:	45	I will dwell among the *I-s*
Lev	25:	42	the *I-s* are my servants,
Nu	14:	2	the *I-s* grumbled against Moses
	20:	13	where the *I-s* quarrelled
Dt	34:	8	The *I-s* grieved for Moses
Jos	7:	1	But the *I-s* were unfaithful
Jdg	2:	11	the *I-s* did evil in the eyes
1Ki	8:	9	made a covenant with the *I-s*
	19:	10	*I-s* have rejected your covenant,
2Ki	17:	7	because the *I-s* had sinned
Eze	2:	3	I am sending you to the *I-s*,
Hos	3:	1	as the LORD loves the *I-s*,
	3:	5	the *I-s* will return
Ro	9:	27	the *I-s* be like the sand
	10:	1	prayer to God for the *I-s* is
2Co	3:	7	the *I-s* could not look steadily
	11:	22	Are they *I-s*? So am I.

J

Jerusalem

Jos	15:	63	the Jebusites, who were living in *J*
2Sa	5:	6	The king and his men marched to *J*
2Ki	21:	12	going to bring such disaster on *J*
	23:	27	I will reject *J*, the city I chose,
	24:	14	He carried all *J* into exile:
2Ch	9:	1	she came to *J* to test him
	12:	7	wrath will not be poured out on *J*
	33:	4	'My Name will remain in *J* for ever
	36:	19	and broke down the wall of *J*;
Ezr	7:	13	who volunteer to go to *J* with you,
Ne	1:	3	The wall of *J* is broken down,
	11:	2	who volunteered to live in *J*
Ps	51:	18	build up the walls of *J*
	79:	1	they have reduced *J* to rubble

	122:	3	*J* is built like a city
	122:	6	Pray for the peace of *J:*
	128:	5	may you see the prosperity of *J*
	137:	5	If I forget you, *J,*
SS	3:	5	Daughters of *J,* I charge you
Isa	2:	3	the word of the LORD from *J*
	40:	2	Speak tenderly to *J,*
	65:	19	I will rejoice over *J*
Jer	26:	18	*J* will become a heap of rubble,
Eze	16:	2	'Son of man, confront *J*
	24:	2	king of Babylon has laid siege to *J*
Joel	2:	32	in *J* there will be deliverance,
	3:	17	*J* will be holy;
Mic	4:	2	the word of the LORD from *J*
Zec	8:	8	I will bring them back to live in *J*
Mt	2:	1	Magi from the east came to *J*
	3:	5	People went out to him from *J*
	21:	10	When Jesus entered *J,* the whole
	23:	37	'*J, J,* you who kill
Mk	10:	33	'We are going up to *J,*' he said,
Lk	2:	22	Mary took him to *J* to present him
	2:	43	the boy Jesus stayed behind in *J,*
	19:	41	As he approached *J* and saw the city
	21:	20	'When you see *J* being surrounded
	21:	24	*J* will be trampled on
	24:	47	to all nations, beginning at *J*
Jn	4:	20	where we must worship is in *J.*
	5:	1	Jesus went up to *J*
Ac	1:	8	and you will be my witnesses in *J,*
	11:	2	So when Peter went up to *J,*
Ro	15:	26	among the Lord's people in *J*
1Co	16:	3	and send them with your gift to *J*
Gal	1:	18	after three years, I went up to *J*
	4:	26	But the *J* that is above is free,
Heb	12:	22	living God, the heavenly *J,*
Rev	21:	2	I saw the Holy City, the new *J,*

Jew, -s

Ezr	6:	14	the elders of the *J-s*
Ne	4:	1	He ridiculed the *J-s*
Est	3:	13	kill and annihilate all the *J-s* –
	4:	14	deliverance for the *J-s* will arise
Da	3:	8	came forward and denounced the *J-s*
Mt	2:	2	who has been born king of the *J-s?*
	27:	11	'Are you the king of the *J-s?*'
	27:	29	'Hail, king of the *J-s!*'
Jn	4:	9	*J-s* do not associate with Samaritans
	4:	22	for salvation is from the *J-s*
	8:	31	To the *J-s* who had believed him,
	12:	11	the *J-s* were going over to Jesus
Ac	10:	28	for a *J* to associate with or visit a Gentile
	14:	1	number of *J-s* and Greeks believed
	18:	4	trying to persuade *J-s* and Greeks
	21:	39	'I am a *J,* from Tarsus in Cilicia,
Ro	1:	16	first to the *J,* then to
	2:	29	a person is a *J* who is one inwardly;
	3:	29	Or is God the God of *J-s* only?
	10:	12	no difference between *J* and Gentile
	15:	8	has become a servant of the *J-s*
1Co	1:	23	a stumbling-block to *J-s*
	9:	20	To the *J-s* I became like a *J,*
Gal	2:	8	Peter as an apostle to the *J-s,*
	3:	28	There is neither *J* nor Gentile,
Rev	3:	9	claim to be *J-s* though they are not

joy

Ne	8:	10	the *j* of the LORD is your strength
Ps	16:	11	fill me with *j* in your presence,
	51:	12	the *j* of your salvation
	98:	4	Shout for *j* to the LORD,
Isa	12:	3	With *j* you will draw water
	55:	12	You will go out in *j*
Lk	6:	23	Rejoice in that day and leap for *j*

Jn	15:	11	so that my *j* may be in you
	16:	20	but your grief will turn to *j*
Ro	14:	17	peace and *j* in the Holy Spirit
Gal	4:	15	What has happened to all your *j*?
	5:	22	the fruit of the Spirit is love, *j,*
Php	1:	4	I always pray with *j*
	1:	25	your progress and *j* in the faith
1Th	1:	6	with the *j* given by the Holy Spirit
Heb	12:	2	For the *j* that was set before him
1Pe	1:	8	an inexpressible and glorious *j*
1Jn	1:	4	this to make our *j* complete
Jude	:	24	without fault and with great *j*

Judah

2Sa	3:	10	David's throne over Israel and *J*
1Ki	1:	35	ruler over Israel and *J.*
	4:	20	The people of *J* and Israel
	14:	22	*J* did evil in the eyes of the LORD.
2Ch	11:	14	and came to *J* and Jerusalem
	11:	17	They strengthened the kingdom of *J*
	12:	12	Indeed, there was some good in *J*
	17:	9	They taught throughout *J,*
	24:	18	God's anger came on *J*
	24:	24	Because *J* had forsaken the LORD,
	25:	22	*J* was routed by Israel,
	28:	19	The LORD had humbled *J*
	29:	21	for the sanctuary and for *J.*
Ne	6:	7	"There is a king in *J!*"
Ps	60:	7	*J* is my sceptre
	76:	1	God is renowned in *J;*
	78:	68	but he chose the tribe of *J,*
	114:	2	*J* became God's sanctuary,
Isa	3:	8	Jerusalem staggers, *J* is falling;
	7:	17	since Ephraim broke away from *J*
	11:	12	assemble the scattered people of *J*
	37:	31	a remnant of the house of *J*
	40:	9	say to the towns of *J,*
Jer	3:	7	her unfaithful sister *J* saw it
	14:	19	Have you rejected *J* completely?
	23:	6	In his days *J* will be saved
	24:	5	I regard as good the exiles from *J,*
	30:	3	I will bring my people Israel and *J*
	31:	24	People will live together in *J*
	33:	7	I will bring *J* and Israel back
La	1:	3	*J* has gone into exile.
	1:	15	trampled Virgin Daughter *J*
Eze	48:	7	'*J* will have one portion;
Da	1:	6	chosen were some from *J:* Daniel,
Hos	1:	7	I will show love to the house of *J;*
	6:	4	What can I do with you, *J?*
Am	2:	5	I will send fire on *J*
Zec	2:	12	LORD will inherit *J* as his portion
	14:	14	*J* too will fight at Jerusalem.
Mal	2:	11	*J* has been unfaithful.

judge, -s, -ing, -d

Ge	18:	25	Will not the *J* of all the earth
Ex	2:	14	'Who made you ruler and *j* over us?
Dt	1:	17	Do not show partiality in *j-ing;*
Jdg	2:	16	Then the LORD raised up *j-s,*
Ps	98:	9	for he comes to *j* the earth.
Isa	11:	4	but with righteousness he will *j*
Mt	7:	1	Do not *j,* or you too will be *j-d*
Lk	18:	2	'In a certain town there was a *j*
Jn	5:	24	life and will not be *j-d*
	7:	24	Stop *j-ing* by mere appearances,
Ro	2:	16	day when God *j-s* people's secrets
	14:	10	why do you *j* your brother
1Co	6:	2	the Lord's people will *j* the world?
	11:	32	*j-d* in this way by the Lord,
2Ti	4:	1	who will *j* the living and the dead,
Heb	12:	23	have come to God, the *J* of all,

1Pe	4:	5	ready to *j* the living and the dead
Rev	20:	12	dead were *j-d* according to what

judgment

Mt	11:	24	bearable for Sodom on the day of *j*
Jn	5:	22	has entrusted all *j* to the Son,
	9:	39	Jesus said, 'For *j* I have come
	12:	31	Now is the time for *j* on this world
	16:	8	about sin and righteousness and *j:*
Ro	14:	13	stop passing *j* on one another.
1Co	11:	29	eats and drinks *j* on themselves
2Co	5:	10	appear before the *j* seat of Christ,
1Ti	3:	6	fall under the same *j* as the devil
Heb	9:	27	die once, and after that to face *j*
1Pe	4:	17	*j* to begin with God's household;
2Pe	3:	7	being kept for the day of *j*
Rev	14:	7	because the hour of his *j* has come.

just, -ly, -ice

Ps	37:	28	For the LORD loves the *j*
	140:	12	the LORD secures *j-ice* for the poor
Pr	17:	23	to pervert the course of *j-ice*
Isa	42:	1	he will bring *j-ice* to the nations
Am	5:	24	But let *j-ice* roll on like a river,
Mic	6:	8	To act *j-ly* and to love mercy
Mt	12:	18	will proclaim *j-ice* to the nations
Lk	11:	42	neglect *j-ice* and the love of God.
Jn	5:	30	my judgment is *j*, for I seek not
Ac	17:	31	he will judge the world with *j-ice*
1Jn	1:	9	he is faithful and *j*

justify, -ies, -ied

Ps	51:	4	and *j-ied* when you judge
Isa	53:	11	my righteous servant will *j* many,
Lk	10:	29	But he wanted to *j* himself,
	18:	14	went home *j-ied* before God.
Ro	3:	24	and are *j-ied* freely by his grace
	4:	5	trusts God who *j-ies* the ungodly,
	5:	1	we have been *j-ied* through faith,
	5:	9	have now been *j-ied* by his blood,
	8:	30	those he called, he also *j-ied;*
	8:	33	It is God who *j-ies*
	10:	that you believe and are *j-ied*,
Gal	2:	16	not *j-ied* by the works of the law,
	3:	8	God would *j* the Gentiles by faith,
Tit	3:	7	having been *j-ied* by his grace,

k

keep, -ing, -er

Ge	4:	9	'Am I my brother's *k-er*?
	31:	49	the LORD *k* watch between you and me
Ex	20:	6	who love me and *k* my commandments
	20:	8	the Sabbath day by *k-ing* it holy
Nu	6:	24	'The LORD bless you and *k* you
2Ki	23:	3	follow the LORD and *k* his commands,
1Ch	10:	13	he did not *k* the word of the LORD,
Ps	17:	8	*K* me as the apple of your eye;
	19:	11	in *k-ing* them there is great reward
	34:	13	*k* your tongue from evil
	121:	7	The LORD will *k* you from all harm –
Ecc	12:	13	fear God and *k* his commandments,
Isa	26:	3	You will *k* in perfect peace
Jer	17:	22	but *k* the Sabbath day holy,
Mt	10:	10	for the worker is worth his *k*
	19:	17	to enter life, *k* the commandments.
	24:	42	'Therefore *k* watch,
	26:	40	'Couldn't you men *k* watch with me
Lk	17:	33	Whoever tries to *k* their life
Jn	12:	25	will *k* it for eternal life
	12:	47	hears my words but does not *k* them,
	14:	15	'If you love me, *k* my commands

Ac	20:	28	*K* watch over yourselves
1Co	1:	8	He will also *k* you firm to the end,
Gal	5:	25	let us *k* in step with the Spirit
Eph	4:	3	to *k* the unity of the Spirit
Heb	13:	1	*K* on loving one another as brothers
1Jn	5:	3	love for God: to *k* his commands.
	5:	21	*k* yourselves from idols
Jude		21	*k* yourselves in God's love
		24	who is able to *k* you from stumbling
Rev	22:	9	all who *k* the words of this scroll.

kept

Dt	7:	8	the LORD loved you and *k* the oath
1Ki	8:	20	'The LORD has *k* the promise he made
	11:	11	not *k* my covenant and my decrees,
Ps	130:	3	If you, LORD, *k* a record of sins,
Lk	18:	21	these I have *k* since I was a boy,'
2Ti	4:	7	I have *k* the faith
Heb	13:	4	and the marriage bed *k* pure,
1Pe	1:	4	*k* in heaven for you
Rev	3:	8	yet you have *k* my word

kill, -s, -ed

Ge	4:	8	his brother Abel and *k-ed* him
	37:	18	they plotted to *k* him
Ex	2:	15	he tried to *k* Moses, but Moses fled
	13:	15	LORD *k-ed* the firstborn of both
Lev	24:	21	*k-s* a human being is to be put to death
2Ki	5:	7	Can I *k* and bring back to life?
Ecc	3:	3	a time to *k* and a time to heal,
Jer	18:	23	all their plots to *k* me.
Mt	2:	16	to *k* all the boys in Bethlehem
Mk	3:	4	or to do evil, to save life or to *k*
	12:	7	This is the heir. Come, let's *k* him
Lk	12:	4	do not be afraid of those who *k*
	13:	34	Jerusalem, you who *k* the prophets
Jn	7:	19	Why are you trying to *k* me?
	10:	10	The thief comes only to steal and *k*
Ac	3:	15	You *k-ed* the author of life,
	10:	13	'Get up, Peter. *K* and eat.
	10:	39	*k-ed* him by hanging him on a cross
	16:	27	and was about to *k* himself
2Co	3:	6	for the letter *k-s*, but the Spirit
	6:	9	beaten, and yet not *k-ed*
1Th	2:	15	who *k-ed* the Lord Jesus

kind, -ness, -nesses

Ex	1:	20	God was *k* to the midwives
Ru	1:	8	May the LORD show you *k-ness*,
Pr	19:	17	Whoever is *k* to the poor lends
Isa	63:	7	tell of the *k-nesses* of the LORD,
Hos	11:	4	with cords of human *k-ness*,
Lk	6:	35	because he is *k* to the ungrateful
Ro	2:	4	his *k-ness*, forbearance and patience,
	11:	22	the *k-ness* and sternness of God:
1Co	13:	4	Love is patient, love is *k*.
Gal	5:	22	peace, patience, *k-ness*, goodness,
Eph	4:	32	Be *k* and compassionate

king, -'s, -s

Ge	14:	18	Melchizedek *k* of Salem
Dt	7:	24	will give their *k-s* into your hand,
	28:	36	the *k* you set over you
Jos	8:	23	they took the *k* of Ai alive
Jdg	17:	6	In those days Israel had no *k;*
1Sa	8:	5	now appoint a *k* to lead us,
	10:	24	people shouted, 'Long live the *k*!
	12:	2	Now you have a *k* as your leader.
	12:	12	though the LORD your God was your *k*
	15:	17	The LORD anointed you *k* over Israel
	15:	23	he has rejected you as *k*.
	24:	20	I know that you will surely be *k*
2Sa	2:	4	and there they anointed David *k*
1Ki	1:	30	Solomon your son shall be *k*

Ps	2:	6	'I have installed my *K* on Zion,
	10:	16	The Lord is *K* for ever and ever;
	20:	9	Lord, give victory to the *k*!
	24:	7	that the *K* of glory may come in
	47:	2	the great *K* over all the earth
	48:	2	the city of the Great *K*
	72:	1	Endow the *k* with your justice,
	72:	11	May all *k-s* bow down to him
	74:	12	But God is my *K* from long ago;
	95:	3	the great *K* above all gods
Pr	14:	35	A *k* delights in a wise servant,
	16:	13	*K-s* take pleasure in honest lips;
	19:	12	A *k-'s* rage is like the roar
	20:	28	Love and faithfulness keep a *k* safe
	24:	21	Fear the Lord and the *k*, my son,
Isa	6:	5	and my eyes have seen the *K*,
	44:	6	Israel's *K* and Redeemer,
	52:	15	*k-s* will shut their mouths because
Jer	10:	10	he is the living God, the eternal *K*
Da	1:	19	so they entered the *k-'s* service
Zec	9:	9	See, your *k* comes to you,
	14:	9	Lord will be *k* over the whole earth
Mt	2:	2	who has been born *k* of the Jews?
	21:	5	"See, your *k* comes to you,
	25:	40	'The *K* will reply, "Truly I tell
	27:	37	Jesus, the *k* of the Jews.
Lk	14:	31	suppose a *k* is about to go to war
	19:	38	'Blessed is the *k* who comes
Jn	18:	37	'You say that I am a *k*.
Ac	4:	26	The *k-s* of the earth rise up
	9:	15	to the Gentiles and their *k-s*
	13:	21	Then the people asked for a *k*,
1Ti	1:	17	the *K* eternal, immortal, invisible,
	2:	2	for *k-s* and all those in authority
	6:	15	the *K* of *k-s* and Lord of lords
Heb	7:	2	Melchizedek means '*k* of righteousness'
Rev	19:	16	*k* of *k-s* and lord of lords.
	21:	24	and the *k-s* of the earth will bring

kingdom

Ex	19:	6	you will be for me a *k* of priests
2Sa	7:	12	and I will establish his *k*
1Ch	29:	11	Yours, Lord, is the *k*;
Ps	145:	13	Your *k* is an everlasting *k*,
Da	7:	27	His *k* will be an everlasting *k*,
Mt	3:	2	Repent, for the *k* of heaven has come near
	5:	3	for theirs is the *k* of heaven
	6:	10	your *k* come, your will be done
	6:	33	But seek first his *k*
	7:	21	Lord," will enter the *k* of heaven,
	13:	24	The *k* of heaven is like a man who
	18:	1	the greatest in the *k* of heaven?
	19:	24	is rich to enter the *k* of God.
	24:	14	gospel of the *k* will be preached
	26:	29	new with you in my Father's *k*.
Mk	9:	1	see that the *k* of God has come
Lk	8:	1	the good news of the *k* of God.
Jn	3:	3	no one can see the *k* of God unless
	18:	36	'My *k* is not of this world.
Ac	8:	12	the good news of the *k* of God
	14:	22	hardships to enter the *k* of God,'
Ro	14:	17	For the *k* of God is not a matter
1Co	6:	9	will not inherit the *k* of God?
	15:	50	blood cannot inherit the *k* of God,
Col	1:	13	brought us into the *k* of the Son
2Ti	4:	18	bring me safely to his heavenly *k*.
Heb	12:	28	receiving a *k* that cannot be shaken
2Pe	1:	11	a rich welcome into the eternal *k*
Rev	1:	6	has made us to be a *k* and priests
	12:	10	the power and the *k* of our God,

know, -s, -ing, s o

Ge	3:	5	like God, *k-ing* good and evil.
	22:	12	Now I *k* that you fear God,
Ex	14:	18	Egyptians will *k* that I am the Lord
Dt	7:	9	*K* therefore that the Lord your God
1Sa	3:	7	Now Samuel did not yet *k* the Lord:
2Ch	20:	12	We do not *k* what to do, but our
Ps	46:	10	'Be still, and *k* that I am God;
	51:	3	For I *k* my transgressions,
	73:	11	They say, 'How would God *k*?
	94:	11	The Lord *k-s* all human plans;
	100:	3	*K* that the Lord is God.
	139:	1	You have searched me, Lord, and you *k* me
	139:	23	Search me, God, and *k* my heart;
Isa	1:	3	The ox *k-s* its master,
	40:	21	Do you not *k*? Have you not heard?
Jer	24:	7	I will give them a heart to *k* me,
	29:	11	For I *k* the plans I have for you,'
Eze	6:	10	And they will *k* that I am the Lord;
Mt	6:	3	do not let your left hand *k* what
	6:	8	for your Father *k-s* what you need
	9:	4	*K-ing* their thoughts, Jesus said,
	9:	6	*k* that the Son of Man has authority
	11:	27	No one *k-s* the Son except the
	22:	29	because you do not *k* the Scriptures
	24:	36	about that day or hour no one *k-s*
	25:	12	Truly I tell you, I don't *k* you
	26:	72	with an oath: 'I don't *k* the man!'
Lk	9:	33	He did not *k* what he was saying.
	12:	2	or hidden that will not be made *k-n*
	18:	20	You *k* the commandments:
	23:	34	they do not *k* what they are doing.
Jn	3:	11	we speak of what we *k*,
	6:	64	Jesus had *k-n* from the beginning
	7:	29	but I *k* him because I am from him
	8:	32	Then you will *k* the truth,
	10:	14	I *k* my sheep and my sheep *k* me
	14:	4	You *k* the way to the place where
	16:	15	from me what he will make *k-n* to you
	17:	3	eternal life: that they *k* you,
	21:	17	Lord, you *k* all things; you *k*
	21:	24	We *k* that his testimony is true
Ro	8:	26	We do not *k* what we ought to pray
	8:	28	we *k* that in all things God works
	11:	34	'Who has *k-n* the mind of the Lord?
1Co	13:	9	For we *k* in part and we prophesy
	14:	16	they do not *k* what you are saying
2Co	6:	9	*k-n*, yet regarded as unknown;
	8:	9	For you *k* the grace of our Lord
Gal	4:	9	you *k* God – or rather are *k-n* by
Eph	1:	17	so that you may *k* him better
	3:	19	and to *k* this love that surpasses
Php	3:	10	I want to *k* Christ – yes, to *k*
Col	1:	27	to make *k-n* among the Gentiles
	2:	2	that they may *k* the mystery of God,
2Ti	1:	12	because I *k* whom I have believed,
	3:	15	you have *k-n* the Holy Scriptures,
Tit	1:	16	They claim to *k* God,
1Jn	2:	4	Whoever says, 'I *k* him,'
	2:	5	This is how we *k* we are in him
	3:	24	how we *k* that he lives in us:
	4:	7	born of God and *k-s* God
	5:	13	*k* that you have eternal life
Rev	2:	2	I *k* your deeds, your hard work

knowledge

Ge	2:	9	the tree of the *k* of good and evil
Ps	139:	6	Such *k* is too wonderful for me,
Lk	11:	52	you have taken away the key to *k*.
1Co	8:	1	But *k* puffs up while love builds up.
	12:	8	to another a message of *k*
	13:	8	where there is *k*, it will pass away

2Co	4:	6	light of the *k* of God's glory
Col	1:	10	growing in the *k* of God
1Ti	2:	4	and to come to a *k* of the truth
2Pe	3:	18	grow in the grace and *k* of our Lord

l

laid

Ge	22:	9	son Isaac and *l* him on the altar
Nu	27:	23	Then he *l* his hands on him
Isa	53:	6	the LORD has *l* on him the iniquity
Mk	6:	29	took his body and *l* it in a tomb
	15:	47	mother of Joses saw where he was *l*
	16:	6	See the place where they *l* him
Lk	12:	19	grain *l* up for many years.
	23:	53	one in which no one had yet been *l*
	23:	55	tomb and how his body was *l* in it
Ac	6:	6	prayed and *l* their hands on them
1Ti	4:	14	body of elders *l* their hands on you
1Jn	3:	16	Jesus Christ *l* down his life for us

lamb, -'s, -s

Ge	22:	8	'God himself will provide the *l*
Ex	12:	21	and slaughter the Passover *l*
2Ch	30:	15	They slaughtered the Passover *l*
Isa	11:	6	The wolf will live with the *l*,
	53:	7	was led like a *l* to the slaughter
Lk	22:	7	the Passover *l* had to be sacrificed
Jn	1:	29	*L* of God, who takes away the sin
	21:	15	Jesus said, 'Feed my *l-s*.
Ac	8:	32	as a *l* before its shearer is silent
1Co	5:	7	our Passover *l*, has been sacrificed
1Pe	1:	19	Christ, a *l* without blemish
Rev	5:	6	Then I saw a *L*, looking
	5:	12	'Worthy is the *L*, who was slain,
	7:	17	the *L* at the centre before the throne
	21:	27	written in the *L-'s* book of life

land, -s

Ge	1:	10	God called the dry ground '*l*',
	1:	11	'Let the *l* produce vegetation:
	1:	24	Let the *l* produce living creatures
	12:	1	to the *l* I will show you.
	15:	18	'To your descendants I give this *l*,
	17:	8	The whole *l* of Canaan,
Ex	3:	8	a *l* flowing with milk and honey
Lev	25:	19	Then the *l* will yield its fruit,
	25:	24	provide for the redemption of the *l*
Nu	35:	33	Do not pollute the *l* where you are.
Dt	1:	8	See, I have given you this *l*.
	8:	7	God is bringing you into a good *l* –
	11:	9	you may live long in the *l*
	26:	1	When you have entered the *l*
	29:	27	LORD's anger burned against this *l*,
	30:	5	He will bring you to the *l*
	34:	1	the LORD showed him the whole *l* –
Jos	1:	11	take possession of the *l*
	2:	2	come here tonight to spy out the *l*.
	2:	9	the LORD has given this *l* to you
	2:	24	given the whole *l* into our hands;
	13:	2	'This is the *l* that remains:
	14:	5	So the Israelites divided the *l*,
	14:	15	Then the *l* had rest from war
2Ch	7:	14	and will heal their *l*
	36:	21	The *l* enjoyed its sabbath rests;
Ezr	9:	11	"The *l* you are entering to possess
Ps	37:	11	But the meek will inherit the *l*
	41:	2	among the blessed in the *l*
	60:	2	You have shaken the *l*
	63:	1	in a dry and parched *l*
	65:	9	You care for the *l* and water it;
	67:	6	The *l* yields its harvest;

	80:	9	and it took root and filled the *l*
Eze	37:	21	bring them back into their own *l*
Mt	4:	16	the *l* of the shadow of death
	23:	15	You travel over *l* and sea
	27:	45	darkness came over all the *l*
Ac	4:	34	those who owned *l* or houses

law, -s

Dt	1:	5	Moses began to expound this *l*,
	4:	44	This is the *l* Moses set before
2Ki	22:	8	'I have found the Book of the *L*
Ezr	7:	6	a teacher well versed in the *L*
Ne	8:	9	they listened to the words of the *L*
Ps	1:	2	delight in the *l* of the LORD
	19:	7	The *l* of the LORD is perfect,
	37:	31	The *l* of their God is in their hearts;
	40:	8	your *l* is within my heart.
	119:	18	may see wonderful things in your *l*
	119:	97	Oh, how I love your *l*!
Isa	2:	3	The *l* will go out from Zion,
Jer	31:	33	'I will put my *l* in their minds
Da	6:	8	the *l* of the Medes and Persians,
Mt	5:	17	to abolish the *L* or the Prophets;
	7:	12	sums up the *L* and the Prophets
	22:	36	the greatest commandment in the *L*?
	23:	15	'Woe to you, teachers of the *L*
Lk	2:	23	it is written in the *L* of the Lord,
Jn	1:	17	For the *l* was given through Moses;
Ro	2:	12	All who sin apart from the *l*
	3:	20	through the *l* we become conscious
	3:	28	by faith apart from the works of the *l*
	3:	31	Not at all! Rather, we uphold the *l*
	4:	15	because *l* brings wrath.
	5:	20	*l* was brought in so that the trespass
	6:	15	not under the *l* but under grace?
	7:	7	Is the *l* sin? Certainly not!
	7:	14	We know that the *l* is spiritual;
	8:	2	*l* of the Spirit who gives life
	8:	3	For what the *l* was powerless to do
	10:	4	Christ is the culmination of the *l*
	13:	10	love is the fulfilment of the *l*
1Co	9:	20	I became like one under the *l*
	15:	56	and the power of sin is the *l*
Gal	2:	16	not justified by the works of the *l*,
	3:	13	redeemed us from the curse of the *l*
	3:	24	the *l* was put in charge of us
	4:	4	born of a woman, born under the *l*
	5:	14	*l* is fulfilled in keeping this one command:
	6:	2	you will fulfil the *l* of Christ
1Ti	1:	8	*l* is good if one uses it properly
Heb	7:	19	(for the *l* made nothing perfect),
	8:	10	I will put my *l-s* in their minds
	10:	1	The *l* is only a shadow of the good
Jas	1:	25	the perfect *l* that gives freedom
1Jn	3:	4	Everyone who sins breaks the *l*;

lay, -ing

Ru	3:	14	So she *l* at his feet until morning,
1Sa	3:	15	Samuel *l* down until morning
Ps	5:	3	in the morning I *l* my requests
Isa	28:	16	I *l* a stone in Zion, a tested stone
	52:	10	The LORD will *l* bare his holy arm
Mt	8:	20	of Man has nowhere to *l* his head.
	28:	6	Come and see the place where he *l*.
Jn	10:	15	and I *l* down my life for the sheep.
	15:	13	to *l* down one's life for one's friends.
Ro	9:	33	'See, I *l* in Zion a stone
2Ti	1:	6	through the *l-ing* on of my hands
1Pe	2:	6	I *l* a stone in Zion, a chosen
Rev	4:	10	*l* their crowns before the throne

lead, -s, -er

Dt	3:	28	for he will *l* this people across
1Sa	8:	5	now appoint a king to *l* us,

2Ch	1:	10	that I may *l* this people,
Ps	23:	2	he *l-s* me beside quiet waters
	27:	11	LORD; *l* me in a straight path
SS	2:	4	Let him *l* me to the banqueting hall,
Eze	13:	10	"Because they *l* my people astray,
Mt	6:	13	And *l* us not into temptation.
	7:	14	narrow the road that *l-s* to life,
	9:	18	a synagogue *l-er* came and knelt
Jn	12:	50	his command *l-s* to eternal life.
Ro	2:	4	God's kindness is intended to *l* you
2Co	7:	10	repentance that *l-s* to salvation
Tit	1:	1	the truth that *l-s* to godliness
1Jn	3:	7	do not let anyone *l* you astray.

led

Ge	24:	27	the LORD has *l* me on the journey
1Ki	11:	3	and his wives *l* him astray
2Ch	26:	16	his pride *l* to his downfall.
Ps	77:	20	You *l* your people like a flock
Isa	53:	7	*l* like a lamb to the slaughter,
Hos	11:	4	*l* them with cords of human kindness
Mt	4:	1	Then Jesus was *l* by the Spirit
2Co	7:	9	your sorrow *l* you to repentance.
Gal	5:	18	But if you are *l* by the Spirit,

left

Ge	7:	23	Only Noah was *l*, and those with him
	25:	5	Abraham *l* everything he owned
	39:	12	But he *l* his cloak in her hand
Dt	16:	3	because you *l* Egypt in haste –
Jos	11:	15	he *l* nothing undone of all that
Ru	1:	3	and she was *l* with her two sons
1Ki	19:	10	I am the only one *l*, and now they
2Ch	32:	31	God *l* him to test him and to know
Hag	2:	3	"Who of you is *l* who saw this house
Mt	4:	20	they *l* their nets and followed him
	8:	15	the fever *l* her, and she got up
Mk	1:	42	Immediately the leprosy *l* him
	10:	28	We have *l* everything to follow you
Lk	5:	11	*l* everything and followed him
	17:	34	one will be taken and the other *l*
Jn	6:	12	Gather the pieces that are *l* over.
Ac	16:	18	At that moment the spirit *l* her

lie, -s, -d

Nu	23:	19	God is not human, that he should *l*,
Ps	88:	7	Your wrath *l-s* heavily on me;
Jer	5:	31	the prophets prophesy *l-s*,
	23:	14	they commit adultery and live a *l*.
Ac	5:	3	you have *l-d* to the Holy Spirit
	5:	4	You have not *l-d* just to human beings
Ro	1:	25	exchanged the truth about God for a *l*,
Heb	6:	18	it is impossible for God to *l*,
1Jn	1:	6	yet walk in the darkness, we *l*
Rev	14:	5	No *l* was found in their mouths;

life

Ge	2:	9	of the garden were the tree of *l*
Ex	21:	23	you are to take *l* for *l*
Dt	30:	15	I set before you today *l* and
Ps	16:	11	make known to me the path of *l*;
	91:	16	With long *l* I will satisfy him
	103:	15	The *l* of mortals is like grass
Pr	19:	23	The fear of the LORD leads to *l*;
Isa	53:	12	he poured out his *l* unto death,
Da	12:	2	will awake: some to everlasting *l*,
Mt	6:	25	do not worry about your *l*,
	7:	14	narrow the road that leads to *l*,
	16:	25	to save their *l* will lose it,
	25:	46	but the righteous to eternal *l*.'
Mk	10:	17	what must I do to inherit eternal *l*
	10:	45	to give his *l* as a ransom for many.
Jn	1:	4	that *l* was the light of all mankind.
	3:	16	shall not perish but have eternal *l*

	5:	24	but has crossed over from death to *l*
	6:	35	'I am the bread of *l*.
	10:	10	I have come that they may have *l*,
	10:	28	I give them eternal *l*,
	11:	25	'I am the resurrection and the *l*.
	14:	6	the way and the truth and the *l*.
	15:	13	to lay down one's *l* for one's friends
	17:	3	is eternal *l*: that they know you,
	20:	31	you may have *l* in his name
Ac	3:	15	You killed the author of *l*,
	5:	20	people all about this new *l*.
	13:	48	who were appointed for eternal *l*
	17:	25	he himself gives everyone *l* and
Ro	4:	25	raised to *l* for our justification.
	5:	10	shall we be saved through his *l*
	6:	22	and the result is eternal *l*
	6:	23	the gift of God is eternal *l*
	8:	6	mind governed by the Spirit is *l*
	8:	38	neither death nor *l*, neither angels
2Co	3:	6	kills, but the Spirit gives *l*
	4:	11	so that his *l* may also be revealed
Gal	2:	20	The *l* I now live in the body, I live
Php	2:	16	as you hold firmly to the word of *l*.
	4:	3	whose names are in the book of *l*
Col	3:	3	your *l* is now hidden with Christ
	3:	4	When Christ, who is your *l*, appears
1Ti	4:	16	Watch your *l* and doctrine closely.
	6:	19	take hold of the *l* that is truly *l*
2Ti	3:	12	to live a godly *l* in Christ Jesus
Tit	1:	2	in the hope of eternal *l*,
Jas	1:	12	will receive the crown of *l*
1Jn	1:	1	proclaim concerning the Word of *l*
	3:	14	we have passed from death to *l*,
	5:	12	Whoever has the Son has *l*;
	5:	20	He is the true God and eternal *l*
Rev	2:	7	the right to eat from the tree of *l*
	2:	10	and I will give you *l* as your victor's crown
	13:	8	written in the Lamb's book of *l*
	21:	27	written in the Lamb's book of *l*
	22:	17	the free gift of the water of *l*

lift, -ing, -ed

Ps	24:	7	*L* up your heads, you gates;
	40:	2	He *l-ed* me out of the slimy pit,
	121:	1	I *l* up my eyes to the mountains –
	134:	2	*L* up your hands in the sanctuary
Isa	52:	13	he will be raised and *l-ed* up
Lk	24:	50	*l-ed* up his hands and blessed them
Jn	3:	14	Just as Moses *l-ed* up the snake
	12:	32	when I am *l-ed* up from the earth,
1Ti	2:	8	to pray, *l-ing* up holy hands

light

Ge	1:	3	And God said, 'Let there be *l*,'
Ex	13:	21	in a pillar of fire to give them *l*,
Ps	19:	8	giving *l* to the eyes.
	27:	1	The LORD is my *l* and my salvation –
	36:	9	in your *l* we see *l*.
	119:105		and a *l* for my path.
	119:130		The unfolding of your words gives *l*
Isa	9:	2	in darkness have seen a great *l*;
	42:	6	and a *l* for the Gentiles
	60:	1	'Arise, shine, for your *l* has come,
Mt	4:	16	in darkness have seen a great *l*;
	5:	14	'You are the *l* of the world.
Lk	11:	34	your whole body also is full of *l*.
Jn	1:	4	and that life was the *l* of all mankind
	1:	8	he came only as a witness to the *l*.
	1:	9	The true *l* that gives *l* to
	3:	19	people loved darkness instead of *l*
	8:	12	he said, 'I am the *l* of the world.
Ac	9:	3	suddenly a *l* from heaven flashed
	13:	47	have made you a *l* for the Gentiles

2Co 4:   6 *l* of the knowledge of God's glory
     6: 14 what fellowship can *I* have with
    11: 14 masquerades as an angel of *l*
Eph 5:   8 Live as children of *l*
1Ti 6: 16 and who lives in unapproachable *l*,
1Pe 2:   9 of darkness into his wonderful *l*
1Jn 1:   5 God is *l*;
     1:   7 But if we walk in the *l*, as he is
Rev 22:   5 for the Lord God will give them *l*.

lion, -'s, -s, -s'

Jdg 14:   6 so that he tore the *l* apart
Ps 22: 21 Rescue me from the mouth of the *l-s*
Pr 28:   1 the righteous are as bold as a *l*
Isa 11:   7 the *l* will eat straw like the ox
Da   6:   7 shall be thrown into the *l-s'* den
     7:   4 'The first was like a *l*,
Am   3:   8 The *l* has roared – who will not fear
2Ti 4: 17 I was delivered from the *l-'s* mouth
Heb 11: 33 who shut the mouths of *l-s*
1Pe 5:   8 prowls around like a roaring *l*
Rev 5:   5 the *L* of the tribe of Judah,

lips

Ps 51: 15 Open my *l*, Lord, and my mouth
   141:   3 keep watch over the door of my *l*
Pr 13:   3 Those who guard their *l* preserve their lives
Isa 6:   5 For I am a man of unclean *l*,
    28: 11 with foreign *l* and strange tongues
Mt 15:   8 These people honour me with their *l*
    21: 16 'From the *l* of children and infants
1Co 14: 21 and through the *l* of foreigners
Col 3:   8 filthy language from your *l*
Heb 13: 15 fruit of *l* that openly profess his name

listen, -s, -ing, -ed

Ge   3: 17 'Because you *l-ed* to your wife
1Sa 3: 10 Speak, for your servant is *l-ing*.
1Ki 4: 34 came to *l* to Solomon's wisdom,
2Ki 21:   9 But the people did not *l*.
Ne   8:   9 they *l-ed* to the words of the Law
Ps 81: 11 'But my people would not *l* to me;
    86:   6 Lord; *l* to my cry for mercy
Pr 12: 15 but the wise *l* to advice
Mt 18: 17 If they still refuse to *l*,
Mk   9:   7 my Son, whom I love. *L* to him!
Lk   8: 18 consider carefully how you *l*.
    10: 16 'Whoever *l-s* to you *l-s* to me;
    10: 39 who sat at the Lord's feet *l-ing*
Jn 10: 27 My sheep *l* to my voice;
Jas 1: 19 everyone should be quick to *l*,
     1: 22 Do not merely *l* to the word,

live, -s, -ing

Ge   2:   7 and the man became a *l-ing* being
     3: 22 and *l* for ever.
Ex 20: 12 so that you may *l* long in the land
    33: 20 for no one may see me and *l*.
Nu 21:   8 bitten can look at it and *l*.
Dt   8:   3 man does not *l* on bread alone
2Sa 22: 47 The Lord *l-s*! Praise be to my Rock!
2Ch 23: 11 and shouted, 'Long *l* the king!
Job 14: 14 If someone dies, will they *l* again?
    19: 25 I know that my redeemer *l-s*,
    28: 13 in the land of the *l-ing*
Ps 15:   1 Who may *l* on your holy mountain?
    18: 46 The Lord *l-s*! Praise be
   118: 17 I will not die but *l*,
   133:   1 when God's people *l* together in unity
Pr 21:   9 Better to *l* on a corner of the roof
Ecc 9:   4 a *l* dog is better off than a dead
     9:   5 the *l-ing* know that they will die,
Isa 6:   5 I *l* among a people of unclean lips,

    11:   6 The wolf will *l* with the lamb,
    26: 19 But your dead will *l*,
    55:   3 listen, that you may *l*.
Jer 10: 10 the *l-ing* God, the eternal King.
Eze 20: 11 who obeys them will *l*.
    37:   3 'Son of man, can these bones *l*?'
Am   5:   6 Seek the Lord and *l*,
Hab 2:   4 the righteous person will *l* by his faithfulness
Zec 2: 11 I will *l* among you
Mt   4:   4 "Man shall not *l* on bread alone,
     4: 16 the people *l-ing* in darkness
    16: 16 the Son of the *l-ing* God.
    22: 32 God of the dead but of the *l-ing*.
Lk 10: 28 'Do this and you will *l*.
Jn   4: 50 'your son will *l*.'
     5: 25 and those who hear will *l*
     6: 51 I am the *l-ing* bread
     6: 57 and I *l* because of the Father,
     7: 38 rivers of *l-ing* water will flow
    14: 17 for he *l-s* with you
Ac 17: 28 "For in him we *l* and move
Ro   1: 17 'The righteous will *l* by faith.
     6:   8 we believe that we will also *l*
     6: 10 the life he *l-s*, he *l-s* to God
     8: 11 his Spirit who *l-s* in you
    12:   1 your bodies as a *l-ing* sacrifice,
    12: 16 *L* in harmony with one another.
    14:   8 If we *l*, we *l* to the Lord;
    14:   9 Lord of both the dead and the *l-ing*
1Co 7: 15 God has called us to *l* in peace
2Co 5:   7 we *l* by faith, not by sight
     6: 16 God has said: 'I will *l* with them
Gal 2: 20 I no longer *l*, but Christ *l-s* in me
     3: 11 'the righteous will *l* by faith.
     5: 25 Since we *l* by the Spirit,
Eph 4: 17 must no longer *l* as the Gentiles do
     5: 15 Be very careful, then, how you *l* –
Php 1: 21 For to me, to *l* is Christ
Col 1: 10 you may *l* a life worthy of the Lord
1Th 1:   9 to serve the *l-ing* and true God
     4:   1 how to *l* in order to please God,
     5: 13 *L* in peace with each other
1Ti 2:   2 we may *l* peaceful and quiet *l-s*
     6: 16 who *l-s* in unapproachable light,
2Ti 1: 14 the Holy Spirit who *l-s* in us
     2: 11 we will also *l* with him
     3: 12 to *l* a godly life in Christ Jesus
Heb 7: 24 because Jesus *l-s* for ever,
     7: 25 he always *l-s* to intercede for them
     9: 14 that we may serve the *l-ing* God
    10: 31 into the hands of the *l-ing* God
    10: 38 my righteous one will *l* by faith.
    12: 14 Make every effort to *l* in peace
1Pe 1: 17 *l* out your time as foreigners here
     2:   4 come to him, the *l-ing* Stone –
     2: 12 *L* such good *l-s* among the pagans
     2: 24 die to sins and *l* for righteousness
     4:   5 to judge the *l-ing* and the dead
2Pe 3: 11 ought to *l* holy and godly *l-s*
1Jn 2:   6 whoever claims to *l* in him
     2: 25 loves their brother and sister *l-s*
     2: 14 the word of God *l-s* in you,
     3: 16 lay down our *l-s* for our brothers,
     3: 24 keeps God's commands *l-s* in him,
     4: 13 we know that we *l* in him
     4: 16 Whoever *l-s* in love *l-s* in God,
Rev 1: 18 I am the *L-ing* One;
    10:   6 he swore by him who *l-s* for ever
    12: 11 they did not love their *l-s* so much

long

Ge	8: 22	'As *l* as the earth endures,
Ex	17: 11	As *l* as Moses held up his hands,
	20: 12	so that you may live *l* in the land
1Ki	3: 14	I will give you a *l* life.
1Ch	29: 28	enjoyed *l* life, wealth and honour.
Ps	6: 3	How *l*, LORD, how *l*
	44: 22	your sake we face death all day *l*;
	63: 4	I will praise you as *l* as I live,
	91: 16	With *l* life I will satisfy him
Isa	65: 2	All day *l* I have held out my hands
Mt	5: 21	it was said to the people *l* ago,
	24: 48	"My master is staying away a *l* time
Lk	15: 20	while he was still a *l* way off
Jn	9: 4	As *l* as it is day,
Ro	8: 36	your sake we face death all day *l*;
	10: 21	All day *l* I have held out my hands
1Co	11: 14	if a man has *l* hair,
Eph	3: 18	how wide and *l* and high and deep
	6: 3	and that you may enjoy *l* life
Heb	3: 13	as *l* as it is called 'Today,

long, -s, -ing, -ed

Ps	61: 4	I *l* to dwell in your tent for ever
	119: 20	consumed with *l-ing* for your laws
	119:174	I *l* for your salvation, LORD,
Pr	13: 12	a *l-ing* fulfilled is a tree of life
Isa	30: 18	the LORD *l-s* to be gracious to you;
Mt	13: 17	righteous people *l-ed* to see what you
	23: 37	I have *l-ed* to gather your children
Ro	15: 23	*l-ing* for many years to visit you
2Co	5: 2	we groan, *l-ing* to be clothed
Php	1: 8	God can testify how I *l* for all
	4: 1	sisters, you whom I love and *l* for
2Ti	4: 8	all who have *l-ed* for his appearing
Heb	11: 16	were *l-ing* for a better country –
1Pe	1: 12	angels *l* to look into these things

look, -s, -ing, -ed

Ge	4: 4	The LORD *l-ed* with favour on Abel
	19: 26	But Lot's wife *l-ed* back,
Ex	2: 25	So God *l-ed* on the Israelites
	3: 6	because he was afraid to *l* at God
1Sa	16: 7	but the LORD *l-s* at the heart.'
Job	31: 1	not to *l* lustfully at a young woman.
Ps	34: 5	Those who *l* to him are radiant;
	105: 4	*L* to the LORD and his strength;
	145: 15	The eyes of all *l* to you,
Isa	42: 18	'Hear, you deaf; *l*, you blind,
	51: 1	*l* to the rock from which you were
Jer	6: 16	'Stand at the crossroads and *l*;
Da	8: 15	stood one who *l-ed* like a man
Hab	1: 13	Your eyes are too pure to *l* on evil
Zec	12: 10	*l* on me, the one they have pierced,
Mt	5: 28	anyone who *l-s* at a woman lustfully
	6: 16	'When you fast, do not *l* sombre
	18: 12	to *l* for the one that wandered off
	25: 36	I was ill and you *l-ed* after me,
	28: 5	I know that you are *l-ing* for Jesus
Mk	1: 37	'Everyone is *l-ing* for you!
	7: 34	He *l-ed* up to heaven
	10: 21	Jesus *l-ed* at him and loved him.
	13: 21	"*L*, here is the Messiah!" or, "*L*,
	16: 6	are *l-ing* for Jesus the Nazarene
Lk	2: 45	back to Jerusalem to *l* for him
	13: 6	and he went to *l* for fruit on it
	18: 13	He would not even *l* up to heaven,
	22: 61	turned and *l-ed* straight at Peter.
	24: 5	you *l* for the living among the dead
	24: 39	*L* at my hands and my feet.
Jn	1: 36	he said, '*L*, the Lamb of God!
	6: 40	everyone who *l-s* to the Son
	7: 34	You will *l* for me, but you will not

	12: 45	The one who *l-s* at me is seeing
	19: 37	*l* on the one they have pierced.
	20: 15	Who is it you are *l-ing* for?'
Ac	1: 11	you stand here *l-ing* into the sky?
Heb	13: 14	*l-ing* for the city that is to come
Jas	1: 23	who *l-s* at his face in a mirror
1Jn	1: 1	which we have *l-ed* at and our hands
Rev	5: 6	Then I saw a Lamb, *l-ing* as if it

LORD, -'s (Yahweh)

Ge	2: 4	when the *L* God made the earth
	2: 7	the *L* God formed a man
	2: 22	Then the *L* God made a woman
	3: 1	the wild animals the *L* God had made
	4: 26	began to call on the name of the *L*
	10: 9	He was a mighty hunter before the *L*
	15: 6	Abram believed the *L*,
	18: 14	Is anything too hard for the *L*?
Ex	3: 2	the angel of the *L* appeared to him
	3: 15	"The *L*, the God of your fathers –
	6: 3	but by my name the *L* I did not
	9: 12	But the *L* hardened Pharaoh's heart
	9: 29	know that the earth is the *L*-'s
	10: 2	that you may know that I am the *L*.
	15: 2	The *L* is my strength and my defence;
	15: 3	the *L* is his name
	20: 2	'I am the *L* your God, who brought
	20: 5	I, the *L* your God, am a jealous God
	20: 7	shall not misuse the name of the *L*
	29: 46	will know that I am the *L* their God
Lev	19: 2	I, the *L* your God, am holy
	25: 38	I am the *L* your God, who brought
Nu	6: 24	'The *L* bless you and keep you
	14: 18	'The *L* is slow to anger,
	15: 41	I am the *L* your God, who brought
	22: 22	angel of the *L* stood in the road
Dt	1: 32	you did not trust in the *L* your God
	1: 36	he followed the *L* wholeheartedly.
	4: 24	*L* your God is a consuming fire,
	4: 31	the *L* your God is a merciful God
	5: 2	The *L* our God made a covenant
	6: 4	The *L* our God, the *L* is one
	6: 5	Love the *L* your God
	10: 20	Fear the *L* your God and serve him.
	11: 1	Love the *L* your God
	28: 1	If you fully obey the *L* your God
	31: 6	for the *L* your God goes with you;
	31: 8	The *L* himself goes before you
Jos	1: 9	the *L* your God will be with you
	23: 10	the *L* your God fights for you,
Jdg	6: 10	I said to you, "I am the *L* your God
	7: 18	"For the *L* and for Gideon."
1Sa	1: 28	So now I give him to the *L*.
	7: 12	'Thus far the *L* has helped us.'
2Sa	22: 7	In my distress I called to the *L*;
	22: 32	For who is God besides the *L*?
1Ki	5: 5	a temple for the Name of the *L*
	18: 21	If the *L* is God, follow him;
	18: 24	I will call on the name of the *L*.
1Ch	16: 8	praise to the *L*, call on his name;
	16: 29	Ascribe to the *L* the glory
	17: 20	'There is no one like you, *L*,
	17: 26	You, *L*, are God!
Ezr	3: 11	they sang to the *L*: 'He is good;
Job	1: 8	Then the *L* said to Satan,
	1: 21	*L* gave and the *L* has taken away;
Ps	1: 2	whose delight is in the law of the *L*
	16: 8	I keep my eyes always on the *L*.
	18: 2	The *L* is my rock, my fortress
	19: 7	The law of the *L* is perfect,
	19: 14	*L*, my Rock and my Redeemer
	21: 13	Be exalted in your strength, *L*;

	23:	1	The *L* is my shepherd,
	23:	6	dwell in the house of the *L* for
	24:	1	The earth is the *L-'s*,
	25:	1	In you, *L* my God, I put my trust
	27:	8	Your face, *L*, I will seek
	31:	23	Love the *L*, all his faithful people!
	34:	3	Glorify the *L* with me:
	46:	7	The *L* Almighty is with us;
	92:	1	It is good to praise the *L*
	95:	3	For the *L* is the great God,
	96:	1	Sing to the *L* a new song;
	96:	7	Ascribe to the *L*,
	96:	9	Worship the *L* in the splendour
	97:	1	The *L* reigns, let the earth be glad
	98:	1	Sing to the *L* a new song,
	99:	1	*L* reigns, let the nations tremble;
	100:	2	Worship the *L* with gladness;
	103:	1	Praise the *L*, my soul;
	110:	1	The *L* says to my lord:
	111:	10	The fear of the *L* is the beginning
	115:	1	Not to us, *L*, not to us
	118:	14	The *L* is my strength and my defence;
	118:	24	The *L* has done it this very day;
	118:	26	he who comes in the name of the *L*.
	121:	2	My help comes from the *L*,
	139:	1	You have searched me, *L*
Pr	1:	7	The fear of the *L* is the beginning
	6:	16	six things the *L* hates,
	8:	13	To fear the *L* is to hate evil;
	11:	1	The *L* detests dishonest scales,
	15:	3	The eyes of the *L* are everywhere,
	16:	9	the *L* establishes their steps
	16:	20	blessed is the one who trusts in the *L*
	18:	10	The name of the *L* is a fortified tower
Isa	6:	3	Holy, holy, holy is the *L* Almighty
	11:	2	Spirit of the *L* will rest on him –
	25:	8	The Sovereign *L* will wipe away
	40:	3	prepare the way for the *L*;
	43:	3	For I am the *L* your God,
	45:	5	I am the *L*, and there is no other;
	50:	5	The Sovereign *L* has opened my ears;
	51:	11	Those the *L* has rescued will return.
	51:	15	For I am the *L* your God,
	55:	6	Seek the *L* while he may be found;
	59:	1	the arm of the *L* is not too short
	59:	19	people will fear the name of the *L*,
	60:	1	the glory of the *L* rises upon you
Jer	9:	24	I am the *L*, who exercises kindness,
	17:	10	'I the *L* search the heart
	17:	13	*L*, you are the hope of Israel;
	32:	27	'I am the *L*, the God of all mankind
La	3:	25	The *L* is good to those whose hope
Eze	7:	27	Then they will know that I am the *L*
	23:	49	will know that I am the Sovereign *L*
Hos	6:	1	'Come, let us return to the *L*.
	10:	12	for it is time to seek the *L*,
Joel	1:	15	the day of the *L* is near;
Am	1:	2	'The *L* roars from Zion
	5:	8	the *L* is his name
	5:	18	you who long for the day of the *L*!
Jnh	1:	9	'I am a Hebrew and I worship the *L*
Mic	6:	8	And what does the *L* require of you?
Na	1:	3	The *L* is slow to anger but great
Hab	1:	12	*L*, are you not from everlasting?
Zec	14:	20	holy to the *L* will be inscribed
Mal	1:	2	'I have loved you,' says the *L*.
	3:	6	'I the *L* do not change.

lord, -'s, -s

Ge	18:	31	so bold as to speak to the *L*,
Ex	4:	13	'Pardon your servant, *L*. Please send
Dt	10:	17	God of gods and *L* of *l-s*,

Jos	3:	13	the Lord – the *L* of all the earth
Ne	4:	14	Remember the *L*, who is great
Ps	8:	1	Lord, our *L*, how majestic is
	16:	2	I say to the Lord, 'You are my *L*;
	90:	1	*L*, you have been our dwelling-place
	110:	1	The Lord says to my *l*:
Isa	6:	1	I saw the *L* seated on a throne,
	7:	14	the *L* himself will give you a sign:
Da	2:	47	God of gods and the *L* of kings
	9:	4	'*L*, the great and awesome God,
Mic	4:	13	the *L* of all the earth
Zec	4:	14	serve the *L* of all the earth.
Mt	3:	3	"Prepare the way for the *L*,
	4:	7	not put the *L* your God to the test.
	7:	21	everyone who says to me, "*L, L*,"
	12:	8	the Son of Man is *L* of the Sabbath.
	22:	37	"Love the *L* your God with all your
	22:	44	"The *L* said to my *L*:
Lk	1:	28	The *L* is with you.
	4:	12	not put the *L* your God to the test.
	6:	46	'Why do you call me, "*L, L*,"
	10:	39	Mary, who sat at the *L-'s* feet
	19:	34	They replied, 'The *L* needs it.'
	24:	34	'It is true! The *L* has risen and
Ac	2:	21	calls on the name of the *L* will be
	2:	25	"I saw the *L* always before me.
	2:	34	"The *L* said to my *L*:
	9:	5	'Who are you, *L*?' Saul asked.
	9:	42	and many people believed in the *L*
	16:	31	'Believe in the *L* Jesus,
Ro	10:	9	with your mouth, 'Jesus is *L*,'
	11:	34	'Who has known the mind of the *L*?
1Co	1:	31	'Let the one who boasts boast in the *L*
	4:	5	wait until the *L* comes.
	8:	5	many 'gods' and many '*l-s*'
	8:	6	there is but one *L*, Jesus Christ,
	11:	20	it is not the *L-'s* Supper you eat
	11:	23	the *L* Jesus, on the night he was
	11:	26	you proclaim the *L-'s* death
	12:	3	'Jesus is *L*,'
	15:	57	victory through our *L* Jesus Christ
	16:	22	If anyone does not love the *L*,
2Co	1:	14	in the day of the *L* Jesus
	3:	17	Now the *L* is the Spirit,
	5:	6	in the body we are away from the *L*
	12:	1	visions and revelations from the *L*
Eph	4:	5	one *L*, one faith, one baptism
	5:	10	find out what pleases the *L*
	6:	10	Finally, be strong in the *L*
Php	2:	11	acknowledge that Jesus Christ is *L*,
	4:	1	stand firm in the *L* in this way,
	4:	4	Rejoice in the *L* always.
Col	1:	10	live a life worthy of the *L*
	3:	17	all in the name of the *L* Jesus
	3:	24	It is the *L* Christ you are serving.
	4:	17	ministry you have received in the *L*.
1Th	3:	12	May the *L* make your love increase
	4:	16	For the *L* himself will come down
	5:	2	day of the *L* will come like a thief
	5:	28	The grace of our *L* Jesus Christ
2Th	2:	1	the coming of our *L* Jesus Christ
	3:	3	But the *L* is faithful,
1Ti	6:	15	King of kings and *L* of *l-s*
2Ti	2:	19	'The *L* knows those who are his,
	4:	22	The *L* be with your spirit.
Heb	12:	14	holiness no one will see the *L*.
	13:	6	'The *L* is my helper;
Jas	4:	10	Humble yourselves before the *L*,
1Pe	1:	25	the word of the *L* endures for ever.
	3:	15	in your hearts revere Christ as *L*
2Pe	1:	11	the eternal kingdom of our *L*
	1:	16	coming of our *L* Jesus Christ

	3:	9	The *L* is not slow in keeping his
Jude		14	the *L* is coming with thousands
Rev	1:	10	On the *L-'s* Day I was in the Spirit
	4:	8	holy, holy is the *L* God Almighty,
	19:	16	king of kings and *l* of *l-s*.
	22:	20	Come, *L* Jesus

love, -s, -ing, -d

Ge	4:	1	Adam made *l* to his wife Eve,
	22:	2	your only son, whom you *l* –
Lev	19:	18	but *l* your neighbour as yourself.
Dt	6:	5	*L* the LORD your God with all your
	7:	8	it was because the LORD *l-d* you
	30:	16	I command you today to *l* the LORD
1Ch	16:	34	his *l* endures for ever
Ne	9:	17	slow to anger and abounding in *l*.
Ps	13:	5	But I trust in your unfailing *l*;
	26:	3	mindful of your unfailing *l*
	31:	23	*L* the LORD, all his faithful people!
	57:	10	For great is your *l*,
	63:	3	Because your *l* is better than life,
	92:	2	proclaiming your *l* in the morning
	106:	1	he is good; his *l* endures for ever
	116:	1	I *l* the LORD, for he heard my voice
	136:	1	His *l* endures for ever.
	145:	8	slow to anger and rich in *l*
Pr	10:	12	*l* covers over all wrongs
SS	2:	4	and let his banner over me be *l*
	8:	7	Many waters cannot quench *l*;
Isa	5:	1	I will sing for the one I *l* a song
Jer	31:	3	*l-d* you with an everlasting *l*;
Hos	6:	4	Your *l* is like the morning mist,
	11:	1	When Israel was a child, I *l-d* him
Joel	2:	13	slow to anger and abounding in *l*,
Mic	6:	8	To act justly and to *l* mercy
Mal	1:	2	'I have *l-d* you,' says the LORD.
Mt	3:	17	'This is my Son, whom I *l*;
	5:	44	But I tell you, *l* your enemies
	5:	46	If you *l* those who *l* you,
	17:	5	'This is my Son, whom I *l*;
	22:	37	*L* the Lord your God with all your
	22:	39	"*L* your neighbour as yourself.
Lk	10:	27	"*L* the Lord your God
Jn	3:	16	For God so *l-d* the world
	11:	36	'See how he *l-d* him!
	13:	23	the disciple whom Jesus *l-d*,
	13:	34	command I give you: *l* one another.
	13:	35	my disciples, if you *l* one another.
	14:	15	'If you *l* me, keep my commands
	14:	21	The one who *l-s* me will be *l-d*
	15:	9	'As the Father has *l-d* me,
	15:	12	*l* each other as I have *l-d* you.
	15:	13	Greater *l* has no one than this:
	21:	17	'Simon son of John, do you *l* me?'
Ro	5:	5	because God's *l* has been poured out
	5:	8	God demonstrates his own *l* for us
	8:	28	for the good of those who *l* him,
	8:	37	conquerors through him who *l-d* us.
	8:	39	to separate us from the *l* of God
	12:	9	*L* must be sincere.
	13:	9	'*L* your neighbour as yourself.
1Co	2:	9	God has prepared for those who *l*
	8:	3	whoever *l-s* God is known by God
	13:	4	*L* is patient, *l* is kind.
	13:	13	But the greatest of these is *l*.
	16:	14	Do everything in *l*
2Co	5:	14	For Christ's *l* compels us,
	9:	7	for God *l-s* a cheerful giver
Gal	2:	20	faith in the Son of God, who *l-d* me
	5:	6	faith expressing itself through *l*
	5:	22	the fruit of the Spirit is *l*,
Eph	1:	4	In *l* he predestined us

	2:	4	because of his great *l* for us, God
	3:	18	high and deep is the *l* of Christ,
	4:	15	speaking the truth in *l*,
	5:	25	Husbands, *l* your wives,
	5:	25	just as Christ *l-d* the church
Php	1:	9	that your *l* may abound more
Col	1:	8	your *l* in the Spirit
	3:	14	And over all these virtues put on *l*
1Ti	6:	10	For the *l* of money is a root of
2Ti	4:	10	because he *l-d* this world, has
Heb	13:	1	Keep on *l-ing* one another
Jas	2:	8	'*L* your neighbour as yourself,'
1Pe	1:	8	you have not seen him, you *l* him;
	2:	17	*l* the family of believers,
	4:	8	Above all, *l* each other deeply,
	4:	8	*l* covers over a multitude of sins.
2Pe	1:	17	'This is my Son, whom I *l*;
1Jn	3:	1	See what great *l* the Father
	3:	16	This is how we know what *l* is:
	4:	8	God is *l*.
	4:	10	This is *l*: not that we *l-d* God,
	4:	19	We *l* because he first *l-d* us.
	5:	3	this is *l* for God: to keep
Jude		21	keep yourselves in God's *l*
Rev	2:	4	you have forsaken the *l* you had
	3:	19	whom I *l* I rebuke and discipline.

m

made

Ge	1:	7	So God *m* the vault
	1:	16	God *m* two great lights –
	1:	31	God saw all that he had *m*,
	2:	3	the seventh day and *m* it holy,
	2:	22	Then the LORD God *m* a woman
	3:	1	animals the LORD God had *m*.
	6:	6	regretted that he had *m* human beings
	9:	6	the image of God has God *m* mankind
	15:	18	the LORD *m* a covenant
Ex	20:	11	six days the LORD *m* the heavens
	24:	8	that the LORD has *m* with you
	32:	4	*m* it into an idol cast
Lev	16:	34	atonement is to be *m* once a year
Dt	32:	6	who *m* you and formed you
2Ki	19:	15	You have *m* heaven and earth
2Ch	2:	12	God of Israel, who *m* heaven
Job	31:	1	'I *m* a covenant with my eyes
Ps	8:	5	You have *m* them a little lower
	73:	28	I have *m* the Sovereign LORD my
	95:	5	The sea is his, for he *m* it,
	98:	2	LORD has *m* his salvation known
	100:	3	the LORD is God. It is he who *m* us,
	139:	14	I am fearfully and wonderfully *m*;
Ecc	3:	11	He has *m* everything beautiful
Isa	43:	7	whom I formed and *m*.
Jer	11:	10	broken the covenant I *m*
	32:	17	you have *m* the heavens
Eze	33:	7	I have *m* you a watchman
Mal	2:	15	Has not the LORD *m* the two of you one
Mt	5:	13	how can it be *m* salty again?
	19:	4	Creator "*m* them male and female"
Mk	2:	27	'The Sabbath was *m* for man,
Lk	3:	5	every mountain and hill *m* low.
Jn	1:	3	Through him all things were *m*;
	1:	10	the world was *m* through him,
	1:	18	with the Father, has *m* him known
Ac	17:	24	'The God who *m* the world
	17:	26	From one man he *m* all the nations
Ro	1:	23	immortal God for images *m* to look
1Co	12:	14	the body is not *m* up of one part
Heb	1:	2	through whom also he *m* the universe.

2: 7 You *m* them a little lower
2: 9 Jesus, who was *m* lower
Jas 3: 9 been *m* in God's likeness
Rev 14: 7 Worship him who *m* the heavens,

make, -s, -ing

Ge 1: 26 'Let us *m* mankind in our image,
2: 18 I will *m* a helper suitable
9: 12 sign of the covenant I am *m-ing*
12: 2 'I will *m* you into a great nation
28: 3 bless you and *m* you fruitful
Ex 6: 3 LORD I did not *m* myself fully known
20: 4 shall not *m* for yourself an image
20: 23 do not *m* any gods to be
25: 17 '*M* an atonement cover of pure gold
32: 10 I will *m* you into a great nation.
32: 23 '*M* us gods who will go before us.
34: 10 'I am *m-ing* a covenant with you.
Lev 17: 11 the blood that *m-s* atonement
20: 8 the LORD, who *m-s* you holy
Nu 6: 25 LORD *m* his face shine on you
21: 8 '*M* a snake and put it up
Ps 2: 8 I will *m* the nations
4: 8 for you alone, LORD, *m* me dwell
19: 7 *m-ing* wise the simple
23: 2 *m-s* me lie down in green pastures,
46: 8 streams *m* glad the city of God,
106: 8 to *m* his mighty power known
110: 1 until I *m* your enemies a footstool
139: 8 if I *m* my bed in the depths,
Ecc 5: 4 When you *m* a vow to God,
Isa 6: 10 *m* their ears dull and close
8: 14 a rock that *m-s* them fall.
40: 3 *m* straight in the desert
44: 9 All who *m* idols are nothing,
49: 6 *m* you a light for the Gentiles,
Jer 31: 31 I will *m* a new covenant
32: 40 I will *m* an everlasting covenant
Hos 13: 2 they *m* idols for themselves
Joel 2: 19 will I *m* you an object of scorn
Hab 3: 2 in our time *m* them known;
Mt 3: 3 *m* straight paths for him.'
Lk 20: 43 until I *m* your enemies a footstool
Jn 1: 23 "*M* straight the way for the Lord."
5: 18 *m-ing* himself equal with God
Ac 2: 35 I *m* your enemies a footstool
Ro 9: 23 *m* the riches of his glory known
1Co 3: 6 but God has been *m-ing* it grow
3: 7 God, who *m-s* things grow
2Co 5: 9 we *m* it our goal to please him,
2Ti 3: 15 able to *m* you wise for salvation
Heb 1: 7 'He *m-s* his angels spirits,
1: 13 until I *m* your enemies a footstool
1Pe 2: 8 a rock that *m-s* them fall.'

man, -'s, -kind

Ge 1: 26 God said 'Let us make *m-kind* in our image
2: 7 formed a *m* from the dust
2: 15 The LORD God took the *m*
2: 18 not good for the *m* to be alone.
2: 20 So the *m* gave names to
2: 24 For this reason a *m* will leave
2: 25 *m* and his wife were both naked,
5: 1 God created *m-kind* ... in the likeness of God
Dt 8: 3 to teach you that *m* does not live on bread alone
8: 5 as a *m* disciplines his son,
2Sa 12: 7 to David, 'You are the *m*!
1Ki 18: 44 'A cloud as small as a *m's* hand
Job 5: 7 *m* is born to trouble as as surely as sparks fly
38: 3 Brace yourself like a *m*;

Ps 8: 4 what is *m-kind* that you are mindful of them
22: 6 But I am a worm and not a *m*,
Ecc 7: 28 I found one upright *m* among
Isa 6: 5 For I am a *m* of unclean lips,
53: 3 rejected by *m-kind*, a *m* of suffering,
Jer 17: 5 Cursed is the one who trusts in *m*
Eze 37: 3 'Son of *m*, can these bones live?
Da 7: 13 was one like a son of *m*, coming
Hos 11: 9 For I am God, and not a *m*—
Mt 1: 19 her husband was a righteous *m*
4: 4 'It is written: "*M* shall not live on bread alone,
7: 24 a wise *m* who built his house
10: 35 to turn ' "a *m* against his father,
12: 29 enter a strong *m-'s* house
19: 3 'Is it lawful for a *m* to divorce
19: 26 'With *m* this is impossible, but with God
Mk 2: 27 "The Sabbath was made for *m*, not *m* for the
Lk 5: 8 I am a sinful *m*!
16: 22 The rich *m* also died
Jn 1: 4 that life was the light of all *m-kind*
1: 6 There was a *m* sent from God
4: 18 the *m* you now have is not
4: 29 see a *m* who told me everything
11: 1 a *m* named Lazarus was ill.
Ac 4: 12 no other name under heaven given to *m-kind*
12: 22 'This is the voice of a god, not of a *m*'
17: 26 From one *m* he made all the nations
Ro 5: 12 entered the world through one *m*,
7: 24 What a wretched *m* I am!
1Co 11: 8 *m* did not come from woman,
13: 11 I became a *m*, I put the ways
15: 21 resurrection of the dead comes also through a *m*
Gal 6: 7 mocked. A *m* reaps what he sows
Eph 5: 31 'For this reason a *m* will leave
Php 2: 8 being found in appearance as a *m*,
2Th 2: 3 the *m* of lawlessness is revealed,
1Ti 2: 5 one mediator between God and *m-kind*, the *m* Christ
Heb 2: 6 testified: 'What is *m-kind* that you
Rev 1: 13 someone like a son of *m*,

marry, -ies, -ied

Ezr 10: 10 you have *m-ied* foreign women,
Isa 62: 4 and your land will be *m-ied*
Hos 1: 3 So he *m-ied* Gomer
Mt 1: 18 pledged to be *m-ied* to Joseph,
5: 32 anyone who *m-ies* a divorced woman
19: 9 and *m-ies* another woman commits
22: 25 The first one *m-ied* and died,
Lk 20: 1 'I have just got *m-ied*, so
Ro 7: 2 *m-ied* woman is bound to her husband
1Co 7: 33 a *m-ied* man is concerned about
1Ti 4: 3 They forbid people to *m*
5: 14 So I counsel younger widows to *m*,

master, -'s, -s, -s', -ed

2Ki 2: 3 to take your *m* from you today?'
Isa 1: 3 The ox knows his *m*, the donkey
Mal 1: 6 honours his father, and a slave his *m*
Mt 6: 24 'No one can serve two *m-s*.
10: 24 nor a servant above his *m*
15: 27 that fall from their *m-'s* table.
23: 8 for you have only one *M*
24: 46 that servant whose *m* finds him
Jn 13: 16 no servant is greater than his *m*,
15: 15 a servant does not know his *m-'s*
Ro 6: 14 For sin shall no longer be your *m*,
14: 4 To their own *m*, servants stand or fall.

1Co	6:	12	I will not be *m-ed* by anything
Eph	6:	5	Slaves, obey your earthly *m-s*
Col	3:	22	your earthly *m-s* in everything;

meet, -s, -ing, -ings

Ex	19:	17	out of the camp to *m* with God,
	28:	43	they enter the tent of *m-ing*
1Ki	18:	19	Israel to *m* me on Mount Carmel.
Ps	42:	2	When can I go and *m* with God
Am	4:	12	Israel, prepare to *m* your God.
Mt	25:	1	went out to *m* the bridegroom
Mk	5:	2	came from the tombs to *m* him
Jn	12:	13	out to *m* him, shouting, 'Hosanna!
Ac	2:	46	to *m* together in the temple courts.
	4:	31	where they were *m-ing* was shaken.
Ro	16:	5	the church that *m-s* at their house.
1Co	11:	17	your *m-ings* do more harm than good
Php	4:	19	And my God will *m* all your needs
1Th	4:	17	in the clouds to *m* the Lord
Heb	10:	25	not giving up *m-ing* together,
Jas	2:	2	Suppose a man comes into your *m-ing*

men

Pr	20:	29	glory of young *m* is their strength,
Isa	40:	30	young *m* stumble and fall
Da	1:	17	young *m* God gave knowledge
	3:	25	I see four *m* walking around
Joel	2:	28	your old *m* will dream dreams,
Ac	1:	10	suddenly two *m* dressed in white
	2:	17	your young *m* will see visions,
	2:	23	with the help of wicked *m*,
1Co	13:	1	the tongues of *m* or angels

mercy, -iful

Ex	33:	19	have *m* on whom I will have *m*,
Dt	4:	31	the LORD your God is a *m-iful* God;
Ps	40:	11	Do not withhold your *m* from me,
	51:	1	Have *m* on me, O God,
Da	9:	9	our God is *m-iful* and forgiving,
Hos	6:	6	For I desire *m*, not sacrifice,
Mic	6:	8	To act justly and to love *m*
Mt	5:	7	for they will be shown *m*
	9:	13	"I desire *m*, not sacrifice."
Lk	1:	50	*m* extends to those who fear him,
	18:	13	"God, have *m* on me, a sinner."
Ro	9:	15	I will have *m* on whom I have *m*
	9:	16	desire or effort, but on God's *m*
	11:	32	so that he may have *m* on them all
	12:	1	sisters, in view of God's *m*,
Eph	2:	4	God, who is rich in *m*
Heb	4:	16	we may receive *m* and find grace
Jas	2:	13	judgment without *m* will be shown
1Pe	1:	3	great *m* he has given us new birth
Jude		22	Be *m-iful* to those who doubt;

message

Isa	53:	1	Who has believed our *m* and to whom
Mt	13:	19	hears the *m* about the kingdom
Jn	12:	38	'Lord, who has believed our *m*
Ro	10:	16	'Lord, who has believed our *m*?
	10:	17	faith comes from hearing the *m*,
1Co	1:	18	the *m* of the cross is foolishness
	2:	4	My *m* and my preaching were not
	2:	6	a *m* of wisdom among the mature,
2Co	1:	18	*m* to you is not 'Yes' and 'No'
	5:	19	to us the *m* of reconciliation
Col	3:	16	the *m* of Christ dwell among you richly
Heb	2:	2	the *m* spoken through angels was binding,
2Pe	1:	19	We also have the prophetic *m*

messiah, -s

Mt	1:	1	Jesus the *M* the son of David
	2:	4	where the *M* was to be born
	16:	16	'You are the *M*, the Son of
	16:	20	not to tell anyone that he was the *M*

	24:	5	claiming, "I am the *M*,"
	24:	24	false *m-s* and false prophets
	26:	63	Tell us if you are the *M*
Mk	1:	1	the good news about Jesus the *M*
Lk	2:	11	he is the *M*, the Lord
	24:	26	Did not the *M* have to suffer
Jn	1:	20	confessed freely, 'I am not the *M*.
	1:	41	'We have found the *M*'
	4:	25	'I know that *M*' (called Christ)
	11:	27	'I believe that you are the *M*,
Ac	2:	36	whom you crucified, both Lord and *M*
	17:	3	proving that the *M* had to suffer

might, -y

Ge	10:	9	a *m-y* hunter before the LORD;
Dt	10:	17	the great God, *m-y* and awesome,
2Sa	1:	25	How the *m-y* have fallen in battle!
Ps	24:	8	The LORD strong and *m-y*,
	106:	2	proclaim the *m-y* acts of the LORD
Isa	9:	6	Wonderful Counsellor, *M-y* God,
	11:	2	the Spirit of counsel and of *m*,
	62:	8	right hand and by his *m-y* arm:
Da	11:	3	Then a *m-y* king will arise,
Zep	3:	17	the *M-y* Warrior who saves.
Zec	4:	6	'Not by *m* nor by power, but by
Mt	26:	64	at the right hand of the *M-y* One
Lk	1:	49	the *M-y* One has done great things
	1:	51	He has performed *m-y* deeds with
Ac	13:	17	with *m-y* power he led them out
Eph	1:	19	same as the *m-y* strength
	6:	10	in the Lord and in his *m-y* power
Col	1:	11	according to his glorious *m*
1Pe	5:	6	under God's *m-y* hand,
Rev	5:	2	I saw a *m-y* angel proclaiming

mind, -s, -ful

Nu	23:	19	that he should change his *m*.
1Sa	15:	29	does not lie or change his *m*;
Ps	8:	4	mankind that you are *m-ful* of them,
	110:	4	sworn and will not change his *m*:
Isa	26:	3	keep in perfect peace those whose *m-s*
Mt	22:	37	all your soul and with all your *m*.
Ro	1:	28	God gave them over to a depraved *m*,
	8:	6	The *m* governed by the flesh is death,
	8:	7	*m* governed by the flesh is hostile to God;
	11:	34	'Who has known the *m* of the Lord?
	12:	2	by the renewing of your *m*.
1Co	2:	9	what no human *m* has conceived –
	2:	16	Who has known the *m* of the Lord
2Co	4:	4	blinded the *m-s* of unbelievers,
Php	3:	19	Their *m* is set on earthly things.
	4:	7	guard your hearts and your *m-s*
Col	3:	2	Set your *m-s* on things above,
Heb	2:	6	'What is mankind that you are *m-ful*
	7:	21	sworn and will not change his *m*:

miracle, -s, -ulous

Ps	77:	14	You are the God who performs *m-s*;
Mt	7:	22	in your name perform many *m-s*?
Ac	2:	22	accredited by God to you by *m-s*,
	19:	11	God did extraordinary *m-s* through
1Co	12:	10	to another *m-ulous* powers,
	12:	29	Are all teachers? Do all work *m-s*
2Co	12:	12	apostle, including signs, wonders and *m-s*
Gal	3:	5	his Spirit and work *m-s* among you
Heb	2:	4	signs, wonders and various *m-s*,

money

Pr	13:	11	Dishonest *m* dwindles away,
Ecc	5:	10	loves *m* never has enough;
Isa	55:	1	you who have no *m*, come, buy
	55:	2	Why spend *m* on what is not bread,
Mt	6:	24	You cannot serve both God and *M*
	26:	9	sold at a high price and the *m*

Lk	3:	14	'Don't extort *m* and don't accuse
Jn	2:	14	sitting at tables exchanging *m*
	12:	6	as keeper of the *m* bag,
Ac	4:	37	*m* and put it at the apostles' feet
	8:	20	'May your *m* perish with you,
1Co	16:	2	*m* in keeping with your income,
1Ti	3:	3	not quarrelsome, not a lover of *m*
	6:	10	For the love of *m* is a root
Heb	13:	5	lives free from the love of *m*

morning

Ge	1:	5	and there was *m* – the first day
Ex	12:	10	Do not leave any of it till *m;*
Job	38:	7	while the *m* stars sang together
Ps	30:	5	but rejoicing comes in the *m*
Isa	14:	12	fallen from heaven, *m* star,
La	3:	23	They are new every *m;* great is
Mt	16:	3	in the *m*, "Today it will be stormy,
Ac	2:	15	It's only nine in the *m*
2Pe	1:	19	the *m* star rises in your hearts
Rev	22:	16	and the bright *M* Star.

mortal, -s

Ge	6:	3	they are *m;* their days will be
Job	4:	17	Can a *m* be more righteous than God?
	14:	1	'*M-s*, born of woman, are of few days
Ps	56:	4	What can mere *m-s* do to me?
Mal	3:	8	'Will a mere *m* rob God?
Ro	1:	23	made to look like a *m* human being
	6:	12	do not let sin reign in your *m* body
	8:	11	give life to your *m* bodies
1Co	15:	54	and the *m* with immortality,
2Co	5:	4	*m* may be swallowed up by life

mother, -'s, -s

Ge	2:	24	man will leave his father and *m*
	3:	20	become the *m* of all the living
Ex	20:	12	'Honour your father and your *m*,
Job	1:	21	'Naked I came from my *m-'s* womb,
Ps	27:	10	Though my father and *m* forsake me,
	51:	5	from the time my *m* conceived me
	139:	13	knit me together in my *m-'s* womb
Isa	49:	15	'Can a *m* forget the baby at
	66:	13	As a *m* comforts her child,
Mt	1:	18	*m* Mary was pledged to be married
	10:	35	a daughter against her *m*,
	10:	37	loves their father or *m* more than me
	12:	48	'Who is my *m*, and who
	15:	4	"Honour your father and *m*"
	19:	5	man will leave his father and *m*
Jn	3:	4	a second time into their *m-'s* womb
	19:	27	the disciple, 'Here is your *m.*'
Eph	5:	31	a man will leave his father and *m*
	6:	2	'Honour your father and *m*' –
1Ti	5:	2	older women as *m-s*, and younger
Heb	7:	3	Without father or *m*,

mountain, -s

Ge	8:	4	ark came to rest on the *m-s*
Ps	2:	6	my king on Zion, my holy *m*
	18:	7	the foundations of the *m-s* shook;
	24:	3	Who may ascend the *m* of the LORD?
	90:	2	Before the *m-s* were born
	121:	1	I lift up my eyes to the *m-s* –
Isa	40:	4	every *m* and hill made low;
	40:	12	weighed the *m-s* on the scales
	52:	7	beautiful on the *m-s* are the feet
Da	2:	35	struck the statue became a huge *m*
Hos	10:	8	say to the *m-s*, 'Cover us!'
Mic	4:	1	the last days the *m* of the LORD's
Mt	4:	8	devil took him to a very high *m*
	17:	1	led them up a high *m* by themselves
	17:	20	you can say to this *m*,
	24:	16	in Judea flee to the *m-s*

Jn	4:	20	Our ancestors worshipped on this *m*,
1Co	13:	2	I have a faith that can move *m-s*,
Heb	12:	18	come to a *m* that can be touched
Rev	6:	16	called to the *m-s* and the rocks,

mouth, -s

Ps	19:	14	May these words of my *m* and
	22:	15	tongue sticks to the roof of my *m;*
	40:	3	He put a new song in my *m*,
	119:	103	sweeter than honey to my *m*
Isa	40:	5	For the *m* of the LORD has spoken.
	53:	7	yet he did not open his *m;*
	55:	11	my word that goes out from my *m:*
Eze	3:	3	tasted as sweet as honey in my *m*
Da	6:	22	he shut the *m-s* of the lions.
Mt	4:	4	that comes from the *m* of God."
	12:	34	*m* speaks what the heart
	13:	35	'I will open my *m* in parables,
	15:	11	someone's *m* does not defile them,
Ac	11:	8	or unclean has ever entered my *m*.
Ro	3:	14	'Their *m-s* are full of cursing
	10:	9	if you declare with your *m*,
Jas	3:	10	Out of the same *m* come praise and
1Pe	2:	22	no deceit was found in his *m*.
Rev	1:	16	*m* was a sharp, double-edged sword.
	3:	16	I am about to spit you out of my *m*

n

name, -'s, -s

Ge	2:	19	to see what he would *n* them;
	12:	2	I will make your *n* great,
	12:	8	called on the *n* of the LORD
Ex	3:	13	they ask me, "What is his *n*?"
	20:	7	not misuse the *n* of the LORD.
Dt	18:	19	the prophet speaks in my *n*.
	32:	3	I will proclaim the *n* of the LORD.
Jdg	13:	18	'Why do you ask my *n*? It is beyond
2Sa	7:	9	Now I will make your *n* great,
	7:	13	who will build a house for my *N*,
1Ki	5:	5	a temple for the *N* of the LORD
2Ki	21:	4	'In Jerusalem I will put my *N*.
1Ch	16:	29	the glory due to his *n;*
Job	1:	21	may the *n* of the LORD be praised.
Ps	8:	1	how majestic is your *n* in all
	23:	3	right paths for his *n-'s* sake.
	29:	2	LORD the glory due to his *n;*
	34:	3	let us exalt his *n* together
	102:	15	will fear the *n* of the LORD,
	103:	1	inmost being, praise his holy *n*
Pr	18:	10	*n* of the LORD is a fortified tower;
	22:	1	A good *n* is more desirable than
	30:	9	so dishonour the *n* of my God
Isa	59:	19	people will fear the *n* of the LORD,
Da	2:	20	Praise be to the *n* of God for ever
	12:	1	everyone whose *n* is found written
Joel	2:	32	who calls on the *n* of the LORD
Mal	1:	11	*n* will be great among the nations,
Mt	1:	21	you are to give him the *n* Jesus,
	6:	9	hallowed be your *n*
	7:	22	did we not prophesy in your *n*
	18:	5	in my *n* welcomes me
	18:	20	two or three come together in my *n*,
	28:	19	baptising them in the *n* of
Jn	1:	12	to those who believed in his *n*,
	3:	18	in the *n* of God's one and only Son
	5:	43	I have come in my Father's *n*,
	10:	3	He calls his own sheep by *n*
	12:	28	Father, glorify your *n*!'
	14:	14	ask me for anything in my *n*,
	14:	26	the Father will send in my *n*,

	20:	31	you may have life in his *n*
Ac	2:	21	everyone who calls on the *n* of
	3:	6	In the *n* of Jesus Christ
	3:	16	It is Jesus' *n* and the faith that
	4:	12	there is no other *n* under heaven given
	5:	41	suffering disgrace for the *N*
	9:	15	to proclaim my *n* to the Gentiles
	10:	43	forgiveness of sins through his *n*.
Ro	10:	13	'Everyone who calls on the *n* of
1Co	1:	2	call on the *n* of our Lord Jesus
Php	2:	9	him the *n* that is above every *n*
	2:	10	at the *n* of Jesus every knee
Col	3:	17	all in the *n* of the Lord Jesus,
2Ti	2:	19	who confesses the *n* of the Lord
Heb	1:	4	the *n* he has inherited is superior
	2:	12	will declare your *n* to my brothers
	12:	23	whose *n-s* are written in heaven.
1Jn	2:	12	forgiven on account of his *n*
	3:	23	his command: to believe in the *n*
Rev	2:	3	have endured hardships for my *n*,
	20:	15	Anyone whose *n* was not found written
	21:	27	*n-s* are written in the Lamb's

nation, -s

Ge	12:	2	'I will make you into a great *n*
	18:	18	all *n-s* on earth will be blessed
Ex	34:	24	I will drive out *n-s* before you
Dt	17:	14	king over us like all the *n-s*
	28:	64	will scatter you among all *n-s*,
1Sa	8:	5	such as all the other *n-s* have.
Ps	2:	1	Why do the *n-s* conspire
	2:	8	Ask of me, and I will make the *n-s*
	22:	28	and he rules over the *n-s*
	33:	12	Blessed is the *n* whose God is
	46:	10	I will be exalted among the *n-s*,
	67:	2	your salvation among all *n-s*
	99:	1	The LORD reigns, let the *n-s*
Pr	11:	14	For lack of guidance a *n* falls,
Isa	14:	12	you who once laid low the *n-s*
	40:	15	*n-s* are like a drop in a bucket;
	63:	6	I trampled the *n-s* in my anger;
	65:	1	a *n* that did not call on my name,
Jer	1:	5	you as a prophet to the *n-s*.
	2:	11	has a *n* ever changed its gods?
	6:	22	a great *n* is being stirred up
	29:	14	will gather you from all the *n-s*
Eze	11:	17	I will gather you from the *n-s*
	39:	21	display my glory among the *n-s*,
Hag	2:	7	I will shake all *n-s*,
Zec	14:	2	I will gather all the *n-s*
Mal	1:	11	name will be great among the *n-s*,
	3:	12	all the *n-s* will call you blessed,
Mt	12:	18	will proclaim justice to the *n-s*
	24:	7	*N* will rise against *n*,
	24:	9	you will be hated by all *n-s*
	24:	14	as a testimony to all *n-s*,
	25:	32	All the *n-s* will be gathered
	28:	19	go and make disciples of all *n-s*,
Mk	11:	17	a house of prayer for all *n-s*"?
Jn	11:	51	Jesus would die for the Jewish *n*
Ac	2:	5	Jews from every *n* under heaven
	4:	25	'Why do the *n-s* rage
	10:	35	accepts from every *n* the one
	14:	16	he let all *n-s* go their own way
	17:	26	From one man he made all the *n-s*
Ro	4:	17	made you a father of many *n-s*.'
Gal	3:	8	'All *n-s* will be blessed
1Ti	3:	16	was preached among the *n-s*,
1Pe	2:	9	a royal priesthood, a holy *n*,
Rev	5:	9	language and people and *n*

nature

Ro	1:	20	his eternal power and divine *n* –
	2:	14	by *n* things required by the law,
Php	2:	6	who, being in very *n* God,
2Pe	1:	4	participate in the divine *n*

need, -s, -ed, -y

Ps	40:	17	me, I am poor and *n-y*;
Pr	14:	21	the one who is kind to the *n-y*
Isa	11:	4	will judge the *n-y*,
	58:	11	he will satisfy your *n-s*
Am	8:	6	the *n-y* for a pair of sandals,
Mt	6:	2	'So when you give to the *n-y*,
	6:	8	your Father knows what you *n*
Ac	2:	45	to give to anyone who had *n*
	17:	25	as if he *n-ed* anything,
1Co	12:	21	say to the hand, 'I don't *n* you!'
Eph	4:	28	something to share with those in *n*
Php	4:	19	my God will meet all your *n-s*
1Jn	3:	17	sees a brother or sister in *n* but has no

neighbour, -'s

Ex	20:	16	false testimony against your *n*
	20:	17	not covet your *n-'s* house.
Lev	19:	18	love your *n* as yourself.
Jer	31:	34	No longer will they teach their *n*,
Mt	5:	43	"Love your *n* and hate your enemy.
	19:	19	"love your *n* as yourself."
Lk	10:	29	he asked Jesus, 'And who is my *n*?
Ro	13:	10	Love does no harm to its *n*.
Gal	5:	14	'Love your *n* as yourself.'
Heb	8:	11	No longer will they teach their *n*,

new

Ps	40:	3	He put a *n* song in my mouth,
	90:	5	like the *n* grass of the morning
	96:	1	Sing to the LORD a *n* song;
Ecc	1:	9	there is nothing *n* under the sun
Isa	43:	19	See, I am doing a *n* thing!
	65:	17	create *n* heavens and a *n* earth.
Jer	31:	31	'when I will make a *n* covenant
Eze	11:	19	put a *n* spirit in them;
	36:	26	I will give you a *n* heart
Mt	9:	17	pour *n* wine into old wineskins.
Lk	22:	20	'This cup is the *n* covenant
Jn	13:	34	'A *n* command I give you:
1Co	11:	25	'This cup is the *n* covenant
2Co	5:	17	in Christ, the *n* creation has come:
Gal	6:	15	what counts is the *n* creation
Eph	4:	24	put on the *n* self, created to be
Heb	8:	8	I will make a *n* covenant
	9:	15	the mediator of a *n* covenant,
2Pe	3:	13	to a *n* heaven and a *n* earth,
1Jn	2:	8	I am writing you a *n* command;
Rev	21:	1	I saw 'a *n* heaven and a *n* earth,
	21:	2	the Holy City, the *n* Jerusalem,
	21:	5	'I am making everything *n*!'

news

2Ki	7:	9	This is a day of good *n*
Pr	15:	30	good *n* gives health to the bones.
Isa	52:	7	feet of those who bring good *n*,
	61:	1	anointed me to proclaim good *n*
Mt	4:	23	the good *n* of the kingdom,
Mk	1:	14	proclaiming the good *n* of God
	1:	15	Repent and believe the good *n*!'
Lk	2:	10	I bring you good *n* of great joy
Ac	17:	18	*n* about Jesus and the resurrection
Ro	10:	15	feet of those who bring good *n*!

night, -s

Ge	1:	5	the darkness he called '*n*'.
	7:	4	for forty days and forty *n-s*,
Ex	13:	21	and by *n* in a pillar of fire
	34:	28	forty *n-s* without eating bread

1Ki	19:	8	forty *n-s* until he reached Horeb,
Ps	1:	2	meditates on his law day and *n*
	19:	2	*n* after *n* they display
	30:	5	weeping may remain for a *n,*
	90:	4	or like a watch in the *n*
	121:	6	harm you by day, nor the moon by *n*
Mt	4:	2	and forty *n-s,* he was hungry
	12:	40	and three *n-s* in the belly
	24:	43	time of *n* the thief was coming,
Lk	12:	20	This very *n* your life will be
Jn	3:	2	He came to Jesus at *n* and said,
1Co	11:	23	Jesus, on the *n* he was betrayed,
2Co	6:	5	hard work, sleepless *n-s* and hunger
1Th	2:	9	we worked *n* and day in order not
	5:	2	will come like a thief in the *n*
2Ti	1:	3	*n* and day I constantly remember
Rev	14:	11	There will be no rest day or *n* for
	22:	5	There will be no more *n.*

nothing

Job	1:	9	'Does Job fear God for *n?*'
Ps	34:	9	for those who fear him lack *n*
	49:	17	will take *n* with him when they die,
	73:	25	earth has I desire besides you
Ecc	1:	9	there is *n* new under the sun
Isa	40:	17	all the nations are as *n;*
	53:	2	*n* in his appearance that we should
Jer	32:	17	*N* is too hard for you
La	1:	12	'Is it *n* to you, all you who
Mt	10:	26	there is *n* concealed that will not
Lk	23:	41	But this man has done *n* wrong.
Jn	1:	3	without him *n* was made that has
	6:	63	the flesh counts for *n.*
	15:	5	apart from me you can do *n.*
Ac	20:	24	I consider my life worth *n* to me;
Ro	14:	14	*n* is unclean in itself.
1Co	2:	2	know *n* while I was with you except
	13:	2	but do not have love, I am *n*
Php	2:	7	made himself *n* by taking the very
1Ti	6:	7	For we brought *n* into the world,
Heb	4:	13	*N* in all creation is hidden
Rev	21:	27	*N* impure will ever enter it,

O

obey, -ing, -ed

Ex	12:	24	'*O* these instructions as a lasting
Lev	18:	4	You must *o* my laws and be careful
Dt	11:	32	be sure that you *o* all the decrees
	28:	2	if you *o* the LORD your God:
Jos	1:	7	Be careful to *o* all the law
1Sa	15:	22	To *o* is better than sacrifice,
2Ki	18:	12	because they had not *o-ed* the LORD
Ps	119:	57	I have promised to *o* your words
Mt	8:	27	Even the winds and the waves *o* him!
	28:	20	to *o* everything I have commanded
Mk	1:	27	orders to evil spirits and they *o*
Jn	17:	6	and they have *o-ed* your word.
Ac	5:	29	'We must *o* God rather than human
	5:	32	whom God has given to those who *o*
Ro	2:	13	but it is those who *o* the law
	6:	12	so that you *o* its evil desires
	6:	17	you have come to *o* from your heart
Gal	5:	7	to keep you from *o-ing* the truth
Eph	6:	1	Children, *o* your parents
Heb	5:	9	eternal salvation for all who *o* him

offer, -ing, -ings, -ed

Ge	8:	20	he sacrificed burnt *o-ings* on it
	22:	7	is the lamb for the burnt *o-ing?*
1Co	31:	54	He *o-ed* a sacrifice there
Ex	29:	18	a burnt *o-ing* to the LORD

2Sa	24:	24	burnt *o-ings* that cost me nothing.
Ps	4:	5	*O* the sacrifices of the righteous
	40:	6	Sacrifice and *o-ing* you did not
	51:	16	not take pleasure in burnt *o-ings*
Isa	1:	13	Stop bringing meaningless *o-ings!*
	53:	10	LORD makes his life an *o-ing* for sin,
Hos	14:	2	that we may *o* the fruit of our lips
Mal	3:	8	we robbing you?" 'In tithes and *o-ings*
Mt	5:	23	if you are *o-ing* your gift
	27:	34	There they *o-ed* Jesus wine to drink
Ro	6:	13	Do not *o* any part of yourself
	12:	1	*o* your bodies as a living sacrifice,
	15:	16	become an *o-ing* acceptable to God,
1Co	9:	18	gospel I may *o* it free of charge,
	10:	20	of pagans are *o-ed* to demons,
Eph	5:	2	fragrant *o-ing* and sacrifice to God
Php	2:	17	poured out like a drink *o-ing*
	4:	18	They are a fragrant *o-ing,*
2Ti	4:	6	being poured out like a drink *o-ing*
Heb	5:	1	to *o* gifts and sacrifices for sins
	5:	7	he *o-ed* up prayers and petitions
	7:	27	once for all when he *o-ed* himself
	9:	14	who through the eternal Spirit *o-ed*
	10:	5	he said: 'Sacrifice and *o-ing*
	11:	4	Abel brought God a better *o-ing*
	13:	15	continually *o* to God a sacrifice
Jas	2:	21	he *o-ed* his son Isaac on the altar
	5:	15	And the prayer *o-ed* in faith

oil

Ex	29:	7	Take the anointing *o* and anoint him
1Sa	16:	13	took the horn of *o* and anointed him
1Ki	1:	39	Zadok the priest took the horn of *o*
	17:	16	and the jug of *o* did not run dry,
Ps	23:	5	You anoint my head with *o;*
	45:	7	by anointing you with the *o* of joy
	89:	20	my sacred *o* I have anointed him
	133:	2	like precious *o* poured on the head,
Mt	6:	17	when you fast, put *o* on your head
	25:	4	The wise, however, took *o* in jars
Mk	6:	13	anointed with *o* many people
Lk	7:	46	You did not put *o* on my head,
	10:	34	bandaged his wounds, pouring on *o*
Jas	5:	14	pray over them and anoint them with *o*

one

Ge	2:	24	and they will become *o* flesh
	11:	1	Now the whole world had *o* language
Dt	6:	4	the LORD our God, the LORD is *o*
Ps	27:	4	*O* thing I ask from the LORD,
Ecc	4:	9	Two are better than *o,*
Isa	40:	26	brings out the starry host *o* by *o*
	43:	15	I am the LORD, your Holy *O,*
	47:	4	is the Holy *O* of Israel
Eze	34:	23	I will place over them *o* shepherd
	37:	17	join them together into *o* stick
	39:	7	I the LORD am the Holy *O* in Israel
Mt	19:	17	'There is only *O* who is good.
Mk	12:	29	the Lord our God, the Lord is *o.*
	15:	27	*o* on his right and *o* on his left
Lk	23:	35	he is God's Messiah, the Chosen *O.*
Jn	1:	18	God, but the *o* and only Son
	6:	69	you are the Holy *O* of God.
	17:	22	that they may be *o* as we are *o*
	19:	36	Not *o* of his bones will be broken,
Ac	1:	17	He was *o* of our number
	3:	14	the Holy and Righteous *O*
	4:	32	*o* in heart and mind.
	13:	35	not let your holy *o* see decay.
	17:	26	From *o* man he made all the nations
Ro	5:	15	the trespass of the *o* man,
	12:	5	we, though many, form *o* body,
1Co	10:	17	Because there is *o* loaf,

	12: 13	baptised by *o* Spirit
	12: 20	many parts, but *o* body
	12: 26	If *o* part suffers,
2Co	5: 14	*o* died for all, and therefore all
Gal	3: 28	for you are all *o* in Christ Jesus.
Eph	2: 15	*o* new humanity out of the two,
	4: 4	*o* body and *o* Spirit,
	4: 5	*o* Lord, *o* faith, *o* baptism
	4: 6	*o* God and Father of all,
	5: 31	and the two will become *o* flesh.'
Php	2: 2	*o* in spirit and of *o* mind
	3: 13	But *o* thing I do:
1Th	5: 24	The *o* who calls you is faithful
1Ti	2: 5	there is *o* God and *o* mediator
Heb	11: 17	to sacrifice his *o* and only son
1Jn	2: 20	anointing from the Holy *O*,
Rev	11: 17	the *O* who is and who was,

open, -s, -ed

Ge	3: 7	the eyes of both of them were *o-ed*,
1Ki	8: 29	your eyes be *o* towards this temple
Ps	51: 15	*O* my lips, Lord,
	81: 10	*O* wide your mouth and I will fill
	119: 18	*O* my eyes that I may see
Pr	31: 20	She *o-s* her arms to the poor
Mt	7: 7	and the door will be *o-ed* to you
	13: 35	'I will *o* my mouth in parables,
Lk	10: 38	Martha *o-ed* her home to him
	24: 31	eyes were *o-ed* and they recognised
	24: 45	Then he *o-ed* their minds
Jn	9: 10	'How then were your eyes *o-ed*?'
Ac	7: 56	I see heaven *o* and the Son of Man
	10: 11	He saw heaven *o-ed*
	16: 14	The Lord *o-ed* her heart to respond
	26: 18	to *o* their eyes and turn them
Ro	3: 13	'Their throats are *o* graves;
2Co	2: 12	the Lord had *o-ed* a door for me
Col	4: 3	God may *o* a door for our message,
Heb	10: 20	a new and living way *o-ed* for us
Rev	3: 20	hears my voice and *o-s* the door,
	5: 2	to break the seals and *o* the scroll

order, -s, -ly

Ex	1: 22	Then Pharaoh gave this *o* to all
Job	38: 12	you ever given *o-s* to the morning,
Ps	110: 4	for ever, in the *o* of Melchizedek.
Isa	38: 1	the Lord says: put your house in *o*,
Mt	2: 16	he gave *o-s* to kill all the boys
Mk	9: 9	Jesus gave them *o-s* not to tell
Lk	1: 3	to write an *o-ly* account for you,
	4: 36	he gives *o-s* to evil spirits
	11: 25	the house swept clean and put in *o*
Ac	5: 28	We gave you strict *o-s* not to teach
1Co	14: 40	be done in a fitting and *o-ly* way
Heb	5: 6	for ever, in the *o* of Melchizedek.
Rev	21: 4	the old *o* of things has passed away

overcome, -came

Ge	32: 28	with God and with humans and have *o*.
Hos	12: 4	with the angel and *o-came* him;
Mt	16: 18	the gates of Hades will not *o* it
Mk	9: 24	I do believe; help me *o* my unbelief
Jn	16: 33	But take heart! I have *o* the world.
Ro	12: 21	but *o* evil with good
1Jn	2: 13	because you have *o* the evil one.
	5: 4	victory that has *o* the world, even

P

palace

2Sa	5: 11	and they built a *p* for David
2Ch	2: 12	a temple for the Lord and a *p*

Ps	45: 15	they enter the *p* of the king
Jer	22: 5	that this *p* will become a ruin."
	22: 13	builds his *p* by unrighteousness
Da	1: 4	qualified to serve in the king's *p*.
	4: 29	the roof of the royal *p* of Babylon
Mk	15: 16	led Jesus away into the *p*
Php	1: 13	throughout the whole *p* guard

parent, -s

Ex	20: 5	for the sin of the *p-s* to the third
Eze	18: 2	"The *p-s* eat sour grapes,
Mal	4: 6	hearts of the *p-s* to their children
Mt	10: 21	children will rebel against their *p-s*
Lk	1: 17	to turn the hearts of the *p-s*
	2: 41	Every year Jesus' *p-s* went to Jerusalem
	21: 16	You will be betrayed even by *p-s*
Jn	9: 3	Neither this man nor his *p-s* sinned
Eph	6: 1	obey your *p-s* in the Lord
2Ti	3: 2	disobedient to their *p-s*

pass, -ing, -ed

Ex	12: 13	I see the blood, I will *p* over you.
	34: 6	And he *p-ed* in front of Moses,
Ps	84: 6	they *p* through the Valley of Baka
	90: 9	our days *p* away under your wrath;
Isa	43: 2	When you *p* through the waters,
La	1: 12	Is it nothing to you, all you who *p*
Mt	24: 35	but my words will never *p* away
	27: 39	Those who *p-ed* by hurled insults
Lk	10: 31	he *p-ed* by on the other side
	18: 37	'Jesus of Nazareth is *p-ing* by.
Ro	15: 24	to see you while *p-ing* through
1Co	10: 1	they all *p-ed* through the sea
	13: 8	there is knowledge, it will *p* away
	15: 3	what I received I *p-ed* on to you
Jas	1: 10	they will *p* away like a wild flower
1Jn	3: 14	we have *p-ed* from death to life,
Rev	21: 4	old order of things has *p-ed* away.

patient, -ly, -nce

Ps	40: 1	I waited *p-ly* for the Lord;
Pr	14: 29	Whoever is *p* has great understanding,
Isa	7: 13	Will you try the *p-nce* of my God
Ro	2: 4	his kindness, forbearance and *p-nce*,
	8: 25	we wait for it *p-ly*
1Co	13: 4	Love is *p*, love is kind.
Gal	5: 22	fruit of the Spirit is … *p-nce*,
Eph	4: 2	be *p*, bearing with one another
1Th	5: 14	help the weak, be *p* with everyone.
Jas	5: 7	Be *p*, then, brothers and sisters
1Pe	3: 20	God waited *p-ly* in the days of Noah
2Pe	3: 15	our Lord's *p-nce* means salvation,
Rev	13: 10	This calls for *p* endurance

pay, -ment

Ge	23: 13	I will *p* the price of the field.
Ex	30: 12	*p* the Lord a ransom for his life
Lev	26: 43	They will *p* for their sins
Mt	17: 24	your teacher *p* the temple tax?
	18: 34	until he should *p* back all he owed
	20: 2	He agreed to *p* them a denarius
	22: 17	Is it right to *p* the poll-tax to Caesar
Lk	3: 14	be content with your *p*.
	19: 8	I will *p* back four times the amount
	23: 2	opposes *p-ment* of taxes to Caesar
Ac	22: 28	to *p* a lot of money for my citizenship
Ro	13: 7	if you owe taxes, *p* taxes;

peace, -loving

Nu	6: 26	his face towards you and give you *p*
Jdg	6: 24	and called it The Lord Is *P*.
1Ch	22: 9	son who will be a man of *p*
Ps	29: 11	the Lord blesses his people with *p*
	37: 37	a future awaits those who seek *p*

119:165 Great *p* have those who love your
            law
    122:   6 Pray for the *p* of Jerusalem:
Isa   9:   6 Everlasting Father, Prince of *P*
     26:   3 You will keep in perfect *p* those
     48: 22 'There is no *p* ... for the wicked.
Jer   6: 14 "*P, p*," they say, when there
Mt   10: 34 I did not come to bring *p*,
Lk   2: 14 and on earth *p* to those on whom
      2: 29 now dismiss your servant in *p.*
Jn   14: 27 *P* I leave with you; my *p* I give
     16: 33 so that in me you may have *p.*
     20: 19 Jesus ... said, '*P* be with you!'
Ro   5:   1 *p* with God through our Lord Jesus
      8:   6 by the Spirit is life and *p.*
     12: 18 live at *p* with everyone.
1Co   7: 15 God has called us to live in *p*
Gal   5: 22 love, joy, *p*, patience, kindness,
Eph   2: 14 For he himself is our *p*,
      6: 15 that comes from the gospel of *p.*
Php   4:   7 And the *p* of God, which transcends
Col   1: 20 by making *p* through his blood,
      3: 15 Let the *p* of Christ rule in your
1Th   5: 13 Live in *p* with each other
Heb 12: 14 Make every effort to live in *p*
     13: 20 may the God of *p*, who through
Jas   3: 17 first of all pure; then *p-loving*,
1Pe   3: 11 they must seek *p* and pursue it

people, -s
Ge   4: 26 At that time *p* began to call
     12:   1 'Go from your country, your *p*
     49: 33 and was gathered to his *p*
Ex   3:   7 the misery of my *p* in Egypt.
      7: 16 let my *p* go,
     33:   3 you are a stiff-necked *p*
Nu   22: 11 "A *p* that has come out of Egypt
Dt   7:   6 For you are a *p* holy to the LORD
     32:   9 For the LORD's portion is his *p,*
2Ki 15: 29 and deported the *p* to Assyria
1Ch 17: 21 And who is like your *p* Israel –
2Ch   2: 11 'Because the LORD loves his *p,*
      7:   5 and all the *p* dedicated the temple
      7: 14 if my *p*, who are called by my name,
     36: 16 the LORD was aroused against his *p*
Ezr   4: 12 the *p* who came up to us
Ps   2:   1 and the *p-s* plot in vain
     22: 22 I will declare your name to my *p*
     28:   8 The LORD is the strength of his *p,*
     44: 12 You sold your *p* for a pittance,
     57:   9 I will sing of you among the *p-s*
     67:   5 May the *p-s* praise you, God;
     68: 18 you received gifts from *p,*
     77: 14 display your power among the *p-s*
     77: 20 You led your *p* like a flock
     90:   3 You turn *p* back to dust, saying,
     94: 14 For the LORD will not reject his *p;*
     95:   7 and we are the *p* of his pasture,
     96: 10 he will judge the *p-s* with equity
    100:   3 we are his *p*, the sheep
    111:   9 He provided redemption for his *p;*
    133:   1 when God's *p* live together in unity
Pr   14: 34 but sin condemns any *p.*
Isa   5: 13 Therefore my *p* will go into exile
      6:   5 I live among a *p* of unclean lips,
      6: 10 Make the heart of this *p* calloused;
      9:   2 The *p* walking in darkness
     11: 12 he will assemble the scattered *p*
     12:   6 sing for joy, *p* of Zion,
     29: 13 'These *p* come near to me
     40:   1 Comfort, comfort my *p,*
     40:   6 'All *p* are like grass,

     40:   7 Surely the *p* are grass
     49: 13 For the LORD comforts his *p*
     52:   6 Therefore my *p* will know my name;
     53:   8 for the transgression of my *p*
     62: 12 They will be called the Holy *P,*
Jer   4: 22 'My *p* are fools; they do not know
      4: 25 I looked, and there were no *p;*
     31:   7 "LORD, save your *p*, the remnant
     32: 38 They will be my *p*, and I will be
     33:   6 I will heal my *p*
Eze 39:   7 my holy name among my *p* Israel.
Da   5: 21 He was driven away from *p*
      7: 27 the holy *p* of the Most High.
     11: 32 but the *p* who know their God will
Hos   1: 10 said to them, "You are not my *p*",
      2: 23 will say to those called "Not my *p*"
Am   9: 14 I will bring my *p* Israel back
Hag   2:   4 Be strong, all you *p* of the land,"
Zec   2: 11 and will become my *p.*
Mt   4: 19 send you out to fish for *p*
      5: 47 And if you greet only your own *p*
      9: 17 Neither do *p* pour new wine
     24: 30 the *p-s* of the earth will mourn.
Mk   5: 20 And all the *p* were amazed
      7:   6 "These *p* honour me with their lips,
      8: 24 'I see *p*; they look like trees
     10: 13 *P* were bringing little children
Lk   1: 17 to make ready a *p* prepared
      1: 68 he has come to his *p* and redeemed
      2: 10 joy that will be for all the *p*
      5: 10 from now on you will fish for *p.*
     18: 11 I am not like other *p* – robbers,
Jn   3: 19 but *p* loved darkness instead of
     11: 50 that one man die for the *p*
     12: 32 will draw all *p* to myself.
Ac   7:   3 "Leave your country and your *p*,"
      7: 51 'You stiff-necked *p*!
     15: 14 a *p* for his name from the Gentiles
     18: 10 because I have many *p* in this city.
     28: 26 "Go to this *p* and say,
Ro   1: 18 all the godlessness and wickedness of *p*
      8: 27 Spirit intercedes for God's *p*
      9: 33 a stone that causes *p* to stumble
     10: 21 to a disobedient and obstinate *p.*
     11:   1 did God reject his *p*? By no means!
     12: 13 Share with the Lord's *p* who are in need.
     12: 16 associate with *p* of low position.
     15: 10 'Rejoice, you Gentiles, with his *p.*
     15: 11 let all the *p-s* extol him.
1Co   6:   2 the Lord's *p* will judge the world
     10:   7 'The *p* sat down to eat and drink
2Co   1:   1 together with all his holy *p*
      4: 15 reaching more and more *p*
      6: 16 and they will be my *p.*
Eph   1: 18 glorious inheritance in his holy *p*
      4:   8 and gave gifts to his *p.*
Php   2: 29 and honour *p* like him
1Th   5: 26 Greet all God's *p* with a holy kiss
1Ti   1:   3 you may command certain *p*
      2:   4 who wants all *p* to be saved
      2:   6 as a ransom for all *p*
      2: 10 who is the Saviour of all *p*,
Tit   2: 14 a *p* that are his very own,
Heb   2: 17 atonement for the sins of the *p*
      4:   9 a Sabbath-rest for the *p* of God
      5:   3 as well as for the sins of the *p*
      9: 27 Just as *p* are destined to die once,
     10: 30 'The Lord will judge his *p.*
     13: 12 to make the *p* holy
1Pe   1: 24 'All *p* are like grass,
      2:   9 But you are a chosen *p*,
      2: 10 but now you are the *p* of God;

2Pe	3:	11	what kind of *p* ought you to be?
Jude		3	entrusted to God's holy *p*
Rev	2:	2	you cannot tolerate wicked *p,*
	5:	8	which are the prayers of God's *p*
	13:	7	every tribe, *p,* language and nation
	18:	4	"Come out of her, my *p,*
	19:	8	the righteous acts of God's holy *p*
	21:	3	They will be his *p,*

perfect, -ing, -er

Dt	32:	4	He is the Rock, his works are *p,*
2Sa	22:	31	'As for God, his way is *p:*
Ps	19:	7	The law of the LORD is *p,*
Isa	26:	3	You will keep in *p* peace
Mt	5:	48	Be *p,* therefore,
Ro	12:	2	his good, pleasing and *p* will
2Co	7:	1	*p-ing* holiness out of reverence for
	12:	9	for my power is made *p* in weakness.
Heb	7:	19	(for the law made nothing *p*),
	7:	28	Son, who has been made *p* for ever
	9:	11	the greater and more *p* tabernacle
	10:	14	by one sacrifice he has made *p*
	12:	2	the pioneer and *p-er* of faith,
	12:	23	the spirits of the righteous made *p*
Jas	1:	25	whoever looks intently into the *p* law
1Jn	4:	18	But *p* love drives out fear,

perish, -ing, -able

Ge	6:	17	Everything on earth will *p*
Lk	13:	3	you repent, you too will all *p.*
	21:	18	But not a hair of your head will *p*
Jn	3:	16	shall not *p* but have eternal life
	10:	28	and they shall never *p;*
1Co	1:	18	foolishness to those who are *p-ing,*
	15:	42	The body that is sown is *p-able,*
2Co	4:	3	it is veiled to those who are *p-ing*
2Pe	3:	9	not wanting anyone to *p,*

persecute, -d, -ion

Mt	5:	10	Blessed are those who are *p-d*
	5:	44	and pray for those who *p* you
	10:	23	When you are *p-d* in one place,
	13:	21	or *p-ion* comes because of the word,
Jn	15:	20	If they *p-d* me, they will *p* you
Ac	8:	1	*p-ion* broke out against the church
	9:	4	'Saul, Saul, why do you *p* me?
	22:	4	I *p-d* the followers of this Way
Ro	8:	35	Shall trouble or hardship or *p-ion*
	12:	14	Bless those who *p* you;
2Ti	3:	12	life in Christ Jesus will be *p-d,*

Pharaoh, -'s

Ge	12:	15	And when *P's* officials saw her,
	41:	1	*P* had a dream: he was standing
	41:	14	So *P* sent for Joseph,
	44:	18	you are equal to *P* himself
	47:	10	Then Jacob blessed *P* and went out
Ex	1:	19	The midwives answered *P,*
	2:	5	*P-'s* daughter went down to the Nile
	3:	10	I am sending you to *P*
	7:	1	See, I have made you like God to *P*
	7:	13	Yet *P-'s* heart became hard
	9:	12	But the LORD hardened *P-'s* heart
	14:	17	And I will gain glory through *P*
1Ki	3:	1	Solomon made an alliance with *P*
Ps	135:	9	against *P* and all his servants
Ac	7:	13	and *P* learned about Joseph's family
	7:	21	*P-'s* daughter took him and brought

Philistine, -s

Ge	21:	34	stayed in the land of the *P-s*
Jdg	3:	31	who struck down six hundred *P-s*
	14:	1	and saw there a young *P* woman
	16:	9	'Samson, the *P-s* are upon you!'
	16:	30	'Let me die with the *P-s!'*

1Sa	4:	1	went out to fight against the *P-s.*
	4:	17	'Israel fled before the *P-s,*
	13:	5	The *P-s* assembled to fight Israel,
	17:	4	Goliath ... came out of the *P* camp.
	23:	2	'Shall I go and attack these *P-s?'*
2Sa	5:	19	'Shall I go and attack the *P-s?*
	8:	1	David defeated the *P-s* and subdued
2Ch	26:	6	He went to war against the *P-s*
Isa	2:	6	practise divination like the *P-s*

plant, -s, -ed

Ge	1:	11	seed-bearing *p-s* and trees
	9:	20	proceeded to *p* a vineyard
Ps	1:	3	is like a tree *p-ed* by streams
	80:	15	the root your right hand has *p-ed,*
Jer	1:	10	and overthrow, to build and to *p.*
	17:	8	like a tree *p-ed* by the water
Mt	13:	6	sun came up, the *p-s* were scorched,
	15:	13	'Every *p* that my heavenly Father
1Co	3:	8	one who *p-s* and the one who waters
	15:	37	you do not *p* the body that will be,
Jas	1:	21	humbly accept the word *p-ed* in you,

please, -s, -ing, -d

Lev	1:	9	an aroma *p-ing* to the LORD
1Ki	3:	10	The Lord was *p-d* that Solomon
Ps	104:	34	May my meditation be *p-ing* to him,
	115:	3	he does whatever *p-s* him
Pr	15:	8	the prayer of the upright *p-s* him
Jer	6:	20	your sacrifices do not *p* me.
Mic	6:	7	Will the LORD be *p-d* with thousands
Mt	3:	17	whom I love; with him I am well *p-d*
Jn	3:	8	The wind blows wherever it *p-s.*
	5:	30	for I seek not to *p* myself but him
Ro	12:	1	sacrifice, holy and *p-ing* to God —
	15:	2	Each of us should *p* our neighbours
1Co	7:	32	how he can *p* the Lord
2Co	5:	9	So we make it our goal to *p* him,
Gal	1:	10	Or am I trying to *p* people?
	6:	8	whoever sows to *p* the Spirit,
Eph	5:	10	find out what *p-s* the Lord.
Php	4:	18	acceptable sacrifice, *p-ing* to God
Col	1:	19	God was *p-d* to have all his fullness
1Th	2:	4	We are not trying to *p* people but God,
Heb	11:	6	faith it is impossible to *p* God,
	13:	21	work in us what is *p-ing* to him,
2Pe	1:	17	whom I love; with him I am well *p-d*

poor

Dt	15:	11	There will always be *p* people
Ps	34:	6	*p* man called, and the LORD heard
	82:	3	uphold the cause of the *p*
	113:	7	He raises the *p* from the dust
Pr	19:	17	is kind to the *p* lends to the LORD,
	31:	20	She opens her arms to the *p*
Isa	25:	4	You have been a refuge for the *p,*
	61:	1	to proclaim good news to the *p.*
Am	2:	7	They trample on the heads of the *p*
Mt	5:	3	'Blessed are the *p* in spirit,
	11:	5	the good news is proclaimed to the *p*
	26:	11	The *p* you will always have with you
Lk	4:	18	to proclaim good news to the *p*
2Co	8:	9	yet for your sake he became *p,*
Gal	2:	10	should continue to remember the *p,*

possess, -ing, -ed, -ion, -ions

Ge	15:	7	this land to take *p-ion* of it.
	17:	8	I will give as an everlasting *p-ion*
Ex	19:	5	you will be my treasured *p-ion.*
Dt	1:	8	Go in and take *p-ion* of the land
	8:	1	and may enter and *p* the land that
1Ch	28:	8	that you may *p* this good land
Da	7:	18	the kingdom and will *p* it for ever
Mt	19:	21	go, sell your *p-ions* and give

Mk	1:	23	who was *p-ed* by an evil spirit
Lk	12:	15	in an abundance of *p-ions.*
	19:	8	give half of my *p-ions* to the poor,
Jn	10:	21	sayings of a man *p-ed* by a demon.
1Co	13:	3	If I give all I *p* to the poor
2Co	6:	10	nothing, and yet *p-ing* everything
	12:	14	what I want is not your *p-ions* but
Heb	10:	34	had better and lasting *p-ions*
1Pe	2:	9	holy nation, God's special *p-ion*
1Jn	3:	17	If anyone has material *p-ions*

pour, -s, -ed

1Sa	10:	1	oil and *p-ed* it on Saul's head
2Ki	3:	11	to *p* water on the hands of Elijah.
Ps	22:	14	I am *p-ed* out like water,
	62:	8	*p* out your hearts to him,
	133:	2	like precious oil *p-ed* on the head,
Isa	53:	12	he *p-ed* out his life unto death,
Eze	39:	29	I will *p* out my Spirit on the house
Joel	2:	28	I will *p* out my Spirit on all
Mt	26:	28	which is *p-ed* out for many
Lk	5:	37	no one *p* new wine into old
Ac	2:	17	I will *p* out my Spirit on all
Ro	5:	5	because God's love has been *p-ed* out
2Ti	4:	6	*p-ed* out like a drink offering,
Tit	3:	6	whom he *p-ed* out on us generously
Rev	16:	1	Go, *p* out the seven bowls of God's

power, -s, -ful, -less

Ex	9:	16	that I might show you my *p*
Jdg	14:	19	of the LORD came upon him in *p.*
1Ch	29:	11	greatness and the *p* and the glory
2Ch	20:	6	*P* and might are in your hand,
Ps	63:	2	and beheld your *p* and your glory
	90:	11	If only we knew the *p* of your anger!
Zec	4:	6	nor by *p*, but by my Spirit,'
Mt	24:	30	Son of Man coming ... with *p*
Mk	5:	30	Jesus realised that *p* had gone out
Lk	1:	35	*p* of the Most High will overshadow
	4:	14	to Galilee in the *p* of the Spirit,
	24:	49	been clothed with *p* from on high.
Ac	1:	8	receive *p* when the Holy Spirit
	4:	33	With great *p* the apostles continued
Ro	1:	16	the *p* of God that brings salvation
	5:	6	we were still *p-less*, Christ died
	8:	38	present nor the future, nor any *p-s*
	9:	17	that I might display my *p* in you
1Co	1:	18	are being saved it is the *p* of God.
	1:	24	Christ the *p* of God and the wisdom
	6:	14	By his *p* God raised the Lord
2Co	4:	7	this all-surpassing *p* is from God
	12:	9	my *p* is made perfect in weakness.'
	13:	4	weakness, yet he lives by God's *p.*
Eph	1:	19	his incomparably great *p* for us
	6:	12	against the *p-s* of this dark world
Php	3:	10	know the *p* of his resurrection
Col	2:	15	disarmed the *p-s* and authorities,
1Th	1:	5	simply with words but also with *p*,
2Ti	3:	5	form of godliness but denying its *p*
Heb	1:	3	all things by his *p-ful* word.
	7:	16	the *p* of an indestructible life
1Pe	1:	5	who ... are shielded by God's *p*
Jude		25	be glory, majesty, *p* and authority,
Rev	4:	11	to receive glory and honour and *p*,
	5:	12	Worthy is the Lamb ... to receive *p*
	20:	6	The second death has no *p* over them

praise, -ing, -d

Ex	15:	2	He is my God, and I will *p* him
Dt	10:	21	He is your *p*; he is your God,
2Sa	22:	47	'The LORD lives! *P* be to my Rock!
1Ch	16:	8	Give *p* to the LORD,
	16:	25	is the LORD and most worthy of *p*;
	29:	10	David *p-d* the LORD in the presence

2Ch	20:	22	As they began to sing and *p*,
Ne	8:	6	Ezra *p-d* the LORD, the great God;
Job	1:	21	may the name of the LORD be *p-d.*
Ps	8:	2	the *p* of children and infants
	22:	3	Holy One; you are the *p* of Israel.
	51:	15	and my mouth will declare your *p*
	96:	4	is the LORD and most worthy of *p*;
	100:	4	thanksgiving and his courts with *p*
	103:	1	my inmost being, *p* his holy name
	108:	3	*p* you, LORD, among the nations;
	135:	3	LORD is good; sing *p* to his name,
	144:	1	*P* be to the LORD my Rock;
	146:	2	I will *p* the LORD all my life;
	150:	6	that has breath *p* the LORD.
Pr	27:	21	people are tested by their *p.*
Isa	61:	3	and a garment of *p* instead of
Da	2:	19	Then Daniel *p-d* the God of heaven
Mt	11:	25	'I *p* you, Father, Lord of heaven
	21:	16	and infants you have ordained *p*"?
Lk	2:	13	appeared with the angel, *p-ing* God
Jn	12:	43	loved human *p* more than *p* from God
Ac	10:	46	speaking in tongues and *p-ing* God.
Ro	2:	29	Such a person's *p* is not from other people,
1Co	4:	5	each will receive their *p* from God
2Co	1:	3	*P* be to the God and Father of our
Eph	1:	6	to the *p* of his glorious grace,
	1:	12	might be for the *p* of his glory.
Heb	13:	15	offer to God a sacrifice of *p* –
Jas	5:	13	happy? Let them sing songs of *p*
1Pe	2:	9	declare the *p-s* of him who called
Rev	5:	13	and to the Lamb be *p* and honour

pray, -s, -ing, -ed

Ge	20:	17	Then Abraham *p-ed* to God,
Nu	21:	7	So Moses *p-ed* for the people
Dt	4:	7	God is near us whenever we *p* to him
Jdg	16:	28	Then Samson *p-ed* to the LORD,
2Sa	15:	31	So David *p-ed*, 'LORD, turn
1Ki	8:	30	when they *p* towards this place.
	18:	36	Elijah stepped forward and *p-ed:*
2Ch	7:	1	When Solomon finished *p-ing*,
	7:	14	humble themselves and *p* and seek
Da	6:	13	He still *p-s* three times a day.
Mt	6:	5	'And when you *p*, do not be like
	6:	9	'This, then, is how you should *p*:
	26:	36	while I go over there and *p.*
	26:	41	'Watch and *p* so that you will not
Lk	6:	12	and spent the night *p-ing* to God
	11:	1	Jesus was *p-ing* in a certain place.
	18:	1	should always *p* and not give up.
	18:	10	Two men went up to the temple to *p*,
Ac	10:	9	Peter went up on the roof to *p*
	12:	5	the church was earnestly *p-ing*
Ro	8:	26	do not know what we ought to *p* for,
1Co	14:	14	For if I *p* in a tongue,
Eph	6:	18	be alert and always keep on *p-ing*
1Th	5:	17	*p* continually,
Jas	5:	14	elders of the church to *p* over them
Jude		20	and *p-ing* in the Holy Spirit

prayer, -s

2Ch	7:	12	I have heard your *p* and have chosen
Ps	61:	1	Hear my cry, O God; listen to my *p*
Mk	9:	29	This kind can come out only by *p.*
Lk	19:	46	"My house will be a house of *p*";
Ac	2:	42	to the breaking of bread and to *p*
2Co	1:	11	as you help us by your *p-s.*
Php	4:	6	in every situation, by *p* and petition,
Col	4:	2	Devote yourselves to *p*,
1Th	1:	2	mention you in our *p-s*
1Ti	2:	1	*p-s* ... be made for all people
Jas	5:	16	*p* of a righteous person is powerful
Rev	5:	8	which are the *p-s* of God's people

preach, -ing, -ed

Ezr 6: 14 the *p-ing* of Haggai the prophet
Mt 4: 17 From that time on Jesus began to *p*,
24: 14 gospel of the kingdom will be *p-ed*
Ro 1: 15 why I am so eager to *p* the gospel
10: 14 can they hear without someone *p-ing*
1Co 1: 21 foolishness of what was *p-ed* to
1: 23 but we *p* Christ crucified:
9: 16 Woe to me if I do not *p* the gospel!
1Th 2: 9 we *p-ed* the gospel of God to you
1Ti 4: 13 devote yourself ... to *p-ing* and
5: 17 whose work is *p-ing* and teaching
2Ti 4: 2 *p* the word;

prepare, -d

Ex 23: 20 bring you to the place I have *p-d*
Ps 23: 5 You *p* a table before me
Isa 40: 3 calling: 'In the wilderness *p* the way
Mal 3: 1 my messenger, who will *p* the way
Mt 3: 3 "*P* the way for the Lord,
11: 10 who will *p* your way before you.
25: 34 *p-d* for you since the creation
26: 12 she did it to *p* me for burial
Jn 14: 3 And if I go and *p* a place for you,
1Co 2: 9 God has *p-d* for those who love him
Eph 2: 10 which God *p-d* in advance for us
2Ti 4: 2 be *p-d* in season and out of season;
Heb 10: 5 but a body you *p-d* for me
1Pe 3: 15 Always be *p-d* to give an answer

presence

Ge 4: 16 So Cain went out from the LORD's *p*
Ex 25: 30 Put the bread of the *P*
1Sa 2: 21 Samuel grew up in the *p* of the LORD
Ps 16: 11 you will fill me with joy in your *p*
23: 5 in the *p* of my enemies.
51: 11 Do not cast me from your *p*
139: 7 Where can I flee from your *p*
Lk 1: 19 Gabriel. I stand in the *p* of God,
Ac 2: 28 you will fill me with joy in your *p*
1Th 3: 13 holy in the *p* of our God and Father
2Ti 4: 1 In the *p* of God and of Christ Jesus
Heb 9: 24 now to appear for us in God's *p*
1Jn 3: 19 we set our hearts at rest in his *p*
Jude 24 before his glorious *p* without fault
Rev 20: 11 earth and the heavens fled from his *p*,

priest, -s, -hood

Ge 14: 18 He was *p* of God Most High
Ex 3: 1 his father-in-law, the *p* of Midian,
19: 6 a kingdom of *p-s* and a holy nation.
28: 1 so that they may serve me as *p-s*
Lev 21: 7 because *p-s* are holy to their God
Nu 10: 8 the *p-s*, are to blow the trumpets.
Jos 3: 8 the *p-s* who carry the ark
1Sa 1: 3 the two sons of Eli, were *p-s*
2: 35 raise up for myself a faithful *p*,
Ezr 7: 12 Ezra the *p*, teacher of the Law
Ps 99: 6 Moses and Aaron were among his *p-s*,
132: 9 *p-s* be clothed with your righteousness;
Mt 8: 4 But go, show yourself to the *p*
26: 3 Then the chief *p-s* and the elders
Ac 9: 14 with authority from the chief *p-s*
Heb 3: 1 acknowledge as our apostle and high *p*
4: 14 since we have a great high *p*
6: 20 He has become a high *p* for ever,
7: 1 king of Salem and *p* of God
7: 17 declared: 'You are a *p* for ever,
7: 26 Such a high *p* truly meets our need –
9: 11 when Christ came as high *p*
10: 21 a great *p* over the house of God
13: 11 The high *p* carries the blood
1Pe 2: 5 spiritual house to be a holy *p-hood*
2: 9 a chosen people, a royal *p-hood*,
Rev 1: 6 a kingdom and *p-s* to serve his God
20: 6 but they will be *p-s* of God

prison, -ers

Ps 142: 7 Set me free from my *p*,
146: 7 The LORD sets *p-ers* free
Isa 42: 7 to free captives from *p*
Mt 25: 36 I was in *p* and you came to visit me
Lk 4: 18 to proclaim freedom for the *p-ers*
Ac 16: 23 flogged, they were thrown into *p*,
Heb 13: 3 remember those in *p*
Rev 2: 10 the devil will put some of you in *p*

proclaim, -s, -ed

Ex 33: 19 and I will *p* my name, the LORD,
2Sa 1: 20 *p* it not in the streets of Ashkelon
Ps 6: 5 Among the dead no one *p-s*
19: 1 the skies *p* the work of his hands
Isa 52: 7 who *p* peace, who bring good tidings
61: 1 to *p* freedom for the captives
Mt 11: 5 the good news is *p-ed* to the poor
12: 18 he will *p* justice to the nations
Lk 4: 18 to *p* freedom for the prisoners
Ac 13: 38 forgiveness of sins is *p-ed* to you
Ro 15: 19 fully *p-ed* the gospel of Christ
1Co 11: 26 *p* the Lord's death until he comes
Col 1: 28 We *p* him, admonishing and teaching
4: 3 that we may *p* the mystery of Christ
1Jn 1: 3 We *p* to you what we have seen

promise, -s, -d

Ge 21: 1 LORD did for Sarah what he had *p-d*
50: 24 the land he *p-d* on oath to Abraham,
Ex 3: 17 And I have *p-d* to bring you up
Dt 6: 18 good land that the LORD *p-d* on oath
Jos 23: 15 good things the LORD your God has *p-d*
2Sa 7: 25 keep for ever the *p* you have made
1Ki 6: 12 the *p* I gave to David your father
Ps 119:116 Sustain me ... according to your *p*,
Lk 24: 49 send you what my Father has *p-d*;
Ac 1: 4 wait for the gift my Father *p-d*,
2: 39 The *p* is for you and your children
Ro 4: 16 Therefore, the *p* comes by faith,
9: 8 but it is the children of the *p*
2Co 1: 20 no matter how many *p-s* God has made
7: 1 since we have these *p-s*,
Gal 3: 14 might receive the *p* of the Spirit.
Eph 1: 13 with a seal, the *p-d* Holy Spirit
2: 12 to the covenants of the *p*, without
Heb 6: 15 Abraham received what was *p-d*
10: 23 for he who *p-d* is faithful
2Pe 1: 4 his very great and precious *p-s*,
3: 9 Lord is not slow in keeping his *p*,
1Jn 2: 25 what he *p-d* us – eternal life

prophesy, -ies, -ing, -ied

Nu 11: 25 Spirit rested on them, they *p-ied*
1Ki 18: 29 they continued their frantic *p-ing*
Eze 37: 4 '*P* to these bones and say to them,
Mt 7: 22 Lord, did we not *p* in your name
26: 68 '*P* to us, Messiah. Who hit you?
Lk 1: 67 with the Holy Spirit and *p-ied*
Jn 11: 51 he *p-ied* that Jesus would die
Ac 2: 17 Your sons and daughters will *p*,
21: 9 four unmarried daughters who *p-ied*
1Co 13: 9 we know in part and we *p* in part
14: 4 but the one who *p-ies* edifies the church

prophet, -s

Ge 20: 7 for he is a *p*,
Ex 7: 1 your brother Aaron will be your *p*
Nu 11: 29 that all the LORD's people were *p-s*
Dt 13: 5 *p* or dreamer must be put to death
18: 18 will raise up for them a *p* like you
34: 10 no *p* has risen in Israel like Moses

1Sa	19:	24	'Is Saul also among the *p-s*?
1Ki	19:	10	and put your *p-s* to death
1Ch	16:	22	do my *p-s* no harm.
2Ch	24:	19	Although the LORD sent *p-s*
	36:	16	scoffed at his *p-s* until the wrath
Jer	1:	5	appointed you as a *p* to the nations
	7:	25	I sent you my servants the *p-s*
	14:	14	*p-s* are prophesying lies in my name
	29:	19	and again by my servants the *p-s*.
Am	7:	14	neither a *p* nor the son of a *p*
Zec	7:	12	through the earlier *p-s*.
Mal	4:	5	'See, I will send the *p* Elijah
Mt	1:	22	the Lord had said through the *p*
	2:	23	what was said through the *p-s:*
	3:	3	was spoken of through the *p* Isaiah:
	5:	12	they persecuted the *p-s* who were
	5:	17	come to abolish the Law or the *P-s;*
	7:	15	'Watch out for false *p-s*.
	13:	57	A *p* is not without honour except.
Ac	7:	37	'God will raise up for you a *p* like me
Ro	1:	2	promised beforehand through his *p-s*
	11:	3	'Lord, they have killed your *p-s*
1Co	12:	28	first of all apostles, second *p-s*,
	12:	29	Are all apostles? Are all *p-s*?
	14:	32	The spirits of *p-s* are subject
Eph	2:	20	foundation of the apostles and *p-s*,
	4:	11	gave the apostles, the *p-s*
Tit	1:	12	One of Crete's own *p-s* has said
Heb	1:	1	through the *p-s* at many times
2Pe	3:	2	spoken in the past by the holy *p-s*
1Jn	4:	1	because many false *p-s* have gone
Rev	16:	13	out of the mouth of the false *p*

punish, -ed, -ment

Ge	15:	14	But I will *p* the nation they serve
2Sa	7:	14	I will *p* him with a rod wielded
Ezr	9:	13	you have *p-ed* us less than our sins
Pr	16:	22	but folly brings *p-ment* to fools
Isa	13:	11	I will *p* the world for its evil,
Jer	21:	14	I will *p* you as your deeds deserve,
Am	3:	2	therefore I will *p* you
Mt	25:	46	they will go away to eternal *p-ment*
2Th	1:	9	*p-ed* with everlasting destruction
1Jn	4:	18	because fear has to do with *p-ment*.
Jude		7	suffer the *p-ment* of eternal fire

pure, -ity

2Sa	22:	27	to the *p* you show yourself *p*,
Ps	19:	9	The fear of the LORD is *p*,
	51:	10	Create in me a *p* heart, O God,
	119:	9	How can a young person stay on the path of *p-ity?*
Hab	1:	13	Your eyes are too *p* to look on evil
Mt	5:	8	Blessed are the *p* in heart,
2Co	11:	2	present you as a *p* virgin to him
Php	2:	15	blameless and *p*, 'children of God
	4:	8	whatever is right, whatever is *p*,
Tit	1:	15	To the *p*, all things are *p*,
Heb	13:	4	and the marriage bed kept *p*,
Jas	3:	17	comes from heaven is first of all *p*

r

raise, -ing, -d

Mt	10:	8	those who are ill, *r* the dead,
	16:	21	on the third day be *r-d* to life
	27:	52	who had died were *r-d* to life
Jn	2:	19	I will *r* it again in three days.
	6:	40	I will *r* them up at the last day.
Ac	2:	24	But God *r-d* him from the dead,
	13:	34	God *r-d* him from the dead
	17:	31	proof of this to everyone by *r-ing*

Ro	4:	24	who believe in him who *r-d* Jesus
	4:	25	to death for our sins and was *r-d*
	8:	11	the Spirit of him who *r-d* Jesus
	10:	9	believe in your heart that God *r-d*
1Co	15:	4	he was buried, that he was *r-d*
	15:	14	And if Christ has not been *r-d*,
	15:	20	But Christ has indeed been *r-d*
	15:	35	'How are the dead *r-d*?
	15:	43	it is *r-d* in glory;
	15:	52	the dead will be *r-d* imperishable,
Eph	2:	6	And God *r-d* us up with Christ

rebel, -s, -led, -lion

Dt	13:	5	for inciting *r-lion* against the LORD
1Sa	15:	23	for *r-lion* is like the sin of
Ps	78:	56	they put God to the test and *r-led*
Mt	10:	21	children will *r* against their
	26:	55	'Am I leading a *r-lion*,
Ro	13:		whoever *r-s* against the authority
2Th	2:	3	the *r-lion* occurs and the man of
Heb	3:	8	hearts as you did in the *r-lion*,
	3:	16	Who were they who heard and *r-led*?
Jude		11	been destroyed in Korah's *r-lion*

receive, -s, -d

Ecc	11:	1	after many days you may *r* a return
Mt	7:	8	For everyone who asks *r-s;*
	10:	8	Freely you have *r-d*, freely give
	13:	20	word and at once *r-s* it with joy
	21:	22	If you believe, you will *r*
Jn	1:	12	Yet to all who did *r* him, to those
	16:	15	the Spirit will *r* from me
	16:	24	Ask and you will *r*,
	20:	22	'R the Holy Spirit
Ac	2:	38	you will *r* the gift of the Holy
	3:	21	Heaven must *r* him until
	19:	2	'Did you *r* the Holy Spirit
	20:	35	more blessed to give than to *r*."
Ro	5:	11	we have now *r-d* reconciliation
	8:	15	you *r-d* brought about
1Co	4:	7	do you have that you did not *r*?
	11:	23	I *r-d* from the Lord what I also
Gal	3:	2	did you *r* the Spirit by the works
Col	2:	6	as you *r-d* Christ Jesus as Lord,
Heb	4:	16	we may *r* mercy and find grace
Jas	4:	3	When you ask, you do not *r*,
1Pe	5:	4	you will *r* the crown of glory

redeem, -s, -ed, -er

Ex	6:	6	*r* you with an outstretched arm
Job	19:	25	I know that my *r-er* lives,
Ps	19:	14	LORD, my Rock and my *R-er*
	49:	7	No one can *r* the life of another
	49:	15	God will *r* me from the realm
	103:	4	who *r-s* your life from the pit
Isa	41:	14	your *R-er*, the Holy One of Israel
	43:	1	'Do not fear, for I have *r-ed* you;
Lk	1:	68	come to his people and *r-ed* them
	24:	21	one who was going to *r* Israel.
Gal	3:	13	Christ *r-ed* us from the curse
	4:	5	to *r* those under the law,
1Pe	1:	18	*r-ed* from the empty way of life

redemption

Ps	111:	9	He provided *r* for his people;
Lk	2:	38	forward to the *r* of Jerusalem.
	21:	28	because your *r* is drawing near.
Ro	3:	24	freely by his grace through the *r*
	8:	23	the *r* of our bodies
1Co	1:	30	our righteousness, holiness and *r*
Eph	1:	7	we have *r* through his blood,
	1:	14	until the *r* of those who are God's
	4:	30	you were sealed for the day of *r*.

Col	1: 14	in whom we have r,
Heb	9: 12	so obtaining eternal r

reign, -s, -ed

Ex	15: 18	The LORD r-s for ever and ever.
Ps	9: 7	The LORD r-s for ever;
	93: 1	LORD r-s, he is robed in majesty;
	97: 1	LORD r-s, let the earth be glad;
	99: 1	LORD r-s, let the nations tremble;
Isa	9: 7	He will r on David's throne
	32: 1	a king will r in righteousness
	52: 7	'Your God r-s!
Lk	1: 33	r over the house of Jacob for ever;
Ro	5: 14	death r-ed from the time of Adam
	5: 21	just as sin r-ed in death,
	6: 12	not let sin r in your mortal body
1Co	15: 25	For he must r until
2Ti	2: 12	we will also r with him.
Rev	5: 10	and they will r on the earth.

reject, -s, -ed

1Sa	8: 7	it is not you they have r-ed,
	15: 23	the LORD, he has r-ed you as king.
2Ki	17: 20	LORD r-ed all the people of Israel;
Ps	27: 9	Do not r me or forsake me,
	118: 22	The stone the builders r-ed
Isa	53: 3	He was despised and r-ed by mankind,
Mt	21: 42	"The stone the builders r-ed
Mk	8: 31	suffer many things and be r-ed
Jn	3: 36	whoever r-s the Son will not see
Ac	4: 11	"the stone you builders r-ed,
Ro	11: 1	did God r his people?
1Pe	2: 7	'The stone the builders r-ed

rejoice, -s, -ing, -d

1Sa	2: 1	'My heart r-s in the LORD;
Ps	13: 5	my heart r-s in your salvation,
Pr	5: 18	r in the wife of your youth
Hab	3: 18	yet I will r in the LORD,
Zec	9: 9	R greatly, Daughter Zion!
Mt	5: 12	R and be glad, because great
Lk	1: 47	my spirit r-s in God my Saviour
	10: 20	do not r that the spirits submit
	15: 7	there will be more r-ing in heaven
Jn	8: 56	Your father Abraham r-d
1Co	13: 6	but r-s with the truth
Php	3: 1	my brothers and sisters, r in the Lord!
	4: 4	R in the Lord always.
1Th	5: 16	R always,
1Pe	1: 6	In all this you greatly r,

remain, -s, -ed

2Ch	33: 4	'My Name will r in Jerusalem
Ps	30: 5	weeping may r for a night,
Isa	62: 1	for Jerusalem's sake I will not r
Hag	1: 4	while this house r-s a ruin?
Mt	26: 63	But Jesus r-ed silent.
Jn	1: 32	as a dove and r on him
	3: 36	God's wrath r-s on them.
	6: 56	and drinks my blood r-s in me,
	15: 4	R in me, as I also r in you.
	15: 9	Now r in my love
Ac	14: 22	encouraging them to r true
Ro	13: 8	Let no debt r outstanding,
1Co	7: 20	Each person should r in the situation
	13: 13	three r: faith, hope and love.
	14: 34	Women should r silent
Php	1: 24	that I r in the body
2Ti	2: 13	he r-s faithful,
Heb	1: 11	They will perish, but you r;
	4: 9	There r-s, then, a Sabbath-rest
Rev	2: 13	Yet you r true to my name.

remember, -s, -ed

Ge	9: 15	I will r my covenant

Ex	2: 24	he r-ed his covenant with Abraham,
	20: 8	'R the Sabbath day
Ne	5: 19	R me with favour, my God,
Ps	42: 4	I r as I pour out my soul:
	63: 6	On my bed I r you;
	103: 14	he r-s that we are dust.
	137: 1	wept when we r-ed Zion
Ecc	12: 1	R your Creator in the days
Isa	17: 10	you have not r-ed the Rock,
	43: 25	r-s your sins no more
	64: 9	do not r our sins for ever.
Hab	3: 2	in wrath r mercy
Mt	5: 23	at the altar and there r that
Lk	17: 32	R Lot's wife!
	23: 42	r me when you come into your
2Ti	1: 3	I constantly r you in my prayers
	2: 8	R Jesus Christ,
Heb	8: 12	will r their sins no more.
	13: 7	R your leaders, who spoke

repent, -s, -ed

Job	42: 6	r in dust and ashes.
Eze	14: 6	what the Sovereign LORD says: r!
Mt	3: 2	'R, for the kingdom of heaven
	4: 17	'R, for the kingdom of heaven
	11: 21	they would have r-ed long ago
	12: 41	r-ed at the preaching of Jonah,
	21: 32	you did not r and believe him
Mk	1: 15	R and believe the good news!'
Lk	13: 3	unless you r, you too
	15: 7	heaven over one sinner who r-s
	17: 3	if they r, forgive them
Ac	2: 38	'R and be baptised,
	17: 30	all people everywhere to r
Rev	2: 5	R and do the things you did at

repentance

Isa	30: 15	In r and rest is your salvation,
Mt	3: 8	Produce fruit in keeping with r
	3: 11	'I baptise you with water for r.
Lk	5: 32	the righteous, but sinners to r.
	24: 47	r for the forgiveness of sins will be
Ac	5: 31	to r and forgive their sins
	20: 21	they must turn to God in r
Ro	2: 4	intended to lead you to r
2Co	7: 10	Godly sorrow brings r
2Ti	2: 25	that God will grant them r
Heb	6: 1	laying again the foundation of r
	6: 6	to be brought back to r.
2Pe	3: 9	but everyone to come to r

rescue, -s, -ed

Ps	22: 8	let the LORD r him.
Da	6: 16	whom you serve continually, r you!
	6: 27	He r-s and he saves;
Mt	27: 43	Let God r him now
Ac	12: 11	Lord sent his angel and r-d me
Ro	7: 24	Who will r me from this body
Gal	1: 4	gave himself for our sins to r us
Col	1: 13	he has r-d us from the dominion
1Th	1: 10	who r-s us from the coming wrath

rest, -s, -ed

Ge	2: 2	on the seventh day he r-ed
	8: 4	ark came to r on the mountains
1Ki	5: 4	God has given me r on every side,
Ps	62: 1	Truly my soul finds r in God;
	91: 1	r in the shadow of the Almighty
	95: 11	"They shall never enter my r.
Pr	6: 10	little folding of the hands to r
Isa	11: 2	Spirit of the LORD will r on him −
	30: 15	repentance and r is your salvation,
	62: 7	give him no r till he establishes

Mt 10: 13 let your peace r on it;
11: 28 I will give you r
11: 29 you will find r for your souls
12: 43 through arid places seeking r
Mk 6: 31 to a quiet place and get some r.'
Lk 2: 14 to those on whom his favour r-s.
23: 56 r-ed on the Sabbath in obedience
Ac 2: 3 came to r on each of them
2: 26 my body also will r in hope
1Co 2: 5 faith might not r on human wisdom,
2Co 12: 9 Christ's power may r on me
Heb 3: 11 "They shall never enter my r."
4: 11 make every effort to enter that r,
Rev 14: 13 'they will r from their labour,

resurrection
Mt 22: 28 at the r, whose wife will she be
Lk 14: 14 repaid at the r of the righteous.
Jn 11: 24 he will rise again in the r
11: 25 'I am the r and the life.
Ac 4: 33 to testify to the r of the Lord
17: 18 good news about Jesus and the r
Ro 1: 4 in power by his r from the dead:
6: 5 united with him in a r like his
1Co 15: 12 there is no r of the dead
15: 21 the r of the dead comes also
Php 3: 10 power of his r and participation
2Ti 2: 18 the r has already taken place,
Heb 11: 35 that they might gain an even better r
Rev 20: 5 This is the first r

return, -s, -ing, -ed
Ge 3: 19 r to the ground, since from it
1Ki 17: 21 let this boy's life r to him!
Job 7: 9 goes down to the grave does not r
Ps 90: 3 'R to dust, you mortals.
126: 6 will r with songs of joy,
Pr 26: 11 As a dog r-s to its vomit,
Isa 10: 21 A remnant will r,
35: 10 those the Lord has rescued will r.
55: 11 it will not r to me empty,
Jer 3: 12 "R, faithless Israel,"
Hos 6: 1 'Come, let us r to the Lord.
Joel 2: 12 'r to me with all your heart,
Mal 3: 7 and I will r to you,'
Mt 2: 12 they r-ed to their country
10: 13 let your peace r to you
24: 46 finds him doing so when he r-s
Jn 13: 3 from God and was r-ing to God
1Pe 2: 25 you have r-ed to the Shepherd
2Pe 2: 22 'A dog r-s to its vomit,'

reveal, -ed
Nu 12: 6 I ... r myself to them in visions,
Isa 40: 5 glory of the Lord will be r-ed,
53: 1 has the arm of the Lord been r-ed
Mt 11: 27 to whom the Son chooses to r him
Lk 10: 21 and r-ed them to little children.
Jn 1: 31 that he might be r-ed to Israel.
17: 6 'I have r-ed you to those whom you
Ro 1: 17 the righteousness of God is r-ed
1: 18 The wrath of God is being r-ed
8: 19 for the children of God to be r-ed
1Co 2: 10 God has r-ed them to us
2Th 1: 7 Lord Jesus is r-ed from heaven
2: 3 man of lawlessness is r-ed,
1Pe 5: 1 share in the glory to be r-ed

revelation, -s
Pr 29: 18 Where there is no r, people
Hab 2: 2 Write down the r and make it plain
Lk 2: 32 a light for r to the Gentiles
Ro 16: 25 the r of the mystery hidden
1Co 14: 6 I bring you some r or knowledge

14: 26 a word of instruction, a r,
2Co 12: 1 I will go on to visions and r-s
12: 7 these surpassingly great r-s,
Gal 1: 12 I received it by r from Jesus
Eph 3: 3 the mystery made known to me by r,

reward
Ge 15: 1 your shield, your very great r.
Ps 19: 11 in keeping them there is great r
127: 3 offspring a r from him
Isa 40: 10 See, his r is with him,
Mt 5: 12 great is your r in heaven,
6: 4 done in secret, will r you
16: 27 he will r each person according to
1Co 3: 14 the builder will receive a r.
Eph 6: 8 the Lord will r each one
Col 3: 24 inheritance from the Lord as a r.
Rev 22: 12 My r is with me,

rich, -es
Ps 49: 6 boast of their great r-es
Pr 8: 18 With me are r-es and honour,
22: 1 more desirable than great r-es;
Isa 53: 9 and with the r in his death,
Mt 19: 24 who is r to enter the kingdom
27: 57 there came a r man from Arimathea,
Lk 1: 53 but has sent the r away empty
8: 14 choked by life's worries, r-es and
16: 19 'There was a r man who was dressed
Ro 9: 23 make the r-es of his glory known
11: 33 Oh, the depth of the r-es
2Co 8: 9 he was r, yet for your sake
Eph 2: 4 God, who is r in mercy
3: 8 the boundless r-es of Christ,
Php 4: 19 according to the r-es of his glory
Jas 2: 6 Is it not the r who are exploiting

right
Ge 18: 25 the Judge of all the earth do r?'
Dt 12: 25 what is r in the eyes of the Lord
2Sa 23: 5 'If my house were not r with God,
Ps 9: 4 For you have upheld my r
19: 8 The precepts of the Lord are r,
51: 4 you are r in your verdict
Pr 16: 25 a way that appears to be r,
21: 2 think their own ways are r,
Isa 7: 15 reject the wrong and choose the r
Eze 18: 21 just and r, that person will surely live;
33: 16 They have done what is just and r;
Da 4: 37 everything he does is r
Hos 14: 9 The ways of the Lord are r;
Jnh 4: 4 'Is it r for you to be angry?
Mt 11: 19 wisdom is proved r by her deeds.
15: 7 Isaiah was r when he prophesied
20: 15 I have the r to do what I want
Lk 7: 29 acknowledged that God's way was r,
Jn 1: 12 he gave the r to become children
Ac 4: 19 Which is r in God's eyes:
6: 2 'It would not be r for us
10: 35 who fears him and does what is r
Ro 5: 6 You see, at just the r time,
9: 21 Does not the potter have the r
1Co 9: 4 Don't we have the r to food
Php 4: 8 whatever is r, whatever is pure,
1Pe 2: 14 to commend those who do r
3: 14 should suffer for what is r,
1Jn 3: 10 who does not do what is r

right
Ex 15: 6 Your r hand, Lord, was majestic
Dt 5: 32 turn aside to the r or to
Ps 16: 8 With him at my r hand,
16: 11 eternal pleasures at your r hand

	73:	23	you hold me by my *r* hand
	110:	1	'Sit at my *r* hand until
	110:	5	The LORD is at your *r* hand;
	139:	10	your *r* hand will hold me fast
Isa	30:	21	you turn to the *r* or to the left,
	62:	8	The LORD has sworn by his *r* hand
Zec	3:	1	Satan standing at his *r* side
Mt	5:	29	If your *r* eye causes you to stumble,
	5:	39	slaps you on the *r* cheek,
	6:	3	left hand know what your *r* hand
	22:	44	'Sit at my *r* hand until
	25:	33	the sheep on his *r* and the goats
	26:	64	Son of Man sitting at the *r* hand
	27:	38	one on his *r* and one on his left.
Mk	10:	37	'Let one of us sit at your *r*
Ac	2:	25	Because he is at my *r* hand,
	2:	33	Exalted to the *r* hand of God,
	2:	34	'Sit at my *r* hand
	5:	31	God exalted him to his own *r* hand
	7:	56	Son of Man standing at the *r* hand
Ro	8:	34	is at the *r* hand of God and
Gal	2:	9	the *r* hand of fellowship
Eph	1:	20	seated him at his *r* hand
Col	3:	1	Christ is, seated at the *r* hand
Heb	1:	3	he sat down at the *r* hand
	10:	12	sins, he sat down at the *r* hand

righteous, -ness

Ge	6:	9	Noah was a *r* man, blameless among
	15:	6	he credited it to him as *r-ness*
	18:	26	'If I find fifty *r* people
Ps	1:	5	sinners in the assembly of the *r*
	9:	8	He rules the world in *r-ness*
	19:	9	and all of them are *r*
	34:	19	*r* person may have many troubles,
	37:	25	I have never seen the *r* forsaken
	85:	10	*r-ness* and peace kiss each other
	106:	31	credited to him as *r-ness*
Pr	11:	30	fruit of the *r* is a tree of life,
	14:	34	*R-ness* exalts a nation, but sin
	18:	10	the *r* run to it and are safe.
Isa	11:	5	*R-ness* will be his belt
	32:	17	fruit of that *r-ness* will be peace
	41:	10	uphold you with my *r* right hand
	45:	21	a *r* God and a Saviour;
	59:	17	put on *r-ness* as his breastplate,
	61:	10	arrayed me in a robe of his *r-ness*,
	64:	6	our *r* acts are like filthy rags;"
Jer	33:	16	The LORD Our *R* Saviour."
Eze	33:	13	*r* person that they will surely live,
Am	5:	24	*r-ness* like a never-failing stream
Hab	2:	4	*r* person will live by his faithfulness
Mal	4:	2	the sun of *r-ness* will rise
Mt	1:	19	Joseph her husband was a *r* man
	5:	6	who hunger and thirst for *r-ness*,
	5:	20	unless your *r-ness* surpasses that
	6:	33	first his kingdom and his *r-ness*,
	9:	13	I have not come to call the *r*
	13:	49	separate the wicked from the *r*
	25:	46	the *r* to eternal life.
Jn	16:	8	in the wrong about sin and *r-ness*
Ro	1:	17	in the gospel the *r-ness* of God
	3:	10	'There is no one *r*, not even one
	3:	21	the *r-ness* of God has been made known
	3:	25	did this to demonstrate his *r-ness*,
	4:	3	it was credited to him as *r-ness*.
	4:	13	the *r-ness* that comes by faith
	5:	7	will anyone die for a *r* person,
	5:	17	grace and of the gift of *r-ness*
	5:	19	the many will be made *r*
	8:	4	that the *r* requirement of the law

	10:	4	*r-ness* for everyone who believes
	14:	17	but of *r-ness*, peace and joy
1Co	1:	30	our *r-ness*, holiness and
2Co	5:	21	we might become the *r-ness* of God.
Gal	3:	11	'the *r* will live by faith.
Eph	6:	14	the breastplate of *r-ness* in place,
Php	3:	9	not having a *r-ness* of my own
2Ti	3:	16	correcting and training in *r-ness*
	4:	8	crown of *r-ness*, which the Lord,
Heb	10:	38	my *r* one will live by faith.
Jas	2:	23	it was credited to him as *r-ness*,
	3:	18	reap a harvest of *r-ness*
1Pe	3:	18	the *r* for the unrighteous,
1Jn	3:	7	The one who does what is right is *r*,

rise, -s, -n

Nu	24:	17	a sceptre will *r* out of Israel.
Ps	2:	2	kings of the earth *r* up
	44:	26	*R* up and help us; redeem us
	127:	2	In vain you *r* early and stay up
	139:	2	You know when I sit and when I *r*;
Isa	60:	1	the glory of the LORD *r-s* upon you
Mal	4:	2	the sun of righteousness will *r*
Mt	5:	45	He causes his sun to *r* on the evil
	11:	11	not *r-n* anyone greater than John
	24:	7	Nation will *r* against nation,
	27:	63	"After three days I will *r* again.
	28:	6	He is not here; he has *r-n*,
Lk	16:	31	even if someone *r-s* from the dead.
Jn	5:	29	done what is good will *r* to live,
	11:	23	'Your brother will *r* again.'
Ac	4:	26	kings of the earth *r* up
1Th	4:	16	and the dead in Christ will *r* first
2Pe	1:	19	the morning star *r-s* in your hearts

rock, -s

Ge	49:	24	the Shepherd, the *R* of Israel
Ex	17:	6	Strike the *r*, and water will come
	33:	22	in a cleft in the *r* and cover you
Dt	32:	4	He is the *R*, his works are perfect,
	32:	18	You deserted the *R*, who fathered
	32:	31	their *r* is not like our *R*,
1Sa	2:	2	there is no *R* like our God
Ps	18:	2	The LORD is my *r*, my fortress
Isa	51:	1	to the *r* from which you were cut
Jer	23:	29	hammer that breaks a *r* in pieces
Da	2:	34	a *r* was cut out, but not by human
Mt	7:	24	who built his house on the *r*
	16:	18	Peter, and on this *r* I will build
	27:	60	tomb that he had cut out of the *r*.
Ro	9:	33	and a *r* that makes them fall,
1Co	10:	4	drank from the spiritual *r*
1Pe	2:	8	and a *r* that makes them fall.
Rev	6:	16	to the mountains and the *r-s*,

ruin, -s, -ed

Ps	73:	18	you cast them down to *r*
Pr	10:	8	a chattering fool comes to *r*
	18:	24	come to *r*, but there is a friend
SS	2:	15	little foxes that *r* the vineyards,
Isa	6:	5	'Woe to me!' I cried. 'I am *r-ed*!
Jer	9:	11	I will make Jerusalem a heap of *r-s*
Hag	1:	4	while this house remains a *r*?
Mt	12:	25	divided against itself will be *r-ed*
Ac	15:	16	Its *r-s* I will rebuild,
1Ti	6:	9	plunge people into *r* and destruction

rule, -s, -r, -rs

Ge	1:	26	they may *r* over the fish
	3:	16	husband, and he will *r* over you.
	4:	7	to have you, but you must *r* over it.
1Ki	8:	16	chosen David to *r* my people Israel.
Ps	2:	2	the *r-rs* band together against
	8:	6	You made them *r-rs* over the works

Pr	8:	15	By me kings reign and *r-rs*
Isa	29:	13	based on merely human *r-s*
Mic	5:	2	who will be *r-r*over Israel,
Mt	2:	6	least among the *r-rs* of Judah;
	15:	9	teachings are merely human *r-s*
	20:	25	the *r-rs* of the Gentiles lord it
1Co	2:	8	None of the *r-rs* of this age
Gal	6:	16	mercy to all who follow this *r* –
Eph	1:	21	far above all *r* and authority,
	2:	2	the *r-r*of the kingdom of the air,
	6:	12	but against the *r-rs*,
Col	3:	15	Let the peace of Christ *r*
Rev	2:	27	will *r* them with an iron sceptre

S

Sabbath

Ex	20:	8	'Remember the *S* day by keeping
Ne	13:	15	treading winepresses on the *S* and
Isa	58:	13	keep your feet from breaking the *S*
Mt	12:	1	through the cornfields on the *S*.
	12:	8	the Son of Man is Lord of the *S*.
	12:	10	'Is it lawful to heal on the *S*?
Jn	5:	16	doing these things on the *S*,
Ac	16:	13	On the *S* we went outside the city
	17:	2	and on three *S* days he reasoned
Col	2:	16	New Moon celebration or a *S* day

sacrifice, -s, -d

Ge	22:	2	*S* him there as a burnt offering
Ex	12:	27	"It is the Passover *s* to the LORD,
1Sa	15:	22	To obey is better than *s*,
1Ki	18:	36	time of *s*, the prophet Elijah
Ps	4:	5	Offer the *s-s* of the righteous
	40:	6	*S* and offering you did not desire
	51:	17	My *s*, O God, is a broken spirit;
Hos	6:	6	For I desire mercy, not *s*,
Mal	1:	8	When you offer blind animals for *s*,
Mt	9:	13	"I desire mercy, not *s*."
Ac	15:	29	abstain from food *s-d* to idols,
Ro	3:	25	Christ as a *s* of atonement,
	12:	1	offer your bodies as a living *s*,
1Co	5:	7	our Passover lamb, has been *s-d*
	8:	1	Now about food *s-d* to idols:
Heb	7:	27	He *s-d* for their sins once
	9:	28	Christ was *s-d* once to take away
	10:	5	said: 'S and offering you did not
	10:	18	*s* for sin is no longer necessary
1Pe	2:	5	spiritual *s-s* acceptable to God
1Jn	2:	2	the atoning *s* for our sins,

salvation

Ex	15:	2	he has become my *s*.
2Sa	22:	3	my shield and the horn of my *s*.
Ps	13:	5	my heart rejoices in your *s*
	27:	1	The LORD is my light and my *s* –
	51:	12	Restore to me the joy of your *s*
Isa	12:	3	draw water from the wells of *s*
	30:	15	'In repentance and rest is your *s*,
	59:	17	the helmet of *s* on his head;
Jnh	2:	9	*S* comes from the LORD.
Lk	1:	69	He has raised up a horn of *s*
	19:	9	'Today *s* has come to this house,
Ac	4:	12	*S* is found in no one else,
Ro	1:	16	it is the power of God that brings *s*
2Co	6:	2	now is the day of *s*,
Eph	6:	17	Take the helmet of *s*
Php	2:	12	work out your *s* with fear
2Ti	3:	15	make you wise for *s* through faith
Tit	2:	11	grace of God has appeared that offers *s*
Heb	2:	3	if we ignore so great a *s*?
1Pe	1:	10	Concerning this *s*, the prophets,

| 2Pe | 3: | 15 | our Lord's patience means *s*, |
| Rev | 7: | 10 | 'S belongs to our God, |

save, -s, -d

Ps	6:	4	*s* me because of your unfailing love
	39:	8	*S* me from all my transgressions;
	68:	20	Our God is a God who *s-s*;
Isa	45:	22	'Turn to me and be *s-d*,
	59:	1	LORD is not too short to *s*,
Mt	1:	21	because he will *s* his people
	10:	22	stands firm to the end will be *s-d*
	16:	25	to *s* their life will lose it,
	19:	25	'Who then can be *s-d*?
Lk	7:	50	'Your faith has *s-d* you;
	19:	10	to seek and to *s* what was lost.
Jn	3:	17	but to *s* the world through him
	10:	9	enters through me will be *s-d*.
Ac	4:	12	by which we must be *s-d*.
	16:	31	be *s-d* – you and your household.
Ro	10:	13	name of the Lord will be *s-d*.
1Co	1:	18	to us who are being *s-d* it is the
	3:	15	but yet will be *s-d* –
	9:	22	possible means I might *s* some
Eph	2:	5	it is by grace you have been *s-d*
1Ti	1:	15	into the world to *s* sinners –
	2:	4	who wants all people to be *s-d*
Heb	7:	25	he is able to *s* completely those

saviour

Dt	32:	15	rejected the Rock their *S*
Ps	25:	5	you are God my *S*,
Isa	43:	11	apart from me there is no *s*
	62:	11	"See, your *S* comes! See, his reward
Lk	1:	47	my spirit rejoices in God my *S*
	2:	11	town of David a *S* has been born
Jn	4:	42	really is the *S* of the world.
Php	3:	20	we eagerly await a *S* from there,
1Ti	1:	1	by the command of God our *S*
	2:	3	good, and pleases God our *S*
	4:	10	God, who is the *S* of all people,
Tit	3:	4	love of God our *S* appeared,
2Pe	1:	1	our God and *S* Jesus Christ
1Jn	4:	14	his Son to be the *S* of the world
Jude		25	to the only God our *S* be glory,

scripture, -s

Mt	22:	29	because you do not know the *S-s*
	26:	54	how then would the *S-s* be
Lk	4:	21	'Today this *s* is fulfilled
	24:	32	opened the *S-s* to us?
Jn	5:	39	You study the *S-s* diligently
	10:	35	the *S* cannot be broken
Ac	1:	16	the *S* had to be fulfilled
	17:	11	examined the *S-s* every day
Ro	15:	4	endurance taught in the *S-s*
1Co	15:	3	for our sins according to the *S-s*
Gal	3:	8	*S* foresaw that God would justify
1Ti	4:	13	to the public reading of *S*,
2Ti	3:	15	you have known the holy *S-s*,
	3:	16	All *S* is God-breathed and is useful
2Pe	1:	20	no prophecy of *S* came about by

sea

Ex	14:	22	went through the *s* on dry ground,
Ps	107:	23	Some went out on the *s* in ships;
	139:	9	I settle on the far side of the *s*
Ecc	11:	1	Ship your grain across the *s*;
Isa	11:	9	as the waters cover the *s*
Hab	2:	14	as the waters cover the *s*
Mt	21:	21	"Go, throw yourself into the *s*,"
	23:	15	land and *s* to win a single convert
1Co	10:	1	they all passed through the *s*
Jas	1:	6	doubts is like a wave of the *s*,

Jude	13	They are wild waves of the *s*,
Rev	20: 13	The *s* gave up the dead
	21: 1	and there was no longer any *s*

see, -s, -ing, -n

Ge	16: 13	'You are the God who *s-s* me,'
Ex	16: 7	will *s* the glory of the LORD,
	33: 20	'you cannot *s* my face,
Jdg	13: 22	'We have *s-n* God!
Job	19: 26	in my flesh I will *s* God
Ps	27: 13	I will *s* the goodness of the LORD
	34: 8	Taste and *s* that the LORD is good;
	37: 25	I have never *s-n* the righteous
	119: 18	that I may *s* wonderful things
	139: 24	*S* if there is any offensive way
Isa	6: 5	my eyes have *s-n* the King,
	6: 9	be ever *s-ing*, but never perceiving
	9: 2	have *s-n* a great light;
	52: 10	will *s* the salvation of our God
	53: 10	he will *s* his offspring
Mt	4: 16	have *s-n* a great light;
	5: 8	pure in heart, for they will *s* God
Lk	2: 30	my eyes have *s-n* your salvation
Jn	1: 14	We have *s-n* his glory,
	1: 18	No one has ever *s-n* God,
	17: 24	and to *s* my glory,
	20: 29	'Because you have *s-n* me,
Ac	1: 11	you have *s-n* him go into heaven.
	2: 31	nor did his body *s* decay.
Ro	8: 24	hope that is *s-n* is no hope at all.
1Co	2: 9	What no eye has *s-n*, what no ear has heard,
1Ti	3: 16	was *s-n* by angels,
Heb	2: 9	But we do *s* Jesus,
1Jn	1: 1	we have *s-n* with our eyes,
	3: 2	we shall *s* him as he is.

seek, -s

Dt	4: 29	if from there you *s* the LORD
2Ch	7: 14	humble themselves and pray and *s*
Ps	27: 8	Your face, LORD, I will *s*
Isa	55: 6	*S* the LORD while he may be found;
	65: 1	found by those who did not *s* me.
Jer	45: 5	Should you then *s* great things
Mt	6: 33	But *s* first his kingdom
	7: 7	*s* and you will find;
Lk	19: 10	Son of Man came to *s* and to save
Jn	4: 23	worshippers the Father *s-s*
Ac	17: 27	God did this so that they would *s*
Ro	3: 11	no one who *s-s* God
	10: 20	found by those who did not *s* me;

send, -s, -ing

Ps	43: 3	*S* me your light and your faithful care
Isa	6: 8	'Here am I. *S* me!'
Mal	3: 1	'I will *s* my messenger,
Mt	4: 19	I will *s* you out to fish
	5: 45	*s-s* rain on the righteous
	9: 38	*s* out workers into his harvest
	10: 16	I am *s-ing* you out like sheep
Lk	24: 49	*s* you what my Father has promised;
Jn	3: 17	did not *s* his Son into the world
	14: 26	Spirit, whom the Father will *s*
	16: 7	I will *s* him to you
	20: 21	I am *s-ing* you.
Ro	8: 3	God did by *s-ing* his own Son

sent

Ex	3: 14	"I am has *s* me to you."
Isa	55: 11	the purpose for which I *s* it.
	61: 1	He has *s* me to bind up
Da	3: 28	has *s* his angel and rescued
Mt	10: 40	welcomes the one who *s* me.
	15: 24	'I was *s* only to the lost sheep
	22: 3	He *s* his servants to those

Mk	9: 37	welcome me but the one who *s* me.
Lk	1: 26	God *s* the angel Gabriel
Jn	1: 6	a man *s* from God whose name
	6: 44	the Father who *s* me draws them,
	17: 3	Jesus Christ, whom you have *s*.
Ro	10: 15	preach unless they are *s*?
Gal	4: 4	time had fully come, God *s* his Son,
2Pe	2: 4	but *s* them to hell,
1Jn	4: 10	he loved us and *s* his Son

servant, -s

1Sa	2: 9	guard the feet of his faithful *s-s*
	3: 9	'Speak, LORD, for your *s*
2Sa	11: 21	your *s* Uriah the Hittite is dead."
2Ki	17: 13	through my *s-s* the prophets.
Job	1: 8	'Have you considered my *s* Job?
Ps	19: 11	By them your *s* is warned;
	34: 22	The LORD redeems his *s-s*;
	134: 1	Praise the LORD, all you *s-s* of the LORD
Isa	41: 9	"You are my *s*"; I have chosen you
	42: 1	'Here is my *s*, whom I uphold,
	52: 13	See, my *s* will act wisely;
	53: 11	my righteous *s* will justify many,
Am	3: 7	revealing his plan to his *s-s*
Mt	8: 8	say the word, and my *s* will
	10: 24	nor a *s* above his master
	12: 18	'Here is my *s* whom I have chosen,
	20: 26	great among you must be your *s*
	23: 11	greatest among you will be your *s*
	25: 21	"Well done, good and faithful *s*!
	26: 51	struck the *s* of the high priest,
Lk	1: 38	'I am the Lord's *s*,'
	1: 54	He has helped his *s* Israel,
	17: 10	"We are unworthy *s-s*;
Jn	12: 26	where I am, my *s* also will be.
	13: 16	no *s* is greater than their master,
	15: 15	I no longer call you *s-s*,
Ac	4: 27	conspire against your holy *s* Jesus,
	12: 13	a *s* named Rhoda came to
Ro	13: 4	is God's *s* for your good.
	14: 4	to judge someone else's *s*?
1Co	3: 5	what is Paul? Only *s-s*,
	4: 1	to regard us: as *s-s* of Christ
2Co	4: 5	ourselves as your *s-s* for Jesus'
Php	2: 7	taking the very nature of a *s*,
Col	1: 23	I, Paul, have become a *s*
2Ti	2: 24	the Lord's *s* must not be quarrelsome
Heb	1: 7	his *s-s* flames of fire.
	3: 5	Moses was faithful as a *s*

serve, -s, -ing, -d

Ge	25: 23	the elder will *s* the younger.
Dt	6: 13	Fear the LORD your God, *s* him only
Jos	24: 15	this day whom you will *s*,
1Ki	18: 15	the LORD Almighty lives, whom I *s*,
Ps	2: 11	*S* the LORD with fear and celebrate
Da	3: 17	the God we *s* is able to deliver us
Mt	4: 10	Lord your God, and *s* him only."
	6: 24	'No one can *s* two masters.
	20: 28	Son of Man did not come to be *s-d*,
Ac	17: 25	he is not *s-d* by human hands,
Ro	1: 25	worshipped and *s-d* created things
	9: 12	'The older will *s* the younger.
	12: 7	if it is *s-ing*, then *s*;
1Co	9: 7	Who *s-s* as a soldier at his own
Php	3: 3	we who *s* God by his Spirit,
Col	3: 24	the Lord Christ you are *s-ing*
1Th	1: 9	to God from idols to *s* the living
1Ti	3: 10	let them *s* as deacons
Heb	1: 14	ministering spirits sent to *s*
	7: 13	has ever *s-d* at the altar

1Pe	4:	10	gift you have received to *s* others,
Rev	22:	3	his servants will *s* him

seven, -s

Ge	7:	2	Take with you *s* pairs of every kind
Jos	6:	4	march round the city *s* times,
Da	4:	25	*S* times will pass by for you
	9:	24	'Seventy "*s-s*" are decreed
Mt	18:	21	sins against me? Up to *s* times?
	22:	25	Now there were *s* brothers
Mk	16:	9	out of whom he had driven *s* demons
Rev	1:	12	I turned I saw *s* golden lampstands
	6:	1	opened the first of the *s* seals.
	17:	9	The *s* heads are *s* hills

share, -d

Ge	21:	10	that woman's son will never *s*
Pr	21:	9	*s* a house with a quarrelsome wife
Isa	58:	7	Is it not to *s* your food
Mt	25:	21	Come and *s* your master's happiness!
Lk	3:	11	'Anyone who has two shirts should *s*
	15:	12	"Father, give me my *s*
Jn	13:	18	"He who *s-d* my bread has lifted up
Ac	4:	32	they *s-d* everything they had
Ro	8:	17	if indeed we *s* in his sufferings
Gal	4:	30	slave woman's son will never *s*
	6:	6	should *s* all good things
Eph	4:	28	they may have something to *s*
Col	1:	12	you to *s* in the inheritance

sheep, -'s

Nu	27:	17	not be like *s* without a shepherd.
1Sa	15:	14	'What then is this bleating of *s*
Ps	100:	3	his people, the *s* of his pasture
Isa	53:	6	We all, like *s*, have gone astray,
	53:	7	a *s* before its shearers is silent,
Zec	13:	7	and the *s* will be scattered.
Mt	7:	15	They come to you in *s-'s* clothing,
	9:	36	like *s* without a shepherd
	10:	6	to the lost *s* of Israel
	25:	33	He will put the *s* on his right
	26:	31	*s* of the flock will be scattered.
Jn	10:	2	is the shepherd of the *s*
	10:	7	I am the gate for the *s*
	10:	11	lays down his life for the *s*
	10:	26	because you are not my *s*
	21:	17	'Feed my *s*
Ac	8:	32	led like a *s* to the slaughter,
Ro	8:	36	considered as *s* to be slaughtered.
Heb	13:	20	that great Shepherd of the *s*

shepherd, -s

Ps	23:	1	The LORD is my *s*,
	80:	1	Hear us, *S* of Israel,
Isa	40:	11	He tends his flock like a *s:*
Eze	34:	2	prophesy against the *s-s* of Israel;
Lk	2:	8	there were *s-s* living out
Jn	10:	2	who enters by the gate is the *s*
	10:	11	'I am the good *s.*
Ac	20:	28	Be *s-s* of the church of God,
Heb	13:	20	that great *S* of the sheep
1Pe	5:	4	And when the Chief *S* appears,

show, -s, -ed, -n

Ex	33:	18	'Now *s* me your glory.
Ps	18:	25	To the faithful you *s* yourself
	25:	4	*S* me your ways, LORD,
Joel	2:	30	I will *s* wonders in the heavens
Mic	6:	8	He has *s-n* you, O mortal,
Mal	1:	6	who *s* contempt for my name.
Mt	4:	8	and *s-ed* him all the kingdoms
	5:	7	for they will be *s-n* mercy
	22:	19	*S* me the coin used for paying
Lk	12:	5	I will *s* you whom you should fear:
Jn	5:	20	Son and *s-s* him all he does.

	14:	8	'Lord, *s* us the Father
Ac	2:	19	I will *s* wonders in the heavens
Ro	9:	22	choosing to *s* his wrath
1Co	12:	31	I will *s* you the most excellent
Eph	2:	7	might *s* the incomparable riches
Jas	2:	18	I will *s* you my faith by what
1Pe	2:	17	*S* proper respect to everyone,

sight

Ex	3:	3	go over and see this strange *s* –
Ps	19:	14	of my heart be pleasing in your *s*,
	51:	4	done what is evil in your *s;*
	90:	4	A thousand years in your *s*
	116:	15	in the *s* of the LORD is the death
Mt	11:	5	the blind receive *s*, the lame walk,
Ac	22:	13	"Brother Saul, receive your *s!*"
Ro	3:	20	declared righteous in God's *s*
2Co	5:	7	we live by faith, not by *s.*
Heb	4:	13	creation is hidden from God's *s.*

sign, -s

Ge	9:	13	it will be the *s* of the covenant
Isa	7:	14	Lord himself will give you a *s*
Mt	12:	39	generation asks for a *s!*
	16:	3	interpret the *s-s* of the times
	24:	3	what will be the *s* of your coming
Jn	2:	11	the first of the *s-s* through which
	6:	30	'What *s* then will you give
	20:	30	Jesus performed many other *s-s*
Ac	2:	19	wonders in the heavens above and *s-s*
	4:	30	to heal and perform *s-s* and wonders
	5:	12	apostles performed many *s-s*
Ro	15:	19	by the power of *s-s* and wonders,
1Co	1:	22	Jews demand *s-s*
2Th	2:	9	power through *s-s* and wonders
Rev	13:	13	performed great *s-s*,

silver

Ps	115:	4	But their idols are *s* and gold,
Pr	8:	10	Choose my instruction instead of *s*,
	22:	1	to be esteemed is better than *s*
Am	2:	6	They sell the innocent for *s*,
Hag	2:	8	"The *s* is mine and the gold
Zec	11:	12	they paid me thirty pieces of *s*
Mt	26:	15	counted out for him thirty pieces of *s*
Lk	15:	8	a woman has ten *s* coins and loses
Ac	3:	6	'*S* or gold I do not have,
1Pe	1:	18	with perishable things such as *s*

sin, -s, -ning, -ned, -ful

Ge	4:	7	*s* is crouching at your door;
	39:	9	a wicked thing and *s* against God?
Nu	14:	18	abounding in love and forgiving *s*
	32:	23	sure that your *s* will find you out
Dt	5:	9	punishing the children for the *s*
2Ch	6:	36	for there is no one who does not *s*
	7:	14	forgive their *s* and will heal
Job	1:	22	Job did not *s* by charging God
Ps	4:	4	Tremble and do not *s;*
	19:	13	servant also from wilful *s-s;*
	32:	1	whose *s-s* are covered
	51:	3	my *s* is always before me
	51:	4	Against you, you only, have I *s-ned*
	66:	18	If I had cherished *s* in my heart,
	103:	3	who forgives all your *s-s* and heals
	103:	10	not treat us as our *s-s* deserve
	119:	11	that I might not *s* against you
Isa	1:	18	'Though your *s-s* are like scarlet,
	6:	7	taken away and your *s* atoned for.
	53:	10	LORD makes his life an offering for *s*
	53:	12	For he bore the *s* of many,
	59:	2	your *s-s* have hidden his face
Jer	31:	30	everyone will die for their own *s;*
Eze	18:	20	The one who *s-s* is the one

Mt	1: 21	save his people from their *s-s.*
	9: 5	"Your *s-s* are forgiven,"
	18: 15	'If your brother or sister *s-s,*
Lk	11: 4	Forgive us our *s-s,*
	15: 18	Father, I have *s-ned*
Jn	1: 29	who takes away the *s* of the world
	8: 7	'Let any one of you who is without *s*
	8: 34	everyone who *s-s* is a slave to *s*
	16: 8	the world to be in the wrong about *s*
Ac	2: 38	for the forgiveness of your *s-s.*
	7: 60	do not hold this *s* against them.'
	10: 43	receives forgiveness of *s-s*
Ro	1: 24	God gave them over in the *s-ful*
	3: 23	all have *s-ned* and fall short
	5: 12	just as *s* entered the world
	6: 1	Shall we go on *s-ning,*
	6: 12	do not let *s* reign
	6: 23	For the wages of *s* is death,
	8: 2	free from the law of *s* and death
	14: 23	does not come from faith is *s*
1Co	15: 56	The sting of death is *s,*
2Co	5: 21	God made him who had no *s* to be *s*
Eph	2: 1	dead in your transgressions and *s-s*
Heb	1: 3	provided purification for *s-s,*
	4: 15	just as we are — yet he did not *s*
	8: 12	will remember their *s-s* no more.
	9: 28	to take away the *s-s* of many;
Jas	5: 16	Therefore confess your *s-s*
	5: 20	and cover over a multitude of *s-s.*
1Pe	2: 22	'He committed no *s,*
	2: 24	He himself bore our *s-s'* in his body
	3: 18	Christ also suffered once for *s-s,*
	4: 8	covers over a multitude of *s-s*
1Jn	1: 7	his Son, purifies us from all *s*
	1: 8	If we claim to be without *s,*
	1: 9	If we confess our *s-s,*
	2: 2	the atoning sacrifice for our *s-s,*
	3: 4	Everyone who *s-s* breaks the law;
	3: 5	And in him is no *s.*
	3: 9	No one who is born of God will continue to *s,*

sister, -s
See also under **brother,** *for references to brother(s) and/or sister(s)*

Ge	20: 2	said of his wife Sarah, 'She is my *s*
	26: 7	his wife, he said, 'She is my *s*
	30: 1	she became jealous of her *s.*
	34: 13	their *s* Dinah had been defiled,
Ex	15: 20	Miriam the prophet, Aaron's *s,*
2Sa	13: 1	Tamar, the beautiful *s* of Absalom
SS	4: 9	You have stolen my heart, my *s*
	8: 8	We have a little *s,*
Mt	13: 56	Aren't all his *s-s* with us?
Lk	10: 40	don't you care that my *s* has left
Jn	11: 1	Bethany, the village of Mary and her *s*
1Ti	5: 2	women as *s-s,* with absolute purity

slave, -s, -ry

Ge	21: 10	'Get rid of that *s* woman
Dt	5: 15	Remember that you were *s-s*
Mal	1: 6	and a *s* his master.
Mt	20: 27	to be first must be your *s*
Jn	8: 34	everyone who sins is a *s* to sin
Ro	6: 6	we should no longer be *s-s* to sin
	7: 25	in my mind am a *s* to God's law,
1Co	9: 27	a blow to my body and make it my *s*
Gal	3: 28	Jew nor Gentile, neither *s* nor free,
	4: 30	rid of the *s* woman and her son,
	5: 1	burdened again by a yoke of *s-ry*
Eph	6: 5	*S-s,* obey your earthly masters

son, -s, -ship

Ge	17: 19	Sarah will bear you a *s,*
	22: 2	'Take your *s,* your only *s,*
Ex	4: 22	Israel is my firstborn *s*
	11: 5	Every firstborn *s* in Egypt will die
2Sa	19: 4	'O my *s* Absalom! O Absalom,
Ps	2: 7	'You are my *s;* today I have become
	2: 12	Kiss his *s,* or he will be angry
Pr	10: 1	A wise *s* brings joy
Isa	7: 14	to a *s,* and will call him Immanuel
	9: 6	to us a *s* is given,
Eze	37: 3	'*S* of man, can these bones live?
Da	7: 13	one like a *s* of man,
Hos	11: 1	out of Egypt I called my *s.*
Joel	2: 28	*s-s* and daughters will prophesy,
Mal	1: 6	'A *s* honours his father,
Mt	1: 21	She will give birth to a *s,*
	2: 15	'Out of Egypt I called my *s.*
	3: 17	'This is my *S,* whom I love;
	4: 3	'If you are the *S* of God,
	8: 20	the *S* of Man has nowhere
	9: 6	you to know that the *S* of Man
	9: 27	'Have mercy on us, *S* of David!
	10: 37	anyone who loves their *s* or daughter
	11: 19	The *S* of Man came eating
	11: 27	No one knows the *S* except the
	12: 8	*S* of Man is Lord of the Sabbath.
	14: 33	'Truly you are the *S* of God.
	16: 16	Messiah, the *S* of the living God.
	20: 28	*S* of Man did not come to be served
	22: 42	the Messiah? Whose *s* is he?'
	24: 27	the coming of the *S* of Man
	25: 31	the *S* of Man comes in his glory,
	27: 43	he said, "I am the *S* of God."
	27: 54	'Surely he was the *S* of God!'
Lk	1: 31	conceive and give birth to a *s,*
	1: 32	called the *S* of the Most High.
	1: 35	will be called the *S* of God
	15: 19	worthy to be called your *s;*
Jn	1: 49	'Rabbi, you are the *S* of God;
	3: 14	the *S* of Man must be lifted up,
	3: 16	he gave his one and only *S,*
	3: 36	believes in the *S* has eternal life,
	5: 19	the *S* can do nothing by himself;
	6: 53	eat the flesh of the *S* of Man
	8: 36	So if the *S* sets you free,
	10: 36	because I said, "I am God's *S*"
	17: 1	Glorify your *S,* that your *S*
	20: 31	Jesus is the Messiah, the *S* of God,
Ac	2: 17	*s-s* and daughters will prophesy,
	7: 56	I see heaven open and the *S* of Man
	13: 33	'You are my *s;* today I have become
Ro	8: 3	God did by sending his own *S*
	8: 29	conformed to the image of his *S,*
	8: 32	He who did not spare his own *S,*
2Co	6: 18	you will be my *s-s* and daughters,
Gal	2: 20	I live by faith in the *S* of God,
	4: 5	receive adoption to *s-ship.*
Eph	1: 5	for adoption to *s-ship*
1Th	1: 10	to wait for his *S* from heaven,
Heb	1: 2	he has spoken to us by his *S,*
	1: 3	*S* is the radiance of God's glory
	12: 5	'My *s,* do not make light
	12: 8	not legitimate, not true *s-s* and
1Jn	2: 23	who denies the *S* has the Father;
	4: 9	his one and only *S* into the world
	5: 5	who believes that Jesus is the *S*
	5: 11	this life is in his *S.*
	5: 12	He who has the *S* has life;
Rev	1: 13	someone like a *s* of man,

soul, -s

Dt	6:	5	heart and with all your *s*
Ps	19:	7	perfect, refreshing the *s*.
	23:	3	he refreshes my *s*.
	42:	1	so my *s* pants for you, my God
	42:	11	Why, my *s*, are you downcast?
	103:	2	Praise the LORD, my *s*,
Mt	10:	28	body but cannot kill the *s*.
	11:	29	you will find rest for your *s-s*.
	16:	26	yet forfeit their *s*?
	22:	37	heart and with all your *s*
Lk	1:	46	'My *s* glorifies the Lord
1Th	5:	23	May your whole spirit, *s* and body
Heb	4:	12	even to dividing *s* and spirit,
1Pe	1:	9	the salvation of your *s-s*

speak, -s, -ing

Ex	33:	11	would *s* to Moses face to face,
Dt	18:	20	a prophet who presumes to *s*
1Sa	3:	10	'*S*, for your servant is listening.
Isa	65:	24	still *s-ing* I will hear
Jer	1:	6	'I do not know how to *s*;
Mt	12:	34	mouth *s-s* what the heart
	13:	13	why I *s* to them in parables:
Lk	6:	26	Woe to you when everyone *s-s* well
Jn	3:	11	we *s* of what we know,
	8:	44	When he lies, he *s-s* his native
	9:	21	he will *s* for himself.
	12:	49	I did not *s* on my own,
Ac	2:	4	began to *s* in other tongues
	4:	20	we cannot help *s-ing* about
	10:	46	they heard them *s-ing* in tongues
	13:	46	'We had to *s* the word of God
Ro	7:	1	I am *s-ing* to those who know the law –
	9:	1	I *s* the truth in Christ –
1Co	2:	6	We do, however, *s* a message
	13:	1	If I *s* in the tongues of men or
	14:	35	for a woman to *s* in the church
Eph	4:	15	Instead, *s-ing* the truth in love,
	5:	19	*S* to one another with psalms,
Heb	11:	4	by faith Abel still *s-s*,
	12:	24	blood that *s-s* a better word

spirit, -'s, -s

Ge	1:	2	the *S* of God was hovering
	6:	3	'My *S* will not contend with humans
1Sa	16:	15	an evil *s* from God is tormenting
	28:	8	'Consult a *s* for me,' he said,
1Ki	22:	23	the LORD has put a lying *s*
2Ki	2:	9	a double portion of your *s*,'
Ps	51:	10	renew a steadfast *s* within me
	51:	11	or take your Holy *S* from me
	139:	7	Where can I go from your *S*?
Isa	42:	1	I will put my *S* on him
	57:	15	one who is contrite and lowly in *s*,
	61:	1	*S* of the Sovereign LORD is on me,
Eze	36:	26	new heart and put a new *s* in you;
Joel	2:	28	I will pour out my *S* on all people.
Zec	4:	6	but by my *S*," says the LORD
Mt	1:	18	pregnant through the Holy *S*
	3:	11	baptise you with the Holy *S*
	3:	16	he saw the *S* of God descending
	5:	3	'Blessed are the poor in *s*,
	12:	31	blasphemy against the *S* will not
	26:	41	The *s* is willing, but
	27:	50	in a loud voice, he gave up his *s*.
	28:	19	of the Son and of the Holy *S*
Lk	1:	17	in the *s* and power of Elijah,
	1:	35	The Holy *S* will come on you,
	2:	26	revealed to him by the Holy *S*
	4:	1	Jesus, full of the Holy *S*,
	4:	18	'The *S* of the Lord is on me,
	11:	13	the Holy *S* to those who ask him!

Jn	1:	32	'I saw the *S* come down from heaven
	3:	5	born of water and the *S*
	3:	34	God gives the *S* without limit
	4:	24	God is *s*, and his worshippers
	14:	26	the Advocate, the Holy *S*,
	16:	13	when he, the *S* of truth, comes,
	20:	22	'Receive the Holy *S*
Ac	1:	5	baptised with the Holy *S*.
	1:	8	receive power when the Holy *S*
	2:	4	them were filled with the Holy *S*
	2:	38	receive the gift of the Holy *S*
	7:	51	You always resist the Holy *S*!
	15:	28	It seemed good to the Holy *S*
	19:	2	'Did you receive the Holy *S*
Ro	5:	5	into our hearts through the Holy *S*,
	8:	2	law of the *S* who gives life
	8:	6	the mind governed by the *S*
	8:	9	does not have the *S* of Christ,
	8:	10	the *S* gives life because
	8:	16	The *S* himself testifies
	8:	26	the *S* helps us in our weakness.
	14:	17	peace and joy in the Holy *S*
1Co	2:	4	a demonstration of the *S-'s* power
	2:	10	God has revealed them to us by his *S*.
	2:	11	thoughts except their own *s*
	2:	14	discerned only through the *S*
	6:	19	your bodies are temples of the Holy *S*
	12:	1	about the gifts of the *S*,
	12:	3	speaking by the *S* of God says,
	12:	10	another distinguishing between *s-s*
	12:	13	we were all baptised by one *S*
	14:	14	if I pray in a tongue, my *s* prays,
2Co	1:	22	his *S* in our hearts as a deposit,
	3:	6	letter kills, but the *S* gives life.
	3:	17	Now the Lord is the *S*,
Gal	4:	6	God sent the *S* of his Son
	5:	16	walk by the *S*,
	5:	22	the fruit of the *S* is love,
	5:	25	let us keep in step with the *S*.
	6:	1	you who live by the *S* should restore
Eph	1:	13	a seal, the promised Holy *S*
	4:	30	do not grieve the Holy *S* of God,
	6:	17	and the sword of the *S*, which is
1Th	5:	19	Do not quench the *S*.
2Ti	1:	7	*S* God gave us does not make us timid
Heb	1:	7	'He makes his angels *s-s*,
	9:	14	who through the eternal *S* offered
1Pe	3:	19	proclamation to the imprisoned *s-s*
2Pe	1:	21	were carried along by the Holy *S*.
1Jn	4:	1	do not believe every *s*, but test
Rev	22:	17	The *S* and the bride say, 'Come!'

spiritual

Ro	7:	14	We know that the law is *s*;
	12:	11	keep your *s* fervour, serving the
1Co	1:	7	you do not lack any *s* gift
	2:	13	explaining *s* realities with
Eph	1:	3	every *s* blessing in Christ
	6:	12	against the *s* forces of evil
1Pe	2:	2	crave pure *s* milk,

spoke, -n

Ex	20:	1	And God *s* all these words
Nu	12:	2	LORD *s-n* only through Moses?'
Dt	5:	4	LORD *s* to you face to face out
Job	38:	1	the LORD *s* to Job out of the storm
	40:	6	the LORD *s* to Job out of the storm
Ps	33:	9	For he *s*, and it came to be;
	73:	15	If I had *s-n* out like that
Am	3:	8	The Sovereign LORD has *s-n* –
Mt	3:	3	This is he who was *s-n* of
	22:	1	Jesus *s* to them again in parables,
Lk	24:	25	all that the prophets have *s-n*

Jn	7:	46	'No one ever *s* the way this man
	12:	41	he saw Jesus' glory and *s* about him
Ac	2:	31	he *s* of the resurrection
	18:	9	the Lord *s* to Paul in a vision:
2Co	4:	13	'I believed; therefore I have *s-n*.
Heb	1:	2	he has *s-n* to us by his Son,
	13:	7	who *s* the word of God to you.
2Pe	1:	21	though human, *s* from God

stand, -s, -ing

Ex	3:	5	where you are *s-ing* is holy ground.
	14:	13	'Do not be afraid. *S* firm
Jos	10:	12	'Sun, *s* still over Gibeon,
2Ch	20:	17	*s* firm and see the deliverance
Ps	1:	1	or *s* in the way that sinners
	1:	5	wicked will not *s* in the judgment,
	24:	3	Who may *s* in his holy place
	119:	89	it *s-s* firm in the heavens
	130:	3	sins, Lord, who could *s*
Jer	6:	16	'*S* at the crossroads and look;
Mal	3:	2	Who can *s* when he appears?
Mt	10:	22	one who *s-s* firm to the end
	12:	25	divided against itself will not *s*
Lk	1:	19	I *s* in the presence of God,
Jn	1:	26	among you *s-s* one you do not know
	3:	18	does not believe *s-s* condemned
Ac	1:	11	'why do you *s* here looking into
	7:	56	Son of Man *s-ing* at the right hand
Ro	5:	2	this grace in which we now *s*.
	9:	11	God's purpose in election might *s*
	14:	4	To their own master they *s* or fall.
	14:	10	all *s* before God's judgment seat
1Co	10:	12	if you think you are *s-ing* firm,
2Co	1:	21	both us and you *s* firm in Christ.
Eph	6:	11	take your *s* against the devil's
2Ti	2:	19	God's solid foundation *s-s* firm,
1Pe	5:	9	Resist him, *s-ing* firm
Rev	3:	20	I *s* at the door and knock.
	5:	6	*s-ing* in the centre before the throne,

stone, -s

Ex	24:	12	give you the tablets of *s*
Dt	19:	14	move your neighbour's boundary *s*
Jos	4:	6	"What do these *s-s* mean?
1Sa	17:	40	five smooth *s-s* from the stream,
Ps	91:	12	strike your foot against a *s*
	118:	22	The *s* the builders rejected
Isa	8:	14	a *s* that causes people to stumble
	28:	16	'See, I lay a *s* in Zion,
Mt	4:	3	tell these *s-s* to become bread.
	4:	6	strike your foot against a *s*."
	7:	9	asks for bread, will give him a *s*
	21:	42	"The *s* the builders rejected
Jn	8:	7	the first to throw a *s* at her.
	8:	59	to *s* him, but Jesus hid himself,
Ac	4:	11	"the *s* you builders rejected,
Ro	9:	33	a *s* that causes people to stumble
2Co	3:	3	not on tablets of *s* but on tablets
1Pe	2:	4	the living *S* – rejected by humans
	2:	7	who believe, this *s* is precious.
Rev	2:	17	I will also give that person a white *s*

stood

Nu	22:	22	angel of the Lord *s* in the road
Jos	3:	17	*s* on dry ground,
	10:	13	So the sun *s* still,
Ps	33:	9	he commanded, and it *s* firm
Lk	4:	16	He *s* up to read,
	18:	11	The Pharisee *s* by himself and prayed
Jn	20:	19	Jesus came and *s* among them
Ac	27:	23	whom I serve *s* beside me
2Co	13:	7	will see that we have *s* the test
2Ti	4:	17	But the Lord *s* at my side

Heb	10:	33	you *s* side by side with those
Jas	1:	12	because, having *s* the test,

strength

Ex	15:	2	The Lord is my *s* and my defence;
1Sa	23:	16	helped him to find *s* in God.
	30:	6	David found *s* in the Lord his God
Ne	8:	10	the joy of the Lord is your *s*.
Ps	28:	7	The Lord is my *s* and my shield;
	46:	1	God is our refuge and *s*,
Isa	12:	2	the Lord, is my *s* and my defence;
	30:	15	in quietness and trust is your *s*,
	40:	31	The Lord will renew their *s*.
Mk	12:	30	your mind and with all your *s*.
1Co	1:	25	God is stronger than human *s*
Eph	1:	19	power is the same as the mighty *s*
Php	4:	13	through him who gives me *s*

strong

Jos	1:	6	Be *s* and courageous,
Ps	24:	8	The Lord *s* and mighty,
	61:	3	a *s* tower against the foe
Joel	3:	10	Let the weakling say, 'I am *s*!
Mt	12:	29	enter a *s* man's house
Ro	15:	1	We who are *s* ought to bear
1Co	1:	27	the world to shame the *s*
2Co	12:	10	when I am weak, then I am *s*
Eph	6:	10	Finally, be *s* in the Lord
2Ti	2:	1	be *s* in the grace

stumble, -s, -ing, -d

2Sa	6:	6	ark of God, because the oxen *s-d*
Isa	8:	14	a stone that causes people to *s*
	40:	30	young men *s* and fall
Mt	5:	29	If your right eye causes you to *s*,
	11:	6	does not *s* on account of me.
Ro	9:	33	a stone that causes people to *s*
1Co	10:	32	Do not cause anyone to *s*
Jas	2:	10	keeps the whole law and yet *s-s*
	3:	2	We all *s* in many ways.
1Pe	2:	8	'A stone that causes people to *s*
Jude		24	who is able to keep you from *s-ing*

suffer, -s, -ing, -ings, -ed

Isa	53:	3	a man of *s-ing*, and familiar with pain.
	53:	11	After he has *s-ed*, he will see
Mt	16:	21	go to Jerusalem and *s* many things
Lk	24:	26	Messiah have to *s* these things
Ac	5:	41	counted worthy of *s-ing* disgrace
Ro	5:	3	we also glory in our *s-ings*,
	8:	18	our present *s-ings* are not worth
1Co	12:	26	If one part *s-s*, every part
2Ti	2:	3	Join with me in *s-ing*, like a good
Heb	13:	12	Jesus also *s-ed* outside the city
1Pe	2:	20	if you *s* for doing good
	3:	18	Christ *s-ed* once for sins,
	4:	16	if you *s* as a Christian,

sun

Jos	10:	13	So the *s* stood still,
Ps	121:	6	the *s* will not harm you by day,
Ecc	1:	9	there is nothing new under the *s*
Isa	60:	19	The *s* will no more be your light
Joel	2:	31	The *s* will be turned to darkness
Mal	4:	2	the *s* of righteousness will rise
Mt	5:	45	He causes his *s* to rise
	17:	2	His face shone like the *s*,
	24:	29	"the *s* will be darkened,
Ac	2:	20	The *s* will be turned to darkness
Eph	4:	26	*s* go down while you are still angry

sword, -s

Ge	3:	24	flaming *s* flashing back and forth
Jdg	7:	14	other than the *s* of Gideon
1Sa	17:	45	come against me with *s* and spear

Isa	2:	4	beat their *s-s* into ploughshares
Joel	3:	10	Beat your ploughshares into *s-s*
Mic	4:	3	beat their *s-s* into ploughshares
Zec	13:	7	'Awake, *s*, against my shepherd,
Mt	10:	34	come to bring peace, but a *s*
	26:	51	companions reached for his *s*,
Lk	2:	35	a *s* will pierce your own soul too.
Ro	8:	35	nakedness or danger or *s*
	13:	4	not bear the *s* for no reason
Eph	6:	17	and the *s* of the Spirit,
Heb	4:	12	Sharper than any double-edged *s*,
Rev	1:	16	was a sharp, double-edged *s*.
	19:	15	Coming out of his mouth is a sharp *s*

t

take, -s, -n

Ge	2:	15	and *t* care of it.
	2:	22	the rib he had *t-n* out of the man,
	3:	22	and *t* also from the tree of life
	15:	7	this land to *t* possession of it.
	22:	17	Your descendants will *t* possession
Ex	3:	5	'*T* off your sandals,
	21:	23	you are to *t* life for life,
	29:	20	*t* some of its blood and put it
Lev	10:	17	given to you to *t* away the guilt
	14:	24	The priest is to *t* the lamb
	24:	14	'*T* the blasphemer outside the camp
	25:	17	Do not *t* advantage of each other,
Dt	1:	8	Go in and *t* possession of the land
	12:	32	do not add to it or *t* away from it.
	31:	26	'*T* this Book of the Law
Jos	6:	6	'*T* up the ark of the covenant
Job	1:	21	LORD gave and the LORD has *t-n* away
	27:	8	when God *t-s* away their life
Ps	16:	1	for in you I *t* refuge.
	25:	18	and *t* away all my sins.
	51:	11	or *t* your Holy Spirit from me.
	89:	33	I will not *t* my love from him,
	109:	8	another *t* his place of leadership
Pr	23:	11	he will *t* up their case against you
Isa	6:	7	your guilt is *t-n* away
Jer	27:	22	"They will be *t-n* to Babylon
Eze	36:	24	I will *t* you out of the nations;
Jnh	4:	3	Now, LORD, *t* away my life,
Zec	3:	4	'See, I have *t-n* away your sin,
Mt	1:	20	do not be afraid to *t* Mary
	2:	20	Get up, *t* the child and his mother
	9:	6	*t* your mat and go home.
	9:	15	bridegroom will be *t-n* from them;
	10:	9	silver or copper to *t* with you
	10:	38	Whoever does not *t* up their cross
	11:	29	*T* my yoke upon you and learn
	13:	12	what they have will be *t-n* from them
	15:	26	not right to *t* the children's bread
	24:	20	flight will not *t* place in winter
	25:	3	but did not *t* any oil with them.
	26:	26	'*T* and eat; this is my body.'
	26:	42	for this cup to be *t-n* away unless
Mk	6:	50	'*T* courage! It is I.
Lk	12:	19	*T* life easy; eat, drink
	17:	35	one will be *t-n* and the other left.
	24:	51	and was *t-n* up into heaven.
Jn	1:	29	Lamb of God, who *t-s* away the sin
	10:	18	No one *t-s* it from me,
	11:	39	'*T* away the stone,' he said.
Ac	1:	2	the day he was *t-n* up to heaven,
2Co	3:	14	only in Christ is it *t-n* away.
	12:	8	pleaded with the Lord to *t* it away
Eph	6:	16	*t* up the shield of faith,
	6:	17	*T* the helmet of salvation

Php	3:	12	but I press on to *t* hold of that
Col	2:	14	*t-n* it away, nailing it to the cross
1Ti	6:	12	*T* hold of the eternal life
Heb	10:	4	of bulls and goats to *t* away sins.
1Jn	3:	5	so that he might *t* away our sins.
Rev	3:	11	so that no one will *t* your crown.
	22:	19	And if any one of you *t-s* words away

teach, -es, -ing, -ings

Dt	4:	9	*T* them to your children
Ps	32:	8	I will instruct you and *t* you
	51:	13	I will *t* transgressors your ways,
	90:	12	*T* us to number our days,
Isa	2:	3	He will *t* us his ways,
Jer	31:	34	No longer will they *t* their
Mt	5:	2	and he began to *t* them.
	28:	20	and *t-ing* them to obey everything
Lk	11:	1	'Lord, *t* us to pray,
	12:	12	for the Holy Spirit will *t* you
Jn	8:	31	'If you hold to my *t-ing*,
	14:	26	will *t* you all things
Ro	12:	7	if it is *t-ing*, then *t*;
Col	3:	16	dwell in you richly as you *t*
2Th	2:	15	hold fast to the *t-ings* we passed on
1Ti	2:	12	I do not permit a woman to *t*
	3:	2	respectable, hospitable, able to *t*,
2Ti	3:	16	and is useful for *t-ing*, rebuking,
Heb	8:	11	No longer will they *t* their
	13:	9	by all kinds of strange *t-ings*.
1Jn	2:	27	But as his anointing *t-es* you
2Jn	9		continue in the *t-ing* of Christ

teacher, -s

Ps	119:	99	I have more insight than all my *t-s*
Mt	10:	24	student is not above the *t*,
	23:	10	for you have one *T*, the Messiah
Jn	3:	2	you are a *t* who has come from God.
	13:	13	'You call me "*T*" and "Lord",
	20:	16	'Rabboni!' (which means '*T*')
1Co	12:	28	second prophets, third *t-s*,
Eph	4:	11	the evangelists, the pastors and *t-s*
Heb	5:	12	by this time you ought to be *t-s*,
Jas	3:	1	of you should become *t-s*,
2Pe	2:	1	there will be false *t-s* among you.

temple, -s

1Ki	6:	1	he began to build the *t* of the LORD
	6:	9	So he built the *t* and completed it,
	8:	10	the cloud filled the *t* of the LORD
	8:	27	How much less this *t* I have built!
	9:	7	reject this *t* I have consecrated
2Ch	6:	2	have built a magnificent *t* for you,
Ezr	1:	2	to build a *t* for him at Jerusalem
	6:	15	The *t* was completed
Ps	5:	7	I bow down towards your holy *t*
	11:	4	The LORD is in his holy *t*;
	68:	29	Because of your *t* at Jerusalem
Isa	37:	14	he went up to the *t* of the LORD
	64:	11	Our holy and glorious *t*,
Jer	7:	4	'This is the *t* of the LORD,
	52:	13	He set fire to the *t* of the LORD,
Eze	43:	5	the glory of the LORD filled the *t*
Jnh	2:	4	look again towards your holy *t*.
Hab	2:	20	The LORD is in his holy *t*;
Hag	2:	18	foundation of the LORD's *t* was laid
Zec	6:	12	and build the *t* of the LORD.
	8:	9	so that the *t* may be built.
Mal	3:	1	you are seeking will come to his *t*;
Mt	4:	5	on the highest point of the *t*.
	12:	6	one greater than the *t* is here.
	23:	16	You say, 'If anyone swears by the *t*
Mk	15:	38	curtain of the *t* was torn in two
Lk	1:	9	to go into the *t* of the Lord
	2:	37	She never left the *t*

	2: 46	they found him in the *t* courts,
	18: 10	'Two men went up to the *t* to pray,
	19: 45	Jesus entered the *t* courts,
Jn	2: 15	and drove all from the *t* courts,
	2: 20	forty-six years to build this *t*,
	2: 21	the *t* he had spoken of was his body
Ac	3: 1	to the *t* at the time of prayer –
	5: 25	in the *t* courts teaching the people
	17: 24	not live in *t-s* built by human hands
1Co	3: 16	that you yourselves are God's *t*
	6: 19	your bodies are *t-s* of the Holy Spirit
2Co	6: 16	For we are the *t* of the living God.
Eph	2: 21	to become a holy *t* in the Lord.
Rev	11: 19	Then God's *t* in heaven was opened,
	15: 8	And the *t* was filled with smoke
	21: 22	I did not see a *t* in the city,

ten, -th

Ge	14: 20	Abram gave him a *t-th* of everything
	18: 32	the sake of *t*, I will not destroy
Ex	34: 28	of the covenant – the *T* Commandments
Ps	91: 7	*t* thousand at your right hand,
SS	5: 10	ruddy, outstanding among *t* thousand
Da	7: 24	The *t* horns are *t* kings
Mt	23: 23	You give a *t-th* of your spices –
	25: 1	will be like *t* virgins who took
	25: 28	to the one who has *t* bags
Lk	15: 8	suppose a woman has *t* silver coins
	17: 12	*t* men who had leprosy met him.
Heb	7: 2	and Abraham gave him a *t-th*
Rev	13: 1	It had *t* horns and seven heads,

tent, -s, -maker

Ge	13: 12	and pitched his *t-s* near Sodom
Ex	29: 44	I will consecrate the *t* of meeting
	33: 7	Moses used to take a *t* and pitch it
	40: 34	the cloud covered the *t* of meeting,
Dt	31: 15	Then the LORD appeared at the *t*
Jdg	4: 21	Heber's wife, picked up a *t* peg
2Sa	7: 2	while the ark of God remains in a *t*
2Ch	10: 16	To your *t-s*, Israel!
Ps	19: 4	he has pitched a *t* for the sun
	104: 2	stretches out the heavens like a *t*
Isa	54: 2	'Enlarge the place of your *t*,
Ac	18: 3	and because he was a *t-maker*
2Co	5: 4	For while we are in this *t*,
2Pe	1: 13	as I live in the *t* of this body

test, -ed

Ge	22: 1	Some time later God *t-ed* Abraham.
Dt	6: 16	not put the LORD your God to the *t*
Ps	95: 9	where your ancestors *t-ed* me;
	139: 23	*t* me and know my anxious thoughts.
Mt	4: 7	not put the Lord your God to the *t*.
	19: 3	Pharisees came to him to *t* him.
2Co	13: 6	that we have not failed the *t*
1Th	5: 21	*t* them all; hold on to what
Heb	3: 9	your ancestors *t-ed* and tried me
Jas	1: 12	because having stood the *t*,
1Jn	4: 1	but *t* the spirits to see whether

thank, -s, -ful

Ps	7: 17	I will give *t-s* to the LORD
Mt	15: 36	and when he had given *t-s*,
	26: 26	and when he had given *t-s*
Ro	7: 25	*T-s* be to God, who delivers me
1Co	11: 24	when he had given *t-s*, he broke it
	15: 57	But *t-s* be to God! He gives us the
2Co	2: 14	*t-s* be to God, who always leads us
	9: 12	in many expressions of *t-s* to God
	9: 15	*T-s* be to God for his indescribable
Eph	5: 20	always giving *t-s* to God the Father
1Th	5: 18	give *t-s* in all circumstances;
Heb	12: 28	let us be *t-ful*, and so worship God

thousand, -s

Ex	34: 7	maintaining love to *t-s*,
1Sa	21: 11	"Saul has slain his *t-s*, and David
1Ki	19: 18	Yet I reserve seven *t* in Israel –
Ps	50: 10	and the cattle on a *t* hills
	90: 4	a *t* years in your sight are like
Mt	14: 21	of those who ate was about five *t*
Heb	12: 22	You have come to *t-s* upon *t-s*
2Pe	3: 8	the Lord a day is like a *t* years,
Rev	5: 11	angels, numbering *t-s* upon *t-s*
	20: 2	and bound him for a *t* years

three

Ge	6: 10	Noah had *t* sons:
	18: 2	Abraham looked up and saw *t* men
Ex	23: 14	*T* times a year you are to celebrate
Ecc	4: 12	A cord of *t* strands
Da	6: 13	He still prays *t* times a day.
Jnh	1: 17	the fish *t* days and *t* nights
Mt	12: 40	For as Jonah was *t* days and *t*
	18: 20	For where two or *t* come together
	26: 34	you will disown me *t* times.
	27: 40	the temple and build it in *t* days,
	27: 63	"After *t* days I will rise again.
Mk	9: 5	Let us put up *t* shelters –
1Co	13: 13	And now these *t* remain:
2Co	12: 8	*T* times I pleaded with the Lord
1Ti	5: 19	it is brought by two or *t* witnesses
Heb	10: 28	the testimony of two or *t* witnesses
1Jn	5: 7	For there are *t* that testify

throne, -s

2Sa	7: 16	your *t* shall be established
Ps	93: 2	Your *t* was established long ago;
Isa	6: 1	I saw the Lord ... seated on a *t*,
	9: 7	He will reign on David's *t*
Mt	5: 34	by heaven, for it is God's *t*
	19: 28	Son of Man sits on his glorious *t*,
	19: 28	me will also sit on twelve *t-s*,
Lk	1: 32	give him the *t* of his father David
Heb	1: 8	But about the Son he says, 'Your *t*
	4: 16	approach God's *t* of grace
Rev	4: 9	thanks to him who sits on the *t*
	20: 11	Then I saw a great white *t*

throw, -n

Ex	4: 3	The LORD said, 'T it on the ground
Jos	24: 23	'*t* away the foreign gods
Mal	3: 10	if I will not *t* open the floodgates
Mt	4: 6	*t* yourself down. For it is written:
	5: 30	cut it off and *t* it away.
	7: 6	do not *t* your pearls to pigs.
Jn	8: 7	without sin be the first to *t* a stone
	9: 35	heard that they had *t-n* him out
	21: 6	'*T* your net on the right side
Heb	10: 35	So do not *t* away your confidence;
	12: 1	*t* off everything that hinders
Rev	20: 15	was *t-n* into the lake of fire

time, -s

Ge	4: 26	At that *t* people began to call
2Sa	11: 1	at the *t* when kings go off to war,
Est	4: 14	for such a *t* as this?
Ps	9: 9	a stronghold in *t-s* of trouble.
	10: 1	you hide yourself in *t-s* of trouble
	31: 15	My *t-s* are in your hands;
	34: 1	I will extol the LORD at all *t-s;*
	59: 16	my refuge in *t-s* of trouble.
	119:164	Seven *t-s* a day I praise you
Pr	17: 17	A friend loves at all *t-s,*
Ecc	3: 1	There is a *t* for everything,
	3: 2	a *t* to be born and a *t* to die,
Da	2: 21	He changes *t-s* and seasons;

6: 13 He still prays three *t-s* a day.
8: 17 vision concerns the *t* of the end.
12: 4 until the *t* of the end.
12: 7 for a *t*, *t-s* and half a *t*.
Mic 5: 2 from of old, from ancient *t-s*.
Mt 13: 21 they last only a short *t*.
16: 3 interpret the signs of the *t-s*.
24: 10 At that *t* many will turn away
25: 5 bridegroom was a long *t* in coming,
26: 34 you will disown me three *t-s*.
Mk 1: 15 'The *t* has come,' he said.
Lk 19: 8 I will pay back four *t-s* the amount
21: 24 until the *t-s* of the Gentiles
Jn 12: 31 Now is the *t* for judgment
Ac 1: 7 'It is not for you to know the *t-s*
3: 19 that *t-s* of refreshing may come
3: 21 the *t* comes for God to restore
26: 28 Do you think that in such a short *t*
Ro 5: 6 You see, at just the right *t*,
9: 9 'At the appointed *t* I will return
2Co 6: 2 In the *t* of my favour I heard you,
Gal 4: 4 But when the set *t* had fully come,
2Th 2: 6 he may be revealed at the proper *t*.
1Ti 6: 15 God will bring about in his own *t* –
2Ti 3: 1 terrible *t-s* in the last days.
Heb 9: 28 and he will appear a second *t*,
10: 12 offered for all *t* one sacrifice
1Pe 1: 5 to be revealed in the last *t*.
1: 20 but was revealed in these last *t-s*
Rev 12: 14 for a *t*, *t-s* and half a *t*,

today

Dt 27: 1 these commands that I give you *t*
30: 15 See, I set before you *t* life
Ps 2: 7 *t* I have become your father.
95: 7 *T*, if only you would hear his voice,
Mt 6: 11 Give us *t* our daily bread
Lk 2: 11 *T* in the town of David a Saviour
12: 28 which is here *t*, and tomorrow is
23: 43 *t* you will be with me in paradise.
Heb 1: 5 *t* I have become your Father'?
3: 7 '*T*, if you hear his voice,
3: 13 as long as it is called '*T*,'
13: 8 same yesterday and *t* and for ever.
Jas 4: 13 listen, you who say, '*T* or tomorrow

tongue, -s

Ps 137: 6 my *t* cling to the roof of my mouth
Pr 10: 19 but the prudent hold their *t-s*.
Isa 28: 11 with foreign lips and strange *t-s*
45: 23 by me every *t* will swear.
Ac 2: 4 and began to speak in other *t-s*
1Co 12: 10 another the interpretation of *t-s*.
13: 1 If I speak in the *t-s* of men or
14: 2 who speaks in a *t* does not
14: 21 'With other *t-s* and through
14: 39 and do not forbid speaking in *t-s*.
Php 2: 11 every *t* acknowledge that Jesus Christ
Jas 3: 6 The *t* also is a fire,
1Pe 3: 10 must keep their *t* from evil

took

Ge 2: 15 The LORD God *t* the man and put him
2: 21 he *t* one of the man's ribs
5: 24 was no more, because God *t* him away
2Sa 6: 6 reached out and *t* hold of the ark
7: 8 I *t* you from the pasture, from
Ps 68: 18 you *t* many captives;
Isa 53: 4 Surely he *t* up our pain
Mt 2: 14 got up, *t* the child and his mother
4: 5 the devil *t* him to the holy city
8: 17 'He *t* up our infirmities
26: 26 Jesus *t* bread, and when he had
26: 27 Then he *t* the cup, and when

Mk 9: 36 *t* a little child whom he placed
Lk 24: 1 the women *t* the spices
Jn 6: 11 Jesus then *t* the loaves, gave
19: 27 this disciple *t* her into his home
1Co 11: 23 the night he was betrayed, *t* bread
11: 25 after supper he *t* the cup,
Eph 4: 8 he *t* many captives
Php 3: 12 for which Christ Jesus *t* hold of me

touch, -es, -ed

Ge 3: 3 you must not *t* it, or you will die.
Ex 29: 37 and whatever *t-es* it will be holy
Nu 4: 15 they must not *t* the holy things
Mt 8: 3 Jesus reached out his hand and *t-ed*
8: 15 He *t-ed* her hand and the fever
Lk 8: 45 'Who *t-ed* me?' Jesus asked.
24: 39 It is I myself! *T* me and see;
Col 2: 21 Do not taste! Do not *t*!'
Heb 12: 18 to a mountain that can be *t-ed*
1Jn 1: 1 looked at and our hands have *t-ed* –

tree, -s

Ge 2: 9 the *t* of life
2: 17 *t* of the knowledge of good and evil
Ps 1: 3 is like a *t* planted by streams
Pr 3: 18 She is a *t* of life to those
Isa 55: 12 all the *t-s* of the field will clap
Jer 17: 8 like a *t* planted by the water
Mt 3: 10 axe has ... to the root of the *t-s*
7: 18 A good *t* cannot bear bad fruit,
Mk 8: 24 they look like *t-s* walking around.
Rev 2: 7 the right to eat from the *t* of life
22: 2 of the river stood the *t* of life,

trouble, -s, -d

Jos 7: 25 Why have you brought this *t* on us?
1Sa 1: 15 'I am a woman who is deeply *t-d*.
Job 5: 7 man is born to *t* as surely as
Mt 6: 34 Each day has enough *t* of its own.
26: 37 he began to be sorrowful and *t-d*
Jn 14: 1 'Do not let your hearts be *t-d*.
16: 33 In this world you will have *t*.
Ro 8: 35 Shall *t* or hardship or persecution
2Co 1: 4 who comforts us in all our *t-s*,
4: 17 For our light and momentary *t-s*
Php 4: 14 was good of you to share in my *t-s*.
Heb 12: 15 no bitter root grows up to cause *t*
Jas 5: 13 Is anyone among you in *t*?

trust, -s, -ed

Ps 22: 8 'He *t-s* in the LORD,' they say,
125: 1 Those who *t* in the LORD are like
Pr 3: 5 *T* in the LORD with all your heart
Isa 26: 3 steadfast, because they *t* in you.
30: 15 in quietness and *t* is your strength
Mt 27: 43 He *t-s* in God. Let God rescue him
Lk 16: 10 can be *t-ed* with very little can
Jn 14: 1 *T* in God; *t* also in me.
Ro 4: 5 *t-s* God who justifies the ungodly,
1Co 9: 17 discharging the *t* committed to me.
13: 7 It always protects, always *t-s*,
Heb 2: 13 And again, 'I will put my *t* in him
1Pe 2: 6 the one who *t-s* in him will never

truth, -s

Job 42: 7 because you have not spoken the *t*
Jn 3: 21 whoever lives by the *t* comes into
4: 23 worship the Father in the Spirit and in *t*
8: 32 know the *t*, and the *t* will set
14: 6 I am the way and the *t* and the life
16: 13 he will guide you into all the *t*.
17: 17 your word is *t*.
18: 38 'What is *t*?' retorted Pilate.
Ro 1: 25 exchanged the *t* about God for a lie,
1Co 5: 8 unleavened bread of sincerity and *t*.

	13: 6	in evil but rejoices with the *t*.
Eph	4: 15	speaking the *t* in love,
	6: 14	belt of *t* buckled round your waist,
1Ti	3: 15	the pillar and foundation of the *t*.
2Ti	2: 15	correctly handles the word of *t*.
	3: 7	able to come to a knowledge of the *t*
Heb	5: 12	the elementary *t-s* of God's word
Jas	5: 19	one of you should wander from the *t*
1Jn	1: 8	and the *t* is not in us.
	2: 20	and all of you know the *t*.

turn, -s, -ing, -ed

Ex	32: 12	*T* from your fierce anger; relent
Lev	19: 4	"Do not *t* to idols or make metal
	19: 31	"Do not *t* to mediums
Dt	5: 32	do not *t* aside to the right
	30: 10	and *t* to the LORD your God with all
2Sa	22: 29	the LORD *t-s* my darkness into light
2Ki	13: 6	they did not *t* away from the sins
2Ch	7: 14	and *t* from their wicked ways,
	7: 19	'But if you *t* away and forsake
	12: 12	the LORD's anger *t-ed* from him,
Ps	25: 16	*T* to me and be gracious to me,
	30: 11	You *t-ed* my wailing into dancing;
	34: 14	*T* from evil and do good;
Pr	15: 1	A gentle answer *t-s* away wrath,
	22: 6	they are old they will not *t* from it
Isa	6: 10	and *t* and be healed.
	45: 22	'*T* to me and be saved,
	53: 6	each of us has *t-ed* to our own way
	55: 7	Let them *t* to the LORD, and he will
La	5: 15	our dancing has *t-ed* to mourning.
Eze	3: 19	they do not *t* from their wickedness
	18: 21	'But if a wicked person *t-s* away
Mal	4: 6	He will *t* the hearts of the parents
Mt	10: 35	I have come to *t*' "a man against
	13: 15	and *t*, and I would heal them."
Lk	1: 17	to *t* the hearts of the parents
	6: 29	on one cheek, *t* ... the other also
Jn	6: 66	many of his disciples *t-ed* back
	16: 20	but your grief will *t* to joy.
Ac	3: 19	Repent, then, and *t* to God,
	15: 19	the Gentiles who are *t-ing* to God
	28: 27	and *t*, and I would heal them."
2Co	3: 16	But whenever anyone *t-s* to the Lord
1Th	1: 9	how you *t-ed* to God from idols

U

understand, -s, -ing

Job	42: 3	I spoke of things I did not *u*,
Ps	32: 9	or the mule, which have no *u-ing*
	73: 16	When I tried to *u* all this,
Pr	2: 2	applying your heart to *u-ing* –
	3: 5	lean not on your own *u-ing*;
Isa	6: 9	"Be ever hearing, but never *u-ing*;
	11: 2	the Spirit of wisdom and of *u-ing*,
	40: 28	and his *u-ing* no one can fathom.
Mt	13: 13	hearing, they do not hear or *u*.
Lk	24: 45	opened their minds so they could *u*
Ac	8: 30	'Do you *u* what you are reading?'
Ro	7: 15	I do not *u* what I do.
1Co	14: 2	no one *u-s* them; they utter mysteries
2Co	6: 6	in purity, *u-ing*, patience
Eph	4: 18	They are darkened in their *u-ing*
	5: 17	but *u* what the Lord's will is
Php	4: 7	which transcends all *u-ing*,
Col	2: 2	the full riches of complete *u-ing*,
Heb	11: 3	By faith we *u*
Jas	3: 13	Who is wise and *u-ing* among you?
2Pe	2: 12	blaspheme in matters they do not *u*.

	3: 16	some things that are hard to *u*,
1Jn	5: 20	has come and has given us *u-ing*,

V

valley, -s

2Sa	15: 23	The king also crossed the Kidron *V*,
Ps	23: 4	I walk through the darkest *v*
	84: 6	As they pass through the *V* of Baka
SS	2: 1	rose of Sharon, a lily of the *v-s*
Isa	40: 4	Every *v* shall be raised up
Joel	3: 14	in the *v* of decision!
Zec	14: 5	flee by my mountain *v*
Lk	3: 5	Every *v* shall be filled in
Jn	18: 1	disciples and crossed the Kidron *V*

vision, -s

Ge	15: 1	of the LORD came to Abram in a *v*:
1Sa	3: 1	there were not many *v-s*.
Eze	1: 1	heavens were opened and I saw *v-s*
	40: 2	In *v-s* of God he took me
Da	1: 17	And Daniel could understand *v-s*
	7: 2	Daniel said: 'In my *v* at night
Lk	24: 23	they had seen a *v* of angels,
Ac	2: 17	your young men will see *v-s*,
	9: 10	The Lord called to him in a *v*,
	10: 3	in the afternoon he had a *v*.
	16: 9	During the night Paul had a *v*
	26: 19	I was not disobedient to the *v*
2Co	12: 1	I will go on to *v-s* and revelations
Rev	9: 17	horses and riders I saw in my *v*

voice

Ps	19: 4	their *v* goes out into all the earth
	95: 7	Today, if only you would hear his *v*,
Isa	6: 8	Then I heard the *v* of the Lord
	30: 21	your ears will hear a *v* behind you
	40: 3	A *v* of one calling: 'In the wilderness
Mt	3: 3	'A *v* of one calling in the wilderness,
	3: 17	And a *v* from heaven said,
Jn	5: 28	in their graves will hear his *v*
	10: 3	and the sheep listen to his *v*.
Ac	9: 4	He fell to the ground and heard a *v*
Ro	10: 18	'Their *v* has gone out into all
Heb	3: 15	'Today, if you hear his *v*,
	12: 26	At that time his *v* shook the earth,
2Pe	1: 18	We ourselves heard this *v* that came
Rev	1: 10	and I heard behind me a loud *v*
	3: 20	If anyone hears my *v* and opens the

W

wait, -s, -ing, -ed

Ps	27: 14	take heart and *w* for the LORD.
	40: 1	I *w-ed* patiently for the LORD;
	130: 6	watchmen *w* for the morning,
La	3: 26	*w* quietly for the salvation
Mk	15: 43	*w-ing* for the kingdom of God,
Lk	2: 25	*w-ing* for the consolation
Jn	3: 29	bridegroom *w-s* and listens
Ac	1: 4	*w* for the gift my Father promised,
	6: 2	in order to *w* on tables.
Ro	8: 19	creation *w-s* in eager expectation
1Th	1: 10	to *w* for his Son from heaven,

walk, -s, -ing, -ed

Ge	3: 8	*w-ing* in the garden in the cool
	5: 24	Enoch *w-ed* faithfully with God;
	17: 1	*w* before me faithfully and be blameless.
Lev	26: 12	I will *w* among you and be your God,
Ps	1: 1	does not *w* in step with the wicked

	23:	4	I w through the darkest valley
Isa	9:	2	The people w-ing in darkness
	30:	21	'This is the way; w in it.'
	40:	31	they will w and not be faint.
Am	3:	3	Do two w together unless
Mic	6:	8	to love mercy and to w humbly
Mt	9:	5	or to say, "Get up and w"?
Jn	8:	12	will never w in darkness,
Ac	3:	6	name of Jesus Christ of Nazareth, w
2Co	6:	16	'I will live with them and w among
1Jn	1:	6	fellowship with him yet w in
	1:	7	But if we w in the light,
Rev	2:	1	and w-s among the seven golden

want, -s, -ing, -ed

1Sa	8:	19	'We w a king over us.
Da	5:	27	scales and found w-ing.
Jn	17:	24	I w those you have given me
	21:	18	went where you w-ed;
Ro	1:	13	I do not w you to be unaware,
	7:	16	I do what I do not w to do,
	9:	18	whom he w-s to have mercy,
Php	3:	10	I w to know Christ
1Th	4:	13	we do not w you to be uninformed
1Ti	2:	4	who w-s all people to be saved
2Ti	3:	12	who w-s to live a godly life
Jas	4:	2	you cannot get what you w,
2Pe	3:	9	not w-ing anyone to perish,

wash, -ing, -ed

Ps	51:	7	w me, and I shall be whiter
Mt	6:	17	oil on your head and w your face,
	15:	2	They don't w their hands before
	27:	24	he took water and w-ed his hands
Jn	13:	5	began to w his disciples' feet,
Ac	22:	16	be baptised and w your sins away,
1Co	6:	11	were w-ed, you were sanctified,
Eph	5:	26	cleansing her by the w-ing
Tit	3:	5	through the w-ing of rebirth
Rev	7:	14	they have w-ed their robes

watch, -es, -ful, -man

Ps	1:	6	the LORD w-es over the way of
	90:	4	or like a w in the night.
	121:	4	he who w-es over Israel
Eze	33:	6	if the w-man sees the sword
Mt	7:	15	'W out for false prophets.
	24:	42	'Therefore keep w, because
	26:	41	'W and pray so that you will not
Lk	2:	8	keeping w over their flocks
Ac	20:	28	Keep w over yourselves and all
Php	3:	2	W out for those dogs,
Col	4:	2	being w-ful and thankful
1Ti	4:	16	W your life and doctrine closely.
Heb	13:	17	they keep w over you as those who

water, -s, -ed

Ex	7:	20	struck the w of the Nile,
	14:	16	to divide the w so that
Ps	1:	3	a tree planted by streams of w,
	23:	2	he leads me beside quiet w-s,
	42:	1	deer pants for streams of w,
SS	8:	7	Many w-s cannot quench love;
Isa	12:	3	draw w from the wells of salvation.
	32:	2	like streams of w in the desert
	40:	12	measured the w-s in the hollow
	43:	2	When you pass through the w-s,
	55:	1	who are thirsty, come to the w-s;
	58:	11	a spring whose w-s never fail.
Eze	36:	25	I will sprinkle clean w on you,
Hab	2:	14	as the w-s cover the sea.
Mt	3:	11	I baptise you with w for repentance
	14:	29	walked on the w and came towards
	27:	24	he took w and washed his hands

Mk	9:	41	gives you a cup of w in my name
Lk	16:	24	dip the tip of his finger in w
Jn	1:	26	'I baptise with w,' John replied
	3:	5	born of w and the Spirit.
	4:	11	Where can you get this living w?
	4:	14	drinks the w I give them will
	5:	7	when the w is stirred.
	7:	38	rivers of living w will flow
	19:	34	a sudden flow of blood and w.
1Co	3:	6	Apollos w-ed it, but God has
Eph	5:	26	washing with w through the word,
1Ti	5:	23	Stop drinking only w,
Heb	10:	22	our bodies washed with pure w.
1Pe	3:	21	this w symbolises baptism
2Pe	2:	17	These people are springs without w
	3:	5	the earth was formed out of w
1Jn	5:	6	the one who came by w and blood −
Rev	1:	15	like the sound of rushing w-s.
	21:	6	To the thirsty I will give w
	22:	17	the free gift of the w of life.

way, -s

Ex	33:	13	teach me your w-s so I may
Dt	1:	33	and to show you the w you should go
	32:	4	and all his w-s are just.
1Sa	12:	23	I will teach you the w that is good
2Sa	22:	31	As for God, his w is perfect:
Ps	1:	1	stand in the w that sinners take
	1:	6	the LORD watches over the w of the
	25:	9	right and teaches them his w.
	32:	8	teach you in the w you should go;
	37:	5	Commit your w to the LORD;
	51:	13	I will teach transgressors your w-s
	139:	3	you are familiar with all my w-s
	139:	24	if there is any offensive w in me,
Pr	3:	6	in all your w-s submit to him,
	14:	12	w that appears to be right, but
	22:	6	Start children off on the w they should go
	30:	19	the w of an eagle in the sky,
Isa	30:	21	'This is the w; walk in it.'
	40:	27	'My w is hidden from the LORD;
	53:	6	each of us has turned to our own w;
	55:	7	Let the wicked forsake their w-s
	55:	8	neither are your w-s my w-s,
Eze	33:	11	turn from their w-s and live.
Mt	3:	3	"Prepare the w for the Lord, make
Jn	14:	6	'I am the w and the truth and the
Ac	9:	2	any there who belonged to the W,
1Co	10:	13	he will also provide a w out
	12:	31	will show you the most excellent w.
Col	1:	10	and please him in every w:
Heb	4:	15	tempted in every w, just as we are
	10:	20	by a new and living w opened for us
Jas	3:	2	We all stumble in many w-s.

weak, -er, -ness, -nesses

Ps	82:	3	Defend the w and the fatherless;
Mt	26:	41	is willing, but the flesh is w.
Ac	20:	35	of hard work we must help the w,
Ro	8:	26	Spirit helps us in our w-ness.
	14:	1	Accept the one whose faith is w,
1Co	1:	27	chose the w things of the world
	9:	22	To the w I became w,
	11:	30	many among you are w and ill,
	15:	43	it is sown in w-ness,
2Co	12:	9	my power is made perfect in w-ness.
Heb	4:	15	to feel sympathy for our w-nesses,
1Pe	3:	7	with respect as the w-er partner

whole

Ex	19:	5	the w earth is mine,
Nu	14:	21	glory of the LORD fills the w earth
Ps	48:	2	the joy of the w earth,
	72:	19	may the w earth be filled

Isa	6:	3	the w earth is full of his glory.
Mal	3:	10	the w tithe into the storehouse,
Mt	5:	29	your w body to be thrown into hell.
	6:	22	your w body will be full of light.
	16:	26	to gain the w world, yet
	24:	14	be preached in the w world
Mk	15:	33	darkness came over the w land
Ac	20:	27	to proclaim to you the w will
Ro	3:	19	w world held accountable to God.
	8:	22	the w creation has been groaning
1Co	5:	6	little yeast leavens the w batch
Gal	5:	3	he is required to obey the w law.
Eph	2:	21	the w building is joined together
1Th	5:	23	May your w spirit, soul and body
Jas	2:	10	whoever keeps the w law
1Jn	2:	2	for the sins of the w world.
	5:	19	the w world is under the control

wicked, -ness

Ge	6:	5	how great the w-ness of
2Sa	13:	12	Don't do this w thing.
Ps	1:	1	walk in step with the w
	1:	6	way of the w leads to destruction
	5:	4	not a God who is pleased with w-ness
	9:	17	The w go down to the realm
	27:	2	When the w advance against me
	73:	3	when I saw the prosperity of the w.
Pr	10:	27	the years of the w are cut short.
Isa	48:	22	peace,' says the LORD, 'for the w
	53:	9	assigned a grave with the w,
	55:	7	Let the w forsake their ways
Eze	3:	18	w person, "You will surely die,"
	18:	21	if a w person turns away
Mt	12:	39	'A w and adulterous generation
	12:	45	other spirits more w than itself,
	13:	49	separate the w from the righteous
	24:	12	w-ness, the love of most will grow
Ac	24:	15	of both the righteous and the w.
Ro	1:	18	the godlessness and w-ness of people
1Co	5:	8	leavened with malice and w-ness,
2Ti	2:	19	Lord must turn away from w-ness.
Tit	2:	14	to redeem us from all w-ness
Heb	1:	9	righteousness and hated w-ness;
	8:	12	I will forgive their w-ness
Rev	2:	2	you cannot tolerate w people,

widow, -s, -s'

Dt	10:	18	the fatherless and the w,
Isa	1:	17	plead the case of the w.
Mt	22:	24	his brother must marry the w
Mk	12:	40	They devour w-s' houses
	12:	42	w came and put in two very small
Lk	18:	5	this w keeps bothering me,
Ac	6:	1	their w-s were being overlooked
1Co	7:	8	to the unmarried and the w-s I say:
1Ti	5:	3	those w-s who are really in need.
Jas	1:	27	to look after orphans and w-s

wife

Ge	2:	24	united to his w,
	38:	8	'Sleep with your brother's w
Ex	20:	17	covet your neighbour's w,
Ps	128:	3	Your w will be like a fruitful vine
Pr	5:	18	rejoice in the w of your youth.
	27:	15	A quarrelsome w is like the dripping
	31:	10	A w of noble character
Ecc	9:	9	Enjoy life with your w,
Mal	2:	15	unfaithful to the w of your youth.
Mt	1:	20	to take Mary home as your w,
	5:	31	"Anyone who divorces his w
	19:	3	for a man to divorce his w
	22:	28	whose w will she be of the seven,
Lk	17:	32	Remember Lot's w!
	18:	29	left home or w or brothers

1Co	5:	1	a man has his father's w.
	7:	3	fulfil his marital duty to his w,
	7:	14	sanctified through his w,
Eph	5:	23	husband is the head of the w
1Ti	3:	2	faithful to his w,
Rev	21:	9	the bride, the w of the Lamb.

wilderness

Ex	3:	18	take a three-day journey into the w
	16:	32	bread I gave you to eat in the w
Nu	32:	13	wander in the w for forty years,
Dt	8:	16	He gave you manna to eat in the w,
Ps	78:	19	'Can God really spread a table in the w
Isa	40:	3	A voice of one calling: 'In the w
Mt	3:	1	Baptist came, preaching in the w
	3:	3	'A voice of one calling in the w,
	4:	1	led by the Spirit into the w
Jn	3:	14	Moses lifted up the snake in the w
1Co	10:	5	bodies were scattered over the w
Heb	3:	8	during the time of testing in the w
Rev	12:	6	The woman fled into the w

will

Ps	40:	8	desire to do your w, my God;
Isa	53:	10	it was the LORD's w to crush him
Mt	6:	10	your kingdom come, your w be done
	7:	21	the one who does the w of my Father
	26:	39	Yet not as I w, but as you w.
Lk	12:	47	servant who knows the master's w
Jn	1:	13	a husband's w, but born of God.
	4:	34	to do the w of him who sent me
Ac	4:	28	w had decided beforehand
Ro	8:	20	the w of the one who subjected it,
	12:	2	to test and approve what God's w is
Eph	1:	11	with the purpose of his w,
	5:	17	understand what the Lord's w is.
Php	2:	13	it is God who works in you to w
1Th	4:	3	It is God's w that you should be
Heb	10:	7	I have come to do your w, my God."
Jas	4:	15	say, 'If it is the Lord's w,
2Pe	1:	21	had its origin in the human w
1Jn	2:	17	does the w of God lives for ever.

wind, -s

Ex	14:	21	sea back with a strong east w
Ps	1:	4	chaff that the w blows away.
	103:	16	w blows over it and it is gone,
Ecc	2:	11	a chasing after the w;
Hos	8:	7	sow the w and reap the whirlwind.
Mt	7:	25	the w-s blew and beat against
	8:	26	rebuked the w-s and the waves,
	11:	7	A reed swayed by the w?
Jn	3:	8	The w blows wherever it pleases.
Ac	2:	2	the blowing of a violent w
Eph	4:	14	blown here and there by every w
Jas	1:	6	blown and tossed by the w.

wine, -press, -skins

Ps	60:	3	given us w that makes us stagger.
	104:	15	w that gladdens human hearts,
Pr	20:	1	W is a mocker and beer
	23:	31	Do not gaze at w when it is red,
Isa	55:	1	buy w and milk without money
Mt	9:	17	pour new w into old w-skins
	21:	33	a wall around it, dug a w-press
	27:	34	they offered Jesus w to drink,
Jn	2:	9	water that had been turned into w.
Ac	2:	13	'They have had too much w.'
Ro	14:	21	not to eat meat or drink w
Eph	5:	18	Do not get drunk on w,
1Ti	3:	8	not indulging in much w,
Rev	14:	10	drink of the w of God's fury,

	4: 12	the w of God is alive and active.
	12: 24	speaks a better w than the blood
Jas	1: 18	birth through the w of truth,
	1: 22	Do not merely listen to the w,
1Pe	1: 25	the w of the Lord endures for ever.
	3: 1	any of them do not believe the w,
2Pe	3: 5	long ago by God's w the heavens
1Jn	1: 1	proclaim concerning the W of life.
	2: 14	the w of God lives in you,
Rev	1: 2	that is, the w of God
	3: 8	yet you have kept my w
	12: 11	by the w of their testimony;
	22: 19	takes w-s away from this scroll of

work, -s, -er, -ers

Ge	2: 2	God had finished the w
	2: 15	in the Garden of Eden to w it
	29: 18	'I'll w for you seven years
Ex	20: 9	labour and do all your w,
Dt	5: 14	On it you shall not do any w,
	32: 4	the Rock, his w-s are perfect,
Ps	8: 3	heavens, the w of your fingers,
	8: 6	rulers over the w-s of your hands;
	19: 1	skies proclaim the w of his hands.
	90: 17	establish the w of our hands
	104: 23	Then people go out to their w,
	107: 24	They saw the w-s of the Lord,
	139: 14	your w-s are wonderful,
	145: 4	commends your w-s to another;
	145: 10	All your w-s praise you, Lord
Pr	8: 22	forth as the first of his w-s,
Mt	9: 37	but the w-ers are few.
	10: 10	for the w-er is worth his keep.
	20: 4	go and w in my vineyard,
Lk	13: 14	'There are six days for w.
Jn	4: 34	and to finish his w.
	5: 17	'My Father is always at his w
	6: 27	Do not w for food that spoils,
	6: 29	'The w of God is this: to believe
	14: 11	believe on the evidence of the w-s
	17: 4	by finishing the w you gave me
Ro	4: 2	Abraham was justified by w-s,
	4: 4	Now to the one who w-s,
	7: 21	So I find this law at w:
	8: 28	in all things God w-s for the good
	11: 6	then it cannot be based on w-s;
1Co	3: 13	their w will be shown for what it is,
	12: 11	the w of one and the same Spirit,
	12: 29	Do all w miracles?
	15: 58	fully to the w of the Lord,
2Co	4: 12	death is at w in us,
Gal	3: 5	his Spirit and w miracles
Eph	1: 11	the plan of him who w-s out
	2: 2	the spirit who is now at w
	2: 9	gift of God – not by w-s,
	2: 10	in Christ Jesus to do good w-s,
	4: 12	his people for w-s of service,
Php	1: 6	he who began a good w in you
	2: 12	continue to w out your salvation
Col	3: 23	w at it with all your heart,
2Th	2: 7	lawlessness is already at w;
	3: 10	'The one who is unwilling to w
1Ti	5: 17	those whose w is preaching
	5: 18	w-er deserves his wages.'
2Ti	3: 17	equipped for every good w.
	4: 5	do the w of an evangelist,
Heb	1: 10	heavens are the w of your hands.
1Jn	3: 8	to destroy the devil's w.
Rev	2: 2	I know your deeds, your hard w

world, -ly

Ge	11: 1	the whole w had one language
Ps	9: 8	rules the w in righteousness

	24: 1	the w, and all who live in it;
	50: 12	w is mine, and all that is in it.
Mt	4: 8	all the kingdoms of the w
	5: 14	'You are the light of the w.
	16: 26	to gain the whole w, yet
	24: 14	preached in the whole w
Mk	16: 15	'Go into all the w and preach
Lk	2: 1	taken of the entire Roman w.
Jn	1: 10	He was in the w,
	1: 29	who takes away the sin of the w
	3: 16	For God so loved the w
	4: 42	the Saviour of the w.'
	8: 12	'I am the light of the w.
	14: 30	the prince of this w is coming.
	15: 18	'If the w hates you, keep in mind
	16: 33	In this w you will have trouble.
	17: 11	I will remain in the w no longer,
	17: 16	They are not of the w, even as I
	17: 18	As you sent me into the w, I have
	17: 21	be in us so that the w may believe
	18: 36	'My kingdom is not of this w.
Ac	17: 6	have caused trouble all over the w
	17: 24	'The God who made the w
	17: 31	will judge the w with justice
Ro	1: 20	creation of the w God's invisible
	5: 12	sin entered the w through one man,
1Co	3: 19	the wisdom of this w is foolishness
	6: 2	the Lord's people will judge the w?
2Co	5: 19	God was reconciling the w
Eph	1: 4	before the creation of the w
	6: 12	against the powers of this dark w
1Ti	1: 15	Jesus came into the w to save
	6: 7	we brought nothing into the w,
2Ti	4: 10	because he loved this w,
Tit	2: 12	'No' to ungodliness and w-ly
Heb	9: 26	since the creation of the w.
Jas	4: 4	friendship with the w means enmity
1Pe	1: 20	before the creation of the w,
2Pe	3: 6	the w of that time was deluged
1Jn	2: 2	also for the sins of the whole w.
	2: 15	Do not love the w or anything in
	2: 17	The w and its desires pass away,
Rev	11: 15	'The kingdom of the w has become
	13: 8	slain from the creation of the w.

worship, -s, -ped

Ge	22: 5	We will w and then
Ex	7: 16	they may w me in the wilderness.
	20: 5	not bow down to them or w them;
1Ch	16: 29	W the Lord in the splendour of his
Ps	29: 2	w the Lord in the splendour
	95: 6	Come, let us bow down in w,
	100: 2	W the Lord with gladness;
Isa	44: 17	he bows down to it and w-s.
Da	3: 6	Whoever does not fall down and w
Mt	2: 2	have come to w him.
	4: 9	if you will bow down and w me.'
	15: 9	They w me in vain;
	28: 17	they w-ped him; but some doubted.
Jn	4: 21	a time is coming when you will w
Ro	1: 25	and w-ped and served created
	12: 1	this is your true w.
Heb	1: 6	'Let all God's angels w him.'

worth, -y

Ps	48: 1	Lord, and most w-y of praise,
Pr	31: 10	She is w far more than rubies.
Mt	10: 10	worker is w his keep.
	10: 31	you are w more than many sparrows.
	10: 37	mother more than me is not w-y
Mk	1: 7	sandals I am not w-y to stoop down
Lk	15: 19	w-y to be called your son;
Ro	8: 18	sufferings are not w comparing

Eph	4:	1	to live a life w-y of the calling
Php	1:	27	in a manner w-y of the gospel
	3:	8	surpassing w of knowing Christ
1Ti	3:	8	to be w-y of respect, sincere,
	5:	17	w-y of double honour,
1Pe	1:	7	faith – of greater w than gold,
Rev	4:	11	'You are w-y, our Lord and God,
	5:	12	'W-y is the Lamb, who was slain

wrath

Ps	2:	12	his w can flare up in a moment.
	90:	11	Your w is as great as the fear
Pr	15:	1	A gentle answer turns away w,
Isa	63:	3	trod them down in my w;
Eze	7:	19	in the day of the LORD's w.
Hab	3:	2	in w remember mercy.
Zep	2:	2	of the LORD's w comes upon you.
Mt	3:	7	to flee from the coming w?
Jn	3:	36	God's w remains on them.
Ro	1:	18	The w of God is being revealed
	5:	9	saved from God's w through him!
Eph	2:	3	by nature deserving of w.
1Th	1:	10	rescues us from the coming w.
	5:	9	God did not appoint us to suffer w
Rev	6:	16	from the w of the Lamb!
	19:	15	fury of the w of God Almighty.

write, -ten, -r

Dt	6:	9	W them on the door-frames
	10:	4	tablets what he had w-ten before,
	28:	58	which are w-ten in this book,
Jos	1:	8	to do everything w-ten in it.
	23:	6	to obey all that is w-ten
Ps	40:	7	it is w-ten about me in the scroll.
	45:	1	tongue is the pen of a skilful w-r
Pr	7:	3	w them on the tablet of your heart.
Jer	31:	33	and w it on their hearts.
Da	12:	1	name is found w-ten in the book –
Mal	3:	16	A scroll of remembrance was w-ten
Lk	10:	20	your names are w-ten in heaven.'
	24:	44	fulfilled that is w-ten about me
Jn	8:	6	Jesus bent down and started to w
	20:	31	are w-ten that you may believe
Ro	2:	15	requirements of the law are w-ten
1Co	10:	11	were w-ten down as warnings for us
2Co	3:	3	w-ten not with ink
Heb	10:	7	it is w-ten about me in the scroll
	10:	16	I will w them on their minds.'
	12:	23	whose names are w-ten in heaven.
Jude		4	whose condemnation was w-ten about
Rev	1:	19	'W, therefore, what you have seen

	2:	17	with a new name w-ten on it,
	21:	27	names are w-ten in the Lamb's

wrong, -s, -ed, -doers, -doing

Ex	23:	2	Do not follow the crowd in doing w.
Job	1:	22	by charging God with w-doing.
Ps	119:104		I hate every w path.
Lk	23:	41	this man has done nothing w.'
Ro	13:	4	if you do w, be afraid,
1Co	6:	7	Why not rather be w-ed?
	6:	9	w-doers will not inherit the kingdom
	13:	5	it keeps no record of w-s.
Heb	8:	7	nothing w with that first covenant,
1Pe	2:	20	you receive a beating for doing w

y

year, -s

Ge	6:	3	a hundred and twenty y-s.
	41:	29	Seven y-s of great abundance
Lev	16:	34	atonement is to be made once a y
	25:	11	fiftieth y shall be a jubilee
Ps	90:	4	A thousand y-s in your sight
	90:	10	days may come to seventy y-s,
Isa	6:	1	In the y that King Uzziah died,
	61:	2	to proclaim the y of the LORD's
Joel	2:	25	the y-s the locusts have eaten –
Lk	4:	19	the y of the Lord's favour.'
	12:	19	plenty of grain laid up for many y-s.
	13:	8	"leave it alone for one more y,
Heb	9:	7	and that only once a y,
	10:	1	repeated endlessly y after y,
Jas	4:	13	a y there, carry on business
2Pe	3:	8	a day is like a thousand y-s,
Rev	20:	4	with Christ for a thousand y-s.

young, -er

Ps	37:	25	I was y and now I am old,
	119:	9	How can a y person stay
Pr	20:	29	glory of y men is their strength,
Isa	40:	30	y men stumble and fall;
Jer	1:	6	I am too y.
La	3:	27	to bear the yoke while he is y.
Lk	15:	13	the y-er son got together
Ac	2:	17	your y men will see visions,
Ro	9:	12	'The older will serve the y-er.'
1Ti	4:	12	down on you because you are y,
	5:	1	Treat y-er men as brothers,
1Pe	5:	5	you who are y-er, submit

FOR FURTHER READING

A one-volume handbook on the Bible has a number of limitations. The most important of these is space: the discussion of the meaning and relevance of any given biblical passage is limited severely by the restricted space. Another difficulty is raised by the author of a commentary. No matter how good the commentator, readers will want to have access to other viewpoints. For this reason, it is a good idea to build up a library of commentaries on Scripture. Guidance on this is provided in this section of this book. Many of these are now available in electronic format.

However, other books are also useful in helping people gain more from reading Scripture. Gordon D. Fee and Douglas Stuart's *How to Read the Bible for All Its Worth*, 3rd ed. (Grand Rapids: Zondervan, 2003), is strongly recommended to all interested in getting the most out of their reading of the Bible.

Several sets of commentaries are of interest. The Tyndale Old Testament commentaries and the Tyndale New Testament commentaries (Downers Grove, Ill.: InterVarsity Press; Nottingham, UK: Inter-Varsity Press) are excellent 'starter' commentaries, and well worth purchasing. They include contributions by leading biblical scholars, pitched at a level suitable for the serious reader who is not (yet!) a biblical scholar.

The Bible Speaks Today series (Downers Grove, Ill.: InterVarsity Press; Nottingham, UK: Inter-Varsity Press) is less concerned with issues of scholarship, and focuses on the relevance of the text to the situation of today. It is an excellent addition to the bookshelf of any serious student of the Bible, and is especially helpful in the preparation of addresses and sermons.

The Word Biblical Commentary (Plano, Tex.: Thomas Nelson) offers a scholarly yet generally accessible perspective on the texts and themes of biblical commentaries.

The Classic Biblical Commentary series (Wheaton, Ill.: Crossway Books) aims to make available some of the best commentaries of the past, edited with the needs of modern readers in mind. This series draws on the great expositors of the past, such as C. H. Spurgeon and J. C. Ryle, who still merit a hearing today.

The New International Biblical Commentary (Peabody, Mass.: Hendrickson) is also recommended. Currently in fourteen volumes, it uses transliterated Greek, for the serious student who does not as yet know New Testament Greek.

The New Cambridge Bible Commentary (Cambridge: Cambridge University Press), now in the process of appearing, will offer a more scholarly approach that will appeal to readers wishing to explore some of the historical and theological issues noted in this introduction in more detail.

Volumes in all the series mentioned above give suggestions for more detailed commentaries that can be used for further study.

Many resources are now available online, including the texts of many translations of the Bible, as well as study guides.

Matthew Henry's Commentary, a classic devotional commentary (1706) is widely available: see, for example, http://www.biblestudytools.com/commentaries/matthew-henry-complete, updated to contemporary language by Martin H. Manser (http://zondervan.com/9780310499497). Other classic commentaries by John Calvin, John Wesley and C. H. Spurgeon are available at (http://www.biblestudytools.com/commentaries) and elsewhere. See also http://deeperstudy.com/link/commentaries.html and http://www.bible-researcher.com/links20.html.

The Christian Classics Ethereal Library offers free access to many classic Christian texts, including many commentaries on the Bible: see http://www.ccel.org.

Electronic versions of the text of the NIV, with many other translations and the original Hebrew and Greek texts of the Bible, are widely available online and in software packages. Online parallel versions of the Bible, which allow users to study the biblical text using multiple translations, include the free *Online Parallel Bible* (http://bible.cc). Widely used packages include *Bibleworks* (http://www.bibleworks.com) and *Logos* (http://www.logos.com). These can be used on many digital platforms.

ACKNOWLEDGEMENTS

The author wishes to acknowledge the use of the following previously published material in the *NIV Bible Handbook*.

Bible book outlines are taken from the *NIV Thematic Study Bible* ed. Alister McGrath (Hodder & Stoughton, 1996).

'The Significance of the Resurrection' is adapted from *Crash Course on Christian Teaching*, Martin Manser (Hodder & Stoughton, 1998).

'People of the Bible' and 'Places of the Bible' are taken from the *NIV Comprehensive Concordance* ed. Martin Manser (Hodder & Stoughton, 2001).

'The Twelve Disciples of Jesus' copyright © Hodder & Stoughton.

'A hymn about Christ'; 'The man of lawlessness'; 'Old Testament allusions'; 'A fascination with numbers'; 'Psalms can help you when you are feeling...'; 'Key themes in Proverbs'; 'Visions in Daniel' and 'The Day of the Lord' copyright © Martin Manser.

'God spoke to them through Romans' is taken from *Four weeks with Romans* ed. Martin Manser, (Creative Publishing, 1984) used by permission of Creative Publishing.

'Can we trust what the Bible says?', 'How can we get the best from reading the Bible?' and all feature panels written by Mike Beaumont copyright © Hodder & Stoughton.